CONTEMPORARY'S
GED

Coordinating Editor
Patricia Mulcrone, Ed.D.
Professor/Chair
Adult Educational Development
William Rainey Harper College
Palatine, Illinois

Reviewers
Kathryn Coleman
GED Instructor
Kishwaukee College
Malta, Illinois

Mary Ann Corley, Ph.D.
GED Administrator
Baltimore, Maryland

Mary Kay Gray
GED Coordinator
Mott Adult High School
Flint, Michigan

Carrie Robinson
Assistant Professor
Staten Island Community College
Staten Island, New York

CB
CONTEMPORARY BOOKS

Library of Congress Cataloging-in-Publication Data

GED : how to prepare for the high school equivalency examination.—Newly rev.
    p.   cm.
    Rev. ed. of: Contemporary's new GED. © 1985.
    ISBN 0-8092-2598-0
    1. General educational development tests—Study guides.   I. Contemporary
Books, Inc.   II. Contemporary's new GED.
LB3060.33.G45G14   1994
373.12'62—dc20   94-1956
                                                    CIP

Contributing Writers

Reading Skills
Noreen Giles
Patricia Mulcrone

Test 1: Writing Skills
Karen A. Fox
Judith Gallagher

Test 2: Social Studies
Dan M. Fox
Karen Gibbons
Virginia Lowe

Test 3: Science
Bruce R. Brown
Robert P. Mitchell

Test 4: Literature and the Arts
Karen A. Fox
Noreen Giles
Anne V. McGravie

Test 5: Mathematics
Jerry Howett
Janice Phillips

Published by Contemporary Books
A division of NTC/Contemporary Publishing Group, Inc.
4255 West Touhy Avenue, Lincolnwood (Chicago), Illinois 60646-1975 U.S.A.
Copyright © 1994 by NTC/Contemporary Publishing Group, Inc.
Printed in the United States of America
International Standard Book Number: 0-8092-2598-0

98 99 00 01 02 03 CU 19 18 17 16 15 14 13 12 11 10 9 8 7 6 5 4 3 2 1

CONTENTS

ACKNOWLEDGMENTS

Article on page 13 from the *Chicago Tribune*. Copyright 1986 by Reuters. Reprinted by permission.

Cartoon on page 14 by Jim Morin. Copyright 1992 by the *Miami Herald*. Reprinted by permission.

Excerpt on page 16 from *Indian Oratory: Famous Speeches by Noted Indian Chieftains* by W. C. Vanderwerth. Copyright 1971 by the University of Oklahoma Press. Reprinted by permission.

Cartoon on page 19 by Larry Wright, © 1986. Reprinted by permission of the *Detroit News*, a Gannett newspaper.

Map on page 21 from *World Geography* by Preston E. James and Nelda Davis, © 1985. Reprinted by permission of the Glencoe division of the Macmillan/McGraw-Hill School Publishing Company.

Excerpt on page 39 from *Song of Solomon* by Toni Morrison. Permission granted by International Creative Management, Inc. Copyright 1977 by Toni Morrison.

Poem on page 39, "Tom Merritt," in *Spoon River Anthology* by Edgar Lee Masters. Originally published by the Macmillan Company. Permission by Ellen C. Masters.

Excerpt on pages 40–41 from *Pygmalion* in *Four Modern Plays* by George Bernard Shaw. Reprinted by permission of The Society of Authors Ltd.

Excerpt on page 209 from "The Night the Ghost Got In," © 1961 by James Thurber. From *My Life and Hard Times*, published by Harper & Row.

Excerpt on pages 209–210 from *Seize the Day* by Saul Bellow. Copyright 1956, 1974, renewed by Saul Bellow. Used by permission of Viking Penguin, a division of Penguin Books USA Inc.

Review on page 212, "Game Shows," by Dorothy Scheuer in *Senior Scholastic Magazines*. Reprinted by permission of Scholastic Inc. © 1982.

Cartoon on page 236 by Dana Summers, © 1983, Washington Post Writers Group, reprinted by permission.

Cartoon on page 237 by Don Wright, © 1992 the *Palm Beach Post*, reprinted by permission.

Excerpt on page 249 from "The Sacred Rac" in *Learning About Peoples and Cultures* by Patricia Hughes Ponzi, © 1972.

Article on page 252, "He's Reborn After 51 Years in an Attic," by Jack Mabley. Copyright December 18, 1986, Chicago Tribune Company, all rights reserved. Used by permission.

Excerpt on page 265 from *The Shaping of Colonial Virginia* by Thomas J. Wertenbaker, © 1958.

Cartoon on page 317 by Hugh S. Haynie. Reprinted by permission. Copyright by the *Courier-Journal*, Louisville Times Company, and Hugh S. Haynie.

Cartoon on page 325 by Arthur Bok, © 1993. Reprinted by permission of the *Akron Beacon Journal*.

Excerpt on page 456 from "A Certain Beginning" by Kim Chi-won in *Words of Farewell: Stories by Korean Women Writers*. Copyright 1989 by Kim Chi-won. Reprinted by permission of Seal Press.

Excerpt on page 458 from *Of Mice and Men* by John Steinbeck. Copyright 1937, renewed © 1965 by John Steinbeck. Used by permission of Viking Penguin, a division of Penguin Books USA Inc.

x ACKNOWLEDGMENTS

Excerpt on page 460 from *The Woman Warrior* by Maxine Hong Kingston. Copyright 1975, 1976 by Maxine Hong Kingston. Reprinted by permission of Alfred A. Knopf, Inc.

Excerpt on page 463 reprinted by permission of Faber and Faber Ltd. and The Putnam Publishing Group from *Lord of the Flies* by William Golding. Copyright 1954 by William Golding; renewed 1982.

Excerpt on page 466 from "The Short Happy Life of Francis Macomber." Reprinted by permission of Charles Scribner's Sons, an imprint of Macmillan Publishing Company, from *The Short Stories of Ernest Hemingway*. Copyright 1936 by Ernest Hemingway; renewal © 1964 by Mary Hemingway.

Excerpt on page 467 from "The Possibility of Evil" by Shirley Jackson. Copyright 1965 by Stanley Edgar Hyman. Reprinted by permission of Brandt & Brandt Literary Agents, Inc.

Excerpt on page 470 from "Everything That Rises Must Converge" in *The Complete Stories* by Flannery O'Connor. Copyright 1961, 1965 by the Estate of Mary Flannery O'Connor. Reprinted by permission of Farrar, Straus & Giroux, Inc.

Excerpt on page 472 from *The Bell Jar* by Sylvia Plath. Copyright 1971 by Harper & Row Publishers, Inc. Reprinted by permission of HarperCollins Publishers, Inc.

Story on pages 476–478, "The Sniper," in *Spring Sowing* by Liam O'Flaherty, reprinted by permission of Harcourt Brace & Company.

Review on page 482 by Anne Whitehouse. Copyright 1993 by the New York Times Company. Reprinted by permission.

Poem on page 483, "Oh, When I Was in Love with You," from *The Collected Poems of A. E. Housman* by A. E. Housman. Copyright 1939, 1940, © 1965 by Henry Holt and Company, Inc. Copyright 1967, 1968 by Robert E. Symons. Reprinted by permission of Henry Holt and Company, Inc.

Excerpt on page 484 from "Southbound on the Freeway" by May Swenson. Copyright 1963 and renewed 1991. Used by permission of The Literary Estate of May Swenson.

Poem on page 486, "On Being a Woman," in *The Portable Dorothy Parker* by Dorothy Parker. Introduction by Brendan Gill. Copyright 1928, renewed © 1956 by Dorothy Parker. Used by permission of Viking Penguin, a division of Penguin Books USA Inc.

Poem on page 487, "History." Copyright 1977 by Gary Soto. Used by permission of Gary Soto.

Poem on page 489, "maggie and milly and molly and may," is reprinted from *Complete Poems, 1904–1962* by E. E. Cummings. Edited by George J. Firmage, by permission of Liveright Publishing Corporation. Copyright 1923, 1925, 1926, 1931, 1935, 1938–1940, 1944–1962 by E. E. Cummings. Copyright 1961, 1963, 1966–1968 by Marion Morehouse Cummings. Copyright 1972–1991 by the Trustees for the E. E. Cummings Trust.

Poem on page 490, "Jazz Fantasia," in *Smoke and Steel* by Carl Sandburg, © 1920 by Harcourt Brace & Company and renewed 1948 by Carl Sandburg, reprinted by permission of the publisher.

Poem on page 491, "My Papa's Waltz," © 1942 by Hearst Magazines, Inc., from *The Collected Poems of Theodore Roethke* by Theodore Roethke. Used by permission of Doubleday, a division of Bantam Doubleday Dell Publishing Group, Inc.

Poem on page 493, "Memory," by Trevor Nunn in *Cats: The Book of the Musical*, incorporating lines from "Rhapsody on a Windy Night" in *Collected Poems 1909–1962* by T. S. Eliot, © 1936 by Harcourt Brace & Company, © 1964, 1963 by T. S. Eliot, reprinted by permission of the publisher.

Poem on page 493, "Memory," from *Cats: The Book of the Musical*. Words by Trevor Nunn after T. S. Eliot. Reprinted by permission of Faber and Faber Ltd. © 1981 by Trevor Nunn/Set Copyrights Ltd.

Poem on page 494, "The Negro Speaks of Rivers," in *Selected Poems* by Langston Hughes. Copyright 1926 by Alfred A. Knopf, Inc., and renewed 1954 by Langston Hughes. Reprinted by permission of the publisher.

Excerpt on page 495 from "Chicago" in *Chicago Poems* by Carl Sandburg, reprinted by permission of Harcourt Brace & Company.

Poem on pages 496–497 from *The Poetry of Robert Frost* edited by Edward Connery Latham. Copyright 1923, © 1969 by Henry Holt and Company, Inc. Copyright 1942, 1951 by Robert Frost. Copyright 1970 by Lesley Frost Ballantine. Reprinted by permission of Henry Holt and Company, Inc.

Excerpt on page 497 from "An Indian Summer Day on the Prairie" in *Collected Poems of Vachel Lindsay* (New York: Macmillan, 1925).

Poem on page 497, "Dreams," in *The Dream Keeper and Other Poems* by Langston Hughes. Copyright 1932 by Alfred A. Knopf, Inc., and renewed 1960 by Langston Hughes. Reprinted by permission of the publisher.

Poem on page 498, "Barter." Reprinted by permission of Macmillan Publishing Company from *Collected Poems of Sara Teasdale* (New York: Macmillan, 1937).

Poem on page 499, "Wind and Silver," from "What's O'Clock" in *The Complete Poetical Works of Amy Lowell*. Copyright 1955 by Houghton Mifflin Company, © renewed 1983 by Houghton Mifflin Company, Brinton P. Roberts, and G. D'Andelot Belin, Esquire. Reprinted by permission of Houghton Mifflin Company. All rights reserved.

Poem on page 499, "Because I Could Not Stop for Death," by Emily Dickinson. Reprinted by permission of the publishers and the Trustees of Amherst College from *The Poems of Emily Dickinson*, Thomas H. Johnson, ed., Cambridge, Mass.: The Belknap Press of Harvard University Press, © 1951, 1955, 1979, 1983 by the President and Fellows of Harvard College.

Poem on page 501, "The Man from Washington," by James Welch in *Tales from American Authors* edited by Natachee Scott Momaday. Used by permission of editor.

Review on page 502 by Stephen C. Levi, October 1992. Reprinted by permission of *Small Press Review*.

Excerpt on pages 512–513 from *'night, Mother* by Marsha Norman. Copyright 1983 by Marsha Norman. Reprinted by permission of Hill and Wang, a division of Farrar, Straus & Giroux, Inc.

Excerpt on pages 514–515, *I Never Sang for My Father*, by Robert Anderson. Reprinted by permission of International Creative Management.

Excerpt on page 519 from *Parent Effectiveness Training* by Dr. Thomas Gordon. Copyright 1970 by Dr. Thomas Gordon. Reprinted by permission of David McKay Co., a division of Random House, Inc.

Excerpt on page 523 from *Hard Times* by Studs Terkel. Copyright 1970 by Studs Terkel. Reprinted by permission of Pantheon Books, a division of Random House, Inc.

Excerpt on pages 525 from *Nigger: An Autobiography* by Dick Gregory. Copyright 1964 by Dick Gregory Enterprises, Inc. Used by permission of the publisher, Dutton, an imprint of New American Library, a division of Penguin Books USA Inc.

Essay on pages 531–532, "The Computer Is Down." Reprinted by permission of The Putnam Publishing Group from *You Can Fool All of the People All of the Time* by Art Buchwald. Copyright 1985 by Art Buchwald.

Excerpt on page 533 from "The Dark Side of the Boom" by Mary S. Glucksman. Reprinted by permission of *Omni*, © 1991, Omni Publications International, Ltd.

Excerpt on page 535 from "Red Jacket Speech" in *A Treasury of Great American Speeches* by Charles Hurd, editor. Copyright 1959 by Hawthorn Books; 1987 by Charles Hurd. Used by permission of the publisher, Dutton, an imprint of New American Library, a division of Penguin Books USA Inc.

Review on page 539 reprinted by permission of *People Weekly* © 1993 Time Inc.

Review on page 541 of the book *The Pentagon Catalog*. Reviewed by Clarence Petersen. Copyright June 15, 1986, Chicago Tribune Company, all rights reserved, used by permission.

Review on page 545 reprinted by permission from *TV Guide*® *Magazine*. Copyright 1993 by News America Publications, Inc.

Excerpt on page 759 from *Scholastic Update*, December 1, 1986, vol. 119, no. 7. Reprinted by permission of Scholastic, Inc.

Excerpt on page 761 from the *News-Sun*, © 1985. Reprinted by permission of the *News-Sun*, Waukegan, Illinois.

Excerpt on page 763 from "Giving Children a Good Start" by Carol A. Emig, © 1986. Reprinted by permission of the author.

Illustration on page 767 from *Scholastic Update*, March 21, 1986, vol. 118, no. 14. Reprinted by permission of Scholastic, Inc.

Excerpt on page 768 from "Still at the Bottom of the Ladder" by Mary Elson. Copyright 1987, Chicago Tribune Company, all rights reserved, used by permission.

Map of Mexico on page 770 from *World Geography Workbook* by Preston E. James and Nelda Davis, © 1985. Reprinted by permission of the Glencoe division of the Macmillan/McGraw-Hill School Publishing Company.

Cartoon on page 772 by Rob Rogers, *Pittsburgh Press*, © 1992. Reprinted by permission of UFS, Inc.

Table on page 773 from *World Geography Workbook* by Preston E. James and Nelda Davis, © 1985. Reprinted by permission of the Glencoe division of the Macmillan/McGraw-Hill School Publishing Company.

Cartoon on page 774 by Mike Thompson, the *State Journal-Register*, © 1993. Reprinted by permission of Copley News Service.

Excerpt on page 801 from "American History" by Judith Ortíz-Cofer. Reprinted by permission of the author.

Excerpt on page 802 from *Medal of Honor Rag*, © 1977, 1983 by Tom Cole. Reprinted by permission of Lois Berman, The Little Theatre Building.

Excerpt on page 803 from "Suburban Prophecy" in *The Collected Poems of Howard Nemerov*. University of Chicago Press, 1977. Reprinted by permission of the author.

Excerpt on page 805 from "Narrow 'Realism' Misses the Point of Real Vision" in *Pieces of Eight* by Sydney J. Harris. Copyright 1982 by Houghton Mifflin Co. Reprinted by permission of Houghton Mifflin Co. All rights reserved.

Excerpt on page 807 from *Main Street* by Sinclair Lewis, © 1920 by Harcourt Brace & Company and renewed 1948 by Sinclair Lewis, reprinted by permission of the publisher.

Excerpt on pages 809–810 from "Beauty Marks." Copyright 1986 Time Inc. Reprinted by permission.

Cartoon on page 852 by Dan Wasserman, © 1986, *Boston Globe*. Distributed by Los Angeles Times Syndicate. Reprinted by permission.

Graphic on page 856, "Amount Spent on TV Ads," © 1992, Time Inc. Reprinted by permission.

Cartoon on page 862 by Tom Toles, © 1991, the *Buffalo News*. Reprinted by permission of Universal Press Syndicate. All rights reserved.

Cartoon on page 867 by Jorgensen, copyright 1992, Extra Newspaper Features. Reprinted by permission.

Excerpt on page 868 from *Newsweek*, May 14, © 1993, Newsweek, Inc. All rights reserved. Reprinted by permission.

Map and key on page 869 from *U.S. News & World Report*, © January 28, 1991. Reprinted by permission of *U.S. News & World Report*.

Excerpt on page 899 from *Gather Together in My Name* by Maya Angelou. Copyright 1974 by Maya Angelou. Reprinted by permission of Random House, Inc.

Excerpt on page 900 from "Girls of Summer" by Marie Brenner. Copyright 1993 by The New York Times Company. Reprinted by permission.

Excerpt on pages 901–902 from *There Will Come Soft Rains* by Ray Bradbury. Reprinted by permission of Don Congdon Associates, Inc. Copyright 1950, renewed 1977 by Ray Bradbury.

Excerpt on page 903 from "Reunion" in *The Brigadier and the Golf Widow*, © 1964 by John Cheever, reprinted by permission of Wylie, Aitken & Stone, Inc.

Excerpt on page 904 from "He" in *Flowering Judas and Other Stories*, © 1930 and renewed 1958 by Katherine Anne Porter, reprinted by permission of Harcourt Brace & Company.

Poem on page 905, "25th High School Reunion," by Linda Pastan in *The Five Stages of Grief*. Reprinted by permission of W. W. Norton & Company, Inc.

Excerpt on pages 906–907 from *The House of Ramon Iglesia*. Copyright 1983 by Jose Rivera.

Review on pages 907–908, " 'White Rose' Celebrates Anti-Nazi Heroes," by Lawrence Bommer, theater critic for the *Chicago Tribune*. Reprinted by permission of the author.

Review on page 909 of the book *In My Place*. Reprinted by permission of Phoebe-Lou Adams, *The Atlantic Monthly*.

The editor has made every effort to trace the ownership of all copyrighted material, and necessary permissions have been secured in most cases. Should there prove to be any question regarding the use of any material, regret is here expressed for such error. Upon notification of any such oversight, proper acknowledgment will be made in future editions.

TO THE STUDENT

If you're studying to pass the GED Tests, you're in good company, In 1994, the most recent year for which figures are available, over 750,000 people took the tests. Of this number, nearly 450,000 actually received their certificates. Why do so many people choose to take the GED Tests? Some do so to get a job or to get a better one than they already have. Others take the tests so that they can go on to college or vocational school. Still others pursue their GED diplomas to feel better about themselves or to set good examples for their children.

Americans and Canadians alike, from all walks of life, have passed their GED Tests and obtained diplomas. Some well-known graduates include country music singers Waylon Jennings and John Michael Montgomery, comedian Bill Cosby, Olympic gold medalist Mary Lou Retton, former New Jersey Governor James J. Florio, Wendy's Old-Fashioned Hamburgers founder Dave Thomas, Delaware State Senator Ruth Ann Minner, U.S. Senator Ben Nighthorse Campbell of Colorado, motion picture actor Kelly McGillis, Famous Amos Chocolate Chip Cookies creator Wally Amos, *Parade* magazine editor Walter Anderson, NBA referee Tommy Nuñez, and Triple Crown winner jockey Ron Turcotte.

This book has been designed to help you, too, succeed on the test. It will provide you with instruction in the skills you need to pass, background information on key concepts in the subject areas of writing skills, social studies, science, literature and the arts, and mathematics, and plenty of practice with the kinds of test items you will find on the real test.

WHAT DOES GED STAND FOR?

GED stands for the Tests of General Educational Development. The GED Test is a national examination developed by the GED Testing Service of the American Council on Education. The credential received for passing the test is widely recognized by colleges, training schools, and employers as equivalent to a high school diploma.

While the GED Test measures skills and knowledge normally acquired in four years of high school, much that you have learned informally or through other types of training can help you pass the test.

The GED Test is available in English, French, and Spanish and on audio-cassette, in Braille, and in large print.

WHAT SHOULD I KNOW TO PASS THE TEST?

The GED Test consists of five examinations in the areas of writing skills, social studies, science, literature and the arts, and mathematics. The chart on the next page outlines the main content areas, the breakdown of questions, and the time allowed per test.

THE GED TESTS			
Test	*Minutes*	*Questions*	*Percentage*
1: Writing Skills Part 1: Conventions of English	75	55	Sentence Structure 35% Usage 35% Mechanics 30%
Part 2: The Essay	45	1 topic	
2: Social Studies	85	64	History 25% Economics 20% Political Science 20% Geography 15%* Behavioral Sciences 20%*
3: Science	95	66	Life Sciences 50% Physical Sciences 50%
4: Literature and the Arts	65	45	Popular Literature 50% Classical Literature 25% Commentary 25%
5: Mathematics	90	56	Arithmetic 50% Algebra 30% Geometry 20%

*In Canada, 20% of the test is based on Geography and 15% on Behavioral Sciences.

On all five tests, you are expected to demonstrate the ability to think about many issues. You also are tested on knowledge and skills you have acquired from life experiences, television, radio, books and newspapers, consumer products, and advertising. In addition to the above information, keep these facts in mind:

1. Three of the five tests—Literature and the Arts, Science, and Social Studies—require that you answer questions based on reading passages or interpreting cartoons, diagrams, maps, charts, and graphs in these content areas. Developing strong reading and thinking skills is the key to succeeding on these tests.

2. The Writing Skills Test requires you to be able to detect and correct errors in sentence structure, grammar, punctuation, and spelling. You also will have to write a composition of approximately 200 words on a topic familiar to most adults.

3. The Mathematics Test consists mainly of word problems to be solved. Therefore, you must be able to combine your ability to perform computations with problem-solving skills.

WHO MAY TAKE THE TESTS?

In the United States, Canada, and many territories, people who have not graduated from high school and who meet specific eligibility requirements (age, residency, etc.) may take the tests. Since eligibility requirements vary, it would be useful to contact your local GED testing center or the director of adult education in your state, province, or territory for specific information.

WHAT IS A PASSING SCORE ON THE GED?

Again, this varies from area to area. To find out what you need to pass the test, contact your local GED testing center. However, you must keep two scores in mind. One score represents the minimum score you must get on each test. For example, if your state requires minimum scores of 40, you must get at least 40 points on every test. Additionally, you must meet the requirements of a minimum average score on all five tests. For example, if your state requires a minimum average score of 45, you must get a total of 225 points to pass. The two scores together, the minimum score and the minimum average score, determine whether you pass or fail the GED Test.

To understand this better, look at the scores of three people who took the test in a state that requires a minimum score of 40 and a minimum average score of 45 (225 total). Ann and Willie did not pass, but Ramon did. See if you can tell why.

	Ann	*Willie*	*Ramon*
Test 1	44	42	43
Test 2	43	43	48
Test 3	38	42	47
Test 4	50	40	52
Test 5	50	40	49
	225	207	239

Ann made the total of 225 points but fell below the minimum score on Test 3. Willie passed each test but failed to get the 225 points needed; just passing the individual tests was not enough. Ramon passed all the tests and exceeded the minimum score. Generally, to receive a GED credential, you must correctly answer half or a little more than half of the questions on each test.

MAY I RETAKE THE TEST?

You are allowed to retake some or all of the tests. Again, the regulations governing the number of times that you may retake the tests and the time you must wait before retaking them are set by your state, province, or territory. Some states require you to take a review class or to study on your own for a certain amount of time before taking the test again.

HOW CAN I BEST PREPARE FOR THE TEST?

Many libraries, community colleges, adult education centers, churches, and other institutions offer GED preparation classes. Some television stations broadcast classes to prepare people for the test. If you cannot find a GED preparation class locally, contact the director of adult education in your state, province, or territory or call the GED Hotline (800-62-MY-GED). This hotline will give you telephone numbers and addresses of adult education and testing centers in your area. The hotline is staffed 24 hours a day, seven days a week.

IF I STUDY ON MY OWN,
HOW MUCH TIME SHOULD I ALLOW TO PREPARE?

It depends on your readiness in each of the five subject areas; however, you should probably allow three to six months to do the following:

1. Read the introductory section of the book.

2. Take and score the five Pre-Tests. Decide which areas you need to focus on the most. Use the Countdown Checklist on pages xxi–xxii to help you plan your study program.

3. Complete the Reading Skills section of the book.

4. Read and complete the exercises in those areas that you decided to focus on.

5. Take the Post-Tests to determine how much improvement you've made.

6. Take the Practice Tests to determine whether you're ready for the real test.

7. Review the test-taking tips below.

8. Contact the GED Administrator or the director of adult education in your state, province, or territory and arrange to take the GED.

TEST-TAKING TIPS FOR SUCCESS

1. **Prepare physically.** Get plenty of rest and eat a well-balanced meal before the test so that you will have energy and will be able to think clearly. Last-minute cramming will probably not help as much as a relaxed and rested mind.

2. **Arrive early.** Be at the testing center at least 15 to 20 minutes before the starting time. Make sure you have time to find the room and to get situated. Keep in mind that many testing centers refuse to admit latecomers.

3. **Think positively.** Tell yourself you will do well. If you have studied and prepared for the test, you should succeed.

4. **Relax during the test.** Take half a minute several times during the test to stretch and breathe deeply, especially if you are feeling anxious or confused.

5. **Read the test directions carefully.** Be sure you understand how to answer the questions. If you have any questions about the test or about filling in the answer form, ask before the test begins.

6. **Know the time limit for each test.** Some testing centers allow extra time, while others do not. You may be able to find out the policy of your testing center before you take the test, but always work according to the official time limit. If you have extra time, go back and check your answers.

7. **Have a strategy for answering questions.** You should read through the reading passages, or look over the materials, once and then answer the questions that follow. Read each question two or three times to make sure you understand it. It is best to refer back to the passage or illustration in order to confirm your answer choice. Don't try to depend on your memory of what you have just read or seen. Some people like to guide their reading by skimming the questions before reading a passage. Use the method that works best for you.

8. **Don't spend a lot of time on difficult questions.** If you're not sure of an answer, go on to the next question. Answer easier questions first and then go back to the harder questions. However, when you skip a question, be sure that you have skipped the same number on your answer sheet. Although skipping difficult questions is a good strategy for making the most of your time, it is very easy to get confused and throw off your whole answer key.

   Lightly mark the margin of your answer sheet next to the numbers of the questions you did not answer so that you know what to go back to. To prevent confusion when your test is graded, be sure to erase these marks completely after you answer the questions.

9. **Answer every question on the test.** If you're not sure of an answer, take an educated guess. When you leave a question unanswered, you will always lose points, but you can possibly gain points if you make a correct guess.

   If you must guess, try to eliminate one or more answers that you are sure are not correct. Then choose from the remaining answers. Remember, you greatly increase your chances if you can eliminate one or two answers before guessing. Of course, guessing should be used only when all else has failed.

10. **Clearly fill in the circle for each answer choice.** If you erase something, erase it completely. Be sure that you give only one answer per question; otherwise, no answer will count.

11. **Practice test-taking.** Use the exercises, reviews, and especially the Post-Tests and Practice Tests in this book to better understand your test-taking habits and weaknesses. Use them to practice different strategies such as skimming questions first or skipping hard questions until the end. Knowing your own personal test-taking style is important to your success on the GED Test.

HOW TO USE THIS BOOK

1. You do not have to work through all of the five sections in this book. In some areas you are likely to have stronger skills than in others. However, before you begin this book you should take the Pre-Tests. These will give you a preview of what the five tests include, but more important, they will help you to identify which areas you need to concentrate on most. Use the **Evaluation Charts** at the end of the Pre-Tests to pinpoint the types of questions you answered incorrectly and to determine what skills you need extra work in.

2. Complete the sections of the book that the Pre-Tests indicate you need to review. However, to prepare yourself best for the test, work through the entire book.

3. After you have worked through the subject areas that needed strengthening as indicated by the Pre-Test scores, you should take the Post-Tests and Practice Tests at the end of this book. These tests will help you determine whether you are ready for the actual GED Test and, if not, what areas of the book you need to review. The Evaluation Charts are especially helpful in making this decision.

4. If you determine that you need still more practice at the GED level in answering the kinds of questions to be found on the GED Test, we recommend that you work through Contemporary's satellite series, available for each of the five GED subject areas:

> Test 1: Writing Skills
> Test 2: Social Studies
> Test 3: Science
> Test 4: Literature and the Arts
> Test 5: Mathematics

Additional titles that Contemporary offers for effective test preparation in math and writing include *The GED Math Problem Solver* and *The GED Essay*.

This book has a number of features designed to help make the task of preparing for the actual GED Test easier as well as effective and enjoyable:

- A special essay section helps to prepare you for the Writing Skills portion of the GED Test.

- A preliminary reading skills section of two chapters isolates the four thinking skills—comprehension, application, analysis, and evaluation—and provides plenty of practice in using these skills; it also provides practice in interpreting graphics and illustrations (these make up at least one-third of the Science and Social Studies Tests and a good portion of the Mathematics Test).

- Skill builders, hints, and tips help you increase your proficiency in the Writing Skills, Reading, and Literature and the Arts sections.

- A variety of exercise types maintain interest—matching, fill-in-the-blank, true-false, multiple-choice, and short essay questions.

- Writing across the curriculum—writing activities in science, social studies, and literature help you practice the skills introduced earlier in the Writing Skills section.

- U.S. history and science "trivia"—fascinating little-known facts add spice to the reading activities and exercises.

- Full-length Post-Tests and Practice Tests that are simulated GED Tests present questions in the format, level of difficulty, and percentages you will find on the actual tests.

- An answer key (coded by skill level) for each section explains the correct answers for the exercises.

- Evaluation charts for the Pre-Tests, Post-Tests, and Practice Tests help pinpoint weaknesses and refer you to specific pages for review.

- Hundreds of questions for strengthening your reading, writing, and thinking skills are provided.

Contemporary Books publishes a wide range of materials to help you prepare for the tests. These books are designed for home study or classroom use. Our GED preparation books are available through schools and bookstores and directy from the publisher. Our toll-free number is (800) 621-1918. For the visually impaired, a large-print version is available. For further information, call Library Reproduction Service (LRS) at (800) 255-5002.

COUNTDOWN CHECKLIST

This checklist will assist those who are studying on their own in planning their course of preparation for the GED examination. It will also be helpful as a guide in GED review classes. It is designed to help students spread out their study, pace themselves wisely, and be prepared for the GED Test.

Step 1

- Begin your review by taking and checking the Pre-Tests on pages 1–53. Take one Pre-Test at a time. Read as much as you can in your spare time.

Step 2

- Read and study the Reading Skills section—Chapters 1 and 2, pages 189–237. In addition, do as much extra reading as you can.

- If you think you need extra reading help, consider taking a reading test and a reading course at a local school or adult education center.

Step 3

- Go over the Evaluation Charts on the Pre-Tests, circling those areas in which you had the most trouble.

- Divide the instructional material into about ten weeks of work, focusing on those areas in which you need the most time to prepare.

- Below, fill in the pages you plan to complete each week. As you complete each assignment, check it off.

Week 1: pages _____   Week 6: pages _____
Week 2: pages _____   Week 7: pages _____
Week 3: pages _____   Week 8: pages _____
Week 4: pages _____   Week 9: pages _____
Week 5: pages _____   Week 10: pages _____

Step 4

- Take and check the Post-Tests and Practice Tests on pages 737–926.

- Based on where you had trouble, target pages you still need to review. Plan a three-week course to get yourself completely ready to take the **GED** Test.

  Week 1: pages _____
  Week 2: pages _____
  Week 3: pages _____

The night before the test—

- Review the test-taking tips on pages xviii–xix.

- Relax. Don't study.

- Get a good night's sleep.

The day of the test—

- Eat a good breakfast, but don't eat heavily.

- Think positively and relax.

- Leave yourself plenty of time to get there; arrive 15–20 minutes early.

Finally, we'd like to hear from you. If our materials have helped you to pass the test or if you feel that we can do a better job preparing you, write to us at the address on the back of the book to let us know. We hope you enjoy studying for the GED Test with our materials and wish you the greatest success.

The Editors

Pre-Tests

The Pre-Tests will help you determine what you need to study in this book. They are half-length tests in the format and level of difficulty of the real GED Test. The results of these tests, along with the Countdown Checklist on pages xxi–xxii, will help you map out a plan of study. We recommend the following approach to the Pre-Tests.

1. Take only one Pre-Test at a time. Don't attempt to do all of the tests at one sitting. Read the directions before you start a test. Use the answer sheets at the beginning of each test to mark your choices.

2. After you finish each Pre-Test, check the answers in the answer key and fill in the Evaluation Chart for that test. An answer key and an Evaluation Chart follow each test. For all of the questions that you miss, read explanations of the correct answers.

3. Based on the information in the Evaluation Charts, you may choose to do one of two things:

   • If you miss half or more of the questions in a Pre-Test, you should work through the entire subject area.
   • If you miss fewer than half of the questions, focus on particular areas of the test that gave you difficulty.

4. Even if you do well on a subject area Pre-Test, for best results you will want to review the chapters on Critical Thinking Skills, beginning on page 189, and Interpreting Graphs and Illustrations, beginning on page 223.

The order of the Pre-Tests and the time allotted for each is listed below.

Time Allowed for Each Test		
Writing Skills	Part 1	75 minutes
	Part 2	45 minutes
Social Studies		85 minutes
Science		95 minutes
Literature and the Arts		65 minutes
Mathematics		90 minutes

Although these are Pre-Tests, you should give them your best effort. If an item seems difficult, mark it and come back later. Always answer every question—even if you have to make an "educated guess." Sometimes you may know more than you give yourself credit for. Also, on the real GED Tests a blank counts as a wrong answer. It's always wise to answer every question as best you can.

PRE-TEST 1: WRITING SKILLS
Part 1: Conventions of English

Part 1 of the Writing Skills Pre-Test consists of 30 multiple-choice questions. The questions are based on paragraphs that contain numbered sentences. Most sentences contain errors, but a few may be correct as written. Read the paragraphs and then answer the questions based on them. For each item, choose the answer that would result in the best rewriting of the sentence or sentences. The best answer must be consistent with the meaning and tone of the rest of the paragraph.

Answer each question as carefully as possible, choosing the best of five answer choices and blackening in the grid. If you find a question too difficult, do not waste time on it. Work ahead and come back to it later when you can think it through carefully.

When you have completed the test, check your work with the answers and explanations at the end of the section.

Use the Evaluation Charts on page 11 to determine which areas you need to review most.

PRE-TEST 1: WRITING SKILLS ANSWER GRID

1 ① ② ③ ④ ⑤   9 ① ② ③ ④ ⑤   17 ① ② ③ ④ ⑤   24 ① ② ③ ④ ⑤

2 ① ② ③ ④ ⑤   10 ① ② ③ ④ ⑤   18 ① ② ③ ④ ⑤   25 ① ② ③ ④ ⑤

3 ① ② ③ ④ ⑤   11 ① ② ③ ④ ⑤   19 ① ② ③ ④ ⑤   26 ① ② ③ ④ ⑤

4 ① ② ③ ④ ⑤   12 ① ② ③ ④ ⑤   20 ① ② ③ ④ ⑤   27 ① ② ③ ④ ⑤

5 ① ② ③ ④ ⑤   13 ① ② ③ ④ ⑤   21 ① ② ③ ④ ⑤   28 ① ② ③ ④ ⑤

6 ① ② ③ ④ ⑤   14 ① ② ③ ④ ⑤   22 ① ② ③ ④ ⑤   29 ① ② ③ ④ ⑤

7 ① ② ③ ④ ⑤   15 ① ② ③ ④ ⑤   23 ① ② ③ ④ ⑤   30 ① ② ③ ④ ⑤

8 ① ② ③ ④ ⑤   16 ① ② ③ ④ ⑤

Choose the best answer to each question that follows.

Questions 1–9 refer to the following passage.

(1) Most fire-related death's result from household fires, yet many people do not have fire extinguishers in their homes. (2) There is smoke detectors in many homes to warn residents of a fire, but fire extinguishers can actually help people fight fires. (3) In most cases, everyone should evacuate a home when a fire has started or the smoke alarm sounds. (4) Someone outside the home should call the fire department. (5) However, if a fire extinguisher is handy, a quick-thinking person often can use them to put out a small fire. (6) There are several types of fire extinguishers on the market, and each are suitable for particular types of fire. (7) Most extinguishers come with instructions, they are very easy to operate. (8) Fire departments may be contacted for training in operating extinguishers. (9) A person should keep in mind some basic safety rules when you are deciding whether or not to use a fire extinguisher. (10) Buying a fire extinguisher knowing how to use it, and placing it in a location familiar to all family members can help protect families against fire.

1. Sentence 1: **Most fire-related death's result from household fires, yet many people do not have fire extinguishers in their homes.**

   What correction should be made to this sentence?

   (1) replace *death's* with *deaths*
   (2) change *result* to *results*
   (3) remove the comma after *fires*
   (4) change *have* to *has*
   (5) replace *their* with *there*

2. Sentence 2: **There is smoke detectors in many homes to warn residents of a fire, but fire extinguishers can actually help people fight fires.**

   Which of the following is the best way to write the underlined portion of this sentence? If you think the original is the best way, choose option (1).

   (1) There is
   (2) Their is
   (3) They're is
   (4) There are
   (5) Their are

3. Sentences 3 and 4: **In most cases, everyone should evacuate a home when a fire has started or the smoke alarm sounds. Someone outside the home should call the fire department.**

   The most effective combination of sentences 3 and 4 would contain which of the following groups of words?

   (1) sounds, and someone
   (2) sounds and call
   (3) sounds, or someone
   (4) sounds unless someone
   (5) sounds and should call

4. Sentence 5: **However, if a fire extinguisher is handy, a quick-thinking person often can use them to put out a small fire.**

   Which of the following is the best way to write the underlined portion of this sentence? If you think the original is the best way, choose option (1).

   (1) them
   (2) him
   (3) it
   (4) they
   (5) theirs

5. Sentence 6: **There are several types of fire extinguishers on the market, and each are suitable for particular types of fire.**

   What correction should be made to this sentence?

   (1) replace *There are* with *There is*
   (2) remove the comma after *market*
   (3) replace *and* with *or*
   (4) replace *each are* with *each is*
   (5) change the spelling of *particular* to *particuler*

6. Sentence 7: **Most extinguishers come with instructions, they are very easy to operate.**

   Which of the following is the best way to write the underlined portion of this sentence? If you think the original is the best way, choose option (1).

   (1) instructions, they are
   (2) instructions and are
   (3) instructions, are
   (4) instructions and they are
   (5) instructions; and are

7. Sentence 8: **Fire departments may be contacted for training in operating extinguishers.**

   What correction should be made to this sentence?

   (1) replace *departments* with *Departments*
   (2) replace *may be* with *were*
   (3) change the spelling of *operating* to *opperating*
   (4) replace departments with department's
   (5) no correction is necessary

8. Sentence 9: **A person should keep in mind some basic safety <u>rules when you are deciding</u> whether or not to use a fire extinguisher.**

   Which of the following is the best way to write the underlined portion of this sentence? If you think the original is the best way, choose option (1).

   (1) rules when you are deciding
   (2) rules when deciding
   (3) rules you decide
   (4) rules when you decided
   (5) rules. You are deciding

9. Sentence 10: **Buying a fire extinguisher knowing how to use it, and placing it in a location familiar to all family members can help protect families against fire.**

   What correction should be made to this sentence?

   (1) insert a comma after *extinguisher*
   (2) change *placing* to *place*
   (3) replace *members* with *member's*
   (4) insert a comma after *help*
   (5) change the spelling of *families* to *familys*

Questions 10–19 refer to the following passage.

(1) A european concept in overnight lodging known as "bed and breakfast" is becoming popular in the United States. (2) Private citizens act as hosts and rent out spare bedrooms in there homes. (3) The hosts provide a home-cooked breakfast and a bedroom appropriatly designed to offer their guests privacy in a cozy setting. (4) While most American travelers expect to find lodging in a hotel or motel, the recent popularity of bed and breakfasts offer a new alternative to travelers. (5) Staying in a private home offers travelers a more personal atmosphere; as a result, they feel pampered and enjoy visiting with the hosts. (6) Saying that they feel safer and like being treated as guests, the bed and breakfast hosts make them feel at home. (7) Travelers can learn much about the history and people of the local area; for example, visitors currently stayed on Wisconsin dairy farms and in restored log cabins in Kentucky. (8) If travelers cannot afford a long trip, they can still enjoy a peaceful getaway weekend as houseguests. (9) The hosts also benefit from running such a business because they can stay at home, make money, and meeting a variety of people. (10) Most State tourism departments and some travel agencies have bed and breakfast listings.

10. Sentence 1: **A european concept in overnight lodging known as "bed and breakfast" is becoming popular in the United States.**

What correction should be made to this sentence?

(1) change *european* to *European*
(2) replace *known* with *is known*
(3) replace *is* with *are*
(4) replace *States* with *states*
(5) no correction is necessary

11. Sentence 2: **Private citizens act as hosts and rent out spare bedrooms in there homes.**

What correction should be made to this sentence?

(1) replace *citizens* with *citizen's*
(2) change *act* to *acted*
(3) change *rent* to *renting*
(4) add a comma after *hosts*
(5) replace *there* with *their*

12. Sentence 3: **The hosts provide a home-cooked breakfast and a bedroom appropriatly designed to offer their guests privacy in a cozy setting.**

What correction should be made to this sentence?

(1) change *provide* to *provides*
(2) insert a comma after *breakfast*
(3) change the spelling of *appropriatly* to *appropriately*
(4) replace *designed* with *design*
(5) no correction is necessary

13. Sentence 4: **While most American travelers expect to find lodging in a hotel or motel, the recent popularity of bed and breakfasts offer a new alternative to travelers.**

What correction should be made to this sentence?

(1) change *expect* to *expects*
(2) remove the comma after *motel*
(3) change *offer* to *offers*
(4) replace *new* with *knew*
(5) replace *to* with *too*

14. Sentence 5: **Staying in a private home offers travelers a more personal atmosphere; as a result, they feel pampered and enjoy visiting with the hosts.**

    If you rewrote sentence 5 beginning with

    Because staying in a private home offers travelers a more personal atmosphere,

    the next word should be

    (1) as
    (2) feeling
    (3) hosts
    (4) they
    (5) the

15. Sentence 6: **Saying that they feel safer and like being treated as guests, <u>the bed and breakfast hosts make them feel at home.</u>**

    Which of the following is the best way to write the underlined portion of this sentence? If you think the original is the best way, choose option (1).

    (1) the bed and breakfast hosts make them feel at home.
    (2) feeling at home with the bed and breakfast hosts.
    (3) the bed and breakfast hosts feel at home with travelers.
    (4) are the bed and breakfast hosts feeling at home.
    (5) the travelers feel at home with the bed and breakfast hosts.

16. Sentence 7: **Travelers can learn much about the history and people of the local area; for example, visitors currently stayed on Wisconsin dairy farms and in restored log cabins in Kentucky.**

    What correction should be made to this sentence?

    (1) replace *can* with *did*
    (2) remove the comma after *example*
    (3) replace *stayed* with *can stay*
    (4) add a comma after *farms*
    (5) no correction is necessary

17. Sentence 8: **If travelers cannot afford a long trip, they can still enjoy a peaceful getaway weekend as houseguests.**

    If you rewrote sentence 8 beginning with

    Travelers who cannot afford a long trip

    the next word should be

    (1) they
    (2) can
    (3) if
    (4) a
    (5) enjoying

18. Sentence 9: **The hosts also benefit from running such a business because they can stay at home, make money, <u>and meeting</u> a variety of people.**

    Which of the following is the best way to write the underlined portion of this sentence? If you think the original is the best way, choose option (1).

    (1) and meeting
    (2) and meet
    (3) to meet
    (4) and be meeting
    (5) get to meet

19. Sentence 10: **Most State tourism departments and some travel agencies have bed and breakfast listings.**

    What correction should be made to this sentence?

    (1) change *State* to *state*
    (2) change *tourism* to *Tourism*
    (3) insert a comma after *departments*
    (4) insert a comma after *agencies*
    (5) change *have* to *has*

Questions 20–30 refer to the following passage.

(1) Recently, educators exammined the effectiveness of computer instruction in American schools. (2) The educators were dismayed to find the issue of sexism and immediately analyzed the results. (3) The studies revealing that, for various reasons, girls spent less time working with computers than boys. (4) By the 1980s many American schools had began to offer computer classes or clubs. (5) Only half as many girls as boys were enrolled in computer-programming classes. (6) Schools with computer clubs and camps reported that membership consisted of many more boys than girls. (7) Some educators were frustrated because they have not become as interested in using computers.

(8) One factor to explain this discrepancy was that many of the early computer games were similar to the Space Invader video games that girls viewed as boys games. (9) Researchers also speculate that some teachers might have given boys more computer time because parents and teachers expected boys to need computers for future careers. (10) Some schools, especially at the elementary level, had only a few computers, so teachers had to choose the students which got to use them. (11) Not surprisingly, boys will be more likely to be chosen to use computers than girls. (12) Because of these findings, educators have recommended that teachers and parents encourage girls to use computers by providing opportunities and exposure to the machines.

20. Sentence 1: **Recently, educators exammined the effectiveness of computer instruction in American schools.**

What correction should be made to this sentence?

(1) replace *educators* with *educator's*
(2) change the spelling of *exammined* to *examined*
(3) replace *computer* with *computer's*
(4) change *schools* to *Schools*
(5) no correction is necessary

21. Sentence 2: **The educators were dismayed to find the issue of sexism and immediately analyzed the results.**

If you rewrote sentence 2 beginning with

Dismayed to find the issue of sexism,

the next words should be

(1) the American schools
(2) their analysis
(3) the educators
(4) computers
(5) the results

22. Sentence 3: **The studies revealing that, for various reasons, girls spent less time working with computers than boys.**

Which of the following is the best way to write the underlined portion of this sentence? If you think the original is the best way, choose option (1).

(1) studies revealing
(2) studies' revelations
(3) studies revealed
(4) studies will reveal
(5) revealing studies

23. Sentence 4: **By the 1980s many American schools had began to offer computer classes or clubs.**

What correction should be made to this sentence?

(1) replace *American* with *american*
(2) change *had began* to *had begun*
(3) replace *classes* with *class's*
(4) change *clubs* to *Clubs*
(5) no correction is necessary

24. Sentences 5 and 6: **Only half as many girls as boys were enrolled in computer-programming classes. Schools with computer clubs and camps reported that membership consisted of many more boys than girls.**

The most effective combination of sentences 5 and 6 would include which of the following groups of words?

(1) classes, schools
(2) classes in schools
(3) classes; furthermore, schools
(4) classes, or schools
(5) classes; however, schools

25. Sentence 7: **Some educators were frustrated because they have not become as interested in using computers.**

Which of the following is the best way to write the underlined portion of this sentence? If you think the original is the best way, choose option (1).

(1) they
(2) educators
(3) computers
(4) girls
(5) boys

26. Sentence 8: **One factor to explain this discrepancy was that many of the early computer games were similar to the Space Invader video games that girls viewed as boys games.**

What correction should be made to this sentence?

(1) add a comma after *was*
(2) change *were* to *was*
(3) replace *girls* with *girls'*
(4) change the spelling of *viewed* to *veiwed*
(5) replace *boys* with *boys'*

27. Sentence 9: **Researchers also speculate that some teachers might have given boys more computer time because parents and teachers expected boys to need computers for future careers.**

Which of the following is the best way to write the underlined portion of this sentence? If you think the original is the best way, choose option (1).

(1) expected
(2) will have expected
(3) expecting
(4) will expect
(5) will be expecting

28. Sentence 10: **Some schools, especially at the elementary level, had only a few computers, so teachers had to choose the students which got to use them.**

What correction should be made to this sentence?

(1) change the spelling of *especially* to *especialy*
(2) remove the comma after *level*
(3) remove the comma after *computers*
(4) replace *which* with *who*
(5) no correction is necessary

29. Sentence 11: **Not surprisingly, <u>boys will be</u> more likely to be chosen to use computers than girls.**

Which of the following is the best way to write the underlined portion of this sentence? If you think the original is the best way, choose option (1).

(1) boys will be
(2) boys' will be
(3) boys are
(4) boys' were
(5) boys were

30. Sentence 12: **Because of these <u>findings, educators</u> have recommended that teachers and parents encourage girls to use computers by providing opportunities and exposure to the machines.**

Which of the following is the best way to write the underlined portion of this sentence? If you think the original is the best way, choose option (1).

(1) findings, educators
(2) findings educators
(3) findings; educators
(4) findings. Educators
(5) findings, and educators

Answers begin on page 10.

Part 2: The Essay

Directions: This part of the test is designed to find out how well you write. The test has one question that asks you to present an opinion on an issue or to explain something. In preparing your answer to this question, you should take the following steps:

1. Read all of the information accompanying the question.

2. Plan your answer carefully before you write.

3. Use scratch paper to mark any notes.

4. Write your answer on a separate sheet of paper.

5. Read carefully what you have written and make any changes that will improve your writing.

6. Check your paragraphing, sentence structure, spelling, punctuation, capitalization, and usage and make any necessary corrections.

Take 45 minutes to plan and write on the following topic. Write legibly and use a ballpoint pen.

Topic

People decide to obtain a GED certificate for a wide variety of reasons. Some are interested in changing jobs, while others simply want to finish something they started a long time ago.

Why have you decided to study for the GED? Explain your decision and what you hope to gain by it. Be sure to give examples and to be specific.

Information on evaluating your essay is on page 11.

PRE-TEST 1: WRITING SKILLS ANSWER KEY
Part 1: Conventions of English

1. **(1)** The plural of *death* is *deaths*. No possession (*death's*) is shown.
2. **(4)** The subject is *detectors*, so the verb must agree with the plural subject.
3. **(1)** The new sentence would read, "In most cases, everyone should evacuate a home when a fire has started or the smoke alarm sounds, and someone outside the home should call the fire department."
4. **(3)** The pronoun *them* incorrectly refers to the singular noun *extinguisher*. The pronoun *it* is singular.
5. **(4)** The indefinite pronoun *each* is always singular, so the verb must agree with a singular subject.
6. **(2)** The original sentence is a comma splice. It incorrectly joins two complete thoughts with only a comma. Only choice (2) is punctuated correctly.
7. **(5)** No correction is necessary.
8. **(2)** This choice eliminates the incorrect pronoun *you*, which does not fit in the passage.
9. **(1)** This sentence contains a series of three items that should be separated by commas.
10. **(1)** The word *European* is derived from the name of a continent, *Europe*, so it should always be capitalized.
11. **(5)** The possessive pronoun *their* should be used here to show that the homes belong to the hosts.
12. **(3)** Keep a silent *e* when adding *ly* to *appropriate*.
13. **(3)** The subject, *popularity*, is singular, so the verb must agree with a singular subject: *popularity offers*.
14. **(4)** The new sentence would read, "Because staying in a private home offers travelers a more personal atmosphere, they feel pampered and enjoy visiting with the hosts."
15. **(5)** The phrase *Saying that they feel safer and like being treated as guests* describes the travelers, not the hosts. Choice (5) puts the phrase next to *travelers*.
16. **(3)** This sentence, as well as the passage as a whole, is written in present tense: travelers *can stay*.
17. **(2)** The new sentence would read, "Travelers who cannot afford a long trip can still enjoy a peaceful getaway weekend as houseguests."
18. **(2)** Each of the parts of the series, *can stay at home, make money,* and *meet a variety of people,* must be parallel in wording.
19. **(1)** The term *state tourism departments* is not the name of a specific agency. *State* should not be capitalized.
20. **(2)** This commonly misspelled word has one *m*, not two.
21. **(3)** The new sentence would read, "Dismayed to find the issue of sexism, the educators immediately analyzed the results."
22. **(3)** The original sentence is a fragment because the verb, *revealing*, requires a helping verb. The verb form *revealed* is complete.
23. **(2)** The past participle of the irregular verb *begin* is *begun*: *had begun*.
24. **(3)** The new sentence would read, "Only half as many girls as boys were enrolled in computer-programming classes; furthermore, schools with computer clubs and camps reported that membership consisted of many more boys than girls."
25. **(4)** The pronoun *they* is vague. It should be replaced by *girls* to make the meaning of the sentence more clear.
26. **(5)** The plural possessive, *boys'*, should be used to show that the sentence means "games for boys."
27. **(1)** There is no error.
28. **(4)** The pronoun *who* should be used to refer to people.
29. **(5)** The passage as a whole is written in the past tense, so *were* is correct.
30. **(1)** There is no error.

Use the answer key on page 10 to check your answers to the Pre-Test. Then find the item number of each question you missed and circle it on the chart below to determine the writing content areas in which you need more practice. Pay particular attention to areas where you missed half or more of the questions. The page numbers for the content areas are listed below on the chart. For those questions that you missed, review the skill pages indicated.

PRE-TEST 1: WRITING SKILLS EVALUATION CHART

Content Area	Item Number	Review Pages
Nouns, Pronouns	1, 26	60–64, 80–92
Verbs	23, 29	65–76
Subject-Verb Agreement	2, 5, 13	76–79
Pronoun Reference	4, 8, 25, 28	82–92
Sentence Fragments	22	93–98
Sentence Combining	3, 6, 14, 17, 21, 24	95–107
Sequence of Tenses	16	109–110
Misplaced/Dangling Modifiers	15	111–112
Parallel Structure	18	112–116
Capitalization	10, 19	117–119
Punctuation	9	119–125
Spelling	11, 12, 20	126–141
No Error	7, 27, 30	—

Part 2: The Essay

If possible, give your essay to an instructor to evaluate. That person's opinion of your writing will be useful in deciding what further work you need to write a good essay.

If, however, you are unable to show your work to someone else, you can try to evaluate your own essay. If you can answer *yes* to the five questions in the Essay Evaluation Checklist, your essay would *probably* earn an upper half score (4, 5, or 6) on Part 2 of the Writing Skills Test. If you receive any *no* answers on your evaluation checklist, you should read your essay carefully to see how it could be improved and review Chapter 4 of the Writing Skills section.

Essay Evaluation Checklist

YES   NO

____ ____ 1. Does the essay answer the question asked?

____ ____ 2. Does the main point of the essay stand out clearly?

____ ____ 3. Does each paragraph contain specific examples and details that help prove the main point?

____ ____ 4. Can you follow how the writer has arranged and linked ideas in sentences and paragraphs?

____ ____ 5. Is the writer's control of grammar and usage effective enough so that you were able to read the essay easily and smoothly?

PRE-TEST 2: SOCIAL STUDIES

The Social Studies Pre-Test consists of 30 multiple-choice questions. Some of the questions are based on maps, charts, graphs, cartoons, and reading passages.

Answer each question as carefully as possible, choosing the best of five answer choices and blackening in the grid. If you find a question too difficult, do not waste time on it. Work ahead and come back to it later when you can think it through carefully.

When you have completed the test, check your work with the answers and explanations at the end of the section.

Use the Evaluation Chart on page 24 to determine which areas you need to review most.

PRE-TEST 2: SOCIAL STUDIES ANSWER GRID

1 ① ② ③ ④ ⑤	9 ① ② ③ ④ ⑤	17 ① ② ③ ④ ⑤	24 ① ② ③ ④ ⑤
2 ① ② ③ ④ ⑤	10 ① ② ③ ④ ⑤	18 ① ② ③ ④ ⑤	25 ① ② ③ ④ ⑤
3 ① ② ③ ④ ⑤	11 ① ② ③ ④ ⑤	19 ① ② ③ ④ ⑤	26 ① ② ③ ④ ⑤
4 ① ② ③ ④ ⑤	12 ① ② ③ ④ ⑤	20 ① ② ③ ④ ⑤	27 ① ② ③ ④ ⑤
5 ① ② ③ ④ ⑤	13 ① ② ③ ④ ⑤	21 ① ② ③ ④ ⑤	28 ① ② ③ ④ ⑤
6 ① ② ③ ④ ⑤	14 ① ② ③ ④ ⑤	22 ① ② ③ ④ ⑤	29 ① ② ③ ④ ⑤
7 ① ② ③ ④ ⑤	15 ① ② ③ ④ ⑤	23 ① ② ③ ④ ⑤	30 ① ② ③ ④ ⑤
8 ① ② ③ ④ ⑤	16 ① ② ③ ④ ⑤		

Choose the best answer to each question that follows.

Questions 1–3 are based on the following news report.

KAMPALA, Uganda [Reuters]—A young boy with all the behavioral traits of a monkey has been found living wild in the jungle of the notorious Luwero Triangle, site of massacres and killings during Uganda's civil war.

The boy, believed to be 5 to 7 years old, shuns human company and moves by jumping from place to place like a monkey with his fists clenched. If he is approached, he scratches. When he is still, he squats on his rump. He eats grass or anything else he can find.

Last September, Ugandan government troops retreating from a rebel army found him living with monkeys. He is now at the Naguru orphanage in Kampala, where nurses have given him the name Robert.

Staffers at the orphanage believe Robert lost his parents when he was about a year old during the fighting in the Luwero area and was mothered by a [primate] chimpanzee or a gorilla.

He is about 2½ feet tall and weighs 22 pounds. He grunts and squeals but does not speak.

Theresa Nansikombi, who runs the orphanage, said that when Robert was brought to Naguru he fled from humans, cried all the time and tried to hide his face.

"He ate anything and still does— grass, clothes, blankets and sheets— even stones," she said.

"He looks miserable all the time."

1. The findings in this case support the belief that

    (1) humans can survive in only one environment or culture
    (2) people know what skills and tools are necessary to survive
    (3) humans are descended directly from the monkeys
    (4) human behavior is not instinctive; it is learned
    (5) primates are the only species to teach their young

2. Robert was raised by the monkeys because he

    (1) ran away from home
    (2) lost his parents during a war
    (3) was intentionally abandoned
    (4) was kidnapped and later abandoned
    (5) chose to be raised by them

3. This passage illustrates how Robert has learned certain behaviors from the primates. Which one of the following is an example of a learned, not an instinctive, behavior.

    (1) Babies tend to respond to bright colors.
    (2) Babies babble and squeal before they can talk.
    (3) Infants can be taught to swim because they have not yet learned to fear water.
    (4) Children like security blankets because the blankets give them comfort.
    (5) Infants tend to put objects they can grasp into their mouths.

4. American consumers are not spending their money as freely as they have in the past. As a result, sales of personal computers have been affected. According to the dynamics of supply and demand, what will happen to the price of computers? The price will

    (1) increase to make up for the loss in profits
    (2) remain the same because the cost to manufacture computers stays the same
    (3) decrease to encourage consumers to buy them
    (4) increase in order for manufacturers to improve the quality of computers
    (5) remain the same because fewer computers will be available for sale

Questions 5 and 6 are based on the following cartoon.

Morin
Miami Herald

5. The cartoonist is suggesting that

(1) terrorists have bigger and better weapons than ever before
(2) terrorists deliberately use the media to publicize and promote their causes
(3) terrorists cover their faces because they are afraid to be identified by the media
(4) to terrorists, the media is the real enemy
(5) terrorists want to dominate the world

6. In recent years, the media has been criticized for "glamorizing" certain news events such as terrorist activities. Some people feel that this excessive coverage contributes to an increase in the number of incidents. The media's handling of which of the following could be criticized largely for the same reasons?

(1) the AIDS epidemic affecting Americans
(2) the bloody casualties suffered in Central America
(3) anti-apartheid violence in South Africa
(4) teen suicides in recent years
(5) widespread drug busts in major cities

Questions 7–9 are based on the bar graph below.

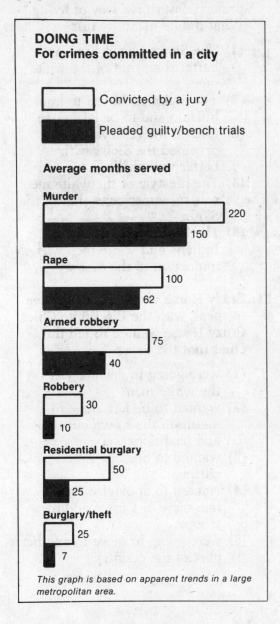

DOING TIME
For crimes committed in a city

☐ Convicted by a jury

■ Pleaded guilty/bench trials

Average months served

Murder
220
150

Rape
100
62

Armed robbery
75
40

Robbery
30
10

Residential burglary
50
25

Burglary/theft
25
7

This graph is based on apparent trends in a large metropolitan area.

7. Which of the following statements is best supported by the information in the graph?

   (1) Accused criminals are better off insisting on their right to a jury trial.
   (2) In this city, accused criminals are better off pleading guilty and accepting a bench trial presided over by a judge.
   (3) Juries do not understand the impact of their decisions.
   (4) Criminal courts in this city are harsher on criminals than in most other cities.
   (5) Criminal courts in this city are more lenient with convictions than in most cities.

8. What values are being given priority by juries in criminal cases in this city?

   (1) the punishment of the criminal over the safety of the community
   (2) the needs of the criminal over the advice of the judge
   (3) the life of the criminal over the needs of the community
   (4) the safety of the community over sympathy for the criminal
   (5) the rights of the criminal over a strict interpretation of the law

9. If defendants have knowledge of the information in the graph, it is reasonable to predict that

   (1) the number of jury trials will increase
   (2) the number of jury trials will remain the same
   (3) the number of bench trials will increase
   (4) juries will give lighter sentences
   (5) judges presiding over bench trials will give harsher sentences

Questions 10 and 11 are based on the following passage.

"We Preferred Our Own Way of Living"

My friend, I do not blame you for this. Had I listened to you this trouble would not have happened to me. I was not hostile to the white men. Sometimes my young men would attack the Indians who were their enemies and took their ponies. They did it in return.

We had buffalo for food, and their hides for clothing and for our teepees. We preferred hunting to a life of idleness on the reservation, where we were driven against our will. At times we did not get enough to eat, and we were not allowed to leave the reservation to hunt.

We preferred our own way of living. We were no expense to the government. All we wanted was peace and to be left alone. Soldiers were sent out in the winter, who destroyed our villages.

Then "Long Hair" (Custer) came in the same way. They say we massacred him, but he would have done the same thing to us had we not defended ourselves and fought to the last. Our first impulse was to escape with our squaws and papooses, but we were so hemmed in that we had to fight.

After that I went up on the Tongue River with a few of my people and lived in peace. But the government would not let me alone. Finally, I came back to the Red Cloud Agency. Yet I was not allowed to remain quiet.

I was tired of fighting. I went to the Spotted Tail Agency and asked that chief and his agent to let me live there in peace. I came here with the agent (Lee) to talk with the Big White Chief, but was not given a chance. They tried to confine me. I tried to escape, and a soldier ran his bayonet into me.

I have spoken.

10. Crazy Horse, chief of the Sioux Indians in the 1870s, said, "We preferred our own way of living." What did he mean by this?

(1) The Sioux way of life was better than that of the white men.
(2) The Sioux preferred to hunt buffalo and to be left alone.
(3) Life on the reservation provided the Sioux with a better way of life.
(4) The lifestyle of the white men was far superior to that of the Sioux.
(5) The hostility between the Indians and white men was important to the Sioux.

11. Crazy Horse went with agent Lee to speak with the Big White Chief. Crazy Horse wanted to tell the chief that the Sioux

(1) were going to declare war on the white men
(2) wanted to be left alone to maintain their own culture and traditions
(3) wanted to become American citizens
(4) wanted to apologize for the massacre of Custer and his troops
(5) were going to move to another part of the country

Questions 12–14 are based on the following passage.

The great rule of conduct for us in regard to foreign nations is, in extending our commercial relations, to have with them as little *political* connection as possible. So far as we have already formed engagements, let them be fulfilled with perfect good faith. Here let us stop.

Europe has a set of primary interests which to us have none or a very remote relation. Hence she must be engaged in frequent controversies, the causes of which are essentially foreign to our concerns. Hence, therefore, it must be unwise in us to implicate ourselves by artificial ties in the ordinary vicissitudes [changes] of her politics or the ordinary combinations and collisions of her friendships or enmities. . . .

It is our true policy to steer clear of permanent alliances with any portion of the foreign world. . . .

from George Washington's
Farewell Address

12. Which one of the following statements reflects George Washington's attitude as expressed in this address?

The United States should

(1) offer its assistance wherever needed in the world
(2) avoid becoming involved in world political affairs
(3) stay out of European affairs while assisting other areas of the world
(4) become as politically connected with Europe as possible
(5) support policies that would increase the territory under its control

13. Based on this quote, Washington may be described *best* as a(n)

(1) patriot
(2) imperialist
(3) isolationist
(4) colonialist
(5) expansionist

14. Based on his address, what would George Washington think of America's position today as a world power? He would think that the United States

(1) has been successful in leaving other nations alone
(2) has achieved its primary goal of being a world power
(3) should continue to control the other nations of the world
(4) has become involved in affairs that are none of America's business
(5) has not changed much from the time when he was president

Question 15 is based on the following chart.

THE RELATIONSHIP BETWEEN INCOME AND EDUCATION, 1990	
Level of Education	**Median Income**
Elementary 8 years or less	$14,336
High School 1 to 3 years 4 years	$17,155 $21,642
College 1 to 3 years 4 years	$26,094 $32,056

Source: U.S. Bureau of the Census

15. Which of the following conclusions is supported by the chart?

(1) No relationship exists between education level and income.
(2) All people with an elementary school education will earn at least $14,336 per year.
(3) A college education is required to earn over $26,000 per year.
(4) Education alone determines a person's income.
(5) People who have more education are more likely to earn a higher income.

Question 16 is based on the paragraph below.

The Monroe Doctrine demanded that Europe stay out of the affairs of the Americas. President Theodore Roosevelt used the doctrine to support a position on imperialism that he called the "Roosevelt Corollary." It stated that the United States had a right to move into areas of the Americas needing our civilizing power.

16. In which incident would Roosevelt have used the corollary to defend his actions?

(1) his approval of England's colonization of India and Egypt

(2) the United Nations' participation in a conference to end French-German rivalry in Morocco

(3) his support for the Open Door policy for trade with China

(4) his negotiating an informal understanding between the United States and Japan to end unwanted immigration

(5) the aiding of Panamanian rebels against the Colombian government

---

17. Before the Civil War, Virginia was united; however, in 1863, West Virginia chose to become independent. Which is the most reasonable cause of West Virginia's secession from the rest of the state?

(1) The state was too large for only one legislature.

(2) West Virginia was defeated by the North early in the war.

(3) Richmond, Virginia, became the capital of the Confederacy.

(4) There were no slave owners in West Virginia.

(5) Political differences existed between western Virginia and the eastern part of the state.

Questions 18 and 19 are based on the following graph and passage.

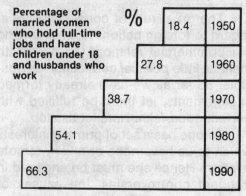

Percentage of married women who hold full-time jobs and have children under 18 and husbands who work	%		
		18.4	1950
		27.8	1960
	38.7		1970
54.1			1980
66.3			1990

Source: Scholastic Update Magazine

The way a male or female acts or is expected to act in society is called a *role*. The traditional role in the American family for the husband has been breadwinner while the wife's role has been homemaker. According to the bar graph above, however, family roles are changing.

18. Which of the following is *least likely* to be considered a cause of the changing role of married women in the family?

(1) increased expenses requiring a second income in many families

(2) more women wanting careers in addition to raising a family

(3) the lack of respect accorded the traditional role of homemaker

(4) increased availability of day care centers and professional baby-sitters

(5) more job opportunities for women than ever before

19. According to the bar graph, during which time period was there the greatest increase in the percentage of married women in the work force?

(1) Before 1950

(2) 1950–1960

(3) 1960–1970

(4) 1970–1980

(5) 1980–1990

Questions 20 and 21 are based on the following cartoon.

LARRY WRIGHT
Courtesy Detroit News

20. Which of the following would most likely agree with the cartoonist's viewpoint?

(1) an opponent of high-rise office development

(2) a conservative politician who is concerned about too many government regulations

(3) the surgeon general who lobbied in favor of printed warnings on cigarette packages

(4) a liberal politician who believes the government should protect the interests of its citizens

(5) a congressman who favors mandatory seat belt laws in all fifty states

21. The main idea the cartoonist is expressing is that the FDA

(1) should be abolished because it violates civil liberties

(2) is experiencing a hiring freeze and is firing longtime employees

(3) has gone to ridiculous extremes in safeguarding the public against potentially harmful products

(4) has control over too many products sold to consumers

(5) focuses too much on products the public considers harmless

---

22. Between 1935 and 1957, the birth rate rose from 16.9 to 25 per 1,000 people. The most likely cause of this "baby boom" was

(1) the return of young American soldiers from war

(2) the growth of the urban/ suburban areas after World War II

(3) the increased mobility of the American family of the 1950s

(4) the continuing expansion of the middle class and its new wealth

(5) the relaxing of moral sanctions against artificial birth control methods

23. Increased personal income lets people purchase more goods and services. For example, spending for houses and cars increases as people feel comfortable in making long-term investments. In such a climate, business would likely

(1) increase production to provide greater quantities of goods

(2) lower the sales tax on the products

(3) spend less money on new equipment and machinery

(4) sell the products to foreign nations

(5) distribute the products equally throughout the country

Questions 24 and 25 are based on the following graph.

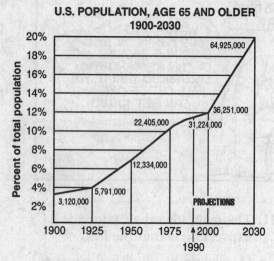

U.S. POPULATION, AGE 65 AND OLDER 1900-2030

24. The number of people in the United States over the age of 65 is increasing dramatically. Which one of the following governmental programs would be most directly affected by this growth?

   (1) veterans' benefits
   (2) national defense
   (3) job training and employment programs
   (4) food stamps
   (5) social security

25. The largest increase in the number of people in the U.S. age 65 years and older occurred during which of the following time periods?

   (1) 1900–1925
   (2) 1925–1950
   (3) 1950–1975
   (4) 1975–1990
   (5) 1990–2000

Questions 26 and 27 are based on the following passage.

In 1992, Australia's Prime Minister, Paul Keating, urged that the country cut its remaining political ties with Britain and become a republic instead of a commonwealth. Britain is no longer a major factor in Australia's economic security. Today, almost half of Australia's exports go to Asia, and Asian immigration to Australia is on the rise. With a declining economy, Australians must decide where their best interests lie.

26. Based on the information in the passage, you can conclude that

   (1) Paul Keating is in favor of continued commonwealth status.
   (2) Australia's economy will most likely improve if it develops further relations with Asia.
   (3) Australia is isolated to maintain its economy.
   (4) Politics has nothing to do with geographical location.
   (5) Many Australians agree with the prime minister.

27. The decision facing the Commonwealth of Australia is most similar to

   (1) the decision to transfer Hong Kong from British rule to Chinese rule
   (2) the decision of the Commonwealth of Kentucky to join the United States
   (3) the decision to adopt Guam as a territory of the United States
   (4) the decision of Puerto Rico about whether to request statehood or remain a commonwealth
   (5) the decision of the thirteen original American colonies to form a new nation

Questions 28 and 29 are based on the following map.

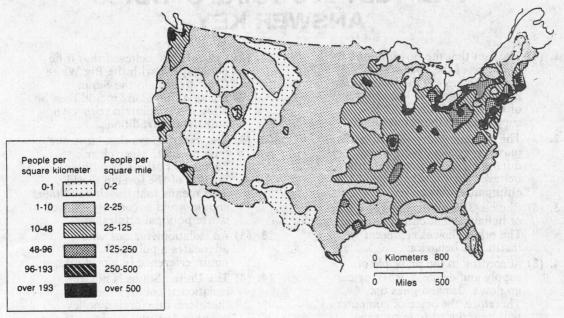

People per square kilometer		People per square mile
0-1	⋯⋯	0-2
1-10		2-25
10-48		25-125
48-96		125-250
96-193		250-500
over 193		over 500

0   Kilometers   800

0   Miles   500

28. Based on the map, which one of the following pairs of cities has over 500 people per square mile?

   (1) Miami/Los Angeles
   (2) Houston/New York
   (3) Atlanta/Boston
   (4) Chicago/San Francisco
   (5) Detroit/Dallas

29. The region of the country with the greatest population density is the

   (1) Midwest
   (2) Southwest
   (3) Northwest
   (4) Southeast
   (5) Northeast

Question 30 is based on the following passage.

   Vice President Andrew Johnson succeeded Lincoln as president after Lincoln's assassination. Johnson was from Tennessee and was the only southern senator not to join the Confederacy when war broke out. Lincoln had trusted him totally, but many in Congress did not. In spite of Johnson's refusal to join the Confederacy, his every action appeared to be suspiciously pro-South to them.

30. Which of the following actions of Johnson's does *not* support these congressmen's opinion of him?

   (1) his issuing a proclamation forgiving most Confederates
   (2) his demand that Confederate states ratify the Thirteenth Amendment abolishing slavery
   (3) his veto of the civil rights bill that guaranteed rights to freed slaves
   (4) his veto of the Freedman's Bureau bill that had been approved without the input of the southern states
   (5) his opposition to the Fourteenth Amendment that toughened Congress's stand against former Confederate loyalists

Answers begin on page 22.

PRE-TEST 2: SOCIAL STUDIES ANSWER KEY

1. (4) The fact that the boy imitated the behavior of the apes with which he lived supports the belief that human behavior is learned. None of the other choices can be supported by the information.

2. (2) The passage states that Robert's parents probably were killed during Uganda's civil war. It is believed that he was raised by a chimpanzee or gorilla.

3. (3) Choice (3) is an example of a type of behavior that can be learned. The other choices represent instinctive behavior.

4. (3) According to the principle of supply and demand, when prices go down, demand goes up. Therefore, the price of computers will be reduced to encourage more people to buy them.

5. (2) Terrorist acts get wide publicity. For this reason, terrorists are perceived as using the media to promote their causes.

6. (4) Psychologists have noted that incidents of teenage suicides increase after the reporting of such acts. This is the only case shown in which the glamour attached to an act leads to increased incidence.

7. (2) The graph shows that the average number of months served by criminals convicted by a jury is greater than the sentence imposed by a judge at a bench trial. Therefore, you can conclude that accused criminals are better off pleading guilty and accepting a bench trial instead of a jury trial.

8. (4) The longer sentences imposed by juries suggest that they value the community's safety over mercy for the criminal.

9. (3) If bench trials continue to provide shorter sentences than jury trials for convicted criminals, then you could predict that more defendants will demand bench trials and that the number of bench trials will increase.

10. (2) The Sioux were content with their lifestyle and did not want the white men to interfere with them, as suggested by choice (2).

11. (2) Crazy Horse believed that if he could speak with the Big White Chief to explain the Sioux position, the Sioux would then be allowed to maintain their own culture and traditions.

12. (2) The excerpt says that "It is our true policy to steer clear of permanent alliances with any portion of the foreign world. . . ." This means that the United States should avoid becoming involved in world political affairs.

13. (3) An isolationist is one who advocates a policy of noninterference in world affairs.

14. (4) The United States is not an isolationist country today; therefore, our foreign policy position does not conform to the spirit of isolationism expressed in Washington's address.

15. (5) The chart indicates a higher income as the level of education increases.

16. (5) Like the Monroe Doctrine, the Roosevelt Corollary applied only to countries in the Americas; Panama and Colombia are located in Central and South America respectively.

17. (5) West Virginia was different from eastern Virginia in culture, religion, nationality, and economy. Therefore, it is most reasonable to conclude that West Virginia seceded from the rest of the state because of political differences.

18. (3) Choices (1), (2), (4), and (5) are all plausible reasons for married women joining the work force. Choice (3) is least likely to be a reasonable explanation for married women entering the work force.

19. (4) Between 1970 and 1980, the percentage of married women who work increased by 15.4 percent—from 38.7 to 54.1 percent.

20. (2) The FDA is a government agency that protects consumers. In the cartoon, the cartoonist is criticizing the tendency for regulators to "go overboard." Of all the choices, a conservative politician who is concerned about too much government regulation would most likely agree with the cartoonist's viewpoint.

21. (3) It is obvious that a person who falls out of a tall building can die. The FDA's proposal to ban the construction of tall buildings for this reason can be viewed as ridiculous. None of the other choices is suggested by the cartoon.

22. (1) Quick marriages after soldiers returned from war is the most reasonable explanation for the surge in births. Choices (2), (3), and (4) did not contribute directly to the baby boom. Choice (5) is not a reasonable explanation.

23. (1) When consumers spend more money, businesses capitalize on the increased spending by producing more goods to sell.

24. (5) The social security program would be the most affected because it provides payments to the retired and the elderly.

25. (3) From 1950 to 1975, the population of Americans 65 years of age and older increased from 12,334,000 to 22,405,000—an increase of over 10,000,000 people.

26. (2) The passage states that almost half of Australia's exports already go to Asia. Further relations with Asia would most probably improve the economy.

27. (5) Both Australia and the thirteen original American colonies were dominated by another nation. Like the colonies, Australia wants to be politically and economically independent. By becoming a republic, Australia would also become an independent nation. The other choices involve incorporation of one country into another.

28. (4) Chicago, located at the southern tip of Lake Michigan, and San Francisco, located along the central Pacific coast, make up the only pair of cities that has over 500 people per square mile.

29. (5) The areas of the country with the greatest number of people per square mile are represented in black. The northeastern part of the country has more black areas than any other.

30. (2) Johnson's demand that the states ratify an amendment abolishing slavery was not a pro-southern action, while all of the other choices could be interpreted as being pro-southern.

Use the answer key on pages 22–23 to check your answers to the Pre-Test. Then find the item number of each question you missed and circle it on the chart below to determine the reading skill and content areas in which you need more practice. Pay particular attention to areas where you missed half or more of the questions. The reading skills are covered on pages 187–243. The page numbers for the content areas are listed below on the chart. Knowledge of reading skill and content area–based questions is absolutely essential for success on the GED Social Studies Test. The numbers in boldface are questions based on graphics. For those questions that you missed, review the skill pages indicated.

PRE-TEST 2: SOCIAL STUDIES EVALUATION CHART

Skill Area/ Content Area	Comprehension (pages 189–195)	Application (pages 195–199)	Analysis (pages 200–210)	Evaluation (pages 211–222)
Behavioral Sciences (pages 247–262)	25	3, **24**	2, 22	1, 18
U.S. History (pages 263–300)	10, 11	13, 16	14, 17	12, 30
Political Science (pages 301–318)	7, 21	6	5, 9	8, 20
Economics (pages 319–332)	19	23	4	**15**
Geography (pages 333–342)	29	27	**28**	26

PRE-TEST 3: SCIENCE

The Science Pre-Test consists of 30 multiple-choice questions. Some of the questions are based on charts, graphs, diagrams, and reading passages.

Answer each question as carefully as possible, choosing the best of five answer choices and blackening in the grid. If you find a question too difficult, do not waste time on it. Work ahead and come back to it later when you can think it through carefully.

When you have completed the test, check your work with the answers and explanations at the end of the section.

Use the Evaluation Chart on page 34 to determine which areas you need to review most.

PRE-TEST 3: SCIENCE ANSWER GRID

1 ① ② ③ ④ ⑤   9 ① ② ③ ④ ⑤   17 ① ② ③ ④ ⑤   24 ① ② ③ ④ ⑤

2 ① ② ③ ④ ⑤   10 ① ② ③ ④ ⑤   18 ① ② ③ ④ ⑤   25 ① ② ③ ④ ⑤

3 ① ② ③ ④ ⑤   11 ① ② ③ ④ ⑤   19 ① ② ③ ④ ⑤   26 ① ② ③ ④ ⑤

4 ① ② ③ ④ ⑤   12 ① ② ③ ④ ⑤   20 ① ② ③ ④ ⑤   27 ① ② ③ ④ ⑤

5 ① ② ③ ④ ⑤   13 ① ② ③ ④ ⑤   21 ① ② ③ ④ ⑤   28 ① ② ③ ④ ⑤

6 ① ② ③ ④ ⑤   14 ① ② ③ ④ ⑤   22 ① ② ③ ④ ⑤   29 ① ② ③ ④ ⑤

7 ① ② ③ ④ ⑤   15 ① ② ③ ④ ⑤   23 ① ② ③ ④ ⑤   30 ① ② ③ ④ ⑤

8 ① ② ③ ④ ⑤   16 ① ② ③ ④ ⑤

Choose the best answer to each question that follows.

Question 1 is based on the following passage.

Our blood consists of a liquid, the straw-colored *plasma*, in which are suspended red blood cells, white blood cells, and *platelets*. Red blood cells are used to transport oxygen throughout the body. The different types of white blood cells are used to fight infections. Platelets are important in blood clotting.

1. Based on the passage above, which of the following blood components would be used to repair an open wound?

   (1) plasma and white blood cells
   (2) red blood cells
   (3) white blood cells
   (4) platelets
   (5) white blood cells and platelets

Questions 2 and 3 are based on the following information.

The leaf is a flat organ composed of two layers of photosynthetic cells sandwiched between the epidermal, or outer, layers. The epidermal layers are coated with a waxy covering called the *cuticle*, which prevents the loss of gas and water. Tiny holes, called *stomata*, provide openings for the entry of carbon dioxide and the exit of oxygen.

2. Based on the information above, the leaf "breathes" through its

   (1) photosynthetic cells
   (2) veins
   (3) cuticle
   (4) epidermal layers
   (5) stomata

3. Stomata in plants are most similar to which of the following?
   A. lungs in mammals
   B. pores in animal skin
   C. gills in fish

   (1) A
   (2) B
   (3) C
   (4) A and B
   (5) B and C

Questions 4 and 5 are based on the table below.

Energy Expenditure	
Activity	**Calories per Hour**
sitting at rest	15
walking	130–200
running	500–900
bicycling	240
swimming	200–700
writing	20

4. According to the table above, which of the people listed below would need to consume 720 calories to maintain body weight after three hours of his or her chosen activity?

   (1) a runner
   (2) a bicyclist
   (3) an office worker
   (4) a writer
   (5) a swimmer

5. For a person concerned with weight loss, which would be the most efficient weight-loss exercise for the time spent?

   (1) bicycling
   (2) swimming
   (3) walking
   (4) writing
   (5) running

Question 6 is based on the following illustration.

| S | N | | N | S |

6. As the two bar magnets above are brought closer together, what do you predict will happen?

   (1) They will attract each other.
   (2) They will repel each other.
   (3) They will cancel out each other's magnetic field.
   (4) They will create an alternating current.
   (5) Nothing will happen.

Questions 7–10 are based on the following passage.

Charles Darwin proposed the theory of natural selection in 1859. The theory holds that those species that are best adapted to the conditions under which they live will survive, and those that are not adapted will perish.

An example of this theory is illustrated by the experience of the peppered moth that was once common near Manchester, England, an industrial city.

Before the industrial revolution, the light-colored form of this moth was common and the dark-colored form was rare. As Manchester's environment became increasingly polluted, however, the tree trunks on which the peppered moth lived became blackened by soot. The light-colored form of the moth stood out against the dark tree trunks and was eaten by birds, which destroyed 99 percent of the light-colored moths.

In the absence of the light-colored moths, the rare dark moths became more common and filled the vacancy left by the light-colored moths. In the 1950s, however, Manchester's industries were cleaned up, the tree trunks became lighter, and the light-colored moth became the more common type again.

7. Based on the passage above, the cause of the light-colored moth's disappearance was

   (1) an inability to tolerate a polluted environment
   (2) the birds' preference for its taste
   (3) an insecticide that killed it
   (4) the reduced number of eggs laid by female moths
   (5) its inability to blend in with its environment

8. Which of the following was *not* a factor in the disappearance of the light-colored moth?

   (1) the industrial pollution found near Manchester
   (2) the presence of moth-eating birds
   (3) the change in the color of the tree trunks
   (4) the interbreeding of light-colored moths with dark-colored moths
   (5) the moth's inability to adapt to a changing environment

9. Based on the information in the passage, you can infer that

   (1) forms of life in a community are influenced by nature's laws
   (2) human activity can have significant ecological impact on an environment
   (3) Darwin's theory works only under ideal circumstances
   (4) all forms of life must fend for themselves
   (5) moths can thrive under the worst conditions

10. Which of the following trees would have bark most favorably suited to the light-colored moth, enabling it to blend in with its surroundings?

    (1) elm
    (2) pine
    (3) paper birch
    (4) red maple
    (5) oak

11. Acetylsalicylic acid (aspirin) is known to retard the blood-clotting process. This can have both positive and negative effects. One positive application of this knowledge is the use of aspirin to

(1) relieve pain
(2) reduce inflammation
(3) reduce the possibility of stroke
(4) act as a stimulant
(5) stop bleeding

Questions 12–14 are based on the following passage.

There is, perhaps, no part of the world where the early geological periods can be studied with so much ease and precision as in the United States. Along the northern border between Canada and the United States, there runs a low line of hills known as the Laurentian Hills. Insignificant in height, nowhere rising more than two thousand feet above the level of the sea, these are nevertheless the first mountains that broke the uniform level of Earth's surface and lifted themselves above the waters. Their low stature, as compared with that of other, loftier mountain ranges, is in accordance with an invariable rule by which the relative age of mountains may be estimated. The oldest mountains are the lowest, while the younger and more recent ones tower above their elders and are usually more jagged and dislocated.

12. In the United States, early geological periods

(1) can be studied only along the country's northern border
(2) can be studied only in the Rocky Mountains
(3) can be studied easily and precisely
(4) are not as visible as in the rest of the world
(5) can be studied only in the Appalachian Mountains

13. The relationship between low mountain ranges and high mountain ranges can be described *best* in terms of

(1) old age and youth
(2) the Laurentian Hills
(3) the Swiss Alps and the Himalayas
(4) dislocation and thickness
(5) their location in either Canada or the United States

14. The Appalachian Mountains are lower than the Rocky Mountains. Therefore, based on the passage, the Appalachian Mountains would be

(1) younger than the Rocky Mountains
(2) older than the Rocky Mountains
(3) the same age as the Rocky Mountains
(4) more scenic than the Rocky Mountains
(5) more torn and dislocated than the Rocky Mountains

Question 15 is based on the information and table below.

Heat is able to pass from one molecule to another. This is called *heat conduction*. In the table that follows, the numbers (called coefficients) indicate the relative rates of heat transfer in the materials listed.

HEAT CONDUCTION COEFFICIENTS

Material	Coefficient
silver	100
copper	92
aluminum	50
iron	11
glass	0.20
water	0.12
wood	0.03
air	0.006
perfect vacuum	0

15. The table identifies the best conductors as

    (1) gases
    (2) natural materials
    (3) metals
    (4) liquids
    (5) compounds

Question 16 is based on the following passage.

Tsunamis are seismic sea waves that may be produced by earthquakes, volcanic eruptions, or submarine landslides. They travel at speeds from 500 to 800 kilometers per hour and in the open ocean may be only 30 to 60 centimeters in height. However, as they approach land they are compressed and may reach 30 meters in height.

16. Tsunamis would be very dangerous to humans because of the potential for causing

    (1) earthquakes
    (2) severe flooding
    (3) submarine landslides
    (4) fault lines
    (5) volcanic eruptions

Questions 17 and 18 are based on the following passage.

Loess is a deposit of windblown dust that slowly blankets large areas and often covers existing landforms. A distinctive sedimentary deposit, loess was laid down long ago. It may cover as much as one-tenth of Earth's surface and is particularly widespread in semi-arid regions along the margins of great deserts. The equatorial tropics and the areas once covered by continental glaciers are free of loess.

17. A nation in which loess would likely be found today is

    (1) Republic of the Congo
    (2) Iceland
    (3) Japan
    (4) United States
    (5) Ecuador

18. The equatorial tropics are free of loess most probably because of the absence of which of the following?

    (1) sun
    (2) aridity
    (3) rain
    (4) glaciers
    (5) running water

Question 19 is based on the diagram below.

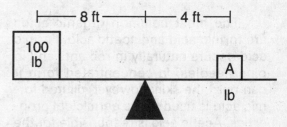

19. In order to balance the lever in the diagram above, how much must object A weigh?

    (1)   50 pounds
    (2)   100 pounds
    (3)   200 pounds
    (4)   500 pounds
    (5) 1,000 pounds

Question 20 is based on the following information.

The Fathometer is a device used for determining ocean depths. It operates by sending sound waves under water. A sudden pulse of sound is transmitted by a ship and then picked up again after it has been reflected, or echoed, from the sea bottom, and the elapsed time is recorded. Knowing the time and the speed of sound waves through water, the depth of the sea at any point may be computed, often to the nearest foot.

20. From the information in the passage, you can conclude that

    (1) the depth of the ocean is already known
    (2) the speed at which underwater sound waves travel from the ocean's surface to the bottom remains constant
    (3) Fathometers show only approximate depths and are, therefore, unreliable
    (4) Fathometers work best in shallow waters
    (5) Fathometers operate on scientific and not mathematical principles

Questions 21–23 are based on the following information.

The most common organic acids are formic acid and acetic acid. Formic acid occurs naturally in red ants and in pine needles. In concentrated form it can burn the skin; however, diluted formic acid is used for its germicidal properties. Acetic acid is responsible for the sour taste of pickles and sharp odors that can burn the nostrils. Cider vinegar contains 3 to 6 percent acetic acid and is made by the natural oxidation of apple cider.

21. The main idea of the passage above is that

    (1) organic acid can be both harmful and beneficial
    (2) formic acid is a part of vinegar
    (3) pine needles contain acetic acid
    (4) undiluted formic acid is used as a germicide
    (5) apple cider turns into formic acid

22. Which of the following organic acids occurring in low concentrations is essential to humans but is highly dangerous when humans are exposed to high concentrations of it?

    (1) citric acid found in citrus fruits
    (2) lactic acid found in milk products
    (3) hydrochloric acid found in the stomach's gastric juices
    (4) oxalic acid found in rhubarb leaves
    (5) folic acid, a form of Vitamin B used to treat anemia

23. The passage supports the statement that

    (1) all acids are harmful to humans
    (2) only organic acids are useful to humans
    (3) organic acids in diluted form are useful to humans
    (4) inorganic acids in diluted form are useful to humans
    (5) only diluted inorganic acids are beneficial to humans

Question 24 is based on the following passage.

In a normal person, glutamic acid, a protein-based acid, is found in hemoglobin; however, in persons who have sickle-cell anemia, valine is found in the hemoglobin instead of glutamic acid. This mutation becomes part of the genetic code and is passed on from generation to generation. Sickle-cell anemia occurs in about 10 percent of African-Americans in the United States and in approximately 25 percent of native African blacks.

24. The facts in this passage support which of the following?

(1) Sickle-cell anemia is not a serious health problem in the United States.
(2) Sickle-cell anemia is gradually declining worldwide.
(3) Sickle-cell anemia is related to the physical environment.
(4) Sickle-cell anemia cannot be cured by means of drugs or medication.
(5) Sickle-cell anemia has been discovered only recently.

---

25. Which of the following represents the three states of matter?

(1) water, vinegar, and vegetable oil
(2) rocks, water, and sand
(3) salt, pepper, and sugar
(4) air, helium, and carbon dioxide
(5) ice, water, and water vapor

Questions 26–28 are based on the chart below.

TRANSFUSION RELATIONSHIP		
Blood Type	Can Receive Blood from	Acts as Donor to
O	O	O, A, B, AB
A	A, O	A, AB
B	B, O	B, AB
AB	O, A, B, AB	AB

26. What type(s) of blood can be given to a person with blood type A?

(1) only type O
(2) only types O and A
(3) only types O and B
(4) only types A and AB
(5) any blood type

27. If a person with blood type AB wishes to donate blood, those with which blood type(s) may receive the blood?

(1) only type O
(2) only types O and B
(3) only types B and AB
(4) only type AB
(5) all types of blood

28. Which of the following blood types can be regarded as a universal donor?

(1) O
(2) A
(3) B
(4) AB
(5) all blood types

Question 29 is based on the following information.

An unusual flowering plant is the *hydrangea*, a shrub that produces showy flowers in the shape of a pom-pom. The hydrangea is unusual in that the color of its flower indicates the type of soil in which it grows. An acidic soil produces a pink bloom, and an alkaline soil produces a blue flower.

29. The characteristic of a change in color is most similar to which of the following tests?

    A. the pH test for alkalinity and acidity
    B. the iodine test for the presence of starch
    C. the litmus-paper test

    (1) A
    (2) B
    (3) C
    (4) A and B
    (5) A and C

Question 30 is based on the following information.

Have you ever wondered how a photograph is made? What actually happens when you push that button to record an image?

When you push the button on a camera, the shutter opens, allowing light to strike the film in the camera. The film is usually coated with silver bromide. The light rays strike the film and reduce the silver bromide, making it less stable.

In black-and-white film, the silver bromide particles that are struck by light turn black when the film is developed. Particles that have not been struck by light will not change. Since the chemical reduction depends on the intensity of light, the film becomes a detailed chemical picture of the object photographed. The developing process converts the chemical pictures into film negatives.

30. What could you conclude if a negative turned out completely black?

    (1) The silver and bromide had been resynthesized into silver bromide.
    (2) The light rays were not strong enough to reduce the silver bromide.
    (3) The film was too old to use.
    (4) The film had not been developed.
    (5) The film had been overexposed to light.

Answers begin on page 33.

PRE-TEST 3: SCIENCE ANSWER KEY

1. **(5)** The passage says that white blood cells fight infections and that platelets are important in clotting of blood. Fighting infections and blood clotting are two processes needed to repair a wound.

2. **(5)** According to the passage, the only opening in the leaf is the stomata. This must be the "mouth" through which a plant breathes.

3. **(2)** Pores, tiny openings in the skin's epidermis, allow the skin to breathe, thus serving a function similar to the stomata in plant leaves.

4. **(2)** A bicyclist would consume approximately 720 calories in three hours ($240 \times 3 = 720$).

5. **(5)** Running consumes the most calories per hour, so it is the most efficient weight-loss activity among those listed.

6. **(2)** Like charges repel; unlike charges attract. The north poles of each magnet are alike, so they will repel each other.

7. **(5)** According to the passage, the light-colored moth was preyed upon by birds when it was no longer able to blend in with the soot-darkened tree trunks on which it lived.

8. **(4)** The interbreeding of light-colored moths with dark-colored moths was not mentioned in the passage.

9. **(2)** The industrial pollution in Manchester that darkened the tree trunks was caused by humans.

10. **(3)** Of the trees listed, the paper birch has the lightest bark, which would enable the light-colored peppered moth to blend in with the environment.

11. **(3)** Since aspirin retards clotting, it is used to reduce the possibility of a stroke, which is caused by the arteries in the brain being blocked by clotted blood.

12. **(3)** The passage says that the early geological periods can be studied with ease and precision.

13. **(1)** The passage describes the relationship between old age and youth; the low mountains are the oldest, and the high mountains are the youngest.

14. **(2)** The Appalachian Mountains are lower than the Rocky Mountains; therefore, the Appalachian Mountains are older.

15. **(3)** The metals silver, copper, aluminum, and iron have the highest heat conduction coefficients; therefore, they are the best conductors among the materials listed.

16. **(2)** Tsunamis are giant waves of water. They would create severe flooding and damage in populated coastal areas.

17. **(4)** Of the countries listed, only the United States has semiarid regions bordering the desert.

18. **(2)** The passage says that loess is widespread in semiarid regions along the margins of great deserts. The tropics are not semiarid but are extremely humid.

19. **(3)** If object A is half as far away from the middle of the lever as the 100-pound weight, then to balance, it must weigh twice as much, or 200 pounds.

20. **(2)** Sound waves must travel at a constant speed through the sea in order for the principle under which a Fathometer works to be valid.

21. **(1)** The passage shows how organic acids can be both beneficial and harmful. Diluted formic acid has germicidal properties, but concentrated formic acid is corrosive and burns. Acetic acid is beneficial because it is used to make pickles but is harmful because its sharp odors can irritate the nostrils.

22. **(3)** Diluted hydrochloric acid is found in the stomach's gastric juices, but undiluted hydrochloric acid is harmful when humans are exposed to it.

23. **(3)** The passage demonstrates how organic acids are beneficial to humans. Examples of beneficial organic acids are formic acid, which can be used as a germicide, and acetic acid, which is used in the processing of cucumbers to make pickles.

24. **(4)** Since sickle-cell anemia is genetic, it has no medical cure. Only a change in genetic material would eliminate the disease.

25. **(5)** The three states of matter are solid, liquid, and gas. Ice is a solid, water is a liquid, and water vapor is a gas.

26. **(2)** Look across the row that starts with blood type A. You can see that a person with blood type A can receive blood from blood types O and A.

27. **(4)** Look across the row on the table that starts with blood type AB. You can see that a person with blood type AB can act as a donor only to a person with blood type AB.

28. **(1)** Since people with blood type O can donate blood to people of all blood types, a person with blood type O is known as a universal donor.

29. **(3)** The characteristic of the hydrangea is most similar to the litmus-paper test. According to the litmus-paper test, acids turn the coloring matter in the litmus paper red, and bases or alkalies turn it blue.

30. **(5)** The last paragraph states that reduced particles of silver bromide turn black when film is developed. If a negative is completely black, then all of the silver bromide must have been reduced by light, indicating overexposure.

Use the answer key on pages 33–34 to check your answers to the Pre-Test. Then find the item number of each question you missed and circle it on the chart below to determine the reading skill and content areas in which you need more practice. Pay particular attention to areas where you missed half or more of the questions. The reading skills are covered on pages 187–243. The page numbers for the content areas are listed below on the chart. Knowledge of reading skill and content area–based questions is absolutely essential for success on the GED Science Test. The numbers in boldface are questions based on graphics. For those questions that you missed, review the skill pages indicated.

PRE-TEST 3: SCIENCE EVALUATION CHART

Skill Area/ Content Area	Comprehension (pages 189–195)	Application (pages 195–199)	Analysis (pages 200–210)	Evaluation (pages 211–222)
Biology (pages 355–374)	1	4, 7, 9, 30	3, 10, **26, 27, 28**	5, 8
Earth Science (pages 375–398)	12, 16	13, 14, 18	17	
Chemistry (pages 399–418)	21	2	11, 22, 29	23, 24
Physics (pages 419–440)	15, 25	**6, 19**		20

PRE-TEST 4: LITERATURE AND THE ARTS

The Literature and the Arts Pre-Test consists of 24 multiple-choice questions. These questions are based on passages of fiction and nonfiction prose, poetry, drama, and commentaries on literature and the arts.

Answer each question as carefully as possible, choosing the best of five answer choices and blackening in the grid. If you find a question too difficult, do not waste time on it. Work ahead and come back to it later when you can think it through carefully.

When you have completed the test, check your work with the answers and explanations at the end of the section.

Use the Evaluation Chart on page 44 to determine which areas you need to review most.

PRE-TEST 4: LITERATURE AND THE ARTS ANSWER GRID

1 ① ② ③ ④ ⑤   7 ① ② ③ ④ ⑤   13 ① ② ③ ④ ⑤   19 ① ② ③ ④ ⑤

2 ① ② ③ ④ ⑤   8 ① ② ③ ④ ⑤   14 ① ② ③ ④ ⑤   20 ① ② ③ ④ ⑤

3 ① ② ③ ④ ⑤   9 ① ② ③ ④ ⑤   15 ① ② ③ ④ ⑤   21 ① ② ③ ④ ⑤

4 ① ② ③ ④ ⑤   10 ① ② ③ ④ ⑤   16 ① ② ③ ④ ⑤   22 ① ② ③ ④ ⑤

5 ① ② ③ ④ ⑤   11 ① ② ③ ④ ⑤   17 ① ② ③ ④ ⑤   23 ① ② ③ ④ ⑤

6 ① ② ③ ④ ⑤   12 ① ② ③ ④ ⑤   18 ① ② ③ ④ ⑤   24 ① ② ③ ④ ⑤

Read each excerpt and choose the best answer to each question.

Questions 1–4 refer to the following biographical sketch.

HOW DID ELVIS PRESLEY ACHIEVE RECOGNITION?

Success often comes to those with humble beginnings. Elvis Aron Presley was born on January 8, 1935, in Tupelo, Mississippi. He first
5 sang in a church choir and taught himself to play the guitar, but he never learned to read music. By 1953, he had moved to Memphis, Tennessee, graduated from high
10 school, and enrolled in night school to become an electrician. That year, at Sun Records, Presley recorded a personal record for his mother, a song that was heard by the com-
15 pany's president. As a result of the president's recognition, Presley's first record, "That's All Right, Mama," was cut in 1954.

He toured the South, and in
20 1955 five of his records were released simultaneously. His first national television appearance was that year on Jackie Gleason's "The Stage Show," but Presley became
25 known for his appearance on "The Ed Sullivan Show," where the young singer gyrated as he sang "rock 'n' roll" music. During the live television performance, Presley was photo-
30 graphed only from the waist up because his motions were considered obscene.

"Elvis the Pelvis" began his film career in 1956 with *Love Me Tender*
35 and signed a long-term film contract. The movie critics were not always kind, but teenagers flocked to Presley's films. Within a few short years, Presley had established a ca-
40 reer that would span twenty-five years of ups and downs and make him one of the most popular entertainers in history. Long after his untimely death at age 42, Presley
45 would be remembered as "The King of Rock 'n' Roll."

1. The author uses the phrase *ups and downs* to refer to Presley's

   (1) use of drugs, "uppers and downers"
   (2) gyrations as he performed
   (3) the best of rock 'n' roll music
   (4) successes and disappointments in his career
   (5) increasing and decreasing finances

2. The last sentence reveals that the author's attitude toward Presley is one of

   (1) indifference
   (2) admiration
   (3) disgust
   (4) disbelief
   (5) sarcasm

3. The main idea of the sketch is that

   (1) there has always been obscenity on television
   (2) singers are more successful if they appear in films
   (3) celebrities are usually more famous after their death
   (4) success always comes to those who work hard
   (5) opportunity and luck are often as important as hard work

4. The statement that "success often comes to those with humble beginnings" would apply best to which of the following historical figures?

   (1) multimillionaire Pierre DuPont
   (2) John F. Kennedy
   (3) Franklin D. Roosevelt
   (4) Abraham Lincoln
   (5) oil billionaire J. Paul Getty

Questions 5–10 refer to the following excerpt from a short story.

WHAT DOES GOLDIE KRAMER WANT?

"Are you ready to be a citizen of the United States of America?" His voice was suddenly stern.

5 She became rigid. "Sure, sure, Judge!" Her hand jerked. "Of course, I want to be a citizner." Tears welled in her eyes.

"Do you understand what is meant by the Constitution?"

10 Fear blanched her face. *Constitution*! She wanted to talk but couldn't.

He looked at her keenly. "Constitution. Do you know what that 15 means?"

Her eyes wandered from his face to the flag, to the clerk, to the bailiff. Where was Krakauer? Where was Slemo Marcus? She looked at 20 the pictures of Washington and Lincoln on the wall behind the bench. "Ye-ye-yeah!" she stuttered.

She saw the clerk smiling, and she remembered. "Oh, Constitu-25 tion!" she cried. "Constitution! Judge, I'm surprised! Constitution is the laws of the land. 'We, the People of the United States because we want to make a perfect govern-30 ment—' We have Congress, is Senators, two to a State, and Representatives, lots of them, and a President, a Supreme Court—" She tittered. "Oh Judge, I been studying the 35 Constitution. Ask me anything, Judge!"

He brushed at his mouth and chin. "So you know the Constitution, Goldie Kramer? Good. Now 40 tell me what is the capital of the United States?"

Again she was horror-stricken. She heard Jacob Krakauer harumphing at her side. "Vashington," 45 she replied nervously. Her fingers knit together and her lips quivered to pronounce the name: "Washington."

"Who makes the laws? Do you 50 know that?"

Her tongue was thick and her knees were trembling. "Congress makes the laws."

"What does the Supreme Court 55 do?"

"You want," she began timidly, "I should say the truth?"

He nodded. His eyes crinkled.

"Then, Judge, if it's the truth—60 the Supreme Court they say if the law that Congress makes is any good."

The gavel rapped as an audible chuckling rattled about the bench. 65 "Goldie Kramer, what do you know about the President?"

She beamed. "Oh, the President is thirty-five years old. At least. He has a job four years. Maybe 70 more if the people want him. He works hard, Judge. Then he becomes an ex-President."

Gravely the Judge studied his papers. He spoke briefly to the wit-75 nesses. "That's all, Goldie Kramer."

She frowned. "That is all you are going to ask me, Judge?"

"That's all."

"But I learned so much, Judge!" 80 She gestured excitedly. Krakauer and Marcus nudged her, but she ran on. "For three months now I studied and you don't ask me—"

The Judge pulled at his ear. 85 "Very good, Goldie Kramer. One more question. Do you love this country?"

She smiled. "Oh, Judge, what a question! Do I love it? Who wouldn't 90 love such a country? Forty years I been here. My oldest boy he died in France. My grandson will fly an airplane soon for the Army." Her dark eyes flashed. "Judge, even if you 95 gave me some other countries, gave them to me free—just like that—I wouldn't take them. But America, Judge—America is for me—and me, I'm for America!"

100 The courtroom applauded. The Judge smiled.

—Louis Zara, excerpted from "The Citizner," 1946

5. If you were to make a film of the excerpt, which of the following locales would make the best setting?

   (1) a criminal courtroom
   (2) a naturalization court
   (3) an Ellis Island immigration processing office
   (4) a police station
   (5) U.S. Senate chambers

6. Goldie Kramer is a

   (1) recent immigrant to the United States
   (2) Native American
   (3) citizen seeking employment outside the United States
   (4) U.S. resident seeking citizenship
   (5) grandmother seeking custody of her grandson

7. Goldie can best be described as

   (1) anxious and emotional
   (2) self-assured and calm
   (3) overly confident
   (4) defeated and troubled
   (5) lighthearted and eager

8. " 'But I learned so much, Judge!' She gestured excitedly. Krakauer and Marcus nudged her, but she ran on." The author includes this to show that

   (1) the judge was angered by Goldie's behavior
   (2) her friends encouraged her to continue speaking
   (3) the tension was increasing in the room
   (4) Goldie was too frightened to speak
   (5) her friends were trying to silence her

9. A writer may use different methods to create characters and make them come to life. Which of the five methods below is *not* used in the excerpt above?

   (1) showing the character's actual speech patterns
   (2) showing what others say about the character
   (3) revealing the character's private thoughts
   (4) describing the character
   (5) showing the character in action

10. The title of the excerpt is "The Citizner." Although no such word exists, it is, nevertheless, an appropriate title. The author most likely chose such a title mainly to

   (1) arouse the reader's curiosity
   (2) test the reader's knowledge of standard English
   (3) impart a lighthearted tone to a serious subject
   (4) show that Goldie Kramer needs to learn to speak English
   (5) ridicule the entire naturalization process

Questions 11–13 refer to the following excerpt from a novel.

HOW DOES THE PERSON FEEL?

Once again he did his Christmas shopping in a Rexall drugstore. It was late, the day before Christmas Eve, and he hadn't had the spirit or
5 energy or presence of mind to do it earlier or thoughtfully. Boredom, which had begun as a mild infection, now took him over completely. No activity seemed worth the doing,
10 no conversation worth having. The fluttery preparations at home seemed fake and dingy. His mother was going on as she did every year about the incredible price of trees
15 and butter. As though their tree would be anything other than it had always been: the huge shadowy thing in a corner burdened with decorations she had had since she was
20 a girl. As if her fruitcakes were edible, or her turkey done all the way to the bone. His father gave them all envelopes of varying amounts of money, never thinking that just once
25 they might like something he actually went into a department store and selected.

—Toni Morrison, excerpted from *Song of Solomon*, 1977

11. The son waits until the last minute to do his Christmas shopping because he

(1) is following the example set by his father
(2) couldn't go shopping until he received his paycheck
(3) hasn't any idea what to buy for his parents
(4) doesn't really care what gifts he buys
(5) spent all his money on a Christmas tree

12. The character's attitude is one of

(1) sadness and resentment
(2) suspense and fear
(3) cheerfulness
(4) peace and tranquility
(5) nostalgia

13. Which of the following methods does the author rely on most heavily in creating character in this excerpt?

(1) showing the character's actual speech patterns
(2) showing what other characters say about the character
(3) revealing the character's private thoughts
(4) describing the character's physical features
(5) showing the character in action

Questions 14–17 refer to the following poem.

WHAT HAPPENED TO TOM MERRITT?

Tom Merritt

At first I suspected something—
She acted so calm and absent-minded.
And one day I heard the back door shut,
As I entered the front, and I saw him slink
5 Back of the smokehouse into the lot,
And across the field.
And I meant to kill him on sight.
But that day, walking near Fourth Bridge,
Without a stick or a stone at hand,
10 All of a sudden I saw him standing,
Scared to death, holding his rabbits,
And all I could say was, "Don't, Don't, Don't,"
As he aimed and fired at my heart.

—Edgar Lee Masters, 1915

14. Who is the speaker of this poem?

(1) Merritt's wife
(2) a murderer
(3) Tom Merritt
(4) God
(5) the sheriff

15. "At first I suspected something—
    She acted so calm and absent-
    minded. And one day I heard the
    back door shut . . ." (lines 1–3)
    The poet introduces the poem
    with these lines to show us that
    Tom Merritt

    (1) was a very suspicious person
    (2) was sure that his wife was ill
    (3) had suspected that his wife
        was losing her mind
    (4) had suspected that his wife
        was seeing another man
    (5) was sure that his wife still
        loved him

16. The poem mainly uses which of
    the following techniques?

    (1) rhyme—the repetition of two
        or more vowel sounds
    (2) verse—a division of a poem
        into distinct parts
    (3) rhythm—an emphasis
        on certain words or
        syllables (beat)
    (4) free verse—the absence
        of rhyme and a regular
        rhythmic pattern
    (5) personification—the
        attributing to an animal or
        thing some human activity
        or quality

17. "Don't, Don't, Don't . . ." (line 12)
    The way in which the poet
    presents these words implies
    that Tom

    (1) did not want to hurt the other
        man
    (2) tried to annoy the other man
    (3) begged the man to stop seeing
        Tom's wife
    (4) turned to run away from the
        other man
    (5) was shot before he finished
        the statement

Questions 18–20 refer to the following
excerpt from a play.

WHAT DOES HIGGINS THINK OF WOMEN?

PICKERING: Excuse the straight question, Higgins. Are you a man of
good character where women are
concerned?

HIGGINS: [*Moodily.*] Have you ever met a
man of good character where
women are concerned?

PICKERING: Yes: very frequently.

HIGGINS: [*Dogmatically, lifting himself
on his hands to the level of the piano, and sitting on it with a bounce.*]
Well, I haven't. I find that the moment I let a woman make friends
with me, she becomes jealous, ex-
acting, suspicious, and a damned
nuisance. I find that the moment I let
myself make friends with a woman, I
become selfish and tyrannical.
Women upset everything. When you
let them into your life, you find that
the woman is driving at one thing
and you're driving at another.

PICKERING: At what, for example?

HIGGINS: [*Coming off the piano rest-
lessly.*] Oh, Lord knows! I suppose
the woman wants to live her own
life; and the man wants to live his;
and each tries to drag the other on
to the wrong track. One wants to go
north and the other south; and the
result is that both have to go east,
though they both hate the east wind.
[*He sits down on the bench at the
keyboard.*] So here I am, a con-
firmed old bachelor, and likely to remain so.

PICKERING: [*Rising and standing over him gravely.*] Come, Higgins! You know what I mean. If I'm to be in this business I shall feel responsible for that girl. I hope it's understood that no advantage is to be taken of her position.

HIGGINS: What! That thing! Sacred, I assure you. [*Rising to explain.*] You see, she'll be a pupil; and teaching would be impossible unless pupils were sacred. I've taught scores of American millionairesses how to speak English: the best looking women in the world. I'm seasoned. They might as well be blocks of wood. I might as well be a block of wood.

—George Bernard Shaw, excerpted from *Pygmalion*, 1913

18. Higgins's negative attitude toward women is based on his

(1) recent divorce
(2) lack of contact with women
(3) desire to meet beautiful women
(4) previous experience with women
(5) upcoming marriage

19. "One wants to go north and the other south; and the result is that both have to go east, though they both hate the east wind."

The playwright includes this reference to show that

(1) relationships are stronger if both parties sacrifice
(2) couples often come from different regions of the country
(3) compromise can have negative effects upon a relationship
(4) trust is the most important element of a relationship
(5) women have equal rights in all relationships

20. The playwright uses the image of blocks of wood to show Higgins's

(1) strictness as a teacher
(2) dislike of inflexibility
(3) pride in his teaching skills
(4) will to "break" his clients
(5) lack of emotions toward his clients

Questions 21–24 refer to the following excerpt from a commentary.

DOES TV STEREOTYPE?

Hispanics may be the fastest-growing minority group in the USA, but they are sorely underrepresented on prime-time television.

5 While 9% of the U.S. population is Hispanic, only 2% of prime-time characters were during a week surveyed by *USA TODAY.* Asians and Native Americans also were un-
10 derrepresented, with Asians 1% of TV's players vs. 3% of the U.S. population and Native Americans .4% of TV's characters vs. 1% in real life.

The problem lies in percep-
15 tions, says Ray Blanco of the National Hispanic Academy of Media Arts & Sciences.

"People tend to think that all Hispanics don't speak English, only
20 watch Spanish-language TV and don't have a disposable income, which is not the case," Blanco says.

Hispanic roles that do exist, Blanco adds, often reinforce derog-
25 atory stereotypes.

Actor Marco Sanchez agrees.

"I can't tell you how frustrating it was to go on auditions and know I'd be considered for one of four
30 roles: the drug dealer, the gang member, the lover or the streetwise youth with a heart of gold."

Sanchez, the son of Cuban im-migrants, says his mother sug-
35 gested he change his name, "but I refused to compromise a part of myself to get a job."

—Donna Gable, excerpted from "TV's Limited Visions of Hispanics," August 30, 1993, *USA Today*

21. According to the excerpt, the fastest-growing minority group in the United States is

    (1) Hispanics
    (2) Asians
    (3) Native Americans
    (4) Cubans
    (5) African Americans

22. Which of the following statements best sums up the main idea of the excerpt?

    (1) It's a myth that Hispanics don't watch programs broadcast in English.
    (2) Prime-time TV programs tend to ignore or stereotype minorities.
    (3) Native Americans and Asians are underrepresented on television.
    (4) There are not enough good roles on television for Cuban actors.
    (5) The perception that TV does not represent all Americans is mistaken.

23. The mother of actor Marco Sanchez suggested that he change his name because

    (1) casting agents found it hard to remember
    (2) people kept misspelling and mispronouncing the name
    (3) it was not an appropriate name for a stage and screen star
    (4) people kept mistaking him for someone with a similar name
    (5) it limited the kinds of characters he was allowed to play

24. If Marco Sanchez were offered the following roles, which would he most likely pick?

    (1) a drug dealer in a made-for-TV movie
    (2) the lead in a Shakespearean comedy
    (3) a gang leader on a weekly drama series
    (4) a streetwise youth in a feature film
    (5) the love interest of a married woman in a soap opera

    Answers begin on page 43.

PRE-TEST 4: LITERATURE AND THE ARTS ANSWER KEY

1. **(4)** The term *ups and downs* refers to high and low points in the entertainer's long career.

2. **(2)** The word *King* implies admiration. The entire passage discusses Presley's early career and the attitude throughout is one of admiration.

3. **(5)** Although hard work is important, being in the right place at the right time also contributes to success. Presley's move to Memphis and his recognition by the record company president were circumstances that were crucial to his success.

4. **(4)** "Humble beginnings" suggests a lack of wealth and influence. Abraham Lincoln, who was born in a log cabin and became president, is the only choice listed who rose from humble beginnings. All the other men were born into wealthy families.

5. **(2)** The judge is asking Goldie questions required of one seeking U.S. citizenship, as would be done in a naturalization court.

6. **(4)** Goldie has been living in the United States for forty years and is asking to become a U.S. citizen.

7. **(1)** Goldie expresses fear, panic, relief, and excitement. Her lips quiver and her knees tremble, but she beams with pride.

8. **(5)** Goldie studied hard for the interrogation and is upset that the judge is not asking her more questions. Her friends do not want her to offend the judge, so they attempt to stop her.

9. **(2)** The writer employs all of the methods listed except showing what other characters say about Goldie.

10. **(3)** Many people take the naturalization process very seriously. The author appears to treat a serious proceeding lightheartedly. While the title does arouse the reader's curiosity, it goes beyond arousing curiosity to establish a lighthearted mood.

11. **(4)** Lines 4–6 say that he "hadn't had the spirit or energy or presence of mind to do it [shop] earlier or thoughtfully." In other words, the son doesn't care what he buys.

12. **(1)** The character is depressed and resents his parents' activities.

13. **(3)** The excerpt is based almost entirely on the private thoughts of the character; none of the other methods is used.

14. **(3)** The title and the reference to the other characters implies that Tom, a dead man, is speaking as "I."

15. **(4)** Her strange behavior and someone's leaving his house aroused his suspicion.

16. **(4)** The poem is written in free verse; there is no rhyme or regular rhythmic pattern.

17. **(5)** The sentence *"Don't"* is unfinished. We assume Tom was killed.

18. **(4)** Higgins refers to "the moment I let a woman make friends with me" and "the moment I let myself make friends with a woman," so we know he has had some experience.

19. **(3)** The reference to directions implies that couples settle for a new direction neither one wants.

20. **(5)** Blocks of wood do not feel or express emotions.

21. (1) The first sentence states that Hispanics are "the fastest-growing minority group in the USA."

22. (2) The first two paragraphs present statistics that show minorities are underrepresented on prime-time TV. The last six paragraphs are about the problem of "derogatory stereotypes."

23. (5) In lines 26–32, Sanchez complains that, as a Cuban-American, he was offered only stereotypical roles. He then goes on to explain that his mother suggested that he change his name. The implication is that Sanchez's Hispanic name was keeping him from being offered a wide variety of roles.

24. (2) In lines 26–32, Sanchez says, "I can't tell you how frustrating it was to go on auditions and know I'd be considered for one of four roles: the drug dealer, the gang member, the lover or the streetwise youth with a heart of gold." Sanchez would probably welcome the opportunity to play against these stereotypes in a Shakespeare comedy.

Use the answer key on pages 43–44 to check your answers to the Pre-Test. Then find the item number of each question you missed and circle it on the chart below to determine the reading skill and content areas in which you need more practice. Pay particular attention to areas where you missed half or more of the questions. The reading skills are covered on pages 187–243. The page numbers for the content areas are listed below on the chart. Knowledge of reading skill and content area–based questions is absolutely essential for success on the GED Literature and the Arts Test. For those questions that you missed, review the skill pages indicated.

PRE-TEST 4: LITERATURE AND THE ARTS EVALUATION CHART

Skill Area/ Content Area	Comprehension (pages 189–195)	Application (pages 195–199)	Analysis (pages 200–210)
Prose Fiction (pages 453–482)	6, 7, 11	5	8, 9, 10, 12, 13
Poetry (pages 483–502)	14, 17		15, 16
Drama (pages 503–518)	18		19, 20
Nonfiction Prose (pages 519–536)	1, 3	4	2
Commentaries (pages 537–546)	21, 22	24	23

PRE-TEST 5: MATHEMATICS

The Mathematics Pre-Test consists of 40 items. It offers you the opportunity to test both your computational and problem-solving skills. These are not multiple-choice items so you will have to work as accurately and carefully as possible. Be sure to use any diagrams or charts that are provided with the problems.

Use the Evaluation Chart on page 53 to determine which areas you need to review most.

PRE-TEST 5: MATHEMATICS ANSWER GRID

1 _____	11 _____	21 _____	31 _____
2 _____	12 _____	22 _____	32 _____
3 _____	13 _____	23 _____	33 _____
4 _____	14 _____	24 _____	34 _____
5 _____	15 _____	25 _____	35 _____
6 _____	16 _____	26 _____	36 _____
7 _____	17 _____	27 _____	37 _____
8 _____	18 _____	28 _____	38 _____
9 _____	19 _____	29 _____	39 _____
10 _____	20 _____	30 _____	40 _____

You may find these formulas useful in solving some of the following problems.

FORMULAS

Description	Formula
AREA (A) of a:	
square	$A = s^2$ where s = side
rectangle	$A = lw$ where l = length, w = width
triangle	$A = \frac{1}{2}bh$ where b = base, h = height
circle	$A = \pi r^2$ where $\pi \cong 3.14$, r = radius
PERIMETER (P) of a:	
square	$P = 4s$ where s = side
rectangle	$P = 2l + 2w$ where l = length, w = width
circle—circumference (C)	$C = \pi d$ where $\pi \cong 3.14$, d = diameter
VOLUME (V) of a:	
cube	$V = s^3$ where s = side
rectangular container	$V = lwh$ where l = length, w = width, h = height
Pythagorean theorem	$c^2 = a^2 + b^2$ where c = hypotenuse, a and b are legs of a right triangle
distance (d) between two points in a plane	$d = \sqrt{(x_2 - x_1)^2 + (y_2 - y_1)^2}$ where (x_1, y_1) and (x_2, y_2) are two points in a plane
slope of a line (m)	$m = \frac{y_2 - y_1}{x_2 - x_1}$ where (x_1, y_1) and (x_2, y_2) are two points in a plane

Solve each problem.

1. Subtract 386 from 72,000.

2. Divide 5310 by 9.

3. In a recent village election, six precincts recorded the following voter turnout.

Precinct	Number of Voters
#26	168
#15	240
#10	195
#7	180
#21	312
#25	87

What was the average number of voters per precinct?

4. Find 1.43 plus .5.

5. What is .38 divided by .4?

6. Corey needs $120 to buy a new coat. She has saved the money she received from four dividend checks of $16.75 each. How much more money must she add to those savings to pay for the coat?

7. $1\frac{1}{4}$
   $-\frac{3}{4}$

8. $4\frac{1}{5} \times \frac{1}{2} =$

Questions 9 and 10 are based on the chart below, which compares the growth of four local companies.

	Sales	
	1989	**1993**
Magic Marketing	$323,000	$904,400
Futures International	$630,000	$925,000
Townley Agency	$264,000	$1,497,000
Billings Printing	$2,000,000	$6,000,000

9. Billings Printing's 1993 sales were what percent of its 1989 sales?

10. If Magic Marketing continues to have approximately the same rate of growth for the 4 years to 1997, what will be the projected sales in 1997 (to the nearest 500,000 dollars)?

11. Martha had $12\frac{2}{3}$ yards of drapery material. She used $\frac{3}{4}$ of it to make the drapes for her family room. How much does she have left to make matching throw pillows?

12. On the first day of their vacation, the Morales family drove 312 miles in 6 hours. At that rate, how far will they travel the next day if they drive for 8 hours?

13. During the last winter carnival, the local college students built a 30-foot snowman out of 100 tons of snow. How much snow will be needed to build a 36-foot snowman this year?

14. Find 72% of $350.

15. Find the length of the diagonal brace used to reinforce the barn door.

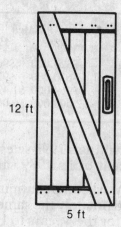

12 ft

5 ft

16. Nick's time card shows his hours for one week. If he works 8 hours per day before earning overtime, find Nick's total pay before deductions.

PHILLIPS CORPORATION time card		
Name: Nick Acino **SS #:** 002-00-0021		
Date	**From**	**To**
7/8	8:30 A.M.	4:30 P.M.
7/9	8:30 A.M.	5:15 P.M.
7/10	8:00 A.M.	4:30 P.M.
7/11	8:30 A.M.	6:00 P.M.
7/12	8:30 A.M.	4:45 P.M.
Total Regular Hours _____ at $8.40		
Overtime Hours _____ at $12.60 (over 40 hours)		

17. In the formula for the circumference of a circle, the d stands for the diameter, which is twice the radius, r. If $\pi \cong 3.14$ and $r = 3$ m, choose the expression below that could be used to find the circumference of the circle.

(1) (3.14)(3)
(2) (3.14)(6)
(3) (3.14)(1.5)
(4) (3.14)(3²)
(5) not enough information is given

18. Write 273,000 in scientific notation.

19. There were many increases in gasohol sales over a nine-year period. What is the difference between the smallest annual increase and the largest annual increase?

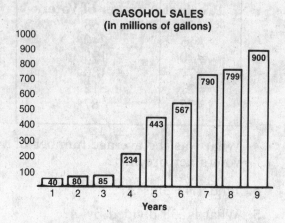

GASOHOL SALES
(in millions of gallons)

20. Find the number of square *yards* of sod needed to cover the circular putting green shown below. (*Hint*: 9 sq ft = 1 sq yd)

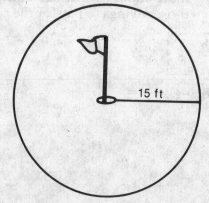

15 ft

21. Margaret wants to put a wallpaper border around her bedroom walls. The room is a rectangle 15 feet by 20 feet. How many complete *yards* of the wallpaper must she buy?

22. How much sand is needed to fill a sandbox 8 feet by 6 feet to a depth of 18 inches?

23. Find the measure of angle x in the illustration below.

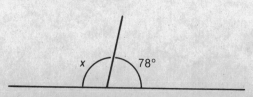

x 78°

24. Main Street and Union Avenue are parallel roads as shown below.

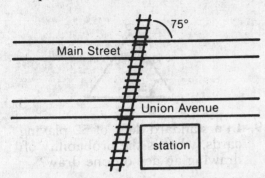

The railroad tracks cut across both streets. What is the angle measure of the land on which the station rests, based on the information given in the diagram above?

25. Solve for x: $14 = \frac{x}{5}$

26. Solve for x: $4x - 9 = 7$

27. Solve for x: $3(x - 2) - 3 = x + 5$

28. Evaluate: $-4 + (-3) - (-2)$

29. Find the average temperature of most of Illinois for the frigid day reported on this weather map.

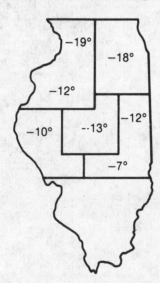

30. If $x = -2$ and $y = 5$, find the value of the expression $5y - 3x^2$.

31. Miguel has fourteen coins in his pocket. He has one more dime than quarters and three more nickels than dimes. How many of each coin does he have?

32. Using the diagram below, find the measure of angle A.

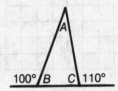

33. If 6 inches of decorative ribbon costs $3.25, how much does a yard cost?

34. If one kilogram = 2.2 pounds, does a 3-kilogram roast beef weigh more or less than a 6-pound roast?

35. To find the height of the evergreen in his backyard, Doug sketched the information shown here.

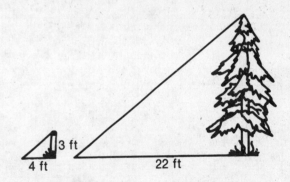

He placed a yardstick parallel to the tree and compared its shadow on the ground with the length of the shadow of the tree. How tall is the tree?

Questions 36 and 37 are based on this drawing.

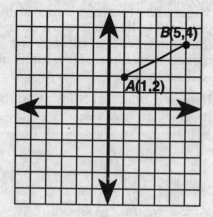

36. Find the length of the line segment from point *A* to point *B*.

37. Find the slope of the line *AB*.

38. Look at the triangle below. What is the measure of $\angle b$?

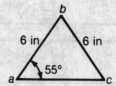

39. In a standard deck of 52 playing cards, what is the probability of drawing an ace on one draw?

40. Evaluate:

$$\sqrt{25} + (4 \times 3)^2 - (5 \times 2)$$

Answers begin on page 51.

PRE-TEST 5: MATHEMATICS ANSWER KEY

1. 71,614
$$\begin{array}{r} 72{,}000 \\ -386 \\ \hline 71{,}614 \end{array}$$

2. 590
$$\begin{array}{r} 590 \\ 9)\overline{5310} \\ \underline{-45} \\ 81 \\ \underline{81} \\ 00 \end{array}$$

3. 197 voters
Find the total:
$168 + 240 + 195 + 180 + 312 + 87 = 1182$
Find the average:
$1182 \div 6 = 197$

4. 1.93
$$\begin{array}{r} 1.43 \\ +\ .5 \\ \hline 1.93 \end{array}$$

5. .95
$$\begin{array}{r} .95 \\ .4)\overline{3.80} \\ \underline{3\ 6} \\ 20 \\ \underline{20} \\ 0 \end{array}$$

6. $53
First, find the total in checks:
$\$16.75 \times 4 = \$67$
Then, find the difference:
$\$120 - \$67 = \$53$

7. $\frac{1}{2}$
$$1\tfrac{1}{4} = \tfrac{5}{4}$$
$$-\ \tfrac{3}{4} = \tfrac{3}{4}$$
$$\tfrac{2}{4} = \tfrac{1}{2}$$

8. $2\frac{1}{10}$
$4\tfrac{1}{5} \times \tfrac{1}{2} =$
$\tfrac{21}{5} \times \tfrac{1}{2} = \tfrac{21}{10} = 2\tfrac{1}{10}$

9. 300%
Write a ratio:
$\dfrac{\$6\ \text{million}}{\$2\ \text{million}} = \tfrac{3}{1}$
Change the ratio to a percent:
$\tfrac{3}{1} = 300\%$

10. $2.5 million
First compare 1993 to 1989:
$\dfrac{\$904{,}400}{\$323{,}000} = 2.80 = 280\%$

*Then multiply 1993 sales by 280%
to find the 1997 projection:*
$\$904{,}400 \times 2.8 = \$2{,}532{,}320$

Then round to the nearest $500,000:
$\$2{,}500{,}000$

11. $3\frac{1}{6}$ yards
First, find $\frac{3}{4}$ of the material:
$12\tfrac{2}{3} \times \tfrac{3}{4} = \tfrac{38}{3} \times \tfrac{3}{4} = \tfrac{38}{4} = 9\tfrac{1}{2}$
Then, find the difference:
$$12\tfrac{2}{3} = 12\tfrac{4}{6}$$
$$-\ 9\tfrac{1}{2} = 9\tfrac{3}{6}$$
$$3\tfrac{1}{6}\ \text{yd}$$

12. 416 miles
$\dfrac{312\ \text{miles}}{6\ \text{hours}} = \dfrac{x}{8\ \text{hours}}$
$= \dfrac{312 \times 8}{6} = 416$

13. 120 tons
$\dfrac{30\ \text{feet}}{100\ \text{tons}} = \dfrac{36\ \text{feet}}{x}$
$= \dfrac{36 \times 100}{30} = \dfrac{3600}{30} = 120$

14. $252
$\dfrac{x}{\$350} = \dfrac{72}{100}$
$= \dfrac{\$350 \times 72}{100} = \dfrac{\$25{,}200}{100} = \$252$
or
$350 \times .72 = 252$

15. 13 feet
$c^2 = a^2 + b^2$
$c^2 = 12^2 + 5^2$
$c^2 = 144 + 25$
$c^2 = 169$
$c = \sqrt{169} = 13$

16. $373.80
Find Nick's hours, including overtime:
$8 + 8\tfrac{3}{4} + 8\tfrac{1}{2} + 9\tfrac{1}{2} + 8\tfrac{1}{4} = 43$
40 hours regular; 3 hours overtime
Find Nick's total pay:
$$\begin{array}{r} 40 \times \$\ 8.40 = \$336.00 \\ +\ \ 3 \times \$12.60 = \$\ 37.80 \\ \hline \$373.80 \end{array}$$

17. (2) (3.14)(6)
The formula for circumference is
$C = \pi d$; $d =$ twice the radius or
$2 \cdot 3 = 6$
$C = \pi d$
$= (3.14)(6)$

18. 2.73×10^5

19. 218 million gallons
Smallest increase:
85 million $-$ 80 million $=$ 5 million
Largest increase:
$790 - 567 = 223$ million
Find the difference:
$223 - 5 = 218$ million

20. **78.5 sq yd** $A = \pi r^2$
$A = \pi(15)^2$
$A = 3.14 \cdot 225$
$A = 706.5$ sq ft
$A = 706.5 \div 9 = 78.5$ sq yd

21. **24 yd** $P = 2l + 2w$
$P = 2(20) + 2(15)$
$P = 40 + 30 = 70$ ft
$(1 \text{ yd} = 3 \text{ ft})$
$P = 70 \div 3 = 23\frac{1}{3}$ yards needed,
so she must buy 24 yards

22. **72 cu ft** $V = lwh$
$V = 8 \cdot 6 \cdot 1\frac{1}{2}$ (18 in $= 1\frac{1}{2}$ ft)
$V = 72$ cu ft

23. **102°** $180° - 78° = 102°$

24. **105°** The angle above the station is 75°, the same as the angle above Main Street. To find its supplement:
$180° - 75° = 105°$

25. $x = $ **70** $14 = \frac{x}{5}$
$14 \cdot 5 = x$
$70 = x$

26. $x = $ **4** $4x - 9 = 7$
$4x = 7 + 9$
$4x = 16$
$x = \frac{16}{4} = 4$

27. $x = $ **7** $3(x - 2) - 3 = x + 5$
$3x - 6 - 3 = x + 5$
$3x - 9 = x + 5$
$3x - x - 9 + 9 = x - x + 5 + 9$
$2x = 14$
$x = 7$

28. **−5** $-4 + (-3) - (-2)$
$-4 - 3 + 2$
$-7 + 2 = -5$

29. **−13°**
Find the total:
$-19°$
$-12°$
$-18°$
$-10°$
$-13°$
$-12°$
$-7°$
$\overline{-91°}$
Find the average:
$-91° \div 7 = -13°$

30. **13** $5y - 3x^2$
$5(5) - 3(-2)^2$
$25 - 3(4)$
$25 - 12 = 13$

31. **3 quarters, 4 dimes, 7 nickels**
Let $x = $ quarters
$x + 1 = $ dimes
$x + 1 + 3 = $ nickels
$x + x + 1 + x + 1 + 3 = 14$
$3x + 5 = 14$
$3x = 14 - 5$
$3x = 9$
$x = \frac{9}{3} = 3$
$x = 3$ quarters
$x + 1 = 4$ dimes
$x + 4 = 7$ nickels

32. **30°** $\angle C = 180° - 110° = 70°$
$\angle B = 180° - 100° = 80°$
$\angle A = 180° - (80° + 70°) = 30°$

33. **$19.50**
Find 1 ft of ribbon:
(6 in $= \frac{1}{2}$ ft)
$2 \times \$3.25 = \$6.50$
Find 1 yd of ribbon:
(3 ft = 1 yd)
$3 \times \$6.50 = \$19.50$

34. **more**
$\dfrac{1 \text{ kg}}{2.2 \text{ lb}} = \dfrac{3 \text{ kg}}{x \text{ lb}}$

$= \dfrac{3 \times 2.2}{1} = 6.6 \text{ lb}$

Therefore, the 3-kg roast weighs more than the 6-lb roast.

35. **$16\frac{1}{2}$ feet** $\dfrac{3}{4} = \dfrac{x}{22}$

$= \dfrac{22 \times 3}{4} = \dfrac{66}{4} = 16\frac{1}{2}$

36. **$2\sqrt{5}$** $d = \sqrt{(x_2 - x_1)^2 + (y_2 - y_1)^2}$
$= \sqrt{(5 - 1)^2 + (4 - 2)^2}$
$= \sqrt{4^2 + 2^2}$
$= \sqrt{16 + 4}$
$= \sqrt{20} = \sqrt{4 \cdot 5} = 2\sqrt{5}$

37. $\dfrac{1}{2}$ $\dfrac{y_2 - y_1}{x_2 - x_1}$

$\dfrac{4 - 2}{5 - 1} = \dfrac{2}{4} = \dfrac{1}{2}$

38. **70°**
First, find $\angle c$:
The measure of angle c is 55° since both side ab and side bc are 6 inches.
Then, find $\angle b$:
$180° - 2(55°) =$
$180° - 110° = 70°$

39. $\dfrac{1}{13}$ $\dfrac{4 \text{ aces}}{52 \text{ cards}} = \dfrac{1}{13}$

40. **139** $\sqrt{25} + (4 \times 3)^2 - (5 \times 2)$
$5 + 12^2 - 10$
$5 + 144 - 10 = 149 - 10 = 139$

Use the answer key on pages 51–52 to check your answers to the Pre-Test. Then find the item number of each question you missed and circle it on the chart below to determine the mathematics content areas in which you need more practice. Pay particular attention to areas where you missed half or more of the questions. The page numbers for the content areas are listed below on the chart. The numbers in boldface are questions based on graphics. For those questions that you missed, review the skill pages indicated.

PRE-TEST 5: MATHEMATICS EVALUATION CHART

Skill Area/ Content Area	Item Number	Review Pages
Whole Numbers & Problem Solving	1, 2	559–572
Decimals	4, 5, 6	573–586
Fractions	7, 8, 11	587–604
Ratio & Proportion	**10**, 12, 13	605–610
Percent	**9**, 14	611–620
Measurement	**16**, 33, 34	621–636
Graphs, Statistics & Probability	**3**, **19**, **29**, 39	637–648
Numeration	18, 40	649–656
Geometry	**15**, 17, **20**, 21, 22, **23**, **24**, **32**, **35**, **38**	657–674
Algebra	25, 26, 27, 28, 30, 31, **36**, **37**	675–710

Test 1: Writing Skills

The GED Writing Skills Test consists of two parts. Each part is discussed separately below.

Part 1: Conventions of English

What's on the test?

Part 1 is a multiple-choice test of 55 questions. You will have 75 minutes to answer these questions. In this part, several passages will be followed by questions about the sentences within the passage. Some questions will ask you to locate errors in the passage, while other questions may ask you to restate an idea in different words. The questions will test your knowledge of sentence structure, grammar and usage, punctuation, spelling, and capitalization.

Part 1 of the test can be broken down into the following content areas:

Sentence Structure	35%
Usage	35%
Mechanics	30%

What kinds of questions are on the test?

Three types of questions will appear on the GED Writing Skills Test. In the *sentence correction* type, you'll see a sentence followed by the question, "What correction should be made to this sentence?" The five answer choices will focus on different parts of the sentence and deal with different grammar and usage issues.

Example   Sentence 1: **Time flies, when you're having fun.**

What correction should be made to this sentence?

(1) replace *flies* with *flys*
(2) remove the comma after *flies*
(3) replace *you're* with *your*
(4) insert a comma after *having*
(5) no correction is necessary

Note that this question tests your understanding of spelling, comma rules, possessives, and contractions. The correct answer is (2) remove the comma after *flies*.

In another question type, *sentence revision*, a sentence from the passage will be given with a part underlined. You will need to choose the best way to rewrite that underlined portion. The first answer choice in this question type is always the original version of the sentence, and this version is sometimes the correct answer.

Example Sentence 2: **Frustration is an emotion we all have to deal <u>with, the</u> question is how to handle it well.**

Which of the following is the best way to rewrite the underlined portion of this sentence? If you think the original is the best way to write the sentence, choose option (1).

(1) with, the
(2) with the
(3) with and the
(4) with. The
(5) with however the

This question tests your understanding of sentence structure and combining. Choice (4) is the best way to write these two sentences. The other choices create incorrect sentence structures.

The last question type, *construction shift*, asks you to choose the best way to rewrite a sentence or combine two sentences. In this type of question, *the original sentences contain no error*. Your job is to understand how the ideas are related in a sentence and which of the answer choices has the same meaning as the original sentence.

Example Sentence 3: **Although the female candidate ran a good race, she didn't receive enough votes.**

If you rewrote sentence 3 beginning with

The female candidate ran a good race,

the next word should be

(1) and
(2) which
(3) but
(4) so
(5) to

As you can see, the original sentence has no error. To answer this question, you must see the contrasting relationship between the two ideas of the sentence, then choose (3) but, the word that correctly shows this contrast.

Part 2: The Essay

You will be given 45 minutes to complete Part 2 of the Writing Skills Test. In this part, you will be given a topic and told to write a composition of about 200 words. You will not be given a choice of topics, but you will not need any special information or knowledge in order to write the essay. The topic will draw on your general knowledge and ask you to explain something about a common issue or problem. In this part of the Writing Skills Test, you should be able to plan and organize your thinking on an issue, and you should be able to communicate these thoughts clearly on paper.

1
BASIC ENGLISH USAGE

What Is Standard English?

We first learn language by listening to people speak. As children, our only language is a spoken one. We learn the meaning of words such as *me* and *cookie*, and we learn to put these ideas together to communicate a need. "Me cookie" might be easily understood by family and friends to mean "I would like a cookie."

As we grow older, we learn that there is a right and a wrong way to say things. By hearing others speak, we understand that "Me want go outside" is unacceptable English. While someone may understand what we mean by this phrase, it is still an incorrect use of the English language. Gradually, through speaking and listening, we learn what is acceptable and unacceptable in our language.

The Writing Skills Test examines your knowledge of standard written English, language that is acceptable at all times and places. It is the language of all kinds of communication, such as in books, newspapers, and magazines, as well as in school and business. In general, when you read something in print, you are reading standard English. When someone gives a prepared presentation or speech, the speaker usually uses standard English.

Nonstandard English does not follow the rules of grammar and usage. In casual conversation, we may use nonstandard English. In fact, incorrect expressions we use in our daily speech may sound "right" to our ears because we are used to hearing them. In this chapter, you'll learn how to correct many common usage errors we make in both speech and writing—problems with pronouns and verb tenses, for example. Of course, whether or not you follow all the rules of standard English in conversation, you will need to know these rules for the Writing Skills Test.

Writing in Complete Sentences

One major difference between spoken and written English is that we do not always speak in complete sentences. For example, in a telephone conversation you might mix complete sentences with *fragments*, groups of words that are not complete sentences. In the following conversation, the fragments are in bold type.

RIPOFF'S APPLIANCE COMPANY: Good morning. This is Ripoff's. You buy 'em, then try 'em.

CUSTOMER: Do you sell air conditioners?

RIPOFF'S: **Yeah, sometimes.**

CUSTOMER: Do you have any in stock now?

RIPOFF'S: **Might have some.**

CUSTOMER: Where is your store located?

RIPOFF'S: **On Airport Road. Next to the Wal-Mart.**

As you will learn in Chapters 1 and 2, a complete sentence has the following three characteristics.

CHARACTERISTICS OF A COMPLETE SENTENCE

1. A complete sentence contains a *complete thought*. It does not leave unanswered questions.

2. A complete sentence must have a *subject* that tells whom or what the sentence is about.

3. A complete sentence must have a *predicate* that tells what the subject is or does.

Look at the following sentences. The subjects and predicates are labeled for you. Compare these sentences with the characteristics listed in the box.

Subject	Predicate
Ripoff's Appliance Co. /	is located on Airport Road next to the Wal-Mart.
We /	sell air conditioners sometimes.
The warehouse /	might have some.

For practice in working with subjects and predicates, try matching a subject from the left column with a predicate from the right. Notice that you are connecting *whom* or *what* the sentence is about with what this subject *is* or *does*.

Subject	Predicate
The carpenter	malfunctioned and exploded.
The Hawaiian Islands	has six nieces and a nephew.
Some of the equipment	are full of tourists.
The unexpected tornado	built four bookshelves.
My Aunt Louise	destroyed fifty homes.

While we often *speak* without including both a subject and a predicate in our sentences, we must always *write* in complete sentences—sentences containing both a subject and a predicate. Complete sentences are a feature of standard written English that will be important on the Writing Skills Test, both Part 1 and Part 2.

EXERCISE 1: SUBJECTS AND PREDICATES

Directions: The following trivia quiz is based on Academy Award winners. Match the following actors, actresses, and movies (Column 1) with what they were or did (Column 2). As you work through the exercise, notice that you are connecting subjects and predicates to make *complete sentences.* The first one is done for you.

Column 1

g 1. The first Academy Awards

_____ 2. Julie Andrews

_____ 3. Katharine Hepburn and Spencer Tracy

_____ 4. Dustin Hoffman and Tom Cruise

_____ 5. *Gone With the Wind, Stagecoach,* and *The Wizard of Oz*

_____ 6. Awards for "Best Film," "Best Actor," "Best Actress," and "Best Director"

_____ 7. *Terminator 2*

_____ 8. Clint Eastwood

Column 2

(a) costarred in *Rain Man,* "Best Film" of 1988.

(b) were nominated for "Best Film" in 1939.

(c) acted together for the last time in 1967's *Guess Who's Coming to Dinner?*

(d) were given to *Silence of the Lambs* in 1991.

(e) finally won an Academy Award for directing *Unforgiven* in 1992.

(f) won the award for Special Effects in 1991.

(g) went to films made in 1927 and 1928.

(h) won an award for her performance in *Mary Poppins* in 1964.

Answers are on page 179.

Parts of Speech

Subjects and predicates are built from the *parts of speech*. You will not have to define or explain these terms on the Writing Skills Test, but a knowledge of these major parts of speech and their functions will help you understand how standard English is put together. You'll be studying the following parts of speech closely in this book.

BASIC PARTS OF SPEECH		
Part of Speech	**Function**	**Examples**
noun	names person, place, thing, or idea	**John** drove to **Milwaukee** to give a **speech** about **democracy**.
pronoun	replaces a noun	**Somebody** showed **him** and **me** a picture of **it**.
verb	shows action or state of being (is, are, was, were, being, be, been)	Jim **is** tall. He **plays** basketball. Lew **looked** for a job.
conjunction	joins words and groups of words	Meg was here, **but** she left. Misha **and** I got home at noon.

Other parts of speech used all the time include adverbs and adjectives. However, in this book we will focus on the points covered on Part 1 of the Writing Skills Test.

What Is a Noun?

A *noun* names a person, place, thing, or idea. Whether or not you realize it, you are very familiar with nouns. Complete the lists of nouns under each of the following headings.

entertainers (people)

a. Bill Cosby

b. _____

c. _____

types of buildings (places)

a. school

b. _____

c. _____

grocery list (things)

a. tomatoes

b. _____

c. _____

qualities of a good leader (ideas)

a. patience

b. _____

c. _____

People, places, and things are usually easy to recognize as nouns. Sometimes ideas are a little harder. Read the following words carefully to get a better sense of this category of nouns: *democracy, capitalism, courage, love, time, anger.*

Noun as a Subject

A noun can be the *subject* of a sentence. Think of the subject as the main noun or the *actor* in the sentence. Ask yourself this question to find the subject of a sentence: "Who or what is doing something or being described in this sentence?"

The following sentence contains several nouns, but only one is the subject. Which one?

The **movers** packed the **truck** with **furniture** such as **beds**, **chairs**, and **tables**.

All of the nouns are in bold type. If you ask yourself, "What is this sentence about?" you might answer, "A truck of furniture." But if you ask, "Who or what is doing something?" your answer will be "movers." The noun *movers* is the subject of this sentence.

EXERCISE 2: NOUNS AND SUBJECTS

Directions: Underline all of the nouns in each of these sentences; then label the subject of each sentence with an *S.*

Example: Since August, my brother has lived in the green house at the end of

the block.

1. Bud missed the bus and had to take a cab to the concert.

2. Because of her poor health, Sheila will move to Arizona.

3. Did Mary apply for the new position at the bank?

4. The men stopped off for a drink on their way home.

5. Our children do their own laundry and clean the house.

6. Here is your pickle.

Answers are on page 179.

Singular and Plural Nouns

Singular means "one" (single). *Plural* means "more than one." You are probably familiar with the most common way to form plural nouns: adding an *s* to the end of the noun. Sounds simple, right? Not always. There are several ways to form plural nouns, as you'll see now.

Rules for forming plurals often depend on combinations of *vowels* and *consonants* at the ends of words. You may know that all the letters of the alphabet are divided into these two groups. The vowels are *a, e, i, o,* and *u* (and sometimes *y*). All the other letters are consonants.

Study the following rules for forming plurals correctly and practice each one as you go.

Rules for Forming Plural Nouns

★ **1. Add *s* to most nouns.**

cup ⟶ cups

boy ⟶ _____

desk ⟶ _____

pencil ⟶ _____

★ **2. Add *es* to words ending with *s, sh, ch, x,* and *z.***

boss ⟶ bosses

bush ⟶ _____

church ⟶ _____

fox ⟶ _____

★ **3. Add *s* to nouns ending in *y* if a vowel comes before the *y.***

driveway ⟶ driveways

bay ⟶ _____

toy ⟶ _____

valley ⟶ _____

★ **4.** **Change the *y* to *i* and add *es* to a word ending in *y* if a consonant comes before the *y*.**

> candy ⟶ candies
>
> lady ⟶ _____
>
> party ⟶ _____
>
> company ⟶ _____

★ **5.** **Change the *f* to *v* and add *es* to <u>some</u> words ending in *f* or *fe*.**

> loaf ⟶ loaves
>
> leaf ⟶ _____
>
> half ⟶ _____
>
> wife ⟶ _____

For most words ending in *f* or *ff* simply add an *s*.

> chief ⟶ chiefs
>
> staff ⟶ _____
>
> roof ⟶ _____
>
> bluff ⟶ _____

★ **6.** **A few nouns do not change form when they are made plural.**

> deer ⟶ deer
>
> sheep ⟶ _____
>
> moose ⟶ _____

★ **7.** **A few nouns are made plural by changing their spelling.** You probably know the plurals of the words below, but if you don't, you can find them in any dictionary.

> goose ⟶ geese
>
> man ⟶ _____
>
> child ⟶ _____
>
> mouse ⟶ _____
>
> foot ⟶ _____

These rules cover most plural forms, but not all. Whenever you're not sure how to form a plural, look up the singular word in the dictionary. The plural will sometimes be listed there.

EXERCISE 3: PLURAL NOUNS

Directions: Write the correct plural forms of each of the following words.

Singular	Plural	Number of Rule That Applies
1. country	_____	_____
2. home	_____	_____
3. business	_____	_____
4. alloy	_____	_____
5. car	_____	_____
6. factory	_____	_____
7. race	_____	_____
8. life	_____	_____
9. woman	_____	_____
10. dish	_____	_____

Answers are on page 179.

Possessive Nouns

Many people confuse possessive nouns and plural nouns. Look at *neighbors* and *neighbor's* in the following sentences. Which shows ownership, or possession?

My neighbors have loud parties on the weekends.
My neighbor's car had to be dragged out of the ditch.

In the second sentence, *neighbor's* shows possession—the neighbor owns a car. Notice the possessive ending: *'s.*

Study the following rules for forming possessive nouns, filling in the blanks for practice as you go.

Rules for Forming Possessive Nouns

★ 1. Add ⌐'s⌐ to form most singular possessive nouns.

desk of the secretary —→ the secretary's desk

policy of the state —————→ _____

gift of my niece —————→ _____

friend of Laurie —————→ _____

★ **2. Add ⎡'⎤ to plural nouns to form most plural possessive nouns.**

decision of the managers → the managers' decision

union of teachers ⟶ _____

house of the Joneses ⟶ _____

shirts of the babies ⟶ _____

★ **3. Add ⎡'s⎤ to plural nouns that do not end in s.**

department for children → children's department

magazine for women ⟶ _____

eggs of geese ⟶ _____

hoofprints of deer ⟶ _____

BE CAREFUL NOT TO USE 's TO FORM PLURALS.

INCORRECT: I saw three bus's at the station.

CORRECT: I saw three buses at the station.

EXERCISE 4: POSSESSIVE NOUNS

Directions: Insert apostrophes wherever they belong in the following sentences. Remember, not all nouns ending in *s* are possessive.

Example: The girls' meeting ended when their votes had been counted.

1. My cats favorite food never stays long in her dish.

2. Over the past two years, the Wagners house has become worn around the doors and windows.

3. Childrens pants and toddlers playsuits are marked down at Emilys favorite shop.

4. The presidents plan to restrict imports was abandoned due to several allies protests.

5. For days after the volcanos eruption, ashes and dust in the atmosphere partially blocked the suns rays.

Answers are on page 179.

What Is a Verb?

The daily news consists of events—actions—that have taken place locally, nationally, or internationally. Read the following headlines and choose the appropriate word to complete each one.

President _____ Legislation   Marries

Hurricane _____ Florida Coastline Rise

Starlet _____ Prince!   Signs

Jaycees _____ Raymond   Elect

Insurance Rates _____   Demolishes

In any sentence, the **verb** is the key word that names what the subject is or does. The two types of verbs are **action verbs** and **linking verbs**. The words in the blanks above are action verbs, words that show action. Some verbs show mental action (*think, believe, wish*), and others show physical action (*run, leave, swim*).

While an action verb tells what the subject is doing, linking verbs do not express action. Instead, they link the subject to words that describe the subject. No action is shown in the following sentences, but the subjects, *Joel* and *We*, are connected to words that describe them, *tall* and *angry*.

Joel **is** tall.

We **are** angry.

Is and *are* are forms of the most common linking verb, the verb *to be*. Forms of *to be* as well as some other common linking verbs are shown in the box below.

COMMON LINKING VERBS

is, am, are, was, were, be, being, been, appear, seem, become

---

For practice in using linking verbs, fill in the blanks in the sentences below with forms of the linking verbs in the box.

She _____ calm during the GED test.

David _____ very nervous about his job interview.

I _____ tired of exercising.

Victor _____ bored during dance class.

Tenses of Regular Verbs

When you read, you are generally aware that what you are reading about either has already happened, is happening now, or will happen in the future. One of the ways writers let you know when events take place is through *verb tense*.

PAST: Yesterday Brandon **wanted** to play outside.

PRESENT: Today Brandon **wants** to play outside.

FUTURE: Tomorrow Brandon **will want** to play outside.

Some verb tenses are formed using a single word, such as *wants*. Other tenses require a verb phrase, such as *will want*. In the verb phrase *will want*, *want* is the **base verb** and *will* is a **helping verb**. To form all verb tenses, you need the base verb. For some, you also need to use helping verbs, as you will see as you review the verb tenses.

Knowing how to form different verb tenses correctly is very important for the Writing Skills Test. **Regular verbs** are verbs that form the simple past tense and the **past participle** (used to form the perfect tenses) by adding *ed* to the base verb. Naturally, the tenses of regular verbs are the easiest to master. However, knowing how to form the different tenses won't help you very much unless you know when to use the different tenses. As you study verb forms, take careful note of when they are used.

The Simple Tenses

The **simple present** tense is used for something that is happening now, something that happens regularly, or something that is always true. The simple present is the base form of the verb unless the subject is *he, she, it,* or a singular noun. For these subjects, add *s* (or *es* if the verb ends in a hissing sound such as *s, sh, ch, x,* and *z*).

I **look** terrible today.

Gary **washes** his car every morning.

The sun **rises** in the east.

The **simple past** tense shows action that occurred in the past. To form the simple past of any regular verb, add *ed* to the base verb.

Wilson **dunked** his cat in the bathtub last night.

The **simple future** tense shows action that will happen in the future. Form the simple future for any subject by using *will* with the base verb.

Tomorrow Becky Brown **will learn** to juggle.

EXERCISE 5: THE SIMPLE TENSES

Directions: Fill in the correct simple tense form of the verb indicated in parentheses. Time clues such as *yesterday, today,* and *tomorrow* in the sentences will help you decide whether to use past, present, or future.

Example: (mix) Last night Mr. Fricks _____ *mixed* _____ the batter for his son's birthday cake.

1. (walk) Next week Fred _____ to work while his car is being fixed.

2. (appear) Right now the store manager _____ very distressed.

3. (plant) In March of 1994 Rayleen _____ those daffodils.

4. (play) Tomorrow night Brian and his buddies _____ Go Fish and drink orange juice until bedtime.

5. (love) Cats _____ tuna fish.

Answers are on page 179.

The Continuing Tenses

The *continuing tenses* show action continuing in the past, present, or future, as in the following examples.

PAST: The crew **was working** on the roof all last week.

PRESENT: Right now the children **are watching** a dreadful TV show.

FUTURE: I **will be knitting** this sweater for months.

As you can see, the continuing tenses are formed by combining helping verbs with the base form of the verb plus *ing*. The following chart shows how to form all the continuing tenses.

CONTINUING TENSES			
Present continuing	I he, she, it* we, you, they**	am is are	I am looking. He is looking. You are looking.
Past continuing	I, he, she, it* we, you, they**	was were	I was looking. We were looking.
Future continuing	all subjects	will be	They will be looking.
*or any singular noun **or any plural noun			

EXERCISE 6: THE CONTINUING TENSES

Directions: Fill in the correct continuing tense form of the verb indicated in parentheses. Time clues such as *yesterday*, *today*, and *tomorrow* in the sentences will help you decide whether to use past, present, or future.

Example: (print) Wannamaker's Copy Shop ___*is printing*___ the programs today.

1. (lick) At the moment, my brother _____ his ice cream cone frantically.

2. (bark) Now that blasted dog _____ again!

3. (cook) By next month I _____ in the kitchen of my own restaurant.

4. (pick) The workers _____ that big crop of beans for the next two weeks.

5. (sleep) On yesterday's show, Tad _____ during the fight between Hillary and Roy.

Answers are on page 179.

The Perfect Tenses

The *perfect tenses* show action completed before or continuing to a specific time. These tenses are used to show more specific time relationships than the simple or continuing tenses.

The *present perfect* tense shows that an action started in the past and either continues into the present or has just been completed.

Al **has fished** in this river since 1920.

The Barhams **have repaired** their back porch.

The *past perfect* tense shows that an action was completed before a specific time in the past.

By midnight last Tuesday, the boys **had washed** forty-six cars.

The *future perfect* tense shows that an action will be completed by a specific time in the future.

By 4:00 tomorrow, I **will have mowed** every blade of this grass.

PERFECT TENSES			
Present perfect	he, she it* I, you, we, they**	has have	She has looked. You have looked.
Past perfect	all subjects	had	We had looked.
Future perfect	all subjects	will have	They will have looked.

*or any singular noun   **or any plural noun

EXERCISE 7: THE PERFECT TENSES

Directions: Fill in the correct perfect tense form of the verb indicated in parentheses. Pay careful attention to the meaning of each sentence before you decide whether to use the past, present, or future perfect.

Example: (paint) Merle Watson recently __*has painted*__ his house lavender with purple trim.

1. (walk) I _____ my dog by bedtime tonight.

2. (curl) My daughter _____ her hair every day since her seventh birthday.

3. (order) By 9:00 last night, Palmer already _____ several rounds of cocoa for everyone.

4. (attend) Lucy is enrolled in a Lamaze class. She _____ every session so far.

5. (work) Before going into the army, Warren _____ in a fish canning factory.

6. (mail) By next October, Ms. Eggebraaten _____ Christmas gifts to her relatives in Europe.

7. (miss) In the last twenty-five years, Ginger _____ the company picnic only once.

8. (travel) Before coming to Chicago last summer, I _____ throughout the Midwest.

Answers are on page 179.

Spelling Regular Verb Forms

So far you have been writing different forms of verbs by adding *ed* or *ing* to the base verb. However, not all verbs change form so simply. Following are five rules for adding *ed* and *ing* that cover all regular verbs. Study each rule.

★ 1. **When *ed* and *ing* are added to most regular verbs, the spelling of the base verb does not change.**

watch ⟶ watched, watching

walk ⟶ walked, walking

reach ⟶ _____ , _____

jump ⟶ _____ , _____

kick ⟶ _____ , _____

★ 2. **If the base verb ends in *y* preceded by a consonant, change the *y* to *i* when adding *ed*, but keep the *y* when adding *ing*.**

rely ⟶ relied, relying

cry ⟶ cried, crying

marry ⟶ _____ , _____

study ⟶ _____ , _____

carry ⟶ _____ , _____

★ 3. **If the base verb ends with a silent *e*, drop the *e* before adding *ed* or *ing*.**

like ⟶ liked, liking

memorize ⟶ memorized, memorizing

live ⟶ _____ , _____

hope ⟶ _____ , _____

★ 4. **If the base verb ends in *ie*, drop the silent *e* when adding *ed*, but change the *ie* to *y* when adding *ing*.**

tie ⟶ tied, tying

die ⟶ _____ , _____

lie ⟶ _____ , _____

★ 5. **If the base verb ends in a single vowel and a single consonant other than *h*, *w*, or *x*, and if the accent falls on the last (or only) syllable of the verb, double the final consonant of the base verb when adding *ed* or *ing*. Otherwise, keep the normal spelling.**

refer ⟶ referred, referring

relax ⟶ relaxed, relaxing

commit ⟶ _____ , _____

prefer ⟶ _____ , _____

rot ⟶ _____ , _____

EXERCISE 8: REGULAR VERB REVIEW

Directions: This exercise tests your understanding of simple, continuing, and perfect tenses. Fill in the blank in each sentence with the correct form of the base verb indicated. Be sure to spell all the verb forms correctly. Read each sentence carefully for clues to the correct tense.

1. (wait) At the time of my arrival last week, Wendell _____ at the wrong bus station.

2. (enter) Someday Reba _____ the glamorous world of TV game shows.

3. (sketch) On her way home from work every day, Fairbanks _____ the other passengers on the train.

4. (plunge) By 8:00 this morning, I already _____ into my projects for the day.

5. (wait) I _____ for this moment for many a year.

6. (lie) By the end of his term two years from now, the executive _____ to his staff about many major issues.

7. (ship) Yesterday afternoon Debra secretly _____ the documents from her office mailroom.

8. (study) For the next few months, I _____ math.

9. (feel) Currently Henry _____ miserable because of his girlfriend's betrayal.

10. (seem) Today Ray _____ to have given up any hope of his friend's survival.

11. (live) Since the day she was born, Therese Ruffing _____ in Texas.

12. (decide) Last night Mary Beth _____ to name her daughter Esmerelda Ophelia after her husband's mother.

Answers are on page 180.

Irregular Verbs

English would be a much easier language to write if all verbs shifted to different tenses according to the regular patterns you have just been studying. However, many English verbs are irregular—they do not change according to these regular patterns. When you study irregular verbs, you need to learn the simple present, the simple past, and the past participle, which is used to form the perfect tenses.

Have, Do, and *Be*

Make sure you know the three most common irregular verbs: *have, do,* and *be.* If you are not sure of the forms of these verbs in the following box, you should memorize them.

	Present	Past	Past Participle
I, you, we, they** he, she, it*	have has	had	had
I, you, we, they** he, she, it*	do does	did	done
I he, she, it* you, we, they**	am is are	was were	been
*or any singular noun **or any plural noun			

The most common mistake people make with irregular verbs is confusing the past participle with the simple past tense. Remember, the past participle is used to form the perfect tenses, so a helping verb (*has, have,* or *had*) must always be used with a past participle.

INCORRECT: I done my chores.

CORRECT: I did my chores.

CORRECT: I have done my chores.

Other Common Irregular Verbs

On the following two pages is a list of the simple present, simple past, and past participle forms of common irregular verbs. Verbs that follow similar patterns are grouped together. You may already use most of these verbs correctly. Study this list by following these steps:

1. Cover the second and third columns of the list.

2. Read the simple present form in a short sentence using *I* as the subject. *I fall.*

3. Test to see if you know the simple past form by putting the sentence in the past tense. *I fell.*

4. Test to see if you know the past participle by putting the sentence in the present perfect. *I have fallen.*

5. Check your answers against the forms listed in the second and third columns.

6. Study the forms you missed by repeating the sentences over and over in each tense until you have memorized them.

Present	Past	Past Participle
cost	cost	cost
put	put	put
read	read	read
set	set	set
bring	brought	brought
buy	bought	bought
think	thought	thought
catch	caught	caught
teach	taught	taught
lay (put or place)	laid	laid
pay	paid	paid
say	said	said
send	sent	sent
feel	felt	felt
keep	kept	kept
leave	left	left
mean	meant	meant
meet	met	met
sleep	slept	slept
build	built	built
get	got	got, gotten
lose	lost	lost
find	found	found
feed	fed	fed
hold	held	held
lead	led	led
hear	heard	heard
sell	sold	sold
tell	told	told
understand	understood	understood
make	made	made
fall	fell	fallen
choose	chose	chosen
speak	spoke	spoken
take	took	taken
drive	drove	driven
eat	ate	eaten
give	gave	given
ride	rode	ridden
write	wrote	written

Present	Past	Past Participle
begin	began	begun
drink	drank	drunk
ring	rang	rung
sing	sang	sung
draw	drew	drawn
grow	grew	grown
know	knew	known
throw	threw	thrown
become	became	become
come	came	come
run	ran	run
see	saw	seen
go	went	gone
lie	lay	lain

There are many more irregular verbs than the ones on this list. Whenever you are unsure of the simple past or past participle of an irregular verb, look up the base verb in the dictionary. The forms of the verb will be listed there.

Correct Verb Tense in a Passage

On the Writing Skills Test, you will have to be able to correct verb tense in the context of a whole passage. Not every sentence in a passage will contain clues such as *at the present* or *next week* to tell you what tense to use. Read the following paragraph and cross out the two incorrect verbs. Write the correct form in the margin.

> Melissa had a hard time sleeping last night. It was her first night alone in her new apartment. The tap in the bathroom drips constantly. The refrigerator rattled and hummed. The neighbors' dog barked all night long. The streetlight was shining in her eyes. Finally she goes to sleep around 3:00 A.M.

Did you change *drips* to *dripped* and *goes* to *went?* The passage as a whole is written in the past tense. Notice the words *last night* in the first sentence. In the following GED practice exercise, make sure that you choose consistent verb tenses to correct the passage. First, identify the tense of the paragraph. Then, identify verbs. Next, determine which are similar and which are different. Finally, change those that need to be changed.

EXERCISE 9: VERBS

Directions: Read the following passage and answer the questions. Be sure that all verb tenses are correct and that verb forms are spelled correctly.

> (1) Videocassette recorders (VCRs) give TV watchers more choice in television programs. (2) Many viewers taped shows to watch later. (3) For example, people who work during the day had recorded daytime news programs, talk shows, movies, and soap operas. (4) Parents make collections of children's shows to give their children "rainy day" entertainment. (5) Sometimes a family has went out for the evening. (6) However, their VCR kept them from missing their favorite prime time shows. (7) Because of VCRs, TV viewers will be seeing more good television.

1. Sentence 2: **Many viewers taped shows to watch later.**

Which of the following is the best way to write the underlined portion of this sentence? If you think the original is the best way to write the sentence, choose option (1).

(1) taped
(2) tapped
(3) tape
(4) had tapped
(5) had taped

2. Sentence 3: **For example, people who work during the day had recorded daytime news programs, talk shows, movies, and soap operas.**

Which of the following is the best way to write the underlined portion of this sentence? If you think the original is the best way to write the sentence, choose option (1).

(1) had recorded
(2) record
(3) will be recording
(4) will have recorded
(5) recorded

3. Sentence 4: **Parents make collections of children's shows to give their children "rainy day" entertainment.**

Which of the following is the best way to write the underlined portion of this sentence? If you think the original is the best way to write the sentence, choose option (1).

(1) make
(2) were making
(3) were makeing
(4) made
(5) will be making

4. Sentence 5: **Sometimes a family has went out for the evening.**

Which of the following is the best way to write the underlined portion of this sentence? If you think the original is the best way to write the sentence, choose option (1).

(1) has went
(2) has gone
(3) will have gone
(4) went
(5) goes

5. Sentence 6: **However, their VCR <u>kept</u> them from missing their favorite prime time shows.**

   Which of the following is the best way to write the underlined portion of this sentence? If you think the original is the best way to write the sentence, choose option (1).

   (1) kept
   (2) keeps
   (3) keeped
   (4) had kept
   (5) keepes

6. Sentence 7: **Because of VCRs, TV viewers <u>will be seeing</u> more good television.**

   Which of the following is the best way to write the underlined portion of this sentence? If you think the original is the best way to write the sentence, choose option (1).

   (1) will be seeing
   (2) will have seen
   (3) are seeing
   (4) will be seen
   (5) had seen

Answers are on page 180.

Subject-Verb Agreement

As adults, we get a great deal of pleasure when someone agrees with us. When we express our opinions, we get support from others saying, "I agree. That's right." Agreement between people makes everything easier.

Agreement also makes the English language easier to understand. When you are writing, it is important to make subjects agree with verbs. ***Subject-verb agreement*** means that you have chosen the correct verb form to match the number and person of the subject. In this section you will learn how to make sure you have this agreement.

The Basic Pattern

If the subject of a present-tense verb is *he, she, it,* or any singular noun (except *I* or *you*), the verb must end in *s* or *es*. Verbs ending in a hissing sound (*s, sh, ch, x,* and *z*) take an *es* ending.

Note that the forms of irregular verbs for *he, she,* and *it* always end in *s*. Test this for yourself by looking back at the forms of *have, do,* and *be* on page 72.

In the following examples, are the subjects singular or plural? Fill in the correct form of the verb *walk* in each sentence.

The elderly women _____ in the mall every day.

The elderly woman _____ in the mall every day.

You should have written *walk* in the first sentence because the subject, *women,* is plural. The subject of the second sentence, *woman,* is singular, so the correct verb is *walks.*

Subject-Verb Agreement Problems

You have to worry about subject-verb agreement only in the present tense, with one exception. The irregular verb *be* changes form for different subjects in the past tense as well. You can review this pattern in the chart on page 72.

Keep subject-verb agreement in mind when you see contractions. If you have trouble figuring out the correct form, take the contraction apart. For example, *doesn't* means *does not*, and *don't* means *do not*.

INCORRECT: She don't (do not) care.

CORRECT: She doesn't (does not) care.

1. Compound Subjects

The following rules apply to compound subjects and verbs.

★ **If the parts of a compound subject are connected by *and*, the subject is always plural and the verb does not end in *s*.**

Mr. Tidwell and his daughter **row** the boat together.

★ **If the parts of a compound subject are connected by *or* or *nor*, the verb agrees with the part of the subject closer to it.**

Mr. Tidwell or his daughters (row, rows) the boat.
His daughters or Mr. Tidwell (row, rows) the boat.

In the first sentence, the verb must agree with *daughters*. You should have chosen *row*. In the second, the verb must agree with *Mr. Tidwell*. You should have chosen *rows*.

2. Inverted Order

In three common types of sentences, the verb comes before the subject. Underline the subject of each of the following sentences; then underline the correct verb.

(Is, Are) the twins hiding in the garage?

Here (goes, go) the Bensons on their way to the races.

In the storeroom (sits, sit) an almond-colored refrigerator.

If you have trouble finding the subject of these sentences, mentally rearrange the word order:

The twins (is, are) hiding in the garage.

The Bensons (goes, go) here on their way to the races.

An almond-colored refrigerator (sits, sit) in the storeroom.

You should have chosen *twins are* for the first example, *Bensons go* for the second, and *refrigerator sits* for the third.

EXERCISE 10: SUBJECT-VERB AGREEMENT
Directions: Underline the subject; then underline the correct verb in parentheses.

1. Down the street (runs, run) the racers in the Boston Marathon.

2. Neither her sons nor Letitia (visits, visit) the dentist often.

3. Time and money (was, were) all he lacked.

4. (Wasn't, Weren't) the secretary really paid $25 per hour?

5. (Has, Have) your mother given away her old clothes?

6. A sandwich and a glass of juice (is, are) plenty of lunch for me.

7. Here (lies, lie) the remains of my dog Roberta.

Answers are on page 180.

3. Interrupting Phrases
The subject and verb of a sentence are often separated by two types of phrases: prepositional phrases, and phrases that add information to the subject. Neither type of phrase affects agreement between subject and verb.

Some of the most common prepositions are *of, in, for, to, from, with, on,* and *by.* The prepositional phrases in the following example sentences are in bold type. They are not part of the subject. Underline the subject and then underline the correct verb.

> The papers **on the desk** (is, are) very important.
>
> The bushel **of peaches** (has, have) been sold.

You should have chosen *papers are* and *bushel has.*

Other interrupting phrases may seem to make the subject plural, but they do not. They often start with words such as *as well as, in addition to,* and *like.* These phrases are set off by commas. Underline the subject and then underline the verb in the following examples.

> Clay, along with his parents, (is, are) headed for the game.
>
> Marcia, like her coworkers, (is, are) going on strike.

You should have chosen *Clay is* and *Marcia is.*

4. Indefinite Pronouns

There are three groups of indefinite pronouns. Some are always singular, some are always plural, and some can be either singular or plural depending on their antecedents (see page 82). Singular indefinite pronouns almost always end in *one* or *body*.

INDEFINITE PRONOUNS			
Singular		**Plural**	**Singular or Plural** *(depending upon their use)*
everyone	everybody	both	some
someone	somebody	few	any
no one	nobody	many	none
anyone	anybody	several	most
one	each (one)		all
either (one)	neither (one)		

Underline the indefinite pronoun in the following sentences and then underline the correct verb.

Each of the children (is, are) here.

Some of the cake (tastes, taste) stale.

Most of the cookies (looks, look) burned.

You should have chosen *Each is, Some tastes,* and *Most look.* Did the interrupting phrase *of the children* throw you off in the first sentence? *Each* is always singular, no matter what comes between it and the verb. In the second sentence, *Some* refers to the singular noun *cake,* making the indefinite pronoun singular. In the third sentence, *most* refers to the plural noun *cookies,* making the indefinite pronoun plural. See the section on antecedents beginning on page 82.

EXERCISE 11: MORE SUBJECT-VERB AGREEMENT

Directions: Underline the subject; then underline the correct verb in parentheses for each sentence.

1. Mrs. Bundt, along with her children, (attends, attend) the Lutheran church.

2. Each of the captains (receives, receive) the award.

3. Some of the students (was, were) absent.

4. A breakfast of cereal and toast (keeps, keep) me going all day.

5. If anyone (wants, want) to go, call me!

6. Most of the figures (is, are) accurate.

7. The new property tax, like our other taxes, (is, are) unreasonably high.

8. None of the water (is, are) fit to drink.

Answers are on page 180.

What Is a Pronoun?

A *pronoun* is a word that replaces and refers to a noun. Usually, you use pronouns to avoid repeating the same nouns over and over. Instead of saying, "Jane told Bob Bob was a liar, and Bob told Jane Jane was a liar, too," you would say, "Jane told Bob he was a liar, and he told her she was a liar, too." *He, she,* and *her* are pronouns.

Types of Personal Pronouns

In the following chart are three important groups of pronouns. Each group has different functions in a sentence.

Subject Pronouns	Object Pronouns	Possessive Pronouns	
act as the subject of a verb	*never act as the subject of a verb*	*show ownership* (appear with another noun)	(stand alone)
I	me	my	mine
you	him	your	yours
he	her	his	his
she	us	her	hers
it	them	its	—
we	whom	our	ours
they		their	theirs
who		whose	whose

Subject and Object Pronouns

The following hints will help you decide when to use subject and object pronouns.

HINT 1: Ask yourself whether the pronoun is the subject of a verb.

In the following sentence, what is the verb? Will the pronoun be the subject of that verb?

Rebecca brought the flowers to (they, them).

In this sentence, the verb is *brought.* The subject of *brought* is *Rebecca,* so the pronoun will not be the subject. The object pronoun *them* is correct.

> **HINT 2:** Cross out any nouns connected to the pronoun with *and*. Then look
> at the pronoun alone to see if it is the subject of a verb.

Which pronoun is correct in the following example?

Bill and (they, them) went to a movie.

Cross out *Bill and*. Will the pronoun be the subject of the verb *went*? Which is correct, *they went to a movie* or *them went to a movie*? The correct pronoun is *they*.

EXERCISE 12: PRONOUN FORM

Directions: Replace the parts of each sentence in bold type with the correct pronoun. Read the sentence carefully to determine whether to use a subject, object, or possessive pronoun. Remember that there are two types of possessive pronouns.

Example: **The** ~~children's~~ *Their* hair is the same color as ~~Tom's~~ *his*.

1. **Jeanette** is going to the circus with **Sandy and Lucy**.

2. Give the pearls to **Mother and me**.

3. John and **John's** friends left the meeting.

4. **Phil and I** read **Kate's** paper with great delight.

5. Nancy was planning to bring her husband, so I brought **my husband**.

Answers are on page 180.

Possessives and Contractions

A possessive noun such as *Gerald's* shows ownership. So does the possessive pronoun *his*, which you could use to substitute for *Gerald's*. However, unlike the possessive noun, the possessive pronoun does not contain an apostrophe ('). If you remember that no possessive pronouns contain apostrophes, you should be able to avoid confusing the possessive pronouns and their sound-alike contractions.

Possessive Pronoun	Sound-Alike Contraction
its	it's (it is)
theirs	there's (there is)
their	they're (they are)
your	you're (you are)
whose	who's (who is)

If you can't decide whether to use a contraction in a sentence, try substituting the two words that the contraction stands for.

I can't believe (your, you're) going to do that!

Test the sentence with *you are*, the two words that *you're* stands for: *I can't believe you are going to do that!* The sentence makes sense, so the contraction *you're* is the correct choice.

(Whose, Who's) house do you think this is, young lady?

Test the sentence with *Who is*: *Who is house do you think this is, young lady?* The sentence makes no sense, so the possessive pronoun *whose* is the correct choice.

EXERCISE 13: POSSESSIVE PRONOUNS AND CONTRACTIONS

Directions: Underline the correct word to complete each sentence.

1. (Your, You're) not ready to move out of the house at age twelve.

2. (Theirs, There's) no one here by that name, Officer.

3. I have given up hope that (your, you're) father will ever stop telling bad jokes.

4. (Whose, Who's) coat is lying in the back corner of the bar?

5. (Its, It's) not likely that Reginald will ever darken (its, it's) door again.

6. (Their, They're) going on a vacation to Alaska.

Answers are on page 180.

Identifying Antecedents

The noun that a pronoun replaces and refers to is called its **antecedent**. The relationship between a pronoun and its antecedent must be clear and correct. There are several specific pronoun problems that you are likely to find on the Writing Skills Test. But before you turn to those problems, first practice identifying the antecedents of pronouns in correctly written sentences.

Draw an arrow from the pronoun in this sentence to its antecedent.

Jenny told Bob how much she loves roses.

Did you draw the arrow from *she* to *Jenny*? The pronoun *she* replaces and refers to the noun *Jenny*.

Pronouns often refer to antecedents in other sentences. Draw arrows from *him* in the second sentence and *they* in the third sentence to their antecedents.

Jim has the children for the weekend. I'll be getting them back from him Sunday night. Then they'll be with me all week.

Did you choose *Jim* as the antecedent for *him* and *children* for *they?*

EXERCISE 14: IDENTIFYING ANTECEDENTS

Directions: In the following paragraph, the pronouns are numbered. Fill in the correct antecedent for each pronoun. The first two are done for you.

Murray and Dee went to church yesterday with their new baby Marissa
                                                    1

for the first time. Upon getting her out of the car, they were surrounded by
                                  2   3

eager friends who wanted to see Marissa. Finally the three of them escaped
              4   5

to the nursery. Marissa seemed to like her temporary crib and the bubble
                                        6

mobile that dangled above it. The nursery worker was nervous about having
                           7

such a young baby to care for, though. He asked Murray and Dee where they
                                            8   9

would be sitting during the service in case he needed to find them.
                                           10   11

Pronoun	Antecedent	Pronoun	Antecedent
1. their	*Murray and Dee*	7. it	
2. her	*Marissa*	8. He	
3. they		9. they	
4. who		10. he	
5. them		11. them	
6. her			

Answers are on page 180.

Pronoun-Antecedent Agreement

Relative Pronouns

Relative pronouns (*who*, *which*, and *that*) are often used to link two ideas in a sentence.

> The eggs that I bought yesterday were brown.
>
> The man who came to dinner was her future son-in-law.
>
> This suitcase, which I have had since 1970, is falling apart.

These relative pronouns must agree with their antecedents according to the following rules.

★ 1. *Who* (*whom*, *whose*) can refer only to humans.

★ 2. The relative pronoun *which* can refer only to nonhumans.

★ 3. *That* can refer to either humans or nonhumans.

Look again at the three example sentences above. Draw an arrow from each relative pronoun to its antecedent.

You should have marked *eggs* as the antecedent of *that*, *man* as the antecedent of *who*, and *suitcase* as the antecedent of *which*.

EXERCISE 15: RELATIVE PRONOUNS

Directions: Underline the antecedent for the relative pronoun in each sentence. Then underline the correct relative pronoun in parentheses.

Example: This exercise, (who, which) is not hard, is quite short.

1. The woman (who, which) is sitting on the floor is the photographer.

2. The door (who, that) is slightly ajar leads to the chamber of horrors.

3. Time, (who, which) waits for no man, waits for no woman either.

4. Dorothy, (who, which) is friends with Glenda, would like to move back to Kansas.

5. The people (that, which) answer the phone there sound as though they have been dead for years.

Answers are on page 180.

Agreement in Number

In the following sentence, the pronoun *they* is used because its antecedent, *cities*, is plural.

> Cities often use tax incentives to stimulate the economic growth they need.

Is *they* used correctly in the next example sentence also? Decide if *they* agrees in number with its antecedent.

> Birmingham used tax incentives to stimulate the economic growth they needed.

Here the plural pronoun *they* incorrectly refers to *Birmingham*, a singular noun. The singular pronoun *it* should be used instead:

> Birmingham used tax incentives to stimulate the economic growth it needed.

As you check for pronoun agreement errors on the GED Writing Skills Test, keep in mind that the antecedent of a pronoun is not always in the same sentence as the pronoun. Find the pronoun in the following passage that does not agree in number with the rest of the passage and correct it.

> Word processors are miracles of technology. Because of them, correction fluid no longer stains the clothing and fingers of typists. They have eliminated typing and retyping drafts of the same material. Its quiet clicking has replaced the noisy thudding of typewriters. Many of them even check grammar and spelling.

Did you find the singular possessive pronoun *its*? The rest of the pronouns in the passage are plural—*they* and *them* are used to refer to *word processors*. Therefore, *its* should be replaced with *their*.

Compound Antecedents

The antecedent of a pronoun is not always a single noun. Sometimes the antecedent is made up of two nouns connected by *and, or,* or *nor*. In this example, the two nouns in the antecedent are connected by *and*. The pronoun is plural.

> **Mark and Tim** showed up for **their** swim team practice.

And makes a *compound antecedent* (an antecedent of more than one noun) plural. Use a plural pronoun to refer to a compound antecedent joined by *and*.

When a compound antecedent is joined by *or* or *nor*, the rule is different. *Or* and *nor* separate the nouns in a compound antecedent. The pronoun must agree with the closest noun in the antecedent.

> Either **Mark or his brothers** will show up for **their** swim practice.

> Either **his brothers or Mark** will show up for **his** swim practice.

In the first example above, *his brothers* is closest to the pronoun, so the pronoun is plural, *their*. In the second example, *Mark* is closest to the pronoun, so the pronoun is singular, *his*.

EXERCISE 16: AGREEMENT IN NUMBER
PART A
Directions: Underline the antecedent of the pronoun; then underline the singular or plural pronoun in parentheses that agrees with it.

Example: Every <u>boy</u> must be checked by (<u>his</u>, their) physician before entering the program.

1. Japan has greatly increased (its, their) industrial capacity.

2. Either Allison or Muriel will give up (her, their) turn at bat.

3. Neither Bobby nor the twins have told us (his, their) new address.

4. Neither the hamsters nor the dog has been fed (its, their) breakfast.

5. This company has sold (its, their) holdings in South Africa.

PART B
Directions: Cross out incorrect pronouns in this passage and write in correct ones, making sure the pronouns agree in number.

Over the last twenty years, Knoxville's population center, once clustered around their small downtown area, has shifted westward. However, their downtown area may become more important again in future years. Many of the city's older buildings are being restored, and its newer downtown buildings are lovely too.

Answers are on page 180.

More than One Antecedent

The meaning of a pronoun is unclear if the pronoun can refer to more than one antecedent. In the following example, whose dress is it?

Jane told Mary about her dress.

Because two females are mentioned in the same sentence, the pronoun *her* is confusing. Here is one way the sentence could be corrected:

Jane told Mary about Mary's dress.

Or, depending on the intended meaning of the original sentence, it might be rewritten this way:

Jane told Mary about Jane's dress.

Now look at another example. Whom does *they* seem to be referring to?

I invited my best friends and my family to the party, but they couldn't come.

The writer does not clearly tell you whether both her best friends and her family couldn't come, just her family, or just her best friends. In this case, she may have to do a little more rewriting to make the sentence clear, depending on her actual meaning. On a piece of scratch paper, jot down a possible revision of the sentence.

Here is one way to correct the problem:

I invited my best friends and my family to the party, but none of the people I invited could come.

No Antecedent

Some pronouns are used without any antecedent at all. The pronouns *it, this,* and *they* commonly appear without an antecedent. Here's an example:

VAGUE: When I went to the public library, they told me I needed two pieces of identification to get a library card.

CLEAR: When I went to the public library, **a librarian** told me I needed two pieces of identification to get a library card.

The following sentences contain a very common example of a pronoun with no antecedent. Circle the vague pronoun. On a piece of scratch paper, rewrite the sentence it appears in to make the meaning clear.

Joe drove sixteen hours in one day to get home for Christmas. As soon as he walked in the door, his mother started nagging him to pay some bills and buy the Christmas tree. This gave him a bad headache.

Did you circle *This*? You might have revised the last sentence several ways. One possibility would be *Her nagging gave him a bad headache.*

EXERCISE 17: CLARIFYING ANTECEDENTS

Directions: Read the following sentences carefully, looking for confusing pronoun reference. If a sentence or group of sentences is written clearly and does not need to be revised, write C in the blank. If revision is needed, write X in the blank and revise on a separate sheet of paper.

Example: ___X___ When I went to the hospital, they gave me eighteen stitches.

When I went to the hospital, the doctor gave me eighteen stitches.

_____ **1.** I wrote to Ken and his sisters, but they did not respond.

_____ **2.** They say that drinking peppermint tea is good for an upset stomach.

_____ **3.** Herd the sheep away from the cattle and feed them.

_____ **4.** Dion asked Tony if he thought he would win the contest.

_____ **5.** When the quarterback made the touchdown in the final seconds of the game, it went wild in the stands.

———— **6.** Sam thought he left his checkbook at home but later couldn't find it.

———— **7.** Darleen never wants to go out anymore, and she is not eating or sleeping well. This worries her husband.

———— **8.** Mr. Olivetti followed Dominick into his storeroom.

———— **9.** Many people drink too much on New Year's Eve and then try to drive home. This drinking and driving makes the roads dangerous for everyone on that holiday night.

Possible answers are on page 181.

Keeping Track of Person

Read this paragraph and try to keep track of the pronouns.

> A person should register to vote as soon as you turn eighteen. He should realize that it is your right to vote in a democracy. To register, he must be a U.S. citizen and a resident of the area in which you vote. Two convenient places he can register to vote are his local library and your post office.

The pronouns in this paragraph are all mixed up between *he* and *you.* The pronouns are all singular, so they agree in number, but they shift in **person** (from *you* to *he* and back again). Within a passage, the pronouns should not shift from one person to another.

First person: I, me, my, mine, we, us, our, ours

Second person: you, your, yours

Third person: he, she, it, him, her, his, hers, its, they, them, they, theirs

Here is one way to correct the paragraph:

> You should register to vote as soon as you turn eighteen. You should realize that it is your right to vote in a democracy. To register, you must be a U.S. citizen and a resident of the area in which you vote. Two convenient places you can register to vote are your local library and your post office.

EXERCISE 18: AGREEMENT IN PERSON

Directions: Find which of the pronouns in bold type need to be corrected in the following passage.

> Most of us think that having running water and electricity is normal. As a result, **you** might be surprised at the simple mud huts many Africans live in. Even when **you** are out of work here, **we** can get help from government agencies, including welfare or unemployment income. **We** may not all have lives of luxury, but **you** easily forget that people in many other countries feel lucky to earn only pennies per day.

Answers are on page 181.

EXERCISE 19: SENTENCE STRUCTURE

Directions: The following items are based on paragraphs that contain numbered sentences. Some of the sentences may contain errors in usage. A few sentences, however, may be correct as written. Read the paragraph and then answer the items based on it. For each item, choose the answer that would result in the most effective writing of the sentence or sentences. The best answer must be consistent with the meaning and tone of the rest of the paragraph.

> (1) One of our most popular American artists are Norman Rockwell, who was a painter. (2) His paintings show such detail that some people have mistaken it for photography. (3) His paintings were on the cover of *The Saturday Evening Post* magazine for several years, and you collected those covers. (4) Although he is no longer alive, those masterpieces of his lives on in art galleries, in bookstores, and even on calendars and greeting cards.

1. Sentence 1: **One of our most popular American artists are Norman Rockwell, who was a painter.**

   What correction should be made to this sentence?

   (1) change *our* to *ours*
   (2) change *are* to *is*
   (3) replace *who* with *which*
   (4) change *was* to *were*
   (5) no correction is necessary

2. Sentence 2: **His paintings show such detail that some people have mistaken <u>it</u> for photography.**

   Which of the following is the best way to write the underlined portion of this sentence? If you think the original is the best way to write the sentence, choose option (1).

   (1) it
   (2) its
   (3) they
   (4) them
   (5) him

3. Sentence 3: **His paintings were on the cover of *The Saturday Evening Post* magazine for several years, and you collected those covers.**

What correction should be made to this sentence?

(1) change *paintings* to *painting's*
(2) change *were* to *was*
(3) change *you* to *people*
(4) change *collected* to *collecting*
(5) no correction is necessary

4. Sentence 4: **Although he is no longer alive, those masterpieces of his lives on in art galleries, in bookstores, and even on calendars and greeting cards.**

What correction should be made to this sentence?

(1) replace *he* with *they*
(2) change *is* to *are*
(3) change the spelling of *alive* to *alife*
(4) change *lives* to *live*
(5) change the spelling of *galleries* to *gallerys*

(1) Born in Boston in 1857, Fannie Farmer was a famous woman who's accomplishments benefit us today. (2) In high school, a stroke will cause her to end her formal education. (3) While recovering, she helped with household duties and begun to cook. (4) Fannie's cooking was noticed by her parents, which enrolled her in the Boston Cooking School. (5) Upon Fannie's graduation, they asked her to stay on as an assistant director. (6) Within two years, she had become the school's director. (7) In 1902 she left and openned Miss Farmer's School of Cookery, a school that trained housewives. (8) She also taught a course in invalid cooking at Harvard for a year. (9) In addition, she and her sister writed a regular column for ten years in *Woman's Home Companion*. (10) Still popular among best-selling cookbooks today are her *Boston Cooking School Cookbook*, which is now known as *The Fannie Farmer Cookbook*. (11) Moreover, the cup or teaspoon that we measure with got its standard size from Fannie Farmer.

5. Sentence 1: **Born in Boston in 1857, Fannie Farmer was a famous woman who's accomplishments benefit us today.**

What correction should be made to this sentence?

(1) change *was* to *were*
(2) change *woman* to *women*
(3) replace *who's* with *whose*
(4) change *benefit* to *benefited*
(5) change *us* to *we*

6. Sentence 2: **In high school, a stroke <u>will cause</u> her to end her formal education.**

Which of the following is the best way to write the underlined portion of this sentence? If you think the original is the best way, choose option (1).

(1) will cause   **(2)** may cause   **(3)** causing   **(4)** were causing   **(5)** caused

7. Sentence 3: **While recovering, she helped with household duties and begun to cook.**

   What correction should be made to this sentence?

   (1) change the spelling of *recovering* to *recoverring*
   (2) change *she* to *her*
   (3) change the spelling of *duties* to *dutys*
   (4) change *begun* to *began*
   (5) no correction is necessary

8. Sentence 4: **Fannie's cooking was noticed by her parents, which enrolled her in the Boston Cooking School.**

   What correction should be made to this sentence?

   (1) change *was* to *were*
   (2) change *parents* to *parent's*
   (3) replace *which* with *who*
   (4) change the spelling of *enrolled* to *enroled*
   (5) no correction is necessary

9. Sentence 5: **Upon Fannie's graduation, <u>they</u> asked her to stay on as an assistant director.**

   Which of the following is the best way to write the underlined portion of this sentence? If you think the original is the best way, choose option (1).

   (1) they   **(2)** the staff   **(3)** their   **(4)** there   **(5)** them

10. Sentence 6: **Within two years, she had become the school's director.**

    What correction should be made to this sentence?

    (1) change *years* to *year's*
    (2) change *she* to *her*
    (3) change *had become* to *has become*
    (4) change *school's* to *schools*
    (5) no correction is necessary

11. Sentence 7: **In 1902, she left and openned Miss Farmer's School of Cookery, a school that trained housewives.**

    What correction should be made to this sentence?

    (1) change the spelling of *left* to *leaved*
    (2) change the spelling of *openned* to *opened*
    (3) change *Farmer's* to *Farmers'*
    (4) replace *that* with *who*
    (5) change *housewives* to *housewive's*

12. Sentence 9: **In addition, she and her sister writed a regular column for ten years in *Woman's Home Companion*.**

    What correction should be made to this sentence?

    (1) change *she* to *her*
    (2) change *writed* to *wrote*
    (3) change *years* to *years'*
    (4) change *Woman's* to *Womans'*
    (5) no correction is necessary

13. Sentence 10: **Still popular among best-selling cookbooks today are her *Boston Cooking School Cookbook*, which is now known as *The Fannie Farmer Cookbook*.**

    What correction should be made to this sentence?

    (1) change *are* to *is*
    (2) change *which* to *who*
    (3) change *is* to *are*
    (4) change *known* to *knowed*
    (5) no correction is necessary

    Answers are on page 181.

2
SENTENCE STRUCTURE

In Chapter 1, you learned a lot about the parts of speech that make up our language. For example, you know what a verb is, and you know to watch out for certain trouble areas in using pronouns. As you saw in the very beginning of Chapter 1, the reason we study these parts of speech so carefully is that they help us to communicate in standard English sentences.

In this chapter, you will examine the uses and purposes of a complete sentence. You will also study a variety of ways to write and combine sentences. These skills will help you to recognize and correct errors on the multiple-choice part of the Writing Skills Test as well as to write well on the GED Writing Sample.

Three Characteristics of a Sentence

One of the first topics you reviewed in writing skills was the characteristics of a complete sentence. You saw that a sentence must contain a subject, the person or thing doing something or being described in a sentence. A sentence must also have a predicate, which contains the verb or verbs in a sentence and tells what the subject is or does. The subject and predicate are the two main parts of a complete sentence. Together they must express a complete thought.

A group of words that does not meet these requirements is a fragment. Can you identify the fragments in the following conversation?

(1) DAD: Where's John?

(2) SIS: Went to a job interview.

(3) DAD: Who drove him?

(4) SIS: His friend Jean.

(5) DAD: What did he wear?

(6) SIS: Your new gray suit.

(7) DAD: He'd better land this one!

The fragments are lines (2), (4), and (6). Have you ever had a conversation like this? When reading each line above, you could tell what was going on because of the lines before and after it. When you read line (2), *Went to a job interview*, you knew whom Sis was talking about because you also read Dad's line above.

However, what if each of these lines stood on its own—without any other lines to help you interpret its meaning? Would you still understand its meaning? The lines that have meaning on their own are complete sentences. The lines that do not make sense by themselves are fragments. For example, look at line (4).

His friend Jean.

What about Jean? This group of words has no predicate to tell you what the subject is or does. To make this fragment a complete sentence, the writer must add a predicate:

His friend Jean **drove him to the interview**.

Now look at line (2):

Went to a job interview.

Who went to a job interview? This group of words is a fragment because it doesn't have a subject to tell you who is performing the action in the sentence. The writer must add a subject to make a complete sentence:

John went to a job interview.

In a certain type of sentence, the subject may be hard to recognize. In a command or an instruction, the subject of the sentence is understood to be *you*. In the following sentence, the subject performing the action is the person being spoken to.

Go down the hall and turn left.

(You) go down the hall and turn left.

In addition to having a subject and predicate, a sentence must express a complete thought. What is the problem with the following sentence?

Caleb driving to the city.

In the sentence above, the verb is not complete. You could correct the sentence by writing *Caleb is driving to the city.*

Sentence fragments are often difficult to detect because they make sense when read with the sentences around them. When proofreading a passage or your own writing for sentence fragments, make sure each group of words has meaning when standing alone. You might want to check this by reading backward, sentence by sentence, in order to see each sentence in isolation.

EXERCISE 1: REWRITING FRAGMENTS
PART A

Directions: Write *S* in front of complete sentences and *F* in front of fragments. Rewrite each fragment as a complete sentence on a separate sheet of paper, making sure each has a subject and a predicate and expresses a complete thought.

Examples: _____F_____ An elderly clerk.

An elderly clerk gave me my change.

_____S_____ Turn on the TV to channel 8.

_____ **1.** The pickup truck.

_____ **2.** Joseph is a man with many dreams.

_____ **3.** Called your house last night.

_____ **4.** Anxious for some news, the inmate.

_____ **5.** Life, with its many disappointments.

_____ **6.** Go to bed.

_____ **7.** To pitch like Dwight Gooden and hit like Ryne Sandberg.

_____ **8.** He knows the answer.

_____ **9.** Movies shown at 5:00 P.M. daily.

_____ **10.** Add ½ teaspoon of cinnamon and stir the batter.

Possible answers are on page 181.

PART B

Directions: Rewrite the following paragraph, fixing all of the sentence fragments. You can fix these fragments by adding a missing subject or predicate, or by joining two fragments together.

> When President John F. Kennedy was inaugurated in 1960, he stated, "Ask not what your country can do for you; ask what you can do for your country." His philosophy did much for U.S. citizens and underdeveloped areas of the world. For example, the Peace Corps. This program sent volunteers. Into underdeveloped areas of the world. The volunteers educated the citizens of those countries in basic survival skills. The main goal was for the countries to become more self-sufficient. And also relations between the U.S. and these countries to be improved.

Possible answers are on page 182.

Sentence Combining

If you wanted to make one sentence out of these two simple sentences, how would you do it? Try writing both ideas in one sentence.

> Those nails are for the paneling.
>
> The others can be used for hanging pictures.

The most common way to combine sentences like these is to use the joining word *and*. In the combined sentence that follows, notice that a comma is necessary before the joining word—where the period was in the first sentence. The wording of the two original sentences is unchanged.

> Those nails are for the paneling, and the others can be used for hanging pictures.

The combined sentences you have just seen are made up of two independent clauses joined by a comma plus *and*. A *clause* is a group of words that contains a subject and a verb. An *independent clause* can stand on its own as a complete sentence: it has a subject and a predicate, and it expresses a complete thought.

The following joining words, or *coordinating conjunctions*, are used with a comma to combine independent clauses: *and, but, or, nor, for, so, yet*. Notice that the joining words have different meanings. The word *and* does not mean the same as *but* or *so*, for example.

In the two examples that follow, notice the difference in meaning because of the conjunctions used. The first sentence implies that Jacob really does not want to go out because it is raining, but he must. The second sentence implies that Jacob has to go out because it is raining.

It is raining, but Jacob has to go out.

It is raining, so Jacob has to go out.

The chart below shows the different coordinating conjunctions and their meaning in a sentence.

Coordinating Conjunction	Meaning
and	adds information
but yet	shows an opposite
or	shows a choice
nor	rejects both choices
for	links effect to cause
so	links cause to effect

EXERCISE 2: CONJUNCTIONS

Directions: Choose a logical conjunction from the chart above to connect each pair of sentences. Then, on a separate sheet of paper, rewrite them as one sentence. Be sure to punctuate each new sentence correctly.

Example: I don't want to work. I need a job.

I don't want to work, but I need a job.

1. We are planning a Fourth of July picnic. We hope all of you can attend.

2. He did not study for his driver's test. He passed it.

3. Al has always wanted his own business. He opened a restaurant.

4. You may have some strawberry pie. You may have some cherry pie.

5. I can do most of my own plumbing. I cannot do the electrical work.

6. Karen is not allowed any hard exercise. She is recovering from an operation.

Answers are on page 182.

Clues About Commas

Don't use a comma every time you see a coordinating conjunction such as *and* or *but*. So far you have learned that a comma is needed when two complete thoughts are joined. If a coordinating conjunction does *not* connect two complete thoughts, do not use a comma.

NO COMMA NEEDED: Sue and Bruce are married.
                               S   V

All of us went but Maureen.
S   V

They built a patio and enclosed it with shrubs.
S   V   V

COMMA NEEDED: Sue is married, but Tina is not.
(two complete thoughts)   S V   S V

Most of the girls went, but Maureen stayed home.
S   V   S   V

They built a patio, but they did not build a deck.
S   V   S   V

Can you see the difference between the two sets of sentences? The second set needs a comma because the conjunction is joining two complete thoughts; in each sentence there are two subject-verb pairs. In the first set of sentences, there is only one subject-verb pair.

EXERCISE 3: USING COMMAS CORRECTLY

Directions: Place commas where they are needed in the following sentences, according to the rule you have just learned. Some of the sentences are correct as written.

1. She took off her coat and hung it in the closet.

2. She took off her coat and she hung it in the closet.

3. Jorge called Marie but he did not call Clara.

4. Jorge called Marie but not Clara.

5. Our daughter has a learning disability but is doing well in school.

6. Our daughter has a learning disability but she is doing well in school.

7. We visited my Aunt Nancy for we had not seen her in a while.

8. The mayor was popular with both senior citizens and young people.

Answers are on page 182.

Run-ons and Comma Splices

"You should see Brooke, my fifteen-year-old daughter her hair is pink and seventeen different lengths it is hideous she has the wildest haircut I've ever seen."

If you let punctuation be your clue, you can count only one sentence in the quote above. *You* begins with a capital letter, and a period follows *seen*. However, how many complete thoughts does the sentence above contain, and what are they?

There are actually four complete thoughts, ending in *daughter, lengths, hideous,* and *seen.* The sentence is one long **run-on.** When two or more sentences are joined without correct punctuation or conjunctions, the result is a run-on—the words run on (and on and on). You can correct run-ons by dividing them into separate sentences or combining the ideas with proper punctuation and conjunctions. Here is a corrected version:

"You should see Brooke, my fifteen-year-old daughter. Her hair is pink and seventeen different lengths, and it is hideous. She has the wildest haircut I've ever seen."

Another type of error, a **comma splice**, results when two complete sentences are joined by a comma without a conjunction, as in this example:

"She did this right before our big family reunion, all of my relatives are going to think she is a creature from outer space."

A comma splice can be separated into two sentences, or a logical conjunction can be placed after the comma:

"She did this right before our big family reunion. All of my relatives are going to think she is a creature from outer space."

"She did this right before our big family reunion, so all of my relatives are going to think she is a creature from outer space."

EXERCISE 4: RUN-ONS AND COMMA SPLICES

Directions: Some of the following sentences are run-ons or comma splices. If a sentence is correct as written, write *C* in the space. Rewrite incorrect sentences on a separate sheet of paper. Either divide them into separate sentences or combine them correctly using a comma with *and, but, for, or, nor, so,* or *yet.*

———— **1.** My pet peeve is waiting in long lines.

———— **2.** Kyle broke his leg he was taken to the emergency room.

———— **3.** Pass the donuts, I'm starving!

———— **4.** Is a storm "watch" less serious than a storm "warning"?

———— **5.** The make of her car is a Buick, the model is a Century.

———— **6.** I'll have a ham on rye with mayonnaise, please.

_____ 7. We attended the Special Olympics at my niece's school.

_____ 8. Of course this is my sweater, I've had it for years.

_____ 9. Dion won every swimming event in the meet we were proud of him.

_____ 10. I'd rather have hay fever than food allergies, at least I can eat!

Answers are on page 182.

EXERCISE 5: RUN-ONS AND COMMA SPLICES

Directions: The following paragraph contains some run-ons and comma splices. Read each sentence carefully to determine if it is written correctly. On a separate sheet of paper, rewrite the paragraph, correcting all the run-ons and comma splices. Either separate the incorrect sentences into two sentences or combine them using a comma with *and, but, or, for, nor, so,* or *yet.*

My cousin Ernie loves solving brainteasers, doing magic tricks, and playing mathematical games. He subscribes to several magazines they are filled with puzzles. In one trick, Ernie challenges his friends to cut a hole in an index card that is big enough to put a person's head through! His friends always try, he watches and laughs. Then Ernie cuts the card into a long strand and places it over his head. Who knows, maybe someday he will be performing the card trick on TV he certainly works hard at his craft.

Possible answers are on page 182.

EXERCISE 6: SENTENCE STRUCTURE PRACTICE

Directions: The following paragraph may contain any type of error you have studied so far in writing skills. Make sure each sentence is complete and correct.

(1) Recently psychologists have been researching birth order, their research suggests that personality and intelligence are based partly on where a child ranks in the family. (2) One of their theories is that the first child receives more of the parents' attention than later children so first-borns tend to be more intellectual. (3) First-borns often pattern their behavior after they're parents and other adults. (4) Later children must share their parents with the oldest child they pattern their behavior after the older siblings and peers. (5) Some theories suggesting that the later children are happier than first-borns. (6) Several books have been published on the subject, but many people soon may be applying birth-order theories to their own families.

1. Sentence 1: **Recently psychologists have been researching birth <u>order, their</u> research suggests that personality and intelligence are based partly on where a child ranks in the family.**

   Which of the following is the best way to write the underlined portion of this sentence? If you think the original is the best way, choose option (1).

   (1) order, their
   (2) order, or their
   (3) order their
   (4) order. Their
   (5) order and their

2. Sentence 2: **One of their theories is that the first child receives more of the parents' attention than later children so first-borns tend to be more intellectual.**

What correction should be made to this sentence?

(1) change *is* to *are*
(2) change *theories* to *theory's*
(3) change *receives* to *received*
(4) change *parents'* to *parent's*
(5) insert a comma after *children*

3. Sentence 3: **First-borns often pattern their behavior after they're parents and other adults.**

What correction should be made to this sentence?

(1) change *pattern* to *patterned*
(2) replace *their* with *they're*
(3) replace *they're* with *their*
(4) change *parents* to *parents'*
(5) no correction is necessary

4. Sentence 4: **Later children must share their parents with the oldest <u>child they</u> pattern their behavior after the older siblings and peers.**

Which of the following is the best way to write the underlined portion of this sentence? If you think the original is the best way, choose option (1).

(1) child they
(2) child, and they
(3) child and they
(4) child, and
(5) child and, they

5. Sentence 5: **Some theories <u>suggesting</u> that the later children are happier than first-borns.**

Which of the following is the best way to write the underlined portion of this sentence? If you think the original is the best way, choose option (1).

(1) suggesting
(2) were suggesting
(3) suggest
(4) suggested
(5) will suggest

6. Sentence 6: **Several books have been published on the subject, but many people soon may be applying birth-order theories to their own families.**

What correction should be made to this sentence?

(1) change *published* to *publishing*
(2) remove the comma after *subject*
(3) replace *but* with *so*
(4) change *may be* to *were*
(5) no correction is necessary

Answers are on page 182.

Using Longer Conjunctions

You have now learned one way to combine two independent clauses, by using a comma and a coordinating conjunction such as *and* or *but*. The following example shows another method. Note the punctuation and conjunction in the new sentence.

Rachel has a lot of friends in New Jersey.   She decided to move there.

Rachel has a lot of friends in New Jersey; **therefore,** she decided to move there.

Conjunctions such as *however* and *therefore* are called ***conjunctive adverbs***. Knowing this term is not important for the Writing Skills Test, but understanding this type of conjunction can help you on both sections of the test. Below is a list of some conjunctive adverbs and their meanings:

Conjunctive Adverb	Meaning
moreover furthermore in addition	adds related information (like *and*)
however nevertheless on the other hand	shows a contrast (like *but*)
therefore consequently	links cause to effect (like *so*) explains relationship between two ideas
otherwise	shows an alternative (like *or*)
for instance for example	gives specifics to illustrate a general idea
then	shows time order

When you are combining two independent clauses with this type of conjunction, the wording of the two clauses does not change. After the first clause comes a semicolon (;), then the conjunctive adverb, then a comma, then the second clause. The exception to the rule is that no comma is needed after *then*. Study the punctuation carefully in the following examples.

Barbara is from Iowa; **however,** she now lives in Illinois.
Barbara moved to Illinois; **then** she moved to New York.

When using this type of conjunction, you should always do two things:

1. **Choose the conjunction that has the correct meaning.** The chart above can help you learn what words to use and when to use them.

2. **Use the correct punctuation.** A semicolon comes *before* all conjunctive adverbs. A comma comes *after* all conjunctive adverbs except *then*.

EXERCISE 7: CONJUNCTIVE ADVERBS

Directions: Choose the correct conjunction to complete each sentence. Be sure the meaning of the conjunction relates the clauses logically.

1. He was qualified for the job; _____, he got it.

   (a) therefore   **(b)** however   **(c)** instead

2. The steak is very good; _____, you might prefer the chicken.

   (a) consequently   **(b)** on the other hand   **(c)** for example

3. The company is in financial trouble; _____, workers may be laid off.

   (a) nevertheless   **(b)** however   **(c)** as a result

4. Jason has been taking piano lessons for years; _____, he does not play well.

   (a) however   **(b)** consequently   **(c)** moreover

5. Jeri may run for councilperson; _____, she may someday become mayor.

   (a) otherwise   **(b)** furthermore   **(c)** for instance

Answers are on page 183.

EXERCISE 8: ERRORS WITH CONJUNCTIVE ADVERBS

Directions: Correct the errors in the following sentences by crossing out mistakes and inserting corrections. Check the punctuation carefully and make sure that the meaning of the conjunction logically links the two clauses. Some sentences may be correct as written.

Example: We saw several interesting sights during the tour; ~~nonetheless~~ *therefore,* I enjoyed it very much.

1. The snowstorm worsened; nevertheless we postponed our trip.

2. Two of the students studied hard; therefore, they failed the test.

3. The dishwasher is broken, in addition the freezer won't stay cold.

4. Mrs. Jones felt ill; however, she called a doctor.

5. Jane has so many talents; otherwise, she sings in a professional choir, weaves detailed tapestries, and can play an excellent game of tennis.

Possible answers are on page 183.

EXERCISE 9: COMBINING SENTENCES

Directions: Combine each pair of sentences **two different ways**, using any correct sentence structure. Be sure to punctuate your new sentences correctly and to use logical conjunctions. Use the charts on pages 96 and 101 to help you.

1. The salesperson was very polite. She listened to my complaints.

2. The music was terrible. We decided to dance.

3. We bought the house in 1975. We sold it in 1980 for twice the price.

4. My friends give me advice. I do not always listen to them.

5. I could drive you to work in the morning. You could take the subway.

Possible answers are on page 183.

Joining Dependent and Independent Clauses

So far you have practiced combining independent clauses with two types of conjunctions. A third type of conjunction makes one clause "dependent" on the other and shows the relationship between the two clauses. Look at the two short sentences and the combined sentence in the following example. Notice that the wording of the original sentences has not changed.

Dirk ran on the ice. He fell.

Because Dirk ran on the ice, he fell.

The ***dependent clause*** is *Because Dirk ran on the ice.* This clause is dependent because it is not a complete thought on its own—it needs the independent clause that follows it. The conjunction *because* makes the clause dependent and shows the relationship between the two ideas.

The meanings of conjunctions like *because* are very important. On page 104 is a list of some common ***subordinating conjunctions***, grouped according to meaning.

Conjunction	Meaning
before after while when whenever until	shows time relationship
because since so that	shows cause or effect
if unless	shows the condition under which something will happen
though although even though	shows a contrast
as though as if	shows similarity
where wherever	shows place

The clauses in a sentence using one of these conjunctions can be moved around. When the dependent clause comes first, a comma separates the two clauses. When the independent clause comes first, no comma is needed.

> After the fog lifted, the planes were no longer grounded.

> The planes were no longer grounded after the fog lifted.

Take care to choose a conjunction that logically relates the two ideas you want to combine. In the first of the following sentences, the conjunction used, *because*, makes the sentence very confusing. In the second sentence, *although* shows that the two ideas contrast.

> NONSENSE: Because I was hungry, I didn't bother to eat.

> MAKES SENSE: Although I was hungry, I didn't bother to eat.

EXERCISE 10: DEPENDENT CLAUSES
PART A

Directions: Using the list of conjunctions above, fill in the blank with an appropriate word. There are several possible answers in each case. Choose one that makes sense to you.

1. _____ Ray was afraid of water, he took swimming lessons.

2. _____ she already knows the words to the song, she can teach us.

3. I'm not going to the class reunion _____ my closest friends won't be there.

4. _____ we left the meeting, we went for pizza.

5. Celia stayed with her mother _____ the nurse returned.

Possible answers are on page 183.

PART B

Directions: Complete the following sentences with suitable dependent clauses, using the conjunction indicated. Be sure to punctuate the sentences correctly.

Example: (after) Margaret Kingsbury was born on Tuesday.

Margaret Kingsbury was born on Tuesday *after* **her mother had put in a full day at the office.**

OR

After **her mother had put in a full day at the office,** Margaret Kingsbury was born on Tuesday.

1. (since) we knew the food at the cafe was good

2. (before) the family bought a new mini-van

3. (whenever) Eliot has nightmares

4. (even though) I ordered a pepperoni pizza

5. (unless) Duane will paint the porch steps

Possible answers are on page 183.

PART C

Directions: Combine each pair of sentences by changing one of them into a dependent clause using one of the conjunctions listed on page 104. Be sure to place a comma after introductory dependent clauses.

Example: Russell attempted to bribe a police officer. Russell was arrested.

When he attempted to bribe a police officer, **Russell was arrested.**

1. We arrived at the church late. We missed their wedding ceremony.

2. Bonnie said that she was not tired. She fell asleep at 7:00 P.M.

3. I left my umbrella at home. I was soaked from the unexpected thunderstorm.

4. Rose was angry with her babysitter. She said she would not hire the young girl again.

5. We drove into the parking lot. We noticed that the store was closed.

Answers are on page 183.

Sentence Combining on the GED Test

One kind of question on the Writing Skills Test will require you to change the structure of a sentence or to combine two sentences without changing the meaning. The original sentence or sentences will contain no error. To answer the question correctly, you will have to figure out which of the answer choices will result in a new sentence that has the same meaning as the original.

There are two types of these questions. Read through the following examples and explanations carefully to become familiar with each.

Sentence 1: **Though city law does not allow pets to run loose, unleashed dogs are frequently seen on the streets.**

If you rewrote Sentence 1 beginning with

City law does not allow pets to run loose;

the next word should be

(1) otherwise
(2) furthermore
(3) then
(4) nevertheless
(5) therefore

To find the correct answer, test each of the answer choices. Which of the following new sentences is correct?

Choice 1: City law does not allow pets to run loose; otherwise, unleashed dogs are frequently seen on the streets.

Choice 2: City law does not allow pets to run loose; furthermore, unleashed dogs are frequently seen on the streets.

Choice 3: City law does not allow pets to run loose; then unleashed dogs are frequently seen on the streets.

Choice 4: City law does not allow pets to run loose; nevertheless, unleashed dogs are frequently seen on the streets.

Choice 5: City law does not allow pets to run loose; therefore, unleashed dogs are frequently seen on the streets.

Choice 4 is correct. Use of the conjunction *nevertheless* shows the contrast between the two ideas in the original sentence. Can you see that none of the other choices make sense?

Sentences 2 and 3: **These dogs are hungry strays. They knock over garbage cans and scavenge in parks.**

The most effective combination of these sentences would include which of the following groups of words?

(1) Because these dogs
(2) Unless these dogs
(3) Although these dogs
(4) In order that these dogs
(5) Until these dogs

Once again, test each answer choice in a new sentence. The first two are done for you. On a piece of scratch paper, write out the other three. Which one is correct?

Choice 1: Because these dogs are hungry strays, they knock over garbage cans and scavenge in parks.

Choice 2: Unless these dogs are hungry strays, they knock over garbage cans and scavenge in parks.

Choice 1 is correct. The conjunction *because* shows the cause-and-effect relationship between the original sentences.

In the rest of the GED practice exercises, you'll see more questions like these.

EXERCISE 11: STRUCTURE AND USAGE

Directions: Read the following paragraph and look for errors in sentence structure and usage. The questions that follow will require you to correct errors as well as choose correct ways of rewriting portions of the paragraph.

(1) Some American consumers are able to save some of their earnings after the bills have been paid and the groceries have been purchased. (2) Many of these people find security in opening a savings account. (3) For others, saving is not as exciting as investing their extra cash. (4) While some bought bonds as a safe way of investing, other investors choose to buy stock in a corporation. (5) Ownership in a corporation is represented by the number of shares of stock a person owns, however, by buying stock, a person becomes an owner of the business. (6) When a corporation is successful, its stockholders reap the benefits. (7) They are paid a share of the increased profits in addition, the value of their stock increases. (8) If the business is not a success stockholders may see the value of their stock decrease. (9) If the value decreases enough, he may lose their entire investment. (10) Because investing money can be risky, a new investor should get some reliable advice.

1. Sentence 1: **Some American consumers are able to save some of their earnings after the bills have been paid and the groceries have been purchased.**

Which of the following is the best way to write the underlined portion of this sentence? If you think the original is the best way, choose option (1).

(1) earnings after the
(2) earnings, after the
(3) earnings; after the
(4) earnings after, the
(5) earnings; however, the

2. Sentences 2 and 3: **Many of these people find security in opening a savings account. For others, saving is not as exciting as investing their extra cash.**

The most effective combination of these two sentences would include which of the following groups of words?

(1) Because many of these people
(2) When many of these people
(3) Although many of these people
(4) If many of these people
(5) As though many of these people

3. Sentence 4: **While some bought bonds as a safe way of investing, other investors choose to buy stock in a corporation.**

What correction should be made to this sentence?

(1) replace *while* with *if*
(2) change *bought* to *buy*
(3) remove the comma after *investing*
(4) change *choose* to *chose*
(5) no correction is necessary

4. Sentence 5: **Ownership in a corporation is represented by the number of shares of stock a person <u>owns, however,</u> by buying stock, a person becomes an owner of the business.**

Which of the following is the best way to write the underlined portion of this sentence? If you think the original is the best way, choose option (1).

(1) owns, however, by
(2) owns; however, by
(3) owns, however by
(4) owns; therefore, by
(5) owns, therefore, by

5. Sentence 6: **When a corporation is successful, its stockholders reap the benefits.**

What correction should be made to this sentence?

(1) replace *When* with *Then*
(2) change *is* to *are*
(3) remove the comma after *successful*
(4) replace *its* with *it's*
(5) no correction is necessary

6. Sentence 7: **They are paid a share of the increased <u>profits in addition, the</u> value of their stock increases.**

Which of the following is the best way to write the underlined portion of this sentence? If you think the original is the best way, choose option (1).

(1) profits in addition, the
(2) profits, in addition the
(3) profits; in addition, the
(4) profits for example, the
(5) profits; for example, the

7. Sentence 8: **If the business is not a success stockholders may see the value of their stock decrease.**

What correction should be made to this sentence?

(1) replace *if* with *though*
(2) insert a comma after *success*
(3) change *stockholders* to *stockholders'*
(4) change *may see* to *are seeing*
(5) replace *their* with *his*

8. Sentence 9: **If the value decreases enough, he may lose their entire investment.**

   What correction should be made to this sentence?

   (1) remove the comma after *enough*
   (2) replace *he* with *they*
   (3) change *lose* to *lost*
   (4) replace *their* with *his*
   (5) no correction is necessary

9. Sentence 10: **Because investing money can be risky, a new investor should get some reliable advice.**

   If you rewrote sentence 10 beginning with *Investing money can be risky*, the next word should be

   (1) but
   (2) nor
   (3) yet
   (4) as
   (5) so

Answers are on page 184.

Sequence of Tenses

The following sentence is made up of two independent clauses, so it has two subjects and two verbs in it. Look at the verbs carefully. What mistake did the writer make?

> The student reads the chapter, but he was unable to answer the test questions.

The verb *reads* is in the present tense, and *was* is in the past tense. Are you confused about when the action took place? Here is one way the sentence could be corrected, putting the first clause in the past, showing that the student has already read the chapter, and the second clause in the present, showing that right now the student can't answer the questions:

> past   present
> The student **read** the chapter, but he **is** unable to answer the test questions.

Another possible correction puts the first clause in the past perfect and the second in the simple past. This combination of tenses shows that the action in the past perfect took place before the action in the simple past:

> past perfect   simple past
> The student **had read** the chapter, but he **was** unable to answer the test questions.

Before you move on in this section, review the verb tenses and their explanations on pages 66–69. Understanding when each tense is used will help you combine different tenses correctly. Also study the following list of special helping verbs. Be careful to note which are used to indicate the past and which indicate present or future.

- If one clause is in the present tense, use one of the helping verbs from the "present or future" column in the other clause.

- If one clause is in the past tense, use one of the helping verbs from the "past" column in the other clause.

Past	Present or Future
could	can
should	shall
would	will
might	may
had to	must

In the following exercise, be careful to choose a logical tense as you choose each verb.

EXERCISE 12: CORRECT VERB SEQUENCE

Directions: In the following sentences, underline the correct verb in parentheses.

1. We had heard the bell, so we (were waiting, will wait) for class to begin.

2. If the nominating committee votes, Greg (became, will become) president.

3. When Connie applied for the job, she (should take, should have taken) her references along with her.

4. Everyone who attended the retirement dinner (was wearing, will wear) formal attire.

5. If Mary is smart, she (will call, called) her boss about the problem.

6. Eileen was really sorry that she (had slept, is sleeping) through the movie.

7. Members of the audience are cheering the dramatic ending because they (enjoy, have enjoyed) the play.

8. Will you make the beds while Bob (has swept, sweeps) the floor?

9. If we had sold the house, we (could have moved, can move) earlier.

10. If I miss work again, I (would lose, may lose) my job.

Answers are on page 184.

Dangling and Misplaced Modifiers

Another way to combine sentences is to use ***modifying phrases***, phrases that describe or add information. A correct sentence will always (1) make clear exactly what a modifying phrase modifies and (2) place the modifying phrase as close as possible to the word it modifies.

Look at the two combinations of the following pair of sentences. What is the difference between the correct and incorrect examples?

We heard the guard dog. The dog was growling loudly.

INCORRECT: Growling loudly, we heard the guard dog.

CORRECT: We heard the guard dog growling loudly.

In the incorrect sentence, the modifer *Growling loudly* is misplaced. The sentence implies that *we* were growling loudly, rather than the dog. In the correct sentence, the modifier *growling loudly* is placed next to the word it modifies, *dog*.

On a piece of scratch paper, rewrite the following sentence. Place the modifier as close as possible to the word it modifies.

The deer crossed in front of the driver with huge antlers.

The misplaced modifier is *with huge antlers*. It should be placed next to *deer*:

The deer with huge antlers crossed in front of the driver.

In addition to being misplaced, modifiers also may "dangle." A sentence with a ***dangling modifier*** contains no word for the modifier to modify. What is the difference between the correct and incorrect examples below?

INCORRECT: Stepping on the brakes too fast, the car slid.

CORRECT: When I stepped on the brakes too fast, the car slid.

The incorrect sentence contains a dangling modifier, *Stepping on the brakes too fast.* The sentence does not tell you *who* stepped on the brakes too fast. In the correct sentence, the dangling modifier has been changed to a dependent clause containing the subject *I.*

On a piece of scratch paper, rewrite the following sentence containing a dangling modifier. Make sure that your new sentence contains a word for the dangler to modify.

An accident was reported while watching the news.

The dangler is *while watching the news.* Here are two possible corrections to this sentence:

While watching the news, I heard an accident reported.

An accident was reported while I was watching the news.

EXERCISE 13: DANGLING AND MISPLACED MODIFIERS

Directions: Underline the modifying phrase in each of the following sentences. On a separate sheet of paper, rewrite each sentence that contains a dangling or misplaced modifier.

Example: <u>Wearing gloves</u>, the parrot perched on the hand of the trainer.

The parrot perched on the hand of the trainer wearing gloves.

1. Nailed to the wall, Rich saw the "No Smoking" sign.

2. The child called for his mother who wanted a toy.

3. While taking a shower, the telephone rang.

4. Driving to work, my papers blew out the window.

5. A bath felt good after working all day.

6. When traveling through Colorado, my luggage was lost on the train.

7. Wearing her wedding gown, we'll certainly be able to recognize the bride!

8. We heard the dog under the table whining for food.

Answers are on page 184.

Parallel Structure

In geometry, *parallel* lines are lines that are the same form. They are always the same distance apart, and they go in the same direction.

In sentences, two or more elements that have the same function must be written in the same form to be considered "parallel."

NOT PARALLEL: She prefers dancing, singing, and to act.

PARALLEL: She prefers dancing, singing, and acting.

Do you see the difference? Underline the three parallel parts in the second sentence above. In the first sentence, *to act* is not the same form as the two *ing* words it is joined to. To make the form parallel, change *to act* to *acting*.

Underline the incorrect part of the following sentence. On a piece of scratch paper, rewrite the sentence using parallel structure.

The model is tall, slim, and has attractive looks.

The corrected sentence would read like this: *The model is tall, slim, and attractive.*

EXERCISE 14: PARALLEL STRUCTURE
Part A

Directions: Cross out the word or phrase that is not parallel to the others. Replace it with an appropriate word or phrase.

Example: (a) knitting
(b) reading
(c) to ~~sew~~
(d) painting

___*sewing*___

1. (a) sad
(b) happiness
(c) afraid
(d) lonely

_____

2. (a) heart was thumping
(b) ears were pounding
(c) palms were perspiring
(d) shaky knees

_____

3. (a) being honest
(b) courage
(c) strength
(d) pride

_____

4. (a) set the table
(b) cook the beans
(c) pour the drinks
(d) slicing the roast

_____

5. (a) homemaker
(b) mother
(c) manager
(d) is a married woman

_____

Answers are on page 184.

PART B

Directions: In the blank, write the letter of the correct sentence from each pair.

_____ 1. (a) Karla told Rita to get in the truck, start the engine, and that she should shift gears.
(b) Karla told Rita to get in the truck, start the engine, and shift gears.

_____ 2. (a) Thomas Edison invented the electric light bulb, and he started motion pictures, and the phonograph.
(b) Thomas Edison invented the electric light bulb, the motion picture, and the phonograph.

_____ 3. (a) His friends respect Tony because of his sincerity, honesty, and kindness.
(b) His friends respect Tony because of his sincerity, honesty, and he is kind to people.

_____ 4. (a) To have a good job, live alone, and enjoy herself are Vicki's goals.
(b) To have a good job, be living alone, and enjoy herself are Vicki's goals.

_____ 5. (a) I promise to be loving, cherish, and honor you.
(b) I promise to love, cherish, and honor you.

Answers are on page 184.

EXERCISE 15: STRUCTURE AND USAGE

Directions: Read the following paragraph, checking for errors in:

- sequence of tenses

- misplaced and dangling modifiers

- parallel structure

- sentence structure and usage errors

Then answer the questions that follow.

(1) As the rest of our family gathered around to play trivia games, our youngest children felt left out of the fun, ages five and six. (2) Feeling sorry for them, new questions are being written by us that young children can answer. (3) We try to think of questions that they would find interesting and challenging but not to frustrate them. (4) Now when we play, we asked them to state the three colors of the American flag or recite the Pledge of Allegiance. (5) Also questions about the cartoons they watch. (6) We ask them about subjects they have learned about in school. (7) Other questions draw on information in the books we read to them. (8) Making up questions for the little children has become part of the game for the rest of us!

1. Sentence 1: **As the rest of our family gathered around to play trivia games, our youngest children felt left out of the fun, ages five and six.**

   Which of the following is the best way to write the underlined portion of this sentence? If you think the original is the best way, choose option (1).

   (1) our youngest children felt left out of the fun, ages five and six
   (2) their youngest children felt left out of the fun, ages five and six
   (3) our youngest children, ages five and six, felt left out of the fun
   (4) their youngest children, ages five and six, felt left out of the fun
   (5) our youngest, ages five and six, children felt left out of the fun

2. Sentence 2: **Feeling sorry for them, new questions are being written by us that young children can answer.**

   Which of the following is the best way to write the underlined portion of this sentence? If you think the original is the best way, choose option (1).

   (1) new questions are being written by us
   (2) new questions written by us
   (3) new questions have been written by us
   (4) we are writing new questions
   (5) they are writing new questions

3. Sentence 3: **We try to think of questions that they would find interesting and challenging but not to frustrate them.**

   Which of the following is the best way to write the underlined portion of this sentence? If you think the original is the best way, choose option (1).

   (1) to frustrate them
   (2) frustrating them
   (3) to frustrating them
   (4) frustrated
   (5) frustrating

4. Sentence 4: **Now when we play, we asked them to state the three colors of the American flag or recite the Pledge of Allegiance.**

   What correction should be made to this sentence?

   (1) change *play* to *played*
   (2) remove the comma after *play*
   (3) change *asked* to *ask*
   (4) change *recite* to *reciting*
   (5) no correction is necessary

5. Sentence 5: **Also questions about the cartoons they watch.**

   Which of the following is the best way to write the underlined portion of this sentence? If you think the original is the best way, choose option (1).

   (1) Also questions
   (2) We may also ask questions
   (3) They may also ask questions
   (4) We also asked questions
   (5) Also question them

6. Sentences 6 and 7: **We ask them about subjects they have learned about in school. Other questions draw on information in the books we read to them.**

The most effective combination of these sentences would include which of the following groups of words?

(1) subjects they have learned about in school and information
(2) subjects they have learned about in school but draw on
(3) subjects they have learned about in school; instead, we
(4) If we ask them about subjects they have learned about in school
(5) subjects they have learned about in school, not information

7. Sentence 8: **Making up questions for the little children has become part of the game for the rest of us!**

Which of the following is the best way to write the underlined portion of this sentence? If you think the original is the best way, choose option (1).

(1) Making up questions for the little children
(2) For the little children, making up questions
(3) Because we are making up questions for the little children
(4) If we make up questions for the little children
(5) Making up questions for the little children, we

Answers are on page 184.

3
MECHANICS

When we read, we rely on the signals of capitalization and punctuation to help us understand the writing. We also must be able to recognize the words by accurate spelling. We have all read, or tried to read, writing that contains so many mistakes that it is impossible to read—writing that, unfortunately, fails in its purpose: to communicate.

In this chapter, you will review skills that help make writing easier to read—capitalization, punctuation, and spelling. These skills will be tested in multiple-choice questions on Part 1 of the Writing Skills Test, and they will also help you write your essay correctly for Part 2. There are rules for capitalization and punctuation that are not covered in this book. The material you will see in this chapter focuses on those issues that may appear on the Writing Skills Test. If you would like more information on other issues, a grammar book will be a big help to you.

As you work through the rest of this book, work to improve your handwriting. Make capital letters big and make sure your punctuation marks are clear. Other people read your writing—write for them as well as for yourself.

Capitalization

Always capitalize *proper nouns*, or names. The naming process is similar for all nouns. When a child is born, we use the common noun *baby* or *infant*. Then the parents name the baby *Jennifer* or *Michael*, proper nouns. We name our pets; some people even name their cars (or at least call the car names when it doesn't start!).

As a society, we start organizations and businesses and name them. We build schools, visit historical sites, and live in towns and states. All of these particular people, places, and things have names that need capital letters. A good question to ask yourself when you are deciding whether to capitalize is "Am I naming someone or something?"

In each blank in the following chart, write a proper noun and be sure to capitalize it.

Common Nouns (General)	Proper Nouns (Specific)
woman	Bette Midler
man	George Washington
college	_____
street	_____
nation	_____
language	_____
holiday	_____
doctor	_____

The chart asks you to think consciously of specific names. Although several rules follow that explain in more detail some of the types of nouns that are capitalized, the rules still fall under the basic rule of "If it's a name, capitalize it."

Other Capitalization Rules

★ **1. Capitalize a word used as a person's title.**

> Representing the state of Illinois is **Senator** Paul Simon.
>
> Our most experienced physician, **Doctor** Kundrat, will see you now.

Don't capitalize these words when they are used as general labels.

> The **senator** will meet with the press at 10:00.
>
> I went to see the **doctor** about a lingering cough.

★ **2. Capitalize the specific names of places. Also capitalize words derived from the specific names of places.**

> My **Russian** boyfriend likes **French** dressing on his salad.
>
> **Washington Square** in **New York City** is the setting of a famous novel.
>
> Julian took **Highway 66** to **North Avenue**.

Don't capitalize general geographical terms.

> We drove **east** until we came to a four-lane highway.
>
> This **country** is the most beautiful I have ever seen.
>
> The **town square** was lit with colorful paper lanterns.

★ **3. Capitalize names of special days and words used as part of a date.**

> My sister was born on **Independence Day**.
>
> The celebration was held on **Monday, January** 22nd.

Don't capitalize the names of seasons unless they are part of the specific name of an event or place.

> A fund-raiser for the group home will be held in the **spring**.
>
> The **Spring** Fling was a fund-raiser for the group home.

If you're not sure whether to capitalize something, the dictionary can help. For example, use your dictionary to look up *civil war*. You'll find a definition for the general term, using no capital letters. You may also find an entry for the specific war fought between the Union and the Confederacy in the 1860s—the Civil War—using capital letters.

EXERCISE 1: CAPITALIZATION RULES

Directions: Rewrite the following sentences, putting in capital letters where they belong and taking out those that are incorrect. The number of errors each sentence has is in parentheses.

1. The mayor of chestortown requested assistance from governor kelly. (3 errors)

2. My favorite time of Fall is thanksgiving. (2 errors)

3. Candy's doctor sent her to get a second opinion from doctor Schwartz. (1 error)

4. We will meet on wednesday, august 9, at lincoln center in memphis, tennessee. (6 errors)

5. Leading sunday services at st. gregory's cathedral will be father McMillan. (5 errors)

6. Drive North to baker avenue, then turn left at Kennedy highway. (4 errors)

7. My german lessons are helping me prepare for my european trip next Spring. (3 errors)

8. Marissa's birthday is christmas day, so her parents will surprise her with a party in january. (3 errors)

9. The ohio river is a beautiful river. (2 errors)

10. This Summer the band will be on the Road for a long tour. (2 errors)

Answers are on page 184.

Punctuation

As you know from all your work in writing, every sentence ends with a period, a question mark, or an exclamation point (!). Watch out for end punctuation that is missing or incorrect. As you learned in the sections about sentence fragments, the fact that a group of words ends with a period or a question mark does not mean it is a complete sentence.

INCORRECT: Cleaned the garage.

CORRECT: Peter cleaned the garage.

INCORRECT: The man running the roulette wheel?

CORRECT: Who is the man running the roulette wheel?

The Comma

You have already learned some comma rules in Chapter 2, "Sentence Structure." Now you will review those rules (the first two rules in the following list) as well as learn new ones. Keep in mind that commas are used for specific reasons. *Extra* commas are just as incorrect as missing ones!

Comma Rules

★ 1. **Use a comma with a coordinating conjunction to join two independent clauses.**

> Buying a new car can be exciting, but it can also be expensive.

Remember that an independent clause is a complete thought. If the second part of the sentence is not a complete thought, do *not* separate it from the first part with a comma.

INCORRECT: Jill finished her exams, and went home for Christmas.

CORRECT: Jill finished her exams and went home for Christmas.

★ 2. **Put a comma after introductory dependent clauses.**

> While she was waiting for a ride to work, Lavonna read the newspaper.

Remember that, if the dependent clause follows the independent clause, no comma is needed.

INCORRECT: I would take a class, if I had time.

CORRECT: I would take a class if I had time.

Now practice Rules 1 and 2. Insert commas wherever they are needed in the following sentences.

> After Jim gave permission Lana went out on his bike.
>
> I see my brothers whenever they are in town.
>
> Rex crawled under the bed and showed no interest in food.
>
> Tracy called the toddler but she could not coax him to come out.

You should have placed a comma after *permission* in the first sentence and after *toddler* in the fourth sentence. No commas are needed in the second and third sentences.

You can review this material further on pages 95–96 and 103–104.

★ 3. **Use commas to set off three types of phrases.**

   (1) Introductory or interrupting phrases:

> **As usual,** no one wants to take out the garbage.
>
> Dora's job involves counseling parents, **for instance**.
>
> The goal, **of course,** is to score the most touchdowns.

The phrases in bold type above introduce or interrupt the main flow of the sentence. Notice that these phrases *never* contain the subject or verb of a sentence. They simply add an additional thought to the sentence.

(2) Modifying phrases:

Chattering happily, the children rode off to the picnic.

Our vacation was spent in New Mexico, my favorite state.

Alan Morse, the manager of our plant, is ill.

Notice that each of the above phrases set off by commas describes, or modifies, another word in the sentence.

(3) Adverb phrases:

We could, on the other hand, eat at McDonald's.

However, the team needs a better defense.

Mrs. Mugford, in addition, is a member of the lunch committee.

Notice that the adverb phrases above are not joining two complete sentences. Instead, they simply add some new meaning to the sentence. Can you see why the sentence below is incorrect?

INCORRECT: Nancy lost her glove, however, her son found it.

Simply using commas in this sentence is not correct because the adverb *however* is joining two complete sentences. As you learned in Chapter 2, this sentence should be punctuated like this:

CORRECT: Nancy lost her glove; however, her son found it.

Now practice Rule 3. Place commas wherever they are needed in the following sentences and cross them out if they are not needed. Be sure to place commas both before and after phrases that interrupt a sentence.

Mosquitoes I think are the worst part of camping.

Unlike her sister Mary asks men out frequently.

For heaven's sake stop making that terrible noise!

Joan, is leaving our firm, I'm sorry to say.

Afraid for her daughter Mrs. Donovan moved quickly toward her.

Nevertheless I'll need some additional income.

The huge blimp, sailed slowly overhead.

In the first sentence, commas are needed before *I* and after *think*. You should have placed commas after *sister* and *sake* in the second and third sentences. The comma after *Joan* in the fourth sentence should be crossed out. In the fifth sentence, add a comma after the modifying phrase *Afraid for her daughter*. In the sixth sentence, place a comma after the word *Nevertheless*. Finally, in the last sentence, take out the comma after *blimp*. Remember that you should never put a comma between a subject and a verb.

★ **4. Use commas to separate items in a *series* (a list of three or more items, actions, or descriptions).** Notice that each of the following series is in parallel structure.

> Children love to eat pizza, hot dogs, and peanut butter.
>
> Sid jogs, lifts weights, and plays handball.
>
> The young, tall, and talented athlete won the contest.

No comma comes before the first item in a series or after the last item.

INCORRECT: You'll find, potatoes, green beans, and lettuce, in that bag.

CORRECT: You'll find potatoes, green beans, and lettuce in that bag.

Do not use commas to separate only two items.

INCORRECT: George types, and takes dictation.

CORRECT: George types and takes dictation.

Now practice Rule 4. Place commas wherever they are needed in the following sentences.

> We traveled through Austria Germany Switzerland and Italy.
>
> The sleigh went over the river and through the woods.
>
> Dopey Sleepy and Doc were three of the seven dwarfs.
>
> My father did all the cooking cleaning and sewing.

In the first sentence, commas are needed after *Austria, Germany,* and *Switzerland.* The second sentence does not need any commas. In the third sentence, commas are needed after *Dopey* and *Sleepy.* In the fourth sentence, commas are needed after *cooking* and *cleaning.* Check your work carefully to make sure you did not add extra commas.

EXERCISE 2: USING COMMAS

Directions: Insert commas wherever they are needed in the body of the following letter. (You should insert nine commas.)

> Dear Mom,
>   Because I do not have enough money I will not be coming home for spring vacation. Unfortunately I need to stay here in Des Moines and work. I did not of course waste my money but I did not allow enough in my budget for an airline ticket. You will understand that I can't come I know. I'd really love to be home in March but I can't afford a ticket until June. Please call Sue Pam and Linda for me and relay the message.
>
>   Love always,
>   Dawn

Answers are on page 185.

Other Punctuation Marks

You have practiced using two other punctuation marks in this book, the semicolon and the apostrophe. Let's review these before you move on to Exercises 3 and 4, which require you to use all these types of punctuation correctly.

Semicolon

Use a semicolon to separate two independent clauses joined by a conjunctive adverb (*however, consequently, moreover, therefore,* etc.)

I will check your files; however, your account seems to be in order.

Notice that this sentence structure also requires a comma following the conjunctive adverb.

You can review this sentence structure, including a list of conjunctive adverbs, on page 101.

Apostrophe

★ 1. **Use an apostrophe to show possession.**

add 's to all singular nouns
to plural nouns not ending in *s*

add ' to plural nouns ending in *s*

I ran into a child's bicycle in the driveway.

The children's bicycles are in the basement.

My three brothers' rooms are always neat and clean.

★ 2. **Use an apostrophe to replace missing letters in contractions.**

They're going to lunch at the Ritz-Carlton.

Lisa doesn't have time for a man like you.

You can review contraction-possessive pronoun confusion on pages 81–82 and subject-verb agreement with contractions on page 77.

EXERCISE 3: PUNCTUATION REVIEW

Directions: Each sentence below contains *one* error in punctuation. Find and correct each error.

Example: Kate finds that ~~its~~ *it's* very difficult to study at home, so she studies at the library.

1. To strip the paint from the woodwork, you will need, a gallon of stripper, old rags, a scraper, a paintbrush, steel wool, and a mask to protect you from the fumes.

2. Mr. Rider my insurance agent, called with information about a rate increase.

3. She hasn't returned the dresses to the store, because she lost the receipt.

4. I love to stay up late and watch old movies, however, I have difficulty getting up in the morning.

5. In spite of her parents protests, Charleen has moved in with her boyfriend.

Answers are on page 185.

EXERCISE 4: STRUCTURE, USAGE, AND MECHANICS

Directions: Read the following paragraph and answer the questions. You'll need to watch for all the types of errors you've studied in writing skills.

(1) Americans are moving to the Sun Belt, an area made up of southern and Western states. (2) Since World War II, many industries have relocated in States such as Nevada, Arizona, Colorado, Utah, and Florida. (3) As a result these states have steadily grown in population. (4) Industries' reasons for moving south and west include cheaper labor, lower taxes, milder weather, lower living costs, and a large market. (5) It's understandable that some industries prefer the climate of the Sun Belt to the long, cold winters of the northeastern and midwestern states the area called the Frost Belt. (6) Traditionally, older citizens have retired to states such as Arizona and Florida because of the climate. (7) Even younger Americans now are seeking the appealing weather and more relaxed lifestyles of the Sun Belt. (8) By the year 2000, the interests of the Sun Belt is expected to play a major part in national decision making as the states gain economic and political power.

1. Sentence 1: **Americans are moving to the Sun Belt, an area made up of southern and Western states.**

What correction should be made to this sentence?

(1) change *Sun Belt* to *sun belt*
(2) remove the comma after *Belt*
(3) change *southern* to *Southern*
(4) change *Western* to *western*
(5) change *states* to *States*

2. Sentence 2: **Since World War II, many industries have relocated in States such as Nevada, Arizona, Colorado, Utah, and Florida.**

What correction should be made to this sentence?

(1) remove the comma after *II*
(2) change *have* to *has*
(3) change *States* to *states*
(4) insert a comma after *as*
(5) no correction is necessary

3. Sentence 3: **As a result these states have steadily grown in population.**

What correction should be made to this sentence?

(1) insert a comma after *result*
(2) change *states* to *States*
(3) insert a comma after *states*
(4) change *have* to *had*
(5) change the spelling of *grown* to *growed*

4. Sentence 4: **Industries' reasons for moving south and west include cheaper labor, lower taxes, milder weather, lower living costs, and a large market.**

What correction should be made to this sentence?

(1) change *Industries'* to *Industries*
(2) change *south* to *South*
(3) change *west* to *West*
(4) insert a comma after *include*
(5) no correction is necessary

5. Sentence 5: **It's understandable that some industries prefer the climate of the Sun Belt to the long, cold winters of the northeastern and midwestern states the area called the Frost Belt.**

What correction should be made to this sentence?

(1) change *It's* to *Its*
(2) change *prefer* to *preferred*
(3) change *Sun Belt* to *sun belt*
(4) change *midwestern* to *Midwestern*
(5) insert a comma after *states*

6. Sentences 6 and 7: **Traditionally, older citizens have retired to states such as Arizona and Florida because of the climate. Even younger Americans now are seeking the appealing weather and more relaxed lifestyles of the Sun Belt.**

The most effective combination of these sentences would include which of the following groups of words?

(1) climate, so younger
(2) climate, but younger
(3) climate; for example, younger
(4) climate, or younger
(5) climate and now are seeking

7. Sentence 8: **By the year 2000, the interests of the Sun Belt is expected to play a major part in national decision making as the states gain economic and political power.**

What correction should be made to this sentence?

(1) remove the comma after *2000*
(2) change *interests* to *interests'*
(3) change *is* to *are*
(4) change *states* to *States*
(5) insert a comma after *economic*

Answers are on page 185.

Spelling

If we ol speld wurds lik tha sound, our riting mite look lik this!

Unfortunately, spelling English the way it sounds doesn't work very well most of the time, as you know. Don't despair.

Becoming a better speller is a goal of many adults. When we think of ourselves as "writers," we often think first of our spelling. In fact, many people think too much about spelling. There is much more to good writing than accurate spelling. Think of spelling as frosting on a cake. After hours of preparing and baking a delicious cake, we want the cake to be topped with frosting. Like frosting, accurate spelling reflects the writer's concern about the final product.

The GED Testing Service has provided you with a list of "frequently misspelled words" (see pages 128–131), words that the general public often misspells. This master list is the basis for the spelling errors you'll have to correct on the Writing Skills Test. The following pages are designed to help you study the words. The rules presented here apply to the words on the list, and almost all of the examples used in the practice exercises are from the list.

General Hints for Improving Your Spelling

1. **Use a dictionary.** There are many different kinds of dictionaries. A salesperson at a bookstore can help you choose a good one.

2. **Read.** You can learn much about spelling by reading material like newspapers, magazines, and books—you'll see common words used correctly over and over.

3. **Write.** You'll be able to practice what you've learned through writing and experimenting with new words.

4. **Record words that cause you difficulty in reading and writing.** Read over them and copy them a few times. Train yourself to spell them correctly.

5. **Make up memory tricks for words you find hard.** For example, *Wednesday* is pronounced "Wensday." Say to yourself WED-NES-DAY each time you write it. Which capital/capitol is a building? The capitol has a dome.

6. **Learn basic rules** that apply to many words on the master list and in everyday use. You'll find helpful spelling rules on pages 132–136.

7. **Don't overemphasize the importance of spelling.** There are a lot of other important topics to study as well. You don't have to be able to spell every word on the master list in order to pass the Writing Skills Test.

Getting to Know the Master List

The following hints will help you study the master list of commonly misspelled words on pages 128–131.

1. Make a few copies of the list so that you can underline, cut, check off, etc. Post the list where you will see the words often. Cut a copy of the list into many shorter lists. Divide and conquer!

2. Arrange for a friend or relative to dictate words to you. Try writing the word a few times as someone else reads it. If you are enrolled in a class, set up a time to meet with a classmate or a study group.

3. Remember, there are probably many words on the list that you *do* know how to spell. You may find that you're a better speller than you thought you were. Be positive! Check off the words you can spell; then attack the ones that are left.

4. Build your vocabulary. Most words on the list are common in daily life. There are, however, many words that you may not use in your own writing and speech. As you learn new words, try to use them. Knowing and practicing the meaning will help you keep the correct spelling fresh in your mind.

EXERCISE 5: THE MASTER LIST

Directions: Use the master spelling list on pages 128–131 to complete this exercise.

1. Find and list the nine entries that are capitalized.

2. There are many numbers on the list. Practice writing each of them. Then fill in the blanks with the missing word in the following sequences.

    (a) third, _____, fifth

    (b) eleventh, _____, thirteenth

    (c) seven, _____, nine

    (d) eleven, _____, thirteen, _____

3. Fill in the following blanks with amounts and measures from the list.

    (a) a coin worth twenty-five cents _____

    (b) a piece of paper worth one hundred cents _____

    (c) twelve of something make a _____

    (d) sixteen _____ make a pound

    (e) four quarts make a _____

4. Find and list the four entries that are written as two separate words.

5. There are seven words on the list that start with *q*. What letter usually follows *q* in a word?

6. Which two words contain apostrophes?

7. Find the other forms of the following words on the master list. Look carefully; different forms have different spellings that change their alphabetical order.

Example: dependent   independence   independent

(a) advise _____ _____

(b) argue _____ _____

(c) bury _____ _____

(d) know _____ _____ _____

   (**HINT:** Look for one of the forms of *know* in the *a* listings.)

(e) decide _____ _____

(f) commit _____ _____

(g) marry _____ _____

(h) occur _____ _____

(i) please _____ _____

(j) possess _____ _____

(k) prefer _____ _____ _____

Answers are on page 185.

Master List of Frequently Misspelled Words

All misspelled words on the GED Test will be taken from the following master list. Other forms of most of these words, including plurals and forms requiring suffixes, also may be tested.

A	across	almost	appearance	associate
a lot	address	already	appetite	association
ability	addressed	although	application	attempt
absence	adequate	altogether	apply	attendance
absent	advantage	always	appreciate	attention
abundance	advantageous	amateur	appreciation	audience
accept	advertise	American	approach	August
acceptable	advertisement	among	appropriate	author
accident	advice	amount	approval	automobile
accommodate	advisable	analysis	approve	autumn
accompanied	advise	analyze	approximate	auxiliary
accomplish	advisor	angel	argue	available
accumulation	aerial	angle	arguing	avenue
accuse	affect	annual	argument	awful
accustomed	affectionate	another	arouse	awkward
ache	again	answer	arrange	B
achieve	against	antiseptic	arrangement	bachelor
achievement	aggravate	anxious	article	balance
acknowledge	aggressive	apologize	artificial	balloon
acquaintance	agree	apparatus	ascend	bargain
acquainted	aisle	apparent	assistance	basic
acquire	all right	appear	assistant	beautiful

because	cigarette	courage	disastrous	exceed
become	circumstance	courageous	discipline	excellent
before	citizen	course	discover	except
beginning	clothes	courteous	discriminate	exceptional
being	clothing	courtesy	disease	exercise
believe	coarse	criticism	dissatisfied	exhausted
benefit	coffee	criticize	dissection	exhaustion
benefited	collect	crystal	dissipate	exhilaration
between	college	curiosity	distance	existence
bicycle	column	cylinder	distinction	exorbitant
board	comedy	**D**	division	expense
bored	comfortable	daily	doctor	experience
borrow	commitment	daughter	dollar	experiment
bottle	committed	daybreak	doubt	explanation
bottom	committee	death	dozen	extreme
boundary	communicate	deceive	**E**	**F**
brake	company	December	earnest	facility
breadth	comparative	deception	easy	factory
breath	compel	decide	ecstasy	familiar
breathe	competent	decision	ecstatic	fascinate
brilliant	competition	decisive	education	fascinating
building	compliment	deed	effect	fatigue
bulletin	conceal	definite	efficiency	February
bureau	conceit	delicious	efficient	financial
burial	conceivable	dependent	eight	financier
buried	conceive	deposit	either	flourish
bury	concentration	derelict	eligibility	forcibly
bushes	conception	descend	eligible	forehead
business	condition	descent	eliminate	foreign
C	conference	describe	embarrass	formal
cafeteria	confident	description	embarrassment	former
calculator	congratulate	desert	emergency	fortunate
calendar	conquer	desirable	emphasis	fourteen
campaign	conscience	despair	emphasize	fourth
capital	conscientious	desperate	enclosure	frequent
capitol	conscious	dessert	encouraging	friend
captain	consequence	destruction	endeavor	frightening
career	consequently	determine	engineer	fundamental
careful	considerable	develop	English	further
careless	consistency	development	enormous	**G**
carriage	consistent	device	enough	gallon
carrying	continual	dictator	entrance	garden
category	continuous	died	envelope	gardener
ceiling	controlled	difference	environment	general
cemetery	controversy	different	equipment	genius
cereal	convenience	dilemma	equipped	government
certain	convenient	dinner	especially	governor
changeable	conversation	direction	essential	grammar
characteristic	corporal	disappear	evening	grateful
charity	corroborate	disappoint	evident	great
chief	council	disappointment	exaggerate	grievance
choose	counsel	disapproval	exaggeration	grievous
chose	counselor	disapprove	examine	grocery

guarantee
guess
guidance
H
half
hammer
handkerchief
happiness
healthy
heard
heavy
height
heroes
heroine
hideous
himself
hoarse
holiday
hopeless
hospital
humorous
hurried
hurrying
I
ignorance
imaginary
imbecile
imitation
immediately
immigrant
incidental
increase
independence
independent
indispensable
inevitable
influence
influential
initiate
innocence
inoculate
inquiry
insistent
instead
instinct
integrity
intellectual
intelligence
intercede
interest
interfere
interference
interpreted

interrupt
invitation
irrelevant
irresistible
irritable
island
its
it's
itself
J
January
jealous
journal
judgment
K
kindergarten
kitchen
knew
knock
know
knowledge
L
labor
laboratory
laid
language
later
latter
laugh
leisure
length
lesson
library
license
light
likelihood
likely
literal
literature
livelihood
loaf
loneliness
loose
lose
losing
loyal
loyalty
M
magazine
maintenance
maneuver
marriage
married

marry
match
material
mathematics
measure
medicine
million
miniature
minimum
miracle
miscellaneous
mischief
mischievous
misspelled
mistake
momentous
monkey
monotonous
moral
morale
mortgage
mountain
mournful
muscle
mysterious
mystery
N
narrative
natural
necessary
needle
negligence
neighbor
neither
newspaper
newsstand
niece
noticeable
O
o'clock
obedient
obstacle
occasion
occasional
occur
occurred
occurrence
ocean
offer
often
omission
omit
once

operate
opinion
opportune
opportunity
optimist
optimistic
origin
original
oscillate
ought
ounce
overcoat
P
paid
pamphlet
panicky
parallel
parallelism
particular
partner
pastime
patience
peace
peaceable
pear
peculiar
pencil
people
perceive
perception
perfect
perform
performance
perhaps
period
permanence
permanent
perpendicular
perseverance
persevere
persistent
persuade
personality
personal
personnel
persuade
persuasion
pertain
picture
piece
plain
playwright
pleasant

please
pleasure
pocket
poison
policeman
political
population
portrayal
positive
possess
possession
possessive
possible
post office
potatoes
practical
prairie
precede
preceding
precise
predictable
prefer
preference
preferential
preferred
prejudice
preparation
prepare
prescription
presence
president
prevalent
primitive
principal
principle
privilege
probably
procedure
proceed
produce
professional
professor
profitable
prominent
promise
pronounce
pronunciation
propeller
prophecy
prophet
prospect
psychology
pursue

pursuit	responsibility	significant	sweet	unusual
Q	restaurant	similar	syllable	useful
quality	rhythm	similarity	symmetrical	usual
quantity	rhythmical	sincerely	sympathy	**V**
quarreling	ridiculous	site	synonym	vacuum
quart	right	soldier	**T**	valley
quarter	role	solemn	technical	valuable
quiet	roll	sophomore	telegram	variety
quite	roommate	soul	telephone	vegetable
R	**S**	source	temperament	vein
raise	sandwich	souvenir	temperature	vengeance
realistic	Saturday	special	tenant	versatile
realize	scarcely	specified	tendency	vicinity
reason	scene	specimen	tenement	vicious
rebellion	schedule	speech	therefore	view
recede	science	stationary	thorough	village
receipt	scientific	stationery	through	villain
receive	scissors	statue	title	visitor
recipe	season	stockings	together	voice
recognize	secretary	stomach	tomorrow	volume
recommend	seize	straight	tongue	**W**
recuperate	seminar	strength	toward	waist
referred	sense	strenuous	tragedy	weak
rehearsal	separate	stretch	transferred	wear
reign	service	striking	treasury	weather
relevant	several	studying	tremendous	Wednesday
relieve	severely	substantial	tries	week
remedy	shepherd	succeed	truly	weigh
renovate	sheriff	successful	twelfth	weird
repeat	shining	sudden	twelve	whether
repetition	shoulder	superintendent	tyranny	which
representative	shriek	suppress	**U**	while
requirements	siege	surely	undoubtedly	whole
resemblance	sight	surprise	United States	wholly
resistance	signal	suspense	university	whose
resource	significance	sweat	unnecessary	wretched
respectability				

EXERCISE 6: THE DICTIONARY

Directions: Below are some words on the list that may be unfamiliar to you. It is difficult to learn how to spell words that you may not use or hear very often (or at all). Use a dictionary to check the meanings and pronunciations of these words. Then use each one in a sentence that demonstrates its meaning.

auxiliary	negligence
ecstasy	perseverance
exorbitant	prevalent
flourish	suppress
hideous	tyranny

Possible answers are on page 185.

Helpful Spelling Rules

You have already studied rules for spelling noun plurals on pages 60–63 and rules for spelling verb forms on pages 70–72. You may want to review these sections now, since you'll need to know them for the exercises in this chapter. Knowing these rules for adding plural and verb endings will also help you learn the rules for adding suffixes, since they are very similar.

Compound Words

Compound words are formed by combining two or more words. When you form a compound word, never change the spelling of the original words.

The following are compound words from the master spelling list. Write them in the blanks.

day + break = daybreak   over + coat = _____

news + stand = _____   news + paper = _____

him + self = _____   it + self = _____

police + man = _____   room + mate = _____

Be careful of words that look like compound words but cannot be divided into two words:

almost	already	although	altogether
always	careful	mournful	pastime

Also remember the words you have found on the list that are written separately—*a lot, all right, post office.*

The IE/EI Rules

Learn the following rhyme to help you remember when you put *i* before *e*: "I before E except after C or when sounding like A as in *neighbor* and *weigh*."

Study the following rules and fill in two more examples of your own for each one.

★ 1. Most of the time, *i* comes before *e*.

chief believe _____ _____

★ 2. After the letter *c*, *e* comes before *i*, except when *ci* together makes a *sh* sound as in *conscience*.

receive perceive _____ _____

★ 3. When the sound is a long *a*, *e* comes before *i*.

eight vein _____ _____

Now practice the rules by circling the error in each of the following groups:

1. (a) weird   2. (a) eight   3. (a) conceit   4. (a) peice
   (b) breif   (b) seize   (b) ceiling   (b) belief
   (c) foreign   (c) view   (c) believe   (c) reign
   (d) leisure   (d) reciept   (d) receive   (d) thief
   (e) mischief   (e) either   (e) seige   (e) priest

Answers: 1. b   2. d   3. e   4. a

Adding Prefixes

When a prefix is added to a word, the spelling of the prefix and the spelling of the base word always remain the same.

Here is a list of some prefixes used in words on the master spelling list and their meanings.

Prefix	Meaning	Examples
anti	against	antiseptic
auto	self	automobile
bene	good	benefit
co, com, con, cor	together	corroborate conversation
de	down	descend, descent
dis	not, away	disappear, disapprove
ex	out of	exceed
fore	front	forehead
im, in	in, into	immigrant, interrupt

Prefix	Meaning	Examples
in, ir	not	independent, irrelevant
mis	wrong	misspell, mistake
pre	before	prejudice
trans	across	transferred
un	not	undoubtedly, unnecessary, unusual

Practice adding common prefixes by filling in the blanks:

bi + cycle   = *bicycle*

dis + appoint   = _____

dis + satisfied   = _____

in + competent   = _____

in + convenient   = _____

ir + relevant   = _____

ir + resistible   = _____

un + acceptable   = _____

un + natural   = _____

Adding Suffixes

Most of the time, when a suffix is added to a base word, the spelling of the base word and the spelling of the suffix remain the same. However, the spelling of the base word is altered in some cases, according to the following rules.

★ **1. If a word ends in a silent *e* and the suffix begins with a vowel, drop the silent *e*.**

appreciate + ation = appreciation

indispense + able = _____

coarse + est = _____

continue + ous = _____

Exceptions: Words that end in *ge* or *ce* must keep the final *e* to maintain the "soft" *g* (like *j*) and *c* (like *s*) sounds.

change + able = changeable

notice + able = _____

advantage + ous = _____

peace + able = _____

★ 2. **Keep a silent _e_ at the end of the base word when adding a suffix that begins with a consonant.**

        care + ful = careful

        extreme + ly = _____

        advertise + ment = _____

Exceptions:

        argue + ment = argument

        true + ly = truly

        judge + ment = judgment

★ 3. **When adding a suffix to a word ending in _y_ preceded by a consonant, change the _y_ to _i_ before adding the suffix. However, if the suffix begins with _i_, keep the _y_.**

        marry + age = marriage

        apply + ing = applying

        easy + er = _____

        bury + al = _____

        carry + ing = _____

        heavy + est = _____

If a base word ends in _y_ preceded by a vowel, the spelling never changes when a suffix is added.

        employ + er = employer

        employ + ment = employment

★ 4. **The final consonant of a base word must be doubled if _all_ of the following are true:**

- the base word ends in a single vowel and single consonant other than _h_, _w_, or _x_

- the accented syllable of the base word is on the last (or only) syllable

- the suffix begins with a vowel

Double the final consonant:

        prefer + ed = preferred

        permit + ing = _____

        transfer + ed = _____

Don't double the final consonant:

        benefit + ed = benefited

        counsel + or = _____

Sometimes the addition of a suffix shifts the accent to a different syllable. Don't double the final consonant unless the accent remains on the final syllable.

prefer + ence = **preference** (accent shifts)

occur + ence = oc**cur**rence (accent stays the same)

con**fer** + ence = _____

Tricky Vowels and Consonants

Below are some words that are often difficult to spell because of the placement or use of vowels. Some of the vowels are silent. Some sound like *e* instead of *a*. Some use *y* as a vowel. Look up the correct spelling of each word on the master spelling list; then write out the entire word for practice.

av__nue	be__utiful	b__ild
cafet__ria	conce__l	cr__stal
enco__raging	envelop__	g__idance
g__arantee	man__uver	misc__llaneo__s
persev__rance	pers__ade	sep__rate
specim__n	so__l	synon__m
t__ranny	tong__e	

Here are words that contain silent consonants. Look up the correct spelling of each word on the master spelling list; then write out the entire word for practice.

ans__er	autum__	colum__
campai__n	dou__t	ex__aust
ex__ibit	__new	__nock
__now	li____t	mor__gage
of__en	__sychology	recei__t
ri____t	r__ythmical	s__issors
si____t	solem__	strai____t

Watch out for combinations of letters that make different sounds. All the following words contain a consonant combination that makes an *f* sound. Look up the correct spelling of each on the master spelling list; then write out the entire word for practice.

enou____	lau____	pro____ecy
pro____et	so____omore	tele____one

For further work on combinations of letters, search the master list for words containing an *sh* sound and practice writing each one. There are several ways this sound can be spelled. To get you started, here are the first three words:

accompli____	accumula____on	affec____onate

EXERCISE 7: SPELLING LIST REVIEW

Directions: Be sure you have studied all the words on the master spelling list before you do this exercise. Place the letter of the word containing an error in the blank. If all the words are correct, write *f* in the blank.

_____ 1. (a) annually   (d) bacheler
         (b) recipe   (e) college
         (c) shining   (f) *no error*

_____ 2. (a) truely   (d) mathematics
         (b) anxiously   (e) temperature
         (c) holidays   (f) *no error*

_____ 3. (a) believed   (d) cheifly
         (b) vicinity   (e) transferred
         (c) applies   (f) *no error*

_____ 4. (a) scarcely   (d) judgment
         (b) procede   (e) all right
         (c) incidentally   (f) *no error*

_____ 5. (a) between   (d) unnecessarily
         (b) employee   (e) restarant
         (c) loneliness   (f) *no error*

_____ 6. (a) panicky   (d) February
         (b) critisize   (e) privilege
         (c) heroine   (f) *no error*

_____ 7. (a) knowledge   (d) stomach
         (b) obedient   (e) significant
         (c) adviseable   (f) *no error*

_____ 8. (a) burial   (d) occuring
         (b) obstacle   (e) technical
         (c) pronunciation   (f) *no error*

_____ 9. (a) exceptionaly   (d) leisure
         (b) possession   (e) preferred
         (c) appreciation   (f) *no error*

_____ 10. (a) persuading   (d) committee
          (b) arguement   (e) piece
          (c) commitment   (f) *no error*

Answers are on page 186.

Sound-Alike Words

Hear is a list of pears of words ewe knead too no.

Here is a list of pairs of words you need to know.

If you read both of these statements aloud, you will hear the same sounds. However, the words that sound alike, *Hear/Here, pears/pairs, ewe/you, knead/need, to, too,* and *two,* and *no/know,* have different meanings and spellings. Many pairs and groups of sound-alike words can be found on the master spelling list.

You have already studied some especially troublesome sound-alike words—the possessives and contractions. Review the material on pages 81–82 to refresh your memory.

Following are more pairs and groups of sound-alike words. Many of them sound exactly alike, such as *to, too,* and *two.* Others should not sound alike if you pronounce them carefully, such as *advice* and *advise.*

Read the explanations of the differences between the sound-alikes; then practice by filling in the blanks with the correct words.

accept (receive)
except (excluding; to leave out)

Everyone _____ Bryan will _____ an award.

advice (recommendation)
advise (recommend)

Samuel will _____ me, and I will follow his

_____ .

affect (act upon)
effect (result)

The medication will _____ me. I hope it doesn't cause any bad

side _____ s.

altogether (entirely)
all together (gathered in the same place)

I'm not _____ sure that the children were

_____ .

already (previously)
all ready (completely prepared)

We are _____ dressed and _____ for the party.

capital (city that is the official seat of a government)
capitol (building in which a state legislature works)
(*Capital* is also used in other ways: capital letters, capital in the bank.)

We visited the _____ building in Springfield, our state

_____ .

choose (pick)
chose (picked)

I'll _____ this dessert today. I _____ cake

yesterday.

coarse (rough)
course (plan of action; part of a meal; class)

When I took a woodworking _____, I learned to turn

_____ planks into fine furniture.

conscience (sense of right and wrong)
conscious (being aware)
conscientious (thorough, responsible)

Herb's _____ bothered him because he had not been

_____ of his daughter's problems. Normally he is a very

_____ father.

desert (dry region; pronounced DEH-zert)
desert (abandon; pronounced duh-ZERT)
dessert (last course of a meal)

Don't _____ your family in the hot, dry _____!

Save some pie or other type of _____ for me.

know (be aware of)
no (negative)

_____, I don't _____ the answer.

knew (was aware of)
new (not old)

I _____ I'd need a _____ coat before winter

came.

loose (not tight)
lose (misplace; fail to win)

The clasp on your key chain is _____. Tighten it, or you may

_____ your keys.

personal (individual)
personnel (relating to a group of workers)

Melinda had an appointment with the _____ director of her com-

pany. She arranged for a leave of absence for _____ reasons.

principal (main; head of a school)
principle (rules, facts, laws)

The _____ reason I called was to arrange a meeting with the

_____ of Jefferson School. I'd like to teach a course about the

_____s of physics.

quiet (silent)
quite (very)
quit (stop)

Please be _____. I'm _____ ill, so

_____ making so much noise.

to (preposition; word before a verb)
too (more than enough, very; also)
two (2)

I'd like _____ hamburgers. She went _____ the

store. Bud likes _____ swim. It's _____ cold in

here. I want _____ go on vacation, _____.

weak (not strong)
week (seven days)

After being hospitalized for a _____, Gloria felt very

_____.

weather (outdoor conditions)
whether (if)

She didn't know _____ she was going to the picnic. Rain was predicted in the _____ forecast.

EXERCISE 8: SOUND-ALIKE WORDS

Circle the error in each sentence; then write the correct word in the blank.

Example: The whole team worked hard all (weak) to build morale and break the

Olympic record. ____week____

1. The teachers knew that the principle's attitude was affected by the grievance they

had filed. _____

2. If you choose to accept his advise and seek the job, you should apply at the per-

sonnel office. _____

3. Tim knows that Shari is quite bored with the coarse. _____

4. The counselor's advice was not all together sound, so I chose to ignore her

suggestions. _____

5. World peace is an issue we senators hear quite a lot about. Here inside the capitol

we are conscience of world affairs. _____

6. He ate a whole pie for dessert. Now he's quiet affected by his

actions. _____

7. I no the picnic will be tomorrow, whether the weather is good or

not. _____

8. All of us except Charlie have all ready chosen to work for the reelection of the

school board members. _____

Answers are on page 186.

EXERCISE 9: STRUCTURE, USAGE, SPELLING, AND MECHANICS

Directions: Read the following paragraph, looking for errors in capitalization, punctuation, spelling, and other types of errors you have studied in writing skills. Then answer the questions that follow.

(1) Every April, American taxpayers, surrounded by expense records, receipts, and canceled checks, cuddle up with their calculaters to figure out their yearly income taxes. (2) Taxpayers study their Internal Revenue Service instructions in order to fill out their tax forms accurately. (3) People want to pay the least possible amount of money but they must avoid mistakes and stay within the law. (4) Over the years, wealthy taxpayers have found several loopholes that seem unfair to others; consequently Americans have cried out annually for changes in the tax laws. (5) Private citizens also have criticized businesses for using loopholes in the laws to their advantage, the loopholes allow companies to pay fewer taxes and maintain higher profits. (6) As a result of years of discussion and debate over the tax dilemma, Congress passed the Tax Reform Act of 1986, which radically changed the way americans pay their income taxes. (7) One reason that the new law, in effect after 1988 was fairer is that it forced businesses to pay taxes on more of their profits. (8) Insted of adding exceptions and deductions, the new law eliminated hundreds of them. (9) Of course, taxpayers had to become competent in analyzing the new forms and learn the new rules for dependints, retirement benefits, and interest. (10) Taxpayers do not enjoy losing their personal income but they may part more easily with their hard-earned dollars if they think the tax laws are fair.

1. Sentence 1: **Every April, American taxpayers, surrounded by expense records, receipts, and canceled checks, cuddle up with their calculaters to figure out their yearly income taxes.**

   What correction should be made to this sentence?

   (1) change *April* to *april*
   (2) change *American* to *american*
   (3) change the spelling of *receipts* to *reciepts*
   (4) remove the comma after *checks*
   (5) change the spelling of *calculaters* to *calculators*

2. Sentence 2: **Taxpayers <u>study their</u> Internal Revenue Service instructions in order to fill out their tax forms accurately.**

   Which of the following is the best way to write the underlined portion of this sentence? If you think the original is the best way, choose option (1).

   (1) study their
   (2) studied their
   (3) will study their
   (4) study there
   (5) study his

3. Sentence 3: **People want to pay the least possible amount of money but they must avoid mistakes and stay within the law.**

   What correction should be made to this sentence?

   (1) change the spelling of *People* to *Poeple*
   (2) insert a comma after *money*
   (3) insert a comma after *but*
   (4) insert a comma after *mistakes*
   (5) no correction is necessary

4. Sentence 4: **Over the years, wealthy taxpayers have found several loopholes that seem unfair to others; consequently Americans have cried out annually for changes in the tax laws.**

   What correction should be made to this sentence?

   (1) remove the comma after *years*
   (2) change the spelling of *several* to *sevral*
   (3) insert a comma after *consequently*
   (4) change *Americans* to *americans*
   (5) change the spelling of *annually* to *annualy*

5. Sentence 5: **Private citizens also have criticized businesses for using loopholes in the laws to their advantage, the loopholes allow companies to pay fewer taxes and maintain higher profits.**

   Which of the following is the best way to write the underlined portion of this sentence? If you think the original is the best way, choose option (1).

   (1) their advantage, the
   (2) its advantage, the
   (3) their advantage. The
   (4) its advantage. The
   (5) their advantage the

6. Sentence 6: **As a result of years of discussion and debate over the tax dilemma, Congress passed the Tax Reform Act of 1986, which radically changed the way americans pay their income taxes.**

   What correction should be made to this sentence?

   (1) change the spelling of *dilemma* to *dilema*
   (2) remove the comma after *dilemma*
   (3) change *Congress* to *congress*
   (4) replace *which* with *who*
   (5) change *americans* to *Americans*

7. Sentence 7: **One reason that the new law, in effect after 1988 was fairer is that it forced businesses to pay taxes on more of their profits.**

   What correction should be made to this sentence?

   (1) change the spelling of *effect* to *affect*
   (2) insert a comma after *1988*
   (3) change the spelling of *businesses* to *buisnesses*
   (4) replace *their* with *they're*
   (5) no correction is necessary

8. Sentence 8: **Insted of adding exceptions and deductions, the new law eliminated hundreds of them.**

What correction should be made to this sentence?

(1) change the spelling of *Insted* to *Instead*
(2) insert a comma after *exceptions*
(3) remove the comma after *deductions*
(4) change the spelling of *eliminated* to *elimanated*
(5) no correction is necessary

9. Sentence 9: **Of course, taxpayers had to become competent in analyzing the new forms and learn the new rules for dependints, retirement benefits, and interest.**

What correction should be made to this sentence?

(1) change the spelling of *competent* to *competant*
(2) change the spelling of *analyzing* to *analizing*
(3) insert a comma after *forms*
(4) change the spelling of *dependints* to *dependents*
(5) insert a comma after *for*

10. Sentence 10: **Taxpayers do not enjoy losing their personal income but they may part more easily with their hard-earned dollars if they think the tax laws are fair.**

What correction should be made to this sentence?

(1) change the spelling of *losing* to *loosing*
(2) change the spelling of *personal* to *personel*
(3) insert a comma after *income*
(4) change the spelling of *dollars* to *dollers*
(5) insert a comma after *dollars*

Answers are on page 186.

4
PREPARING FOR THE GED WRITING SAMPLE

Usage, sentence structure, and mechanics are all crucial to communicating successfully with others in writing. However, these surface features of writing are not the whole story. A written composition may present accurate usage, contain no errors in mechanics, have well-structured, complete sentences, and *say nothing*. Good writing must *say something*—convey an explanation, present an opinion with logical and accurate support, or describe someone or something.

The writing process can be compared to an exercise workout: you go through a series of steps to reach the desired result. The five steps of the writing process are 1. Prewriting 2. Drafting 3. Revising 4. Editing 5. Publishing. A writing "workout" is an exercise program for our minds, helping us clarify our thoughts and get them on paper for our readers.

THE 45-MINUTE WORKOUT

Exercise for the Body

1. **Plan.** Arrange a time and place to exercise.

2. **Warm up** by stretching your muscles.

3. **Organize your exercises:** sit-ups, then jogging, etc.

4. **Use those muscles!** Keep moving! Don't give up!

5. **Cool down.** You've worked hard; relax your muscles.

Exercise for the Mind

1. **Prewriting.** Brainstorm for a topic, using mapping, clustering, organizing strategies.

2. **Drafting.** Write first draft based on prewriting activities.

3. **Revising.** Write second draft. Do a self-check based on what you like or dislike about the writing.

4. **Editing.** Check mechanics, spelling, punctuation, and grammar.

5. **Publishing.** Write for a purpose—family stories, the GED Essay Test.

As you can see, a good writing workout follows a series of steps. Throughout the rest of your work in writing skills, you'll practice these steps: prewriting, writing, revising, editing, and publishing. These writing steps will be very useful to you when you take the Writing Skills Test, so be sure to practice each one fully and carefully.

Warming Up to Writing

Think of the kinds of writing you already do. Underline any of these that you have written in your daily life. Add other kinds of writing you do.

1. *Lists*—grocery lists, meal planning or menu lists, errand lists, "Things to Do" lists, gift lists, _____

2. *Notes*—notes to family members, co-workers, children's teachers; notes inside of greeting cards; memos; postcards sent from vacation spots; _____ _____

3. *Letters*—friendly letters, business letters, letters of application for jobs, letters to the editors of newspapers or magazines, _____

4. *Diary or journal*—personal diary, daily written journal entries, notes to children in baby books, _____

5. Other types of writing that you do: _____

Building Material for Writing

Keeping informed and writing about your daily experiences, thoughts, and conversations will help you build your resources for writing.

1. *Keep a journal.* Write about whatever is on your mind or whatever happens to you. You'll have a record of your ideas and experiences.

2. *Think about discussions you have with others.* How do you verbally convince or persuade others? Try writing a few of your arguments in your journal or in letters.

3. *Read with a writer's point of view.* Look at how newspaper and magazine articles are written. Notice how the main ideas are developed, how paragraphs are organized, and what clues help you read and understand the articles.

4. *Try writing something you haven't before.*
   • If you always call relatives or friends, surprise them with a letter.
   • Write down stories you want to remember about your children or family; start a memory journal.

EXERCISE 1: WARMING UP

1. Write a note to someone or a journal entry of four or five sentences.

2. Think of a memorable day in your life and write a few lines describing the day or event.

3. Choose an article of at least five paragraphs in a newspaper or magazine. First read it to see what information you can learn from it. Then read it carefully once again to see how the information is ordered and structured. Jot down, in note form, what the main idea is.

Answers will vary.

Topic, Audience, and Purpose

The *topic* is the subject of your writing—what you are writing about. If you write a letter to a landlord, the topic may be "high rent," "longer lease," or "broken appliance." If you are writing an essay on marriage for a class or an organization, the topic may be "some reasons why most teenage marriages fail," "trust in a marriage," or "second marriages."

Once you have a topic, you need to determine your *purpose*. What point do you want to make? Why are you writing? Are you writing to tell a story? to describe? to inform? to persuade? If you are writing a letter of complaint to the credit department of a store, then your purpose is to state the problem, explain your opinion, and offer a solution. If you are writing an essay, you might describe a situation, inform about an issue, or state your opinion and support it.

Your purpose also depends on who is reading your writing—the *audience*. While diaries and journals are personal, most other types of writing are meant to be read. For example, you might write a letter of application to a personnel director, a note to the newspaper carrier, a report to a club or class, or an essay for an instructor to grade. An essay is usually meant for "general readership." It is written so that anyone reading it can understand it. Most of us write reports or essays with the idea that "someone out there" will be reading them. Keeping your readers in mind will help you make good word choices and use appropriate support for your ideas.

EXERCISE 2: TOPIC, AUDIENCE, AND PURPOSE

Directions: Read the following ending paragraph from a short letter and identify the writer, the topic, the purpose, and the reader (audience).

> For these reasons, I am asking that Erik be excused from your class next Friday. I hope that this absence will not hurt his progress in your history class. Please send homework with him.
>
> Thank you.

1. Who is the writer?

2. What is the topic?

3. What is the purpose?

4. Who is the reader?

Answers are on page 186.

Prewriting Paragraphs

There are many types of writing. However, being able to write a good paragraph is helpful in almost any kind of writing. Writing a good paragraph requires you to think clearly and organize your thoughts—the best writing practice you can get. Have you ever helped people move from one home to another? If they are packed and organized, the hard part is done before you come to carry boxes and furniture to the truck. Writing is the same way. If you plan and organize your ideas before you write, the writing itself is much easier and the end product is better.

Brainstorming for Paragraphs

You have taken a major step in the writing process. You have considered your topic, purpose, and audience. Now what? Once you have determined what point you want to make, you need to come up with ideas to put into your paragraph. This process is often called **brainstorming**.

To brainstorm, simply list rapidly all the ideas you can think of about your topic. Don't stop to edit or evaluate your ideas; don't worry about spelling or try to write complete sentences. A "whirlwind" of ideas should come to you as you think about the ways that you can support your topic. Write down all of your ideas—you want quantity now. You'll have time to think about quality later.

Here's an example of brainstorming:

Topic: garage sales

Topic sentence: It takes a lot of organization to get ready for a garage sale.

Brainstorm list:
sorting and pricing items
clean the garage
watching my kids and keeping the dog in the yard
cleaning out the closets and the basement before
keeping the neighbor's kids out of my yard
borrow tables
taking out an ad in the newspaper
friends always ask to sell their stuff
I hate the cleanup afterward!
making and posting signs

Some of these ideas are very useful. You can see that the writer wrote down every idea, even the problems with the neighbor's kids and dog. Not all of these ideas will be used in the paragraph, but all were part of the brainstorming process. Writing down everything helped keep the writer's thoughts and pencil flying.

EXERCISE 3: BRAINSTORMING

Directions: Choose *two* of the following topics. Make a brainstorm list of at least six items for each one. Don't worry about spelling, wording, or whether the ideas are relevant. Just write down all of your ideas. Spend at least five minutes on each topic.

Be sure to save your work! In fact, you will want to save all the work you do in this chapter as you will have many opportunities to work on it later.

1. fashion fads

2. my favorite television show

3. the worst job I ever had

Answers will vary.

Structure of a Paragraph

A paragraph is a group of sentences written about one topic or main idea. A paragraph has two very important components: a *topic sentence* and *supporting sentences*. The topic sentence states the main idea of the paragraph and often appears at the beginning. The supporting sentences back up and explain the main idea—giving evidence, examples, and reasons. A paragraph may also have a *concluding sentence*, which sums up or restates the main idea.

In the following example, notice that the first sentence is the topic sentence. It "sets the stage" for the paragraph. The supporting sentences explain the main idea, and the concluding sentence summarizes without repeating.

Karate lessons have really improved Jay's self-esteem. He is a small boy and not very athletically inclined, but after watching and loving the Karate Kid movies, he became interested in karate. He has taken lessons now for six months and feels very good about himself. As he advances in the classes, he gains confidence and seems to relate better to his friends. Jay is now more self-assured as he works toward his goal—a black belt!

Writing the Topic Sentence

The topic sentence is the most important sentence of a paragraph. It is often the first sentence of the paragraph, and it states the purpose of your piece of writing. Think of the topic sentence as an "umbrella" sentence. The supporting sentences should all belong under the main idea stated in the topic sentence.

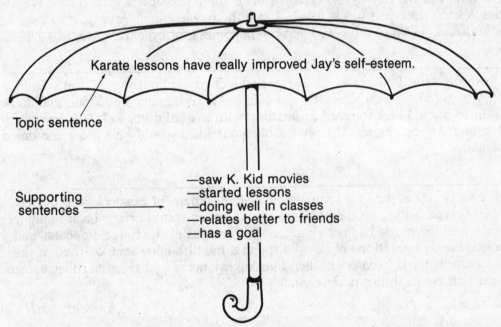

Karate lessons have really improved Jay's self-esteem.

Topic sentence

Supporting sentences →

—saw K. Kid movies
—started lessons
—doing well in classes
—relates better to friends
—has a goal

Make sure your topic sentences state the subject of your paragraphs and the point you want to make. In the previous example, the subject of the paragraph is Jay's karate lessons. However, the writer also makes an important point in the topic sentence—that the lessons are improving Jay's self-esteem. When you are writing your own topic sentences, ask yourself these questions:

1. What is the topic?

2. What do I want to say about the topic?

EXERCISE 4: WRITING TOPIC SENTENCES
PART A

Directions: Write a topic sentence for a paragraph on each of the following topics. Make sure your topic sentence tells what point you would make about the topic. Remember, you need only write the topic sentence, not the whole paragraph.

1. birthday parties

2. the president of the United States

3. the kitchen in my new apartment

4. noise pollution

5. weather forecasting

Possible answers are on page 186.

PART B

Directions: Each of these paragraphs needs a good topic sentence. Read the supporting and concluding sentences; then write a topic sentence.

1. _____

The first record I ever bought was his "Fingertips," which he recorded when he was "Little Stevie Wonder." I've collected his singles and albums since the 1960s. His *Songs in the Key of Life* is my favorite and a classic. I watched the "We Are the World" video just to see Stevie. I saw the movie *Jungle Fever* just to hear his soundtrack. His music has brought me happiness for over thirty years.

2. _____

On sunny days, I have a lot of energy and feel good about myself. I'm usually easy to get along with when the sun shines. When it rains, I feel blue and do not want to work. I look forward to sledding with my children, so I'm happy when it snows. As you can see, if I never looked outside, I would be a more contented person.

3. _____

Buying tickets at the gate reminds me of the excitement I experienced at the yearly event. Sitting on the horse on the merry-go-round brings back many memories, and the music has not changed. The aromas of the fudge, popcorn, and cotton candy remind me of how I'd spend a month's allowance on food at the amusement park. Even now, when I get up my nerve and ride the roller coaster, I get sick. Some things never change!

Answers will vary.

Selecting and Organizing Ideas

Now that you have determined what stand you will take or what viewpoint you will present, worked on collecting ideas, and written your topic sentence, you need to select the ideas you will use. Can you use all of the ideas on your brainstorm list, or should you cross out some? You want to eliminate irrelevant ideas, ideas that do not support your topic sentence. For example, in the garage sale brainstorm on page 148, the item "I hate the cleanup afterward" is irrelevant because it does not support the topic sentence—"It takes a lot of organization to get ready for a garage sale." Go back and find at least two other items in the brainstorm list that do not support the topic sentence.

After you have eliminated irrelevant ideas, you have a list of ideas that you can use in a paragraph. But what order will you write them in? Every topic and every paragraph is different, so there's no one way to put ideas in order. You have to think carefully about what order of ideas will make your paragraph easy to understand. You can put things in time order, least-to-most-important order, or another order that works for your subject.

Here is the brainstorm list from page 148 with the irrelevant ideas eliminated. The remaining ideas are numbered in the order that the writer performs the tasks—time order.

2 sorting and pricing items

4 clean the garage

1 cleaning out the closets and the basement before

5 borrow tables

3 taking out an ad in the newspaper

6 making and posting signs

EXERCISE 5: SELECTING AND ORGANIZING IDEAS

Directions: Take out your brainstorm lists from Exercise 3, page 148. Eliminate irrelevant ideas from each list and number the ideas in logical order.

Be sure to save your work. You will need it in Exercise 6.

Answers will vary.

Writing a Rough Draft

You have worked through much of the process. You understand topic, purpose, and audience. You've brainstormed ideas. You've written topic sentences. You've chosen relevant ideas and put them in order. Now you're ready to create a paragraph—a first draft.

As you write, use your numbered brainstorm list as a guide. You don't have to follow it exactly, of course. But if you have done a good job of prewriting, you have already done most of the work—all that's left is turning the items on your list into supporting sentences and adding a concluding sentence.

Remember that you are writing a rough draft. Your paragraph does not have to be perfect on the first try. Just work on getting the ideas on paper. You can polish the writing and make corrections later. If you leave space between lines and wide margins, you'll be able to make changes more easily. As you write a draft, keep in mind the following features of a paragraph:

1. The first word is indented. Look at the first word of each paragraph in this book to see what *indented* means.

2. A paragraph has a topic sentence that tells a main idea.

3. A paragraph has several sentences that support the topic sentence.

EXERCISE 6: WRITING A ROUGH DRAFT

Directions: Choose *one* of your lists from Exercises 3 and 5. Write a rough draft of a paragraph. Be sure to save your work; you will need it in Exercise 8.

Answers will vary.

EXERCISE 7: PRACTICING THE WRITING PROCESS

Directions: Choose *two* of the following topics. For each,

- write a topic sentence that tells the main point you will make about the topic in a paragraph

- brainstorm ideas to support your topic sentence

- select and order the ideas you want to use in a paragraph

- write a rough draft of each paragraph

Be sure to save your work. You will be working on your paragraphs again in Exercise 8.

1. your favorite type of car

2. your least favorite musician or rock group

3. the quality of the schools in your area

4. a friend or relative whom you admire

Answers will vary.

Revising Your Rough Draft

Once you have drafted a paragraph, it's a good idea to take a break from it for a while—a couple of hours, if possible, so you can see it with a fresh eye when you revise. When you take it up again, think about what you wanted to say. Then read your paragraph as if you were the audience. Did you fully develop your main idea? Is your topic sentence clear and supported? Is there a closing sentence? Ask yourself these questions:

- What's good about my paragraph?

- What don't I like about my paragraph?

- What can I do to improve my paragraph?

This step in the writing process is called *revising*. The revision process is a "second chance." It is an opportunity to move words and sentences, add ideas, remove or rewrite irrelevant sentences, and clarify confusingly worded sentences. Rather than copying your paragraph over, use the spaces between the lines and the margins on each side to make changes. Don't worry about mechanical errors yet. You will have a chance to edit later.

To get an idea of what revising is all about, look at the following sample rough draft. It needs some work. What would you do to strengthen it?

Thanksgiving is a day to relax. The rest of our family usually sleeps late. Mom or Dad gets up at 6:00 A.M. to prepare the turkey, then the dutiful parent goes back to bed. Because our aunts, uncles, and cousins bring food, there are only last-minute preparations, so there is plenty of time to sit and talk or play cards. Little children run all over, making it difficult to have a quiet conversation. After a big meal at 1:00 and a long afternoon of visiting, we are all thankful for our time spent together.

Two changes that would strengthen the paragraph would be (1) reverse the second and third sentences and (2) eliminate or revise the sentence "Little children run all over, making it difficult to have a quiet conversation." This sentence does not support the topic sentence; it is an irrelevant idea.

EXERCISE 8: REVISING A ROUGH DRAFT

Directions: Choose *two* of the paragraphs you wrote in Exercises 6 and 7. Revise each one, making sure that your main idea is stated clearly and well supported.

Be sure to save your work. You will need it in Exercise 9.

Answers will vary.

Editing

Now that you have revised your paragraph, you will want to refine it by making corrections in usage, sentence structure, and mechanics. You have done a lot of editing in previous chapters, so you have some experience in looking for errors. In the example below, see how the writer has used markings to indicate corrections neatly and carefully.

About a week before the sale date, I call the newspaper, and list the items in an ~~advertizement~~ *advertisement*. The ~~hole~~ *whole* family helps me clean the garage for the sale.

The day before the sale, I borrow tables and arrange all of the items.

EXERCISE 9: EDITING PRACTICE

Directions: Edit all the paragraphs you have written so far in this chapter, looking for errors in usage, sentence structure, and mechanics.

Answers will vary.

Four Types of Writing

Now that you have practiced the writing process, you are ready to put your skills to work for different purposes. The following pages present four types of writing and new skills to help you organize and develop each type.

Type of Writing	Purpose
Narrative	to narrate, or tell a story
Descriptive	to describe something
Informative	to inform or explain with facts
Persuasive	to persuade the reader to agree

Narrative Writing

The purpose of narrative writing is to tell a story, usually in time order. You have probably heard someone tell the punch line of a joke, then say, "Wait a minute! I left out a part!" If a joke or story is not told in the correct sequence, the listener or reader will not understand the story. Read the following paragraph and notice that the narrator, a police officer, relates in time order the events of a typical domestic call.

> One of the most difficult aspects of my job is answering the domestic dispute call. Many of these disputes involve violence, often a man beating a woman or children. When my partner and I arrive, we first check for weapons. Next we quickly decide which person is the aggressive one. We may then try to avoid arrest by counseling all members of the household. If necessary, my partner or I take one of the people outside to calm down. Because the victims are often too afraid to sign a complaint against the abusers, we may leave the home not knowing if the people living there are safe. For these reasons, the domestic call is one of the most frustrating for police officers.

Words that help you follow the sequence of ideas in a paragraph are *transitions*. The following words are helpful in narrative writing because they indicate time order.

after	before	then
during	finally	when
first	second	later
meanwhile	next	now

Scan the example paragraph about domestic dispute calls, underlining transition words that show time order.

You should have underlined *When, first, Next,* and *then*.

EXERCISE 10: PRACTICING NARRATIVE WRITING

Directions: Choose *one* of the following topics and write a narrative paragraph. Be sure your paragraph has a topic sentence and presents events in correct time order. Use transition words to help your reader follow the flow of your ideas.

1. Tell a story about an unusual experience in a supermarket. Write a true story or make one up.

2. Tell a story about an occasion you remember clearly from your childhood.

Answers will vary.

Descriptive Writing

Writing that draws a mental picture for the reader is descriptive writing. A writer may use all five senses, describing how something looks, smells, feels, tastes, and sounds. It's very important to include specific details in descriptive writing to ensure that the reader can "picture" what is described.

Here is a sample of descriptive writing. What is the problem with it?

> Rich and Heather have a new baby. She was born on November 10, and they named her Meghan. She is a pretty baby and is really large. They sent some pictures of her at a few days old. She sure is cute.

This paragraph is vague. We know that Meghan is pretty and large, but we have no idea what she actually looks like. Notice how the following improved paragraph gives us many more specific details.

> Meghan Brady Marmor appeared on November 10 as a nine-pound, round-faced, dark-eyed, gorgeous little girl. Her parents, Rich and Heather, proudly sent us pictures of their first daughter. Her wispy wheat-colored hair peeked out from a green hooded sleeper. Like most newborns, she has no neck, and her cheeks look as if they were formed from the soft material of a Cabbage Patch Doll. Because she is so big, she does not look like a fragile infant. Instead, she looks like a miniature toddler, very alert and ready to take on the world.

TIP: When you write, avoid vague, overused words such as *very, nice, pretty, good, great, bad,* etc. Instead, use more specific words that tell the reader exactly what you mean. Try to avoid flowery and repetitive language.

EXERCISE 11: USING DESCRIPTIVE WRITING

Directions: Rewrite the following vague, dull sentences. Load them with interesting, specific details. Use your imagination!

Example: We bought a nice car.

> We finally bought a luxurious, full-sized family car, which is metallic gray with a dark blue interior and loaded with extras like cruise control, stereo and cassette player, and power locks and windows.

1. I got a great job.

2. That is a good dessert.

3. It's a funny movie.

4. Those are happy children.

5. He's a neat guy.

6. She gave a hard test.

Answers will vary.

EXERCISE 12: WRITING A DESCRIPTIVE PARAGRAPH

Directions: Choose *one* of the following situations and write a descriptive paragraph. Be sure to use specific details to draw a picture for the reader.

1. You're supposed to meet an old family friend at the airport. She has not seen you since you were five. Write a note describing yourself and what you'll be wearing so she will know you at the airport.

2. Joe, a co-worker, needs a ride home from work. You tell him to meet you at your car in the parking lot. Where is your car, and what does it look like?

Answers will vary.

Informative Writing

Informative writing presents facts. The writer's opinion is not included. A very common example of informative writing is the news story, which explains something to the reader. Other common examples of informative writing are recipes and instructions for assembling toys and furniture.

Many writers present information to (1) explain the causes of an effect or (2) explain the effects of a cause. Read the following paragraphs carefully to see how each is organized according to cause and effect. The first paragraph states an effect in the topic sentence (in bold type). The supporting sentences give causes.

> **There are several reasons why Nora decided to become a physical therapist.** First, she was injured as a child and had to undergo months of therapy for an injured leg. While in high school, she volunteered in a children's hospital, and her major in college was premedicine. Consequently, her friend, a doctor, suggested that she take classes in physical therapy. Nora finally graduated and has a career as a therapist.

Identify the causes of Nora's becoming a physical therapist:

(1)   (2)   (3)   (4)

The following paragraph gives a *cause* in the topic sentence. The supporting sentences list the effects.

> **The Wilsons recently filed for divorce.** As a result, the family home will be sold, and a property settlement must be decided. Mrs. Wilson, who has worked part-time for several years, may seek full-time employment. Since the separation, Mr. Wilson has moved into an apartment, while Mrs. Wilson and the children are living with her sister. The Wilsons' lives have certainly changed in the last two months.

Identify the effects of the Wilsons' divorce:

(1)   (2)   (3)   (4)   (5)

TIP: Be careful not to confuse causes and effects in your writing. If you are asked to discuss the causes, check your writing to be sure you didn't also include effects.

Transition Words in a Cause-Effect Paragraph

In the two example cause-effect paragraphs, you may have noticed transition words that signaled both time order and cause-effect relationships. Review the list of time order transition words on page 154 and study the cause-effect transition words below. Then underline the transition words in the two paragraphs above.

as a result	because	consequently
for	for this reason	if . . . then
then	therefore	thus

EXERCISE 13: INFORMATIVE WRITING—CAUSE AND EFFECT

Directions: Choose *one* of the following topics and write a paragraph showing the causes or effects.

1. Write a paragraph explaining why you decided to prepare for the GED Test. (Your paragraph should discuss the *causes*.)

2. Write a paragraph explaining how studying for the GED Test has affected your life. (Your paragraph should discuss the *effects*.)

Answers will vary.

Persuasive Writing

Persuasive writing expresses an opinion. The writer's purpose is to "sell" a particular point of view or line of reasoning to the reader. A persuasive writer must be able to state an opinion, then focus on clear and logical reasons.

Stating an Opinion

Two writers were asked to write a paragraph in response to the following topic:

Should the town of Northpark approve a tax increase to pay for expanding the community college? State your opinion clearly and give solid reasons.

Which of the following opening paragraphs do you think is the more persuasive?

A tax increase to pay for expansion of the community college might be a good idea, but there are good reasons to vote against it, too. It's a very tough issue to decide.

A tax increase to pay for expansion of the community college now will help our town meet the demands of the future. Though it will be costly, an improved community college is an excellent idea.

The second one is much stronger because it states a clear point of view. The writer of the first paragraph would have a tough time convincing anyone to vote either for or against the tax increase! The writer of the second paragraph takes a firm position on the issue.

Giving Supporting Reasons

Once a writer has a good topic sentence for a persuasive paragraph, she needs some supporting reasons. *Why* would expansion of the community college benefit the community in the future? Look at the writer's brainstorm list on page 158. Cross out ideas that are *not* good reasons to support the writer's opinion.

Topic sentence: A tax increase to pay for expansion of the community college now will help our community meet the demands of the future.

Brainstorm list:

1. people won't have to go out of town for so many educational programs

2. most people won't vote for a tax increase

3. new industries coming into area will require new training programs

4. classes already overcrowded; enrollment rising

5. can always enroll in programs in nearby counties

You should have crossed out items 2 and 5. Item 5 is not relevant to the topic sentence, so including it in the paragraph would distract the reader from the writer's opinion. Item 2 argues against the writer's opinion instead of supporting it.

EXERCISE 14: WRITING PERSUASIVE PARAGRAPHS

Directions: Choose *one* of the following topics and write a persuasive paragraph. Be sure that your topic sentence states a clear position and that your supporting sentences are good reasons to back up your opinion.

1. When a man or woman runs for public office, his or her personal life often becomes front-page news. Sometimes a candidate's private life even affects his or her chances of winning an election. Does the public have a right to know about the private lives of political figures?

2. Although it has negative effects on the body, caffeine is found in many beverages consumed daily by both adults and children—soft drinks, tea, and coffee. Do you think people should be prevented from drinking beverages containing caffeine?

Answers will vary.

Comparison/Contrast Development

A useful technique for organizing ideas in many persuasive paragraphs is *comparison/contrast*. Look at how one writer handled the question "Which type of animal makes a better pet in the city, a dog or a cat?"

Topic sentence: A cat makes a better pet than a dog does for people who live in the city.

cats	dogs
use litter pan indoors	have to be walked outdoors
good company without being demanding	have to be played with frequently
don't need a lot of space	need large area to run

This chart, comparing the traits of cats and dogs, lists the writer's ideas in a useful form. The following paragraph is based on the ideas in the chart. You may notice the use of some transition words that signal comparison/contrast relationships between ideas. Underline these words as you read.

A cat makes a better pet than a dog does for people who live in the city. While a cat can use a convenient indoor litter pan, dogs have to be walked outdoors several times every day. Cats are good company, but they are not demanding. Dogs, on the other hand, need to be played with frequently, or they will be unhappy. Cats don't need a lot of space to run and play, but dogs need a large area to run in and take up a lot of space in a city apartment. A cat is the right choice for a city person who wants a pet's companionship.

You might have underlined *while, but,* and *on the other hand.*

> **TIP:** When you are comparing and contrasting two things, use a chart to list your ideas. Put related ideas about the two things across from each other, as the writer did in the above example.

EXERCISE 15: USING COMPARISON/CONTRAST TO PERSUADE

Directions: Choose *one* of the following topics and use comparison/contrast development to write a persuasive paragraph.

1. Choose two states or towns you are familiar with. Decide which of the two states or towns is a nicer place to live and write a paragraph persuading others that you have made the right choice.

2. Choose two television programs that come on the air at the same time and decide which you would rather watch. Write a paragraph convincing others to choose the same program you chose.

Answers will vary.

The Four Types of Writing

Notice that the methods of development you studied (time order, cause-effect, and comparison/contrast) can be helpful with all the types of writing. For example, time order can be very useful in informative writing when you are asked to give the steps in a process. Comparison/contrast can help you develop descriptive paragraphs if you have to describe more than one thing. And discussing the causes or effects of something may help you persuade readers to agree with you on an issue.

The following writing ideas and topics are listed under the headings of four types of writing: narrative, descriptive, informative, and persuasive. You may return to these suggested topics often in order to gain new ideas for journal writing, classroom assignments, and essay writing.

Narrative Writing
Tell a story about

(1) the best day of your life (or worst day)
(2) your first kiss
(3) your biggest mistake
(4) the first time you met _____ (spouse, close friend)
(5) your greatest accomplishment

Descriptive Writing

Use vivid description and specific language to describe

(1) a room in your home
(2) a beautiful view
(3) the fronts of two buildings
(4) a photograph, painting, or poster displayed in your home
(5) the physical appearance of a person you know well

Informative Writing

Explain carefully to your readers

(1) the importance of proper nutrition
(2) how to paint a room
(3) the steps in a simple recipe
(4) some tips for reducing utility costs in the home
(5) some simple fire safety rules

Persuasive Writing

State your opinion and give strong supporting reasons why your readers should agree with you about

(1) your annual raise
(2) an aspect of tobacco smoking or regulation of it
(3) prayer in the public schools
(4) drug testing
(5) nuclear arms reduction

Writing an Essay

You have been studying the writing process, the steps needed to develop a good paragraph. The same process is used for all types of writing. If you can write a good paragraph, you can apply that ability to longer pieces of writing.

There are many similarities between paragraphs and essays. The goals of writing a paragraph and an essay are the same:

- to discuss one main idea

- to provide plenty of support for the idea

- to stay on topic throughout the piece

The structure of an essay is also similar to that of a paragraph:

Paragraph	Essay
Topic sentence	Introductory paragraph
Supporting sentences	Body paragraphs
Concluding sentence	Concluding paragraph

As you read the following descriptions of the parts of an essay, think of a paragraph s-t-r-e-t-c-h-e-d.

- The *introductory paragraph* contains the *thesis statement*, which tells the reader the main idea, or purpose, of your essay. The introduction should also preview the major points you will be making to support your thesis statement.

- The main part of your essay is the *body*. As the supporting sentences of a paragraph support your topic sentence, the body paragraphs of an essay support your thesis statement. Each major supporting idea is developed in a paragraph. In your body paragraphs, you may want to use cause-effect, comparison/contrast, or sequence of events to organize your ideas.

- The *concluding paragraph* of an essay should contain a reworded version of the thesis statement to remind the reader of your main point. You can expand on your conclusion by asking yourself, "What do I want to suggest, recommend, or make sure my reader knows before I close my essay?"

Prewriting for an Essay

The way to get started on writing an essay is the same as getting started on a paragraph: write a statement that tells what point you are going to make in your writing; then brainstorm ideas to support your point. You can then use the ideas in your brainstorm list to write the body of your essay. Here's how one writer got started:

Thesis statement: Our elementary school needs more crossing guards.

Brainstorm list:

> busy streets, more traffic
> new mall on Oak St. four blocks away
> Lincoln St./Davis Ave. is a dangerous intersection
> Plum St./Morton St. dangerous too
> some children leave school at noon for lunch
> morning kindergartners leave at 11:30
> afternoon kids come at 12:15
> parents or senior citizens might be free at noon

Once you have written a thesis statement and brainstormed ideas to use in your body paragraphs, you can start organizing. Though there are many possibilities for organizing the ideas in any essay, outlining is one useful method.

TIP: When organizing ideas for an essay, make groups of ideas that you can turn into paragraphs when you draft the essay. Give each group a heading that you can turn into the topic sentence of the paragraph.

Read the following outline, based on the brainstorming list you just saw. The writer has grouped details and examples under main headings that tell how each paragraph will develop a single idea supporting the thesis statement.

Paragraph 1: Introduction
Thesis statement: Our elementary school needs more crossing guards.

Paragraph 2: two dangerous intersections a few blocks from school
  A. one at Lincoln St. and Davis Ave.
  B. another at Plum St. and Morton St.
  C. high-speed traffic through these intersections

Paragraph 3: many children leave and return to school at the noon hour
  A. the morning kindergartners leave at 11:30
  B. some students go home for lunch at 12:00 and return
  C. the afternoon kindergartners arrive at 12:15

Paragraph 4: increase in traffic this year due to the new shopping mall near the school
  A. new mall is on Oak St., four blocks from school
  B. busy streets, more traffic everywhere because of mall

Paragraph 5: Conclusion—For these reasons, I recommend that the principal request at least four more guards.
  A. parents or senior citizens might be free at noon
  B. school must make sure children are safe

Having finished the outline showing the organization of his essay ideas, the writer has completed a large part of the job. With the outline in hand, drafting the actual essay should be a straightforward task of turning the parts of the outline into sentences and paragraphs.

EXERCISE 16: PREWRITING FOR AN ESSAY

Directions: Choose *one* of the following topics and follow these steps in prewriting for an essay on that topic:

- Write a thesis statement that clearly states the main point of your essay.

- Brainstorm ideas to support your thesis statement. Keep in mind that you'll need plenty of ideas—enough to fill a whole essay of about five paragraphs.

- Read over your brainstorm list carefully. Cross out ideas that do not truly support your thesis statement.

- Organize your list into groups of related items that can be developed into well-unified paragraphs when the essay is written. Use an outline or any other method of organization you are comfortable with.

1. Think of a problem in your neighborhood or town, such as the need for organized neighborhood watches, a park or other recreational facility that needs improvement, etc. Prewrite an essay about the problem.

2. What has been the best period of your life, and why? Prewrite an essay describing the time of your life when you were happiest and explaining why you were happiest then. (You could choose to write about your life right now.)

Be sure to save your work; you will need it in Exercise 17.

Answers will vary.

Drafting an Essay

With your paragraphs planned and outlined, you can draft your essay. All of the prewriting steps lead to the rough draft, which you don't have to get right the first time, since you will be revising and editing it. Leave wide margins and space between lines to make changes later.

> **TIP:** When writing a rough draft, keep your outline plan next to you. Use words and phrases from the plan as the basis for your sentences.

Begin to develop your own personal writing process as you practice writing these longer pieces. Many experienced writers complete the introduction and conclusion after they have written the body paragraphs. You are not breaking any rules of writing if you start with the body paragraphs, write a strong conclusion, then go back and add a general introduction to your thesis statement.

Next, you will read the rough draft of the essay on the crossing guard topic. The thesis statement is in bold type. As you read the rough draft, notice that the writer did not stick strictly to the outline; instead, he used it as a guide, changing wording in several places. You might notice places where the writer's thoughts are hard to follow. Underline these sections and try to think of changes that would improve them.

OUTLINE

Paragraph 1: Introduction
Thesis: Our elementary
      school needs more
      crossing guards.

Paragraph 2: two dangerous
      intersections
A. Lincoln and Davis
B. Plum and Morton
C. high-speed traffic

Paragraph 3: children leave
      and return at noon
A. morning kindergart-
    ners leave at 11:30
B. students go home for
    lunch and return
C. afternoon kindergart-
    ners arrive at 12:15

Paragraph 4: increase in traffic
A. new mall on Oak
B. more traffic

Paragraph 5: Conclusion—
    For these reasons, I
    recommend that the
    principal request at least
    four more guards.
A. parents or senior citizens
B. school must ensure safety

Many parents of children attending Jefferson School are concerned about the safety of their children walking to and from school. Although older students act as crossing guards before and after school, they can't do the whole job. Unguarded intersections near the school, noon hour comings and goings, and the general increase in traffic from the new mall all make walking dangerous, especially for young children. **Our elementary school needs more crossing guards.**

We should hire guards to cover two very dangerous intersections located a few blocks from school. One is the intersection of Lincoln Street and Davis Avenue, where there is a "Yield" sign that drivers often miss. The other is at Plum Street and Morton Street, where there have been several accidents recently. An alert adult crossing guard is needed at each of the intersections whenever children are crossing.

Many children leave and return to school at the noon hour. When morning kindergartners are dismissed at 11:30, many five-year-olds walk home. There are no crossing guards on duty anywhere. At 12:00, many students go home for lunch and return around 12:45. The afternoon kindergartners arrive between noon and 12:15, so there are many children crossing unguarded intersections. Many parents drive their kids to school.

There has been an increase in traffic this year due to the new Oak Street Mall, four blocks from school. The traffic count is up in all areas of our neighborhood.

For these reasons, the principal should request that the school board hire at least four more crossing guards. Some parents are willing to volunteer temporarily, but we feel that the school district should provide the funds for ensuring the safety of the students over the long term.

Now that you have read the rough draft once, go back and study it again for a few moments. Notice how the introduction previews the arguments the author will raise in the body paragraphs: dangerous intersections, noon hour comings and goings, and increased traffic from the new mall. Then each of the body paragraphs takes up one of these arguments. Also notice that the conclusion contains a reworded version of the thesis statement.

EXERCISE 17: DRAFTING AN ESSAY

Directions: Write a rough draft of the essay you planned in Exercise 16. Use your plan as a guide, but make any improvements you can in organization as you write. You may also think of new ideas to add.

Be sure to save your draft. You will need it in Exercise 18.

Answers will vary.

Revising the Essay

Before you revise, take a break from the writing process. Leave the essay alone for a day or two—or at least several hours. You want to be able to look at your own writing as objectively as you can, so you will benefit by getting away from the essay for a while.

When you revise, read first as a reader. Read as if you are seeing the essay for the first time. What does it say to you? Then read as the writer. What can be rewritten or rearranged so that the ideas are clear and the purpose is supported? You can change the order of sentences or paragraphs, add or delete material, rewrite sentences, insert transition words, etc. At this stage, don't worry about looking for errors in usage, sentence structure, or mechanics. You'll come to that step last.

Checklist for Revising an Essay

1. Does the introduction preview my body paragraphs?

2. Does my thesis statement give my essay a clear purpose?

3. Are my ideas arranged logically in body paragraphs that support my thesis statement?

4. Will my reader be able to understand how my ideas fit together and support your thesis statement?

5. Are there any irrelevant ideas?

6. What's good about my essay?

7. What don't I like about my essay?

8. What can I do to improve my essay?

Now look at two ways the writer of the essay on crossing guards improved his writing in the revision stage. First look at the last sentence of the third paragraph of the essay.

> Many children leave and return to school at the noon hour. When morning kindergartners are dismissed at 11:30, many five-year-olds walk home. There are no crossing guards on duty anywhere. At 12:00, many students go home for lunch and return around 12:45. The afternoon kindergartners arrive between noon and 12:15, so there are many children crossing unguarded intersections. **Many parents drive their kids to school.**

The last sentence seems irrelevant because there is no transition between it and the rest of the paragraph. Here is a possible revision for the last sentence:

> Many parents drive their kids to school at noon, creating even more dangerous traffic in the area for the children who are walking.

Notice how the revised sentence makes the flow of the writer's thoughts clearer. The original wording did not show the relationship between the ideas.

Another problem spot in the essay is the fourth paragraph. The two sentences in the paragraph are not clearly related. In addition, the paragraph as a whole lacks strong supporting ideas. Here is the original version of the fourth paragraph, followed by a revised version:

> There has been an increase in traffic this year due to the new Oak Street Mall, four blocks from school. The traffic count is up in all areas of our neighborhood.

> This year the new Oak Street Mall, located four blocks from Jefferson School, opened for business. It has caused an increase in traffic throughout our neighborhood, but especially around the school. Much of the traffic going to and from the mall comes from the main highway, then down Oak Street. Since many of our students cross Oak Street, additional crossing guards are needed to cover more intersections along this busy street.

EXERCISE 18: REVISING AN ESSAY

Directions: Revise the essay you drafted in Exercise 17, page 164. Use the revising checklist on page 164 to guide you in looking for ways to improve your writing.

Be sure to save your work; you will be using it again in Exercise 19.

Answers will vary.

Editing Your Essay

Editing means checking for surface errors in your writing—misspelled words, comma splices, incorrectly capitalized words, etc. If the appearance of your paper distracts from your purpose, your reader will not be able to appreciate fully what you have written. Even minor errors can cause confusion for the reader and make your ideas hard to understand.

Learn to edit neatly. Cross out errors and print corrections above them or draw arrows into the margin and write the correction there. Use a caret (∧) to show where something should be inserted. Use a paragraph symbol (⁊) if you forgot to indent a paragraph or want to break one paragraph into two.

Last $\overset{S}{\cancel{S}}$pring I registered for some $\overset{C}{\cancel{C}}$ollege $\overset{courses}{\cancel{coarses.}}$ Then I was switched to the night shift at work,$\overset{so}{\wedge}$I couldn't go.

Notice how the small marks help keep the paper neat.

TIP: Many writers read their papers backward, word by word, to look for spelling errors. It's also helpful to read backward sentence by sentence while checking for fragments.

EXERCISE 19: EDITING YOUR ESSAY

Directions: Edit the essay you have been working on, checking for surface errors. The following questions should help remind you what to look for.

1. Are all the sentences complete thoughts?

2. Are your verbs correct? Are they consistent throughout your paragraphs?

3. Do pronouns refer correctly and clearly to their antecedents?

4. Have you combined ideas correctly, using the different types of conjunctions such as *and, therefore,* and *because*?

5. Have you used punctuation, especially commas and apostrophes, correctly?

6. Have you used capital letters correctly?

7. Are all the words spelled correctly? Use a dictionary to look up any you are unsure of.

Answers will vary.

Writing the GED Test Essay

Preparing for the GED essay is similar to training for a test of any skill. You must practice ahead of time so that when you are finally sitting at the testing site with your pen, scratch paper, writing booklet, and the topic in front of you, you will know what to do. The rest of this chapter provides you with plenty of explanations and practice exercises—your training program. As you practice, remember what you have already learned in this chapter about writing paragraphs and essays and apply that knowledge to the testing situation. Keep the writing process in mind: *prewriting, drafting, revising, editing,* and *publishing.*

Common Questions About the GED Essay

1. How much time will I have? How long should the essay be? Tell me the specifics!

The directions for Part 2 of the Writing Skills Test will present the essay topic and tell you to spend up to forty-five minutes writing an essay of about 200 words. The figure of 200 words is given *only as a guideline*; you will not be penalized if you write more words or fewer words—as long as you express your ideas well. The directions will also remind you to plan, revise, and edit your essay. You will need to use a ballpoint pen to write your answer in the test booklet. You'll be given scratch paper, but your notes will not be scored.

2. Why is there an essay on the GED Test?

Many educators and employers feel that writing is an important skill needed by every adult. In fact, some states require that seniors pass a writing test before they can receive a high school diploma. For the GED tests to truly represent a high school education, GED examinees also need to show that they can write. While the multiple-choice part of the test shows whether you can edit what another person has written, only by actually writing an essay can you show that you have learned to write.

3. What is the essay topic like?

You will be asked to present an opinion or explanation of an issue with which all adults are familiar. You will be expected to support your explanation with appropriate and specific reasons, details, and examples. The topic will be broad enough that many approaches to the essay will be possible, and no particular answer will be required or expected. In other words, there is no "right answer" on the GED Essay Test. You will see several examples of GED-type essay topics in this section.

4. How will the essays be scored?

Readers trained in standards developed by the GED Testing Service will read and score your essay on a scale of 1–6. The readers evaluate the essay for its overall effectiveness; in fact, your paper can contain some errors and still receive a high score. To score well, you should be able to plan an essay that effectively supports a central idea. You should also be able to use correct grammar and spelling most of the time.

5. What are the standards for the scores?

Here are descriptions of papers at each level of the scoring guide.

6 Papers show a clear organizational plan. Writers are able to support well-reasoned views with thorough, specific, and relevant detail. The papers are interestingly written and contain few errors.

5 Papers are well organized, and ideas are supported convincingly, but they are not as smoothly written as 6 papers. These essays are generally correct but contain some errors.

4 Papers show that writers organized their ideas and provided some support for their views. They contain more errors, but the errors do not prevent readers from understanding the essays.

3 Papers are somewhat organized or developed, but in a limited and unconvincing way. Use of standard English is weak, and essays fail to accomplish their writers' purposes.

2 Papers lack a clear purpose. They are disorganized, and little or no support is given for the writers' ideas. Errors in standard English are frequent and may prevent readers' understanding these essays.

1 Papers show no purpose or organization. Writers are unable to express themselves in correct English.

NOTE: Papers that are blank, illegible, or written on a topic other than the one assigned cannot be scored, and a Writing Skills Test composite score cannot be reported.

6. **What should I study in order to prepare for the essay?**

The best preparation is to write, write, and write. Spend your study time learning the writing process and how to put it to work in a test situation. Practice writing timed essays and plan how you will use your time when you take the test.

Making the Most of Your Time

One of the steps you should take in preparing for the GED essay is learning to adapt the writing process to the testing situation. You have practiced all the steps in the writing process before, but you need to have a strategy for using your time well when you take the test. Study the following description of how you might approach the essay. Think about how you could adapt this strategy to suit *your* writing style.

Prewrite (5–10 minutes): Study the topic, think about the choices you have and the different directions you might take, then jot down a thesis statement for your essay. Quickly brainstorm ideas to support your thesis statement. Organize your brainstorm list by numbering ideas, drawing arrows between ideas that belong together, or using any other workable method. You may even want to jot down a rough outline. Be sure you have a clear idea of how your ideas will be organized *before* you begin drafting your essay.

Draft (25–30 minutes): Neatly write a rough copy in ink, keeping in mind that you won't have time to recopy the essay. Leave wide margins so that you can go back and add ideas and make corrections. As you write, be sure to keep the overall organizational plan of your essay in mind.

Revise and edit (5–10 minutes): Read over your essay. Look for changes you can make that will make your ideas clearer to the reader, such as adding paragraph breaks or transition words. Make sure you have included a clear thesis statement in your introduction and that your supporting paragraphs are relevant and well organized. Then correct spelling, punctuation, and other mechanical errors.

Understanding the Topic

According to the GED Testing Service, "Examinees will be provided with a single topic which asks them to present an opinion or an explanation regarding a situation about which adults would be expected to have some general knowledge."

The topic will briefly identify an issue or situation. You will need to give an explanation of it, then back up your explanation with specific details, reasons, and examples.

Study this sample topic, which is similar to the type of topic you may see on the Writing Skills Test. Underline important words that tell you what to write about.

> Many of today's divorced parents are choosing joint custody of their children. The parents feel that the children benefit from being with each parent.
>
> What are the effects of joint custody on children of divorced parents? You may describe the positive effects, the negative effects, or both. Be sure to support your views with specific reasons and examples.

Many words in the topic are important. The term *joint custody* tells you what the subject of your essay must be. The word *effects* (both *positive effects* and *negative effects*) tells you more about your subject. Finally, you are told to use *specific reasons and examples.*

Notice that you are given three choices about the types of effects to describe in your essay:

1. describe the positive effects

2. describe the negative effects

3. describe both the positive and negative effects

Now that you have all this information from the topic, you can start thinking about how to approach the essay. Jot down a thesis statement you could use to tell your readers the main point of an essay on this topic. Make sure you have a couple of ideas in mind that could support your thesis statement.

Here is how one writer decided to write her essay:

Thesis statement: Joint custody has several positive effects on children, although no one usually thinks of them.

Supporting ideas: child gets to see each parent separately for a solid block of time; parents are happier and will share happiness with child; child gets to see and learn about two different lifestyles.

Notice that this writer chose to discuss *only positive effects.* You might have a different plan, and as a writer, you have this choice. However, with this topic, remember that you *must* discuss effects—not causes or anything else.

Take a look at another GED-type essay topic. Underline the key words that tell you what the topic is and what you are being asked to write.

> Some people feel very lucky to be born the sex that they are. Others feel that being a woman or being a man has too many drawbacks, and they may wish that they were born the opposite sex.
>
> Write a composition of about 200 words explaining the advantages or disadvantages or both of being the sex that you are. Support your ideas with specific examples.

With this topic, you are not being asked to discuss causes or effects. Instead, you are being asked to discuss *advantages* or *disadvantages* or *both*. These are key words that you should underline. Take a minute to think about how you might answer this topic. Then write a thesis statement that will tell your reader the main point of your essay.

Here is how one writer chose to write his essay:

Thesis statement: On the whole, the advantages of being a man outweigh the disadvantages.

Supporting ideas: physically able to do some things that women can't do; don't have to worry about sex discrimination as women do; I think being a father is easier than being a mother; I get a lot of satisfaction from being the main provider for my family

Remember that this is only *one* of *many* ways to respond to this topic. You may choose to write about disadvantages. You may also choose to talk about *both* the advantages and disadvantages. The important thing is that you support your ideas clearly. You'll learn more about supporting ideas later in the chapter.

In the following exercise, you'll see two other possible GED-type topics. These topics will suggest different types of ideas and different choices. Practice studying essay topics carefully so you can be flexible when you take the Writing Skills Test.

EXERCISE 20: UNDERSTANDING THE TOPIC

Directions: Study the following sample topics. First underline key words and phrases in each one. Then answer the questions following. By doing this, you will begin to understand what GED essay topics actually require of the writer.

TOPIC A

Some people think youth is the best part of life; others prefer the stability and privileges that come with age.

Write a composition of about 200 words discussing the advantages, disadvantages, or both of being your age. Be sure to support your views with specific reasons and examples.

1. What must be the *subject* of this essay topic?

2. What three choices does the topic give you?

3. Write a thesis statement that you could use in an essay on this topic. Then jot down at least two specific reasons or examples that would support your thesis statement.

TOPIC B

In spite of research proving the bad effects of tobacco, many people continue to puff or chew regularly on various forms of it, especially cigarettes.

In a composition of about 200 words, explain why people use tobacco. Be sure to support your views with specific reasons and examples.

4. What must be the subject of this essay topic?

5. This essay topic is asking you to explain a cause-effect relationship. Are you being asked to provide causes or effects in your essay?

6. Write a thesis statement that you could use in an essay on this topic. Then jot down at least two specific ideas that would support your thesis statement. (Make sure your thesis statement and your ideas reflect the correct cause-effect relationship.)

Answers are on page 186.

Ideas for Your Essay

Imagine that you open your essay booklet and find the following topic:

As citizens living in a democracy, we have the right to vote, yet voting records indicate that many of us do not go to the polls.

In a composition of about 200 words, explain why many citizens do not vote. Be sure to support your views with specific reasons and examples.

Perhaps you have never considered this topic before. You may never have even thought about why people don't vote. You may think, "I don't know why people don't vote. I have no ideas about this topic!"

Although you may not have thought about a topic before, the chances are good that you can come up with plenty of good ideas if you think in a productive way. The more practice you get writing with GED-type topics, the more comfortable you will be when you receive the actual test topic. You will have a *plan* for how you will think of ideas to include.

One effective way to generate ideas is to use *idea circles*. Here is how they work:

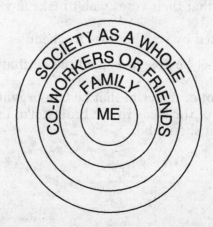

For the topic on page 171, you must identify reasons why people do not vote.

- Start at the inside circle. Do you vote? If you never vote, or you vote only part of the time, what stops you? Jot down these reasons.

- If you need more ideas, move to the next circle. Think of your family or other people you live with. If they didn't vote in the last election, why do you suppose they made that choice? Jot down whatever reasons you come up with.

- Moving to the next circle, what about your co-workers or friends—probably some of them do not vote. Why not? You may not know for sure what all their reasons are, but you probably have a pretty good idea of some of them. Jot these ideas down.

- Finally, if you feel you still need more ideas, you may want to think about what you have heard about society as a whole. Have you ever heard a newscaster say something like "Voter turnout is expected to be low today because freezing rain is in the forecast"? Or perhaps you read something in a newspaper or magazine that mentioned voting. What other reasons can you think of that explain why a lot of people don't vote? Sometimes just common sense can help you.

You can use this method of questioning yourself to generate ideas for almost any essay topic. Just imagine different groups of people, starting with yourself, and think about how the topic relates to each group. You don't even have to use all the circles—just go far enough so that you are comfortable with the ideas you have.

Of course, you may not need this technique to generate ideas. You may have a method of your own, such as simple brainstorming, that works just fine. However, if your mind just "goes blank" at the sight of a new writing topic, picturing these idea circles might help you get started on the GED Essay Test.

Here's an example showing how one writer used three of the circles to brainstorm ideas for the voting essay:

me—if I don't like any of the candidates, I don't bother to vote

my parents—never bother to vote

       don't seem interested in politics

       maybe feel that their votes won't make any difference

people in general—affected by weather, work schedules, child care

       may not be able to make time on that certain day

This writer has quite a lot of material that he can organize into an essay. He may not even want to use all of the ideas in the brainstorm list, depending on what he decides his main point should be.

Now take a look at how another writer took the *same topic* and came up with completely different ideas.

me—Last year I didn't vote because I moved and forgot to register

hard to know who to vote for—all politicians so much alike

my two best friends—too lazy

society as a whole—some never get around to registering, then can't vote even if they want to

may not realize how much politicians' work affects their lives

This writer has thought of a lot of reasons why people don't vote, and in her essay she may decide to use all or some of them. Notice that her ideas are quite different from those of the other writer, but both lists will make fine essays.

EXERCISE 21: USING THE IDEA CIRCLES

Directions: Use the idea circles to generate ideas on the following topics. Spend about five minutes brainstorming on each topic.

1. In the last twenty years, the roles of women have changed greatly. The changes in the roles of women affect all members of a family.

How have these changes in women's roles affected families? You may describe the positive effects, the negative effects, or both. Be sure to support your views with specific reasons and examples.

2. People who live in small towns or in the country often think that city living is glamorous and exciting, but city dwellers are just as likely to envy their suburban or country friends.

In a composition of about 200 words, discuss the advantages, disadvantages, or both of living in a big city *or* living in the country. Be sure to support your views with specific reasons and examples.

Answers will vary.

Using Examples

The instructions for the GED essay tell you to use *specific examples* to make your point. What does this mean, and where do you find examples? To see how useful examples can be, read the following paragraph.

> Many people don't vote because of the weather. They also might not vote because it is hard to find time.

Now read this paragraph that includes some good examples:

> Many people don't vote because of the weather. For example, if it is snowing and icy outside, a person may not go out to vote for fear he will get into a car accident. Another person just might not feel like going out on a rainy day. Other people don't vote because it's hard to find time. Between work and getting kids to and from school and dealing with traffic jams, many people just cannot fit another event into their busy schedules.

Can you see that the first paragraph made two very general statements? Although he gives two good reasons why people don't vote, the writer could use some examples that *show* the reader what he means. The second paragraph does just that. Instead of just giving the reason "weather," the writer gives an example of *how* weather can affect people's voting habits. Furthermore, this writer gives an example of *how* it can be hard to find time to vote. As a reader, you can really understand the writer's reasoning because he has given such clear examples.

When you are faced with a GED essay topic, remember to give examples that *show* the reader what you are talking about. Watch out for general statements in your writing and add an idea or two that can support those statements. If you have trouble thinking of examples, you might try using the "idea circles" again. This technique is useful whenever you find yourself stuck for an idea.

EXERCISE 22: USING SPECIFIC EXAMPLES

Directions: Add one or two specific examples to each of the following general statements made in a GED essay. Use the idea circles if you have trouble thinking of ideas. The first one is done as an example.

1. People don't vote because they are lazy.

   For example, if I have to get up an hour early just to get to the polling place, I probably will sleep in instead.

   In addition, smart voting requires a citizen to read a newspaper or pay attention to campaigns, and most people don't have the energy for this extra work.

2. Some people don't vote because they can't find an appealing candidate.

3. America does not have a good voter turnout because people don't believe that voting can improve their situation.

4. Many people fail to vote because elections are held too often.

Answers will vary.

Drafting Your Essay

Once you have a plan for what you will include in your essay, you'll need to communicate these ideas in essay form. Remember what you have already learned about writing a rough draft. In addition, use these hints:

Suggestions for Drafting a GED Test Essay

☑ 1. Write an introductory paragraph that contains your thesis statement and tells your reader what main points you will be making in your body paragraphs.

☑ 2. As you write, illustrate general statements with specific examples. You can draw from your personal experience, things you have read or seen on television, experiences of your friends and family members, etc. Use the idea circles if they have helped you in the past.

☑ 3. Leave wide margins around your writing so you'll have space to make corrections and add words after you have drafted your essay.

☑ 4. Write steadily. You will use your time better if you fully develop your major points than if you agonize over grammar and sentence structure. The readers who score your paper do not expect perfect papers.

☑ 5. Write a conclusion that contains a reworded version of your thesis statement and reminds your readers of your main points.

EXERCISE 23: DRAFTING A TEST ESSAY

Directions: Go back to your brainstorm lists from Exercise 21, page 173. Select the one you would like to continue to work with. Allow yourself 25 minutes of uninterrupted time and draft the essay. You may want to refer to the suggestions above as you write.

Be sure to save your work, since you'll need it in Exercise 24.

Answers will vary.

Revising and Editing a Test Essay

When you have finished drafting your test essay, check the time. You may not be able to make many changes. However, if you have a strategy planned, you can improve your paper in a short amount of time. By knowing your own writing strengths and weaknesses, you can prepare yourself to use those last few minutes well. A revising and editing checklist follows. Which tend to be *your* problem areas? Perhaps the most important revising and editing issues for you are not even on the checklist. Take a few minutes now to jot down some things you might want to be looking for in those final minutes. You won't be able to remember a lot of items, so choose ones that most apply to you.

Revising and Editing Checklist
Organization and Content

1. Does your introductory paragraph contain a thesis statement that tells the reader the main point of your essay?
2. Will the reader be able to see how each body paragraph develops an idea that supports the main point?
3. Did you illustrate general statements with specific reasons and examples?
4. Did you include a reworded version of your thesis statement in your concluding paragraph?

Proofreading

1. Check to make sure all your sentences are complete thoughts.
2. Make sure that commas are used correctly and not overused.
3. Check to be sure that connecting words like *and, but, because, then,* and *however* are used logically.
4. Check spelling by reading the essay backward.
5. Look for sound-alike words such as *their/there* and *its/it's* and make sure the spelling you chose is correct.
6. Check your verbs carefully, making sure you used tenses logically and formed them correctly. Check subject-verb agreement.

Improving the Essay

Now that you have an idea of what you will be looking for when you revise your test essay, look at an example of what one writer did in this situation. Here is another sample paragraph from the essay on the voting topic. The writer made some changes to improve the organization and content of the essay and also corrected some mechanical errors. Note the neat, clear markings he used to show the changes. Look carefully at each change to see how it improves the paragraph.

Even someone who is interested in politics may not care much about
voting, ~~B~~ecause it's so hard to tell which candidates to vote for. Occasionally
one candidate may stand out as really interested in improving the ~~comunity,~~ *community*
or taking care of *important* issues ~~that are important~~ *like the arms race*. However, they usually seem pretty
much the same, no matter what political party is backing them. They spend
their time raising money *for fancy TV ads* and insulting their opponents. If voters knew what
candidates ~~realy~~ *really* wanted to accomplish in office, they would be more likely to
vote.

Now that you have given some thought to revising and editing in the testing situation, it's your turn to try it. Before you start the following exercise, be sure you have made a list of about five items that you want to be sure to check for in your GED Test essay. The items should be problem areas that you are likely to encounter in *your* writing. And keep in mind that your GED essay does not have to be a perfect paper. Your essay should simply be the best writing you can produce in forty-five minutes.

EXERCISE 24: REVISING AND EDITING A TEST ESSAY

Directions: Revise and edit the essay you drafted in Exercise 23, page 175. Spend about five minutes, no more than ten. Use your checklist to prioritize your time. Keep in mind that you don't have to produce a perfect paper. If you're not sure of the spelling of a word or perfect punctuation, that's OK.

Answers will vary.

Sample Topics for Practice

Here are some more essay topics that are similar to the ones that may be used as Part 2 of the Writing Skills Test. When you write essays based on these topics, use the skills you have been learning and manage your time carefully. Use the idea circles if they have been useful to you in the past. Remember that you should spend about forty-five minutes on your essay.

1. Equal rights and opportunities for women mean equal responsibilities. Some people feel that women should be drafted to serve in the military just as men are. Others feel that women should be exempt from required military service.

   Should women be drafted into the military? State your opinion and be sure to support it with specific reasons, details, and examples.

2. Leadership is a quality most of us admire. A president, governor, or mayor must be able to lead and inspire to be effective.

   Identify one or more personality traits that you feel leaders should have and explain the importance of the trait(s). Be sure to support your views with specific reasons and examples.

3. Personal qualities such as generosity, good humor, and selfishness are among the things that make us like or dislike a person.

   Identify a quality that you either admire or dislike in a person and explain why it affects you. Be specific and use examples to support your views.

4. Many people find that holidays are difficult times as well as joyous ones. Sad and lonely experiences may be as common for some people as parties and family gatherings are for others.

   Why do people often feel unhappy emotions during holidays? In answering this question, state your views clearly, and be sure to use specific examples and reasons.

5. In our society, the eight-hour work day and two-day weekend are considered very important. Even those of us who work the hours of three to eleven instead of nine to five, or who take off Monday and Wednesday instead of Saturday and Sunday, usually work about forty hours in a week. In contrast, workers 100 years ago often put in fourteen-hour days six days a week.

   What advantages does the forty-hour work week give us? Be specific, and use examples to support your views.

6. Frustration and anger are emotions that all people feel at one time or another. However, some people are able to recognize and control their feelings, while others resort to unkind actions and even violence when they are angry.

Why are some people able to control themselves and their actions better than other people? Be specific with your ideas, and use good, clear examples to support them.

7. It has been said that reading can open up a whole new world for a person. Do you agree with this idea? State your opinion, and support it clearly with details and examples.

8. To the surprise of many, daytime and nighttime soap operas have always attracted large and faithful audiences. Soap opera fans say that these shows ease loneliness and help them cope with problems in their own lives. Critics of soap operas, however, see little value in such shows.

Do you think soap operas can be valuable to people? State your opinion and support it with specific reasons, examples, and details.

TEST 1: WRITING SKILLS ANSWER KEY

CHAPTER 1: BASIC ENGLISH USAGE

Exercise 1: Subjects and Predicates
pages 58–59

1. **(g)** The first Academy Awards went to films made in 1927 and 1928.

2. **(h)** Julie Andrews won an award for her performance in *Mary Poppins* in 1964.

3. **(c)** Katharine Hepburn and Spencer Tracy acted together for the last time in 1967's *Guess Who's Coming to Dinner?*

4. **(a)** Dustin Hoffman and Tom Cruise costarred in *Rain Man*, "Best Film" of 1988.

5. **(b)** *Gone with the Wind, Stagecoach,* and *The Wizard of Oz* were nominated for "Best Film" in 1939.

6. **(d)** Awards for "Best Film," "Best Actor," "Best Actress," and "Best Director" were given to *Silence of the Lambs* in 1991.

7. **(f)** *Terminator 2* won the award for Special Effects in 1991.

8. **(e)** Clint Eastwood finally won an Academy Award for directing *Unforgiven* in 1992.

Exercise 2: Nouns and Subjects
pages 60–61

The nouns in each of the sentences are listed below, and the subject is in bold type. If you are confused about the subject in the following sentences, remember to ask yourself, "Who or what is doing something or being described in this sentence?"

1. **Bud**, bus, cab, concert
2. health, **Sheila**, Arizona
3. **Mary**, position, bank
4. **men**, drink, way, home
5. **children**, laundry, house
6. **pickle**

Exercise 3: Plural Nouns
page 63

1. countries	4	6. factories	4
2. homes	1	7. races	1
3. businesses	2	8. lives	5
4. alloys	3	9. women	7
5. cars	1	10. dishes	2

Exercise 4: Possessive Nouns
page 64

Corrections are in bold type.

1. My **cat's** favorite food never stays long in her dish.

2. Over the past two years, the **Wagners'** house has become worn around the doors and windows.

3. **Children's** pants and **toddlers'** playsuits are marked down at **Emily's** favorite shop.

4. The **president's** plan to restrict imports was abandoned due to several **allies'** protests.

5. For days after the **volcano's** eruption, ashes and dust in the atmosphere partially blocked the **sun's** rays.

Exercise 5: The Simple Tenses
pages 66–67

Verb	Time Clue
1. will walk	Next week
2. appears	Right now
3. planted	In March of 1975
4. will play	Tomorrow night
5. love	(statement is always true)

Exercise 6: The Continuing Tenses
page 68

Verb	Time Clue
1. is licking	At the moment
2. is barking	Now
3. will be cooking	By next month
4. will be picking	for the next two weeks
5. was sleeping	On yesterday's show

Exercise 7: The Perfect Tenses
page 69

Verb	Time Clue
1. will have walked	by bedtime
2. has curled	every day since her seventh birthday
3. had ordered	By 9:00 last night
4. has attended	so far
5. had worked	Before going into the army
6. will have mailed	By next October
7. has missed	In the last twenty-five years
8. had traveled	Before coming to Chicago last summer

Exercise 8: Regular Verb Review
page 71

Verb	Time Clue
1. was waiting	At the time of my arrival last week
2. will enter	Someday
3. sketches	every day
4. had plunged	By 8:00 this morning
5. have waited	this moment
6. will have lied	By the end of his term two years from now
7. shipped	Yesterday afternoon
8. will study or will be studying	For the next few months
9. feels or is feeling	Currently
10. seems	Today
11. has lived	Since the day she was born
12. decided	Last night

Exercise 9: Verbs
pages 74–76

1. (3) The first sentence in this paragraph is correct, and it is in the present tense. So, the passage as a whole must be in the present tense. Sentences 1–5 should be in the simple present, and Sentence 6 should be in the present continuing.
2. (2)
3. (1)
4. (5)
5. (2)
6. (3)

Exercise 10: Subject-Verb Agreement
page 78

Subject	Verb
1. racers	run
2. Letitia	visits
3. Time and money	were
4. secretary	Wasn't
5. mother	Has
6. A sandwich and a glass of juice	are
7. remains	lie

Exercise 11: More Subject-Verb Agreement
page 79

Subject	Verb
1. Mrs. Bundt	attends
2. Each	receives
3. Some	were
4. breakfast	keeps
5. anyone	wants
6. Most	are
7. tax	is
8. None	is

Exercise 12: Pronoun Form
page 81

1. **She** is going to the circus with **them**.
2. Give the pearls to **us**.
3. John and **his** friends left the meeting.
4. **We** read **her** paper with great delight.
5. Nancy was planning to bring her husband, so I brought **mine**.

Exercise 13: Possessive Pronouns and Contractions
page 82

1. **You're** not ready to move out of the house at age twelve.
2. **There's** no one here by that name, Officer.
3. I have given up hope that **your** father will ever stop telling bad jokes.
4. **Whose** coat is lying in the back corner of the bar?
5. **It's** not likely that Reginald will ever darken **its** door again.
6. **They're** going on a vacation to Alaska.

Exercise 14: Identifying Antecedents
page 83

Pronoun	Antecedent
3. they	Murray and Dee
4. who	eager friends
5. them	Murray, Dee, and Marissa
6. her	Marissa
7. it	crib
8. He	nursery worker
9. they	Murray and Dee
10. he	nursery worker
11. them	Murray and Dee

Exercise 15: Relative Pronouns
page 84

1. woman who
2. door that
3. Time, which
4. Dorothy, who
5. people that

Exercise 16: Agreement in Number
page 86
Part A

Antecedent	Pronoun
1. Japan	its
2. Muriel	her
3. twins	their
4. dog	its
5. company	its

Part B

Corrections are in bold type.

Over the last twenty years, Knoxville's population center, once clustered around **its** small downtown area, has shifted westward. However, **its** downtown area may become more important again in future years. Many of the city's older buildings are being restored, and its newer downtown buildings are lovely too.

Exercise 17: Clarifying Antecedents pages 87–88

The following sentences are *possible* revisions. The words in bold type replace the confusing pronoun or pronouns. Remember that your sentences can be different and still be correct. When checking your work, be sure that you have replaced all vague pronouns.

1. **X** I wrote to Ken and his sisters, but **Ken and his sisters** did not respond.
2. **X** **Experts on home remedies** say that drinking peppermint tea is good for an upset stomach.
3. **X** Herd the sheep away from the cattle and feed **the sheep.**
4. **X** Dion asked Tony if **Tony** thought **Dion** would win the contest.
5. **X** When the quarterback made the touchdown in the final seconds of the game, **the crowd** went wild in the stands.
6. **C**
7. **X** Darleen never wants to go out anymore, and she is not eating or sleeping well. This **behavior** worries her husband.
8. **X** Mr. Olivetti followed Dominick into **Dominick's** storeroom.
9. **C**

Exercise 18: Agreement in Person page 89

Corrections are in bold type.

Most of us think that having running water and electricity is normal. As a result, **we** might be surprised at the simple mud huts many Africans live in. Even when **we** are out of work here, we can get help from government agencies, including welfare or unemployment income. We may not all have lives of luxury, but **we** easily forget that people in many other countries feel lucky to earn only pennies per day.

Exercise 19: Sentence Structure pages 89–92

1. (2) The verb *is* must agree with the singular subject *One*.
2. (4) The object pronoun *them* must agree with its antecedent *paintings*.
3. (3) Pronouns in a passage should not shift from one person to another. *You* does not fit here because the writer is not talking directly to the reader.
4. (4) The verb *live* must agree with the plural subject *masterpieces*.
5. (3) If you substitute *who is* for *who's*, the sentence doesn't make sense. The possessive pronoun *whose* is correct.
6. (5) This verb should be in the past tense since the entire passage describes past events.
7. (4) *Began* is the correct simple past tense form of the irregular verb *begin*. *Begun* is the past participle.
8. (3) The relative pronoun *who* must be used when referring to people.
9. (2) Replace *they* with *the staff* to avoid a confusing pronoun reference.
10. (5) no correction is necessary
11. (2) When *ed* is added to most verbs, including *open*, the spelling of the base verb does not change.
12. (2) The past tense of *write* is *wrote*. *Writed* is not a correct verb form.
13. (1) The verb *is* must agree with the singular subject *Boston Cooking School Cookbook*.

CHAPTER 2: SENTENCE STRUCTURE

Exercise 1: Rewriting Fragments pages 94–95

Part A

The following are *possible* revisions of these fragments. Remember, your answers can be different and still be correct. When checking your answers, be sure your revised sentences contain a subject and predicate and express a complete thought.

1. **F** The pickup truck that I borrowed from George is now dented.
2. **S**
3. **F** Luis called your house last night.
4. **F** Anxious for some news, the inmate waited by the window for his lawyer.

5. **F** Life, with its many disappointments, is still worth living.

6. **S** (In a command or instruction, the subject is understood to be *you*.)

7. **F** You can't teach someone to pitch like Dwight Gooden and hit like Ryne Sandberg.

8. **S**

9. **F** Movies are shown at 5:00 P.M. daily.

10. **S** (In a command or instruction, the subject is understood to be *you*.)

Part B

Corrected sentences are in bold type. Remember, your revised sentences can be different and still be correct.

When President John F. Kennedy was inaugurated in 1960, he stated, "Ask not what your country can do for you; ask what you can do for your country." His philosophy did much for U.S. citizens and underdeveloped areas of the world. **For example, the Peace Corps sent volunteers into underdeveloped areas of the world.** The volunteers educated the citizens of those countries in basic survival skills. The main goal was for the countries to become more self-sufficient. **A second goal was to improve relations between the U.S. and these countries.**

Exercise 2: Conjunctions
pages 96–97

The correct conjunction and punctuation are in bold type. More than one conjunction may be correct in some sentences.

1. We are planning a Fourth of July picnic, **and** we hope all of you can attend.

2. He did not study for his driver's test, **but** he passed it.

3. Al has always wanted his own business, **so** he opened a restaurant.

4. You may have some strawberry pie, **or** you may have some cherry pie.

5. I can do most of my own plumbing, **but** I cannot do the electrical work.

6. Karen is not allowed any hard exercise, **for** she is recovering from an operation.

Exercise 3: Using Commas Correctly
page 97

Remember, a comma is needed only when two complete thoughts are joined by a coordinating conjunction such as *and* or *but*. If you use a comma, make sure the ideas you join have both a subject and a predicate.

1. She took off her coat and hung it in the closet.

2. She took off her coat, and she hung it in the closet.

3. Jorge called Marie, but he did not call Clara.

4. Jorge called Marie but not Clara.

5. Our daughter has a learning disability but is doing well in school.

6. Our daughter has a learning disability, but she is doing well in school.

7. We visited my Aunt Nancy, for we had not seen her in a while.

8. The mayor was popular with both senior citizens and young people.

Exercise 4: Run-ons and Comma Splices
pages 98–99

1. C

2. Kyle broke his leg, so he was taken to the emergency room.
   OR:
   Kyle broke his leg. He was taken to the emergency room.

3. Pass the donuts. I'm starving!

4. C

5. The make of her car is a Buick, and the model is a Century.
   OR:
   The make of her car is a Buick. The model is a Century.

6. C

7. C

8. Of course this is my sweater. I've had it for years.

9. Dion won every swimming event in the meet, so we were proud of him.
   OR:
   Dion won every swimming event in the meet. We were proud of him.

10. I'd rather have hay fever than food allergies. At least I can eat!

Exercise 5: Run-ons and Comma Splices
page 99

The sentences in bold type show possible ways to correct the run-ons and comma splices in this paragraph. They have been separated into two sentences or combined using a comma with *and, but, or, for, nor, so,* or *yet.*

My cousin Ernie loves solving brainteasers, doing magic tricks, and playing mathematical games. **He subscribes to several magazines. They are filled with puzzles.** In one trick, Ernie challenges his friends to cut a hole in an index card that is big enough to put a person's head through! **His friends always try, and he watches and laughs.** Then Ernie cuts the card into a long strand and places it over his head. **Who knows? Maybe someday he will be performing the card trick on TV. He certainly works hard at his craft.**

Exercise 6: Sentence Structure Practice
pages 99–100

1. (4) Comma splices can be corrected by making two complete sentences.

2. (5) When the conjunction *so* is used to combine two complete thoughts, you must place a comma before it.

3. (3) The possessive pronoun *their*, not its sound-alike contraction *they're*, is correct here.

4. (2) Run-ons can be corrected by joining the two complete thoughts with a conjunction (*and*) and a comma.

5. (3) The present-tense verb *suggest* is correct because the passage is in the present tense.

6. (3) The coordinating conjunction *so* links cause ("books have been published on the subject") to effect ("people soon may be applying birth-order theories to their families").

Exercise 7: Conjunctive Adverbs
page 102
The conjunctive adverb is in bold type.

1. (a) He was qualified for the job; **therefore**, he got it.

2. (b) The steak is very good; **on the other hand,** you might prefer the chicken.

3. (c) The company is in financial trouble; **as a result,** workers may be laid off.

4. (a) Jason has been taking piano lessons for years; **however**, he does not play well.

5. (b) Jeri may run for councilperson; **furthermore**, she may someday become mayor.

Exercise 8: Errors with Conjunctive Adverbs
page 102
The correct conjunctive adverb and punctuation are in bold type. More than one conjunctive adverb may be correct in some sentences.

1. The snowstorm worsened; **therefore,** we postponed our trip.

2. Two ot the students studied hard; **however,** they failed the test.

3. The dishwasher is broken; **in addition,** the freezer won't stay cold.

4. Mrs. Jones felt ill; **consequently,** she called a doctor.

5. Jane has so many talents; **for example,** she sings in a professional choir, weaves detailed tapestries, and can play an excellent game of tennis.

Exercise 9: Combining Sentences
page 103
The following are *possible* combinations of these sentences. Remember, your answers can be different and still be correct. When checking your answers, be sure that your punctuation is correct and that your conjunction is logical.

1. (a) The salesperson was very polite, so she listened to my complaints.
(b) The salesperson was very polite; therefore, she listened to my complaints.

2. (a) The music was terrible, but we decided to dance.
(b) The music was terrible; nevertheless, we decided to dance.

3. (a) We bought the house in 1975, and we sold it in 1980 for twice the price.
(b) We bought the house in 1975; then we sold it in 1980 for twice the price.

4. (a) My friends give me advice, but I do not always listen to them.
(b) My friends give me advice; however, I do not always listen to them.

5. (a) I could drive you to work in the morning, or you could take the subway.
(b) I could drive you to work in the morning; otherwise, you could take the subway.

Exercise 10: Dependent Clauses
pages 104–105
Remember, your answers can be different from those in bold type and still be correct.

Part A
1. Even though Ray was afraid of water, he took swimming lessons.

2. Since she already knows the words to the song, she can teach us.

3. I'm not going to the class reunion **because** my closest friends won't be there.

4. After we left the meeting, we went for pizza.

5. Celia stayed with her mother **until** the nurse returned.

Part B
The dependent clause in each of the following sentences is in bold type.

1. Since the tables were always full, we knew the food at the cafe was good.

2. The family bought a new mini-van **before they went on vacation**.

3. Whenever he reads science fiction books, Eliot has nightmares.

4. I ordered a pepperoni pizza **even though I ate an hour ago**.

5. Unless he finds another job, Duane will paint the porch steps.

Part C
The subordinating conjunction in each sentence is in bold type.

1. Because we arrived at the church late, we missed their wedding ceremony.

2. Even though Bonnie said that she was not tired, she fell asleep at 7:00 P.M.

3. Because I left my umbrella at home, I was soaked from the unexpected thunderstorm.

4. Since Rose was angry with her babysitter, she said she would not hire the young girl again.

5. When we drove into the parking lot, we noticed that the store was closed.

Exercise 11: Structure and Usage pages 107–109

1. **(1)** No correction is necessary.

2. **(3)** The subordinating conjunction *although* shows the contrast in this sentence between "people who open savings accounts" and "people who invest."

3. **(2)** The passage as a whole is in the present tense, so change *bought* to *buy*.

4. **(4)** When combining two independent clauses with a conjunctive adverb, a semicolon should be placed before the conjunctive adverb and a comma placed after it. Also, be sure to choose the most logical conjunctive adverb. *Therefore* is correct because it links a cause to an effect.

5. **(5)** No correction is necessary.

6. **(3)** When combining two independent clauses with a conjunctive adverb, a semicolon should be placed before the conjunctive adverb and a comma placed after it.

7. **(2)** When a dependent clause comes first in a sentence, a comma must separate the two clauses.

8. **(2)** The passage as a whole refers to a group of people—stockholders. The plural subject pronoun *they* is correct.

9. **(5)** The coordinating conjunction *so* links cause to effect in this sentence.

Exercise 12: Correct Verb Sequence page 110

1. were waiting
2. will become
3. should have taken
4. was wearing
5. will call
6. had slept
7. have enjoyed
8. sweeps
9. could have moved
10. may lose

Exercise 13: Dangling and Misplaced Modifiers page 112

The modifying phrase in each of the following sentences is in bold type and is in its correct place—nearest to the word it modifies.

1. Rich saw the "No Smoking" sign **nailed to the wall**.

2. The child **who wanted a toy** called for his mother.

3. **While I was taking a shower,** the telephone rang.

4. My papers blew out the window **while I was driving to work**.

5. A bath felt good **after I had worked all day.**

6. **When I was traveling through Colorado,** my luggage was lost on the train.

7. We'll certainly be able to recognize the bride **wearing her wedding gown!**

8. We heard the dog **whining for food** under the table.

Exercise 14: Parallel Structure pages 113–114
Part A
1. **(b)** happy
2. **(d)** knees were shaking
3. **(a)** honesty
4. **(d)** slice the roast
5. **(d)** married woman
Part B
1. (b) 2. (b) 3. (a) 4. (a) 5. (b)

Exercise 15: Structure and Usage pages 114–116

1. **(3)** The modifier *ages five and six* should be placed next to *children*, the word it modifies.

2. **(4)** The dangling modifier in this sentence incorrectly implies that *new questions* were feeling sorry for the children.

3. **(5)** *Frustrating* is correct because it is parallel to *interesting* and *challenging*.

4. **(3)** The passage as a whole is in the present tense, so change *asked* to *ask*.

5. **(2)** This fragment is missing a subject and a verb. Choice (2) is correct because the subject pronoun *we* agrees with the rest of the passage and because the verb *ask* is in the present tense, as is the rest of the passage.

6. **(1)** The conjunction *and* joins two related ideas.

7. **(1)** No correction is necessary.

CHAPTER 3: MECHANICS
Exercise 1: Capitalization Rules page 119

1. The mayor of Chestortown requested assistance from Governor Kelly.

2. My favorite time of fall is Thanksgiving.

3. Candy's doctor sent her to get a second opinion from Doctor Schwartz.

4. We will meet on Wednesday, August 9, at Lincoln Center in Memphis, Tennessee.

5. Leading Sunday services at St. Gregory's Cathedral will be Father McMillan.

6. Drive north to Baker Avenue, then turn left at Kennedy Highway.

7. My German lessons are helping me prepare for my European trip next spring.

8. Marissa's birthday is Christmas Day, so her parents will surprise her with a party in January.

9. The Ohio River is a beautiful river.

10. This summer the band will be on the road for a long tour.

Exercise 2: Using Commas
page 122

Dear Mom,

Because I do not have enough money, I will not be coming home for spring vacation. Unfortunately, I need to stay here in Des Moines and work. I did not, of course, waste my money, but I did not allow enough in my budget for an airline ticket. You will understand that I can't come, I know. I'd really love to be home in March, but I can't afford a ticket until June. Please call Sue, Pam, and Linda for me and relay the message.

Love always,
Dawn

Exercise 3: Punctuation Review
pages 123–124

1. To strip the paint from the woodwork, you will need a gallon of stripper, old rags, a scraper, a paintbrush, steel wool, and a mask to protect you from the fumes.

2. Mr. Rider, my insurance agent, called with information about a rate increase.

3. She hasn't returned the dresses to the store because she lost the receipt.

4. I love to stay up late and watch old movies; however, I have difficulty getting up in the morning.

5. In spite of her parents' protests, Charleen has moved in with her boyfriend.

Exercise 4: Structure, Usage, and Mechanics
pages 124–125

1. **(4)** Don't capitalize general directions.

2. **(3)** Don't capitalize general geographical terms.

3. **(1)** Use a comma to set off introductory phrases like *as a result.*

4. **(5)** No correction is necessary.

5. **(5)** Use a comma to set off a modifying phrase added at the end of a sentence.

6. **(2)** The coordinating conjunction *but* is correct because it shows the contrast between two ideas.

7. **(3)** The verb *are* agrees with the plural subject *interests.*

Exercise 5: The Master List
pages 127–128

1. American, August, December, English, February, January, Saturday, United States, Wednesday

2. **(a)** fourth
   (b) twelfth
   (c) eight
   (d) twelve, fourteen

3. **(a)** quarter
   (b) dollar
   (c) dozen
   (d) ounces
   (e) gallon

4. a lot, all right, post office, United States

5. u

6. it's, o'clock

7. **(a)** advisor, advisable
   (b) arguing, argument
   (c) burial, buried
   (d) acknowledge, knew, knowledge
   (e) decision, decisive
   (f) commitment, committed
   (g) marriage, married
   (h) occurred, occurrence
   (i) pleasant, pleasure
   (j) possession, possessive
   (k) preference, preferential, preferred

Exercise 6: The Dictionary
page 132

The following are *possible* sentences. Be sure your sentences have a subject and predicate and that they express a complete thought.

1. When the **auxiliary** system at the plant failed too, the engineers knew they had a real problem.

2. Pat enters a state of **ecstasy** whenever she eats a hot fudge sundae.

3. The cost of the ultrasuede coat was **exorbitant.**

4. Tulips **flourish** when they receive direct sunlight.

5. Timothy's monster mask for Halloween is **hideous.**

6. The cause of many household fires is pure **negligence.**

7. It takes great **perseverance** to finish a marathon race.

8. Heavy accents are **prevalent** in the deep South.

9. If the mayor and his wife **suppress** this information, they will be criticized sharply.

10. In response to unfair laws imposed by the British, Boston lawyer James Otis in 1763 said, "Taxation without representation is a form of **tyranny**."

Exercise 7: Spelling List Review
page 137

1. d **3.** d **5.** e **7.** c **9.** a

2. a **4.** b **6.** b **8.** d **10.** b

Exercise 8: Sound-Alike Words
page 141

The corrected word in each of the following sentences is in bold type.

1. The teachers knew that the **principal's** attitude was affected by the grievance they had filed.

2. If you choose to accept his **advice** and seek the job, you should apply at the personnel office.

3. Tim knows that Shari is quite bored with the **course**.

4. The counselor's advice was not **altogether** sound, so I chose to ignore her suggestions.

5. World peace is an issue we senators hear quite a lot about. Here inside the capitol we are **conscious** of world affairs.

6. He ate a whole pie for dessert. Now he's **quite** affected by his actions.

7. I **know** the picnic will be tomorrow, whether the weather is good or not.

8. All of us except Charlie have **already** chosen to work for the reelection of the school board members.

Exercise 9: Structure, Usage, Spelling, and Mechanics
pages 142–144

1. (5) The correct spelling is *calculators*.

2. (1) No correction is necessary.

3. (2) A comma is needed when a coordinating conjunction such as *but* connects two complete thoughts.

4. (3) When a conjunctive adverb joins two independent clauses, a comma is needed after the conjunction.

5. (3) This comma splice can be corrected by separating the two thoughts into two sentences.

6. (5) *Americans* is always capitalized because it is derived from the name of a specific place.

7. (2) Use a comma to set off an interrupting phrase in a sentence.

8. (1) The correct spelling is *Instead*.

9. (4) The correct spelling is *dependents*.

10. (3) A comma is needed when two complete thoughts are joined by a coordinating conjunction such as *but*.

CHAPTER 4: PREPARING FOR THE GED WRITING SAMPLE
Exercise 2: Topic, Audience, and Purpose
page 147

1. a parent

2. a child's absence from class

3. to ask that Erik be excused from class next Friday

4. a teacher

Exercise 4: Writing Topic Sentences
page 150
Part A

The following are *possible* topic sentences. Make sure your topic sentences state the subject of your paragraph and the point you would make about the subject.

1. My husband and I always tried to give our daughter memorable **birthday parties**.

2. Few people in the world have more power and responsibility than **the president of the United States.**

3. **The kitchen in my new apartment**, with its wood floors, flowered wallpaper, and small pantry, is nicer than any kitchen I've ever had.

4. Sometimes the ringing phones and computer printers in my office seem louder than any **noise pollution**.

5. Since **weather forecasting** is such an unpredictable science, I've stopped listening to forecasts.

Exercise 20: Understanding the Topic
pages 170–171

1. The subject of this essay must be your age.

2. You can discuss the advantages, disadvantages, or both of being your age.

3. Sample thesis statement: *There are far more advantages to being twenty-three years old than there are disadvantages.*
   - I am in extremely good health.
   - I don't yet have many of the responsibilities that will come later in life.

4. The subject of this essay must be why people use tobacco.

5. You are being asked to provide *causes*, or reasons why people smoke.

6. Sample thesis statement: *The reasons that people continue to risk their health by using tobacco are both personal and cultural.*
   - People think that smoking reduces stress.
   - People believe advertisements that suggest that cigarettes will make them more sophisticated, popular, and athletic.

Reading Skills for the GED

Developing strong reading and reasoning skills is key to your success on the GED Tests. This section focuses on skills that are used on all of the tests and particularly in the content areas of science, social studies, and literature and the arts. These skills are called *comprehension, application, analysis, synthesis,* and *evaluation.*

If these words sound unfamiliar to you, don't be concerned. The purpose of this section is to give you practice in four of these five skill areas. You encountered the synthesis level of critical thinking skills in the Writing Skills section of this book. Synthesis involves putting elements together to create a whole as in a piece of writing. In the Writing Skills section, you were asked to write an essay on a given subject that included an introduction, body, and conclusion.

Writing activities are included in the Science, Social Studies, and Literature and the Arts sections of this book. By writing paragraphs to answer the variety of questions asked, you will be strengthening your skills in synthesis.

The reading skills mentioned above can be understood as layers of a pyramid. Each higher-level skill rests on the skill that precedes it. Each skill is a stepping-stone to a higher one. Memory (knowledge), sometimes referred to as *recall,* is the foundation of the pyramid. At the memory level, you recall facts. *Memory* helps you answer the questions *who, what, when, where,* and *how.*

Other tests that you took in school may have focused heavily on memory-based questions in which you had to recall facts. On the GED Tests, however, you will have to manipulate, or work with, the information that you read and that you hold in your memory. The questions on the GED will test your ability to comprehend, apply, analyze, and evaluate what you read. The thinking skill pyramid is illustrated below.

PYRAMID OF THINKING SKILLS

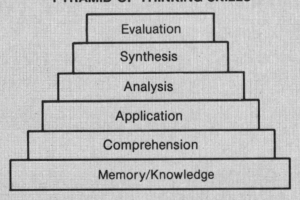

| Evaluation |
| Synthesis |
| Analysis |
| Application |
| Comprehension |
| Memory/Knowledge |

The next two chapters will help you develop the critical thinking skills and interpret the types of illustrations you will see on the GED Tests.

1
CRITICAL THINKING SKILLS

Comprehension— Understanding What You Read

When you *comprehend* something, you understand what you read. You show your understanding by being able to interpret or explain in your own words what something means. This skill involves putting one meaning into other words, identifying the main idea or key thought, and making inferences (sometimes referred to as *reading between the lines*).

When you *paraphrase*, you explain something so that another person can understand it. We are all familiar with slang—informal language used by a particular group. When you paraphrase slang spoken by a teenager to a member of an older generation, you do not repeat the message word for word; instead, you give the intended meaning. And that meaning does not last very long because slang words go out of style after a short period of time. Consider the example below, in which a teenager is speaking slang to an adult who may not comprehend the language of teenagers.

> *Teenager:* Your new shades are smooth.
> *Adult's literal translation:* Your new sunglasses have an even surface.
> *Intended meaning:* Your new sunglasses look good.

If you were paraphrasing the teen's statement, a word-for-word interpretation would not get the meaning across. You would have to explain *in other words* what the teen intended. Only by giving such an explanation could you show that you comprehended, or understood, what was said.

Idiomatic expressions, like slang, do not follow the rules of grammar, so it is difficult to translate them. However, we use them every day, and the English language would be much poorer without them. Common examples of idiomatic expressions are *get rid of, put up with, in the wink of an eye*, and *frog in my throat*. To understand the expression *frog in my throat*, we associate the sound of the person's voice with another concept familiar to us: the croaking sound made by a frog.

As you will find later, in the Literature and the Arts section, writers frequently use descriptive language and idiomatic expressions to make their writing more vibrant and vivid. You will often find yourself relying on your senses to understand what the writer is trying to say. The paragraph in the following exercise includes idiomatic expressions.

EXERCISE 1: UNDERSTANDING IDIOMATIC EXPRESSIONS

Directions: Read the following paragraph and paraphrase the numbered words or phrases by writing the intended meaning for each. The first one is done for you.

Carmen really needed to <u>brush up on</u> her Spanish. If she didn't <u>get cold</u>
(1)

<u>feet</u> and wasn't <u>broke</u> by the end of the month, she was going to Mexico. <u>Her</u>
(3)

<u>heart was set</u> on a trip, but she was <u>up to her ears in</u> work at the real estate

office. She had talked until she was <u>blue in the face</u> trying to persuade her

mother to <u>keep an eye on</u> the kids. As usual, Carmen had <u>bitten off more than</u>

<u>she could chew</u>. How could she continue working just to <u>make ends meet</u> and

plan for a trip? It <u>crossed her mind</u> just to <u>throw in the towel</u> and <u>hang around</u>

<u>the house</u> during her vacation week.

1. *review* _____   7. _____

2. _____   8. _____

3. _____   9. _____

4. _____   10. _____

5. _____   11. _____

6. _____   12. _____

Answers are on page 238.

Identifying the Main Idea

Another way you might show your comprehension of material is to **summarize**, or restate, the main idea. The main idea sums up what the writer is trying to get across. For example, if you answer the phone at work for an absent co-worker, and the caller gives you a long story about the reason for the call, you generally won't write down every word the caller says. You will summarize the message or simply write down the key thought or purpose of the call. You also might jot down key words or summarize main ideas when you take class notes.

In a paragraph, the main idea is often stated first. Details that support the main idea are included in the sentences that follow. Occasionally, writers put the main idea in the middle or at the end of a paragraph. Then the author must ensure that enough supporting details are included before or after to "add up" to the main point the writer is trying to make. Read the following paragraph and identify the sentence that states the main idea.

Michael Jordan and Bo Jackson have gotten a lot more publicity these days than such trailblazers as the late U.S. Supreme Court justice Thurgood Marshall and the medical research pioneer Dr. Jane C. Wright. So historians at the Du Sable Museum of African American History in Chicago want to make sure that—besides athletes and entertainers—African-Americans' positive contributions to society are represented and respected. They aim to teach young African-Americans more about their own history and to show them that there are plenty of strong role models in different professions. To quote one recent visitor: "If they knew some of the things the pioneers of our people did, they'd have a better chance of being more successful in life." Through creative displays and educational tours, the museum succeeds in portraying these values.

The main idea here appears in the middle of the paragraph: "They aim to teach young African-Americans more about their own history and to show them that there are plenty of strong role models in different professions." Can you see how the sentences before it and the sentences that follow it all add up to the main idea?

And just as a paragraph has a main or central idea, a longer passage or article has a main idea. Read the following passage to identify the main idea. Where is it stated in the passage?

Weather is one of many variables that affect the nation's agricultural economy, and it is the most unpredictable. Northern farmers who hope for record harvests have frequently seen crops wiped out by droughts, seeds washed away by torrential rains, and early spring planting plans thwarted by frozen ground. You might think that a farmer's problems are solved by lots of sunshine, plentiful rain, and year-round warm temperatures. Well, think again! In recent years, orange growers in Florida have had their hopes dashed by unexpected subfreezing temperatures. These cold temperatures have resulted in reduced harvests.

The higher prices we must pay at the market for reduced crops cannot make up for the dollars lost because of Mother Nature's whims. The old adage that "we can only *talk* about the weather" accurately indicates just how powerless we are in controlling the forces of nature.

Which of the following sentences states the main idea of this passage?

(1) Man can't control the weather.
(2) Weather can have a serious effect on a nation's farm economy.
(3) A farmer's life can be very difficult.
(4) Man must strive to overcome all odds.
(5) The farmer is the backbone of the American economy.

The answer is (2). The main idea of the passage is stated in the introductory sentence: "Weather is one of many variables that affect the nation's agricultural economy, and it is the most unpredictable." The passage goes on to explain how acts of nature affect the productivity of farmers. Choice (1) gives support for the main idea. Choices (3) and (4) are true statements that can be inferred after having read the passage. Choice (5) is not expressed at all in the passage.

Read the passage below to find the main idea. Where is it placed in the paragraph?

> In Africa, UNICEF (United Nations International Children's Emergency Fund) has helped provide emergency food supplies, water, and medicine for starving and malnourished children and adults in the nations of Angola, Ethiopia, Sudan, Zimbabwe and Somalia.
>
> UNICEF was also active in Latin America. In Mexico, it provided resources to help earthquake victims. It aided Colombians after a devastating volcanic eruption. In fact, UNICEF has worked hard on a number of international causes during the last decade.

The main idea is stated in the last sentence of the passage: "In fact, UNICEF has worked hard on a number of international causes during the last decade." The main idea is stated only after supporting details have built a case for it:

> In Africa, UNICEF . . .
> + In Mexico, it provided . . .
> + It aided Colombians . . .
> _____
> **UNICEF worked hard on a number of international causes.**

In certain cases, an author may not directly state the main idea in a sentence or paragraph. Readers must always consider all of the important details to determine the main idea of a paragraph. Often they must make an inference or "read between the lines" to decide what the main idea is. Before readers come to any conclusion about the main idea, however, they must decide whether or not the main idea is stated. Read the passage below. Decide what the main idea is.

> The years pass and Abe Lincoln grows up, at 17 standing six feet, nearly four inches, long-armed with rare strength in his muscles. At 18 he could take an ax at the end of the handle and hold it out from his shoulders in a straight horizontal line, easy and steady. He could make his ax flash and bite into a sugar maple or a sycamore, one neighbor saying, "He can sink an ax deeper into wood than any man I ever saw."
>
> *The Prairie Years*, Carl Sandburg

The main idea—that Abe Lincoln was physically strong at a young age—must be inferred from the details provided. To determine the main idea, you have to find the key ideas:

> at 17 standing six feet, nearly four inches
> + long-armed with rare strength in his muscles
> + could take an ax at the end of the handle and hold it out from his shoulders in a straight horizontal line, easy and steady
> + can sink an ax deeper into wood than any man
> _____
> **Abe Lincoln was physically strong at a young age** (or something similar).

Theme is another way that a writer can express a main idea. In one section on the Literature and the Arts Test, you will learn about a story's theme. An author does not directly state the theme in a story or novel. The reader must infer the main idea by putting together the details of plot, character, and setting that are shown in the story. The next exercise provides practice in reading between the lines to determine the main idea.

EXERCISE 2: READING BETWEEN THE LINES

Directions: Read the passage and answer the questions that follow.

The Priceless Gift

A young boy's dramatic adventure unfolds several years before the Soviet Union breaks up into the Commonwealth of Independent States. Picture a little Ukrainian boy coming to the United States with his parents. His parents decide to return to the Soviet Union, but he refuses to accompany them. Six years later, the boy, now twelve years old, receives a gift. The gift is something that native-born American children take for granted. It's a gift for a young boy who rode his bicycle to a relative's house and hid there for five days to avoid leaving the United States against his will. But this gift is wrapped in yards of legal red tape.

Before the boy earned the gift, he had to ignore the wishes of his parents and his native country. He had to learn to accept a whole new way of life without his parents and brother. He had to learn the English language and learn the ways of elementary school students in Chicago. He had to get used to grocery stores with plenty of food, unrestricted movement on the streets, and the option of celebrating religious holidays. He had to attempt to lead a normal life in spite of all the media attention. He knew the gift could not be bought with money; it was priceless.

1. The unstated main idea of the passage is that

   (1) teenage boys usually need to break with their parents
   (2) the boy earned the right to become a U.S. citizen
   (3) the boy was wrong to hide from his parents
   (4) the wrapped gift was delivered on the boy's birthday
   (5) the boy disliked Soviet schools

2. Which of the following details does *not* help you arrive at the main idea?

   (1) The boy was a twelve-year-old student in Chicago.
   (2) The gift was tied with yards of legal red tape.
   (3) Native-born Americans take this gift for granted.
   (4) The gift could not be bought with money.
   (5) The boy had to become used to living in the United States.

Answers are on page 238.

SKILL BUILDER: IDENTIFYING THE MAIN IDEA

1. Circle key words in a sentence. What words are absolutely necessary to get the message across?

2. Identify key ideas contained in a paragraph; key ideas are groups of key words. List what these ideas have in common; this is the main idea.

3. Notice headlines and titles; they usually contain key ideas.

Restating Information

When you paraphrase, or restate information, you use different words and phrases to express the same idea. Here are two examples of restated information:

Original

That author's enlightening new book gives deep insights into the nature of human relationships.

Previous experience with preschool education is more of a determinant of success in elementary education than socioeconomic status.

Restatement

There is a lot to be learned about personal relationships from this author's new book.

Going to preschool will have a positive effect on a child's elementary school education. This is a more important factor than whether the child comes from a rich or poor family.

On the GED Tests, you may be required to show how well you comprehend something by recognizing a restatement of a phrase, a sentence, or an idea.

EXERCISE 3: RESTATING IDEAS

Directions: Rewrite the following sentences in your own words.

1. One type of behavior is known as *stimulus-response*. According to this principle, an organism will respond in some way when acted on by a stimulus.

   Restatement: _____

   _____

2. It was no easy task to draw up a new constitution for the young United States. A split soon developed between the Federalists, who wanted a strong central government with authoritative control over the states, and the anti-Federalists, who were afraid the individual people and states would lose their freedoms under one central government.

   Restatement: _____

   _____

   _____

3. A consumer would be foolhardy to assume that the mere assertion of a product's quality is proof enough. Consumers should not spend a great deal of money purchasing a new car without researching it in an authoritative source on car performance and standards.

   Restatement: _____

   _____

   _____

4. All payments received will be applied first to the fees, if any, billed to your account by us, next to billed and unpaid finance charges, and then to billed and unpaid purchases and advances in the order determined by us.

   Restatement: _____

   _____

   _____

5. The manufacturer warrants that if anything goes wrong with your television set within ninety days—and it's our fault—we will pay our authorized Servicenter only for the labor to repair it in that shop. Transportation to and from the Servicenter is your responsibility. After the ninety-day warranty expires, all labor charges are your responsibility.

Restatement: _____

_____

_____

Possible answers are on page 238.

Application—Applying What You Read

One of the most important outcomes of an education is the ability to apply what you have learned. For example, police cadets must be able to apply to test situations knowledge of the laws they have learned before they can be awarded their badges. Paramedics must be able to perform CPR (cardiopulmonary resuscitation) and other procedures before they can earn their certificates.

On the GED Tests, you will have to use information given to you and apply it in a problem-solving situation. The information that you will be given may be in the form of a definition, scientific theory, or principle. You will encounter application questions primarily in the areas of science and social studies; however, the Literature and the Arts Test will contain some as well.

To practice your skill in applying definitions, read the following passage about forms of drama and answer the questions that follow.

> The major forms of drama are the comedy and the tragedy. **Comedies** generally are light and amusing. They usually begin in humorously difficult situations and always end happily. Not all comedies are funny and lighthearted, although the majority are. Types of comedy include **slapstick**, a form of physical comedy that includes pratfalls and pie-in-the-face acts. **Farce** is a type of comedy that features exaggerated circumstances, improbable plots, and foolish action and dialogue.
>
> **Tragedies** often begin happily and always end in disaster. The main character is usually good but loses to an opponent in a conflict and is either ruined or killed. The major reason for the main character's failure is the tragic flaw—the human weakness that has made the tragic hero or heroine vulnerable.
>
> Somewhere between comedy and tragedy lies **melodrama**, a type of drama that relies on sentimentality, exaggerates emotion, and provides thrilling action.

Based on the information in the passage, answer the following questions.

1. The boisterous humor featured by comedians such as the Three Stooges, Jerry Lewis, and Charlie Chaplin would be classified *best* as

   (1) comedy
   (2) tragedy
   (3) slapstick
   (4) farce
   (5) melodrama

2. A movie produced by Mel Brooks or Woody Allen and featuring actors such as Chevy Chase, Robin Williams, and Gene Wilder involved in outlandish circumstances would probably be classified *best* as

    (1) comedy
    (2) tragedy
    (3) slapstick
    (4) farce
    (5) melodrama

3. One of the most popular television programs of the last decade was "Cheers." This classic look at the human condition from the points of view of the lively characters in a Boston barroom would be described *best* as

    (1) comedy
    (2) tragedy
    (3) slapstick
    (4) farce
    (5) melodrama

4. Shows such as "Picket Fences," "All My Children," and "In the Heat of the Night" would fall into the category of

    (1) comedy
    (2) tragedy
    (3) slapstick
    (4) farce
    (5) melodrama

The answer to question 1 is **(3)**. Slapstick is defined in the passage as physical comedy characterized by pratfalls, pie-in-the-face acts, and other behavior demonstrated by the Three Stooges, Jerry Lewis, and Charlie Chaplin.

The answer to question 2 is **(4)**. The passage defines farce as a form of comedy featuring exaggerated circumstances and unbelievable plots. Actors such as Chevy Chase, Robin Williams, and Gene Wilder frequently perform in farces.

The answer to question 3 is **(1)**. The passage describes a comedy as light and amusing. "Cheers" featured humorous exchanges between Sam and the regulars of the barroom.

The answer to question 4 is **(5)**. The passage describes melodrama as a form of drama that relies on sentimentality, exaggerated emotion, and thrilling action. "In the Heat of the Night" is action-oriented, and "All My Children," a soap opera, and "Picket Fences," a drama, rely on sentimentality and exaggerated emotion.

Application in Social Studies and Science

The Social Studies and Science Tests will challenge your ability to apply given ideas in different situations using an item format similar to the one on the next page. In this type of item, certain categories are defined and specific situations are given. Some of the categories may seem very similar, so you will need to read each category *very carefully* to understand the differences among them.

EXERCISE 4: APPLICATION IN SOCIAL STUDIES

Directions: Read the definitions below and answer the questions that follow.

Propaganda is information provided in such a way as to influence or slant the opinion or feelings of the audience that receives the message. Listed below are five techniques used by propagandists.

name-calling—attaching an unfavorable name to an idea, a person, or a group so as to influence the attitude of the audience against the idea or position

glittering generalities—high-sounding but general and vague terms used to influence positively the feelings of the audience toward a subject

bandwagoning—advising people to do something because "everyone" does it, because it is popular, or because it is the "in" thing to do

transferring—associating the respect, prestige, or power of one person or object with another person so that the audience is influenced favorably

card-stacking—choosing only specific, favorable points that support a cause and ignoring the unfavorable points

1. In the 1992 presidential election, vice presidential candidate Albert Gore came to be known by his opponents as "Mr. Ozone" because of his efforts to educate the public about threats to the environment. Those who criticized him were employing the propaganda technique of

    (1) name-calling
    (2) glittering generalities
    (3) transferring
    (4) bandwagoning
    (5) card-stacking

2. A presidential candidate on the campaign stump who takes credit for increasing employment, lowering taxes, and improving trade relationships but ignores his foreign policy failures is guilty of engaging in

    (1) name-calling
    (2) glittering generalities
    (3) transferring
    (4) bandwagoning
    (5) card-stacking

3. After a tense night of police and gang clashes, fire has broken out in several stores on the street. Gang members begin to raid the supermarkets and appliance stores. More people on the streets join in the looting. As local residents are awakened and look out their windows, people in the streets call out, "Come on and grab what you can get. Hey, we're all getting free stuff. All the guys in the neighborhood are taking stuff. Get in on the free loot."

    What means of propaganda did the crowds use to justify their criminal acts?

    (1) name-calling
    (2) glittering generalities
    (3) transferring
    (4) bandwagoning
    (5) card-stacking

4. The local school council is proposing to adopt a measure to keep kids in school for an extra half hour each day. Parents and community leaders favor the idea, but the teachers aren't convinced. The president of the national teachers' association is known to oppose the plan. Staff teachers appeal to the council to drop the plan, arguing that if their national leader is against it, shouldn't they all fight it?

What propaganda technique is illustrated here?

(1) name-calling
(2) glittering generalities
(3) transferring
(4) bandwagoning
(5) card-stacking

Answers are on page 238.

EXERCISE 5: APPLICATION IN SCIENCE

Directions: Read the definitions below and answer the questions that follow.

The human body is composed of several systems that keep it functioning. Though each system may be viewed separately, it is closely related to the others in the body—so much so that a problem in one system invariably affects another. Defined below are five of at least ten systems that make up the human body.

excretory system—the system that excretes or expels water and salts from the body; it includes the urinary system, in which the kidneys, ureters, urethra, and bladder play vital roles

endocrine system—the system made up of glands such as the pituitary, thyroid, and adrenal, which secrete body fluids, stimulating cells and regulating the body's development

lymphatic system—the system that circulates lymph (a pale fluid) to the body's tissues, bathing the cells; lymphocytes found in the system produce antibodies that help fight bacterial infections

digestive system—the system that processes and distributes nutrients from food; composed chiefly of the esophagus, stomach, liver, and large and small intestines

muscular system—the system composed of the three types of tissue that enable the body and its parts to move

1. AIDS (acquired immunodeficiency syndrome) is a disease that inhibits the body's ability to fight off infections. AIDS would interfere mainly with the proper functioning of which system?

(1) excretory
(2) endocrine
(3) lymphatic
(4) digestive
(5) muscular

2. The skin (the body's largest organ) may be defined loosely as belonging to this system since, through perspiration, wastes are removed from the body.

    (1) excretory
    (2) endocrine
    (3) lymphatic
    (4) digestive
    (5) muscular

3. The sudden growth spurt characteristic of adolescents may be attributed to the operation of which of the body's systems?

    (1) excretory
    (2) endocrine
    (3) lymphatic
    (4) digestive
    (5) muscular

4. Saliva, needed by the body to perform the first step in the operation of one of the bodily systems, is an integral component of which system?

    (1) excretory
    (2) endocrine
    (3) lymphatic
    (4) digestive
    (5) muscular

Answers are on page 238.

SKILL BUILDER: ANSWERING APPLICATION QUESTIONS

To answer application questions, use the process of elimination. Go through each category to rule out ones that do *not* fit the question. In this way, you should be able to find the correct choice.

Analysis—Analyzing What You Read

When you analyze something, you take it apart. You examine the elements to understand better what makes up its whole.

On the GED Tests you will be expected to analyze complete passages in the areas of social studies, science, and literature and the arts. You will look at specific ideas and pieces of information to understand better the point being made by a writer, graphic artist, or cartoonist.

The Social Studies and Science Tests will test your ability to

- distinguish facts from opinions and hypotheses
- recognize unstated assumptions
- draw conclusions

On the Literature and the Arts Test you will be required to identify

- elements or techniques of style and structure
- the techniques used to produce a particular effect
- the effects produced by the use of different techniques

Distinguishing Facts from Opinions and Hypotheses

Some of the material you will read on the GED Tests will be based on facts, opinions, or hypotheses. *Facts* can be proved to be true by using one or more of the five senses. Newspapers and magazine articles are based largely on facts.

Opinions are beliefs that may or may not be supported by facts. Opinions express feelings or ideas and are influenced greatly by one's background, values, and outlook on life. For example, editorials and columns in newspapers generally present a writer's opinions along with the facts.

Hypotheses are educated guesses that are made to explain a phenomenon or an event. Hypotheses may be proved or disproved by the passage of time or the acquiring of additional information. The statements below show how facts, opinions, and hypotheses differ.

- It is a fact that Pittsburgh has more bridges than any other major American city because of the meeting of two rivers—the Allegheny and the Monongahela—to form the Ohio. This fact can be proved by acquiring data on bridges in U.S. cities.

- It is an opinion that Pittsburgh is the most desirable place to live in the United States. This is a statement that is based on a person's values, background, and outlook on life.

- It is a hypothesis that Pittsburgh will experience a 15 percent decrease in population over the next five years because of the decline in smokestack industries there. More time and information will be needed to prove or disprove this hypothesis.

EXERCISE 6: FACTS, OPINIONS, AND HYPOTHESES

Directions: Read each group of statements below. Write *F* for the ones that express a fact, *O* for the ones that express an opinion, and *H* for the ones that express a hypothesis.

1. ____ **(a)** Our city is a great place to live.

   ____ **(b)** If the present trend continues, our city's population will reach 70,000 by the year 2000.

   ____ **(c)** The population of our city is 58,000.

2. ____ **(a)** Several million legal abortions have been performed.

   ____ **(b)** When birth control clinics are established at all inner-city high schools, the number of abortions in the city will decline by 50 percent.

   ____ **(c)** Antiabortion activists believe abortion is murder.

3. ____ **(a)** With her teaching methods, Mrs. Smith's class will experience an across-the-board increase in test scores by the year's end.

   ____ **(b)** Mrs. Smith is an outstanding teacher.

   ____ **(c)** The Board of Education has agreed to rehire Mrs. Smith for another year.

4. ____ **(a)** If you're patriotic, you'll buy only American-made cars.

   ____ **(b)** There continues to be a market for foreign-made cars.

   ____ **(c)** The number of Americans buying foreign-made cars will jump 20 percent when import quotas are lifted.

5. ____ **(a)** Marianne wallpapered the dining room herself.

   ____ **(b)** The wallpaper in the dining room will last two years longer than the wallpaper in the living room if Marianne uses premixed paste.

   ____ **(c)** Marianne should have hired a professional paperhanger to wallpaper the dining room.

Answers are on page 239.

EXERCISE 7: MORE ON FACTS, OPINIONS, AND HYPOTHESES

Directions: Read the passage and the statements that follow. Then write *F* if the statement is a fact stated in or supported by the passage, *O* if it is an opinion, and *H* if it is a hypothesis.

Hispanic influence is expanding in the United States of America. In fact, people of Hispanic origin are the second-fastest-growing minority in the United States, making up nearly 9 percent of the population. Demographers—people who study and report vital statistics on population groups—estimate that by the year 2020 Hispanic-Americans will become the nation's largest minority.

Where do they come from, and where do they live? Many Hispanic-Americans come from Mexico, frequently settling in San Antonio or Los Angeles. Those who come from Cuba often make Miami their home. New York and Chicago have large Hispanic populations from Puerto Rico.

Hispanic culture is expanding, too. After struggling for many years to achieve status, Hispanic-American culture is becoming more widely accepted in the United States. For instance, Hispanic artists and entertainers and Hispanic foods have become popular in many cities across the nation. Even more significant, however, is that Hispanic-Americans are being elected or appointed to political office and other important positions. Robert Martinez, the former governor of Florida, and Lauro Cavazos, formerly the Secretary of Education, for example, have earned respected leadership roles in government.

In 1993, President Bill Clinton named two Hispanics to his White House Cabinet: Henry Cisneros, Secretary of Housing and Urban Development (HUD), and Federico Peña, Secretary of Transportation. Although some people criticized Clinton for being influenced by activists who demanded more minorities, he said, "I can say with pride that I believe this Cabinet and these other appointees represent the best in America."

_____ **1.** By the year 2020, Hispanic-Americans will be the United States' largest minority.

_____ **2.** Hispanic-American artists owe their success to great struggles.

_____ **3.** Many Hispanic-Americans came from Cuba and Puerto Rico.

_____ **4.** President Clinton appointed two Hispanic-Americans to his 1993 Cabinet.

_____ **5.** The 1993 Cabinet appointees are the most effective leaders in America.

_____ **6.** Twenty years from now, Hispanic-Americans will live and work in every city in the United States.

_____ **7.** People who come here from Mexico help to advance our culture.

Answers are on page 239.

Hypotheses and the Scientific Method

Formulating a hypothesis is an important step in the scientific method. The scientific method is a system of investigation on which all scientific inquiry is based. Most science courses offer at least a bare summary of the procedure. It can be reduced to six steps:

1. Identify and state the problem.
2. Collect information.
3. Make a hypothesis.
4. Make a prediction on the basis of the hypothesis.
5. Make observations and perform experiments to test the hypothesis.
6. Draw a conclusion.

In step 1, the scientist identifies a problem that needs to be solved or a question that must be answered. Step 2 requires that the scientist gather as much information about the problem as possible. At step 3, the scientist makes an educated guess that might explain the reason for the problem or answer the question. The scientist then predicts what the outcome of the experiment or observation will be if the hypothesis is correct, step 4. During step 5, the scientist observes or experiments to test the hypothesis. According to step 6, if the results confirm the scientist's prediction, the hypothesis is correct. If they don't, the hypothesis must be changed or thrown out.

When the results of an experiment or observation can be explained by a hypothesis, a *theory* is formed. When a theory has few exceptions, it is called a *law*.

Let's look at a situation to which we might apply these six steps to solve a problem.

> We went to fish at our favorite lake, but the fishing was terrible. The water was very clear, and we didn't see any plants growing at the bottom of the lake at all. We were told a few weeks earlier that there had been a heavy die-off of fish. We called the Environmental Protection Agency. Agency officials said that they think the lake is a victim of acid rain. Water tests and an examination of frozen fish samples confirmed the belief that the high level of acidity in the lake had killed all life.

The situation described above can be investigated by following the six steps of the scientific method.

1. *Problem:* The fishing at our favorite lake was terrible.

2. *Information (observable facts):* The water was clear, there were no plants, and there was a recent die-off of fish.

3. *Hypothesis:* The lake may be a victim of acid rain.

4. *Prediction:* If the lake is acidic, a pattern will show up in water and fish samples.

5. *Experiment:* All tests prove positive for the characteristics of acid rain; our results agree with our prediction.

6. *Conclusion:* The lake has been affected by acid rain.

In following the scientific method, a scientist must be objective. The results of the experiment must not be influenced in any way by the scientist's hunches or beliefs. The results of the experiment must speak for themselves. For this reason, experiments involving the scientific method require the use of controls so that the outcome is not biased by the experimenter's expectations.

EXERCISE 8: HYPOTHESES AND THE SCIENTIFIC METHOD

Directions: Read the passage below. Then fill in the steps of the scientific method with the correct information from the passage.

The shipbuilding industry was a significant part of New England's economy. An important but hazardous mineral used in shipbuilding is asbestos. Asbestos is used widely for fireproofing and insulating. However, workers exposed to asbestos fibers for long periods of time are known to have a higher-than-average risk of getting lung cancer.

In the late 1950s, doctors were getting an unusual number of asbestos-related cancer cases. Two distinct forms of cancer were dominant—cancer of the abdominal lining and cancer of the bronchial tubes. Doctors who treated these diseases noticed that not all of the workers exposed to asbestos contracted bronchiogenic cancer. Physicians who compiled case histories for cancer patients found nothing in the records that would seem to cause one group of men over another to get the deadly disease.

A research team at one medical center, however, suspected that another factor—cigarette smoking—might increase a worker's chances of getting cancer of the bronchial tubes. They suggested that, if those suffering with this type of cancer were polled, the results would indicate that they were heavy cigarette smokers. When the team surveyed this group of cancer patients, it found that, indeed, a very high percentage were cigarette smokers.

1. *Problem:* _____

_____

2. *Information (observable facts):* _____

_____

3. *Hypothesis:* _____

_____

4. *Prediction:* _____

_____

5. *Observation (perform experiment):* _____

_____

6. *Conclusion:* _____

_____

Answers are on page 239.

EXERCISE 9: MORE ON HYPOTHESES AND THE SCIENTIFIC METHOD

Directions: Read the passage below. Then fill in the steps of the scientific method with the correct information from the passage.

We've long known that what vegetation grows in rain forests is determined partly by the climate there. However, recent scientific studies and computer simulations of rain forest weather reveal an interesting twist: the weather in tropical rain forests is determined partly by the vegetation that grows there.

Rain forests are being destroyed to grow food crops, to provide land for cattle grazing, and to provide settlement areas to ease population density. In the Amazon rain forests, evaporation from plants and soil accounts for half of all the water that falls. The removal of vegetation from the ecosystem may disrupt the water cycle, causing less water to be evaporated.

Some scientists believed that if they could perform a mathematical analysis of the climate and create the conditions of the South American rain forest, their results would show that removing plant growth would affect the weather, which would in turn affect future growth.

Using supercomputers and analyzing the climate, researchers were able to simulate the rain forest environment. Their projections showed that turning the South American rain forest into cattle pasture would reduce rainfall by 25 percent and increase average temperatures in the area by 5°F. This would also lengthen the dry season.

The result of this experiment was the knowledge that clearing away the rain forest would affect the weather, making it unlikely that forest plants could ever grow there again.

1. *Problem:* _____

   _____

2. *Information (observable facts):* _____

   _____

3. *Hypothesis:* _____

   _____

4. *Prediction:* _____

   _____

5. *Observation (experiment):* _____

   _____

6. *Conclusion:* _____

   _____

Answers are on page 239.

Drawing Conclusions Through
Inductive and Deductive Reasoning

The scientific method is based on logical reasoning. When you draw conclusions that support evidence gathered in an investigation, you are following logic. Two methods of reasoning that are involved in logic are inductive reasoning and deductive reasoning.

Inductive reasoning involves drawing a conclusion by going from the specific to the general. In following induction, you observe the behavior or characteristics of members of a class or group and then apply this information to the unobserved members of the group. In other words, you ***generalize*** about the other members of the group. To see how a scientist follows inductive reasoning, read the following passage:

> Scientific evidence from field studies of golden eagles indicates that the pesticide DDT is threatening the existence of our birds of prey. Raptors such as hawks and eagles provide a service by controlling rodents that damage our food crops. Although DDT does not poison the birds directly, it can interfere with their metabolism, causing them to produce eggs with thinner shells that break easily. Also, the birds' ability to store toxic materials in the fatty tissues weakens the offspring, increasing mortality.
>
> A specific statement that can be made from this study is that DDT is threatening golden eagles (birds of prey).

Based on this observation, scientists can generalize that other birds of prey living in the same region as golden eagles are similarly threatened by DDT.

Deductive reasoning involves drawing a conclusion by applying a generalization to a specific example or case. In the case above, scientists who have found that our birds of prey are threatened by DDT may infer that bald eagles, red-tailed hawks, falcons, great horned owls, and other raptors in the area are also being threatened.

For a valid conclusion to be drawn, the generalization must be known, accepted, and true. If the generalization is faulty, it cannot be applied to a specific example.

EXERCISE 10: DEDUCTIVE REASONING

Directions: Read the generalization, then write *yes* for each conclusion that is valid based on the generalization, and *no* for each that is not.

Generalization: A stroke is a condition in which there is lessening or loss of consciousness, sensation, and motion caused by the rupture or obstruction of an artery of the brain.

Conclusions:

_____ **1.** A cerebral hemorrhage occurs when a defective brain artery bursts; therefore, a cerebral hemorrhage often can lead to a stroke.

_____ **2.** An embolism is the sudden blockage of a blood vessel by a mass or an air bubble in the blood; therefore, an embolism in the brain can lead to a stroke.

_____ **3.** A tumor is a mass of tissue that does not swell and that rises from tissue that already exists; therefore, brain tumors generally lead to a stroke.

_____ **4.** An aneurysm is a permanent, abnormal, blood-filled swelling of a vessel; therefore, the rupture of an aneurysm can cause a stroke.

_____ **5.** Phlebitis is the inflammation of a vein; varicose veins are abnormally swollen or dilated veins; therefore, phlebitis and varicose veins can lead to a stroke.

Answers are on page 240.

SKILL BUILDER: INDUCTIVE/DEDUCTIVE REASONING QUESTIONS

To answer these questions, ask yourself
- Is the generalization accepted by most people?
- Is it true, based on your experience and knowledge?
- Were a great number of subjects observed?
- Are you aware of any exceptions to the rule?

Faulty Reasoning and Unstated Assumptions

Writers and speakers may not always follow logic in expressing their views. Sometimes, they make statements or write essays that are based on information that is not true. They often do this to influence the opinions of their audience.

Propagandists are especially guilty of this practice. If an assumption is faulty, a writer's or speaker's entire argument can be faulty. One indication of an informed mind is the ability to recognize when a faulty assumption is being made. Read the statement below and consider the assumption being made.

All who receive welfare benefits under the AFDC (Aid to Families with Dependent Children) program should be forced to do community work if they want to keep their benefits.

An assumption that the speaker has made is that everyone who receives welfare benefits under AFDC is able to work. This is not necessarily the case for all recipients. In fact, according to statistics, most of the recipients are actually children who, of course, cannot go to work.

EXERCISE 11: FAULTY REASONING AND UNSTATED ASSUMPTIONS

Directions: Read the statements below to detect the assumption made by the writer. Then complete the statements that follow by filling in the blank with the appropriate word or words. *Note:* You may uncover underlying assumptions that are not included in the answer key.

1. All unwed mothers should be forced to complete high school before receiving any welfare benefits.

   The speaker assumes that all unwed mothers are _____

   _____ .

2. All foreign-born doctors practicing in the United States should have their licenses reviewed annually and should undergo frequent competency exams.

   The speaker assumes that foreign-born doctors are less _____
   than American-born doctors.

3. All polling places in the inner city should have pollwatchers to guard against vote fraud.

   The writer assumes that vote fraud is _____ in the inner city.

4. All cars over five years of age should undergo mandatory emissions tests.

   The speaker assumes that older cars tend to cause more _____
   than newer cars.

5. In professional and collegiate sports, all athletes should undergo mandatory drug testing.

   The speaker assumes that professional and collegiate athletes are guilty of

   _____ .

   Answers are on page 240.

SKILL BUILDER: RECOGNIZING FAULTY REASONING AND UNSTATED ASSUMPTIONS

Be suspicious of blanket statements that include *all* people or things in a category. Such statements are often faulty since there are exceptions to every rule.

Analysis in Literature and the Arts

The Literature and the Arts Test will tap your skill in analyzing excerpts from fiction, nonfiction, and drama, as well as poetry. You will be required to identify techniques of style and to be able to understand how a writer's technique contributes to the overall effect of a piece of literature.

Style is the writer's way of using language to express an idea. Style varies among individual writers, as do their personalities. Style is established by the writer's choice of words and helps to create *tone*, the attitude an author conveys toward the subject and reader. An example of how tone is used is shown in the following statement:

Thanks a lot!

Spoken in one tone of voice, the statement can be taken as a compliment; however, if spoken in another tone, it can be taken as an insult, proving that it's not *what* you say but *how* you say it. You will learn more about style and tone in the Literature and the Arts section.

Read the following excerpt to determine the tone the writer is using. Is it serious, sentimental, or humorous? Could the passage be characterized as slapstick, tragedy, melodrama, or farce?

. . . The ghost that got into our house on the night of November 17, 1915, raised such a hullabaloo of misunderstandings that I am sorry that I didn't just let it keep on walking, and go to bed. Its advent caused my mother to throw a shoe through a window of the house next door and ended up with my grandfather shooting a patrolman. I am sorry, therefore, that I ever paid any attention to the footsteps.

from "The Night the Ghost Got In" by James Thurber

The tone may be described as humorous. The reader can infer the tone by the author's use of language. "The ghost . . . raised such a hullabaloo of misunderstandings . . ." lets us know that this is not the opening of a horror story about ghosts. The improbable actions triggered by the ghost's appearance include the mother's throwing a shoe through a neighbor's window and the grandfather's shooting a patrolman.

The passage could be characterized as farce, a form of comedy featuring exaggerated circumstances and unbelievable plots. A ghost getting into a house and causing the grandfather to shoot a patrolman would be unbelievable to many.

EXERCISE 12: STYLE AND TONE

Directions: Read the passage and answer the questions that follow.

"Ah, Father, Father!" said Wilhelm. "It's always the same thing with you. Look how you lead me on. You always start out to help me with my problems, and be sympathetic and so forth. It gets my hopes up and I begin to be grateful. But before we're through I'm a hundred times more depressed than before. Why is that? You have no sympathy. You want to shift all the blame on to me. Maybe you're wise to do it." Wilhelm was beginning to lose himself. "All you seem to think about is your death. Well, I'm sorry. But I'm going to die too. And I'm your son. It isn't my fault in the first place. There ought to be a right way to do this, and be fair to each other. But what I want to know is, why do you start up with me if you're not going to help me? What do you want to know about my problems for, Father? So you can lay the whole responsibility on me—so that you won't have to help me? D'you want me to comfort you for having such a son?" Wilhelm had a great knot of wrong tied tight within his chest, and tears approached his eyes but he didn't let them out. He looked shabby enough as it was. His voice was thick and hazy, and he was stammering and could not bring his awful feelings forth.

from *Seize the Day*, by Saul Bellow

1. The author's style suggests that Wilhelm is

   (1) talking too fast
   (2) suffering emotionally
   (3) getting ready for a fight
   (4) showing maturity and wisdom
   (5) acting responsibly

2. The overall tone of the excerpt is

   (1) nostalgic
   (2) mocking
   (3) tragic
   (4) angry
   (5) sentimental

3. In this excerpt, the author's style can be described as

   (1) formal
   (2) poetic
   (3) romantic
   (4) realistic
   (5) imaginative

4. The author portrays a father-and-son relationship that has a history of

   (1) conflict
   (2) physical violence
   (3) acceptance
   (4) understanding
   (5) mutual cooperation

5. Wilhelm may best be described as a man who

   (1) struggles with external and internal conflicts
   (2) lives in a world rich in fantasy
   (3) knows exactly what he wants and how to get it
   (4) turns his emotions on and off at will
   (5) hates his family

Answers are on page 240.

Evaluation—Evaluating What You Read

When you *evaluate* something, you make a judgment. You decide how well or poorly an idea or object meets certain standards. For example, when you evaluate a movie, you judge it according to the quality of its acting, directing, cinematography, sound track, and other standards. Standards by which a judgment is made are called *criteria*. Criteria may be either subjective or objective.

Objective criteria are standards that are not affected by an individual's personal tastes, beliefs, or opinions about what is being judged. *Subjective* criteria are standards that *are* affected by an individual's personal tastes, beliefs, or opinions.

For example, tests like true/false and multiple-choice exams, in which there is a single correct answer for each question, can be evaluated objectively. The correctness of the answer choice is not open to dispute; if the answer is debatable, then the question itself is not valid. On the other hand, an essay exam, one in which students have to interpret and answer questions using their own words, is open to subjective evaluation. The teacher who grades the test has to decide in his or her own mind whether or not the student answered the question adequately. For this reason, essay examinations are very difficult to grade, and instructors must establish clear-cut guidelines by which the exam is to be evaluated.

The following situation illustrates the difference between objective and subjective criteria. Read the paragraph and answer the questions that follow.

A young couple is purchasing their first home. They have two small school-age children. They must consider several factors in the decision to buy a home. They have drawn up a list of criteria by which to judge the prospective neighborhood for the home. In the space provided, write *O* if the standard is objective and *S* if it is subjective.

_____ **1.** the peacefulness of the community during the day

_____ **2.** the closeness, in walking distance, to the nearest school

_____ **3.** the attractiveness of the other homes on the block

_____ **4.** the community's tax rate compared to other communities

_____ **5.** the success of the community's recreational programs

_____ **6.** the performance of the school district on national standardized tests

_____ **7.** the quality of the municipal services the community offers

You should have identified the objective standards as numbers 2, 4, and 6. Each of these criteria can be evaluated by information that can be collected or measured objectively. The subjective criteria are numbered 1, 3, 5, and 7. These criteria are subjective because personal opinion, not objective facts, affects how a person views the community in this regard. What may be described as peaceful, attractive, successful, and of good quality varies from person to person. In fact, the husband and wife themselves may not even agree on these points.

EXERCISE 13: EVALUATING IDEAS

Directions: Read the following television commentary and answer the questions that follow.

They're fast, they're fun, they're not terribly difficult, and you could get a chance to win a lot of money or prizes. They're TV game shows, and they've been a staple of the daytime schedule since television began.

Game shows are remarkably good at offering something for everyone. Contestants can be famous for a day and get the thrill of competing. Studio and home audiences can share in the excitement and play along. Producers, whose hardest job is coming up with the idea for the game in the first place—and then selling it to a network or group of stations—can settle back and make money.

Mark Goodson, of Mark Goodson–Bill Todman Productions, has been the brains behind some of the most popular TV game shows, like "To Tell the Truth," "The Price Is Right," "Password," "Match Game," "Family Feud," and "Child's Play," where adults try to guess the secret word from clues given by six- to eight-year-olds.

Goodson says creating a game show is tricky. "You have to come up with a simple concept that is also novel and involving," he explains. There are other "rules" that must be followed as well. "Good game shows have at least three things in common," Goodson says. "First, there's an element of suspense, because we don't know who is going to win. Second, everyone can participate—even the audience can guess at the answers. And third, the viewers can identify with the contestants. They start thinking, 'I could do better than that guy.'"

Sometimes the viewers think they could do better than the show *host*. "People write in all the time asking to be the host of a game show," Goodman laughs. "That shows how successful we are in making it look simple. After all, they wouldn't [have asked] to replace Richard Burton in *Hamlet*, would they?" But hosting a game show isn't as easy as it looks, either. "The principal requirement is the hardest to explain," Goodman says. "It's a technical skill, an ability to be an emcee [master of ceremonies], like an ability to do acrobatics or play tennis. It's also important to be able to think on your feet, to be charming, and to have a good sense of humor. But that indescribable skill is the most important thing. . . ."

from "Game Shows: They're More Than Just 'Child's Play' "
by Dorothy Scheuer

1. The writer lists at least six adjectives as standards that game shows must meet. These standards are

(1) _____

(2) _____

(3) _____

(4) _____

(5) _____

(6) _____

2. Many of the criteria that successful game shows must follow are also necessary ingredients for successful

A. poetry
B. fiction—novels and short stories
C. essays

(1) A
(2) B
(3) C
(4) A and B
(5) B and C

3. Which of the following is also a requirement for a successful game show and is supported by the article?

(1) the low budget compared to other TV programs
(2) the time slot in which game shows are scheduled
(3) the technical and personal abilities of the host
(4) the age of the emcee
(5) the number of markets in which the show airs

4. The article quotes Mark Goodson as saying "The principal requirement is the hardest to explain. It's a technical skill, an ability to be an emcee [master of ceremonies], like an ability to do acrobatics or play tennis. It's also important to be able to think on your feet, to be charming, and to have a good sense of humor. But that indescribable skill is the most important thing. . . ."

This quote suggests that the main requirement for hosting a game show

(1) is based on objective and measurable characteristics
(2) is based on subjective and nonmeasurable characteristics
(3) is a God-given gift
(4) is impossible to learn
(5) does not come across effectively on the television screen

5. Which of the following statements is supported by the information in the article?

(1) Practically anybody can host a game show.
(2) Game shows have had a long history in television.
(3) Game shows are not as profitable for producers as they are for contestants.
(4) Game shows are relatively new in television.
(5) The best game shows are difficult and challenging.

Answers are on page 240.

SKILL BUILDER: ANSWERING EVALUATION QUESTIONS

To answer evaluation questions:
1. Determine the standards or criteria for judging an idea.
2. Decide how closely the idea or object meets the established criteria.

Adequacy of Facts

Before you reach a decision or draw a conclusion, you need to evaluate the information that is available. You need to ask yourself, "Is there enough information to make this decision?" or "Is this decision supported adequately by the facts?"

When you don't have all the facts, you can't make an informed decision. Suppose you were interested in an issue in your community, such as "Should a low-rent apartment building be torn down to make room for a new high-rise building?" To be able to judge how you feel about the issue, you need to know all the facts. You need to know

1. How many people will be affected by tearing down the building?

2. What kinds of rents will be charged in the new building?

3. Will the construction company hire community residents to work on the project?

All of these facts (and others) will help you decide where you stand on the issue.

Similarly, when you answer questions on the GED Tests, you may need to determine whether there is enough information to support the writer's conclusion or point of view.

EXERCISE 14: ADEQUACY OF FACTS

Directions: Read the following commentary by a newspaper columnist about the construction of a high-rise building in the community. Then put an *F* next to the charges that the commentator has supported with facts and an *N* next to charges for which he has not cited any evidence.

A high-rise apartment building is being constructed in South Rochelle, but neither renters nor community businesses will benefit from this new venture. It will not increase much-needed rental properties because the building will consist solely of resident-owned condominiums. The developers, who have already shown their contempt for local residents, will certainly not try to involve local business in the project. Undoubtedly, they will go outside of the community for the labor and materials that they need.

This problem could have been prevented, but the newly elected mayor and her staff refused three different offers to meet with community organizations on this issue. The fat cats from the construction company must have lined the coffers of her campaign chest to influence the mayor to disregard the wishes of her constituents.

_____ 1. The high-rise will not create more rental units in the community.

_____ 2. The developers will not utilize community labor or businesses.

_____ 3. The mayor refused to meet with community members.

_____ 4. The construction company has lined the coffers of the mayor's campaign.

Answers are on page 240.

Roles of Values and Beliefs

When people make decisions, they are, in part, influenced by facts. But we all have deeply held values and personal beliefs that influence our decision making. Many of the literature selections that you read on the GED Tests will consist of commentaries—writers' opinions of various types of literary and artistic works. These commentaries are based on the writers' own values. In social studies and science-related issues, you will see that personal values have a big impact on decision making.

The following situation reflects a conflict between two different sets of values.

Industrial waste from the Nelson Corporation is polluting the local lake. The corporation claims that if it has to spend a lot of money on water pollution cleanup, it will have to lay off several hundred community workers.

What values are in conflict here? If you think something like *interest in public health and safety vs. commitment to community employment*, you are correct. The following exercise examines the role of values and beliefs.

EXERCISE 15: THE ROLE OF VALUES AND BELIEFS

Directions: In each situation described below, there is a conflict between two competing sets of values. On the lines following each paragraph, write the two values that are in conflict.

1. Myrna wants to marry Sam, settle down, and have a family. However, she knows that while her family likes Sam personally, family members object to the marriage because Sam's religious background is different from their own.

Myrna has to choose between ＿＿＿＿＿＿＿＿＿＿＿＿＿＿＿ and

＿＿＿＿＿＿＿＿＿＿＿＿＿＿＿.

2. The government of New Zealand has a dilemma. On the one hand, its citizens demand that no ships with nuclear weapons dock in its ports. On the other hand, it is afraid of alienating its trading partner and military ally, the United States.

The government of New Zealand must choose between ＿＿＿＿＿＿＿＿＿＿

and ＿＿＿＿＿＿＿＿＿＿＿＿＿＿.

3. One of the most controversial areas of scientific research is genetic engineering. Advocates of genetic engineering maintain that they will be able to prevent many genetically based birth defects such as Down's syndrome and sickle-cell anemia. Opponents of genetic engineering warn that this research tampers with nature and will lead to attempts to create a genetically "pure" master race.

A scientist who is approached to do genetic research must choose between

＿＿＿＿＿＿＿＿＿＿＿＿＿＿＿ and ＿＿＿＿＿＿＿＿＿＿＿＿＿＿＿.

Answers are on page 240.

Recognizing Organizational Patterns

Textbooks and reading passages in social studies and science are organized according to certain patterns. Also, literary works such as novels, short stories, plays, and forms of nonfiction are based on organizational patterns. Three common patterns used in writing are cause and effect, comparison and contrast, and sequence or time order.

Organizational patterns can be the framework for entire books as well as single paragraphs. For example, a chapter in U.S. history may be organized in a time-order pattern, and another may be organized to show causes and effects. Single paragraphs within those chapters may be organized in the same way. Often, there is a mixing of these three patterns within both single paragraphs and longer selections. However, generally you can see a predominant pattern within paragraphs of longer selections.

Cause and Effect

The *cause and effect* pattern shows a relationship between events. We connect causes with effects every day. For example, members of the baby boom generation, who had delayed starting their families, are now parents of school-age children. This change in the American family unit has caused an increase in school enrollment and has slowed the school closings that were characteristic of the 1970s and 1980s. Several results came from the single cause: increase in family size. Some are shown below.

Cause	Effect
1. increase in number of children	increase in enrollments
2. increase in school enrollments	greater need for teachers

What effect might come from the cause shown below? Write one.

Cause	Effect
3. greater need for teachers	_____
	_____
	_____

You may have written "higher salaries for teachers" since a low supply (in this case teachers) leads to higher salaries. You can probably think of other causes and effects stemming from this occurrence. For example, higher salaries for teachers (cause) might mean that more people will enter the field of education (effect). Also, more students becoming teachers (cause) results in increased enrollments in departments of education at universities (effect).

As demonstrated here, events can sometimes lead to a chain of cause-and-effect relationships. Understanding cause and effect helps us understand everyday events and plan our actions in accordance with them.

Usually, effects *follow* causes in time. However, sometimes an effect appears in a sentence *before* the cause, even though the effect follows the cause in time. The statement below is an example of this inverted relationship:

    effect

Depression, which is twice as common in women as in men, is believed to

                cause

come from biochemical changes.

Rewrite the sentence above with the cause coming before the effect.

_____

_____

You should have written something like *Biochemical changes are believed to cause depression, which is twice as common in women as in men.*

> ### SKILL BUILDER: RECOGNIZING CAUSE-AND-EFFECT RELATIONSHIPS
> The cause-and-effect relationship is frequently signaled by key words such as *because, since, therefore, as a result, consequently, accordingly, if . . . then, led to, brought about, the outcome was, the end result was,* and *was responsible for.*

EXERCISE 16: CAUSE AND EFFECT

Directions: Read the passage below. Then write the letter of each effect in the space next to its cause.

    In 1961, during the cold war, the Peace Corps was established by President John Kennedy because he saw a need to expose U.S. citizens to citizens of developing Third World nations. The achievement of world peace and friendship were the intended goals of the humanitarian efforts of American volunteers.

    The Peace Corps was such a success that in 1964 VISTA (Volunteers in Service to America) was founded to foster goodwill among different cultures *within* the United States. A decline in federal funding, however, contributed to the abandonment of VISTA in the early 1980s.

    In 1993, President Clinton hoped to introduce a form of mandatory community service for young Americans, especially as a means of repaying millions of dollars worth of college loans.

Cause	Effect
_____ **1.** Kennedy's belief in a need to expose Americans to Third World nations	**(a)** beginning of VISTA in 1964
_____ **2.** the success of the Peace Corps	**(b)** discontinuation of VISTA in the 1980s
_____ **3.** a decline in federal funding	**(c)** would help to repay expensive tuition loans
_____ **4.** the concept of mandatory community service for all young Americans	**(d)** establishment of the Peace Corps in 1961

Answers are on page 241.

EXERCISE 17: ORGANIZING PARAGRAPHS

Directions: Read the effects below. Then write *yes* for the possible causes around which a paragraph could be organized and *no* for those that could not be a paragraph topic.

1. **Effect:** The population of the world has continued to grow rapidly.

   _____ **(a)** Birth control devices are not available in some parts of the world.

   _____ **(b)** Most of the world's population subsists on vegetables and grains.

   _____ **(c)** Mankind's ability to grow more food and fight disease has improved.

2. **Effect:** Gasoline prices increased 35 cents per gallon.

   _____ **(a)** New energy sources were uncovered.

   _____ **(b)** Refinery costs rose by 21 percent.

   _____ **(c)** The cost of crude oil remained the same.

3. **Effect:** Congress passed legislation to stop pollution of our major waterways.

   _____ **(a)** The quality of water tested in rivers near major cities was poor.

   _____ **(b)** Conservation groups in favor of the act sent petitions with thousands of signatures to their senators.

   _____ **(c)** The president, during a campaign speech, said that he favored an anti–water pollution act.

Answers are on page 241.

Comparison and Contrast

A writer uses the comparison/contrast pattern to explain or show the similarities and differences among ideas, people, or things. A writer who points out how two or more things are alike is making a *comparison*; one who points out how they are different is using *contrast*.

EXERCISE 18: COMPARISON AND CONTRAST

Directions: Read the following passage in which the writer compares and contrasts two modern presidents—Franklin D. Roosevelt and Ronald Reagan. Then fill in the blanks with the appropriate comparison and contrast phrases. The first two are done for you. As you are reading, keep in mind the following: does the writer compare these two presidents first or contrast them?

During the presidential campaign of 1980, Ronald Reagan lauded Franklin Delano Roosevelt as his political hero. On the face of it, this fact is hard to believe, given the sharp differences between the two.

President Roosevelt, a liberal Democrat, founded the social security system to provide a worry-free retirement for the nation's elderly. President Reagan, a conservative Republican, was criticized for trying to weaken the program. President Roosevelt's New Deal legislation provided for the regulation of banks and other financial institutions; under the Reagan administration, these institutions were greatly deregulated. President Roosevelt's administration set the minimum-wage law; President Reagan's administration favored abandoning it for teenagers. Labor organizations were encouraged under the Roosevelt administration and thrived; labor organizations were weakened and threatened under the Reagan administration.

Despite these differences, there are striking similarities between the two men. Roosevelt, an extremely popular leader, became president in the midst of economic despair. Reagan, an equally popular leader, became president when the country was suffering from a *malaise* and economic problems. Roosevelt was a persuasive politician and a strong communicator; Reagan's nickname was the "Great Communicator" because of his skill in handling the media. Both men were reelected to the presidency after huge landslides. The legislation of the New Deal affected the lives of many Americans, and as of the 1990s the effects of the "Reagan Revolution" seem likely to have a similar impact, for better or worse, on generations to come.

Roosevelt, a man from a wealthy background who became a champion of the "little people," is considered one of America's few great presidents. Will Ronald Reagan, a man from a modest background who became the "champion of big business," be accorded the same honor? Only time will tell.

Contrasting Words and Phrases (Differences)

Roosevelt

1. *liberal Democrat*
2. *founded social security*
3. _____
4. _____
5. _____
6. _____
7. _____

Reagan

1. *conservative Republican*
2. *criticized for weakening it*
3. _____
4. _____
5. _____
6. _____
7. _____

Comparative Words and Phrases (Similarities)

1. *Both were popular presidents.*
2. *Both came to power after economic problems.*
3. _____
4. _____
5. _____

Answers are on page 241.

SKILL BUILDER: IDENTIFYING COMPARISON AND CONTRAST PATTERNS

Words and phrases that signal comparisons include *like, likewise, also, similarly, on the one hand, in the same way* or *fashion*, and *compared to.*

Words and phrases that signal contrasts include *however, but, on the other hand, differently, on the contrary, while, although, yet, conversely, on the other side of the coin, versus, in contrast to*, and *either . . . or.*

EXERCISE 19: CONTRAST IN AN ESSAY

Directions: Read the following essay and list the four pairs of contrasting phrases contained in it. *Hint:* It helps to underline them as you read.

Television as a medium is a mixed blessing. Many people hold opposing views toward this powerful fixture in the American home. For some, it is a tasteful and exciting way to entertain; for others, an insult to standards of good taste. Television can be a captivating means to teach the young or a mindless, uninspiring babysitter. For some, the "tube" can bring important and accurate news of the moment, but for others it can spew trivia and "happy talk" that does not match the quality of newspapers and magazines.

While television commercials make a healthy contribution to society by helping consumers make intelligent buying decisions, commercials also plant seeds of dissatisfaction in viewers, making them crave what the advertisers sell.

1. _____ vs. _____

2. _____ vs. _____
   _____   _____

3. _____ vs. _____
   _____   _____

4. _____ vs. _____

Sequence

Often, writers organize their works on the basis of *sequence*, sometimes known as *time order*. With this pattern of organization, events follow a series. Sequence is especially common in social studies when a writer describes historical events. It is also used widely in science writing to outline the steps in an experiment. Sequence is used as a pattern of organization in literature as well. In novels, short stories, and plays, plot events must follow a sequence. Often, this sequence has a cause-and-effect pattern.

SKILL BUILDER: RECOGNIZING SEQUENCE IN A PASSAGE

Some words and phrases that signal sequence include *on* (*a certain date— e.g., January 1*), *not long after, now, before, next, then, when, first, second,* and *third.*

EXERCISE 20: RECOGNIZING SEQUENCE

An *allegory* is a story in which the characters are symbolic; that is, they stand for abstract qualities. The plot events in an allegory reveal a truth or generalization about life. An example of a symbol would be a lion (concrete object) standing for courage (abstract quality).

Directions: Read the following summary of the famous short story "The Devil and Daniel Webster" by Stephen Vincent Benét. Then write *1* for the event that occurs first, *2* for the event that occurs second and so on.

The tale begins in New Hampshire during the time of Daniel Webster, a great lawyer and orator who aspired to be president of the United States. A local farmer, Jabez Stone, gets tired of poor crops and lack of prosperity. Enter the stranger, a lawyer, Mr. Scratch, who offers Stone a trade guaranteed to make him prosperous. Mr. Scratch then draws up a contract. Jabez Stone pricks his finger and signs with his blood. Afterward, every year for six years, the stranger visits Stone to remind him of the contract.

On the seventh year, the stranger comes to collect. Jabez Stone pleads for and receives a three-year extension. After the years pass, it is time for him to surrender the deed. Jabez Stone then goes to Daniel Webster to ask him to plead his case. When Daniel Webster visits Stone, the stranger appears.

The two argue strongly, but the stranger demands his due. Daniel Webster then asks for a trial including a courtroom, judge, and jury. Twelve men enter who have come from afar and who have the "fires of hell still upon them."

After Daniel Webster pleads the case all night, the defense rests. The jury finds for the defendant, Jabez Stone, and the judge and jury leave. Finally, the stranger signs a document promising never to bother Jabez Stone and is never seen in New Hampshire again.

_____ 1. The stranger visits Jabez Stone to remind him of his contract.

_____ 2. Twelve men with the "fires of hell still upon them" hear the case.

_____ 3. Jabez Stone tires of his lack of prosperity.

_____ 4. Daniel Webster argues with Mr. Scratch at Stone's house.

_____ 5. Jabez Stone strikes a bargain with Mr. Scratch and signs in blood.

_____ 6. Daniel Webster agrees to plead Jabez Stone's case.

_____ 7. Mr. Scratch leaves New Hampshire and is never seen again.

_____ 8. Mr. Scratch finally comes to collect from Jabez Stone.

_____ 9. The jury rules in favor of Jabez Stone.

_____ 10. Stone pleads for and gets a three-year extension.

Answers are on page 241.

EXERCISE 21: SYMBOLS IN ALLEGORY

Directions: Fill in the blanks with the correct answer from the plot summary of "The Devil and Daniel Webster."

1. The devil is _____.

2. Jabez Stone's selling his soul to the devil is demonstrated by Stone's agreement

   to _____.

3. Jabez Stone's death sentence is represented by the devil coming to collect after

   _____.

4. The twelve men who have come from hell are the _____

   _____.

5. The fight between good and evil is shown by _____

   arguing with _____.

Answers are on page 241.

2
INTERPRETING GRAPHS AND ILLUSTRATIONS

About one-third of the questions on the Science, Social Studies, and Mathematics Tests will be based on graphics. Many of the exercises later in this book are based on illustrations. Throughout this book and on the GED Test, you will need to understand how a writer uses pictorial information to support a point. The types of graphics that will appear on the test include graphs, maps, tables, and editorial cartoons.

To read and interpret graphic materials, you must pay close attention to all of the information that is given in both pictures and words. This means that you must look at how the material is labeled and the types of figures and numbers used. You may be asked to locate a particular number or fact, or you may be required to make an interpretation such as stating the main idea, reading between the lines, or drawing a conclusion.

Interpreting Graphs

A graph is a simple and clear way of presenting facts. Reading passages that include a lot of facts and figures can be difficult to understand, so writers often include graphs to help the reader understand the subject better. The types of graphs that are used to present information pictorially are pictographs, line graphs, bar graphs, and circle or pie graphs.

Pictographs

Pictographs are the simplest form of graphs. *Pictographs* use symbols to show how certain quantities of a thing compare. Some common symbols used in pictographs represent people, cars, houses, and dollars. Whole symbols and partial symbols may be used in a pictograph. Like all graphs, pictographs have a *title* that gives the main idea.

A *key* that shows the amount that each symbol stands for is always provided to help the reader interpret the graph. The pictograph on page 224 illustrates the growth of the world's population, estimated from the year A.D. 1.

WORLD POPULATION GROWTH A.D. 1 TO 1992

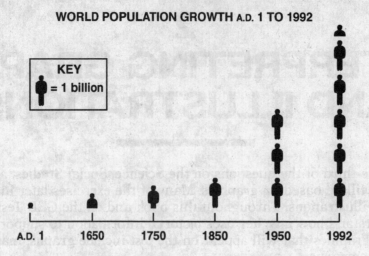

Source: *The World Almanac and Book of Facts, 1993 edition*

What was the world's population in 1650?

Look at the key. It indicates that the symbol of one person stands for 1 billion people. The symbol representing the population for the year 1650 is one-half of a person; therefore, the population of the world was approximately **half a billion (500,000,000) people**.

The greatest increase in the world's population occurred during which time period?

According to the pictograph,

- between A.D. 1 and 1650, world population grew from 200 million to 500 million;
- between 1650 and 1750, the world's population grew from 500 million to 725 million;
- from 1750 to 1850, population increased from 725 million to 1 billion people;
- from 1850 to 1950, the number of people in the world went from 1 billion to 3 billion;
- finally, between 1950 and 1992, the world's population grew from 3 billion to almost 5.5 billion.

Therefore, the greatest total increase in the number of people in the world occurred **between 1950 and 1992**.

Line Graphs

Line graphs are generally used to show a relationship among two or more things. They are used particularly to show a change in the quantity of something in relation to dates, years, or fixed amounts. Line graphs are especially helpful in showing trends at a glance. Look at the line graph below.

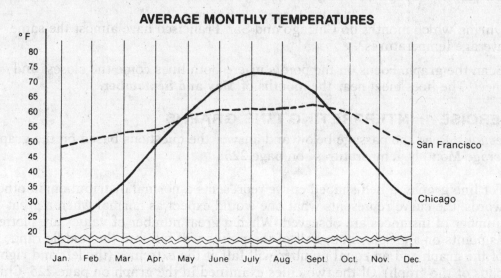

AVERAGE MONTHLY TEMPERATURES

Notice that the graph has a title, "Average Monthly Temperatures." This tells you the topic. The labels at the ends of the lines tell you that the cities San Francisco and Chicago are being compared.

The graph has numbers going up the left side of the graph (the *vertical axis*); these numbers are temperatures in degrees Fahrenheit. Also, the graph shows the twelve months of the year going across the bottom (the *horizontal axis*). The "picture" on the graph is created by connecting the points that stand for temperatures during each month of the year. As each point is connected, a line is formed; this is why such a graph is known as a *line graph*. Let's answer some questions based on this graph.

1. What is the temperature of San Francisco in July? Is it colder or warmer than Chicago's?

   To find the answer, place your finger at the point indicating July on the broken line representing San Francisco. Now look to the left at the vertical axis.

   The answer is 60 degrees Fahrenheit—the temperature for San Francisco in July.

   Follow the same procedure for Chicago. (The solid line represents Chicago.)

   The answer is about 72 degrees Fahrenheit; therefore, **it is colder in San Francisco than in Chicago at that same time of the year**. Notice that you may need to approximate values on line graphs—your answers may fall between the labeled points on the vertical axis.

2. Which city has the greater range in temperature; that is, which has the greater extreme from the lowest temperature to the highest?

   To find the answer, scan the graph to find the lowest point for each city. The lowest temperature would occur during January. Compare this temperature with the highest point for each city. The highest temperature would occur during July for Chicago and September for San Francisco.

The lowest average temperature in January for San Francisco is nearly 50 degrees; the highest average temperature in September is nearly 60 degrees. The lowest average temperature in January for Chicago is nearly 25 degrees; the highest average temperature in July is nearly 75 degrees. The extreme from 25 degrees to 75 degrees is greater than that from 50 degrees to 60 degrees. Therefore, **Chicago has the greater range in temperature**.

3. During which months do Chicago and San Francisco have almost the same average temperatures?

Scan the graph. Focus on the points where both lines come the closest and meet. The lines meet near the months of **May and September**.

EXERCISE 1: INTERPRETING LINE GRAPHS

Directions: Read the passage below and answer the questions based on the graph "Average Monthly Temperatures" on page 225.

1. For line graphs, a bell-shaped curve represents a normal distribution; in other words, the curve represents what one would expect as normal when a great number of instances are observed. When a great number of values are plotted as points on a graph, about half of the points will fall into the middle range of the graph and an equal number will fall at the extremes (the left and right ends of the graph). Of the two cities examined in the graph on page 225, Chicago's temperatures generally follow a bell-shaped curve. This fact suggests that

   A. San Francisco's average temperature distribution is not considered normal compared to that of most U.S. cities.

   B. Chicago's average temperature distribution is likely to be more representative of other U.S. cities than San Francisco's.

   C. Chicago's average temperature distribution is considered abnormal.

   D. San Francisco enjoys better weather than most other cities.
       (1) A
       (2) B
       (3) A and B
       (4) D
       (5) A and C

2. Which of the following cities is *most* likely to have an average temperature distribution more like Chicago's than San Francisco's?

   (1) Los Angeles
   (2) Miami
   (3) Detroit
   (4) Anchorage
   (5) New Orleans

Answers are on page 241.

EXERCISE 2: MORE ON INTERPRETING LINE GRAPHS

Directions: Study the graph below and answer the questions that follow.

PAPER INDUSTRY PROFITS/LOSSES

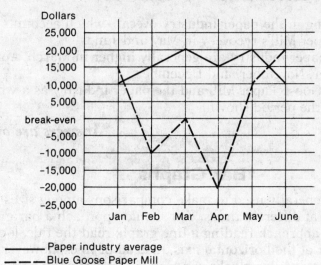

_____ Paper industry average
– – – – Blue Goose Paper Mill

1. During how many months shown on the graph did the Blue Goose Paper Mill lose money?

(1) none   **(2)** 1   **(3)** 2   **(4)** 3   **(5)** 4

2. In which month(s) did the Blue Goose Paper Mill exceed the industry average in profits?

(1) January only
(2) February, March, April, and May
(3) June only
(4) February and April
(5) January and June

3. During the six-month period, the paper industry as a whole showed

(1) profits and losses similar to that of the Blue Goose Paper Mill
(2) average profits of between $10,000 and $20,000 per month
(3) signs of a dangerous financial crisis
(4) greater losses than the Blue Goose Paper Mill
(5) better profits than in the previous six-month period

4. In which month was there the greatest difference between the industry's average profit/loss and that of the Blue Goose Paper Mill?

(1) January
(2) February
(3) March
(4) April
(5) June

5. Which of the following statements best summarizes the data on the graph?

(1) The paper industry as a whole was profitable every month, but the Blue Goose Paper Mill showed wide variations from month to month.

(2) The Blue Goose Paper Mill will probably fold as a result of its heavy losses.

(3) Profits are rising in the paper industry overall, which accounts for the Blue Goose Paper Mill's recovery in May and June.

(4) Profits in the paper industry are generally higher in March, April, and May than in October, November, and December.

(5) Both the Blue Goose Paper Mill and the paper industry as a whole lost money during the period shown.

Answers are on page 241.

Bar Graphs

Bar graphs are generally used to make comparisons among sizes or quantities of similar items at different times. You should approach a bar graph the same way you would approach reading a line graph: read the title, look at the vertical axis, and look at the horizontal axis. Instead of lines, however, a bar graph uses bars or rectangular blocks running either vertically or horizontally. Sometimes a bar graph includes a key. The key is used when two or more sets of information are being compared as in Exercise 4 on pages 229–230.

Look at the bar graph below, "Number of Persons 65+: 1900–2050"

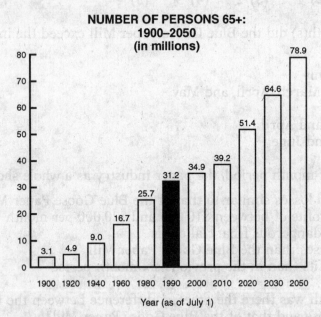

NUMBER OF PERSONS 65+:
1900–2050
(in millions)

Year (as of July 1)

Note: Increments in years on horizontal scale are uneven.

Based on data from U.S. Bureau of the Census

In what year is the percentage of persons 65 and over expected to double the figure shown for 1980?

Looking at the graph, you can see that the percentage of persons 65 years and older in 1980 was 25.7 percent of the population. If this figure is doubled, the percentage will be 51.4 percent. The year for which the percentage of persons 65+ reaches 51.4 is **2020** on the graph.

EXERCISE 3: INTERPRETING BAR GRAPHS

Directions: Answer the following question based on the preceding graph and the information provided below.

The growth of America's older population is expected to slow somewhat during the 1990s but is expected to increase rapidly after the year 2000. Which of the following implications can be drawn from these facts?

A. A relatively small number of babies were born during the Depression years of the 1930s; these people will be turning 65 in the 1990s.

B. A relatively large number of Americans born during the 1930s were killed in the Korean War.

C. A relatively large number of babies were born between the years 1940 and 1960; these people, called the *baby boom generation*, will be turning 65 between 2005 and 2025.

(1) A   **(2)** B   **(3)** C   **(4)** A and C   **(5)** B and C

Answer is on page 242.

EXERCISE 4: MORE ON READING BAR GRAPHS

Directions: Study the bar graph below and answer the questions that follow.

MARITAL STATUS OF PERSONS 65+: 1990

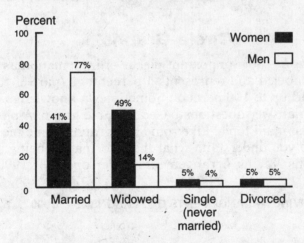

Based on data from U.S. Bureau of the Census

1. The figures in the bar graph tend to support the fact that

   (1) men 65 years or older were three times as likely to be married as women 65 years or older
   (2) women 65 years or older were twice as likely to be married as men 65 years or older
   (3) men 65 years or older were nearly twice as likely to be married as women 65 years or older
   (4) the percentages of older men and women who were likely to be married are equal
   (5) more women 65 years or older were married than men who were 65 years or older

2. From the percentages of older men and women who were widowed as of 1990, we can infer that

(1) older men who were married outlived their wives
(2) older women who were married outlived their husbands
(3) older men who were widowed represented the smallest segment of the older population
(4) the percentage of older women who were widowed was higher than the number of married, single, and divorced women combined
(5) the percentage of older men who were widowed was lower than the number of single and divorced men combined

3. Which of the following statements was true in 1990 according to the graph?

A. Nearly half of all older women were widows.
B. More than three-fourths of all older men were widowers.
C. More than three-fourths of all older men were married.
D. Half of all older women were married.

(1) A and B
(2) A and C
(3) B and D
(4) C and D
(5) D

Answers are on page 242.

Circle Graphs

Circle or *pie graphs* show important pieces of information as parts of a whole. Each slice is labeled and represents a percentage (part of the whole). All of the slices must add up to 100 percent. Sometimes a knowledge of basic arithmetic is necessary to answer questions based on a pie graph. A pie graph has a title that gives you the main topic. Like some bar graphs, some pie graphs also provide a key to help you understand what the information being shown means. Look at the pie graphs "Living Arrangements of Persons 65+: 1990."

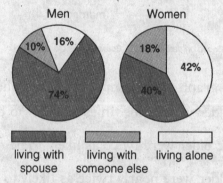

LIVING ARRANGEMENTS OF PERSONS 65+: 1990

Based on data from U.S. Bureau of the Census

What percentage of men 65 years and older live in a family or group setting?

To answer this question, you must look at the pie graph labeled "Men" and look at the key. The key distinguishes among those men living with a spouse, those living with someone else, and those living alone. Add the percentage of men living with a spouse (74%) to those living with someone else (10%) to determine the total number living in a family or group setting—**84 percent.**

Do more older men than older women live in family settings?

Follow the same procedure with the pie graph labeled "Women." Add the percentage of those living with spouses (40%) to the percentage living with someone else (18%). Then compare the figure for men with the one for women (84% to 58%). The answer is **yes**; more men live in family or group settings than women— 26 percent more.

EXERCISE 5: READING PIE GRAPHS

Directions: Compare the information in the bar graph titled "Marital Status of Persons 65+: 1990" on page 229 with the information in the pie graph "Living Arrangements of Persons 65+: 1990" on page 230, then answer the question below:

Generally, the facts in the pie graph "Living Arrangements of Persons 65+"

(1) dispute the figures contained in the "married" category of the graph "Marital Status of Persons 65+"

(2) have no relationship at all to the figures in the "married" category of the graph "Marital Status of Persons 65+"

(3) support the figures shown in the "married" category of the graph "Marital Status of Persons 65+"

(4) show that the divorced men and women whose numbers are illustrated in the bar graph are living alone

(5) demonstrate that all the people living in group facilities are widowed

Answer is on page 242.

Maps

Maps are another way of presenting pictorial information. Maps can provide a variety of information about a place. Like graphs, maps have a title that tells you what the focus of the map is. A *key* or *legend* explains the symbols that the map contains. Maps that require you to measure a distance have a scale of miles that you can use as a guide to find the distance between two points. Before you answer questions pertaining to a map, take time to study the map and the key that goes with it.

The map on page 232 is a demographic map. A *demographic* map shows the distribution of a certain segment of a population. The map on the next page shows the percentage change of the U.S. population 65 years or older between the years 1980 and 1990.

According to the map, how many states experienced the greatest percentage change in population from 1980 to 1990?

To answer this question, consult the key to find out which code stands for the greatest percentage change. The code with the greatest percentage change is 20 percent or more. Note the particular shading for that code and count the number of states that are filled in with exactly that shading. You will find that **six states** experienced 20 percent change in population or more. These states are California, Nevada, Arizona, Alaska, Florida, and New Hampshire.

POPULATION CHANGE, 1980–1990

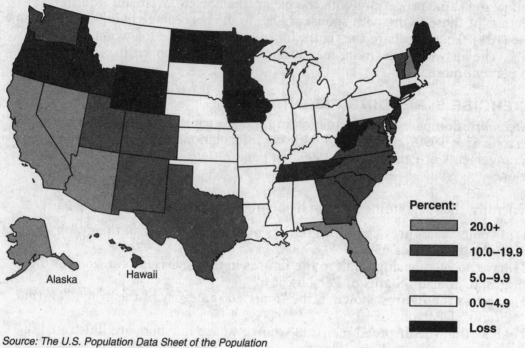

Percent:

	20.0+
	10.0–19.9
	5.0–9.9
	0.0–4.9
	Loss

Source: The U.S. Population Data Sheet of the Population Reference Bureau, Inc., Ninth Edition

EXERCISE 6: INTERPRETING MAPS

Directions: Look at the map above and answer the following questions.

1. The map could be used to support which of the following facts?

    (1) Florida's climate and lifestyle are more desirable than Alaska's.
    (2) The same number of states lost population as gained.
    (3) The smallest percentage of change occurred primarily in the north and central parts of the United States.
    (4) Alaska experienced an economic boom in the 1980s.
    (5) Hawaii and Alaska are farther away than any of the other states.

2. How many states experienced the moderate percentage growth of 5–9.9 percent?

    (1) eleven
    (2) four
    (3) twenty-two
    (4) eight
    (5) five

3. For the entire United States, the percentage change in population between 1980 and 1990 was 9.9 percent. How many states were above the national average in percentage change?

    (1) thirteen
    (2) seven
    (3) four
    (4) nineteen
    (5) six

4. Which statement can be inferred from the information given in the map?

   (1) Generally, the midwestern and central states have a fairly stable population.
   (2) Everyone who moves to a different state wants a warmer climate.
   (3) More states had 10–19.9 percent population growth than experienced less than 5 percent growth.
   (4) California farmers cannot grow the same kinds of crops in the Midwest as they can produce in their own state.
   (5) Fewer states gained population than lost population.

5. Which category of states among the five percentage groups on the population change map has no state bordering an ocean?

   (1) 5–9.9 percent
   (2) Loss
   (3) 0–4.9 percent
   (4) 10.0–19.9 percent
   (5) 20+ percent

Answers are on page 242.

Tables

A *table* is an organization of many facts into a small space. Tables are used to keep scores in games, list train schedules, assign work tasks, compare weather reports, and so on. A table has a title at the top. The separate columns and rows within it are also labeled so that you will know what information the table contains. Look at the table below.

**MARRIAGES AND DIVORCES
IN THE UNITED STATES
(Per 1,000 People)**

Year	Marriages	Divorces
1930	9.2	1.6
1940	12.1	2.0
1950	11.1	2.6
1960	8.5	2.2
1970	10.6	3.5
1980	10.6	5.2
1990	9.8	4.7

The title tells you that the table is about the number of marriages and divorces per 1,000 people in the United States. The row headings give the decades (beginning with 1930 and ending with 1990). The column headings give the number of marriages and the number of divorces. Study the table and answer the following questions.

During which decades was the number of marriages stable?

Stable means showing no change. If you scan the table to find the decades during which the number of marriages per 1,000 people remained unchanged, you will see that in the decades **1970 and 1980** the number of marriages per 1,000 people was 10.6.

Between which decades was there a decrease in both the number of marriages and the number of divorces per 1,000 people?

If you examine each ten-year interval, you will notice that **between 1950 and 1960** and **between 1980 and 1990** both the number of marriages and the number of divorces decreased. In the year 1950, the number of marriages was 11.1; it decreased to 8.5 by 1960. In the year 1950, the number of divorces was 2.6; it decreased to 2.2 by 1960. In the year 1980, the number of marriages was 10.6; it decreased to 9.8 by 1990. In the year 1980, the number of divorces was 5.2; it decreased to 4.7 by 1990.

EXERCISE 7: READING TABLES

Directions: Look at the table below and answer the questions that follow.

FORECAST OF POPULATION INCREASE, 1975–2000
(In Millions)

	Population		Increases, 1975–2000	
	1975	2000	Absolute	Percent
Anglo-America	242	295	53	22
Europe	474	540	66	14
former Soviet Union	254	314	60	24
Oceania	21	33	12	57
Subtotal	991	1,182	191	19
Latin America	328	610	282	86
Asia	2,407	3,800	1,393	58
Africa	420	830	410	98
Subtotal	3,155	5,240	2,085	66
World Total	4,146	6,422	2,276	55

1. According to the table, which area of the world will have the largest absolute increase in population between 1975 and 2000?

   (1) Anglo-America
   (2) former Soviet Union
   (3) Latin America
   (4) Asia
   (5) Africa

2. By what percentage is the population of the world projected to increase between 1975 and 2000?

   (1) 19
   (2) 2,276
   (3) 55
   (4) 191
   (5) 22

3. Which area of the world is projected to have the smallest percentage population increase between 1975 and 2000?

   (1) Anglo-America
   (2) Asia
   (3) Europe
   (4) Oceania
   (5) Africa

4. Which area of the world is projected to nearly double its population between 1975 and 2000?

   (1) Africa
   (2) former Soviet Union
   (3) Anglo-America
   (4) Asia
   (5) Europe

5. Which two areas expect the lowest percentage increase?

   (1) Oceania and Asia
   (2) former Soviet Union and Anglo-America
   (3) Latin America and Africa
   (4) Anglo-America and Europe
   (5) Asia and Africa

Answers are on page 243.

Editorial Cartoons

An *editorial cartoon* expresses the opinion of the cartoonist toward a political or social issue. Editorial cartoons often caricature (depict in cartoon figures) politicians or statesmen. The caricatures usually exaggerate a feature of the person being illustrated. For example, Ronald Reagan's dark hair, Jimmy Carter's toothy smile, and President Bill Clinton's full face and chin have been widely caricatured.

Political symbols are often used as well. For example, the donkey represents the Democratic party, an elephant represents the Republican party, a bearded man dressed in stars and stripes (Uncle Sam) represents the United States, a dove represents peace, and a hawk represents war. Cartoonists often use humor to express their opinions on important issues affecting our country and world.

Look at the political cartoon below. Notice that the cartoon is divided in half. The top half shows a line of unemployed people waiting to apply for benefits. Many of the people are complaining about the lack of jobs and criticizing the government and its leaders.

The bottom half of the cartoon, however, shows an empty polling place on election day. By placing the two illustrations together, the cartoonist is making a statement suggesting that, while citizens are quick to criticize the government, when it comes to making their voices heard at the ballot box they are silent— they don't show up to vote.

The exercise on page 237 will give you a chance to practice your skill in interpreting editorial cartoons.

DANA SUMMERS
Courtesy The Sentinel

EXERCISE 8: INTERPRETING EDITORIAL CARTOONS

Directions: Study the cartoon below and answer the questions that follow.

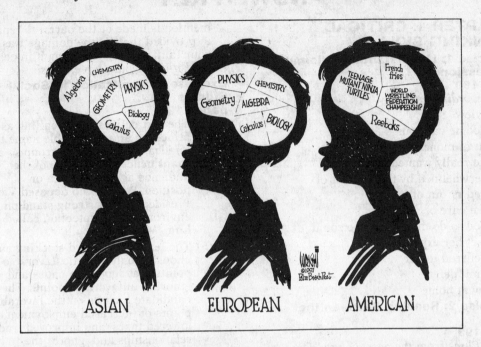

1. The cartoon appeared in 1992 during a long period of public dissatisfaction with American education. How do you think the cartoonist would like to influence our thinking about education?

   (1) We ought to work toward making American schools better by keeping Europeans and Asians out.
   (2) We ought to try to stimulate American students' interests in the same educational pursuits as their Asian and European counterparts.
   (3) We should emphasize athletics more in American schools because things such as tennis shoes and sports competitions are typically American.
   (4) European and Asian students should be urged to compete harder in sports.
   (5) European and Asian students should be encouraged to participate more in sports and entertainment.

2. The cartoonist is suggesting that

   (1) Asian, European, and American students think about similar problems
   (2) American and Asian students compete heavily with European students
   (3) the brains of students everywhere are about the same size
   (4) the minds of American students are centered on trivial interests compared to the minds of Asian and European students
   (5) Physics and biology are more important than chemistry and algebra

3. From your understanding of the cartoon, what inferences can you make about American culture?

   (1) We need a lot more Asian and European teachers to set standards.
   (2) Families ought to go to classes and try to learn together.
   (3) Our society needs to stress academics more than athletics.
   (4) European and American students are behind Asians in academic achievement.
   (5) Education will be at its best if we all cooperate and work together.

Answers are on page 243.

READING SKILLS FOR THE GED ANSWER KEY

CHAPTER 1: CRITICAL THINKING SKILLS

Exercise 1: Understanding Idiomatic Expressions
page 190
Exact wording may vary.

1. review
2. become cautious
3. out of money
4. She really wanted to go
5. overwhelmed by the amount of
6. tired *or* out of breath
7. take care of
8. tried to do more than she could
9. meet her expenses
10. occurred to her
11. admit defeat
12. stay at home

Exercise 2: Reading Between the Lines
page 193

1. (2) Clues from the passage are "The gift is something that native-born American children take for granted"; "[he] hid there for five days to avoid leaving the United States against his will"; and "this gift is wrapped in yards of legal red tape."

2. (1) There are thousands of twelve-year-old elementary school boys in Chicago. However, this does not help you determine that he was seeking U.S. citizenship. Choices (2), (3), (4), and (5) do lead to that conclusion.

Exercise 3: Restating Ideas
pages 194–195
Answers will vary.

1. Another way to express the principle of stimulus-response is to say that if you touch or attack something, it will react.

2. The dispute over the Constitution developed between the Federalists, who wanted a strong central government, and the anti-Federalists, who feared it.

3. Don't buy a new car without checking it out in a car magazine or consumer guide.

4. When you make a payment on your credit card, the money pays off any amounts that you owe in fees and finance charges first. After those charges are fully paid, the remaining amount you paid goes toward the actual things you bought and charged.

5. The company promises that if anything goes wrong with your TV set within 90 days after you buy it, the manufacturer will pay for the cost of the labor (no mention is made of the parts) to repair it, provided that (1) the damage was not your fault and (2) you bring it in or send it in at your own expense.

Exercise 4: Application in Social Studies
pages 197–198

1. (1) The text defines name-calling as attaching an unfavorable name to an idea, a person, or a group so as to influence the attitude of the audience against an idea or position. People who opposed Vice President Gore's strong stand on environmental protection called him "Mr. Ozone."

2. (5) The text defines card-stacking as choosing only specific, favorable points that support a cause and ignoring unfavorable points. The candidate focuses on the favorable points of increased employment, lowered taxes, and improved trade relationships and ignores the unfavorable issue of foreign policy failures.

3. (4) The text defines bandwagoning as advising people to do something because "everyone" does it. Neighbors were being urged to join the gang's illegal looting because everybody else was doing it.

4. (3) The teachers who oppose the extended school day are trying to influence the local council by associating their own views with the prestige of the national association's president.

Exercise 5: Application in Science
pages 198–199

1. (3) Of the five systems described, only the lymphatic system produces lymphocytes, whose antibodies help fight bacterial infections.

2. (1) According to the definition, the excretory system excretes or expels water and salts from the body. Perspiration is a form of water; therefore, the skin loosely belongs to the excretory system.

3. (2) According to the definition, the endocrine system is made up of glands that secrete body fluids that regulate the body's development. A teen's growth spurt can be explained by hormones released by the endocrine system.

4. (4) According to the definition, the digestive system processes and distributes nutrients from food. The first step in processing food involves moistening by saliva.

Exercise 6: Facts, Opinions, and Hypotheses
page 201
1. (a) **O** The statement is based on personal values.
   (b) **H** More time and information are needed to prove the statement.
   (c) **F** The statement can be proved by obtaining census data.
2. (a) **F** The statement can be proved by acquiring data.
   (b) **H** Time and data are needed to prove this statement.
   (c) **O** The statement reflects the personal beliefs of a certain group.
3. (a) **H** Time and data are needed to prove this prediction.
   (b) **O** The statement expresses personal beliefs.
   (c) **F** The statement is a fact that can be proved.
4. (a) **O** The statement expresses a personal belief based on certain values.
   (b) **F** The statement is a fact that can be proved by obtaining data on foreign car purchases.
   (c) **H** Time and data about foreign car purchases are needed to prove or disprove the statement.
5. (a) **F** The statement can be proved.
   (b) **H** The passage of time will help to prove or disprove the statement.
   (c) **O** The statement expresses a personal belief; the word *should* indicates that an opinion is being expressed.

Exercise 7: More on Facts, Opinions, and Hypotheses
page 202
1. **H** The passage estimates that by 2020 Hispanic-Americans will become the nation's largest minority. This is a hypothesis that can be proved only with the passage of time.
2. **O** The statement that Hispanic-American artists owe their success to great struggles is not mentioned in the passage. This is an opinion, not something that can be proved or disproved.
3. **F** The passage states that Hispanic-Americans came from Cuba and Puerto Rico.
4. **F** The passage states that President Clinton appointed two Hispanics to his White House Cabinet.
5. **O** The statement that the 1993 Cabinet appointees are the most effective leaders in America is a personal opinion. Others may agree or disagree.

6. **H** The prediction that twenty years from now Hispanic-Americans will live and work in every city in the United States can be proved only when statistics are gathered twenty years from now.
7. **O** The statement that people who come here from Mexico help to advance our culture is an opinion since it's based on a person's beliefs. Other people may believe differently about the statement.

Exercise 8: Hypotheses and the Scientific Method
page 204
Exact wording may vary.
1. *Problem:* Certain workers in the shipbuilding industry were developing cancer of the bronchial tubes.
2. *Information:* Not all the workers exposed to asbestos fibers developed cancer of the bronchial tubes.
3. *Hypothesis:* Cigarette smoking might increase a worker's chances of getting cancer of the bronchial tubes.
4. *Prediction:* If patients suffering from cancer of the bronchial tubes were polled, the results would indicate that they were heavy cigarette smokers.
5. *Observation:* The poll revealed that a very high percentage of the cancer patients were smokers.
6. *Conclusion:* Asbestos workers who are heavy cigarette smokers are more likely to get cancer of the bronchial tubes than those who are not.

Exercise 9: More on Hypotheses and the Scientific Method
page 205
Exact wording may vary.
1. *Problem:* Rain forests are being destroyed.
2. *Information:* In the Amazon rain forest, evaporation from plants and soil accounts for half of all the water that falls there.
3. *Hypothesis:* The removal of plants from the ecosystem may disrupt the cycle, causing less water to be evaporated.
4. *Prediction:* If scientists could create the conditions of the rain forest, their results would show that removing plants would affect the weather and, in turn, future plant growth.
5. *Observation:* The experiment showed that clearing the rain forest land would reduce rainfall by 25 percent and increase average temperatures by 5°F.
6. *Conclusion:* Clearing away the rain forest would affect the weather, making future growth of rain forest plants unlikely.

**Exercise 10: Deductive Reasoning
pages 206–207**

1. **yes** A cerebral hemorrhage results from the bursting (rupture) of a brain artery.

2. **yes** An embolism results from the blockage (obstruction) of a blood vessel; if the embolism is found in an artery of the brain, it can lead to a stroke.

3. **no** A tumor is not a rupture or an obstruction of an artery of the brain.

4. **yes** An aneurysm is a blood-filled swelling of a vessel (artery). The rupture of an aneurysm can lead to a stroke.

5. **no** Phlebitis results from the swelling of a vein, not an artery of the brain.

**Exercise 11: Faulty Reasoning and Unstated Assumptions
page 208**

Exact wording may vary.

1. high school dropouts *or* high school age *or* teenagers
2. competent *or* qualified
3. widespread *or* common *or* rampant
4. air pollution
5. drug abuse *or* taking drugs

**Exercise 12: Style and Tone
pages 209–210**

1. **(2)** Wilhelm tells his father, "You always start out to help me with my problems, and be sympathetic. . . . It gets my hopes up and I begin to be grateful. But before we're through I'm a hundred times more depressed than before." The author uses this style of dialogue to show that Wilhelm is suffering emotionally.

2. **(3)** " 'It's always the same. . . . Look how you lead me on. . . . There ought to be a right way to do this, and be fair to each other. . . . why do you start up with me if you're not going to help me?' . . . Wilhelm had a great knot of wrong tied tight within his chest, and tears approached his eyes but he didn't let them out." These words suggest a tragic tone.

3. **(4)** The dialogue in this excerpt conveys a real-life situation.

4. **(1)** The son's desperate tone and the choice of words in the excerpt indicate that the relationship has had a history of conflict.

5. **(1)** Wilhelm has a knot "tied tight within his chest," he's stammering, and he's unable to express his real feelings. This suggests that he is struggling with external and internal conflicts— with himself and with his father.

**Exercise 13: Evaluating Ideas
pages 212–213**

1. The writer describes good game shows as simple, novel, involving, suspenseful, participatory, and fostering viewer identification.

2. **(2)** Of the three forms of literature shown, fiction—novels and short stories—shares many criteria with good game shows. The criteria that they share are novelty, involvement, suspense, and participation. Also, readers of novels and short stories must be able to identify with the characters.

3. **(3)** The article says that hosting a game show requires both technical and personal skills. The other choices are not mentioned in the article.

4. **(2)** The quote refers to characteristics that are hard to explain and describe, such as the ability to think on your feet, as well as having charm and a good sense of humor. All of these qualities may be described as subjective, nonmeasurable characteristics.

5. **(2)** The only statement that is supported by the article is that game shows have had a long history in television.

**Exercise 14: Adequacy of Facts
page 214**

1. **F** The writer has supported his view that the building will not open up any new rental units. He cites the fact that it will consist solely of resident-owned condominiums rather than rental units.

2. **N** The writer assumes that the development company will not use local workers or business, but he provides no evidence.

3. **F** The writer cites evidence that the mayor and her staff refused three times to meet with community groups.

4. **N** The writer assumes, but does not support his allegation, that the construction company has influenced the mayor with cash donations.

**Exercise 15: The Role of Values and Beliefs
page 215**

Exact wording may vary.

1. Myrna has to choose between her desire to marry Sam on the one hand and her loyalty to her own family on the other.

2. The government of New Zealand must choose between its opposition to nuclear war and weapons and its loyalty to a trading partner and military ally.

3. A scientist who is approached to do genetic research must choose between the chance of advances in preventing birth defects and the possible danger of contributing to the creation of a "genetically superior" master race.

Exercise 16: Cause and Effect
pages 217–218
1. (d)   **2.** (a)   **3.** (b)   **4.** (c)

Exercise 17: Organizing Paragraphs
page 218
1. (a) yes   **2.** (a) no   **3.** (a) yes
    (b) no   (b) yes   (b) yes
    (c) yes   (c) no   (c) yes

Exercise 18: Comparison and Contrast
pages 219–220
Differences

Roosevelt	*Reagan*
1. liberal Democrat	**1.** conservative Republican
2. founded social security	**2.** criticized for weakening it
3. passed laws to regulate financial institutions	**3.** passed laws to deregulate financial institutions
4. set minimum-wage law	**4.** favored abandoning the minimum-wage law for teenagers
5. encouraged labor unions	**5.** weakened and threatened labor unions
6. champion of "little people"	**6.** champion of "big business"
7. had a wealthy background	**7.** had a modest background

Similarities
1. Both were popular presidents.
2. Both came to power after economic problems.
3. Both were persuasive politicians and strong communicators.
4. Both were reelected to office after landslides.
5. Both oversaw legislation that greatly affected the lives of Americans.

Exercise 19: Contrast in an Essay
page 220
1. tasteful and exciting *vs.* insult to standards of good taste
2. captivating means to teach the young *vs.* mindless, uninspiring babysitter
3. can bring important, accurate news *vs.* can spew trivia and "happy talk"
4. commercials help consumers make intelligent buying decisions *vs.* plants seeds of dissatisfaction

Exercise 20: Recognizing Sequence
pages 221–222
1. 3   **3.** 1   **5.** 2   **7.** 10   **9.** 9
2. 8   **4.** 7   **6.** 6   **8.** 5   **10.** 4

Exercise 21: Symbols in Allegory
page 222
1. Mr. Scratch, the stranger
2. sign a contract with Mr. Scratch
3. the tenth year
4. jury
5. Daniel Webster, Mr. Scratch

CHAPTER 2: INTERPRETING GRAPHS AND ILLUSTRATIONS
Exercise 1: Interpreting Line Graphs
page 226
1. (3) The passage says that a bell-shaped curve represents a normal distribution of information. Chicago's average temperature distribution conforms to a bell-shaped curve, but San Francisco's does not. Therefore, San Francisco's average temperature distribution is not considered representative of most U.S. cities (choice A). Moreover, if Chicago's average temperature distribution is considered to be normal, it is more likely to be representative of other U.S. cities than is San Francisco (choice B).

2. (3) Among the cities listed, Detroit, located in the Midwest, is the city closest to Chicago. Therefore, its climate would be most like Chicago's. Los Angeles, Miami, and New Orleans have higher average temperatures. Anchorage, located in Alaska, would have a lower average temperature than Chicago.

Exercise 2: More on Interpreting Line Graphs
pages 227–228
1. (3) For February and April, the points for the Blue Goose Paper Mill are below the break-even point, indicating a loss for the Blue Goose Paper Mill.

2. (5) At the beginning of January and June, the points for the Blue Goose Paper Mill are above the points for the industry average.

3. (2) The points for the paper industry average are all between $10,000 and $20,000.

4. (4) The widest distance between the point for the industry average and the point for the Blue Goose Paper Mill for the same month is in April, when there was a difference of $35,000.

5. (1) This is the only statement you can prove by using the data on the graph. The paper industry average remains consistently between $10,000 and $20,000, and the Blue Goose Paper Mill shows several large increases and decreases.

**Exercise 3: Interpreting Bar Graphs
page 229**

(4) Two implications can be drawn from the two sets of facts: during the 1990s the growth of America's older population is expected to slow, and after the year 2000 it is expected to increase rapidly. The implications are (1) that the relatively small number of babies born during the Depression years explains the reduced number of older Americans in the 1990s, and (2) the large number of babies born between the years 1940 and 1960 explains the increased number of older Americans expected after the year 2000.

**Exercise 4: More on Reading Bar Graphs
pages 229–230**

1. (3) According to the graph, 41 percent of women 65 years of age and older were married and 77 percent of men 65 years of age and older were married. The latter figure represents nearly double the percentage of married women 65 years of age and older.

2. (2) The figures in the graph show that the percentage of older women who were widowed (49%) is greater than the percentage of older men who were widowed (14%); therefore, you can infer that older women who were married outlived their husbands.

3. (2) The graph shows that nearly half (49%) of all older women in 1990 were widows and that more than three-fourths (77%) of all older men were married.

**Exercise 5: Reading Pie Graphs
page 231**

(3) The figures in the bar graph show that, in 1990, 77 percent of men 65 years of age and older were married; the figures in the pie graph show that 74 percent of men 65 years of age and older were living with a spouse. Moreover, the figures in the bar graph show that, in 1990, 41 percent of women 65 years of age and older were married; the figures in the pie graph show that 40 percent of women 65 years of age and older were living with a spouse. Therefore, the figures in the pie graph generally support those found in the bar graph.

**Exercise 6: Interpreting Maps
pages 232–233**

1. (3) Look at the key code that stands for the smallest percentage of change (0–4.9 percent) and note where most of the states with this shading are located. Many of them are in the central and northern parts of the country.

2. (4) Find the code that represents the 5–9.9 percent change and count the number of states filled in with that shading. Eight states show 5–9.9 percent change: Maine, Rhode Island, Connecticut, New Jersey, Minnesota, Tennessee, Idaho, and Oregon.

3. (4) If the national average is 9.9 percent, then all states in the 10–19.9 percent category and all states in the 20+% category must be counted above the average. Nineteen states are above the national average in percent of population change: New Hampshire, Vermont, Delaware, Maryland, Virginia, North Carolina, South Carolina, Florida, Georgia, Texas, Colorado, New Mexico, Arizona, Utah, Nevada, Washington, California, Alaska, and Hawaii.

4. (1) The category 0–4.9 percent change indicates stability. This means that few people have moved in or moved out. These states are Massachusetts, New York, Pennsylvania, Ohio, Indiana, Illinois, Michigan, Wisconsin, Missouri, South Dakota, Nebraska, Kansas, Kentucky, Alabama, Mississippi, Arkansas, Louisiana, Oklahoma, and Montana.

5. (2) By checking the states that border coastlines and then looking at all the others, you can see that the group coded "Loss" does not have any ocean borders. These states include Iowa, North Dakota, District of Columbia, West Virginia, and Wyoming.

Exercise 7: Reading Tables
pages 234–235

1. **(4)** Looking down the column headed "Increases, Absolute," you will find that the highest number in the column is for Asia.

2. **(3)** The bottom row of the chart gives you the world total in all the categories. The forecasted total percentage increase is 55.

3. **(3)** Look down the column labeled "Percent" to find the lowest number. The smallest increase is 14 percent, on the line for Europe.

4. **(1)** Look at both columns under "Population." Under the year 2000, find the number that is almost double the 1975 number for the same country. Africa shows a 1975 population of 420 million. That number is nearly doubled, to 830 million, for the year 2000.

5. **(4)** Look down the "Percent" column for the lowest numbers: Anglo-America, 22 percent, and Europe, 14 percent.

Exercise 8: Interpreting Editorial Cartoons
page 237

1. **(2)** Asian and European students have a reputation for doing well academically, while American students lag behind. The cartoonist is implying that we should try to get American students to think more about math and science.

2. **(4)** The cartoonist is contrasting what is going on in the minds of American students with what is going on in the minds of Asian and European students. The cartoon shows the brains of Asian and European students filled with important school subjects, while American students' brains are filled with thoughts of sports, food, and entertainment.

3. **(3)** Since Asian and European students often do better in school than American students, our society should stress academics more than sports.

Test 2: Social Studies

The GED Social Studies Test consists of multiple-choice questions. These questions require you to know some of the basic social studies concepts that will be covered in this book. However, the test emphasizes your ability to think about these concepts. You will not have to recall an isolated fact or date as on some other tests. Rather, you will read a passage or look at an illustration and answer questions based on it. To answer successfully, you will need to

▶ have an understanding of basic social studies concepts

▶ be able to interpret illustrations and reading passages

▶ be able to show that you can

  • understand what you read
  • apply information to a new situation
  • analyze relationships among ideas
  • make judgments about the material presented

Actually, you already use all of these different kinds of thinking skills in daily life. In this section, we will help you to apply these skills to social studies materials.

How many questions are on the test?

There are 64 multiple-choice questions, and you will be given 85 minutes to complete the test. About two-thirds of the questions will be based on reading passages of up to 250 words each, and one-third will be based on visuals—maps, charts, graphs, or political cartoons. (If you need practice in interpreting visual materials, you might want to review Chapter 2 on pages 223–237 of the Reading Skills section.) To get an idea of what the test is like, look at the Practice Test at the end of this book. This Practice Test is based on the real GED Test. In fact, all of the multiple-choice questions in this section are sample GED questions.

What's on the test?

The GED Social Studies Test can be broken down into the content areas it covers and the skills it tests. The following subjects make up the content of the test:

* Behavioral Science	20%
* U.S. History	25%
Political Science	20%
Economics	20%
* Geography	15%

* In Canada, 25% of the test is Canadian history, 15% is behavioral science, and 20% is geography.

These essential social studies concepts are covered in Chapters 1–5 of this section. However, keep in mind that a given question may draw from a number of these subjects. It's difficult to discuss society or people without touching on a number of topics. For example, a question on the U.S. Constitution may draw from material covered in both political science and history.

Also remember that you are being tested on your ability to think through certain ideas and concepts. You will be asked to do more than just find an answer that was given in a passage.

Thinking skills that you will be tested on include

Understanding Ideas	20%
Applying Ideas	30%
Analyzing Ideas	30%
Evaluating Ideas	20%

Chapter 1 of the Reading Skills section of this book (on pages 189–222) focuses on these thinking skills, and all of the activities and questions in this section will help you practice answering these types of questions. If you have not already worked through the Reading Skills section, you might want to go back and complete the exercises in that section. The more practice you have had in answering the four categories of questions, the better prepared you will be to answer questions in this section and on the actual test.

1
WHAT ARE THE BEHAVIORAL SCIENCES?

Behavioral science is the area in social studies that concerns how human beings behave as individuals and within groups and cultures. The Social Studies Test will include questions on three subjects in behavioral science: anthropology, sociology, and psychology.

Although each subject overlaps the others to some extent, this book examines each one individually. Each of the behavioral sciences focuses on a specific aspect of humankind. Anthropology addresses the question *Who are humans?* Sociology answers the question *To what groups do people belong?* and psychology deals with the complex question *How do people think and behave?*

Anthropology—Who Are Humans?

Have you ever wondered about the human race in general—about who we are, where we came from, how we are alike, and how we are different? *Anthropology* is the science that tries to answer these and many other questions about human origins and civilizations.

The word *anthropology* comes from two Greek words: *anthropos* meaning "man" and *logos* meaning "study of." Of course, the study of "man" includes all of humankind, men and women.

Anthropology has two branches: physical anthropology and cultural anthropology. *Physical anthropologists* study human ancestry to understand how humans have biologically adapted to a variety of environments found throughout the world.

Cultural anthropologists study how people live in groups and how they have developed the tools of culture such as language, religion, and technology in order to survive. *Culture* is the shared, learned behavior that people develop from group experiences.

Research in the field of anthropology has led to many surprising discoveries about humans and their adaptation to their environment. For example, in India in 1913, the "wolf children" were found. They were two ten-year-old boys who lived with three wolves. The boys would eat only raw food. They never smiled or talked. They avoided humans, but allowed a dog to eat with them. Even after they were captured by hunters, the children could not be taught any human behaviors and died a short time later.

A physical anthropologist might ask these questions about this phenomenon:

- How did humans survive among wolves?

- How did the boys' bodies adapt to the wolves' way of life?

- How were they accepted and raised by these animals?

A cultural anthropologist might ask:

- How could two boys learn to live with wolves?
- How did the human beings communicate with these animals?

Although each observes human behavior from different perspectives, both the physical and cultural anthropologist raise and answer questions that contribute to our overall knowledge about human beings in their varying environments.

EXERCISE 1: PHYSICAL AND CULTURAL ANTHROPOLOGY

Directions: Write *P* in front of the topic that a physical anthropologist would study and *C* in front of the topic a cultural anthropologist would study.

_____ 1. fossils of bones of prehistoric people

_____ 2. discovery of crude tools for digging

_____ 3. hieroglyphics found on the walls of an Egyptian cave

_____ 4. a people's preference for raw meat

_____ 5. rites of manhood in African tribes

Answers are on page 343.

Culture

Culture consists of the knowledge, beliefs, and learned human behavior shared by a group of people. It includes the way we think, feel, and behave as we adapt to our environment. Humans can adapt to many environments that lower animals cannot. This is because we have the intelligence and creativity to develop culture.

In fact, humans *must* create culture in order to adapt and survive. For a culture to continue to exist, it must satisfy certain basic needs of its members. These needs, common to all cultures, are called **cultural universals**. Among them are food, shelter, language, family, belief system, economic system, and political system.

Customs

We study various cultures so that we may increase our understanding of other people throughout the world. We study their *customs*, the patterns of behavior shared by the members of a specific culture. The customs are based upon the values that each culture believes to be important. For example, eating with a knife and fork is an established custom in our society. In the United States, family, school, and church are the major institutions that transmit culture to young people.

Values, Ethnocentrism, and Cultural Relativity

Values are beliefs that direct and influence behavior. For example, a fundamental value in American life is the belief that all people are created equal. Values can include freedom, equality, fairness, and individualism.

While observing other cultures, anthropologists are careful not to judge the culture they study according to their own values. Judging another culture according to one's own values is called *ethnocentrism*. For example, an American who condemns child-rearing practices in Asia because they are different from ours is practicing ethnocentrism. Anthropologists attempt to study each culture realizing that each is different yet satisfying to its members.

The opposite of ethnocentrism is *cultural relativity*, judging each culture by using that particular culture's values. Recognizing differences among cultures increases our understanding of the varieties of ways in which people can adapt to the environment.

EXERCISE 2: ETHNOCENTRISM

Directions: Read the following humorous cultural study to see how others might view an aspect of American culture. Then answer the questions that follow.

THE SACRED RAC

An Indian anthropologist, Chandra Thapar, made a study of foreign cultures that had customs similar to those of his native land.

One culture in particular fascinated him because it reveres one animal as sacred, much as the people in India revere the cow.

The tribe Dr. Thapar studied is called the Asu and is found on the American continent north of the Tarahumara of Mexico. Though it seems to be a highly developed society of its type, it has an overwhelming preoccupation with the care and feeding of the rac—an animal much like a bull in size, strength, and temperament.

In the Asu tribe, it is almost a social obligation to own at least one if not more racs. Anyone not possessing at least one is held in low esteem by the community because he is too poor to maintain one of these beasts properly. Some members of the tribe, to display their wealth and social prestige, even own herds of racs.

Unfortunately the rac breed is not very healthy and usually does not live more than five to seven years. Each family invests large sums of money each year to keep its rac healthy.

There are rac specialists in each community, perhaps more than one if the community is particularly wealthy. These specialists, however, due to the long period of ritual training they must undergo and to the difficulty of obtaining the right selection of charms to treat the rac, demand costly offerings whenever a tribesman must treat his ailing rac.

At the age of sixteen in many Asu communities, many youths undergo a puberty rite in which the rac figures prominently. The youth must petition a high priest in a grand temple. He is then initiated into the ceremonies that surround the care of the rac and is permitted to keep a rac.

1. Who are the tribe called Asu? What clues helped you to decide?

_____

_____

2. What is the sacred "rac"? What clues helped you to make this inference?

_____

_____

3. What is the rite that is so important to the sixteen-year-olds?

_____

_____

Answers are on page 343.

Answers are on page 343.

EXERCISE 3: VALUES, ETHNOCENTRISM, AND CULTURAL RELATIVITY

Directions: Based on the passage "The Sacred Rac," choose the best answer for each statement or question that follows.

1. The passage is being used to illustrate the pitfalls of

(1) ethnocentrism
(2) cultural relativism
(3) cultural diffusion
(4) natural selection
(5) cultural universal

2. This study of the customs of the Asu is intended to show

(1) how strange human societies can become
(2) that all cultures have the same customs and beliefs
(3) that the Asu are normal and caring people
(4) what the Asu society would look like to most other cultures
(5) that Asu society is no better or worse than any other society

Answers are on page 343.

WRITING ACTIVITY 1

What differences in culture have you observed among Americans of ethnic groups other than your own? Choose one group and write two paragraphs describing a cultural difference in the area of dress, family relationships, child-rearing, or any other aspect with which you are familiar.

Sociology—To What Groups Do People Belong?

People belong to many different groups. You may be a parent, a spouse, a brother, or a sister. Unless you live alone and are a hermit, or you intensely dislike other human beings, you are a friend. You obviously are a student, because you are studying for the GED Test. All of these roles that you play indicate your membership in different groups.

Sociology studies how humans interact with other humans. We develop relationships and learn to behave in accordance with the beliefs and values of the society in which we live.

Sociologists define a *group* as two or more persons who communicate with each other. Merely being together, however, does not constitute a group relationship. All of the people on a bus or in a room are not considered a group unless they interact—unless they communicate with one another.

Types of Groups

Sociologists divide groups into two categories based upon the group's influence on the individual. *Primary groups* are most important and immediate to a person. Your family is the most primary of all groups. Most people have close, personal relationships with family members. From this group, you form your habits, beliefs, and attitudes. Though not quite as close as your family, personal friends with whom you share intimacies also are members of the primary group to which you belong.

Group relationships that are less personal and exert less influence on an individual are called *secondary groups*. The people you work with or the other students in your class are examples of secondary groups to which you belong. Your communication with co-workers and fellow students tends to be specific and brief. These relationships are usually temporary and impersonal. However, when you work as a team with the same people over a period of time, relationships with co-workers can begin to resemble those with close friends or family.

EXERCISE 4: PRIMARY AND SECONDARY GROUPS

Directions: Write *P* in the space if the situation describes a primary group and *S* if it describes a secondary group.

_____ **1.** all the members of a fan club

_____ **2.** students in math class

_____ **3.** family

_____ **4.** people in a town of 200

_____ **5.** your daughter's closest playmates

Answers are on page 343.

WRITING ACTIVITY 2

Write two paragraphs describing the primary and secondary groups to which you belong. What makes these groups primary and secondary in your life?

Social Institutions

An institution is a system organized by society to provide for its members' basic needs. The major function of most institutions is to transmit to citizens their culture's customs and values. In advanced societies, institutions are of five major types: family, religious, economic, political, and educational. The most important of these is the family.

Socialization and the Family

The family is the first group to which we belong. The most important function of a family is reproduction of the species. For a society to survive, new members must be continually added. After a child is born, the family is responsible for protecting and caring for the child and teaching him or her the appropriate customs and behaviors. This teaching process is called *socialization*.

Humans must learn to be human. The wolf children described in the anthropology section were biologically human. However, they had never been socialized as humans and, as a result, never adjusted to human society. On occasion, newspapers and magazines report cases of people being raised without contact with other humans. An article by Jack Mabley from the *Chicago Tribune* recounts one such story.

EXERCISE 5: SOCIALIZATION AND THE FAMILY

Directions: Read the passage below and answer the questions that follow.

HE'S REBORN AFTER 51 YEARS IN AN ATTIC
by Jack Mabley

ALTON, IL—The neighbors thought the old man lived alone. But when he died, and they went through the house, they heard the noise in the attic.

They found this creature—a human being. Hairy, filthy, crawling on his hands and knees, eyes like gray marbles. They carried him out of the house, placed him upright in the back seat of a car, and drove him to Alton State Hospital.

He was taken to Holly Center, a building housing mentally retarded adults. They cleaned him up and started the long, arduous process of reclaiming this human soul.

I asked Peggy Barr, the Holly administrator, if they measured his IQ when he came. "No," she said. "There was nothing to measure. He was zero. No response. He was still crawling. To get him off the floor we tied him to a chair. He couldn't feed himself. Apparently he had been eating off the floor from a pan, like a dog. We had to start toilet training him. He was 51 years old, we found. We don't know how long he'd been in that attic. Maybe all his life. He'd never had any medical or dental attention. The doctors marveled that he'd survived at all. When we got him there was just no response. He couldn't distinguish between a table and a person. They were just objects he could dimly see.

"It was hard to get a response from him. Apparently his toys in the attic had been a coat hanger and a spoon. We'd hit them together, to see if he'd respond, and he did. Not immediately. But he'd hear the sound, and in a moment look around. He learned to recognize his name. Then he was walking by himself. Our greatest day came when he got up and very slowly, very tentatively, walked over to the window, pulled back the curtain, and looked out. We all felt like cheering."

1. Based on the information above, which of the following explains why the fifty-one-year-old man behaved as he did?

   (1) his extreme isolation from other humans
   (2) the fact that he was born mentally retarded
   (3) the lack of medical attention
   (4) repeated physical punishment by his family
   (5) his fear of people

2. Which hypothesis might best explain why the fifty-one-year-old man survived among humans and the "wolf boys" could not?

   (1) The "wolf boys" had a physical disease; the man did not.
   (2) The man lived in a house; the boys were exposed to the elements.
   (3) The man had a stronger constitution than the boys.
   (4) The man had experienced some human contact during his early life; the boys had none.
   (5) The man's diet was better than the boys' since they ate only meat.

Answers are on page 343.

Nuclear and Extended Families

The structure that the family takes depends upon the customs and values of the society. Traditionally, the family structure in the United States has been nuclear. A ***nuclear*** family is centered around a father, mother, and children. Other societies are based upon what is called an extended family structure. In the ***extended*** family, the nuclear family has been extended to include grandparents, great-grandparents, and sometimes other relatives. In the extended family structure, all adults are responsible for the care and upbringing of all of the children.

EXERCISE 6: NUCLEAR AND EXTENDED FAMILIES

Directions: Write *N* in the space if the situation below describes a nuclear family and *E* if it describes an extended family.

_____ **1.** In the countries of Japan, India, Iran, Turkey, and Africa, the family unit consists of three generations living together.

_____ **2.** The dominant culture of the United States dictates that in most cases only two generations—parents and their children—live together as a family unit.

_____ **3.** Chinese, Moslem, and Hindu cultures dictate that a newly married couple establish residence with the husband's family.

_____ **4.** The Hopi, Navajo, and Iroquois Indians require that a newly married couple establish residence with the wife's family.

_____ **5.** In general, the size of the family varies only in the number of siblings it contains.

Answers are on page 343.

The Changing American Family

Several trends in society have changed the nature of the American family. The divorce rate has increased significantly. Statistics show that more and more children come from single-parent homes. Also, economic pressures have encouraged and even forced some mothers to work to supplement or replace the income of the father. Since more educational and career opportunities have become available to women, some mothers have chosen to have careers in addition to raising children. Thus, the role of women in American society has changed dramatically during the past quarter century.

EXERCISE 7: THE CHANGING AMERICAN FAMILY

Directions: Based on the pictograph, choose the best answer for each of the following questions.

A CRYING NEED FOR HELP

WOMEN IN LABOR FORCE WITH CHILDREN UNDER SIX (Spouse present)

WOMEN IN LABOR FORCE WITH CHILDREN UNDER SIX (No spouse present)

1. Based on the information in the pictograph, the period that shows the greatest amount of increase of *married* women workers with children under six is

   (1) 1960–1965 **(2)** 1965–1970 **(3)** 1975–1980 **(4)** 1980–1985 **(5)** 1985–1990

2. Based on the graph, which of the following is a fact?

   (1) More single mothers are employed than mothers with spouses.
   (2) More than 26 million families require daycare.
   (3) There were nearly 3 million working mothers in 1960.
   (4) The daycare needs of America's families are being met.
   (5) Because more women are working, the divorce rate has skyrocketed.

3. Which of the following is the most likely explanation for the sharp increase in two-job families during the years 1975–1980?

   (1) fewer school-age children at home, permitting more women to work
   (2) less job discrimination against women
   (3) higher cost of living for families
   (4) increased acceptance of working mothers in society
   (5) lowered wages for male breadwinners

Answers are on page 344.

Social Structure

Many societies are divided into categories called social classes. Members of a *social class* possess similar levels of prestige. *Stratification* refers to the way that society is divided into classes. Placement of people into social classes is based upon society's values and behaviors.

In the United States, the social classes are based upon economic values—how much one earns. The upper, middle, and lower classes are distinguished by the wealth and power of the individuals. The upper class is far more wealthy and powerful than the lower class.

Social class is an example of *ascribed* (automatically attained) *status* since one is born into it, but it is not permanent. As one moves upward from one level to a higher one, the new social class is considered an *achieved* (earned) *status*. Some societies prohibit this social mobility (change in status).

In India, for example, the social structure is called a caste system. One way to remember the meaning of *caste* is to compare it with the type of cast used for a broken limb. Neither permits movement. The caste system in India works the same way. People are born into one of the five levels (classes) of the caste system. They are prohibited from changing levels. Thus, the ascribed status will remain for the rest of that person's life, regardless of any attempt to rise above it. Like the three basic levels of social class in America, the five levels in India are based upon society's values and customs.

EXERCISE 8: SOCIAL STRATIFICATION

Directions: Read the statements below. Write *CL* in the space if it describes a class system and *CA* if it describes a caste system.

_____ 1. promotes ambition and self-improvement

_____ 2. encourages achieved status

_____ 3. has strict social structure

_____ 4. makes available many job choices

_____ 5. is characterized by five levels

Answers are on page 344.

WRITING ACTIVITY 3

Controversy surrounds the issue of exactly how much social mobility exists in American society. The "American dream" is that anyone who works hard can succeed economically in this country. Is the American dream being realized? If not, why not? Write two or three paragraphs defending your position on this question. Be sure to include specific examples to support your position.

Psychology—How Do People Think and Behave?

Psychology, the study of human behavior, attempts to answer the questions that concern why human beings think and behave as they do. Three of the components psychologists study and analyze are thinking and learning processes, personality, and social environment.

The Thinking and Learning Process

Because people must learn to be human, learning is the basis for human behavior. According to the behaviorist school of psychology, *learning* is a permanent change in behavior that results from past experience.

Psychologists have identified many ways by which humans learn. Each of the ways represents an increasing level of sophistication by the learner. On the most basic level, people learn to respond to a stimulus (an event that causes a response or reaction). This is called *conditioning*. More sophisticated forms of learning involve reasoning and working out solutions to problems.

EXERCISE 9: TYPES OF LEARNING

Directions: Read the definitions and apply them to the four questions that follow.

classical conditioning—After a stimulus has been introduced several times, a person learns to respond in a certain way. Some reinforcement (either a reward or a punishment) is part of the conditioning process.

operant conditioning—Learning results from interacting with the environment. In operant conditioning there is no direct stimulus. People do things because they want to gain something or to avoid some outcome.

trial-and-error learning—A person solves a problem after trying several possibilities and finally arrives at the right answer or achieves the goal.

cognitive perception—Learning is the result of a logical thought process. The mind takes in information, reorganizes it, and adapts the information to fit a new situation.

maze learning—Learning requires a series of responses in order for the goal to be reached. The responses are often made by trial and error, but maze learning also requires that an individual follow a logical thought process in solving a problem.

1. An infant cries when she wakes up in a dark room. At the sound of the baby's voice, the father goes to the room, picks her up and turns on the light. The baby stops crying. The father continues this for several weeks. One night, he turns on the light before he picks up the baby. To his surprise, the baby stops crying. Thus, turning on the light has caused the same response as picking up the baby. This is an example of

    (1) classical conditioning
    (2) operant conditioning
    (3) trial-and-error learning
    (4) cognitive perception
    (5) maze learning

2. A child is told that birds fly. While playing outside, the child sees an airplane fly overhead. Based on his stored knowledge, the child tells his mother that he has seen a bird. His mother tells him, "No, dear, that's an airplane," and explains the differences between the two. The next time he sees an object flying, he will be able to know whether it is an airplane or a bird. This is an example of

(1) classical conditioning
(2) operant conditioning
(3) trial-and-error learning
(4) cognitive perception
(5) maze learning

3. A pigeon receives food after it presses a bar in its cage. Thereafter, whenever the pigeon is hungry, it presses the bar. This is an example of

(1) classical conditioning
(2) operant conditioning
(3) trial-and-error learning
(4) cognitive perception
(5) maze learning

4. If you are buying a pair of shoes for a child and no measuring tool is available, the child could try on shoes of several sizes until one pair fits. This is an example of

(1) classical conditioning
(2) operant conditioning
(3) trial-and-error learning
(4) cognitive perception
(5) maze learning

Answers are on page 344.

EXERCISE 10: MODES OF LEARNING

Directions: Choose the best answer to complete the statement below.

Many experiments in classical conditioning mainly involve animals and humans at the very early stages in life. This suggests that

(1) classical conditioning is useless in helping us learn about human behavior
(2) classical conditioning is useful only for training animals like guide dogs for the blind
(3) adults cannot be conditioned to do anything
(4) after a certain stage in life, cognitive perception becomes a much more important component of how humans learn
(5) it is against the law for adults to be involved in experimentation of any kind

Answer is on page 344.

Personality

To a great degree, our personality influences how we behave. *Personality* can be summed up as the traits a person exhibits in the way he or she behaves, adjusts, and relates to others and the environment.

Because no two people are exactly alike, it follows that no two personalities can be duplicates. There are, however, similarities in behaviors among people, and it is these similarities that psychologists study to better understand human behavior.

The study of personality is so complex that even psychologists do not all agree about how this facet of human behavior can be explained. Briefly described in this section are four theories that psychologists rely on to understand personality: psychoanalytic theory, superiority and compensation theory, anxiety theory, and self-actualization theory.

Psychoanalytic Theory

Developed by Sigmund Freud, the psychoanalytic theory was the first proposed theory of personality. According to Freud's theory, much of personality comes from unconscious instincts and desires. We are unaware of them because they are hidden from us. Freud labeled the three parts that make up the personality: the id, the ego, and the superego. The *id* is pleasure-seeking and can cause trouble in its drive to satisfy the needs of food, sex, and self-protection. The *ego* acts as a check on the id's search for pleasure. The *superego* represents the conscience. It stops us from doing things that satisfy the id but hurt society.

Freud also believed that personalities are developed during childhood. Childhood experiences influence our thoughts, feelings, and behaviors throughout our lives. Freud attributes some neurotic adult behavior to difficulty experienced during formative stages like toilet-training.

EXERCISE 11: PSYCHOANALYTIC THEORY

Directions: Read the situation and answer the questions that follow.

Otto likes to have a beer with the boys at the neighborhood bar every Friday after work. Greta, his wife, does not like him to drink because he has an ulcer and because he is abusive to her when he comes home drunk. One evening after work, Otto meets his drinking buddies and has a couple of drinks but takes care not to get "plastered." He leaves the bar early and on his way home feels guilty for stopping off. He buys Greta a bunch of roses from a roadside vendor.

1. What drive represents the id in this case?

_____

_____

_____

2. What action represents the functioning ego?

_____

_____

_____

3. What represents the superego?

_____

_____

_____

Answers are on page 344.

Superiority and Compensation Theory

Alfred Adler believed personality is shaped by a striving for superiority and that the failure of people to be as strong or as powerful as they would like to be can result in a feeling of inferiority.

According to Adler, awareness of one's weakness makes a person strive especially hard to overcome it. This explains why some people become experts in areas where they felt weak. An example is Teddy Roosevelt's drive for physical fitness after having been a sickly child. Like Freud, Adler attributes some adult problems to feelings of inadequacy in childhood.

Anxiety Theory

A third theory of personality, developed by Karen Horney, holds that people become anxious when they worry about not becoming who they want to be. To lessen the anxiety, they adopt behaviors or needs to help them adjust. This theory explains how adults develop neurotic needs—learned needs—to reduce anxiety. An example of a neurotic need is a woman's washing her hands several times a day, even when they are not dirty. According to Horney, this need was likely formed in childhood by a parent's overwhelming emphasis on the child's cleanliness.

Self-Actualization Theory

Still another theory to explain personality is the self-actualization theory developed by Abraham Maslow. According to Maslow, the human personality is motivated to satisfy certain needs in life. These needs are expressed in the form of a hierarchy—they are ranked in order of importance to people.

At the bottom of the pyramid are the *physiological* (survival) needs—food, shelter, and clothing. They are the most basic needs. Immediately above them are the *safety and security* needs—needs based on the desire for order and predictability. Third from the bottom is the need for *belongingness*—the need to develop social attachments. Next is the need for *esteem*—recognition and respect from others. The highest human need is the need to fulfill one's potential, to realize one's fullest capabilities—*self-actualization*.

Maslow believed that appeals to the higher-order needs are the most motivational for human beings. Failure to satisfy these needs is an important cause of frustration and unhappiness. The diagram illustrates Maslow's hierarchy.

**MASLOW'S HIERARCHY
OF HUMAN NEEDS**

Need for Self-Actualization

Esteem Needs

Belongingness Needs

Safety and Security Needs

Physiological (Survival) Needs

EXERCISE 12: SELF-ACTUALIZATION THEORY

Directions: Choose the best answer for the following question.

Commercial advertisers base their television appeals on satisfying certain needs. For example, a popular toothpaste commercial implies that the particular brand will increase a person's popularity because of the brighter smile that results from using the product. Which need from Maslow's hierarchy does such a commercial appeal to?

(1) self-actualization
(2) belongingness
(3) esteem
(4) both 1 and 2
(5) both 2 and 3

Answer is on page 344.

Defense Mechanisms

Compensation was described as a part of Adler's theory of personality. A person compensates for a shortcoming by striving hard to overcome it. There are many other ways in which people seek to overcome a weakness or adjust to problems in their lives. *Defense mechanisms* are devices adopted to reduce frustration in achieving one's goals. Some of them include:

repression—keeping thoughts buried, that, if admitted, might arouse anxiety

Mary doesn't like dentists' drills, so she conveniently "forgets" her two o'clock dental appointment.

projection—hiding the source of the conflict by blaming others

Jim needs an "A" on the math test to pass the course. He'd like to cheat, but his conscience won't let him. Instead, he accuses innocent students of cheating.

displacement—substituting one object or goal with another

Ralph gets angry with his boss, but is afraid to tell him off. Instead, he comes home and picks a fight with his wife.

rationalization—assigning the reason for failure to reach a goal to something else. This is the most commonly used defense mechanism.

Hector wasn't good enough to make the basketball team's first string, so he blames the coach for being prejudiced against him.

reaction formation—completely disguising a motive by showing behavior that is the exact opposite of the motive

Deep down, June hates her father, but she appears to be overly concerned about his comfort and health.

EXERCISE 13: DEFENSE MECHANISMS
Directions: Reread the definitions on page 260 and choose the best answer for each of the following situations.

1. According to the "sour grapes" fable, a fox wanted a cluster of grapes that was out of his reach. Because he couldn't get the grapes, he turned away from them saying that they were sour and not worth having anyway. The defense mechanism described is

   (1) repression
   (2) projection
   (3) displacement
   (4) rationalization
   (5) reaction formation

2. Years after it happened, Tyrone still refuses to discuss a boating accident in which he was a passenger and in which his identical twin brother was killed. The defense mechanism described is

   (1) repression
   (2) projection
   (3) displacement
   (4) rationalization
   (5) reaction formation

3. Michael, angry because his team lost the football game, kicks his dog when it runs up to him. The defense mechanism described is

   (1) repression
   (2) projection
   (3) displacement
   (4) rationalization
   (5) reaction formation

Answers are on page 344.

Social Environment

People behave differently when they are alone from when they are in a group. Social environment greatly influences how humans behave. *Social psychologists* study the effects of groups on individuals. Social psychologists are concerned with two areas: social attitudes and group behavior.

Social attitudes involve the actions, beliefs, and feelings of people toward groups and classes of people. By studying attitudes, social psychologists are able to understand how people are attracted to one another and how they are repelled by one another.

Group behavior involves the different ways individuals behave in groups. An example of the influence of the group on individual behavior is the adolescent peer group. After a child reaches a certain age, his or her peer group becomes more important to him or her than the family. The peer group provides the child with a sense of identity and belonging. Parents must compete for influence with the peer group. Often, the parents lose. Children who resist the lure of the peer group often suffer rejection or ridicule.

Social psychologists have found that when people become members of certain types of groups, they become anonymous—they lose their individual identity—and become part of the crowd. This "loss of identity" enables them to do things that they would not ordinarily do as individuals. Two examples of groups in which people do things they would not ordinarily do are mobs and vigilante groups. A positive example of a group in which people lose their individual identities is a group of rescuers working together to help victims of an earthquake.

EXERCISE 14: SOCIAL ENVIRONMENT

Directions: Choose the best answer for the following question.

Which of the following best explains why individuals in groups often behave differently from when they are alone?

(1) People are easily influenced and are always looking for a cause.
(2) People in crowds never feel individually responsible for their actions.
(3) When caught up in a crowd, people lose their sense of who they really are.
(4) People want most to be accepted; therefore, they will do anything to gain the acceptance of the group.
(5) A group setting gives individuals the license to do whatever they have longed to do without being individually held accountable.

Answer is on page 344.

2
U.S. HISTORY— WHAT IS OUR PAST?

Why study the past? We study the past because each of us is a result of those who came before. By understanding their triumphs and failures, we can better understand events that take place in our society today and better prepare ourselves for the future.

History is more than a collection of facts. It is largely a recording of cause-and-effect relationships. Historians study these connections between events.

This chapter is an overview and will highlight the most important events in U.S. history. In this chapter, you will follow historical events from the beginning of this country to the present. You will learn not only *what* happened but will be better able to understand *why* it happened.

A New Nation in a New World

No American holiday recognizes the contribution of the Norwegian Vikings, but 400 years before Columbus set sail, the Vikings landed on North America's shores at what is now Newfoundland. They were the first Europeans to reach North America.

Columbus Day, celebrated on the second Monday in October, honors a hero's mistake. Sailing from Spain in 1492 to search for gold and other treasures from the East, Columbus followed a "shortcut" and landed in North America on the island now made up of Haiti and the Dominican Republic. Thinking he was in India, he called the native Americans "Indians," a name that remains today.

Columbus's error, however, opened the doors for later exploration of the New World. Amerigo Vespucci, for whom America is named, and Ferdinand Magellan, who sailed around the world, were among our continent's most notable early explorers.

As Spain grew in wealth and power because of settlements in what is now Central and South America, France ventured north to Canada. England settled on the coastland between the areas claimed by Spain and France.

By the late 1500s and into the early 1600s, England and Spain fought for control of the southern territory of North America, which included what is now Florida. England's victory led to further colonization in an area that became the east coast of the United States.

As more and more English people came to the colonies to start a new life, England began to acquire more land. In the mid-1700s, England and France fought over the land in the north and central parts of North America. Again, England won and gained total control over the land from Georgia to Maine. This area became known as the thirteen colonies. See the map on the next page.

EXERCISE 1: DISCOVERY, EARLY EXPLORATION, AND COLONIZATION

Directions: Using the map, choose the best answer for each question or statement.

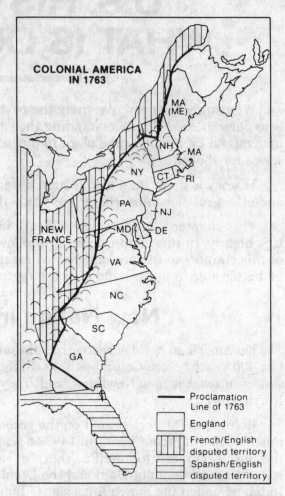

1. From the details in the map, it is clear that the New England state Maine was

   (1) not discovered by the English
   (2) owned and controlled by the French
   (3) owned and controlled by Spain
   (4) a part of Canada
   (5) originally part of Massachusetts (MA)

2. Which of the following can be proved by the map to be false?

   (1) Georgia was the last colony to become a state.
   (2) Pennsylvania was the most powerful colony.
   (3) In the 1700s, France gave up all interest in the New World.
   (4) England controlled much of the Eastern Seaboard.
   (5) The first colonists in New York were Dutch.

COLONIAL AMERICA IN 1763

Proclamation Line of 1763

England

French/English disputed territory

Spanish/English disputed territory

Answers are on page 344.

DID YOU KNOW THAT: The oldest European settlement in the New World is St. Augustine, Florida, settled by the Spanish in 1565?

The Thirteen English Colonies

Each of the thirteen colonies was governed by a council or governor who was appointed by the King of England. These leaders were to control the colonies in the name of the King. Because colonists came from many areas, they brought with them differing customs, religious beliefs, and dialects. This diversity of people made each colony unique and difficult to govern.

Coming to a strange land and trying to make a new start was difficult for the colonists. However, the Pilgrims at Plymouth Colony (Massachusetts) survived the first difficult year and in celebration observed the first Thanksgiving, during which they gave thanks for new opportunities and new freedoms.

In the new land, economic opportunities opened up because of the vast expanse of land available for farming. In the northern colonies, the abundance of natural resources permitted the development of industries such as shipbuilding and iron mining. Fur trading and fishing also were significant industries. Though individual ambition and effort were rewarded, the King ruled supreme and taxed the colonists for what he believed was his rightful share of earnings.

Although the colonists retained much of their cultural traditions and customs, they were forced to make changes as they adapted to a new environment. Thus, a new identity emerged for them. This sense of belonging was described by historian Thomas Wertenbaker in his book *The Shaping of Colonial Virginia*.

EXERCISE 2: THE THIRTEEN ENGLISH COLONIES

Directions: Read the following passage from Wertenbaker's book and choose the answer that best completes each statement.

The bulk of immigrants to Virginia were poor men seeking to better their condition in a new country. Many came as indentured workers who placed their signatures to contracts to work for four years in the tobacco fields in return for their passage across the Atlantic; other thousands paid their fare in advance and so entered the colony as freemen. . . . Most of them, indentured workers and freemen alike, sooner or later acquired small plantations and became members of the yeoman class. A few acquired wealth. Many went into trades to become carpenters, or bricklayers, or blacksmiths, or coopers, or saddlers, or wheelwrights. . . .

Among the thousands of Englishmen who left their homes to seek their fortunes in Virginia, there were no dukes, no earls, rarely a knight, or even a son of a knight. They were, most of them, ragged farm workers, deserters from the manor, ill-paid day laborers, yeomen who had been forced off their land . . . youthful tradesmen tempted by the cheapness of land or by the opportunities for commerce, now and then a lad who had taken a mug of doctored grog and awakened to find himself a prisoner aboard a tobacco ship. But Virginia claimed them all, moulded them into her own pattern, made them Virginians.

1. Indentured workers are

    (1) skilled craftspeople who began their own businesses
    (2) dentists who worked for free
    (3) people who agreed to work in return for a ticket to the New World
    (4) criminals who were sentenced to work in the tobacco fields
    (5) wealthy plantation owners who hired the workers for their fields

2. The purpose of this passage is to show that

    (1) the immigrants were no better off in Virginia than they had been in England
    (2) colonists who came to Virginia came of their own free will
    (3) Virginia was the best colony in which to settle for economic growth
    (4) regardless of their background, colonists who settled in Virginia developed a common bond
    (5) Virginia was a rich colony that had great political power

Answers are on page 345.

WRITING ACTIVITY 1

According to the information in this section, "Because colonists came from many areas, they brought with them differing customs, religious beliefs, and dialects. This diversity of people made each colony unique and difficult to govern." Does the fact that the United States is more diverse today than 200 years ago make the country difficult to govern? In two or three paragraphs, explain whether or not you think the country is difficult to govern because of the diversity of ethnic groups. Be sure to support your position with facts.

The Quest for Independence

Soon after the end of the French and Indian War in 1763, England needed to finance its huge war debt. As a result, the British Parliament and King George III passed the Stamp Act of 1765 and the Townshend Acts of 1767. The Stamp Act required all official documents in the colonies to bear a purchased British stamp. The Townshend Acts placed large duties on glass, lead, and tea. The colonists were outraged by these taxes and rebelled against them by dumping tea into Boston Harbor. This incident is usually referred to as the "Boston Tea Party." The English Parliament punished them by passing laws the colonists called the Intolerable Acts, which sought to further establish the authority of the Crown.

The colonists were quick to respond. In September 1774, at the First Continental Congress, representatives from all thirteen colonies demanded that the Intolerable Acts be repealed. Moreover, the colonists demanded to be treated fairly and given the same rights as all other English citizens. However, the King and Parliament refused.

Battles between British soldiers and colonists had already taken place by May 1775 when the Second Continental Congress was formed.

Inspired by colonist Thomas Paine's pamphlet "Common Sense," in which he explained why separation from England was necessary, Thomas Jefferson drafted the Declaration of Independence. This important document justified the need for a revolution by listing grievances that the colonists had against King George III. The declaration was approved by the Second Continental Congress on July 4, 1776.

Patriotism does not come without sacrifice. The Revolutionary War was a long and costly conflict for both sides. The fighting ended in 1781 when the British troops surrendered to the army of the Thirteen United States. Finally, in 1783, the Treaty of Paris was signed. In addition to gaining its independence, the new American nation was granted all the land west to the Mississippi River, north to the Great Lakes, and south to Florida.

DID YOU KNOW THAT: The first man to die in the fight for American independence was Crispus Attucks, a free African-American?

EXERCISE 3: THE REVOLUTIONARY WAR

Directions: Match the cause in the left column with its effect in the right column.

_____ **1.** the Townshend Acts   **a.** First Continental Congress

_____ **2.** the Intolerable Acts   **b.** Revolutionary War

_____ **3.** the Declaration of Independence   **c.** Declaration of Independence

_____ **4.** king's refusal to compromise   **d.** Boston Tea Party

_____ **5.** end of the Revolutionary War   **e.** signing of the Treaty of Paris

Answers are on page 345.

EXERCISE 4: THE QUEST FOR INDEPENDENCE

Directions: Choose the best answer for each of the following questions.

1. The purpose of the First Continental Congress was to

(1) ask the British king for the colonies' independence
(2) demand the repeal of the Intolerable Acts
(3) form a militia to fight the British soldiers
(4) write the Declaration of Independence
(5) name George Washington as commander-in-chief of the militia

2. The fight of the American colonists against Great Britain can be compared with which event of the twentieth century?

(1) the British invasion of the British-owned Falkland Islands causing a war with Argentina in 1982
(2) India's rebellion against British domination in 1947
(3) the resistance of Afghanistan rebels against the U.S.S.R.
(4) the American support of the Contras in their fight against the Sandinistas
(5) the attack on Pearl Harbor by the Japanese in 1941

Answers are on page 345.

DID YOU KNOW THAT: Three of the thirteen original states—Virginia, Massachusetts, and Pennsylvania—are officially called commonwealths as opposed to states, and that Kentucky is also a commonwealth?

The Beginning of American Government

To prevent the abuses the colonies suffered under the king, a central government was formed. It operated under the Articles of Confederation. Some of its powers under the Articles of Confederation are outlined here.

Powers of the States

The thirteen states had the power to

- levy taxes
- regulate business and commerce
- decide whether to support the decisions of the central government

Powers of the Central Government

The central government had the power to

- make treaties with other nations
- govern Indian affairs
- declare war
- develop a postal service

Within the framework of this new system of government, each of the thirteen states was determined to maintain its sovereignty. This posed a serious problem for the new nation because it limited the powers of the central government in dealing with major issues. These issues were: Who would regulate trade? Who should print money? Who should defend the new nation?

Realizing that the country might collapse if something was not done to address these issues, a convention to amend the Articles of Confederation was called in Philadelphia in May 1787. The result was the creation of the Constitution—the document by which we have been governed for the past 200 years.

EXERCISE 5: THE BEGINNING OF AMERICAN GOVERNMENT

Directions: Read the following statements. Write *T* before each true statement and *F* before each false statement.

_____ **1.** The Articles of Confederation gave the central government the power to levy taxes.

_____ **2.** After the Revolution, the power of the government was divided between the states and the central government.

_____ **3.** As a document, the Articles of Confederation was inadequate in addressing issues that were common to the thirteen states.

_____ **4.** The general feeling of the citizens was that the Articles of Confederation gave too much power to the central government.

_____ **5.** The Articles of Confederation and the Constitution are two names for the same document.

Answers are on page 345.

The U.S. Constitution and Federalism

The challenge facing the Constitutional Convention was to develop a written document that would give the central government more power while allowing the states to retain their sovereignty. To accomplish this, the Constitution was written to create a federal system of government. Under *federalism*, a union is formed by the states, which gives supreme decision-making authority to a central government.

Although the Constitution established the framework for American democracy, its acceptance was no easy accomplishment. Several disputes arose between those who wanted a strong central government with authoritative control over the states (the Federalists) and those who feared that the individual states would lose their freedom under a strong central government (the anti-Federalists).

The Federalists were largely members of the merchant class who favored commercial and industrial expansion. The anti-Federalists were largely farmers who favored individual liberties and did not believe strongly in territorial expansion. Two historical figures whose policies reflected these opposing positions were Alexander Hamilton (a Federalist) and Thomas Jefferson (an anti-Federalist).

The disputes that arose out of the Constitutional Convention and their compromises are illustrated in the chart on the next page.

DISPUTES AND COMPROMISES
AT THE CONSTITUTIONAL CONVENTION

Dispute:	Should the states be governed by a strong central government (Federalists' view)
	or
	Should the new government be based on the sovereignty of the states (anti-Federalists' view)?
Compromise:	1. President was to be elected by electoral college; the Senate, by the state legislatures (this was later changed by the Seventeenth Amendment, adopted in 1913); and House of Representatives, by the people.
	2. Bill of Rights—first ten amendments were added to the Constitution later to guarantee individual rights.
Dispute:	Should the makeup of Congress be based on each state's population (large states' view)
	or
	Should all states have equal representation (small states' view)?
Compromise:	Bicameral legislature (two houses in Congress)
	1. Members of House of Representatives were based on each state's population.
	2. Senate would have two delegates from each state. (This was called the "Great Compromise.")
Dispute:	Should slaves be counted in the population (southern slave states' view)
	or
	Should slaves be excluded from the population count (northern industrialized states' view)?
Compromise:	1. Slave importation would be allowed until at least 1808.
	2. Slaves would be counted as three-fifths of the population only for the purposes of representation and for assessing taxes; however, they were not permitted to vote.

EXERCISE 6: DISPUTES AND COMPROMISES

Directions: Based on the preceding chart, choose the best answer for each of the following questions.

1. Counting slaves as only three-fifths of the population was favorable to the northern states because it

   (1) limited the number of senators to represent the South
   (2) limited the South's number of seats for the House of Representatives
   (3) was based on the amount of property for taxing purposes
   (4) kept slavery from spreading
   (5) equalized the number of representatives for both the North and South

2. The anti-Federalists like Thomas Jefferson were motivated by certain concerns about government. Which of the following beliefs most likely shaped their opinions?

   (1) the likelihood that England would regain control over the colonies
   (2) the necessity for a strong central government to pull the new nation together
   (3) the greater likelihood of individual liberties being protected under local and state governments than under a national government
   (4) the feeling that slavery should be expanded throughout the states so that laws would be uniform for North and South
   (5) the belief that there was no need for a central government because each state could make its own laws

3. Most likely, a Federalist would have been a member of which of the following occupations?

   (1) a New York banker
   (2) a Virginia farmer
   (3) a Massachusetts commercial shipper
   (4) both (1) and (2)
   (5) both (1) and (3)

4. Today, many southern conservatives—Democrats and Republicans alike—are strong supporters of states' rights. These Americans would likely have been supporters of

   (1) anti-federalism
   (2) federalism
   (3) republicanism
   (4) democracy
   (5) colonialism

Answers are on page 345.

DID YOU KNOW THAT: Jefferson's vice president, Aaron Burr, killed his political rival, Federalist Alexander Hamilton, in a duel, and also tried to persuade the western states to secede from the Union?

WRITING ACTIVITY 2

The chart on page 269 cites the positions of southern and northern states about counting slaves as a part of the population. Write a paragraph telling why you think the South wanted slaves counted and the North did not.

Domestic and Foreign Policy

The years between 1701 and 1850 saw the United States expand geographically. Between 1791 and 1796, Vermont, Kentucky, and Tennessee were admitted to the Union under the administration of George Washington.

In 1802, under President Thomas Jefferson, Ohio was admitted to the Union, but the largest acquisition of land for the United States occurred with the Louisiana Purchase in 1803. By paying only $15 million for the territory, Jefferson doubled the size of the country. He subsequently appointed Lewis and Clark to explore the territory acquired. *Manifest Destiny*—the drive to extend the U.S. borders to the Pacific Ocean—became a rallying cry. The map on page 273 shows the territory acquired under the terms of the Louisiana Purchase.

The War of 1812

In 1812, the United States declared war against Great Britain. The war was declared in part because England allegedly interfered with U.S. trade with other European nations and because it aided the Indians in their uprisings in the West. As part of its strategy to cripple the U.S. economy, Britain imposed a blockade of U.S. ships going to France and forced American seamen to join its navy.

Despite successful military campaigns, the United States did not win the unpopular war, and in 1814 the war ended with the signing of the Treaty of Ghent. The Federalists, who were pro-British in foreign affairs, lost political strength and declined as an important voice in U.S. politics.

Westward expansion continued because of the victories over the Indians. Also, the United States began to industrialize and manufacture its own goods because of the shortages created by the British blockade during the war. As a result, a new sense of nationalism developed as the country turned its focus inward.

EXERCISE 7: THE WAR OF 1812

Directions: Choose the best answer for each of the following questions.

1. Which event contributed to the sense of nationalism in the United States after the War of 1812?

   (1) the spirit of Manifest Destiny that caught fire during the early 1800s
   (2) the need to manufacture its own goods because of the British naval blockade
   (3) the scapegoating of the Federalists as traitors
   (4) both 1 and 2
   (5) both 2 and 3

2. Which of the following could explain why the Federalists were pro-British and, therefore, did not support "Mr. Madison's War"?

   (1) The Federalists did not vote for President Madison and had a personal vendetta against him.
   (2) Madison declared war against Great Britain without consulting with the U.S. Congress.
   (3) The Federalists were mainly merchants and shipowners who feared that their trade with other European nations would suffer.
   (4) The Federalists did not believe that the United States had a navy strong enough to challenge the British.
   (5) The Federalists knew that taxes would have to be raised to support a war, and they were against higher taxes.

Answers are on page 345.

The Era of Good Feelings and the Monroe Doctrine

The strong sense of nationalism that developed after the War of 1812 was bolstered by President Monroe's proclamation to the world that European powers would no longer be allowed to colonize the Americas and the United States would remain neutral in European conflicts. Known as the *Monroe Doctrine*, this foreign policy statement marked the emergence of the United States as a world power.

Because of the western expansion into land acquired by the United States through the Louisiana Purchase and the continuing economic development in the East, the years under President Monroe were known as the Era of Good Feelings.

EXERCISE 8: THE ERA OF GOOD FEELINGS AND THE MONROE DOCTRINE

Directions: Choose the answer that best completes the following statement.

The situation that best represents an attempt to enforce the principles of the Monroe Doctrine would be

(1) the dispatch of American soldiers to Grenada to protect American medical students
(2) the U.S. bombing of Libya in retaliation for Libyan terrorist attacks against Americans
(3) the sending of arms to the Nicaraguan Contras in their guerilla war against the Sandinistas
(4) the American blockade of Cuba to prevent Soviet ships from entering the Western Hemisphere
(5) the sending of an American delegation to the Philippines to certify the results in the election between Corazon Aquino and Ferdinand Marcos

Answer is on page 345.

Jacksonian Democracy and the Mexican War

The Era of Good Feelings did not survive Monroe's term, for, after he left office, sectionalism became a problem for the nation. *Sectionalism* refers to the political, cultural, and economic differences among regions of the country—in this case the agricultural South and West and the industrial Northeast. The conflicting demands that each section put upon the government were the cause of great political turmoil.

The first U.S. president elected to office as a result of these factional differences was Andrew Jackson. A southerner and war hero, Jackson was considered to be a *populist*, a man who represented the interests of the common people. He believed that all people, not just the propertied few, should have a voice in deciding how the government should be run.

As the champion of the common people, Jackson opposed the establishment of a national bank, because he believed that it would only benefit the wealthy and because he feared the eastern merchants and industrialists would control it. Under Jacksonian democracy, farmers and craftspeople gained a louder voice in government than they had under previous administrations. Despite pressure to annex Texas, Jackson refused, fearing a war with Mexico.

President James Polk, Jackson's successor, had no such fear, and Congress, agreeing to the demands of the citizens of the territory, annexed Texas in 1845. Thus the expansionist fervor in the United States was renewed. When President Polk was unable to purchase the territory that included New Mexico and California, the United States declared war on Mexico as a result of a territorial dispute between the two countries.

The Treaty of Guadalupe Hidalgo that ended the war resulted in the Mexican Cession in 1848. The Mexican government gave to the United States the land that would later become California, Utah, Nevada, and parts of Colorado, New Mexico, Arizona, and Wyoming. Thus, the United States had set its continental boundaries. The following map shows the boundaries of the United States by 1853.

EXPANSION OF THE UNITED STATES, 1783–1853

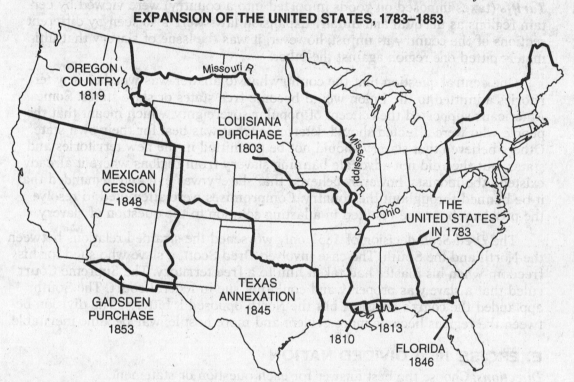

EXERCISE 9: JACKSONIAN DEMOCRACY AND THE MEXICAN WAR

Directions: Choose the best answer for each question or statement.

1. When Andrew Jackson, a southerner, was inaugurated, the shocked eastern establishment treated the invitees to his inauguration with contempt. Which twentieth-century president and his advisors were largely disliked by Washington society because he was considered an outsider?

    (1) John Kennedy
    (2) Gerald Ford
    (3) Jimmy Carter
    (4) Ronald Reagan
    (5) Dwight Eisenhower

2. The attitude toward Jackson described in the previous question is based on

    (1) racism
    (2) populism
    (3) colonialism
    (4) sectionalism
    (5) federalism

Answers are on page 345.

DID YOU KNOW THAT: Andrew Jackson lived with a bullet in his lung for forty years and that the bullet was a result of his being shot in a duel to defend his wife's honor?

Times of Internal Strife

By the 1850s, all the land that made up today's continental United States was under the control of the federal government. Sectionalism persisted, however, as citizens seemed more loyal to their own region than to the Union as a whole. *Tariffs* (taxes imposed on goods imported into a country) were viewed by certain regions as unequal and unfair. Expansion laws were also seen by different sections of the country as unjust; however, it was the issue of slavery that ultimately pitted one region against the other.

One central question that the country had to answer was whether new territories admitted to the Union would become free states or slave states. Some Americans supported the concept of popular sovereignty, which meant that the people who were affected should determine what was best for their own state. Others believed that slavery should not be permitted in the new territories and states, but they did not advocate banning slavery from regions where it already existed. Abolitionists, however, believed that slavery was evil and demanded that it be banned throughout the country. Compromises were attempted to resolve the problem, but none resulted in a lasting solution to the question of slavery.

The *Dred Scott* decision of 1857 only worsened the strained relations between the North and the South. The case involved Dred Scott, a slave who sued for his freedom when his master had taken him to a free territory. The Supreme Court ruled that a slave was property and could not sue in federal court. The South applauded the court's decision, but the North opposed it bitterly. The division between the regions became more evident and more hostile; war became inevitable.

EXERCISE 10: A DIVIDED NATION

Directions: Choose the best answer for each question or statement.

1. A referendum is a political procedure that allows voters to approve or disapprove of a measure proposed by the voters themselves or by the legislature. This method is most similar to which of the following proposed solutions to the issue of slavery?

   (1) abolitionism
   (2) compromise
   (3) popular sovereignty
   (4) secession
   (5) territorial balance

2. The passage cites the *Dred Scott* decision as a decisive event leading to the Civil War. The values upheld by the Supreme Court's decision were that

   (1) slavery was inhuman
   (2) states had more rights than people
   (3) new states could permit slavery
   (4) slavery could only be maintained in the South
   (5) human beings could be treated as property

Answers are on page 346.

The Nation Goes to War

In 1860, when Abraham Lincoln was elected president, he promised to restrict slavery to the states where it already existed. The Southern states, feeling that they were being treated unfairly, feared that they would eventually be dominated by the North. They voted to secede from the United States and to form their own government—the Confederate States of America.

South Carolina was first to secede in 1860, and by February 1861 Georgia, Florida, Alabama, Mississippi, Louisiana, and Texas seceded. Richmond, Virginia, was chosen as the Confederate capital and Jefferson Davis elected president of the Confederacy. In response, President Lincoln determined that the only way to preserve the Union was through the use of force. The South was disobeying the laws of the land. Lincoln believed that if the South did not follow the law, any state that chose to disagree with a national decision would feel that it could simply ignore the law. The Confederacy's firing on Fort Sumter in April 1861 opened the bloodiest war in the nation's history.

EXERCISE 11: THE VOTE ON SECESSION

Directions: Based on the following map, match the state in the left column with its description in the right column.

VOTE ON SECESSION IN THE SOUTH

☒ Overwhelmingly for secession

☐ Overwhelmingly against secession

_____ **1.** Virginia
a. As a "border state," it remained in the Union despite being a slave state.

_____ **2.** Texas
b. As a solid Southern slave state, it voted overwhelmingly to secede from the Union.

_____ **3.** Kentucky
c. This state split in two over the issue of secession, with the western part loyal to the Union.

_____ **4.** Mississippi
d. The entire state seceded from the Union even though only its eastern part voted to do so.

Answers are on page 346.

The Civil War

The nation could not exist half slave and half free, and the war that settled the question lasted four years. Most of the war was fought in the South. The North had the advantage of a larger army because of its greater population, an ability to manufacture goods needed for the war effort because of its industrialization, an excellent transportation system, and an abundance of natural resources.

The South, on the other hand, had the advantage of a greater familiarity with battle sites, as the war was fought on its soil, and great confidence in its outstanding military leaders.

In 1862, President Lincoln issued the ***Emancipation Proclamation***. The document ordered the freeing of slaves in those slave states that were not border states loyal to the Union. As a result, the Union army's ranks grew by 180,000 former slaves who fought against the rebels.

The war ended on April 9, 1865, when Confederate General Robert E. Lee surrendered. However, the task ahead for President Lincoln and the citizens of the Union was enormous. The division between the North and the South had to be mended, and the devastated South had to be rebuilt. The South's readmission to the Union would prove to be difficult.

EXERCISE 12: NORTH VS. SOUTH

Directions: In the spaces below, write *N* if the description applies to the North and *S* if it applies to the South.

_____ **1.** outstanding field generals

_____ **2.** better transportation network

_____ **3.** greater population

_____ **4.** forces increased by former slaves

_____ **5.** greater familiarity with battle sites

Answers are on page 346.

EXERCISE 13: THE NATION GOES TO WAR

Directions: Choose the best answer for each of the following questions.

1. Which of the following *best* explains why Lincoln limited the Emancipation Proclamation to the Confederate states?

(1) Confederate states would have the most to lose if slavery were weakened.
(2) The Confederate states had a large number of loyal slaves who supported their cause.
(3) President Lincoln did not want to alienate border states that held slaves but that were loyal to the Union.
(4) He wanted to punish the Confederate states for leaving the Union.
(5) The border slave states made a secret pact to join the Confederacy if he freed their slaves.

2. What effect did the Emancipation Proclamation have on the outcome of the war?

(1) It made the South more determined to win the war; therefore, the South won most of the battles that followed the proclamation.
(2) The South gained a reliable source of soldiers in the freed slaves.
(3) It officially ended the war, because the question of slavery for which the war was fought was no longer an issue.
(4) It made President Lincoln one of the most popular presidents in American history.
(5) It gave the Union army a military advantage because many former slaves fought on the side of the North.

Answers are on page 346.

DID YOU KNOW THAT: The military draft was started during the Civil War, or that President Lincoln suffered from frequent bouts of depression throughout his life?

Reconstruction

Lincoln's plan for reuniting the nation included allowing the South to regain citizenship rights and statehood. However, he did not live to see the plan, known as Reconstruction, carried out. While attending a play five days after the war was over, Abraham Lincoln was assassinated by a Confederate sympathizer.

He was succeeded by a Tennesseean, Andrew Johnson, who, though he supported the Union, was mistrusted by Congress as being pro-South. This mistrust contributed to Johnson's becoming the only U.S. president to be impeached—charged with official misconduct. However, the Senate failed by one vote to convict Johnson. Therefore, he was not removed from office.

By 1870, the Fourteenth Amendment was ratified, guaranteeing citizenship to blacks, and the Fifteenth Amendment the same year gave blacks the right to vote. Despite these gains, racial issues and their resulting problems would remain in the South for years.

EXERCISE 14: RECONSTRUCTION

Directions: Read the following passage and then choose the best answer for each question.

Strangers from the North who moved to the South after the Civil War to help the freed slaves find their place in society were called Carpetbaggers by the Southerners. These Northerners brought no more than they could carry in carpetbags—the first suitcases made from pieces of carpet. Many Southerners felt that they only came to profit from the opportunities that arose during the rebuilding of the South.

1. You can infer from the above information that the strangers were called Carpetbaggers because they

(1) were primarily salesmen
(2) did not intend to stay long
(3) were wealthy landowners
(4) were poor and illiterate
(5) did not like uncomfortable surroundings

2. History has shown that the Southerners' resentment of Carpetbaggers was justified in many cases. Which of the following is an example of corruption on the part of these Carpetbaggers?

(1) support of fraudulent bond schemes
(2) concern about the education of freed slaves
(3) attempt to register former slaves as voters
(4) contempt for former Confederate leaders of the South
(5) ability to buy land in the reconstructed South

Answers are on page 346.

DID YOU KNOW THAT: President Andrew Johnson was a tailor, and that when he died he was buried, as he requested, wrapped in the American flag and with his head resting on a copy of the U.S. Constitution?

The Rise of Industrial America

With the Industrial Revolution, America's position as a world power was cemented further. The *Industrial Revolution* was the change in the economy's character from a manual means of production to a mechanical one. Goods were mass-produced by machinery rather than crafted by hand. Because of this change in production methods, more products could be produced at lower costs.

Great Britain generally is credited as the place of origin of the Industrial Revolution. Advantages that Great Britain had were

- an abundance of mineral resources

- access to waterways for transporting products

- a compact size that encouraged consumerism within the country

- a ready market in the New World because of the demand for manufactured goods

- a large middle class that could afford commercially manufactured goods

- a comparatively free and literate society responsive to change

Although the Industrial Revolution began in Great Britain, the United States, with its abundant natural resources and growing population, became the world's industrial leader by the turn of the century. The number of factories in the United States grew, attracting people from rural areas who could earn more money working in factories than on farms. As a result, the population of the cities grew. With increased earnings, people could buy more goods and improve the quality of their lives. This consumer demand encouraged existing businesses to expand, new products to be created, and new industries to be developed.

EXERCISE 15: THE INDUSTRIAL REVOLUTION

Directions: Choose the best answer to each of the following questions.

1. Based on the preceding information, what can you infer about the relationship between a country's size and the development of industry at the beginning of the Industrial Revolution?

   (1) A small population adapted more easily to change than a larger one did.
   (2) A small area containing a large population gave manufacturers more opportunities to sell their goods.
   (3) The larger the population of a country, the more likely it was to resist change.
   (4) The smaller the population of a country, the less likely it was to purchase manufactured goods.
   (5) A large population spread over a large area presented more opportunity for industrialization.

2. Russia and Japan both had the potential at the turn of the century to become industrial giants. Japan succeeded eventually, but Russia still lags far behind. Which of the following would be a logical explanation for this difference between the two countries?

   (1) Japan has had an abundance of natural resources, while Russia has had relatively few.
   (2) Russia has had a long history of economic and social restraint, while Japan has encouraged technological and economic changes.
   (3) Russia has encouraged small groups of highly educated scientists and technicians, while Japan has not.
   (4) Japan has had a large and growing population, while Russia is a small country and is limited in its potential for growth.
   (5) Russia has had a system of serfdom under a tyrannical czar, while Japan has had a large proportion of poor peasants.

Answers are on page 346.

Growth of Big Business

Rapid and widespread industrialization led directly to the development of big business. As one company bought another related company, large corporations began to control the marketplace. This was true especially in the steel, railroad, and oil industries.

Working conditions for employees deteriorated as businesses ran unchecked by the government, and power became concentrated in the hands of a few powerful industrialists. The government practice of noninterference in the affairs of business is termed *laissez-faire* business policy.

EXERCISE 16: GROWTH OF BIG BUSINESS

Directions: Place a check before each of the following actions that represents economic activity *without* government intervention.

———— **1.** The Federal Communications Commission (FCC) requires AT&T to divest—break up into smaller companies.

———— **2.** A large company hires and pays unskilled workers whatever the market will bear and is not brought into court for violating the minimum wage law.

———— **3.** The FCC requires a newspaper owner in Baltimore to sell one of its newspapers when it buys a local television station.

———— **4.** A credit card company charges its customers whatever amount of interest it wants to.

———— **5.** The USDA closes a dairy when it is found guilty of selling tainted butter.

Answers are on page 346.

Urbanization and Social Change

Urbanization is the shift of the population away from rural areas and to cities where most of the jobs are. Before industrialization, only one out of every six Americans lived in the cities.

By 1890, one-third of the population lived in the cities. Cities such as New York, Chicago, and Philadelphia had populations of more than one million people. These cities were railway centers that provided transportation for people, supplies, and manufactured goods.

Businesses and factories found an abundant labor supply in the cities. The tremendous number of immigrants who entered the United States from 1870 to 1900 flooded the job market. Their willingness to work long hours for less money forced native American workers to accept the same conditions.

Immigrants were often prevented from living in certain areas or from applying for certain jobs. Some Americans wanted to protect themselves from these "others." Yet people continued to come to the cities, bringing with them different cultures and backgrounds. Thus, cities became true melting pots of American society.

Urbanization changed the face of the country socially, economically, and politically. The following bar graph shows the gradual shift of the nation's population from rural to urban areas.

AMERICA BECOMES URBANIZED

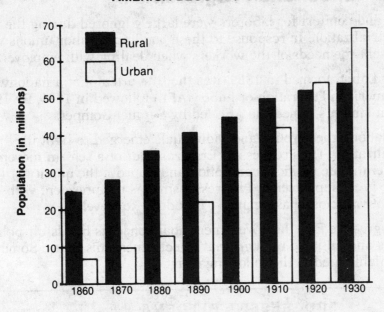

EXERCISE 17: AMERICA BECOMES URBANIZED

Directions: Based on the bar graph above, answer the following questions.

1. What was the first decade in which more people lived in urban areas than in rural areas? _____

2. In what decade was the total population of the country approximately 50 million? _____ .

3. The population of the country in 1860 was approximately how many million people? _____

4. By 1930, the number of people living in urban areas was approximately how many million? _____

Answers are on page 346.

EXERCISE 18: URBANIZATION AND SOCIAL CHANGE

Directions: Choose the answer that best completes the statement below.

The figures in the bar graph support the fact that the United States reached half its present population of 248 million (based on the 1990 census) by

(1) 1890   **(2)** 1900   **(3)** 1910   **(4)** 1920   **(5)** 1930

Answer is on page 346.

WRITING ACTIVITY 3

Do Americans accept immigrants more readily today than in the nineteenth century? Write two or three paragraphs supporting your position. Be sure to include examples to support your point of view.

Labor and Progressivism

Health, safety, and comfort for laborers were largely ignored during the period of rapid industrialization. In response to these conditions, labor unions were organized to represent the needs of the workers when dealing with employers.

The Knights of Labor, formed in 1869, was the first attempt at a nationwide labor union. The American Federation of Labor (AFL) followed in 1881. By 1904, more than a million laborers joined the AFL led by Samuel Gompers.

In addition to labor, other groups and individuals emerged to fight the abuses of industrialization. The Progressive Era arose out of a reform movement whose goal was to eliminate political corruption and improve the quality of life for Americans. One great supporter of Progressivism was the president with whom the movement was closely associated—Theodore Roosevelt.

During the Progressive Era, the government abandoned its hands-off policy toward big business and initiated reforms that affect Americans today. Some of these reforms are highlighted in the following chart.

PROGRESSIVE REFORMS
Sherman Anti-Trust Act—outlawed monopolies
Hepburn Act—gave Interstate Commerce Commission increased authority to regulate the nation's railroads
Pure Food and Drug Act—set standards for production and sale of foods and drugs
United States Department of Agriculture (USDA)—began inspecting meat
Child labor laws—prohibited child labor
Minimum wage and worker's compensation laws—improved working conditions and wages

EXERCISE 19: THE PROGRESSIVE ERA

Directions: Read the passage below and choose the best answer.

The Sherman Anti-Trust Act outlawed price-fixing (the agreement between companies to set their prices), underproduction of goods, market sharing, and any other form of monopolizing among producers of a similar product. However, public utilities such as gas, electric power, and water companies are exempted from these restraints. These government-sanctioned monopolies are permitted to exist so that essential services are not duplicated and natural resources are not wasted.

According to the Sherman Anti-Trust Act, an example of an illegal monopoly is

(1) the existence of only one power company in a city, giving consumers no choice of whom to obtain service from
(2) a large commercial bank that has branches located throughout the city in direct competition with other banks
(3) a hamburger chain's restaurants, all of which belong to the same system of franchises
(4) oil manufacturers in a state that agree on a minimum price to set for gasoline
(5) a local telephone company that sets minimum and maximum rates for customers in a particular service area

Answer is on page 346.

EXERCISE 20: WOMEN'S SUFFRAGE

Directions: The two passages that follow represent two views of the women's suffrage movement—the movement to secure for women the right to vote. Read each passage and answer the questions that follow.

Although only a working woman, I have by hard work and close economy accumulated a small property that I find I have the privilege to pay taxes for, but have no right to vote for men that tax me. I also find that I am taxed for said property as much again as what many men are that have political influence. Last year I appealed against the enormous tax the assessor put on my property. But I could get no resolution because I have no political influence.

—Mrs. Callor, Jersey City, New Jersey

I intend to vote for woman suffrage in New Jersey because I believe that the time has come to extend that privilege and responsibility to the women of the state; but I shall vote, not as a leader of my party in the nation, but only upon my private conviction as a citizen of New Jersey called upon by the legislature of the state to express his conviction at the polls. I think that New Jersey will be greatly benefited by the change. My position with regard to the way in which this great question should be handled is well known. I believe that it should be settled by the states and not by the national government, and that in no circumstances should it be made a party question: and my view has grown stronger at every turn of the agitation.

—A press release by President Woodrow Wilson,
October 6, 1915

1. Which statement summarizes the main idea of both passages?

   (1) It is time for women to be granted the right to vote.
   (2) Though it is a good idea, women are not yet ready to vote.
   (3) Only educated women who own property should vote.
   (4) Most women have always been treated as equals of men.
   (5) Most women would not vote even if given the right.

2. Who does President Wilson believe should make the decision regarding women's suffrage?

   (1) the Congress of the United States
   (2) the voters nationwide
   (3) the voters of each state
   (4) the U.S. Supreme Court
   (5) the women's suffrage movement

3. By Mrs. Callor's statement, you can tell that she has assumed that

   (1) women should not have the right to vote
   (2) she has no power because she cannot vote
   (3) she should not have to pay taxes
   (4) she should not have to work
   (5) President Wilson will help her

Answers are on page 346.

The United States as a World Power

From the time it had achieved its independence from England, the United States stayed out of the affairs of other countries. This policy of *isolationism* prevented the United States from forming alliances with other countries.

In 1867, the United States bought the territory of Alaska from Russia against the wishes of most Americans. The purchase turned out to be a good investment, however, because of Alaska's many natural resources. Also, because Alaska was the first land acquired that was outside the boundaries of the continental United States, the purchase marked the beginning of a new foreign policy. The United States was no longer an isolationist country.

Another motive for the United States to become less isolationist was the need to develop more markets for its manufactured goods. U.S. ships sailed the Pacific Ocean carrying goods to Japan and China. These ships often docked in many island ports along the way to buy supplies and to make repairs. By the late 1890s, the U.S. government had taken possession of a number of Pacific islands for their easy access and available resources. This marked America's emergence as an *imperialist* country—a nation that controls other territories or nations.

The Spanish-American War

America's emergence on the world scene was strengthened by the Spanish-American War. The United States supported rebels who revolted against Spain.

The battleship *Maine* was sent to Cuba to protect American citizens there. It exploded, killing 260 American sailors, and Spain was held responsible. The United States declared war against Spain in 1898 and won the war in four months. Under the terms of the peace treaty, the United States gained control of Guam, Puerto Rico, and the Philippines. These new territories and the islands in the Pacific increased the number of territories under American control.

EXERCISE 21: THE UNITED STATES BECOMES A WORLD POWER

Directions: Choose the best answer to each of the following questions.

1. Which of the following foreign policy actions today is a direct result of early American imperialist policy?

   (1) America's military support of Israel in the Middle East
   (2) the implicit support of apartheid in South Africa by some large American corporations
   (3) America's establishment of military bases in the Philippines' Subic Bay
   (4) the stationing of American troops in West Germany
   (5) America's patrolling of waters off the Libyan coast

2. From the end of the Civil War until the Spanish-American War in 1898, most Americans were isolationists. Which is the most likely cause of such widespread desire for withdrawal from international concerns?

   (1) the lack of information about events taking place in foreign lands
   (2) the desire to expand U.S. boundaries farther across the continent into Canada and Mexico
   (3) the disillusionment with foreign allies who had refused to take sides during the Civil War
   (4) the nation's preoccupation with reconstruction and industrialization after the Civil War
   (5) the resentment toward the new immigrants flooding the country

Answers are on page 347.

World War I

Conflicts over boundary lines and power struggles among European countries resulted in a war that, by its end, included twenty-seven nations. For this reason, it was called a world war.

The nations divided themselves into two rival groups—the Central Powers and the Allied Powers. The Central Powers included Germany, Austria-Hungary, Bulgaria, and Turkey. The Allied Powers included Great Britain, France, Russia, Belgium, and Italy.

The United States tried to remain neutral during the early years of the war that had begun in 1914. In 1917, however, in response to German attacks on ships carrying American citizens, the United States declared war.

The war resulted in many changes in the United States. Factories shifted their production to the manufacture of needed military weapons and supplies. Women and older children replaced draftees as factory workers. Shipyards built only naval vessels. To conserve food for the soldiers, the U.S. government restricted the consumption of meat and bread to particular days.

Strengthened by the United States' entrance in the war on their side, the Allies drove the Central Powers back to their own boundaries. When the Allies broke through the German lines, the Germans conceded defeat.

The Treaty of Versailles, signed in early 1919, officially ended the war. One condition of the treaty was that the League of Nations be established to maintain peace throughout the world. Congress did not want the United States to become involved in European affairs again, so the country did not join the League of Nations, contributing to the organization's decline. After the war, the United States returned to a policy of isolationism, and domestic issues became the focus of the postwar period.

EXERCISE 22: WORLD WAR I

Directions: Fill in the following blanks.

The United States became involved in the war in 1917 by joining the side of the

(1) _____. To rapidly increase the size of the U.S. Army, the Selective Service Act was passed. This act permitted the military to **(2)** _____ men

between the ages of 18 and 45. The **(3)** _____

ended the war in early 1919. Congress did not want the United States to join the

(4) _____. As a result of this sentiment, the United States

adopted its former foreign policy of **(5)** _____.

Answers are on page 347.

DID YOU KNOW THAT: President Woodrow Wilson was president of Princeton University before becoming president of the United States?

The Roaring Twenties

"Back to Normalcy" was the goal and slogan of President Warren G. Harding. The twenties, however, were anything but normal as Harding, relying on the poor advice of cabinet officers, became entangled in the financial oil lease scandal of Teapot Dome. The scandal disgraced the entire administration.

Also during the twenties, the Immigration Acts of 1921 and 1924 were enacted to preserve jobs for American workers. These acts strictly limited the number of immigrants that could enter the United States.

From Prosperity to Despair

Harding's successor, Calvin Coolidge, believed in few government regulations. He reduced government spending and lowered taxes. As a result, the people had more money to spend, and businesses were able to expand. This period in U.S. history was called the Golden Twenties because of the prosperity the nation enjoyed. The period was characterized by speculation (taking unwise risks in investments hoping to increase gains), bootlegging (the manufacture and purchase of illegal liquor, the sale of which was banned by the Eighteenth Amendment), and an emphasis on materialism.

Unfortunately, by the end of the decade, the Golden Twenties became tarnished as the stock market fell in 1929. Businesses failed and the unemployment rate soared while Herbert Hoover, elected president in 1928, continued the policies introduced by Coolidge. President Hoover believed in individual opportunity, free enterprise, and little government regulation. He maintained that if government left business alone, the country would quickly recover from the economic depression. By 1932, however, the number of unemployed workers reached 11 million. The U.S. economy required drastic measures in order to recover.

In 1932, the voters overwhelmingly elected Democrat Franklin D. Roosevelt president on his campaign promise to give Americans a "New Deal."

EXERCISE 23: THE ROARING TWENTIES

Directions: Using the graph below, answer the questions that follow.

This graph illustrates how effective the Immigration Acts of 1921 and 1924 were in controlling the number of immigrants entering the United States.

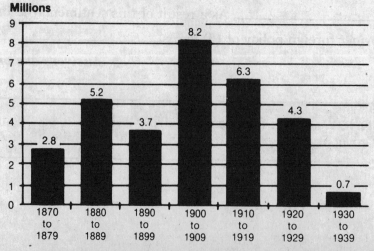

IMMIGRANTS ARRIVING IN THE U.S.

Source: U.S. Department of Commerce. Bureau of the Census

1. The largest number of immigrants to enter the country occurred in which decade? _____

2. Which was the first full decade to be affected by the Immigration Act? _____

3. How many persons emigrated to the United States during that decade? _____

Answers are on page 347.

DID YOU KNOW THAT: During the Depression, Americans in the Southwest ate armadillos (which taste like pork)? The armadillos were called "Hoover hogs."

The Thirties and Forties

The goals of the New Deal were to bring relief to people who were in need, to direct the recovery of the economic system, and to establish reforms that would prevent another depression from occurring.

Roosevelt's programs radically changed governmental policy. Within his first 100 days in office, he persuaded Congress to approve an unprecedented number of bills to address the nation's economic crisis. Many of the agencies created during the New Deal remain today. Most notable are the social security system and the Federal Housing Administration.

Roosevelt's actions reversed the economic and emotional climate of the country. Voters reelected him by the largest margin (up to that time) in U.S. history.

EXERCISE 24: THE NEW DEAL
Directions: Match the group in the left column with the New Deal legislation it would have most likely supported in the right column.

_____ 1. sharecroppers

_____ 2. unemployed laborers

_____ 3. the elderly

_____ 4. environmentalists

_____ 5. bankers

a. National Industrial Recovery Act

b. Federal Deposit Insurance Corporation

c. Civilian Conservation Corps

d. Agricultural Adjustment Act

e. Social Security Act

Answers are on page 347.

DID YOU KNOW THAT: Presidents Franklin D. Roosevelt and Theodore Roosevelt were cousins; that William Henry Harrison and Benjamin Harrison were grandfather and grandson; and that John Adams and John Quincy Adams were father and son?

World War II

Because of isolationist foreign policy and concern about the Depression, the United States chose to ignore the conflicts that were brewing in Europe and Asia. The struggle for power and territorial conquest brought Germany's dictator Adolf Hitler into conflict with Great Britain and France.

Japan, too, showed military aggression, especially toward China. Elsewhere in Europe, Spain was experiencing a bloody civil war, and Italy had invaded Ethiopia.

When Germany invaded Poland in 1939, Great Britain and France declared war. The United States tried to remain neutral, but its neutrality was being challenged and its security threatened. By 1940, Italy and Germany had joined the Axis forces, later to be joined by Japan in 1941.

On December 7, 1941, the Japanese Air Force attacked Pearl Harbor, an American naval base on the island of Hawaii. This attack on Americans forced the United States to declare war on Japan. The United States joined Great Britain, the Soviet Union, and France as the Allied Forces.

World War II was truly a global war. Battles were fought in Europe, North Africa, Asia, and on many Pacific Ocean islands. During the six years of the war, millions of lives were lost and millions of dollars were spent. One month before massive Allied military efforts forced Germany to surrender, President Franklin Roosevelt died.

Vice President Harry Truman succeeded him. Truman was determined to end the war with Japan very quickly. The dropping of atomic bombs on Hiroshima and Nagasaki brought a quick surrender from Japan on September 2, 1945.

In February 1945 President Roosevelt, Great Britain's Winston Churchill, and Russia's Joseph Stalin had met in the Soviet Union in the city of Yalta. Under the Yalta Agreement, Germany was divided into four zones under the control of Great Britain, the Soviet Union, France, and the United States, and the United Nations was established as a world organization to maintain world peace.

Although the war ended many years ago, its scars remain. In addition to the death of thousands of people and the radioactive fallout from the dropping of the atomic bombs in Japan, the extermination of six million Jews—known as the Holocaust—is a continual reminder of the war's atrocities.

EXERCISE 25: WORLD WAR II

Directions: Write *T* in the space if the statement is true and *F* if it is false.

———— **1.** Territorial aggression by the Axis Powers was a leading cause of World War II.

———— **2.** The Allied Powers included Germany, Italy, and Japan.

———— **3.** Japan's bombing of Pearl Harbor ended the United States' neutrality.

———— **4.** The Axis Powers included Great Britain, France, and the United States.

———— **5.** The United Nations is a league of nations determined to defend its members in the face of war.

Answers are on page 347.

EXERCISE 26: U.S. FOREIGN POLICY POSITIONS

Directions: Use the following definitions to answer the questions below.

Listed are five foreign policy positions followed by U.S. leaders during the 20th century.

isolationism—the policy of noninterference in world affairs

imperialism—the policy of one nation controlling other territories or nations

anti-imperialism—the policy of rejecting a nation's practice of controlling another territory

jingoism—extreme nationalism marked by frequent use of warlike rhetoric

internationalism—a policy of cooperation among different nations of the world

1. Lecturer and writer John Fiske believed in Charles Darwin's theory of natural selection. According to the theory, the strongest and best adjusted members of a group survive certain conditions. In his lectures, Fiske stated that it was the "white man's burden" to "civilize" underdeveloped countries of the world. Based on this view, Fiske would be described best as

   (1) an isolationist
   (2) an imperialist
   (3) an anti-imperialist
   (4) a jingoist
   (5) an internationalist

2. Two days after Japan attacked Pearl Harbor, FDR made the following statement: "In the past few years and most violently in the past few days, we have learned a terrible lesson. We must begin the great task that is before us by abandoning once and for all the illusion that we can ever again isolate ourselves from the rest of humanity." In the statement, Roosevelt is expressing the ideas of

   (1) an isolationist
   (2) an imperialist
   (3) an anti-imperialist
   (4) a jingoist
   (5) an internationalist

Answers are on page 347.

The Atomic Age

The end of the war marked the end of the cooperative relationship between the United States and the Soviet Union. President Truman, perceiving communism to be a serious threat to democracy, formulated the Truman Doctrine. With the *Truman Doctrine*, he announced that the United States would support free peoples who resist attempted control by armed minorities from within or by foreign powers from without. Thus, a U.S. policy of containment of communism was put into words.

EXERCISE 27: THE TRUMAN ERA

Directions: Place a check mark before each situation that represents an attempt to enforce the principles of the Truman Doctrine.

———— **1.** the sending of American troops to South Vietnam to preserve democracy and prevent an invasion from North Vietnam

———— **2.** the provision of financial and military aid to the Philippines to put down left-wing insurgents

———— **3.** the decision by the U.S. Congress to approve economic sanctions against South Africa

———— **4.** the American blockade of Cuba to prevent Soviet ships from entering the Western Hemisphere

———— **5.** U.S. support of the Polish Solidarity movement's rebellion against the communist government of Poland

Answers are on page 347.

> **DID YOU KNOW THAT:** President Truman was a haberdasher (owner of a men's clothing store) before he became president?

The Korean War

At the end of World War II, the Soviet Union and the United States (who were allies at the time) agreed that the nation of Korea should be free from Japanese control. To protect this freedom, the Soviet Union occupied the northern half, while the United States occupied the southern half.

By 1950, however, a "cold war" between the two nations had developed, and neither country trusted the other. Each feared that the other would try to take control of Korea.

South Korea held public elections to determine its leadership, while a communist government was established in North Korea. Armies representing the North and the South were stationed along the border.

When a North Korean army crossed the border into the South, President Truman committed U.S. troops and asked for troop support from the United Nations.

President Truman claimed that the Korean conflict was a "U.N." war and never asked Congress for a formal declaration of war. Despite this, the United States suffered 137,000 casualties; the U.N.'s losses were 263,000. It was not until 1953, under newly elected president Dwight D. Eisenhower, that a treaty was signed. The original boundary between North and South Korea was reinstated. However, tensions between the two countries still exist today.

EXERCISE 28: THE KOREAN WAR

Directions: Choose the best answer for each of the following questions.

1. The undeclared war in Korea most closely resembled the situation of

   (1) World War I
   (2) World War II
   (3) the Spanish-American War
   (4) the Vietnam War
   (5) the Civil War

2. Which of the following is an opinion about the Korean War?

   (1) Dwight Eisenhower finally ended American military action in Korea.
   (2) The Soviet Union and the United States mistrusted each other's intentions in Korea.
   (3) The Korean conflict was an extension of American policy to contain communism.
   (4) Our government has no right to make soldiers fight in an undeclared war.
   (5) After the war, the boundary between the two countries was reinstated.

Answers are on page 347.

The Eisenhower Years

The end of the Korean War marked only the end of armed conflict. The United States and the Soviet Union, neither trusting the other, increased their military forces, and both developed the hydrogen bomb. This nuclear weapon was far more powerful than the atomic bomb. The mistrust between the two superpowers continued the *Cold War*—a war of words and beliefs—the Soviet Union pushing communism and the United States spreading its influence.

Also, during the 1950s, Senator Joseph McCarthy used the country's hatred and fear of communism to his political advantage. He accused hundreds of government officials, prominent businesspeople, and entertainers of being part of a communist plot to take over the country. Although he ruined many people, his charges were never proved. However, his reputation was so badly damaged that he lost all of his influence and power.

EXERCISE 29: THE EISENHOWER YEARS

Directions: Choose the best answer to the following question.

Under McCarthyism, hundreds of innocent Americans were wrongly accused of being communist sympathizers and suffered public humiliation and the loss of their jobs. Which earlier event created a similiar hysteria in the United States?

(1) the Stock Market Crash of 1929
(2) the Civil War
(3) John Brown's raid at Harper's Ferry
(4) the San Francisco earthquake of the 1920s
(5) the Salem witchcraft trials

Answer is on page 347.

Space Exploration and Social Change

President Eisenhower's second term was marked by economic development and social change. Important technological advances encouraged America's involvement in the exploration of space. In 1957, the launching of the first man-made satellite (Sputnik) by the Soviet Union inaugurated the entry of the United States into the space race.

Also during the Eisenhower administration, the modern civil rights movement began as a direct result of the famous U.S. Supreme Court decision *Brown* v. *Topeka Board of Education.* In the case, the court ruled that "separate educational facilities are inherently unequal." This ruling was resisted in many school districts throughout the South. The most celebrated case occurred in Little Rock, Arkansas, when black students were refused entry to all-white Central High School. President Eisenhower sent federal troops to ensure the students' safety. Later, the Civil Rights Act of 1957 established the Civil Rights Commission to investigate illegal voting requirements based on race, national origin, or religion.

EXERCISE 30: SPACE EXPLORATION AND SOCIAL CHANGE

Directions: Choose the answer that best completes the following statement.

The *Brown* v. *Topeka Board of Education* decision is significant today because it

(1) sanctioned segregated schools
(2) allowed Eisenhower to set a precedent by sending out federal troops
(3) serves as the legal basis for school busing to achieve desegregation
(4) permitted blacks to attend private schools
(5) helped to increase Eisenhower's personal popularity

Answer is on page 347.

The Sixties

John F. Kennedy, the first Catholic and the youngest man to be *elected* president, brought great promise to the office. Kennedy's challenge to America is capsulized in the quote delivered at his inauguration: "Ask not what your country can do for you, ask what you can do for your country."

Youth rallied to his call as Kennedy established the Peace Corps and VISTA (Volunteers in Service to America) to share America's wealth and knowledge with underprivileged nations.

The U.S. space program helped symbolize Kennedy's vision of a "new frontier" as the Mercury Seven astronauts ushered in the era of U.S. manned space flights.

In 1961, the Soviet Union began supplying nuclear missiles to pro-Soviet Cuba, located just 90 miles off the Florida coast. President Kennedy established a naval blockade to prevent any Soviet ships from reaching Cuba. He demanded that the missile site already established be dismantled and the missiles be removed. Soviet Premier Khrushchev, not wanting to risk war, agreed to withdraw all of the missiles from Cuba.

On the domestic front, President Kennedy continued Eisenhower's policy of guaranteeing civil rights to the nation's black minority. In 1963, a civil rights commission found that voting rights of blacks were still being denied. Also that year, the Rev. Martin Luther King, Jr., led a series of nonviolent protests throughout the South, culminating in the historic march on Washington that August. President Kennedy's death by an assassin's bullet in November 1963 prevented many of his social programs from becoming a reality. The mantle of leadership passed to Kennedy's vice president, Texan Lyndon B. Johnson.

EXERCISE 31: KENNEDY'S NEW FRONTIER

Directions: Choose the answer that best completes each statement below.

1. The Soviet Union's attempt to establish a missile base in Cuba may be interpreted as a direct violation of

   (1) the Declaration of Independence
   (2) the Truman Doctrine
   (3) the Monroe Doctrine
   (4) the Strategic Arms Limitation Talks (SALT)
   (5) the U.S. Constitution

2. Based on the information in the passage, you can conclude that

   (1) the Soviet Union sought to control Cuba
   (2) the Soviet Union planned an attack on the United States from Cuba
   (3) Cuba and the United States enjoyed friendly relations
   (4) Cuba, a communist country, was an ally of the Soviet Union
   (5) Cuba planned to attack the United States

Answers are on page 347.

DID YOU KNOW THAT: President Kennedy's PT boat was cut in two by a Japanese destroyer during World War II, and he swam for fifteen hours guiding members of his crew to nonhostile land?

Johnson's Great Society

Lyndon Baines Johnson pursued the policy of fulfilling his predecessor's dreams, and, in the course, realized many of his own. A skillful politician, LBJ pushed bills through Congress in numbers that had not been seen since the New Deal. The social legislation he introduced became the basis for his "Great Society."

In 1964, he pushed through Congress the most significant achievement of his career—the Civil Rights Act. The law forbade racial discrimination in circumstances where federal funds were used.

Despite Johnson's domestic achievements in the area of civil rights, his foreign policy—particularly with regard to the Vietnam War—proved to be his undoing. Under Johnson, the Vietnam War, an inherited problem, was escalated in 1965. The number of American soldiers fighting in the undeclared war grew from 25,000 in 1963 to more than 500,000 American soldiers by 1968.

In the United States, public controversy over the war painfully divided the society. Supporters maintained that the war was necessary to contain communism and protect democracy in the Far East. Critics maintained that the war was essentially a civil war in which outsiders did not belong.

Antiwar protests occurred on college campuses across the nation. Draft resisters fled to Canada to avoid having to serve in the war. President Johnson continued to seek a military end to the war, but because of the division within the country, in 1968 he chose not to seek reelection to the presidency. His decision not to run opened the door to new leadership and a new direction for the American people.

EXERCISE 32: JOHNSON'S GREAT SOCIETY

Directions: Choose the answer that best completes the following statement.

Based on the preceding text, the Johnson administration's greatest single achievement was the

(1) active pursuit of world peace
(2) escalation of war in Vietnam
(3) successful containment of communism throughout the world
(4) successful passage of legislation to guarantee the rights of blacks and the disadvantaged
(5) withdrawal of troops from Vietnam

Answer is on page 348.

DID YOU KNOW THAT: Before he became a lawyer and politician, President Johnson was a schoolteacher?

The Nixon Era

In the extremely close presidential election of 1968, Republican Richard M. Nixon defeated Hubert Humphrey, Johnson's vice president. Many people attributed Humphrey's loss to his early support for the Vietnam War.

Nixon continued Johnson's earlier bombing strategy to force a surrender in Vietnam. He ordered troops into Cambodia, a military move that was unpopular with the American people. He did, however, gradually withdraw troops and negotiate a pullout by March 1973. The agreement to end the war included a ceasefire, U.S. withdrawal of all military troops, and a release of all prisoners captured during the war.

After the Vietnam pullout, Nixon was extremely popular among the American voters and was at the peak of his political career. To his credit, he enjoyed many achievements as a world statesman.

His policy of *détente* (the easing of tensions between nations) helped to establish the first SALT (Strategic Arms Limitation Talks) agreement. Both countries agreed to limit the number of missiles each could have. He was the first American president ever to visit the People's Republic of China, which he traveled to in 1972. In the Middle East, the United States had become a major peacekeeping influence. As a result of these successes, Nixon won the presidential election of 1972 with one of the largest margins in modern history.

Overshadowing all of these achievements in Nixon's career, however, was his involvement in the Watergate scandal that began in June 1972. The scandal involved the break-in of the Democratic Committee Headquarters, whose offices were located in the Watergate Hotel. Nixon's part in the attempted coverup led to his resignation in 1974. Thus, he became the first U.S. president to ever resign from office to escape the threat of impeachment proceedings. Vice President Gerald Ford succeeded Nixon and finished his term. Ford lost to Democrat Jimmy Carter in the 1976 election.

EXERCISE 33: THE NIXON ERA

Directions: Choose the best answer to each of the following questions.

1. Of President Nixon's foreign policy initiatives, for which will history likely credit him most?

   (1) ordering of troops into Cambodia
   (2) negotiating peace in the Middle East
   (3) reestablishing relations with the People's Republic of China
   (4) ordering the bombing of Hanoi
   (5) ending the Cold War with Russia

2. Which of the following opinions is best supported by the evidence presented in the passage?

   (1) Political spying is a common practice in American politics.
   (2) Nixon's military strategy brought about victory in Vietnam.
   (3) Nixon's aides broke the law for the good of the country.
   (4) A serious character flaw cost Nixon the presidency.
   (5) The President of the United States is not above the law.

Answers are on page 348.

Ending the 20th Century

Jimmy Carter, elected president in 1976, was considered a Washington "outsider" because he had never held a national political office. A peanut farmer and former governor of Georgia, Carter was seen by the public as a fresh change from the distrust of Washington government officials that was created by the Watergate scandal. One of Carter's chief goals was to regain the public's confidence in its leadership.

Carter may have been a new face, but the problems he confronted were the same old ones. Inflation, fueled by the increases in oil prices set by oil-exporting nations, rose steeply. In the meantime, the worsening situation in the Middle East added impetus to the effort of the United States to conserve energy.

In spite of the problems that beset his administration, Carter experienced some triumphs. He was instrumental in framing a peace treaty between Egypt and Israel; he was a driving force in establishing full diplomatic relations with mainland China; he signed a second SALT (Strategic Arms Limitation Talks) treaty with the Soviet Union; and he successfully returned control of the Panama Canal to Panama.

The event that many believe damaged Carter's image as an effective president was the takeover of the American embassy in Teheran, Iran, in which more than sixty Americans were held as hostages by militant Iranians. Most of the hostages remained in captivity for fifteen months despite an attempt to free them. They were finally released on the day of the inauguration of President Ronald Reagan.

EXERCISE 34: CARTER AND THE MIDDLE EAST

Directions: Choose the best answer for each of the following questions.

1. For which of the following actions will former President Jimmy Carter likely be remembered most favorably?

    (1) formally recognizing the African nation of Zimbabwe
    (2) allowing the shah of Iran to seek refuge in the United States
    (3) negotiating with Egypt and Israel for reconciliation between the two nations
    (4) framing a treaty to return the Canal Zone to Panama
    (5) coming to the White House on an anti-Washington platform

2. President Carter's part in relinquishing U.S. control of the Canal Zone to Panama would likely be described as a victory for

    (1) isolationism
    (2) imperialism
    (3) anti-imperialism
    (4) jingoism
    (5) conservatism

Answers are on page 348.

Reagan and the New Conservatism

At the age of sixty-nine, Ronald Reagan was the oldest man to be elected president of the United States. Before he became America's fortieth president, he had been a movie actor and governor of California. His conservative political philosophy and his ability to communicate with people made him a popular president.

Under Reagan, conservatism reigned as his administration sought to correct the problem of inflation, which he attributed to the overspending of the sixties. In an effort to reduce federal spending, many of the social programs implemented during the sixties were cut drastically. The Reagan administration expected the states, local governments, and private industry to replace those programs that were cut by the federal government.

The thrust of American foreign policy under Reagan was anticommunism. The administration supported the efforts of anticommunist rebels throughout the world. Much of the money saved by cutting domestic programs was redirected into the Defense Department. Both the increase in terrorist activity during the eighties and the Soviet military buildup were used to justify the Reagan administration's hard-line defense policies.

EXERCISE 35: REAGAN AND THE NEW CONSERVATISM

Directions: Choose the best answer for the following question.

Which of the following actions best exemplifies the main thrust of Reagan's foreign policy?

(1) giving aid to anticommunist rebels in Nicaragua, Afghanistan, and Angola
(2) setting up summit talks with Soviet leader Mikhail Gorbachev
(3) refusing to intervene in the Philippine elections of 1986 between dictator Ferdinand Marcos and Corazon Aquino
(4) arranging peace talks between Israel and the PLO (Palestine Liberation Organization)
(5) stationing U.S. troops in Lebanon

Answer is on page 348.

Bush and the "New World Order"

Vice president under Ronald Reagan for eight years, George Bush was elected president in 1988. Bush promised to carry on many of Reagan's conservative policies.

Political changes throughout the world during the Bush administration gave rise to Bush's phrase "a new world order." In 1989, communism collapsed in Eastern Europe. In February of 1991, the United States led worldwide efforts against Iraq in the Persian Gulf War. Later that same year, America's Cold War rival, the Soviet Union, disbanded as a result of economic and political turmoil.

Meanwhile, the U.S. economy dipped into recession in the early 1990s. The deepening recession seemed to defy attempts to resuscitate the economy and became a major issue in the 1992 presidential campaign.

Bush's strength was in foreign affairs. The American people began to feel he had ignored domestic policy. In the months before the 1992 election, the Gross National Product (GNP, the amount of all goods and services a nation produces in one year) dropped and the unemployment rate rose.

Bush's challengers focused on the economy, an issue that lost the Republicans their hold on the presidency. Ross Perot, the self-made millionaire and independent candidate, appealed to many Americans' discontent. Democrat William (Bill) Clinton, who promised tax cuts, creation of jobs, and health-care reform, won the election. Free from the threat of the Cold War, Americans had become more concerned about economic recovery than about the state of the rest of the world.

EXERCISE 36: BUSH'S "NEW WORLD ORDER"

Directions: Write *F* in the space if the statement is a fact and *O* if it is an opinion.

_____ **1.** The fall of the Soviet Union shows that communism won't work anywhere.

_____ **2.** Economic troubles in the United States can become a political issue.

_____ **3.** Now that the Cold War is over, the CIA (Central Intelligence Agency) should disband.

_____ **4.** During the Bush administration, momentous changes occurred worldwide.

_____ **5.** Bush let the United States slip into recession.

Answers are on page 348.

Clinton—the First Baby-Boom President

The first of the baby-boom generation to hold the nation's highest office, Bill Clinton had run as a "New" Democrat. Clinton was seen as a moderate, moving away from the old image of a tax-and-spend big government. At age forty-six, he had already been governor of Arkansas for twelve years. Clinton projected himself as an outsider, a man of the people, and a force for change.

During the first 100 days of his tenure, a time period made famous by Franklin Roosevelt, Clinton found that campaign promises were difficult to keep. Reducing the federal deficit proved more complicated than he had expected. Because of Republican opposition, Clinton's first job-stimulus bill never reached a vote. In creating a budget proposal, he was accused of reverting to too much spending and too many new taxes. He also encountered controversy over his first nominee for attorney general, his attempt to drop the ban on homosexuals in the military, and the appointment of his wife, Hillary Rodham Clinton, to head the health-care task force.

His commitment to represent America's diversity through Cabinet appointments fared better. Well-qualified minorities and women played active roles in White House decisions. Tough-minded Janet Reno became the first woman attorney general, and highly regarded Ruth Bader Ginsberg was Clinton's first Supreme Court appointment.

Inexperienced in foreign policy, Clinton faced a number of major foreign-affairs crises. He continued Bush's military strategy in Iraq and, despite his preelection stand, upheld Bush's policy of denying asylum to Haitian refugees. Clinton granted a limited economic aid package to financially troubled Russia in hopes of preventing the return of hard-line communists. In urging military intervention in the ongoing Bosnian civil war, the president of four months ran into opposition from a reluctant Congress and a hesitant NATO.

EXERCISE 37: CLINTON—THE FIRST BABY-BOOM PRESIDENT

Directions: Choose the best answer for each of the following questions.

1. What do Bill Clinton's initial experiences in office suggest about the presidency?

   (1) Former governors make good presidents.
   (2) The presidency is more complex than candidates expect.
   (3) Presidents don't need to know much about foreign affairs.
   (4) There are few surprises for a newly elected president.
   (5) The presidency is overrated by the American people.

2. With which of the following statements would Bill Clinton most likely agree?

   (1) The Congress is easy to please.
   (2) Women have no real place in government.
   (3) Economic recovery is simply a matter of getting down to business.
   (4) The hardest part of being president is getting elected.
   (5) Thinking about tomorrow's problems is easier than creating today's solutions.

3. With which of the former presidents did Bill Clinton have the most in common?

(1) Jimmy Carter
(2) Ronald Reagan
(3) George Bush
(4) Franklin Roosevelt
(5) Richard Nixon

4. According to the passage, which of the following was Clinton's most successful action during his first few months in office?

(1) nominating Janet Reno attorney general
(2) proposing his first job-stimulus bill
(3) urging military intervention in Bosnia
(4) appointing the head of the health-care task force
(5) including new spending in the budget proposal

Answers are on page 348.

3
POLITICAL SCIENCE— HOW ARE PEOPLE GOVERNED?

Human beings are social animals; therefore, people must live in groups. To maintain order in society, governments with rules and laws are established to meet the needs of the individuals who make up society. Important functions of government include making decisions, resolving conflicts, and providing necessary services. **Political scientists** analyze the organization and management of government within a society.

Types of Political Systems

Several types of political systems exist in the world. The differences among political systems chiefly concern the way the government acquires and uses its authority.

Under a **dictatorship**, a single leader completely controls the political, social, and economic aspects of life in a country. The dictatorships of Adolf Hitler in Germany and Benito Mussolini in Italy are historical examples of one individual holding complete political power. Modern-day examples of dictatorships include Libya under Colonel Muammar Gadhafi and the Philippines when ruled by Ferdinand Marcos.

A **monarchy** is a political system in which the power to rule is held by a royal family. This power is passed within the family from one generation to the next. In the past, **absolute monarchies** were headed by a king or queen who had final say in governmental decision making. Today, however, monarchs are bound by the laws of a constitution and have limited authority, as is the case in Great Britain. Queen Elizabeth II of England is primarily a ceremonial leader; governmental decisions are made by a parliament headed by a prime minister.

In a **democracy**, the head of the government is chosen by the people he or she governs. The leader's decisions must meet the approval of the people.

Two types of democracies exist today—the pure democracy and the representative democracy. In a **pure democracy**, the people make the decisions directly. This is impractical with a large population, however, and is usually found only in small towns. The town meeting (still used in parts of New England) is an example of a pure democracy.

For large populations, such as that of the United States, a representative democracy is used. In a **representative democracy**, the people elect representatives to determine policies for the entire population. Thus, the representatives remain accountable to the people.

Sometimes nations are governed by a few leaders who form a group. Such a government by the few is called an **oligarchy**.

An oligarchy is similar to a dictatorship in that government officials are not elected by the people and often come to power after a revolution. A group of persons controlling a government after a revolutionary seizure of power is called a *junta* (*hoon-tuh*). Communist countries such as the former Soviet Union and the People's Republic of China are modern-day examples of oligarchies.

EXERCISE 1: METHODS OF OBTAINING POWER

Directions: Listed are five ways by which goverment leaders may assume power. Read the definitions and apply them to the questions that follow.

ancestry—The leader comes from a family that has led the country for many generations.

divine right—The leader claims to have been placed in his or her position by God.

conquest—The leader acquires territory through military domination.

revolution—The leader comes to power as a result of an overthrow of the earlier political system.

popular vote—The leader is chosen by the vote of the people he or she is to govern.

1. The French, inspired in part by the revolt of the thirteen colonies against England, replaced their monarchy with a republic. The new leader came to power by

   (1) ancestry
   (2) divine right
   (3) conquest
   (4) revolution
   (5) popular vote

2. Austria maintained its independence in the face of World War II until Hitler's army occupied the small nation and forced it to join the Third Reich. Hitler acquired power over Austria by

   (1) ancestry
   (2) divine right
   (3) conquest
   (4) revolution
   (5) popular vote

3. President Corazon Aquino of the Philippines outpolled former president Ferdinand Marcos in the election of 1986. Aquino won the presidency through

   (1) ancestry
   (2) divine right
   (3) conquest
   (4) revolution
   (5) popular vote

Answers are on page 348.

The U.S. Federal Government

The U.S. Constitution is based on the idea of federalism. Under *federalism*, the authority of the government is divided between the states and a central government. The central government is further divided into three branches: the *legislative*, which makes the laws; the *executive*, which carries out the laws; and the *judicial*, which interprets the laws. Under this separation of powers, no one part of government is able to dominate another. Each branch of government is able to exert its authority to prevent another branch from becoming too powerful.

The Legislative Branch: Maker of Laws

The legislative branch of the government is outlined in Article One of the Constitution. The U.S. legislature, called the U.S. Congress, is made up of two houses—the House of Representatives and the Senate. The House of Representatives is called the lower house, and the Senate is called the upper house.

In the House of Representatives, each state's number of representatives is based on its population in relationship to the population of the entire country. Smaller states have fewer representatives than larger states. To determine the correct number of representatives a state should have, a *census*, or counting of the population, occurs every ten years. In the Senate, each state is equally represented with two senators each.

Representatives are chosen by popular election and serve for two years. Senators are chosen by popular election also, although under the original Constitution they were chosen by the state legislatures. Senators serve six-year terms.

The U.S. Congress has the power to

- levy and collect taxes
- borrow money
- regulate commerce
- coin money
- declare war
- provide and maintain an army and navy

- approve treaties (Senate only)
- impeach the president (House only)
- introduce bills other than tax bills
- introduce a revenue or tax bill (House only)
- approve presidential appointments (Senate only)
- admit new states to the Union

These powers are called *enumerated* powers because they are listed in Article One of the U.S. Constitution. In addition to enumerated powers, the Constitution provides for powers that are not listed. The *elastic clause* enables the legislative branch to stretch its authority to meet the needs of specific situations that the Founding Fathers could not foresee.

EXERCISE 2: LEGISLATIVE REPRESENTATION

Directions: Choose the best answer for each of the questions below.

1. Which of the following states is likely to have the least number of representatives in the House?

   (1) Texas
   (2) New York
   (3) Rhode Island
   (4) California
   (5) Georgia

2. Although New Jersey is smaller in size than Wyoming and Nevada, it has a larger number of representatives. Based on this fact, which of the following can you infer to be true?

   (1) New Jersey has a dwindling population.
   (2) New Jersey is primarily an urban, industrial state.
   (3) New Jersey is a densely populated state.
   (4) Both (1) and (2)
   (5) Both (2) and (3)

3. Arizona, one of the fastest-growing Sunbelt states, is attracting residents from the industrial Northeast. Based on this fact, which of the following hypotheses could be true?

   (1) The number of senators for Arizona will need to be increased.
   (2) The number of representatives for Arizona will need to be adjusted to reflect the increase in population.
   (3) The number of representatives for the states in the Northeast that are losing residents will need to be adjusted.
   (4) Both (1) and (2)
   (5) Both (2) and (3)

Answers are on page 348.

EXERCISE 3: THE LEGISLATIVE BRANCH

Directions: Write *C* in the space if the action listed is an example of a power stated in the U.S. Constitution and listed on page 303. Write *E* in the space if it is an example of an application of the elastic clause, which allows Congress to stretch its authority to meet needs not mentioned in the Constitution.

_____ 1. Congress approved economic sanctions against the apartheid regime of South Africa.

_____ 2. Congress reformed the nation's tax structure in 1986.

_____ 3. Congress admitted Hawaii as the fiftieth state of the Union.

_____ 4. The Senate approved President Bush's appointment of Clarence Thomas as an Associate Justice of the U.S. Supreme Court.

_____ 5. The 99th Congress introduced legislation to abolish the mandatory retirement age for workers.

Answers are on page 349.

The Executive Branch: Enforcer of the Laws

Article Two of the U.S. Constitution outlines the powers of the executive branch of the U.S. government. The executive branch consists of the president, vice president, and all of the agencies and departments that are necessary to administer and enforce the laws of the country. As described in Article Two of the U.S. Constitution, the president

- is commander-in-chief of the armed forces
- has power to grant reprieves and pardons for offenses against the United States
- may appoint judges to the U.S. Supreme Court and ambassadors with the approval of the Senate
- may nominate and appoint major executive officers
- may veto (refuse to approve) bills sent by Congress

Just as the legislative branch has powers not provided for in the Constitution, so too does the president. This vagueness of executive authority has allowed each president to shape the office to his own personality. "Strong" presidents, to some extent, have dominated the legislative branch and have relied less on the advice of their cabinets and direction from Congress. Strong presidents frequently use their veto power. "Weak" presidents, on the other hand, have made the office subordinate to the legislature, have relied more on their cabinets, and have been less authoritative. Generally speaking, however, the office of president has been one of increasing authority.

The president serves for four years and is limited to serving a maximum of two terms. The vice president serves if the president becomes disabled or dies in office before completing the term. The president and vice president are chosen by popular vote, but the electoral college later officially certifies the results of the popular election. The *electoral college* consists of a group of electors from each state who, a month after the general election, cast votes for the president and vice president. To be officially elected president, a candidate must receive a majority of the electoral votes. Originally established to serve as a check and balance against an unsound decision made by the voters, the electoral college today is a target of much criticism. Many politicians believe that the institution has outlived its usefulness and should be abolished.

In general, the candidate who receives the majority of a state's popular vote almost always receives the state's electoral votes. In only two instances in U.S. history has a candidate received the majority of the popular vote but lost the election because of the electoral vote. This occurred in the election of 1876 in which Rutherford B. Hayes was chosen as president even though his opponent, Samuel Tilden, received the majority of the popular vote. This also happened in the election of 1888, when Benjamin Harrison was elected president even though his opponent, Grover Cleveland, received the majority of the popular vote.

306 TEST 2: SOCIAL STUDIES

EXERCISE 4: THE EXECUTIVE BRANCH

Directions: Choose the best answer for each question below.

1. "Strong" presidents have been described as dominating the legislative branch and making the office of the presidency self-directing. "Weak" presidents have made the office more reliant on and subordinate to the legislature. Which of the following early presidents *best* fits the description above of a strong president?

    (1) President Madison, a statesman who declared war on Britain in 1812 only after popular demand called for it.
    (2) President John Adams, who believed that the governing representatives should be "the rich, the well-born, and the able."
    (3) President Thomas Jefferson, who opposed the Louisiana Purchase and the first Bank of the United States on the grounds that the Constitution did not provide for it.
    (4) President James Monroe, who advanced the idea of the Monroe Doctrine on the advice of his secretary of state, John Quincy Adams.
    (5) President Andrew Jackson, who made unprecedented use of his veto power and who relied little on Congress and his cabinet in making his decisions.

2. Based on what you read in the section on U.S. history, which of the following twentieth-century presidents may be best described as "weak" when he got embroiled in the Teapot Dome scandal by relying on the poor advice of his subordinates?

    (1) Theodore Roosevelt
    (2) Franklin D. Roosevelt
    (3) Woodrow Wilson
    (4) Harry Truman
    (5) Warren G. Harding

3. In the early years before political parties were established, the second highest vote-getter in a presidential election automatically became vice president. This was changed later when parties were founded and candidates for president and vice president ran together on a ticket. Which of the following is the *best* explanation as to why the policy for electing the vice president was changed?

    (1) The Constitution required that candidates for the offices of president and vice president be from the same party.
    (2) The country was better served when the candidates for president and vice president came from different regions of the country.
    (3) Before the system was changed, it was easier to cheat a candidate out of the presidency.
    (4) Too many unqualified candidates for the presidency were running for office; the new system guaranteed the candidates would be better qualified.
    (5) The new system prevented the vice president (who often had opposing political views) from obstructing the president's ability to govern.

Answers are on page 349.

WRITING ACTIVITY 1

The electoral college system was created as a way to check potentially "unsound" decisions made by the voting public. Should the president and vice president of the United States be elected by direct popular vote or by the electoral college system as is currently the case? Write one or two paragraphs defending your point of view.

The Judicial Branch: Interpreter of the Laws

Article Three of the Constitution describes the Supreme Court of the United States. The purpose of the Supreme Court is to rule on the constitutionality of certain laws passed by Congress, the president, and the states themselves. The authority to decide whether or not a law is in keeping with the spirit of the Constitution is called *judicial review*.

The Supreme Court is composed of nine justices appointed for life by the president. The head of the court is called the *chief justice*. The judicial branch of the federal government consists of the U.S. Supreme Court, the eleven Circuit Courts of Appeal distributed throughout the country, and approximately ninety federal District Courts.

Some of the powers vested in the Supreme Court are the powers to

- rule on cases involving a state and citizens of another state
- rule on controversies between two or more states
- rule on cases between citizens of different states
- rule on cases between a state and its citizens, and a foreign state and its citizens
- rule on conflicts arising on the high seas
- rule on conflicts over patents and copyrights

In carrying out its rulings, a decision is reached when a majority of the justices of the Supreme Court agree. When all nine justices are present and vote, a majority decision requires at least five votes.

EXERCISE 5: THE JUDICIAL BRANCH

Directions: Choose the best answer to complete each of the following statements.

1. Chief Justice Charles Evans Hughes wrote in 1907, "The Constitution is what the Judges say it is." This quote best defines the Supreme Court's power of

   (1) checks and balances
   (2) ignoring the decisions made by the legislative branch
   (3) being "above the law"
   (4) judicial review
   (5) judicial restraint

2. The purpose of the quote is to

   (1) define the role of the Supreme Court
   (2) show that the Supreme Court is the final authority on the Constitution's meaning
   (3) show how arrogant former Chief Justice Hughes was
   (4) both (1) and (2)
   (5) both (2) and (3)

Answers are on page 349.

EXERCISE 6: STATES' VS. INDIVIDUALS' RIGHTS

Throughout the history of the U.S. Supreme Court, the court has had to decide whether or not it should preserve and uphold the federal system (which included supporting the authority of the individual states) or uphold the rights of the individual. Supreme Court justices who lean toward upholding the rights of the states are described as exercising *judicial restraint*.

Directions: For each of these landmark cases, write *I* if it is a victory for the rights of the individual.

_____ 1. the case of *Plessy* v. *Ferguson* (1896), in which the Supreme Court upheld a lower-court decision that ruled that separate but equal facilities for blacks and whites were correct and legal

_____ 2. the case of *Roe* v. *Wade* (1973), in which the court ruled that states could not prohibit abortion under certain conditions during the first six months of pregnancy

_____ 3. the case of *Dred Scott* v. *Sanford* (1857), in which the Supreme Court agreed with a lower court that freeing Dred Scott would be depriving his owner of personal property without due process of law

_____ 4. the case of *Miranda* v. *Arizona* (1966), in which the court ruled that a person accused of a crime must be informed of his or her rights or any resulting confession would be invalid

_____ 5. the case of *Brown* v. *Board of Education* (1954), in which the court ruled that separate facilities for the races were not equal and therefore were unconstitutional

Answers are on page 349.

WRITING ACTIVITY 2

One example of a president's use of implied powers is the replacement of retiring Supreme Court justices with judges sympathetic to the appointing president's political views. For example, Presidents Reagan and Bush, both conservatives, appointed conservative judges to the Supreme Court to fill vacancies. Do you think it is an abuse of presidential authority to appoint only judges who agree with the president's political philosophy? Write two or three paragraphs defending your point of view.

System of Checks and Balances

The framers of the Constitution understood that the powers of the three branches had to be balanced so that no one center of power dominated the other two. To prevent this from happening, the U.S. Constitution allows for certain actions by one branch to restrain the activities of another. One such restraint is the ability of the president to refuse approval of (veto) a bill sent from Congress.

However, Congress could still pass the bill into law by a majority vote of its members. This procedure is called *overriding a veto*. Finally, if the issue is brought to the Supreme Court, the court can still declare the law unconstitutional. This happens if the justices conclude that the law contradicts the principles of the Constitution. The following diagram shows how a bill is enacted into law.

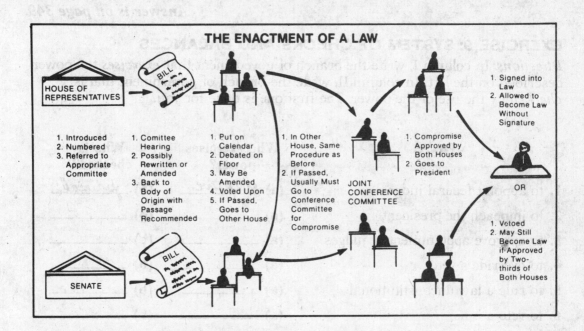

THE ENACTMENT OF A LAW

EXERCISE 7: THE ENACTMENT OF A LAW

Directions: Choose the best answer for the following question.

Which statement is best supported by the preceding chart?

(1) Bills justified by the elastic clause in the Constitution must be introduced directly by the president.

(2) Before being sent to the president, a bill must be approved in identical form by both houses of Congress.

(3) A filibuster on certain bills may not take place in either house.

(4) A bill introduced in the Senate may be changed by the House but not the other way around.

(5) The president must sign all bills for them to become law.

Answer is on page 349.

EXERCISE 8: FILIBUSTER

Directions: Read the passage below and answer the question that follows.

In 1957, Senator Strom Thurmond of South Carolina talked for more than twenty-four hours to delay the vote on the first civil rights law to be proposed since shortly after the Civil War. Thurmond's filibuster did not prevent passage of the bill, and the Civil Rights Act became law that year.

The best explanation of a filibuster is

(1) a twenty-four-hour delay of a vote to give legislators a chance to discuss a bill
(2) an opportunity to propose a bill on a topic that has been long ignored
(3) a monologue aimed at convincing legislators to vote for passage of a bill
(4) political lobbying to get others to vote either for or against a bill
(5) marathon talking for the purpose of preventing passage of a bill into law

Answer is on page 349.

EXERCISE 9: SYSTEM OF CHECKS AND BALANCES

Directions: In column I, write the branch of government that *exercises* the power described on the left. In column II, write the branch of government that is *checked* by the use of the power. The first one is done for you.

Power	I Who exercises power?	II Who is checked?
1. to appoint federal judges	(a) *executive*	(b) *judicial*
2. to impeach the president	(a) _____	(b) _____
3. to approve appointment of judges	(a) _____	(b) _____
4. to override a veto	(a) _____	(b) _____
5. to rule a law unconstitutional	(a) _____	(b) _____
6. to veto a bill	(a) _____	(b) _____

Answers are on page 349.

State and Local Governments

State Government

Article Four of the U.S. Constitution defines the role of the states. The structure of the state government resembles that of the federal government. The executive authority of the state is the governor. Like the president, the governor has veto power.

The legislative branch, which makes the laws, is composed of two houses in all states except Nebraska. Each state has its own court system, which includes trial courts, appellate courts, and a state supreme court. Also, each state has its own written constitution (most of which are based on the U.S. model).

The state constitution outlines the powers and duties of the various state officials and agencies. Like the federal governmental system on which they are based, the fifty states have a system of checks and balances among the three branches of government.

Most criminal codes and civil laws are established by state law. The state also establishes laws for contracts, chartering businesses, and marriage and divorce. Another responsibility of state government is to charter local governments. The powers of municipalities—villages, towns, and cities—are outlined and defined in a charter approved by the state.

EXERCISE 10: POWERS OF STATE GOVERNMENT

Directions: In the spaces provided, write *S* if the power belongs to the states, *F* if it belongs to the federal government, and *B* if it belongs to both.

_____ **1.** vetoing a bill by the chief executive

_____ **2.** passing laws that provide for the welfare of its citizens

_____ **3.** declaring war against a foreign country

_____ **4.** setting import quotas and duties

_____ **5.** establishing a legal age for drinking alcoholic beverages

_____ **6.** setting up guidelines for chartering a business

Answers are on page 349.

Local Government

While the structure and organization of the federal and state governments are similar, local governments can be quite different. Local governments are usually one of three types: mayor-council, council-manager, and commission.

Under the *mayor-council* form of municipal government, the mayor is the executive and is elected by the voters. The council is the legislature; each council member represents a ward or district established by legal boundaries.

Under the *council-manager* form of government, members of the council are elected by the people. The duties of the council are to make policies, set goals, and provide leadership. The council hires a manager to oversee the day-to-day operations of the government and carry out the policies set by the council.

Under the *commission* form of government, commissioners are elected by the people. Their job is to make policies and to run a specific department of the city or county. For example, one commissioner may be in charge of public safety (fire, police, civil defense), while another commissioner may be in charge of public works (water, sewers, roads).

All municipalities receive most of the money to operate from local taxes, fees, and service charges. The following graphs show the sources of income for cities and how they are allocated.

EXERCISE 11: CITY INCOME AND EXPENDITURES

Directions: Read the two graphs and fill in the blanks in the following sentences.

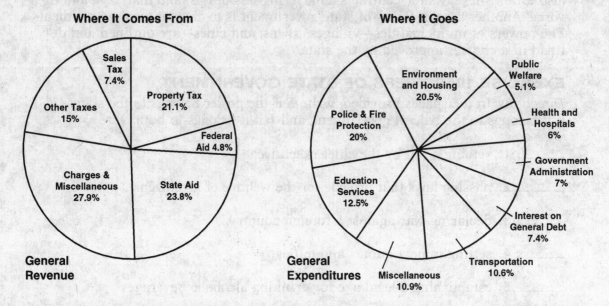

THE CITY DOLLAR
(23 largest cities)

1. The income that a government receives is called _____,

   and the money it spends is called _____.

2. In the graph, the largest source of income for the city is _____.

3. The largest percentage of the city dollar goes to _____.

Answers are on page 349.

EXERCISE 12: CITY BUDGETING

Directions: Choose the best answer for the following question.

If federal aid were cut to 3 percent and state aid remained the same, what options would the city have to make up for the loss in revenue?

(1) borrow money from a more prosperous state
(2) increase revenue by raising local taxes or fees
(3) decrease expenditures by cutting programs
(4) both (1) and (2)
(5) both (2) and (3)

Answer is on page 350.

WRITING ACTIVITY 3

What type of structure does your local government have? Write two to three paragraphs describing your municipal government's structure. State whether or not you think the form is effective and explain why. If you think it is not effective, tell what form you would replace it with.

The U.S. Political System

The voting public has been viewed as holding a range of positions on political issues. These political positions are illustrated as occupying one of five segments of a spectrum. The segments are generally referred to as political labels. To win an election, each political party must obtain the majority of the votes cast. Since most American voters occupy the middle of the spectrum, both political parties must appeal to this group of voters to win.

The following illustration shows the five political positions.

THE POLITICAL CONTINUUM

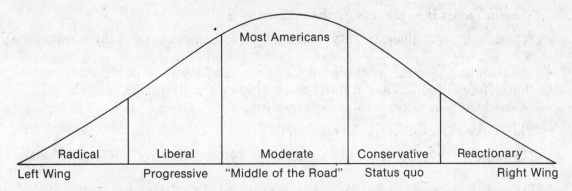

radical: one who advocates sweeping changes in laws and methods of government with little delay

liberal: one who advocates political change in the name of progress, especially social improvement through governmental action

moderate: one who believes in avoiding extreme changes and measures in laws and government

conservative: one who advocates maintaining the existing social order and believes that change, if any, should be gradual

reactionary: one who resists change and usually advocates a return to an earlier social order or policy

EXERCISE 13: THE POLITICAL SPECTRUM

Directions: Read the passage and, using the definitions above, identify the political position of each of the quotes that follow the passage.

> An issue in American life that has generated many positions and has divided the population is bilingualism. Many Americans are concerned that we are quickly becoming a bilingual country—the primary and secondary languages being English and Spanish. Americans have varying opinions about the increasing concessions made to our Spanish-speaking minority.

1. "We might as well accept the fact that Hispanic-Americans are here to stay and are significant contributors to our American way of life. Instead of criticizing them for speaking in their native tongue, the government should improve bilingual programs to make it easier for Hispanics to learn English."

The speaker is best expressing the opinion of a

(1) radical   **(2)** liberal   **(3)** moderate   **(4)** conservative   **(5)** reactionary

2. "Let's not lose our heads. We don't need harsher laws, nor do we need to spend more money. The current strategies to bring Hispanics into the mainstream of American society by helping them to overcome language barriers are sufficient. We just need to work harder at them."

The speaker is best expressing the opinion of a

(1) radical   (2) liberal   (3) moderate   (4) conservative   (5) reactionary

3. "I'm tired of seeing my tax dollars spent to make it easier for people too lazy to learn the language. Every public sign written in Spanish should be taken down—my Italian parents didn't have it that easy back in the thirties. Then these people would have to learn English—they'd have to sink or swim."

The speaker is best expressing the opinion of a

(1) radical   (2) liberal   (3) moderate   (4) conservative   (5) reactionary

4. "English has been the primary language here and always will be. I suggest that before Hispanics are granted citizenship or are given jobs, they should be made to pass a test on standard English."

The speaker is expressing the opinion of a

(1) radical   (2) liberal   (3) moderate   (4) conservative   (5) reactionary

5. "Unless the laws that treat Mexicans as second-class citizens because of their inability to speak the language are changed immediately, starting tomorrow, Mexicans should stop picking lettuce, washing dishes, and sweeping floors—doing the dirty work at low pay that other Americans think they are above doing."

The speaker is expressing the opinion of a

(1) radical   (2) liberal   (3) moderate   (4) conservative   (5) reactionary

Answers are on page 350.

WRITING ACTIVITY 4

Do you consider yourself a radical, liberal, moderate, conservative, or reactionary? Based on the definitions provided, write one or two paragraphs describing your political orientation.

Political Parties

A *political party* is a group whose goal is to influence public policy by getting its candidates elected to office. Although the U.S. Constitution makes no provision for political parties, they serve a useful function in our democracy. Political parties

- define the issues and propose possible solutions for governmental problems

- act as another check in our governmental system of checks and balances by monitoring the policies of the party in power

- enable citizens to become involved in the governmental apparatus

- help to keep the number of candidates running for public office manageable

For over a century, there have been two major political parties in the United States—the Democrats and the Republicans.

The differences between the Democratic and Republican parties tend to center around domestic, economic, and social issues as well as foreign policy. Most fundamentally, however, the two parties differ in their views of the role of government in solving problems.

In general, the Democratic party favors a strong federal government at the expense of the sovereign rights of the states; advocates government regulation of big business; endorses labor unions; and champions the rights of the disadvantaged and minorities.

The Republican party, on the other hand, favors stronger state authority at the expense of the federal government; advocates free enterprise; supports checks on labor unions; and believes in maintaining the status quo (keeping things as they are).

There are exceptions to these generalizations, of course, and in recent years, the distinctions between the two parties are becoming increasingly blurred.

EXERCISE 14: POLITICAL PARTIES

Directions: Write *D* in the space provided if the statement generally applies to the Democratic party's philosophy and *R* if it generally applies to the Republican party's philosophy.

_____ **1.** favors having state and local governments solve their own problems

_____ **2.** supports labor unions and the right of their members to strike

_____ **3.** represents the interests of big business

_____ **4.** advocates spending large amounts of money for welfare and other social services

_____ **5.** more often supports "guns" (defense spending) over "butter" (domestic spending)

Answers are on page 350.

WRITING ACTIVITY 5

Are you a Republican, Democrat, or an independent? Write two or three paragraphs describing your party affiliation or why you have none. List reasons why you are loyal to that party or political orientation.

Pressure Groups

Once public officials are elected, they are under constant pressure exerted by individuals, businesses, governmental agencies, and others who make up their constituency. *Pressure groups* are organized groups not associated with a political party, who actively seek to influence public opinion, policies, and actions. The attempt to influence legislation is called *lobbying*. Lobbyists constantly watch for bills that may affect the group or groups they represent.

For example, when the automobile emission-control law was being proposed, lobbyists for the automobile manufacturers worked hard to ensure that the law would be reasonable, not too costly, and not disruptive to automobile production.

Political Action Committees, known as PACs, seek to influence public officials directly. PACs contribute to legislators' campaign funds in the hope of obtaining favorable votes on legislation important to the committees.

Individuals, too, can influence their elected representatives by signing petitions, embarking on letter-writing campaigns, and staging public demonstrations against unpopular policies. Each of these methods is one more informal check in our governmental system of checks and balances.

WRITING ACTIVITY 6

Do you think special interest groups such as PACs have too much influence on legislators (and, indirectly, on the American political process)? Write two or three paragraphs defending your point of view.

The Electoral Process

Both the Democratic and Republican parties maintain national party headquarters and staffs. Every four years, a national convention is held to nominate a presidential candidate who must have won a majority of delegates in the primaries that precede the nominating convention. A political *primary* enables members of a party to express their preference for a candidate to run in the general election. In most primary elections, the candidate must receive a *plurality* (more votes than any other candidate) to win. Primaries may be open or closed. In an *open primary* voters need not declare their party affiliations. In a *closed primary* voters must declare whether they are Republicans or Democrats.

At the nominating convention, each state sends a designated number of delegates, who are local and state party representatives, to help select the party's nominee. At the end of a week-long forum in which the issues are discussed and speeches are delivered, the delegates vote to choose the party's nominee and to approve the party's platform. The *platform* is a formal declaration of the principles on which the party stands.

After the candidates from each party campaign for office, the general election is held. In the general election, the winner must receive a *majority* of the votes cast.

Once elected, public officials are responsible to a *constituency*—the people who elected them to office. The elected official is obligated to faithfully serve this group of people. For the president of the United States, of course, the constituency is the entire American population.

EXERCISE 15: ELECTING A PRESIDENT

Directions: Match each definition on the right with the correct term on the left.

_____ 1. plurality   **a.** declaration of a party's stand on the issues

_____ 2. primary   **b.** the people a public official represents

_____ 3. platform   **c.** more than half of the votes cast in an election

_____ 4. majority   **d.** party election to select a candidate to run in the general election

_____ 5. constituency   **e.** more votes than any other candidate (but not more than half)

Answers are on page 350.

EXERCISE 16: THE DEMOCRATIC PRIMARY

Directions: Look at the cartoon and answer the questions that follow.

HUGH HAYNIE
Louisville Courier-Journal
©Los Angeles Times Syndicate

"Okay . . . are there any other Democratic presidential candidates who'd like t'be in the group picture?"

1. The cartoon supports the cartoonist's belief that

   (1) in presidential politics, the Democratic party is never to be taken seriously
   (2) anybody can run in the Democratic presidential primary
   (3) in the Democratic party, only familiar figures seek the nomination for the presidency
   (4) Democratic presidential candidates are well known for fighting among themselves
   (5) the Democratic party is seldom united during a presidential campaign

2. Based on the cartoon, the cartoonist would likely agree with which of the following opinions?

   (1) The Democratic party is more "democratic" than the Republican party.
   (2) The Democratic party is more popular than the Republican party.
   (3) The Republican party will win elections more often because it usually unites behind one candidate.
   (4) The Republican party should field as many presidential candidates as the Democratic party.
   (5) It is ridiculous for the Democratic party to allow such a large number of candidates to seek the office of president.

Answers are on page 350.

EXERCISE 17: THE ELECTORAL PROCESS

Directions: Choose the best answer for the following question.

Based on the definition of a closed primary, which of the following practices is generally true in order for the results to be valid?

(1) Republicans and Democrats alike can vote in any primary they choose.
(2) Voters should declare their party affiliations (Republican or Democrat) and vote in the respective primary.
(3) Voters need not declare whether or not they are Republican or Democrat when they vote in a primary.
(4) Voters should bypass the primary and only vote in the general election.
(5) Voters should not be eligible to vote in primaries; primaries are only for party regulars on the local and state levels.

Answer is on page 350.

The Impact of the Media

Another significant force in the modern American political process is the media. Television, radio, newspapers, and magazines are all part of the media. Television by far has the greatest influence on the American voter, as evidenced by the huge sums of campaign money spent on television. Close elections may be won or lost on the basis of a candidate's media campaign.

Some political observers believe that television is undermining the American democratic process since only those who have the money to finance huge publicity campaigns are able to run for office. This makes it nearly impossible for candidates who are not wealthy to run for office.

EXERCISE 18: THE IMPACT OF THE MEDIA

Directions: Read the passage and answer the question that follows.

> Some people say that public opinion polls should not be taken close to an election because the results might influence the voters. For example, during the 1980 election in which President Carter lost to Ronald Reagan, the outcome was predicted by television networks before the polls closed. Informal surveys, *exit polls*, were being conducted outside the voting areas, and vote percentages for each candidate were projected from them.

Which of the following *best* explains how the televised poll results could have affected the election's outcome?

(1) Carter's supporters who had not yet voted did not bother to when they saw the lopsided results.
(2) When it became known that Carter was trailing Reagan, more of Carter's supporters rushed out to vote than would have otherwise.
(3) Backers of Reagan who had not yet voted did not think it necessary to vote since he was far ahead.
(4) Happy about the obvious victory, Reagan supporters came out in even greater numbers to vote.
(5) Voters who were previously undecided finally decided to join the winning team and vote for Reagan.

Answer is on page 350.

4
ECONOMICS—HOW ARE PEOPLE'S NEEDS MET?

"Man does not live by bread alone," it says in Deuteronomy, a book of the Bible. This means that there is more to human survival than meeting the needs of food, shelter, and clothing. However, economists might add, "But man lives by bread first of all." For before humans can satisfy their emotional and spiritual needs, they must first meet the physical needs of survival.

Economists study how a society meets its unlimited material needs with its limited resources. The limitation of resources requires that people make choices about what needs to satisfy.

Societies also must make choices. Every society must answer three basic questions when determining the type of economic system under which it will operate. These questions are:

- *What should be produced?* What do members of a society need and want?

- *How should it be produced?* Should each person make his or her own goods, or should businesses or government manufacture them for the entire society?

- *How should the product be distributed?* Should the products be given to everyone equally or only to those who can afford to buy them?

To answer these questions, each government must first identify its goals and values and then determine what resources are available to produce what the society needs.

Factors of Production

Economists have identified three vital factors of production: natural resources, capital, and labor.

Natural resources are the raw materials needed to produce goods. Trees must be available for the production of wood and paper products. Automobiles can be built only if ore can be mined to make the necessary steel.

Each society lacks some resources and, therefore, cannot produce certain goods. For example, the Dani tribe of New Guinea lives in a tropical climate on a remote mountain range. Their huts, weapons, and tools are built of wood because that is what natural resource is available. Nothing is made of metal because ore is not one of their natural resources.

A second factor of production is capital. *Capital*, as it is referred to here, is any equipment, factories, or machines that are used to produce other goods or to provide services. Capital also may be defined as money invested in an enterprise. A sewing machine used in the manufacture of dresses or shirts is an example of capital, as is an entire lumber mill that covers a square mile of land.

The third factor of production is labor. *Labor* is made up of the people who do the work. They run the assembly lines, plant the crops, build the buildings, drive the trucks, and sell the merchandise. For example, the seamstresses who cut and sew the patterns to make the dresses and shirts are considered to be labor.

History has shown that no matter how carefully and efficiently an economy manages the factors of production, they remain scarce as compared to the ever-increasing demands society makes upon them.

EXERCISE 1: FACTORS OF PRODUCTION

Directions: In each example, write *N* if the factor of production refers to natural resources, *C* if it refers to capital, and *L* if it refers to labor.

_____ **1.** the seals, Arctic foxes, and walruses hunted by the Eskimos

_____ **2.** the tools a plumber uses in practicing the trade

_____ **3.** diamonds unearthed from the mines of South Africa

_____ **4.** farmers who plant the spring corn crop

_____ **5.** conveyor belts used in the packing houses to carry meat

Answers are on page 350.

WRITING ACTIVITY 1

Multinational corporations are corporations that cross national boundaries in their manufacturing and sales operations. In recent years, large American corporations have established operations in areas of the world where production costs and labor are cheaper than in the United States. Do you agree or disagree with this business practice? Whom do you think this affects? Does it affect them positively or negatively? Defend your point of view in two or three paragraphs.

Economics and Government

A nation's system of government often determines the type of economic system under which the nation will operate. For example, the U.S. system of government is founded on the principle of individual freedom. This belief in the importance of individual freedom contributed greatly to the establishment of capitalism as the economic form under which the American economy operates.

Capitalism

Capitalism is an economic system based on the private ownership of the resources of production. Investment decisions are made by the individual or corporation rather than by the government. The production, distribution, and prices of goods and services are determined by competition in a free market. The government intervenes only when necessary to protect the public interest.

Other governments place the importance of the collective (all the people) above the individual. This emphasis on the collective permitted the emergence of economic systems that are alternatives to capitalism. Two such types are socialism and communism.

Socialism

Under *socialism*, the most important industries and services are publicly and cooperatively owned. These industries, which may be steel production, banking and finance, public transportation, or health are controlled with the goal of providing equal opportunity for all.

In socialist economies, ownership of private property is permitted; however, owners of businesses together with the government decide what goods and services are produced, how they are produced, and who should get them. The economy of Sweden is a socialist economy.

Communism

A third economic order does not permit private ownership of property and the means of production at all. Under *communism*, the government, described as the community, owns the property and distributes the society's goods in accordance with the "common good." The government decides what goods and services are produced and who should get them. The economies of the People's Republic of China and Cuba operate under the principles of communism, as did the economy of the former Soviet Union.

None of these three economic systems exists in pure form. That is, no *completely* capitalist, socialist, or communist economy exists in the modern world. In its operation, each of the economic systems incorporates some aspect of another.

The term *mixed economy* is used to describe the U.S. economy, since some government regulation of private enterprise exists. For example, the Food and Drug Administration ensures that any new medicine or drug that is marketed in the United States has been properly tested before it is sold to the public.

EXERCISE 2: ECONOMIC SYSTEMS

Directions: Choose the best answer to complete each of the following statements.

1. The quote "From each according to his ability, to each according to his need" best describes the economic system of

   (a) capitalism
   (b) socialism
   (c) mixed economy

2. The quote "In the area of economics, the government that governs least governs best" best describes the economic system of

   (a) capitalism
   (b) socialism
   (c) communism

Answers are on page 350.

EXERCISE 3: ECONOMIC SYSTEMS AND GOVERNMENTS

Directions: The diagram below shows the continuum of economic systems. Look at the diagram and answer the questions that follow it.

THE CONTINUUM OF ECONOMIC SYSTEMS

MARKET   Capitalism   Socialism   Communism   COMMAND

1. According to the continuum of economic systems, which of the following conclusions may be drawn?

    (1) Communism is the best example of the market system.
    (2) Capitalism is the best example of the command system.
    (3) Socialism is the opposite of capitalism.
    (4) Capitalism is the opposite of communism.
    (5) Capitalism is better than any other system represented.

2. Which of the following situations *best* supports the statement "Each of the economic systems incorporates some aspect of the other"?

    (1) In socialist Sweden, SAAB, the automobile manufacturer, is owned and run by the government.
    (2) In Cuba, the government-controlled media schedules the broadcasting for all television and radio programs.
    (3) In the United States, a dairy manufacturer is told by a government agency what percentages of milk and cream a product sold as ice cream must contain.
    (4) In the People's Republic of China, all of the nation's farms are nationalized, and young people are forced to work them.
    (5) In the United States, major air carriers engage in a "price war" to attract passengers during the peak vacation season.

Answers are on page 351.

WRITING ACTIVITY 2

Great Britain has a national health-care system in which the costs for medical treatment are paid for by the government. In the United States, national health-care insurance has become an issue of heated political debate. Do you support such a program or not? Write an essay of two or three paragraphs defending your position for or against national health insurance paid by the government.

Supply and Demand

The foundation of American capitalism is supply and demand. *Supply* is the quantity of goods and services available for sale at all possible prices. *Demand* is the desire to buy the product or service and the ability to pay for it.

Producers or suppliers are in business to make a profit. Therefore, they supply goods and services at a price. They must charge prices high enough to cover their costs for production and earn a profit for themselves. Consumers who are willing and able to buy these goods and services create a demand.

The amount of production (supply) of an item and its price depend on the cost of production and the demand in the marketplace. In general, producers seek the highest possible prices to maximize their profits. Consumers seek the lowest possible prices to keep money in their pockets. These opposing goals of producers and consumers significantly affect prices in the marketplace.

Price and Supply—The Producer's View

In general, the higher the price, the greater the number of companies that supply a product or service. A high-priced item or service that yields a large profit will attract many producers who will compete with one another for a share of the market. This applies chiefly to manufactured goods and to services. Precious minerals and metals such as diamonds and gold command higher prices than more common minerals and metals because they are scarce and more cannot be made.

A good example of the relationship between price and supply is the running shoes phenomenon. When they were introduced to the buying public, running shoes bearing the trademarks of such companies as Nike and Reebok created great demand. Consumers—adults and teens—paid higher prices for the labels than they ordinarily might have for other brands. As a result, several competitors entered the market (increasing the supply) seeking to make money on the product. Each running shoe manufacturer fought to capture a share of the market.

When too many producers compete in the marketplace, however, supply exceeds demand because buyers cannot or will not buy all of the goods offered for sale. As a result, a surplus occurs and prices fall. Producers no longer reap the profits necessary for them to compete successfully. Some businesses streamline their operations, and others are forced out of business.

Price and Supply—The Consumer's View

From the consumer's viewpoint, the higher the price, the lower the demand; the lower the price, the greater the demand. If prices for running shoes became too high, consumers might stop buying them and revert to wearing offbrands. On the other hand, when prices for an item fall too low and consumer demand exceeds the producer's ability to provide the product, a shortage in supply occurs. As a result, prices rise higher, and in extreme cases, the product is rationed. Under rationing, the quantity of the item sold is restricted.

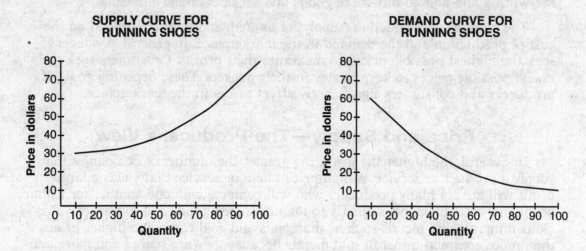

As shown in the graph on the left, as the price of running shoes goes up, the quantity supplied increases. In this graph, producers cannot supply running shoes at a price of $20. However, as the price increases to $30, about ten pairs of running shoes are available for purchase. According to this graph, what would happen to the supply if the price were $60?

You're right if you said that there would be about 80 pairs of running shoes available for purchase.

As shown in the graph on the right, as the price of running shoes goes down, the quantity demanded rises. At $60 each, the demand would be for ten pairs. If the price were lowered to $30, the demand would increase to about 45 pairs. According to this graph, if the price rose to $70 per pair, would demand increase or decrease?

Since the graph shows no values for $70 per pair, you can infer that there is no demand for running shoes at this price.

EXERCISE 4: SUPPLY AND DEMAND IN THE U.S. ECONOMY

Directions: Study the cartoon and answer the following questions.

1. One proposal to cover the costs of President Clinton's health-care package was to impose "sin taxes" and value-added taxes on tobacco and alcohol. Which of the following does the cartoonist suggest might result from these taxes?

    (1) high prices the consumer could not afford to pay
    (2) a greater demand for both tobacco and alcohol
    (3) a lower demand for health-care services
    (4) an increased demand for bartenders who can handle large amounts of money
    (5) a reduction in the number of people who can afford to pay their taxes

2. The cartoonist would most likely agree with which of the following statements?

    (1) Added taxes on alcohol and tobacco would be a fair way to raise money.
    (2) Excessive taxation is creating a nation of alcoholics.
    (3) Americans already feel the burden of paying high taxes.
    (4) Alcohol already costs too much.
    (5) Smoking should be banned in bars.

Answers are on page 351.

Supply and Equilibrium

To produce exactly the amount that consumers are willing to buy, producers must determine at what point supply equals demand. Economists call this point the **equilibrium**. Equilibrium occurs when the supply and demand curves intersect. This establishes the market price for a product or service.

When the price is greater than the equilibrium, demand falls and there is more of a product or service than people want to buy. This is called a **surplus**. When the price falls below the equilibrium, demand increases, exceeding supply, and a **shortage** in the product or service occurs.

The following graph illustrates the equilibrium.

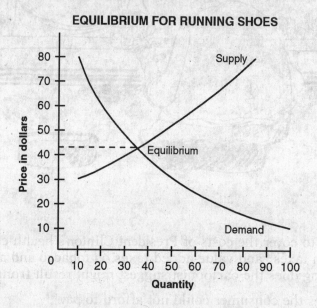

EQUILIBRIUM FOR RUNNING SHOES

What is the price at which the supply of running shoes equals demand? The equilibrium point on the graph indicates that this is about $42.

EXERCISE 5: SUPPLY, DEMAND, AND EQUILIBRIUM

Directions: Study the graph and answer the following questions or statements.

1. According to the graph, the market price of these video-cassette recorders would be about

   (1) $500
   (2) $400
   (3) $300
   (4) $200
   (5) $100

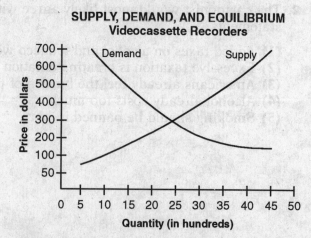

SUPPLY, DEMAND, AND EQUILIBRIUM
Videocassette Recorders

2. If the market price for videocassette recorders fell to $150, what would be the likely result?

(1) Demand would decrease.
(2) Supply would remain the same.
(3) Demand would increase.
(4) Producers would not be able to satisfy demand.
(5) The supply would become scarce.

3. In recent years, Korea has developed the technology to manufacture and import to the United States electronic equipment such as videocassette recorders. If demand for VCRs were low, what impact would Korea's entrance into the market have on the sale of VCRs in the United States?

(1) Prices for VCRs would increase because the supply would be greater.
(2) Prices for VCRs would decrease because the supply would be greater.
(3) A surplus of VCRs might result.
(4) Both 1 and 2
(5) Both 2 and 3

Answers are on page 351.

Economic Growth

Economic growth is a major goal of an economic system. In a growing economy, there is an increasing capacity to produce more goods and services. During periods of great economic growth, consumers are increasingly able to buy these goods and services. An economy's growth must occur at a steady and controllable pace.

This process may be likened to blowing up a balloon. If a balloon is inflated too quickly, it may burst; if it is inflated too slowly, it may never reach its full capacity. Similarly, the American economy must grow evenly, or problems will occur. The following diagram illustrates what economists call the **business cycle**.

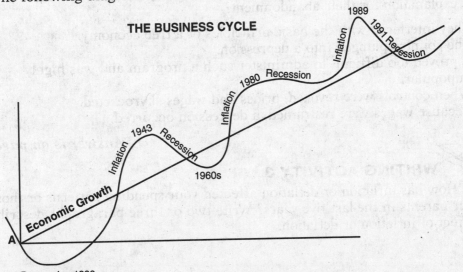

THE BUSINESS CYCLE

Line A is the goal of economic growth—what economists believe is a healthy level of producing goods and services. Comparing the blowing up of a balloon with the growth of the economy, the line represents the level at which air should be blown into the balloon. If too much air is blown into the balloon, it becomes overinflated. When not enough air is in the balloon, it is underinflated or deflated.

Inflation and Its Effects

When too much money and credit are available and too few goods are available to satisfy demand, the dollar loses its value and the prices of goods increase. The country begins a period of inflation. (Notice the upward slope of the line.)

For consumers to be able to keep pace with the rise in the cost of goods, their wages must increase. For producers to pay the increased wages, they must produce more goods and charge higher prices for them. This chainlike pattern in which wage increases feed on price increases is called an *inflationary spiral*. An "inflation psychology" sets in as consumers rush to make major purchases because they believe that prices will only increase.

For inflation to fall, demand must be decreased and credit restricted. However, one result of curbing high inflation is an economic recession. The United States experienced just this situation in the early 1980s when inflation raged out of control and the Federal Reserve System acted to control it.

Deflation and Its Effects

When too little money and credit are available, and more goods are available than necessary to satisfy demand, the dollar gains value and the prices of goods decrease. Under these circumstances, the economy enters a period of deflation. Because goods remain unsold, producers' profits fall. Falling profits lead to layoffs. Unless the situation is corrected, a recession occurs, and if the recession is prolonged, a depression can result. The United States experienced this condition during the Great Depression of the 1930s.

EXERCISE 6: ECONOMIC GROWTH

Directions: Choose the best answer for the following question.

During a period of severe inflation in 1973–1974, the Nixon administration implemented wage and price controls for a brief period. The controls were soon revoked, however, and did not break the inflationary spiral. Which is the most likely explanation for their abandonment?

(1) They interfered with the basic principles of a free economy.
(2) The country plunged into a depression.
(3) It proved too difficult to administer such a program and was highly unpopular.
(4) When controls were revoked, prices and wages skyrocketed.
(5) Because wages were restrained, a depression occurred.

Answer is on page 351.

WRITING ACTIVITY 3

How has inflation or deflation affected your spending patterns or those of your parents in the last five years? Write two or three paragraphs describing the effect of inflation or deflation.

Measurement of Economic Growth

Economic indicators are statistics that show economic experts how the economy is performing. Among the more commonly used economic statistics are stock market trading, unemployment percentages, number of housing starts, and the gross national product (GNP).

One of the most important measurements of economic growth, the *GNP* represents the total amount of all goods and services produced in one year.

Economists measure GNP in current dollars and again in constant dollars. *Current* dollars indicate the actual dollar value of goods. *Constant* dollars take into account the change in prices over the years because of inflation. In measuring the nation's GNP, economists measure current dollars against constant dollars during a given year. In recent years, economists have used 1987 as the base year with which to compare current GNP dollars. The following graph measures the GNP from 1977 to 1991.

EXERCISE 7: THE GNP AS A MEASURE OF ECONOMIC GROWTH

Directions: Study the graph and choose the *best* answer to complete each statement.

1. According to the graph, the constant-dollar GNP grew between the years

   (1) 1978 and 1980
   (2) 1980 and 1982
   (3) 1982 and 1989
   (4) 1988 and 1991
   (5) 1990 and 1991

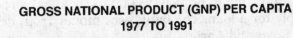

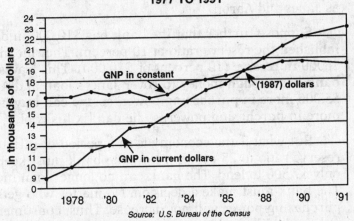

GROSS NATIONAL PRODUCT (GNP) PER CAPITA 1977 TO 1991

Source: U.S. Bureau of the Census

2. The steep increase in the line that indicates GNP in current dollars may be attributed to

   (1) deflation
   (2) a recession
   (3) inflation
   (4) a depression
   (5) a booming economy

3. The GNP in constant dollars fell during the years 1979–1980, 1981–1982, and 1990–1991. These periods may best be described as

   (1) depressions
   (2) recessions
   (3) deflations
   (4) inflations
   (5) economic booms

Answers are on page 351.

Money and Monetary Policy

Money is the medium of exchange accepted by a society in payment for goods and services. The nation's money supply consists mainly of coins, bills, and checking and savings deposits.

The U.S. Federal Reserve Board is responsible for setting the nation's *monetary policy*—the regulation of the nation's supply of money and credit in order to keep the economy in balance. Through the nation's banking system, the Federal Reserve Board controls the availability of credit to consumers primarily in two ways—by determining the reserve ratio and by setting the discount rate.

The Reserve Ratio

Every lending institution—banks and savings and loan associations—must hold on to a certain amount of its deposits. This amount that cannot be lent out is called the *reserve ratio*. Most banks are members of the nation's Federal Reserve System (the Fed). By controlling the reserve ratio, the Fed determines the amount of money banks are able to lend.

Suppose, for example, Janet wants to borrow $5,000 to buy a new car, and Aaron wants to borrow $3,000 to fix a leaky roof. They go to the same bank and apply for a loan. The bank uses money from depositors to lend to customers such as Janet and Aaron.

Suppose further that the bank has $10,000 in deposits and the Fed has established the reserve ratio at 10 percent. That means that the bank must keep $1,000 in reserve (10 percent of $10,000). This leaves the bank $9,000 to lend. The bank has enough money to cover Janet's loan and Aaron's loan. Janet now has $5,000 more in purchasing power, so she can buy her car. Aaron now has $3,000 more in purchasing power, so he can fix his roof.

But what if the economy is in a period of inflation? The Fed might raise the reserve ratio to 25 percent. Now the bank must keep on deposit $2,500, leaving only $7,500 to lend. The bank can no longer loan money to both Janet and Aaron. The bank must make a decision. No matter who gets the loan, the other person's purchasing power will not increase. Thus, consumers' demand has been lowered indirectly. When this process is implemented nationwide, the impact on the economy is significant, chiefly because less money is available to lend.

The Discount Rate

A second way in which the Fed influences the nation's economy is through the discount rate. The *discount rate* is the rate of interest the Fed charges member banks to borrow money.

Banks make money by charging a higher interest rate on loans than they pay to those who deposit money into checking and savings accounts. Suppose, for example, that Jake deposits $100 in the bank at a 6 percent interest rate. If he leaves the funds on deposit for one year, he can collect $106 from the bank. This includes his $100 deposit plus the $6 in interest the bank owes him. During this time, however, the bank lends $100 to Samantha for a year. The bank charges her 15 percent interest. After one year, Samantha owes the bank $115. The bank then gives Jake his $106. The profit to the bank is $9. Obviously, the more money a bank has to lend, the more profit it can make.

To have more money to meet demand, banks often borrow from the Federal Reserve System. The bank then lends the money to its customers (borrowers) at a higher rate.

The Fed adjusts the discount rate to affect the supply of money. For example, if the discount rate is 5 percent, consumer banks might lend it out for 10 percent. If the discount rate were raised to 15 percent, consumer banks might charge 20 percent. Thus, you can see the impact a changing discount rate has on the availability of credit in the U.S. economy.

EXERCISE 8: MONEY AND MONETARY POLICY

Directions: Circle *T* if the statement is true or *F* if it is false.

T F **1.** The role of the Fed is to serve as a clearinghouse for all banks in one region.

T F **2.** Two ways in which the Federal Reserve influences the money supply are coining money and setting the prime rate.

T F **3.** Purchasing power is increased through the banking system by banks lending funds from deposited money after first setting aside required reserves.

T F **4.** Most banks belong to the Federal Reserve System.

T F **5.** The prime rate is the interest rate the Fed charges member banks to borrow money.

Answers are on page 351.

Government and Fiscal Policy

While the U.S. Federal Reserve Board directly influences the supply of money and credit in the economy, the government, through its fiscal policy, also indirectly affects the nation's economic condition.

In establishing *fiscal policy*, the president proposes an annual budget to the Congress. As Congress determines what programs are needed, it must also consider how these programs will be funded. Raising taxes is the simplest and most common answer.

Consumers and businesses pay these taxes to the government. The government, in turn, spends the money on programs designed to help the citizens and the country, such as interstate highways, the space program, and the military.

By deciding whether to raise or lower taxes and whether to increase or decrease spending, the government is controlling a major part of the money supply. For example, during inflationary times, the government might exercise fiscal policy by taking money out of the pockets of consumers by increasing taxes. During periods of deflation, the government might put more money in the hands of consumers by cutting spending and lowering taxes.

If the government spends less than it collects in taxes, a *budget surplus* results. If the government spends more than it collects, the condition is called *deficit spending*. A *balanced budget* results when the income from taxes equals the money spent on programs.

EXERCISE 9: FISCAL AND MONETARY POLICY

Directions: Circle the correct answer choice in parentheses.

1. During a recession, to put more money in circulation, the president and Congress should (increase/decrease) government spending while (raising/lowering) taxes.

2. During an inflationary period, the Fed should (increase/decrease) the money in circulation by (raising/lowering) the discount rate while (increasing/decreasing) the reserve ratio.

3. When the government spends more money than it receives in taxes, there is a (budget surplus/budget deficit).

Answers are on page 351.

5
GEOGRAPHY—WHERE DO PEOPLE LIVE?

Like the lower animals, humans are first, last, and always creatures of the land. However, humans differ from the lower animals in their ability to adapt to a variety of environments. This adaptability explains why there is no part of the globe that has not been visited by people and few regions where humans do not live.

Geographers study the physical features of the earth and the ways in which humans have adapted to these features.

In their investigation of the surfaces and regions of the earth, geographers rely on two basic tools. A *globe* is a spherical representation of the earth that shows the continents, countries, and waterways in their true proportions. Globes are not easily portable, however, so mapmakers draw *maps*, which are flat representations of the earth's regions.

Geographers generally use five kinds of maps:

topographical maps—show physical land features (hills, mountains, plains) of an area

population maps—illustrate the distribution of people throughout the world

world maps—illustrate the continents, oceans, seas, and rivers of the world

political maps—outline borders between countries or states and show trade relationships among countries

weather maps—show current or forecasted weather as well as the climate of a particular region

EXERCISE 1: MAPS

Directions: Complete the following statements about the five types of maps.

1. The regions of Asia that receive more than seventy-five inches of rain per year would be best illustrated on a

    (1) topographical map
    (2) population map
    (3) world map
    (4) political map
    (5) weather map

2. The best map for showing the borders of the fifty states in the United States would be a

    (1) topographical map
    (2) population map
    (3) world map
    (4) political map
    (5) weather map

3. A map that would show the highest elevation of the Wasatch Mountain Range in Utah would be a

    (1) topographical map
    (2) population map
    (3) world map
    (4) political map
    (5) weather map

Answers are on page 351.

Symbols and Legends

So that you can read a map, mapmakers provide symbols and a legend or key that tells what the symbols stand for.

For example, on a political map, a star usually indicates a state's or nation's capital. On a population map, the number of people who live in a given city is indicated by the size of the dot that locates the city. (Larger dots indicate cities with large populations; small dots indicate cities with small populations.)

On road maps, a scale of miles is often provided in the legend. A scale of miles is most commonly shown in inches. For example, the legend on a map scale might read "One inch equals 50 miles." An example of a scale is shown below.

You can measure distance with a ruler or with a strip of paper that has a straight edge. Lay a strip of paper against the map to make a straight line between the two points you are interested in. Mark off the two points on the paper's edge, and lay the paper strip against the scale of miles. The distance between the two points will be the number of miles from one place to another.

EXERCISE 2: MEASURING DISTANCE

Directions: Study the map and answer the questions that follow.

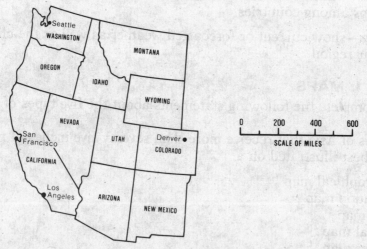

1. According to the map shown here, approximately how far is Denver from San Francisco? _____

2. Approximately how long is the state of Wyoming from north to south? _____

3. Approximately how far is the west coast of California from the easternmost boundary of Colorado? _____

Answers are on page 352.

Latitude and Longitude

The *equator*, an imaginary line that circles the earth's center, divides the earth into two *hemispheres*, or halves. The land and water above the equator lie in the Northern Hemisphere; the land and water below the equator are known as the Southern Hemisphere. North America, Central America, and a small part of South America lie in the Northern Hemisphere.

The distance from the equator is measured on maps and globes by degrees of latitude. Lines of *latitude* are parallel lines that measure distance north or south of the equator in degrees. These lines increase in 20-degree increments. The equator is located at 0 degrees latitude, the North Pole at 90 degrees north latitude, and the South Pole at 90 degrees south latitude. Most of the continental United States lies between 25 and 50 degrees north latitude.

Lines of *longitude* are lines that measure distances in degrees east and west of the *prime meridian*, an imaginary line running through Greenwich, England, that divides the world into the Eastern and Western Hemispheres. The prime meridian is located at 0 degrees longitude. There are 180 degrees east of the prime meridian and 180 degrees west of it, for a total of 360 degrees around the earth. Most of the United States, including Alaska and Hawaii, lies between 65 and 125 degrees west longitude.

The lines of latitude and longitude cross each other to form what is called a *grid*. To locate a particular place on a globe or map, you must find the point where two lines intersect. The number of degrees latitude and longitude indicate the location. For example, in the grid diagram below, the island of Madagascar, located off the southeast coast of Africa, is located at approximately 20 degrees south latitude and 45 degrees east longitude.

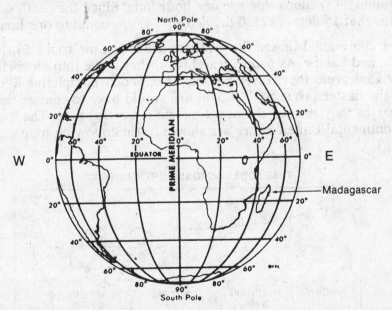

Based on the grid, what continent is found at 50 degrees north latitude and 0 degrees longitude?

You should have answered *Europe*. The point where the 50-degree-north line of latitude meets the 0-degree line of longitude is the continent of Europe; Europe is located directly north of Africa.

EXERCISE 3: THE LATITUDE AND LONGITUDE GRID

Directions: Choose the best answer for each of the following questions, which are based on the grid on page 335.

1. Which of the following is at 15 degrees north latitude and 20 degrees east longitude?

   (1) northern Europe
   (2) eastern South America
   (3) western Africa
   (4) southern Asia
   (5) central Africa

2. Which of the following countries is located nearest 30 degrees south latitude and 20 degrees east longitude?

   (1) Italy
   (2) Chile
   (3) Egypt
   (4) South Africa
   (5) England

Answers are on page 352.

Time Zones

A *time zone* is a geographical region within which the same standard time is used. To establish time zones for the entire world, geographers have divided the earth into 24 sections that are one hour long. Since the earth is 360 degrees, this means that 15 degrees (360 divided by 24) are equal to one hour of a day.

In the continental United States, there are four time zones: Eastern, Central, Mountain, and Pacific. As people travel west, they move into an earlier time zone for every 15 degrees they travel. For example, people completing a journey west through the Eastern time zone at 5:00 P.M. would have to change their watches to 4:00 P.M. as they entered the next time zone, Central time. The four time zones for the continental United States are shown in the following map.

TIME ZONES ACROSS NORTH AMERICA

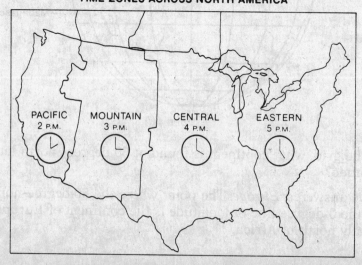

EXERCISE 4: TIME ZONES

Directions: Choose the best answer for each question.

1. According to the map, what time is it in Los Angeles when it is midnight in Philadelphia, Pennsylvania?

   (1) 9:00 A.M.
   (2) 9:00 P.M.
   (3) 3:00 P.M.
   (4) 3:00 A.M.
   (5) 2:00 A.M.

2. What time is it in Denver when it is noon in Milwaukee?

   (1) 10:00 A.M.
   (2) 12:00 P.M.
   (3) 11:00 A.M.
   (4) 1:00 P.M.
   (5) 9:00 A.M.

3. The lines marking the four time zones are irregular. All of Indiana except a tiny section of northwest Indiana lies in the Eastern time zone. Which of the following is the most reasonable explanation for why northwest Indiana lies in the Central time zone?

   (1) The people in northwest Indiana voted to be included in the Central time zone.
   (2) The time zones must be evenly divided; in order to obtain an even division of time zones in the United States, part of Indiana was placed in the Central time zone.
   (3) Western Kentucky and western Tennessee, the states south of Indiana, are located in the Central time zone; therefore, northwest Indiana had to comply with the rule.
   (4) Northwest Indiana was once a part of northeast Illinois, which is why the region has a different time zone from the rest of the state.
   (5) Northwest Indiana is considered to be part of Chicago's metropolitan area; therefore, for economic reasons it lies in the same time zone as Chicago.

4. Which group would likely benefit the most from northwest Indiana's falling within the Central time zone?

   (1) people who travel to and from Chicago frequently
   (2) northwest Indiana's schoolchildren
   (3) merchants and businesspeople in northwest Indiana
   (4) both 1 and 3
   (5) both 2 and 3

Answers are on page 352.

Earth's Topography

The physical features of the earth also can affect a region's climate. In general, geographers divide the earth into flatlands (plains) and highlands (mountains, hills, and plateaus).

Plains typically are areas with little or no land elevation and few trees. *Hills* are elevations of less than 1,000 feet that have sides sloping up to flat or rounded tops. *Plateaus* are lower than hills, rise sharply above the level of the neighboring areas, and have elevations lower than 500 feet and broad, flat tops. *Mountains* are elevations of over 1,000 feet, usually with steep, rocky inclines on all sides and pointed or rounded tops.

Plains regions have a uniform climate characterized by hot, dry weather during the summer and very cold temperatures during the winter. Because plains are frequently treeless, there are no barriers against the cold air that sweeps across them during the winter. Hills and plateaus generally share the same climate characteristics of the plains near which they are located. Mountains often act as boundaries between different climate regions. The lower slopes of the mountains usually share the climate of the surrounding area, but the higher up one goes, the colder the air gets. Also, mountains are often snowcapped because the colder air above them is unable to hold moisture. It falls to the earth as snow.

Mapmakers illustrate the varying heights and shapes of land masses by using *contour lines*, lines that show elevations in numbers of feet or meters. The closer together the contour lines, the steeper the incline. The base line for determining the height of highlands is *sea level*. An example of a contour map follows.

CONTOUR MAP

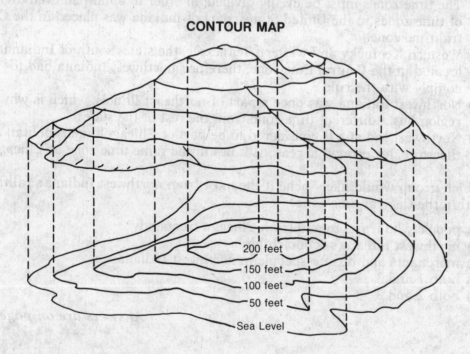

200 feet
150 feet
100 feet
50 feet
Sea Level

What would this land form be classified as—a hill, plain, mountain, or plateau?

___

Because the land mass is lower than 1,000 feet and has a rounded top, it would be classified as a *hill*.

EXERCISE 5: U.S. TOPOGRAPHY

Directions: Choose the best answer for the statement and questions below.

1. Based on the information in the passage, it is reasonable to conclude that during the winter it is likely to be colder in

   (1) Wisconsin than in Minnesota
   (2) Nebraska than in New Jersey
   (3) Florida than in California
   (4) Washington than in Oregon
   (5) New York than in Connecticut

2. Based on its location, which of the following cities in the United States is at the highest altitude?

   (1) Detroit
   (2) Boston
   (3) Denver
   (4) Los Angeles
   (5) Memphis

3. Low-lying land is often subject to flooding because the area has no elevation. Land that lies below sea level acts as a bowl that collects water. As a result, an effective pumping system is needed to handle flooding. Which of the following cities best meets this description?

   (1) Las Vegas
   (2) New York City
   (3) New Orleans
   (4) Atlanta
   (5) Phoenix

Answers are on page 352.

EXERCISE 6: THE INDIAN PENINSULA

Directions: Study the map and answer the questions that follow.

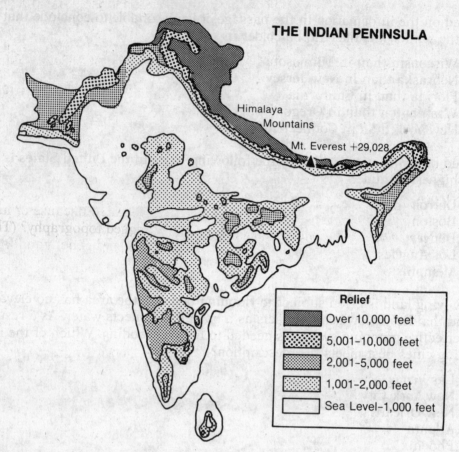

THE INDIAN PENINSULA

Himalaya Mountains

Mt. Everest +29,028

Relief

■	Over 10,000 feet
▦	5,001–10,000 feet
▦	2,001–5,000 feet
▦	1,001–2,000 feet
□	Sea Level–1,000 feet

1. What is the highest point in the Himalaya Mountains?

   (1) 6,000 feet
   (2) 10,300 feet
   (3) 19,861 feet
   (4) 29,028 feet
   (5) 33,411 feet

2. The majority of the land shown on the map may be generally described as being at an elevation of

   (1) over 10,000 feet
   (2) between 5,000 and 10,000 feet
   (3) between 2,000 and 5,000 feet
   (4) between 1,000 and 2,000 feet
   (5) between sea level and 1,000 feet

Answers are on page 352.

WRITING ACTIVITY 1

   In one or two paragraphs, describe the topography of the area in which you live. Do you live near mountains, hills, plains, or plateaus? Describe how the topography of your region affects the climate.

Population Distribution

Population demographics is the study of numbers and locations of people in a region. Climate and topography are two factors that affect where people live in the world.

Most of the world's population lives in the temperate zones because humans cannot survive very long in regions with extreme cold or intense heat. Also, regions with plains allow for a greater and more even distribution of population than regions that are mountainous. In mountainous regions, people tend to inhabit the land at the foot of the mountains or in the valleys.

EXERCISE 7: POPULATION DISTRIBUTION

Directions: Choose the best answer for each question below.

1. Which of the following western states is sparsely populated because of its extremes in temperature and altitudes as well as its rugged topography? (This state also has to import much of its food because the land is not good for farming.)

    (1) California
    (2) Washington
    (3) Oregon
    (4) Nevada
    (5) Colorado

2. Of the following states, which would most likely have the *least* even distribution of population because of its land features?

    (1) Georgia
    (2) New Jersey
    (3) Kansas
    (4) West Virginia
    (5) Michigan

Answers are on page 352.

Other Factors Affecting Population Distribution

Other factors can affect the population of an area. For instance, the location of jobs is one such factor. In the early history of the United States, agricultural areas were the major population centers because most of the jobs were in farming. With the beginning of the Industrial Revolution, the situation reversed, and cities, where the factories were, replaced rural areas as the nation's centers of population.

Another factor is the overall quality of life that a region provides. In the 1950s, for example, suburbs displaced big cities as the most popular places to live. The relative safety of the suburbs, their cleanliness, their better schools, and their wide-open spaces are all benefits that have attracted people and jobs away from the cities. While the population shift to the suburbs has provided Americans with an alternative lifestyle to city living, there have been problems.

Discrimination in the establishment of many suburbs has resulted in all-white or nearly all-white towns circling large minority-dominated cities. This pattern has been lamented often by social observers like writer Vance Packard. In his book *A Nation of Strangers*, Packard criticizes the uniformity of classes and colors that is characteristic of the suburbs.

EXERCISE 8: OTHER FACTORS AFFECTING POPULATION DISTRIBUTION

Directions: Read the following quote from Packard's book and choose the best answer for each question.

> Some social stratification (by income and ethnic background) is probably inevitable in any complex society. But we miss much of life's richness if we fail to take affirmative action against the current trend among developers to lay us all out with "our own kind" of people.

1. Which of the following statements supports the opinion expressed by Vance Packard?

   (1) The advantages of suburban living far outweigh the disadvantages.
   (2) Wealthy communities are safe because they can afford to pay for high levels of police protection, unlike big, poor cities.
   (3) Housing patterns based on income, class, and ethnic background are inevitable.
   (4) Children exposed to only one kind of people grow up crippled in their understanding of the world.
   (5) Big cities are to blame for driving white residents out, forcing them to live in the suburbs.

2. Vance Packard's argument could be used to support which of the following measures?

   (1) restrictive covenants—clauses in property deeds that keep certain people from buying homes in a community
   (2) separate suburbs established for specific ethnic and minority groups
   (3) the rehabilitation of the housing stock in the central areas of big cities
   (4) the practice of busing minority children from the big cities to the suburbs that have the best schools
   (5) the enforcement of fair-housing laws allowing for more ethnically diverse communities

Answers are on page 352.

TEST 2: SOCIAL STUDIES ANSWER KEY

CHAPTER 1: BEHAVIORAL SCIENCES

Exercise 1: Physical and Cultural Anthropology
page 248
Application

1. **P** Fossils or bones represent the physical aspect of human beings.

2. **C** Tools represent technology, a cultural aspect of human beings.

3. **C** Hieroglyphics (writings) on walls represent the cultural aspect.

4. **C** Eating habits represent the cultural aspect.

5. **C** Rites of manhood represent the cultural aspect.

Exercise 2: Ethnocentrism
pages 249–250
Analysis

Exact wording of responses may vary.

1. The tribe Asu represents the U.S.A., spelled backward. Clues are location on the American continent north of Mexico and highly developed society.

2. The sacred "rac" is the word *car* spelled backward. Some clues are: social obligation to own at least one rac (car); racs (cars) do not live more than five to seven years; there are rac (car) specialists in each community.

3. The rite that is so important to sixteen-year-olds is obtaining their driver's licenses.

Exercise 3: Values, Ethnocentrism, and Cultural Relativity
page 250
Application

1. **(1)** According to the essay preceding the passage, ethnocentrism is the judging of another culture by one's own values. Dr. Thapar is showing how Americans' reliance on the car appears to another culture.

Analysis

2. **(4)** The study of this aspect of American culture is intended to show how the role of the car in American society would appear to others not familiar with our culture.

Exercise 4: Primary and Secondary Groups
page 251
Application

1. **S** There need not be personal contact among members of a fan club.

2. **S** The math class is a secondary group because the interaction is brief and general.

3. **P** Your family is the most primary of all groups.

4. **S** You may know all of the townspeople, but you do not have a close relationship with each of them.

5. **P** Children who play together frequently develop a close bond—a feature of a primary group.

Exercise 5: Socialization and the Family
pages 252–253
Comprehension

1. **(1)** The passage suggests that the lack of socialization or extreme isolation from other humans is the cause of the man's behavior. None of the other choices is supported by the passage.

Analysis

2. **(4)** The hypothesis that the man experienced some human contact and the boys did not best explains why he survived among humans. Choice (1) is not stated. Choice (2) has nothing to do with their survival after human contact was made. Choices (3) and (5) are not supported.

Exercise 6: Nuclear and Extended Families
page 253
Application

1. **E** Three generations indicate that the parents, children, and grandparents live together; this describes an extended family.

2. **N** Two generations entail the parents and their children living together; this describes a nuclear family.

3. **E** According to the passage, an extended family includes relatives other than the husband, wife, and children, all of whom live together.

4. **E** According to the passage, an extended family includes relatives other than the husband, wife, and children, all of whom live together.

5. **N** A nuclear family may include no children, or it may include a few or many living together under one roof.

344 TEST 2: SOCIAL STUDIES

Exercise 7: The Changing American Family
page 254
Comprehension
1. **(4)** The increase for the years 1980–1985 is 1.2 million; the amount of increase for the others is less.

Evaluation
2. **(3)** This is the only fact supported by the graph. There were about 3 million (2.5 with spouses and .42 without spouses) working mothers in 1960. Choices (1) and (2) are not supported by the graph, and choices (4) and (5) are opinions.

Analysis
3. **(3)** The most likely explanation for the sharp increase in two-job families during the years 1975–1980 is inflation and the higher cost of living for families. The other choices are less supportable by the passage and pictograph.

Exercise 8: Social Stratification
page 255
Application
1. **CL** A class system enourages self-improvement and achievement.
2. **CL** Achieved status is permissible under the class system.
3. **CA** A caste system is strict and rigid.
4. **CL** Job choices are open in a class system.
5. **CA** The caste system is characterized by five levels.

Exercise 9: Types of Learning
pages 256–257
Application
1. **(1)** The baby learns to respond (stop crying) when it associates the light (stimulus) with being picked up and comforted (reward).
2. **(4)** The child makes a logical thought process and adapts information to distinguish between the bird and the airplane.
3. **(2)** The pigeon gains something (food) after it interacts with an element in its environment (presses a bar in its cage).
4. **(3)** Trying several alternatives to arrive at the right answer or solution to a problem (finding the right shoe size) demonstrates trial-and-error learning.

Exercise 10: Modes of Learning
page 257
Analysis
(4) The fact that experiments in classical conditioning are performed only on lower animals and very young children suggests that as humans get older, cognitive perception becomes much more important in their ability to learn. Choices (1) and (2) wrongly state that classical conditioning is not important in helping to understand human behavior. Choices (3) and (5) are not true.

Exercise 11: Psychoanalytic Theory
pages 258–259
Comprehension
1. Otto's habit of stopping off for a drink after work represents the **id**.
2. Otto's limiting himself to two drinks and his leaving the bar before he gets drunk represent his **ego**.
3. The guilt Otto experiences on his way home represents the **superego**.

Exercise 12: Self-Actualization Theory
page 260
Comprehension
(5) The need for personal popularity is directly related to one's need to belong and the need for recognition and respect from others.

Exercise 13: Defense Mechanisms
page 261
Application
1. **(4)** The fox makes an excuse (the grapes were sour anyway) for his failure to reach them. This is an example of rationalization.
2. **(1)** By refusing to discuss the boating accident that causes him anxiety, Tyrone is demonstrating repression.
3. **(3)** Michael directs his anger at his dog instead of directing it at the real cause of his team's loss. This demonstrates displacement.

Exercise 14: Social Environment
page 262
Analysis
(3) According to the passage, people lose their individual identities when they become part of a group. This means that they lose their sense of who they really are.

CHAPTER 2: U.S. HISTORY
Exercise 1: Discovery, Early Exploration, and Colonization
page 264
Comprehension
1. **(5)** Two places on the map are labeled MA (Massachusetts), but one has ME (Maine) written in it. This indicates that Maine was originally a part of Massachusetts.

Evaluation

2. (3) The map shows the area west of the 13 colonies to be disputed by France and Britain. Therefore, the map indicates that France still had interest in the New World. The other choices, whether true or untrue, cannot be supported by the information in the map.

Exercise 2: The Thirteen English Colonies
page 265
Comprehension

1. (3) The passage states that "indentured workers placed their signatures to contracts to work for four years in the tobacco fields in return for their passage across the Atlantic."

2. (4) The passage states that "Virginia claimed them all, moulded them into her own pattern, made them Virginians." This suggests that colonists who settled Virginia developed a common bond.

Exercise 3: The Revolutionary War
page 267
Analysis

1. d   2. a   3. b   4. c   5. e

Exercise 4: The Quest for Independence
page 267
Comprehension

1. (2) The passage states that the purpose of the First Continental Congress was to demand the repeal of the Intolerable Acts.

Application

2. (2) India's rebellion against British domination is the only event shown that can be compared to the American colonists' fight against the British. India was once a British colony until it revolted against British domination and gained its independence in 1947.

Exercise 5: The Beginning of American Government
page 268
Comprehension

1. F   2. T   3. T   4. F   5. F

Exercise 6: Disputes and Compromises
pages 269–270
Analysis

1. (2) Counting slaves as only three-fifths of the population was favorable to the northern states because it meant that the South would have fewer representatives in the House of Representatives.

Evaluation

2. (3) The passage and the chart indicate that the anti-Federalists feared strong, centralized control. You could conclude that this was because they believed that individual liberties were more likely to be protected under a local than a central authority.

Application

3. (5) The passage states that the Federalists were largely members of the merchant class who favored commercial and industrial expansion. A banker and shipper would fit this category.

4. (1) According to the passage, anti-Federalists were largely farmers who favored individual liberties and feared authoritative control by a central government. Similarly, today's southern conservatives of both parties favor state sovereignty over federal sovereignty.

Exercise 7: The War of 1812
page 271
Comprehension

1. (4) According to the passage, the events that contributed to the United States' sense of nationalism after the War of 1812 were the westward expansion (Manifest Destiny) and the increased need to manufacture its own goods because of the British naval blockade.

Analysis

2. (3) The Federalists, who were merchants and shipowners, feared that the war would interrupt their trade with other European nations.

Exercise 8: The Era of Good Feelings and the Monroe Doctrine
page 272
Application

(4) The only situation listed that represents an attempt to enforce the principles of the Monroe Doctrine is the American blockade of Cuba, in which the United States prevented foreign involvement in the Western Hemisphere.

Exercise 9: Jacksonian Democracy and the Mexican War
page 273
Application

1. (3) Jimmy Carter, a newcomer to Washington, is the only president listed who experienced a reception similar to Andrew Jackson's.

2. (4) Because easterners disliked southerners in each of these cases, the attitude may be described as one of sectionalism.

Exercise 10: A Divided Nation
page 274
Application
1. **(3)** Popular sovereignty permitted the people to approve or disapprove of a legislative action; therefore, of the choices given, popular sovereignty is the most similar to a referendum.

Evaluation
2. **(5)** When the Supreme Court ruled that Dred Scott could be returned to his master, it was upholding the practice of treating slaves as personal property.

Exercise 11: The Vote on Secession
page 275
Comprehension
1. **(c)** Virginia split in two over the issue of secession, with the western part (now known as West Virginia) loyal to the Union.

2. **(d)** Texas seceded from the Union despite the fact that only the eastern part of the state voted to do so.

3. **(a)** Kentucky was a border state that remained with the Union despite being a slave state.

4. **(b)** Mississippi is a solidly southern state that voted overwhelmingly to secede from the Union.

Exercise 12: North vs. South
page 276
Comprehension
1. S   2. N   3. N   4. N   5. S

Exercise 13: The Nation Goes to War
pages 276–277
Analysis
1. **(3)** Of the choices given, it is reasonable to assume that Lincoln did not issue an order for emancipation for the entire country out of loyalty to the four border states. Those states remained in the Union despite being slave states.

2. **(5)** The passage says, "As a result, the Union army's ranks grew by 180,000 former slaves who fought against the rebels." This was a considerable contribution to the Union's forces.

Exercise 14: Reconstruction
pages 277–278
Comprehension
1. **(2)** The passage suggests that the Carpetbaggers, who brought only what they could carry, did not intend to stay in the South.

2. **(1)** The only choice listed that is an example of corruption is the Carpetbaggers' support of fraudulent bond schemes.

Exercise 15: The Industrial Revolution
page 279
Analysis
1. **(2)** The passage cites Great Britain's advantages of "a compact size that encouraged consumerism within the country" and "a large middle class that could afford commercially manufactured goods."

Evaluation
2. **(2)** Choices (1), (3), (4), and (5) are not true. Russia has more natural resources than Japan; Japan has encouraged groups of scientists and technicians; Russia is much larger than Japan; and Japan does not have a large population of poor peasants.

Exercise 16: Growth of Big Business
page 280
Application
(2) and **(4)** The situations that represent economic activity without government intervention are (2) and (4). Choices (1), (3), and (5) all represent a government agency directing a business to do something.

Exercise 17: America Becomes Urbanized
page 281
Comprehension
1. 1920
2. 1880
3. 30 million
4. 70 million

Exercise 18: Urbanization and Social Change
page 281
Evaluation
(5) In 1930, the height of the bar for America's rural population is at about 52 million people; the bar for the urban population is at about 68 million people. The total population (rural and urban) was about 120 million, which is about half of the current population of 248 million.

Exercise 19: The Progressive Era
page 282
Application
(4) Agreement by oil manufacturers on a minimum price to set for gasoline is an example of price-fixing, an act outlawed by the Sherman Anti-Trust Act.

Exercise 20: Women's Suffrage
page 283
Comprehension
1. **(1)** Both readings reflect the belief that women should be given the right to vote.

2. (3) The passage states, "I believe it [this great question] should be settled by the states and not by the national government."

Analysis

3. (2) Mrs. Callor is complaining that while she works and pays taxes, she cannot vote for the men who decide what her taxes should be. Furthermore, she cannot get any results from her complaints about her taxes. In both cases, she is assuming that without the right to vote she is powerless.

Exercise 21: The United States Becomes a World Power
page 284
Analysis

1. (3) The Philippines were ceded to the United States under the terms of the treaty that ended the Spanish-American War; therefore, the U.S. establishment of military bases there is a result of a policy of expanding American control over other areas.

2. (4) The most likely explanation for America's isolationist position from the end of the Civil War until the Spanish-American War is that the country was preoccupied with healing its wounds and rebuilding the South after the Civil War.

Exercise 22: World War I
page 285
Comprehension

(1) Allies

(2) draft

(3) Treaty of Versailles

(4) League of Nations

(5) isolationism

Exercise 23: The Roaring Twenties
pages 286–287
Comprehension

1. 1900–1909

2. 1930–1939

3. 700,000 or 0.7 million

Exercise 24: The New Deal
page 287
Application

1. d   2. a   3. e   4. c   5. b

Exercise 25: World War II
page 288
Comprehension

1. T   2. F   3. T   4. F   5. F

Exercise 26: U.S. Foreign Policy Positions
page 289
Application

1. (2) An imperialist believes in controlling other territories or nations.

2. (5) An internationalist believes in cooperating with the nations of the world.

Exercise 27: The Truman Era
page 290
Application

(1) and **(2)** The situations that represent attempts to enforce the principles of the Truman Doctrine are (1), (2). Choice (3) has nothing to do with resisting communist takeover. Choice (4) involves the U.S.S.R.'s attempt to establish missile bases in Cuba, a country that had already become communist. Choice (5) involves U.S. support for a democratic movement against a communist government.

Exercise 28: The Korean War
page 291
Application

1. (4) The undeclared war in Vietnam most closely resembled the situation of the Korean War. Both were undeclared wars that resulted from the U.S. policy of trying to contain communism.

Analysis

2. (4) The belief that the U.S. government should not commit soldiers to an undeclared war represents an opinion and not a fact.

Exercise 29: The Eisenhower Years
page 291
Application

(5) The Salem witchcraft trials are the only historical event listed in which hysteria resulted in innocent people being wrongly accused and persecuted.

Exercise 30: Space Exploration and Social Change
page 292
Analysis

(3) The *Brown* v. *Topeka Board of Education* decision is significant today because it ruled that "separate but equal" educational facilities could no longer exist. This serves as the legal basis for school busing to achieve desegregation.

Exercise 31: Kennedy's New Frontier
page 293
Application

1. (3) The Soviet attempt to establish a missile base in Cuba may be interpreted as a direct violation of the principles of the Monroe Doctrine, which opposed foreign interference in the affairs of the Western Hemisphere.

Analysis

2. (4) From reading the passage, it may be assumed that Cuba, a communist nation, was an ally of the Soviet Union.

**Exercise 32: Johnson's Great
Society
page 294
Comprehension**
(4) The passage states that the most
significant achievement of former
President Johnson was the passage of
the Civil Rights Act.

**Exercise 33: The Nixon Era
page 295
Evaluation**
1. (3) Of former President Nixon's foreign
policy initiatives, history will likely
credit him most for reestablishing
relations with the People's Republic
of China. The other choices can be
eliminated either because they are
not true or are not achievements.

2. (5) The opinion best supported by the
evidence presented in the passage
is that "The president of the United
States is not above the law." It was
President Nixon's involvement in the
coverup of the break-in and the
subsequent threat of impeachment
action that led to the first
presidential resignation in U.S.
history.

**Exercise 34: Carter and the Middle
East
page 296
Evaluation**
1. (3) Of all the choices, Jimmy Carter
will be remembered most favorably
for his efforts to reconcile Egypt
and Israel. Choices (1) and (5) are
acts by Carter, but they lack the
significance of the Mideast peace
accords. Choices (2) and (4) were
actions that were unpopular with
large segments of the American
people.

Application
2. (3) Anti-imperialists reject the policy
of one nation controlling another
nation or territory. Although the
United States helped to build the
Panama Canal, it is in territory that
belongs to Panama. Therefore, anti-
imperialists would favor the United
States' relinquishing control of the
canal.

**Exercise 35: Reagan and the New
Conservatism
page 297
Evaluation**
(1) President Reagan's foreign policy is
characterized generally as one of
anticommunism. Giving support to
anticommunist rebels in Nicaragua,
Angola, and Afghanistan is an
expression of this policy.

**Exercise 36: Bush's "New World
Order"
page 298
Analysis**
1. O   2. F   3. O   4. F   5. O

**Exercise 37: Clinton—The First
Baby-Boom President
pages 299–300
Application**
1. (2) According to the passage, Clinton
"found that campaign promises
were difficult to keep." His
experience as governor, choice (1),
did not necessarily make him a
better president. Clinton's problems
included foreign affairs (3) and
often were a surprise (4).

Evaluation
2. (5) As a candidate, Clinton could think
about tomorrow's problems without
solving them, but as president, he
had to act immediately on today's
problems. Clinton's solutions did
not always please the Congress
(1) or lead easily to economic
recovery (3). He appointed women
to public office (2).

Application
3. (1) Like Carter, Clinton was a former
Democratic governor who was
regarded as a Washington
"outsider." They both faced
economic and political problems
that had begun in a previous
administration.

Evaluation
4. (1) The passage implies that Clinton's
appointment of Janet Reno was well
received. The other choices refer to
unpopular or problem-ridden
decisions.

CHAPTER 3: POLITICAL
SCIENCE
**Exercise 1: Methods of Obtaining
Power
page 302
Application**
1. (4) France's overthrow of the
monarchy in favor of a republican
form of government is an example
of a revolution.

2. (3) Because Hitler overpowered Austria
militarily, the method used to gain
power is conquest.

3. (5) The people elected Corazon Aquino
president of the Philippines; this is
an example of a leader coming to
power through popular vote.

**Exercise 2: Legislative
Representation
page 304
Application**
1. (3) Rhode Island is the smallest state
among those represented; therefore,
it is likely to have the fewest
representatives in the House.

Analysis

2. (5) Since the number of representatives a state has is based on its population, you can infer that New Jersey, in spite of its small size, is densely populated. Dense populations are characteristic of urban, industrialized states.

3. (5) Because the number of a state's representatives is based on its population, and because Arizona is gaining residents at the expense of states in the Northeast, the number of representatives for both Arizona and northeastern states will need to be adjusted.

**Exercise 3: The Legislative Branch
page 304
Application**

1. E The power to impose economic sanctions is not stated in the Constitution; therefore, the elastic clause applies.

2. C The power to pass tax laws is stated in the Constitution.

3. C The power to admit a state is stated in the Constitution.

4. C The power to approve presidential appointments is stated in the Constitution.

5. C The power to introduce legislation is stated in the Constitution.

**Exercise 4: The Executive Branch
page 306
Application**

1. (5) The passage states that strong presidents frequently use their veto power and attempt to dominate the legislature. The actions of Andrew Jackson best fit that description.

2. (5) Based on the information in the chapter on U.S. history, President Warren G. Harding may be described as a weak president; his reliance on the advice of his subordinates led to the Teapot Dome Scandal.

Analysis

3. (5) The vice president carries out many functions for the executive branch as a whole. Therefore, when the president and vice president are from differing political parties, the president's effectiveness and ability to govern can suffer.

**Exercise 5: The Judicial Branch
page 307
Comprehension**

1. (4) The practice of deciding on the constitutionality of a law (which the Supreme Court does) is called the power of judicial review.

2. (4) The quote both defines the role of the Supreme Court and affirms that the court is the final authority on the Constitution's meaning.

**Exercise 6: States' vs. Individuals' Rights
page 308
Application**

2. I In prohibiting states from outlawing abortions under certain conditions, the Supreme Court upheld the rights of the individual.

4. I In ruling that an accused must be informed of his or her rights, the Supreme Court supported the rights of the individual.

5. I In ruling that separate facilities for the races were not equal, the Supreme Court upheld the rights of the individual.

**Exercise 7: The Enactment of a Law
page 309
Evaluation**

(2) Choice (2) is supported by the part of the chart that shows that a bill must go to a conference committee for compromise. The chart does not indicate that a bill may be introduced directly by the president. A filibuster is an acceptable means by which a vote on a bill may be delayed. Bills introduced by *either* house may be amended as shown in the illustration. The chart shows that bills may become law without the president's signature if approved by two-thirds of both houses.

**Exercise 8: Filibuster
page 310
Comprehension**

(5) The passage says that "Senator Thurmond talked for more than 24 hours to delay the vote." This is the same as talking for the purpose of trying to prevent passage of a bill into law.

**Exercise 9: System of Checks and Balances
page 310
Comprehension**

1. (a) executive   (b) judicial
2. (a) legislative   (b) executive
3. (a) legislative   (b) executive
4. (a) legislative   (b) executive
5. (a) judicial   (b) legislative
6. (a) executive   (b) legislative

**Exercise 10: Powers of State Government
page 311
Application**

1. B   2. B   3. F   4. F   5. S   6. S

**Exercise 11: City Income and Expenditures
page 312
Comprehension**

1. revenue; expenditures
2. charges and miscellaneous
3. environment and housing

Exercise 12: City Budgeting
page 312
Analysis
(5) The only ways for a city to make up
for lost revenue are to raise taxes or
fees and to decrease expenditures.
Borrowing from a more prosperous
state is not a plausible alternative.

Exercise 13: The Political Spectrum
pages 313–314
Application
1. (2) Because the speaker advocates
social improvement (improved
bilingual programs) through
governmental action, the speaker
may be classified as a liberal.
2. (3) Because the speaker believes in
avoiding extreme changes in laws
and government ("we don't need
harsher laws"), the speaker may be
classified as a moderate.
3. (5) Because the speaker advocates
a return to an earlier policy (the
absence of public signs written
in Spanish), the speaker may be
classified as a reactionary.
4. (4) Because the speaker advocates
maintaining the existing social
order ("English has been the
primary language here and always
will be."), the speaker may be
classified as a conservative.
5. (1) Because the speaker advocates
swift, sweeping changes in laws, the
speaker may be classified as a
radical.

Exercise 14: Political Parties
page 315
Application
1. **R** Republicans generally favor stronger
state and local authority.
2. **D** Democrats generally endorse the
efforts of labor unions.
3. **R** Republicans advocate free
enterprise (big business operating
without restraint).
4. **D** Democrats support government
expenditures for the disadvantaged
and minorities.
5. **R** Republicans tend to favor defense
spending at the expense of domestic
spending.

Exercise 15: Electing a President
page 317
Comprehension
1. e   2. d   3. a   4. c   5. b

Exercise 16: The Democratic
Primary
page 317
Evaluation
1. (2) The picture is crowded with several
well-known cartoon figures. This
suggests that anybody can run in
the Democratic presidential
primary.

2. (5) By making the Democratic
presidential candidates cartoon
characters, the cartoonist is
ridiculing the Democratic party's
practice of allowing large numbers
of candidates to seek office.

Exercise 17: The Electoral Process
page 318
Evaluation
(2) Because the purpose of a closed
primary is to give members of a party
an opportunity to express their
preference for a candidate to run in a
general election, it follows that voters
must declare their party affiliation;
otherwise, the purpose of a primary
election is defeated.

Exercise 18: The Impact of the
Media
page 318
Analysis
(1) The best choice is (1), which is based
on the hypothesis that the early
announcements of Reagan's victory
discouraged Carter's supporters from
voting. Choice (2) is contrary to the
facts in the passage because Carter
lost overwhelmingly. Choices (3), (4),
and (5) are not plausible reasons that
motivate people to vote.

CHAPTER 4: ECONOMICS
Exercise 1: Factors of Production
page 320
Application
1. **N** Seals, Arctic foxes, and walruses are
found in nature; Eskimos produce
goods from them.
2. **C** A plumber's tools are equipment
used to provide a service.
3. **N** Diamonds are raw materials found
in nature.
4. **L** Farmers who plant crops are
laborers.
5. **C** Conveyor belts are used in the
production of other goods.

Exercise 2: Economic Systems
page 321
Comprehension
1. (b) The quote "From each according
to his ability, to each according
to his need" reflects the socialist
goal of working together to provide
equal opportunity for all.
2. (a) The quote "In the area of
economics, the government that
governs least governs best" reflects
the capitalist feature of
government's noninterference in
business.

Exercise 3: Economic Systems and Governments
page 322
Comprehension
1. **(4)** Because capitalism and communism occupy the extremes of the continuum, you can conclude that they are opposites.

Application
2. **(3)** An aspect of a U.S. dairy manufacturer's operations (capitalist system) is dictated by a government agency's requirement (a feature of a socialist system).

Exercise 4: Supply and Demand in the U.S. Economy
page 325
Evaluation
1. **(1)** The bartender's bill, as a result of added taxes, is ridiculously high, suggesting that the overburdened taxpayer won't find any relief.
2. **(3)** The customer has just come from paying his income taxes and wants a drink to take his troubles away.

Exercise 5: Supply, Demand, and Equilibrium
pages 326–327
Comprehension
1. **(3)** The point where the lines intersect is at $300.

Analysis
2. **(3)** As the price decreases, the demand increases.
3. **(5)** With a greater supply brought about by the entrance of Korea into the market and a low demand for VCRs, the supply would exceed demand, resulting in a surplus.

Exercise 6: Economic Growth
page 328
Analysis
(3) The only plausible reason given for the abandonment of wage and price controls is that the program proved too difficult to administer and was highly unpopular. Choice (1) is incorrect because it was known before the controls were implemented that they would interfere with the basic principles of a free economy. Choice (2) is not true; choice (4) is a result of the revoking of the controls and not an explanation for their abandonment. Choice (5) is incorrect because even though wages were decreased, a depression did not occur.

Exercise 7: The GNP as a Measure of Economic Growth
page 329
Comprehension
1. **(3)** The span of years between 1982 and 1989 is the only period in which the slope of the line increases steadily.

Analysis
2. **(3)** Current dollars represent the current price of something. Inflation (an increase in prices) explains the steep increase in current dollar GNP shown on the graph.
3. **(2)** A falling constant dollar GNP indicates a period of poor economic growth, a recession. During the years 1979–1980, 1981–1982, and 1990–1991, the United States experienced recessions.

Exercise 8: Money and Monetary Policy
page 331
Comprehension
1. **F** According to the passage, the role of the Fed is to regulate the nation's supply of money and credit.
2. **F** The two primary ways in which the Federal Reserve influences the money supply are by setting the reserve ratio and the discount rate.
3. **T**
4. **T**
5. **F** The **discount rate** is the interest rate the Fed charges member banks to borrow; the prime rate, not mentioned in the passage, is the rate banks charge to their best customers.

Exercise 9: Fiscal and Monetary Policy
page 332
Comprehension
1. **decrease; lowering** To stimulate the economy during a recession, the government should decrease government spending while lowering taxes. Both actions put more money into the hands of consumers.
2. **decrease; raising; increasing** Inflation is an increase in the amount of money in circulation. To reduce inflation, the Fed reduces the amount of money in circulation by raising the discount rate. This makes it more costly for banks to borrow from the Fed. By increasing the reserve ratio, the Fed reduces the amount of money a bank can lend.
3. **budget deficit** When operating at a budget deficit, the government is spending more money than it takes in.

CHAPTER 5: GEOGRAPHY
Exercise 1: Maps
pages 333–334
Application
1. **(5)** A weather map shows the climate of a particular region, including its precipitation.
2. **(4)** A political map outlines the borders between states.
3. **(1)** A topographical map shows the physical land features of an area.

Exercise 2: Measuring Distance
page 334
Comprehension
1. about 900 miles
2. about 300 miles
3. about 1,100 miles

Exercise 3: The Latitude and Longitude Grid
page 336
Comprehension
1. (5) central Africa
2. (4) South Africa

Exercise 4: Time Zones
page 337
Application
1. (2) Los Angeles falls within the Pacific time zone, which is three hours earlier than the Eastern time zone, in which Philadelphia falls.
2. (3) Denver falls within the Mountain time zone, which is one hour earlier than the Central time zone, in which Milwaukee falls.

Analysis
3. (5) Northwest Indiana is economically tied to the Chicago metropolitan area; therefore, for economic reasons it falls within the Central time zone.
4. (4) Groups that benefit most from northwest Indiana's placement within the Central time zone are commuters who work in Chicago and live in northwest Indiana and the merchants and businesspeople in northwest Indiana who transact business with Chicagoans.

Exercise 5: U.S. Topography
page 339
Analysis
1. (2) Nebraska is located in the plains region—an area described in the text as having very cold temperatures during the winter.
2. (3) Denver (whose nickname is the "Mile High City") is located in the Rocky Mountains of Colorado. None of the other cities listed is located in a mountainous region.
3. (3) New Orleans is the only city represented that lies below sea level and experiences flooding because of its proximity to the Mississippi River. Las Vegas is located in a desert; Phoenix is located in a dry region of the country. Neither New York nor Atlanta is subject to flooding, as neither lies below sea level.

Exercise 6: The Indian Peninsula
page 340
Comprehension
1. (4) Mt. Everest, the highest mountain in the world, is also the highest point in the Himalaya Mountains at 29,028 feet above sea level.
2. (5) A glance at the map of the Indian Peninsula shows that the elevation for the majority of the land is between sea level and 1,000 feet. In the key, white space indicates this level of elevation.

Exercise 7: Population Distribution
page 341
Analysis
1. (4) Nevada, one of the least populous of the fifty states, is characterized by extremes in temperatures and altitude and rugged topography and has soil poorly equipped for farming. Because of climate and topography, neither California, Washington, Oregon, nor Colorado is as sparsely populated as Nevada.
2. (4) West Virginia is mainly mountainous, a characteristic that precludes an even distribution of the state's population.

Exercise 8: Other Factors Affecting Population Distribution
page 342
Evaluation
1. (4) The quote states, "We miss much of life's richness if we fail to take affirmative action against the current trend among developers to lay us all out with 'our own kind' of people." This opinion is similar to the opinion that children exposed to only one kind of people grow up crippled in their understanding of the world.
2. (5) Fair-housing laws that provide for more ethnically diverse communities are the only example of affirmative action that is related to changing housing patterns.

Test 3: Science

The GED Science Test consists of multiple-choice questions. These questions require you to know basic science concepts that will be covered in this section of the book. However, the test emphasizes your ability to think about these concepts. You will not be required to recall an isolated fact as you might have on some other tests. Rather, you will read a passage or look at an illustration and answer questions based on it. To answer successfully, you will need to

▶ have an understanding of basic science concepts

▶ be able to interpret illustrations and reading passages

▶ be able to show that you can
  • understand what you read
  • apply information to a new situation
  • analyze relationships among ideas
  • make judgments about the material presented

Actually, you already use all of these different kinds of thinking skills in daily life. In this section, we will help you to apply these skills to science materials.

How many questions are on the test?

There are 66 multiple-choice questions, and you will be given 95 minutes to complete the test. About two-thirds of the questions will be based on reading passages of up to 250 words each, and one-third will be based on visuals—diagrams, charts, or graphs. (If you need practice in interpreting visual materials, you might want to review Chapter 2 on pages 223–237 of the Reading Skills section.) To get an idea of what the test is like, look at the Practice Test at the end of this book. This Practice Test is based on the real GED Test. In fact, all of the multiple-choice questions in this section are sample GED questions.

What's on the test?

The GED Science Test can be broken down into the content areas it covers and the skills it tests. The following subjects make up the content of the test:

Life Sciences	50%
Biology	
Physical Sciences	50%
Earth Science	
Chemistry	
Physics	

These essential science areas are covered in Chapters 1–4 of this section. However, keep in mind that a given question may draw from a number of these subjects. It's difficult to discuss society or people without touching on a number of topics. For example, a question on air pollution may draw from material covered in both biology and chemistry.

Also remember that you are being tested on your ability to think through certain ideas and concepts. You will be asked to do more than just find an answer that was given in a passage.

Thinking skills that you will be tested on include

Understanding Ideas	20%
Applying Ideas	30%
Analyzing Ideas	30%
Evaluating Ideas	20%

Chapter 1 of the Reading Skills section of this book (on pages 189–222) focuses on these thinking skills, and all of the activities and questions in this section will help you practice answering these types of questions. If you have not already worked through the Reading Skills section, you might want to go back and complete the exercises in that section. The more practice you have had in answering the four categories of questions, the better prepared you will be to answer questions in this section and on the actual test.

1
BIOLOGY—THE STUDY OF LIVING THINGS

"How did life begin on Earth?" "Does life exist on Venus or Mars?" "Have UFOs (unidentified flying objects) ever brought alien beings to Earth?" Questions such as these fascinate people everywhere. In fact, all human beings seem to have a natural curiosity about life—both life on Earth and the possibility of life on other planets.

The scientific study of all life forms is known as *biology*. Biologists are interested in how living things grow, how they change over time, and how they interact with one another and with their environment. Of particular interest are the characteristics that all living things have in common. All living things react to stimuli, take in food and use it to grow, eliminate wastes, and reproduce. The starting point for any systematic study of biology is an examination of the basic unit of life, the cell.

The Cell, the Basis of Life

The *cell* is the smallest unit of living material capable of carrying on the activities of life. Like the bricks of a building, cells are the "building blocks" of an organism.

Cells were first observed in 1665 by Robert Hooke, who, with the aid of a crudely made microscope, examined a slice of cork. The tiny compartments he saw reminded him of the little rooms, or cells, of a monastery. By 1839 it had been proposed that all living things are made up of cells, and by 1855 it was theorized that cells can be produced only from existing cells. These breakthroughs supported the belief that life is a continuous process.

Cells vary widely in size and appearance. It is the number of cells in an organism, however, and not the size, that determines the size of an organism. The cells of an ant, a human being, and a whale are of equal size. The whale is larger because its genetic pattern dictates that a larger number of cells be produced.

An "average" cell measures about 10 micrometers (1/25,000 inch) in diameter. This means that a parade of 25,000 typical cells end to end would measure only one inch.

Types of Cells

Two kinds of cells are known to exist—plant cells and animal cells. One difference between the two is that the plant cell has a cell wall that protects it, and an animal cell does not. Also, plant cells contain *chloroplasts*, structures active in the food-making process, while animal cells do not.

Both plant and animal cells are surrounded by a delicate boundary, the **cell membrane**. The cell membrane

- preserves the cell by acting as a barrier between it and the outside environment
- helps the cell maintain its shape
- regulates molecular traffic passing into and out of the cell

The following illustration shows the differences between the plant cell and animal cell:

CELL STRUCTURE

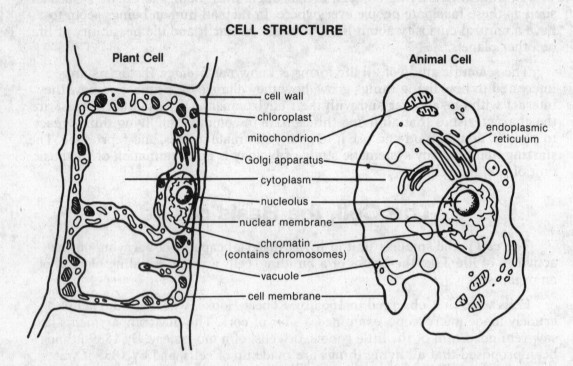

Plant Cell   Animal Cell

cell wall
chloroplast
mitochondrion
Golgi apparatus
cytoplasm
nucleolus
nuclear membrane
chromatin
(contains chromosomes)
vacuole
cell membrane
endoplasmic reticulum

Cell Structure

Within the cell membrane is **protoplasm**, a jellylike substance that forms the largest component of the cell. The protoplasm lying between the nuclear membrane and the cell membrane is called **cytoplasm**.

A highly specialized and complex structure, the cell has its own control center, transportation system, power plants, factories for making needed materials, and even a reproductive blueprint, or chemical recipe.

Most of the organelles (little organs) performing these functions are located within the cytoplasm. Resembling an intricate tunnel system, the **endoplasmic reticulum** serves as a network for transporting materials from one part of the cell to another or from the cell to the environment. The power plants of the cell are the **mitochondria**, the sites where the cell releases energy for cellular work. Mitochondria are abundant in highly active cells that produce energy for important life processes. For example, more than 1,000 mitochondria have been counted in a single liver cell.

Located in stacks of platelike membranes at one side of the nucleus is another organelle: the *Golgi apparatus*. The Golgi apparatus functions as a packaging plant. Proteins and carbohydrates are gathered together and enclosed in a membranous sac. In gland cells, the Golgi apparatus is responsible for releasing the gland's hormones into the body.

Of all the structures within the cell, the most important is the *nucleus*, the control center of the cell. The nucleus is surrounded by a double nuclear membrane. Pores in the nuclear membrane permit the passage of molecules between the cytoplasm and the nucleus. Within the *nucleus* are the *chromosomes* and the *nucleolus*. Each chromosome contains several hundred *genes*, which contain DNA, a molecular acid that carries instructions on how the organism should develop. While the chromosomes serve as a "chemical recipe" for the cell, the genes might be considered individual ingredients.

The nucleolus is rich in RNA, an acid that is essential in the chemical activity of the cell. The nucleolus contains sections of chromosomes that are believed to be important in the manufacture of protein.

EXERCISE 1: CELL STRUCTURE

Directions: Match the terms on the right with the mechanical function they perform on the left by writing the letter of the correct term in the space provided.

_____ **1.** power plant of cell; enables cell to breathe

_____ **2.** regulator of traffic passing into and out of cell

_____ **3.** control center for cell

_____ **4.** means of transportation for material within cell

_____ **5.** packager of proteins and carbohydrates

_____ **6.** factory where RNA ingredients are assembled and stored

(a) nucleus

(b) endoplasmic reticulum

(c) mitochondrion

(d) Golgi apparatus

(e) cell membrane

(f) nucleolus

Answers are on page 441.

EXERCISE 2: CELLS

Directions: Choose the best answer for each of the following questions.

1. The main purpose of the reading passage is to point out that

(1) all living things are made of cells
(2) the nucleus is the control center of the cell
(3) there are differences between plant and animal cells
(4) the cell is a highly organized, complex structure with subsystems of its own
(5) the Golgi apparatus functions as a packaging plant in the cell

2. One of the many functions of cells in the stomach lining is to slowly release quantities of stomach acid into the stomach chamber. From the passage, we can infer that the part of the cell that is involved in this function is the

   (1) endoplasmic reticulum
   (2) Golgi apparatus
   (3) nucleus
   (4) nucleolus
   (5) chromosome

3. We can conclude from the passage that the largest number of mitochondria would be found in the cells of the

   (1) hair   (2) skin   (3) heart   (4) smooth muscles   (5) sense organs

4. In plant cells, chloroplasts are active in the chemical processes required to make food. Animal cells have no chloroplasts. Based on this, we can conclude that

   (1) plant cells are more complex than animal cells
   (2) plant cells and not animal cells generate chemical reactions
   (3) animal cells prey upon plant cells as a food source
   (4) animal cells are more complex than plant cells
   (5) animals must obtain food from outside sources

5. According to the passage, mitochondria are the power plants that produce energy for important life processes in the animal cell and are responsible for cellular respiration. What part of a plant cell serves a similar function?

   (1) cell wall
   (2) nucleus
   (3) nucleolus
   (4) chromosome
   (5) chloroplast

Answers are on page 441.

DID YOU KNOW THAT: The single-celled organism *euglena* has both plant and animal features? It contains chlorophyll, which only plants have, and has no cell wall, a feature of an animal cell. Also, it moves—another characteristic of animals.

Cells and Active Transport

Every cell has a membrane that selectively permits the passage of certain molecules in and out of the cell.

The movement of molecules through the cell membrane without any effort on the cell's part is achieved by diffusion. *Diffusion* is the movement of molecules from an area of high concentration to an area of low concentration. Vibrating molecules are propelled away from one another after they collide. It is through this process that odors can fill a large room in a short period of time.

Diffusion is important in higher organisms. In the human body, for example, oxygen moves from the air sacs in the lungs through cell membranes and into the blood through diffusion.

A cell's cytoplasm contains many substances in varying degrees of concentration. These concentrations differ sharply from those in the fluid surrounding the cell. Such differences are so essential that the cell can die if the differences are not maintained. Given the opportunity, diffusion would quickly eliminate these critical differences. Therefore, the cell must be able to negate, and sometimes even reverse, the process of diffusion. This is accomplished by active transport. During *active transport*, the cell moves materials from an area of low concentration to an area of high concentration. This work requires energy.

EXERCISE 3: CELLS AND ACTIVE TRANSPORT

Directions: In the blank spaces below, supply the words that correctly complete each statement.

1. Diffusion is the movement of molecules from an area of

_____ concentration to an area of _____

concentration.

2. In active transport, materials are moved from an area of

_____ concentration to an area of _____

concentration.

3. Diffusion may be described as the _____ of active transport.

Answers are on page 441.

EXERCISE 4: DIFFUSION AND OSMOSIS

Directions: Choose the best answer for each of the following questions.

1. In the human body, the process of diffusion

  (1) allows for concentrations of materials where needed in the body, through stockpiling
  (2) regulates blood flow
  (3) allows an even distribution of substances throughout all cells of the body
  (4) comes into play in times of extreme illness
  (5) plays an insignificant role in the body's functioning

2. *Osmosis* may be described as a process by which water in a solution is able to move through the cell membrane from a *lower* concentration to a *higher* one in order to maintain balance on either side of the membrane. If the salt solution in blood plasma surrounding red blood cells is higher than the solution inside the cells, which is most likely to occur?

  A. Water will leave the cell and pass into the blood plasma.
  B. Water will leave the blood plasma and pass into the cell.
  C. The cell will shrink because of a loss of water.

  (1) A   **(2)** B   **(3)** C   **(4)** A and B   **(5)** A and C

Answers are on page 441.

Mitosis—Cell Division

One quality of an organism is that it has the capacity to grow. As a cell grows, its cell membrane becomes unable to provide oxygen and nutrients for the interior of the cell and wastes are unable to leave the cell. In addition, a nucleus can control only so much cytoplasm. Therefore, when a cell reaches its limit in size, it must divide, or undergo a process called mitosis.

Mitosis is the process by which cells reproduce themselves by division. In a multicellular organism, mitosis leads to tissue growth and maintenance. In a single-celled organism, mitosis results in two new genetically identical independent organisms. Mitosis can be divided into four stages or phases, as shown below.

Stage 1: Prophase

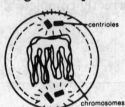

Just before prophase begins, genetic material in the nucleus is duplicated (doubled). Then, as prophase begins, the nuclear membrane and nucleolus disappear. The genetic material, which has not been easy to view, now becomes evident as long, threadlike bodies, the chromosomes. As prophase continues, centrioles appear at opposite ends of the cells and small fibers start to form between them.

Stage 2: Metaphase

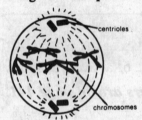

During metaphase, the next phase in the sequence, the spindle fibers attach themselves to the genetic material at the center of the chromosomes (centromeres). The chromosomes are now quite thick and visible. They begin to line up at the equator of the cell.

Stage 3: Anaphase

During the third stage, anaphase, the centromeres divide, and the duplicate pairs of chromosomes separate. The separate pairs then repel each other and move toward the poles of the cell.

Stage 4: Telophase

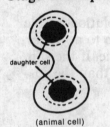

When the chromosomes arrive at the poles, telophase begins. In telophase, the nuclei re-form, the chromosomes gradually become less visible, and the cell separates to form two new cells. The daughter cells are genetically and physically identical to the parent cell except for size.

In single-cell organisms, cell division results in two new individuals. In complex organisms made of more than one cell, the new daughter cells form a subsystem of the parent cell. In many organisms, cell reproduction is at its peak while the organism grows. As the organism ages, the process is limited to the replacement of old and damaged cells.

EXERCISE 5: MITOSIS

Directions: Match the phase of mitosis shown on the left with its description shown on the right.

_____ **1.** prophase

_____ **2.** metaphase

_____ **3.** anaphase

_____ **4.** telophase

(a) chromosomes become easily visible

(b) chromosomal material lines up at the center of the cell

(c) cell divides to form two new cells

(d) pairs of chromosomes move to opposite poles

Answers are on page 441.

DID YOU KNOW THAT: Brain cells are the only cells in the body that cannot replace themselves and that, from the moment of birth, the average human *loses* brain cells?

Meiosis—Reproductive Cell Division

Each organism has a chromosome number that is characteristic of that organism. For example, all of the cells in the human body contain forty-six chromosomes except for the *gametes* (the reproductive cells). The reproductive cells (sperm and egg) cannot carry the same number of chromosomes as those of other parts of the body. If they did, the offspring that would result from the union of the egg and sperm would have twice the normal amount of genetic material after cell division. In animals, this would result in the termination of the embryo early in development. To prevent this, the sex cells undergo meiosis, a special division process.

Meiosis is a process in which a parent cell undergoes two special types of cell division that result in the production of four gametes (reproductive cells). Each gamete has half the number of chromosomes of the original parent cell. The two stages of meiosis are illustrated below.

MEIOSIS I

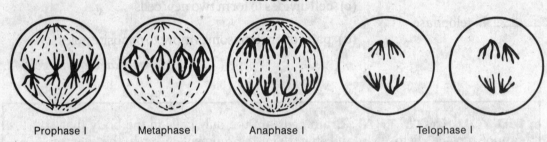

| Prophase I | Metaphase I | Anaphase I | Telophase I |

As the preceding diagram shows, the chromosome pairs come together to exchange genes. This process is called crossing over. *Crossing over* ensures a recombination of genetic material. Later, the pairs separate and one of each pair moves to a new cell. During Telophase I, the cytoplasm divides and two daughter cells are formed. Each daughter cell is called a *haploid* cell, a cell that contains half the number of chromosomes of the original parent cell.

MEIOSIS II

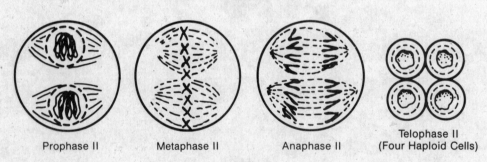

| Prophase II | Metaphase II | Anaphase II | Telophase II (Four Haploid Cells) |

(*Note:* Only one daughter cell from Meiosis I is shown here.)

In Meiosis II, the chromosomal material combines, separates, and moves to new cells, resulting in four reproductive cells. In humans, when two haploid cells (a sperm and egg, each containing twenty-three chromosomes) unite in fertilization, they form a *diploid* cell, a cell containing forty-six chromosomes. The fertilized cell contains forty-six chromosomes, or twenty-three pairs—half from the mother and half from the father.

EXERCISE 6: MEIOSIS

Directions: Number the steps in meiosis in the order in which they occur.

_____ Two new cells divide, resulting in four reproductive cells.

_____ Chromosome pairs come together.

_____ Chromosome pairs separate and each moves to a new cell.

_____ Chromosomes exchange genes.

Answers are one page 441.

EXERCISE 7: CELL DIVISION

Directions: Choose the best answer for each of the following questions.

1. The method of reproduction that provides for the most variety in offspring is

   (1) asexual (nonsexual) reproduction
   (2) mutative reproduction
   (3) sexual reproduction
   (4) cloning
   (5) cellular reproduction

2. Without the process of meiosis, we can infer that offspring from sexual reproduction (if they survived) would

   (1) have twice the assigned number of chromosomes
   (2) have a high degree of genetic variety
   (3) be identical
   (4) produce cells with a haploid chromosomal number
   (5) have a number of mutations

3. A human cell that contains half the normal number of chromosomes is the

   (1) brain cell
   (2) egg cell
   (3) skin cell
   (4) hair cell
   (5) heart cell

4. Cancer is a condition in which cells that serve no function in the body invade healthy ones. Based on this, we can conclude that malignant cancer cells

   (1) do not reproduce by mitosis
   (2) divide by meiosis
   (3) divide more unpredictably than normal cells
   (4) divide less frequently than benign cells
   (5) are parasites and do not reproduce by division at all

Answers are on page 441.

DID YOU KNOW THAT: The reproductive cells of children born with Down's syndrome contain forty-seven instead of the normal forty-six chromosomes? Scientists attribute this to a defect in genetic communication.

Genetics and Heredity

Heredity is the term used to describe the passing of traits from parents to off-spring. Every species has its own set of traits that it transmits to its offspring. *Genetics* is the study of how traits are passed on. *Geneticists*, the scientists who study heredity, have found that hereditary information of an organism is carried by the chromosomes of the cell nucleus.

Genes map out all our inherited traits. Every human receives two genes for each trait—one from the mother and one from the father. Genes may be dominant or recessive. The dominant gene will always appear in an offspring, if present. For example, since brown eye color is a dominant trait, 90 percent of human beings have brown eyes. If two dominant genes are inherited, the resulting trait will be a combination of the two inherited characteristics. For example, pink flowers result from the inheritance of a dominant gene for red and a dominant gene for white.

Sexual reproduction ensures that the offspring is composed of genetic material from both parents. This genetic material is thoroughly remixed with every fertilization so that, with the exception of identical twins, no two offspring of the same parents are similar genetically.

Gender and Mutations

Whether a mother gives birth to a boy or girl is determined by the "X" and "Y" chromosomes. A person receives two sex chromosomes—one from the father's sperm cell and one from the mother's egg cell. Egg cells contain a single "X" chromosome. Male sperm cells may contain either an "X" or a "Y" chromosome. If two "X" chromosomes unite, a female will result. If the sperm reaching the egg has a "Y" chromosome, a male will be produced. The sperm cells, then, carry the chromosome that determines the *gender* of offspring.

Sometimes a mistake occurs in the genetic makeup of a chromosome during cell duplication. This change in the genes is called a *mutation* and may be passed on to offspring. Many of these mutations are harmful. Two mutations in humans are Down's syndrome, which results in brain damage, and muscular dystrophy, a disease that causes muscles to waste away.

EXERCISE 8: GENETICS AND HEREDITY

Directions: Study the diagram and choose the best answer for the questions that follow.

HOW EYE COLOR IS INHERITED

G = Dominant Green Eye Gene

B = Dominant Brown Eye Gene

b = Recessive Blue Eye Gene

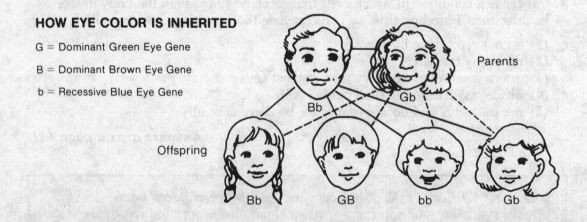

1. According to the diagram, what percentage of this couple's children might have blue eyes?

(1) 75 percent
(2) 50 percent
(3) 0 percent
(4) 25 percent
(5) 100 percent

The following question is *not* based on the preceding diagram.

2. The Jones family has had four children, all girls. The fifth child born is a boy. This change is the result of

(1) conception classes taken by the parents
(2) the timing of the fertility cycles
(3) the father's contribution of a "Y" chromosome
(4) the mother's contribution of a "Y" chromosome
(5) the "law of averages" finally catching up

3. Which of the following can be supported by information in the preceding passage?

A. The father's chromosomes determine the sex of the offspring.

B. The father's genetic makeup determines eye and hair color.

C. Mutations are caused by mistakes in genetic makeup.

(1) A
(2) B
(3) C
(4) A and B
(5) A and C

Answers are on page 441.

DID YOU KNOW THAT: Some conditions in humans are sex-linked; that is, they are inherited through chromosomal genes carried by one of the sexes? For example, color blindness (the inability to distinguish colors such as red and green) is most often found in males. Hemophilia, the inability of the blood to clot properly, is another condition found almost exclusively in males.

WRITING ACTIVITY 1

In one form of genetic engineering, human parenting is made to be dependent on uniting individuals with certain traits, such as blond hair, blue eyes, above-average intelligence, etc. The theory is that the genes the offspring inherit will also carry these traits. Write an essay of two or three paragraphs expressing your opinion for or against this form of genetic engineering.

Growth, Energy, and Living Things

Some of the characteristics that distinguish living things from nonliving things are the capacities for growth, food consumption, and release of energy for cellular work. Important biological processes involved in these functions are the nitrogen cycle, photosynthesis, and cellular respiration.

The Nitrogen Cycle

Nitrogen, which makes up nearly 80 percent of Earth's atmosphere, is an essential ingredient for living tissues. Human beings and other animals depend on plants as a source of nitrogen. Plants cannot manufacture nitrogen themselves, so to obtain it they must depend on other organisms.

Free nitrogen, however, cannot be used by organisms, so it must combine with other elements to form *nitrates* that can be used. Plants absorb these nitrates to manufacture *amino acids*, which are essential components of protein needed by living cells. Amino acids are used to manufacture both proteins and nucleic acids that are absorbed by man.

The conversion of free nitrogen into a combined form is called *nitrogen fixing*. This is best achieved by certain bacteria—microorganisms and decomposers—that live in the soil. These microorganisms live in special sacs, called *nodules*, on the roots of legumes—plants such as alfalfa, peas, and beans. The microorganisms produce *nitrogenase*, an enzyme that is essential to nitrogen fixing.

Scientists believe that all of the nitrogen in Earth's atmosphere has been fixed and liberated many times. At any one time, probably only a few pounds of nitrogenase exist on our planet. This small amount, however, is enough to sustain all life on Earth.

EXERCISE 9: THE NITROGEN CYCLE

Directions: Choose the best answer for each of the following questions.

1. *Symbiosis* describes the relationship between two organisms that are different but that live together for their mutual benefit. The microorganisms that live in the nodules attached to legumes may be described as symbiotic. Another example of a symbiotic relationship would be

   (1) bacteria that can live only in the stomachs of hoofed animals and that help the animals digest food
   (2) bees that make their hives in caves, thereby providing a ready source of food for bears
   (3) soldier ants that live and work together in colonies
   (4) tapeworms that live in the intestines of humans
   (5) scavengers such as vultures that feed on the carcasses of dead animals

2. Which of the following foods, known for its high protein content, obtains this characteristic from the nitrogen-fixing process?

   (1) chicken　　(2) beef　　(3) peanuts　　(4) wheat germ　　(5) milk

3. Which of the following farming procedures best illustrates the process of nitrogen fixing?

(1) rotating a crop of cotton one year with a crop of beets
(2) irrigating the land with more modern methods
(3) using more advanced equipment to plow the land
(4) rotating the planting of cotton one year with a crop of soybeans
(5) using airplanes to spray the crops with insecticides

Answers are on page 442.

> **DID YOU KNOW THAT:** Alfalfa, a popular nitrogen-fixing plant, is able to survive dry climates and long periods of drought and that its roots can penetrate seventeen feet into the ground to reach moist earth and water?

Photosynthesis

Plants can live without human beings, but human beings cannot live without plants. Plants provide the oxygen we need to breathe and the nutrients we need to thrive. Green plants are self-sufficient because they are able to make their own food, while humans and lower animals must obtain their food to live.

Photosynthesis is the food-making process by which green plants convert the light from the sun into usable chemical energy. Photosynthesis can be understood as a process involving several steps.

The first step is the capture of energy by the plant. In most plants the process of photosynthesis takes place within the *chloroplasts*, where chlorophyll molecules absorb light. *Chlorophyll* is the substance that gives plants their green color.

Using the energy that chlorophyll releases from sunlight, the plant splits water into its two components—oxygen and hydrogen. The oxygen is released to the atmosphere, and hydrogen recombines with carbon dioxide to produce carbohydrate molecules (a form of starch) in the plant.

EXERCISE 10: PHOTOSYNTHESIS

Directions: Choose the best answer for each of the following questions.

1. Which of the following may we conclude about plants and the process of photosynthesis?

A. Plants that do not possess chlorophyll must use a process other than photosynthesis to produce the energy they need.

B. Photosynthesis is used by plants to make energy because it is the simplest method available.

C. Plants that do not use the process of photosynthesis are parasites; they must obtain food from another source.

(1) A　　**(2)** B　　**(3)** C　　**(4)** A and B　　**(5)** A and C

Question 2 is based on the information in the following passage.

> Some plants have leaves in which chlorophyll is lacking in some parts and is present in others. A coleus plant, with its brightly colored leaves, is one example. In an experiment in which the pigment (color) of the coleus leaf is removed, an iodine solution will identify places where starch is present by turning that part of the leaf brown.

2. Which of the following would you predict to happen to a coleus leaf in such an experiment?

   (1) The areas that turn brown will be areas where the leaf was green originally.
   (2) The leaf would not turn brown at all.
   (3) The areas that turn brown are the areas where the leaf was not green.
   (4) The entire leaf would turn brown.
   (5) Only half the leaf would turn brown.

Answers are on page 442.

DID YOU KNOW THAT: Some algae (green plants that inhabit the ocean) are found at depths where light is nonexistent? Because light is necessary for photosynthesis, scientists are puzzled as to how these algae photosynthesize.

Cellular Respiration

Cellular respiration is the complex series of chemical reactions by which a cell releases the energy trapped inside glucose molecules. *Glucose*, a form of sugar, is the end product of the process of photosynthesis. The process of cellular respiration, then, is the reverse of photosynthesis.

During cellular respiration, cells (plant or animal) break down the glucose so that energy is released for cellular work. Because the energy cannot be free-floating in the cell, it is repackaged and stored.

Cellular respiration occurs in three stages, beginning with the breakdown of a molecule of glucose and ending with the energy needed for the cell to perform its work. Energy that is not used is released in the form of heat.

EXERCISE 11: CELLULAR RESPIRATION

Directions: Choose the best answer for each of the following questions.

1. The function of cellular respiration is to

   (1) release water in the cell
   (2) produce oxygen for the cell
   (3) create energy from a cell fuel source
   (4) consume carbon dioxide
   (5) help in photosynthesis

2. From the information about cellular respiration, we can infer that

    (1) in plants, photosynthesis must always precede cellular respiration
    (2) no relationship exists between photosynthesis and cellular respiration
    (3) photosynthesis and respiration share many processes
    (4) cellular respiration occurs only in animal cells
    (5) plants do not perform cellular work

3. The rate of cellular respiration in humans can be measured by the amount of carbon dioxide exhaled. Which of the following would you expect to be true about the rate of cellular respiration for a group of students who are the same age, height, and weight?

    (1) Africans would have a higher rate of cellular respiration than Asians
    (2) boys would have a higher rate of cellular respiration than girls
    (3) girls would have a higher rate of cellular respiration than boys
    (4) athletes would tend to have higher rates of cellular respiration than nonathletes
    (5) nonathletes would have higher rates of cellular respiration than athletes

4. Which of the following procedures would be *most effective* in proving your hypothesis in the preceding example?

    (1) measuring the amounts of carbon dioxide exhaled by the students immediately after they wake up
    (2) measuring the amounts of carbon dioxide exhaled by every student after vigorous exercise
    (3) measuring the amounts of carbon dioxide exhaled by one student at rest and another student after vigorous exercise
    (4) measuring the amounts of carbon dioxide exhaled by half the students at rest and half the students after vigorous exercise
    (5) taking a reading of all of the students' blood pressures

Question 5 is based on the following passage.

> Glucose, a form of carbohydrate, is the body's main fuel source; however, it cannot get into the cells without insulin, a hormone secreted by the body. Diabetes mellitus is a condition in which the body either
>
> 1. does not produce enough insulin to break down glucose, or,
>
> 2. does not effectively use the insulin it produces to break down the glucose into a form cells can use.
>
> To correct this problem, some diabetics must take additional insulin.

5. By which of the following methods can *all* diabetics control the condition and avoid experiencing heart disease and blindness that can result from diabetes?

A. regulating their intake of glucose (sugars and carbohydrates)

B. increasing the levels of insulin in the body by taking insulin injections

C. maintaining a reasonable exercise regimen to keep weight down

    (1) A   **(2)** B   **(3)** C   **(4)** A and B   **(5)** A and C

Answers are on page 442.

Diversity of Life

The planet Earth is home to well over a million different kinds of living organisms. These organisms range from the lowest form—bacteria—to the highest form—*Homo sapiens*. Their habitats range from the ocean depths to mountain peaks, from subzero cold to boiling mud pots.

We take for granted this abundance and diversity of life until we are warned that one member of life's family faces extinction. Many years ago in the United States, the passenger pigeon became extinct. The same fate nearly happened to the whooping crane. Today, the panda (found mainly in China) is threatened with extinction.

Humanity, as the natural steward of Earth's life forms, has the important responsibility of overseeing this inventory of life. The job of categorizing the kinds of living things has been made easier by a system of classification.

Classification of Organisms

The classification system for living things moves from the general to the specific. Each downward step in the classification system provides more detail about the organism that is classified.

The **kingdom** is the broadest grouping. Within each kingdom, the organisms with the greatest similarities are grouped further into a **phylum**. Below the phylum is the **class**. The class is followed by an **order**, a **family**, a **genus**, and a species. The **species** is the final category of classification. The classification of the human (*Homo sapiens*) is illustrated in the following chart.

TAXONOMY OF HUMAN CLASSIFICATION

Category	Taxon	Characteristics
Kingdom	Animalia	Is multicellular, cannot make its own food, is able to move
Phylum	Chordata	Has a notochord (skeletal rod) and hollow nerve cord
Class	Mammalia	Has hair or fur, female secretes milk to nourish young
Order	Primate	Has flattened fingers for grasping, keen vision, poor sense of smell
Family	Hominidae	Walks on two feet, has flat face, eyes facing forward, color vision
Genus	Homo	Has long childhood, large brain, speech ability
Species	Sapiens	Has reduced body hair, high forehead, prominent chin

EXERCISE 12: CLASSIFICATION OF ORGANISMS

Directions: Read the definitions and apply them to the questions that follow.

Listed below, from lowest to highest, are the five kingdoms that all living organisms are classified into.

kingdom monera—simple one-celled, mobile organisms lacking organelles, some of which can produce their own food (example: bacteria)

kingdom protista—single-celled, mobile organisms having a more complex cell structure than monera (example: paramecia)

kingdom fungi—multicellular, lacks chlorophyll, cannot move, obtains food from other organisms (example: mushroom)

kingdom plantae—multicellular, has chlorophyll, produces its own food, has no mobility (example: moss)

kingdom animalia—multicellular, capable of moving by itself and obtaining its own food (example: bird)

1. Streptococcus is a single-celled organism that has no organelles and that occurs in a sequence of chains. It causes strep throat when it invades the throat. In which kingdom would it be classified?

    (1) monera   **(2)** protista   **(3)** fungi   **(4)** plantae   **(5)** animalia

2. Mold is a parasite that grows on bread, cheese, or other organic foods. It lacks chlorophyll and obtains nutrients from the host. In which kingdom would it be classified?

    (1) monera   **(2)** protista   **(3)** fungi   **(4)** plantae   **(5)** animalia

3. The amoeba is a one-celled organism with very few organelles. It changes its shape and moves with the aid of pseudopods, or "false feet." In which kingdom would it be classified?

    (1) monera   **(2)** protista   **(3)** fungi   **(4)** plantae   **(5)** animalia

Answers are on page 442.

DID YOU KNOW THAT: We are losing as many as one species per day and that the rate of extinction today is 400 times faster than in previous centuries?

Evolution and Natural Selection

Among all cultures of human beings, there is some explanation for the origin of humankind. In many cultures, the theory of Divine Creation is the most widely accepted explanation for the origin of Earth and its creatures. This belief holds that a supreme being created the world and its varied forms of life.

A scientific explanation that has wide currency is the theory of *evolution*. Proposed in 1859 by Charles Darwin in his book *On the Origin of Species*, the theory holds that all forms of life developed gradually (over 600 million years) from different and often much simpler ancestors. These forms of life adapted over the years to meet the demands of their environment. Thus, all lines of descent can be traced back to a common ancestral organism. As offspring differed from their parents, generations with characteristics that were less and less alike resulted. Ultimately, new species were formed from the diverse offspring because these new characteristics were inheritable.

The new characteristics of the offspring are explained by a process called natural selection. According to *natural selection*, the species that are best adapted to the conditions under which they live survive, and those that do not adapt perish. This theory is also known as the "survival of the fittest."

Darwin's theories were considered bizarre for his time. The creationist theory had held that all species had been created and remained unchanged since the beginning of time. It had widespread acceptance and, until Darwin's discovery, remained unchallenged. Darwin demonstrated that evolution is an ongoing process whose final outcome has not yet been determined.

EXERCISE 13: EVOLUTION AND NATURAL SELECTION

Directions: Choose the best answer for each question below.

1. An unusual member of the animal kingdom is the duckbill platypus—an animal that has many characteristics of birds, mammals, and reptiles. Found in Australia and Tasmania, the animal has a ducklike bill, has webbed and clawed feet, is covered with thick fur, and reproduces by laying eggs.

   Which of the following hypotheses related to Darwin's theory of evolution could be applied to the platypus?

   (1) The platypus is the result of the interbreeding of three distinct animal classes.
   (2) The platypus is the earliest living member of the mammalian family.
   (3) The platypus developed independently in a closed environment during the early history of mammals.
   (4) The platypus was not subject to the influences described in Darwin's theory.
   (5) Mammal life originated in Australia and Tasmania hundreds of millions of years ago.

Questions 2 and 3 refer to the following passage.

Mammals are placed in two groups—*placental* (having a placenta that nourishes the fetus) and *marsupial* (having a pouch in which the young are nourished and carried). Most of the world's marsupials are found on the continent of Australia and the islands nearby, where few placental mammals lived during the early history of the continents.

2. Which of the following hypotheses *best* suggests why marsupials are found primarily in and around Australia?

A. Australia, a subcontinent, became isolated from the other six continents millions of years ago.

B. Marsupials didn't have to compete with placental mammals for survival.

C. Australia is the only continent that has the climate to support marsupials.

(1) A   **(2)** B   **(3)** C   **(4)** A and B   **(5)** A and C

3. The presence of which of the following marsupials native to North America would dispute the belief that all marsupials originated in Australia?

(1) koala
(2) kangaroo
(3) opossum
(4) wombat
(5) bandicoot

4. Based on the preceding information about how marsupials differ from placental mammals, we can infer that

(1) marsupials are less biologically advanced than placental mammals
(2) placental mammals are more primitive than marsupials
(3) marsupials cannot survive in areas other than Australia and North America
(4) marsupials are the oldest forms of life on Earth
(5) marsupials descended from the reptiles

5. Which of the following mammals *best* exhibits a physical adaptation to environmental conditions?

(1) cow
(2) lion
(3) mouse
(4) seal
(5) bear

Answers are on page 442.

DID YOU KNOW THAT: The oldest living thing in the United States is the General Sherman tree, an evergreen that grows in the Sequoia National Park? It is nearly 4,000 years old.

WRITING ACTIVITY 2

In 1925, a Tennessee science teacher, John Scopes, was tried in court for teaching the theory of evolution—the belief that humans and apes descended from common ancestors. At the time, a Tennessee statute forbade the teaching of any theory that contradicted the story of Divine Creation as depicted in the Bible. Should states have the authority to dictate what beliefs teachers should impart to their students? Write an essay of two or three paragraphs defending your point of view.

Ecology and Ecosystems

The science of *ecology* involves the interrelationship of a living organism with its nonliving environment. Ecology is a young science. The word *ecology* comes from the Greek word *oikos*, meaning "house" or "dwelling." Ecology, then, is the study of how we live on the planet Earth. The ecologist studies the relationships between the component organisms and their environments. A self-supporting environment is called an *ecosystem*. The photosynthetic producers, the consumers, decomposers, and their environment constitute an ecosystem.

In a typical ecosystem, the primary producers are the green plants that derive their energy from the sun. A primary consumer would be a rabbit that feeds on the leaves of the green plant. A secondary consumer in this ecosystem would be a fox that preys on the rabbit. A tertiary, or third-level, consumer would be the buzzard that feeds on the carcass that the fox leaves behind. Finally, decomposers—the bacteria and fungi that feed on the scraps left by the buzzard—provide the nitrates necessary for the green plants, the first link in this chain.

The ecological balance of a community is delicate. The removal of one key element can destroy a system, sometimes permanently.

The following passage describes an imbalance in a particular ecosystem.

EXERCISE 14: ECOLOGY AND ECOSYSTEMS

Directions: Read the passage and in the blanks below write the correct element in the ecosystem described in the passage.

At the turn of the century, ranchers moved onto the grassy Kaibab Plateau in northern Arizona. They were attracted by the fine grazing areas and abundance of deer for hunting. Fearing that the mountain lion, another inhabitant of the region, would prey on the cattle and deer, the ranchers waged a campaign to eradicate the cat from the plateau. They were successful in their effort, and mountain lions disappeared within a few years.

Their success produced catastrophic ecological results, however. Increased numbers of deer, along with herds of cattle that grazed on the land, denuded it. Soon, heavy rains caused major erosion, and the land was reduced to a fraction of its usefulness. This problem has occurred repeatedly where humans have manipulated an ecosystem without considering the possible consequences.

1. primary producer _____

2. primary consumers _____ and _____

3. tertiary consumer _____

4. The destruction of the _____ led to the increase of grazing by _____ and _____, which led to _____ of the land and its eventual _____ by heavy rains.

Answers are on page 443.

DID YOU KNOW THAT: Scientists estimate that it takes between 500 and 600 years to make a one-inch layer of topsoil?

2
EARTH SCIENCE—THE STUDY OF EARTH

Some of the most dramatic scientific discoveries in recent years have taken place in the field of earth science. *Earth science* is the study of the planet Earth and its origin and development. It differs from the life sciences in that it focuses on nonliving rather than living things. Earth science is a very broad field that covers the subjects of astronomy, geology, meteorology, and oceanography.

Astronomy—The Study of Heavenly Bodies

The beginning of any study of Earth generally lies in astronomy, one of the oldest of all sciences. *Astronomers* study the size, movements, and composition of the heavenly bodies. By observing the stars, planets, comets, and other objects in space, astronomers hope to understand how our planet was created and how it evolved. A number of important theories have been advanced to explain the beginning of Earth and the universe in which it lies. Two related theories are the big bang theory and the pulsation theory.

The Big Bang and Pulsation Theories

The leading theory to explain the origin of the universe is the *big bang theory*. According to this theory, a "cosmic egg" made up of dust and gas containing all the matter in the universe exploded. This explosion occurred 15 to 20 billion years ago, creating the basic atoms, elements, and heavenly bodies of the universe. The big bang theory is widely accepted because it accounts for the apparent expansion of the universe and the background radiation found in outer space.

A further refinement of the big bang theory was the development of the *pulsation theory*. According to this theory, the universe will expand to a certain point and then begin to contract. This contraction will continue until the cosmic egg is again achieved, when another "big bang" will create expansion in the universe.

As scientists can never know for certain how the universe came to be, theories such as these help to explain their observations.

Stars and Galaxies

The big bang theory also explains how stars are formed. According to supporters of the theory, the energy from the bang was so powerful that matter lighter than air remained suspended in space (just as the energy from an explosion releases particles that remain in the atmosphere). Eventually, the force of gravity exerted itself, and the matter was drawn, along with helium and hydrogen gases, into dark, cloudlike formations. The gaseous matter became compressed, and the colliding of the compressed particles produced heat. A star developed when the temperature reached 15 million degrees centigrade—the temperature at which nuclear reactions begin.

The lifetime of a star ranges from a few hundred thousand years to billions of years. Most stars eventually use up their supply of hydrogen, contract to a smaller size, and then explode. The explosion results in clouds of dust and gas. Some stars eventually contract to black holes—stars of very small size that have gravitational fields so strong that not even light escapes from them.

Most stars exist within a very large formation called a *galaxy*. Hundreds of millions of galaxies are believed to exist in the universe. The stars of a galaxy may be so closely packed together that we can see them only as a blur of light rather than as individual stars.

Our galaxy, the Milky Way, is a spiral galaxy, as are 80 percent of all galaxies. The Milky Way is composed of at least 100 billion stars and enough matter, in the form of dust and gas, to create millions of additional suns. The following illustration shows the Milky Way Galaxy.

THE MILKY WAY GALAXY

Sun's Position

EXERCISE 1: THE BIG BANG THEORY

Directions: Choose the best answer for the following question.

Which of the following facts support the big bang theory's explanation of the creation of the universe?

(1) The universe is constantly expanding.
(2) The universe has no beginning or end.
(3) Background radiation is found throughout the universe.
(4) Both 1 and 2
(5) Both 1 and 3

Answer is on page 443.

EXERCISE 2: STARS AND GALAXIES

Directions: Number the steps of star formation in the correct sequence, with *1* representing the first step and *4* the last.

_____ Heat is produced by the colliding of molecules.

_____ Fifteen million degrees centigrade is reached, and visible light is emitted.

_____ Dust and gas move throughout the universe.

_____ Gas and dust become compressed because of gravitational forces.

Answers are on page 443.

DID YOU KNOW THAT: In 1987, astronomers reported observing starlight from a new galaxy and that they have evidence that planets are taking shape around stars other than our own?

The Sun and the Solar System

The Sun is the star at the center of our solar system, and, despite its importance to our world, it is really only an "average" star when compared to others in our galaxy. It is average in age (4 to 5 billion years old), size (860,000 miles in diameter or about 100 times Earth's diameter), and heat intensity (its surface temperature is about 6,000 degrees centigrade).

Other members of the solar system include the nine planets, seven of which have one or more satellites (moons), and 1,600 large asteroids located between Mars and Jupiter.

The inner planets (Mercury, Venus, Earth, and Mars) are small, with high densities and few satellites. The outer planets (Jupiter, Saturn, Uranus, and Neptune) are large gas giants and have many moons. Pluto is so far away that all we can tell is that it is not similar to other outer planets.

The planets are believed to have begun as clumps of matter within the dust cloud that formed the Sun. They were too small to achieve the conditions needed to become stars. Instead, they cooled and became the planets as we know them. Our space probes have reached all except the most distant outer planets, and it appears that Earth is the only inhabited body in our solar system.

The following illustration shows our solar system.

OUR SOLAR SYSTEM

EXERCISE 3: THE SOLAR SYSTEM

Directions: Choose the best answer for each question below.

1. The "Goldilocks problem" in astronomy (in which one of the eight planets other than Earth is too hot to support life and the other too cold to support life) applies to which two planets?

    (1) Pluto and Neptune
    (2) Mars and Saturn
    (3) Mercury and Venus
    (4) Venus and Mars
    (5) Jupiter and Uranus

2. The Earth's sister planets are Venus and Mars. Scientists most likely have designated these two as sister planets because

    (1) life has been proven to exist on Venus and Mars
    (2) all three planets share the same orbit
    (3) both planets show evidence of having had Earthlike climates sometime in the distant past
    (4) both planets are the two closest to the Sun
    (5) all three planets are the exact same age and size

Answers are on page 443.

EXERCISE 4: THE PLANETS

Directions: Based on the information in the table, complete each of the following statements by writing the name of the correct planet in the blank.

Planet	Length of Year	Rotates on Its Axis Every	Number of Satellites	Distance from Sun (miles)
Mercury	88 days	58 days	0	36 million
Venus	225 days	243 days	0	67 million
Earth	365.26 days	23.9 hours	1	93 million
Mars	686.98 days	24.6 hours	2	142 million

1. The length of the day is approximately the same on _____ and _____.

2. Of the planets listed, based on Earth years, you would age at the slowest rate on _____.

3. Of the planets listed, based on Earth years, you would age at the fastest rate on _____.

4. Of the planets listed, _____ rotates on its axis most slowly.

5. Mars takes a little more than three times longer to revolve around the Sun than _____.

Answers are on page 443.

EXERCISE 5: THE SUN AND SOLAR SYSTEM

Directions: Choose the best answer for the following question, based on the table on page 378.

There appears to be a relationship between the distance of these planets from the Sun and

(1) the amount of time it takes for the planet to rotate on its axis
(2) the number of satellites or moons it has
(3) the time it takes the planet to revolve around the Sun
(4) both 1 and 2
(5) both 2 and 3

Answer is on page 443.

DID YOU KNOW THAT: Venus rotates backward with respect to the Sun, so that from Venus the Sun would appear to rise in the west and set in the east?

WRITING ACTIVITY 1

Solar energy is being considered seriously as an alternative form of energy in American life. To what extent is solar energy being explored and applied where you live? If it is not being applied, what are the likely reasons? Write a paragraph describing the role solar energy plays where you live.

Geology—The Study of Earth's Formation

Earthquakes! Floods! Volcanic eruptions! The occurrence of each of these natural disasters is evidence that, far from being the steady ground on which we stand, Earth is changing constantly.

Today's Earth is not the same as the Earth of a thousand years ago; nor will it be the same a thousand years from today. *Geologists* study the features of Earth and how they affect its development. In this century alone, geologists have made significant discoveries that have revolutionized the entire field of earth science. Probably the most significant of all findings made in recent history has been the formulation of the theory of plate tectonics, a theory that explains the development of mountains and ocean trenches and the occurrence of earthquakes and volcanic eruptions.

Continental Drift and Plate Tectonics

Scientists have long observed that accurately drawn maps of Africa and South America suggest that the two continents once fit together. Based on this observation, geologists formulated the *theory of continental drift*. According to the theory, all seven continents formed a supercontinent millions of years ago. It broke apart and split into the land masses that are recognized today as the seven continents.

Despite this appearance that the continents interlock like pieces of a puzzle, scientists could not explain why the continents drifted apart. The *theory of plate tectonics*, advanced in the 1960s, provided an explanation of the phenomenon.

According to the theory, Earth is made up of the crust, mantle, outer core, and inner core, as depicted in the following picture:

EARTH'S STRUCTURE

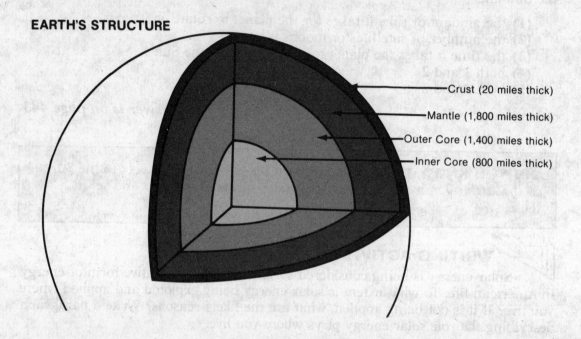

Crust (20 miles thick)
Mantle (1,800 miles thick)
Outer Core (1,400 miles thick)
Inner Core (800 miles thick)

The crust and upper mantle are made up of about twenty plates. These plates may be likened to plates floating on the surface of water in a vast sink. They move very slowly—approximately one-half to four inches per year. Attached to the surface of these plates are the continents and the ocean floor. As the plates slowly move, they carry the continents with them. Geologists believe that the plates move because currents of partially molten rock in the mantle carry them.

This motion of the plates appears to explain the formation of mountains and ocean trenches and the occurrence of earthquakes and volcanoes. For example, when two plates collide, one plate piles atop another, forming a mountain. When one plate is forced down into the mantle of another, a trench occurs. A volcano is created when the heat beneath the surface of Earth melts the plate material that was forced into the trench and sends the molten rock to the surface. An earthquake is formed by the shifting and breaking of the surface rocks when two plates slide past each other.

The vibrations caused by the slippage of plates are called *seismic waves*. The strength of these waves is measured by a device called a seismograph and then rated on the Richter scale. Earthquakes measuring more than 4.5 on the Richter scale are considered potentially dangerous.

EXERCISE 6: PLATE TECTONICS

Directions: Choose the best answer for the following question.

According to the passage, the theory of plate tectonics helps explain which of the following?

A. the Earth's gravitational pull

B. earthquakes, volcanoes, and mountains

C. the theory of continental drift

   (1) A
   (2) B
   (3) C
   (4) A and B
   (5) B and C

Answer is on page 443.

EXERCISE 7: EARTHQUAKES

Directions: Choose the best answer for the question below, based on the following map.

U.S. EARTHQUAKE ZONES AND SEISMIC RISK

Potential for Damage
0—None
1—Minor
2—Moderate
3—Major

Which of the following statements about earthquakes is supported by the map?

   (1) California is the only state in which residents might expect major earthquake damage.
   (2) Texas and Florida are the only states that do not have to worry about earthquakes.
   (3) The potential for moderate to major earthquake damage is greatest on the West Coast.
   (4) Most of the continental United States is not affected by earthquakes.
   (5) Earthquakes are the most dangerous phenomenon on Earth.

Answer is on page 443.

EXERCISE 8: CONTINENTAL DRIFT

Directions: Read the following passage and choose the best answer for each question.

Ascension Island is a small volcanic island located in the south Atlantic halfway between Africa and South America. It is a famous breeding ground for sea turtles. Giant green turtles each year swim 2,000 miles from the coast of South America to lay their eggs on Ascension Island. This phenomenon has puzzled scientists for years.

1. Which of the following geological hypotheses best explains the behavior of the giant sea turtles?

   A. Ascension Island is the only place in the world where turtle eggs can survive.

   B. Predators, like alligators that live on the coast of South America, eat turtle eggs, forcing the sea turtles to migrate.

   C. The turtles laid their eggs on Ascension Island millions of years ago before the continents of Africa and South America became separated.

   (1) A   **(2)** B   **(3)** C   **(4)** A and B   **(5)** B and C

2. The behavior of the sea turtles, the location of South America with respect to Africa, and the theory of continental drift all point to what possibility about the Atlantic Ocean?

   (1) It was once a river.
   (2) It has always been the size it is today.
   (3) It has moved from its original position on Earth.
   (4) It did not exist when giant sea turtles laid their eggs millions of years ago.
   (5) It was probably once a narrow sea between Africa and South America before the sea floor spread apart.

Answers are on page 443.

DID YOU KNOW THAT: The coastal areas of the continents surrounding the Pacific Ocean are collectively called the Ring of Fire because more than three-fourths of the world's earthquakes occur there?

Geologic Time

What is a long period of time to you? Without any reference point, your answer might vary from an hour to a century. If you were told to measure time in relation to your own life, you might consider fifty years to be a long time. In geology, however, fifty years is not very long, since geologic time extends back nearly five billion years, when geologists believe Earth was formed.

We owe our concept of *absolute time*—time not influenced by man's arbitrary reference points—to geology. Geologists are able to fix periods of time by studying the rocks found in Earth's crust. These rocks serve as records of time.

The rocks found in Earth's crust are of three types, described according to their origins. These rocks are igneous, metamorphic, and sedimentary. *Igneous* rocks are formed when molten rock (magma) hardens. Just below igneous rock are *metamorphic* rocks, which have been changed by high pressure and temperature within the crust. The rocks that undergo metamorphosis are mainly igneous rocks. *Sedimentary* rocks are deposited near Earth's surface by wind, water, and ice. In sedimentary rock, the oldest layers are on the bottom and the youngest are on the top.

Instruments for Measuring Time

We have determined which rocks are older than others, but how do we find out how old that is? Radiometric measurement is one tool that scientists use to measure absolute time. In *radiometric measurement*, geologists measure the rate of radioactive decay in the minerals found in the rock. Over the last century, scientists have learned that radioactive substances will change, or decay, into nonradioactive substances over a period of time. This method is valid for matter up to 50,000 years in age. Radiometric dating works well with samples of igneous and sedimentary rocks because it measures the radioactivity of minerals created when the rocks were formed. For metamorphic rock, however, the age of the original rock and the age of metamorphism are difficult to pinpoint.

In addition to radiometric dating, the principle of *faunal succession* is used to determine the age of sedimentary rock. With this method, geologists examine the types of animal fossils found in layers of sedimentary rock. Igneous and metamorphic rock rarely contain fossils. Scientists have found that certain layers of rock will contain certain kinds of fossils, no matter where in the world the rock is located. Moreover, scientists have found that certain fossils are always found at lower layers than others, indicating that a sequence exists to the evolution of organisms.

EXERCISE 9: MEASURING GEOLOGIC TIME

Directions: Choose the best answer for each of the following questions.

1. Based on the information in the preceding passage, which correctly describes the placement of the three types of rocks?

   (1) Igneous is located at the surface, metamorphic in the middle, and sedimentary on the bottom.
   (2) Sedimentary is located at the surface, metamorphic in the middle, and igneous at the bottom.
   (3) Metamorphic is located at the surface, sedimentary in the middle, and igneous at the bottom.
   (4) Igneous is located at the surface, sedimentary in the middle, and metamorphic at the bottom.
   (5) Sedimentary is located at the surface, igneous in the middle, and metamorphic at the bottom.

2. Dating metamorphic and igneous rocks presents problems for scientists because

   A. they almost never contain fossils

   B. for metamorphic rocks, the age of the original rock and date of metamorphism are more difficult to pinpoint

   C. neither type of rock can be dated radiometrically

   (1) A
   (2) B
   (3) C
   (4) A and B
   (5) A and C

3. Trilobite fossils are found at a depth of 18 meters in a rock bed, and coral fossils are found at 14 meters. Which of the following is likely to be true about each organism?

   (1) Coral is older than trilobites.
   (2) Coral and trilobites are the same age.
   (3) Coral and trilobites share a common ancestry.
   (4) Trilobites are more advanced than corals.
   (5) Trilobites are older than corals.

Answers are on page 443.

Minerals and Rocks

Just as cells are the building blocks of living organisms, minerals are the building blocks of rocks. A *mineral* is a natural, inorganic solid with a specific composition and structure. All specimens of a given mineral share certain physical properties. Some physical properties of minerals are crystalline form, hardness, color, and cleavage (the way they break).

More than 95 percent of Earth's crust is made up of the minerals formed from the elements oxygen and silicon. The following chart shows the eight main elements, including their percent of the crust's weight and volume.

Element	Percent of Crust's Mass (weight)	Percent of Crust's Volume (space)
Oxygen	46.71	94.24
Silicon	27.69	0.51
Aluminum	8.07	0.44
Iron	5.05	0.37
Calcium	3.65	1.04
Sodium	2.75	1.21
Potassium	2.58	1.85
Magnesium	2.08	0.27

EXERCISE 10: MINERALS AND ROCKS

Directions: Choose the best answer for the questions below.

1. According to the information in the table, which element represents less of the crust's weight but occupies over three times the space of silicon, a major component of the crust?

   (1) sodium
   (2) calcium
   (3) potassium
   (4) magnesium
   (5) iron

2. Which of the following elements also represents less weight than silicon but takes up more space?

   (1) aluminum
   (2) oxygen
   (3) magnesium
   (4) sodium
   (5) iron

3. The implication from the facts in the preceding table is that the two elements that represent less weight than silicon but occupy more space

   (1) are denser than silicon
   (2) combine more often with oxygen than silicon
   (3) represent a greater percentage of the crust's weight
   (4) weigh less than oxygen
   (5) cannot be compressed as easily as silicon

4. Which of the following best explains why oxygen, a gas, is the largest component of Earth's crust?

   (1) Oxygen gives Earth's crust its lightness.
   (2) Oxygen is the most abundant element in the world.
   (3) Oxygen is found in plants, and plants are significant parts of Earth's crust.
   (4) Oxygen is needed to sustain all life on Earth.
   (5) Oxygen is capable of combining with most of the elements in Earth's crust.

Answers are on page 444.

DID YOU KNOW THAT: The softest mineral known to man is talc, from which talcum powder is made, and the hardest is the diamond? Diamonds are so hard that they can be cut only by another diamond.

The Changing Earth

Another process that contributes to the changing face of Earth is erosion. *Erosion* is the wearing away of Earth's surface. Erosion has occurred throughout time and will continue as long as dry land exists. You can see the process of erosion at work when you water your lawn. Under the pressure of a steady stream of water, loose soil is moved from a higher elevation to a lower one. The chief agents that cause erosion are gravity, wind, ice, and water.

The pull of *gravity* makes surface material move downward. Downslope movements may be rapid or very slow. They may involve only the surface material, or they may involve the bedrock underneath. Houses built on hills can contribute to soil movements because the weight of the homes may add to the gravitational force. For this reason, knowledge about erosional processes must be considered by homebuilders.

Wind contributes to the erosional process by carrying surface material from one location to another. Erosion occurs when rock particles wear away surface material much like the process involved in sandblasting, in which sand blown at high rates of speed wears away a brick's veneer.

Glaciers, huge sheets of ice that can move slowly over land, pick up and carry rocks and soil with them. When they pass through river valleys, they deepen them. Mountain glaciers, coupled with the downward force of gravity, create avalanches that can cause great erosional damage.

Of all the erosional agents, running water is the most powerful. Rivers, working with the force of gravity, are devastating in their erosional impact. The action of rivers flowing against the land has formed gorges as large as the Grand Canyon. As rivers erode land, they carry deposits with them. *Deltas* are formed at the mouths of rivers that empty into a lake or ocean. The soil that is carried along a river and deposited at its mouth is the richest and most fertile of all soils. The Nile and Mississippi rivers have formed deltas that are noted for their rich soil, making these regions highly desirable for agriculture.

EXERCISE 11: THE CHANGING EARTH

Directions: Choose the best answer for the following questions.

1. Which of the following procedures followed by a farmer is *not* related directly to preventing erosion?

    (1) planting grass in gullies to act as a filler
    (2) planting crops in alternate rows (strip farming)
    (3) contour plowing around a hill
    (4) planting new trees to replace those that die
    (5) planting more seeds than are necessary to yield a bountiful crop

2. The force of erosion is counteracted by the effects of changes in Earth's surface. Which of the following internal forces interrupt the external forces of erosion?

A. forces that cause volcanoes

B. forces that cause ocean trenches

C. forces that create mountains

(1) A
(2) B
(3) C
(4) A and B
(5) A and C

Answers are on page 444.

DID YOU KNOW THAT: Many lakes were formed by large holes dug by glaciers? These holes were later filled with water and became lakes.

WRITING ACTIVITY 2

What evidence of erosion can you see in the region where you live? Write two or three paragraphs describing how erosion has affected your community.

Oceanography—The Study of Earth's Oceans

Observed from space, Earth has been described as a big blue marble. The one feature that contributes to this description is water—it covers nearly 71 percent of Earth's surface. Water dominates our lives. For those who live near bodies of water, water provides recreation, food, and a means of transportation. Earth scientists who study large bodies of water are called *oceanographers*.

From their studies of the oceans, oceanographers have made many discoveries that help them to understand and explain phenomena they observe on Earth. For example, the theory of plate tectonics was further substantiated by the finding that a ridge encircling the globe lies under the ocean—the *oceanic ridge*. This ridge circles the globe like the seam of a baseball. Numerous openings have been photographed along the crest of this ridge. Evidence from the pictures provided the basis for the theory that magma forces itself up from the ridges, pushes the ocean plates apart, cools, and forms new rock that becomes part of the ocean plate.

The last twenty-five years have yielded many fascinating findings about the ocean, the last frontier on our planet. The advances in ocean technology, like those in space technology, are the chief reasons for our increased knowledge about the ocean. Inventions such as sonar (an underwater ranging device), deep-diving submarines, and remote-control cameras have aided in our exploration of the oceans.

The Oceans' Beginning

Oceanographers are not sure how Earth's oceans began. Many believe that the oceans were formed by the release of water bound up in rocks of Earth's interior. Evidence from some of the most ancient sedimentary rocks suggests that the original sediments forming the rocks were deposited in water.

While scientists are not certain about the beginning of Earth's oceans, they do know that the volume of water covering Earth is affected by the formation of glaciers and the melting of huge blocks of ice covering Earth's surface. The graph below illustrates the change in sea level during the past 20,000 years. (Glaciers covered much of Earth 20,000 years ago.)

EXERCISE 12: CHANGE IN SEA LEVEL

Directions: Choose the best answer for each of the following questions.

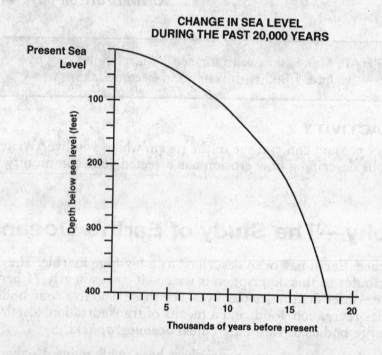

1. Based on the graph, Earth's sea level was at its lowest approximately

   (1) 1,000 years ago
   (2) 5,000 years ago
   (3) 10,000 years ago
   (4) 15,000 years ago
   (5) 18,000 years ago

2. Which of the following are best supported by the graph and the fact that the formation of glaciers significantly affects the level of Earth's oceans?

   A. The period when sea level was lowest was the period when glaciers were at their peak.

   B. The period when sea level was highest was the period after the glaciers had been melted for thousands of years.

   C. The period when sea level was at its lowest was the period when glaciers had been melted for thousands of years.

   D. The period when sea level was at its highest was the period when ice covered Earth.

   (1) A and B
   (2) A and C
   (3) B and C
   (4) A and D
   (5) B and D

Answers are on page 444.

EXERCISE 13: THE OCEANS' BEGINNING

Directions: Choose the best answer for the questions below.

DISTRIBUTION OF WATER ON EARTH

Type of Water	Relative % of abundance
Seawater	86.5
Lakes, rivers	0.03
Continental Ice	1.3
Water vapor in atmosphere	0.001
Water in sediments and sedimentary rocks	12.2
Total	100

1. Which of the following sources yields the smallest amount of water throughout Earth?

   (1) seawater
   (2) lakes and rivers
   (3) continental ice
   (4) water vapor in the atmosphere
   (5) water in sediments and sedimentary rocks

2. The presence of 12 percent of water in sediments and in sedimentary rocks lends support to the theory of

   (1) continental drift
   (2) plate tectonics
   (3) how Earth's sea level has risen over time
   (4) the origin of the oceans
   (5) faunal succession

Answers are on page 444.

DID YOU KNOW THAT: All the oceans except the North Pacific are divided in the center by an almost continuous system of mountains?

The Oceans' Tides

One phenomenon of the oceans that can be easily observed is the occurrence of tides. *Tides* result from the rising and falling of the ocean's surface caused by the gravitational pull of the Sun and the Moon on Earth. The Moon is the most dominant factor in causing tides because of its closeness to Earth.

When the Moon is directly overhead, the ocean beneath it tends to bulge up, causing a tide. On the opposite side of Earth, the oceans experience a lesser bulge. As Earth rotates once every twenty-four hours, it experiences two high tides and two low tides. The position of the Moon in relation to the Sun and Earth determines the period and height of the tides. *Spring tides* are tides of greater-than-average range. *Neap tides* are tides of smaller-than-average range. The illustration in the exercise below shows a spring tide and a neap tide.

EXERCISE 14: THE OCEANS' TIDES

Directions: Choose the best answer for the following questions.

SPRING AND NEAP TIDES

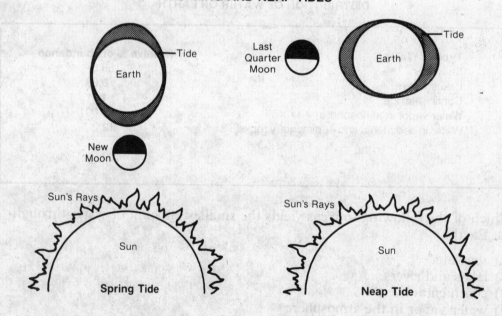

1. Spring tides are tides of greater-than-average range. During which two phases of the Moon is the gravitational pull of the Moon together with the Sun likely to be greatest, causing a spring tide?

    A. first quarter—when the Moon is to the right side of Earth

    B. full moon—when Earth is between the Sun and the Moon

    C. last quarter—when the Moon is to the left side of Earth, as shown

    D. new moon—when the Moon is between Earth and the Sun

    (1) A and B   **(2)** A and C   **(3)** A and D   **(4)** B and C   **(5)** B and D

2. Neap tides are tides of smaller-than-average range. During which two periods of the Moon is the gravitational pull of the Moon negated by the Sun, causing a neap tide?

A. first quarter—when the Moon is to the right side of Earth

B. full moon—when Earth is between the Sun and the Moon

C. last quarter—when the Moon is to the left side of Earth, as shown

D. new moon—when the Moon is between Earth and the Sun

(1) A and B
(2) A and C
(3) B and C
(4) B and D
(5) A and D

Questions 3 and 4 are based on the following explanation

   Syzygy (siz'-e-je) is the term that describes a rare alignment of the Sun, Moon, and Earth that causes extraordinarily high tides. This phenomenon occurred during the period from December 30, 1986, to January 4, 1987. It aggravated the severe storms that occurred along the Atlantic Coast. Three coinciding events occurred during this five-day period.

A. The Moon's orbit was closest to Earth—about 223,000 miles instead of 240,000 miles.

B. The Moon was directly between Earth and the Sun, causing a new moon.

C. Earth's orbit was the closest to the Sun—91½ million miles, instead of the normal 93 million miles.

3. The occurrence of which of the preceding events best explains why the tide was higher than normal?

(1) A
(2) B
(3) C
(4) A and B
(5) A and C

4. Conditions under which the Moon's orbit is farthest from Earth, Earth is between the Sun and the Moon, and Earth's orbit is farthest from the Sun would likely result in

(1) the same effect as syzygy
(2) unusually low tides
(3) neap tides
(4) spring tides
(5) unusually high tides

Answers are on page 444.

DID YOU KNOW THAT: There are areas in the world that have no tides, such as the Mediterranean Sea, the Baltic Sea, the Adriatic Sea, and the Gulf of Mexico?

WRITING ACTIVITY 3

Does water play a significant role in the region where you live? Write two or three paragraphs describing the importance of water in the areas of recreation, food, economics, transportation, and weather.

Meteorology—The Study of Earth's Atmosphere

Just as land and water constitute significant parts of Earth, so does the *atmosphere*—the invisible layer of air that envelops Earth. Scientists believe that it is primarily because of our atmosphere that life exists on Earth and not on neighboring planets such as Mars and Venus.

Meteorologists study Earth's atmosphere to understand and predict the weather. The atmosphere is not one distinct air mass that surrounds Earth; it is composed of several layers of air that begin at specific altitude ranges. Meteorologists have identified four layers of Earth's atmosphere. In ascending order (from lowest to highest) they are the troposphere, stratosphere, ionosphere, and exosphere. Each of these four layers serves a specific purpose in helping to sustain life on Earth.

The *troposphere* lies closest to Earth. It extends upward about seven to ten miles. Earth's weather occurs in this layer of the atmosphere, and it contains almost all of the clouds. The *tropopause* is the boundary where the troposphere ends and the stratosphere begins.

The *stratosphere* begins somewhere between seven and ten miles and extends upward about thirty miles. It is a uniform layer of air with little vertical air movement. Airplane travel in this layer is generally smooth and visibility always clear.

Beginning after the stratosphere, the *ionosphere* extends upward about 300 miles. The air in the ionosphere is extremely thin, and air particles are electrified. Through the ionosphere, radio waves are transmitted great distances around Earth.

The *exosphere* is the highest layer of the atmosphere. It is characterized by extreme heat during the day when the Sun's direct rays reach it and extreme cold at night when it is shielded from the Sun's direct rays.

EXERCISE 15: LAYERS OF EARTH'S ATMOSPHERE

Directions: Choose the best answer for each of the following questions after reading the passage below and studying the accompanying diagram.

At different altitudes of Earth's atmosphere we are able to observe different phenomena. Also, scientists are able to use different technologies to explore and understand Earth and the regions in outer space.

1. *Noctilucent* clouds, spectacular clouds that can be seen only at dusk, appear shortly after sunset. At which atmospheric level are these clouds visible?

   (1) exosphere
   (2) troposphere
   (3) stratosphere
   (4) ionosphere
   (5) tropopause

2. "D" layer radio waves that are transmitted around the world may be found at

   (1) the upper range of the stratosphere
   (2) the lower range of the stratosphere
   (3) the lower range of the ionosphere
   (4) the upper range of the ionosphere
   (5) the upper range of the troposphere

3. The illustration suggests that the peak of Mt. Everest

   A. is at times hidden by clouds

   B. extends beyond the tropopause

   C. lies in the troposphere

   (1) A
   (2) B
   (3) C
   (4) A and B
   (5) A and C

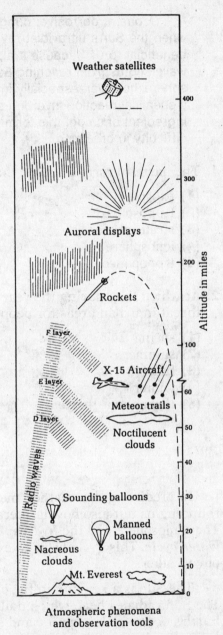

Atmospheric phenomena and observation tools

Answers are on page 444.

EXERCISE 16: OZONE IN THE ATMOSPHERE

Directions: Read the following passage and choose the best answer for each of the questions that follow.

> *Ozone*, a corrosive, pungent, and toxic gas, occurs in the atmosphere when the Sun's ultraviolet rays cause ionization in oxygen atoms. Ozone is beneficial to us because it absorbs ultraviolet rays, preventing these lethal wavelengths from reaching Earth's surface. At lower levels in Earth's atmosphere, however, especially in large urban areas, ozone can be created from a chemical reaction involving solar heat and the exhaust from cars. The chief ingredient of smog, this form of ozone is harmful to humans and can cause difficulty in breathing.

1. The harmful form of ozone that can be seen as smog is formed in the

   (1) exosphere
   (2) troposphere
   (3) stratosphere
   (4) ionosphere
   (5) tropopause

2. At which time during the year does the ozone level present a particular health threat in urban areas for people with respiratory problems?

   (1) spring
   (2) summer
   (3) fall
   (4) winter
   (5) throughout the year

Answers are on page 444.

The Water Cycle

In predicting the weather, meteorologists must consider not just the air surrounding us but also how it interacts with the water that covers Earth's surface. The atmosphere and the **hydrosphere** (the watery portion of Earth) create the **water cycle**. This cycle helps to explain precipitation, an important element in our weather.

The Sun is a key link in the chain of events that makes up the water cycle. The Sun radiates heat, which daily evaporates millions of tons of water from Earth's oceans, lakes, rivers, and streams into the air. As moist air rises, it slowly cools. Finally, it cools so much that the humidity (the amount of water vapor the air is holding) reaches 100 percent. At this point, the water vapor condenses and clouds form. Depending on the temperature and other conditions, either rain or snow falls as precipitation when the clouds can't hold all of the water. The rain or snow eventually flows to the ocean, and the cycle is completed again. The illustration on the next page shows the water cycle.

THE WATER CYCLE

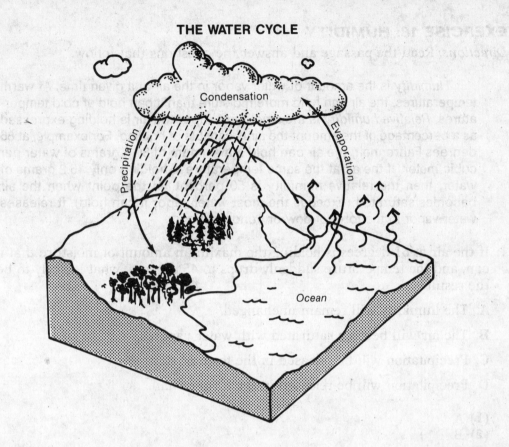

Condensation

Evaporation

Precipitation

Ocean

EXERCISE 17: THE WATER CYCLE

Directions: Number the steps of the water cycle in the correct sequence, with *1* representing the first step and *5* the last. The first one is done for you.

_____ Rain or snow returns water to the ocean.

_____ Condensation occurs, forming clouds.

__*1*__ The Sun radiates heat.

_____ Precipitation in the form of rain or snow occurs.

_____ Water evaporates into the atmosphere.

Answers are on page 444.

DID YOU KNOW THAT: The sky is blue because sunlight diffuses or scatters the rays of the colors found in the atmosphere's gases? Of all the colors in the rainbow, blue, purple, and violet have shorter rays than the other colors. So these three colors are diffused many more times and, therefore, dominate the sky.

EXERCISE 18: HUMIDITY

Directions: Read the passage and answer the questions that follow.

> *Humidity* is the amount of water vapor in the air at a given time. At warm temperatures, the air can hold more moisture than it can hold at cold temperatures. *Relative humidity* is the amount of vapor the air is holding expressed as a percentage of the amount the air is capable of holding. For example, at 86 degrees Fahrenheit, the air can hold a maximum of 30.4 grams of water per cubic meter. If the air at the same temperature is holding only 15.2 grams of water, then the relative humidity is 50 percent. At the point when the air becomes saturated (exceeds the most water vapor it can hold), it releases water vapor in the form of dew or condensation.

1. If the air at 61 degrees is holding the maximum amount of moisture that it can, and the temperature suddenly drops to 45 degrees, what is likely to be the result?

   A. The humidity will remain unchanged.

   B. The air will become saturated with water vapor.

   C. Precipitation will be released in the form of rain.

   D. Precipitation will be released in the form of hail.

   (1) A
   (2) B
   (3) C
   (4) B and C
   (5) B and D

2. During subfreezing days in many parts of the country, the indoor relative humidity decreases when homes are heated. Furniture and skin dry out, and static electricity increases. For health reasons, doctors recommend the use of humidifiers. Which of the following best explains the lack of humidity in the air indoors?

   A. The amount of water vapor in the air goes down.

   B. The water vapor in the air evaporates.

   C. The water vapor present in the air at lower temperatures is less than the amount that heated indoor air can hold.

   (1) A
   (2) B
   (3) C
   (4) A and B
   (5) B and C

3. What indoor relative humidity range would probably be comfortable when the outside temperature and humidity levels are extremely low?

(1) 1 to 5 percent
(2) 10 to 15 percent
(3) 30 to 40 percent
(4) 75 to 80 percent
(5) 90 to 100 percent

Answers are on page 445.

DID YOU KNOW THAT: When the humidity is high, wood, skin, and hair absorb moisture and expand and that blond human hair increases its length by 2½ percent as the relative humidity increases from 0 to 100 percent?

Air Masses, Fronts, and Weather

Another key element in determining Earth's weather is an air mass. Basically, an air mass may be either warm or cold. Cold air masses tend to be unstable and turbulent and move faster than warm air masses. The clouds that are formed by cold air masses are *cumulus clouds*—puffy, cottonlike clouds. During warm weather, when cold air masses bring precipitation, it is likely to be in the form of thundershowers. Warm air masses are usually stable, and the wind that accompanies them is steady. Clouds that are formed by warm air masses are *stratus clouds*—low-lying, level clouds that in warm weather bring precipitation in the form of drizzle.

A *front* occurs when two air masses collide and a boundary between the two masses forms. The weather for the land below is affected. Fronts may be either weak or strong. Strong fronts generally bring precipitation.

When cold air acts like a plow and pushes warm air back, a *cold front* forms. If the cold air retreats, and the warm air pushes it away, a *warm front* occurs. Sometimes, the boundary between the two air masses does not move, and the front becomes stationary. *Stationary fronts* bring conditions similar to those brought by warm fronts. However, precipitation that results is usually milder and lasts longer.

An understanding of the behavior of air masses and fronts helps weather forecasters predict weather conditions for a particular region with reasonable accuracy.

EXERCISE 19: AIR MASSES, FRONTS, AND WEATHER

Directions: Choose the best answer for the following questions.

1. Which of the following changes in the weather can occur when a strong warm air mass displaces a cold air mass?

   (1) Cumulus clouds may form, winds become gusty, and thunderstorms may result.
   (2) Stratus clouds may form, winds may become steady, and drizzling occurs.
   (3) Stratus clouds may form, winds become turbulent, and thunderstorms may result.
   (4) Cumulus clouds may form, winds become steady, and thundershowers may result.
   (5) The sky remains cloudless, and no winds or precipitation occurs.

2. A region experiences a steady drizzle for two days straight after having had cool, clear weather for several days before. Which of the following fronts is likely to have caused these weather conditions?

   (1) A weak cold front has moved in.
   (2) A weak warm front has moved in.
   (3) A stationary front has moved in.
   (4) A stationary front is slowly departing.
   (5) A strong warm front has moved in.

3. Based on the preceding passage, which of the following has *no* relation to the action of fronts in causing weather changes?

   (1) the temperature of the air mass
   (2) the speed at which the air mass moves
   (3) the strength of the air mass
   (4) the stability of the winds that accompany the air mass
   (5) the direction in which the air mass moves

Answers are on page 445.

DID YOU KNOW THAT: The winds of hurricanes can reach 230 miles per hour and that the amount of energy a hurricane can release in a day if harnessed could supply electricity to the United States for about six months?

WRITING ACTIVITY 4

What is the general pattern of weather for the region where you live? In two or three paragraphs, describe the area where you live on the basis of its atmospheric conditions (pollution level), level of precipitation, humidity, and frequency in frontal activity.

3
CHEMISTRY—THE STUDY OF MATTER

Hardly a single moment occurs in our lives that is not affected by a chemical process. Our homes, schools, and places of employment are composed of glass, steel, plaster, insulation, and paint—items that are chemically based. Our cars run on a chemical—fuel. Much of our clothing is synthetic—composed of man-made chemical fibers. Our medicine is manufactured from chemicals developed in laboratories. Even many of our food products include chemical additives. *Chemistry* is the branch of science that concerns the composition, structure, and properties of matter as well as the changes it undergoes.

Matter is any substance that occupies space and has mass. Your chair, desk, and table are composed of matter. Even the air you breathe is composed of matter. Matter exists in four states—as solids, liquids, gases, and as plasma, an ionized gas of which the Sun is made. The starting point for a systematic study of chemistry generally begins with an examination of the basic unit of matter, the atom.

The Atom, the Basis of Matter

In biology, cells are the building blocks for living organisms; in chemistry, atoms are the building blocks for matter. The *atom* is the smallest particle of an element that has the properties of that element. An *element* is a substance that occurs in nature and that cannot be broken down into a simpler substance. Nearly 100 fundamental substances known as elements are known to occur in nature. A few elements have been produced synthetically by man.

Atoms also form molecules. A *molecule* is the smallest part of a compound that can exist by itself. A molecule consists of two or more atoms joined together chemically.

The belief that all elements are composed of atoms was first proposed in the early nineteenth century by John Dalton, an English chemist. At that time, only a few elements were known to exist. According to Dalton's theory, an atom cannot be made, destroyed, or divided, and atoms of the same element are alike. This became known as *atomic theory*. Atomic theory had to be modified later when physicists discovered that the nucleus of an atom can be split by bombarding it with neutrons, a process known as *nuclear fission*.

A Russian chemist, Dmitri Mendeleyev, constructed a table by which he calculated the atomic weights of the different elements. This table is known as the *periodic table*. The elements are identified by symbols taken largely from Latin names for the elements. Hydrogen is the lightest known element, so the weights of all the other elements are based on the weight (mass) of hydrogen. Hydrogen was given the atomic mass of 1 and assigned the atomic number 1. An atom of oxygen, an abundant gas on Earth, has a mass 16 times that of a hydrogen atom;

therefore, oxygen was given an atomic mass of 16. Oxygen is the eighth lightest element and is assigned the atomic number 8. Dalton's and Mendeleyev's discoveries were the most significant in the field of chemistry since that of Lavoisier, a French chemist who identified oxygen as the key element that supports combustion. An example of the periodic table is illustrated on page 404.

Atomic Structure

Scientists have learned a great deal about atoms since Dalton's time. For example, an atom is composed of a nucleus with electrons that surround it. The *nucleus*, located in the center of the atom, is made up of protons and neutrons. A *proton* is a positively charged particle. An element's atomic number is determined by the number of protons it has. Since hydrogen has only one proton in its nucleus, it has an atomic number of 1. A *neutron* has a mass nearly equal to a proton's but has no charge at all. The nucleus has a positive charge determined by the number of protons it contains. The nucleus provides the mass number for an element.

An *electron* is a negatively charged particle. Electrons occupy an orbit, or shell, that surrounds the nucleus. Each shell can hold only a fixed number of electrons. It is the number of shells that distinguishes one element from another. The greater the number of shells with orbiting electrons an element has, the greater its atomic number.

At one time, electrons were thought to orbit the nucleus like the planets orbit the Sun; however, this belief has not proved to be true. The following illustration shows the structure of an atom.

THE HELIUM ATOM

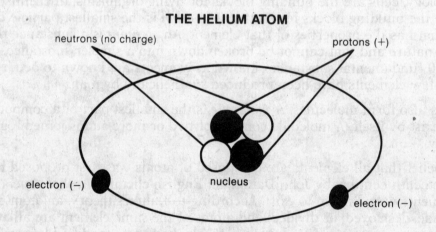

EXERCISE 1: ATOMIC STRUCTURE

Directions: Match the terms on the right with the correct description on the left by writing the correct letter of the term in the space provided.

_____ 1. the second lightest element; contains two protons in its nucleus

_____ 2. a negatively charged particle

_____ 3. the part of an atom that determines an element's mass

_____ 4. a particle that has no charge

_____ 5. a positively charged particle

_____ 6. an element containing eight protons in its nucleus

a. oxygen

b. neutron

c. proton

d. helium

e. electron

f. nucleus

Answers are on page 445.

EXERCISE 2: NUCLEAR ENERGY

Directions: Read the passage below and choose the best answer for each of the following questions. You may need to refer to the periodic table shown on page 404.

Nuclear energy may be released in two ways: by fission and by fusion. Nuclear *fission* involves the splitting of the nucleus of a heavy chemical element by bombardment with neutrons. Nuclear *fusion* involves the uniting of two nuclei of an element at high temperatures and pressure to form the nucleus of a new, heavier, element. In each process, nuclear energy is released.

1. Based on the information in the passage and the atomic masses shown in the periodic table, energy from nuclear fusion would be released when

   (1) uranium nuclei are fused to make plutonium
   (2) hydrogen nuclei are fused to make oxygen
   (3) oxygen nuclei are fused to make helium
   (4) hydrogen nuclei are fused to make helium
   (5) helium nuclei are fused to make hydrogen

2. Energy from nuclear fission would be released in the splitting of the nucleus of which element?

   A. plutonium

   B. hydrogen

   C. oxygen

   (1) A
   (2) B
   (3) C
   (4) A and B
   (5) A and C

Answers are on page 445.

EXERCISE 3: ISOTOPIC ELEMENTS

Directions: Read the passage and table below and choose the best answer for the statements that follow.

Sometimes the number of neutrons in the atom of an element varies. This can affect the mass number of an element. For example, the element carbon has six protons in its nucleus, but it can also have as few as six or as many as seven neutrons in its nucleus. An element that can vary in the number of neutrons in its nucleus is described as being *isotopic*. Thus, two isotopes of carbon exist—carbon 12 and carbon 13, and they have different chemical properties. Of the two, carbon 12 is the more common.

Element	Atomic Number	Mass Number
Hydrogen	1	1.01
Helium	2	4.00
Lithium	3	6.94
Beryllium	4	9.01
Boron	5	10.81

1. The only element in the preceding chart that could have an isotope of mass number 6 and whose two nuclei might be fused to form carbon 12 would be

   (1) hydrogen
   (2) helium
   (3) lithium
   (4) beryllium
   (5) boron

2. Deuterium and tritium are two isotopes that have mass numbers of 2 and 3 respectively. Of the two isotopes, tritium is especially radioactive. Based on the preceding chart, you could infer that these elements used in nuclear fusion are different forms of

   (1) hydrogen
   (2) helium
   (3) lithium
   (4) beryllium
   (5) boron

Answers are on page 445.

DID YOU KNOW THAT: The hydrogen bomb, created by the fusion of deuterium or tritium nuclei to form a helium atom, is far more explosive and destructive than an atomic bomb, created from the splitting of a uranium or plutonium atom?

WRITING ACTIVITY 1

As fossil fuels become scarce, our modern world is growing increasingly dependent on new energy sources. As a result, many energy producers have turned to nuclear energy as a source for generating electricity in heavily populated regions. The nuclear reactors that generate this energy pose considerable risks, as demonstrated by nuclear disasters such as those at Three Mile Island and Chernobyl. Are the risks to human life worth the benefits that nuclear energy provides? In two or three paragraphs, defend your position.

Elements and Periodicity

The periodic table organizes elements based on their atomic and physical properties. The table relates the properties of the elements to their atomic numbers. Elements in the same row (across) have the same number of shells containing a varying number of electrons. Elements in the same column (down) have the same number of electrons in their outermost shell.

In classifying elements according to physical properties, scientists consider color, odor, taste, density, boiling point, solubility (ability to dissolve), malleability (capability of being shaped by beating), and hardness. Out of these properties arose the three broad groupings that chemists have used to categorize all of the elements—metals, nonmetals, and metalloids.

Metals conduct heat and electricity well, melt at high temperatures, and have a high density and brilliant luster. Examples of these elements are sodium, gold, and aluminum.

Nonmetals melt at low temperatures, have low luster, are less dense than metals, and are poor conductors of heat and electricity. Examples of these elements are carbon, sulfur, and oxygen.

Metalloids have properties of metals and nonmetals. Antimony and arsenic are examples of metalloids.

According to the periodic law, as the atomic number increases for elements in a column, similar properties occur regularly and to a greater degree. For example, the metals with the atomic numbers 3, 11, and 19—lithium, sodium, and potassium—are all chemically active metals. In many cases, the greater the atomic number, the higher the degree of certain properties. While the second member of this group, sodium, is chemically active, rubidium, the fourth member, is so highly active that it bursts into flame upon exposure to air.

PERIODIC TABLE OF THE ELEMENTS

Legend:
- Atomic Number
- Symbol (*man made)
- Name
- Mass Number (number of protons and neutrons)

Example:
- ⑥ C Carbon 12

Period																		
1	① H Hydrogen 1																	② He Helium 4
2	③ Li Lithium 7	④ Be Beryllium 9											⑤ B Boron 11	⑥ C Carbon 12	⑦ N Nitrogen 14	⑧ O Oxygen 16	⑨ F Fluorine 19	⑩ Ne Neon 20
3	⑪ Na Sodium 23	⑫ Mg Magnesium 24											⑬ Al Aluminum 27	⑭ Si Silicon 28	⑮ P Phosphorus 31	⑯ S Sulfur 32	⑰ Cl Chlorine 35	⑱ Ar Argon 40
4	⑲ K Potassium 39	⑳ Ca Calcium 40	㉑ Sc Scandium 45	㉒ Ti Titanium 48	㉓ V Vanadium 51	㉔ Cr Chromium 52	㉕ Mn Manganese 55	㉖ Fe Iron 56	㉗ Co Cobalt 59	㉘ Ni Nickel 59	㉙ Cu Copper 64	㉚ Zn Zinc 65	㉛ Ga Gallium 70	㉜ Ge Germanium 73	㉝ As Arsenic 75	㉞ Se Selenium 79	㉟ Br Bromine 80	㊱ Kr Krypton 84
5	㊲ Rb Rubidium 85	㊳ Sr Strontium 88	㊴ Y Yttrium 89	㊵ Zr Zirconium 91	㊶ Nb Niobium 93	㊷ Mo Molybdenum 96	㊸ Tc* Technetium 98	㊹ Ru Ruthenium 101	㊺ Rh Rhodium 103	㊻ Pd Palladium 106	㊼ Ag Silver 108	㊽ Cd Cadmium 112	㊾ In Indium 115	㊿ Sn Tin 119	51 Sb Antimony 122	52 Te Tellurium 128	53 I Iodine 127	54 Xe Xenon 131
6	55 Cs Cesium 133	56 Ba Barium 137	57 La Lanthanum 139	72 Hf Hafnium 178	73 Ta Tantalum 181	74 W Tungsten 184	75 Re Rhenium 186	76 Os Osmium 190	77 Ir Iridium 192	78 Pt Platinum 195	79 Au Gold 197	80 Hg Mercury 201	81 Tl Thallium 204	82 Pb Lead 207	83 Bi Bismuth 209	84 Po Polonium 209	85 At Astatine 210	86 Rn Radon 222
7	87 Fr Francium 223	88 Ra Radium 226	89 Ac Actinium 227	104 Rf* Rutherfordium 261	105 Ha* Hahnium 262	106 Unh* Unnilhexium 263	107 Uns* Unnilseptium 262	108 Uno* Unniloctium	109 Une* Unnilennium	110 Uun* Unununium								

Rare Earth Elements

Lanthanide Series	58 Ce Cerium 140	59 Pr Praseodymium 141	60 Nd Neodymium 144	61 Pm* Promethium 145	62 Sm Samarium 150	63 Eu Europium 152	64 Gd Gadolinium 157	65 Tb Terbium 159	66 Dy Dysprosium 163	67 Ho Holmium 165	68 Er Erbium 167	69 Tm Thulium 169	70 Yb Ytterbium 173	71 Lu Lutetium 175
Actinide Series	90 Th Thorium 232	91 Pa Protactinium 231	92 U Uranium 238	93 Np* Neptunium 237	94 Pu* Plutonium 244	95 Am* Americium 243	96 Cm* Curium 247	97 Bk* Berkelium 247	98 Cf* Californium 251	99 Es* Einsteinium 252	100 Fm* Fermium 257	101 Md* Mendelevium 258	102 No* Nobelium 259	103 Lr* Lawrencium 260

EXERCISE 4: ELEMENTS AND PERIODICITY

Directions: Choose the best answer for each of the following questions.

1. The metals copper, silver, and gold are in the same family (column), having atomic numbers of 29, 47, and 79 respectively. According to the principle of periodic law, of the three metals, gold would have the highest degree of which *physical* property?

   (1) value
   (2) rarity
   (3) volatility
   (4) malleability
   (5) scarcity

2. Radon is in the same family as helium, neon, argon, krypton, and xenon. Which of the following facts would help you to determine that radon has a greater density than the other elements in the same family?

   A. Radon is found in the ground while the others are not.

   B. Radon has a higher atomic number than the other elements in its family.

   C. Radon poses potential health problems for people in areas where great concentrations are found in the ground.

   (1) A
   (2) B
   (3) C
   (4) A and B
   (5) B and C

Answers are on page 445.

DID YOU KNOW THAT: Silver has the greatest ability to conduct heat and electricity of any substance, but it is not used for this purpose because it is so expensive?

WRITING ACTIVITY 2

In recent years, the dangers radon gas poses to humans have been widely publicized in certain parts of the country. Radon poses such a potential health hazard that buyers of homes in certain areas where concentrations of the gas are high are advised to have readings done to measure the level of radon in the ground beneath the home's foundation.

Is radon or some other material in the ground perceived as a threat in the area in which you live? Whether or not such a threat is present in your area, write two or three paragraphs describing what you think the government should do about such dangers.

Elements and Chemical Reactions

You are involved in a variety of chemical reactions every day. Do you cook your food or heat your home with gas? Did you use a battery-powered object today? Have you cleaned your oven or bathroom fixtures with a cleaning agent? All of these activities and countless others, including those taking place within your body, are dependent upon chemical reactions.

Each chemical reaction has two components: a reactant and a product. A *reactant* is the substance or substances that enter into the reaction. The *product* is the substance or substances that result from the reaction. A chemical reaction may be either a *combination reaction*, in which two elements or substances are combined, or a *decomposition reaction*, in which an element or substance is broken down.

Chemical reactions are written in a shorthand called a *chemical equation*. A chemical formula uses symbols for elements and shows the number of atoms for each element of a substance. For example, the chemical reaction that produces water would be written:

$$2H_2 + O_2 \longrightarrow 2H_2O$$

When you read a chemical equation, the large number tells how many molecules (structures containing more than one atom) are present. When only a single molecule or atom is present, the number *1* is not written. The smaller subscript number tells how many atoms of an element are present in each molecule.

The equation for water says that two molecules of hydrogen gas (H_2) plus one molecule of oxygen gas (O_2) combine to form two molecules of water (H_2O). Notice that one molecule of hydrogen gas (H_2) contains two atoms of hydrogen, and one molecule of oxygen gas (O_2) contains two atoms of oxygen. Each molecule of water (H_2O) contains two atoms of hydrogen and one atom of oxygen.

The chemical reaction in which one atom of carbon unites with two atoms of oxygen to form carbon dioxide would be written:

$$C + O_2 \longrightarrow CO_2$$

This equation says that one molecule of carbon plus one molecule of oxygen (two atoms of oxygen) combine to form one molecule of carbon dioxide (CO_2).

All chemical reactions are governed by the *Law of Conservation of Matter*. This law holds that matter can neither be created nor destroyed in a chemical reaction. A chemical equation adheres to this law; it shows the same number of atoms on both sides of the arrow for each element involved in a reaction. For example, the following chemical reaction occurs when methane gas (CH_4) is burned with oxygen:

$$CH_4 + 2O_2 \longrightarrow CO_2 + 2H_2O$$

Methane gas burns with oxygen to form carbon dioxide and water vapor; specifically, one molecule of carbon dioxide and two molecules of water.

Notice that the reaction begins with one carbon atom (C) and ends with one carbon atom (C). The reaction begins with four hydrogen atoms (H_4) and ends with four hydrogen atoms ($2H_2$ or $2 \times 2 = 4$). The reaction begins with four oxygen atoms ($2O_2 = 2 \times 2 = 4$) and ends with 4 oxygen atoms ($O_2 + 2O = 4$).

When the number of atoms of each element is equal on both sides of the equation, we say that the equation is **balanced**.

EXERCISE 5: BALANCED EQUATIONS

Directions: Identify each of the following equations as either balanced or unbalanced by writing *B* or *U* in the space provided.

_____ **1.** $N_2 + O_2 \longrightarrow 2NO$

_____ **2.** $Fe + HCl \longrightarrow FeCl_3 + H_2$

_____ **3.** $2H + O \longrightarrow H_2O$

_____ **4.** $ZnCO_2 \longrightarrow ZnO + CO_2$

_____ **5.** $C + 2S \longrightarrow CS_2$

Answers are on page 445.

EXERCISE 6: CHEMICAL REACTIONS

Directions: Choose the best answer for each of the following questions.

1. When iron is exposed to moist air, it rusts. **Rust** is the common name for ferric oxide, formed by two iron atoms and three oxygen atoms. The correct chemical formula for rust would be:

   (1) Fe_3O_2
   (2) FeO
   (3) Fe_2O_3
   (4) Fe_2O_2
   (5) $2FeO_3$

2. The chemical reaction that gives soda pop (a carbonated beverage) its fizz results from dissolving a molecule of carbon dioxide into a molecule of water. Which of the following represents the chemical equation for the process?

   (1) $CO_3 + H_2O \longrightarrow H_2CO_4$
   (2) $CO_2 + H_2O \longrightarrow H_2CO_3$
   (3) $CO + H_2O \longrightarrow H_2CO_2$
   (4) $CO_2 + H_2O \longrightarrow H_2CO_2$
   (5) $CO + 2H_2O \longrightarrow H_4CO_2$

3. The reactants and products of a chemical reaction

   (1) always double in mass
   (2) must always balance
   (3) never equal each other in mass
   (4) always need a catalyst
   (5) must triple themselves to balance

Questions 4 and 5 refer to the following passage.

A *physical change* is a change that does not produce a new substance. For example, when you saw wood or dissolve salt in water you are not changing the chemical composition of the substances. However, a new substance *is* formed when a *chemical change* takes place. The result is a change in the chemical composition of a substance. Some common chemical changes include the burning of wood and the rusting of metal on a car.

In an experiment concerning physical and chemical changes, you add 10 g of copper sulfate to 100 ml of water. You heat the solution over a low flame and stir. After the solution cools, you place a piece of aluminum foil in the copper sulfate solution. After 24 hours, the solution has changed from deep blue to a very light blue, and the aluminum has acquired a deep copper coating.

4. Which of the following pieces of information would you need to prove that a chemical change had occurred?

   (1) whether the copper sulfate solution had been heated
   (2) whether the solution had been stirred
   (3) whether twenty-four hours had passed
   (4) whether the aluminum had acquired a copper coat
   (5) whether the aluminum was breakable

5. Which hypothesis best explains what happened in the experiment?

   (1) The experiment failed.
   (2) Aluminum and copper were incorrectly mixed.
   (3) The copper sulfate solution and aluminum produced a new substance.
   (4) The copper sulfate solution caused a temporary change in the appearance of the aluminum.
   (5) The aluminum caused the copper sulfate to turn blue.

Answers are on page 446.

DID YOU KNOW THAT: Yeast makes dough rise because yeast (a fungus) attacks the starch in the flour, changing it into sugar? The sugar changes to alcohol and carbon dioxide gas. Then the carbon dioxide bubbles up through the dough to make it rise.

Elements in Combination

Compounds are formed when two or more elements combine in a chemical reaction. The resulting product usually has different properties from either of the component elements. Compounds, when formed, can be broken down into simpler substances only by chemical action.

For example, water, the most commonly known compound, is composed of two atoms of hydrogen and one atom of oxygen. When water is subjected to extreme temperatures, it can be reduced to its component elements—hydrogen and oxygen—and its liquid characteristic is lost.

Mixtures are substances that are formed when two or more elements or compounds are mixed in different proportions. The resulting product retains the properties of the combining elements. In most mixtures the combining ingredients can be separated easily. For example, gunpowder is a mixture of charcoal (a form of carbon), sulfur, and potassium nitrate (a compound of potassium and nitrogen). When mixed, the three ingredients form gunpowder, a highly explosive substance. These three ingredients can be identified by their different colors in this mixture.

A *solution* is a mixture formed when a solid, liquid, or gaseous substance is dissolved in a liquid. The substance that is dissolved into the liquid is called the *solute*. The liquid in which the substance is dissolved is called the *solvent*. One of the characteristics that distinguishes a solution from a mixture is that a solution is homogeneous—the same throughout. An *aqueous* solution features water as the solvent. A *tincture* has alcohol as the solvent, such as the antiseptic tincture of iodine. Sometimes a solution is formed when a substance is dissolved in a gas or solid.

When metals are combined in varying proportions, they often form *alloys*. In an alloy, each metal dissolves into the other at high temperatures. Common examples of alloys are brass (copper and zinc), bronze (copper, tin, and other elements), and steel (iron, carbon, and other elements). An *amalgam* is formed when a metal is dissolved into mercury, a liquid metal. Amalgams are used chiefly in making tooth cements.

EXERCISE 7: TYPES OF SUBSTANCES

Directions: Listed below are five kinds of substances known to scientists. Read the definitions and apply them to the questions that follow.

compound—a substance that is composed of two or more elements, in specific proportions, but has properties different from the combining elements

mixture—a substance that is composed of two or more elements or other substances but that keeps the properties of the combining ingredients

solution—a homogeneous substance formed by dissolving a solid, liquid, or gas into a liquid

alloy—a substance formed by the combination of metals in which one metal dissolves into another at high temperatures

amalgam—an alloy that includes mercury and that is usually soft and may be liquid

1. Table salt—sodium chloride, one of the most common substances occurring in nature—is best classified as

    (1) a compound
    (2) a mixture
    (3) a solution
    (4) an alloy
    (5) an amalgam

2. Solder is a substance formed by the combination of tin and lead at low melting points. It is used in electronics for fusing metals. Solder may be best described as

   (1) a compound
   (2) a mixture
   (3) a solution
   (4) an alloy
   (5) an amalgam

3. Air is composed of nitrogen (78 percent), oxygen (21 percent), argon (0.93 percent), carbon dioxide (0.03 percent), and other gases (0.04 percent). Air may be *best* described as

   (1) a compound
   (2) a mixture
   (3) a solution
   (4) an alloy
   (5) an amalgam

4. Mercurochrome is a red, antiseptic liquid in which mercuric acetate, dibromin, and fluorescein are dissolved. Based on this composition, it may be best described as

   (1) a compound
   (2) a mixture
   (3) a solution
   (4) an alloy
   (5) an amalgam

Answers are on page 446.

EXERCISE 8: COMPOUNDS AND MIXTURES

Directions: Choose the best answer for the following question.

There is enough information in the preceding passage to support which of the following statements?

A. Compounds may contain mixtures but mixtures may not contain compounds.

B. Mixtures may contain compounds but compounds may not contain mixtures.

C. Solutions may contain compounds and mixtures.

(1) A
(2) B
(3) C
(4) A and B
(5) B and C

Answer is on page 446.

DID YOU KNOW THAT: When copper combines with water it forms *verdigris*, a poisonous deposit that gives the gutters or rain troughs you see on old buildings their greenish color?

WRITING ACTIVITY 3

The defoliant Agent Orange, used to remove leaves from trees, contains the deadly chemical contaminant *dioxin*, a carbon compound. A link has been discovered between Agent Orange and the cancer found in some returning Vietnam veterans. The United Nations has attempted to ban all uses of chemical warfare. Do you agree with the UN's position on chemical warfare, or do you believe that "all is fair in war" and that a country can use whatever means it deems necessary to defeat its opponent? Take a position and write an essay of two or three paragraphs to support it.

Chemical Bonding

When compounds are made, a bond is formed between two or more elements. A *bond* is a force that holds together two atoms, two ions (electrically charged particles), two molecules, or a combination of these. Bonding may result from either the transfer or the sharing of electrons between atoms.

When electrons are transferred from one atom to another, an *ionic bond* is formed. In the following example, an ionic bond is formed when an electron from a sodium atom is transferred to the outermost shell of a chlorine atom. The result is the common compound table salt.

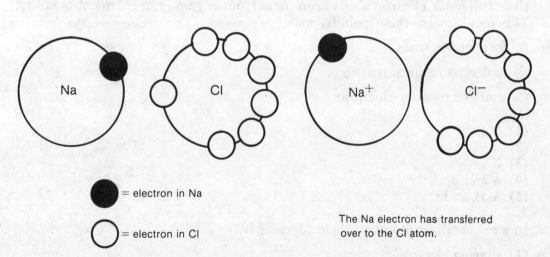

SODIUM AND CHLORINE ATOMS

SODIUM CHLORIDE

● = electron in Na

○ = electron in Cl

The Na electron has transferred over to the Cl atom.

In the preceding example, both sodium and chlorine are electrically neutral (have no charge); however, when the sodium atom loses its electron, it becomes positively charged. Opposite charges attract, forming a bond. Ionic compounds such as salt typically have high melting and boiling points, are flammable, conduct electricity when dissolved in water, and exist as solids at room temperatures.

When two or more different atoms of elements share electrons to form a molecule, a *covalent* bond is formed. In the following illustration, a covalent bond is formed when two atoms of hydrogen are bonded to one atom of oxygen to form the compound water.

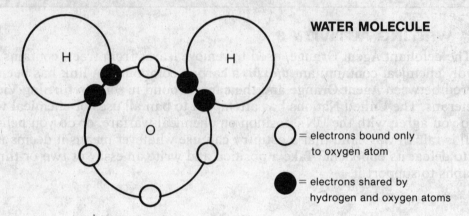

WATER MOLECULE

○ = electrons bound only to oxygen atom

● = electrons shared by hydrogen and oxygen atoms

In covalent bonding, the outermost shell of the element with the greatest number of electrons is filled to capacity at eight electrons. Once the combining element achieves eight electrons in its outermost ring, it cannot combine with another element. Covalent compounds such as water typically have low melting and boiling points, are nonflammable, have poor conductivity, and exist as gases and liquids.

EXERCISE 9: COMPOUNDS AND CHEMICAL BONDING

Directions: Choose the best answer for each of the following questions.

1. The inert gases—helium, neon, argon, krypton, xenon, and radon—all have eight electrons in their outermost ring. These gases are called inert because their full outer electron shells keep them from engaging in chemical bonding. This fact explains their inability to

   A. form compounds

   B. undergo chemical reactions

   C. share or transfer electrons

   (1) A
   (2) B
   (3) C
   (4) A and B
   (5) A, B, and C

2. In ionic bonding, atoms are held together by

   (1) sharing electrons
   (2) transferring electrons
   (3) chemical attraction
   (4) temperature
   (5) magnetic fields

3. In covalent bonding, atoms are held together by

  (**1**) sharing electrons
  (**2**) transferring electrons
  (**3**) chemical attraction
  (**4**) temperature
  (**5**) magnetic fields

Answers are on page 446.

DID YOU KNOW THAT: Before helium was used to fill airships (blimps), hydrogen, a highly flammable gas, was used? The cause of the change was the *Hindenburg* disaster, in which hydrogen ignited and caused an explosion in which many people died. This prompted the use of helium to fill lighter-than-air vehicles. Helium, an inert gas, is nonflammable.

Acids, Bases, and Salts

Many compounds that result from ionic and covalent bonding are categorized as acids or bases. An *acid* is a covalent compound that produces hydrogen ions when dissolved in water. Acids have a sour taste. Common acids are acetic acid (the main component of vinegar), citric acid (found in citrus fruits), lactic acid (found in milk), and hydrochloric acid, a component of stomach acid used in digestion.

A *base* is a compound that forms hydroxide ions when dissolved in water. Bases are able to take a proton from an acid or to give up an unshared pair of electrons to an acid. Bases are described as alkaline because they dissolve in water and have a slippery feel. Many hydroxides are bases. Household cleaning agents such as ammonia, borax, lye, and detergents are common examples of bases.

When an acid combines with a base, a salt is formed and water is released because the metal found in the base replaces the hydrogen contained in the acid. Inorganic acids, bases, and inorganic salts can conduct electricity when dissolved in water.

Chemists apply the *litmus test* to a substance to determine whether or not it is an acid or base. Litmus paper is a colored paper that changes color when exposed to an acid or base. An acid turns blue litmus paper red, and a base turns red litmus paper blue.

EXERCISE 10: CHEMICAL FIRST AID

Directions: Read the passage below and choose the best answer for each of the following questions.

Many common household cleaning products are poisons; therefore, the labels of many products must contain an antidote to be administered in case the product is swallowed accidentally. These antidotes may be emetics (agents that cause the substance to be expelled from the body), neutralizers (agents that cancel out the effect of the substance swallowed), or diluents (agents that dilute the substance swallowed).

1. A person accidentally swallows ammonia. The first-aid instructions on the label tell you to administer two tablespoons of vinegar in two glasses of water or a glass of orange or lemon juice. The effect of this action would be that

   (1) the person would expel the ammonia
   (2) the ammonia would be changed into an acid
   (3) the ammonia would change into a salt by neutralization
   (4) the ammonia would be changed into a base
   (5) the ammonia would be diluted by the water and voided by the body

2. Which of the following antidotes would likely have a similar effect if vinegar or citrus juice were not available?

   (1) water
   (2) bread
   (3) milk
   (4) raw egg white
   (5) vegetable oil

3. If a person accidentally swallowed a toilet bowl cleaner that contained phenol, a corrosive acid, it would probably be *best* to first

   (1) induce vomiting immediately
   (2) administer milk of magnesia (magnesium hydroxide)
   (3) dilute the poison with plenty of water
   (4) dilute the poison with plenty of milk
   (5) administer plenty of lemon or orange juice

4. The antidote administered in the preceding case would be best described as

   (1) a diluent
   (2) an emetic
   (3) a reactant
   (4) a neutralizer
   (5) a catalyst

Answers are on page 446.

EXERCISE 11: ACIDS, BASES, AND SALTS

Directions: The questions are based on the following explanation and scale. Read the information and choose the best answer for each question.

The designation pH (*potential for Hydrogen*-ion formation) is a value by which certain substances are classified according to acidity or alkalinity. The pH scale ranges from 0 to 14, with the value 7 representing neutrality. The pH scale is illustrated below.

pH SCALE

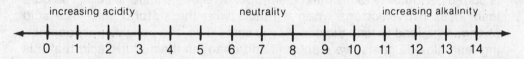

1. According to the pH scale, acetic acid, a very mild acid, would most likely be found between

   (1) 7 and 8
   (2) 0 and 1
   (3) 2 and 3
   (4) 4 and 5
   (5) 10 and 11

2. Oxalic acid, a strong, poisonous acid found in the leaves of rhubarb that is used as a bleaching agent, would most probably fall between

   (1) 9 and 10
   (2) 1 and 2
   (3) 5 and 6
   (4) 6 and 7
   (5) 13 and 14

3. Based on the pH scale, water would be found

   (1) between 0 and 1
   (2) between 3 and 4
   (3) at 7
   (4) at 14
   (5) between 5 and 6

4. Which of the following could be used to prove that a substance is an acid?

   A. The substance has a pH above 7.

   B. The substance is sour or caustic.

   C. It neutralizes a base to form a salt and water.

   (1) A
   (2) B
   (3) C
   (4) A and B
   (5) B and C

Answers are on page 446.

EXERCISE 12: A CAR BATTERY

Directions: Read the passage below and answer the questions.

Acids, bases, and inorganic salts (salts obtained from nonliving things) are effective conductors of electricity. The common car battery demonstrates an electric current generated by the chemical action between an acid and a metal.

In a car battery, pure lead (the negative post) and lead dioxide (the positive post) are submerged in sulfuric acid (the conductor). Distilled water is added periodically to maintain the proper level of the sulfuric acid. The pure lead loses two electrons when it reacts with the sulfuric acid—the acid changes the lead to lead dioxide. At the same time, the positive post containing lead dioxide gains two electrons and changes the sulfuric acid that it is submerged in to lead sulfate (a salt) and water. The current that makes the car start results from the flow of electrons from the lead dioxide to the lead through the sulfuric acid to the starter switch, all of which makes a complete circuit. A diagram of a car battery is shown below.

CAR BATTERY

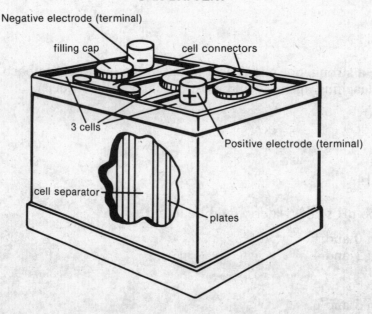

1. An *electrolyte* is an inorganic compound that will conduct an electric current when dissolved in water. What is an electrolyte in the preceding example?

   A. lead dioxide

   B. sulfuric acid

   C. distilled water

   (1) A
   (2) B
   (3) C
   (4) A and B
   (5) B and C

2. A substance is *oxidized* when it loses electrons. In the preceding example, which of the following compounds is oxidized?

   (1) lead
   (2) lead dioxide
   (3) lead sulfate
   (4) water
   (5) sulfuric acid

3. A substance is *reduced* when it gains electrons. In the preceding example, which of the following compounds is reduced?

   (1) lead
   (2) lead dioxide
   (3) lead sulfate
   (4) water
   (5) sulfuric acid

4. The substances that oxidize and reduce other substances are called *oxidizing agents* and *reducing agents*. In the preceding example, the oxidizing and reducing agents, in correct order, are

   (1) lead dioxide and water
   (2) sulfuric acid and lead dioxide
   (3) lead and sulfuric acid
   (4) lead sulfate and lead dioxide
   (5) sulfuric acid and water

5. Based on the preceding example, you can conclude that in a car battery, chemical energy is converted into electrical energy by

   (1) nuclear fission
   (2) nuclear fusion
   (3) oxidation-reduction
   (4) ionic bonding
   (5) covalent bonding

6. Which of the following compounds would *not* adequately serve as an electrolyte?

   (1) sodium chloride (salt)
   (2) sulfuric acid
   (3) citric acid
   (4) sodium hydroxide
   (5) hydrochloric acid

7. Which of the following can you conclude to be true when a battery is discharged and can no longer generate a current?

   A. The sulfuric acid can no longer oxidize the lead.

   B. The lead dioxide can no longer reduce the sulfuric acid.

   C. The battery has run out of sulfuric acid.

   (1) A
   (2) B
   (3) C
   (4) A and B
   (5) A and C

Answers are on page 447.

Reaction Rate, Catalysts, and Equilibrium

Chemical reactions occur at different rates determined by the conditions under which reactions occur. Sugar dissolves more quickly in hot water than in cold. White phosphorus bursts into flame when exposed to the air. Carbon monoxide from car exhaust remains in the atmosphere for up to two-and-a-half years before it is changed into carbon dioxide.

Reactions such as these may be speeded up or slowed down when another substance is introduced. A *catalyst* is a substance that increases the rate of a chemical reaction but itself remains chemically unchanged. Many finely divided metals act as catalysts. For example, today's cars are equipped with a catalytic converter, a device that contains finely divided platinum, a metal. The function of the converter is to change harmful carbon monoxide and unburned gasoline vapor into harmless carbon dioxide and water vapor and reduce the amount of nitrogen oxides released into the air. Platinum in this case is a catalyst because it speeds up the process but remains unchanged.

Some catalysts have a negative effect. A negative catalyst slows down the chemical reaction. Negative catalysts are often inhibitors, such as the chemicals used in undercoating a car to retard the rusting process.

A given set of reactants may react to form more than one product. Often, the by-products react to form the original reactants. When the rate of forward reaction balances the rate of reverse reaction, *chemical equilibrium* occurs. For example, the carbon monoxide in car exhaust enters the atmosphere and reacts with oxygen to form carbon dioxide. The carbon dioxide is broken down by sunlight into the original reactant—carbon monoxide. This reaction represents chemical equilibrium because the reaction reverses itself. Chemical reactions such as these create a cycle.

EXERCISE 13: REACTION RATE, CATALYSTS, AND EQUILIBRIUM

Directions: Choose the best answer for the following questions.

1. Lipase is an enzyme produced by the liver that helps in the digestion of fats by speeding up the rate at which lipids (fats) are changed into fatty acids and glycerol. Based on this description, we can conclude that an enzyme is

   (1) a product in a chemical reaction
   (2) a negative catalyst
   (3) a biological catalyst
   (4) both a product in a chemical reaction and a negative catalyst
   (5) both a product in a chemical reaction and a biological catalyst

2. Which of the following processes illustrates chemical equilibrium?

   A. bonding

   B. photosynthesis

   C. respiration

   (1) A
   (2) B
   (3) C
   (4) A and B together
   (5) B and C together

Answers are on page 447.

4
PHYSICS—THE STUDY OF HOW MATTER BEHAVES

"What makes the world go 'round?" is a question people have asked for thousands of years. In answer to this question, scientists long ago formulated laws that explain not only how Earth revolves around the Sun but also how other forms of matter behave in the physical world.

Physics is the branch of science that concerns the behavior of matter in our world—the forces that cause matter to behave as it does. Physics helps us to understand how things work.

The scope of physics is so broad that the other branches of science studied earlier in this book cannot be fully understood without some knowledge of its basic laws. For example, physics helps to explain how cellular molecules can move from a lower concentration in an organism to a higher one, how ocean tides occur, and how matter exists in the states of a solid, liquid, or gas.

The preceding examples from biology, earth science, and chemistry all illustrate some force at work on a body. A *force* shows the presence of energy in an environment. *Energy* is the capacity to do work. The area of physics that deals with forces, energy, and their effect on bodies is *mechanics*.

Mechanics

The study of mechanics was one of the first sciences developed. Ancient Greek philosopher and scientist Aristotle theorized that heavy bodies fall faster than light bodies. This theory was proved false in the early 17th century by Italian scientist and mathematician Galileo, who dropped items of different weights from the leaning tower of Pisa. The force acting upon the objects was not fully understood, however, until Sir Isaac Newton, an Englishman, formulated laws of gravity and motion that explained how different forces act on objects.

The Force of Gravity

Gravity is the most commonly experienced of all forces in nature. The presence of gravity was first proposed by Newton when he observed the motion of an apple falling from a tree. Based on the simple observation, he developed the *Law of Universal Gravitation*, which holds that every body having a mass exerts an attractive force on every other body having a mass in the universe. The strength of the force depends on the masses of the objects and the distance between them. (*Mass* is the measure of the amount of matter in an object.) Thus, the apple's falling to earth illustrates the gravitational pull (attraction) of the larger Earth on the smaller apple. The Law of Universal Gravitation also explains how the planets, attracted by the much larger Sun, remain in their orbits as they revolve around it.

Newton's Three Laws of Motion

Newton proposed other laws of motion to explain the relationship between force and motion. They are the Law of Inertia, the Law of Applied Force, and the Law of Action and Reaction.

According to the *Law of Inertia*, a body remains at rest or continues in a state of uniform motion unless a force acts on it. For example, when you drive a car and suddenly jam on the brakes, you continue to move forward. This is because your body's tendency is to remain in the same state of uniform motion (moving forward). The brakes were applied to the car, so its uniform motion was changed.

The *Law of Applied Force* holds that a body's change in speed and direction is proportional to the amount of force applied to it. For example, the vanes on a windmill, which move by the force of the wind, will accelerate according to the speed and direction of the wind that drives them.

Newton's third law, the *Law of Action and Reaction*, maintains that for every action there is an equal but opposite reaction force. For example, a gun's muzzle kicks backward when a bullet is discharged from it.

Newton's laws of motion help us to explain all known occurrences involving force in the field of mechanics.

EXERCISE 1: LAWS OF FORCE AND MOTION

Directions: In the space provided, write *G* if the example illustrates Newton's Law of Universal Gravitation, *I* if it applies to the Law of Inertia, *AF* if it applies to the Law of Applied Force, and *AR* if it applies to the Law of Action and Reaction.

_____ **1.** A motorboat moves forward because its propeller rapidly throws water backward.

_____ **2.** A jet, upon landing, lowers the flaps on its wings. The flaps create drag, a force that reduces lift and helps the plane to slow down.

_____ **3.** A rocket is propelled upward by the powerful downward discharge of exhaust gases.

_____ **4.** A bullet discharged into the air eventually falls to the ground.

_____ **5.** A pendulum in a grandfather clock, once set in motion, continues to swing, thereby regulating the clock's movement.

Answers are on page 447.

EXERCISE 2: THE FORCE OF GRAVITY

Directions: Read the paragraph below and answer the question that follows.

An astronaut weighs in before blast-off. He weighs only a fraction of his original weight when he steps on a scale on the moon. Journeying to Jupiter, he finds that his weight has increased several times over his original weight. These changes in weight may be explained *best* by

(1) the amount of force each planet produced as the astronaut weighed himself
(2) the distance from the Sun of the planetary bodies on which he weighed himself
(3) changes in the atmospheric pressure on the different heavenly bodies
(4) the amount of calories consumed during the flight
(5) the duration of time that elapsed between weigh-ins

Answer is on page 447.

EXERCISE 3: MECHANICS, FORCE, AND MOTION

Directions: Read the passage below and answer the questions that follow.

In an experiment, a *vacuum* is created when all air is removed from a tube. A coin and bits of confetti are released in the vacuum at the same time. They fall at the same rate and reach the bottom at the same time.

1. The results of this experiment prove that

A. in a vacuum, the rate of acceleration is the same for all objects regardless of weight

B. outside a vacuum, air resistance is what makes different objects fall at different rates

C. gravity has no effect at all on objects that fall in a vacuum

(1) A
(2) B
(3) C
(4) A and B
(5) B and C

2. The experiment described above serves to support

(1) Aristotle's theory of falling objects
(2) Galileo's findings about falling objects
(3) Newton's Law of Inertia
(4) Newton's Law of Applied Force
(5) Newton's Law of Action and Reaction

Answers are on page 448.

DID YOU KNOW THAT: Of all the forces present in our physical world, gravity is considered by scientists to be the weakest?

Work, Energy, and Power

Everyone knows what work is. Work is the labor put forth to do a job. Whether it is typing a letter, sawing wood, or providing a needed service, most of us are familiar with work.

In physics, work has a different meaning. **Work** occurs when a force succeeds in moving an object it acts upon. For example, a person who lifts a fifty-pound weight one foot off the floor is performing work. For work to be performed, the movement of the object must be in the same direction as the force—in this case vertical. Work may be expressed as any force unit times any distance unit and may be written as follows:

$$W = F \times D$$

The amount of work done is the amount of force multiplied by the distance moved. In the preceding example, fifty foot-pounds of work is done when fifty pounds are lifted one foot:

$$50 \text{ lb} \times 1 \text{ ft} = 50 \text{ ft lb}$$

Energy is required to do work. In the example above, muscular energy is illustrated in the form of a body that is capable of doing work. Energy may be classified as either kinetic or potential energy. **Kinetic energy** is energy possessed by a body in motion. The form of energy shown by a moving train is kinetic energy. **Potential energy** is energy that is stored or is available for use by a body. For example, coal has potential energy that is released only when it is burned. A boulder positioned on a hilltop has potential energy before it is released. When the boulder is pushed, its potential energy becomes kinetic.

Power is the rate at which work is done. Power is generally measured in horsepower, which is equal to 550 foot-pounds per second or 33,000 foot-pounds per minute.

The Law of Conservation of Energy

In chemistry, the Law of Conservation of Matter governs all chemical reactions. The law holds that matter can be neither created nor destroyed in a chemical reaction. The same principle applies to the expenditure of energy. The **Law of Conservation of Energy** holds that all the energy of the universe is conserved. The capacity for energy to do work can be changed from one kind to another, but it cannot be lost. This principle can be illustrated in the following example of energy generated from a waterfall:

Water possesses *potential energy*. When water moves rapidly in a downward motion, drawn by the pull of gravity, the potential energy is changed into *kinetic energy*. Kinetic energy from a waterfall can be harnessed to power a turbine, a rotary engine, creating *rotational energy*. This rotational energy is sufficient to generate *electrical energy*, which in turn is converted into *light* and *heat* energy, which we use in our home. As this chain shows, the initial potential energy was not lost but was changed into five different forms.

EXERCISE 4: FORMS OF ENERGY

Directions: In the space provided, write *K* if the example demonstrates kinetic energy and *P* if it demonstrates potential energy.

_____ **1.** a strong west wind blowing across a region

_____ **2.** a stick of unlit dynamite

_____ **3.** a tightly coiled spring

_____ **4.** a moving car

_____ **5.** a steaming kettle

Answers are on page 448.

EXERCISE 5: TYPES OF ENERGY

Directions: Defined below are five types of energy that can perform work. Read the definitions and apply them to the questions that follow.

nuclear energy—energy obtained from splitting an atom or fusing more than one atom

chemical energy—energy obtained from the reaction of two or more substances combining with one another

electrical energy—energy obtained from an electric current

solar energy—energy obtained from the Sun's heat

steam energy—energy derived from steam pressure

1. Energy that is radiated to Earth and is the means of sustaining all forms of life is

  (1) nuclear energy
  (2) chemical energy
  (3) electrical energy
  (4) solar energy
  (5) steam energy

2. Energy that results from the fission of uranium-235 nuclei that is used to generate electrical power is

  (1) nuclear energy
  (2) chemical energy
  (3) electrical energy
  (4) solar energy
  (5) steam energy

3. Energy that results from the ignition of a gas and air mixture and that powers a car is

  (1) nuclear energy
  (2) chemical energy
  (3) electrical energy
  (4) solar energy
  (5) steam energy

Answers are on page 448.

Simple Machines

Many jobs require that greater amounts of energy be expended at a faster rate than human muscle power can provide. A *machine* is a device that transmits or multiplies force. A machine operates on the principle of a little force being applied through a great distance and a great resistance being overcome through a short distance.

A *lever* is a simple machine used to perform work by lifting a great weight. A lever is just a bar that is free to pivot on its support (called a *fulcrum*). Through the use of a lever, for example, a one-thousand-pound weight can be lifted with relatively little effort (force).

THE LEVER—A SIMPLE MACHINE

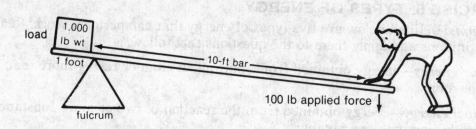

The illustration above shows that it would take 100 pounds of force for a person to lift a 1,000-pound weight positioned 1 foot from the fulcrum when the lever bar is 10 feet long. This may be expressed as follows:

$$1,000 \text{ lb} \times 1 \text{ ft} = 100 \text{ lb} \times 10 \text{ ft}$$

In this case, a relatively small force (100 lb) applied at a great distance from the object (10 ft) is able to overcome great resistance (1,000 lb). According to this principle, the greater the distance between the fulcrum and the applied force, the less force required to perform the work.

The wheelbarrow and the crowbar are two simple machines that operate on the principle of the lever. Other simple machines include the pulley and the inclined plane. All machines are classified as being either simple or complex. Complex machines are made of more than one simple machine.

EXERCISE 6: SIMPLE MACHINES

Directions: Choose the best answer for the following questions.

1. According to the principle that a little force applied through a great distance can overcome great resistance, which is likely to happen if the lever bar in the preceding illustration is increased to 20 feet in length and the weight remains at the end of the bar?

   (1) The effort to lift the weight would increase to 150 pounds of applied force.
   (2) The effort to lift the weight would remain at 100 pounds of applied force.
   (3) The effort would be decreased by half, to 50 pounds of applied force.
   (4) The resistance of the weight would double.
   (5) The resistance of the weight would triple.

2. Which of the following variables has *no* direct bearing on the lever's effectiveness in performing work?

(1) the length of the bar
(2) the distance from the fulcrum of the object being lifted
(3) the shape of the fulcrum
(4) the weight of the load
(5) the distance of the object being lifted from the point where the force is applied

Answers are on page 448.

The Nature of Heat and Energy

One of the world's most valuable commodities is invisible. It cannot be held in our hands or manufactured in a factory. Yet it is necessary to all living things. It warms our homes, cooks our food, and helps to generate electricity through nuclear fission. This valuable commodity is heat.

In the early nineteenth century, heat was thought to be a fluid substance that moved from a hot to a cold object. Today, however, we know that heat is the result of the random motion of molecules. It is nothing more than energy itself. One theory of physics that has contributed greatly to our understanding of the phenomenon of heat is kinetic theory, a basic theory that explains how different states of matter can exist.

The Kinetic Theory of Matter

According to the *kinetic theory of matter*, matter exists in three states—as solids, liquids, or gases. A fourth state, *plasma*, is an ionized gas; the Sun is made up of plasma. The form, or phase, of matter is determined by the motion of the molecules within it.

Solids are composed of atoms or molecules in limited motion. These atoms or molecules are in direct contact with one another, allowing for little or no space available for random movement. The attractive forces of the particles keep the solid intact and give the solid its definite shape and structure.

In *liquids*, individual atoms or molecules are able to move past one another into new positions, giving this form of matter its fluidity. Cohesive forces hold liquids intact.

Gases are substances in which the individual atoms or molecules are in constant random motion. The motion, or kinetic energy, increases along with an increase in temperature. Molecules are unable to hold together, and this property gives gases the ability to flow or spread out to fill the container in which they are placed.

Heat, Temperature, and the States of Matter

The state of matter depends on its heat content. *Temperature* is a measure of heat intensity. The change from one state of matter to another involves the addition or subtraction of a certain amount of heat per gram of substance. For example, at 32 degrees Fahrenheit, water, a liquid, changes to ice, a solid. When the temperature is raised above 32 degrees Fahrenheit, the ice changes to water, a liquid. At temperatures at or above 212 degrees Fahrenheit, the boiling point of water, it changes to steam, a gaseous state. Impurities in water affect its freezing point.

Certain materials expand when their temperature is raised and shrink when it is lowered. Liquids expand more noticeably than solids, but gases expand even more. The mercury thermometer employs this principle. Mercury, an element that expands uniformly over a wide range of temperatures, is placed in a bulb attached to a glass tube. Changes in temperature become apparent as the mercury expands and contracts.

Temperature can be measured in degrees centigrade or degrees Fahrenheit. On the centigrade (or Celsius) scale, 0 degrees represents the freezing point of water, and 100 degrees is the boiling point. On the Fahrenheit scale, 32 degrees represents the freezing point of water, and 212 degrees is the boiling point. While temperature is measured in degrees by thermometer, heat is measured by the calorie or British Thermal Unit (BTU). A *calorie* is the amount of heat needed to raise one gram of water one degree centigrade. The BTU is the amount of heat required to raise one pound of water 1 degree Fahrenheit.

EXERCISE 7: KINETIC THEORY OF MATTER

Directions: In the space provided, write *T* if the statement is true or *F* if it is false.

_____ 1. There is more rigid molecular structure in a solid than in a gas.

_____ 2. Molecules in a gas are close together and exhibit little motion.

_____ 3. An increase in temperature decreases the molecular motion of a gas.

_____ 4. Molecules moving past each other in a liquid give it fluidity.

_____ 5. The presence or absence of heat has no connection with the state of matter of a substance.

Answers are on page 448.

EXERCISE 8: KINETIC THEORY AND MOTION

Directions: Choose the best answer for the following questions.

1. In an experiment, a drop of blue ink is placed on the surface of a glass of water. In a few minutes, the drop of ink is dispersed throughout the water, turning it light blue. The results of the experiment prove that

   (1) ink molecules have less density than water molecules
   (2) a new compound is formed by the combination of ink and water
   (3) heat causes the ink molecules to disperse
   (4) molecules of ink and molecules of water are in constant motion
   (5) the molecules of ink are in motion, but the molecules of water are not

2. If the water were heated, and the ink were not, which of the following would likely be the effect?

   (1) The movement of the water molecules would be slowed, and it would take longer for the color to change.
   (2) The movement of the ink molecules would be speeded up, and the water would change color more quickly.
   (3) The movement of the water molecules would be speeded up, causing the ink molecules to be dispersed more quickly.
   (4) The movement of the ink molecules would be slowed, and the water would change color more slowly.
   (5) Heating would have no effect on the rate of change.

Answers are on page 448.

EXERCISE 9: THE THERMOSTAT

Directions: Read the passage below and answer the questions that follow.

A *thermostat* is a device for regulating the temperature of a heating or cooling system. In a thermostat, a strip of steel and a strip of brass, both of equal length, are welded together in the shape of a question mark. When heated, brass expands nearly 50 percent more than steel. As the metals expand and contract with the application and removal of heat, the tail end of the thermostat trips an electrical switch that turns a furnace or an air conditioner on or off. The temperature at which the thermostat is set determines the point at which the system goes on or off, based on a change in temperature.

1. The principle under which a thermostat operates is the same under which

   (1) ink disperses throughout a liquid
   (2) a gas expands to fill the container in which it is held
   (3) the level of mercury rises or falls in a glass tube
   (4) a chemical reaction occurs when two substances combine
   (5) a pendulum swings when set into motion

2. In operating an air conditioner, the thermostat is set for 70° so that when the temperature rises above 70° the air conditioner goes on. Which of the following is likely to occur when the temperature inside remains below seventy?

   (1) The brass strip will expand and turn the heating system on.
   (2) The steel strip will contract and turn the air conditioner on.
   (3) The brass strip will expand and turn the air conditioner on.
   (4) The brass strip will contract and turn the air conditioner off.
   (5) The thermostat will not trigger the air conditioner to go on.

Answers are on page 448.

EXERCISE 10: HEAT AND TEMPERATURE

Directions: Read the passage below and answer the question that follows.

Different materials expand at different degrees of temperature change and in different percentages of their length, volume, or surface. In the preceding example, brass expands lengthwise 50 percent more than steel when heat is applied. Buckling can occur when a material such as asphalt used for road surfaces reacts to changes in temperature, causing potholes. This is one of the reasons for the widespread use of reinforced concrete (concrete with a steel framework) on road surfaces rather than asphalt and the use of reinforced concrete in high-rise apartment construction.

The widespread use of reinforced concrete in construction suggests that

A. concrete and steel expand and contract at nearly the same temperatures

B. reinforced concrete expands at temperatures much higher than ordinary asphalt and does not buckle

C. reinforced concrete does not expand and contract at all

(1) A   **(2)** B   **(3)** C   **(4)** A and B   **(5)** B and C

Answer is on page 448.

DID YOU KNOW THAT: A steel bridge one mile long changes in length by more than four feet when there is a change in temperature from 40 degrees below zero in winter to 100 degrees in summer?

The Nature of Waves

You may not realize how important waves and wave action are to your life. Consider the following example. After a long day at work, you come home to a darkened apartment. You turn on the lights and put your favorite tape on the stereo. After washing up, you go to the refrigerator, take out the leftovers, and reheat them in your microwave oven. When dinner is over, you wash the dishes, turn off the stereo, and turn on the television for an evening of entertainment. After a couple of hours in front of the set, you go to bed, where you fall asleep to the gentle motion of your waterbed.

Each of the preceding activities is dependent on the existence of waves. A *wave* is a periodic or harmonic disturbance in space or through a medium (water, for instance) by which energy is transmitted. Water, sound, and light all travel in waves.

In the preceding example, the illumination the lamp provides comes from light waves (a form of electromagnetic waves); the music emanating from the stereo comes from sound waves; the powers to preserve your food and warm it come from electromagnetic waves; the power that transmits signals to your TV set comes from radio waves (another form of electromagnetic waves); and the energy that gives your waterbed its soothing motion comes from water waves.

Types and Properties of Waves

Waves transmit energy in different ways, and all phases of matter transmit waves. An example of a solid transmitting wave energy is an earthquake that takes place when rocks are under pressure and snap or slide into new positions. Waves that are felt and seen in water are examples of a liquid transmitting wave energy. Gases also transmit wave energy, as in an explosion, when heat, sound, and light waves are generated.

Two basic types of waves exist—longitudinal waves and transverse waves. A *longitudinal* wave is one in which the particles of the medium move back and forth in the same direction as the wave itself moves. An example of a longitudinal wave is a sound wave that occurs when a tuning fork is tapped, as shown below.

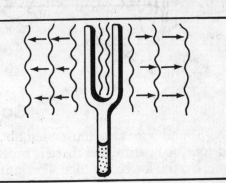

LONGITUDINAL WAVE

When a tuning fork is tapped, the prongs move from right to left in a rapid periodic motion. A sound wave is produced, and it moves parallel (right and left) to the moving prong.

A *transverse* wave is one in which the particles of the medium move at right angles to the direction of the wave's movement. An example of a transverse wave is one that occurs when a pebble is tossed into a still pond. Light travels in transverse waves. An example of a transverse wave is shown below.

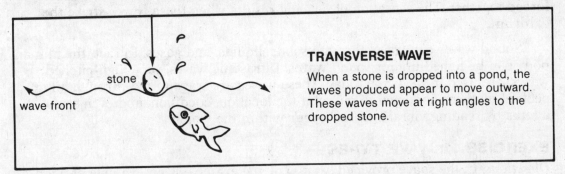

TRANSVERSE WAVE

When a stone is dropped into a pond, the waves produced appear to move outward. These waves move at right angles to the dropped stone.

Waves have two components, a crest and a trough. A *crest* is the point of highest displacement in a wave, and the *trough* is the point of lowest displacement. Crests and troughs are easily visible in water waves. The following illustration shows the crest and trough of a wave.

Two specific characteristics of a wave are length and frequency. **Wavelength** is defined as the distance between two successive wave crests or two successive wave troughs. Wave *frequency* is the number of wave crests that pass a given point per second. Therefore, the shorter the wavelength, the higher the wave frequency. In fact, a wave's speed equals the wavelength times the wave frequency. Wavelength is illustrated in the diagram below.

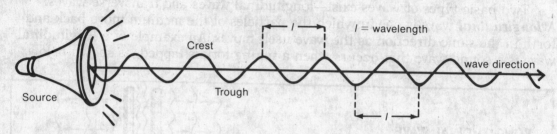

SOUND WAVE

Sound Waves

Sound waves, as illustrated above, are longitudinal waves. A musical pitch, or tone, is heard when there is a definite frequency to a wave. The lower the frequency, the lower the tone. For example, the frequency of a bass speaker in a stereo is lower than a tweeter, or high-frequency speaker, because the low-pitched sound of the bass results from a lower number of vibrations per second.

A sound wave is a wave of compression. It begins at a source—in the case above, a horn speaker. The speaker vibrates, compressing the air in front of it, and, like a spring, pushes it away. As the wave passes, the air molecules are forced together. The sensation of hearing results when these waves strike the eardrum.

Sound waves can travel through solids, liquids, and gases. In fact, the human body can be a medium for sound waves. Ultrasonic waves, very high-pitched waves, are used in medicine today. These waves are transmitted through an expectant mother's abdomen to pinpoint the location, condition, and even sex of a fetus by reading vibrations that occur within the womb.

EXERCISE 11: WAVE TYPES

Directions: In the space provided, write *L* if the example is an example of a longitudinal wave and *T* if it is an example of a transverse wave.

———— **1.** a wave that can be seen when a loose rope held end to end is jerked at one end

———— **2.** a noise caused by the detonation of an atomic bomb

———— **3.** the hum created when an arrow is released from a bow

———— **4.** waves created on the surface of boiling soup

———— **5.** waves that appear on the surface of the ocean

Answers are on page 449.

EXERCISE 12: PROPERTIES OF WAVES

Directions: Look at the illustration below and answer the question that follows.

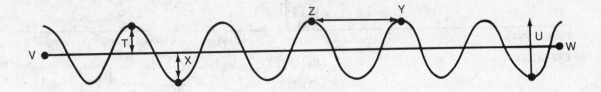

According to the illustration above, which points could be used to measure wavelength?

(1) T and Y
(2) X and Y
(3) Z and Y
(4) V and W
(5) T, X, and U

Answer is on page 449.

DID YOU KNOW THAT: Sound travels through air more slowly than it does through water, wood, or steel? Air molecules are not as closely packed together as water, wood, or steel molecules. Therefore, the sound waves lose much of their energy when passing through air.

The Nature of Light

Light is so ordinary to us that we take it for granted, yet light is so vital a part of life that neither plants nor animals could exist without it. Light produces heat, color, and the conditions that make vision possible. In fact, ancient scientists believed that light and vision were practically the same and that all light originated in the eye when contact was made with observed objects. Today, of course, we know this is not true.

Physicists define *light* as a form of electromagnetic energy that stimulates sensitive cells of the retina of the human eye to cause perception of vision. Electromagnetic energy can be expressed in wavelength ranges along a continuum, or spectrum. Light occupies the center of a spectrum that ranges from the low end (gamma rays) to the high end (radio waves). The other rays that occupy the electromagnetic spectrum are x-rays, ultraviolet rays, and infrared rays. Ultraviolet rays are invisible and are chiefly responsible for sunburn and tan. Heat-emitting objects such as the sun, an electric heater, and a radiator send out infrared rays that can be detected only by certain sensitive instruments. An illustration of the electromagnetic spectrum is shown on page 432.

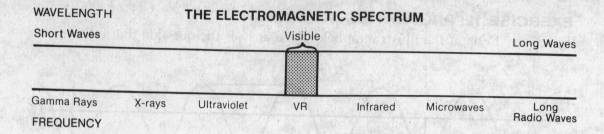

WAVELENGTH   **THE ELECTROMAGNETIC SPECTRUM**

Short Waves   Visible   Long Waves

Gamma Rays   X-rays   Ultraviolet   VR   Infrared   Microwaves   Long Radio Waves

FREQUENCY

The visible rays of the spectrum are recognized by the human eye as color. In order, these colors are red, orange, yellow, green, blue, indigo (deep blue), and violet. The shortest wavelengths that we can see are those we call violet; the longest ones we call red.

Two theories about the nature of light exist: the wave theory and the particle theory. These theories seem to oppose each other, but really just focus on different properties of light. According to the **wave theory of light**, light is a luminous energy emitted by a light source and travels through space as a transverse wave. According to the **particle theory of light**, light energy is both radiated (transmitted) and absorbed as tiny packets, or bundles, and not as continuous waves. Atoms and molecules are able to emit or absorb light energy in specific amounts.

EXERCISE 13: ANCIENT THEORY OF LIGHT

Directions: The ancients believed that light and vision were the same and that light originated in the eye. Write *S* in the space if the statement would support the ancients' beliefs and *D* if the statement would disprove the theory.

———— **1.** Glowing bodies are clearly perceived in total darkness by the human eye.

———— **2.** Extremely bright light can cause blindness in humans.

———— **3.** Nocturnal animals such as bats, opossums, and raccoons see better at night than during the day; their eyes are more keenly suited to darkness than to light.

———— **4.** Light exists despite the inability of the blind to observe it.

———— **5.** Although they can no longer see it, people who have lost their sense of sight nevertheless know that light exists.

Answers are on page 449.

EXERCISE 14: THE PHOTOELECTRIC PRINCIPLE

Directions: Read the passage below and answer the question that follows.

The electric eye, or photoelectric cell, is a mechanism used to open and close a garage door when a beam of light is activated or broken. The principle of the electric eye is based on the photoelectric effect. The photoelectric effect occurs when a beam of light strikes certain metals, causing electrons to be knocked out of the metal, producing an electric current. This is how it happens: Light falling on the inside of a bulb coated with an active substance causes electrons to be emitted. The electrons are attracted to a positively charged electrode positioned in the center of the bulb like a filament. An electric current results when the electrons (negatively charged particles) are attracted to the positively charged particles of the electrode. It is observed that electrons will be knocked loose only when a certain light energy is reached. The current can then be controlled by changes in light intensity. It appears that electrons are able to absorb only a certain amount of light at one time. When light shines on the electric eye, a current is established and the door moves. When the beam of light is broken, the door stops.

The principle of the electric eye acts to

    A. support the wave theory of light that light comes only from a luminous source

    B. dispute the belief that all light exists only as a continuous wave

    C. support the particle theory of light, which states that light energy is transmitted in packets and bundles and not as waves

    (1) A   **(2)** B   **(3)** C   **(4)** A and B   **(5)** B and C

Answer is on page 449.

EXERCISE 15: THE PHOTOELECTRIC EFFECT

Directions: Write *Yes* in the space provided if the example demonstrates the use of the photoelectric effect described in Exercise 14 and *No* if it doesn't.

_____ **1.** a light sensor in an outdoor light that causes the light to come on when dusk approaches and turn itself off when daylight begins

_____ **2.** an automatic door at a supermarket that opens when the rubber tread is stepped on

_____ **3.** an ultrasonic remote control device that turns a televison set on or off when a button is touched

_____ **4.** the sound of a film is controlled by markings on the side of a filmstrip that establish a current when exposed to the projector's lamp

_____ **5.** an elevator door remains open when a beam is broken by a hand placed in front of it

Answers are on page 449.

Properties of Light Waves

    Waves of light can be affected in at least five different ways: by reflection, refraction, diffraction, interference, and polarization. ***Reflection*** of light rays occurs when light waves strike a surface and bounce back or are returned at an angle. An example is light bouncing off a mirror. The angle of light and the type of reflecting surface produce different types of reflection.

    Refraction occurs when light rays appear to bend as they pass from one medium to another. For example, when a straw is held upright in a glass of water, it looks broken. This is because light rays travel faster in air than in water. The light ray changes its path and bends when it passes through water.

Diffraction results when light waves bend according to their wavelengths as they pass near the edge of an obstacle or through a small opening. Longer waves bend more than shorter ones. For example, holding a phonograph record edgewise toward a white light will produce an iridescent (rainbow) pattern on the record's surface. This occurs because the wavelengths of light are bent, or diffracted, by the grooves (obstacles) on the record's surface.

Interference of light rays occurs when two or more light waves come together, interfering with each other. When light waves interfere, an alternating pattern of lightness and darkness occurs because the rays displace each other and cancel each other out. For example, if you hold your thumb and index finger together and look through the opening at a bright light, you will see alternating patterns of light and darkness—interference.

Polarization of light waves occurs when they are caused to vibrate on one plane, usually horizontal or vertical. A *polarizer* is a material that will block all light except waves that vibrate in a particular plane. A light wave that travels at a vertical angle can be prevented from traveling at a horizontal angle by a polarizer. Reflection alone is capable of polarizing light. The ability of light waves to be polarized suggests that light waves are transverse waves and not longitudinal waves as sound waves are. Longitudinal waves cannot be polarized.

EXERCISE 16: PROPERTIES OF LIGHT WAVES

Directions: Defined below are five changes that light waves can undergo. Read the definitions and apply them to the questions that follow.

reflection—the angular return of a light wave that occurs when it strikes a shiny surface

refraction—the apparent bending of light waves as they pass from one medium to another

diffraction—the bending of light waves according to their wavelengths as they pass near the edge of an obstacle or through a small opening

interference—the altering of brightness of light rays that occurs when they interfere with each other, causing reinforcement and cancellation

polarization—the restriction of light waves to a particular plane, horizontal or vertical

1. A coin lying at the bottom of a pool is located at a different point from where the eye perceives it to be. The light rays from the coin bend as they pass from water to air. This demonstrates

    (1) reflection **(2)** refraction **(3)** diffraction **(4)** interference **(5)** polarization

2. Rays of light striking a polished piece of chrome appear to bounce off its surface. This demonstrates

    (1) reflection **(2)** refraction **(3)** diffraction **(4)** interference **(5)** polarization

Answers are on page 449.

EXERCISE 17: WAVE PROPERTIES

Directions: Read the passage below and choose the best answer for the following question.

On bright sunny days, sunlight is reflected from a concrete road surface and from a large body of water. This light is polarized horizontally. When we look at these surfaces without wearing sunglasses or polarized glasses, we experience glare from the reflection. Wearing polarized sunglasses prevents the reflected light from striking our eyes and causing glare. Which of the following best describes the action of the polarized glasses?

(1) The lenses are polarized horizontally, cutting off the reflected light rays.
(2) The lenses are polarized vertically, cutting off the reflected light rays.
(3) The lenses act as a mirror, reflecting all light.
(4) The lenses act as a refractor, bending the light rays.
(5) The lenses absorb the light rays.

Answer is on page 449.

DID YOU KNOW THAT: Stars appear to twinkle because the light rays from the stars are bent several times by layers of moving air before they reach our atmosphere.

The Nature of Electricity

Electricity is another invisible but vital form of energy that we often take for granted. Without electricity, however, our lives would be paralyzed. To appreciate our near total dependence on this form of energy, we need only to consider what happens when a power failure occurs overnight.

Our clock radios don't function, so we oversleep. Unless we're wearing a watch, we don't know the correct time. Refrigerated food that doesn't spoil can't be cooked if we depend on a microwave oven or an electric stove. Trains powered by electric rails can't run, elevators in high-rises get stuck, and business comes to a standstill because typewriters, computers, and other office machines powered by electricity cannot operate. If the power outage continues into the night, we use flashlights, if we have them, or rely on candles and kerosene lamps to find our way around.

The more urbanized we become, the more dependent on electricity we are. Nuclear energy, despite its potential hazards, has emerged in recent years as an important source for generating the electrical power we need. Physicists define *electricity* as a form of energy that results from the flow of loose electrons—electrons weakly bound to atoms. Electricity is closely related to magnetism; therefore, the attractive force of magnetism must be discussed in order to understand electrical energy better.

Magnetism and Electrical Charges

Magnetism has been known to humankind for a long period of time. The ancient Greeks discovered that a rock called ***magnetite*** was able to attract iron, and the Chinese experimented and found that a piece of free-hanging magnetite would always align itself in a northerly-southerly direction. These early discoveries led to the invention of the compass to help direct ships.

You have probably observed that a magnet dipped into a pile of iron filings will attract the metal to each end. These points of attraction at opposite ends of a magnet are called its ***poles***. Magnets have a north and a south pole, also called a positive and a negative pole. The opposite poles of two different magnets (a north pole and a south pole) will attract each other. Correspondingly, similar poles (two north or south poles) will repel each other. The space around magnets is called a ***magnetic field***. Only a few natural and manmade materials can be magnetized—iron, steel, nickel, cobalt, and some alloys. A magnet, with its poles and lines of force, is illustrated below.

MAGNET AND LINES OF FORCE

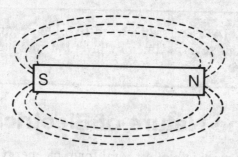

Magnetic Lines of Force

Every magnetic substance contains domains, groups of molecules with attractive forces. Before a substance is magnetized, these domains are arranged randomly so that the field of one domain is canceled out by the field of another. When the substance is magnetized, the domains line up parallel to the lines of force, with all north poles facing the same direction. This makes a permanent magnet out of a material in which the domains are too weak to disarrange themselves. The illustration on page 437 shows the difference between a magnetized and an unmagnetized substance.

In most elements, the atoms possess a slight magnetic field because of their spinning electrons. However, the fields cancel each other out because the atoms rotate and spin in different directions. In a magnet, whole groups of atoms line up in one direction and increase each other's magnetic effect rather than cancel it out. These magnetic concentrations are called ***magnetic domains***.

Static Electricity and Magnetism

If you have ever shocked yourself in dry weather after walking across a carpet and touching an object, you have experienced static electricity. ***Static electricity*** is a stationary electrical charge caused by the friction of two objects, one positively charged and the other negatively charged.

Static electricity operates on the same principle as magnetism. The rubbing of the carpet by your shoes causes your body to become electrified. The shock you feel is caused by your negatively charged body being neutralized by the positive charge of the object you touch. Upon contact, your body is no longer charged. Static electricity is stored and does not move. The charged object must be brought into contact with another object that has an opposite charge for electrical shock to occur.

MAGNETIZED AND UNMAGNETIZED IRON ATOMS

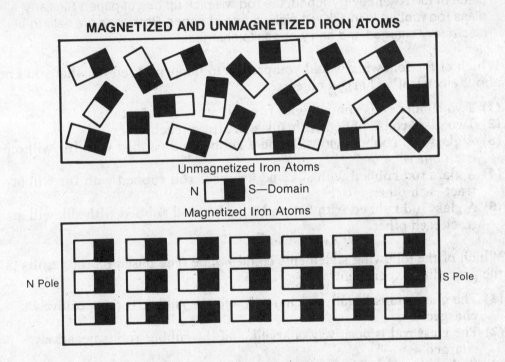

Unmagnetized Iron Atoms

N ☐ ■ S—Domain

Magnetized Iron Atoms

N Pole S Pole

EXERCISE 18: ELECTRICITY AND MAGNETISM

Directions: Choose the best answer for the questions below. The first question is based on the following paragraph.

Earth itself is surrounded by a magnetic field. This may be because of strong electric currents in Earth's core and the rotation of Earth. The north magnetic pole is located in Canada; the south magnetic pole is in nearly the opposite location. The strong magnetic attraction of these poles tends to align the needle of a compass in a northerly-southerly direction.

1. Based on the preceding passage, a compass will tell direction because

    (1) the whole Earth acts as a magnet
    (2) the Chinese discovered the magnetic poles
    (3) the Greeks discovered the magnetic poles
    (4) large iron deposits are located in Canada
    (5) the magnetic attraction of Earth is increasing

2. Which of the following would be attracted to either pole of a magnet?

   (1) a piece of aluminum
   (2) a piece of brass
   (3) a piece of tin
   (4) an unmagnetized piece of cobalt
   (5) a magnetized piece of cobalt

Answers are on page 449.

EXERCISE 19: LIKE AND UNLIKE CHARGES

Directions: Read the following passage and answer the questions.

   In an experiment, a rod made of hard rubber is rubbed vigorously with a piece of fur. After being rubbed, the rod will pick up bits of paper. Similarly, a glass rod rubbed with silk will pick up bits of paper. Both rods are said to be electrically charged and carry opposite charges.

1. Which of the following would you predict to happen based on what you know about electrically charged objects?

   (1) Two rubber rods rubbed with fur will attract each other.
   (2) Two glass rods rubbed with silk will attract each other.
   (3) A glass rod rubbed with silk and a rubber rod rubbed with fur will repel each other.
   (4) A glass rod rubbed with silk and a rubber rod rubbed with fur will attract each other.
   (5) A glass rod rubbed with fur and a rubber rod rubbed with silk will attract each other.

2. Which of the following statements could *not* be true based on the results of the preceding experiment?

   (1) The glass rod is negatively charged, and the rubber rod is positively charged.
   (2) The glass rod is positively charged, and the rubber rod is negatively charged.
   (3) Both rods carry the same electrical charge.
   (4) Both rods have different electrical charges.
   (5) Both rods have been magnetized.

3. Which of the following would be true in the above experiment?

   A. The fur would attract the rubber rod.

   B. The fur would repel the rubber rod.

   C. The silk would attract the glass rod.

   D. The silk would repel the glass rod.

   (1) A   **(2)** B   **(3)** C   **(4)** A and C   **(5)** A and D

Answers are on page 449.

DID YOU KNOW THAT: A permanent magnet made of cobalt, nickel, and aluminum (alnico) can hold up to sixty times its own weight? A one-pound magnet can lift a sixty-pound child suspended in a steel harness.

Electric Currents

Can you imagine one of our modern electric appliances being run by static electricity? It would take forever just to toast a slice of bread! A charge would have to be built up on the toaster by rubbing it, and it would discharge immediately upon touch.

Early scientists who experimented with electric charges found that charges could move easily through certain materials called *conductors*. As you learned in the chemistry section, metal was found to be a good conductor of electricity, as were salt solutions, acids, and hot gases. Other materials such as rubber were found not to conduct charges at all. These materials are called *insulators*.

An *electric current* is created by an electric charge in motion. In a solid conductor, such as wire, the current is a stream of moving electrons. In a liquid or gas, the current may be positively and negatively charged atoms—ions.

An electric current flowing through a solid conductor can be compared to the flow of water through the pipes in your plumbing system. An electric current moves slowly—about a hundredth of an inch per second. Although our lights come on instantly when a switch is turned on, it is not because the electrons race through the wires; it is because the wires are always filled with electrons just as a water pipe is always filled with water.

Electromagnets

An *electromagnet* is a core of soft magnetic material surrounded by a coil of wire. An electric current is passed through the wire to magnetize the core when a switch is flicked or a button pushed. The device then has the power to attract iron objects. When the switch is turned off, the attraction is broken.

Electromagnets are used in radios and an ordinary doorbell. In the doorbell, when the bell is pushed, the core is magnetized and attracts the clapper, causing the bell to sound. An electromagnet has obvious advantages over a permanent magnet in that an electromagnet can be turned on or off at will, and its attractive force can be increased by changing the amount of electricity sent to the coil. Modern electromagnets can lift up to 50,000 pounds of scrap iron and steel. They are used extensively in loading and transportation.

EXERCISE 20: CONDUCTORS AND INSULATORS

Directions: In the blanks below, write *C* if the material is a conductor of electricity and *I* if it is an insulator.

_____ **1.** leather   _____ **6.** glass

_____ **2.** porcelain   _____ **7.** salt water

_____ **3.** silver   _____ **8.** distilled water

_____ **4.** copper   _____ **9.** sulfuric acid

_____ **5.** wood   _____ **10.** plastic

Answers are on page 449.

EXERCISE 21: ELECTROMAGNETS

Directions: Choose the best answer for the following question.

A radio with a strong electromagnet would *not* be placed near the navigation instruments on a plane or ship because

(1) the radio wouldn't work because of electrical interference
(2) the radio couldn't be heard clearly because of static
(3) the accuracy of the compass would be affected by the magnetic field established by the radio's electromagnet
(4) the radio's electromagnet would cause all the navigation instruments to malfunction
(5) the radio would draw too much electrical energy, causing the electrical system of the ship or plane to discharge

Answer is on page 449.

DID YOU KNOW THAT: An electric eel can generate enough electricity to knock down a full-grown horse or drive a small motor? A large electric eel can discharge up to 600 volts of electricity.

TEST 3: SCIENCE ANSWER KEY

CHAPTER 1: BIOLOGY

Exercise 1: Cell Structure
page 357
Comprehension
1. c   2. e   3. a   4. b   5. d   6. f

Exercise 2: Cells
pages 357–358
Comprehension
1. (4) Choices (1), (2), (3), and (5) are not the main idea. They are details that support the key idea that the cell is a highly organized, complex structure.

Analysis
2. (1) The passage states that the endoplasmic reticulum serves as a network for transporting materials from one part of the cell to another or from the cell to the environment.

3. (3) According to the passage, mitochondria are abundant in highly active cells that produce energy for important life processes. The heart, which pumps blood throughout the body, is the most active of the choices listed.

4. (5) Chloroplasts are important in the food-making process for plants. Since animal cells have no chloroplasts, you can infer that animals must obtain their own food.

Application
5. (5) The organelle present in plants but not in animals that produces energy for important life processes is the chloroplast.

Exercise 3: Cells and Active Transport
page 359
Comprehension
1. high/low
2. low/high
3. reverse *or* opposite

Exercise 4: Diffusion and Osmosis
page 359
Analysis
1. (3) According to the passage, diffusion is the passage of molecules from an area of high concentration to an area of low concentration. This process allows for an even distribution of substances throughout all the cells of the body.

2. (5) In osmosis, water moves from a *lower* concentration to a *higher* one. The salt solution in the blood plasma is higher; therefore, the cell will lose water. If it loses water, it will shrink.

Exercise 5: Mitosis
page 361
Comprehension
1. a   2. b   3. d   4. c

Exercise 6: Meiosis
page 363
Comprehension
4, 1, 3, 2

Exercise 7: Cell Division
page 363
Comprehension
1. (3) Because of the exchange and recombination of chromosomal material, the method of reproduction that allows for the most variety is sexual reproduction.

Analysis
2. (1) The purpose of meiosis is to reduce the number of chromosomes in reproductive cells so that when sperm and egg unite, they create the proper number of chromosomes for the species. You can infer that without meiosis, offspring would have twice the assigned number of chromosomes.

Comprehension
3. (2) An egg cell is a reproductive cell. Only reproductive cells have a haploid number of chromosomes.

Analysis
4. (3) Because cancerous cells spread to invade healthy cells, you can conclude that cancer cells divide more unpredictably than normal cells.

Exercise 8: Genetics and Heredity
pages 364–365
Comprehension
1. (4) The diagram shows only one child out of four that does not have a dominant green eye gene or a dominant brown eye gene. This is the only child that will have blue eyes; therefore, the chances are that 25 percent of the children will have blue eyes.

Analysis
2. (3) The "Y" chromosome that determines a child's sex is carried by the father.

Evaluation
3. (5) Both A and C are supported by information in the reading. Choice B is not true.

**Exercise 9: The Nitrogen Cycle
pages 366–367
Analysis**
1. (1) The only case that shows a mutually beneficial relationship between two different organisms is that of bacteria that live in the stomachs of hoofed animals and at the same time help the animals digest food.

Comprehension
2. (3) Nitrogen fixing is described as the process by which legumes form nitrates in the soil. Peanuts are the only legume among the choices listed.

Application
3. (4) Soybeans are legumes and are important in the nitrogen-fixing process. The introduction of soybeans into the crop rotation process improves the possibility of replenishing the supply of nitrogen.

**Exercise 10: Photosynthesis
pages 367–368
Analysis**
1. (5) Plants that do not possess chlorophyll must use a process other than photosynthesis to obtain the energy they need. One such process is parasitism, in which one organism feeds off another.
2. (1) Green pigment indicates the presence of chlorophyll. The areas of the coleus leaf that were green originally contained starch, which is produced through photosynthesis. Therefore, the starch turns brown when iodine is applied.

**Exercise 11: Cellular Respiration
pages 368–369
Comprehension**
1. (3) According to the passage, cellular respiration is the series of chemical reactions by which a cell releases the energy trapped inside glucose molecules.

Analysis
2. (1) Glucose molecules must be present for cellular respiration to occur. Since glucose molecules are the end product of photosynthesis in plants, you can infer that photosynthesis must precede cellular respiration.

Application
3. (4) The more active a person is, the more energy he or she expends and the more carbon dioxide he or she exhales. Athletes are more active than most people; therefore, they would have higher rates of cellular respiration.

Evaluation
4. (4) The rate of cellular respiration is affected by whether or not a person is at rest or is physically active. Choices (3) and (4) include both criteria; however, in choice (4) the greater number of students tested provides more reliable data.

Analysis
5. (5) The passage describes two types of diabetics—those whose bodies do not produce enough insulin and those whose bodies cannot effectively use the insulin produced. The passage states further that *some* diabetics must take additional insulin. Since not all diabetics are required to increase their insulin intake, the only precautions that would apply to *both* categories of diabetics is regulating their glucose intake and maintaining a reasonable exercise regimen.

**Exercise 12: Classification of Organisms
page 371
Application**
1. (1) Streptococcus is a single-celled organism of the bacteria family and fits in the kingdom monera.
2. (3) Mold lacks chlorophyll and obtains food from another organism. It is classified in the kingdom fungi.
3. (2) An amoeba is a single-celled organism that can move and has a more complex cell structure than monerans. It is classified in the kingdom protista.

**Exercise 13: Evolution and Natural Selection
pages 372–373
Application**
1. (3) According to the passage, certain forms of life adapted to meet the demands of the environment. The fact that the duckbill platypus is found only in and around Australia supports the hypothesis that the platypus developed independently in a closed environment during the early history of mammals.
2. (4) That Australia became isolated from the other six continents millions of years ago (choice A), and that marsupials didn't have to compete with placental mammals (choice B), are two facts that together help to explain why marsupials are found primarily around Australia. Choice C is not true, since marsupials survive in zoos throughout the world.
3. (3) The opossum is the only marsupial listed that is native to North America.

Analysis

4. (1) Choice (1) is the best answer because choices (3), (4), and (5) are not true. Choice (2) is not true because the highest forms of animal life are placental mammals.

Evaluation

5. (4) Of the choices listed, the seal is the only mammal listed whose body is adapted for living in water—an environment that is not typically one that mammals live in.

Exercise 14: Ecology and Ecosystems
page 374
Application

1. grass
2. cattle and deer
3. mountain lion

Analysis

4. The destruction of the **mountain lion** led to the increase of grazing by **deer** and **cattle**, which led to **denuding** of the land and its eventual **erosion** by heavy rains.

CHAPTER 2: EARTH SCIENCE

Exercise 1: The Big Bang Theory
page 376
Comprehension

(5) The passage states that the big bang theory accounts for both the expansion of the universe and the presence of background radiation.

Exercise 2: Stars and Galaxies
page 377
Comprehension

3, 4, 1, 2

Exercise 3: The Solar System
page 378
Application

1. (4) According to the story of Goldilocks and the Three Bears, Goldilocks tried one bowl of porridge that was too cold, another that was too hot, and a third that was just right. This corresponds to Mars being too cold, Venus too hot, and Earth just right to support life.

Analysis

2. (3) Choice (1) is not true. Earth is the only planet known to support life. You can see from the illustration of the solar system that choices (2) and (4) are not true. The exact age of the planets cannot be determined, choice (5). Choice (3) is the only reasonable explanation.

Exercise 4: The Planets
page 378
Comprehension

1. Earth, Mars
2. Mars
3. Mercury
4. Venus
5. Venus

Exercise 5: The Sun and Solar System
page 379
Analysis

(5) Based on the facts in the chart, the farther away from the Sun these planets are, the greater number of moons they have and the longer they take to revolve around the Sun.

Exercise 6: Plate Tectonics
page 381
Comprehension

(5) In the passage, the occurrence of earthquakes, volcanoes, and mountains and the theory of continental drift are explained by the theory of plate tectonics.

Exercise 7: Earthquakes
page 381
Evaluation

(3) The map shows the potential for most moderate and major earthquake damage occurring on the West Coast. Choices (1), (2), and (4) are directly contradicted by the map. Choice (5) is an opinion, not a fact.

Exercise 8: Continental Drift
page 382
Analysis

1. (3) This choice reflects an understanding of continental drift. Choice (A) is untrue, and choice (B) is not a good explanation.

2. (5) This is the best choice because it takes into account both the theory of continental drift and the behavior of sea turtles.

Exercise 9: Measuring Geologic Time
pages 383–384
Comprehension

1. (5) The text states that sedimentary rocks are deposited near Earth's surface and that metamorphic rock is located just below igneous rock.

2. (4) According to the passage, metamorphic and igneous rock rarely contain fossils, and it is difficult to determine the age of original rock in metamorphic rocks. Igneous rock is capable of being dated radiometrically although metamorphic rock is not.

Analysis

3. (5) The trilobite rocks are likely to be older than the coral because the greater the depth at which a fossil is found, the older it is likely to be.

Exercise 10: Minerals and Rocks
page 385
Analysis

1. **(3)** Potassium, which makes up 1.85 percent of Earth's crust, is the only element that occupies three times more space than does silicon.

2. **(4)** The other choices given either weigh more or take up less space than silicon.

Comprehension

3. **(5)** If an element weighs more than another but takes up less space, it is highly compressible, a property of silicon.

Analysis

4. **(5)** The fact that oxygen combines with most of Earth's elements explains why it constitutes such a great part of Earth's crust. Choices (1), (2), and (3) are not true. Choice (4) has no relation to the issue of the composition of Earth's crust.

Exercise 11: The Changing Earth
pages 386–387
Application

1. **(5)** Choice (5) is a procedure most farmers follow to increase their chances of a bountiful harvest and has nothing to do with preventing erosion.

Comprehension

2. **(5)** Forces that cause volcanoes and mountains both result in an uplifting of Earth's surface; ocean trenches do not.

Exercise 12: Change in Sea Level
pages 388–389
Comprehension

1. **(5)** According to the graph, nearly 18,000 years ago the depth of the oceans was at almost 400 feet below sea level, its lowest level.

Evaluation

2. **(1)** Glaciers covered the earth 20,000 years ago, and sea level was at its lowest—400 feet. Today, glaciers no longer cover Earth, and sea level is at its highest according to the graph.

Exercise 13: The Oceans' Beginning
page 389
Comprehension

1. **(4)** At 0.001 percent, water vapor in the atmosphere yields the lowest amount of water on Earth.

Analysis

2. **(4)** According to the text, many scientists believe that oceans were formed by the release of water bound up in Earth's interior.

Exercise 14: The Oceans' Tides
pages 390–391
Analysis

1. **(5)** According to the illustration, the Moon is in a direct line with the Sun and receives the Sun's greatest attractive force. The periods when this occurs are at full moon and new moon.

2. **(2)** According to the illustration, the Moon is at a right angle to the Sun and the rays are indirect, striking only a portion of the Moon's surface. This corresponds to the periods of first quarter moon and last quarter moon.

3. **(5)** The two conditions that are more pronounced during unusually high tide are the Moon's closeness to Earth and Earth's closeness to the Sun. These two conditions increase the gravitational pull of the Moon and the Sun on Earth.

Application

4. **(2)** The opposite condition of syzygy results in unusually low tides because the gravitational pull of the Moon and the Sun on Earth is at its weakest.

Exercise 15: Layers of Earth's Atmosphere
page 393
Comprehension

1. **(4)** The ionosphere extends from 30 miles to 300 miles in Earth's atmosphere. Noctilucent clouds are found at heights above 50 miles.

2. **(3)** "D" radio waves are found at the same level as noctilucent clouds—in the lower ionosphere.

3. **(5)** Clouds (located in the troposphere) shown at the same level as Mt. Everest's peak suggest that the peak may be hidden by clouds.

Exercise 16: Ozone in the Atmosphere
page 394
Analysis

1. **(2)** Smog is visible and, therefore, lies in the troposphere, the level of the atmosphere closest to Earth.

2. **(2)** Ozone is formed by heat and the exhaust from cars. The heat during hot summer days contributes to the formation of ozone.

Exercise 17: The Water Cycle
page 395
Comprehension

5, 3, 1, 4, 2

Exercise 18: Humidity
pages 396–397
Analysis

1. **(4)** According to the passage, warm air holds more moisture than cold air; therefore, when the temperature drops, the colder air cannot hold the amount of moisture that the warmer air held. As a result, the saturation point is reached and excess humidity is released as rain.

2. **(3)** At a given time, water vapor in the air is constant. Cold air can hold less moisture than warm air. When air is heated, it has the capacity to hold more water. If moisture is not added to the air, the humidity level goes down.

3. **(3)** Choices (1) and (2) are too low for comfort; choices (4) and (5) too high for comfort.

Exercise 19: Air Masses, Fronts, and Weather
page 398
Comprehension

1. **(2)** According to the passage, warm fronts bring low-lying clouds, steady winds, and drizzling rain.

2. **(3)** According to the passage, a stationary front lingers and brings conditions similar to those of a warm front.

Evaluation

3. **(5)** The passage discusses all of the properties affecting fronts except the direction in which the air mass moves.

CHAPTER 3: CHEMISTRY
Exercise 1: Atomic Structure
page 401
Understanding Ideas
1. d   2. e   3. f   4. b   5. c   6. a

Exercise 2: Nuclear Energy
page 401
Application

1. **(4)** The passage states that fusion involves the uniting of two nuclei of a chemical element at high temperatures and pressures to form a new element. Hydrogen, the lightest element, is the only one listed whose nuclei when fused can form the second lightest element—helium.

2. **(1)** The passage states that fission involves the splitting of the nucleus of a heavy element. Plutonium is not a gas and, therefore, is the only heavy element shown.

Exercise 3: Isotopic Elements
page 402
Application

1. **(3)** According to the chart, lithium's atomic mass is 6.94. Of all the elements shown, it would be the most likely to have an isotope of 6. If two lithium isotopes are fused, the atomic mass of the new element would be 12—the atomic mass of carbon 12.

2. **(1)** According to the passage, an isotope is a form of an element that varies in the number of neutrons in its nucleus. The only element represented that is capable of doubling or tripling its mass to achieve a final mass of 2 or 3 would be hydrogen, with an atomic mass of 1.01.

Exercise 4: Elements And Periodicity
page 405
Application

1. **(4)** The passage states that as the atomic number increases for elements in a column, similar chemical properties occur regularly and to a greater degree. The only *physical* property that gold would have a higher degree of would be malleability because it is a soft and workable metal. Choices (1), (2), and (5) are not physical properties. Choice (3) is not true of gold or the other metals.

Evaluation

2. **(4)** The fact that radon is found in the ground (choice A) suggests that it is denser and weighs more than the others. Also, the fact that it has a higher atomic number (choice B) indicates that its properties, including weight and density, are greater than those of other elements in its family.

Exercise 5: Balanced Equations
page 407
Comprehension

1. **B**—The reaction begins and ends with two atoms of nitrogen (N) and two atoms of oxygen (O).

2. **U**—The reaction begins with one atom of iron (Fe), one atom of hydrogen (H), and one atom of chlorine (Cl). However, it ends with one atom of iron, two atoms of hydrogen, and three atoms of chlorine. Therefore, it is not balanced.

3. **B**—The reaction begins and ends with two atoms of hydrogen (H) and one atom of oxygen (O).

4. **U**—The reaction begins with one atom of zinc (Zn), one atom of carbon (C), and two atoms of oxygen (O). It ends with one atom of zinc, one atom of carbon, and three atoms of oxygen.

5. **B**—The reaction begins and ends with one atom of carbon (C) and two atoms of sulfur (S).

Exercise 6: Chemical Reactions
pages 407–408
Analysis

1. **(3)** None of the other formulas indicate two iron atoms and three oxygen atoms.

2. **(2)** None of the others are balanced equations indicating one molecule of carbon dioxide (CO_2) and one molecule of water (H_2O). Choice (4) starts with carbon dioxide and water but does not result in a balanced equation.

Comprehension

3. **(2)** According to the passage, a chemical equation is balanced when it follows the Law of Conservation of Matter, which states that matter can neither be created nor destroyed in a chemical reaction.

Evaluation

4. **(4)** The fact that there is a copper coating on the aluminum is the only evidence cited that can prove that a chemical change has taken place.

Analysis

5. **(3)** The appearance of a new substance is best explained by the occurrence of a chemical change.

Exercise 7: Types of Substances
pages 409–410
Application

1. **(1)** Salt is a compound composed of elements sodium and chlorine and has properties different from each.

2. **(4)** Solder is an alloy composed of two metals—tin and lead—with one dissolved into the other.

3. **(2)** Air is a mixture composed of at least four gases. Each gas retains its own distinct properties.

4. **(3)** Mercurochrome is a solution composed of three compounds dissolved in a liquid.

Exercise 8: Compounds and Mixtures
page 410
Evaluation

(2) Compounds are substances that are composed of two or more elements in which the elements lose their original properties, so only statement B is correct. In a mixture, the combining elements do not lose their original properties. Therefore, by definition, a compound cannot contain a mixture (statement A). Statement C can be eliminated because a solution is a mixture; it does not contain mixtures.

Exercise 9: Compounds and Chemical Bonding
pages 412–413
Comprehension

1. **(5)** The inert gases are incapable of forming compounds, undergoing chemical reactions, and sharing or transferring electrons, all of which involve some form of chemical bonding.

2. **(2)** The passage says that ionic bonding is achieved by the transfer of electrons.

3. **(1)** The passage says that a covalent bond is one in which atoms are held together by sharing electrons.

Exercise 10: Chemical First Aid
page 414
Analysis

1. **(3)** The passage on page 413 says that when an acid combines with a base a salt is formed. In this case, the base is ammonia, and the acid is vinegar, orange juice, or lemon juice.

2. **(3)** Milk is the only substance listed that contains acid—lactic acid.

3. **(2)** The acid must be neutralized—changed into a salt and water. A base such as milk of magnesia is the only antidote listed that can neutralize the acid phenol.

4. **(4)** The action of the milk of magnesia would neutralize the acid, changing it into a salt and water.

Exercise 11: Acids, Bases, and Salts
page 415
Analysis

1. **(4)** Acetic acid, a mild acid contained in vinegar, would be found at the acidic end of the pH scale closest to neutrality—between the values 4 and 5. Choices (1) and (5) represent alkalinity, not acidity, and choices (2) and (3) represent high acidity.

2. (2) Oxalic acid, described as a strong, poisonous acid, would be found at the lower end of the pH scale nearest increasing acidity—between 1 and 2. Choice (1) represents low alkalinity, choice (3) low acidity, choice (4) low acidity approaching neutrality, and choice (5) high alkalinity.

3. (3) Water is neither acidic nor alkaline; therefore, it would be neutral on the pH scale.

Evaluation

4. (5) A substance is an acid if it tastes sour (choice B) or neutralizes a base (choice C). An acid has a pH reading under 7, so choice A is eliminated.

Exercise 12: A Car Battery
pages 416–417
Application

1. (2) In the example, sulfuric acid, a conductor of electricity, is dissolved in water.

2. (1) The passage says that the lead loses two electrons when it reacts with sulfuric acid; therefore, lead is oxidized.

3. (2) The passage says that lead dioxide gains two electrons, so it is the substance that is reduced.

4. (2) Sulfuric acid is an oxidizing agent because it causes the lead in the battery to lose electrons. The lead dioxide is a reducing agent because it causes the sulfuric acid to gain electrons.

5. (3) Oxidation-reduction is a process in which one substance loses electrons and the other gains electrons to convert chemical energy into electrical energy. The other choices do not reflect this process. Nuclear fission and nuclear fusion, choices (1) and (2), involve the splitting and the uniting of the nuclei of atoms. Ionic bonding and covalent bonding, choices (4) and (5), are processes that create compounds by either the transferring or sharing of electrons.

Analysis

6. (3) Citric acid (obtained from fruits) is the only organic compound listed. Organic compounds do not conduct electrical currents.

7. (4) A battery is completely discharged when the sulfuric acid is no longer capable of oxidizing lead, and the lead dioxide is no longer able to reduce the sulfuric acid; thus the oxidation-reduction process that causes an electric current to flow cannot occur.

Exercise 13: Reaction Rate, Catalysts, and Equilibrium
page 418
Analysis

1. (3) A catalyst is an agent that speeds up a chemical reaction but that is not affected by the reaction itself. Lipase speeds up the rate at which fats are changed into fatty acids. Because lipase is found in the body, it may be described as a biological catalyst. A negative catalyst (choice B) inhibits, or slows down, a chemical reaction.

Application

2. (5) According to the passage, chemical equilibrium occurs when the rate of forward reaction balances the rate of reverse reaction. In photosynthesis (B), plants take in water and carbon dioxide from the air to make starch with the sun's help. The by-product oxygen is released. The reverse of this process is respiration (C), the taking in of oxygen by animals and the combining of oxygen with starch to form carbon dioxide and water, which the plants use for photosynthesis. Thus, the forward reaction of photosynthesis is balanced by the reverse reaction of respiration, resulting in chemical equilibrium.

CHAPTER 4: PHYSICS
Exercise 1: Laws of Force and Motion
page 420
Application
1. AR   **2.** AF   **3.** AR   **4.** G   **5.** I
Exercise 2: The Force of Gravity
page 421
Comprehension
(1) Weight is a function of the attractive force of one object on another. According to the passage, the strength of the force depends on the masses of the objects. Since Jupiter is larger than Earth, the attractive force must be greater. This would result in an increase in the astronaut's weight relative to his weight on Earth.

Exercise 3: Mechanics, Force, and Motion
page 421
Evaluation
1. **(4)** Air does not exist in a vacuum. Both the coin and the confetti fall at the same rate even though the coin is heavier. This proves that weight has less to do with the rate of acceleration of falling objects than air resistance. Outside a vacuum, the coin would fall faster than the confetti, which would flutter because of the air resistance. Choice C is incorrect because *all* falling objects are affected by the force of gravity.
2. **(2)** By dropping items of different weights from the leaning tower of Pisa, Galileo proved that falling objects fell at the same rate of speed.

Exercise 4: Forms of Energy
page 423
Application
1. K   2. P   3. P   4. K   5. K

Exercise 5: Types of Energy
page 423
Application
1. **(4)** The Sun radiates energy to Earth; its warmth and light sustain all life on Earth.
2. **(1)** Nuclear energy results from the splitting of an atom of a heavy chemical element such as U-235.
3. **(2)** Gas and air are mixtures. When they are ignited, combustion, a chemical process, occurs.

Exercise 6: Simple Machines
pages 424–425
Analysis
1. **(3)** According to the passage, the greater the distance between the fulcrum and the applied force, the less the force required to perform the work. If the distance is increased to 20 feet, then the effort would be halved:
100 ÷ 2 = 50 pounds of applied force.

Evaluation
2. **(3)** The shape of the fulcrum is the only variable not cited in the passage that would have any bearing on the lever's effectiveness.

Exercise 7: Kinetic Theory of Matter
page 426
Comprehension
1. T   2. F   3. F   4. T   5. F

Exercise 8: Kinetic Theory and Motion
pages 426–427
Evaluation
1. **(4)** The dispersion of the ink throughout the water, turning it light blue, proves that the molecules of ink and water are in constant motion and intermingle. Choices (1) and (2) cannot be proved by observation alone. Choice (3) is incorrect because the variable of heat is not introduced. Choice (5) is incorrect since all liquids are fluid because their molecules are able to move past each other.

Analysis
2. **(3)** According to the passage, heat causes molecules to speed up and materials to expand. Choice (3) is the only one that correctly shows an effect of heating the water.

Exercise 9: The Thermostat
page 427
Application
1. **(3)** The passage states that certain materials expand when their temperatures are raised and shrink when they are lowered. The expansion and contraction of the brass strip in the thermostat is similar to the rising and falling of mercury in a thermometer.

Analysis
2. **(5)** If the thermostat is set for 70°, this means that when the room temperature rises above seventy degrees, the air conditioner will come on; when the temperature reaches seventy degrees, the air conditioner will go off. If the temperature remains below seventy degrees, the thermostat will not trigger the air conditioner to go on.

Exercise 10: Heat and Temperature
page 428
Analysis
(4) Reinforced concrete could not maintain its durability if the two materials, concrete and steel, expanded and contracted at different temperatures—so choice A is correct. Also, because reinforced concrete does not buckle as asphalt does, you can infer that reinforced concrete must expand at a higher temperature than asphalt—so choice B is correct. Choice C is not true since steel is known to expand and contract.

Exercise 11: Wave Types
page 430
Application
1. T   2. L   3. L   4. T   5. T

Exercise 12: Properties of Waves
page 431
Comprehension
(3) The passage states that wavelength is the distance between two successive wave crests or troughs. Points Z and Y are two successive wave crests.

Exercise 13: Ancient Theory of Light
page 432
Evaluation
1. S   2. D   3. D   4. D   5. D

Exercise 14: The Photoelectric Principle
pages 432–433
Evaluation
(5) The passage states that an active substance emits electrons when light falls on it. Light intensity determines the strength of the current generated by the emission of electrons. This suggests that light energy is transmitted in packets or bundles and disputes the belief that light exists only as a continuous wave.

Exercise 15: The Photoelectric Effect
page 433
Evaluation
1. Yes   2. No   3. No   4. Yes   5. Yes

Exercise 16: Properties of Light Waves
page 434
Application
1. (2) Refraction is the bending of light waves as they pass from one medium to another—in this case, from water to air.
2. (1) Reflection is the return of a light wave when it strikes a shiny surface.

Exercise 17: Wave Properties
page 435
Comprehension
(2) Polarization is the restriction of light waves to a particular plane, horizontal or vertical. In this case, the lenses are polarized vertically, restricting the penetration of the horizontally polarized light from the water and concrete surfaces.

Exercise 18: Electricity and Magnetism
pages 437–438
Analysis
1. (1) According to the information in the text, the strong magnetic attraction coming from Earth's core tends to align the compass' needle in a northerly-southerly direction.

Comprehension
2. (4) A magnetized object will attract either end of an unmagnetized object made of iron, steel, nickel, or cobalt, but will attract only the opposite pole of another magnetized object. Aluminum, brass, and tin cannot be attracted.

Exercise 19: Like and Unlike Charges
page 438
Analysis
1. (4) An electrically charged rubber rod and glass rod will attract each other because they carry opposite charges.

Evaluation
2. (3) The experiment states that the rods carry opposite charges. Therefore, they cannot carry the same charge.
3. (4) In order for fur to magnetize a rubber rod and silk to electrify a glass rod, an attractive force between the respective materials must exist.

Exercise 20: Conductors and Insulators
page 440
Application
1. I   3. C   5. I   7. C   9. C
2. I   4. C   6. I   8. I   10. I

Exercise 21: Electromagnets
page 440
Analysis
(3) The only plausible reason listed for a radio's not being placed near navigational instruments is that the radio's electromagnet would exert an attractive force on the compass of a ship or plane, thus throwing it off course. Choices (1) and (2) have nothing to do with navigational instruments. Choices (4) and (5) are neither plausible nor true.

Test 4:
Literature and the Arts

The GED Literature and the Arts Test consists of prose passages of about 200 to 400 words, poetry passages of about 8 to 25 lines, and drama excerpts. Each passage is followed by multiple-choice questions. These questions require you to interpret selections from popular literature, classical literature, and commentaries about literature and the arts. (All of these types of literature are covered in this book.) To answer successfully, you will need to

▶ understand what you read

▶ apply information to a new situation

▶ analyze elements of style and structure in passages

Actually, you already use many of these different kinds of reading and thinking skills in daily life. In this section, we will help you learn to apply these skills to literature and commentaries on the arts.

How many questions are on the test?

There are 45 multiple-choice questions, and you will be given 65 minutes to complete the test. Each passage on the literature test is preceded by a purpose question. This question is *not* a title for the passage. Rather, it is intended to help you focus your reading of the piece. To get an idea of what the test is like, look at the Practice Test at the end of this book. The Practice Test is based on the real GED Test. In fact, all of the multiple-choice questions in this section are sample GED questions.

What's on the test?

The GED Literature and the Arts Test can be broken down into the content areas it covers and the skills it tests. The following subjects make up the content of the test:

Popular Literature	50%
Classical Literature	25%
Commentaries about Literature and the Arts	25%

These content areas are covered in Chapters 1–4 of this section. There you will find selections of fiction, poetry, drama, nonfiction, and articles about literature and the arts.

Also remember that you are being tested on your ability to think through certain ideas and concepts. You will be asked to do more than just find a statement or quotation that was given in a passage.

Thinking skills that you will be tested on include:

Understanding Ideas	60%
(Literal and Inferential Comprehension)	
Applying Ideas	15%
Analyzing Ideas	25%

Chapter 1 of the Reading Skills section of this book (on pages 189–222) focuses on these thinking skills, and all of the activities and questions in this section will help you to practice answering these types of questions. If you have not already worked through the Reading Skills section, you might want to go back and complete the exercises in that section. The more practice you have had in answering the three categories of questions, the better prepared you will be to answer questions in this section and on the actual test.

1
INTERPRETING PROSE FICTION

The fiction passages presented on the Literature and the Arts Test are taken from either novels or short stories. Both novels and short stories usually present imaginary people and events that imitate life. Novels and short stories are written in *prose*—ordinary spoken language—and share common literary devices and techniques. These devices and techniques will be explored in this section.

By reading fiction, you can enjoy stories about interesting people and situations and gain a greater understanding of life. Your understanding of literature will also aid you as a moviegoer and television viewer, for many characteristics of literature can be applied to films and TV.

Although many elements in fiction are common to both the novel and the short story, there are basic differences between the two forms.

The Novel and the Short Story

The *novel* is a long, book-length story. Often, the novelist writes a story that involves several characters and events in their lives. A skillful novelist brings together characters, their adventures, and their struggles, and weaves them into one main plot.

The *short story* is also a work that deals with imaginary characters, locations, or events, but the story is much shorter than a novel. Moreover, a short story usually focuses on fewer characters and on one event. By narrowing the focus, the short-story writer achieves a single effect.

Edgar Allan Poe, one of America's earliest and best short-story writers, believed that a short story should be read in one sitting. Of course, how long that is depends upon how long you choose to sit and read, but the idea is that a short story should be read in hours, not days or weeks—the length of time it might take to read a novel.

A good short-story writer gets to the point and quickly develops believable characters and events. Like an artist who must create within the limited confines of a canvas, the writer has limited space in which to create a work of art. When you read a piece of fiction, think about its creation. Focus on how the writer expresses ideas as well as on the ideas themselves.

Although novels and short stories are developed around fictional characters, the events that occur may sometimes be based on fact. This is especially true in historical novels. For example, *Gone with the Wind*, one of the most popular novels of this century, describes events in the American Civil War. Novelist Margaret Mitchell used facts about the war, such as the battles, their locations, and the leaders of the North and South. However, Scarlett O'Hara, Rhett Butler, and the plantation home Tara were made up by Mitchell.

Basic Elements of Fiction

The basic elements of fiction are illustrated in the puzzle below. These elements and other literary terms will be explained in this section. As you progress through this section, this diagram will help you to understand the parts (elements) that make up the whole (novel or short story).

BASIC ELEMENTS OF FICTION
The Novel and Short Story

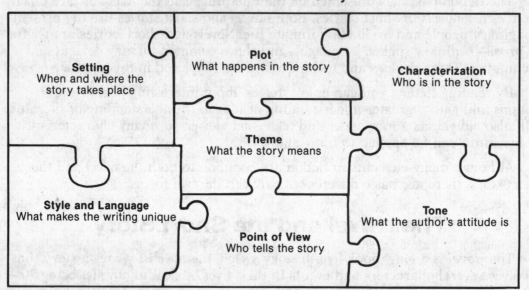

Setting
When and where the story takes place

Plot
What happens in the story

Characterization
Who is in the story

Theme
What the story means

Style and Language
What makes the writing unique

Point of View
Who tells the story

Tone
What the author's attitude is

Setting: When and Where the Story Takes Place

The *setting* of a short story or novel is the time and place in which the action occurs. Time of day or year, conditions, and atmosphere are all part of the setting. Some authors are very direct about revealing their settings. They state early in a work exactly when and where the story is happening:

- He rode into St. Louis at high noon in August 1875.

- 11:00 A.M.—San Francisco, July 1984—at Democratic Convention headquarters.

- The vehicle completed its orbit before landing on the lunar surface. It was A.D. 2021.

Inferring Time and Place

In many stories, the time and place are not directly stated. The reader needs to read between the lines, or look for clues, to identify a specific time and place.

Read the following paragraph to infer setting. Underline all the clues that suggest *time* (when the action takes place) and **location** (where the action takes place).

James saddled the pony and led the new pet around to the side of the porch. He stopped and tied the reins to the tractor so that he could attach a big red bow to the bridle.

Yesterday, he'd bought the saddle, reins and bridle, and the bow at the department store over in Helena. He'd planned well for this surprise.

The sun had barely risen when Angie, barefoot and still dressed in her nightgown, ran out of the old screen door and heard her father say, "Happy tenth birthday, honey!"

1. Does the action take place in a city or on a farm? _____

What details act as clues? _____

2. Does the action take place in the 1860s or 1960s? _____

What details act as clues? _____

3. Does the action take place in the early morning or the late evening? _____

What details act as clues? _____

4. Does the action take place in Montana or in New Jersey? _____

What details act as clues? _____

_____

The action takes place on a farm. You can infer this from the words *tractor* and *barn*. Other helpful clues are "saddled the pony" and "over in Helena." (James had to travel to a city to buy the gifts.) Your second answer should be *1960s*. Tractors and department stores did not exist in the 1860s, so you can assume that the time is sometime during the 1900s. Your third answer should be *early morning*. You can infer time of day by these details: "The sun had barely risen" and "Angie, barefoot and still dressed in her nightgown." The location of the story is Montana; Helena is in Montana. If you had not known already that Helena is in Montana, an atlas or map of the United States could have helped you determine this.

EXERCISE 1: IDENTIFYING SETTING

Directions: Read the passage below and answer the questions that follow.

WHERE ARE YUN-JA AND CHONG-IL?

Yun-ja floated on the blue swells, her face toward the dazzling sun. At first the water had chilled her, but now it felt agreeable, almost responding to her touch. Ripples slapped about her ears, and a breeze brushed the wet tip of her nose. Sailboats eased out of the corner of her eye and into the distance. She heard the drone of powerboats, the laughter of children, and the babble of English, Spanish, and other tongues blending indistinguishably like faraway sounds in a dream. Her only reaction to all this was an occasional blink. She felt drugged by the sun.

Yun-ja straightened herself in the water and looked for Chong-il. There he was, sitting under the beach umbrella with his head tilted back, drinking something. From her distant vantage point, twenty-seven-year-old Chong-il looked as small as a Boy Scout. He reminded her of a houseboy she had seen in a photo of some American soldiers during the Korean War.

—Excerpted from "A Certain Beginning" by Kim Chi-won

1. At the beginning of the excerpt, where is Yun-ja and what is she doing?

_____

What details act as clues? _____

2. Yun-ja is Korean. Is she in a place frequented only by Koreans or a place popular with people from other countries?

_____

What details act as clues? _____

3. Where is Chong-il and what is he doing?

_____

What details act as clues? _____

4. Is the action taking place in the present, the distant future, or the long-ago past?

_____

What details act as clues? _____

5. Is the action taking place during the day or during the evening?

_____

What details act as clues? _____

Answers are on page 547.

Atmosphere as Part of Setting

An important part of setting is *atmosphere*—the sensations and emotions associated with details of the physical setting.

For example, if a story opens with a nighttime setting, a thunderstorm, a castle, and a man approaching the door, the author is creating an atmosphere of mystery or suspense. On the other hand, if a story opens with early morning as the setting and children playing happily in a playground, the atmosphere is different, maybe one of hope. Of course, something shocking could happen, thus changing the atmosphere of the entire story.

EXERCISE 2: ATMOSPHERE AS PART OF SETTING

Directions: Read the passage below and answer the questions that follow.

HOW DOES THIS MAN FEEL?

I've got to hide, he told himself. His chest heaved as he waited, crouching in a dark corner of the vestibule. He was tired of running and dodging. Either he had to find a place to hide, or he had to surrender. A police car swished by through the rain, its siren rising sharply. They're looking for me all over. . . . He crept to the door and squinted through the fogged plate glass. He stiffened as the siren rose and died in the distance.

Yes, he had to hide, but where?

He gritted his teeth. Then a sudden movement in the street caught his attention. . . .

—Excerpted from "The Man Who Lived Underground" by Richard Wright

1. Is the atmosphere of the passage one of fear, optimism, or happiness?

_____

2. Which details help you determine the atmosphere?

_____

_____

Answers are on page 547.

BASIC ELEMENT OF FICTION: SETTING

Time—refers to *when* actions occur, from time of day to time period in history

Place—refers to *where* actions occur, from a specific place, such as a room in a house, to a general place, such as a community, city, or country

Characterization: Who Is in the Story

Characters are the fictional people in a novel or short story. *Characterization* is the method by which a writer creates fictional people who seem lifelike and believable. Writers may use any of these different methods to create character:

- describing the character and his or her actions
- revealing the character's speech patterns
- revealing what other characters say about the character
- revealing the character's unspoken thoughts

EXERCISE 3: INFERRING CHARACTER

Directions: Read the passage below and choose the best answer to each question that follows.

WHAT KIND OF MAN IS SLIM?

A tall man stood in the doorway. He held a crushed Stetson hat under his arm while he combed his long, black, damp hair straight back. Like the others he wore blue jeans and a short denim jacket. When he had finished combing his hair he moved into the room, and he moved with a majesty only achieved by royalty and master craftsmen. He was a jerkline skinner, the prince of the ranch, capable of driving ten, sixteen, even twenty mules with a single line to the leaders. He was capable of killing a fly on the wheeler's butt with a bull whip without touching the mule. There was a gravity in his manner and a quiet so profound that all talk stopped when he spoke. His authority was so great that his word was taken on any subject, be it politics or love. This was Slim, the jerkline skinner. His hatchet face was ageless. He might have been thirty-five or fifty. His ear heard more than was said to him, and his slow speech had overtones not of thought, but of understanding beyond thought. His hands, large and lean, were as delicate in their action as those of a temple dancer.

—Excerpted from *Of Mice and Men* by John Steinbeck

1. The description that best conveys Slim's personality is

    (1) "He was a jerkline skinner."
    (2) "His hands, large and lean, were as delicate in their action as those of a temple dancer."
    (3) "His hatchet face was ageless."
    (4) "he wore blue jeans and a short denim jacket."
    (5) "His authority was so great that his word was taken on any subject."

2. In this excerpt, we learn about Slim's character primarily from

    (1) Slim's actual speech
    (2) other characters' statements about Slim
    (3) Slim's unspoken thoughts
    (4) descriptions of Slim
    (5) scenes showing Slim in action

Answers are on page 547.

Dialogue as an Element of Characterization

In the previous exercise, you learned about a character by reading an extended description of him. Another way an author reveals character is through dialogue. **Dialogue** is conversation among characters in a story. Quoting what a character says allows authors to reveal a character's attitudes, feelings, and true personality in the character's own words rather than through descriptions alone.

In novels and short stories, quotation marks are placed around each speaker's exact words. Usually an author will provide transitions like *he said* and *she replied* to indicate when a character is speaking. For example: Joan said, "Help!"

The following sentences illustrate the difference between a restatement of a person's words and a speaker's exact words:

Restatement: She told me that she would call me for an appointment.

Exact words: "I will call you for an appointment," she said.

In longer conversations, *he said* and *she asked* may not be used in each sentence. Notice that the speakers are identified only once in this passage:

"May I help you?" inquired the eager car salesman.

"I'm looking for a used car, but I can't spend much money," Jill replied.

"I'm sure we can find something in your price range! Step over here, please. I'll show you our newer models. We have some beauties. . . ."

"Uh, I don't have much money—only a few hundred dollars."

"Well, . . . step this way to some of our older, economy cars."

Now read this passage, in which the speakers are not identified. Paragraph indenting and quotation marks show you when a new speaker is talking:

"We were out at Suburban Gardens Mall last night and tried a new Oriental restaurant."

"Really? Was it nice?"

"Yes! It was beautiful. We sat at a hibachi table, and a chef prepared our seafood right in front of us."

"Did the kids like it?"

"Not at first. I had to explain to them that they couldn't order burgers after they finished their egg rolls. My kids have been to so many drive-through fast-food joints that they don't know how to act in a fancy ethnic restaurant."

Who are the two characters in this dialogue? Briefly describe each.

The two characters are probably neighbors, co-workers, or friends. They are familiar with the Suburban Gardens Mall and take their children to drive-through restaurants. Therefore, it is likely that they live in the suburbs. The references to children make it clear that both characters are parents.

EXERCISE 4: IDENTIFYING CHARACTERS THROUGH DIALOGUE
Directions: Read the passage below and answer the questions that follow.

WHO'S TALKING TO WHOM?

"Oh, the shame of it—a whole family of skinny children. And your father—he's so skinny, he's disappearing."

"Don't worry about him, Mama. Doctors are saying that skinny people live longer. Papa's going to live a long time."

"So! I knew I didn't have too many years left. Do you know how I got all this fat? Eating your leftovers. Aiaa, I'm getting so old. Soon you will have no more mother."

"Mama, you've been saying that all my life."

"This time it's true. I'm almost eighty."

"I thought you were only seventy-six."

"My papers are wrong. I'm eighty."

"But I thought your papers are wrong, and you're seventy-two, seventy-three in Chinese years."

"My papers are wrong, and I'm eighty, eighty-one in Chinese years. Seventy. Eighty. What do numbers matter? I'm dropping dead any day now. The aunt down the street was resting on her porch steps, dinner all cooked, waiting for her husband and son to come home and eat it. She closed her eyes for a moment and died. Isn't that a wonderful way to go?"

"But our family lives to be ninety-nine."

"That's your father's family. My mother and father died very young. My youngest sister was an orphan at ten. Our parents were not even fifty."

"Then you should feel grateful you've lived so many extra years."

Excerpted from *The Woman Warrior* by Maxine Hong Kingston

1. What is the relationship of the two speakers in the excerpt?

2. Which character speaks first?

3. Which character thinks that being skinny is healthier than being fat?

4. Which character is blamed for making someone fat?

_____

5. Briefly describe what you think the two characters are like. Base your description on details included in the conversation.

_____

_____

Answers are on page 547.

BASIC ELEMENT OF FICTION: CHARACTERIZATION

You can understand what characters are like by looking for these elements:

- how characters are described
- what characters say to and about each other
- what characters think
- what characters do

Plot: What Happens in the Story

The events that occur in a story make up the *plot*. The plot events occur in some time order, or sequence.

To see how events might follow a logical sequence, arrange the plot events below in order. Place the number *1* in the blank before the first event, *2* in front of the second event, and so on. Notice the cause-and-effect relationship between events: one event leads to another, which leads to another, and so on.

_____ **a.** Then, a small crafts shop was for sale, so we decided to make our move.

_____ **b.** For years, my sisters and I discussed owning our own business.

_____ **c.** We contacted a real estate agent about purchasing the shop.

_____ **d.** With pride, we stood with our families outside of our new shop as the workmen hoisted the sign that read "Pins and Needles."

_____ **e.** First, I read articles about developing a "cottage industry" as we considered opening a store in one of our homes.

The first event, the desire to open a shop, is described in b. Sentence e follows; the sisters think about using one of their homes for a shop. Next, sentence a explains that a crafts shop went on the market. A real estate agent was then contacted (sentence c). Sentence d is the conclusion. The families see the dream come true.

Flashback as an Element of Plot

An author may choose to present events out of order, allowing the reader to piece the events together. One such popular technique is called *flashback*. For example, a novel or film may open with a voice saying, "It all began fifteen years ago when the couple met. . . ." The story then shifts to another scene, fifteen years ago. The events progress in order until, by the end of the story, the characters have returned to the time and place of the opening scene. If you have ever watched television soap operas, you have witnessed this type of scene.

Parts of a Plot

The events that make up a plot may be grouped and labeled according to their function in a story. The diagram illustrates the basic parts of a plot: exposition, conflict, climax, and resolution.

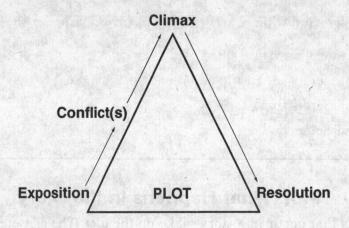

Exposition refers to background information that "sets the stage" for a story. *Conflict*, or friction between opposing characters or forces, is the basis of every plot.

Most stories and novels are centered around one of the following conflicts:

• *Individual vs. self*—inner struggles characters suffer while trying to decide what to do—change jobs, get divorced, have children, tell someone the truth about something.

• *Individual vs. another*—disagreements between characters.

• *Individual vs. society*—struggles against the rules, conventions, or pressures of living with other humans.

• *Individual vs. nature and other forces*—struggles against forces beyond a character's control, such as an earthquake or other natural disaster, or an abstraction like evil.

Another element of plot is *climax*, the point of highest intensity in the plot. The climax of a story occurs when the conflict comes to a head. For example, the climax of many westerns occurs when the hero and villain meet face-to-face in a gun duel. The climax does not always occur at the very end of the story, but it usually occurs in the last part. All of the events and conflicts involving characters must be evident before they can lead to the climax. Mystery stories have very obvious climaxes. All of the clues come together to provide the answer to "Whodunit?"

Following the climax, all of the loose ends are tied together, and readers learn the outcome of the conflict, or **resolution**. The **resolution** of the story is usually its ending.

Bear in mind that novels and stories do not have to follow the traditional plot pattern just described. For example, many stories have open endings in which conflicts are not resolved. And many stories include **subplots**—"stories within stories" that involve conflicts of their own. Nevertheless, it is helpful to know the parts of the traditional plot, because most stories include some form of exposition, conflict, climax, and resolution.

EXERCISE 5: IDENTIFYING DETAILS OF SETTING, PLOT, AND CONFLICT

Directions: Read the passage below and answer the questions that follow.

WHO ARE RALPH AND JACK AND WHAT IS HAPPENING TO THEM?

Ralph cleared his throat.

"Well then."

All at once he found he could talk fluently and explain what he had to say. He passed a hand through his fair hair and spoke.

5   "We're on an island. We've been on the mountain top and seen water all round. We saw no houses, no smoke, no footprints, no boats, no people. We're on an uninhabited island with no other people on it."

Jack broke in.

"All the same you need an army—for hunting. Hunting pigs—"

10   "Yes. There are pigs on the island."

All three of them tried to convey the sense of the pink live thing struggling in the creepers.

"We saw—"

"Squealing—"

15   "It broke away—"

"Before I could kill it—but—next time!"

Jack slammed his knife into a trunk and looked round challengingly.

The meeting settled down again.

"So you see," said Ralph, "we need hunters to get us meat. And another
20   thing."

He lifted the shell on his knees and looked round the sun-slashed faces.

"There aren't any grownups. We shall have to look after ourselves."

The meeting hummed and was silent.

—Excerpted from *Lord of the Flies* by William Golding

1. Which line supports the fact that the plot involves children?

_____

2. Which lines establish the location?

_____

3. What was the "pink live thing struggling in the creepers"?

_____

4. Who is leading the meeting?

_____

5. Name at least two conflicts that are evident here.

_____

_____

6. Put the plot events below in the order in which they happen by writing the number *1* for the event that happened first, *2* for the event that occurred second, and so on.

_____ Jack thrusts his knife into a tree trunk.

_____ Three boys tell of the "pink live thing."

_____ Ralph begins the meeting by telling the boys where they are.

_____ The boys react to the fact that they're without adults.

_____ Ralph states that there are pigs (food) on the island.

Answers are on page 547.

BASIC ELEMENT OF FICTION: PLOT
Traditional plots follow this pattern and sequence:

1. **exposition**, or background information
2. **conflict**, or friction between opposing forces
3. **climax**, or point of highest tension
4. **resolution**, or the outcome of the conflict

WRITING ACTIVITY 1

Lord of the Flies is a novel about British school boys stranded on an island after a plane crash. No adults survive, so the boys are on their own. Golding presents the negative side of human nature, and the novel concerns evil overcoming good. Even without reading the book, you can probably predict some of the conflicts, or problems, that might arise in this situation.

First, list three problems facing the marooned boys. Then resolve the conflicts by writing one paragraph for each problem, suggesting possible solutions.

Point of View: Who Tells the Story

When you read fiction, ask yourself, Through whose eyes, or *point of view*, is the story being told? An author can choose from a variety of ways to tell a story. For example, if you were to write a story about a basketball game, you might choose from the following points of view:

1. *The coach's*—"The fourth quarter began. My team was twelve points down. I had to make a decision—fast!"

2. *The fan's*—"Here I paid big bucks for these tickets, and my team is getting killed! I should have known. . . ."

3. *The guard of the team that's leading*—"Twelve points. We're in good shape! I'll just work the ball around a bit, kill time, and wait for the best shots."

4. *A player sitting on the bench*—"Boy, if I could just convince Coach to let me in. Just once, I'd like to turn a game around. Just once, I'd like to be a hero."

The point of view from which a story is told is important because the reader has to identify with, or "get into the skin of," the character. For this reason, most authors tell their story through the eyes of the *main character*—the character whom the action affects most. Only the thoughts of the main character are revealed when the author chooses this point of view.

A writer, having decided who is to tell, or *narrate*, the story, may relate the events in first person or third person. In *first-person narration*, the word *I* is used, and the narrator speaks directly to the reader. The four points of view above are first-person narration. In his famous novel *The Adventures of Huckleberry Finn*, Mark Twain created Huck Finn as the narrator to tell the story. Huck is the main character, and the story is told through his eyes, using the first-person *I* method.

In *third-person narration*, the story is told by an "outsider"—someone who is not involved in the action—and the main character is referred to as *he* or *she*. There are several different approaches to the third-person point of view, depending on how much the author wants readers—and the main character—to know.

The passage on page 466 is from an Ernest Hemingway short story, "The Short Happy Life of Francis Macomber." In the passage, Macomber hunts and shoots a lion, and Hemingway captures the moment by describing the hunter's activities and the lion's thoughts as the animal is shot. You can tell that the story is told in the third person, because Hemingway uses *he* to refer to both Macomber and the lion. However, the story is unusual in that Hemingway tells us what the lion, rather than the hunter, is thinking.

EXERCISE 6: DETERMINING POINT OF VIEW

Directions: Underline each noun (e.g., *Macomber*) or pronoun (e.g., *he, his,* or *them*) that represents a person or people. Circle each noun or pronoun that refers to the lion. The first three are done for you.

HOW DOES THE LION FEEL?

Macomber stepped out of the curved opening at the side of the front seat, onto the step and down onto the ground. The lion still stood looking majestically and coolly toward this object that his eyes only showed in silhouette, bulging like some super-rhino. There was no man smell carried toward him and he watched the object [jeep], moving his great head a little from side to side. Then watching the object, not afraid, but hesitating before going down the bank to drink with such a thing opposite him, he saw a man figure detach itself from it and he turned his heavy head and swung away toward the cover of the trees as he heard a cracking crash and felt the slam of a .30–06 220-grain solid bullet that bit his flank and ripped in sudden hot scalding nausea through his stomach. He trotted, heavy, big-footed, swinging wounded full-bellied, through the trees toward the tall grass and cover, and the crash came again to go past him ripping the air apart. Then it crashed again and he felt the blow as it hit his lower ribs and ripped on through, blood sudden hot and frothy in his mouth, and he galloped toward the high grass where he could crouch and not be seen and make them bring the crashing thing close enough so he could make a rush and get the man that held it.

Answers are on page 547.

> ### BASIC ELEMENT OF FICTION: POINT OF VIEW
> **First-person narration**—a speaker identified as *I* talks directly to readers
> **Third-person narration**—an unidentified outsider refers to characters as *he* and *she*.

WRITING ACTIVITY 2

Choose one of the four points of view described in the example of the basketball game on page 465. Write a paragraph to finish the story. If you prefer, choose a different point of view for the game. Become the referee, the spouse or child of a player, a sportswriter, even the basketball court, backboard, or ball! Use *I* and write in dialogue what the narrator would see, feel, and think.

Theme: What the Story Means

Behind all of the action in a story or movie is the writer's or director's purpose. The creator of a work wants it to have meaning for the audience. The main idea, or theme, may be an insight into life, a viewpoint about a social issue, a new view of an old problem, or positive or negative looks into human nature.

In successfully written fiction, as in effective films, the theme is rarely stated directly. Instead, it is implied or suggested. The reader or viewer is expected to interpret the meaning from all elements presented.

For example, since the early 1950s, many science fiction writers and filmmakers have given us stories about aliens landing on our planet. A typical plot involves the aliens trying to take over Earth. One human being usually leads a rebellion against them. The theme is fear of the unknown.

BASIC ELEMENT OF FICTION: THEME

- The main idea, or central meaning, of a story
- Often involves an insight into people's lives, or human nature

EXERCISE 7: INFERRING THEME

Directions: Read the passage below and choose the best answer to each question that follows.

WHAT CONCERNS MISS STRANGEWORTH?

After thinking for a minute, she decided that she would like to write another letter, perhaps to go to Mrs. Harper, to follow up the ones she had already mailed. She selected a green sheet this time and wrote quickly: HAVE YOU FOUND OUT YET WHAT THEY WERE ALL LAUGHING ABOUT AFTER YOU LEFT THE BRIDGE CLUB ON THURSDAY? OR IS THE WIFE REALLY ALWAYS THE LAST ONE TO KNOW?

Miss Strangeworth never concerned herself with facts; her letters all dealt with the more negotiable stuff of suspicion. Mr. Lewis would never have imagined for a minute that his grandson might be lifting petty cash from the store register if he had not had one of Miss Strangeworth's letters. Miss Chandler, the librarian, and Linda Stewart's parents would have gone unsuspectingly ahead with their lives, never aware of possible evil lurking nearby, if Miss Strangeworth had not sent letters opening their eyes. Miss Strangeworth would have been genuinely shocked if there *had* been anything between Linda Stewart and the Harris boy, but as long as evil existed unchecked in the world, it was Miss Strangeworth's duty to keep her town alert to it.

—Excerpted from "The Possibility of Evil" by Shirley Jackson

1. The plot concerns Miss Strangeworth's

   (1) preventing others from hearing damaging rumors
   (2) blackmailing others for money
   (3) caring about those around her
   (4) suspecting her husband and Linda Stewart
   (5) sending anonymous warnings to others

2. The conflict of this passage is Miss Strangeworth vs.

   (1) nature
   (2) Mrs. Harper
   (3) herself
   (4) society
   (5) imaginary evil

3. The theme of the passage is best stated in which of these ways?

   (1) It is a citizen's duty to judge the behavior of others.
   (2) What people don't know won't hurt them.
   (3) Regardless of their intentions, some people create pain for others.
   (4) Knowing all the facts is not important when making accusations.
   (5) One should not join organizations if one has something to hide.

Answers are on page 548.

EXERCISE 8: REVIEW OF FIVE FICTION ELEMENTS

Directions: Read the passage below and answer the questions that follow.

HOW DOES IVAN ILYCH FEEL?

Ivan Ilych saw that he was dying, and he was in continual despair.

In the depth of his heart he knew he was dying, but not only was he not accustomed to the thought, he simply did not and could not grasp it. . . .

He could not understand it, and tried to drive this false, incorrect, morbid thought away and to replace it by other proper and healthy thoughts. But that thought, and not the thought only but the reality itself, seemed to come and confront him.

And to replace that thought he called up a succession of others, hoping to find in them some support. He tried to get back into the former current of thoughts that had once screened the thought of death from him. But strange to say, all that had formerly shut off, hidden, and destroyed his consciousness of death no longer had that effect. Ivan Ilych now spent most of his time in attempting to re-establish that old current. He would say to himself: "I will take up my duties again—after all I used to live by them." And banishing all doubts he would go to the law courts, enter into conversation with his colleagues, and sit carelessly as was his wont, scanning the crowd with a thoughtful look and leaning both his emaciated arms on the arms of his oak chair; bending over as usual to a colleague and drawing his papers nearer he would interchange whispers with him, and then suddenly raising his eyes and sitting erect would pronounce certain words and open the proceedings. But suddenly in the midst of those proceedings the pain in his side, regardless of the stage the proceedings had reached, would begin its own gnawing work. Ivan Ilych would turn his attention to it and try to drive the thought of it away, but without success. *It* would come and stand before him and look at him, and he would be petrified and the light would die out from his eyes, and he would begin to ask himself whether *It* alone was true. And his colleagues and subordinates would see with surprise and distress that he, the brilliant and subtle judge, was becoming confused and making mistakes.

—Excerpted from "The Death of Ivan Ilych" by Leo Tolstoy

1. The major conflict developed in the passage is Ivan Ilych's struggle to

(1) restore his health
(2) regain his old job as a judge
(3) come to terms with death
(4) win an important legal case
(5) overcome mental illness

2. The story is told in which of the following points of view?

(1) first person, by Ivan Ilych himself
(2) first person, by Ivan Ilych's colleagues and subordinates
(3) first person, by Leo Tolstoy, the author
(4) third person, by an unnamed outsider
(5) third person, by Ivan Ilych's physician

3. The author develops the character of Ivan Ilych mainly by

(1) revealing what Ilych says to other people
(2) disclosing what Ilych secretly thinks
(3) showing how Ilych interacts with other characters
(4) describing what Ilych looks like
(5) summarizing what other characters think of Ilych

4. Which of the following statements best sums up the theme of the passage?

(1) One cannot comprehend his or her impending death.
(2) People can overcome their fear of death by concentrating on their work.
(3) A positive mental outlook can help a person cope with a terminal illness.
(4) One must expect seriously ill people to become confused and make mistakes.
(5) Healthy people do not understand what it is like to be seriously ill.

5. The setting for the action in the last paragraph is

(1) a crowded courtroom
(2) the waiting room of a doctor's office
(3) the lobby of a medical building
(4) a private room in a hospital
(5) an ambulance's interior

Answers are on page 548.

Tone and Style

Tone: What the Author's Attitude Is

The *tone* of a novel or short story is the overall attitude that an author conveys toward his or her subject. When listening to a person speak, you can infer the person's attitude by the sound of his or her voice. The tone tells you whether the person means to be sarcastic or serious or funny. When reading, you must infer the author's tone.

An author's choice of words and phrasing reflects his or her attitude. What tone is presented in the paragraph below? Write a few words that describe the tone of this passage.

> Our first-born son, "Matt the Mouth," was a wild, oversized, constantly hungry toddler. As he grew, he seemed to dwarf all other children around him. His first word was *cake*, and his first step was taken toward the refrigerator! How that kid loved to eat!

_____

You might have written *funny, humorous, comical, light, nostalgic,* or *mocking.* The author is a parent looking back on a son whose eating habits were memorable. The tone is not one of sadness or resentment, but one of fond yet humorous memories of "Matt the Mouth."

BASIC ELEMENT OF FICTION: TONE
To determine the tone of a passage, ask yourself the following questions:
- What subject is the author describing?
- How does the author feel about the subject?
- What language or descriptive details reveal the author's attitude?

EXERCISE 9: TONE AND CHARACTERIZATION

Directions: Read the passage below and answer the questions that follow.

WHAT IS THE AUTHOR'S TONE?

Her doctor had told Julian's mother that she must lose twenty pounds on account of her blood pressure, so on Wednesday nights Julian had to take her downtown on the bus for a reducing class at the Y. The reducing class was designed for working girls over fifty, who weighed 165 to 200 pounds. His mother was one of the slimmer ones, but she said ladies did not tell their age or weight. She would not ride the buses by herself at night since they had been integrated, and because the reducing class was one of her few pleasures, necessary for her health, and *free*, she said Julian could at least put himself out to take her, considering all she did for him. Julian did not like to consider all she did for him, but every Wednesday night he braced himself and took her.

—Excerpted from "Everything That Rises Must Converge"
by Flannery O'Connor

1. Julian's mother may best be described as a woman who

   (1) subscribes to old-fashioned values and beliefs
   (2) is easy to please
   (3) takes advantage of every opportunity to improve herself
   (4) believes in the equality of all people
   (5) is without an identity of her own

2. "[S]he said Julian could at least put himself out to take her [to her class], considering all she did for him. Julian did not like to consider all she did for him, but every Wednesday night he braced himself and took her." If the author read these lines, how would her voice sound?

   (1) gentle and tolerant
   (2) angry and bitter
   (3) tragic and depressed
   (4) sarcastic and funny
   (5) sweet and resigned

3. The author's attitude is most likely that people like Julian's mother are

   (1) to be laughed at or ridiculed
   (2) to be respected for their high ideals
   (3) to be tolerated and sympathized with
   (4) absolutely wrong in their outlook on life
   (5) morally superior to all other people

Answers are on page 548.

Style and Language: What Makes the Writing Unique

A writer of fiction is a craftsperson. The tools of the trade are words. The effectiveness and success of a piece of literature depend upon the quality of words the writer uses.

Style refers to the author's unique use of the language—the choice and arrangement of words. An author's style may contain long, complex sentences, it may contain everyday spoken language, or it may contain dialect.

Which of the following statements do you consider to be more formal?

a. Joan said she would drop by after she got a bite to eat.
b. Joan stated that she would visit us after her lunch.

Sentence b is stated formally. Sentence a presents the same information worded casually.

Dialect as an Element of Style

Dialect is the pattern of speech characteristic to a certain region. In the United States, we can sometimes tell if people are from the Deep South or New England just by their accents. Regional expressions, word choices, and pronunciations contribute to dialect.

Writers of fiction may have their characters speak in dialects. Mark Twain, for instance, used dialect throughout *The Adventures of Huckleberry Finn* to make the characters more real and believable. Below are two examples of how the dialect of an area and time period are used in novels. The first example is from Nathaniel Hawthorne's *The Scarlet Letter*. The characters are Puritans living around Boston in the 1600s:

> "Pearl! Little Pearl!" cried he, after a moment's pause; then, suppressing his voice, "Hester! Hester Prynne! Are you there?"
>
> "Yes; it is Hester Prynne!" she replied, in a tone of surprise; and the minister heard her footsteps approaching from the sidewalk, along which she had been passing, "It is I, and my little Pearl."
>
> "Whence come you, Hester?" asked the minister. "What sent you hither?"
>
> "I have been watching at a deathbed," answered Hester Prynne—"at Governor Winthrop's deathbed, and have taken his measure for a robe, and am now going homeward to my dwelling."

Notice words such as *whence* ("from where") and *hither* ("here").

The next passage is from Zora Neale Hurston's 1937 novel *Their Eyes Were Watching God*. It is written in a dialect that was spoken by some rural southern African-Americans of the time. As the novel opens, a group of neighbors are gossiping about Janie, a woman who has just returned to the neighborhood she moved away from some time before.

> "What she doin' coming back here in dem overhalls? Can't she find no dress to put on?—Where's dat blue satin dress she left here in?—Where all dat money her husband took and died and left her?—What dat ole forty year ole 'oman doin' wid her hair swingin' down her bak lak some young gal?—Where she left dat young lad of a boy she went off here wid?"

Types of Styles

Authors who publish many works often become known and appreciated for their styles as well as their themes and characters. Hemingway, for example, was trained in writing as a newspaper reporter. He is known for a terse writing style because his ideas are expressed in few words.

On the other hand, Charles Dickens is known for a narrative style characterized by long sentences and vivid descriptions. Edgar Allan Poe used short sentences; the repetition of words; and many dashes, exclamation points, and italics to add emotion and suspense to his stories. He opens "The Tell-Tale Heart" with:

> "True!—nervous—very, very dreadfully nervous I had been and am! but why *will* you say that I am mad?"

In her novel *The Bell Jar*, Sylvia Plath, who was known primarily as a poet, used poetic style and images that appealed to the senses. The following exercise is an example of that style.

EXERCISE 10: IDENTIFYING AN AUTHOR'S STYLE

Directions: Read the passage below. Underline all descriptions and images that appeal to your senses: sight, smell, taste, touch, and especially hearing.

WHAT IMAGES DOES THE WRITER CALL TO MIND?

The soprano screak of carriage wheels punished my ear. Sun, seeping through the blinds, filled the bedroom with a sulphurous light. I didn't know how long I had slept, but I felt one big twitch of exhaustion.

The twin bed next to mine was empty and unmade.

At seven I had heard my mother get up, slip into her clothes and tiptoe out of the room. Then the buzz of the orange squeezer sounded from downstairs, and the smell of coffee and bacon filtered under my door. Then the sink water ran from the tap and dishes clinked as my mother dried them and put them back in the cupboard.

Then the front door opened and shut. Then the car door opened and shut, and the motor went broom-broom and, edging off with a crunch of gravel, faded into the distance.

Answers are on page 548.

WRITING ACTIVITY 3

Rewrite one of the dialect passages on page 471. For *The Scarlet Letter* passage, rewrite the speeches in present-day English. For the passage from *Their Eyes Were Watching God*, change the dialect into modern written English, formalizing the grammar.

Descriptive Language as an Element of Style

Look again at the passage in Exercise 10. Did the screak of wheels actually "punish" the narrator's ear? Was the bed really "unmade"—an unassembled frame and pieces of lumber? When you say you're going to "make" your bed, do you mean you're going to build a bed, using wood, hammer, and nails? Of course not! You mean you're going to rearrange the pillow, blankets, and bedspread to make the bed look neat and tidy. *Figures of speech* like these are not meant to be taken literally. They are expressive ways of describing.

EXERCISE 11: DESCRIPTIVE LANGUAGE

Directions: Match the expression on the left with its meaning on the right by writing the appropriate letter in the space provided.

_____ **1.** She tried to *iron out* her problems.

a. exhausted

_____ **2.** I've complained until I'm *blue in the face,* but no one seems to care.

b. extremely quick

_____ **3.** I still have a lot of packing to do, but I think I'm finally *on top of it!*

c. in control of the situation

_____ **4.** The running back is *like greased lightning.*

d. solve

Answers are on page 548.

Figures of Speech as an Element of Style

You hear figures of speech in spoken English every day. In fiction writing, figurative language is used to create vivid pictures and original descriptions.

There are many kinds of figures of speech. In literature, especially in poetry, you can find specific figures of speech called *similes, metaphors,* and *personification.* A brief explanation of each will help you recognize the use of this type of descriptive language.

A *simile* (sim'-ih-lee) is a comparison that shows a likeness between two unlike things. A simile is introduced by the words *like, than,* or *as.*

Her hair was like woven straw.   She is colder than ice.

Bill is as strong as an ox.

A *metaphor* (met'-uh-for) is a comparison that does not contain *like, than,* or *as.* A metaphor implies that one thing is something else.

The path was a ribbon of moonlight.   All the world is a stage.

Personification (per-sahn-ih-fih-kay'-shun) attributes some human activity or quality to an animal or thing.

The sun smiled down on me.   The leaves awoke and greeted the season.

EXERCISE 12: IDENTIFYING FIGURES OF SPEECH

Directions: As you read the passage below, underline similes, metaphors, and examples of personification. Then choose the best answer to each question that follows the passage.

WHO IS GRANDMA KIRK AND WHAT IS SHE LIKE?

Grandma Kirk was a whisper of a woman—four feet eleven and weighing only ninety pounds—but the strength and determination with which she attacked chickens were admirable (and comical).

5 She would casually approach the chicken-yard like a fox moving in for the kill. Swooping down on a trusting, unsuspecting hen, Grandma would become a cyclone. With two or three crafty twists of her wrist, she would break the hen's neck and would nimbly thrust her prey over a chopping stump for the beheading.

Her ax, a bloody character that seemed to lie in wait for hens, would sever
10 the head. As the hen's body departed from its head, Grandma's strength would give way, and the headless chicken would be released to dance around the yard like a savage in an ancient tribal rite.

Unnerved, Grandma would chase the unruly dancing corpse, grab it, and thrust it into a tub of boiling water. She would then patiently pluck, feather by
15 feather, until the naked bird was ready for roasting pan and family feast.

I think of my grandmother's effort, time, and spirit each time I shop at the local suburban supermarket with its plastic-wrapped parcel of fowl labeled "Combo-Pak." My microwave oven lazily sits waiting for the quick preparation, brief cooking process, and "instant" meal. My family thinks every chicken is
20 equipped with three breasts, four thighs, six legs, and organs wrapped in white paper.

1. "Grandma Kirk was a whisper of a woman" refers to her

(1) sneaky approach
(2) quiet manner
(3) small stature
(4) pride
(5) speech pattern

2. The sentence "Her ax, a bloody character that seemed to lie in wait for hens, would sever the head" (lines 9–10) creates an image that makes the ax seem

(1) old
(2) rusted
(3) bent
(4) alive
(5) useless

3. The tone of this passage is one of

   (1) nostalgia
   (2) distaste
   (3) suspicion
   (4) dread
   (5) mystery

4. The narrator is contrasting Grandma Kirk's killing chickens with

   (1) fox hunting in the wild
   (2) a cyclone's destruction of a village
   (3) modern shopping and cooking practices
   (4) primitive ritual tribal dances
   (5) chopping wood for the winter

5. With which of the following statements would the author of the passage be the most likely to agree?

   (1) In general, food is tastier today than it was a few generations ago.
   (2) Grandma Kirk was a brutal person.
   (3) Supermarkets and microwaves are unnecessary conveniences.
   (4) Years ago, women were not allowed to do physical labor.
   (5) Life today is much easier than it was in our grandparents' day.

Answers are on page 548.

How to Read Fiction on Your Own

You have learned about the basic elements of fiction illustrated in the puzzle on page 454. In both the novel and the short story, the elements contribute to the whole. While your examination of each element of fiction contributes to your understanding, it is the *whole*, not its *parts*, that creates a work of art. Use the tips that follow to guide your reading of literature.

TIPS ON READING FICTION

As you read a story, ask yourself:

- What is the setting?
- What is the atmosphere?
- Who are the characters?
- Are they named or described?
- What is the plot?
- What is the conflict?
- From whose point of view is the story told?
- What are clues to the theme?
- What is the author's style like?
- What is the author's tone?

EXERCISE 13: INTERPRETING A SHORT STORY

Directions: A complete short story (much longer than the passages on the GED Test) follows. Read the story and answer the questions that follow.

WHAT IS THE AUTHOR SAYING ABOUT WAR?

The long June twilight faded into night. Dublin lay enveloped in darkness, but for the dim light of the moon, that shone through fleecy clouds, casting a pale light as of approaching dawn over the streets and the dark waters of the Liffey. Around the beleaguered Four Courts the heavy guns roared. Here and
5 there through the city machine guns and rifles broke the silence of the night, spasmodically, like dogs barking on lone farms. Republicans and Free Staters were waging civil war.

On a rooftop near O'Connell Bridge, a Republican sniper lay watching. Beside him lay his rifle and over his shoulders were slung a pair of field-
10 glasses. His face was the face of a student—thin and ascetic, but his eyes had the cold gleam of the fanatic. They were deep and thoughtful, the eyes of a man who is used to looking at death.

He was eating a sandwich hungrily. He had eaten nothing since morning. He had been too excited to eat. He finished the sandwich, and taking a flask
15 of whiskey from his pocket, he took a short draught. Then he returned the flask to his pocket. He paused for a moment, considering whether he should risk a smoke. It was dangerous. The flash might be seen in the darkness and there were enemies watching. He decided to take the risk. Placing a cigarette between his lips, he struck a match, inhaled the smoke hurriedly and put out
20 the light. Almost immediately, a bullet flattened itself against the parapet of the roof. The sniper took another whiff and put out the cigarette. Then he swore softly and crawled away to the left.

Cautiously he raised himself and peered over the parapet. There was a flash and a bullet whizzed over his head. He dropped immediately. He had
25 seen the flash. It came from the opposite side of the street.

He rolled over the roof to a chimney stack in the rear, and slowly drew himself up behind it, until his eyes were level with the top of the parapet. There was nothing to be seen—just the dim outline of the opposite housetop against the blue sky. His enemy was under cover.

30 Just then an armoured car came across the bridge and advanced slowly up the street. It stopped on the opposite side of the street fifty yards ahead. The sniper could hear the dull panting of the motor. His heart beat faster. It was an enemy car. He wanted to fire, but he knew it was useless. His bullets would never pierce the steel that covered the grey monster.

35 Then round the corner of a side street came an old woman, her head covered by a tattered shawl. She began to talk to the man in the turret of the car. She was pointing to the roof where the sniper lay. An informer.

The turret opened. A man's head and shoulders appeared, looking towards the sniper. The sniper raised his rifle and fired. The head fell heavily on
40 the turret wall. The woman darted toward the side street. The sniper fired again. The woman whirled round and fell with a shriek into the gutter.

Suddenly from the opposite roof a shot rang out and the sniper dropped his rifle with a curse. The rifle clattered to the roof. The sniper thought the noise would wake the dead. He stooped to pick the rifle up. He couldn't lift it.
45 His forearm was dead. "I'm hit," he muttered.

Dropping flat on to the roof, he crawled back to the parapet. With his left hand he felt the injured right forearm. The blood was oozing through the sleeve of his coat. There was no pain—just a deadened sensation, as if the arm had been cut off.

50 Quickly he drew his knife from his pocket, opened it on the breastwork of the parapet and ripped open the sleeve. There was a small hole where the bullet had entered. On the other side there was no hole. The bullet had lodged in the bone. It must have fractured it. He bent the arm below the wound. The arm bent back easily. He ground his teeth to overcome the pain.

55 Then, taking out his field dressing, he ripped open the packet with his knife. He broke the neck of the iodine bottle and let the bitter fluid drip into the wound. A paroxysm of pain swept through him. He placed the cotton wadding over the wound and wrapped the dressing over it. He tied the end with his teeth.

60 Then he lay still against the parapet, and closing his eyes, he made an effort of will to overcome the pain.

In the street beneath all was still. The armoured car had retired speedily over the bridge, with the machine gunner's head hanging lifeless over the turret. The woman's corpse lay still in the gutter.

65 The sniper lay for a long time nursing his wounded arm and planning escape. Morning must not find him wounded on the roof. The enemy on the opposite roof covered his escape. He must kill that enemy and he could not use his rifle. He had only a revolver to do it. Then he thought of a plan.

Taking off his cap, he placed it over the muzzle of his rifle. Then he
70 pushed the rifle slowly upwards over the parapet, until the cap was visible from the opposite side of the street. Almost immediately there was a report, and a bullet pierced the center of the cap. The sniper slanted the rifle forward. The cap slipped down into the street. Then, catching the rifle in the middle, the sniper dropped his left hand over the roof and let it hang, lifelessly. After
75 a few moments he let the rifle drop to the street. Then he sank to the roof, dragging his hand with him.

Crawling quickly to the left, he peered up at the corner of the roof. His ruse had succeeded. The other sniper, seeing the cap and rifle fall, thought that he had killed his man. He was now standing before a row of chimney
80 pots, looking across, with his head clearly silhouetted against the western sky.

The Republican sniper smiled and lifted his revolver above the edge of the parapet. The distance was about fifty yards—a hard shot in the dim light, and his right arm was paining him like a thousand devils. He took a steady aim. His
85 hand trembled with eagerness. Pressing his lips together, he took a deep breath through his nostrils and fired. He was almost deafened with the report and his arm shook with the recoil.

Then, when the smoke cleared, he peered across and uttered a cry of joy. His enemy had been hit. He was reeling over the parapet in his death agony.
90 He struggled to keep his feet, but he was slowly falling forward, as if in a dream. The rifle fell from his grasp, hit the parapet, fell over, bounded off the pole of a barber's shop beneath and then cluttered on to the pavement.

Then the dying man on the roof crumpled up and fell forward. The body turned over and over in space and hit the ground with a dull thud. Then it lay
95 still.

The sniper looked at his enemy falling and he shuddered. The lust of battle died in him. He became bitten by remorse. The sweat stood out in beads on his forehead. Weakened by his wound and the long summer day of fasting and watching on the roof, he revolted from the sight of the shattered
100 mass of his dead enemy. His teeth chattered. He began to gibber to himself, cursing the war, cursing himself, cursing everybody.

He looked at the smoking revolver in his hand and with an oath he hurled it to the roof at his feet. The revolver went off with the concussion, and the bullet whizzed past the sniper's head. He was frightened back to his senses by
105 the shock. His nerves steadied. The cloud of fear scattered from his mind and he laughed.

Taking the whiskey flask from his pocket, he emptied it at a draught. He felt reckless under the influence of the spirits. He decided to leave the roof and look for his company commander to report. Everywhere around was
110 quiet. There was not much danger in going through the streets. He picked up his revolver and put it in his pocket. Then he crawled down through the skylight to the house underneath.

When the sniper reached the laneway on the street level, he felt a sudden curiosity as to the identity of the enemy sniper whom he had killed. He
115 decided that he was a good shot whoever he was. He wondered if he knew him. Perhaps he had been in his own company before the split in the army. He decided to risk going over to have a look at him. He peered around the corner into O'Connell Street. In the upper part of the street there was heavy firing, but around here all was quiet.

120 The sniper darted across the street. A machine gun tore up the ground around him with a hail of bullets, but he escaped. He threw himself face downwards beside the corpse. The machine gun stopped.

Then the sniper turned over the dead body and looked into his brother's face.

—"The Sniper" by Liam O'Flaherty

1. Underline the seven words and phrases below that correctly describe the setting and background for "The Sniper."

rooftop, August, civil war, Dublin, Paris, rural hillside, noon, Ireland, June, city, night, World War II

2. Which word below best describes the overall atmosphere of "The Sniper"?

(1) thrilling **(2)** nostalgic **(3)** lighthearted **(4)** depressing **(5)** tense

3. Match the description on the left with the character on the right. One choice on the right will be used twice.

_____ **(1)** "whirled round and fell with a shriek into the gutter"

_____ **(2)** "The head fell heavily on the turret wall."

_____ **(3)** "seeing the cap and rifle fall, thought that he had killed his man"

_____ **(4)** "paused for a moment, considering whether he should risk a smoke"

a. the sniper

b. the enemy

c. the informer

4. Arrange these events in the order in which they happen in the story by writing *1* in the space before the event that occurred first, *2* before the event that occurred second, and so on.

_____ **a.** The sniper is shot in the arm by his enemy.

_____ **b.** The sniper shoots an old woman, an informer.

_____ **c.** The sniper turns over his victim.

_____ **d.** The sniper drinks whiskey and leaves the roof.

_____ **e.** The sniper eats a sandwich.

5. Does the author reveal all of his characters' thoughts or just the sniper's?

Why? _____

6. Is the point of view first-person narration or third-person narration?

_____

7. The tone of the story may best be described as

(1) matter-of-fact
(2) lighthearted
(3) exaggerated
(4) disrespectful
(5) sarcastic

8. In the spaces below, write *s* if the figure of speech is a simile, *m* if it is a metaphor, or *p* if it represents personification. (See pages 473–474 for definitions of *simile*, *metaphor*, and *personification*.)

_____ **1.** "like dogs barking on lone farms"

_____ **2.** "the steel that covered the grey monster"

_____ **3.** "dull panting of the motor"

_____ **4.** "Morning must not find him"

_____ **5.** "like a thousand devils"

9. Figures of speech such as "grey monster" (line 34) and "like a thousand devils" (line 84) reveal the author's attitude toward

    (1) guns
    (2) soldiers
    (3) brothers
    (4) war
    (5) informers

10. The climax of the plot occurs when the sniper

    (1) sees the armoured car leave
    (2) shoots the old woman
    (3) shoots the enemy on the roof
    (4) climbs down from the roof
    (5) turns over his brother

11. The excerpt "he revolted from the sight of the shattered mass of his dead enemy. His teeth chattered. He began to gibber to himself, cursing the war, cursing himself, cursing everybody" (lines 99–101) illustrates the conflict between the sniper and

    (1) the old woman
    (2) the enemy
    (3) the Republican Army
    (4) himself
    (5) nature

12. The description "The lust of battle died in him. He became bitten by remorse" (lines 96–97) reveal that the

    (1) sniper thinks the enemy may be his brother
    (2) sniper feels guilty about killing his enemy
    (3) sniper fears that he will be shot by another enemy
    (4) sniper could now leave the rooftop
    (5) enemy deserved his fate

13. What is the theme of "The Sniper"?

    (1) A good soldier never feels guilty about killing.
    (2) A sniper must be ready to die for his country.
    (3) The character of a sniper is different from that of other soldiers.
    (4) A civil war is the worst kind of war.
    (5) War often brings out the negative side of human nature.

Answers are on page 549.

WRITING ACTIVITY 4

Choose two of the topics below and write a paragraph on each.

1. What did the sniper do next? Write one more paragraph that could be added to the story.

2. The author was seriously wounded in World War I. How do you think that affected his attitude toward war and influenced his writing? Write a paragraph that expresses your opinion.

3. Write a short story from the enemy's point of view. (Use *I*—first-person narration.) Give your reactions to the sniper's killing of the old woman, the trick used by the sniper, and other major events in the plot.

About Prose Fiction: Commentary

You have learned techniques to help you approach and analyze literature in order to gain an understanding of what you read. You have read samples of fiction and answered questions in order to test your ability to interpret prose fiction.

Sometimes, however, it is useful to read literary criticism *about* fiction. *Criticism* is the art of evaluating and analyzing a work of art or literature. A *critic* is a person who expresses an opinion about or who comments on a work of art or literature. Critics are also known as *reviewers*, persons who review works of literature or art.

Writers of literary criticism analyze a particular work by discussing the elements introduced earlier in this section—setting, plot, characterization, theme, tone, and style and language. Critics read works of fiction, poetry, drama, and nonfiction. They ask such questions as "How did the author create the story?" and "Was the author successful in achieving her goal?"

A critic may write general commentary about fiction and nonfiction in a newspaper or magazine column that appears regularly. A critic may also write reviews of movies, television programs, theater performances, art exhibits, live or recorded musical performances, or dance.

Nearly one-fourth of the questions on the Literature and the Arts Test will deal with commentary. *Commentary* is writing *about* literature and the arts—published comments, reviews, and criticism. You will study commentary in greater depth in the nonfiction section of this book.

EXERCISE 14: COMMENTARY ABOUT FICTION

Directions: Below is a review of a novel. The review is brief and, as many book reviews do, tells a little about the author and his or her career, major events in the plot of the book, and the reviewer's opinion of the book. Read the review and answer the questions that follow.

History Repeats Itself
by Anne Whitehouse
A Review of *The Last Room* by Elean Thomas
Virago/Trafalgar Square, paper, $13.95

The Last Room, the Jamaican writer Elean Thomas's first novel, is about two generations of mothers and daughters. Valerie Barton, nicknamed Putus ("meaning sweet and special"), is the only child and bright hope of her parents. As her mother says, "You wi be the one who bruk dem slavery chain fi-ever." But Putus's father dies, her mother remarries, and the girl is sent away. Befriended by an older man, she becomes pregnant. Young and naive, she does not realize at first that her condition means the death of her hopes. History repeats itself when Putus leaves her own daughter, Icylane, behind in Jamaica to join a man in England whom she will marry. Eighteen years pass. The story continues through Icy, now a civil servant, who goes to England to seek out the mother who abandoned her and who is said to be ill. Throughout the novel, Ms. Thomas makes generous use of dialect, and a glossary of Jamaican terms is provided. Her storytelling only falters with the somewhat disconcerting break between the stories of Putus and Icy; one wants to follow Putus's life as a young woman instead of returning to her decades later, when she has only the remnants of her anger and pride. Nevertheless, *The Last Room* is an affecting novel about hope and disillusionment, expectation and failure.

1. What is the reviewer's opinion of the story?

   (1) Its dialect is confusing.
   (2) The focus should be on Putus.
   (3) Icy is the book's best character.
   (4) The characters should remain in Jamaica.
   (5) The story falters because it's set in England.

2. Which statement best sums up the reviewer's opinion of the author?

   (1) She is a good storyteller.
   (2) She is a beginning writer.
   (3) Her writing is confusing.
   (4) She doesn't know Jamaica.
   (5) She doesn't know England.

3. Which of the following categories does *The Last Room* most likely fall into?

   (1) humorous writing
   (2) detective-mystery
   (3) science fiction
   (4) real-life drama
   (5) light romance

Answers are on page 549.

2
INTERPRETING POETRY

Poetry expresses ideas and emotions in a tightly controlled and structured way. Simply put, poetry is the best words in their best order.

Poetry is compressed. *Imagery* (word pictures that appeal to the five senses) and figures of speech enable the poet to convey ideas in just a few words.

Some poems are written in rhyme, the repetition of a sound at the end of two or more words, like *say* and *hay*. Sound and rhythm, the "beat," arouse feelings and evoke thoughts. All of these characteristics of poetry make it a distinct form of literature.

This chapter will help you to read and appreciate poetry. You will read many poems and examine their use of language, shape, sound, and meaning.

On the Literature and the Arts Test, you will be expected to demonstrate your understanding of a poem's meaning. You should be able to read a poem, spend a few minutes interpreting it, and answer the questions about the theme.

Interpreting Two Poems

The following poems are about human relationships. The first poem is nostalgic—the poet is remembering. The second poem is highly emotional. It is a sonnet, a structured poem that expresses a single emotion or idea.

EXERCISE 1: INTERPRETING TWO POEMS

Directions: Read each poem aloud and answer the questions that follow.

WHAT ARE THE POETS SAYING AND HOW ARE THEY SAYING IT?

Oh, When I Was in Love with You

Oh, when I was in love with you,
    Then I was clean and brave,
And miles around the wonder grew
    How well did I behave.

And now the fancy passes by,
    And nothing will remain,
And miles around they'll say that I
    Am quite myself again.

              —A. E. Housman

Sonnet 43

How do I love thee? Let me count the ways.
I love thee to the depth and breadth and height
My soul can reach, when feeling out of sight
For the ends of Being and ideal Grace.
I love thee to the level of every day's
Most quiet need, by sun and candlelight.
I love thee freely, as men strive for Right;
I love thee purely, as they turn from Praise.
I love thee with the passion put to use
In my old griefs, and with my childhood's faith.
I love thee with a love I seemed to lose
With my lost saints—I love thee with the breath,
Smiles, tears, of all my life!—and, if God choose,
I shall but love thee better after death.

—Elizabeth Barrett Browning

1. The theme of both poems involves

   (1) separation
   (2) love that is not returned
   (3) beauty
   (4) romantic love
   (5) love for one's fellow human being

2. A technique common to both poems is the use of

   (1) personification
   (2) imagery
   (3) rhyme
   (4) simile
   (5) metaphor

Answers are on page 549.

Poems as Riddles

In some ways, reading a poem is much like solving a riddle. The following poem presents a riddle to solve. Read the poem and answer the questions that follow.

Southbound on the Freeway

A tourist came in from Orbitville,
parked in the air, and said:

The creatures of this star
are made of metal and glass.

Through the transparent parts
you can see their guts.

Their feet are round and roll
on diagrams—or long

measuring tapes—dark
with white lines.

They have four eyes.
The two in the back are red.

Sometimes you can see a 5-eyed
one, with a red eye turning

on the top of his head.
He must be special—

the others respect him,
and go slow,

when he passes, winding
among them from behind.

They all hiss as they glide,
like inches, down the marked

tapes. Those soft shapes,
shadowy inside

the hard bodies—are they
their guts or their brains?

—May Swenson

1. Who is the tourist? (Two clues are "from Orbitville" and "parked in the air.")

_____

2. Who are the "creatures of this star"?

_____

3. What are their "feet"?

_____

4. What are "measuring tapes"?

_____

5. Who is the "5-eyed / one, with a red eye"?

_____

6. What observation does the visitor make about this "5-eyed" creature?

_____

7. What are the "soft shapes, / shadowy inside / the hard bodies"?

_____

Were you able to solve the riddle? Did you imagine a UFO looking down at the "creatures of this star"? The creatures are cars; their feet are tires; the measuring tapes are the roads. The five-eyed one is a police car. The tourist observes how the other cars behave when a police car is in traffic: "the others respect him, / and go slow, / when he passes, winding / among them from behind."

The poem captures a certain point of view that is much different from that of a driver in a car. You can now imagine what it must be like to see our driving habits from the viewpoint of someone looking down. If you have ever seen traffic out of an airplane window, then you have a better idea of this viewpoint.

TIPS ON READING POETRY

1. Read the title as a clue to the meaning.

2. Read the whole poem to get the general ideas and mood.

3. Ask yourself, What is this about? What is the poet saying? What does the poem mean? What is the theme?

4. Reread the poem using the punctuation as a guide. (Stop where there's a period or other end mark, not at the end of a line.)

5. Notice how lines are grouped together and if lines are repeated. What is the poet stressing by repeating words and lines?

6. Notice the language used and unusual word choices, comparisons, imagery, and figures of speech.

7. Read the poem aloud so you can hear it, especially if words rhyme.

8. Summarize in your own words what the poem is saying to understand the poem's tone and theme.

The Shape of Poetry

The structure and form of poetry distinguish it from other types of literature. Many poets choose a highly structured format, in which they shape their ideas using rhyme, rhythm, and stanzas. A *stanza* is a group of lines that work together to express an idea. Just as a new paragraph signals that a new idea is beginning in an article, so a new stanza signals that a new idea is being introduced in a poem. Often, stanzas are separated by a blank space.

The following poem by Dorothy Parker contains two stanzas:

On Being a Woman

stanza 1
> Why is it, when I am in Rome,
> I'd give an eye to be at home
> But when on native earth I be,
> My soul is sick for Italy?

stanza 2
> And why with you, my love, my lord,
> Am I spectacularly bored,
> Yet do you up and leave me—then
> I scream to have you back again?

When you sing a song, you may sing a verse, a chorus, the second verse, the same chorus, the third verse, a chorus, etc. A *verse* is any piece of poetry that is arranged in a pattern. Many songs were poems before they were set to music. An example is "The Battle Hymn of the Republic," by Julia Ward Howe.

The term *free verse* refers to verses without a regular rhythmic pattern and usually without rhyme. Much of today's poetry is free verse. Most of the poems in this section are written in free verse.

Capitalization and Punctuation

In poetry, a comma or a dash means "pause." A period means "stop." If the poem contains capitalization and punctuation, it should be read in sentences, not just one line at a time. Sometimes the reader may have to run two or more lines together. For example, in the poem "History," which follows, lines 2–4 are read "morning sunlight lengthened in spears across the linoleum floor."

The use of capital letters in poetry can vary. Sometimes a poet capitalizes each line. Sometimes a poet capitalizes a word for emphasis. Refer to the poems in this section to see how each poet uses capitalization and punctuation.

EXERCISE 2: THE SHAPE OF POETRY

Directions: Read aloud the poem below and answer the questions that follow. Notice the capitalization and punctuation as you read.

HISTORY

Grandma lit the stove.
Morning sunlight
Lengthened in spears
Across the linoleum floor.
Wrapped in a shawl,
Her eyes small
With sleep,
She sliced papas,
Pounded chiles
With a stone
Brought from Guadalajara.

After
Grandpa left for work,
She hosed down
The walk her sons paved
And in the shade
Of a chinaberry,
Unearthed her
Secret cigar box
Of bright coins
And bills, counted them
In English,
Then in Spanish,
And buried them elsewhere.
Later, back
From the market,
Where no one saw her,
She pulled out
Pepper and beet, spines
Of asparagus
From her blouse,
Tiny chocolates
From under a paisley bandana,
And smiled.

That was the '50s,
And Grandma in her 50s,
A face streaked
From cutting grapes
And boxing plums.
I remember her insides
Were washed of tapeworm,
Her arms swelled into knobs
Of small growths—
Her second son
Dropped from a ladder
And was dust.
And yet I do not know
The sorrows
That sent her praying
In the dark of a closet,
The tear that fell
At night
When she touched
Loose skin
Of belly and breasts.
I do not know why
Her face shines
Or what goes beyond this shine,
Only the stories
That pulled her
From Taxco to San Joaquin,
Delano to Westside,
The places
In which we all begin.

—Gary Soto

1. There are eleven lines in the first stanza. How many *sentences* are there? (Notice periods.)

_____

2. List at least three details from the third stanza that describe Grandma's earlier years:

(1) _____

(2) _____

(3) _____

3. In which stanza is she happier? Give the clue word that indicates this mood.

_____

4. Who is the narrator in this poem?

_____

5. What work did Grandma do? List two clues.

_____

Answers are on page 549.

The Sound of Poetry

Poets rely on many devices to communicate their messages to readers. Three common poetic devices are rhyme, rhythm, and alliteration.

Babies and toddlers may be introduced to the literature of their native language through nursery rhymes. **Rhyme** is the repetition, in two or more words, of the stressed vowel sound and of the syllables that follow that sound.

Hickory-dickory-*dock*, the mouse ran up the *clock*.

Jack and *Jill* went up the *hill*.

Some of the poems in this section rhyme: "Sonnet 43," page 484; "Oh, When I Was in Love with You," page 483; "maggie and milly and molly and may," page 489; "Memory," page 493; "Design," pages 496–497. Refer to these poems to see the use of rhyme. Read the poems aloud if necessary.

Just as word choices produce a desired effect in poetry, so does the beat, or rhythm, of a poem. In poetry, **rhythm** is the rise and fall of stressed words and syllables. If the rhythm is regular, or ordered strictly, the poem is said to have **meter**.

The repetition of consonant sounds, usually at the beginning of words, is **alliteration**. "Peter Piper picked a peck of pickled peppers" is an example of alliteration. Nursery rhymes contain much alliteration, and advertising slogans and jingles incorporate this technique frequently.

E. E. Cummings was a poet known for experimenting with the structure of poems. Cummings seldom used traditional capitalization and punctuation in his poetry. In addition, some of his poems present unique syllable divisions. Cummings creatively used language as he explored new forms for poetry. An example of his poetry is in Exercise 3.

EXERCISE 3: THE SOUND OF POETRY

Directions: The poem below presents insights into the characters of four girls. Read the poem and answer the questions that follow. Notice (1) the absence of capitalization in names, (2) the rhythm, (3) alliteration of the letters *s*, *b*, and *m*.

maggie and milly and molly and may

maggie and milly and molly and may
went down to the beach (to play one day)

and maggie discovered a shell that sang
so sweetly she couldn't remember her troubles, and

5   milly befriended a stranded star
whose rays five languid fingers were;

and molly was chased by a horrible thing
which raced sideways while blowing bubbles: and

may came home with a smooth round stone
10   as small as a world and as large as alone.

For whatever we lose (like a you or a me)
it's always ourselves we find in the sea

1. List at least three different examples of alliteration:

   (1) _____

   (2) _____

   (3) _____

2. Cummings uses rhyme in this poem. In lines 5–6 *star* and *were* do not rhyme perfectly, but they do share a similar sound. Which pairs of lines do not rhyme at all?

   _____

3. From a quick reading, you might say that the poem is not structured. Yet there is alliteration, two-line stanzas, rhyme, and rhythm. Read the poem aloud. How many "beats" per line do you hear?

   _____

4. Lines 11–12, which read "For whatever we lose (like a you or a me) / it's always ourselves we find in the sea," contain the theme of the poem. In these lines, the author is expressing which of the following ideas?

   (1) The sea is a source of life and death.
   (2) The sea is the best place for a person to reflect about life.
   (3) Everybody does not have the same respect for the sea.
   (4) The sea and its surroundings can give people a fresh view on life.
   (5) The sea represents all of our moods.

   Answers are on page 549.

Words That Stand for Sounds

Most poetry is written to be read aloud. As the poet writes the words, he or she is aware of the sound of the poem. Many poets use "sound words" to enhance the imagery and message of their poetry. The term *onomatopoeia* (ahn'-uh-mah'-tuh-pee'-uh) refers to the use of words whose sounds imitate their meanings. Sound-imitating words include *buzz, screech, boom,* and *crash.* *Whisper* is also a sound word.

Carl Sandburg wrote the following poem in 1920. Notice the poet's use of the sound words to describe jazz—a new music at the time. Jazz originated in New Orleans, and Sandburg makes reference to its birthplace by mentioning the Mississippi River in the fourth stanza. Notice how the "mood" of the poem changes as does the mood of a jazz tune. Count the number of times you see a word beginning with the letter *s*. Sandburg uses the sounds "s" and "sh" throughout his poem.

EXERCISE 4: WORDS THAT STAND FOR SOUNDS

Directions: Read aloud the poem below and answer the questions that follow.

WHAT JAZZ SOUNDS CAN YOU HEAR?

Jazz Fantasia

Drum on your drums, batter on your banjos, sob on the long cool winding saxophones. Go to it, O jazzmen.

Sling your knuckles on the bottoms of the happy tin pans, let your trombones ooze, and go husha-husha-hush with the slippery sandpaper.

Moan like an autumn wind high in the lonesome treetops, moan soft like you wanted somebody terrible, cry like a racing car slipping away from a motorcycle-cop bang-bang! you jazzmen, bang altogether drums, traps, banjos, horns, tin cans—make two people fight on the top of a stairway and scratch each other's eyes in a clinch tumbling down the stairs.

Can the rough stuff. . . . Now a Mississippi steamboat pushes up the night river with a hoo-hoo-hoo-oo . . . and the green lanterns calling to the high soft white stars . . . a red moon rides on the humps of the low river hills. . . . Go to it, O jazzmen.

1. Sandburg uses alliteration to establish a rhythm in the first stanza. Which words illustrate alliteration?

   (1) *long* and *cool*
   (2) *sob* and *winding*
   (3) *to* and *it*
   (4) *O* and *jazzmen*
   (5) *batter* and *banjos*

2. One descriptive device that Sandburg uses in the third stanza is both a simile *and* an example of personification. Which of the following descriptions represents both of these?

   (1) "high in the lonesome treetops"
   (2) "like a racing car slipping away from a motorcycle-cop"
   (3) "Moan like an autumn wind"
   (4) "make two people fight on the top of a stairway"
   (5) "bang altogether drums, traps, banjos, horns, tin cans"

3. The fiction passage most similar in technique to "Jazz Fantasia" would be the excerpt from

    (1) "The Man Who Lived Underground"
    (2) *Of Mice and Men*
    (3) "The Possibility of Evil"
    (4) *The Bell Jar*
    (5) *Lord of the Flies*

Answers are on page 550.

Interpreting Meaning

When you interpret a poem, you rephrase it, putting the poem into your own thoughts and words. You may simply change words around to make a statement more understandable to you. You may guess at the poet's main purpose and ask yourself, "Why is the poet using this comparison?" or "Why does the poet say this?"

Read the following poem, "My Papa's Waltz," by Theodore Roethke. Then read it again, a stanza at a time. On the lines provided next to each stanza, write a sentence or two summarizing the stanza in your own words. After you write *your* interpretation, read the interpretation provided at the end of the poem. You may agree with the interpretation, or you may not. Remember, there is no single correct interpretation.

My Papa's Waltz

Interpretation

The whisky on your breath
Could make a small boy dizzy;
But I hung on like death:
Such waltzing was not easy.

_____
_____
_____
_____

We romped until the pans
Slid from the kitchen shelf;
My mother's countenance
Could not unfrown itself.

_____
_____
_____
_____

The hand that held my wrist
Was battered on one knuckle;
At every step you missed
My right ear scraped a buckle.

_____
_____
_____
_____

You beat time on my head
With a palm caked hard by dirt,
Then waltzed me off to bed
Still clinging to your shirt.

_____
_____
_____
_____

Interpretation of stanza 1: A man is remembering his father. His father must have been drinking before he began dancing with his son.

Interpretation of stanza 2: The son remembers dancing wildly around the kitchen while his mother watched disapprovingly.

Interpretation of stanza 3: The son remembers being tall enough to notice the battered knuckle of his father and to remember the pain of his ear scraping against his father's belt buckle each time his father stumbled.

Interpretation of stanza 4: His father was dirty from working hard; his hands were still dirty as they danced. The son held on to his father as they waltzed.

This poem might be interpreted in different ways. Use the answers above as guidelines for checking your own.

EXERCISE 5: INFERRING MEANING

Directions: In the blanks below the poem, indicate the line numbers and key words that support the inferences. The first one has been done for you.

Strength

```
     That strong right hand that
     once balanced our
     young sons near the sky,
     once tossed bales of
  5  straw each August,
     once pitched no-hitters
     after Sunday picnics,
     once tenderly stroked
     my once-auburn hair . . .
 10  That hand
     now crudely arches to grasp
     a bamboo cane and
     now trembles as you reverently
     bow your feeble body in prayer
 15  and give thanks for the years
     of that strong right hand.
```

Inferences	Line numbers	Key words
1. The man is a father.	2, 3	our young sons
2. The man prays.		
3. The man was a farmer.		
4. The man is now elderly.		
5. The man was athletic.		

Answers are on page 550.

Inferring Mood

Mood is very important in poetry. When a poet creates a poem, the words chosen help present an overall feeling. The mood may be humorous and light, or it may be somber and serious. Underline the word below that best describes the mood of the poem "My Papa's Waltz," on page 491.

brooding   ecstatic   affectionate   light-hearted

You probably underlined *brooding* since the writer was brooding over the fear of waltzing with his father.

Within a poem, the mood sometimes changes. Read the following song from the musical *Cats*. As you read, identify the mood of each part. Circle the word that most accurately describes the mood of the lines.

Memory

Midnight, not a sound from the pavement.
Has the moon lost her memory?
She is smiling alone.
In the lamp light the withered leaves
    collect at my feet
And the wind begins to moan.

1. (a) optimistic
   (b) lonely
   (c) eager
   _____

Memory. All alone in the moonlight
I can smile at the old days.
I was beautiful then.
I remember the time
    I knew what happiness was,
Let the memory live again. . . .

2. (a) nostalgic
   (b) humorous
   (c) afraid
   _____

Daylight. I must wait for the sunrise
I must think of a new life
And I mustn't give in.
When the dawn comes
    tonight will be a memory, too
And a new day will begin. . . .

3. (a) depressed
   (b) sarcastic
   (c) hopeful
   _____

Touch me. It's so easy to leave me
All alone with the memory
Of my days in the sun.
If you touch me you'll understand
    what happiness is.
Look, a new day has begun.

4. (a) regretful
   (b) content
   (c) confused
   _____

The first part of the song refers to the moon smiling alone and the wind moaning. The word *lonely* (b) most accurately describes the mood. For 2, you should have chosen (a), *nostalgic*, because the cat is smiling and remembering. For the third part, *hopeful* (c) describes the cat anticipating daylight and a new day. The last part sounds final. A new day has begun. *Content* (b) describes the mood. Of course, other word choices that weren't given above may apply, but you should see four different moods in this song.

EXERCISE 6: INTERPRETING A POEM

Directions: Circle the number of the choice that best answers each question.

WHO IS THE NARRATOR OF THE POEM?.

The Negro Speaks of Rivers

I've known rivers:
I've known rivers ancient as the world and
  older than the flow of human blood in
  human veins.

My soul has grown deep like the rivers.

I bathed in the Euphrates when dawns
  were young.
I built my hut near the Congo and it lulled
  me to sleep.
I looked upon the Nile and raised the
  pyramids above it.
I heard the singing of the Mississippi when
  Abe Lincoln went down to New Orleans,
  and I've seen its muddy bosom turn all
  golden in the sunset.
I've known rivers:
Ancient, dusky rivers.

My soul has grown deep like the rivers.

—Langston Hughes

1. "My soul" in the poem refers to the soul of

  (1) the poet himself
  (2) the rivers
  (3) all people of African descent
  (4) Abe Lincoln
  (5) all people

2. The mood of the lines "I heard the singing of the Mississippi when / Abe Lincoln went down to New Orleans, / and I've seen its muddy bosom turn all / golden in the sunset" is one of

  (1) awe
  (2) fear
  (3) dread
  (4) joy
  (5) sorrow

3. Throughout the poem, the poet refers to rivers. He does this to

  (1) emphasize the beauty of rivers
  (2) show rivers as ever-present in African-American history
  (3) share his love for rivers
  (4) give the poem a feeling of tranquillity
  (5) tell why his soul is like a river

Answers are on page 550.

The Language of Poetry

You were introduced to descriptive language in the fiction section of this book. While figures of speech contribute greatly to style in short stories and novels, poetry relies even more heavily on this special language. This is because of the compression of ideas that a poem requires. In this section, you will review some of the devices introduced in the fiction section and analyze how they are used in poems to arouse the mind and emotions.

Imagery

When you use your imagination, you are forming *images*, or pictures, in your mind. A poet relies on readers' ability to create pictures in their minds from the words on a page. For this reason, the poet must choose the perfect word to convey a thought. When a poem appeals to your senses and enables you to imagine a scene, the poem is rich in *imagery*. The following line is an example of imagery:

The noisy raindrops hit the car's hood like thousands of thumbtacks.

Can you "see" the raindrops and "hear" the metallic sound made as they hit the car's hood?

Personification

Recall that *personification* is a form of imagery in which human activities or qualities are attributed to an animal or a thing. In other words, a nonhuman thing comes "alive" as it is given human abilities.

Carl Sandburg used personification to immortalize a city in his famous poem "Chicago." Notice that he addresses the city as a person. Here are the opening lines:

Chicago
Hog Butcher for the World,
Tool Maker, Stacker of Wheat,
Player with Railroads and the Nation's Freight Handler;
Stormy, husky, brawling,
City of the Big Shoulders:

The names he calls the city in the first three lines refer to commerce and industry Chicago was known for. Chicago is personified—made human—when the poet calls it by name.

In the following poem, underline all examples of personification. In what ways is the town human?

Steel Town

August skies accept
your belch of refuse
and ashes are excreted
high above new grass that
timidly borders
your concrete veins,
pulsating to sustain the hectic tempo
of days that too soon expire.
Your structure ages, breathing lessens,
and you remain
a body
with no soul.

You should have underlined the following words as examples of personification: *belch, excreted, timidly, veins, pulsating, expire, ages, breathing,* and *body with no soul.* The poet writes as if the town possesses the human abilities to live and die.

EXERCISE 7: THE LANGUAGE OF POETRY

Directions: Write *imagery* if a line evokes an image or *personification* if it attributes a human quality to an inanimate object.

Line 1: Midnight, not a sound from the pavement.   _____

Line 2: Has the moon lost her memory?   _____

Line 3: She [the moon] is smiling alone.   _____

Line 4: In the lamp light the withered leaves collect at my feet   _____

Line 5: And the wind begins to moan.   _____

Answers are on page 550.

Simile and Metaphor

As described in the fiction section, a **simile** is a comparison of two unlike things. A simile includes the word *like, than,* or *as.* Poet Robert Frost uses similes in the following poem, "Design." Underline the four similes.

Design

I found a dimpled spider, fat and white,
On a white heal-all,[1] holding up a moth
Like a white piece of rigid satin cloth—
Assorted characters of death and blight
Mixed ready to begin the morning right,
Like the ingredients of a witches' broth—
A snow-drop spider, a flower like a froth,

[1]A *heal-all* is a type of plant.

And dead wings carried like a paper kite.
What had that flower to do with being white,
The wayside blue and innocent heal-all?
What brought the kindred spider to that height,
Then steered the white moth thither in the night?
What but design of darkness to appall?—
If design govern in a thing so small.

You should have underlined these similes: "a moth / Like a white piece of rigid satin cloth"; "Like the ingredients of a witches' broth"; "a flower like a froth"; and "dead wings carried like a paper kite."

Recall that a **metaphor** is an implied or suggested comparison between two things. A metaphor does not contain *like, than,* or *as*. With a metaphor, one thing *is* the second thing to which it is being compared.

The day was an unwritten journal page waiting to be filled.

This metaphor presents an image of a blank paper—the day—ready for activities. The day *is* an unwritten journal page.

In this opening stanza of "An Indian Summer Day on the Prairie," by Vachel Lindsay, there are three metaphors. What three comparisons are made?

The sun is a huntress young,
The sun is a red, red joy,
The sun is an Indian girl,
Of the tribe of the Illinois.

The poet compares the sun to a huntress, joy, and an Indian girl. The reader gets a different image of the sun and an idea of the prairie setting.

Note the comparison made in this opening stanza of "Dreams" by Langston Hughes:

Hold fast to dreams
For if dreams die
Life is a broken-winged bird
That cannot fly.

The metaphor of "Life is a broken-winged bird" draws an unusual but very vivid image.

EXERCISE 8: REVIEW OF FIGURATIVE LANGUAGE AND THEME

Directions: Read the poem and answer the questions that follow.

HOW DOES THE SPEAKER VALUE BEAUTY?

Barter

Life has loveliness to sell,
    All beautiful and splendid things,
Blue waves whitened on a cliff,
    Soaring fire that sways and sings,
And children's faces looking up,
Holding wonder like a cup.

Life has loveliness to sell,
    Music like a curve of gold,
Scent of pine trees in the rain,
    Eyes that love you, arms that hold,
And for your spirit's still delight,
Holy thoughts that star the night.

Spend all you have for loveliness,
    Buy it and never count the cost;
For one white singing hour of peace
    Count many a year of strife well lost,
And for a breath of ecstasy
Give all you have been, or could be.

—Sara Teasdale

1. Which of the following lines from the poem is a simile?

   (1) "Life has loveliness to sell"
   (2) "Soaring fire that sways and sings"
   (3) "Holding wonder like a cup"
   (4) "Eyes that love you, arms that hold"
   (5) "Buy it and never count the cost"

2. What does the poet compare music to?

   (1) the scent of pine trees
   (2) the rain
   (3) eyes that love
   (4) arms that hold
   (5) a curve of gold

3. Which of the following lines from the poem is a metaphor?

   (1) "All beautiful and splendid things"
   (2) "Blue waves whitened on a cliff"
   (3) "Spend all you have for loveliness"
   (4) "Holy thoughts that star the night"
   (5) "Count many a year of strife well lost"

Answers are on page 550.

EXERCISE 9: INTERPRETING A POEM

Directions: Read the poem below and answer the questions that follow.

WHAT IS SILVER IN THE POEM?

Wind and Silver

Greatly shining,
The Autumn moon floats in the thin sky;
And the fish-ponds shake their backs and flash their dragon scales
As she passes over them.

—Amy Lowell

1. The fish-ponds are personified. What living creature are the ponds compared to?

_____

2. There is a second instance of personification in the poem. What object is compared to a woman?

_____

Answers are on page 550.

EXERCISE 10: PRACTICE IN INTERPRETING A POEM

Directions: Read the following poem and answer the questions that follow.

WHAT IS THE POET SAYING ABOUT DEATH?

Because I Could Not Stop for Death
Because I could not stop for Death,
He kindly stopped for me;
The carriage held but just ourselves
And Immortality.

We slowly drove, he knew no haste,
And I had put away
My labor, and my leisure too,
For his civility.

We passed the school where children played
At wrestling in a ring;
We passed the fields of gazing grain,
We passed the setting sun.

We paused before a house that seemed
A swelling of the ground;
The roof was scarcely visible,
The cornice but a mound.

Since then 'tis centuries; but each
Feels shorter than the day
I first surmised the horses' heads
Were toward eternity.

—Emily Dickinson

1. Match the stanza on the left with the images on the right by writing the correct letter in the space provided.

    _____ Stanza 1   **a.** images of a school yard, farm, land, dusk

    _____ Stanza 2   **b.** the narrator riding in a carriage with two others

    _____ Stanza 3   **c.** a slow ride as the narrator accepts her fate

    _____ Stanza 4   **d.** the narrator remembering the day of the carriage ride, hundreds of years before

    _____ Stanza 5   **e.** the carriage pausing at a gravesite

2. The poet capitalizes the words *Death* and *Immortality* to illustrate that

    (1) death is a major theme
    (2) they are the chief concerns of a person's life
    (3) they are characters in the poem
    (4) the two words are opponents, one fighting the other
    (5) they are two unexplainable concepts that people must deal with

3. The lines that begin the poem, "Because I could not stop for Death,/ He kindly stopped for me . . ."

    (1) prove that Death is of the male gender
    (2) give human qualities to an abstract state
    (3) show that Death can be postponed if one puts up a fight
    (4) indicate that the suffering poet was relieved of her pain
    (5) imply that the writer of the poem is a woman

4. The title and lines 1–2 imply that the speaker of the poem

    (1) was very ill
    (2) drove the carriage
    (3) stopped at a school yard
    (4) fought death to the last
    (5) died unexpectedly

5. From the last stanza, one can infer that the speaker in the poem

    (1) knows when she is going to die
    (2) feels time moves too slowly
    (3) never looks back at the past
    (4) enjoys carriage rides
    (5) believes in eternal life

Answers are on page 550.

EXERCISE 11: MORE PRACTICE IN INTERPRETING A POEM

Directions: Read the following poem and choose the best answer to each question that follows.

WHO IS THE MAN FROM WASHINGTON AND WHAT IS THE POET SAYING ABOUT HIM?

The Man from Washington

The end came easy for most of us.
Packed away in our crude beginnings
in some far corner of a flat world,
we didn't expect much more
than firewood and buffalo robes
to keep us warm. The man came down,
a slouching dwarf with rainwater eyes,
and spoke to us. He promised
that life would go on as usual,
that treaties would be signed, and everyone—
man, woman, and child—would be innoculated
against a world in which we had no part,
a world of wealth, promise, and fabulous disease.

—James Welch

1. The speaker of the poem is a

    (1) man from Washington
    (2) politician
    (3) white settler
    (4) Native American
    (5) slave

2. The mood of this poem could best be described as one of

    (1) alienation
    (2) hopefulness
    (3) anticipation
    (4) fear
    (5) nostalgia

3. The theme that is reflected in this poem is the

    (1) welcoming of the Puritans by Native Americans
    (2) signing of the treaties between the U.S. government and Native Americans
    (3) mass execution of soldiers in Custer's Last Stand
    (4) destruction of the Native Americans' way of life
    (5) slaughter of the buffalo

Answers are on page 550.

About Poetry: Commentary

On the Literature and the Arts Test, you may be expected to read and answer questions about a review or criticism of poetry.

Below is a sample review of a poetry collection. The review is written by a literary critic whose purpose is to evaluate a volume of poetry. You might see a review of poetry in a literary magazine or the literature section of a news magazine or newspaper.

WHAT IS THE CRITIC'S OPINION?

Whispered Secrets by Ann Fox Chandonnet, Denise Lassaw, Eleanor Limmer, and Joanne Townsend
Sedna Press, $10
Reviewed by Stephen C. Levi

Whispered Secrets was a book long in coming and well worth the wait. In fact, it is unexpectedly refreshing. Allow this reviewer to explain. Sedna Press, as the foreword explains, takes its name from the Eskimo goddess Sedna whose father severed her fingers and then allowed her to sink into the sea. There she created all of the marine life on which the Eskimos lived as well as all storms at sea. She was thus both creator and destroyer.

With such a publishing imprint and four women poets, I was prepared for another manhating, how-I-hurt collection of poetry by bitter women. I was pleasantly surprised. As a unit, the poems form a spear of opinion thrusting forward with a single theme: a woman's personal ownership of herself achieved through self-knowledge and coming to terms with herself and her surroundings. More basically put, the poems carry the message that wealth of spirit comes from knowledge of oneself and understanding that the slings and arrows of outrageous fortune are often gifts which make us stronger.

Further, the four women present their point of view separately. Each poet adds her own special direction of philosophical travel yet, at the same time, collimates [runs parallel] with the bent of the other three. In the end, the collection holds together well and delivers the message clearly.

EXERCISE 12: COMMENTARY ON POETRY
Directions: Choose the best answer for each of the questions.

1. Which of the following statements would the reviewer agree with?

   (1) Women's poetry is almost always objective.
   (2) Hardships can help us face up to our lives.
   (3) Publishers need to have interesting imprints.
   (4) Women poets should always write in groups.
   (5) The goddess Sedna is not a subject for a poem.

2. The reviewer states, "*Whispered Secrets* was a book long in coming and well worth the wait." What is another way of saying the same thing?

   (1) The time put into the book shows in the excellence of the writing.
   (2) The writers took much too long to write the book.
   (3) Readers had to wait a long time to read the book.
   (4) The book would be better if it had come out earlier.
   (5) Waiting for the book made people expect too much.

Answers are on page 551.

3
INTERPRETING DRAMA

Around 1950, the television entered the American living room; as a result, life in America has never been the same. The average American watches several hours of television each day, from movies to soap operas to sitcoms (situation comedies). Turn on your TV at this moment, and on at least one channel you will see drama.

What Is Drama?

Drama is the form of literature designed to be performed in the theater by actors taking on the roles of characters. In many cases, drama closely imitates life because the actors confront real-life situations and come to grips with real-life problems. As you study this chapter, do not think of drama as an unfamiliar form of literature and art. Think of how much you already know about drama from life and from TV.

The requirements for interpreting drama on the GED Test are similar to the requirements for interpreting prose fiction and poetry. For example, on the test, you may be asked to read an excerpt from a play and interpret the meaning or tone of the character's speech.

It is not difficult to read a play, even if you are not accustomed to reading drama. However, as you read a play, you must be able to "see" the action. You must use your imagination and picture the action taking place. You need to read carefully to infer setting, characterization, and theme, just as you do when you read prose and poetry.

Read the following exchange of conversation (dialogue) and try to visualize the action. The words in parentheses—stage directions—are not meant to be read aloud. They are directions to the actors and explanations of "what's happening" as the actors speak.

WHAT DO YOU *HEAR*? WHAT DO YOU *SEE*?

[*The scene begins in a community college parking lot. Glen parks his car as Rob walks by.*]

GLEN: [*Locking his car and putting his keys in his pocket*] Hi! [*Waving to Rob*] Well, this is it, huh?

ROB: Yeah, why else would I be up at 7:30 on a Saturday morning?

GLEN: [*As he joins Rob to walk up the hill to the administration building*] I've done all the right things. I went to bed at ten o'clock, ate a good breakfast, and got here a little early. Now all I have to do is pass this test!

ROB: Not me, man. I partied until one o'clock. I'm too nervous to eat, and I don't think I'm gonna pass. I decided to come anyway, try the test, and see what happens. [*He opens the door for Glen as they enter the building.*] Let's grab a cup of coffee and try to relax. We have a little while before checking in.

GLEN: [*Shaking his head*] Y'know, I've waited ten years to come back to school. [*Getting coffee and sitting down.*] I went to most of the classes, did some studying at home, and finally got enough nerve to register for this test. I just can't believe that by the end of the day I could have earned my GED certificate.

ROB: [*Raising his coffee cup in a toast*] Cheers! Good luck!

GLEN: [*Toasting*] Same to you. See you in real estate class this summer, huh?

ROB: [*Rising from his chair*] Yeah, let's go get 'em. [*They walk toward the testing area.*]

What happened in the scene between Rob and Glen? Could you picture the setting, the two men, and the general theme of this scene? To check your understanding, fill in the blanks with the appropriate words.

Glen and Rob are arriving at a _____ to take their

_____ . _____ is well prepared for the test,

while _____ is less confident. They decide to have

_____ and try to _____ before checking in.

They wish each other _____ and plan to see each other in

_____ . _____ has a better chance of passing

the test.

You could have filled the blanks with these answers: community college, GED Tests, Glen, Rob, coffee, relax, luck, real estate class or the summer, Glen. Most of these answers are stated directly in the reading. If you answered that Glen had a better chance of passing, you *inferred* this information from the fact that Rob had attended a party until one o'clock and Glen had taken his studying very seriously.

If you can imagine where the characters would be taking the test, how they would feel and act, and what the achievement means to them, you can relate to the situation.

How Drama Differs from Other Forms of Literature

Although drama has much in common with the two other forms of literature you have studied—poetry and fiction—each of the three forms of literature treats its subject differently. Illustrated below are differences in the way each form of literature treats the same subject—a marriage proposal.

Prose: The young couple, John and Mary, went for a midnight boat ride on the Mississippi River. John gave Mary a diamond ring, and she accepted his proposal of marriage.

Poetry:	Lovers in the moonlight
	Aboard the Delta Miss
	Exchanged a ring and promises
	And sealed them with a kiss.

Drama: [*John and Mary board the* Delta Miss *for a midnight cruise.*]

JOHN: [*Embracing Mary*] I love you. [*He gives her a package.*]

MARY: [*Surprised*] What's this?

JOHN: It's a symbol of our future together—if you agree to marry me next month.

MARY: [*Opening the package and seeing a diamond ring*] Oh, John!

JOHN: [*Slipping the ring on her finger*] Don't ever take it off.

MARY: No . . . [*flustered*] I mean yes! I mean *no* I won't take it off . . . *Yes*, I'll marry you. [*They kiss.*]

EXERCISE 1: HOW DRAMA DIFFERS

Directions: Reread the three versions of the marriage proposal. Then choose the best answer for each of the following questions.

1. In which of the three versions do the characters seem to come to life?

  (a) prose   **(b)** poetry   **(c)** drama

2. Which version contains concise images and is written in verse?

  (a) prose   **(b)** poetry   **(c)** drama

3. Which example seems the most like real life?

  (a) prose   **(b)** poetry   **(c)** drama

4. Which example relates the exact words and actions of characters?

  (a) prose   **(b)** poetry   **(c)** drama

5. Which version presents a summary of action in sentences?

  (a) prose   **(b)** poetry   **(c)** drama

Answers are on page 551.

Dialogue

In a play, as in other forms of literature, *dialogue* is conversation between characters. When reading dialogue in a novel or short story, it is sometimes difficult to keep track of who is talking, because the speakers are not always identified. In reading drama, however, there are clues to help you keep track of who is speaking.

Clue #1: The speakers are identified in each line that is delivered.

In the scene at the beginning of this section, the clues *GLEN* and *ROB* indicate who is talking. The names and the use of the colon (:) let you know who's speaking.

When only two people are speaking, it is easy to follow, but when three or more characters get involved, you must read more carefully and be aware of which speaker is responding to which other characters.

Clue #2: Punctuation marks are used to begin and end a character's speech.

In the writing skills section of this book, you reviewed punctuation. Notice the end marks, especially for questions (?) and exclamations (!). Punctuation is used in drama to show volume of voice and emotion. Dashes (—) and ellipses (. . .) are also used to show pauses. Dashes are used to show a break in thought, while ellipses indicate that there is a pause in the action or that one character is being interrupted by another character.

Clue #3: Line spacing between lines of dialogue indicates who's speaking.

A more obvious and visual clue that indicates when a different speaker is talking is the "white space" between lines of dialogue.

EXERCISE 2: DIALOGUE AND PUNCTUATION

Directions: Read the dialogue below, noticing the punctuation. Then answer the questions that follow.

> [*The scene begins in a nineteenth-century parlor as Catherine, Edward and Victoria's daughter, enters with tea.*]

CATHERINE: Would you like some tea and . . .

EDWARD: Not now—Can't you see we're talking?

VICTORIA: *You're* talking—I'm not!

EDWARD: Oh—a little irritable, are we?

VICTORIA: No—just bored—with you. . .

CATHERINE: [*Mumbling*] I'm leaving. [*She exits.*]

In the space below, write the name of the character that correctly completes each statement.

1. Catherine interrupts _____ .

2. _____ asks two questions.

3. _____ is rude to Catherine.

4. Victoria is upset with _____ .

Answers are on page 551.

EXERCISE 3: INFERRING MOOD FROM DIALOGUE

Directions: Choose the best answer to the question that follows.

The mood of this scene may *best* be described as

(1) tense   **(2)** happy   **(3)** suspenseful   **(4)** nostalgic   **(5)** humorous

Answer is on page 551.

Stage Directions

Stage directions are used to assist the actors and director in interpreting the writer's intentions and purpose and to help the reader follow the imagined actions. In the brief scene above, the stage directions are "[*The scene begins in a nineteenth-century parlor as Catherine, Edward and Victoria's daughter, enters with tea.*]"; "[*Mumbling*]"; and "[*She exits.*]."

Notice that the playwright inserts the directions within and between the dialogue. In the scene above, the stage directions tell the reader who Catherine is and why she leaves.

There are two play excerpts on the next few pages. The first excerpt relies on your understanding of dialogue, while the second requires you to follow the action as well as the words.

Interpreting a Scene

The scene below has been included to give you practice in reading plays. The more comfortable you are with following the format of a play, the better your understanding of it will be. Read the following play scene and try to imagine the characters, setting, mood, and action. The scene presents facts about the history of drama. If you're studying with a group or a class, perhaps your instructor would like to assign parts as you read the dialogue aloud.

WHO ARE THE CHARACTERS AND WHAT IS TAKING PLACE?

[*The scene is a drama class where students are learning about the history of drama. The teacher is seated on her desktop, referring to her notes as her students ask questions.*]

MISS ANDERSON: You need to take some notes on this, so listen carefully and interrupt me if you have a relevant question . . .

PETE: Anyone have a pen I can borrow? . . . [*Ann, tapping him on the shoulder, hands him one.*] Thanks.

MISS ANDERSON: That's not what I would call a relevant question, Pete. OK . . . Western drama began in Greece about 500 B.C. at the festivals of Dionysus, the god of wine. In early Greek drama, there were few individual actors; instead, a chorus was used to "chant" and recite passages. The spectators sat on the hillside, looking down upon the performance. Later, arenas and the Colosseum were built. There were no costumes or makeup, but robes and masks were worn. These festival plays often lasted three days.

PETE: What a party!

MISS ANDERSON: Well . . . yes, it was a party atmosphere.

LINDA: Were there any stars or famous actors of the time?

MISS ANDERSON: The first actor is believed to be Thespis.

LINDA: Is that why actors are called thespians?

MISS ANDERSON: Yes. If drama students, actors, or crew members earn so many hours of credit in drama, they can join the International Thespian Society.

LARRY: Did they use swords and stuff on stage then, or is that just in movies?

MISS ANDERSON: Later, in Roman theater, there was much violence. It's believed that in the days of gladiators some people were actually killed on stage.

PETE: I can see it now. "This play is rated *R*. Death scenes not for people under seventeen!" [*Laughter from class*]

MISS ANDERSON: Let's go on, please. As drama advanced, the raised stage was developed. The audience sat in front of or around it. In the Middle Ages, plays centered around religion, and traveling actors performed plays on pageant wagons that traveled from village to village throughout Europe.

PETE: Is that where the expression "Let's get this show on the road!" comes from? [*Groans from the teacher and class*]

MISS ANDERSON: Very funny, Pete. By the late 1500s, the Elizabethan era in England gave us William Shakespeare. Drama would never be the same. It became much better.

RICK: Excuse me, what's the big deal about Shakespeare? I can't read or understand his stuff unless a teacher is standing in front of the class "translating" for me. Then I like and understand it.

MISS ANDERSON: Today it *is* necessary to translate Shakespeare because he wrote in the English spoken during his time. But once you study Shakespeare, you'll see that his themes about human nature still apply to us today. In fact, the musical *West Side Story* is based on Shakespeare's play *Romeo and Juliet.* Many of today's soap operas about conflicts between two families reflect some of Shakespeare's themes. Imagine a play such as *Romeo and Juliet*, which includes many characters, an exciting plot, an everlasting theme about love, and all of it written in verse form!

RICK: OK, I'm impressed.

MISS ANDERSON: Also, keep in mind that Juliet and all of the women were played by men.

RICK AND PETE: [*together*] WHAT!?

MISS ANDERSON: That's right. Theater was quite bawdy—obscene. Women were not allowed to act in or to attend many plays, so all of the women's roles were played by boys or men.

PETE: [*Standing and "acting"*] "Romeo, Romeo, wherefore art thou, Romeo?"

RICK: Oh, Juliet. You need a shave. You have to look good for the next scene. [*Laughter from the class*]

MISS ANDERSON: Let's go on, guys. In the next 200 years, theater would evolve to allow the wearing of elaborate costumes and the use of movable scenery, lighting, and indoor theaters. Women were allowed in the audience, then finally in the productions as actresses.

PETE: I have only two lines left on my page. This history of drama is longer than I thought.

> MISS ANDERSON: The first American theater was built in 1716, so I have a lot to tell you about American drama—tomorrow. I will conclude by saying Western drama today is a "mixed bag." It's a product of all that has come before us—classical Greek, Roman, Shakespearean, and experimental. Plays are performed daily in our city theaters, in community playhouses, and on TV. Directors and actors try new approaches and forms . . . [*Bell rings*] Go home and watch TV, and you'll see drama in some form.
>
> PETE: [*Turning*] Here's your pen, Ann. Now, that's my kind of homework assignment! See ya tomorrow, Miss A!

The stage directions that open this scene tell the reader *where* the action takes place and *who* is involved. They set the scene. They establish the *setting*, the drama class. Also, the stage directions set the *mood*. As in prose and poetry, the mood is set early in a work to help determine the attitude the playwright expects from the audience.

The stage directions here include "[*The teacher is seated on her desktop, referring to her notes as her students ask questions.*]"

As in prose literature and poetry, the reader must *infer* character, plot, setting, mood, and theme.

EXERCISE 4: IDENTIFYING CHARACTERS

Directions: Match the character on the right with the appropriate action or description on the left. Base your answers on the classroom scene you just read.

_____ 1. likable "class clown"   **a.** Miss Anderson

_____ 2. asks about early actors   **b.** Pete

_____ 3. asks about violence on stage   **c.** Linda

_____ 4. character who doesn't speak   **d.** Larry

_____ 5. asks about studying Shakespeare   **e.** Ann

_____ 6. leads the discussion   **f.** Rick

Answers are on page 551.

EXERCISE 5: HISTORY OF DRAMA

Directions: Choose the best answer for each question that follows.

1. All of the following facts were presented in the scene *except*:

   (1) Only in the last few hundred years have women been in theater.
   (2) Actors are known as thespians.
   (3) During the Middle Ages, plays centered around religion.
   (4) William Shakespeare's plays are seldom performed today.
   (5) The Greeks performed without costumes or makeup.

2. The mood of the scene may be best described as

   (1) informal (2) serious (3) suspenseful (4) blissful (5) threatening

3. Miss Anderson's approach may be described as

(1) strict   **(2)** unenthusiastic   **(3)** haphazard   **(4)** casual   **(5)** formal

4. Based on her explanations, we can infer that Miss Anderson

(1) has no knowledge of Greek theater
(2) has great admiration for Shakespeare
(3) is angered by Pete's interruptions
(4) sees no link between drama of the past and drama of today
(5) does not like teaching literature at all

5. The purpose of this scene is to

(1) compare and contrast different types of plays
(2) explain why Shakespeare is so important to drama
(3) distinguish between comedy and tragedy
(4) trace the development of Western drama from past to present
(5) show how Miss Anderson handles a difficult situation

Answers are on page 551.

WRITING ACTIVITY 1

Create your own play scene based on a classroom or work experience. Use the speakers' names followed by a colon (:). Insert your own stage directions in brackets. Use four or five exchanges of dialogue to practice with the play format.

From Idea to Production

The ancient Greeks sat on a hillside to watch plays; today we turn on our television sets or attend live productions. We escape for a while as we are entertained by situations that often are more exciting than our own lives.

To appreciate a play or TV drama fully, it helps to know how drama is created and produced. A play is created by a writer (playwright or dramatist). Usually, it is written to be performed, rather than to communicate directly to *readers*. It takes the work of many different people with different talents and skills to put on a performance. Costumers, set designers, makeup artists, and many others contribute.

The diagram below illustrates the process by which a play—an idea in the writer's head—becomes the reality of a live production.

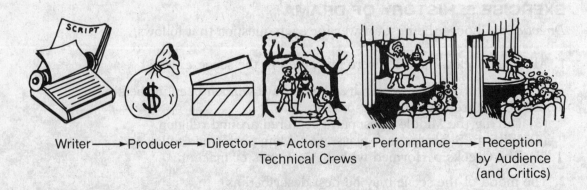

Writer ⟶ Producer ⟶ Director ⟶ Actors / Technical Crews ⟶ Performance ⟶ Reception by Audience (and Critics)

When playwrights or screenplay writers create a script, they visualize their final work as a performance. The producer, who finances the production, chooses a director who will effectively present the raw material—the script. The director casts actors and actresses who fit the characters the writers have created.

Structure of Drama

Like poetry and fiction, drama has structure. A play is composed of *acts*—the major divisions of a dramatic work. Acts are composed of scenes. *Scenes* show an action that occurs in one place among characters.

A *prologue* begins classical drama. Because there was no scenery in early drama, the audience needed to know when and where the story was taking place and what circumstances caused the action. An actor would come on stage and introduce the play by explaining the setting and some of the plot.

The *epilogue* ends classical drama. At the end of the play, an actor would come on stage and deliver a summary poem or speech. Although the prologue and epilogue are not as common in drama today, some television dramas and movies use them to help the audience understand the plot.

Shakespeare developed and refined the structure of drama as we know it today. He presented his plots in five acts. These acts are subdivided into numbered scenes. The diagram below shows the relationship between the acts and the corresponding elements of a traditional plot.

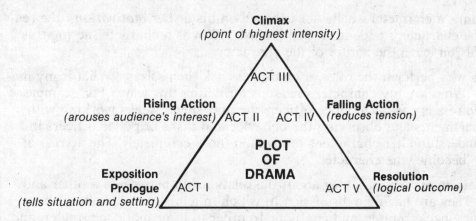

Elements of Drama

Plot, setting, character, and theme are all devices that were introduced and explained in the prose and poetry sections. These elements also apply to drama.

As you can see from the diagram above, the plot in drama is tightly structured. As in a short story, there is *exposition* that orients the audience to the dramatic situation and setting.

The *rising action* is made up of all of the events that create suspense and arouse the audience's interest. We wonder, "What will happen next?" "What will the main character do?" All of these events and conflicts lead to the *climax*, the point of highest intensity in the play.

The *falling action* may be brief. The conclusion or *resolution* is the logical outcome of the plot. As in fiction, the resolution ties up all of the loose ends of the plot.

Characterization

Since characters in plays are intended to be brought to life by actors before a live audience, they are not developed in exactly the same ways as characters in novels and stories. How can you interpret character? One way is by listening to the character's dialogue and watching his or her facial expressions and mannerisms. Another way to interpret character is to be aware of the motivation for the character's actions.

Dialogue and Nonverbal Communication

A writer of fiction need not rely solely on dialogue for the reader to *understand* why characters behave the way they do. The novelist or short story writer can *tell* us how a character thinks and feels and why the character feels that way.

In drama, however, personalities are revealed by what characters say. Thus, dialogue carries greater responsibility for getting the author's point across in drama than in fiction.

Another difference between interpreting character in drama and in prose fiction is that in drama, character is revealed by the actor's **nonverbal communication**—mannerisms, tone of voice, facial expression, and costume. For example, you might be able to infer a character's job by the costume he wears. Or you might infer a character's unspoken thoughts by her tone of voice and facial expressions.

Motivation

In drama, a character's behavior is based on his or her **motivation**—the reasons for the character's actions. You might ask, "Why is a character acting this way?" until you learn the nature of the character.

Actors who perform the roles of characters ask themselves, "What is my motivation?" "What are my character's reasons for acting this way?" For example, if a film actress is cast as a police officer, she may spend weeks working with police departments and observing the behavior and tasks of police officers in order to understand her character's motivation more completely. The actress attempts to "become" the character.

Below is an excerpt of a play about the relationship between a mother and daughter. They are having a discussion in which much is revealed about their personalities, backgrounds, and conflicts. In order to infer mood, character, and form, you must rely on your understanding of dialogue.

EXERCISE 6: UNDERSTANDING CHARACTER

Directions: Read the passage below and answer the questions that follow.

WHAT ARE THE CHARACTERS' PERSONALITIES?

MAMA: Nothing I ever did was good enough for you, and I want to know why.

JESSIE: That's not true.

MAMA: And I want to know why you've lived here this long feeling the way you do.

JESSIE: You have no earthly idea how I feel.

MAMA: Well how could I? You're real far back there, Jessie.

JESSIE: Back where?

MAMA: What's it like over there, where you are? Do people always say the right thing or get whatever they want, or what?

JESSIE: What are you talking about?

MAMA: Why do you read the newspaper? Why don't you wear that sweater I made for you? Do you remember how I used to look, or am I just any old woman now? When you have a fit do you see stars, or what? How did you fall off the horse, really? Why did Cecil leave you? Where did you put my old glasses?

JESSIE: They're in the bottom drawer of your dresser in an old Milk of Magnesia box. Cecil left because he made me choose between him and smoking.

MAMA: Jessie, I know he wasn't that dumb.

JESSIE: I never understood why he hated it so much when it's so good. Smoking is the only thing I know that's always just what you think it's going to be. Just like it was the last time and right there when you want it and real quiet.

MAMA: Your fits made him sick, and you know it.

JESSIE: Say seizures, not fits. Seizures.

MAMA: It's the same thing. A seizure in the hospital is a fit at home.

JESSIE: They didn't bother him at all. Except he did feel responsible for it. It was his idea to go horseback riding that day. It was his idea I could do *anything* if I just made up my mind to. I fell off the horse because I didn't know how to hold on. Cecil left for pretty much the same reason.

—Excerpted from *'night, Mother* by Marsha Norman

1. The relationship between the mother and daughter seems to suffer from

    (1) Jessie's dependence on Mama
    (2) Mama's dependence on Jessie
    (3) a lack of communication
    (4) Jessie's resentment of her mother
    (5) Mama's hatred of Cecil, Jessie's husband

2. Mama may best be described as

    (1) understanding
    (2) vengeful
    (3) supportive
    (4) critical
    (5) selfish

3. Jessie seems to like smoking because

    (1) its effect is something she can depend on
    (2) it irritates her mother
    (3) it makes her feel as strong as Cecil
    (4) she started at a young age
    (5) it calms her nerves

4. Jessie may best be described as

(1) conniving
(2) responsible
(3) out of touch with reality
(4) at odds with her mother
(5) hopeless

5. The mood that this excerpt conveys is one of

(1) despair   (2) happiness   (3) suspense   (4) tension   (5) doubt

Answers are on page 551.

EXERCISE 7: SUPPORTING FACTS AND INFERENCES

Directions: Below is a list of facts and inferences made about Jessie's character. In the spaces provided, write the key words from the passage that support each fact or inference.

1. Jessie has epilepsy. _____

2. Jessie is separated from Cecil. _____

_____

3. Jessie smokes. _____

4. Jessie is confused about what her mother wants to know. _____

_____

5. Mama doesn't believe Jessie's story of how she fell off the horse. _____

_____

Answers are on page 552.

EXERCISE 8: INTERPRETING A SCENE FROM A PLAY

Directions: Read the passage below and answer the questions that follow.

WHAT PROBLEM IS BEING DISCUSSED BY ALICE AND GENE?

ALICE: I'm doing a lot for my kids. I don't expect them to pay me back at the other end. [*Gene wanders around, thinking, scuffing the grass.*] I'm sure we could find a full-time housekeeper. He can afford it.

GENE: He'd never agree.

ALICE: It's that or finding a home. [*Gene frowns.*] Sidney's folks like where they are. Also, we might as well face it, his mind's going. Sooner or later, we'll have to think about powers of attorney, perhaps committing him to an institution.

GENE: It's all so ugly.

ALICE: [*smiling*] Yes, my gentle Gene, a lot of life is.

GENE: Now, look, don't go trying to make me out some soft-hearted . . . [*He can't find the word.*] I know life is ugly.

ALICE: Yes, I think you know it. You've lived through a great deal of ugliness. But you work like a Trojan to deny it, to make it not so. [*After a moment, not arguing*] He kicked me out. He said he never wanted to see me again. He broke Mother's heart over that for years. He was mean, unloving. He beat you when you were a kid. . . . You've hated and feared him all your adult life. . . .

GENE: [*cutting in*] Still he's my father, and a man. And what's happening to him appalls me as a man.

ALICE: We have a practical problem here.

GENE: It's not as simple as all that.

ALICE: To me it is. I don't understand this mystical haze you're casting over it. I'm going to talk to him tomorrow, after the session with the lawyer, about a housekeeper. [*Gene reacts but says nothing.*] Just let me handle it. He can visit us, and we can take turns coming to visit him. Now, I'll do the dirty work. Only when he turns to you, don't give in.

GENE: I can't tell you how ashamed I feel . . . not to say with open arms, "Poppa, come live with me . . . I love you, Poppa, and I want to take care of you." . . . I need to love him. I've always wanted to love him. [*He drops his arms and wanders off.*]

—Excerpted from *I Never Sang for My Father* by Robert Anderson

1. The relationship between Alice and Gene is

   (1) husband and wife
   (2) nurse and doctor
   (3) sister and brother
   (4) close friends
   (5) mother and son

2. Alice would agree with which of the following statements?

   (1) All children should care for their elderly parents.
   (2) Nursing homes are for people who have no children.
   (3) The best situation for the elderly is staying in their own houses.
   (4) Children should get powers of attorney before placing parents in institutions.
   (5) Elderly parents should not expect their children to take care of them.

3. Alice's attitude toward her father is one of

   (1) devotion
   (2) resentment
   (3) undying love
   (4) indifference
   (5) respect

4. Alice is upset by Gene's

   (1) denial of his father's abusive treatment of Gene
   (2) refusal to love and care for his own father
   (3) lack of concern for his father now that his father is old
   (4) carefree attitude toward the situation
   (5) indifference to the feelings of all other family members

5. Gene exhibits all of the following emotions except

    (1) depression
    (2) relief
    (3) disgust
    (4) shame
    (5) frustration

6. The fact that Alice is making the final decision in this situation is shown by the line

    (1) "We have a practical problem here."
    (2) "I'm sure we could find a full-time housekeeper. He can afford it."
    (3) "Sooner or later, we'll have to think about powers of attorney. . . ."
    (4) "Just let me handle it. He can visit us, and we can take turns coming to visit him. Now, I'll do the dirty work."
    (5) "I don't understand this mystical haze you're casting over it."

7. Gene's last speech reveals Gene's

    (1) acceptance of his father's love
    (2) anger with Alice's negative attitude
    (3) eagerness to visit his father and offer to care for him
    (4) guilt that he doesn't love his father
    (5) inability to make decisions that affect his future

Answers are on page 552.

About Drama: Commentary

On the Literature and the Arts Test, you may be required to answer questions about commentary on a film or play. Below is a film review.

EXERCISE 9: INTERPRETING A FILM REVIEW

Directions: Read the review below and answer the questions that follow.

HOW DOES *THE LAST TYCOON* PORTRAY HOLLYWOOD?

Film Review of *The Last Tycoon*

F. Scott Fitzgerald, author of *The Great Gatsby*, has been called the "Poet of the Jazz Age," the 1920s. But he also had something important to say about Hollywood's Golden Age, the 1930s—and he said it in his last book, *The Last Tycoon*. He showed Hollywood as a kind of company town and the heads of
5 studios as absolute rulers. Critic Edmund Wilson has called *The Last Tycoon* the best book ever written about moviemaking.

Somehow, director Elia Kazan and Harold Pinter (who wrote the screenplay) have managed to turn *The Last Tycoon* into a fascinating low-key film. It couldn't have been easy. Fitzgerald died in 1940, leaving only six finished
10 chapters of *The Last Tycoon*. He left notes for some possible endings, and the one Pinter and Kazan chose may not please everybody.

15

20

25

The time is 1933, the place a big Hollywood studio like MGM. Monroe Stahr (Robert De Niro) is the studio production head. Fitzgerald meant Stahr to be based on the late Irving Thalberg, MGM's creative "Boy Wonder." Like Thalberg, Stahr is a human dynamo. He controls every stage of filmmaking. He shows actors how to act, screenwriters how to write, and the studio boss (Robert Mitchum) how to run things.

But Stahr himself is a flawed human being. He sees life as a movie and people as shadows. He even tries to "cast" Kathleen (Ingrid Boulting), the girl he loves, as a reincarnation of his dead wife. But real life keeps getting into the act. People refuse to stay in the roles he has chosen for them. The writers he thinks of as children are ready to strike. His boss resents his arrogance and looks for a way to get rid of him.

The Last Tycoon won't please Hollywood Boosters, but Fitzgerald fans should like it. It pays respect to his work and to his last troubled years as a screenwriter in Hollywood.

1. Lines 7–9, "Elia Kazan and Harold Pinter have managed to turn *The Last Tycoon* into a fascinating low-key film," illustrate the writer's attitude toward Kazan and Pinter, which is one of

   (1) ridicule
   (2) admiration
   (3) envy
   (4) indifference
   (5) disgust

2. Lines 18–19, "He sees life as a movie and people as shadows," is a figure of speech that

   (1) gives an inanimate object human qualities
   (2) compares two unlike things
   (3) suggests one thing is exactly the same thing as another
   (4) hints at an unexpected turn of events
   (5) completely exaggerates the quality of a thing

3. Lines 18–19 also offer support for the statement that Stahr

   (1) is a man with character flaws
   (2) is like Irving Thalberg, the "Boy Wonder"
   (3) is energetic and thoughtful
   (4) treats writers as children
   (5) heads all aspects of production

4. "*The Last Tycoon* won't please Hollywood Boosters" implies that the film will

   (1) be unpopular with most film critics
   (2) be successful as a money-making film
   (3) not win Academy Awards
   (4) offend Fitzgerald's survivors
   (5) offend the producers of Hollywood films

Answers are on page 552.

WRITING ACTIVITY 2

Be the critic—write your own film review. The next time you watch a movie, use the following form to critique the film.

Evaluate the acting, directing, plot, and entertainment value (or lack of it). Indicate in your review who this film would appeal to most. Be sure to provide specific examples from the movie that support your judgment. Try to see the movie through the eyes of a film critic.

The Artists
Read the credits. Know *who* made the film.

1. Director: _____

2. Actors/Actresses: (stars) _____

   _____

   (supporting) _____

   _____

3. Writer and performer of musical score: _____

   _____

The Film Itself

4. In a paragraph or two, what is the plot of the movie?_____

   _____

   _____

   _____

5. Are the actors' and actresses' portrayals believable?_____

6. What do you like about the film?_____

   _____

7. What do you dislike about the film and would like to see improved?_____

   _____

   _____

   _____

8. What is the film's message or theme?_____

9. Who would this film likely appeal to the most?_____

10. Rate the film on a scale of 0 to 5. (0 for poor, 5 for excellent)_____

4
INTERPRETING NONFICTION

Do you read nonfiction? If you read a daily newspaper, you read nonfiction. If you read articles in *People, Newsweek, Sports Illustrated, Ebony*, or *Better Homes and Gardens*, you read nonfiction. If you read articles or books explaining how to diet, strip furniture, or buy a car, you read nonfiction.

Nonfiction is literature that is *not* fiction and is based on fact. The nonfiction author writes about actual people, events, and ideas. The author's purpose may be to inform, instruct, entertain, record, examine, persuade, or analyze. Read the following excerpt about the teen years taken from a nonfiction book about parenting. Then answer the questions that follow the passage. As you read, ask yourself:

- What is the author's purpose for writing the piece?

- What details does he include to support his theory?

WHY DO TEENS REBEL?

I am now convinced that most theories about the "stress and strain of adolescence" have focused incorrectly on such factors as the adolescent's physical changes, his emerging sexuality, his new social demands, his struggle between being a child and an adult, and so on. This period is difficult for children and parents largely because the adolescent becomes so independent of his parents that he can no longer be easily controlled by their rewards and punishments. And since most parents rely so heavily on rewards and punishment, adolescents react with much independent, resistive, rebellious, hostile behavior.

Parents assume that adolescent rebellion and hostility are inevitably a function of this stage of development. I think this is not valid—it is more that the *adolescent becomes more able to resist and rebel*. He is no longer controlled by his parents' rewards because he does not need them so much; and he is immune to threats of punishment because there is little they can do to give him pain or strong discomfort. The typical adolescent behaves as he does because he has acquired enough strength and resources to satisfy his own needs and enough of his own power so that he need not fear the power of his parents.

An adolescent, therefore, does not rebel against his *parents*. He rebels against their *power*. If parents would rely less on power and more on non-power methods to influence their children *from infancy on*, there would be little for the child to rebel against when he becomes an adolescent. The use of power to change the behavior of children, then, has this severe limitation: parents inevitably run out of power, and sooner than they think.

—Excerpted from *Parent Effectiveness Training* by Dr. Thomas Gordon

Place a check mark (✓) before each statement with which the author would likely agree.

_____ **1.** There has been too much focus on parenting techniques and not enough on the teen's development.

_____ **2.** The main factor of the rebellious period is the adolescent's independence of parental control.

_____ **3.** Parents should not assume that a teenager's rebellious behavior is inevitable.

_____ **4.** A teenager no longer needs his or her parents' love.

_____ **5.** Parents should use power to discipline their children.

_____ **6.** Most theories about the "terrible teens" have missed the main point.

_____ **7.** Parents' use of power over children is counterproductive. Although power works for children, it causes problems during adolescence.

_____ **8.** A teenager is rebelling more against the power than the parents.

The author's purpose is clear. By using phrases such as "I am now convinced . . ." and "I think this is not valid," the author is giving his opinion. He is rejecting most other theories about the "terrible teens" and rebellion.

You should have checked off statements 2, 3, 6, 7, and 8. The others (1, 4, 5) are not the views of the author according to the passage.

What is the author's main point? Reread the first two sentences of the last paragraph. These sentences clearly tell the author's purpose—to state why teens rebel.

In this section, you will read a variety of nonfiction excerpts. As in the previous fiction, poetry, and drama sections, you will be asked to interpret meaning, style, tone, and language.

Types of Nonfiction

Nonfiction appears in several forms and covers every conceivable subject. To organize such a wide range of material, libraries use the Dewey decimal system or the Library of Congress system in categorizing their books. Under the Dewey decimal system, main classes of books and other publications are given a three-digit number. For example, nonfiction books that fall within the category of literature are found in the 800s. Under the Library of Congress system, classes of books are given an alphabetical prefix. For example, books that fall under the heading of literature are assigned the letter _P._

Forms of nonfiction include biographies, autobiographies, articles, essays, and speeches. A description and example from each category is represented in this section.

Biography—About People

Most people like to read about other people's lives; consequently, biography is a popular form of nonfiction. A *biography* is a factual book or sketch that records the life of an individual. Biographies are written about historical figures, politicians, sports figures, current and past celebrities, and any other people who might have attracted the public's eye.

Biographers report major events in a person's life and interpret their meaning. A biography is often meant to entertain as well as to educate; you can certainly learn from the experiences of others. Traditionally, biographies were written after someone's death, as a tribute. But today, more and more biographies are written about people who are still alive.

Most major writers and literary figures are subjects of biographies, because critics and readers want to know more about the personal lives of writers and how those events relate to their writings. The passage below is a biographical sketch of a famous essayist.

EXERCISE 1: THE BIOGRAPHY

Directions: Read the biographical sketch below and answer the questions that follow.

WHO WAS HENRY DAVID THOREAU?

Henry David Thoreau was born in Concord, Massachusetts, in 1817. He graduated from Harvard in 1837. The week he graduated, he heard a speech by Ralph Waldo Emerson and became a follower of the famous essayist and poet. Thoreau tried teaching but resigned after objections to his refusal to use corporal punishment; teachers were expected to hit students. In 1839, Thoreau, on a vacation from teaching, journeyed down the Concord River with his brother. The trip resulted in his first book, *A Week on the Concord and Merrimack Rivers*. He and his brother also opened a private school, where he introduced the idea of field trips to study nature.

Philosopher and writer Ralph Waldo Emerson encouraged Thoreau to keep a daily journal and to write poetry and essays. On July 4, 1845, Thoreau began his famous "experiment in living" at Walden Pond. He lived in a cabin in the woods.

He wrote, "I went to the woods because I wished to live deliberately. . . ." The journal entries he wrote while living at Walden Pond were later published and became an American nonfiction classic, *Walden*.

Known as an individualist and nonconformist, someone who did not always go along with the rest of society, Thoreau also wrote the essay "On the Duty of Civil Disobedience." [See pages 529–530.] The essay was written as a result of his one-day imprisonment for refusing to pay a poll tax that helped fund the United States' war with Mexico. He also opposed slavery and did much in 1859 to publicize abolitionist John Brown as a martyr. Thoreau died of tuberculosis in Concord in 1862.

His works, especially "On the Duty of Civil Disobedience," were later read by Mahatma Gandhi of India and Martin Luther King, Jr. Thoreau's ideas of civil disobedience and passive resistance were practiced by both Gandhi and King in their protests against their respective governments. Today, Thoreau is viewed as one of the great thinkers and writers in American history.

1. The biographical sketch of Thoreau does all of the following except

    (1) tell when he lived
    (2) describe some of his beliefs
    (3) name his most important literary works
    (4) criticize his writing style
    (5) summarize his contributions to society

2. It is significant that Thoreau moved to Walden Pond on July 4, 1845, because

    (1) it was his summer vacation from teaching
    (2) he wanted to attract worldwide attention to his cause
    (3) the pond was beautiful in July
    (4) he was hiding from the law
    (5) it was the anniversary of the nation's independence

3. In *Walden*, Thoreau writes: "I went to the woods because I wished to live deliberately, to front only the essential facts of life, and see if I could not learn what it had to teach, and not, when I came to die, discover that I had not lived." If you were to follow Thoreau's advice, you would

    (1) live and work in New York City
    (2) get involved in national politics
    (3) live away from civilization
    (4) take time out to ponder the meaning and beauty of life
    (5) become a stockbroker and make as much money as possible

4. According to the biographical sketch, Thoreau's most influential work is

    (1) the essay "On the Duty of Civil Disobedience"
    (2) the book *A Week on the Concord and Merrimack Rivers*
    (3) the book *Walden*
    (4) his journals
    (5) his poetry

5. Civil disobedience may best be described as

    (1) disregarding all laws passed by one's government
    (2) nonviolent resistance to unjust laws
    (3) breaking any law that one does not like
    (4) living one's life as a free spirit
    (5) a violent attempt to overthrow one's government

6. In the conclusion of *Walden*, Thoreau writes, "If a man does not keep pace with his companions, perhaps it is because he hears a different drummer. Let him step to the music which he hears, however measured or far away." This statement reveals Thoreau's belief in

    (1) laws
    (2) individualism
    (3) conformity
    (4) friendship
    (5) patriotism

Answers are on page 552.

WRITING ACTIVITY 1

Choose one of Thoreau's quotations from questions 3 and 6 in Exercise 1. In a paragraph or two, explain its meaning in your own words.

Oral History—Word of Mouth

Not all biographical works document the life of a famous or distinguished individual. Studs Terkel's book *Hard Times* records facts and impressions about the lives of many different "common people" who were affected by the Great Depression of the 1930s. He interviewed people about their memories of the Depression and recorded their responses as oral history. In the following excerpt from the oral history, he interviews Cesar Chavez, who was, at the time of the interview, the head of the United Farm Workers of America. Chavez recalls what it was like for his family to leave a farm that they owned and become migrant workers.

Many times, nonfiction authors interview their sources, then summarize the interview in their own words. Here, Terkel reports both his questions to Chavez and Chavez's responses.

EXERCISE 2: ORAL HISTORY

Directions: Read the passage below and answer the questions that follow.

WHAT DOES CHAVEZ REMEMBER ABOUT THE DEPRESSION?

[Chavez] We had been poor, but we knew every night there was a bed *there* and that *this* was our room. There was a kitchen. It was sort of a settled life, and we had chickens and hogs, eggs and all those things. But that all of a sudden changed. When you're small, you can't figure these things out. You know something's not right and you don't like it, but you don't question it and you don't let that get you down. You sort of just continue to move.

But this had quite an impact on my father. He had been used to owning the land and all of a sudden there was no more land. What I heard . . . what I made out of conversations between my mother and my father—things like, we'll work this season and then we'll get enough money and we'll go and buy a piece of land in Arizona. Things like that. Became like a habit. He never gave up hope that some day he would come back and get a little piece of land.

I can understand very, very well this feeling. These conversations were sort of melancholy. I guess my brothers and my sisters could also see this very sad look on my father's face.

[Terkel] *That piece of land he wanted . . . ?*

[Chavez] No, never. It never happened. He stopped talking about that some years ago. The drive for land, it's a very powerful drive.

When we moved to California, we would work after school. Sometimes we wouldn't go. "Following the crops," we missed much school. Trying to get enough money to stay alive the following winter, the whole family picking apricots, walnuts, prunes. We were pretty new, we had never been migratory workers.

Write *T* if a statement is true or *F* if it is false.

———— **1.** There were at least five people in Chavez's family.

———— **2.** Chavez is very bitter about his experience.

———— **3.** Chavez's parents were hopeful people.

———— **4.** According to Chavez, children keep going along even when they do not understand what's happening.

———— **5.** Chavez's parents had always been migrant workers.

———— **6.** Being a migrant worker affected Chavez's opportunity to get a good education.

———— **7.** The Great Depression did not greatly affect Chavez's family.

———— **8.** Chavez has trouble remembering much about the Depression.

Answers are on page 553.

WRITING ACTIVITY 2

TV interviews are popular. Programs like "60 Minutes," "Nightline," and "The Oprah Winfrey Show," to name a few, rely on the interview process. Interview an older person whom you know who lived through the Depression. Ask at least five questions, and write up the results of your interview in a question-and-answer format.

Autobiography—About You

Only *you* can write your autobiography, the story of your own life. **Autobiography** is a *self*-biography. Many writers of autobiographies are not professional writers but notable individuals telling their own story. Autobiographies are also known as *memoirs*.

Notable autobiographies include *The Diary of Anne Frank*, a diary of a young Jewish girl who hid from the Nazis in World War II; *Out of Africa*, the autobiography of Isak Dinesen, which was the basis for the film of the same title; and *The Autobiography of Malcolm X*, which served as the basis for Spike Lee's film about Malcolm X.

Like authors of fiction, authors of nonfiction exhibit particular styles. Autobiographies, especially, tend to be written in a less formal style because the writers are revealing the personal details of their lives. In the passage on page 525, Dick Gregory, writer, comedian, and social activist, uses many sentence fragments—quick images to set the mood. Notice his style and the effects he achieves.

EXERCISE 3: AUTOBIOGRAPHY

Directions: Read the passage below and answer the questions that follow.

HOW DOES DICK GREGORY FEEL ABOUT SCHOOL?

The teacher thought I was stupid. Couldn't spell, couldn't read, couldn't do arithmetic. Just stupid. Teachers were never interested in finding out that you couldn't concentrate because you were so hungry, because you hadn't had any breakfast. All you could think about was noontime, would it ever come? Maybe you could sneak into the cloakroom and steal a bite of some kid's lunch out of a coat pocket. A bite of something. Paste. You can't really make a meal of paste, or put it on bread for a sandwich, but sometimes I'd scoop a few spoonfuls out of the paste jar in the back of the room. Pregnant people get strange tastes. I was pregnant with poverty. Pregnant with dirt and pregnant with smells that made people turn away, pregnant with cold and pregnant with shoes that were never bought for me, pregnant with five other people in my bed and no Daddy in the next room, and pregnant with hunger. Paste doesn't taste too bad when you're hungry.

The teacher thought I was a troublemaker. All she saw from the front of the room was a little black boy who squirmed in his idiot's seat and made noises and poked the kids around him. I guess she couldn't see a kid who made noises because he wanted someone to know he was there.

—Excerpted from "Not Poor, Just Broke" in *Nigger—An Autobiography*

1. The author uses the word *pregnant* to mean

   (1) overdue with
   (2) carrying the burden of
   (3) separated from
   (4) expecting a baby
   (5) looking forward to

2. From the author's point of view, the teacher was all of the following *except*

   (1) unaware of his hunger
   (2) insensitive to his real needs
   (3) aware of his disruptive behavior
   (4) uninterested in him
   (5) understanding of his problems

3. The use of the word *pregnant* is effective because the word

   (1) expresses a feeling of expectation
   (2) appeals to mothers
   (3) creates a vivid image in the reader's mind
   (4) is used in a different way than is expected
   (5) contributes to the writer's use of alliteration as a device

4. Cesar Chavez and Dick Gregory were alike in that both men

   (1) lived in fatherless homes
   (2) had their early education interrupted
   (3) had no brothers or sisters
   (4) made names for themselves despite their childhood poverty
   (5) had no faith at all in adults

5. The title of the chapter from which the excerpt comes is, "Not Poor, Just Broke." This title suggests that Gregory

    (1) wasn't poor; he'd just spent his lunch money
    (2) was used to poverty, so it didn't bother him
    (3) supposes that being poor is the same thing as being broke
    (4) believes being broke is better than being poor
    (5) thinks those who are called poor by others don't necessarily consider themselves to be poor

Answers are on page 553.

Journals and Letters

Have you ever kept a diary or journal? Both are daily records of personal activities, events, or reflections. Many people keep records of their lives for themselves or for their children. When people write their autobiographies, they may refer to their diaries or journals as sources of material.

Ralph Waldo Emerson referred to his journals as his "savings banks" in which he deposited his thoughts. Later, he drew out those thoughts and wrote some of his famous speeches, essays, and poems. Below is an entry from one of his journals.

EXERCISE 4: JOURNAL ENTRIES

Directions: Read the passage below and answer the questions that follow.

WHAT IS EMERSON'S ATTITUDE TOWARD LIFE?

November 11, 1842 [age thirty-nine]

Do not be too timid and squeamish about your actions. All life is an experiment. The more experiments you make the better. What if they are a little coarse, and you may get your coat soiled or torn? What if you do fail, and get fairly rolled in the dirt once or twice? Up again you shall never be so afraid of a tumble.

1. Based on the quotation above, with which of the following statements about life might Emerson agree?

    (1) Life is one big bowl of cherries.
    (2) Life is a precious gift not to be wasted.
    (3) Life is one big rat race.
    (4) Life isn't fair.
    (5) Life is a risk; to risk is to be alive.

2. Which of the following occupations is the best expression of Emerson's beliefs?

    (1) philosopher
    (2) writer
    (3) astronaut
    (4) physician
    (5) historian

Answers are on page 553.

Article—Just the Facts, Please

An *article* is a short nonfiction piece, often appearing in a newspaper or magazine. The writer presents facts, usually in an objective manner. *Feature articles* are special attractions that cover topics that have high reader interest. An article may instruct readers in how to do something, or it simply may be entertaining.

The following article about the Vietnam Veterans Parade presents facts in an objective way; the writer's opinions are not included in the article. Read the article and answer the questions that follow.

On Friday, June 13, 1986, approximately 200,000 marchers participated in Chicago's Vietnam Veterans Parade. Along the 2.8-mile route, an estimated 500,000 spectators gathered. For almost five hours, they cheered, hugged, and even walked along with the veterans and the veterans' families.

The parade was the major activity of the four-day reunion for those serving in the controversial war of the 1960s and 1970s. Gen. William Westmoreland, former U.S. wartime commander, was Grand Marshal of the parade. Politicians, older veterans, and ethnic organizations also marched. The parade ended in Grant Park, where the half-size replica of the Vietnam War Memorial was on display. The purpose of the parade was to recognize the veterans for their service in the war.

The tone of this article is *objective*, and the purpose is to convey the facts. What five facts are related in the article above? Answer the questions by filling in the blanks below with the correct words.

1. Who? _____

2. What? _____

3. When? _____

4. Where? _____

5. Why? _____

You should have answered *Who?*—Vietnam veterans; *What?*—Chicago Vietnam Veterans parade; *When?*—June 13, 1986; *Where?*—Chicago; *Why?*—to recognize the veterans for their service in the war. This article is an objective reporting of facts.

Now read the next article on the same subject and answer the questions that follow. This article is said to be a *subjective* account because the writer's opinions are included.

EXERCISE 5: THE ARTICLE AS NONFICTION

Directions: Read the article below and answer the questions that follow.

WHAT IS THE AUTHOR'S VIEW OF THE VIETNAM PARADE?

June 13, 1986—They came from all over America—200,000 heroes strong, with their families. Some veterans were clad in their old uniforms, others in battle fatigues. They marched, those that could, near their buddies in wheelchairs or on crutches. Others rode in VA buses. Some marched with their children, babies born during the war. A few ex-POWs waved at TV cameras. One marcher carried a sign, "Honor the warriors and not the war." And Chicago came out for them—years later than we should've—but we came—for the Vietnam War Vets who were deprived of the "Welcome Home" and "Thank You" they deserved in the 1970s.

The crowd of about 500,000 sat on curbs, ran along, and helped throw tons of confetti on the troops that were led by Gen. William Westmoreland, their commander in Vietnam. On Friday the 13th, thirteen years after the U.S. troops pulled out of Vietnam, the veterans' luck ran high. The much-deserved five-hour parade was part of the four-day observance. It ended in Grant Park, where the marchers and spectators viewed the half-size replica of the Vietnam Memorial of Washington, D.C.

There they paused. There they were quiet. They had marched for themselves, for their families, for those men and women not yet home—the MIAs—for the names on the Wall—for those who weren't there to march. To the veterans who marched, welcome home and thank you.

1. The opening line of the article immediately suggests that the writer

   (1) is a flag-waving patriot
   (2) opposed the Vietnam War
   (3) was a veteran of the war
   (4) felt that the parade was an unnecessary gesture
   (5) holds great admiration for the veterans

2. The author emphasizes the date, Friday the 13th, and the fact that the parade occurred thirteen years after the withdrawal of troops in order to

   (1) show that she is highly superstitious
   (2) indicate that the parade's success had everything possible against it
   (3) prove that the Vietnam veterans have been plagued by bad luck since the days of the war
   (4) show contrast between the success of the parade and the outcome normally associated with the number thirteen
   (5) impress the reader with her memory of important dates

Answers are on page 553.

NEWSPAPER NONFICTION

A good way to prepare for the GED Test is to read a major daily newspaper regularly. Besides practicing your reading and comprehension skills, you can enjoy interesting nonfiction in the form of articles and editorials.

Of the pieces that you just read about the Vietnam Veterans Parade, the first is very similar to what you would find on the front page or in other news sections of the paper. The second piece is similar to what you would find either in a featured writer's weekly column or on the editorial page of the paper because it expresses either one person's opinion or the opinion of the publisher.

As you read your newspaper, use the index to guide you to the articles and learn the differences between objective and subjective reporting.

Essay—One Person's View

An *essay* is a nonfiction work in which an author presents a personal viewpoint on a subject. Traditionally, an essay is a formal piece of writing, an expository piece that "exposes" and analyzes a subject.

Below is an excerpt from a well-known formal essay, "On the Duty of Civil Disobedience," by Henry David Thoreau. As you read it, recall Thoreau's background from page 521. Remember that the essay was written after Thoreau was jailed for refusing to pay a poll tax that he viewed as support for the Mexican War. The essay is personal in that Thoreau uses *I* to explain his views; it is serious in tone, and the vocabulary is somewhat more difficult than today's prose. The ideas put forth in this excerpt of the long essay were shared by civil rights leaders of the 1960s and 1970s, the Nazi-resisters of the 1930s and 1940s, and many other people who chose to disobey unfair rules or laws.

EXERCISE 6: THE FORMAL ESSAY

Directions: Read the passage below and answer the questions that follow.

WHAT IS THE PURPOSE OF GOVERNMENT?

I heartily accept the motto,—"That government is best which governs least;" and I should like to see it acted up to more rapidly and systematically. Carried out, it finally amounts to this, which also I believe,—"That government is best which governs not at all;" and when men are prepared for it, that will be the kind of government which they will have. Government is at best but an expedient; but most governments are usually, and all governments are sometimes, inexpedient. The objections which have been brought against a standing army, and they are many and weighty, and deserve to prevail, may also at last be brought against a standing government. The standing army is only an arm of the standing government. The government itself, which is only the mode which the people have chosen to execute their will, is equally liable to be abused and perverted before the people can act through it. Witness the present Mexican war, the work of comparatively a few individuals using the standing government as their tool; for, in the outset, the people would not have consented to this measure.

This American government,—what is it but a tradition, though a recent one, endeavoring to transmit itself unimpaired to posterity, but each instant losing some of its integrity? It has not the vitality and force of a single living man; for a single man can bend it to his will. It is a sort of wooden gun to the people themselves; and, if ever they should use it in earnest as a real one against each other, it will surely split. . . .

1. The title of the essay implies that a citizen

   (1) is disloyal for disobeying laws
   (2) should serve in the army
   (3) should appreciate U.S. citizenship
   (4) is obligated to break an unjust law
   (5) must vote in all elections

2. In the line "The government itself, which is only the mode which the people have chosen to execute their will," the word *execute* is used to mean

   (1) capital punishment of criminals
   (2) kill during a war
   (3) carry out; perform
   (4) ignore the wishes of
   (5) create; originate

3. Thoreau's view of the army is that the army exists

   (1) for each individual's use
   (2) for the government to use as it wishes
   (3) as a necessary part of democracy
   (4) as the symbol of individual heroism
   (5) independently of the government

4. Thoreau's interpretation of "government" is that the government

   (1) is the people themselves
   (2) is made up of knowledgeable leaders
   (3) is a tool of the standing army
   (4) should give fewer freedoms to its citizens
   (5) encourages individual liberty

5. Emerson said of Thoreau, "No truer American existed than Thoreau." Emerson admired Thoreau's

   (1) undying patriotism
   (2) faith in the justice system
   (3) military mind
   (4) belief in individual liberty
   (5) legislative ability

Answers are on page 553.

EXERCISE 7: REVIEW OF THOREAU

Directions: After reading the biography of Thoreau (p. 521) and the excerpt above, review your knowledge of Thoreau's beliefs. Place a check mark (✓) in front of the actions you think Thoreau would support today.

_____ **1.** antiwar protests

_____ **2.** the military draft

_____ **3.** civil rights demonstrations

_____ **4.** the women's movement

_____ **5.** the end of apartheid in South Africa

_____ **6.** literary censorship

Answers are on page 554.

WRITING ACTIVITY 3

Is it ever right to break a law? If so, under what conditions? Write two or three paragraphs using examples to support your answer.

EXERCISE 8: COMPARING AND CONTRASTING STYLES

As you learned in the section on fiction, *style* refers to the author's unique use of language to express an idea. It is the writer's style that distinguishes a formal from an informal essay. Below are two essays about computers. One is written with a light approach—a conversation between a customer and an airline worker. The other is a discussion of the danger of computers in the workplace. Note the differences in style and approach.

Directions: Read each passage below and answer the questions that follow.

Passage 1

HOW DOES THE WRITER FEEL ABOUT COMPUTERS?

The most frightening words in the English language are, "Our computer is down." You hear it more and more as you go about trying to conduct your business.

The other day I was at the airport attempting to buy a ticket to Washington and the attendant said, "I'm sorry, I can't sell you a ticket. Our computer is down."

"What do you mean your computer is down? Is it depressed?"

"No, it can't be depressed. That's why it's down."

"So if your computer is down just write me out a ticket."

"I can't write you out a ticket. The computer is the only one allowed to issue tickets for the plane." I looked down the counter, and every passenger agent was just standing there drinking coffee and staring into a blank screen.

"What do all you people do?"

"We give the computer the information about your trip, and then it tells us whether you can fly with us or not."

"So when it goes down, you go down with it."

"That's very good, sir. I haven't heard it put that way before."

"How long will the computer be down?" I wanted to know.

"I have no idea. Sometimes it's down for ten minutes, sometimes for two hours. There is no way we can find out without asking the computer, and since it's down it won't answer us."

"Don't you have a backup computer when the main computer goes down?"

"I doubt it. Do you know what one of these things costs?"

"Let's forget the computer. What about your planes? They're still flying aren't they?"

"I couldn't tell without asking the computer, and as I told you—"

"I know, it's down."

—Excerpted from "The Computer Is Down" by Art Buchwald

1. All of the following elements of style are found in this passage *except*

    (1) exaggerated circumstances
    (2) first-person narration
    (3) long explanatory paragraphs
    (4) dialogue
    (5) sarcasm

2. "There is no way we can find out without asking the computer, and since it's down it won't answer us." This statement reveals the airline agent's

    (1) irritation with the customer
    (2) creativity
    (3) ability to deal with crises
    (4) total dependence on the computer
    (5) seniority of position

3. The line that best summarizes the main idea of this passage is

    (1) "What do you mean your computer is down?"
    (2) "So if your computer is down just write me out a ticket."
    (3) "So when it goes down, you go down with it."
    (4) "How long will the computer be down?"
    (5) "Let's forget the computer. What about your planes?"

Passage 2

WHAT IS THIS WRITER'S OPINION OF COMPUTERS?

The millions of people on the bottom levels of electronic hierarchies [computer networks that connect managers with workers] are increasingly likely to spend their days in an isolated no-man's-land, subservient to intelligent information systems that report their progress to unseen supervisors far away. Because computers measure quantity better than quality, such systems tend to reward employees who work faster more than those who work better. There's a sharp rise in loneliness and disconnection as individuals blindly forge ahead. Service people on the telephone or at a cash register curtly terminate attempts at idle conversation because their performance is being electronically monitored. Once judged on their ability to communicate with customers or troubleshoot unexpected situations, they're now evaluated by the number of transactions they complete in a shift or the number of keystrokes required to draft a document. In these "electronic sweatshops," the computers are running the people, not the other way around.

"I think people are going to feel an increased fragmentation of self. They won't be able to hold the pieces together," human resources consultant Philip Nicholson says. "How do you keep a coherent space if you're going in and out of spaces that don't exist?" A graduate of the law-psychiatry program at Stanford University Law School, Nicholson has advocated preventive psychiatry since a Vietnam-era Air Force stint spent designing programs to alleviate drug abuse and race relations problems. He likens the psychic numbing of electronic information overload to symptoms of post-traumatic stress syndrome. In office wars, people become overwhelmed by the sheer amount of information available, internalize the diversity of the world outside, and fear losing control over their own lives.

"You operate from a position of chronic performance anxiety and background stress," Nicholson says. "In fact, I think it fosters a kind of mass self-hypnosis. When you're working on the computer, it's you and the screen and your mind. That's exactly what happens when you go into a hypnotic trance."

—Excerpted from "The Dark Side of the Boom" by Mary S. Glucksman

4. The tone of this passage, as compared to Passage 1, is more

   (1) humorous
   (2) satirical
   (3) conversational
   (4) serious
   (5) informal

5. When the author calls highly computerized offices "electronic sweatshops," she is

   (1) commenting on the amount of heat generated by electronic equipment
   (2) complaining that computers generate fear in the workplace by causing layoffs
   (3) praising computers for making entry-level employees work harder
   (4) saying that computers make workers "sweat it out," or worry excessively
   (5) comparing today's electronic office to the dehumanizing factory of yesterday

6. The main idea, or point, of the excerpt is that electronic offices are

    (1) the wave of the future
    (2) an improvement over old-time offices
    (3) causing psychological problems in workers
    (4) increasing American productivity
    (5) helping people develop their ability to troubleshoot

7. The major purpose of quoting human resources consultant Philip Nicholson is to

    (1) make the article more convincing by including the opinions of an expert
    (2) enliven the article by offering a real-life, concrete example
    (3) balance the article by presenting a different point of view about computers
    (4) develop the ideas in the article in a variety of ways
    (5) tie in problems suffered by vets with problems suffered by office workers

8. Both authors would agree with which of the following statements?

    (1) We would be better off without any computers.
    (2) The airline industry would be safer without computers.
    (3) Computers are a necessary part of human life.
    (4) People should control computers rather than letting computers control them.
    (5) The government should control all computers.

Answers are on page 554.

Speech—Telling It Like It Is

As you can see from what you've read, essays embrace a variety of tones, styles, language, and themes. While an essay is a *written* communication of an opinion or a point of view, a **speech** is a *spoken* communication about a topic.

A speech is similar to the essay in its organization. The speaker should have an interesting introduction, support for the main idea, and a strong conclusion.

Notable speeches include Abraham Lincoln's "Gettysburg Address," John F. Kennedy's "Inaugural Address," and Martin Luther King, Jr.'s "I Have a Dream." King's speech has been publicized, taped, and widely recognized as instrumental in the civil rights movement.

Because speeches are considered to be nonfiction, they can be analyzed by examining tone, style, message, and purpose. The following speech was delivered in 1805 by Sagoyewatha (Red Jacket), chief of the Seneca people and spokesperson for the Iroquois League, a confederation of six Native American nations. This speech was his answer to requests that the Native Americans be baptized into Christianity. As you read, ask yourself these questions: What is the great water? The island? The Book? The Great Spirit?

EXERCISE 9: INTERPRETING A SPEECH

Directions: Read the passage below and answer the questions that follow.

WHY DOES SAGOYEWATHA REJECT THE WHITE PEOPLE'S RELIGION?

Your forefathers crossed the great water and landed on this island. Their numbers were small. They found friends and not enemies. They told us they had fled from their own country for fear of wicked men and had come here to enjoy their religion. They asked for a small seat. We took pity on them, granted their request, and they sat down among us. We gave them corn and meat; they gave us poison in return.

Brother, our seats were once large and yours were small. You have now become a great people, and we have scarcely a place left to spread our blankets. You have got our country, but are not satisfied; you want to force your religion upon us.

Brother, continue to listen. You say that you are sent to instruct us how to worship the Great Spirit agreeably to His mind; and, if we do not take hold of the religion which you white people teach we shall be unhappy hereafter. You say that you are right and we are lost. How do we know this to be true? We understand that your religion is written in a Book. If it was intended for us, as well as you, why has not the Great Spirit given to us, and not only to us, but why did He not give to our forefathers the knowledge of that Book, with the means of understanding it rightly? We only know what you tell us about it. How shall we know when to believe, being so often deceived by the white people?

Brother, you say there is but one way to worship and serve the Great Spirit. If there is but one religion, why do you white people differ so much about it? Why do not all agree, as you can all read the Book?

1. In the lines, "Brother, our seats were once large and yours were small. You have now become a great people, and we have scarcely a place left to spread our blankets," the word *great* refers to white people's

   (1) generosity
   (2) kindness
   (3) increased population
   (4) evil intentions
   (5) honesty

2. The statement quoted in question 1 refers to the Native Americans' loss of

   (1) food   (2) land   (3) blankets   (4) religion   (5) buffalo

3. The statement "They told us they had fled from their own country for fear of wicked men and had come here to enjoy their religion" makes the Native Americans' situation ironic because it refers to the

   (1) English citizens' seeking religious freedom in America
   (2) way the white people had been treated by the Native Americans
   (3) beginning of the Revolutionary War
   (4) settlers' rejecting all religions
   (5) worship of the Great Spirit

4. Sagoyewatha's tone expresses

   (1) faith in the white people
   (2) distrust of the white people
   (3) loyalty to American government
   (4) lack of faith in the Great Spirit
   (5) willingness to convert to Christianity

5. Sagoyewatha demonstrates that he is skeptical about the assertion that there is only one true religion. He points out that

   (1) all white people cannot even agree about the Book
   (2) the Indians cannot read the Book
   (3) the Great Spirit wrote the Book for Indians only
   (4) the Native Americans fear baptism
   (5) the Native Americans will have to move closer to churches

Answers are on page 554.

EXERCISE 10: MORE PRACTICE INTERPRETING SPEECHES

Directions: The following passage is from John F. Kennedy's "Inaugural Address." Read the excerpt and answer the questions that follow.

WHAT DOES THE PRESIDENT ASK OF HIS FELLOW CITIZENS?

In your hands, my fellow citizens, more than mine, will rest the final success or failure of our course. Since this country was founded, each generation of Americans has been summoned to give testimony to its national loyalty. The graves of young Americans who answered the call to service surround the globe.

Now the trumpet summons us again—not as a call to bear arms, though arms we need; not as a call to battle, though embattled we are; but a call to bear the burden of a long twilight struggle, year in and year out, "rejoicing in hope, patient in tribulation," a struggle against the common enemies of man: tyranny, poverty, disease and war itself.

Can we forge against these enemies a grand and global alliance, North and South, East and West, that can assure a more fruitful life for all mankind? Will you join me in this historic effort?

In the long history of the world, only a few generations have been granted the role of defending freedom in its hour of maximum danger. I do not shrink from this responsibility; I welcome it. I do not believe that any of us would exchange places with any other people or any other generation. The energy, the faith, the devotion which we bring to this endeavor will light our country and all who serve it, and the glow from that fire can truly light the world.

And so, my fellow Americans, ask not what your country can do for you; ask what you can do for your country.

My fellow citizens of the world, ask not what America will do for you, but what together we can do for the freedom of man.

1. The tone of the speech can best be characterized as

    (1) sarcastic
    (2) light-hearted
    (3) angry
    (4) uplifting
    (5) sad

2. One of the purposes of the speech is to motivate listeners to

    (1) preserve the right to bear arms
    (2) enlist in the armed services
    (3) serve their country
    (4) take an oath swearing to their national loyalty
    (5) prepare themselves for battle

3. In the speech, Kennedy paints a picture of the United States as a nation that is

    (1) on the brink of world war
    (2) longing to return to the past
    (3) the leading defender of freedom
    (4) struggling to survive
    (5) weakened by citizens whose major interest is self-gain

4. The speech is characterized by all of the following stylistic devices *except*

    (1) a standard, predictable rhythm and the use of rhyme
    (2) the use of the personal pronouns *we* and *us* to build rapport with listeners
    (3) catchy turns of phrase in which subjects and objects are inverted
    (4) the repetition of key words
    (5) questions that invite readers to answer "yes" silently

Answers are on page 554.

Commentary

Commentary is a form of nonfiction in which the writer comments about literature and the arts: film, television, dance, music, art, and theater. A person who writes commentary—a critic—evaluates a work of art and assesses the work's strengths and weaknesses.

You have already seen an example of commentary at the end of each of the fiction, poetry, and drama sections. As a result of reading these commentaries, you already know that a review often discusses the work of art and the artist and presents the critic's opinion of both.

The Style and Language of Commentary

Because a critic or reviewer is both describing and analyzing a work of art, the style and language of commentary is often highly descriptive.

The reader of commentary must be able to analyze style as well as tone to evaluate the reviewer's judgment about a work of art.

Reading on Two Levels

To understand criticism, you must be able to read on two levels. First, you must understand facts about both the work of art and its creator. Then, you have to understand the critic's opinions. Below are the opening lines of a review of a popular nonfiction book.

Father of the Year
by Barbara E. Anderson
A review of *Fatherhood* by Bill Cosby

Every father must read Bill Cosby's *Fatherhood*! Cosby's comedic treatment of such an important role in society entertains while it instructs fathers how to become better at such a formidable job.

Over the years, many of us have bought his albums and have been delighted by his presence in many commercials. For the past few years, Americans have planned their evenings around the popular "Cosby Show," so it should be no surprise that his book is at the top of the best-seller list.

The following facts are covered in the review:

* Title of book being reviewed: *Fatherhood*
* Author of book: Bill Cosby
* Reviewer: Barbara Anderson

In addition to the facts about *Fatherhood*, the reviewer offers her opinion of the book. Choose the number of the answer that best completes the three questions below.

1. Anderson's opinion about *Fatherhood* might *best* be described as

    (1) unfavorable **(2)** lukewarm **(3)** very favorable

2. A reliable clue to Anderson's opinion about the book might be

    (1) her knowledge about Cosby's television exposure
    (2) the title of her review
    (3) her reference to his albums and popular show

3. Anderson's tone might *best* be described as

    (1) academic **(2)** enthusiastic **(3)** humorous

In answering question 1, you should have circled choice (3). Phrases in the review that indicate Anderson's favorable opinion of *Fatherhood* are "Every father must read Bill Cosby's *Fatherhood*"; "Cosby's comedic treatment of such an important role . . . entertains while it instructs"; and "it should be no surprise that his book is at the top of the best-seller list."

In answer to question 2, you should have circled choice (2), since the title of the review, "Father of the Year," best indicates the reviewer's favorable opinion of the book.

In answer to question 3, you should have circled choice (2). The reviewer's statement "Every father must read Bill Cosby's *Fatherhood*" indicates enthusiastic support for the book.

TIPS FOR READING LITERARY CRITICISM

When you read literary criticism, ask yourself these questions:

1. What does the critic say about the author or the author's abilities?

2. What does the critic like about the literary work? What does the critic dislike about the work? Look for words that communicate the critic's feelings about the work.

3. What statements are based on facts about the work? What statements are based on the critic's opinion or personal reaction to the work?

4. Does the critic recommend the work? Does the critic recognize the literary value of the work?

EXERCISE 11: INTERPRETING A BOOK REVIEW

Read the following review of a novel and answer the questions that follow.

A Review of *Looking for Bobby* by Gloria Norris, Knopf, $15.95

    The narrator of this often funny novel, Marianne, is a Mississippi woman just awakening to the fact that although her husband is rich and handsome and practically perfect, their marriage was a mistake. She runs off to New York City, hoping to find her first cousin Bobby. Once when they were children and she was lost on a fox hunting trip, Bobby found her and said, "Even if you were a thousand miles away, I would still be close to you and know what you're thinking. No matter what happens, when we grow up, I'll always be there right by you. All you ever have to do is think about me and I'll be close." The descriptions of Marianne's courtship and marriage, her talkative mother-in-law, and the New Orleans scenes are all wonderful. But problems mount, even for a sympathetic reader, when Marianne, in New York, learns that Bobby has switched from selling stocks to directing a play off-Broadway. A producer's lunch at Sardi's is preposterous, and Bobby and his much discussed charisma become equally unbelievable. Nothing that he does makes him appear to the reader as magnetic as he seems to everyone in the book. Then, thanks to Bobby, Marianne gets into show business and becomes a successful agent. She also bumps into him in Mexico and learns his secret. What she finds out about his past isn't all that surprising—a good therapist ought to be able to straighten him out in a couple of weeks. Norris, who has had several short stories published, is skillful at creating eccentric, oversized characters, but they are a lot more fun in the Deep South than when she wedges them into the tritely portrayed showbiz worlds of New York or Hollywood.

Directions: Write a (+) in the blank if the following statement is a positive opinion, (−) if the statement is a negative opinion, and (*F*) if the statement is only a fact about the novel's plot.

_____ **1.** "The narrator of this often funny novel, Marianne, is a Mississippi woman. . . ."

_____ **2.** "She runs off to New York City, hoping to find her first cousin Bobby."

_____ **3.** "The descriptions of Marianne's courtship and marriage, her talkative mother-in-law, and the New Orleans scenes are all wonderful."

_____ **4.** "But problems mount, even for a sympathetic reader, when Marianne, in New York, learns that Bobby has switched from selling stocks to directing a play off-Broadway."

_____ **5.** "A producer's lunch at Sardi's is preposterous, and Bobby and his much described charisma become equally unbelievable."

_____ **6.** "Nothing that he does makes him appear to the reader as magnetic as he seems to everyone in the book."

_____ **7.** "She also bumps into him in Mexico and learns his secret."

Answers are on page 554.

EXERCISE 12: INTERPRETING A REVIEW OF A NOVEL

Directions: Choose the best answer to each question below.

1. The critic's least favorite character in the book is

    (1) Marianne
    (2) Marianne's husband
    (3) Bobby
    (4) the mother-in-law
    (5) the producer

2. The critic says, "Norris, who has had several short stories published, is skillful at creating eccentric, oversized characters. . . ." In this quotation, the term *oversized* means

    (1) large; overweight
    (2) too many characters for the length of the book
    (3) inappropriate; out of place
    (4) bossy; overbearing; rude
    (5) memorable; unique

3. The critic would agree with which of the following statements?

    (1) Norris should write short stories, not novels.
    (2) A major flaw in the novel is the way the New York scenes are written.
    (3) The most exciting scenes in the novel are set in Mexico.
    (4) *Looking for Bobby* is an exceptionally well-written novel.
    (5) The character of Marianne should be better developed.

4. The reviewer states, "But problems mount, even for a sympathetic reader. . . ." The word *but* indicates

    (1) that the author of the review is not a sympathetic reader
    (2) a shift from praise to criticism of the book
    (3) the reviewer's contempt for the author of the book
    (4) the author's sympathy for Marianne
    (5) a new complication in the plot events

Answers are on page 554.

Satire in Nonfiction

Satire is a literary form that uses ridicule and irony to expose people's faults or behavior. Often utilizing exaggerated characters or circumstances, satire is used in both fiction and nonfiction.

The following piece of commentary is a review of a nonfiction book that was written to poke fun at a department of the U.S. government. The book, written in the form of a catalog, is a satire. The reviewer uses direct quotations from the book to help make his opinion clear to the reader.

EXERCISE 13: REVIEW OF A SATIRE

Directions: Read the following review and answer the questions that follow. Be sure to distinguish facts about the book from the reviewer's opinion about it.

WHAT IS THE REVIEWER'S OPINION ABOUT THIS SATIRE ON PENTAGON SPENDING?

Review of *The Pentagon Catalog: Ordinary Products at Extraordinary Prices*, compiled by Christopher Cerf and Henry Beard
Reviewed by Clarence Petersen, *Chicago Tribune*

"Buy this catalog for only $4.95," begins the irresistible offer on the cover, "and get this $2,043 nut for FREE!" And there, beautifully mounted on the cover, is a shiny hex nut of genuine steel construction, with center hole, threads, six equal sides and beveled edges. I screwed mine onto the rear axle of my bicycle, and you can imagine what this has done for the resale value of an ordinary Schwinn 10-speed. This is a funny book indeed, taken from real life, as well as from congressional investigations, news reports and expert testimony presented on "Donahue," which together have driven Cap Weinberger right up the wall. It offers a slim, durable flat washer for only $387, a deluxe, lightweight toilet seat for only $640.09, a space-age coffeemaker for only $7,622 and a P-3 Orion luncheon refrigerator for only $12,000. "And remember," the catalog promises, "When you buy from us, you're backed by this unique pledge: If you find that any of the products listed in this catalog are offered for sale by a retail outlet or mail-order company at a higher price, bring us that price and we will top it. *We will not be oversold!*"

1. All of the following are sources of information contained in this nonfiction book *except*

    (1) real life
    (2) expert testimony on a television talk show
    (3) news reports
    (4) mail-order catalogs
    (5) congressional investigations

2. The critic thinks the authors of the book are

    (1) too sarcastic
    (2) very funny
    (3) uninformed
    (4) unfair
    (5) too serious

3. The book satirizes, or pokes fun at,

(1) Pentagon spending
(2) TV talk shows
(3) catalogs
(4) the president
(5) the high price of hardware

4. The tone of the book and the style in which it is written are similar to

(1) a television talk show host
(2) a formal speech; a lecture
(3) a forceful advertisement; a sales pitch
(4) the military's approach in recruiting
(5) a soft sell approach to marketing a product

5. The reviewer relies heavily on quotations from the book to

(1) show that he read it
(2) illustrate how ridiculous it is
(3) support his opposition to Pentagon spending
(4) help his readers get a feeling for the book's humor
(5) encourage the readers to order from the catalog

Answers are on page 555.

Interpreting Other Forms of Commentary

The following three reviews are commentaries on music, art, and television. As you read each review, look for specific qualities of the work that each critic is evaluating. Ask yourself:

- What facts about the work itself does the critic include?

- Does the critic like or dislike this work? Why?

- What does the critic say about the background of the artist?

- What is the critic's style? How does he or she present the message?

EXERCISE 14: INTERPRETING MUSICAL COMMENTARY

Directions: Read the music review below and answer the questions that follow.

WHO IS WYNTON MARSALIS, AND WHAT DOES THIS CRITIC THINK OF HIM?

Review of *Hot House Flowers* by Wynton Marsalis
(A Four Star Review) ★★★★

Jazz history can be traced through the arrival of precociously talented trumpet players who revolutionize the way jazz is perceived, both by the public and by the musicians who play it. King Oliver, Louis Armstrong, Roy Eldridge, Dizzy Gillespie, Clifford Brown, Miles Davis, Lee Morgan and Lester Bowie, among others, came on the scene and turned everything upside down by forging new directions or simply making obvious something that had been overlooked. Though he has only made three albums as a leader, Wynton Marsalis has already joined this elite, at least by reputation.

Part of what distinguishes Marsalis is that he has seemingly assimilated jazz history at the tender age of twenty-three. At this point only his beautiful tone and impressive technique are his own, for he has chosen to work, for the most part, in familiar styles. Therein may lie the key to his genius. Marsalis has avoided the trap so many young players fall into of trying to be different just for the sake of being different. Marsalis obviously relishes drawing comparisons to Miles Davis of the fifties on "Melancholis." His specialty is acknowledging such a debt, then playing in such a way as to make it totally an expression of himself. The fact that Wynton Marsalis is also an accomplished classical player may explain in part his understanding of how a tradition can be nurtured rather than just copied.

1. This review reveals the critic's

    (1) dislike of young musicians
    (2) admiration and appreciation of Marsalis
    (3) bias against older, familiar jazz styles
    (4) lack of knowledge about classical jazz musicians
    (5) belief that classical music is better than jazz

2. According to the critic, Marsalis is unique because of his

    (1) application of his own technique to traditional jazz
    (2) mastery of a variety of instruments
    (3) long, established career
    (4) ability to play gospel as well as jazz
    (5) many television performances

3. Besides being a jazz musician, Marsalis also plays

    (1) country
    (2) rock
    (3) gospel
    (4) classical
    (5) rhythm and blues

4. The reviewer states, "a tradition can be nurtured rather than just copied." This statement supports the critic's belief that a musician should

    (1) ignore other musicians in his rise to fame
    (2) improve, not just repeat, the art
    (3) reject all musicians of the past
    (4) experiment with all types of music
    (5) record the music of previous artists

Answers are on page 555.

EXERCISE 15: INTERPRETING A PAINTING

Directions: Read the art review below and answer the questions that follow.

WHAT DOES THE CRITIC SEE IN WYETH'S WORK?

A Review of Artist Andrew Wyeth and His Work
by Frieda Davenport

We can take photographs to "freeze moments" in our memories. We do not consider ourselves artists, for we use the camera to capture the memory for us. When we see a painting which freezes a moment and gives meaning to it, we know art.

Andrew Wyeth, one of the most popular American artists of our time, has the ability to capture moments on canvas. His temperas and watercolors present natural colors—earth tones of browns, greys, and muted shades of pink. He uses white as no other artist has.

Wyeth's subjects and landscapes are rural. His compositions reflect a thoughtful simplicity as if he has created "impressionistic" photographs. Not only is a landscape captured but a subject against a horizon, old farmhouses, bruised buckets, torn lace curtains, and window frames.

To learn about Wyeth is to see one of his paintings—*Christina's World* (1948)—his most well-known work. Christina, an actual friend of his, is in a crawling position with her back to the observer. She leans into, perhaps yearning for, a farmhouse on the horizon. Centered on the painting and on the horizon is an out-shed, a barn, which is to the left of the house.

The three focal points—the girl, the barn, and the farmhouse—are "balanced" on a grassy, barren field. The "plainness" is characteristic of Wyeth. Each time we look at the painting, we are drawn to Christina, the "center" of the painting and of her world.

Wyeth is often categorized as an American Realist, but to label artists is to limit our views of their accomplishments. The simplicity of Wyeth's work discourages complexity of thought, and we are left to thoroughly enjoy the moment that he creates for us.

1. The review discusses all of the following *except*

   (1) the popularity of the artist
   (2) the types of paints and techniques used
   (3) the artist's preference in colors
   (4) a specific painting
   (5) the price of one of Wyeth's paintings

2. The critic is most impressed with Wyeth's

   (1) development of new techniques
   (2) use of earth tones
   (3) fame and fortune
   (4) ability to capture a specific moment
   (5) use of "balance" in the paintings

3. The quality that the critic likes most in *Christina's World* is Wyeth's

(1) accuracy
(2) colors
(3) simplicity
(4) complexity
(5) portrayal of the 1940s

Answers are on page 555.

Interpreting a Television Review

Most of the reviews you have been reading deal with a specific work. The critic reacts to one book, film, or work of art. However, criticism may discuss trends or characteristics of one type of art.

The following television review presents views not only about a specific show but about the nature of TV programming. As you read, look for statements of facts and statements of opinion. Remember that most reviews are persuasive essays. The critic's purpose is illustrated with details and examples. Notice this critic's style, tone, and use of language.

EXERCISE 16: INTERPRETING A TELEVISION REVIEW

Directions: Read the television review below and answer the questions that follow.

HOW DOES THE REVIEWER RATE THE "ALL-TIME BEST" SITCOMS?

"M*A*S*H"

Where "Lucy" created a new comic form for TV, and "All in the Family" used social issues for comic fodder, "M*A*S*H" did what only the greatest— the classic—comedies do: mix hilarity and tragedy, often in equal measure. "M*A*S*H" made us laugh till we cried. And though its anti-war message occasionally got heavy-handed, it was never at the expense of laughter or character. Like all great sitcoms, it succeeded mainly by exploring, indeed celebrating, the chemistry between the characters. The last episode of "M*A*S*H" was the most-watched program in TV history for good reason. Yes, the final episode of "Cheers" may yet rival it, but "M*A*S*H" has an underriding urgency to its comedy—it's about life, death, war, and the redeeming grace of humor—that makes it, in our eyes, the best sitcom in history.

1. If you were retitling the review, which of the following titles would you choose?

(1) Keeping It All in the Family
(2) How "Lucy" Changed Our Viewing
(3) Watching the Last of the Best
(4) Is TV Getting Better or Worse?
(5) Laughing and Crying with a Classic

2. The comment "And though its anti-war message occasionally got heavy-handed" suggests the reviewer's belief that

(1) sitcoms like "M*A*S*H" might sometimes be about war
(2) the sitcom's characters were sometimes interesting
(3) sometimes the show was about hand-to-hand combat
(4) sometimes the message against war was too obvious
(5) the sitcom's characters sometimes got into fights

3. The reviewer would agree that a sitcom that hopes to become the best in history must

(1) contain very powerful anti-war messages
(2) have strong relationships among characters
(3) closely follow the comic form of the "Lucy" show
(4) use "All in the Family" as a writing blueprint
(5) use humor to cover up the tragedy in a story

4. The reviewer's statement that "'M*A*S*H' has an underriding urgency to its comedy" means

(1) stunts with horses were used in the show
(2) the humor in the show was always fast-paced
(3) there was always a deeper reason for the humor
(4) shows were always written at the last minute
(5) there was always someone facing danger

5. You are eager to write a good TV sitcom. After reading the review, which of the following "rules" would you observe?

(1) Being funny is more important than developing good characters.
(2) Good one-liners can make or break a show.
(3) Social issues do not belong on television.
(4) War should be dealt with in a serious way.
(5) Mix humor and tragedy in balanced amounts.

6. What is the tone of the review?

(1) appreciative
(2) questioning
(3) uncomplimentary
(4) irresolute
(5) sarcastic

Answers are on page 555.

TEST 4: LITERATURE AND THE ARTS ANSWER KEY

CHAPTER 1: INTERPRETING PROSE FICTION

Exercise 1: Identifying Setting
page 456
Inferential

1. Yun-ja is in the water, swimming. The clues are "floated on the blue swells," "the water chilled her," and "ripples slapped about her ears."

2. She is in a public place frequented by people from many different countries, as evidenced by the fact that she can hear "the babble of English, Spanish, and other tongues. . . ."

3. Chong-il is relaxing on the beach. Note the clue that reads, "There he [Chong-il] was, sitting under the beach umbrella . . . drinking something."

4. The story is set in the present. The clue is "She heard the drone of powerboats. . . ."

5. The action takes place during the day. The clue is the reference to "the dazzling sun."

Exercise 2: Atmosphere as Part of Setting
page 457
Inferential

1. The atmosphere of the passage is one of fear.

2. The words that indicate fear are *crouching, running, dodging, hide,* and *stiffened.*

Exercise 3: Inferring Character
page 458
Literal

1. (5) Only choice (5) describes Slim's personality; the other choices are physical descriptions.

2. (4) The descriptions of Slim are the only information we have about his character.

Exercise 4: Identifying Characters Through Dialogue
pages 460–461
Literal

1. mother and adult child

2. the mother

3. the adult child

4. the adult child

5. The mother is an elderly Chinese woman who likes to complain. The adult child is a level-headed person who appears to be used to the mother's complaining.

Exercise 5: Identifying Details of Setting, Plot, and Conflict
pages 463–464
Literal

1. Line 22: "There aren't any grownups. We shall have to look after ourselves."

2. Lines 5–7: "We're on an island. . . ."

3. a pig; line 10 states, "There are pigs on the island."

4. Ralph; The line "we need hunters to get us meat" (line 19) and the author's statement that Ralph "looked round the sun-slashed faces" (line 21) suggest that Ralph is leading the meeting.

Inferential

5. Individual vs. nature; the boys have to adapt to the island. Individual vs. society; the boys have to deal with each other without grownups. Individual vs. another; Ralph and Jack are in conflict.

Literal

6. 4, 3, 1, 5, 2

Exercise 6: Determining Point of View
page 466
Application

The words you should have underlined are in italic type and the circled words appear in bold type.

Macomber stepped out of the curved opening at the side of the front seat onto the step and down onto the ground. The **lion** still stood looking majestically and coolly toward this object that **his** eyes only showed in silhouette, bulging like some super-rhino. There was no man smell carried toward **him** and **he** watched the object [jeep], moving **his** great head a little from side to side. Then watching the object, not afraid, but hesitating before going down the bank to drink with such a thing opposite **him**, **he** saw a *man figure* detach *itself* from it and **he** turned **his** heavy head and swung away toward the cover of the trees as **he** heard a cracking crash and felt the slam of a .30–06 220-grain solid bullet that bit **his** flank and ripped in sudden hot scalding nausea through **his** stomach. **He** trotted, heavy, big-footed, swinging wounded full-bellied, through the trees toward the tall grass and cover, and the crash came again to go past **him** ripping the air apart. Then it crashed again and **he** felt the blow as it hit **his** lower ribs and ripped on through, blood sudden hot and frothy in **his** mouth, and **he** galloped toward the high grass where **he** could crouch and not be seen and make *them* bring the crashing thing close enough so **he** could make a rush and get the *man* that held it.

Exercise 7: Inferring Theme
page 467
Inferential

1. **(5)** All of the incidents concern Miss Strangeworth's sending anonymous letters.

2. **(5)** The excerpt concerns Miss Strangeworth's fighting "possible evil lurking nearby."

3. **(3)** While Miss Strangeworth's motives may have seemed good to her, her actions hurt innocent people.

Exercise 8: Review of Five Fiction Elements
pages 468–469
Inferential

1. **(3)** The first two sentences state that "Ivan Ilych saw that he was dying, and he was in continual despair. In the depth of his heart he knew he was dying, but not only was he not accustomed to the thought, he simply did not and could not grasp it."

2. **(4)** Note the use of the word *he* to refer to Ivan Ilych. The third-person narrator is never named and does not take part in the action.

3. **(2)** Most of the passage consists of Ilych's thoughts about death and his desperate attempts to erase the thoughts from his mind.

4. **(1)** As the second sentence states, "[Ilych] simply did not and could not grasp it [his impending death]."

5. **(1)** Paragraph four states that Ilych would "go to the law courts."

Exercise 9: Tone and Characterization
page 470
Analysis

1. **(1)** The passage states that Julian's mother "said ladies did not tell their age or weight" (lines 5–6) and that "she would not ride buses by herself at night since they had been integrated" (lines 6–7). This suggests that Julian's mother subscribes to old-fashioned values.

2. **(4)** The last two sentences point to a funny and sarcastic tone of voice.

3. **(3)** The author seems to feel that people like Julian's mother require tolerance and sympathy.

Exercise 10: Identifying an Author's Style
page 472
Analysis

The descriptions and images that appeal to the senses appear in italic type.

The *soprano screak* of *carriage wheels punished my ear*. Sun, *seeping through the blinds, filled the bedroom* with a *sulphurous light*. I didn't know how long I had slept, but I *felt one big twitch of exhaustion*.

The twin bed next to mine was empty and unmade.

At seven I had *heard my mother get up, slip into her clothes* and *tiptoe out of the room*. Then the *buzz of the orange squeezer sounded* from downstairs, and the *smell of coffee and bacon filtered under my door*. Then the *sink water ran from the tap and dishes clinked* as my mother dried them and put them back in the cupboard.

Then the *front door opened and shut*. Then the *car door opened and shut*, and the *motor went broom-broom* and, edging off with a *crunch of gravel, faded into the distance*.

Exercise 11: Descriptive Language
page 473
Application

1. d   2. a   3. c   4. b

Exercise 12: Identifying Figures of Speech
pages 474–475
Analysis

Words underlined include: *a whisper of a woman* (metaphor)
like a fox moving in for the kill (simile)
Grandma would become a cyclone. (metaphor)
Her ax, a bloody character that seemed to lie in wait for hens, would sever the head. (personification)
like a savage in an ancient tribal rite (simile)
My microwave oven lazily sits waiting (personification)

Analysis

1. **(3)** "Whisper of a woman" is a metaphor referring to her size.

2. **(4)** Personification is used to make the ax seem human.

Inferential

3. **(1)** The author is looking back with nostalgia.

4. **(3)** Grandma's killing of a chicken is contrasted to present-day shopping habits and microwave meals.

5. **(5)** The last paragraph expresses this sentiment.

**Exercise 13: Interpreting a
Short Story
pages 476–480
Literal**
1. rooftop, civil war, Dublin, Ireland,
   June, city, night

Analysis
2. (5) Because of the subject of the
   story, war, the atmosphere may be
   best described as tense.

Literal
3. c, b, b, a

Analysis
4. 3, 2, 5, 4, 1

Inferential
5. The author lets us know the thoughts
   of only the sniper to create an
   atmosphere of suspense.

Analysis
6. Third person; the references *he* and
   they indicate third-person narration
7. (1) The author reports the incidents
   in a controlled and unemotional
   manner.

Application
8. s, m, p, p, s

Inferential
9. (4) The figures of speech "grey
   monster" and "like a thousand
   devils" suggest the author's
   attitude toward the horror of war.

Analysis
10. (3) The point of highest intensity in
    the story is when the sniper kills
    the enemy.

Inferential
11. (4) The lines reflect the sniper's inner
    struggle.
12. (2) To show remorse means to express
    guilt.

Analysis
13. (5) The author explores human
    behavior by showing the sniper's
    character. Because of the sniper's
    "lust for battle," he kills his
    brother.

**Exercise 14: Commentary
About Fiction
page 482
Literal**
1. (2) The review states that "one wants
   to follow Putus's life as a young
   woman instead of returning to her
   decades later. . . ."

Inferential
2. (1) The last sentence of the review
   makes it clear that the reviewer
   admires the writer's story-telling
   abilities.

Application
3. (4) The review of the book indicates
   that it fits only the real-life drama
   category.

CHAPTER 2: INTERPRETING POETRY

**Exercise 1: Interpreting Two Poems
pages 483–484
Inferential**
1. (4) Romantic love is mentioned in both
   poems; it is referred to repeatedly
   in Sonnet 43.

Analysis
2. (3) Both poems include rhyme.
   Rhyming words in "Oh, When I
   Was in Love with You" include *you*
   and *grew*; *brave* and *behave*, and
   remain and *again*; rhyming words
   in Sonnet 43 include *height* and
   sight.

**Exercise 2: The Shape of Poetry
pages 487–488
Literal**
1. There are three sentences; a period
   ends each sentence.
2. The third stanza refers to Grandma's
   life as a younger woman. She had been
   (1) a migrant "cutting grapes and
   boxing plums." (2) She had had
   tapeworm and diseased skin. (3) Her
   son had died. (4) She had been sad
   and had traveled to various locations
   to work in the fields.

Inferential
3. The first stanza tells of her later years,
   of a happier life. At the end of the
   second stanza, Grandma smiles. *Smiled*
   is the clue word that indicates the
   mood of contentment.
4. The narrator is the grandchild of a
   Hispanic migrant farm worker.
5. Grandma was a migrant farm worker.
   The clues are "cutting grapes and
   boxing plums" and "that pulled her
   from Taxco to San Joaquin, Delano
   to Westside."

**Exercise 3: The Sound of Poetry
page 489
Analysis**
1. Some different examples of alliteration
   are:
   (1) "maggie and milly and molly and
       may"
   (2) "a shell that sang / so sweetly
       she . . ."
   (3) "blowing bubbles"
   (4) "smooth round stone / as
       small . . ."
   (You may have found others)
2. Lines 3 and 4 and 7 and 8 do not rhyme
   at all.
3. There are four "beats" per line.

Inferential

4. (4) The author is saying that when we "lose" ourselves at the beach, it's because we become interested in something outside ourselves: the water, the fish, the shells, the sand, etc. This gives us a new view on life.

Exercise 4: Words that Stand for Sounds
pages 490–491
Analysis

1. (5) *b*atter and *b*anjos; alliteration is a repetition of a beginning consonant sound.

2. (3) The word *like* makes a comparison between two things—moan and autumn wind. The sound of the autumn wind is given a human quality.

Application

3. (4) In *The Bell Jar*, Plath uses sound words such as *screak, buzz, clinked,* and *broom-broom.* Examples of alliteration are *soprano screak* and *sun seeping.*

Exercise 5: Inferring Meaning
page 492
Inferential

2. Inference: The man prays./ Line numbers: 13–15/ Key words: *reverently, prayer, give thanks*

3. Inference: The man was a farmer./ Line numbers: 4, 5/ Key words: *tossed bales of straw each August*

4. Inference: The man is now elderly./ Line numbers: 11–12/ Key words: *now crudely arches to grasp a bamboo cane.*/ Line number: 14/ Key words: *bow your feeble body in prayer*

5. Inference: The man was athletic./ Line number: 6/ Key words: *once pitched no-hitters*

Exercise 6: Interpreting a Poem
page 494
Inference

1. (3) The title of the poem, "The Negro Speaks of Rivers," is a clue to the narrator's identity. "My soul" refers to a person of African descent, speaking for the race.

Analysis

2. (4) This is a positive image and probably refers to Lincoln's freeing the slaves. He "heard" the "singing" of the river, and the bosom of the river "turned golden."

3. (2) The poem mentions four great rivers of the world that are associated with African and African-American people: the Euphrates, the Congo, the Nile, and the Mississippi.

Exercise 7: The Language of Poetry
page 496
Analysis
Line 1: *imagery*
Line 2: *personification*
Line 3: *personification*
Line 4: *imagery*
Line 5: *personification*

Exercise 8: Review of Figurative Language and Theme
page 498
Analysis

1. (3) "Holding wonder like a cup"; *like* is a word that identifies a simile.

2. (5) In line 8, the speaker compares music to "a curve of gold."

3. (4) Thoughts are compared to stars.

Exercise 9: Interpreting a Poem
page 499
Analysis

1. fish

2. the moon

Exercise 10: More Practice in Interpreting a Poem
pages 499–500
Literal

1. b, c, a, e, d

Analysis

2. (3) Death and Immortality are characters who ride in the carriage with the narrator.

3. (2) The lines "Because I could not stop for Death, He kindly stopped for me" are an example of personification—giving human qualities to an abstraction.

Inferential

4. (5) The title of the poem and lines 1–2 imply that the narrator of the poem was full of life and died unexpectedly.

5. (5) From the last stanza, we can infer that the poet believes that the narrator was taken from earth but lives on.

Exercise 11: More Practice in Interpreting a Poem
page 501
Inferential

1. (4) The narrator of the poem "The Man from Washington" is a Native American. Clue words to this are: *firewood and buffalo robes, rainwater eyes, treaties signed, a world in which we had no part.*

Analysis

2. (1) The mood of the poem is one of alienation. Clue words are *would be innoculated against a world in which we had no part, a world of wealth, promise, and fabulous disease.*

3. (4) The theme of this poem concerns the loss of self-determination and the way of life for the Native American.

Exercise 12: Commentary on Poetry
page 502
Inferential

1. (2) The reviewer (quoting Shakespeare's *Hamlet*) states "that 'the slings and arrows of outrageous fortune' are often gifts which make us stronger."

2. (1) This is a simpler rewording of the cliché.

CHAPTER 3: INTERPRETING DRAMA

Exercise 1: How Drama Differs
page 505
Analysis

1. (c) Drama shows the words and actions of characters in a real-life setting.

2. (b) The poetry version is written in verse with concise images.

3. (c) We can "see" the setting, the characters and how they react to each other.

4. (c) In drama, character is revealed through dialogue and action.

5. (a) The prose version summarizes the action and is written in simple sentence form.

Exercise 2: Dialogue and Punctuation
page 506
Literal

1. Edward and Victoria; the ellipses indicate that Catherine interrupts Edward's speech.

2. Edward; both of Edward's speeches are questions.

3. Edward; Edward is bothered by Catherine's interruption.

4. Edward; Victoria's tone and responses to Edward indicate that she is upset with him.

Exercise 3: Inferring Mood from Dialogue
page 506
Analysis

(1) The rudeness of Edward toward Catherine, Victoria's responses to Edward, and Catherine's abrupt departure all indicate that the mood of the scene is tense.

Exercise 4: Identifying Characters
page 509
Literal

1. b   2. c   3. d   4. e   5. f   6. a

Exercise 5: History of Drama
pages 509–510
Literal

1. (4) Choices (1), (2), (3), and (5) are stated in the scene. Choice (4) is contrary to the information provided in the scene.

Analysis

2. (1) The setting—Miss Anderson seated on her desktop—and her students' humorous responses indicate that the mood is informal.

3. (4) Miss Anderson's manner and tone in responding to Pete's antics indicate that her approach is casual.

Inferential

4. (2) Miss Anderson's discussion of Shakespeare, especially her remark "and all of it written in verse form," indicates great admiration for Shakespeare.

5. (4) The stage directions that introduce the play state "The scene is a drama class where students are learning about the history of drama." Also, in her dialogue, Miss Anderson describes the origin and progression of Western drama.

Exercise 6: Understanding Character
pages 512–514
Inferential

1. (3) In the scene, Jessie's mother asks her a series of questions, including where Jessie put her glasses. Mama's initial statement, "I want to know why," and Jessie's response, "You have no earthly idea of how I feel," suggest that a lack of communication exists between mother and daughter. None of the other choices are supported adequately by the dialogue in the scene.

2. (4) The scene contains several lines of dialogue in which Mama criticizes Jessie for being ungrateful and distant. Also, Mama blames Jessie for Cecil's leaving.

3. (1) A line of Jessie's dialogue states, "smoking is the only thing I know that's always just what you think it's going to be. Just like it was the last time and right there when you want it and real quiet." This line suggests that Jessie likes smoking because its effect is something she can depend on.

4. (4) Because the dialogue between Jessie and her mother is angry and bitter, we can infer that Jessie is at odds with her mother.

Analysis

5. (4) The angry, accusing tone shown by Jessie's mother and Jessie's responses to her mother suggest a mood of tension.

Exercise 7: Supporting Facts and Inferences
page 514
Inferential

1. Support for the inference that Jessie has epilepsy are the lines of dialogue that refer to "seizures" and "fits." Mama asks Jessie, "When you have a fit do you see stars, or what?" and "Your fits made him sick."

2. Support for the inference that Jessie is separated from Cecil are the following lines: "Why did Cecil leave you?" "Cecil left me because he made me choose between him and smoking." "Cecil left for pretty much the same reason."

3. Support for the fact that Jessie smokes are the lines: "Cecil left me because he made me choose between him and smoking." Also "Smoking is the only thing I know . . ."

4. The inference that Jessie is confused about what her mother wants to know is supported by the lines of dialogue: "Back where?" "What are you talking about?"

5. Support for the inference that Mama doesn't believe Jessie's story about the accident is the line of dialogue, "How did you fall off the horse, really?"

Exercise 8: Interpreting a Scene from a Play
pages 514–516
Inferential

1. (3) Alice's second line of dialogue, in which she suggests finding a home for her senile father (like her husband Sidney did for his parents) and the discussion about powers of attorney imply that she and Gene are sister and brother. Another clue to their relationship comes later in the scene: "He broke Mother's heart over that for years."

Application

2. (5) Alice's first line of dialogue, in which she says "I'm doing a lot for my kids. I don't expect them to pay me back at the other end," suggests that she believes elderly parents should not expect their children to take care of them.

Inferential

3. (2) Alice says in the scene, "He kicked me out. He said he never wanted to see me again. He broke Mother's heart over that for years. He was mean, unloving." These lines of dialogue suggest resentment toward her father.

4. (1) In the scene, Alice says, "You've lived through a great deal of ugliness. But you work like a Trojan to deny it, to make it not so."

5. (2) Based on Gene's dialogue, he is not relieved; he is ashamed that he can't ask his father to live with him.

Literal

6. (4) Alice's last line of dialogue in the exchange tells Gene to let her handle it and not to give in.

7. (4) Gene's line, "I can't tell you how ashamed I feel . . . not to say with open arms, 'Poppa, come live with me. . . . I love you, Poppa, and I want to take care of you,'" indicates that he feels guilty for not loving his father.

Exercise 9: Interpreting a Film Review
pages 516–517
Analysis

1. (2) The fact that the novel *The Last Tycoon* was unfinished and that Pinter and Kazan nevertheless were able to turn the book into a "fascinating low-key film" implies an attitude of admiration.

2. (2) The figure of speech, "He sees life as a movie and people as shadows," is a simile; it uses the word *as* to compare two unlike things. It suggests that life is like a movie and people are like shadows.

Literal

3. (1) The passage states directly that "Stahr himself is a flawed human being."

Inferential

4. (5) Because "Hollywood Boosters" are supporters of Hollywood, and these supporters are likely to be movie producers, the implication is that the film will offend the producers of Hollywood films.

CHAPTER 4: INTERPRETING NONFICTION
Exercise 1: The Biography
pages 521–522
Literal

1. (4) The passage does not comment on Thoreau's writing style.

Analysis

2. **(5)** The significance of Thoreau's move to Walden Pond on July 4 is that the date is the anniversary of the nation's independence. On that date, Thoreau was declaring his own independence.

Application

3. **(4)** While secluded in the woods, Thoreau reflected on the meaning and beauty of life. The other choices have nothing to do with considering the meaning of life.

Literal

4. **(1)** The passage states that the essay "On the Duty of Civil Disobedience" influenced the works of Gandhi and Martin Luther King, Jr.

Inferential

5. **(2)** The passage states that Thoreau was imprisoned for refusing to pay a poll tax that supported the Mexican War. Thoreau's action is an example of nonviolent resistance to an unjust law.

6. **(2)** The quote reflects the ideal of individualism. No other choice listed is supported by the quote.

**Exercise 2: Oral History
pages 523–524
Literal**

1. **T** The passage refers to Chavez's parents and brothers and sisters.

2. **F** The passage relates sadness and hope and Chavez's belief that "you don't let [things] get you down."

3. **T** The passage states that his father never gave up hope.

4. **T** The passage says that when you're small, you don't question things; you continue to move.

5. **F** The last sentence of the passage says that "we had never been migratory workers."

6. **T** The passage states that " 'following the crops,' we missed much school."

7. **F** The entire passage describes the effect the Depression had on Chavez's family.

8. **F** The facts presented in the passage show that the speaker remembers many things about the Depression's impact on his family.

**Exercise 3: Autobiography
pages 525–526
Inferential**

1. **(2)** The word *pregnant* is connected with many unpleasant experiences that the writer faced, suggesting a burden he was carrying.

2. **(5)** The passage describes the teacher as being unaware, insensitive, and uninterested in the author. She is not described as being understanding.

Analysis

3. **(4)** The use of the word *pregnant* to mean "burdened with" is an example of the writer's unique mode of expression.

4. **(4)** The only similarity between Chavez's and Gregory's childhood is that both made successful lives despite their childhood poverty. Choices (1), (2), (3), and (5) are not true of *both* men's childhoods.

5. **(5)** The title suggests that people do not always think of themselves the way others might think of them. The other choices are not supported by the passage.

**Exercise 4: Journal Entries
page 526
Inferential**

1. **(5)** The quote refers to experimenting with life. Experimenting involves taking a risk. The other choices are not supported by the advice in the quote.

Application

2. **(3)** An astronaut's occupation involves a greater degree of physical risk than the other choices provided.

**Exercise 5: The Article as
Nonfiction
page 528
Inferential**

1. **(5)** The reference to the veterans as heroes suggests that the writer holds great admiration for the marchers.

Analysis

2. **(4)** The writer emphasizes the number thirteen to point out the positive outcome despite the parade's association with an unlucky number. The other choices are not supported by the information in the passage.

**Exercise 6: The Formal Essay
pages 529–530
Inferential**

1. **(4)** The word *duty* implies an obligation; therefore, the title suggests that a person is obligated to break an unjust law.

2. **(3)** The government represents the people and is the means by which a people carry out their desires. The other choices do not help to define government in this sense.

3. **(2)** The essay states that "The standing army is only an arm of the standing government."

4. (1) According to the essay, "The government . . . is only the mode which the people have chosen to execute their will."

5. (4) Emerson, who also believed in nonconformity, admired Thoreau's belief in individual liberty.

Exercise 7: Review of Thoreau
page 531
Application

1, 3, 4, and 5   Thoreau would have supported 1, 3, 4, and 5 because they further social justice and individual freedoms. Choices 2 and 6 limit individual freedoms; therefore, Thoreau would not have supported them.

Exercise 8: Comparing and Contrasting Styles
pages 531–534
Analysis

1. (3) The short essay is characterized by all of the choices given except long, explanatory paragraphs.

Inferential

2. (4) The statement and the entire thrust of the passage show the agent's total dependence on the computer.

Literal

3. (3) The agent is completely paralyzed by the situation in which the computer is down.

Analysis

4. (4) Passage 2 lacks the humor of Passage 1.

Inferential

5. (5) *Sweatshop* originally referred to nineteenth- and early twentieth-century factories in which workers labored long hours for low pay in unhealthy work conditions.

6. (3) Throughout the excerpt, the author talks about psychological problems caused by electronic offices—for example, "a rise in loneliness and disconnection" and "fragmentation of self."

Analysis

7. (1) The author briefly describes Nicholas's educational background and experience to let readers know that he is a reliable and expert source of opinion.

Application

8. (4) Both passages illustrate our dependence on and trust in computers. Both writers feel we should retain control over computers.

Exercise 9: Interpreting a Speech
pages 535–536
Inferential

1. (3) Because Sagoyewatha says that "we have scarcely a place left to spread our blankets," he is referring to the growth in numbers of the white population.

Literal

2. (2) *Place* is a clue to the land that Sagoyewatha speaks about.

Inferential

3. (1) The irony is that, while white people left their homeland to seek freedom of religion, they did not respect the Native Americans' choice to worship freely.

Analysis

4. (2) The speech refers to acts of betrayal by the white man; the tone is one of distrust.

Literal

5. (1) The speech concludes with the opinion that, though whites practice one religion, they do not all worship in the same way.

Exercise 10: More Practice Interpreting Speeches
pages 536–537
Analysis

1. (4) As the first speech of his presidency, Kennedy wants to inspire listeners.

2. (3) The most persuasive call to serve the public is in the second to the last paragraph: "ask not what your country can do for you; ask what you can do for your country."

Literal

3. (3) In paragraph 4, Kennedy says that "only a few generations have been granted the role of defending freedom in its hour of maximum danger."

Analysis

4. (1) The speech does not rhyme or display a standardized rhythmic pattern.

Exercise 11: Interpreting a Book Review
pages 539–540
Analysis

1. +   2. F   3. +   4. −   5. −   6. −   7. F

Exercise 12: Interpreting a Review of a Novel
page 540
Inferential

1. (3) The critic says, "Bobby and his much described charisma become equally unbelievable" and "Nothing that he does makes him appear to the reader as magnetic as he seems to everyone in the book."

Analysis

2. **(5)** The only choice that reflects on the author's skillfulness in creating characters are the words *memorable* and *unique*.

Application

3. **(2)** The statements "A producer's lunch at Sardi's is preposterous" and "tritely portrayed show-biz worlds of New York or Hollywood" reflect the critic's view that New York scenes are flawed.

Analysis

4. **(2)** Prior to this comment, the reviewer has said only positive things about the book. This quote indicates a shift to critical comments.

Exercise 13: Review of a Satire
pages 541–542
Literal

1. **(4)** "Mail-order catalogs" is the only choice listed that is not a source for information contained in the book.

2. **(2)** The review states, "This is a funny book indeed. . . ."

3. **(1)** The topic of the book is Pentagon spending.

Application

4. **(3)** The book begins with a forceful sales pitch.

Analysis

5. **(4)** The reviewer uses lots of quotes from the book to give his audience an appreciation of the book's humor.

Exercise 14: Interpreting Musical Commentary
pages 542–543
Inferential

1. **(2)** The reviewer describes Marsalis as belonging to an elite—a superior group. This statement indicates admiration for the musician.

Literal

2. **(1)** The review refers to Marsalis's "beautiful tone and impressive technique."

3. **(4)** The passage states that Marsalis also plays classical music.

Application

4. **(2)** *To nurture* means "to further one's development." This suggests that the critic supports Marsalis's improvement of the tradition.

Exercise 15: Interpreting a Painting
pages 544–545
Literal

1. **(5)** The only topic not discussed in the review is the cost of Wyeth's paintings.

2. **(4)** The review begins by discussing Wyeth's ability to capture a specific moment.

Inferential

3. **(3)** The passage refers to Wyeth's simplicity twice—"a thoughtful simplicity" and "The simplicity of Wyeth's work discourages complexity of thought. . . ."

Exercise 16: Interpreting a Television Review
pages 545–546
Inferential

1. **(5)** The reviewer says of "the classic" "M*A*S*H" it "made us laugh till we cried."

2. **(4)** Choice 4 is the only accurate reworking of the quoted line.

Application

3. **(2)** The reviewer states, "Like all great sitcoms ["M*A*S*H"] succeeded mainly by exploring, indeed celebrating, the chemistry between the characters."

Inferential

4. **(3)** This would seem to be the only correct explanation of the term.

Application

5. **(5)** The reviewer writes " 'M*A*S*H' did what only the greatest—the classic—comedies do: mix hilarity and tragedy, often in equal measure."

Analysis

6. **(1)** The reviewer showed his admiration for all the sitcoms discussed.

Test 5: Mathematics

The GED Mathematics Test consists of multiple-choice questions. Almost all of the questions will be either word problems or based on some graph or other illustration. These math items will test not only your ability to do arithmetic, algebra, and geometry but also your problem-solving skills. To answer successfully, you will need to

▶ estimate an answer

▶ go through several steps to solve a problem

▶ select only the information needed to solve the problem

▶ determine that not enough information is given to get an answer

Actually, you already use these skills in your work with math on the job or at home. In this section, we will give you lots of practice in basic math skills as well as these crucial problem-solving areas.

How many questions are on the test?

There are 56 problems, and you will be given 90 minutes to complete the test. About one-third of the items will be based on diagrams, charts, or graphs. Some of the questions will appear in item sets—a passage or drawing that is followed by 2 or more problems. Some of the problems will not require any computation. Instead, you will have to determine how a problem could be set up to solve it.

To get an idea of what the test is like, look at the Practice Test at the end of this book. This Practice Test is based on the real GED Test.

What's on the test?

The GED Mathematics Test can be broken down into the content areas it covers and the skills it tests. The following subjects make up the content of the test:

Arithmetic	50%
Measurement	
Number Relationships	
Data Analysis	
Algebra	30%
Geometry	20%

The ten chapters in this section will provide you with explanations, examples, and exercises in all of these content areas. Some of the material will be familiar and even seem easy. You will still want to sharpen your skills in those areas. Other areas will be new and difficult and will require concentrated study and repeated practice to learn.

What can help me prepare for the test?

To be successful, you must constantly practice and test each skill as you learn it. Remember, this is a book to work with, not just to read. Learning mathematics is like learning to play the piano; you can read a book about it or watch someone else do it. But until you actually practice it yourself, you won't know how to play a piano or solve a math problem.

The following are some specific suggestions to help you:

1. To learn a new skill, go over the example problems carefully. Try to do the example problems yourself.

2. Learn the rules that are summarized in the boxes in each section. Then try to say the rules out loud and explain how to use them.

3. Check each exercise with the answer key starting on page 712. You need to know right away if you are grasping the skills.

4. Use all of the problem-solving strategies that are provided in this section. In particular, you will find that drawing a picture with the information and estimating an answer will often help you understand a problem that seems confusing.

5. Do your practice work in pencil. Carefully write down all the information that you need to solve a problem.

Getting Rid of "Math Anxiety"

Many people feel that they are just "not good in math." If this is true of you, listed below are some ideas that will help.

1. Accept the fact that while you have some math anxiety, most other people do too.

2. Math requires logic, but often intuition comes first. Don't be afraid to use the ideas that pop into your mind.

3. You can be creative. Solving a problem in a way that's different from what is given in the book is fine too.

4. Estimating answers is helpful with many problems.

5. Use all the tools at hand—your fingers, paper, pencil, pictures—whatever works for you.

6. Have confidence in yourself and your ability to learn math concepts and try new approaches.

1
WHOLE NUMBERS AND PROBLEM SOLVING

Most of the problems on the Mathematics Test are word problems. In this chapter and throughout the math section, you will practice and learn techniques for working with word problems.

Basic to solving all word problems is a good, strong foundation in math facts, mainly the multiplication tables and the addition facts. If you are unsure of any of these facts, now is the time to review and memorize those that give you trouble. Just as you can remember the phone numbers, addresses, and other important numbers in your life, you can remember these facts. Your ability to work with decimals, fractions, and other math skills depends on how quickly and accurately you can do these computations.

Before starting work on problem solving, let's review the basic operations of addition, subtraction, multiplication, and division.

Review of Math Operations

The examples below will help you refresh your memory about the basics of addition, subtraction, multiplication, and division. An *estimate* for each problem is also shown in bold type. In some situations, an estimated (approximate) answer can serve as the final answer. At other times, estimates are used to check the reasonableness of exact answers, including calculator computations.

Example 1 shows how you must *regroup* (*carry*) in some addition problems.

Example 1:

$$
\begin{array}{r}
\overset{2}{4}\overset{2}{8}6 \\
39 \\
1\,725 \\
+\quad 89 \\
\hline
2\,339
\end{array}
$$

regroup to the next column to the left

Estimate:
$$
\begin{array}{r}
500 \\
50 \\
1\,700 \\
100 \\
\hline
2\,350
\end{array}
$$

Example 2 illustrates *regrouping* (*borrowing*) in subtraction.

Example 2:

$$
\begin{array}{r}
\overset{3}{\cancel{4}}\,\overset{10}{\cancel{0}}\,\overset{7}{\cancel{8}}\,\overset{16}{\cancel{8}} \\
-\quad 957 \\
\hline
3\,129
\end{array}
$$

regroup from the next available unit to the left

Estimate:
$$
\begin{array}{r}
4\,000 \\
-1\,000 \\
\hline
3\,000
\end{array}
$$

Example 3 shows both *regrouping* and *indenting* in multiplication.

Example 3:

$$
\begin{array}{r}
\overset{2}{}\overset{1}{4}8 \\
\times\quad 32 \\
\hline
96 \\
144 \\
\hline
1\,536
\end{array}
$$

regroup to the next column to the left

indent rows one column at a time

Estimate: $50 \times 30 = 1500$

For most people, division is the most complicated operation. Example 4 shows the basic steps.

Example 4: $3049 \div 6$

STEP 1. Divide by the number that follows the division sign ($\div$). Divide into the first number that you can. Since 6 won't divide into 3, divide into 30.

```
            ┌─ divisor
            ↓  5
           6) 3049 ←
               dividend ─┘
```

STEP 2. Multiply and subtract. Bring down the next number. If you can't divide into it, write a zero in the answer before you bring down the next number.

```
          50
       6) 3049
        − 30
          04
```

STEP 3. Divide 6 into 49. Multiply. Subtract. Write the *remainder* as a part of your answer.

```
          508 r1
       6) 3049
        − 30
          49
        − 48
           1
```

Estimate: $3000 \div 6 = 500$

▶ **TIP:** There is no *one* correct estimate. Work with numbers that you are comfortable with. Estimates can vary.

Now practice a mixed group of problems to test your understanding of math facts.

EXERCISE 1: WHOLE NUMBERS

Directions: Solve each problem. Find an estimate and an exact answer for each problem. Compare the two answers in each problem. Are they close?

1.
```
    9873
     412
     509
  +   48
```

3.
```
   1276
  −   99
```

5.
```
    268
  ×  47
```

7. $15)\overline{4021}$

2.
```
   3000
  −   56
```

4.
```
    87
  × 95
```

6. $9)\overline{5643}$

8. $72)\overline{36,072}$

Answers are on page 712.

Problem-Solving Skills

In this section, we will discuss a six-step approach for solving word problems. Since most of the problems on the Mathematics Test are word problems, you should be sure to master these skills. When you do a word problem, read it carefully. Sometimes, you will need to read a problem more than once.

The six steps on page 561 will help you understand and solve math word problems.

STEP 1: **QUESTION** Understand what the *question* is asking.

STEP 2: **NECESSARY INFORMATION** Select important *information* to use in solving the problem and organize it.

STEP 3: **OPERATION** Choose the correct arithmetic *operations* (addition, subtraction, multiplication, division).

STEP 4: **ESTIMATION** Estimate an answer. For some problems, an estimate is all you will need.

STEP 5: **CALCULATION** Calculate the operations *accurately*.

STEP 6: **EVALUATION** Reread the problem and evaluate your solution to make sure it answers the question *sensibly*. Use your estimate to check whether your answer makes sense.

Step 1: Question

First, read the entire problem and determine exactly what the question is asking. Below are three sample problems with the question in italic type.

Example 1: In 1930, the attendance at the World Series games was 312,619. At the 1960 World Series games, the attendance was 349,813. *How many more people attended the World Series in 1960 than in 1930?*

Example 2: Two pancakes contain 120 calories. *How many calories did Fred consume* if he had a stack of 6 pancakes for breakfast?

Example 3: *Find the area of a triangle* whose base is 4 inches and whose height is 6 inches.

Your first thought when you solve a problem should be "What am I looking for?" As shown in the three examples, the question can be at the beginning, in the middle, or at the end of a problem.

Step 2: Necessary Information

Every word problem contains a lot of information. You must decide which information is necessary to solve the problem. Keeping the question in mind, go through the problem and select the numbers with their unit labels (for example, choose 5 *apples*, not just the number 5). Be sure you choose only the numbers you need to solve the problem.

The examples below illustrate selecting only the information that is necessary to answer the question.

Example 1: Ellis has been renting an apartment for two years. The first year, his rent was $320 per month. At the beginning of the second year, his landlord raised the monthly rent to $355. How much more was the monthly rent the second year than the first year?

The question: How much more was the monthly rent the second year than the first year?

Needed information: $320 first-year rent, $355 second-year rent

Example 2: An estate of $16,920 was divided between a widow and her three children. The widow received one-half of the estate. The rest was divided equally among the children. What was each child's share?

The question: What was each child's share?

Needed information: $16,920 estate, 3 children, $\frac{1}{2}$ estate for widow

▶ **TIP:** Notice that the information "one-half of the estate" was given in words. Be sure to select *all* information—words and numbers—that you need.

Special Problems

On the Mathematics Test, you will run into two areas of difficulty with selecting the necessary information:

1. extra information
2. not enough information is given

Example 1: For the company picnic, only 20 out of the 30 employees paid the $6 fee. How much did the company collect?

In this problem, the fact that there are 30 employees is not needed to answer the question. You need only 20 × $6 = $120.

Example 2: At the 20%-off sale, Tom bought 6 ties. How much did he pay?

Here, you are given the numbers 20% and 6 ties. However, you are not given the original price of the ties. Since you do not have the information you need, the correct answer is "not enough information is given."

▶ **TIP:** On the GED Test, some problems have "not enough information is given" as a possible answer choice. Be sure you read the problem thoroughly before you choose this as your answer.

EXERCISE 2: UNDERSTANDING THE QUESTION AND SELECTING INFORMATION

Directions: Read the problems below and underline the question. In the space, write *all* of the information you would need to solve the problems. Be sure to write numbers and the labels that go with the numbers. If there is not enough information to solve a problem, write *N* for "not enough information is given." *Do not solve the problems.*

1. Dave worked 8 hours at his regular rate and 2 hours of overtime. If he makes $10.00 per hour and $15.00 for each hour of overtime, how much did Dave make altogether?

Information: _____

2. Mercedes put $150 down and paid $48 a month for 30 months for new furniture. How much did her monthly payments total?

Information: _____

3. When Esther shipped 3 boxes to her mother, she was charged $1.05 per pound. Two of the boxes weighed 12 pounds 3 ounces and 5 pounds 7 ounces. How much was she charged?

Information: _____

4. Over the years, Bensenville received $2.7 million from the state for highway construction, education, and public health. If Bensenville spends $800,000 on education, how much does it spend on public health?

Information: _____

5. Only 7,000 people are registered voters out of an adult population of 12,000. If 3,000 voters are women, how many voters are men?

Information: _____

Answers are on page 712.

Step 3: Operation

Once you are ready to solve a problem, remember that there are only four arithmetic operations from which to choose: addition, subtraction, multiplication, and division. Each problem will contain key words or concepts that will help you decide what to do.

Many times, your intuition will help you determine which operation to choose. This intuition comes from both personal experience and your understanding of math concepts from school.

The following chart will help you decide which operation to use.

When combining amounts	add
When finding the difference between two amounts	subtract
When given one unit of something and asked to find several	multiply
When asked to find a fraction of a quantity	multiply
When given the amount for several and asked for one	divide
When splitting, cutting, sharing, etc.	divide

Notice that there are clue words in the first three examples below that help you decide what to do.

Example 1: During one week, the U.S. Motor Company produced 4821 passenger cars, 7216 trucks, and 596 station wagons. *Altogether*, how many vehicles did the company produce that week?

Question: How many vehicles did the company produce?

Information: 4821 cars, 7216 trucks, 596 station wagons

Operation: "Altogether, how many"—addition

Example 2: The local village borrowed $2,250,000 and has repaid $955,000 of its debt. How much of the debt still *remains unpaid*?

Question: How much debt remains?

Information: $2,250,000; $955,000

Operation: "How much remains"—subtraction

Example 3: How much money will each of 68 stockholders receive if $98,600 is *divided equally* among them?

Question: How much money will each receive?

Information: 68 stockholders; $98,600

Operation: "divided equally"—division

If no clue words appear in the problem, look for the math concept involved in the problem. Use your understanding of the problem to help you choose whether to add, subtract, multiply, or divide.

Example 4: Allan's yearly salary is $20,304. What is his monthly salary?

Question: What is his monthly salary?

Information: $20,304; 1 year

Operation: No key words. However, *monthly* means "each month." There are 12 months in one year. Thus, we choose to divide by 12 to find the salary each month.

EXERCISE 3: CHOOSING THE OPERATION

Directions: Read each problem and decide whether to add, subtract, multiply, or divide. Write the name of the operation only. *Do not solve the problems.*

1. When Myron drove 300 miles on 15 gallons of gas, he tried to figure out how many miles he got per gallon. On the average, how many miles did he get per gallon?

2. Sandy lost 34 pounds on her diet. If her weight is now 123, what was her original weight?

3. Brownsville has 23,340 people, and Sylvan has 23,346. How many more people live in Sylvan than in Brownsville?

4. One package is 100 pounds, and the other is 150 pounds. The weight of the second package is how many times that of the first?

5. Sal's mother sent him to the store to buy 5 feet of ribbon. The clerk wants to know how many inches he needs. How many inches are in 5 feet?

Answers are on page 712.

Step 4: Estimation

After choosing the operation, estimate an answer. Sometimes, an estimate can be the final answer. At other times, use the estimate to check whether your answer makes sense.

Example 1: If you drive 448 miles in 7 hours, what is your average rate of speed?

Question: What is the average speed?

Information: 448 miles; 7 hours

Operation: "average"—divide

Estimation: $420 \div 7 = 60$ miles per hour

Example 2: An auto mechanic receives a salary of $525 each week. Find the auto mechanic's earnings for 4 weeks.

Question: How much does the mechanic earn in 4 weeks?

Information: $525 each week; 4 weeks

Operation: No clue words. The problem gives the salary for one week and asks you to find the amount of several (4)—multiply.

Estimation: $500 × 4 = $2000

Step 5: Calculation

After estimating the answer, solve the problem. Do the computations carefully and accurately. Let's go through the five problem-solving steps for the next two examples:

Example 1: If you drive 448 miles in 7 hours, what is your average rate of speed?

Question: What is the average speed?

Information: 448 miles; 7 hours

Operation: "average"—divide

Estimation: 420 ÷ 7 = 60 miles per hour

Calculation:

$$
\begin{array}{r}
64 \\
7\overline{)448} \\
-42 \\
\hline
28 \\
-28 \\
\hline
0
\end{array}
$$

Example 2: An auto mechanic receives a salary of $525 each week. Find the auto mechanic's earnings for 4 weeks.

Question: How much does the mechanic earn in 4 weeks?

Information: $525 each week; 4 weeks

Operation: No clue words. The problem gives the salary for one week and asks you to find the amount of several (4)—multiply.

Estimation: $500 × 4 = $2000

Calculation:

$$
\begin{array}{r}
\$525 \\
\times\quad 4 \\
\hline
\$2100
\end{array}
$$

Step 6: Evaluation

The final step in solving any problem is to evaluate your answer. Does your solution answer the question? Is your answer a sensible one? Is your calculation close to your estimate?

Look at Example 2 above. Suppose you had misunderstood the problem and had divided instead of multiplying:

$$\$525 \div 4 = \$131.25$$

This *wrong* answer tells you that the mechanic earned $131.25 in 4 weeks. Would it make sense for the mechanic to earn *less* in a month than in a week? No. By seeing whether your answer makes sense, you may be able to catch a mistake.

The following problems will give you a chance to practice the 6-step approach to problem solving.

EXERCISE 4: PROBLEM SOLVING

Directions: Solve the problems. For each problem, draw a chart like this and fill it in as you do the problem.

Question:	Calculation:
Necessary Information:	
Operation:	
Estimation:	
Evaluation—Does the answer make sense?	

1. You are leaving for a three-day minivacation. The odometer on your car reads 49,752 miles. You plan to drive 162 miles the first day, 229 miles the second day, and 375 miles the third day. How many miles do you plan to drive?

2. A contest prize of $12,855 is shared equally by 15 people. What amount does each person receive?

3. How much larger is Canada than the United States? Canada is 3,851,809 square miles, and the United States is 3,675,633 square miles.

4. A buyer for a motel purchased 97 color TVs at $325 each. What is the total cost of the 97 TVs?

5. Marlene pays $2492 each quarter for estimated tax. What total amount does she pay in one year if a quarter year is three months?

6. When Mr. MacDonald died, he left his 588 acre farm to be divided equally among his three children. How many acres did each child inherit?

7. Jose makes $1300 a month. He pays $345 for a month's rent and $90 per week for food. How much does he have left each month after paying for rent and food?

Answers are on page 712.

Multi-Step Problems

Many of the problems you see on the Mathematics Test will take more than one calculation to solve. As with the problems you've already done, use the 6-step process, but identify all the steps you need to take. Make sure that you do all calculations.

Example: The yearly rainfall for four consecutive years in Rockton was 22 inches, 28 inches, 31 inches, and 19 inches. Find the average rainfall over the four-year period.

Question: What is the average rainfall?

Information: 22 in, 28 in, 31 in, and 19 in; 4 years

Operation: STEP 1: To get the total rainfall—add.
STEP 2: To get the average rainfall—divide.

Estimation:

STEP 1	STEP 2
20 in	$100 \div 4 = 25$
30 in	
30 in	
+ 20 in	
100 in	

Calculation:

STEP 1	STEP 2
22 in	25
28 in	4) 100
31 in	8
+ 19 in	20
100 in	20
	0

Does it make sense? It makes sense that the average is within the range of 19–31 inches. And your estimate and calculation are not only close; they're an exact match!

▶ **TIP:** With multi-step problems, after you have finished your calculations, go back and see if your answer to the question makes sense. If you have forgotten a step, this can help you catch yourself and finish the problem correctly.

Using Charts and Diagrams

You have heard the saying "A picture is worth a thousand words." A picture that accompanies a problem can help you "see" how to solve word problems. Sometimes a word problem gives several numbers that could be organized into a chart. Also, drawing a diagram might help you picture the information in a problem so you can "see" what to do. Let's look at a few examples.

Example 1: To better insulate his house, Miguel had to put new weather stripping around the large window in his family room. The window frame measured 5 feet wide and 4 feet high. How many feet of weather stripping did he need for that window?

First draw a diagram of the window. Remember, a window has four sides!

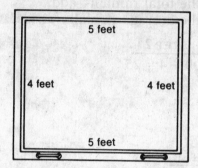

Since Miguel wants to put the weather stripping around the whole window, label all four sides. The diagram helps you see that you have to add all the sides. Miguel needs 18 feet of weather stripping: 5 + 5 + 4 + 4 = 18.

Example 2: A warehouse clerk had a checking account balance of $425.15 before making a deposit of $185.75. The clerk then wrote two checks, one for $43.50 and another for $260.10. Find the current checkbook balance.

Make a box to list the clerk's assets, which include the deposit and account balance. In the second box, list the two checks she wrote. The last box is the current balance, which is the difference between the assets and checks written.

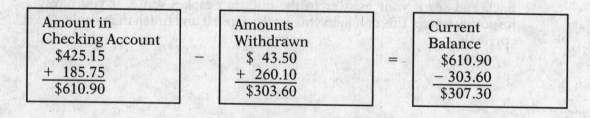

Restating the Problem

The two previous examples show that it helps to restate the problem by organizing the information into charts or diagrams. Another way of restating a problem is to try to put the problem into your own words. Sometimes this means you might actually talk to yourself. As you do this, jot down notes on paper to help you organize your thoughts.

Example: A teacher drives 7 miles one way to school. How many miles does the teacher drive to and from school during one five-day workweek?

After reading the problem, say out loud (or just in your mind) what the problem says. "A teacher drives 7 miles to work. (That means she must drive 7 miles home each day, too.)"

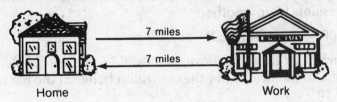

Home   Work

"She works 5 days. (That means she drives 14 miles each day for 5 days.)"
"How many miles does she drive?" $14 \times 5 = 70$ She drives 70 miles in 5 days.

Personalizing a Problem

If you have trouble restating a problem, reread it several times. Think about how you might solve a similar problem in your own life. Many of the problems on the GED Test will involve questions about practical, everyday situations.

Example: The total cost of a computer system is $4830. A down payment of $1500 is made, and the balance is paid in 18 equal monthly payments. Find the monthly payments.

As you read this problem, recall the times you have purchased something and put down a deposit, planning to pay the rest later. You subtracted the deposit from the purchase price to find out how much you still owe.

$4830   purchase price
$- 1500$ deposit
$3330   amount owed

According to the problem, you can pay the amount owed in 18 equal payments. So you have to divide by 18 to find out how much you will pay each month.

$3330 \div 18 = \$185$ per month

Setup Problems

Some problems on the GED will require you to choose a way to solve the problems. These are called *setup problems* because they show a way that a problem could be set up before an answer is found.

Example 1: Tracy will type a 600-word paper and then a 150-word letter. If she types 60 words a minute, how many minutes will it take her to do this work?

(1) $600 \times 150 \times 60$ **(2)** $600 + 150 \times 60$ **(3)** $\frac{600 + 150}{60}$ **(4)** $\frac{60}{600 + 150}$
(5) not enough information is given

To approach a setup problem, you represent the mathematical relations with numbers and symbols for operations. This kind of statement is called an **arithmetic expression**. In the example above, you want to find how many minutes *both* documents will take to type.

total words $= 600 + 150$

words per minute $= 60$

minutes to type $= \dfrac{\text{total words}}{\text{words per minute}} = \dfrac{600 + 150}{60}$

Your answer will be (3). This answer choice indicates that to get a solution you must add the number of words together and then divide the sum by 60.

▶ **TIP:** In the solution on page 569, the *fraction bar* means "divided by." This representation of division is often used in setup problems.

Sometimes you will have to use *parentheses* to separate one part of an arithmetic expression from another.

Example 2: $(200 \times 2) - (40 + 2)$

In the arithmetic expression above, you would solve the problems within the parentheses first and then carry out the operation between the parentheses. This could be solved by

$$\underbrace{(200 \times 2)}_{400} - \underbrace{(40 + 2)}_{42} = 358$$

WRITING ARITHMETIC EXPRESSIONS

1. Write the individual steps of multi-step problems (within parentheses if necessary).

2. Division can be indicated by the division sign ($\div$) or by a fraction bar.

3. Unless otherwise indicated, the order in which an arithmetic expression should be solved is
   a. parentheses or tops of fraction bars first
   b. multiplication or division next
   c. addition or subtraction last

EXERCISE 5: WORD PROBLEMS

Directions: Solve each problem.

1. You just inherited an apartment building. If your income from the building is $5160 per month, what is the building's yearly income?

   (1) $430
   (2) $5,160
   (3) $15,480
   (4) $61,920
   (5) not enough information is given

2. There were 395 people who registered for a tour around the country. If a bus can hold 72 people, how many buses will be needed to accommodate everyone?

   (1) 5
   (2) 6
   (3) 7
   (4) 10
   (5) 50

3. A garment factory completed an order for 500 pairs of pants and was paid $5500. It received $9130 for a second order of the same kind of pants. How many pairs of pants were in the second order?

   (1) 363
   (2) 500
   (3) 830
   (4) 913
   (5) 3630

Questions 4–6 refer to the information below.

High School Student Enrollment

Year	Lincoln	Mead	Sandburg	Austin	Edison
1983	1686	1982	2234	1648	1846
1993	1420	1650	1847	1296	1318

The local high school district has experienced a recent decline in enrollment. The chart above compares enrollment figures between 1983 and 1993 for the five high schools in the district.

4. Which high school had the greatest decline in enrollment?

   (1) Lincoln
   (2) Mead
   (3) Sandburg
   (4) Austin
   (5) Edison

5. What was the total decline in the district during the ten-year period?

   (1) 1865
   (2) 2865
   (3) 7531
   (4) 9396
   (5) not enough information is given

6. What was the average decline per school in the district?

   (1) 373
   (2) 1865
   (3) 1879
   (4) 7531
   (5) 9396

7. Four workers for Transmachine, Inc., must produce 1298 parts in a week's time. If the first worker produces 350 parts, the second worker 375 parts, and the third worker 417 parts, how many parts remain for the fourth worker?

   (1) 39
   (2) 156
   (3) 324
   (4) 610
   (5) 2440

8. Melanie bought a new car. The final price was $12,800. In addition, she purchased the following options: $282 for an AM/FM radio, $252 for power steering, and $156 for rustproofing. The dealer gave her a $500 rebate for the purchase of the new car. If Melanie made a down payment of $3150, what would be her monthly payments if she takes 48 months to pay the remaining balance?

   (1) $186
   (2) $205
   (3) $225
   (4) $267
   (5) $310

9. The manager of a men's shop can buy 80 men's suits for $4800. Each sports jacket will cost the store $23. The manager decides to order 80 men's suits and 25 sports jackets. Which expression shows how to find the total cost of the order?

   (1) (25 × $23)
   (2) (25 + $23) + $4800
   (3) (25 × $23) × $4800
   (4) (25 × $23) + $4800
   (5) $4800 − (25 × $23)

10. A charity organization collected $348,284 in a recent fund-raising drive. Of the amount collected, some was put aside to pay expenses. The remaining money was divided equally among six local charities. What amount did each charity receive?

   (1) $58,041
   (2) $58,047
   (3) $58,053
   (4) $348,284
   (5) not enough information is given

Answers are on page 713.

2
DECIMALS

Maxine's normal temperature is 98.6°. When she had the flu, it rose to 102.4°.

Elena has a new job working as a receptionist. She is paid $6.55 an hour and makes $245.63 a week.

Numbers like 98.6, 102.4, 6.55, and 245.63 are *decimals*. These everyday decimals are already familiar to you. To fully understand and use decimals, it is important to learn about place values first.

Using Decimals

In our number system, we have ten digits: 0, 1, 2, 3, 4, 5, 6, 7, 8, 9. We use these digits to write every number. The place that a digit occupies in a number tells us the value of the digit. This means that each digit has a *place value*.

We can use the chart below to read the place value of numbers. The whole numbers are to the left of the *decimal point*. The decimals, which are parts of a whole, are to the right of the decimal point. Decimals are also called *decimal fractions*. The places to the right of the decimal point are called *decimal places*. Notice that the names of the decimal places end in *th*.

Billions	Hundred Millions	Ten Millions	Millions	Hundred Thousands	Ten Thousands	Thousands	Hundreds	Tens	AND Ones	Tenths	Hundredths	Thousandths	Ten-Thousandths	Hundred-Thousandths	Millionths
							3	2	6.	7	5				

▶ **TIP:** We use the decimal point to separate the whole-number places and the decimal places. The point is read as "and."

Let's consider the number 326.75 from the chart. We can say that

3 is in the hundreds place. Now fill in the blanks below.

2 is in the _____ place.

6 is in the _____ place.

7 is in the _____ place.

5 is in the _____ place.

In the number 326.75, 3 is in the hundreds place, 2 is in the tens place, 6 is in the ones place, 7 is in the tenths place, and 5 is in the hundredths place.

The number 326.75 has two decimal places. The number is read as "326 and 75-hundredths." The .75 is read as "75-hundredths" because we give the entire decimal the name of the last decimal place it occupies. This is also why we read $326.75 as "326 dollars and 75 cents."

READING DECIMALS

1. Read the whole part first.

2. Say "and" for the decimal point.

3. Read the decimal part.

4. Say the place name of the last digit.

▶ **TIP:** If there is no whole number, start at step 3. For instance, .008 is read as eight-thousandths.

Zeros in Decimals

The zero is very important in writing and reading decimal numbers. To see how important zeros are, read the names of each of the mixed decimals below. *Mixed decimals* combine whole numbers with decimal fractions.

12.5   12.05   12.005

The first number is read as "12 and 5-tenths," the second as "12 and 5-hundredths," and the third as "12 and 5-thousandths." You can see that the only digits used to write these numbers are 0, 1, 2, and 5. The actual value of the number depends on the place value of each digit. The zeros in the second two numbers "hold" the number 5 in a specific decimal place—the hundredths place in 12.05 and the thousandths place in 12.005.

EXERCISE 1: READING DECIMALS

Directions: Circle the number on each line that matches the written value. Remember that the word *and* stands for the decimal point.

1. five-hundredths   500   .05   .5

2. six and two-tenths   6.2   .62   .062

3. one hundred and two-thousandths   102.00   100.2   100.002

4. one thousand thirty-two   1032   1.032   .1032

5. four hundred and twenty-five thousandths   400.25   400.025   .0425

6. Write the following in number form:
  (a) seven-tenths
  (b) six and thirty-two thousandths
  (c) two thousand and eight-hundredths
  (d) three hundred five and fifty-six thousandths
  (e) sixty-five ten-thousandths

Answers are on page 713.

Comparing and Ordering Decimals

Sometimes we need to compare decimals to see which one is larger. This is when adding zeros *after* the last decimal digit is most useful. It is easier to compare two numbers that have the same number of decimal places.

Adding zeros to the right of the last decimal digit does not change the value of a number. For example, 12.5, 12.50, and 12.500 all have the same value.

To compare .14 and .126, first add a zero to .14 to make it .140. Now both .126 and .140 are expressed in thousandths and have the same number of decimal places:

$$.14 = .140$$
$$.126 = .126$$

You can now see that 126-thousandths is smaller than 140-thousandths because 126 is less than 140.

Example: Put 4.8, 4.12, 4.2, and 4.1003 in order from the *smallest to the largest*.

STEP 1. Write in zeros so that each number has the same number of decimal places. Then number the mixed decimals in order from the *smallest* to the *largest*.

4.8	= 4.8000	4th
4.12	= 4.1200	2nd
4.2	= 4.2000	3rd
4.1003	= 4.1003	1st

STEP 2. Using your ranking system, put the *original numbers* in order from smallest to largest.

1st	4.1003
2nd	4.12
3rd	4.2
4th	4.8

EXERCISE 2: COMPARING DECIMALS

Directions: Solve each problem.

1. Select the *larger* number in each pair.

   (a) .005; .05 **(b)** 4.10; 4.01 **(c)** .7; .68 **(d)** .5; .51 **(e)** 1.033; 1.03

2. Arrange each set of numbers in size order with the *largest* number first.

   (a) 1.95; 2.105; 2.15 **(b)** .0035; .0503; .005

3. Put these weights in order from the *lightest to the heaviest*.

   14.3 lb   14.03 lb   14.003 lb   14.3033 lb

4. Sarah has to pile these crates in order from the *heaviest on the bottom to the lightest on the top*. What would be the correct order in which to pile the crates? (List them from bottom to top.)

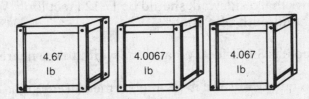

4.67 lb   4.0067 lb   4.067 lb

Answers are on page 713.

Rounding Decimals

We might solve a problem involving money and get an answer like $25.128. Since our money is expressed in hundredths, we must round off the answer to dollars and cents. Following are the steps we use to round off the answer.

Example 1: Round off $25.128 to the nearest cent.

STEP 1. Underline the place value to which you are rounding.

$25.1<u>2</u>8

STEP 2. Identify the digit to the right of the place to which you are rounding.

$25.1<u>2</u>8 ←— number to the right

STEP 3. a) If this digit is 5 or more, increase the digit in the place to which you are rounding by 1 and drop the digits to the right.

$25.1<u>2</u>8 ←— 5 or more
+   1
$25.13

   b) If this digit is less than 5, keep the same digit in the place to which you are rounding and drop the digits to the right.

Example 2: Round 10.0239 to the nearest thousandth.

```
          ┌──── 5 or more
          │
10.0239 rounds to 10.024
     ↑
     └──── thousandth
```

Example 3 shows an application of rounding decimals.

Example 3: A bank computes the interest on Sonya's savings account and finds it to be $37.7034. Round off this interest to the nearest cent.

```
          ┌── less than five
          │
Solution: $37.7034 rounds to $37.70
     ↑
     └── cent
```

EXERCISE 3: ROUNDING DECIMALS

Directions: Solve each problem.

1. A $\frac{3}{8}$ inch drill bit has a diameter of .375 inches. What is the size of the drill bit to the nearest hundredth inch?

2. Today's interest rate is 7.58 percent. What is the interest rate to the nearest tenth of a percent?

3. At the gas station, the pump says the gas costs $1.298 per gallon. In dollars and cents, how much will you pay per gallon?

4. A blueprint shows that a sidewalk should be 17.124 feet long. What is the length to the nearest hundredth of a foot?

5. The width of a boat is 8.275 feet. What is the width to the nearest tenth of a foot?

6. The value of π, a number useful in geometric measurement, is 3.14159. Round off this value to the nearest hundredth.

7. Juanita's temperature was 101.68 degrees. What was her temperature to the nearest degree?

Answers are on page 714.

Adding and Subtracting Decimals

A cashier who adds up your bill is adding decimals. One who makes change is subtracting decimals. This is done the same way as with whole numbers. There are three basic rules to follow:

> **ADDING AND SUBTRACTING DECIMALS**
>
> 1. Line up the decimal points.
> 2. Add or subtract the numbers.
> 3. Bring the decimal point straight down.

Example 1: Add 4.5 and 38.68.

Read this space as a zero. ──────┐   ┌── Line up the decimal points.

$$
\begin{array}{r}
4.5 \\
+\ 38.68 \\
\hline
43.18
\end{array}
$$

▶ **TIP:** If necessary, add zeros to the right of the decimal point to fill in place values. This will help you keep the rows lined up but won't change the value of the numbers.

Example 2: Add 2.1, .48, 38, and .005.

Filled-in zeros will help you line up the columns.

$$
\begin{array}{ll}
2.1 & 2.100 \\
.48 & .480 \\
38. & 38.000 \\
.005 & +\ \ .005 \\
\hline
& 40.585
\end{array}
$$

When you subtract decimals, you may have to fill in zeros to get enough decimal places.

Example 3: Subtract .0856 from 12.1.

$$
\begin{array}{ll}
12.1 & 12.1000 \quad \longleftarrow \text{ Filled-in zeros are necessary.} \\
-\ \ \ .0856 & -\ \ .0856 \\
\hline
& 12.0144
\end{array}
$$

Example 4: Jake gave the cashier $20 to pay for the lunch check of $7.48. How much change did Jake get back?

$$
\begin{array}{ll}
\$20.00 & \$20.00 \\
-\ \ 7.48 & -\ \ 7.48 \\
\hline
& \$12.52
\end{array}
$$

▶ **TIP:** Notice that whole numbers like 20 have an "imaginary" decimal point at the end. You can put in this point when you need it.

EXERCISE 4: ADDING AND SUBTRACTING DECIMALS

Directions: Solve each problem.

1. Add 12.4 and 132.647.

2. Add 5.9, 2.46, 6, 3.07, and .48.

3. Subtract 5.2 from 43.

4. Find the difference between 85.2 and 6.9.

5. Find the distance around the field shown. All distances are in meters.

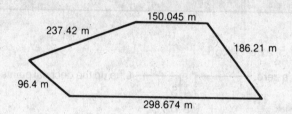

6. Can you balance a checkbook? At the beginning of the week, your balance was $472.24. During the week, you wrote checks for $42.87, $5.93, $10, $17.48, and $38.40. What is your new balance?

7. At the start of a trip, your mileage meter read 25,176.3; at the end of the trip, it read 28,054.1. How far did you travel?

8. Sam bought a sandwich for $4.75, a cup of soup for $.95, and a drink for $.75. How much change did he receive from a ten-dollar bill?

    (1) $2.45
    (2) $2.95
    (3) $3.55
    (4) $4.50
    (5) $5.25

9. Although Jill's temperature is usually 98.6°, it rose to 104.2° when she had a fever. Her medication brought her fever down to 102.8°. By how many degrees did the medication bring it down?

    (1) 0.6
    (2) 1.4
    (3) 1.6
    (4) 2.0
    (5) 2.2

10. A piece of wood was 1.03 inches long. Jill needed to cut some off. First she cut off .2 inch. Then she cut off .15 inch. Which of the expressions below shows how much she cut off?

    (1) (1.03 + .2) + .15
    (2) 1.03 − .2
    (3) 1.03 − .15
    (4) .2 + .15
    (5) .2 − .15

Part of a service order is shown below. Use the information given to answer questions 11 and 12.

LAKE MARINE SERVICE				Date: 8/12	Name: Kim Yang	
Qty.	Part	Amount		Work Performed	Labor Charge	
1	Gear lube	17	50	1. Winterize	70	00
1	Grease	4	95	2. Weld skeg	90	00
1	Oil	6	00	3. Repair ladder	n	c
1	Gas	13	44			
3	Antifreeze	60	75			
				Total Labor	160	00
				Total Parts		
				Tax	2	63
	Total			Invoice Total		

11. Find the total cost of the parts.

12. What is the invoice total for Mr. Yang's boat?

Answers are on page 714.

Multiplying and Dividing Decimals

Decimals are multiplied the same way as whole numbers, and then the decimal point is placed in the answer. There are three rules for multiplying decimals.

MULTIPLYING DECIMALS

1. Multiply the two numbers as whole numbers, ignoring the decimal points.
2. Find the total number of decimal places in the numbers being multiplied.
3. Count the total number of decimal places in the answer, starting from the right, and place the point there.

Example 1: Multiply 3.2 and 4.05.

```
  4.05    two decimal places
× 3.2     one decimal place
  810
12 15
12.960  = 12.96 total of three decimal places (You can drop the last zero.)
```

Example 2: 28 × .06

```
  28    no decimal places
× .06   two decimal places
1.68    total of two decimal places
```

Example 3 shows putting zeros at the beginning of the answer to have enough decimal places.

Example 3: .043 × .0056

$$
\begin{array}{r}
.0056 \quad \text{4 decimal places} \\
\times \quad .043 \quad \text{3 decimal places} \\
\hline
168 \\
224 \\
\hline
2408 \quad \text{You need a total of 7 decimal places.}
\end{array}
$$

In this case, put three zeros at the beginning of the number:

.0002408

▶ **TIP:** Notice that it is easier to multiply if you put the larger number on top.

Dividing Decimals

How many $.59 hamburgers can you buy for $8.00? To answer this question, you have to divide decimals.

There are two basic types of decimal division: (1) division of decimals by whole numbers and (2) division of decimals by decimals. Let's look at examples of each type.

Dividing By A Whole Number

DIVIDING DECIMALS BY WHOLE NUMBERS

1. Divide as though both numbers were whole numbers.

2. Divide by the number that follows the division sign (÷).

3. Place the decimal point in the answer directly above the decimal point in the dividend.

Example 1 shows how to divide a decimal by a whole number.

Example 1: 36.48 ÷ 4

Place decimal point directly above the decimal point in the dividend.

$$
\begin{array}{r}
9.12 \\
4\overline{)\ 36.48} \\
-\ 36 \\
\hline
04 \\
-\ 4 \\
\hline
08 \\
-\ 8 \\
\hline
0
\end{array}
$$

As Example 2 shows, some whole-number problems require you to add a decimal point and zeros.

Example 2: $12 \div 25$

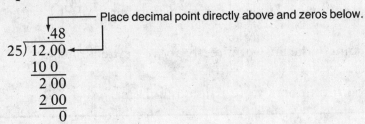

```
         .48  ──── Place decimal point directly above and zeros below.
    25) 12.00 ◄──────
        10 0
         2 00
         2 00
            0
```

Example 3 shows a problem that often causes difficulty. If the first whole number in the divisor doesn't divide into the first number after a decimal point, you *must* put in a zero before continuing your division.

Example 3: $.35 \div 7$

```
        ┌───── Put in the zero after the decimal point.
       .05
    7) .35
```

Dividing By A Decimal

To divide a decimal by a decimal, you have to change the divisor into a whole number. Because you do this, you also have to move the decimal point in the dividend the same number of places.

Example 1: $4.864 \div .32$

```
                                 ┌──── Place the decimal point directly above the decimal point
                      15.2              in the dividend.
 Move the decimal point ──► .32) 4.86 4 ◄── Move the decimal point two places to the right.
 two places to the right.   − 3 2
                              1 66
                            − 1 60
                                6 4
                            −   6 4
                                  0
```

Sometimes, you will have to add zeros to move the decimal point.

Example 2: $25 \div .125$

```
 Move the decimal point           200.
 three places to the right. ──► .125) 25.000 ◄── Add three zeros and move the
                                − 25 0              decimal point three places to the right.
                                   00
                                 −  0
                                    0
                                 −  0
                                    0
```

> ## DIVIDING A DECIMAL BY A DECIMAL
>
> 1. Move the decimal point in the divisor all the way to the right.
>
> 2. Move the decimal point in the dividend the same number of places to the right.
>
> 3. Place the decimal point in the answer directly above the decimal point in the dividend.
>
> 4. Divide as though both numbers were whole numbers.

▶ **TIP:** The easy way to multiply or divide by multiples of ten (10, 100, 1000, etc.) is simply to move the decimal point. When you multiply, you move the decimal point to the right, and when you divide, you move it to the left. In either case, the decimal point moves as many places as there are zeros in the multiple of ten. (As the examples show, you add zeros when necessary.)

For example: $.13 \times 1000 = 130$ $9.5 \div 100 = .095$

3 zeros 3 places   2 zeros 2 places

EXERCISE 5: MULTIPLYING AND DIVIDING DECIMALS

Directions: Solve each problem.

1. Multiply $.342 \times 1.5$.

2. Multiply $46 \times .00034$.

3. Multiply $.8 \times .03$.

4. Multiply $\$6.50 \times 3.5$.

5. Divide 6.005 by .05.

6. $.012 \div 3$

7. Divide 2.8 by .04.

8. Divide 56 by .08.

9. $.38 \times 10$

10. $472 \times 10,000$

11. $.0972 \times 100$

12. $.617 \div 10$

13. $456.12 \div 100$

14. $57 \div 1000$

15. Monica pays $7.85 each month for newspaper home delivery. Which expression shows how much she pays for the newspaper over a year's time?

   (1) $7.85 \times 4 \times 12$
   (2) $(7.85 + 4) \times 12$
   (3) 7.85×12
   (4) 7.85×52
   (5) 7.85×365

16. One stamp costs $.29. How much does a roll of 100 stamps cost?

   (1) $14.50
   (2) $20.00
   (3) $25.00
   (4) $29.00
   (5) $31.00

17. Finishing Touch Decorators can paint 1.5 rooms in an hour. Working 10 hours each day, how many days will it take them to paint a 75-room building?

    (1) 3
    (2) 4
    (3) 5
    (4) 8
    (5) 10

18. At the store, Mike bought a 3.5-pound package of chicken at $1.19 a pound and 2 gallons of milk at $2.30 a gallon. Which expression shows what Mike paid?

    (1) $(3.5 + 1.19) + (2 + 2.30)$

    (2) $(3.5 + 2) + (1.19 + 2.30)$

    (3) $(3.5 \times 1.19) + (2 \times 2.30)$

    (4) $2.5(1.19 + 2.30)$

    (5) $2(1.19 + 2.30)$

Answers are on page 714.

Estimating for Problem Solving

Estimating is a handy tool to use in solving decimal problems. If a problem involves decimals, reread the problem and replace the mixed decimals with whole numbers. This will help you see how to solve the problem. After choosing the correct operations to use, work the problem with the original decimal numbers if an exact answer is necessary.

Example 1: What is the cost of 12.8 gallons of gasoline at $1.19 per gallon?

Estimation: What is the cost of 13 gallons of gasoline at $1 per gallon? Using whole numbers helps us see we should multiply 1×13, which equals 13. Our answer in the original problem should be about $13. The actual answer rounds off to $15.23.

Example 2: Approximately how much did Emil spend on his recent shopping spree? This is what he bought: a blazer, $49.95; slacks, $24.95; shirt, $18.69; tie, $9.75; belt, $12.25; shoes, $34.95.

Estimation: To estimate the answer, round off the numbers.

	Estimate
$49.95 to	50
$24.95 to	25
$18.69 to	20
$ 9.75 to	10
$12.25 to	10
$34.95 to	35
Total	$150

Emil spent approximately $150. The actual amount is $150.54. If Emil wanted to know about how much he spent, an estimate would give him a close enough answer.

Estimating can help you see how to do a problem, provide you with an approximate answer, allow you to choose a multiple-choice answer, or help you double-check your work.

EXERCISE 6: ESTIMATING

Directions: Estimate the answers to the following problems.

1. Dino drove his truck the following distances during the week: Monday, 4.8 miles; Tuesday, 12.3 miles; Wednesday, 74.5 miles; Thursday, 10 miles; and Friday, 8.1 miles. Approximately how far did he travel?

estimation _____

2. Liz had $50 in her purse. She spent $24.75 on cosmetics and $2.50 on a magazine. Approximately how much did she have left from her $50?

estimation _____

3. If a bushel of apples cost $8.95, what will ten bushels cost?

estimation _____

4. How many streamers, each 1.75 feet long, can be cut from a roll of crepe paper 36 feet long?

estimation _____

Answers are on page 715.

EXERCISE 7: DECIMAL WORD PROBLEMS

Directions: Use estimation to help you solve the problems. Sometimes you may need to find the exact amount.

1. You are building a bookcase with shelves that are 3.2 feet long. How many complete shelves can be cut from a 12-foot board?

- **(1)** 2
- **(2)** 3
- **(3)** 4
- **(4)** 5
- **(5)** not enough information is given

2. Mr. Stansky earns a part-time salary of $425 every four weeks. During the past four weeks he also received commissions of $485.75, $399.87, $642.15, and $724.52. What was his total income for the past 4-week period?

- **(1)** $535.46
- **(2)** $669.32
- **(3)** $2252.29
- **(4)** $2256.42
- **(5)** $2677.29

3. On a bicycle road trip, Otis rode 2492 miles in 140 hours. What was his average speed in miles per hour, to the nearest tenth?

- **(1)** .178
- **(2)** 1.78
- **(3)** 17.8
- **(4)** 178
- **(5)** 1780

4. The carat is a unit of measure used to weigh precious stones. It equals 3.086 grains. How many grains does a 2.8-carat diamond weigh?

   (1) 3.086
   (2) 5.886
   (3) 8.6408
   (4) 86.408
   (5) 8640.8

Questions 5 and 6 are based on the table below.

   As an assistant accountant for a computer company, you must calculate each employee's gross earnings, total of deductions, and net pay by using the following table.

Employee No.	Regular Pay	Overtime Pay	Gross Earnings	Social Security Tax (FICA)	Federal Income Tax (FIT)	Total of Deductions	Net Pay
24	237.25	117		26.48	71.26		
35	339.45	71.25		26.93	82.14		
17	265.72	168.75		27.03	86.90		

5. Find the net pay for employee 17 after deductions are taken out.

   (1) $113.93
   (2) $320.54
   (3) $434.47
   (4) $548.40
   (5) not enough information is given

6. How much did employee 24 make per hour?

   (1) $5.93
   (2) $6.42
   (3) $8.85
   (4) $354.25
   (5) not enough information is given

7. A Tercel can be bought for $3500 down and monthly payments of $207.25 for 48 months. What is the total cost of the Tercel?

   (1) $5,987
   (2) $9,948
   (3) $13,448
   (4) $17,795
   (5) not enough information is given

8. If large eggs are on sale for $.69 per dozen, what does one egg sell for to the nearest cent?

    (1) $ .06
    (2) $ .07
    (3) $ .08
    (4) $6
    (5) $7

9. The odometer of your sports car read 7353.2 miles at the start of a trip. When you returned, it read 8747.6 miles, and you had used 86.4 gallons of gasoline. How many miles per gallon did you get? (Round off to the nearest tenth.)

    (1)   1.6
    (2)   16.1
    (3)   16.2
    (4)   18.6
    (5) 1394.4

10. One evening, a waiter received the following tips: $4.25, $3.80, $5.75, $10, $6, $3.70, $4.90. What was his average tip for the evening?

    (1) $3.22
    (2) $5.40
    (3) $5.49
    (4) $38.40
    (5) not enough information is given

Answers are on page 715.

3 FRACTIONS

We encounter fractions in all aspects of life without even thinking about it. "Let me borrow half a dollar." "Cut the pie into eighths so everyone gets a piece." "It's a quarter past seven; I'd better hurry, or I'll be late." "She bought $3\frac{7}{8}$ yards of material."

Forms of Fractions

Fractions represent a part of a whole. The top number is called the **numerator**, and the bottom number is called the **denominator**.

$\dfrac{5}{8}$

numerator
tells how many parts you have

denominator
tells how many parts a whole is divided into

This circle is divided into 8 parts. $\frac{5}{8}$ of this circle is shaded. $\frac{3}{8}$ is not.

There are many types of fractions that you will use in your work:

Proper fractions: The numerator is smaller than the denominator. $\frac{1}{2}, \frac{2}{5}, \frac{1}{7}, \frac{3}{9}$

Improper fractions: The numerator is the same as or larger than the denominator. $\frac{5}{4}, \frac{3}{2}, \frac{7}{3}, \frac{5}{5}$

Like fractions: Fractions have the same denominator. $\frac{1}{8}, \frac{3}{8}, \frac{6}{8}, \frac{9}{8}$

Unlike fractions: Fractions have different denominators. $\frac{1}{4}, \frac{7}{8}, \frac{3}{5}, \frac{9}{2}$

Mixed numbers: The combination of a whole number and a proper fraction. $2\frac{1}{3}, 3\frac{1}{4}, 6\frac{1}{5}$

EXERCISE 1: TYPES OF FRACTIONS

Directions: Based on the information on page 587, name each group of fractions below.

1. $\frac{2}{3}$, $\frac{5}{3}$, $\frac{1}{3}$, $\frac{7}{3}$ _____

2. $1\frac{3}{4}$, $7\frac{1}{5}$, $2\frac{1}{8}$ _____

3. $\frac{9}{3}$, $\frac{10}{5}$, $\frac{4}{2}$, $\frac{6}{6}$ _____

4. $\frac{1}{5}$, $\frac{3}{7}$, $\frac{7}{8}$, $\frac{1}{3}$ _____

5. $\frac{1}{2}$, $\frac{1}{4}$, $\frac{2}{5}$, $\frac{3}{7}$ _____

Answers are on page 715.

Raising and Reducing Fractions

To use fractions easily, you must be able to ***raise*** a fraction to higher terms or to ***reduce*** a fraction to lower terms. In either case, you are changing both the numerator and the denominator of the fraction. When you do either, you are finding an ***equivalent fraction***—a fraction that has the same value. For example, a half-dollar has the same value as two quarters. As equivalent fractions, these can be written as $\frac{1}{2} = \frac{2}{4}$. This relationship can also be shown in pictures.

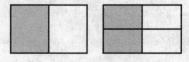

$$\frac{1}{2} = \frac{2}{4}$$

TO RAISE A FRACTION TO HIGHER TERMS
Multiply both the numerator and the denominator by the same number. You will obtain an equivalent fraction.

Example 1: $\dfrac{5\ (\times\ 2)}{8\ (\times\ 2)} = \dfrac{10}{16}$

TO REDUCE A FRACTION TO LOWER TERMS
Divide both the numerator and the denominator by the same number. You will obtain an equivalent fraction. (*Hint:* Look for a number that divides evenly into both.)

Example 2: $\dfrac{12\ (\div\ 4)}{16\ (\div\ 4)} = \dfrac{3}{4}$

A fraction is in the **lowest terms** if there is no whole number that will divide evenly into both the numerator and denominator. For example, $\frac{3}{8}$ is already in lowest terms because there is no whole number other than 1 that divides evenly into 3 and 8. Fraction answers should always be reduced to lowest terms. In fact, all fraction answers for the Mathematics Test will be given in lowest terms.

EXERCISE 2: RAISING AND REDUCING FRACTIONS

Directions: Solve each problem.

1. Raise each fraction to higher terms as indicated.

(a) $\dfrac{3 \ (\times 3)}{8 \ (\times 3)} = \dfrac{}{24}$ (b) $\dfrac{3 \ (\times 5)}{4 \ (\times 5)} = \dfrac{}{20}$ (c) $\dfrac{1 \ (\times 6)}{6 \ (\times 6)} = \dfrac{}{36}$

(d) $\dfrac{3}{7} = \dfrac{}{21}$ (e) $\dfrac{6}{7} = \dfrac{}{28}$ (f) $\dfrac{2}{5} = \dfrac{}{30}$

2. Reduce each fraction to lower terms as indicated.

(a) $\dfrac{12 \ (\div 4)}{16 \ (\div 4)} = \dfrac{}{4}$ (b) $\dfrac{21 \ (\div 7)}{28 \ (\div 7)} = \dfrac{}{4}$ (c) $\dfrac{2 \ (\div 2)}{6 \ (\div 2)} = \dfrac{}{3}$

(d) $\dfrac{40}{50} = \dfrac{}{5}$ (e) $\dfrac{24}{36} = \dfrac{}{3}$ (f) $\dfrac{30}{42} = \dfrac{}{7}$

3. Reduce each of the following fractions to the lowest terms.

(a) $\frac{6}{8}$ (b) $\frac{15}{20}$ (c) $\frac{9}{27}$ (d) $\frac{4}{12}$ (e) $\frac{25}{30}$

Answers are on page 715.

Relating Fractions and Decimals

In many arithmetic problems, you will work with both fractions and decimals. Each fraction can be expressed as a decimal, and vice versa. That's because decimals and fractions each represent parts of a whole.

You can think of decimals as fractions with denominators in powers of 10: 10, 100, 1000, and so on.

For example: one decimal place $= \dfrac{}{10}$

two decimal places $= \dfrac{}{100}$

three decimal places $= \dfrac{}{1000}$

Therefore, $.1 = \frac{1}{10}$ and $.03 = \frac{3}{100}$. Let's review the methods of changing from decimals to fractions and fractions to decimals.

Example 1: Change .75 to a fraction.

STEP 1. Write the number 75 without a decimal point as a numerator. $\dfrac{75}{}$

STEP 2. Write 100, the value of the last decimal place, as a denominator. $\dfrac{75}{100}$ This can be reduced to $\frac{3}{4}$.

Example 2: Change .039 to a fraction.

$.039 = \dfrac{39}{1000}$ ← number without decimal point

← three decimal places are thousandths

CHANGING A DECIMAL TO A FRACTION

1. Write the number without the decimal point. This is your numerator.

2. Make the denominator the value of the last place value in the decimal.

To change a fraction to a decimal, divide the numerator by the denominator. You can do this because a fraction bar also indicates division. In other words, $\frac{5}{8}$ can mean $5 \div 8$ or $8\overline{)5}$.

Example 1:
$$\frac{5}{8} = \begin{array}{r} .625 \\ 8\overline{)5.000} \\ \underline{-48} \\ 20 \\ \underline{-16} \\ 40 \\ \underline{-40} \\ 0 \end{array}$$

Example 2:
$$\frac{2}{3} = \begin{array}{r} .66\frac{2}{3} \\ 3\overline{)2.00} \\ \underline{-18} \\ 20 \\ \underline{-18} \\ 2 \end{array}$$

▶ **TIP:** Example 2 is a repeating decimal. After two decimal places, you can bring up the remainder to be part of a fraction. If necessary, you can round off decimals; for example, $.66\frac{2}{3} = .67$.

CHANGING A FRACTION TO A DECIMAL

Divide the numerator by the denominator. After two decimal places, make a fractional remainder.

You now know three meanings for fractions: $\frac{5}{8}$ means

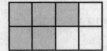

$$5 \div 8$$

5 out of 8 parts   5 out of 8 pieces   5 divided by 8

EXERCISE 3: CHANGING FRACTIONS AND DECIMALS

Directions: Solve each problem.

1. Change the following decimals to fractions. Reduce if necessary.

   (a) $.05 = \frac{}{100}$ **(b)** $.450 = \frac{}{1000}$ **(c)** $.07 = \frac{}{100}$

   (d) $.32$ **(e)** $.005$ **(f)** 3.1

2. Change the following fractions to decimals. Write a fractional remainder after two decimal places.

   (a) $\frac{3}{8}$ **(b)** $\frac{1}{5}$ **(c)** $\frac{4}{9}$ **(d)** $\frac{4}{3}$ **(e)** $\frac{5}{3}$ **(f)** $\frac{5}{6}$

Answers are on page 716.

Relating Mixed Numbers and Improper Fractions

In your work with fractions, you will have to make another type of change. This involves changing mixed numbers to improper fractions, and vice versa.

Example 1: Change $3\frac{7}{8}$ to an improper fraction.

STEP 1. Multiply the whole number by the denominator. $\qquad (3 \times 8) = 24$

STEP 2. Add that to the numerator of the fraction. $\qquad 24 + 7 = 31$

STEP 3. Write the sum over the original denominator. $\qquad 3\frac{7}{8} = \frac{31}{8}$

CHANGING A MIXED NUMBER TO AN IMPROPER FRACTION

1. Multiply the whole number by the denominator. Add that to the numerator of the fraction.

2. Write the sum over the original denominator.

The other skill you need is to be able to change an improper fraction to a mixed number.

Example 2: Change $\frac{11}{5}$ to a mixed number.

STEP 1. Divide the denominator into the numerator.

$$\frac{11}{5} = \begin{array}{r} 2 \\ 5\overline{)11} \\ -10 \\ \hline 1 \end{array}$$

STEP 2. Put the remainder over the denominator.

$$\frac{11}{5} = \begin{array}{r} 2\frac{1}{5} \\ 5\overline{)11} \\ -10 \\ \hline 1 \end{array}$$

CHANGING AN IMPROPER FRACTION TO A MIXED NUMBER

1. Divide the denominator into the numerator to get the whole-number part of the answer.

2. Put the remainder over the denominator to get the fractional part of the mixed number.

EXERCISE 4: CHANGING IMPROPER FRACTIONS AND MIXED NUMBERS

Directions: Solve each problem.

1. Change the following to improper fractions.

(a) $1\frac{5}{9}$ (b) $12\frac{1}{4}$ (c) $3\frac{2}{5}$ (d) $3\frac{1}{4}$ (e) $2\frac{1}{2}$ (f) $6\frac{2}{3}$

2. Change the following to whole or mixed numbers.

(a) $\frac{4}{3}$ (b) $\frac{16}{7}$ (c) $\frac{9}{9}$ (d) $\frac{9}{8}$ (e) $\frac{17}{5}$ (f) $\frac{3}{2}$

Answers are on page 716.

Comparing Numbers

On the GED Test, you may have to compare whole numbers, fractions, or decimals. In arithmetic, we often use a number line to help us "see" the relationships among numbers.

The Number Line

The number line is similar to a ruler except that it has no beginning or end. We indicate this by putting arrows at both ends of the line. We can say that all numbers are represented on this line even though it would be impossible to try to label all of them.

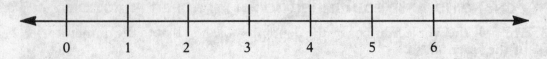

Whole numbers as well as mixed numbers can be represented on the number line.

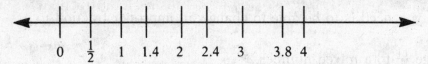

Note that the numbers get larger as you go to the right on the line.

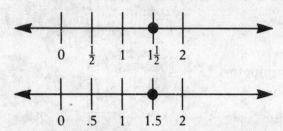

As the illustration shows, the same points can indicate either fractions or decimals. For example, $1\frac{1}{2}$ has the same value as 1.5.

We can use the number line to compare numbers and show their order. If we are given two numbers, then one of three statements must be true:

1. The two numbers are equal.

2. The first is larger than the second.

3. The first is smaller than the second.

There are symbols to indicate these relationships:

Symbol	Meaning	Example
=	is equal to	$4 = 4$
>	is greater than	$7 > 3$
<	is less than	$2 < 9$

▶ **TIP:** The arrow always points to the smaller number.

Comparing Decimals

When you compare decimals, make sure you have the same number of decimal places in each number. Attach as many zeros as needed after the last number in the decimal. Remember that adding zeros to the end of a decimal number does *not* change its value.

Example: Compare .064 and .06.

.064 has 3 decimal places   .064   both now have 3 decimal places

.06 has 2 decimal places   .060

Now both numbers are expressed in thousandths. Because 64 > 60, .064 > .060. So .064 > .06.

Comparing Fractions

To compare fractions, we must make sure that they have the same denominator. This is called the **common denominator**. For instance, we can compare $\frac{3}{16}$ and $\frac{11}{16}$. We know $\frac{11}{16} > \frac{3}{16}$ because 11 is greater than 3. If the fractions that you are comparing have different denominators, you must find a common denominator.

Example 1: Which is larger, $\frac{5}{8}$ or $\frac{1}{2}$?

STEP 1. Look at the larger denominator. If it is evenly divisible by the smaller denominator, use the larger one as the common denominator. $\frac{5}{8}$ $\frac{1}{2}$

STEP 2. Write both fractions with the same denominator. Change one fraction to higher terms.

$$\frac{5}{8} = \frac{5}{8}$$
$$\frac{1\,(\times 4)}{2\,(\times 4)} = \frac{4}{8}$$

STEP 3. Compare and determine which is larger. $\frac{5}{8} > \frac{4}{8}$, so

$$\frac{5}{8} > \frac{1}{2}$$

In some cases, the smaller denominator will not divide into the larger. You can multiply them together if they are small enough to get a reasonable common denominator.

Example 2: Which is larger, $\frac{2}{3}$ or $\frac{3}{4}$?

STEP 1. Multiply the denominators to get a common denominator. $3 \times 4 = 12$

STEP 2. Give them both the same denominator. In this case, it will be 12. Multiply $\frac{2}{3}$ by 4 and $\frac{3}{4}$ by 3.

$$\frac{2\,(\times 4)}{3\,(\times 4)} = \frac{8}{12}$$
$$\frac{3\,(\times 3)}{4\,(\times 3)} = \frac{9}{12}$$

STEP 3. Compare the fractions. $\frac{9}{12} > \frac{8}{12}$, so

$\frac{3}{4}$ is larger than $\frac{2}{3}$.

In other cases, the common denominator you get by multiplying might be too large to work with. In this case, find multiples of both denominators. Use the smallest multiple they have in common as the common denominator.

Example 3: Which is larger, $\frac{5}{12}$ or $\frac{3}{10}$?

STEP 1. Find multiples of both denominators. The smallest multiple of both will be the common denominator.

12: 12, 24, 36, 48, 60
10: 10, 20, 30, 40, 50, 60

STEP 2. Raise both fractions to higher terms. Divide the denominators into 60 to find which numbers to multiply the fractions by: $60 \div 12 = 5$ and $60 \div 10 = 6$.

$\frac{5}{12} \frac{(\times 5)}{(\times 5)} = \frac{25}{60}$

$\frac{3}{10} \frac{(\times 6)}{(\times 6)} = \frac{18}{60}$

STEP 3. Compare the fractions.

$\frac{25}{60} > \frac{18}{60}$, so

$\frac{5}{12}$ is greater than $\frac{3}{10}$.

TO FIND A COMMON DENOMINATOR

Look at the larger denominator.

1. Is it divisible by the other denominator? If so, use the larger number as the common denominator.

2. If not, try multiplying the denominators together.

3. If multiplying results in a very large common denominator, try multiples of both denominators until you find a common multiple.

Comparing Fractions and Decimals

We can compare fractions and decimals, but we must first change the decimal to a fraction or the fraction to a decimal.

Example: Compare $\frac{7}{8}$ and .75.

STEP 1. Change $\frac{7}{8}$ to a decimal.

$\frac{7}{8} = 8\overline{)7.000}^{.875}$

STEP 2. Write .75 with 3 decimal places because .875 has 3 decimal places.

.75 = .750
.875 > .750, so

STEP 3. Compare.

$\frac{7}{8}$ is greater than .75.

▶ TIP: You can also compare by changing a decimal to a fraction. For instance, .75 is $\frac{75}{100}$ or $\frac{3}{4}$. Both fractions would then have to have the same denominator: $\frac{6}{8}$ and $\frac{7}{8}$.

EXERCISE 5: COMPARING NUMBERS

Directions: Solve each problem.

1. Which of the following is larger?

(a) $\frac{7}{8}$ or $\frac{3}{5}$ (b) $\frac{2}{3}$ or $\frac{4}{9}$ (c) $\frac{3}{10}$ or $\frac{3}{4}$

2. Compare using the symbol $>$, $<$, or $=$. For example, $6 \boxed{<} 9$.

(a) $3 \boxed{} 8$

(b) $6 \boxed{} 0$

(c) $\frac{3}{8} \boxed{} \frac{1}{8}$

(d) $\frac{3}{4} \boxed{} \frac{2}{3}$

(e) $2\frac{3}{8} \boxed{} \frac{5}{2}$

(f) $\frac{5}{6} \boxed{} \frac{8}{9}$

(g) $.3 \boxed{} \frac{1}{4}$

(h) $\frac{1}{2} \boxed{} \frac{6}{12}$

(i) $\frac{9}{9} \boxed{} \frac{2}{2}$

(j) $.07 \boxed{} .0873$

(k) $\frac{3}{5} \boxed{} .6$

Answers are on page 717.

Operations with Fractions

Adding and Subtracting Fractions

When you are asked to add or subtract fractions or mixed numbers, you must be sure that the fractions have common denominators. If they don't, then rewrite the fractions with common denominators before adding or subtracting.

Example 1: Add $\frac{3}{8}$ and $\frac{1}{8}$.

STEP 1. Since the denominators are the same, add the numerators.

STEP 2. Reduce the answer.

$$\begin{array}{r} \frac{3}{8} \\ + \frac{1}{8} \\ \hline \frac{4}{8} \frac{(\div 4)}{(\div 4)} = \frac{1}{2} \end{array}$$

Example 2: Add $\frac{1}{10}$ and $\frac{3}{5}$.

STEP 1. Find the common denominator and equivalent fractions.

STEP 2. Add the numerators.

$$\begin{array}{r} \frac{1}{10} = \frac{1}{10} \\ + \frac{3}{5} \frac{(\times 2)}{} = \frac{6}{10} \\ \hline \frac{7}{10} \end{array}$$

Example 3: $\frac{2}{3} + \frac{1}{6} + \frac{3}{4}$

STEP 1. Find the common denominator for all numbers.

STEP 2. Add the numerators and put them over the denominator.

STEP 3. Change the improper fraction to a mixed number.

$$\begin{array}{r} \frac{2}{3} = \frac{8}{12} \\ \frac{1}{6} = \frac{2}{12} \\ + \frac{3}{4} = \frac{9}{12} \\ \hline \frac{19}{12} = 1\frac{7}{12} \end{array}$$

TO ADD FRACTIONS

1. Be sure all fractions have common denominators.

2. Add the numerators.

3. Put the total over the common denominator and be sure the answer is in lowest terms.

You follow the same method for adding mixed numbers. Add the fractions first in case you need to combine your fraction total with the whole numbers.

Example 4: Jorge bought $1\frac{3}{4}$ pounds of chicken and $6\frac{2}{3}$ pounds of ground beef for the picnic. How much did he buy altogether?

STEP 1. Find the common denominator: 12.

STEP 2. Add the fractions. Simplify the improper fraction $\frac{17}{12}$ to the mixed number $1\frac{5}{12}$.

STEP 3. Add $1\frac{5}{12}$ to 7 to get $8\frac{5}{12}$.

$$1\frac{3}{4} = 1\frac{9}{12}$$
$$+ \ 6\frac{2}{3} = 6\frac{8}{12}$$
$$\overline{}$$
$$7\frac{17}{12} = 7 + 1\frac{5}{12} = 8\frac{5}{12}$$

TO ADD MIXED NUMBERS

1. Be sure fractional parts have common denominators.

2. Add the fractional parts. Simplify to a mixed number if necessary.

3. Add the whole numbers.

4. Be sure your answer is in lowest terms.

The process of subtracting fractions is similar to adding fractions.

Example 5: $\frac{7}{16} - \frac{3}{16}$

$$\frac{7}{16}$$
$$- \ \frac{3}{16}$$
$$\overline{\frac{4}{16} = \frac{1}{4}}$$

Example 6: Take $\frac{3}{8}$ from $\frac{11}{12}$.

$$\frac{11}{12} = \frac{22}{24}$$
$$- \ \frac{3}{8} = \frac{9}{24}$$
$$\overline{\frac{13}{24}}$$

TO SUBTRACT FRACTIONS

1. Be sure the fractions have common denominators.

2. Subtract the numerators.

3. Put the difference over the common denominator.

4. Be sure the answer is in lowest terms.

One difference between adding and subtracting mixed numbers is that you might have to regroup to be able to subtract.

Example 7: Miriam needs to lose $9\frac{1}{4}$ pounds. She has already lost $5\frac{3}{4}$ pounds. How much does she have left to lose?

STEP 1. When you write the problem, you see that you can't take $\frac{3}{4}$ from $\frac{1}{4}$. You must regroup 1 from 9. Since 1 can also be written as $\frac{4}{4}$, rewrite the 9 as $8\frac{4}{4}$.

$$9\frac{1}{4} = 8\frac{4}{4} + \frac{1}{4} = 8\frac{5}{4}$$
$$- 5\frac{3}{4} \qquad\qquad = 5\frac{3}{4}$$
$$\overline{\qquad\qquad\qquad 3\frac{2}{4} = 3\frac{1}{2} \text{ pounds}}$$

STEP 2. Add the numerators to get $\frac{5}{4}$.

STEP 3. Subtract the fractions and whole numbers. Reduce the fraction.

▶ **TIP:** To decide how to rewrite a 1 that you regroup, look at the denominator of the fraction being subtracted. For example, if you are subtracting $\frac{3}{8}$, write the 1 as $\frac{8}{8}$, or if you are subtracting $\frac{5}{6}$, write the 1 as $\frac{6}{6}$.

TO SUBTRACT MIXED NUMBERS

1. Whether or not you need to regroup, be sure that the fractions have common denominators.

2. Subtract the fraction. If you have to regroup 1 from a whole number, convert it to an improper fraction with the same denominator and add it to the original fraction (if there is one).

3. Subtract the whole number.

EXERCISE 6: ADDING AND SUBTRACTING FRACTIONS

Directions: Solve each problem.

1. $\frac{1}{9}$
   $+ \frac{5}{9}$

2. $\frac{2}{3}$
   $+ \frac{1}{4}$

3. $\frac{3}{8}$
   $+ \frac{1}{12}$

4. $\frac{5}{6}$
   $+ \frac{1}{6}$

5. $1\frac{5}{12}$
   $+ 6\frac{4}{12}$

6. $4\frac{1}{5}$
   $+ 3\frac{2}{7}$

7. $4\frac{2}{9}$
   $+ 5\frac{1}{9}$

8. $3\frac{7}{8}$
   $2\frac{5}{6}$
   $+ 3\frac{1}{3}$

9. $\frac{9}{10}$
   $- \frac{3}{10}$

10. $\frac{5}{8}$
    $- \frac{1}{2}$

11. $\frac{4}{5}$
    $- \frac{1}{2}$

12. $\frac{12}{18}$
    $- \frac{5}{18}$

13. $4\frac{3}{4}$
    $- 2\frac{7}{8}$

14. $25\frac{1}{6}$
    $- 11\frac{1}{2}$

15. 10
    $- 3\frac{2}{17}$

16. 20
    $- \frac{4}{5}$

Answers are on page 717.

Multiplying Fractions

Unlike adding and subtracting fractions, there is no need for common denominators when you multiply and divide. In some cases, you will just multiply straight across, multiplying numerator by numerator and denominator by denominator.

Example 1: $\frac{3}{4} \times \frac{1}{2} = \frac{3}{8}$

Other problems can be solved more easily by *canceling*—reducing a numerator and a denominator divisible by the same factor.

Example 2: $\frac{6}{15} \times \frac{5}{12}$

STEP 1. The 15 and the 5 can be divided by 5.

$$\frac{6}{\cancel{15}_3} \times \frac{\cancel{5}^1}{12}$$

STEP 2. The 6 and the 12 can be divided by 6.

$$\frac{\cancel{6}^1}{\cancel{15}_3} \times \frac{\cancel{5}^1}{\cancel{12}_2}$$

STEP 3. Multiply straight across. If necessary, reduce the answer. $\frac{1}{3} \times \frac{1}{2} = \frac{1}{6}$

TO MULTIPLY FRACTIONS

1. Reduce numerators and denominators by canceling.

2. Multiply straight across.

3. Be sure your answer is reduced to lowest terms.

You can also cancel with three fractions. Sometimes you have to "jump" over the middle number.

Example 3: $\frac{3}{8} \times \frac{4}{7} \times \frac{5}{9}$

STEP 1. Divide both the 3 and the 9 by 3.

$$\frac{\cancel{3}^1}{8} \times \frac{4}{7} \times \frac{5}{\cancel{9}_3}$$

STEP 2. Divide both the 4 and the 8 by 4.

$$\frac{\cancel{3}^1}{\cancel{8}_2} \times \frac{\cancel{4}^1}{7} \times \frac{5}{\cancel{9}_3} = \frac{5}{42}$$

STEP 3. Multiply straight across.

Example 4 shows a case that involves multiplying mixed numbers.

Example 4: Sarah usually jogs $2\frac{1}{3}$ miles daily. She jogged the full distance on 3 days and $\frac{1}{2}$ the distance on another day. How many miles did she jog in all?

STEP 1. Change all mixed numbers to improper fractions. $\qquad 2\frac{1}{3} \times 3\frac{1}{2} = \frac{7}{3} \times \frac{7}{2}$

STEP 2. Multiply and change the improper fraction back to mixed numbers. $\qquad \frac{7}{3} \times \frac{7}{2} = \frac{49}{6} = 8\frac{1}{6}$

TO MULTIPLY MIXED NUMBERS

1. Change mixed numbers to improper fractions.

2. Reduce numbers divisible by the same number by canceling.

3. Multiply straight across.

4. Be sure your answer is reduced to lowest terms.

▶ **TIP:** Sometimes you may have to multiply a whole number by a fraction or a mixed number. Rewrite the whole number over 1 and then multiply as usual. For example, 4 can be written as $\frac{4}{1}$, so

$$\frac{1}{2} \times 4 = \frac{1}{\cancel{2}} \times \frac{\cancel{4}^{2}}{1} = 2.$$

EXERCISE 7: MULTIPLYING FRACTIONS

Directions: Solve each problem.

1. $\frac{6}{15} \times \frac{5}{12}$

2. $8 \times \frac{3}{4}$

3. $\frac{3}{8} \times \frac{2}{15} \times \frac{6}{7}$

4. $8\frac{1}{6} \times 4$

5. $\frac{5}{9} \times \frac{2}{5}$

6. $2\frac{1}{2} \times 2\frac{1}{3}$

7. $2\frac{3}{4} \times \frac{6}{7}$

8. $1\frac{3}{10} \times 5$

9. $3\frac{3}{8} \times 1\frac{3}{9}$

Answers are on page 718.

Dividing Fractions

Division is the opposite operation of multiplication. For instance, when we divide a number by 2, we are actually multiplying by $\frac{1}{2}$.

$$12 \div 2 = \frac{\cancel{12}^{6}}{1} \times \frac{1}{\cancel{2}_{1}} = \frac{6}{1} = 6$$

The fraction $\frac{1}{2}$ is called the ***reciprocal*** of 2. Two numbers whose product is 1 are reciprocals. Because $5 \times \frac{1}{5} = 1$, the numbers 5 and $\frac{1}{5}$ are reciprocals. To find the reciprocal of a number, you merely invert it, which means you turn it over.

To divide a fraction, follow the method shown below.

Example 1: Divide $\frac{7}{8}$ by $\frac{3}{4}$.

STEP 1. Multiply the first fraction by the reciprocal of the second. $\qquad \frac{7}{8} \div \frac{3}{4} = \frac{7}{8} \times \frac{4}{3}$

STEP 2. Multiply across and change the improper fraction to a mixed number. $\qquad \frac{7}{\cancel{8}_{2}} \times \frac{\cancel{4}^{1}}{3} = \frac{7}{6} = 1\frac{1}{6}$

To divide a mixed number, first change any mixed numbers to improper fractions.

Example 2: What is $4\frac{2}{3} \div 1\frac{1}{2}$?

STEP 1. Change both mixed numbers to improper fractions. $\qquad \frac{14}{3} \div \frac{3}{2}$

STEP 2. Multiply the first fraction by the reciprocal of the second and change improper fractions back to mixed numbers. $\qquad \frac{14}{3} \times \frac{2}{3} = \frac{28}{9} = 3\frac{1}{9}$

TO DIVIDE FRACTIONS OR MIXED NUMBERS

1. Change mixed numbers to improper fractions.

2. Multiply the first fraction by the reciprocal of the second.

3. Change any improper fractions back to mixed numbers.

EXERCISE 8: DIVIDING FRACTIONS

Directions: Solve each problem.

1. $\frac{4}{10} \div \frac{2}{3}$

3. $\frac{3}{7} \div \frac{6}{35}$

5. $1\frac{3}{8} \div 11$

2. $\frac{2}{5} \div 4$

4. $3\frac{2}{3} \div 1\frac{1}{2}$

6. $9 \div 2\frac{1}{2}$

Answers are on page 718.

Simplifying Fraction Problems

The best way to simplify fraction word problems is to *restate* the problem using whole numbers. Many times the fractions scare us off and make it difficult to figure out what to do. Let's look at a few examples of restating fraction problems.

▶ **TIP:** You can always look for key words or basic concepts that indicate the operation to use. A frequently used key word in fraction problems is *of*. A problem may ask you to find "$\frac{1}{2}$ of" something or "$\frac{2}{3}$ of" something. When you find a "part of" something, you multiply.

Example: An upholstery cleaner schedules $1\frac{1}{2}$-hour appointments for each couch to be cleaned. If he works $7\frac{1}{2}$ hours, how many couches will he clean?

Restated replacing fractions with whole numbers: "A cleaner schedules 2-hour appointments for each couch. If he works 8 hours, how many couches will he clean?"

Solution: After restating the problem, it seems more obvious that it is a division problem—the cleaner is splitting his day into smaller segments. Therefore, we would choose to use division in the original problem.

$$7\frac{1}{2} \div 1\frac{1}{2} = \frac{15}{2} \div \frac{3}{2} \qquad \frac{\overset{5}{\cancel{15}}}{\underset{1}{\cancel{2}}} \times \frac{\overset{1}{\cancel{2}}}{\underset{1}{\cancel{3}}} = 5$$

The cleaner will clean 5 couches.

▶ **TIP:** Be sure that the amount that is being divided up comes first in a division problem. In the example above, the $7\frac{1}{2}$-hour period was being divided into $1\frac{1}{2}$-hour segments.

Item Sets

Some problems on the Mathematics Test will be presented as item sets. An item set refers to a lot of information given in a paragraph or two or in an illustration. Then several questions based on that information (usually 3–5) will follow.

▶ **TIP:** The key to solving questions based on item sets is choosing only the information needed to answer that particular question.

The next group of problems follows the item set format. These problems require you to use your skills with whole numbers, decimals, and fractions.

EXERCISE 9: ITEM SETS

Directions: Write the information needed for each problem and then solve the problem.

Questions 1–3 are based on the problem below.

José wants to build bookshelves in his den. He needs 8 shelves, each $5\frac{1}{4}$ feet long. He must buy the lumber for the shelves in 6-foot lengths and then cut the $5\frac{1}{4}$-foot pieces from those lengths. The cost of the lumber is $98\frac{1}{2}$ cents per linear foot.

1. How much will the lumber cost for all of the shelves?

   Information needed:_____

   (1) $5.91   **(2)** $47.28   **(3)** $591   **(4)** $788   **(5)** $1379

2. How many linear feet of lumber will he waste by cutting?

   Information needed:_____

   (1) $\frac{3}{4}$ foot   **(2)** $4\frac{1}{2}$ feet   **(3)** 6 feet   **(4)** 8 feet   **(5)** 10 feet

3. The cost of varnishing all of the shelves will amount to an additional $12. José can buy prevarnished shelves of the correct length ($5\frac{1}{4}$ feet) for $13.95 each. How much will he save by doing the cutting and varnishing himself?

   Information needed:_____

   (1) $52.32   **(2)** $59.28   **(3)** $64.32   **(4)** $99.60   **(5)** $111.60

Questions 4–6 are based on the picture below.

The owner of a campground is planning to add two new roads, Birch Trail and Pine Way. The campground area is $\frac{7}{8}$ mile wide and $\frac{19}{20}$ mile deep.

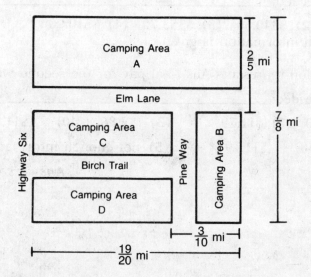

4. What is the length of Pine Way?

   Information needed:_____

   (1) $\frac{1}{8}$ mile   **(2)** $\frac{7}{20}$ mile   **(3)** $\frac{19}{40}$ mile   **(4)** $1\frac{11}{40}$ miles   **(5)** $1\frac{2}{3}$ miles

5. What is the total length of the two new roads?

Information needed:_____

   (1) $\frac{19}{40}$ mile   **(2)** $\frac{13}{20}$ mile   **(3)** $\frac{21}{23}$ mile   **(4)** $1\frac{1}{8}$ miles   **(5)** $1\frac{1}{4}$ miles

6. How wide is Elm Lane?

Information needed:_____

   (1) $\frac{1}{5}$ mile   **(2)** $\frac{2}{5}$ mile   **(3)** $\frac{19}{40}$ mile   **(4)** $\frac{19}{20}$ mile

   (5) not enough information is given

Questions 7–9 are based on the problem below.

> Al Watt gets paid an hourly wage for the first 40 hours he works. He gets $1\frac{1}{2}$ times his hourly wage for any overtime hours past the original 40 hours. The chart below shows his time sheet for the second week in April.

Name	Employee #	Hourly Wage	Hours
Al Watt	08395	$7.86	$43\frac{1}{3}$

7. What is Al's hourly wage per hour of overtime?

Information needed:_____

   (1) $3.93   **(2)** $5.24   **(3)** $11.79   **(4)** $15.72
   (5) not enough information is given

8. What is Al's total pay for the third week in April?

Information needed:_____

   (1) $314.40   **(2)** $340.60   **(3)** $353.70   **(4)** $510.90
   (5) not enough information is given

9. Which expression represents Al's total pay for the second week in April?

Information needed:_____

   (1) $7.86 × 40   **(2)** $11.79 × $\frac{10}{3}$ **(3)** ($7.86 × 40) × ($11.79 × $3\frac{1}{3}$)

   (4) ($7.86 × 40) + ($11.79 × $\frac{10}{3}$)   **(5)** not enough information is given

Answers are on page 718.

The following practice problems are GED-type problems that require you to use your skills with fractions as well as problem solving.

EXERCISE 10: FRACTION REVIEW

Directions: Solve each problem.

1. An $8\frac{3}{8}$-foot post was set $2\frac{3}{4}$ feet into the ground. What is the exact length of the post above ground?

    (1) $5\frac{5}{8}$ ft

    (2) $5\frac{7}{8}$ ft

    (3) 6 ft

    (4) $11\frac{1}{8}$ ft

    (5) not enough information is given

2. If a share of oil stock costs $\$36\frac{1}{4}$, how much do 24 shares cost?

    (1) $1.51

    (2) $\$16\frac{7}{8}$

    (3) $\$60\frac{7}{8}$

    (4) $864

    (5) $870

3. A car averages $22\frac{1}{2}$ miles per gallon of gasoline on a trip. Which of the following shows how many gallons of gasoline the car uses on a 720-mile trip?

    (1) $22\frac{1}{2} + 720$

    (2) $22\frac{1}{2} - 720$

    (3) $720 \div 22\frac{1}{2}$

    (4) $720 \times 22\frac{1}{2}$

    (5) $22\frac{1}{2} \div 720$

4. A dosage of medicine is $\frac{2}{3}$ milliliter. How many dosages can be given from a bottle containing 20 milliliters?

    (1) $13\frac{1}{3}$

    (2) $19\frac{1}{3}$

    (3) 20

    (4) 30

    (5) not enough information is given

5. Find the total weight of 2 cartons including the weight of both the cartons and the contents of the cartons. Each carton contains $16\frac{3}{4}$ pounds of potatoes.

    (1) $8\frac{3}{8}$ lb

    (2) $16\frac{3}{4}$ lb

    (3) $33\frac{1}{2}$ lb

    (4) $18\frac{3}{4}$ lb

    (5) not enough information is given

6. Find the missing length l in the drawing below.

   (1) $4\frac{3}{4}$ in
   (2) $5\frac{3}{4}$ in
   (3) 6 in
   (4) $8\frac{1}{8}$ in
   (5) not enough information is given

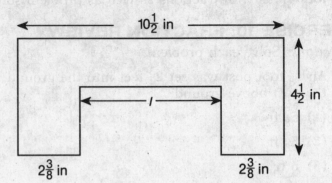

7. The price of round-trip airfare to Dallas is $285. How much will it cost a family of four if the husband pays full fare, the wife pays $\frac{2}{3}$ of full fare, and the two children each pay $\frac{1}{2}$ of the regular price?

   (1) $475
   (2) $570
   (3) $617.50
   (4) $760
   (5) $1140

8. Mr. Cortez owns a $10\frac{1}{2}$-acre tract of land, and he plans to subdivide this tract into $\frac{1}{4}$-acre lots. He must first set aside $\frac{1}{6}$ of the total land for roads. How many lots will this tract yield?

   (1) $1\frac{3}{4}$
   (2) $8\frac{3}{4}$
   (3) 35
   (4) $41\frac{1}{3}$
   (5) 42

9. A carpenter wanted three pieces of wood each $1\frac{5}{8}$ feet long. If he planned to cut them from a 6-foot piece of wood, how much of the piece would be left?

   (1) $1\frac{1}{8}$ ft
   (2) 3 ft
   (3) $4\frac{3}{8}$ ft
   (4) $4\frac{7}{8}$ ft
   (5) not enough information is given

10. A politician wants to get his message to $\frac{2}{3}$ of the population of 48,000 in Springfield. However, his advertising campaign reaches only $\frac{3}{4}$ of the number he intended. How many people does he actually reach?

    (1) 16,000
    (2) 24,000
    (3) 36,000
    (4) 68,000
    (5) 72,000

Answers are on page 718.

4
RATIO AND PROPORTION

Let's move from fractions to ratio and proportion. The word *ratio* basically means fraction, and we can use fractions to set up most ratios that compare two quantities; together, these two ratios are called a *proportion*. A proportion shows that two fractions are equal to each other. In this chapter, we will use proportions to solve many types of problems. In the next chapter, we will use proportions to solve percent word problems.

Ratio

A *ratio* is a mathematical way of comparing two quantities. Some everyday uses of ratio are "Six out of every eight students saw the concert," "I drove 55 miles per hour on the expressway," and "The mixture contains 2 cups of flour for every cup of water."

If the ratio compares two quantities with different units, it is called a *rate*. For example, 55 *miles* per *hour* is a rate. Whether we call the comparison a ratio or a rate, it can be written as a fraction, as a comparison using the word *to*, or as a comparison using a colon. You can set up a ratio whenever you are comparing two numbers.

Example 1: Write a ratio for: Six out of eight students saw the concert.

The ratio is: 6 to 8 OR 6:8 OR $\frac{6}{8}$

$\frac{6}{8}$ can be reduced to $\frac{3}{4}$

▶ **TIP:** The smaller the numbers are, the easier it is to understand the comparison, so it is a good idea to reduce the ratio to lowest terms.

Example 2: "I drove 55 miles per hour."

The rate is: 55 miles to 1 hour OR 55:1 OR $\frac{55}{1}$

The word *per* often tells you to set up a ratio. This ratio is a rate because it compares two different units: *miles* to *hours*.

▶ **TIP:** In a ratio, unlike a fraction, the number 1 is kept in the denominator.

Sometimes it is necessary to change the form of one of the numbers to make a comparison.

Example 3: Eggs cost 72 cents per dozen. What is the cost per egg?

$72:12 = \frac{72}{12} = \frac{6}{1}$

First you had to write 12 for a dozen eggs. When the ratio is reduced, it is 6 to 1, which means each egg costs 6 cents.

EXERCISE 1: RATIO

Directions: Write each comparison as a ratio or a rate in fraction form. Be sure to reduce each fraction completely.

1. 3 miles to 8 miles

2. 30 minutes to 1 hour

3. 27 feet to 18 feet

4. 3 pounds of meat for 4 people

5. 300 miles on 15 gallons of gas

6. 88 feet in 8 seconds

7. $42.21 earned in 7 hours

8. $80 for 12 boards

Answers are on page 719.

Application of Ratio

The real value of ratio on the GED Test is its application to real-life problem solving. For example, "Which is the better buy?" is a question frequently posed by shoppers. These problems can be solved by using ratios to compare the cost per unit of weight for each item.

Example: There are three sizes of Wow Chow on the grocer's shelves. Which is the best buy?

To find the per-unit cost for each item, calculate the ratio of cost to weight. This is represented by the ratio $\frac{cost}{weight}$.

(a) $\frac{\$1.89}{3\,lb} = \frac{\$.63}{1\,lb}$ OR $.63 per lb

(b) $\frac{\$2.95}{5\,lb} = \frac{\$.59}{1\,lb}$ OR $.59 per lb

(c) $\frac{\$11.40}{20\,lb} = \frac{\$.57}{1\,lb}$ OR $.57 per lb

Notice that each ratio was reduced. The 20-lb bag costs 57 cents per pound, the 5-lb bag costs 59 cents per pound, while the 3-lb bag costs 63 cents per pound. The 20-lb bag is the best buy. Now all you would need to decide is how much dog food you *really* want to buy.

Next, let's look at a few application problems involving ratios and rates.

EXERCISE 2: APPLICATION OF RATIOS

Directions: Solve each problem.

Questions 1–3 are based on the information in the table below. Write each ratio as a fraction to compare the expenses.

PAINTERS' WEEKLY WORK EXPENSES				TOTAL
Tools $25	Supplies $120	Transportation $40	Telephone $15	$200

1. Compare the cost of supplies to total expenses.

2. The total expenses are how many times greater than the expense for transportation?

3. Find the ratio of supplies to tools.

4. A company has assets of $6,800,000 and liabilities of $1,700,000. What is the company's ratio of liabilities to assets?

5. In a tennis club of 750 members, 250 members are women. What is the ratio of female members to total membership?

6. You own 300 shares of Consolidated Merchants stock and receive a dividend of $729. What is the dividend per share?

Questions 7 and 8 are based on the information below.

> The Miranda family purchased a 250-pound side of beef and had it packaged. They paid $365 for the side of beef. During the packaging, 75 lb of beef were discarded as waste.

7. How many pounds of beef were packaged?

8. What was the cost per pound for the packaged beef?

Answers are on page 719.

Proportion

A *proportion* is a statement that two ratios (fractions) are equal. The arithmetic statement $\frac{7}{8} = \frac{14}{16}$ is an example of a proportion. In words, it means "7 is to 8 as 14 is to 16." A proportion is true if the *cross products* are equal. Cross products are the numbers that are at opposite corners of the equivalent fractions.

Example 1:

$$\frac{7}{8} = \frac{14}{16}$$

$$\underbrace{7 \times 16}_{112} = \underbrace{8 \times 14}_{112} \qquad \textit{7} \times \textit{16} \text{ and } \textit{8} \times \textit{14} \text{ are cross products.}$$

A useful type of proportion is one in which one of the ratios is not completely known. The missing number is represented by a letter. Example 2 shows how to solve for the letter.

Example 2: If 3 apples cost 50 cents, find the cost of 15 apples at the same rate.
You can write a proportion to represent this.

STEP 1. Set up the proportion where c represents the unknown cost of the apples.

$$\frac{3 \text{ apples}}{\$.50} = \frac{15 \text{ apples}}{c}$$

$$\frac{3}{.50} = \frac{15}{c}$$

STEP 2. Cross multiply the two given numbers.

$$15 \times .50 = \$7.50$$

STEP 3. Divide that answer by the number that is left.

$$\$7.50 \div 3 = \$2.50$$
$$c = \$2.50$$

Therefore, if 3 apples cost 50 cents, 15 apples cost $2.50.

We know this is true because the cross products are equal.

$$\frac{3}{\$.50} = \frac{15}{\$2.50}$$

$$3 \times \$2.50 = 15 \times \$.50$$

$$\$7.50 = \$7.50$$

▶ **TIP:** When setting up a proportion, be sure to set up both fractions in the same way. In this case, we put *apples* over *money* in both fractions. It helps to begin by writing the labels *apples* and c on each fraction to make sure they are both written the same way.

TO SOLVE A PROPORTION

1. Cross multiply two given numbers.

2. Divide that answer by the number that is left in the proportion.

You can also represent the operations to solve a proportion in the following way.

1. Write the proportion.

$$\frac{b}{8} = \frac{5}{20}$$

2. Write the multiplication above a fraction bar. Remember that a fraction bar also means "divided by."

$$8 \times 5$$

3. Write the remaining number under the fraction bar.

$$\frac{8 \times 5}{20}$$

4. Solve by multiplying the top and dividing by the bottom.

$$\frac{40}{20} = 2$$

EXERCISE 3: SOLVING PROPORTIONS

Directions: Solve the following proportions for the missing element in each.

1. $\frac{2}{5} = \frac{m}{10}$ **2.** $\frac{x}{7} = \frac{3}{21}$ **3.** $\frac{5}{y} = \frac{15}{20}$ **4.** $\frac{6}{4} = \frac{12}{z}$ **5.** $\frac{x}{12} = \frac{30}{24}$

Answers are on page 719.

Application of Proportion

As you will see throughout the math section of this book, proportion has a great many applications. If a problem compares two types of quantities and asks for a missing factor, you should consider using a proportion to solve the problem.

Example 1: A 25-acre field yields 350 bushels of wheat. At that rate, how many bushels will a 60-acre field yield?

STEP 1. Set up the proportion, keeping acres on the top and bushels on the bottom.

$$\frac{25 \text{ acres}}{350 \text{ bushels}} = \frac{60 \text{ acres}}{b}$$

$$\frac{25}{350} = \frac{60}{b}$$

STEP 2. Cross multiply and divide by the remaining number.

$$\frac{350 \times 60}{25} = \frac{21{,}000}{25} = 840 \text{ bushels}$$

Therefore, a 60-acre field will yield 840 bushels of wheat.

The most challenging part of setting up a proportion is putting the numbers in the right part of the proportion. Try setting up a proportion to solve the problem below.

Example 2: If a baseball player hits 10 home runs in the first 45 games, at the same rate how many home runs can he expect to hit during the 162-game season?

STEP 1. Gather the given information and identify the unknown quantity.

10 home runs in 45 games.
h home runs in 162 games.

STEP 2. Write a proportion, keeping the labels in the same part of both ratios.

$$\frac{10 \text{ home runs}}{45 \text{ games}} = \frac{h}{162 \text{ games}}$$

STEP 3. Solve.

$$\frac{162 \times 10}{45} = \frac{1620}{45} = 36$$

The player can expect to hit 36 home runs in 162 games.

EXERCISE 4: APPLICATION OF PROPORTION

Directions: Solve each problem.

1. A car travels 96 miles on 8 gallons of gas. How far can the car travel on a full tank of gas that holds 20 gallons?

2. The picture to the right is to be enlarged. If the width of the enlargement will be 8 inches, how high will it be?

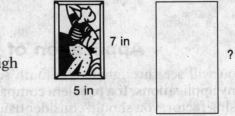

3. At Foster's Department Store, the ratio of managers to salespeople is 2:9. If Foster's currently has 180 salespeople, how many managers are there?

4. On the scale drawing to the right, $\frac{1}{8}$ inch = 1 foot. If the length of a room on the scale drawing is $2\frac{1}{4}$ inches, how long is the actual room?

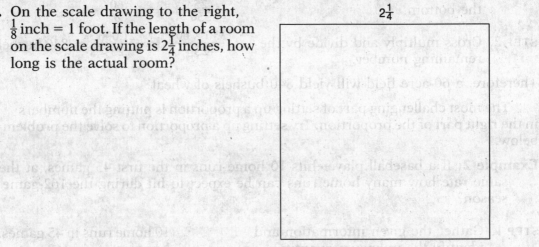

Key: $\frac{1}{8}$ in = 1 ft

5. Two pancakes contain 120 calories. Ellen had a stack of 7 pancakes. How many calories did she have?

Answers are on page 719.

5
PERCENTS

One of the most common and practical applications of math is the study of percents. We are confronted with percents when we buy on installment, pay taxes, get a loan, get discounts on purchases, read major-league baseball standings, or even listen to the weather report.

You might hear on the radio or TV that mortgage loans are at 7.5%. The interest rate on credit cards is 16%. You can finance your new car at 6.9%. The state sales tax is 7%. Crawford's Department Store has 20% off on winter coats this week. Percents are everywhere!

What Are Percents?

Percents, like decimals and fractions, are ways of writing parts of a whole. A percent is a part of a whole that has been divided into 100 equal pieces. Therefore, **percent** means "per hundred."

A percent is written as a number with the sign %. For example, the number 50% means the same as $\frac{50}{100}$ or .50. When you work with percents, you may have to change them to an equivalent decimal or fraction. The chart below shows the relationship among percents, fractions, and decimals. You should memorize this list because these relationships are used over and over again.

Percent	Fraction	Decimal
1%	$\frac{1}{100}$	.01
5%	$\frac{5}{100} = \frac{1}{20}$	.05
10%	$\frac{10}{100} = \frac{1}{10}$	.10
25%	$\frac{25}{100} = \frac{1}{4}$	.25
$33\frac{1}{3}$%	$\frac{33\frac{1}{3}}{100} = \frac{1}{3}$	$.33\frac{1}{3}$
50%	$\frac{50}{100} = \frac{1}{2}$	.50
$66\frac{2}{3}$%	$\frac{66\frac{2}{3}}{100} = \frac{2}{3}$	$.66\frac{2}{3}$
75%	$\frac{75}{100} = \frac{3}{4}$	.75
100%	$\frac{100}{100} = 1$	1.00

▶ **TIP:** Since 100% is one whole, then anything less than 100% is less than one whole. For example, 75% of a quantity is a part of that quantity.

Changing to Fractions and Decimals

Many problems require a change back and forth from fractions to decimals to percents. To change a percent to a fraction or decimal, remember what % means: percent means "per hundred."

$$\% \text{ means } "\times \tfrac{1}{100}, " \text{ and } \% \text{ means } "\times .01."$$

Example 1: Change 13% to an equivalent fraction and to an equivalent decimal.

To a fraction: $13 \times \frac{1}{100} = \frac{13}{1} \times \frac{1}{100} = \frac{13}{100}$

To a decimal: $13 \times .01 = .13$

▶ **TIP:** You will notice that multiplying by .01 moves the decimal point 2 places to the left. $13\% = .13. = .13$

Example 2: Change the following to an equivalent fraction and an equivalent decimal. Be sure to reduce fractions to lowest terms.

80% *To a fraction:* $80 \times \frac{1}{100} = \frac{\overset{4}{\cancel{80}}}{1} \times \frac{1}{\underset{5}{\cancel{100}}} = \frac{4}{5}$

To a decimal: $80 \times .01 = .80 \text{ or } .8$

$33\frac{1}{3}\%$ *To a fraction:* $33\frac{1}{3} \times \frac{1}{100} = \frac{\overset{1}{\cancel{100}}}{3} \times \frac{1}{\underset{1}{\cancel{100}}} = \frac{1}{3}$

To a decimal: $33\frac{1}{3} \times .01 = .33\frac{1}{3}$

150% *To a mixed number:* $150 \times \frac{1}{100} = \frac{\overset{3}{\cancel{150}}}{1} \times \frac{1}{\underset{2}{\cancel{100}}} = \frac{3}{2} = 1\frac{1}{2}$

To a decimal: $150 \times .01 = 1.50 \text{ or } 1.5$

Some percents can be written like this: .6%. This means "six-tenths of one percent" and is less than 1%.

Example 3: Write .6% as a fraction and as a decimal.

As a fraction: First, write the decimal part as a fraction. Then, multiply by $\frac{1}{100}$.
$.6 = \frac{6}{10} = \frac{3}{5}$
$\frac{3}{5} \times \frac{1}{100} = \frac{3}{500}$

As a decimal: Just write the decimal part and multiply by .01. $.6 \times .01 = .006$

▶ **TIP:** Always read a decimal carefully for its meaning. Anything over 100% is *more than one whole*. For example, 200% is the same as 2 times a whole. Thus, 200% of 6 is 12.

Any proper fraction or decimal followed by % means *less than 1%*. For example, $\frac{3}{4}\%$ means "three-quarters of one percent," and .75% means "seventy-five hundredths of one percent," *not* 75%.

EXERCISE 1: CHANGING TO FRACTIONS AND DECIMALS

Directions: Change each percent to an equivalent fraction *and* an equivalent decimal.

1. 87%   **4.** $66\frac{2}{3}\%$ **7.** 18%

2. 40%   **5.** 200%   **8.** .8%

3. 2%   **6.** 12.5%   **9.** $\frac{1}{2}\%$

Answers are on page 720.

Changing to Percents

In some problems, you are given a fraction or a decimal, and you need to change it to a percent. You can do this by dividing by one-hundredth.

- To change a fraction to a percent, multiply by 100 and attach a % sign.

- To change a decimal to a percent, multiply by 100 and attach a % sign.

Example 1: Change $\frac{7}{8}$ to a percent.

$$\frac{7}{8} \times 100 = \frac{7}{8} \times \frac{100}{1} = \frac{700}{8} = 87\frac{1}{2} = 87\frac{1}{2}\%$$

Example 2: Change .3 to a percent.

$$.3 \times 100 = 30 = 30\%$$

Example 3: Change the mixed number 2.04 to an equivalent percent.

$$\frac{2.04}{1} \times \frac{100}{1} = \frac{204}{1} = 204 = 204\%$$

EXERCISE 2: CHANGING TO PERCENTS

Directions: Change the following numbers to equivalent percents.

1. $\frac{3}{5}$ **4.** .0025   **7.** $\frac{9}{10}$

2. .70   **5.** $\frac{3}{8}$ **8.** .625

3. $\frac{1}{3}$ **6.** 4.5   **9.** $2\frac{1}{4}$

Answers are on page 720.

Solving Percent Problems

As you've seen, a percent can be written as a fraction. The percent 25% can be written as $\frac{25}{100}$. From your study of ratio, you also know that $\frac{25}{100}$ means "25 out of 100." Because of this relationship among percents, fractions, and ratios, you can use an interesting method to solve percent word problems.

Using Proportions

A percent word problem can be solved by setting up a proportion. We call this the "PART over WHOLE" method. The proportion below shows how to set up one of these problems.

$$\frac{\text{PART}}{\text{WHOLE}} = \frac{\%\,(\text{PART})}{100\%\,(\text{WHOLE})}$$

You may also see it shown this way:

part	%
whole	100

In the example of 25%, the proportion would look like this:

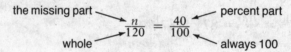

$$\underset{\text{whole}}{\overset{\text{part}}{\frac{25}{100}}} = \underset{\text{always 100\%}}{\overset{\text{percent (part)}}{\frac{25\%}{100\%}}}$$

This proportion shows that the relationship of a part to a whole is the same as the relationship of a percent to 100%. To solve a percent word problem, you must read the problem carefully and first decide whether you are looking for the *percent*, *part*, or *whole*. Use an *n* for the number you are trying to find. Remember, the 100 on the bottom right *never* changes.

To illustrate the use of this method in solving percent problems, we will work through three examples.

Example 1: Find 40% of 120.

Solution: We are looking for a missing PART.

$$\underset{\text{whole}}{\overset{\text{the missing part}}{\frac{n}{120}}} = \underset{\text{always 100}}{\overset{\text{percent part}}{\frac{40}{100}}}$$

Cross multiply: 120 × 40 = 4800

Divide: 4800 ÷ 100 = 48

The missing number is 48. 40% of 120 is 48.

► **TIP:** Sometimes, to find a percent, it may be easier just to change the percent to a decimal or fraction and multiply. For example, to find 40% of 120: 120 × .40 = 48, and 120 × $\frac{2}{5}$ = 48.

Example 2: 18 is what percent of 72?

Solution: We are looking for the PERCENT.

$$\underset{\text{whole}}{\overset{\text{part}}{\frac{18}{72}}} = \underset{\text{always 100}}{\overset{\text{the missing percent}}{\frac{n}{100}}}$$

Cross multiply: 18 × 100 = 1800

Divide: 1800 ÷ 72 = 25

The number is 25%. 18 is 25% of 72.

Example 3: 120% of what number is 60?

Solution: We are looking for the WHOLE.

$$\underset{\text{the missing whole}}{\overset{\text{part}}{\frac{60}{n}}} = \underset{\text{always 100}}{\overset{\text{percent}}{\frac{120}{100}}}$$

Cross multiply: 60 × 100 = 6000

Divide: 6000 ÷ 120 = 50

The missing number is 50. 120% of 50 is 60.

   Notice that in Example 3 the part (60) is larger than the whole (50). This is because the percent is 120%, which is more than 100%.

SOLVING A PERCENT PROBLEM

1. Decide if you are looking for the part, whole, or percent. Use n in place of the missing number.

2. Set up the proportion and put any given numbers and the n in the right place.

$$\frac{\text{Part}}{\text{Whole}} = \frac{\text{Percent}(\%)}{100}$$

3. Cross multiply.

4. Divide.

EXERCISE 3: PERCENT PROBLEMS

Directions: Write down which you are looking for: part, whole, or percent. Then solve each problem.

1. Find 4% of 30.

2. What percent of 56 is 14?

3. 10 is 2.5% of what number?

4. 7% of what amount is 14?

5. What percent of $340 is $30.60?

6. $\frac{1}{2}$% of 62 is what number?

7. What is 120% of 45?

8. 210 is what percent of 600?

9. 16% of what number is 18?

10. 20 is what percent of 5?

Answers are on page 720.

Percent Word Problems

As you know, percents are a part of the math that people do every day—at work, while shopping, or in personal money matters. On pages 617–619, you will study special types of percent problems—finding interest, discounts, and repayments of loans. In general, percent word problems are multi-step problems. You know, of course, that you always multiply and then divide after you have set up a proportion. However, you may also have to perform some addition or subtraction to get a final answer.

The tricky part of percent word problems is to identify what is being asked for. These problems require more careful reading than those in Exercise 3.

Example 1: To pass her science test, Amy must get 75% of the problems correct. Out of 80 questions, how many must she get right to pass?

Given: 75%—the percent
        80—the whole test

Look for: n—the number to get right (the part)

The proportion for this problem reads:

$$\text{part} \rightarrow \frac{n}{80} = \frac{75}{100} \leftarrow \text{percent}$$
$$\text{whole} \qquad\qquad \leftarrow \text{always 100}$$

Example 2: Erica is charged 21% in finance charges for the unpaid balance on her credit cards. If her bank tells her she owes $42 in finance charges, what is her unpaid balance?

The proportion for this problem is:

$$\text{finance charge} \rightarrow \frac{42}{n} = \frac{21}{100} \leftarrow \text{percent}$$
$$\text{balance} \qquad\qquad \leftarrow \text{always 100}$$

Example 3 is a case that needs more than one step to find the answer.

Example 3: A car depreciates (loses value) 20% the first year it is owned. If Elena's car cost her $12,480 when it was new, what was it worth after the first year?

STEP 1. Find the amount of depreciation.

$$\frac{n}{12,480} \times \frac{20}{100}$$

Cross multiply: $12,480 \times 20 = 249,600$

Divide: $249,600 \div 100 = \$2496$ depreciation

STEP 2. Find the value of the car after 1 year.

Subtract: $\$12,480 - \$2496 = \$9984$

EXERCISE 4: PERCENT WORD PROBLEMS

Directions: Solve each problem.

Questions 1–3 refer to the information below.

Jesse takes home $2100 a month. He saves 12% of his earnings, and he spends $420 a month for rent.

1. How much does Jesse save each month?

2. Jesse's rent is what percent of his take-home pay?

3. Jesse's employer has offered him a 5% raise for next year. What will be his monthly take-home pay next year?

4. On her test, Rachel got 26 out of 40 questions right. What percent did she get wrong?

5. Mrs. Rogers put 15% down on her new car. If the down payment was $1800, how much did the car cost?

6. A political campaign conducted a poll to determine how the candidate was doing. The results were as follows. What percent of the voters was undecided?

Allen	Gault	Undecided
200	120	180

7. Employees at Todd's Musicmart get a 20% discount on all purchases. If Hosea buys three cassettes at $7.49 each, what will he have to pay after his employee discount?

Answers are on page 720.

Interest Problems

If you borrow or invest money, you will be dealing with an *interest rate* that is expressed as a percent. Interest rates are calculated on an annual basis. Thus, if the loan is longer or shorter than one year, the amount of interest per year must be multiplied by the length of time.

The length of time of the loan must always be expressed as one year or a part of a year. If the time is given in months, write the months as a fraction comparing the given number of months to 12 months.

For example, 9 months = $\frac{9 \text{ months}}{12 \text{ months}} = \frac{3}{4}$ year

If the time is given in days, change it to a fraction of a year by comparing the given number of days to 360 (approximately the number of days in a year).

For example, 120 days = $\frac{120 \text{ days}}{360 \text{ days}} = \frac{1}{3}$ year

Example 1: To expand one of its factory-outlet stores, a towel manufacturer secures a $2\frac{1}{2}$-year loan for $35,000 at an annual interest rate of 7%. How much interest will the manufacturer pay on the loan?

STEP 1. Find the interest for 1 year. $\frac{n}{35,000} = \frac{7}{100}$

STEP 2. Cross multiply and divide. $\frac{35,000 \times 7}{100} = 2450$

STEP 3. Find the interest for $2\frac{1}{2}$ years. $2450 \times 2\frac{1}{2} = \$6125$

Example 2: Mrs. Barnes borrowed $4000 for 3 years. Find the amount she repaid if the annual rate of interest was 9%.

STEP 1. Find the interest for 1 year.

$$\frac{n}{4000} = \frac{9}{100}$$

$$\frac{9 \times 4000}{100} = \frac{36,000}{100} = 360$$

STEP 2. Find the interest for 3 years.

$$360 \times 3 = 1080$$

STEP 3. Find the amount she repaid.

$$4000 + 1080 = \$5080$$

▶ **TIP:** Some interest problems require you to find only the interest, and others require you to find the total amount of the loan or investment. The total is the amount that you borrowed plus the interest. You must read problems carefully to make sure you understand whether you are being asked for the *interest* or the *amount to pay back* as in Example 2.

Example 3: Marcy borrowed $18,000 for 90 days to buy inventory for her gift shop at an annual rate of 12%. How much interest did she pay?

STEP 1. Find the interest for 1 year.

$$\frac{n}{18,000} = \frac{12}{100}$$

$$\frac{18,000 \times 12}{100} = \frac{216,000}{100} = 2160$$

STEP 2. Find the interest for $\frac{1}{4}$ year.

$$2160 \times \frac{1}{4} = \$540$$

SOLVING INTEREST PROBLEMS

1. Set up a proportion and solve it for the interest.
$$\frac{\text{Interest}}{\text{Original Amount}} = \frac{\text{Percent}}{100}$$

2. To find the total interest, multiply the interest by the length of time of the loan.

3. To find the total amount of the loan or investment, add the original amount to the total interest.

In some cases, you may have to find an amount other than the interest. You can still use the proportional method to find the percent of interest (rate).

Example 4: The yearly income from an investment of $2400 is $192. What is the annual rate of interest?

STEP 1. Write the proportion.

$$\frac{192}{2400} = \frac{n}{100}$$

STEP 2. Solve for the percent.

$$\frac{192 \times 100}{2400} = 8\%$$

▶ **TIP:** A common way to find interest is to use the formula $I = prt$, where p = principal, r = rate, and t = time.

EXERCISE 5: INTEREST PROBLEMS

Directions: Solve each problem.

1. A building contractor borrowed $60,000 for 9 months at an annual interest rate of 8%. What is the interest due on the loan?

   (1) $2400   **(2)** $3600   **(3)** $3900   **(4)** $64,800   **(5)** $72,000

2. To take advantage of a closeout sale, a motel owner borrows $31,000 to buy 124 color television sets. The loan is for 90 days at an annual interest rate of 12.5%. Find the total amount to be repaid.

(1) $968.75 (2) $3,875 (3) $31,968.75 (4) $34,875
(5) not enough information is provided

3. Which expression shows how you find the interest on $1500 at $8\frac{1}{2}\%$ for one year?

(1) $\dfrac{1500 \times 8\frac{1}{2}}{100}$ (2) $\dfrac{1500 \times 100}{8\frac{1}{2}}$ (3) $\dfrac{1500}{100 \div 8\frac{1}{2}}$ (4) $\dfrac{100}{1500 \times 8\frac{1}{2}}$ (5) $\dfrac{100}{1500 \div 8\frac{1}{2}}$

4. Alex borrowed some money for one year at a rate of 8%. If he paid $360 in interest that year, how much did he borrow?

(1) $28.80 (2) $288 (3) $2,880 (4) $4,500 (5) $36,000

5. Ted has already saved $12,000, which he plans to use in building a summer cottage. The lot he wants costs $8500. The builder estimates that it will cost $32,000 to build the house, and Ted expects that there will be additional expenses of $2500. Ted will borrow the additional money he needs from the American Bank. At 10.5%, how much interest will he owe at the end of the first year?

(1) $3255 (2) $4816 (3) $31,000 (4) $34,255 (5) $347,200

Answers are on page 721.

EXERCISE 6: PERCENT REVIEW

Directions: Solve each problem.

1. During a recent shopping spree, Tom and Ali bought some new accessories for their apartment. Ali chose a crocheted throw pillow at $24.95, and Tom purchased a rural landscape painting for $135. How much did they actually spend if they paid 7% sales tax on their purchases?

(1) $11.20
(2) $12.00
(3) $148.75
(4) $159.95
(5) $171.15

2. Paint that regularly sells for $15.90 per gallon is on sale at a 20% discount. Which expression shows how to find the price of the paint after the discount?

(1) $15.90 × .20(15.90)
(2) $15.90 + .20(15.90)
(3) $15.90 − .20(15.90)
(4) $15.90 ÷ .20(15.90)
(5) $15.90 − .20

3. You buy a new car for $12,800 and make a down payment of $2500. If you finance the remainder at 8% annually for three years, how much will you actually pay for the car?

(1) $10,300
(2) $12,190
(3) $9,400
(4) $12,772
(5) $15,272

4. A car dealer is offering a rebate of $750 on any new-car purchase. If the purchase price of a car is $2000 more than it was last year, what is the rate of discount offered by the rebate?

(1) 7.5%
(2) 10%
(3) 13.3%
(4) 75%
(5) not enough information is given

620 TEST 5: MATHEMATICS

5. A real estate agent received a $4\frac{1}{2}\%$ commission on the sale of a condominium. The condominium sold for $48,900. How much did the agent receive?

(1) $1,956
(2) $2,200.50
(3) $19,560
(4) $22,005
(5) not enough information is given

Questions 6–11 refer to the chart below.

Margaret's net earnings (take-home pay) for last year were $24,000. Her expenses for the year were

Food	$3900
Rent	6000
Utilities	2400
Medical	600
Insurance	1500
Car	3800
Clothing	1000
Dues	300
Phone	300
Entertainment	1200
Savings	2400
Miscellaneous	600

6. What percent of her total net income did Margaret spend on rent?

(1) $\frac{1}{4}$ (2) 2.5 (3) 4 (4) 25 (5) 40

7. What is the ratio of savings to total income?

(1) $\frac{1}{24}$ (2) $\frac{1}{10}$ (3) $\frac{10}{1}$ (4) $\frac{24}{1}$ (5) $\frac{21,600}{1}$

8. Entertainment and savings account for what percent of Margaret's expenditures?

(1) 5 (2) 10 (3) 15 (4) 50 (5) 75

9. Assume that insurance costs are expected to rise 6.5% next year. How much will Margaret pay for insurance then?

(1) $6.50 (2) $65.00 (3) $97.50 (4) $1565 (5) $1597.50

10. Margaret's property taxes rose 7% last year. How much of her take-home pay went to property taxes?

(1) $168 (2) $1200 (3) $4800 (4) $6168
(5) not enough information is given

11. Margaret's take-home pay is 67% of her gross pay, which amounts to $35,821. Which expression shows how you would find her take-home pay?

(1) (35,821 + 67) ÷ 100
(2) (35,821 × 67) ÷ 100
(3) (35,821 × 100) ÷ 67
(4) (35,821 + 100) ÷ 67
(5) (35,821 + 100) + 67

Answers are on page 722.

6
MEASUREMENT

What is measurement? What do we do when we measure the length of a room or take the weight of a package? To measure any physical object, we assign both a number and a unit of measurement to it. For instance, a room is 23 feet long, and a package weighs 2 pounds 3 ounces. Units of measurement connect our real world to our number system.

Standard Measurement

The units of measurement below are the ones used most often in the United States. They are often referred to as the *standard* or *American* units of measure.

Units of Length
12 inches (in) = 1 foot (ft)
3 feet = 1 yard (yd)
36 inches = 1 yard
5280 feet = 1 mile (mi)

Units of Capacity
4 quarts (qt) = 1 gallon (gal)
2 pints (pt) = 1 quart
2 cups (c) = 1 pint
8 ounces (oz) = 1 cup

Units of Weight
2000 pounds (lb) = 1 ton (T)
16 ounces = 1 pound

Units of Time
12 months (mo) = 1 year (yr)
52 weeks (wk) = 1 year
365 days (da) = 1 year
7 days = 1 week
24 hours (hr) = 1 day
60 minutes (min) = 1 hour
60 seconds (sec) = 1 minute

Converting Units

In solving measurement problems, it is often convenient to change the units of measure. This is called making a *conversion*. There are two types of conversions. One is a conversion from a large unit to a smaller unit. For example, a weight given in pounds might be converted to ounces. The other is a conversion to a larger unit, such as changing feet (small unit) to yards (larger unit). The following table will be useful in converting units.

CONVERTING UNITS		
To change a large unit to a smaller unit	Multiply ✕	This is because we want *more* of the smaller unit.
To change a small unit to a larger unit	Divide ÷	This is because we want *fewer* of the larger unit.

▶ **TIP:** The diagram below will remind you what to do. For this diagram to work, you always put the larger unit on the left and keep the arrows and signs in the same places.

$$\times$$

larger ⟶ smaller

$$\div$$

This process could be represented with feet and inches. Example 1 changes feet (larger) to inches (smaller).

Example 1: Change 7 feet to inches.

Because we are changing from feet (a large unit) to inches (a smaller unit), we multiply. (Recall: 12 inches = 1 foot.)

12 inches
× 7
——————
84 inches

Example 2: Change 6 tons to pounds.

Because we are changing from a large unit to a smaller unit, we multiply. (Recall: 2000 pounds = 1 ton.)

2000 pounds
× 6
——————
12,000 pounds

Example 3: Change 48 ounces to pints.

Because we are changing from a smaller unit (ounces) to a larger unit (pints), we divide. (Recall: 8 ounces = 1 cup, and 2 cups = 1 pint.)

Before dividing to find the number of pints, we must find the number of ounces in a pint.

First, multiply 8 ounces by 2 cups to get 16 ounces in a pint. $8 \times 2 = 16$

Then, divide 48 ounces by 16 ounces. $48 \div 16 = 3$

There are 3 pints in 48 ounces.

Example 4: Change 20 ounces to pounds.

Because we are changing from a smaller unit to a larger unit, we divide by the number of ounces in a pound.

1
16) 20
− 16
——
4

The answer is 1 pound with 4 ounces left over, which is written as 1 lb 4 oz.

The next example is a practical application of converting measurement.

Example 5: A tailor needs 18 inches of seam tape that costs $1.08 per yard. How much does he pay for the material?

We must convert from inches to yards because the price is given in yards.

Question: How much does he pay?

Information: 18 inches; $1.08 per yard

Operation: Change 18 inches to yards by dividing the number of inches in a yard. Then multiply $1.08 by the number of yards.

Estimation: .50 × $1 = $.50

Calculation:

.5 $1.08
36) 18.0   ×   .5
− 18 0   ——————
—————— $.540 or $.54
0

Evaluation: If 18 inches are half a yard, it makes sense that the tape costs half of the price of a yard. Now let's try a few problems with conversion.

EXERCISE 1: CONVERSIONS

Directions: Make the conversions in the following problems.

1. 5 yards = _____ feet

2. 40 ounces = _____ pounds

3. 96 hours = _____ days

4. 20 quarts = _____ gallons

5. 2 quarts = _____ ounces

6. 2 days = _____ minutes

7. 3 pints = _____ quarts

8. If Pike's Peak is 14,110 feet high, what is its elevation in miles (to the nearest tenth)?

9. If a half-gallon of milk costs 96 cents, what is the cost of an 8-ounce glass of milk?

10. One shrub is to be placed every 15 feet along an expressway. How many shrubs are to be planted along a 2-mile stretch of the expressway?

Answers are on page 722.

Basic Operations with Measurements

We often need to add, subtract, multiply, or divide measurements. Let's review these skills.

Example 1: Add 3 pounds 8 ounces to 15 ounces.

$$
\begin{array}{r}
3 \text{ lb} \quad 8 \text{ oz} \\
+ \qquad 15 \text{ oz} \\
\hline
3 \text{ lb} \ 23 \text{ oz}
\end{array}
$$

Be sure to add ounces to ounces.

Because 23 ounces is more than 16 ounces (1 pound), simplify it by dividing by 16.

$$
\begin{array}{r}
1 \text{ r } 7 = 1 \text{ lb } 7 \text{ oz} \\
16\overline{)23} \\
-16 \\
\hline
7
\end{array}
$$

3 pounds 23 ounces = 3 pounds + 1 pound 7 ounces = 4 pounds 7 ounces

Example 2: Take 5 pounds 7 ounces from 8 pounds 12 ounces.

$$
\begin{array}{r}
8 \text{ lb} \ 12 \text{ oz} \\
- \ 5 \text{ lb} \ \ 7 \text{ oz} \\
\hline
3 \text{ lb} \ \ 5 \text{ oz}
\end{array}
$$

Subtract ounces from ounces.
Then subtract pounds from pounds.

Example 3: Subtract 2 yards 2 feet from 6 yards 1 foot.

$$
\begin{array}{r}
\overset{5}{\cancel{6}} \text{ yd } \overset{4}{\cancel{1}} \text{ ft} \\
- \ 2 \text{ yd } 2 \text{ ft} \\
\hline
3 \text{ yd } 2 \text{ ft}
\end{array}
$$

Regroup 1 yard = 3 feet from the 6 yards. Add the 3 feet to the 1 foot.
Then subtract feet from feet and yards from yards.

Example 4: Multiply 4 feet 8 inches by 3.

    4 ft 8 in   Multiply 3 by 8 inches, then multiply 3 by 4 feet.
      × 3
  12 ft 24 in ← Since 12 inches = 1 foot, simplify the answer.

12 ft 24 in = 12 ft + 2 ft = 14 ft

In some cases, as in Example 5, you will have to change units to the same form before you can do any calculating.

Example 5: Multiply 8 feet by 2 yards.

First change yards to feet, so we are multiplying   2 × 3 = 6 feet
like units. (1 yd = 3 ft) Now multiply

    8 feet
  × 6 feet
  48 square feet
Note: feet × feet = square feet

Example 6: Divide 2 quarts 5 ounces by 3.

     0 qt   23 oz = 1 pt 7 oz
3) 2 qt   5 oz
  − 0
    2 qt = 64 oz ← 3 will not go into 2 quarts. Change 2 quarts to 64 ounces.
        69 oz ← Add 64 ounces to 5 ounces. Then divide by three.
     − 69 oz
       0

BASIC OPERATIONS WITH MEASUREMENTS	
ADDITION	1. Add like units. 2. Write the answer in simplest form.
SUBTRACTION	1. Subtract like units. 2. Regroup units when necessary. 3. Write the answer in simplest form.
MULTIPLICATION	1. Multiply like units if units are involved. 2. Write the answer in simplest form.
DIVISION	1. Divide into the larger unit first. 2. Change the remainder to the smaller unit and add that to any other smaller units. 3. Then divide into the smaller unit. 4. Be sure your answer is in simplest form.

EXERCISE 2: BASIC OPERATIONS WITH MEASUREMENTS

Directions: In the following practice problems, add, subtract, multiply, or divide as indicated. Be sure the final answer is in simplest form. For example, an answer of 15 inches should be changed to 1 foot 3 inches.

1. 9 feet 4 inches − 2 feet 9 inches

2. 1 hour 20 minutes + 3 hours

3. 130 pounds − 8 pounds 4 ounces

4. 5.3 inches × 7

5. 22 feet 6 inches ÷ 3

6. 5 hours 20 minutes ÷ 8

7. What is the difference in weight of two boxes of cereal, one weighing 1 pound 4 ounces and the other weighing 13 ounces?

8. If you divide a 6-foot 8-inch board into four equal lengths, how long will each piece be?

9. Each of 45 delegates to the convention will be given a badge made of a 4-inch piece of ribbon. At 65 cents per yard, how much will the ribbon cost to make the badges?

    (1) $1.80
    (2) $2.40
    (3) $3.25
    (4) $3.60
    (5) $6.50

10. At a price of $415 per ounce, which of the following represents the value of 1 pound 3 ounces of gold?

    (1) 3($415)
    (2) 16($415)
    (3) 3 + 16 + $415
    (4) 19($415)
    (5) $\frac{\$415}{19}$

11. Shane has a part-time job at the local hardware store. He earns $5 per hour. Last week he worked the following times: Monday, 2 hours 30 minutes; Wednesday, 3 hours; Friday, 4 hours 45 minutes; Saturday 7 hours 15 minutes; and Sunday, 4 hours. How much was he paid last week?

    (1) $ 28
    (2) $ 66
    (3) $ 72
    (4) $ 86
    (5) $107.50

Answers are on page 723.

The Metric System

The *metric system* is an international measuring system used to simplify trade and commerce among nations. The basic unit of measure of length is the *meter*. One meter is a little longer than a yard. The basic unit of weight is the *gram*. A paper clip weighs approximately one gram. A more practical comparison to our American system is the kilogram, which is about 2 pounds. The basic liquid measure is a *liter*. A liter has slightly more capacity than a quart.

All units are derived from the basic units of meter (length), gram (weight), and liter (liquid). Prefixes are added to the basic unit to indicate the amount of each unit. For example, the prefix *centi* means one-hundredth; therefore, one centimeter is one-hundredth of a meter, one centigram is one-hundredth of a gram, and one centiliter is one-hundredth of a liter.

Prefix	Meaning
kilo	1000
hecto	100
deca	10
BASIC UNIT	
deci	$\frac{1}{10}$ (.1)
centi	$\frac{1}{100}$ (.01)
milli	$\frac{1}{1000}$ (.001)

The diagram below relates the metric prefixes to the decimal system that you already know.

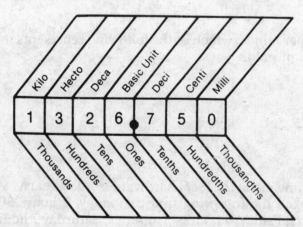

The charts below show the most common units of metric measure.

LENGTH

1 kilometer (km) = 1000 m

1 meter (m) = 1 m

1 centimeter (cm) = .01 m

1 millimeter (mm) = .001 m

WEIGHT

1 kilogram (kg) = 1000 g

1 gram (g) = 1 g

1 milligram (mg) = $\frac{1}{1000}$ g (.001 g)

CAPACITY

1 kiloliter (kl) = 1000 l

1 liter (l) = 1 l

1 milliliter (ml) = $\frac{1}{1000}$ l (.001 l)

Conversion in the Metric System

Conversions between units involve moving the decimal point to the right or left.

As with standard measurement, it is important to remember how to convert. The diagram below represents the conversions.

right (×)

larger ⟵⟶ smaller

left (÷)

The diagram below represents the prefixes from larger to smaller.

kilo	hecto	deca	unit	deci	centi	milli

Example 1: Change 420 meters to kilometers.

STEP 1. Recognize that meters to kilometers is going from a smaller unit to a larger. (1000 meters = 1 kilometer) Draw the arrow to show that.

kilometers ⟵ meters

left (÷)

STEP 2. Since kilo means "thousand," move 3 places.

km hm dam m dm cm mm

420 = .420

Example 2: Convert 4.2 kilograms to grams.

kg hg dag g dg cg mg

3 moves right

4.2 kg = 4.200 g = 4200 g

3 moves right

Example 3: Convert 4 meters 48 centimeters to centimeters.

First, change 4 meters to centimeters.

km hm dam m dm cm mm

2 moves right

4 m = 4.00 cm = 400 cm

Then, add.

400 cm + 48 cm = 448 cm

TO CHANGE METRIC UNITS

1. List the units from largest to smallest.

2. Put a mark at the starting unit.

3. Move by units to the new unit and count the moves right or left.

4. Move the decimal point the same number of places in the same direction.

The following is an example of metric problem solving.

Example 4: On an airplane trip from Chicago to London, you are told that the luggage limit is 20 kilograms. There is an extra charge of $2.80 for every kilogram over that limit. If your luggage weighs 23,000 grams, what additional charge can you expect?

STEP 1. First, change 23,000 grams to kilograms. Then, subtract to find out how much you are over the limit.

kg hg dag g dg cg mg

3 moves left

23,000 g = 23000 kg = 23 kg

23 kg − 20 kg = 3 kg

STEP 2. Since there are 3 extra kilograms, multiply to find the additional charge.

3 × $2.80 = $8.40

EXERCISE 3: METRIC MEASUREMENT

Directions: Convert to the units shown.

1. 500 meters to centimeters

2. 7423 milligrams to grams

3. 50.3 centimeters to millimeters

4. .027 kilograms to grams

5. 1 kiloliter 47 liters to liters

6. 6 meters 42 centimeters to meters

7. Find the length of the shaft illustrated below in meters.

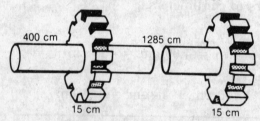

400 cm   1285 cm

15 cm   15 cm

8. The recommended dosage of vitamin C is 857 *milligrams* per day. How many *grams* of vitamin C will Max take in one week if he takes the recommended dosage?

9. Terry competed in a 1000-meter speed-skating race; how many kilometers did he skate?

10. If the speed limit sign in Canada reads 80 kilometers per hour and the speed limit sign in some areas of the United States reads 55 miles per hour, which country allows the motorist to drive at a faster speed? (1 kilometer = .621 mile)

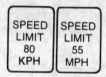

SPEED LIMIT 80 KPH   SPEED LIMIT 55 MPH

11. Which expression can be used to find the cost of .75 kilogram of cheese at the price of $6.40 per kilogram?
    (1) $\dfrac{\$6.40}{.75}$
    (2) .75 × $6.40
    (3) $\dfrac{\$6.40}{2}$
    (4) .75 + $6.40
    (5) $6.40 − .75

12. A yard is approximately .91 meter. A football field is 100 yards long. What is the length of a football field in meters?
    (1) 30
    (2) 49.5
    (3) 91
    (4) 100
    (5) 109

Answers are on page 723.

Special Topics in Measurement

The next several topics will present some tips for solving specific practical problems. We'll look at money problems, time problems, scale drawings, and meter reading. We'll follow these discussions with a variety of problems from these topics.

Money Problems

Some of the ways we handle money include paying bills, making purchases, writing a budget, and writing bills and receipts. Let's look at a few problems that require calculations involving money.

To do these calculations, you will be using the formula $c = nr$. A ***formula*** uses letters to represent rules for finding different quantities or measurements. When you work with formulas, you can substitute different numbers for the letters. You will be learning more about using formulas in Chapter 8.

To find the total cost (c), multiply the number of units (n) by the cost per unit (r). This is written as $c = nr$. (Two letters next to each other in a formula indicate that the two quantities have to be multiplied.) For example, you buy 4 tires at $98 each. To find the total cost of the tires, you must multiply $4 \times \$98 = \$392$.

Example: Margaret bought the following groceries on May 15: $1\frac{1}{2}$ dozen apples at $1.69 per dozen, 2 dozen eggs at 84¢ per dozen, 2 boxes of bran flakes at $3.15 each, 1 pound of margarine at $1.58 per pound, and 3 cans of soup at 79¢ per can. How much change did Margaret receive from a twenty-dollar bill?

STEP 1. Use the formula $c = nr$ to find the total cost of each item she bought. Then add to find the total cost of the purchases.

Apples:	$1\frac{1}{2} \times 1.69 =$	
	$1.5 \times 1.69 =$	
	$2.535 =$	$2.54
Eggs:	$2 \times .84 =$	1.68
Bran flakes:	$2 \times 3.15 =$	6.30
Margarine:	$1 \times 1.58 =$	1.58
Soup:	$3 \times .79 =$	+ 2.37
	Total	$14.47

STEP 2. Subtract to find the change from $20.

$$\begin{array}{r} \$20.00 \\ -\ \ 14.47 \\ \hline \$\ \ 5.53 \end{array}$$

▶ **TIP:** Always round money to the hundredths place. In general, we round upward as opposed to downward. For instance, suppose you want one item and the price is 3 items for $1.24. If you divide $1.24 by 3, you get about $.413. The actual price you would pay for one item is 42¢ even though .413 would normally round to .41.

EXERCISE 4: MONEY PROBLEMS

Directions: Solve each problem.

Question 1 is based on the sales slip below.

Corey's Fashions 579 Mall Drive Elk Grove, Illinois 60007			
Qty.	**Description**	**Unit Price**	**Amount**
1	Dress	$49.95	
2	Shirts	$14.95	
3	Pairs of hose	$ 4.95	
		Subtotal	
		Tax (7%)	
Pay this amount		**Total**	

1. Lola works at Corey's Fashions. Her customer made the purchases shown on the sales slip. How much money should Lola collect from this customer?

    (1) $6.63   **(2)** $66.33   **(3)** $94.70   **(4)** $101.33   **(5)** $196.03

2. Mr. Barnes stocked his garden supply stores with 2 tons of sand in 50-pound bags for $138 per ton. If he sells the entire order of bags of sand for $5.95 per bag, what will be his profit?

    (1) $3.19   **(2)** $69   **(3)** $200   **(4)** $276   **(5)** $470.40

3. You need 48 feet of molding to finish decorating the family room. What is the cost of the molding if each 1-yard length costs 98 cents?

    (1) $3.92   **(2)** $15.68   **(3)** $47.04   **(4)** $392.00   **(5)** $470.00

4. If one serving of ice cream is $1\frac{1}{2}$ cups, how many servings can be made from 3 quarts?

    (1) 2   **(2)** 3   **(3)** 4   **(4)** 8   **(5)** 16

5. Happy Bran cereal costs $1.79 for a 1-pound 9-ounce box; Wheatos cereal in a 12-ounce box costs $1.49; Friendly Flakes costs $2.19 for a 1-pound 13-ounce box; and Sugar Snaps is $2.39 for 1 pound 4 ounces. Which cereal is the most economical purchase?

    (1) Happy Bran   **(2)** Wheatos   **(3)** Friendly Flakes   **(4)** Sugar Snaps
    (5) They are all the same.

6. A famous-brand multisymptom cold reliever costs $6.48 for 36 capsules. The generic equivalent costs $4.32 for 36 capsules. How much money do you save per dose using the generic medicine if each dose is 2 capsules?

    (1) 6¢   **(2)** 12¢   **(3)** 18¢   **(4)** $1.08   **(5)** $2.16

7. First-class postage is \$.29 for up to 1 ounce and \$.23 for each additional ounce. Which of the following represents the cost of sending a 4-ounce envelope by first class?

(1) 4(\$.29)

(2) 4(\$.23)

(3) (\$.29 + \$.23)

(4) \$.29 + 3(\$.23)

(5) $\dfrac{(\$.29 + \$.23)}{2}$

Answers are on page 724.

Time Problems

Many jobs require you to punch in on a time clock when you arrive at work and punch out when you leave. The time card will record a starting time and an ending time.

TIME CLOCK

A.M. means "hours between midnight and noon."

P.M. means "hours between noon and midnight."

Numbers on the left of the colon are hours.   **3:30**   Numbers on the right of the colon are minutes.

Example 1: Tina worked overtime on Thursday. She started at 7:30 A.M. and ended at 6:45 P.M. How long did she work?

STEP 1. Find her morning hours.

$$\begin{array}{r} \overset{11\ \ 60}{\cancel{12:00}} \\ -\ \ 7:30 \\ \hline 4:30 \end{array}$$ or 4 hr 30 min

— Borrow 60 minutes from the hours

STEP 2. Find her afternoon hours.

Noon to 6:45 is 6 hours 45 minutes.

STEP 3. Add the total hours.

$$\begin{array}{r} 4:30 \\ +\ \ 6:45 \\ \hline 10:75 = 11:15 \end{array}$$

— Because 75 minutes is more than 60 minutes (one hour), we simplify that to 1 hour and 15 minutes and add it to 10 hours.

11:15 can be written as *11 hr 15 min* or $11\frac{15}{60} = 11\frac{1}{4}$ *hr.*

HOW TO CALCULATE TIME

1. Find the number of morning hours.

2. Find the number of evening hours.

3. Add the morning hours and evening hours. Be sure to simplify your answer.

Example 2: Kelly's time card showed a starting time of 8:10 A.M. and an ending time of 6:40 P.M. If she gets paid $5.25 per hour straight time and $7.50 per hour overtime (any time more than the straight eight-hour shift), how much did she make that day?

STEP 1. Calculate the work hours. 8:10 A.M. to noon $3\frac{5}{6}$ hours

noon to 6:40 P.M. $+\ 6\frac{2}{3}$ hours

total $10\frac{1}{2}$ hours

STEP 2. Calculate the overtime hours.

$10\frac{1}{2} - 8 = 2\frac{1}{2}$ hours overtime

8 hours at $5.25	$42.00
$2\frac{1}{2}$ hours at $7.50	+ 18.75
Total pay	$60.75

If you know rate and time, you can find distance by using the formula distance (d) equals the rate or speed (r) times the amount of time (t) traveled. This relationship is represented as $d = rt$.

▶ **TIP:** Time must be in hours or parts of an hour because the rate is in miles per hour.

For instance, what if you travel 6 hours at 55 miles per hour? To get the distance traveled, you would multiply $6 \times 55 = 330$. The distance traveled is 330 miles.

On the other hand, you often know the distance to be traveled but have to figure out the length of time required for a trip. Suppose you must travel 726 miles and the legal speed limit is 55 mph. You know the distance and the rate; to find the time, you'll have to divide:

$$726 \div 55 = 13\frac{1}{5} \text{ hours}$$

EXERCISE 5: TIME PROBLEMS

Directions: Solve each problem.

1. The sign on a parking meter states, "12 minutes for a nickel; maximum deposit 75 cents." How many hours can you legally park for the maximum deposit?

    (1) $1\frac{1}{4}$ **(2)** 3 **(3)** $6\frac{1}{4}$ **(4)** $7\frac{1}{2}$ **(5)** 15

2. Roger works the lunch shift from 10:00 A.M. to 2:30 P.M. Monday through Friday each week at $8.00 per hour. Which expression shows how much he earns every four weeks?

    (1) $4\frac{1}{2} + 8 + 5 + 4$

    (2) $(4\frac{1}{2} \times 8) + (5 \times 4)$

    (3) $4\frac{1}{2} \times 8 \times 5 \times 4$

    (4) $4\frac{1}{2}(8 + 5 + 4)$

    (5) $4\frac{1}{2} \times 8$

3. Sonya and Olaf leave home at 8:30 A.M. to begin their driving tour of Wisconsin. At 3:45 P.M., they decide to stop for the day. If they drive a steady 50 miles per hour, how many miles do they drive that day?

    (1) 362.5 **(2)** 387.5 **(3)** 437.5 **(4)** 426.5 **(5)** 600.0

Questions 4–6 refer to the time card below:

MARSHALL MANUFACTURING					
NAME: Tom Wolper SS# 000-45-0000					
Date From To	5/20 8:00 A.M. 4:00 P.M.	5/21 8:00 A.M. 5:30 P.M.	5/22 8:00 A.M. 6:45 P.M.	5/23 8:00 A.M. 4:00 P.M.	5/24 8:00 A.M. 4:30 P.M.
Total Regular Hours _____ at $7.85 Overtime Hours _____ at $12.00 (over 40 hours)					

4. According to his time card, Tom Wolper worked the week of 5/20 to 5/24. How many overtime hours (any time more than the straight eight-hour shift) did he work that week?

   (1) $3\frac{3}{4}$ **(2)** 4 **(3)** $4\frac{1}{4}$ **(4)** $4\frac{1}{2}$ **(5)** $4\frac{3}{4}$

5. What is Tom's full pay before deductions? (Include regular hours and overtime hours.)

   (1) $57 **(2)** $314 **(3)** $351 **(4)** $371 **(5)** $537

6. If state withholding tax is 1%, federal withholding tax is 25%, and social security tax (FICA) is 7%, how much will Tom's take-home pay be after these deductions?

   (1) $122.43 **(2)** $155.82 **(3)** $215.18 **(4)** $248.57 **(5)** $493.43

7. An airplane travels 960 miles per hour. Which expression tells how far it travels in twenty minutes?

   (1) 960×20 **(2)** $960 \times \frac{1}{3}$ **(3)** $\frac{960}{20}$ **(4)** $\frac{3}{960}$ **(5)** $\frac{\frac{1}{3}}{960}$

8. A tornado traveled 75 miles in $2\frac{1}{2}$ hours. Which expression shows how fast the tornado is traveling?

   (1) $2\frac{1}{2} \times 75$

   (2) $75 + 2\frac{1}{2}$

   (3) $75 - 2\frac{1}{2}$

   (4) $2\frac{1}{2} \div 75$

   (5) $75 \div 2\frac{1}{2}$

Answers are on page 724.

Reading and Interpreting Scales and Meters

You often have to read a scale or meter to get information. For instance, a map is a scale drawing you use when you travel. You read a thermometer when you're sick and read an electric meter to check your electric bill. On the next few pages, we'll take a look at some scales and meters.

READING SCALES AND METERS

Follow these tips when you solve problems with scales or meters.

1. Read the labels on the meter carefully.

2. If instructions are included, refer to the meter as you read them.

3. Write down the information you get as you read the meter.

4. Ignore extra information that is not needed for the problem.

Scale Drawings

A map is a drawing of land area. When a map is drawn to scale (in proportion to the land it represents), a *key* is given so you may calculate distances on the map. A key has the information about the ratio for that particular drawing. You can use the scale to set up a proportion to find a distance.

Let's look at the local map below. Answer the following questions while referring to the map. Notice the scale of miles at the top of the map.

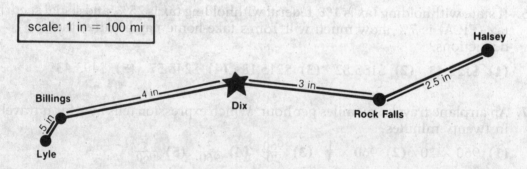

Example 1: If the distance from Halsey to Rock Falls on the map is 2.5 inches, what is the actual distance between Halsey and Rock Falls?

The ratio is 1 inch to 100 miles. If the distance on the map between Halsey and Rock Falls is 2.5 inches, we can set up the following proportion to solve the problem. Notice that we are using a proportion to compare two things (inches to miles).

$$\frac{1 \text{ in}}{100 \text{ mi}} = \frac{2.5 \text{ in}}{n \text{ mi}}$$

Cross multiply: $100 \times 2.5 = 250$

Divide: $250 \div 1 = 250$

The actual distance between Halsey and Rock Falls is 250 miles. (This makes sense because each inch is 100 miles. Since we have more than 2 inches, there are more than 200 miles.)

Example 2: To go by road from Lyle to Halsey, you must go through Billings, Dix, and Rock Falls. How much farther is it from Lyle to Halsey than from Billings to Rock Falls?

STEP 1. Calculate the distance from Lyle to Halsey. Then calculate the distance from Billings to Rock Falls.

.5 in + 4 in + 3 in + 2.5 in = 10 in

4 in + 3 in = 7 in

STEP 2. Subtract to find the difference.

10 in − 7 in = 3 in

STEP 3. Set up and solve a proportion to compare inches to miles. Cross multiply and divide.

$$\frac{1 \text{ in}}{100 \text{ mi}} = \frac{3 \text{ in}}{n \text{ mi}}$$

$$\frac{100 \times 3}{1} = 300$$

It is 300 miles farther from Lyle to Halsey.

Reading Meters

Meters are devices used to measure time, speed, distance, and energy used. You might recognize some meters such as a speedometer, barometer, or thermometer. Meters give us information to solve problems. It's important that you read a meter accurately. Always notice the labels on the meter and read the instructions for use if they are given.

On the next few pages, we'll look at some problems that require meter reading.

The Electric Meter

Appliances such as refrigerators, fans, radios, TVs, and dishwashers require electricity. The electric meter is the instrument that measures the amount of electricity used in kilowatt-hours (kwh).

The numbers above the dial indicate one complete round around the dial. Notice that the numbers may go in different directions around the dial.

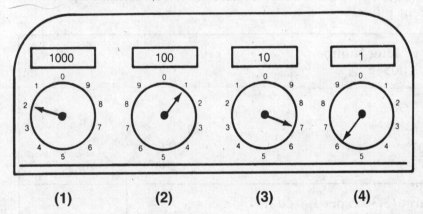

Dial (1) measures the number of 1000 kwh.

Dial (2) measures the number of 100 kwh.

Dial (3) measures the number of 10 kwh.

Dial (4) measures the number of 1 kwh.

(1)   (2)   (3)   (4)

Example: Read the meter above.

Start reading the dials with the left dial. If the pointer is between two numbers, read the *smaller* of the two numbers. Reading the meter above, you get 2176 .

Dial (1)   2   2 × 1000 = 2000

Dial (2)   1   1 × 100 = 100

Dial (3)   7   7 × 10   =   70

Dial (4)   6   6 × 1   =   6

Total kwh used: 2176

EXERCISE 6: SCALES AND METERS

Directions: Solve each problem.

1. The scale on a map is 1 inch = 180 miles. How far apart on this map are two cities if the distance between them is 450 miles?

   (1) 1 in **(2)** $1\frac{1}{2}$ in **(3)** 2 in **(4)** $2\frac{1}{2}$ in **(5)** $3\frac{1}{2}$ in

2. What is the scale for a map in which 2000 miles is represented by 10 inches?

   (1) 1 in = 2 mi **(2)** 1 in = 20 mi **(3)** 1 in = 200 mi **(4)** 1 in = $\frac{1}{2}$ mi **(5)** 1 in = 100 mi

3. Emma's last reading on her electric meter was 3843 kwh. Her new reading is indicated on the meter shown below. If the charge is 12.5¢ per kwh, what is Emma's new electric bill?

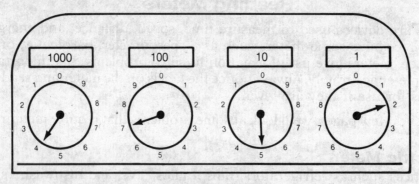

KILOWATT-HOURS

   (1) $113.63 **(2)** $909 **(3)** $2,020 **(4)** $2,562.50 **(5)** $11,362.50

4. Daryl wanted to check his gas bill, shown below. From the information given, find his total current bill.

Your Acct. # 12345678	Meter Number 00386	
METER READINGS		
Current 3380 Previous 3207 100 cu ft 173		
Gas Supply Charge ($.3065 per 100 cu ft)		
Monthly Customer Charge		$ 2.00
Distribution Charge		$19.16
	Subtotal	
	Utility Tax (5%)	
	Total Current Bill	

   (1) $3.71 **(2)** $53.02 **(3)** $74.19 **(4)** $77.89 **(5)** $203.87

Answers are on page 725.

7
GRAPHS, STATISTICS, AND PROBABILITY

Graphs, charts, and statistical tables help us organize information. When you are presented with material that has been organized for you, you must carefully study the details such as the title, subtitle, column and row headings, key (if shown), and type of information given. We call this interpreting the *data*. Statistics is the study of data. With statistics, you organize the data and then draw a conclusion based on them.

Mean and Median

Two common types of statistical problems ask you to find the mean or median of a set of data. The **mean** is the average of the numbers. To find the average, you add the data and then divide by the number of pieces of data.

For instance, Brenda bowled 132, 147, and 108 at the bowling alley last night. To find her mean (average) score, you add:

$$132 + 147 + 108 = 387$$

and then divide by 3 (the number of scores):

$$387 \div 3 = 129$$

Therefore, her average or *mean* bowling score is 129.

The **median** of a set of data is found by arranging the numbers from smallest to largest and then choosing the middle number in the arrangement. That middle number is the median. You would arrange Brenda's three bowling scores to read 108, 132, 147. The middle score is 132, so the median is 132.

TO FIND THE AVERAGE OR MEAN

1. Add the numbers.
2. Divide by the number of numbers.

TO FIND THE MEDIAN

1. Put the numbers in order from lowest to highest.
2. Choose the middle number. (If there are two middle numbers, find the average of the two numbers.)

Example 1: Mr. Parker wants to know his average monthly gas bill. The chart below lists his gas expenses for the last six months of the year. What is his average monthly gas bill?

July	$148.70
August	385.60
September	195.20
October	208.40
November	186.75
December	220.88

Add all six months; the total is $1345.53. Then divide by 6 (the number of months) and get $224.255. Round off the amount to an average of $224.26.

If you want to find Mr. Parker's median gas bill, arrange the amounts in order from smallest to largest. Since there is no middle number, you must find the average of the two middle numbers. The median is $201.80.

STEP 1.	STEP 2.	STEP 3.
148.70	195.20	$201.80
186.75	+ 208.40	2) $403.60
195.20 ⎫ Middle	403.60	
208.40 ⎭		
220.88		
385.60		

Example 2: To get information on the number of evening diners at her Shamrock Inn, Shannon accumulated the following information for the first 17 days of March. What is the median of the number of diners?

35, 37, 43, 28, 32, 38, 45, 21, 26, 27, 44, 46, 29, 39, 42, 86, 117

The median is 38, while the average (mean) is 43.24.

In this case, the median of 38 is a better representation of the normal amount of diners. The average is thrown off by the large crowds on the 17th day, St. Patrick's Day. The median is often used when the mean does not give a true picture because of a few unusually high or low scores.

EXERCISE 1: MEAN AND MEDIAN

Directions: Solve each problem.

1. Your seven salesclerks reported the sales figures at the right during the week of April 19. To the nearest cent, what was the average of the sales figures?

Tom	$4300
Astrid	$5600
Ben	$1875
Josephine	$4250
Wilbur	$2876
Inez	$4108
Zoe	$2983

Questions 2–4 are based on the information below. Round your answer to the nearest whole number.

The scorekeeper for the Union Town basketball team recorded the results of the last six games.

Date	Opponent	Union Town vs. Opponent
12/4	Hinkley	48 to 37
12/6	Barton	45 to 63
12/10	Angel Park	53 to 42
12/12	Eagle Rock	72 to 24
12/18	Bennett	68 to 44
12/20	Alton	74 to 51

2. What is the average number of points scored by the opponent?

3. What is the median score scored by Union Town?

4. What is the average score of Union Town?

5. The prices of identical winter jackets at five local stores are $48.95, $39.95, $44.80, $52.25, and $42.88. What is the median price of that jacket?

Answers are on page 725.

Graphs

Graphs and charts are useful ways of simplifying complicated information by putting it in picture form. We can often understand an entire situation with only a quick look at a graph. By organizing data visually, graphs and charts help us interpret, compare, and analyze numbers. In this section, we'll look specifically at circle graphs, bar graphs, and line graphs.

Circle Graphs

The circle in a *circle graph* represents a whole quantity. For instance, a circle could represent the whole population of the United States or an entire family income. Each circle is then subdivided into sections that represent parts of the whole.

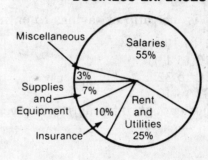

HAMPTON PRODUCTS BUSINESS EXPENSES

The circle at the right represents all of the business expenses of Hampton Products, a small family business. If you add all the sections in the circle, the total is 100%.

Example 1: If Hampton Products' business expenses totaled $125,000 last year, how much were the expenses for rent and utilities? We see from the graph that rent and utilities account for 25% of the total. We need to find 25% of $125,000.

$$\frac{n}{125,000} = \frac{25}{100}$$

$$\frac{125,000 \times 25}{100} = \$31,250$$

Example 2: What is the ratio of insurance costs to the total budget? Set up a ratio of insurance to total.

$$\frac{10\%}{100\%} = \frac{10}{100} = \frac{1}{10}$$

The ratio is 1 to 10. Another way of saying this is $1 out of every $10 spent is used for insurance.

EXERCISE 2: CIRCLE GRAPHS

Directions: Solve each problem.

1. Using the circle graph below and this chart, find the average yearly amount spent on salaries in the three years 1991–1993.

HAMPTON PRODUCTS	
Year	**Total Expenses**
1991	$ 92,000
1992	$156,000
1993	$125,000

HAMPTON PRODUCTS BUSINESS EXPENSES

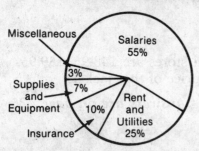

Questions 2–5 are based on the graph below and to the right.

2. How much is spent for car expenses each year?

3. What is the average *monthly* expense for rent?

4. How much is spent on clothing during the year?

    (1) $320 **(2)** $480 **(3)** $800 **(4)** $3200
    (5) not enough information is given

5. What is the ratio of savings to entire income?

    (1) 1 to 10
    (2) 10 to 1
    (3) 10 to 32
    (4) 32 to 10
    (5) not enough information is given

DISTRIBUTION OF A YEARLY INCOME OF $32,000

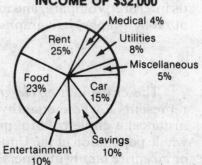

Answers are on page 725.

Bar Graphs

A **bar graph** is an excellent way of comparing amounts. This bar graph shows the distance five experimental cars traveled on one gallon of gas. You can see that Car Z had the highest gas mileage and that Car T traveled 30 miles on a gallon of gas.

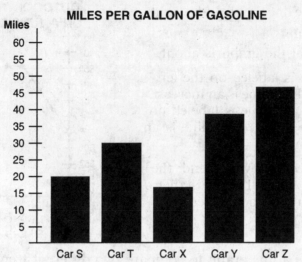

MILES PER GALLON OF GASOLINE

In the bar graph below, compare income with expenses for a particular year.

EXERCISE 3: BAR GRAPHS

Directions: Use the following graph to answer the questions.

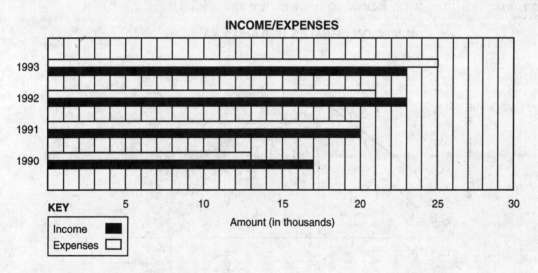

INCOME/EXPENSES

1. What was the income in 1990?

2. What was the average of expenses for the years 1990–1993?

3. In what year did expenses exceed income?

   (1) 1990 **(2)** 1991 **(3)** 1992 **(4)** 1993
   (5) not enough information is given

4. In 1992, what was the difference between income and expenses?

   (1) $200 **(2)** $2,000 **(3)** $20,000 **(4)** $21,000 **(5)** $23,000

Answers are on page 725.

Line Graphs

Line graphs are used to show trends or patterns. On a line graph, each point relates two values. One is the value on the vertical (↕) axis at the left side, and the other is the value on the horizontal (↔) axis at the bottom.

As you look at the line graph at the right, notice the following:

OUTDOOR TEMPERATURES ON A JUNE DAY IN CHICAGO

1. The title tells what the graph is about.

2. The vertical scale is labeled on the left side of the graph. Each line is an increase of 5°. The horizontal scale is labeled on the bottom of the graph. Each line is an increase of 1 hour.

3. The line shows the following trend: the temperature rose until 11:00 A.M., then remained steady until noon. Then the temperature fell.

You can also use a line graph to compare two different trends. Below is an example of this. One trend is shown with a solid line; the other is shown with a broken line. When a graph uses two or more lines, you can compare information from the lines.

EXERCISE 4: LINE GRAPHS

Directions: Use the graph below to answer the questions.

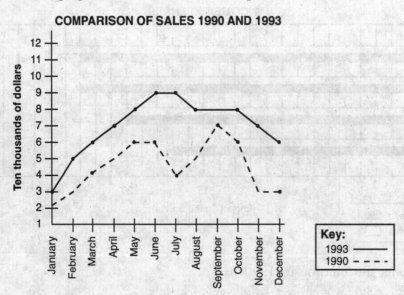

COMPARISON OF SALES 1990 AND 1993

Key:
1993 ———
1990 – – –

1. The title tells us that the graph compares _____ in _____ (year) and _____ (year).

2. The vertical scale is labeled in _____.

3. The horizontal scale is labeled in _____.

4. In June of 1990, sales were about _____.

5. In June of 1993, sales were about _____.

6. The graph shows that both 1990 and 1993 had seasonal highs and lows. In general, 1993 produced considerably _____ sales all year long.

Answers are on page 726.

EXERCISE 5: MIXED GRAPH PRACTICE

Directions: Solve each problem. Questions 1–5 are based on the circle graph below.

1. What is the ratio of savings to earnings?

2. If you make $12,000 per year, what is your monthly take-home pay?

3. If you make $25,000 per year, what is your annual contribution to social security?

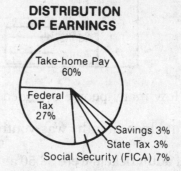

DISTRIBUTION OF EARNINGS

Take-home Pay 60%
Federal Tax 27%
Savings 3%
State Tax 3%
Social Security (FICA) 7%

4. If you wanted to have take-home pay of $20,000, how much would your actual earnings have to be?

5. One year, Mike earned $24,000. The deductions from his paycheck were federal tax, FICA, and state tax. What was his yearly take-home pay?

Questions 6–12 refer to the bar graph below.

6. What is the difference in height between the Empire State Building and the Sears Tower?

7. If a 107-foot TV antenna were erected at the top of the Sears Tower, what would be the total height of the tower?

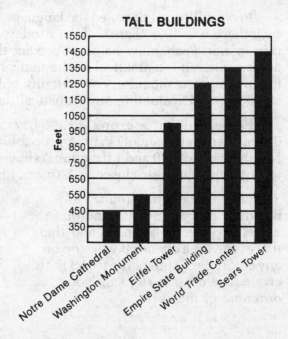

TALL BUILDINGS

Feet: 1550, 1450, 1350, 1250, 1150, 1050, 950, 850, 750, 650, 550, 450, 350

Notre Dame Cathedral, Washington Monument, Eiffel Tower, Empire State Building, World Trade Center, Sears Tower

8. The World Trade Center is how many times as tall as the Washington Monument?

9. The height of Notre Dame Cathedral is approximately what percent of the height of the Sears Tower?

10. What is the average height of these six structures?

11. What is the median height of these six structures?

12. If each floor is about 13 feet tall, about how many floors are in the Sears Tower?

Questions 13–15 refer to the line graph below.

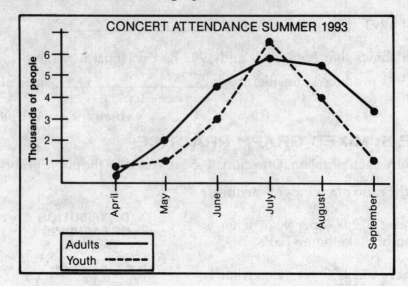

13. How many people attended concerts in June?

14. In which months was youth attendance higher than that for adults?

15. If adult tickets were $8.50 and youth tickets were $5.75, what were the receipts for the concerts held in August?

Answers are on page 726.

Probability

Probability can be called the language of uncertainty. The weather reporter says there is a 40% chance of rain today, but we still don't know if it's going to rain or not. Probability helps us predict the future based on analyzing past performance. It is a practical mathematical tool used in developing mortality rates for insurance companies, constructing polls to assess public opinion during elections, and evaluating any statistical data.

Probability can be expressed as a fraction, ratio, or percent. A probability of 0 means an event cannot occur. A probability of 1 means an event is sure to happen. Numbers between 0 and 1 (fractions) show whether the event is closer to 0 (closer to not happening) or closer to 1 (more likely to happen).

Let's use a game spinner to illustrate probability. Assume that the wheel is perfectly balanced and that there is an even chance it will stop on any color. Each spin of the wheel is an *event*. The color it stops at is an *outcome* of the event.

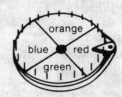

There are four possible outcomes when you spin this wheel: red, blue, green, and orange. A successful event occurs when you spin the wheel and get the color you want. The probability of success is the ratio of the number of successes of an event to the number of possible outcomes of that event. You can express probability in the following fraction or ratio form. Remember, this can also be a percent.

$$\text{Probability} = \frac{\text{Number of Successful Outcomes}}{\text{Number of Possible Outcomes}}$$

Using the spinning wheel, the probability of stopping at red would be $\frac{1}{4}$. While there are four possible outcomes (red, blue, green, or orange), there is only one successful outcome (red). The probability of $\frac{1}{4}$ can also be written as 25%, so you can say there is a 25% chance of landing on red.

Again, using the spinning wheel on page 644, find the probability of landing on *either* red *or* green. Now there are two possible outcomes that would be successful. The probability is:

$$\frac{2}{4} \quad \begin{array}{l}\text{number of successes}\\\text{number of possibilities}\end{array}$$

You can reduce $\frac{2}{4}$ to $\frac{1}{2}$. Thus, the probability of landing on red or green is $\frac{1}{2}$, or 50%.

Probability of 0 or 1

A probability of 0 or 0% means an event will *not* take place. Using the same spinning wheel, the probability of landing on purple is 0, because the number of successful outcomes of purple on this wheel is 0. So we would have $\frac{0}{4} = 0$. There is 0% chance of landing on purple.

A probability of 1 or 100% means an event is *certain* to happen. Let's use the spinning wheel to find the probability of landing on red, green, blue, or orange. The number of successful outcomes is 4, and the number of possible outcomes is 4. Now we have $\frac{4}{4} = 1$.

EXERCISE 6: PROBABILITY

Directions: Solve each problem.

1. If a single card is picked from a deck of 52 playing cards, what is the probability that it is the ace of spades?

2. From the same deck of 52 cards, what is the probability of drawing a heart? Give your answer as a percent. (*Hint:* There are 13 cards in each suit.)

3. In a deck of 52 cards, what is the probability of drawing a king? Give your answer as a fraction.

For questions 4–10, consider the roll of a single die; a single die has six faces as shown:

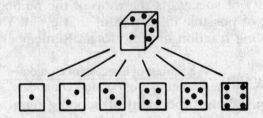

4. What is the probability of rolling a 5?

   (1) $\frac{1}{6}$ **(2)** $\frac{1}{5}$ **(3)** $\frac{1}{3}$ **(4)** $\frac{1}{2}$ **(5)** $\frac{5}{6}$

5. What is the probability of rolling either a 3 or a 4?

   (1) $16\frac{2}{3}\%$ **(2)** 25% **(3)** 30% **(4)** $33\frac{1}{3}\%$ **(5)** 40%

6. What is the probability of rolling an even number?

   (1) $16\frac{2}{3}\%$ **(2)** 20% **(3)** 30% **(4)** $33\frac{1}{3}\%$ **(5)** 50%

7. What is the probability of rolling a number greater than 6?

   (1) 0 **(2)** $\frac{1}{6}$ **(3)** $\frac{1}{3}$ **(4)** $\frac{1}{2}$ **(5)** 1

8. What is the probability of rolling a number less than 5?

   (1) 0% **(2)** 30% **(3)** $33\frac{1}{3}\%$ **(4)** 40% **(5)** $66\frac{2}{3}\%$

9. What is the probability of rolling a number less than 7?

   (1) 0% **(2)** 25% **(3)** 60% **(4)** 70% **(5)** 100%

10. What is the probability that you will read this page in March instead of another month?

    (1) $\frac{1}{25}$ **(2)** $\frac{1}{12}$ **(3)** $\frac{1}{4}$ **(4)** $\frac{1}{3}$ **(5)** not enough information is given

11. What is the probability that your social security number will end in 8?

    (1) $\frac{1}{12}$ **(2)** $\frac{1}{10}$ **(3)** $\frac{1}{8}$ **(4)** $\frac{4}{5}$ **(5)** not enough information is given

12. You flip a coin nine times, and each time it lands on heads. What is the probability it will land on heads the tenth time you flip it?

    (1) $\frac{1}{9}$ **(2)** $\frac{1}{10}$ **(3)** $\frac{1}{2}$ **(4)** $\frac{9}{10}$ **(5)** not enough information is given

13. In every shipment of clay pots, a number of them will be broken. In a recent shipment, 240 out of 960 were cracked. At the same rate, what is the probability of getting pots that are *not* cracked?

    (1) $\frac{1}{24}$ **(2)** $\frac{1}{4}$ **(3)** $\frac{1}{2}$ **(4)** $\frac{3}{4}$ **(5)** not enough information is given

Answers are on page 726.

Dependent Probability

Suppose a box contains two green balls and three red balls. If one ball is drawn from the box, the probability of drawing a green ball is $\frac{2}{5}$ and the probability of drawing a red ball is $\frac{3}{5}$. If you do not replace the ball drawn, there are now only four balls in the box. The probability for the drawing of the next ball now depends on which ball you drew the first time.

Possibility 1: You Drew a Green Ball

If you drew a *green* ball on the first draw, the box now contains one green ball and three red balls. In this situation, the probability of next drawing a green ball is now $\frac{1}{4}$ and the probability of drawing a red ball is $\frac{3}{4}$.

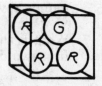

Possibility 2: You Drew a Red Ball

If you drew a *red* ball on the first draw, the box now contains two green balls and two red balls. The probability of drawing a green ball is now $\frac{2}{4}$ or $\frac{1}{2}$, and the probability of drawing a red ball is now $\frac{2}{4}$ or $\frac{1}{2}$.

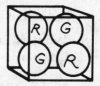

We see that the second draw *depends* on the first draw. This is an example of **dependent probability**.

EXERCISE 7: DEPENDENT PROBABILITY

Directions: Solve each problem.

Questions 1–4 are based on the following situation. Express your answers as fractions. Draw a picture if necessary to help you find the probabilities.

Two cards are drawn in succession from a deck of 52 playing cards without the first card being replaced.

1. Find the probability that the first card drawn is an ace.

2. If the first card drawn was an ace, what is the probability that the second draw is also an ace?

3. What is the probability that the second card drawn is an ace if the first card drawn was not an ace?

4. Suppose the first card drawn is a spade. What is the probability that the second card drawn is a spade?

TEST 5: MATHEMATICS

Questions 5–7 are based on the following situation. Express your answers as fractions.

A committee is to be chosen at random from a group of seven men and three women. The names of the ten people are placed on slips of paper and put in a hat.

5. What is the probability that the first name drawn from the hat will be a woman's?

6. If the first name drawn is a man's, what is the probability that the second name drawn will also be a man's?

7. What is the probability that the third name drawn will be a woman's if the first two draws were also women's names?

Questions 8–10 are based on the following situation. Express your answers as fractions.

A change purse contains 3 nickels, 4 dimes, and 2 quarters.

8. What is the probability that the first coin taken from the purse will be a quarter?

9. If the first coin taken from the purse was a nickel, what is the probability that the next coin will be a quarter?

10. What is the probability that the third coin taken from the purse will be a nickel if the first two coins were also nickels?

Answers are on page 726.

8
NUMERATION

Numeration is the study of number relationships. In this chapter, we'll review powers, roots, and the order of operations. We'll also look at the use of formulas and substitution. We'll conclude the study of arithmetic with a look at number patterns, properties of numbers, ordering of numbers, and scientific notation.

Powers and Roots

Powers

When a number is multiplied by itself, we say that it is *squared*. We show that with a small 2 placed to the upper right of the number. For example, $7^2 = 7 \times 7 = 49$. This means seven squared is 7 times 7, which is 49.

In the expression 7^2, the two is called the *power* or *exponent*, and the seven is called the *base*. It is best to think of the exponent as an instruction. The exponent tells you what to do with the base. When the exponent is 2, the base is squared, and we multiply the base by itself.

Examples: $3^2 = 3 \times 3 = 9$ $9^2 = 9 \times 9 = 81$

$10^2 = 10 \times 10 = 100$ $(\frac{1}{3})^2 = \frac{1}{3} \times \frac{1}{3} = \frac{1}{9}$

Sometimes the exponent is a number other than 2. The exponent tells how many times to multiply the base by itself. For example:

$3^4 = 3 \times 3 \times 3 \times 3 = 81$

$5^3 = 5 \times 5 \times 5 = 125$

$10^6 = 10 \times 10 \times 10 \times 10 \times 10 \times 10 = 1,000,000$

$(\frac{1}{2})^3 = \frac{1}{2} \times \frac{1}{2} \times \frac{1}{2} = \frac{1}{8}$

Here are three special rules you should know.

SPECIAL RULES ABOUT POWERS

1. The number 1 to any power is 1. $1^5 = 1 \times 1 \times 1 \times 1 \times 1 = 1$

2. Any number to the first power is that number. $6^1 = 6$

3. Any number to the zero power is 1. $14^0 = 1$

When we multiply a number by itself, we get a ***perfect square***. For instance, $6^2 = 36$; 36 is a perfect square. Some perfect squares that are helpful to know are listed here.

$1^2 = 1$	$6^2 = 36$	$11^2 = 121$	$20^2 = 400$
$2^2 = 4$	$7^2 = 49$	$12^2 = 144$	$30^2 = 900$
$3^2 = 9$	$8^2 = 64$	$13^2 = 169$	$40^2 = 1600$
$4^2 = 16$	$9^2 = 81$	$14^2 = 196$	$50^2 = 2500$
$5^2 = 25$	$10^2 = 100$	$15^2 = 225$	$100^2 = 10,000$

EXERCISE 1: POWERS

Directions: For each number below, multiply the base by itself the number of times indicated by its exponent.

1. 5^2

2. $\left(\frac{1}{2}\right)^2$

3. 9^3

4. $\left(\frac{3}{4}\right)^3$

5. $(.3)^2$

6. 1^{10}

7. 2^4

8. $(1.2)^2$

9. 4^0

10. 10^4

11. 25^2

12. $(.2)^3$

13. $\left(\frac{2}{3}\right)^2$

14. 3^3

15. 0^2

Answers are on page 727.

Square Roots

The operation opposite of squaring a number is finding the ***square root*** of a number. For instance, $5^2 = 25$, so $\sqrt{25} = 5$. The $\sqrt{\ }$ symbol is called the ***radical symbol***, and it means to find the square root of the number underneath the radical. $\sqrt{36}$ is read, "the square root of 36." Being familiar with perfect squares makes many square roots relatively easy to find. For instance, $\sqrt{100} = 10$ because $10^2 = 100$. $\sqrt{49} = 7$ and $\sqrt{4} = 2$.

If you need to find the square root of a number that is not a perfect square, you can simplify the square root. For instance, $\sqrt{75}$ can be expressed as

$$\sqrt{25 \cdot 3} = \sqrt{25} \cdot \sqrt{3} = 5\sqrt{3}.$$

You choose 25 and 3 because 25 is a perfect square, and you can find its square root.

EXERCISE 2: SIMPLIFYING SQUARE ROOTS

Directions: Simplify the following square roots.

1. $\sqrt{18}$ 2. $\sqrt{48}$ 3. $\sqrt{8}$ 4. $\sqrt{72}$ 5. $\sqrt{27}$

Answers are on page 727.

Approximating Square Roots

Calculators and tables of square roots can help us find the square roots of unfamiliar numbers. If a table or calculator is not available, ***approximation*** is helpful. For example, let's find the square root of 75. To find $\sqrt{75}$, we look at the perfect squares closest to 75. Those are 64 and 81.

$\sqrt{64} = 8$
$\sqrt{75}$ $\quad \Big\{$ Notice that $\sqrt{75}$ is between $\sqrt{64}$ and $\sqrt{81}$.
$\sqrt{81} = 9$

Therefore, $\sqrt{75}$ is between 8 and 9. Because 75 is closer to 81 than to 64, $\sqrt{75}$ is closer to 9. Approximate the answer to be 8.7.

Now let's approximate $\sqrt{40}$.

$\sqrt{36} = 6$
$\sqrt{40}$ $\quad \Big\{$ 40 is closer to 36 than 49.
$\sqrt{49} = 7$ $\quad$ (42 or 43 is about halfway.)

You can approximate $\sqrt{40} \approx 6.3$ (6.2 and 6.4 are also good approximations.)

EXERCISE 3: SQUARE ROOTS

Directions: This is a mixture of square root problems. When finding the square root of a perfect square, give the exact answer. When finding a square root that is not a perfect square, give either an approximate answer or a simplified answer.

1. $\sqrt{81}$ 4. $\sqrt{9}$ 7. $\sqrt{10}$ 10. $\sqrt{90}$ 13. $\sqrt{32}$

2. $\sqrt{1}$ 5. $\sqrt{144}$ 8. $\sqrt{16}$ 11. $\sqrt{225}$ 14. $\sqrt{64}$

3. $\sqrt{28}$ 6. $\sqrt{52}$ 9. $\sqrt{121}$ 12. $\sqrt{400}$ 15. $\sqrt{0}$

Answers are on page 727.

Order of Operations

Accurate calculations depend on careful use of addition, subtraction, multiplication, and division. These are our four main arithmetic operations. Throughout this section, you have been working with arithmetic expressions that combine these operations. The following is a series of steps called *the order of operations*.

THE ORDER OF OPERATIONS

First: Perform all powers and roots as they appear from left to right.

Second: Perform all multiplication and division as they appear from left to right.

Third: Perform all addition and subtraction as they appear from left to right.

Example 1: $4 + 3 \times 2 + 7$

STEP 1. Multiply first. $\qquad\qquad 4 + \underline{3 \times 2} + 7$

STEP 2. Add. $\qquad\qquad\qquad 4 + \quad 6 \quad + 7 = 17$

Example 2: $\quad 15 \; - \; 3 \; \times \; 4 \; + \; 7 \; \times \; 2 \; - \; 5$

$\qquad\qquad\qquad 15 \; - \quad 12 \quad + \quad 14 \quad - \; 5$

$\qquad\qquad\qquad\quad\; 3 \qquad\quad + \quad 14 \quad - \; 5$

$\qquad\qquad\qquad\qquad\quad\;\; 17 \qquad\qquad - \; 5$

$\qquad\qquad\qquad\qquad\qquad\qquad\qquad 12$

Example 3: $\quad 16 \; - \; 4 \; \times \; 2 \; + \; 16 \; \div \; 8$

$\qquad\qquad\qquad 16 \; - \quad 8 \quad + \quad 2$

$\qquad\qquad\qquad\quad\; 8 \qquad\quad + \quad 2$

$\qquad\qquad\qquad\qquad\quad\; 10$

▶ **TIP:** If you do not follow the order of operations, you will *not* get the right answer. For example, in the problem $8 + 2 \times 2$, you should get $8 + 4$ or 12. If you simply worked from left to right, you would *incorrectly* get $8 + 2$ or $10 \times 2 = 20$.

EXERCISE 4: ORDER OF OPERATIONS

Directions: Simplify the following expressions.

1. $7 - 5 + 3 - 5$

2. $8 \times 3 + 5$

3. $8 + 3 \times 5$

4. $6 + 21 \div 3 - 5$

5. $40 \div 2 - 5 \times 3$

6. $3 + 5^2$

7. $15 - 3 + 2^3$

8. $4 + 3^3 + 3 \times 2 - 2^2$

Answers are on page 727.

Parentheses

You will always follow the preceding order of operations when you evaluate an arithmetic expression. However, if a pair of parentheses ( ) is used in the expression, do the work within the parentheses first.

Now our order of operations is

First: Do all work inside parentheses or above and below a fraction bar.

Second: Evaluate powers and square roots.

Third: Multiply and divide.

Fourth: Add and subtract.

Examples:

$4 \times (3 + 5) = 4 \times (8) = 32$ Work inside parentheses first.

$(8^2 + 3) \times (5 + 4) = (64 + 3) \times (5 + 4)$ Work inside parentheses first.
$$= (67) \times (9)$$
$$= 603$$

$\dfrac{10 - 4}{4 - 2} = \dfrac{6}{2}$ Work above and below the fraction bar.

$\qquad\quad = 3$ A fraction bar means divide.

EXERCISE 5: MORE ORDER OF OPERATIONS

Directions: Simplify the following expressions.

1. $2 + 3^2 \times (4 + 5)$

2. $(12 - 5) + (14 - 6)$

3. $49 - (28 - 19)$

4. $8 + 6 \times (10 - 2^2)$

Answers are on page 727.

Formulas

Letters of the alphabet are often used to represent numbers that you need to find. For instance, you may remember the distance formula $d = rt$. The letters d, r, and t are used to represent numbers for distance (d), rate (r), and time (t). Letters used this way are called ***unknowns*** or ***variables***. This use of letters helps us express general relationships about numbers.

Formulas are a way of showing these general relationships. Some common formulas that help us are the area of a circle ($A = \pi r^2$), the perimeter of a rectangle ($P = 2l + 2w$), and the Pythagorean theorem ($c^2 = a^2 + b^2$). The GED Mathematics Test will include a page of formulas that will help you solve some problems on the test. As you read a particular problem, *you* will have to decide which formula will help you solve it. You should become familiar with the formulas on page 711.

Evaluating Formulas

When you replace letters with numbers in a formula, you ***substitute*** numbers for letters.

When you perform mathematical operations on the substituted values, you are ***evaluating*** a formula.

In evaluating formulas, it is very important to follow this order of operations:

1. Solve any expressions in parentheses or above or below a fraction bar.

2. Evaluate powers and roots.

3. Multiply and divide.

4. Add and subtract.

Example 1: The formula for the perimeter (distance around) of a rectangle is $P = 2l + 2w$. Substitute 6 for l (the length) and 5 for w (the width).

STEP 1. Substitute in the formula. $P = 2l + 2w$

$$P = 2(6) + 2(5)$$

STEP 2. Multiply. $P = 12 + 10$

STEP 3. Add. $P = 22$

Example 2: Find the volume of a rectangular box whose length is 7 inches, width is 5 inches, and height is 3 inches.

STEP 1. Find the appropriate formula on the formulas page. $V = lwh$

STEP 2. Substitute the values given. $V = (7)(5)(3)$

STEP 3. Multiply. Notice that the parentheses indicate multiplication. $V = 105$ cubic inches

EXERCISE 6: EVALUATING FORMULAS

Directions: Select the appropriate formula from the formulas page. Substitute the numbers in the problem and evaluate the formulas. The units of your answers are given in parentheses.

1. Find the area of a square if one side (s) is 12 inches. (square inches)

2. Find the volume of a cube if one side (s) is 5 inches. (cubic inches)

3. Find the simple interest if the principal (p) is $800 at ($r$) 12% annually for 3 years (t). (dollars)

4. Find the area of a circle where $\pi \cong$ 3.14 and the radius (r) is 3 inches. (square inches)

5. Find the distance (d) traveled if you are going 38 miles per hour (r) for 2 hours (t). (miles)

6. Find the volume of a cylinder if $\pi \cong$ 3.14, the radius (r) is 6 inches, and the height (h) is 10 inches. (cubic inches)

7. Find the area of a triangle where the base (b) is 12 centimeters and the height (h) is 9 centimeters. (square centimeters)

8. Find the perimeter of a rectangle if the length (l) is 14 feet and the width (w) is 2 yards. (feet)

Answers are on page 727.

Scientific Notation

Our number system is based on multiples of ten. *Scientific notation* uses this idea of a base of 10 to give us a shortened method of writing extremely large or extremely small numbers. The notation is used a lot in science, but we are seeing it more often in everyday life as we use calculators and computers.

We can also express fractional powers of ten using negative exponents. The negative sign is used to indicate the reciprocal. (The reciprocal of 10 is $\frac{1}{10}$.) For instance, $10^{-1} = \frac{1}{10} = .1$.

Let's look at some powers of ten using positive and negative exponents:

$$10^0 = 1$$

$$10^1 = 10 \qquad 10^{-1} = \frac{1}{10} = .1$$

$$10^2 = 100 \qquad 10^{-2} = \frac{1}{10^2} = \frac{1}{100} \text{ or } .01$$

$$10^3 = 1000 \qquad 10^{-3} = \frac{1}{10^3} = \frac{1}{1000} \text{ or } .001$$

$$10^4 = 10,000 \qquad 10^{-4} = \frac{1}{10^4} = \frac{1}{10,000} \text{ or } .0001$$

WRITING A NUMBER IN SCIENTIFIC NOTATION

1. Represent the number as a number or a mixed decimal between 1 and 10.
2. Write a multiplication sign and represent the number's value to the correct power of 10.

You can use scientific notation to write some numbers in shortened form. Simply count the number of positions that the decimal point must be moved to determine the power of 10 to use. The power of 10 is positive for whole numbers and negative for decimals.

Example 1: Express 86,200,000 in scientific notation. (The original decimal point is understood to be at the end of the number.)

STEP 1. Represent the number as a mixed decimal between 1 and 10. Insert the decimal point between 8 and 62 to get 8.62.

$$86,200,000 = 8.62 \times 10^?$$

STEP 2. Count the number of places the decimal point moved to get from 86,200,000 to 8.62. Since the point moved 7 places to the left, the power of 10 is 7.

$$86,200,000 = 8.62 \times 10^7$$
7 places left

Example 2: Express .00098 in scientific notation.

STEP 1. Represent the number as a mixed decimal between 1 and 10. Insert the decimal point between 9 and 8 to get 9.8.

$$.00098 = 9.8 \times 10^{-4}$$
4 places right

STEP 2. Count the number of places the decimal point moved to get from .00098 to 9.8. Since the point moved 4 places to the right, the power of 10 is −4.

EXERCISE 7: SCIENTIFIC NOTATION

Directions: Express each of the numbers below in scientific notation.

1. .0082
2. 500
3. 38,200
4. .58

Each number below is written in scientific notation. Find the actual value.

5. 1.624×10^3
6. 3.12×10^{-1}
7. 8.24×10^0
8. 7.13×10^3

Answers are on page 727.

9
GEOMETRY

Geometry is the study of shapes and the relationships among them. The geometry that you are required to know for the Mathematics Test is fundamental and practical. You will not be asked to "prove" theorems as you would in a formal geometry class. Instead, you will review the basic concepts in geometry and apply them to everyday situations.

Angles

An *angle* is formed when two lines intersect. The point of intersection is called the *vertex* of the angle. On the angle here, point S is the vertex. The two sides are ST and SR.

An angle is named with a small angle symbol ∠ and three points—two on the ends of the angle and one at the vertex: ∠RST. Sometimes, we just name an angle by its vertex, such as ∠S.

An angle is measured in *degrees*. The symbol for degrees is a familiar one from weather reports, such as in 72°.

One complete revolution around a point is 360°. One-fourth of a revolution is 90°. A 90° angle, called a *right angle*, is often used in construction. You can often recognize a right angle because of the small square drawn in the vertex. When two intersecting lines meet at right angles, we say they are *perpendicular lines*. The symbol for perpendicular lines is ⊥.

Special Pairs of Angles

The Mathematics Test will give information about angles and then ask you to use your understanding of their relationships. Let's look at some rules that apply to certain pairs of angles.

Complementary angles are two angles whose sum is 90°. That means the two angles together make a right angle. A 60° angle and a 30° angle are complements of each other because their sum is 90°.

Example 1: What is the complement of a 53° angle?

Solution: 90° − 53° = 37°

Supplementary angles are two angles whose sum is 180°. When the two angles are placed side by side, their sides form a straight line. A 110° angle is the supplement of a 70° angle because their sum is 180°.

Example 2: What is the supplement of a 30° angle?

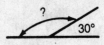

Solution: 180° − 30° = 150°

Vertical angles are formed when two lines intersect. The pair of angles opposite each other are equal. In the picture at right, ∠ABC and ∠DBE are vertical angles. Therefore, ∠ABC is equal to ∠DBE. We write this as ∠ABC = ∠DBE. ∠ABD and ∠CBE are also vertical angles; therefore, ∠ABD = ∠CBE. Sometimes, as in Example 3, you may be given a pair of intersecting lines and the measurement of one angle. From that one angle, you can find the measure of the other angles.

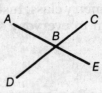

Example 3: Find the measure of ∠EFG.

Solution: ∠EFG and ∠HFJ are vertical angles and, therefore, equal.
∠EFG = 130°

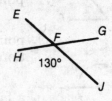

Example 4: Find the measure of ∠GFJ.

STEP 1. Notice that ∠GFJ is the supplement to ∠EFG. Together, they are on a straight line that equals 180°.

STEP 2. Subtract the angle you know from 180°.

180° − 130° = 50°

∠GFJ = 50°

Sometimes, angles are merely parts of a picture in a problem. Knowing these angle relationships (complementary, supplementary, and vertical) can help you solve the problem if you look for a pair of angles formed by intersecting lines.

Example 5: Find the measure of the angle indicated.

The ladder forms a supplementary angle with the ground. To find the missing angle, subtract 45° from 180°.

Solution: 180° − 45° = 135°

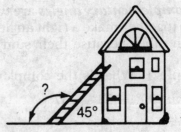

EXERCISE 1: PAIRS OF ANGLES

Directions: Solve each problem.

Use the picture below to answer questions 1–3.

1. Find the measure of ∠DBC.

2. Find the measure of ∠ABE.

3. Find the measure of ∠EBC.

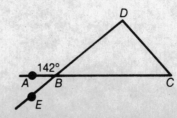

4. Two pieces of a puzzle fit together to form a right angle. If one piece has an angle of 52°, what is the angle of the complementary piece?

5. A carpenter is putting an oak chair rail around a dining room wall. He wants to make sure it fits nicely and looks straight. What is the measure of the angle that will supplement 75° to make a straight, snug fit?

Answers are on page 727.

Triangles

Triangles are the basis of land measurement. Surveyors use triangles to measure a small plot of ground, an entire state or county, or a large body of water. Triangles are used in science, navigation, and building construction. Carpenters use right triangles when no T squares or carpenters' squares are available. Astronomers use triangles to find out how far stars are from Earth. We also find important uses for triangles in maps, scale drawings, and architectural plans.

What Are Triangles?

On the Mathemetics Test, you will find measurement problems concerning triangles. Let's review the basic information about triangles and see how it applies to the type of problem that appears on the GED Test.

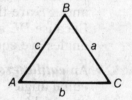

A *triangle* is a closed three-sided figure. The point where the sides meet is called a *vertex*. At each vertex, we find an angle. The figure on the right is called *triangle ABC*, written △*ABC*. It has three angles: ∠*A*, ∠*B*, ∠*C*. The triangle has three sides labeled *a*, *b*, and *c*. We can name a side by using a single letter or by using the letters representing the angles at the endpoints. For example, another name for side *a* is *BC*, for side *b* is *AC*, and for side *c* is *AB*.

The three angles of every triangle add up to 180°. So we say ∠*A* + ∠*B* + ∠*C* = 180°. Use this fact to find the measure of the third angle of a triangle when the measure of the first two angles is known, as in the following example.

Example: Find ∠*C* in the triangle below.

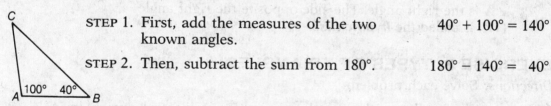

STEP 1. First, add the measures of the two known angles. $40° + 100° = 140°$

STEP 2. Then, subtract the sum from 180°. $180° - 140° = 40°$

▶ **TIP:** When you see a three-sided figure in a drawing, look for a special triangular relationship.

EXERCISE 2: ANGLES IN TRIANGLES

Directions: Find the measurement of the missing angle in each of the following triangles.

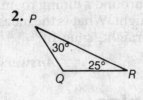

1.

2.

3.

4.

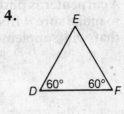

Answers are on page 728.

Types of Triangles

Triangles may be named according to the length of their sides. A triangle may be referred to as *scalene, isosceles,* or *equilateral.*

- A *scalene* triangle has no equal sides and no equal angles. In the figure at right, △*ABC* is scalene. Side *AB* is not equal to side *BC* or to side *AC*.

- An *isosceles* triangle has two equal sides and two equal angles. In △*DEF* in the figure at right, *DF* is the **base** of the triangle, *DE* and *EF* are the **legs** of the triangle, ∠*D* and ∠*F* are the **base angles**, and ∠*E* is the **vertex angle**. Because *DE = EF*, the triangle is isosceles. The two base angles are equal; ∠*D* = ∠*F*.

- An *equilateral* triangle has three equal sides and three equal angles. Because the three angles of the triangle must add up to 180°, each angle must be 60°. △*PQR* is equilateral because *PQ = QR = PR*. It is also true that ∠*P* = ∠*Q* = ∠*R*. (An equilateral triangle is sometimes referred to as an **equiangular** triangle.)

- A right triangle is a special type of triangle that is often used in geometry problems. A **right triangle** has one right angle of 90°. We can recognize right triangles because the right angle looks like a corner. The small box in the corner indicates a right triangle. In △*XYZ* at right, ∠*X* is the right angle. The side opposite the right angle (*YZ*) is called the **hypotenuse**.

EXERCISE 3: TYPES OF TRIANGLES

Directions: Solve each problem.

1. Name each triangle as either a scalene, isosceles, equilateral, or right triangle.

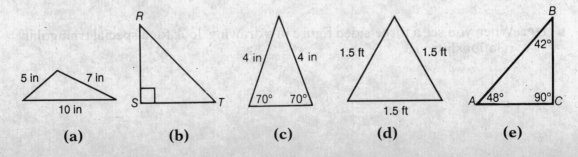

(a)   **(b)**   **(c)**   **(d)**   **(e)**

2. In triangle *RST*, ∠*R* = 70° and ∠*S* = 20°. What kind of triangle is △*RST*?

3. In isosceles triangle *ABC*, the base angles are each 52°. Find the measure of the third angle.

4. A right triangle contains a 60° angle. What is the measure of the third angle?

Answers are on page 728.

Similar Triangles

Similar triangles are figures that have the same shape. We often use similar figures to find hard-to-measure lengths, such as the distance across a lake or the height of a building. ***Similar triangles*** are two triangles whose ***corresponding angles*** are equal and whose ***corresponding sides*** are in proportion.

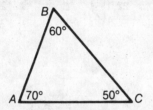 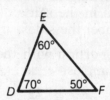

Look at △*ABC* and △*DEF*. They are similar triangles because they have the same shape. We can see that corresponding angles are equal. ∠*A* = ∠*D*, ∠*B* = ∠*E*, and ∠*C* = ∠*F*. Therefore, the two triangles are not the same size, but their sides are in proportion. We write this relationship as

$$\frac{AB}{DE} = \frac{BC}{EF} = \frac{AC}{DF}$$

Example 1: On a sunny day, the village inspector used similar triangles to find the height of a flagpole without climbing it. She found that her 6-foot-tall coworker cast a 10-foot shadow at the same time the flagpole cast a 40-foot shadow. How tall is the flagpole?

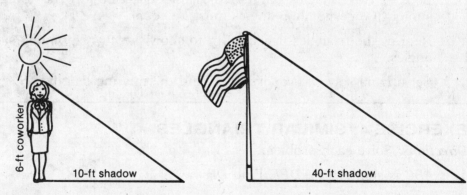

STEP 1. Notice that the coworker and the flagpole are at right angles to the ground. Set up a proportion.

$$\frac{\text{flagpole}}{\text{coworker}} = \frac{\text{flagpole's shadow}}{\text{coworker's shadow}}$$

STEP 2. Fill in the numbers from the problem. Let *f* stand for the flagpole.

$$\frac{f}{6} = \frac{40}{10}$$

STEP 3. Cross multiply and divide.

$$f = \frac{6 \times 40}{10} = \frac{240}{10} = 24 \text{ ft}$$

Another type of problem involving similar triangles is a surveying problem.

Example 2: The figure below shows a method of measuring the width of a river. If measurements are taken along the riverbank as shown, how wide is the river?

STEP 1. Look to see if there are two similar triangles. $\angle B = \angle E$ because they are both right angles, and both angles at point C are the same because they are vertical angles. Since two pairs of angles are the same, the triangles must be similar.

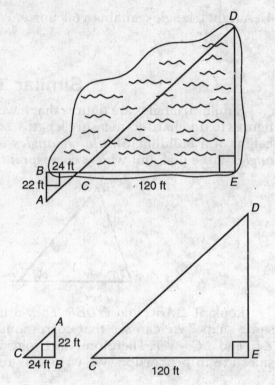

STEP 2. Redraw the triangles by turning them in the same direction. Label the sides.

STEP 3. Set up a proportion with the sides of the angles.

$$\frac{AB}{DE} = \frac{CB}{CE} \qquad \frac{22}{DE} = \frac{24}{120}$$

STEP 4. Cross multiply and divide.

$$DE = \frac{120 \times 22}{24} = \frac{2640}{24} = 110 \text{ ft}$$

▶ **TIP:** Always look for similar triangles when you are comparing two triangles.

SOLVING SIMILAR TRIANGLE PROBLEMS

1. Look for two triangles that have the same shape. Be sure the triangles are similar. Corresponding angles must be equal.

2. Redraw the triangles if necessary to show the corresponding sides and angles.

3. Set up and solve a proportion to find the missing length.

EXERCISE 4: SIMILAR TRIANGLES

Directions: Solve each problem.

1. $\triangle ABC$ is similar to $\triangle DEF$. Find DF.

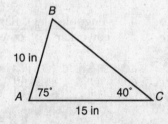
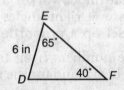

2. An oak tree along a parkway casts an 18-foot shadow at the same time an 8-foot traffic light casts a 12-foot shadow. Find the height of the tree.

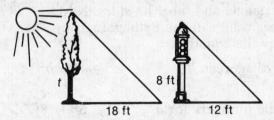

3. Suppose we need to find the distance d across a pond but are unable to swim to the other side and measure the distance directly. We can still find the distance. Find a marker on one side of the pond. On the other side of the pond, place a stake in the ground directly across from the marker. Measure a given distance c on a line perpendicular to the line determined by the marker and the stake. Then form two triangles as in the sketch below.

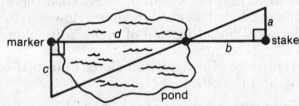

(a) With these measures, what would you do first to determine the distance, d?

(b) Find the distance across the pond if $a = 2$ feet, $b = 6$ feet, and $c = 50$ feet.

4. To find the height of a tower, Melissa held a yardstick perpendicular to the ground. She measured the shadow cast by the tower and the shadow cast by the yardstick. The tower's shadow was 42 feet, and the yardstick's shadow was 4 feet. How tall is the tower?

Answers are on page 728.

The Pythagorean Theorem

Although the **Pythagorean theorem** was developed by the Greek mathematician Pythagoras in about 500 B.C., it is still widely used today. Since the rule applies only to right triangles, the problem has to include a 90° angle or the right angle symbol (⌐) for the Pythagorean theorem to apply. In a right triangle, the side opposite the right angle is called the *hypotenuse*, and the other two sides are called the *legs* of the triangle.

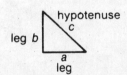

The Pythagorean theorem states that in a right triangle the square of the hypotenuse equals the sum of the squares of the legs. According to the diagram, the Pythagorean theorem is written as $c^2 = a^2 + b^2$. This is put in terms of the right triangle with legs a and b and hypotenuse c.

▶ **TIP:** To use the rule effectively, you need to be familiar with the use of squares and square roots. Refer to pages 649–651 for a review of squares and square roots.

Example 1: Find the length of the hypotenuse of a right triangle with legs 6 inches and 8 inches.

First, draw a right triangle and label its sides. Next, substitute the number values in the Pythagorean theorem and simplify the equation.

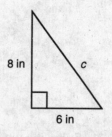

STEP 1. Write the Pythagorean theorem.

$$c^2 = a^2 + b^2$$

STEP 2. Substitute the numbers for a and b (the legs of the triangle).

$$c^2 = 6^2 + 8^2$$

STEP 3. Square the numbers.

$$c^2 = 36 + 64$$

STEP 4. Add the numbers.

$$c^2 = 100$$

STEP 5. Take the square root.

$$c = \sqrt{100} = 10 \text{ in}$$

Example 2 asks us to find the length of a leg when the hypotenuse and one leg are given. We still use the Pythagorean theorem. However, to find a leg rather than the hypotenuse, we subtract instead of add before taking the square root.

Example 2: The hypotenuse of a right triangle is 13 feet. If one leg is 12 feet, what is the length of the other leg?

First sketch a right triangle with a corner to show the right angle and then label its parts. Remember, the hypotenuse is the side opposite the right angle.

STEP 1. Write the Pythagorean theorem.

$$c^2 = a^2 + b^2$$

STEP 2. Substitute the numbers for c and b.

$$13^2 = a^2 + 12^2$$

STEP 3. Square the numbers.

$$169 = a^2 + 144$$

STEP 4. Subtract the numbers when looking for a leg.

$$169 - 144 = a^2$$
$$25 = a^2$$

STEP 5. Take the square root.

$$a = \sqrt{25} = 5 \text{ ft}$$

To solve the next problem, you first have to recognize a right triangle relationship in a familiar figure.

Example 3: A painter is concerned about setting up his equipment too near the street. He leans a 50-foot ladder against the top of a 48-foot building. How far is the bottom of the ladder from the foot of the building?

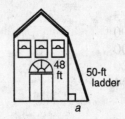

First sketch a picture of the problem and label the parts. A building makes a right angle with the ground. The leaning ladder completes a triangle. Substitute the values in the Pythagorean theorem and simplify the equation.

STEP 1. Write the Pythagorean theorem. $c^2 = a^2 + b^2$

STEP 2. Substitute the numbers for c and b. $50^2 = a^2 + 48^2$

STEP 3. Square the numbers. $2500 = a^2 + 2304$

STEP 4. Subtract the numbers when looking for a leg. $2500 - 2304 = a^2$

STEP 5. Take the square root. $\sqrt{196} = a$ 14 ft $= a$

▶ **TIP:** Always make a sketch when working a geometry problem. If the sketch is a right triangle, consider using the Pythagorean theorem.

SOLVING PYTHAGOREAN THEOREM PROBLEMS

1. Sketch the information in the problem and label the parts.

2. Identify the right angle and then the hypotenuse.

3. Substitute the values into the formula $c^2 = a^2 + b^2$.

4. Square the values.

5. Add if you are looking for the hypotenuse or subtract if you are looking for a leg.

6. Take the square root.

EXERCISE 5: THE PYTHAGOREAN THEOREM

Directions: Solve each problem.

1. In a right triangle whose legs are a and b and whose hypotenuse is c, find the length of the missing side when

   (a) $a = 9$, $b = 12$ **(b)** $b = 4$, $c = 5$ **(c)** $a = 10$, $b = 24$

2. The screen on Alberto's TV has the measurements shown. Find the measure of the diagonal for Alberto's TV.

3. Can 20 inches, 21 inches, and 29 inches be the sides of a right triangle?

4. At summer camp, the swimming course runs the length (*l*) of a small lake. To determine the length of the course, the camp counselors measure the two "dry" legs of a right triangle. What is the length in meters of the swimming course in the figure below?

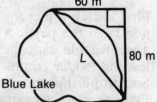

(1) 75
(2) 90
(3) 100
(4) 120
(5) 144

5. A television antenna is 24 feet tall and is held in place by three guy wires (braces) fastened at the top of the antenna and to hooks 7 feet from the base of the tower. If the antenna is installed on a flat roof, how many feet of guy wire are used?

(1) 40
(2) 50
(3) 60
(4) 65
(5) 75

6. A ladder that is 13 feet long is placed against a house. The foot of the ladder is 5 feet from the base of the house. How many feet above the ground does the ladder touch the building?

(1) 10
(2) 12
(3) 15
(4) 16
(5) 20

Answers are on page 728.

Plane Figures

Rectangles and squares are used extensively in the construction of buildings. Floor tile, tabletops, windowpanes, doors, books, and picture frames are a few of the items that often are rectangular or square. The GED Mathematics Test will ask you to recognize these shapes and to solve problems based on them.

Types of Figures

A *rectangle* is a closed four-sided figure. The points where the four sides meet are called *vertices*. At each vertex there is a right angle (90°).

1. The sum of the four angles is 360°.
2. Opposite sides are equal.
3. Opposite sides are parallel.
4. All four angles are equal (90°).

A *parallelogram* is a closed four-sided figure. It has four angles (not necessarily right angles).

> 1. The sum of the four angles is 360°.
> 2. Opposite sides are equal.
> 3. Opposite sides are parallel.
> 4. Opposite angles are equal.

A *square* is a four-sided figure with four right angles.

> 1. All four sides are equal.
> 2. All four angles are equal; each is 90°.
> 3. Opposite sides are parallel.

Circles

Many objects around us are circular: clock faces, wheels, bottle caps, rings, and the pupils of eyes. What makes a circle a circle? In geometry, we define a *circle* as a set of points all the same distance from a center point.

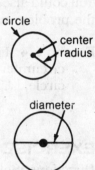

That distance from the center to the circle is called the *radius*. A radius can be drawn from any point on the circle to the center. A *diameter* is a straight line that goes through the center of the circle and has its endpoints on the circle. A diameter is twice as long as a radius.

Measurement of Figures

Perimeter

Perimeter is the distance around a figure. Measuring for a fence around a yard, putting a baseboard around a room, or setting up a baseball diamond are some uses of perimeter. You will find formulas for perimeter on the formulas page of the GED Mathematics Test.

▶ **TIP:** Keep in mind that the perimeter of a figure is the distance all the way around the figure, so you can also *add* all the sides of the figure.

The perimeter of a square is $P = 4s$ where P is the perimeter and s is one side. Since all four sides of a square are equal, multiply one side by 4 to get the total distance around the square.

Example 1: Find the perimeter of this square.

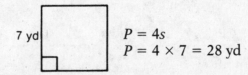

7 yd

$P = 4s$
$P = 4 \times 7 = 28$ yd

The perimeter of a rectangle is $P = 2l + 2w$ where P is the perimeter, l is the length, and w is the width. Since opposite sides of a rectangle are equal, double the length and double the width, then add to find the total distance around the rectangle.

Example 2: Find the
perimeter of this
rectangle.

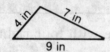

$P = 2l + 2w$
$P = (2 \times 7) + (2 \times 3) = 20$ ft

The perimeter of a triangle is $P = a + b + c$ where P equals the perimeter and a, b, and c are the lengths of the three sides. To find the perimeter, add the lengths of the three sides.

Example 3: Find the
perimeter of this triangle.

$P = a + b + c$
$P = 4 + 7 + 9 = 20$ in

The *circumference* of a circle is the perimeter of (or distance around) a circle. The formula is $C = \pi d$ where C is the circumference, pi or $\pi \cong 3.14$, and d is the diameter. The circumference is equal to approximately 3.14 times the diameter. You could also use $\frac{22}{7}$ for π if the diameter or radius is given as a fraction or when the problem would be easier to solve with $\frac{22}{7}$.

Example 4: Find the
circumference of this
circle.

42 in

$C = \pi d$
$C = \frac{22}{7} \times 42 = 132$ in

EXERCISE 6: PERIMETER

Directions: Solve each problem.

1. A baseball diamond is a square with distances between the bases as shown. How far will the batter run if he hits a home run?

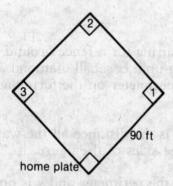

home plate

2. Find, in feet, the amount of framing needed to frame a picture $8\frac{1}{2}$ in by 11 in.

3. How much binding is needed around a triangular sail for the toy sailboat shown below?

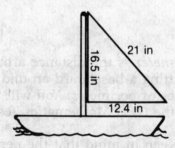

4. A farmer wants to fence a rectangular pasture 400 yards by 224 yards. The cost of fencing is $5.75 per eight-foot section. What will his cost be?

5. Find the perimeter of the figure shown below.

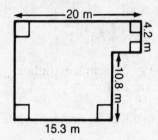

6. How many feet of fencing are needed to fence the yard below?

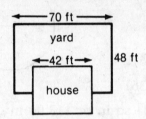

7. To jog 6 miles, how many times must you jog around a city block that is $\frac{1}{4}$ mile long by $\frac{1}{8}$ mile wide?

8. Find the perimeter of the ice-skating rink with the given dimensions. (*Hint*: Think of the rink as made up of a rectangle and 2 half-circles.)

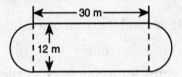

Answers are on page 729.

Area

Area is the amount of surface over a certain region. It can be used to describe the size of farmland, floor space, or a tabletop. Area is measured in square units such as square inches or square feet. Imagine a square one inch on each side. This is a square inch.

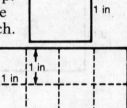

When we are asked to find the area in square inches, we are actually finding the number of squares one inch by one inch that could fit on the surface we are measuring. For example, the rectangle to the right contains 8 square inches of area.

Remember that the formulas page of the GED Test will provide the formulas for the area of the square, the rectangle, and the triangle. All of the formulas appear on page 711 of this book.

▶ **TIP:** Answers in area problems are given in square units, such as square inches or square meters.

The area of a square is $A = s^2$ where A is the area and s is one side. The area equals the side times the side. Given a square with a side of 7 inches, the area equals 7 in × 7 in = 49 square inches.

The area of a rectangle is $A = lw$ where A is the area, l is the length, and w is the width. The area equals the length times the width.

Example 1: How much surface area is the rectangular top of a desk 3 feet by 5 feet?

Solution: The area is $A = lw = 3$ ft × 5 ft = 15 square feet or 15 ft^2

The area of a triangle is $A = \frac{1}{2}bh$ where A is the area, b is the base, and h is the height. To find the area of a triangle, multiply the base by the height and find $\frac{1}{2}$ of that amount.

Example 2: Find the area of a triangle with a base of 6 inches and height of 9
inches.

STEP 1. Multiply the base by the
height.

$$A = \tfrac{1}{2}bh$$

$$A = \tfrac{1}{2}(6 \cdot 9) = \tfrac{1}{2}(54)$$

STEP 2. Divide that by 2 to find $\tfrac{1}{2}$.

$$A = \tfrac{1}{2}(54) = 27 \text{ square inches}$$
or 27 in^2

The area of a circle is $A = \pi r^2$ where A is the area, π is approximately 3.14
or $\tfrac{22}{7}$, and r is the radius.

Example 3: Find the area of a circle whose diameter is 12 inches.

STEP 1. Find the radius.

$$12 \div 2 = 6$$

STEP 2. Substitute numbers in the
formula and do the
calculation.

$$A = \pi r^2$$

$$A = 3.14(6)^2$$

$$A = 3.14(36)$$

$$A = 113.04 \text{ sq in or } 113.04 \text{ in}^2$$

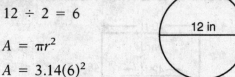

EXERCISE 7: AREA

Directions: Solve each problem. For questions 1–3, find the area of the figures.

1.

14.3 m

9 m

2.

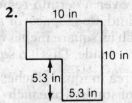

10 in

10 in

5.3 in

5.3 in

(This shape combines a
square and a rectangle.)

3.

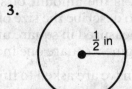

$\tfrac{1}{2}$ in

(Use $\tfrac{22}{7}$ for π.)

4. How many square yards of carpet are needed for a room 30 feet by 15 feet?
   (1 sq yd = 9 sq ft)

5. At $1.15 per square foot, find the rental cost for an office 20 feet by 15 feet.

6. How many square feet is the largest circular rug that can be put on the floor
   of a room 10 feet by 12 feet?

Questions 7–10 are based on the following information and diagram.

The diagram below shows the backyard at the Smith house. In the yard are an 18-foot-diameter swimming pool, an 8-foot square garden, and a 10-foot-by-20-foot patio deck. The rest of the yard is grass-covered.

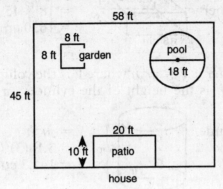

7. How large is the patio?

8. What percentage (to the nearest 1 percent) of the yard is covered by the pool?

9. How many square yards (to the nearest hundredth) of outdoor carpeting are needed to cover the patio?

10. To the nearest whole number, how many times larger is the pool than the garden?

Answers are on page 729.

Volume

Volume is the amount of space that a solid, or a three-dimensional figure, contains. Examples of solids are a rectangular box, a cylinder, and a cube.

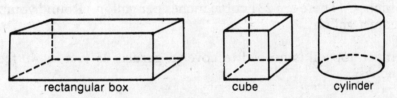

Volume is measured in *cubic units* such as cubic feet, cubic inches, or cubic yards. For example, a cubic inch is a cube with edges of 1 inch each.

The formulas page of the GED Mathematics Test gives formulas for the volume of a cube, a rectangular container, and a cylinder. Let's look at each formula.

The volume of a *cube* is $V = s^3$ where V is the volume and s is the edge of the cube. A die and a square box are examples of cubes. Each edge of the cube has the same length. Thus, the volume of a cube is equal to the edge cubed, or edge times edge times edge.

Example 1: Find the volume of the cube at the right:

$$V = s^3$$
$$= 2 \times 2 \times 2$$
$$= 8 \text{ cu in or } 8 \text{ in}^3$$

2 in

The volume of a ***rectangular container*** is $V = lwh$ where V is the volume, l is the length, w is the width, and h is the height. The volume is equal to the length times the width times the height.

Example 2: What is the volume of the container at the right?

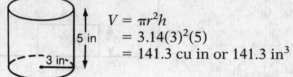

$V = lwh$
$= 18 \times 15 \times 6$
$= 1620 \text{ cm}^3 \text{ or } 1620 \text{ cu cm}$

The volume of a ***cylinder*** is $V = \pi r^2 h$ where V is the volume, r is the radius of the circular base, and h is the height of the cylinder. π is approximately 3.14 or $\frac{22}{7}$.

Example 3: Find the volume of the container at the right.

$V = \pi r^2 h$
$= 3.14(3)^2(5)$
$= 141.3 \text{ cu in or } 141.3 \text{ in}^3$

▶ **TIP:** On the GED Mathematics Test, you may be asked to find the perimeter (or circumference), area, or volume of a figure. However, you may not be told directly *which* measurement you are to find. Keep in mind that the perimeter is what goes around a figure, the area is what covers a figure, and the volume is the capacity of an object. Once you have determined what you are looking for, you can select the right formula from the formulas page.

EXERCISE 8: VOLUME

Directions: Solve each problem.

1. Find the volume of a freezer chest that is 6 feet long, 4 feet deep, and 3 feet wide.

2. How many gallons of water will fill a fish tank that is 18 inches by 12 inches by 48 inches? (There are 231 cubic inches per gallon.) Round your answer to the nearest gallon.

3. How much topsoil is needed to cover a garden 25 feet by 40 feet to a depth of 6 inches?

4. The edge of a small cube is 2 inches, and the edge of a larger cube is 4 inches. What is the ratio of the volume of the small cube to the volume of the larger cube?

5. The farmer's silo has the dimensions shown at the right. What is the volume of the silo? (Use $\frac{22}{7}$ for π.)

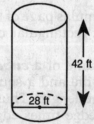

Answers are on page 730.

EXERCISE 9: REVIEW OF GEOMETRY

Directions: Solve each problem. Refer to the formulas on page 711 when necessary.

1. How many feet of weather stripping are needed to frame the two windows with the dimensions indicated?

    (1) 12 **(2)** 15 **(3)** 33 **(4)** 396 **(5)** 4752

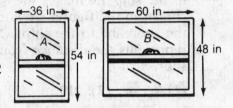

2. The Family Food Co. is redesigning its bran flakes box as shown. Find the capacity of the new box in cubic inches.

    (1) 22 **(2)** 92 **(3)** 115 **(4)** 230 **(5)** 460

3. Family Foods is also redesigning its soup can. Which of the following can be used to find the capacity of the new soup can?

    (1) $(3.14)(1.5)^2(4)$
    (2) $(3.14)(3)(4)$
    (3) $(3.14)(1.5)^2$
    (4) $(3.14)(3)^2$
    (5) not enough information is given

4. The diagonal of a rectangle is 17 inches. If the length of the rectangle is 15 inches, what is the width of the rectangle in inches?

    (1) 4 **(2)** 8 **(3)** 16 **(4)** 32 **(5)** 64

5. A local radio station broadcasts over a 21-mile radius. How many square miles does this cover? (Use $\frac{22}{7}$ for π.)

    (1) 66 **(2)** 441 **(3)** 1386 **(4)** 1764 **(5)** 5542

6. Ramon needs to carpet a room. Carpeting costs \$11.50 per square yard. Disregarding waste, how much will it cost to carpet the room in the diagram?

    (1) \$159.25
    (2) \$207
    (3) \$1380
    (4) \$1601.38
    (5) not enough information is given

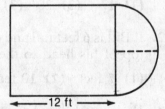

7. Mary planted a triangular flower bed with the dimensions shown at right. What is the area (in square feet) of the garden?

    (1) 37 **(2)** 45 **(3)** 60 **(4)** 120 **(5)** 150

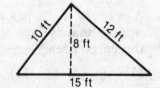

8. An observer on the shore sees a ship anchored off the coast. To find the distance to the ship, he makes the measurements shown in the figure. How far is it from the shoreline to the ship? (Note that d represents the distance from ship to shore.)

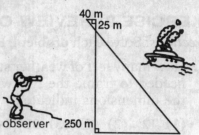

(1) 65 m (2) 210 m (3) 400 m (4) 500 m (5) 10,000 m

9. A right triangle contains a 60° angle. What is the measure of the third angle?

(1) 30° (2) 120° (3) 150° (4) 210° (5) not enough information is given

Use the information below to answer questions 10–12.

Ellen was curious about the height of a radio tower near her house. On a sunny day, her brother Bill stood next to the tower. Both Bill and the tower cast a shadow. The figure at right represents Bill and the tower.

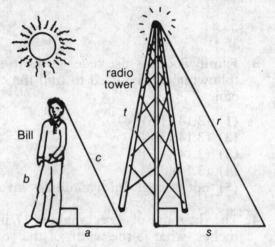

10. Which expression below correctly represents the height of the tower, t?

(1) $t = \dfrac{s \times b}{a}$ (2) $t = a + b + c$ (3) $t = s - r$ (4) $t = \dfrac{a \times b}{s}$ (5) $t = s + a$

11. If Bill is 5 feet tall and casts a 12-foot shadow while the tower casts a 42-foot shadow, how many feet tall is the tower?

(1) $17\frac{1}{2}$ (2) 20 (3) 30 (4) 35 (5) 60

12. If Bill is 6 feet tall and casts an 8-foot shadow, what is the distance from the top of his head to the tip of his shadow?

(1) 7 feet (2) 10 feet (3) 14 feet (4) 50 feet (5) 100 feet

13. How much larger is the supplement of a 57° angle than the complement of a 75° angle?

(1) 18° (2) 105° (3) 108° (4) 123° (5) 228°

14. A delivery truck has a cargo area that is 8 feet by 8 feet by 12 feet. Approximately how many square boxes 2 feet on a side can be loaded into the cargo area?

(1) 48 (2) 96 (3) 160 (4) 768 (5) not enough information is given

15. A circular pond has a circumference of 628 feet. What is the distance in feet from the center to the edge of the pond?

(1) 100 (2) 157 (3) 200 (4) 314 (5) 628

Answers are on page 730.

10
ALGEBRA
___

Algebra, an extension of arithmetic, is an organized system of rules that help us solve problems. Think of algebra as a game. When you first sit down to play, you read the rules and try to understand how to use them.

Every game has its own vocabulary that is defined in the rules. As you actually begin to play the game, you find yourself using the vocabulary of the game and following the rules. The more you play the game, the easier it is to remember both the vocabulary and the rules. Let's start our study of algebra with a look at its special vocabulary.

The Language of Algebra

Algebra uses letters of the alphabet to represent numbers or unknown quantities. These letters are called *variables*. These values are variable because they change from problem to problem. The letters can be capital letters, lowercase letters, or even Greek letters. Some examples are x, t, B, R, and P. *Constants* are fixed numbers. The value of a constant is known and does not change from problem to problem. Some constants are 8, 75, 0, π, and $\sqrt{3}$.

In algebra, we still work with the four operations of addition, subtraction, multiplication, and division. Look at the chart below to see the symbols that are used for these four operations.

TABLE OF OPERATIONS			
Operation	Symbol	Example	Meaning
Addition	+	$5 + x$	5 plus x
Subtraction	−	$8 - x$ $y - 8$	8 minus x y minus 8
Multiplication	· (dot) ( ) parentheses no symbol	$5 \cdot 3$ $10(2)$ xy	5 times 3 10 times 2 x times y
Division	÷ —— (fraction bar)	$x \div y$ $\frac{x}{12}$ $\frac{3}{x}$	x divided by y x divided by 12 3 divided by x

Whenever a number and a variable are multiplied together, the number part is called the ***coefficient*** of the variable. In the expression $7x$, the coefficient of x is 7. The variable x is multiplied by 7.

▶ **TIP:** Whenever the variable is written without a number in front of it, the coefficient is understood to be 1. Therefore, y means $1y$, and the coefficient is 1.

Algebraic Expressions

An ***algebraic expression*** connects variables to variables or variables to constants using the operation signs. For example, $a + 4$, $5 - 3y$, and $\frac{m+n}{4}$ are all algebraic expressions. In the expression $x + 5$, x is the variable that represents the unknown, and 5 is the constant value. The operation is addition.

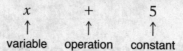

Algebraic expressions contain ***terms***. A term can be a number, a variable, or the multiplication or division of numbers with variables. Some examples of terms are

5 (a number) $7y$ (the product of a number and a variable)

y (a variable) $\frac{y}{3}$ (the quotient of a variable and a number)

In an algebraic expression, terms are separated by + and − signs. The sign before the term belongs to the term.

Examples:

is an expression that contains two terms: $5x$ and $+4y$.

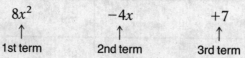

is an expression that contains three terms: $8x^2$, $-4x$, and $+7$.

$$\underset{\substack{\uparrow \\ \text{1st term}}}{\frac{x}{5}} \qquad \underset{\substack{\uparrow \\ \text{2nd term}}}{-2}$$

is an expression that contains two terms: $\frac{x}{5}$ and -2.

▶ **TIP:** Keep the plus or minus sign with the term, as in -2 above. You will learn more about negative numbers on pages 690–696.

EXERCISE 1: TERMS

Directions: Name the terms in the following expressions

1. $4 + x$ **2.** $8x + 7y - 5$ **3.** $2x^2 - \frac{3}{x}$ **4.** $8ab + 12$

Answers are on page 731.

Equations

An algebraic *equation* sets one expression equal to another expression or a value.

$$x + 7 \quad = \quad 10 \qquad\qquad x + 3 \quad = \quad 2x - 9$$

expression   equals   value   expression   equals   expression

---

AN ALGEBRAIC EQUATION ALWAYS HAS THREE PARTS:

1. left-side expression
2. an equal sign (=)
3. right-side expression

The equation $x + 7 = 10$ says that some number (x) added to 7 equals 10. We know that 3 added to 7 equals 10, so 3 is the **solution** of the equation. The solution is the value of the variable that makes the statement true. You **solve** an equation when you find the solution for the variable. On the Mathematics Test, you may have to translate a word problem into an equation. You will also write and interpret your own equations.

Example: $2x + 5 = 17$

This expression means that *a number multiplied by 2 and added to 5 equals 17*. Do you know what the number is? You're right if you said 6, because $2(6) + 5 = 17$.

EXERCISE 2: EQUATIONS

Directions: Write in words what each expression means. Use the words *a number* for any letter as shown in the example above.

1. $5 + 7y = 19$ **2.** $9y = 27$ **3.** $a - 5 = 23$ **4.** $\frac{10}{y} - 5 = 0$ **5.** $\frac{y}{8} = 9$

Answers are on page 731.

Solving One-Step Equations

Among the most important uses of algebra are the solution of equations and the use of equations to solve word problems.

Eyeballing the Solution

Solving an equation means finding the value of the variable that makes the equation true. Some equations will be fairly easy to solve because you know your math facts. If you can just look at the equation and see the answer, you are "eyeballing" the equation.

For example, $x + 3 = 10$ is an algebraic equation. What value of x will make this true? You would choose $x = 7$ because you know $7 + 3 = 10$. Another example is $3x = 15$. What value of x makes this equation true? The answer is 5 because you know $3(5) = 15$.

EXERCISE 3: EYEBALLING

Directions: Solve the following equations by "eyeballing" them. Ask yourself, "What number would make this equation true?" Then choose that number to represent the variable (letter) shown in the problem.

1. $x - 2 = 0$ **3.** $4 + x = 9$ **5.** $x - 5 = 8$ **7.** $5a = 10$

2. $\frac{x}{5} = 2$ **4.** $x + 3 = 8$ **6.** $3x = 9$ **8.** $\frac{36}{x} = 9$

Answers are on page 731.

Algebraic Solutions

Let's look at algebraic methods of solving one-step equations. Before you start solving equations, you must understand a couple of mathematical ideas. First of all, an equation is a perfect balance between what is on the left side of the equal sign and what is on the right side of the equal sign.

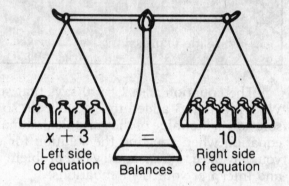

$x + 3$
Left side
of equation

$=$
Balances

10
Right side
of equation

If you make any changes on the left side, you must make the *same* changes on the right side. For instance, if you add 7 to the left side, you must add 7 to the right side for the 2 sides to remain equal. Then you know the result will be true.

Second, your goal in solving an equation is to get the variable all by itself on one side of an equation. Concentrate on the variable. In the equation $x + 3 = 10$, concentrate on the x. Notice that the x is being added to 3. This will tell you how to solve the equation.

▶ **TIP:** Keep the equation in balance and concentrate on the variable.

To solve an equation, perform the opposite operation (called the ***inverse*** operation). Addition and subtraction are opposites, and multiplication and division are opposites. In the equation $x + 3 = 10$, you see that x is being added to three. The opposite of "adding three" is "subtracting three." If you subtract three from both sides, you will get x all by itself.

Example 1: $x + 3 = 10$

STEP 1. Look at x. It is added to 3. $x + 3 = 10$

STEP 2. Subtract 3 from both sides. $x + \underbrace{3 - 3}_{0} = \underbrace{10 - 3}_{7}$

STEP 3. Solve the equation. $x = 7$

WHEN SOLVING AN EQUATION, REMEMBER:

1. Keep the equation in balance.

2. Concentrate on the variable.

3. Perform the opposite operation.

Example 2: $7x = 21$

STEP 1. Look at x. It is multiplied by 7. $\qquad\qquad 7x = 21$

STEP 2. Divide by 7 on both sides. The $\qquad \dfrac{\cancel{7}x}{\cancel{7}} = \dfrac{\cancel{21}^{3}}{\cancel{7}}$
7s on the left side "cancel out."

STEP 3. Solve the equation. $\qquad\qquad\qquad x = 3$

Check the answers to each problem by substituting the answer in the original equation. For example, when we solved $7x = 21$, we got $x = 3$. Check that answer by substituting 3 for x in the original problem.

$\qquad 7x = 21$

$\quad 7(3) = 21$ Substitute 3 for x.

$\quad\ \ 21 = 21$ This is a true statement, so $x = 3$ is the solution for $7x = 21$.

Example 3: $8 = \frac{x}{5}$

STEP 1. Look at x. It is divided by 5. $\qquad\quad 8 = \frac{x}{5}$

STEP 2. Multiply both sides by 5. $\qquad 5 \cdot 8 = \frac{x}{\cancel{5}_{1}} \cdot \cancel{5}^{1}$

$\qquad\qquad\qquad\qquad\qquad\qquad\quad 5 \cdot 8 = x$

STEP 3. Solve the equation. $\qquad\qquad\quad 40 = x$

EXERCISE 4: ONE-STEP EQUATIONS

Directions: Solve for x. Check your answers.

1. $3 + x = 7$ **3.** $2x = 6$ **5.** $5x = 75$ **7.** $x - 3 = 12$

2. $\frac{x}{3} = 12$ **4.** $x - 8 = 0$ **6.** $\frac{x}{4} = 16$ **8.** $\frac{1}{2}x = 14$

Answers are on page 731.

Solving Algebra Word Problems

To use algebra to solve mathematical problems, you have to translate the problem into algebraic language. Let a letter of the alphabet, a variable, represent the unknown quantity. The letters x, y, and z are most often used as variables.

A few English phrases are used repeatedly in algebra problems. Become familiar with the phrases and their algebraic expressions in the chart on page 680.

TRANSLATING EXPRESSIONS

1. First assign a variable to the unknown quantity.

2. Use that variable to write an expression for any other unknown quantity.

3. Identify the phrases that indicate the mathematical operation.

4. Use the operation to write the expression.

Translate: "The square of a number decreased by the number."

1. Let x be the number.
2. The square of a number is x^2.
3. *Decreased by* means "subtract."
4. Write $x^2 - x$.

TRANSLATION CHART		
English Phrase	**Operation**	**Algebraic Expression**
the *sum* of two numbers	+ (add)	$x + y$
five *more than* a number		$x + 5$
a number *increased by* 4		$x + 4$
a number *added to another* number		$x + y$
nine *plus* a number		$9 + x$
the *difference* between two numbers	− (subtract)	$x - y$
seven *decreased by* a number	(Be sure the number subtracted follows the minus sign.)	$7 - x$
a number *reduced by* 4		$x - 4$
three *less than* a number		$x - 3$
six *subtracted* from a number		$x - 6$
six *minus* a number		$6 - x$
the *product* of two numbers	multiply	xy
six *times* a number	( )	$(6)(x)$
twice a number	or ·	$2 \cdot x$
two-thirds of a number	or no sign	$\left(\frac{2}{3}\right)x$ or $\frac{2x}{3}$
double a number		$2x$
one number *multiplied* by another number		xy
the *quotient* of two numbers	divide	$\frac{x}{y}$ $x \div y$
a number *divided by* three	(Be sure the number you are dividing by is below the fraction bar or follows the division symbol.)	$\frac{x}{3}$
seven *divided by* a number		$\frac{7}{x}$
half a number		$\frac{x}{2}$ or $\frac{1}{2}x$
a number *squared*	raise to the second power	x^2
a number *cubed*	raise to the third power	y^3
the *square root* of a number	square root	$\sqrt{x}$

Using the chart as a guide to the examples below, translate the following English phrases into algebraic expressions.

Examples:

four more than a number

$\underbrace{\text{four}}_{4} \quad \underbrace{\text{more than}}_{+} \quad \underbrace{\text{a number}}_{x} \qquad = 4 + x$

six decreased by half a number

$\underbrace{\text{six}}_{6} \quad \underbrace{\text{decreased by}}_{-} \quad \underbrace{\text{half a number}}_{\frac{1}{2}x} \qquad = 6 - \frac{1}{2}x \text{ or } 6 - \frac{x}{2}$

twelve divided by a number squared

$\underbrace{\text{twelve}}_{12} \quad \underbrace{\text{divided by}}_{\div} \quad \underbrace{\text{a number squared}}_{x^2} \qquad = \frac{12}{x^2}$

twice the sum of a number and 4

$\underbrace{\text{twice}}_{2} \quad \underbrace{\text{the sum of a number and 4}}_{(x + 4)} \qquad = 2(x + 4)$

the sum of twice a number and 4

$\underbrace{\text{the sum of}}_{+} \quad \underbrace{\text{twice a number}}_{2x} \quad \underbrace{\text{and 4}}_{4} \qquad = 2x + 4$

EXERCISE 5: TRANSLATING ENGLISH TO ALGEBRA

Directions: Translate the English phrases to algebraic expressions using x and y to stand for the unknown numbers.

1. six minus a number

2. the product of fourteen and a number

3. the difference between two numbers, divided by 3

4. the sum of a number squared and another number squared

5. four times the sum of ten and a number

6. seven less than twice a number

7. the square of a number increased by twelve

8. a number cubed divided by 4

9. the sum of two numbers less 4

10. five times a number divided by twice the same number

Answers are on page 731.

Translating Equations

We can now practice translating an entire sentence into an algebraic equation. Remember, an equation has three parts: left-side expression, equal sign, and right-side expression.

Many key words or phrases indicate "equal." Become familiar with the list below:

equals	is	was
is equal to	are	were
equal to	gives	leaves
the same as	the sum is	makes
the result is	the difference is	yields
the product is	the quotient is	the answer is

TRANSLATING EQUATIONS

1. Assign a variable to the unknown quantity.

2. Write two expressions for the values.

3. Use an equal sign between the expressions.

Example 1: Three times a number is one more than twice the number.

$3x = 1 + 2x$ or $3x = 1 + 2x$

Example 2: Four more than a number equals 15.

$x + 4 = 15$ or $x + 4 = 15$

Example 3: Twice a number reduced by six is equal to 9.

$2x - 6 = 9$ or $2x - 6 = 9$

Example 4: To promote holiday sales, a magazine offers one-year subscriptions for $7 and additional gift subscriptions for $5 each. With a one-year subscription, how many gift subscriptions can you get if you have $42 to spend altogether?

You would let x represent the number of $5 gift subscriptions. Then 5 times x is the cost of the additional subscriptions. The basic statement is

original subscription price plus additional subscription cost is 42

$7 + 5x = 42$ or $7 + 5x = 42$

In Example 4, the variable was identified first. Then, algebraic expressions and the operation were written. Finally, these values were translated into an algebraic equation.

▶ **TIP:** To identify the variable in a word problem, isolate the term or element that you don't know. Then assign a letter to that term.

EXERCISE 6: TRANSLATING SENTENCES TO EQUATIONS

Directions: Translate each sentence to an equivalent algebraic equation as shown above.

1. One-fourth of a number equals 18.

2. Two less than a number is 40.

3. Three times a number increased by 1 is 25.

4. Nine increased by half a number gives a result of 13.

5. The product of six and a number makes 35.

6. The difference between two numbers is 8.

7. Eighteen more than twice a number is 22.

8. A number divided by four yields a quotient of 18.

9. Twice a number, reduced by 3, is equal to 5 times the same number increased by 9.

In questions 10–14 select the equation that could be used to find the unknown in the problem.

10. A man had x dollars. After paying a bill of $48, he had $75 left.

  (1) $x + 48 = 75$ **(2)** $48 - x = 75$ **(3)** $x - 48 = 75$ **(4)** $75 - 48 = x$

11. A golfer had x number of golf balls. After playing eighteen holes of golf, he lost 5 balls and had 19 left. How many balls did he have before he played the eighteen holes of golf?

  (1) $x - 5 = 19$ **(2)** $\frac{x}{5} = 19$ **(3)** $x - 18 = 19$ **(4)** $x + 5 = 19$

12. In a wrestling meet, Mike scored 5 points, which represented one-seventh of his team's final score. What was the final score, x?

  (1) $x + \frac{1}{7} = 5$ **(2)** $x - 5 = \frac{1}{2}$ **(3)** $x - 5 = 7$ **(4)** $\frac{x}{7} = 5$

13. A plumber charges $22 for a house call plus $12 per hour for the time worked. If the charge is $64, how many hours, h, did he work?

  (1) $12 + h + 22 = 64$ **(2)** $12h = 64$ **(3)** $22 + 12h = 64$ **(4)** $\frac{h}{12} + 22 = 64$

14. Sue will not tell her age, x. But in six years, her age will be $\frac{7}{6}$ as much as it is now. How can her age be written?

  (1) $x + 6 = \frac{7}{6}x$ **(2)** $x - \frac{7}{6}x = 1$ **(3)** $\frac{x}{6} = \frac{7}{6}x$ **(4)** $\frac{7}{6}x = 6$

Answers are on page 731.

Solving One-Step Algebra Word Problems

This next exercise combines practice in translating, setting up, and solving one-step algebra problems. Let's look at an example before you begin the exercise.

Example: Sue has x dollars, and Tom has $\frac{2}{3}$ as much money as Sue. If Tom has $48, how much does Sue have?

STEP 1. Translate and set up.
  Tom has $48.

  $\frac{2}{3}$ of Sue's money is $48 $\frac{2}{3}x = 48$

STEP 2. Solve the equation. Divide both sides by $\frac{2}{3}$.

$$\frac{2}{3}x = 48$$

$$\frac{2}{3}x \div \frac{2}{3} = 48 \div \frac{2}{3}$$

$$x = 48 \times \frac{3}{2}$$

$$x = \$72$$

EXERCISE 7: SOLVING ONE-STEP ALGEBRA WORD PROBLEMS

Directions: Solve each problem.

1. If seven less than a number is 8, find the number.

2. Baseballs cost $2.25 each. How many baseballs can you buy for $40.50?

3. Jack saved one-eighth of his allowance. If he saved $2.50, how much is his allowance?

4. Amanda sold her stereo set for $120 less than she paid for it. If she sold the stereo set for $72, what did she originally pay for it?

5. After $5\frac{1}{2}$ feet were cut off a wooden beam, $6\frac{1}{2}$ feet were left. What was the original length of the beam?

6. After José gained 14 pounds, he weighed 172 pounds. What was his original weight?

7. Twelve years from now, Lucille will be 48 years old. How old is she now?

8. By purchasing a fleet of cars for its salespeople, Tower Manufacturing gets a discount of $927 on each car purchased. This is 16% of the regular price. Find the regular price.

Answers are on page 731.

Solving Multi-Step Problems

Many algebraic expressions contain two or more terms. For instance, $2x - 7$ has two terms, and $3x - 9y + 7z$ has three terms. It is best to write algebraic expressions in the simplest form possible. We will cover several steps in simplifying algebraic expressions so that you can solve more complicated algebra word problems.

Simplifying Algebraic Expressions

To simplify an algebraic expression, combine like terms and remove all symbols of grouping such as parentheses and brackets.

Simplifying by Combining Like Terms

Like terms are terms that contain the same variables to the same power.

Examples of like terms: $4x$ $7x$ $12x$ $\quad$ $2xy$ xy $17xy$ $\quad$ $9x^2$ $4x^2$ x^2

Examples of unlike terms: $3x$ $4y$ -2 $2xy$ $\quad$ $3x$ $4y$ $3x^2$ $\quad$ $2x$ -5

We can combine like terms to simplify an expression.

Example 1: $3x + 5x = 8x$ (Just add the coefficients—the numbers.)

Example 2: $7y^2 - 5y^2 = 2y^2$ (You can also subtract coefficients.)

Example 3: $3x^2 + 6y + 2x^2 - 4y = 5x^2 + 2y$

First, combine x^2 terms.　　Then, combine y terms.

$$\begin{array}{r} 3x^2 \\ + 2x^2 \\ \hline 5x^2 \end{array} \qquad\qquad \begin{array}{r} + 6y \\ - 4y \\ \hline + 2y \end{array}$$

Example 4: $2x - 3y - 5y + 2 + 4x - 6 = 6x - 8y - 4$

Combine x terms.　　Combine y terms.　　Combine numbers.

$2x + 4x = 6x$ 　　　$-3y - 5y = -8y$ 　　　$-6 + 2 = -4$

▶ **TIP:** Notice that in Example 4, three of the terms had answers with a minus sign. These are called *negative numbers* and will be discussed on pages 690–691. If the signs of numbers are the same (+ or −), combine the numbers and just attach the sign (+6 and +3 = +9; −6 and −3 = −9). If the signs are different, find the *difference* between the numbers and attach the sign of the *larger* number (−6 + 2 = −4).

EXERCISE 8: COMBINING LIKE TERMS

Directions: Simplify the following expressions by combining like terms.

1. $3x + 12x$

2. $7y - 4y$

3. $2x + 3y + 6y + 7x$

4. $7x^2 + 3x + 4x - 2x$

5. $8x - 3 + 5x$

6. $3x^2 + 14 + 7x + 2x^2 - 5$

7. $4a + 3b - 2a - 3b + a$

8. $x + 2y - y$

9. $9a^2 + 4a + a + 3a^2$

10. $5xy + 7x - 3y - x + 4xy$

Answers are on page 732.

Removing Grouping Symbols

Sometimes algebraic expressions are grouped together. Grouping symbols can be parentheses or brackets. These symbols draw your attention first when you simplify an expression.

Example 1: $3(2x - 4)$

Multiply 3 by $2x$ and 3 by (-4).

$3(2x - 4) = 3(2x) - 3(4) = 6x - 12$

If a plus sign or no sign is in front of parentheses, the terms do not change when you remove the parentheses.

Example 2: $6x + (2x - 7) = 6x + 2x - 7 = 8x - 7$

A minus sign in front of a set of parentheses changes the sign inside to the opposite sign. With a minus and a number, you change the signs, multiply the numbers, and combine like terms.

Changed sign

Example 3: $3x - 2(6x - 4) = 3x - 12x + 8 = -9x + 8$

REMOVING GROUPING SYMBOLS

1. Remove the parentheses or brackets.

2. Distribute the multiplication over every term in the parentheses.

EXERCISE 9: REMOVING GROUPING SYMBOLS

Directions: Simplify the following expressions by removing grouping symbols.

1. $5(3x + 2)$

2. $4(7x - 8)$

3. $6x + 2(12x - 7)$

4. $2(x - 1)$

5. $3(2x + 4 - 3y)$

6. $-6(5x - 12)$

7. $x - 2(9 + 6x)$

8. $2(x - y)$

Answers are on page 732.

Solving Multi-Step Equations

We study multi-step equations because we will use them to solve some algebra word problems on the GED Mathematics Test. To solve multi-step equations, we must take a step-by-step approach as shown below. Always plan to start with step 1 and progress through the following steps in order. But keep in mind that some equations will not need every step.

STEP 1. Simplify expressions on both sides of the equation.

STEP 2. Get all the variables on the left side of the equation using addition or subtraction from the right side.

STEP 3. Concentrate on the variable and *undo addition and subtraction* using the opposite operation.

STEP 4. Concentrate on the variable and *undo multiplication and division* using the opposite operation.

Example 1: $3x + 7 = 13$

STEP 1. Already simplified

STEP 2. Variable already on left side

STEP 3. $\quad 3x + \underbrace{7 - 7}_{0} = 13 - 7$

$$3x = 6$$

STEP 4. $\qquad \dfrac{3x}{3} = \dfrac{6}{3}$

$$x = 2$$

Example 2: $3(x - 2) + 18 = 6 + 2(x + 6)$

STEP 1. $\qquad 3x - 6 + 18 = 6 + 2x + 12$

$$3x + 12 = 2x + 18$$

STEP 2. $\qquad \underbrace{3x - 2x}_{x} + 12 = \underbrace{2x - 2x}_{0} + 18$

$$x + 12 = 18$$

STEP 3. $\qquad x + \underbrace{12 - 12}_{0} = 18 - 12$

$$x = 6$$

EXERCISE 10: SOLVING MULTI-STEP EQUATIONS

Directions: Solve the following equations.

1. $3x + 9 = 15$

2. $2x - 26 = 2$

3. $\frac{x}{3} + 4 = 9$

4. $\frac{4x}{3} - 14 = 14$

5. $8(x - 4) = 0$

6. $2(5x - 11) + 12x = 0$

Answers are on page 732.

Translating in Multi-Step Problems

To set up a multi-step problem, we have to translate from English to algebra.

Remember to check your answer to see if it satisfies the original problem.

Example: Tony worked 35 hours last week and only a few hours this week. He makes $9 per hour, and his paycheck for the two weeks is $477 before deductions. How many hours did he work this week?

STEP 1. Let x be the number of hours he worked this week.

STEP 2. $x + 35$ is the total number of hours worked during both weeks.

$9(x + 35)$ is the amount of money he is paid for working

$x + 35$ hours at $9 per hour.

STEP 3. $9(x + 35) = 477$ (The amount of money he is paid equals $477.)

STEP 4. $\qquad 9(x + 35) = 477$

$$9x + 315 = 477$$

$$9x + \underbrace{315 - 315}_{0} = 477 - 315$$

$$9x = 162$$

$$\frac{9x}{9} = \frac{162}{9}$$

$$x = 18 \text{ hours this week}$$

EXERCISE 11: SETTING UP AND SOLVING MULTI-STEP EQUATIONS

Directions: Solve each problem.

Questions 1 and 2 are based on the following information.

Oscar went on a ski trip for 3 days and 3 nights. His chalet cost him $32 a night, and he paid for a lift ticket each day. His total bill was $123. Find the cost of the daily lift ticket, x.

1. Which equation best describes the problem?

    (1) $x + 96 = 123$
    (2) $3x + 32 = 123$
    (3) $x + 32 = 123$
    (4) $3(x + 32) = 123$
    (5) not enough information is given

2. What is the cost of the daily lift ticket?

    (1) $ 9
    (2) $27
    (3) $30.33
    (4) $41
    (5) $91

Questions 3 and 4 are based on the following information.

The perimeter of a triangle is 56 inches. If one side is 24 inches and the other two sides have the same measure, find the length, x, of one of these two sides.

3. Which equation best describes the problem above?

    (1) $x + 24 = 56$
    (2) $2x + 56 = 24$
    (3) $2x - 24 = 56$
    (4) $2x + 24 = 56$
    (5) $x - 24 = 56$

4. What is the length of one of the two equal sides?

    (1) 16
    (2) 32
    (3) 40
    (4) 80
    (5) 160

Questions 5 and 6 are based on the following information.

Nick's age is six years less than twice Tom's age, x. The sum of their two ages is 42. Find Tom's age.

5. Which equation best describes the problem above?

(1) $2x - 6 = 42$
(2) $x - 6 = 42$
(3) $x + 2x = 42$
(4) $(2x - 6) + x = 42$
(5) not enough information is given

6. What is Tom's age?

(1) 14
(2) 16
(3) 18
(4) 24
(5) not enough information is given

Questions 7 and 8 are based on the following information.

Eric purchased a new car for $10,200. He made a $4800 down payment and agreed to pay the balance in 36 equal monthly payments. How much will he pay each month?

7. Which equation best describes the problem above? Let x be the amount of the monthly payment.

(1) $36x = 10,200$
(2) $36x = 4800$
(3) $36x - 4800 = 10,200$
(4) $4800 - 36x = 10,200$
(5) $4800 + 36x = 10,200$

8. How much will Eric pay each month?

(1) $133.33
(2) $150.00
(3) $283.33
(4) $416.67
(5) $450.00

Questions 9 and 10 are based on the following information.

Twice as many adult tickets for a soccer game were sold as children's tickets. Also, some of the tickets were given free of charge to contest winners. The attendance at the game was 8324 people. How many tickets of each type were sold?

9. Which equation best describes the problem above? Let x be the number of children's tickets sold.

　(1) $x + 2x = 8324$
　(2) $x - 2x = 8324$
　(3) $2(x + 2) = 8324$
　(4) $2(x - 2) = 8324$
　(5) not enough information is given

10. How many adult tickets were sold?

　(1) 2770
　(2) 2775
　(3) 2780
　(4) 4155
　(5) not enough information is given

Answers are on page 732.

Signed Numbers

Number Line

The *number line*, shown below, represents all of the real numbers that we use. In algebra, we use zero and the numbers greater than zero, called the *positive numbers*, but we also use the numbers less than zero, called the *negative numbers*. Signed numbers include all positive numbers, zero, and all negative numbers.

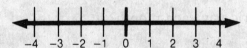

Negative numbers　Zero　Positive numbers

Positive numbers have a plus sign in front of them, like +7, or no sign in front, like 8. Negative numbers have a minus sign in front of them, like −2 (read as "negative two"). The graph of a signed number is a dot on the number line. On the number line below, we see the graph of −3.5, −1, and 3.

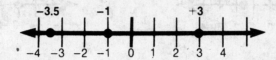

We can use the number line to show the relationship among signed numbers. A number to the right of another number is greater than (>) the other number. A number to the left of another number is less than (<) the other number.

▶ **TIP:** The symbols < and > always point to the smaller number.

$$1 > -3$$

1 is greater than −3 because it is to the right of −3 on the number line.

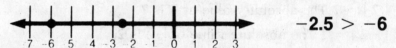

$$-2.5 > -6$$

−2.5 is greater than −6 because it is to the right of −6.

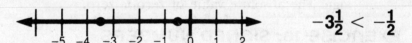

$$-3\tfrac{1}{2} < -\tfrac{1}{2}$$

$-3\tfrac{1}{2}$ is less than $-\tfrac{1}{2}$ because it is to the left of $-\tfrac{1}{2}$.

EXERCISE 12: NUMBER LINE

Directions: Identify the relationships between the numbers graphed below.

1.

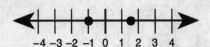

3.

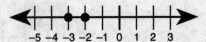

2.

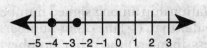

4.

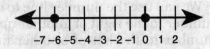

Answers are on page 732.

Absolute Values

The **absolute value** is the distance on the number line between zero and the number. Since distance is always a positive value, the absolute value of a number is always positive or zero. The symbol for absolute value is $|\;\;|$.

$|7| = 7$ The absolute value of 7 is 7.

$|-2| = 2$ The absolute value of -2 is 2.

▶ **TIP:** The absolute value of a positive number is the same positive number. The absolute value of a negative number is the same number but with a positive sign. The absolute value of zero is zero.

EXERCISE 13: SIGNED NUMBERS

Directions: Solve each problem. For questions 1–5, represent the quantities with either positive or negative numbers.

1. a loss of $12

2. a temperature 15° below zero Fahrenheit

3. a three-yard loss on the second down of a football game

4. a credit of $75 on your credit card

5. a stock rise of $4\frac{1}{2}$ points for the week

For questions 6–11, place the correct symbol, < or >, between the pairs of numbers.

6. 7 11

8. -3 1

10. -6 2.4

7. -9 -4

9. 0 -4

11. $-\frac{1}{4}$ $-\frac{1}{2}$

For questions 12–15, find the values.

12. $|9|$

13. $|-\frac{1}{2}|$

14. $|2\frac{1}{3}|$

15. $|-3|$

Answers are on page 732.

Operations with Signed Numbers

Signed numbers can be added, subtracted, multiplied, and divided. Let's use a personal financial situation to understand these operations with signed numbers.

Todd has a part-time job while attending the technical institute. In the month of April, he earns $132, $120, $180, $49, $68, and $75. (These are all positive values.) His total earnings are $624. When we combine all the positive numbers, we get a larger positive number.

During the month of April, Todd pays the following bills: car insurance, $185; gas, $78; lunches, $60; and room and board, $250. (These are all negative values.) His total expenses are $573. When we combine all his bills, we get a larger negative number (which can be written −$573).

To find out how much money Todd has left at the end of April, we have to find the difference between his income (the positive total) and his expenses (the negative total). If his income is larger, he'll have a positive amount left (profit). If his expenses are larger than his income, he'll be in a negative situation. (He'll owe money.) The difference between +624 and −573 is +51. Todd has a profit of $51.

Combining Signed Numbers

The first two rules about combining signed numbers are the same as what we just used to understand Todd's financial situation.

> If the numbers being combined are *all positive* or *all negative*, add the numbers and keep the same sign.

Both positive   Both negative

$+8 + 7 = +15$ $-8 - 7 = -15$

> If two numbers being combined are *opposite* in sign, subtract the numbers and use the sign from the number with the larger absolute value.

Opposite signs   Opposite signs

$-8 + 7 = -1$ $-7 + 8 = +1 \text{ or } 1$

sign of the larger number   sign of the larger number

The next problem contains several numbers. Some of them are positive, and some of them are negative. We'll use both rules to come up with the answer.

Example: $-6 + 1 + 14 - 2 - 8 + 6 - 9$

First, combine the positive numbers. $1 + 14 + 6 = 21$

Then, combine the negative numbers. $-6 - 2 - 8 - 9 = -25$

The difference between 21 and −25 is 4.

The absolute value of −25 (the negative number) is larger, so the answer is −4.

EXERCISE 14: COMBINING SIGNED NUMBERS

Directions: Solve each problem.

1. $7 + 8$ **4.** $6 - 8$ **7.** $140 - 236$ **10.** $-5 - 7 - 1 - 6$

2. $-3 + 2$ **5.** $-3 - 2$ **8.** $-12 + 6 + 3$ **11.** $5.2 - 6.7 + 5.3$

3. $-9 - 8$ **6.** $-127 + 94$ **9.** $16 + 23 - 4$ **12.** $-4.5 - 3.2$

Answers are on page 732.

Eliminating Double Signs

Sometimes, we encounter a number that has two signs in front of it. We always want to *eliminate* double signs. There are two rules for doing this:

ELIMINATING DOUBLE SIGNS

1. If the double signs are the same, replace them with +.

   Examples: $+ (+3) = +3$

   $- (-8) = +8$

   $-4 - (-12) = -4 \underbrace{- (-12)}_{\text{same}} = -4 + 12 = +8$

   (*Note*: a minus sign [−] changes the sign of the negative following number to a positive number [+] as in the last two examples above.)

2. If the double signs are opposite, replace them with −.

   Examples: $+ (-4) = -4$

   $- (+2) = -2$

   $5 + (-7) = \underbrace{5 + (-7)}_{\text{opposite}} = 5 - 7 = -2$

EXERCISE 15: ELIMINATING DOUBLE SIGNS

Directions: Solve each problem.

1. $-6 - (-2)$ **2.** $-6 + (-2) - (-9)$ **3.** $3 - (+8)$

4. A running back on a football team makes the following yardage on six plays: $+23, -4, +8, +3, -6, -2$. What is his total gain or loss?

5. What is his average yardage per play in question 5?

6. What is the drop in temperature if the thermometer goes from 12°F to −7°F?

7. At Arlington Park Race Track, Larry had $140 to begin the day. On the first race, he won $56; on the second race, he lost $14; on the third race, he lost $32; on the fourth race, he lost $18; on the fifth race, he won $26. How much money did he have at the end of the 5 races?

Answers are on page 732.

Multiplying and Dividing Signed Numbers

Let's return to Todd and his finances to understand the multiplication and division of signed numbers. If Todd earns $3 per hour and works 7 hours, then he earns $7 \times \$3$, or $21. A positive number $3 times a positive number 7 is $7 \times 3 = 21$.

If Todd had to pay $3 per day for the past seven days, how much *more* money did he have seven days *ago*? He had $21 *more* dollars 7 days ago than he does now. $(-7)(-3) = 21$ equals a positive number, $21.

Suppose Todd spends $3 each day for lunch. How much does he spend in 7 days? The money *spent* (-3) times the number of days (7) equals $-\$21$. The rules below for multiplying and dividing signed numbers will help you solve problems like those related to Todd's financial situation.

1. If the two numbers being multiplied or divided *have the same sign*

   a. Multiply or divide.

   b. Make the answer *positive*.

Both positive	*Both negative*
$8(7) = 56$	$-8(-7) = 56$
$26 \div 2 = 13$	$-32 \div -16 = 2$

2. If the two numbers being multiplied or divided are *opposite* in sign

   a. Multiply or divide.

   b. Make the answer *negative*.

Opposite in sign	*Opposite in sign*
$-7(8) = -56$	$8(-7) = -56$
$\dfrac{-48}{12} = -4$	$\dfrac{-56}{7} = -8$

MULTIPLYING AND DIVIDING SIGNED NUMBERS

1. When you are multiplying or dividing two numbers with the *same* sign, the answer is *positive*.

2. When you are multiplying or dividing two numbers with *opposite* signs, the answer is *negative*.

When multiplying a string of signed numbers, you may count the number of negative signs to determine whether the answer is positive or negative.

a. Even number of negative signs: answer is positive.

b. Odd number of negative signs: answer is negative.

Example 1: $(-3)(-2)(-1)(-5) = 30$ (4 negative signs, EVEN: answer is +)
$(+6)$ $(+5)$
$(+30)$

Example 2: $(-1)(-5)(-4) = -20$ (3 negative signs, ODD: answer is −)
(5)
-20

EXERCISE 16: MULTIPLYING AND DIVIDING SIGNED NUMBERS

Directions: Solve each problem.

1. $(8)(5)$ **4.** $-22(4)$ **7.** $(-6)(-7)(-2)$ **10.** $\dfrac{-48}{-16}$

2. $12(-12)$ **5.** $-15(-15)$ **8.** $-8(5)(0)$ **11.** $\dfrac{56}{-14}$

3. $-5(6)$ **6.** $(-9)(-4)$ **9.** $-25/5$ **12.** $\dfrac{-50}{-10}$

13. The stock fell $\frac{3}{8}$ point for each day for four consecutive days. What was the total drop for the stock?

14. A-One Sales bought 9 car telephones at a cost of $2476 each. How much does the company owe for the telephones? (Express the answer as a negative number.)

Answers are on page 733.

Inequalities

The relationship between two things is not always equal, so we cannot always use an equation to solve a problem. If the relationship is not equal, we can use *inequalities* such as < (is less than) or > (is greater than) to solve the problem. For example, $x + 3 > 10$ is an algebraic inequality. What value of x would make this a true statement? Several values of x would make this statement true. The letter x could be 8 because $8 + 3 > 10$. It could be 25 because $25 + 3 > 10$. In fact, x could be any number larger than 7. Our solution is $x > 7$.

When you solve any inequality, the set of possible solutions is often infinite. You must be aware of the boundary of the solution. In this case, the boundary is 7; x cannot be 7, but it can be any number larger than 7.

Solving Inequalities

The algebraic methods for solving an inequality are much the same as for algebraic equations.

SOLVING INEQUALITIES

1. Keep the inequality in balance. Whatever operation you perform on one side of the inequality, perform on the other.

2. Concentrate on the variable. Your goal is to get the variable on one side of the equation.

3. Perform the opposite operation. First, do addition or subtraction; then, do multiplication or division.

Example 1: $x + 3 > 10$

Look at x. It is added to 3. Subtract 3 from both sides. The inequality is solved (x is all by itself on the left side of the inequality).

$$x + 3 > 10$$
$$x + \underbrace{3 - 3}_{0} > 10 - 3$$
$$x > 7$$

Check: Choose any number greater than 7. Let's choose 9.

$$x + 3 > 10$$
$$9 + 3 > 10$$
$$12 > 10$$

There is one major rule that you must keep in mind when solving an inequality.

When you multiply or divide both sides of an inequality by a negative number, it changes the direction of the inequality sign.

For example, we know that $8 < 12$.

$$8 < 12$$

If we multiply both sides by -2, we get $8(-2)$, which is -16, and $12(-2)$, which is -24. You know that -16 is greater than -24. So the answer is

$$8(-2) > 12(-2)$$

Notice that the arrow changed direction from less than to greater than.

$$-16 > -24$$

Example 2: $-4x < 12$

Divide both sides by -4. *Notice* that you are dividing by a *negative number*, so change the direction of the inequality sign.

$$-4x < 12$$
$$\frac{-4x}{-4} > \frac{12}{-4}$$
$$x > -3$$

Check: Choose any number greater than -3. Let's choose 0.

$$-4x < 12$$
$$-4(0) < 12$$
$$0 < 12$$

Sometimes, you may see the signs $\leq$ and $\geq$. These mean "less than or equal to" and "more than or equal to," respectively. So, if an answer is $x \geq 3$, this means that the answer is 3 or a number larger than 3.

EXERCISE 17: ONE-STEP INEQUALITIES

Directions: Solve for x. Check your answers.

1. $x - 3 > -5$
2. $5 + x < 7$
3. $-3 + x < -10$

4. $\frac{x}{-3} < 12$
5. $x - 5 \geq -1$
6. $-4x > 8$

7. $x - 7 \leq 0$
8. $70 > 5x$
9. $-4x > -16$

Answers are on page 733.

Factoring

Some problems require factoring algebraic expressions. To *factor* means to find and separate numbers that have been multiplied. An example from arithmetic helps to explain factoring. There are two ways to multiply to get the number 15: $3 \times 5 = 15$ and $15 \times 1 = 15$. We can say that 3 and 5 are factors of 15 and that 1 and 15 are also factors of 15. The factors are the numbers that were multiplied.

Factoring is the process of looking for the factors in a multiplication problem. This process can be used to solve some types of equations and to simplify some expressions. As with arithmetic, an algebraic expression is the answer to a multiplication problem. We must determine what expressions were multiplied to get that answer.

Multiplying Algebraic Expressions

Algebraic expressions can be multiplied together. An algebraic expression may consist of a number (coefficient), a letter (variable), and an exponent. Remember, an exponent is a small raised number to the right of the variable.

When we multiply variables with exponents, the base must be the same. For example, x^2, x^3, and x^5 all have the same base, x. However, x^2 and y^3 have different bases; they are x and y.

MULTIPLYING VARIABLES WITH EXPONENTS

1. Keep the same base.
2. Add the exponents.

Examples: $x^2 \cdot x^3 = x^{2+3} = x^5$ $\qquad$ $x^2 y^3 \cdot x^4 y^5 = x^{2+4} \cdot y^{3+5} = x^6 y^8$

$\qquad$ $y^4 \cdot y^7 = y^{4+7} = y^{11}$ $\qquad$ $x \cdot x^3 = x^1 \cdot x^3 = x^{1+3} = x^4$

▶ **TIP:** The last example shows that the letter x alone is understood to have an exponent of 1. Although no number is written in front of the variables above, the number 1 is understood to be there. The examples below show what you do when there are coefficients in front of the variables.

ONE TERM TIMES ONE TERM

1. Multiply the coefficients.
2. Multiply the variables—keep the same base and add the exponents.

Examples: $4x \cdot 7x^2 = 4 \cdot 7 \cdot x^1 \cdot x^2 = 28x^{1+2} = 28x^3$

$\qquad$ $-3y^2 \cdot 5xy = -3 \cdot 5 \cdot x^1 \cdot y^2 \cdot y^1 = -15x \cdot y^{2+1} = -15xy^3$

ONE TERM TIMES AN EXPRESSION OF TWO OR MORE TERMS

Distribute the multiplication over the expression by multiplying each term.

Examples:
$$5x(2x + 3) = 5x \cdot 2x + 5x \cdot 3$$
$$= 10x^2 + 15x$$

$$-x(2x^2 + 3x - 7) = -x \cdot 2x^2 - x \cdot 3x - x(-7)$$
$$= -2x^3 - 3x^2 + 7x$$

EXERCISE 18: MULTIPLYING ALGEBRAIC EXPRESSIONS

Directions: Solve each problem.

1. $8x \cdot 3x^2$

2. $7xy(-4x)$

3. $(-6ab^2)(3a^2)$

4. $(-5x^2y)(3xy^2)$

5. $2x(x^2 + 1)$

6. $3y(2y^2 - 4y - 7)$

Answers are on page 733.

Finding the Greatest Common Factor

The expression $2x + 10$ has two terms, $2x$ and 10. To factor $2x + 10$, look for the largest number that is a factor of both $2x$ and 10. $\quad 2x = 2 \cdot x \quad\quad 10 = 5 \cdot 2$

Therefore, 2 is a common factor of both $2x$ and 10. In factored form, we write $2x + 10 = 2(x + 5)$.

Example 1: Factor $7x^2 + 14x$

STEP 1. Look for the common factors. 7 and x are common factors in both terms.

$$7x^2 \quad + \quad 14x$$
$$\boxed{7} \cdot \boxed{x} \cdot x + 2 \cdot \boxed{7} \cdot \boxed{x}$$

STEP 2. Write the common factors in front of the rest of the expression.

$$7x(x + 2)$$

To check this factored expression, multiply $7x$ by $x + 2$ to be sure the result is $7x^2 + 14x$. $\quad 7x(x + 2) = 7x^2 + 14x$

Example 2: Factor $65y^3 - 35y^2 + 15y$

The greatest common factor for the terms of this expression is $5y$.

$$65y^3 - 35y^2 + 15y =$$
$$\boxed{5y} \cdot 13y^2 + \boxed{5y} \cdot -7y + \boxed{5y} \cdot 3 =$$
$$5y(13y^2 - 7y + 3)$$

Example 3: Factor $3x^2 + x$

The greatest common factor for the terms of this expression is x.

Note that 1 is a factor of x; x means "1 times x." So if you can't factor a variable any other way, show it as 1 times the variable.

$$3x^2 + x =$$
$$3x(x) + 1(x) =$$
$$x(3x + 1)$$

EXERCISE 19: THE GREATEST COMMON FACTOR

Directions: Write each expression in factored form.

1. $21x^3 - 14x^2$

2. $100a^4 - 16a^2$

3. $121p^5 - 33p^4$

4. $8x^2 - 4$

5. $9x^3y^2 + 36x^2y^3$

6. $100x^5 - 50x^3 + 100x^2$

7. $5x^4 + 25x^3 - 20x^2$

8. $9x^3 - 9x$

Answers are on page 733.

Factoring by Grouping

In an expression of four or more terms, we can use the method of factoring by grouping to factor the expression. We generally separate the four terms of the expression into pairs of terms. Then we factor out the common factor from each pair. If possible, factor the common factor from the results.

Example 1: $x^2 + 5x + 2x + 10$

STEP 1. Separate into pairs of terms.

STEP 2. Factor each pair.

STEP 3. Put the common factor $(x + 5)$ in front.

$\boxed{x^2 + 5x} + \boxed{2x + 10}$

$x(x + 5) + 2(x + 5)$

$(x + 5)(x + 2)$

Example 2: $2y^2 - 8y + 3y - 12$

STEP 1. $\boxed{2y^2 - 8y} + \boxed{3y - 12}$

STEP 2. $2y(y - 4) + 3(y - 4)$

STEP 3. $(y - 4)(2y + 3)$

FACTORING BY GROUPING

1. Separate the four terms into pairs that have common factors.

2. Factor out the common factor from each pair of terms.

3. Put the common factor in front of the other factors.

EXERCISE 20: FACTORING BY GROUPING

Directions: Use grouping to factor the following expressions.

1. $x^2 + 4x + 3x + 12$

2. $x^2 - 2x + 5x - 10$

3. $8y^2 + 6yz + 12yz + 9z^2$

4. $2xy^2 - 8y^2 + x - 4$

Answers are on page 733.

Graphing

In Chapter 7, we saw how graphs can be used to display data visually. Graphs can also be used to represent an equation.

Rectangular Coordinates

To understand the graph of an equation, we must first learn how points are plotted on a grid. The grid is called a **rectangular coordinate plane**. A horizontal number line called the **x-axis** and a vertical number line called the **y-axis** intersect at a point called the **origin**.

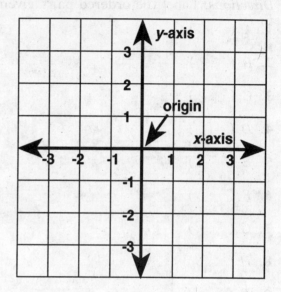

Each point that is graphed is identified by an **ordered pair** of numbers (x,y). The first number in the ordered pair is called the **x-coordinate**, and the second number is called the **y-coordinate**. The order of the coordinates is very important. The x-coordinate is always given first in the ordered pair, and the y-coordinate is always given second.

PLOTTING A POINT WITH THE COORDINATES (x, y)

1. Start at the origin $(0,0)$.

2. If x is positive, move x units to the right.
   If x is negative, move x units to the left.
   If x is 0, make no move.

3. If y is positive, move y units upward.
   If y is negative, move y units downward.
   If y is 0, make no move.

4. Place a point at the location and label it with the positive or negative numbers of the ordered pair (x,y).

Example 1: Plot the point $(3,4)$.

Start at the origin.

x is 3 → move 3 units right.

y is 4 → move 4 units up.

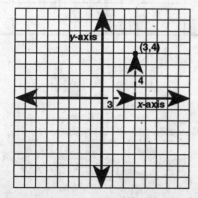

Example 2: Plot the point $(-3,5)$.

Start at the origin.

x is -3 → move 3 units left.

y is 5 → move 5 units up.

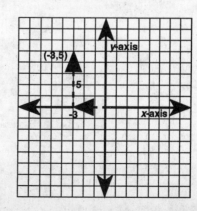

EXERCISE 21: ORDERED PAIRS

Directions: Label the ordered pairs given below.

1. *A* (,)

2. *B* (,)

3. *C* (,)

4. *D* (,)

5. *E* (,)

6. *F* (,)

7. *G* (,)

8. *H* (,)

9. *I* (,)

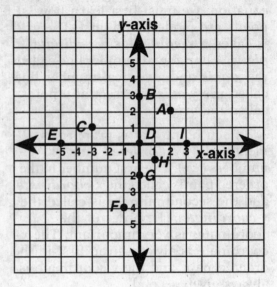

Answers are on page 734.

Distance Between Two Points

There are two methods of finding the distance between two points on a graph. If the two points are on the same horizontal line or the same vertical line, we can simply count the units between the two points.

Counting

To find the distance between point *C* and point *A* as shown at right, count the units from *C* to *A*. The distance is 10 units.

To find the distance between point *A* and point *B* as shown at right, count the units from *A* to *B*. The distance is 7 units.

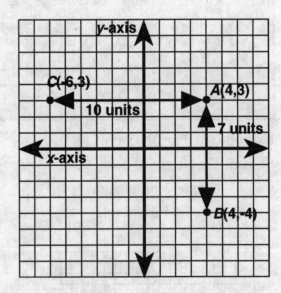

Using a Formula

The second method of finding the distance between two points uses the formula $d = \sqrt{(x_2 - x_1)^2 + (y_2 - y_1)^2}$ for the two points. You will not need to memorize this formula; it will be on the formulas page of the Mathematics Test. We can use this formula to find the distance between *any* two points, whether or not they are on the same horizontal or vertical line.

In the formula, x_1 is the x-coordinate of one graphed point and x_2 is the x-coordinate of the other. Similarly, y_1 is the y-coordinate of the first graphed point and y_2 is the y-coordinate of the other. So, in the coordinates (4,2) and (3,−3)

$$x_1 = 4 \qquad \text{and} \qquad y_1 = 2$$
$$x_2 = 3 \qquad\qquad y_2 = -3$$

Using the figure at right, look at the next examples, which use the distance formula to find the distance between two points.

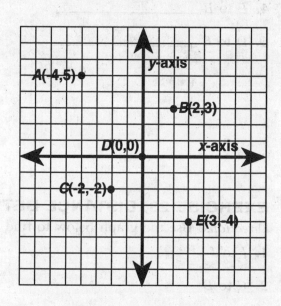

Example 1: Find the distance from A to B.

Point A is (−4,5). Let that be (x_1,y_1). So $x_1 = -4$ and $y_1 = 5$. Point B is (2,3). Let that be (x_2,y_2). So $x_2 = 2$ and $y_2 = 3$.

$d = \sqrt{(x_2 - x_1)^2 + (y_2 - y_1)^2}$

$\quad = \sqrt{(2 - (-4))^2 + (3 - 5)^2}$

$\quad = \sqrt{6^2 + (-2)^2}$

$\quad = \sqrt{36 + 4}$

$d = \sqrt{40}$

Simplify $\sqrt{40}$ to $\sqrt{4 \cdot 10} = 2\sqrt{10}$

Example 2: Find the distance from D to E.

Let $(x_1,y_1) = (0,0)$ and $(x_2,y_2) = (3,-4)$.

$d = \sqrt{(x_2 - x_1)^2 + (y_2 - y_1)^2}$

$\quad = \sqrt{(3 - 0)^2 + (-4 - 0)^2}$

$\quad = \sqrt{3^2 + (-4)^2}$

$\quad = \sqrt{9 + 16}$

$\quad = \sqrt{25}$

$d = 5$

▶ **TIP:** Use the distance formula only if the points are not on a horizontal or vertical line. If the points are on the same horizontal or vertical line, simply count the units between them.

EXERCISE 22: DISTANCE BY COUNTING

Directions: Find the distance
between the following points.

1. *A* to *B* _____

2. *C* to *D* _____

3. *C* to *F* _____

4. *E* to *B* _____

5. *D* to *E* _____

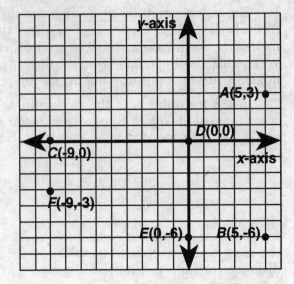

Answers are on page 734.

EXERCISE 23: DISTANCE BETWEEN TWO POINTS

Directions: Use the graph below to find the distances indicated.

1. *I* to *J*

2. *C* to *D*

3. *E* to *F*

4. *G* to *H*

5. *x*-axis to *B*

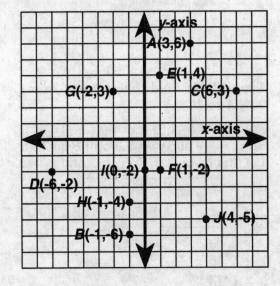

Answers are on page 734.

The Slope of a Line

An equation whose graph is a straight line has a special number associated
with the line. This number is called the *slope* of the line. The slope is actually
the ratio of the change in *y*-values to the change in *x*-values as we go from point
to point on the line.

Look at the graph of the line $2x - 3y = 6$.

As we go from $(-3, -4)$ to $(0, -2)$, there is a 2-unit change in the y values at the same time there is a 3-unit change in the x values.

The slope then is

$$\frac{\text{change in } y}{\text{change in } x} = \frac{2}{3}$$

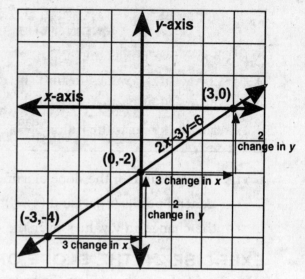

Example 1: Find the slope of the line that contains the points $(-6, -3)$ and $(-2, -1)$.

Change in y: $-3 - (-1) = -3 + 1 = -2$

Change in x: $-6 - (-2) = -6 + 2 = -4$

Slope $= \dfrac{\text{change in } y}{\text{change in } x} = \dfrac{-2}{-4} = \dfrac{1}{2}$

The slope is $\frac{1}{2}$. The line has a positive slope and slants upward.

Example 2: Find the slope of the line graphed below.

Change in $y = 6 - 0 = 6$

Change in $x = 0 - 2 = -2$

Slope $= \dfrac{6}{-2} = -3$

The slope is -3. The line has a negative slope and slants downward.

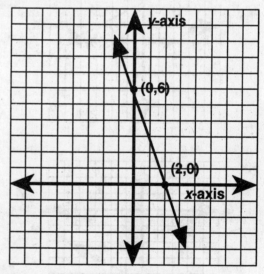

If the slope is a positive number, it represents a line that slants upward from left to right. A line that slants downward is said to have a negative slope. A line that is parallel to the x-axis has a slope of zero. A line that is parallel to the y-axis has no slope.

> **FINDING THE SLOPE OF A LINE**
>
> 1. Choose two points on the line.
> 2. Subtract the y values to find the change in y.
> 3. Subtract the x values to find the change in x.
> 4. Write the slope as the ratio: $\dfrac{\text{change in } y}{\text{change in } x}$

▶ **TIP:** The formula for the slope of a line is given on the formulas page. For two general points (x_1, y_1) and (x_2, y_2), the slope is $\dfrac{y_2 - y_1}{x_2 - x_1}$. This says the slope is the change in y values over the change in x values.

EXERCISE 24: THE SLOPE OF A LINE

Directions: Solve each problem. For questions 1–4, find the slope of the line that contains the two given points.

1. (0,0) and (3,4)

2. (−5,−1) and (6,0)

3. (−9,3) and (9,3)

4. (−1,−2) and (−2,−1)

For questions 5–8, find the slope of the graphed lines.

5.

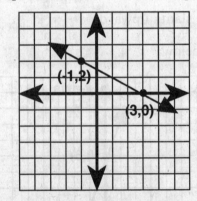

7.

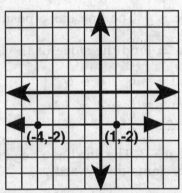

6.

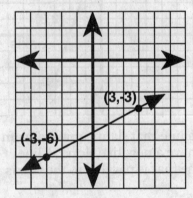

8.

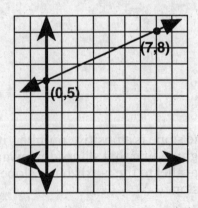

Answers are on page 734.

EXERCISE 25: ALGEBRA REVIEW

Directions: Solve each problem.

1. If a $1400 computer decreases in value $120 per year, which expression shows the value at the end of x years?

   (1) $1400 - (120 + x)$
   (2) $1400 - 120x$
   (3) $1400 - x$
   (4) $1400 + 120x$
   (5) $1400 + x$

2. Joe spent one-third of his monthly salary. After he used $70 more, he had spent half of his salary. Choose the equation that represents this information.

   (1) $3x + 70 = 2x$
   (2) $\frac{1}{3}x = 70 \div \frac{1}{2}x$
   (3) $\frac{1}{3}x - 70 = \frac{1}{2}x$
   (4) $\frac{1}{3}x + \frac{1}{2}x = 70$
   (5) $\frac{1}{3}x + 70 = \frac{1}{2}x$

3. Steve, the local handyman, has a board 42 inches long. He wishes to cut it into three pieces so that one piece is six inches longer than the shortest piece and the third piece is twice as long as the shortest piece. How long should the shortest piece be?

   (1) $4\frac{2}{3}$ in

   (2) $5\frac{1}{4}$ in

   (3) 9 in

   (4) $11\frac{1}{3}$ in

   (5) 12 in

4. The perimeter of a rectangle is 78 meters. The length of the rectangle is 5 meters more than the width. If x is the width of the rectangle, which equation below best describes these relationships?

   (1) $x^2 + 5x = 78$
   (2) $2x + 2(x + 5) = 78$
   (3) $2x + 5 = 78$
   (4) $x + 5 = 78$
   (5) not enough information is given

5. On a cold winter morning, the temperature at 3:00 A.M. was −12°, but it went up 25° by 11:00 A.M. At noon it had risen another 7°. What was the temperature at noon?

    (1) 13°
    (2) 20°
    (3) 30°
    (4) 32°
    (5) 44°

6. If six times a number is subtracted from ten times a number, the result is six less than twice the number. Find the number.

    (1) −3
    (2) $-\frac{4}{3}$
    (3) −1
    (4) $\frac{4}{5}$
    (5) 1

7. If an object is thrown straight up with an initial velocity of 128 feet per second, its height after t seconds is $h = 128t - 16t^2$. Find the height of the object after three seconds.

    (1) 240 ft
    (2) 336 ft
    (3) 1104 ft
    (4) 1120 ft
    (5) 3312 ft

8. Find the value of x in the equation $3x + 2(4 - x) = x - (3x + 1) - 3$.

    (1) −4
    (2) −2.5
    (3) −2
    (4) −1
    (5) 4

9. Find the value of x in the inequality $x + 5 < 13$.

    (1) $x > 8$
    (2) $x > \frac{1}{8}$
    (3) $x < 8$
    (4) $x < \frac{1}{8}$
    (5) $x < 0$

10. On a business trip, Margo traveled to her destination at an average speed of 55 mph. Coming home, her average speed was 45 mph, and the trip took two hours longer. How many hours did she travel altogether?

    (1) 9
    (2) 11
    (3) 20
    (4) 405
    (5) 495

11. A football team gained 17 yards and then lost 4 yards on each of the next two plays. On the 4th play, it passed for a gain of 28 yards. What is its total yardage for the four plays?

    (1) 29
    (2) 37
    (3) 41
    (4) 45
    (5) not enough information is given

12. Frank's car gets 24 miles per gallon of gasoline. Which expression below best shows how to find how many gallons he needs for a trip of 672 miles?

    (1) $\frac{24}{x} = 672$

    (2) $\frac{x}{24} = 672$

    (3) $24x = 672$

    (4) $x + 24 = 672$

    (5) $672 - x = 24$

13. Yesterday, you spent twice as much money as you did today. Altogether you spent $48. How much did you spend yesterday?

    (1) $12
    (2) $16
    (3) $24
    (4) $32
    (5) not enough information is given

14. After Pauly bought some cotton material, she found that she had only $\frac{3}{4}$ of what she needed. How many more yards does she need to buy?

    (1) $\frac{1}{4}$

    (2) $\frac{3}{4}$

    (3) 3

    (4) 4

    (5) not enough information is given

15. Find the distance between line *A* and line *B*.

(1) −16
(2) −8
(3) 8
(4) 12
(5) 16

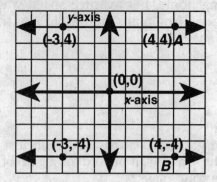

For questions 16 and 17, use the following information.

Foods That Add Calories	
1 slice of cheesecake	+478 calories
1 chocolate sundae	+560 calories
1 soda pop (12 oz)	+105 calories
1 orange juice (8 oz)	+ 96 calories
1 apple (medium)	+ 70 calories
3 chocolate chip cookies	+160 calories

Activities That Take Off Calories	
1 set of tennis	−200 calories
1 hour of swimming	−480 calories
1 mile of walking	−172 calories
1 hour of dancing	−264 calories
1 hour cross-country skiing	−430 calories

16. This afternoon, Fred had a chocolate sundae before playing three sets of tennis. After tennis, he had a glass of orange juice and six cookies. How many calories has he used or gained during the afternoon?

(1) −40 (2) +216 (3) +376 (4) +616 (5) +1416

17. How many miles would you need to walk to work off a slice of cheesecake and two 12-ounce bottles of soda pop?

(1) 2.4 (2) 2.8 (3) 3.4 (4) 4 (5) not enough information is given

18. The slope of the line that contains the points $(-4,3)$ and $(5,2)$ is

(1) $-\frac{1}{9}$ (2) $\frac{1}{9}$ (3) $\frac{1}{5}$ (4) 5 (5) 9

Answers are on page 734.

FORMULAS

Description	Formula
AREA (A) of a:	
square	$A = s^2$ where s = side
rectangle	$A = lw$ where l = length, w = width
parallelogram	$A = bh$ where b = base, h = height
triangle	$A = \frac{1}{2}bh$ where b = base, h = height
circle	$A = \pi r^2$ where $\pi \cong 3.14$, r = radius
PERIMETER (P) of a:	
square	$P = 4s$ where s = side
rectangle	$P = 2l + 2w$ where l = length, w = width
triangle	$P = a + b + c$ where a, b, and c are the sides
circle—circumference (C)	$C = \pi d$ where $\pi \cong 3.14$, d = diameter
VOLUME (V) of a:	
cube	$V = s^3$ where s = side
rectangular container	$V = lwh$ where l = length, w = width, h = height
cylinder	$V = \pi r^2 h$ where $\pi \cong 3.14$, r = radius, h = height
Pythagorean theorem	$c^2 = a^2 + b^2$ where c = hypotenuse, a and b are legs of a right triangle
distance (d) between two points in a plane	$d = \sqrt{(x_2 - x_1)^2 + (y_2 - y_1)^2}$ where (x_1, y_1) and (x_2, y_2) are two points in a plane
slope of a line (m)	$m = \dfrac{y_2 - y_1}{x_2 - x_1}$ where (x_1, y_1) and (x_2, y_2) are two points in a plane
mean	$mean = \dfrac{x_1 + x_2 + \ldots + x_n}{n}$ where the xs are the values for which a mean is desired and n = number of values in the series
median	$median$ = the point in an ordered set of numbers at which half of the numbers are above and half of the numbers are below this value.
simple interest (i)	$i = prt$ where p = principal, r = rate, t = time
distance (d) as function of rate and time	$d = rt$ where r = rate, t = time
total cost (c)	$c = nr$ where n = number of units, r = cost per unit

TEST 5: MATHEMATICS ANSWER KEY

CHAPTER 1: WHOLE NUMBERS AND PROBLEM SOLVING

Exercise 1: Whole Numbers
page 560

Exact answers:

1. 10,842

$$
\begin{array}{r}
{\scriptstyle 1\,1\,2} \\
9873 \\
412 \\
509 \\
+\ \ 48 \\
\hline
10,842
\end{array}
$$

2. 2944

$$
\begin{array}{r}
{\scriptstyle 2\,9\,9\,10} \\
\cancel{3000} \\
-\ \ 56 \\
\hline
2944
\end{array}
$$

3. 1177

$$
\begin{array}{r}
{\scriptstyle 1\,16\,16} \\
1\cancel{276} \\
-\ \ 99 \\
\hline
1177
\end{array}
$$

4. 8265

$$
\begin{array}{r}
{\scriptstyle 6} \\
{\scriptstyle 3} \\
87 \\
\times\ 95 \\
\hline
435 \\
783 \\
\hline
8265
\end{array}
$$

5. 12,596

$$
\begin{array}{r}
{\scriptstyle 2\,3} \\
{\scriptstyle 4\,5} \\
268 \\
\times\ \ 47 \\
\hline
1\,876 \\
10\,72 \\
\hline
12,596
\end{array}
$$

6. 627

$$
\begin{array}{r}
627 \\
9)\overline{5643} \\
\underline{54} \\
24 \\
\underline{18} \\
63 \\
\underline{63} \\
0
\end{array}
$$

7. 268 r1

$$
\begin{array}{r}
268\ \text{r}1 \\
15)\overline{4021} \\
\underline{30} \\
102 \\
\underline{90} \\
121 \\
\underline{120} \\
1
\end{array}
$$

8. 501

$$
\begin{array}{r}
501 \\
72)\overline{36,072} \\
\underline{36\ 0} \\
72 \\
\underline{72} \\
0
\end{array}
$$

Exercise 2: Understanding the Question and Selecting Information
pages 562–563

1. *Question:* How much did Dave make altogether?
Information: 8 hours and 2 hours overtime; $10.00 per hour and $15.00 per hour for overtime.
2. *Question:* How much did her monthly payments total?
Information: $48; 30 months. You don't need her down payment.
3. *Question:* How much was she charged?
Information: N; you do not have enough information because you don't know how much the third box weighs.
4. *Question:* How much does Bensenville spend on public health?
Information: N; you do not have enough information because you don't know how much Bensenville spends on highway construction.
5. *Question:* How many voters are men?
Information: 7,000 registered voters; 3,000 women. You don't need to know the total population of 12,000 to answer the question.

Exercise 3: Choosing the Operation
page 564

1. **Divide;** you have to find an average.
2. **Add;** add the new weight and the amount she lost to find her original weight.
3. **Subtract;** you have to find a difference.
4. **Divide;** to find how many times heavier one package is, you divide.
5. **Multiply;** there will be more inches than feet, so you multiply.

Exercise 4: Problem Solving
page 566

1. *Question:* How many miles do you plan to drive?
Information: 162 miles, 229 miles, 375 miles
Operation: You need to find the combined amount of miles driven—add.
Estimation: 150 + 200 + 400 = 750
Calculation: 162 + 229 + 375 = 766 miles
Evaluation: It makes sense that the total mileage is more than any one distance. Also, the answer is close to the estimate.
2. *Question:* What amount does each person receive?
Information: $12,855; 15 people
Operation: "shared"—divide
Estimation: $15,000 ÷ 15 = $1000
Calculation: 12,855 ÷ 15 = $857
Evaluation: It makes sense that the answer is around but less than the estimate of $1000.

3. *Question:* How much larger is Canada than the United States?
Information: 3,851,809 square miles (Canada); 3,675,633 square miles (U.S.)
Operation: "How much larger"—subtract
Estimation: 3,900,000 − 3,700,000 = 200,000
Calculation: 3,851,809 − 3,675,633 = 176,176 square miles
Evaluation: The answer should be much smaller than the two numbers and close to the estimate.

4. *Question:* What is the cost of 97 TVs?
Information: $325 each; 97 TVs
Operation: from the cost of one to many: multiply
Estimation: $325 × 100 = $32,500
Calculation: 97 × $325 = $31,525
Evaluation: The answer should be almost 100 times $325.

5. *Question:* How much does Marlene pay in estimated tax per year?
Information: $2492 paid each quarter and 4 quarters in a year
Operation: you need to find the amount for all 4 quarters—multiply.
Estimation: $2500 × 4 = $10,000
Calculation: $2492 × 4 = $9968
Evaluation: The answer should be much larger than quarterly tax and close to the estimate.

6. *Question:* How many acres did each child inherit?
Information: 588 acres altogether and 3 children
Operation: The clue word *divided* is provided in the question.
Estimation: 600 ÷ 3 = 200
Calculation: 588 ÷ 3 = 196
Evaluation: The answer should be about a third smaller than the total number of acres.

7. *Question:* How much does he have left each month after paying for rent and food?
Information: $1300 a month in earnings, $345 a month for rent, $90 a week or $360 a month in food.
Operation: How much does he have left means subtract.
Estimation: $1300 − 300 − 400 = $600
Calculation: $1300 − 345 − 360 = $595
Evaluation: The answer should be much smaller than $1300 dollars.

Exercise 5: Word Problems
pages 570–572

1. **(4) $61,920**

$$\begin{array}{r} \$5160 \\ \times\ \ \ 12 \\ \hline 10\,320 \\ 51\,60 \\ \hline \$61,920 \end{array}$$

2. **(2) 6**

$$\begin{array}{r} 5\ r35 \\ 72\overline{)395} \\ 360 \\ \hline 35 \end{array}$$

Because the answer is 5 r35, you will need 6 buses to accommodate the people.

3. **(3) 830**

STEP 1	STEP 2
$ 11 per pair	830 pairs
500)5500	11)9130
500	88
500	33
500	33
0	00

4. **(5) Edison**

$$\begin{array}{r} 1846 \\ -\ 1318 \\ \hline 528 \end{array}$$

5. **(1) 1865**

STEP 1	STEP 2	STEP 3
1686	1420	9396
1982	1650	− 7531
2234	1847	1865
1648	1296	
+ 1846	+ 1318	
9396	7531	

6. **(1) 373**

$$\begin{array}{r} 373 \\ 5\overline{)1865} \\ 15 \\ \hline 36 \\ 35 \\ \hline 15 \\ 15 \\ \hline 0 \end{array}$$

7. **(2) 156**

STEP 1	STEP 2
350	1298
375	− 1142
+ 417	156
1142	

8. **(2) $205**

STEP 1	STEP 2	STEP 3	STEP 4
$12,800	$13,490	$12,990	$205
282	− 500	− 3 150	48)9840
252	$12,990	$9 840	96
+ 156			240
$13,490			240
			0

9. **(4) (25 × $23) + $4800** The cost of the jackets is 25 × $23. Add the cost of the suits: (25 × $23) + $4800.

10. **(5) not enough information is given**
The problem does not tell how much was put aside to pay expenses.

CHAPTER 2: DECIMALS
Exercise 1: Reading Decimals
page 574

1. .05
2. 6.2
3. 100.002
4. 1032
5. 400.025
6. (a) .7
(b) 6.032
(c) 2000.08
(d) 305.056
(e) .0065

Exercise 2: Comparing Decimals
page 575

1. (a) .05 (b) 4.10 (c) .7 (d) .51
(e) 1.033
2. (a) 2.15; 2.105; 1.95
(b) .0503; .005; .0035
3. 14.003; 14.03; 14.3; 14.3033
4. 4.67; 4.067; 4.0067

Exercise 3: Rounding Decimals
page 576
1. .375 rounds to **.38**
2. 7.58 round to **7.6**
3. $1.298 rounds to **$1.30**
4. 17.124 rounds to **17.12**
5. 8.275 rounds to **8.3**
6. 3.14159 rounds to **3.14**
7. 101.68 rounds to **102**

Exercise 4: Adding and Subtracting Decimals
pages 578–579

1. 145.047
```
      12.4
  + 132.647
    145.047
```

2. 17.91
```
   5.9
   2.46
   6
   3.07
 +  .48
  17.91
```

3. 37.8
```
   43.0
 -  5.2
   37.8
```

4. 78.3
```
   85.2
 -  6.9
   78.3
```

5. 968.749 meters
```
    237.42
    150.045
    186.21
    298.674
 +   96.4
    968.749 meters
```

6. $357.56
```
STEP 1        STEP 2
$42.87        $472.24
  5.93      - 114.68
 10.00        $357.56
 17.48
+ 38.40
$114.68
```

7. 2877.8 miles
```
   28,054.1
 - 25,176.3
    2 877.8 miles
```

8. (3) $3.55
```
STEP 1      STEP 2
$4.75       $10.00
  .95      -  6.45
  .75         $3.55
$6.45
```

9. (2) 1.4
```
 104.2°
-102.8°
   1.4°
```
98.6° is unnecessary information.

10. (4) .2 + .15 This is the only expression given that you could solve to find out how much wood she cut off.

11. $102.64
```
$17.50
  4.95
  6.00
 13.44
+60.75
$102.64
```

12. $265.27
```
$160
 102.64
 +  2.63
 $265.27
```

Exercise 5: Multiplying and Dividing Decimals
pages 582–583

1. .513
```
   .342
 ×  1.5
  1710
  342
  .5130 = .513
```

2. .01564
```
   .00034
 ×    46
  00204
  00136
  0.01564
```

3. .024
```
   .03
 × .8
  .024
```

4. $22.75
```
   $6.50
 ×   3.5
  3 250
 19 50
 $22.750 = $22.75
```

5. 120.1
```
        120.1
 .05 ) 6.005
        5
        1 0
        1 0
          0
          0
          05
           5
           0
```

6. .004
```
       .004
 3 ) .012
      0
      01
       0
       12
       12
        0
```

7. 70
```
        70
 .04 ) 2.80
        2 8
         00
          0
          0
```

8. 7 00
```
         700
 .08 ) 56.00
        56
         000
          00
           0
```

9. .38 × 10 = **3.8**
10. 472 × 10,000 = **4,720,000**
11. .0972 × 100 = **9.72**
12. .617 ÷ 10 = **.0617**
13. 456.12 ÷ 100 = **4.5612**
14. 57 ÷ 1000 = **.057**
15. (3) 7.85 × 12
16. (4) $29.00
   $.29 × 100 = 29 = $29.00
17. (3) 5
   STEP 1. 1.5 rooms per hour × 10 hours = 15 rooms per day
   STEP 2. 75 rooms ÷ 15 rooms per day = 5 days
18. (3) (3.5 × 1.19) + (2 × 2.30)

Exercise 6: Estimating
page 584
1. *estimate:* 5 + 12 + 75 + 10 + 8 = **110 miles**
2. *estimate:* $50 − 25 = 25
   $25 − 2.50 = **$22.50**
3. *estimate:* $9 × 10 = **$90**
4. *estimate:* 36 ÷ 2 = **18**

Exercise 7: Decimal Word Problems
pages 584–586
1. **(2) 3**

```
            3.75
3.2 ) 12.0 00
       9 6
       2 4 0
       2 2 4
         1 6 0
         1 6 0
             0
```

3.75 shelves can be cut, but only 3 *complete* shelves can be cut.

2. **(5) $2677.29**

```
    $425.00
     485.75
     399.87
     642.15
   + 724.52
   $2677.29
```

3. **(3) 17.8**

```
           17.8
140) 2492.0
     140
     1092
      980
     1120
     1120
        0
```

4. **(3) 8.6408**

```
    3.086
  ×   2.8
  2 4 688
  6 1 72
  8.6 408
```

5. **(2) $320.54**

Gross Earnings:	Total Deductions:	Net Pay:
$265.72	$27.03	$434.47
+ 168.75	+ 86.90	− 113.93
$434.47	$113.93	$320.54

6. **(5) not enough information is given**
   You cannot calculate the answer because the problem does not contain the number of hours that employee 24 worked.

7. **(3) $13,448**

Total Monthly Payments:	Total Cost:
$207.25	$ 3 500
× 48	+ 9 948
1658 00	$13,448
8290 0	
9948.00	

8. **(1) $.06**

```
       .0575 rounds to .06
12) .6900
    0
    69
    60
    90
    84
    60
    60
     0
```

9. **(2) 16.1**

Miles Traveled:	Miles per Gallon:
8747.6	16.13 rounds to 16.1
− 7353.2	86.4) 1394.4 00
1394.4	864
	530 4
	518 4
	12 0 0
	8 6 4
	3 3 60
	2 5 92
	7 68

10. **(3) $5.49**

STEP 1	STEP 2
4.25	5.485 rounds to $5.49
3.80	7) 38.400
5.75	35
10.00	3 4
6.00	2 8
3.70	60
+ 4.90	56
38.40	40
	35
	5

CHAPTER 3 FRACTIONS
Exercise 1: Types of Fractions
page 588
1. like fractions and improper fractions
2. mixed numbers
3. improper fractions and unlike fractions
4. unlike fractions and proper fractions
5. proper fractions and unlike fractions

Exercise 2: Raising and Reducing Fractions
page 589
1. (a) $\frac{9}{24}$

   (b) $\frac{15}{20}$

   (c) $\frac{6}{36}$

   (d) $\frac{3}{7} \frac{(×3)}{(×3)} = \mathbf{\frac{9}{21}}$

   (e) $\frac{6}{7} \frac{(×4)}{(×4)} = \mathbf{\frac{24}{28}}$

   (f) $\frac{2}{5} \frac{(×6)}{(×6)} = \mathbf{\frac{12}{30}}$

2. (a) $\frac{3}{4}$

(b) $\frac{3}{4}$

(c) $\frac{1}{3}$

(d) $\frac{40}{50}\frac{(\div 10)}{(\div 10)} = \frac{4}{5}$

(e) $\frac{24}{36}\frac{(\div 12)}{(\div 12)} = \frac{2}{3}$

(f) $\frac{30}{42}\frac{(\div 6)}{(\div 6)} = \frac{5}{7}$

3. (a) $\frac{6}{8}\frac{(\div 2)}{(\div 2)} = \frac{3}{4}$

(b) $\frac{15}{20}\frac{(\div 5)}{(\div 5)} = \frac{3}{4}$

(c) $\frac{9}{27}\frac{(\div 9)}{(\div 9)} = \frac{1}{3}$

(d) $\frac{4}{12}\frac{(\div 4)}{(\div 4)} = \frac{1}{3}$

(e) $\frac{25}{30}\frac{(\div 5)}{(\div 5)} = \frac{5}{6}$

Exercise 3: Changing Fractions and Decimals
page 590

1. (a) $\frac{5}{100}\frac{(\div 5)}{(\div 5)} = \frac{1}{20}$

(b) $\frac{450}{1000}\frac{(\div 50)}{(\div 50)} = \frac{9}{20}$

(c) $\frac{7}{100}$

(d) $.32 = \frac{32}{100}\frac{(\div 4)}{(\div 4)} = \frac{8}{25}$

(e) $.005 = \frac{5}{1000}\frac{(\div 5)}{(\div 5)} = \frac{1}{200}$

(f) $3.1 = 3\frac{1}{10}$

2. (a)
$$\begin{array}{r} .37 \\ 8\overline{)3.00} \\ \underline{2\,4} \\ 60 \\ \underline{56} \\ 4 \end{array} = .37\frac{4}{8} = .37\frac{1}{2}$$

(b)
$$\begin{array}{r} .20 \\ 5\overline{)1.00} \\ \underline{1\,0} \\ 00 \\ \underline{0} \\ 0 \end{array} = .2$$

(c)
$$\begin{array}{r} .44 \\ 9\overline{)4.00} \\ \underline{3\,6} \\ 40 \\ \underline{36} \\ 4 \end{array} = .44\frac{4}{9}$$

(d)
$$\begin{array}{r} 1.33 \\ 3\overline{)4.00} \\ \underline{3} \\ 1\,0 \\ \underline{9} \\ 10 \\ \underline{9} \\ 1 \end{array} = 1.33\frac{1}{3}$$

(e)
$$\begin{array}{r} 1.66 \\ 3\overline{)5.00} \\ \underline{3} \\ 2\,0 \\ \underline{1\,8} \\ 20 \\ \underline{18} \\ 2 \end{array} = 1.66\frac{2}{3}$$

(f)
$$\begin{array}{r} .83 \\ 6\overline{)5.00} \\ \underline{4\,8} \\ 20 \\ \underline{18} \\ 2 \end{array} = .83\frac{2}{6} = .83\frac{1}{3}$$

Exercise 4: Changing Improper Fractions and Mixed Numbers
page 591

1. (a) $1\frac{5}{9} = \frac{(1 \times 9) + 5}{9} = \frac{9 + 5}{9} = \frac{14}{9}$

(b) $12\frac{1}{4} = \frac{(12 \times 4) + 1}{4} = \frac{48 + 1}{4} = \frac{49}{4}$

(c) $3\frac{2}{5} = \frac{(3 \times 5) + 2}{5} = \frac{15 + 2}{5} = \frac{17}{5}$

(d) $3\frac{1}{4} = \frac{(3 \times 4) + 1}{4} = \frac{12 + 1}{4} = \frac{13}{4}$

(e) $2\frac{1}{2} = \frac{(2 \times 2) + 1}{2} = \frac{4 + 1}{2} = \frac{5}{2}$

(f) $6\frac{2}{3} = \frac{(6 \times 3) + 2}{3} = \frac{18 + 2}{3} = \frac{20}{3}$

2. (a) $\frac{4}{3} = \begin{array}{r} 1 \\ 3\overline{)4} \\ \underline{3} \\ 1 \end{array} = 1\frac{1}{3}$

(b) $\frac{16}{7} = \begin{array}{r} 2 \\ 7\overline{)16} \\ \underline{14} \\ 2 \end{array} = 2\frac{2}{7}$

(c) $\frac{9}{9} = \begin{array}{r} 1 \\ 9\overline{)9} \\ \underline{9} \\ 0 \end{array} = 1$

(d) $\frac{9}{8} = \begin{array}{r} 1 \\ 8\overline{)9} \\ \underline{8} \\ 1 \end{array} = 1\frac{1}{8}$

(e) $\frac{17}{5} = \begin{array}{r} 3 \\ 5\overline{)17} \\ \underline{15} \\ 2 \end{array} = 3\frac{2}{5}$

(f) $\frac{3}{2} = \begin{array}{r} 1 \\ 2\overline{)3} \\ \underline{2} \\ 1 \end{array} = 1\frac{1}{2}$

Exercise 5: Comparing Numbers page 595

1. (a) $\frac{7}{8} > \frac{3}{5}$ $\frac{7}{8}\,(\times 5) = \frac{35}{40}$
   $\frac{3}{5}\,(\times 8) = \frac{24}{40}$

   (b) $\frac{2}{3} > \frac{4}{9}$ $\frac{2}{3}\,(\times 3) = \frac{6}{9}$
   $\frac{4}{9} = \frac{4}{9}$

   (c) $\frac{3}{4} > \frac{3}{10}$ $\frac{3}{10}\,(\times 4) = \frac{12}{40}$
   $\frac{3}{4}\,(\times 10) = \frac{30}{40}$

2. (a) $3 < 8$

   (b) $6 > 0$

   (c) $\frac{3}{8} > \frac{1}{8}$

   (d) $\frac{3}{4} = \frac{9}{12}$
   $\frac{2}{3} = \frac{8}{12}$
   $\frac{3}{4} > \frac{2}{3}$

   (e) $2\frac{3}{8} = \frac{19}{8}$
   $\frac{5}{2} = \frac{20}{8}$
   $2\frac{3}{8} < \frac{5}{2}$

   (f) $\frac{5}{6} = \frac{15}{18}$
   $\frac{8}{9} = \frac{16}{18}$
   $\frac{5}{6} < \frac{8}{9}$

   (g) $.3 = .30$
   $\frac{1}{4} = .25$
   $.3 > \frac{1}{4}$

   (h) $\frac{1}{2} = \frac{6}{12}$
   $\frac{6}{12} = \frac{6}{12}$
   $\frac{1}{2} = \frac{6}{12}$

   (i) $\frac{9}{9} = 1$
   $\frac{2}{2} = 1$
   $\frac{9}{9} = \frac{2}{2}$

   (j) $.07 = .0700$
   $.0873 = .0873$
   $.07 < .0873$

   (k) $\frac{3}{5} = .6$
   $.6 = .6$
   $\frac{3}{5} = .6$

Exercise 6: Adding and Subtracting Fractions page 597

1. $\frac{2}{3}$ $\frac{1}{9}$
   $+ \frac{5}{9}$
   $\frac{6}{9} = \frac{2}{3}$

2. $\frac{11}{12}$ $\frac{2}{3} = \frac{8}{12}$
   $+ \frac{1}{4} = \frac{3}{12}$
   $\frac{11}{12}$

3. $\frac{11}{24}$ $\frac{3}{8} = \frac{9}{24}$
   $+ \frac{1}{12} = \frac{2}{24}$
   $\frac{11}{24}$

4. 1 $\frac{5}{6}$
   $+ \frac{1}{6}$
   $\frac{6}{6} = 1$

5. $7\frac{3}{4}$ $1\frac{5}{12}$
   $+ 6\frac{4}{12}$
   $7\frac{9}{12} = 7\frac{3}{4}$

6. $7\frac{17}{35}$ $4\frac{1}{5} = 4\frac{7}{35}$
   $+ 3\frac{2}{7} = 3\frac{10}{35}$
   $7\frac{17}{35}$

7. $9\frac{1}{3}$ $4\frac{2}{9}$
   $+ 5\frac{1}{9}$
   $9\frac{3}{9} = 9\frac{1}{3}$

8. $10\frac{1}{24}$ $3\frac{7}{8} = 3\frac{21}{24}$
   $2\frac{5}{6} = 2\frac{20}{24}$
   $+ 3\frac{1}{3} = 3\frac{8}{24}$
   $8\frac{49}{24} = 8 + 2\frac{1}{24} = 10\frac{1}{24}$

9. $\frac{3}{5}$ $\frac{9}{10}$
   $- \frac{3}{10}$
   $\frac{6}{10} = \frac{3}{5}$

10. $\frac{1}{8}$ $\frac{5}{8} = \frac{5}{8}$
   $- \frac{1}{2} = \frac{4}{8}$
   $\frac{1}{8}$

11. $\frac{3}{10}$ $\frac{4}{5} = \frac{8}{10}$
   $- \frac{1}{2} = \frac{5}{10}$
   $\frac{3}{10}$

12. $\frac{7}{18}$ $\frac{12}{18}$
   $- \frac{5}{18}$
   $\frac{7}{18}$

13. $1\frac{7}{8}$ $4\frac{3}{4} = 4\frac{6}{8} = 3\frac{14}{8}$
   $- 2\frac{7}{8} = 2\frac{7}{8} = 2\frac{7}{8}$
   $1\frac{7}{8}$

14. $13\frac{2}{3}$ $25\frac{1}{6} = 25\frac{1}{6} = 24\frac{7}{6}$
   $- 11\frac{1}{2} = 11\frac{3}{6} = 11\frac{3}{6}$
   $13\frac{4}{6} = 13\frac{2}{3}$

15. $6\frac{15}{17}$ $10 = 9\frac{17}{17}$
$\quad\quad\quad - \; 3\frac{2}{17} = 3\frac{2}{17}$
$\quad\quad\quad\quad\quad\quad\quad 6\frac{15}{17}$

16. $19\frac{1}{5}$ $20 = 19\frac{5}{5}$
$\quad\quad\quad - \; \frac{4}{5} = \frac{4}{5}$
$\quad\quad\quad\quad\quad\quad 19\frac{1}{5}$

Exercise 7: Multiplying Fractions
page 599

1. $\frac{6}{15} \times \frac{5}{12} = \frac{1}{6}$
2. $8 \times \frac{3}{4} = \frac{8}{1} \times \frac{3}{4} = \frac{6}{1} = 6$
3. $\frac{3}{8} \times \frac{2}{15} \times \frac{6}{7} = \frac{6}{140} = \frac{3}{70}$
4. $8\frac{1}{6} \times 4 = \frac{49}{6} \times \frac{4}{1} = \frac{98}{3} = 32\frac{2}{3}$
5. $\frac{5}{9} \times \frac{2}{5} = \frac{2}{9}$
6. $2\frac{1}{2} \times 2\frac{1}{3} = \frac{5}{2} \times \frac{7}{3} = \frac{35}{6} = 5\frac{5}{6}$
7. $2\frac{3}{4} \times \frac{6}{7} = \frac{11}{4} \times \frac{6}{7} = \frac{33}{14} = 2\frac{5}{14}$
8. $1\frac{3}{10} \times 5 = \frac{13}{10} \times \frac{5}{1} = \frac{13}{2} = 6\frac{1}{2}$
9. $3\frac{3}{8} \times 1\frac{3}{9} = \frac{27}{8} \times \frac{12}{9} = \frac{9}{2} = 4\frac{1}{2}$

Exercise 8: Dividing Fractions
page 600

1. $\frac{4}{10} \div \frac{2}{3} = \frac{4}{10} \times \frac{3}{2} = \frac{6}{10} = \frac{3}{5}$
2. $\frac{2}{5} \div 4 = \frac{2}{5} \times \frac{1}{4} = \frac{1}{10}$
3. $\frac{3}{7} \div \frac{6}{35} = \frac{3}{7} \times \frac{35}{6} = \frac{5}{2} = 2\frac{1}{2}$
4. $3\frac{2}{3} \div 1\frac{1}{2} = \frac{11}{3} \times \frac{2}{3} = \frac{22}{9} = 2\frac{4}{9}$
5. $1\frac{3}{8} \div 11 = \frac{11}{8} \times \frac{1}{11} = \frac{1}{8}$
6. $9 \div 2\frac{1}{2} = \frac{9}{1} \times \frac{2}{5} = \frac{18}{5} = 3\frac{3}{5}$

Exercise 9: Item Sets
pages 601–602

1. **(2) $47.28**
Information: $.98\frac{1}{2}$, 6 feet; 8 shelves

Cost to make 1 shelf:
$.98\frac{1}{2} \times 6 = \frac{1.97}{2} \times \frac{6}{1} = \$5.91$
Cost of 8 shelves: $\$5.91 \times 8 = \$47.28$

2. **(3) 6 feet**
Information: 6-ft lengths; $5\frac{1}{4}$-ft length; 8 pieces
Amount cut off each: $6 - 5\frac{1}{4} = \frac{3}{4}$ ft
Total amount of waste:
$8 \times \frac{3}{4} = \frac{8}{1} \times \frac{3}{4} = 6$ feet

3. **(1) $52.32**
Information: 8 shelves; $13.95 prevarnished; $12 varnishing; $47.28 (cost of shelves from question 1)
Cost of prevarnished shelves:
$8 \times \$13.95 = \$111.60$
Cost to self-varnish: $\$12 + \$47.28 = \$59.28$
Difference: $\$111.60 - \$59.28 = \$52.32$

4. **(3) $\frac{19}{40}$ mile**
Information: $\frac{7}{8}$ mile; $\frac{2}{5}$ mile (from map)
Length of Pine Way: $\frac{7}{8} - \frac{2}{5} = \frac{35}{40} - \frac{16}{40} = \frac{19}{40}$ mile

5. **(4) $1\frac{1}{8}$ miles**
Information: $\frac{19}{20}$ and $\frac{3}{10}$ for Birch Trail (from map); $\frac{19}{40}$ for Pine Way (from question 4)
Length of Birch Trail: $\frac{19}{20} - \frac{3}{10} = \frac{19}{20} - \frac{6}{20} = \frac{13}{20}$
Total of both roads: $\frac{13}{20} + \frac{19}{40} = \frac{26}{40} + \frac{19}{40} = \frac{45}{40} = 1\frac{5}{40} = 1\frac{1}{8}$ miles

6. **(5) not enough information is given**
You need to know the width of Camping Area A, but this is not given.

7. **(3) $11.79**
Information: $1\frac{1}{2}$ times; $7.86
$\$7.86 \times 1\frac{1}{2} = \frac{7.86}{1} \times \frac{3}{2} = \$11.79$

8. **(5) not enough information is given**
There is no information on the number of hours in the third week; this chart is for the *second* week in April.

9. **(4) ($7.86 × 40) + ($11.79 × $\frac{10}{3}$)**
Information: 40 hr at $7.86; $11.79 overtime rate (from question 7)
Number of hours of overtime:
$43\frac{1}{3} - 40 = 3\frac{1}{3}$ hours
Represent amount at hourly wage: $7.86 × 40
Represent amount at overtime rate: $11.79 × $3\frac{1}{3}$ = $11.79 × $\frac{10}{3}$
Represent total wages:
($7.86 × 40) + ($11.79 × $\frac{10}{3}$)

Exercise 10: Fraction Review
pages 603–604

1. **(1) $5\frac{5}{8}$ ft**
$\quad\quad 8\frac{3}{8} = 8\frac{3}{8} = 7\frac{11}{8}$
$\quad\quad - 2\frac{3}{4} = 2\frac{6}{8} = 2\frac{6}{8}$
$\quad\quad\quad\quad\quad\quad\quad\quad 5\frac{5}{8}$ feet

2. **(5) $870**
$\$36\frac{1}{4} \times 24$
$\frac{145}{4} \times \frac{24}{1} = \$870$

3. **(3) $720 \div 22\frac{1}{2}$**
This expression shows the number of miles divided by miles per gallon. This would give you total gallons.

4. **(4) 30**
$20 \div \frac{2}{3}$
$\frac{20}{1} \times \frac{3}{2} = 30$ doses

5. (5) not enough information is given
You cannot figure this out because you do not know the weight of the cartons.

6. (2) $5\frac{3}{4}$ in

Total of two given widths: $2\frac{3}{8} \times 2 =$
$\frac{19}{8} \times \frac{2}{1} = \frac{38}{8} = 4\frac{6}{8} = 4\frac{3}{4}$

Subtract that from length: $10\frac{1}{2} - 4\frac{3}{4} =$
$10\frac{2}{4} - 4\frac{3}{4} = 9\frac{6}{4} - 4\frac{3}{4} = 5\frac{3}{4}$ in

7. (4) $760

Wife's fare: $285 \times \frac{2}{3} = \frac{285}{1} \times \frac{2}{3} =$
$190

Childrens fare: $2 \times \frac{285}{2} = \$285$

Total fares: $285 + \$190 + \$285 =$
$760

8. (3) 35

Find the $\frac{1}{6}$ for roads: $10\frac{1}{2} \times \frac{1}{6} =$
$\frac{21}{2} \times \frac{1}{6} = \frac{21}{12} =$
$1\frac{9}{12} = 1\frac{3}{4}$ acres

Remaining acreage for lots:
$10\frac{1}{2} = 10\frac{2}{4} = 9\frac{6}{4}$
$- \quad 1\frac{3}{4} = \quad 1\frac{3}{4} = 1\frac{3}{4}$
$\overline{\qquad\qquad\qquad 8\frac{3}{4} \text{ acres}}$

Number of lots: $8\frac{3}{4} \div \frac{1}{4} =$
$\frac{35}{4} \times \frac{4}{1} = 35$ lots

9. (1) $1\frac{1}{8}$

Total amount of wood needed:
$3 \times 1\frac{5}{8} =$
$\frac{3}{1} \times \frac{13}{8} = \frac{39}{8} = 4\frac{7}{8}$ ft

Amount left: $6 \quad = 5\frac{8}{8}$
$\underline{\quad - 4\frac{7}{8} = 4\frac{7}{8}}$
$\qquad\qquad\quad 1\frac{1}{8}$ ft

10. (2) 24,000

First, find $\frac{3}{4}$ of $\frac{2}{3}$:
$\frac{2}{3} \times \frac{3}{4} = \frac{3}{6} = \frac{1}{2}$

Then, find how many people got the message:
$\frac{48,000}{1} \times \frac{1}{2} = 24,000$

CHAPTER 4: RATIO AND PROPORTION

Exercise 1: Ratio
page 606

1. $\frac{3 \text{ miles}}{8 \text{ miles}} = \frac{3}{8}$

2. First, change 1 hour to 60 minutes to make a comparison of like units.
$\frac{30 \text{ minutes}}{1 \text{ hour}} = \frac{30 \text{ minutes}}{60 \text{ minutes}} = \frac{1}{2}$

3. $\frac{27 \text{ feet}}{18 \text{ feet}} = \frac{3}{2}$

4. $\frac{3 \text{ pounds}}{4 \text{ people}} = \frac{3}{4}$

5. $\frac{300 \text{ miles}}{15 \text{ gallons}} = \frac{20}{1}$

6. $\frac{88 \text{ feet}}{8 \text{ seconds}} = \frac{11}{1}$

7. $\frac{\$42.21}{7 \text{ hours}} = \frac{6.03}{1}$

8. $\frac{\$80}{12 \text{ boards}} = \frac{20}{3}$

Exercise 2: Application of Ratios
page 607

1. $\frac{\text{cost of supplies}}{\text{total expenses}} = \frac{\$120}{\$200} \div \frac{40}{40} = \frac{3}{5}$

2. $\frac{\text{total}}{\text{transportation}} = \frac{\$200}{\$40} \div \frac{40}{40} = \frac{5}{1}$

3. $\frac{\text{supplies}}{\text{tools}} = \frac{\$120}{\$25} \div \frac{5}{5} = \frac{24}{5}$

4. $\frac{\text{liabilities}}{\text{assets}} = \frac{\$1,700,000}{\$6,800,000} = \frac{17}{68} \div \frac{17}{17} = \frac{1}{4}$

5. $\frac{\text{women}}{\text{total}} = \frac{250}{750} \div \frac{250}{250} = \frac{1}{3}$

6. $\frac{\text{dividend}}{\text{shares}} = \frac{\$729}{300} = \$2.43$ per share

7.   250 lb of beef
   $\underline{- \quad 75 \text{ lb of waste}}$
   175 lb of packaged beef

8. $\frac{\text{cost}}{\text{lb of packaged beef}} = \frac{\$365}{175}$
$365 \div 175 = 2.085 = $ **$2.09 per lb**

Exercise 3: Solving Proportions
page 609

1. $m = 4$ $\frac{2}{5} = \frac{m}{10}$
$\frac{2 \times 10}{5} = 4$

2. $x = 1$ $\frac{x}{7} = \frac{3}{21}$
$\frac{7 \times 3}{21} = \frac{21}{21} = 1$

3. $y = 6\frac{2}{3}$ $\frac{5}{y} = \frac{15}{20}$
$\frac{20 \times 5}{15} = \frac{100}{15} = 6\frac{2}{3}$

4. $z = 8$ $\frac{6}{4} = \frac{12}{z}$
$\frac{12 \times 4}{6} = \frac{48}{6} = 8$

5. $x = 15$ $\frac{x}{12} = \frac{30}{24}$
$\frac{30 \times 12}{24} = \frac{360}{24} = 15$

Exercise 4: Application of Proportion
page 610

1. **240 miles**
$\frac{96 \text{ miles}}{8 \text{ gallons}} = \frac{m \text{ (number of miles)}}{20 \text{ gallons}}$
$\frac{96 \times 20}{8} = \frac{1920}{8} = 240$ miles

2. **$11\frac{1}{5}$ inches tall**
$\frac{5 \text{ inches wide}}{7 \text{ inches tall}} = \frac{8 \text{ inches wide}}{i \text{ (number of inches)}}$
$\frac{7 \times 8}{5} = \frac{56}{5} = 11\frac{1}{5}$ inches tall

3. **40 managers**
$\frac{2 \text{ managers}}{9 \text{ salespeople}} = \frac{m \text{ (managers)}}{180 \text{ salespeople}}$
$\frac{180 \times 2}{9} = \frac{360}{9} = 40$ managers

4. 18 feet

$$\frac{\frac{1}{8}\text{ inch}}{1\text{ foot}} = \frac{2\frac{1}{4}\text{ inches}}{f\text{ (feet)}}$$

$$\frac{2\frac{1}{4} \times 1}{\frac{1}{8}} = \frac{2\frac{1}{4}}{\frac{1}{8}} = 2\frac{1}{4} \div \frac{1}{8} = \frac{9}{4} \times \frac{8}{1} = 18\text{ feet}$$

5. 420 calories

$$\frac{2\text{ pancakes}}{120\text{ calories}} = \frac{7\text{ pancakes}}{c\text{ (calories)}}$$

$$\frac{120 \times 7}{2} = \frac{840}{2} = 420\text{ calories}$$

CHAPTER 5: PERCENTS

Exercise 1: Changing to Fractions and Decimals
page 613

1. $\frac{87}{100}$ $87 \times \frac{1}{100} = \frac{87}{1} \times \frac{1}{100} = \frac{87}{100}$

   .87 $87 \times .01 = .87$

2. $\frac{2}{5}$ $40 \times \frac{1}{100} = \frac{40}{1} \times \frac{1}{100} = \frac{2}{5}$

   .4 $40 \times .01 = .40 = .4$

3. $\frac{1}{50}$ $2 \times \frac{1}{100} = \frac{2}{1} \times \frac{1}{100} = \frac{1}{50}$

   .02 $2 \times .01 = .02$

4. $\frac{2}{3}$ $66\frac{2}{3} \times \frac{1}{100} = \frac{200}{3} \times \frac{1}{100} = \frac{2}{3}$

   $.66\frac{2}{3}$ $66\frac{2}{3} \times .01 = .66\frac{2}{3}$

5. 2 $200 \times \frac{1}{100} = \frac{200}{1} \times \frac{1}{100} = 2$

   2   $200 \times .01 = 2$

6. $\frac{1}{8}$ $12.5 \times \frac{1}{100} = 12\frac{1}{2} \times \frac{1}{100} =$
   $\frac{25}{2} \times \frac{1}{100} = \frac{1}{8}$

   .125 $12.5 \times .01 = .125$

7. $\frac{9}{50}$ $18 \times \frac{1}{100} = \frac{18}{1} \times \frac{1}{100} = \frac{9}{50}$

   .18 $18 \times .01 = .18$

8. $\frac{1}{125}$ $.8 \times \frac{1}{100} = \frac{8}{10} \times \frac{1}{100} = \frac{2}{250} = \frac{1}{125}$

   .008 $.8 \times .01 = .008$

9. $\frac{1}{200}$ $\frac{1}{2} \times \frac{1}{100} = \frac{1}{200}$

   .005 $\frac{1}{2} \times .01 = .5 \times .01 = .005$

Exercise 2: Changing to Percents
page 613

1. $\frac{3}{5} \times \frac{100}{1} = \frac{300}{5} = 60\%$

2. $.70 \times 100 = 70\%$

3. $\frac{1}{3} \times \frac{100}{1} = \frac{100}{3} = 33\frac{1}{3}\%$

4. $.0025 \times 100 = .25\%$

5. $\frac{3}{8} \times \frac{100}{1} = \frac{300}{8} = 37\frac{1}{2}\%$

6. $4.5 \times 100 = 450\%$

7. $\frac{9}{10} \times \frac{100}{1} = \frac{900}{1} = 90\%$

8. $.625 \times 100 = 62.5\%$

9. $2\frac{1}{4} \times 100 = \frac{9}{4} \times \frac{100}{1} = \frac{900}{4} = 225\%$

Exercise 3: Percent Problems
page 615

1. **1.2**   You are looking for the part:

   $$\frac{n}{30} = \frac{4}{100}$$

   Cross multiply: $30 \times 4 = 120$
   Divide: $120 \div 100 = 1.2$

2. **25%**   You are looking for the percent:

   $$\frac{14}{56} = \frac{n}{100}$$

   Cross multiply: $14 \times 100 = 1400$
   Divide: $1400 \div 56 = 25\%$

3. **400**   You are looking for the whole:

   $$\frac{10}{n} = \frac{2.5}{100}$$

   Cross multiply: $10 \times 100 = 1000$
   Divide: $1000 \div 2.5 = 400$

4. **200**   You are looking for the whole:

   $$\frac{14}{n} = \frac{7}{100}$$

   Cross multiply: $14 \times 100 = 1400$
   Divide: $1400 \div 7 = 200$

5. **9%**   You are looking for the percent:

   $$\frac{30.60}{340} = \frac{n}{100}$$

   Cross multiply:
   $30.60 \times 100 = 3060$
   Divide: $3060 \div 340 = 9$

6. **.31**   You are looking for the part:

   $$\frac{n}{62} = \frac{\frac{1}{2}}{100}$$

   Cross multiply: $62 \times \frac{1}{2} = 31$
   Divide: $31 \div 100 = .31$

7. **54**   You are looking for the part:

   $$\frac{n}{45} = \frac{120}{100}$$

   Cross multiply: $120 \times 45 = 5400$
   Divide: $5400 \div 100 = 54$

8. **35%**   You are looking for the percent:

   $$\frac{210}{600} = \frac{n}{100}$$

   Cross multiply:
   $210 \times 100 = 21,000$
   Divide: $21,000 \div 600 = 35\%$

9. **112.5**   You are looking for the whole:

   $$\frac{18}{n} = \frac{16}{100}$$

   Cross multiply: $18 \times 100 = 1800$
   Divide: $1800 \div 16 = 112.5$

10. **400%**   You are looking for the percent:

    $$\frac{20}{5} = \frac{n}{100}$$

    Cross multiply: $20 \times 100 = 2000$
    Divide: $2000 \div 5 = 400$

Exercise 4: Percent Word Problems
pages 616–617

1. **$252**

   You are looking for the part Jesse saves each month.

   $$\frac{n}{2100} = \frac{12}{100}$$

   Cross multiply: $2100 \times 12 = 25,200$
   Divide: $25,200 \div 100 = \$252$

2. 20%
You are looking for the percent of his income that goes for rent.

$$\frac{420}{2100} = \frac{n}{100}$$

Cross multiply: 420 × 100 = 42,000
Divide: 42,000 ÷ 2100 = 20%

3. $2205
First, find the amount of his raise:

$$\frac{n}{2100} = \frac{5}{100}$$

Cross multiply: 2100 × 5 = 10,500
Divide: 10,500 ÷ 100 = $105
Then, add his raise to his old monthly income:
$2100 + $105 = $2205

4. 35% wrong
You are looking for the percent she got wrong. First, find the percent correct:

$$\frac{26}{40} = \frac{n}{100}$$

Cross multiply: 26 × 100 = 2600
Divide: 2600 ÷ 40 = 65% correct
Then, find the percent she got wrong:
100% − 65% = 35% wrong

5. $12,000
You are looking for the whole cost of the car.

$$\frac{1800}{n} = \frac{15}{100}$$

Cross multiply: 1800 × 100 = 180,000
Divide: 180,000 ÷ 15 = $12,000

6. 36% undecided
First, find the total number of voters:
200 + 120 + 180 = 500
Then, find the percent undecided:

$$\frac{180}{500} = \frac{n}{100}$$

Cross multiply: 180 × 100 = 18,000
Divide: 18,000 ÷ 500 = 36% undecided

7. $17.98
First, find the total cost of the cassettes:
$7.49 × 3 = $22.47
Then, find Hosea's discount:

$$\frac{n}{22.47} = \frac{20}{100}$$

Cross multiply: 22.47 × 20 = 449.40
Divide: 449.40 ÷ 100 = $4.49
Find Hosea's final cost.
$22.47 − $4.49 = $17.98

**Exercise 5: Interest Problems
pages 618–619**

1. (2) $3,600
First, find the interest for 1 year:

$$\frac{n}{60,000} = \frac{8}{100}$$

Cross multiply: 60,000 × 8 = 480,000
Divide: 480,000 ÷ 100 = $4800
Then, find the interest for 9 months:

9 months = $\frac{9}{12} = \frac{3}{4}$ year

$\frac{4800}{1} \times \frac{3}{4}$ = $3600 for 9 months

2. (3) $31,968.75
First, find the interest on the loan for 1 year:

$$\frac{n}{31,000} = \frac{12.5}{100}$$

Cross multiply:
31,000 × 12.5 = 387,500
Divide: 387,500 ÷ 100 = $3875 for 1 year
Then, find the interest for 90 days:

$\frac{90}{360} = \frac{1}{4}$ year

$3875 × $\frac{1}{4}$ = $968.75 for 90 days
Finally, find the total amount to be repaid:
$31,000 + 968.75 = $31,968.75

3. (1) $\dfrac{1500 \times 8\frac{1}{2}}{100}$

This represents how to solve the proportion

$$\frac{n}{1500} = \frac{8\frac{1}{2}}{100}$$

Cross multiply: 1500 × $8\frac{1}{2}$

Divide: (1500 × $8\frac{1}{2}$) ÷ 100 or

$$\frac{1500 \times 8\frac{1}{2}}{100}$$

4. (4) $4,500
Find the whole to find how much he borrowed:

$$\frac{360}{n} = \frac{8}{100}$$

Cross multiply: 360 × 100 = 36,000
Divide: 36,000 ÷ 8 = $4500

5. (1) $3255
First, find the total Ted needs:
$32,000 + $8500 + $2500 = $43,000
Then, find the amount he needs to borrow:
$43,000 − $12,000 saved = $31,000
Finally, find the interest for 1 year:

$$\frac{n}{31,000} = \frac{10.5}{100}$$

Cross multiply:
31,000 × 10.5 = 325,500
Divide: 325,500 ÷ 100 = $3255 interest

Exercise 6: Percent Review
pages 619–620

1. (5) $171.15
First, add the purchases:
$135.00 + $24.95 = $159.95
Then, find the tax:
$$\frac{n}{159.95} = \frac{7}{100}$$
Cross multiply: 159.95 × 7 = 1119.65
Divide: 1119.65 ÷ 100 = 11.1965 =
$11.20 tax
Then, find the total:
$159.95 + $11.20 = $171.15

2. (3) $15.90 − .20(15.90)
This represents the original cost
($15.90) less the 20% discount for the
sale.

3. (5) $15,272
First, find the amount to be financed:
$12,800 − $2500 = $10,300
Then, find one year's interest:
$$\frac{n}{10,300} = \frac{8}{100}$$
Cross multiply: 10,300 × 8 = 82,400
Divide: 82,400 ÷ 100 = $824
Then, find three years' interest:
$824 × 3 = $2472
Finally, find the total, including the
sale price of the car and the interest:
$12,800 + $2472 = $15,272
Note that you were asked to find the
total cost of the car, not the total cost
of the interest.

4. (5) not enough information is given
You are not told the current cost of
the car, so you cannot find the
discount rate.

5. (2) $2,200.50
Find the commission, which is a part
of the sales price.
$$\frac{n}{48,900} = \frac{4\frac{1}{2}}{100}$$
Cross multiply: 48,900 × $\frac{9}{2}$ = 220,050
Divide: 220,050 ÷ 100 = $2200.50

6. (4) 25
$$\frac{rent}{net\ income} = \frac{6000}{24,000} = \frac{1}{4}$$
$$4\overline{)1.00}^{\,.25} = 25\%$$

7. (2) $\frac{1}{10}$
$$\frac{savings}{income} = \frac{2400}{24,000} = \frac{1}{10}$$

8. (3) 15
First, find the total spent on
entertainment ($1200) and savings
($2400):
$1200 + $2400 = $3600
Then, find the percent this is of the
total expenses:
$$\frac{3600}{24,000} = \frac{n}{100}$$
Cross multiply:
3600 × 100 = 360,000
Divide: 360,000 ÷ 24,000 = 15

9. (5) $1597.50
First, find 6.5% of Margaret's
insurance:
$$\frac{n}{1500} = \frac{6.5}{100}$$
Cross multiply: 1500 × 6.5 = 9750
Divide: 9750 ÷ 100 = 97.50
Then, add this to her original
insurance payments:
$1500.00 + $97.50 = $1597.50

10. (5) not enough information is given
You cannot find an answer to this
question. Although you are told that
her property taxes rose 7%, you do
not know how much her property
taxes originally were.

11. (2) (35,821 × 67) ÷ 100
This represents the solution to the
following proportion to find net pay:
$$\frac{n}{35,821} = \frac{67}{100}$$
Cross multiply and divide:
(35,821 × 67) ÷ 100

CHAPTER 6: MEASUREMENT
Exercise 1: Conversions
page 623

1. Convert from a large unit (yards) to a
smaller unit (feet). Multiply 5 by the
number of feet in a yard (3 ft = 1 yd):
3 × 5 = **15 feet**

2. Convert from a small unit (ounces) to a
larger unit (pounds). Divide 40 by the
number of ounces in a pound (16 oz =
1 lb):
40 ÷ 16 = 2.5 or **2$\frac{1}{2}$ pounds**

3. Convert from a small unit (hours) to a
larger unit (days). Divide 96 by the
number of hours in a day (24 hr = 1 day):
96 ÷ 24 = **4 days**

4. Convert from a small unit (quarts) to a
larger unit (gallons). Divide 20 by the
number of quarts in a gallon (4 qt = 1
gal):
20 ÷ 4 = **5 gallons**

5. Convert from a large unit (quarts) to a
smaller unit (ounces). Multiply 2 by the
number of ounces in a quart (32 oz = 1
qt):
32 × 2 = **64 ounces**

6. Convert from a large unit (days) to a
smaller unit (minutes). First, find the
number of minutes in one day (1 day =
24 hr, and 1 hr = 60 min):
24 × 60 = 1440
Then, multiply that total by 2 for 2 days:
1440 × 2 = **2880 minutes**

7. Convert a small unit (pints) to a larger
unit (quarts). Divide 3 by the number of
pints in a quart (2 pts = 1 qt):
3 ÷ 2 = **1.5 quarts**

8. Convert a small unit (feet) to a larger unit (miles). Divide 14,110 by the number of feet in a mile (5280 ft = 1 mi):
14,110 ÷ 5280 = 2.67 = **2.7 miles** (to the nearest tenth)

9. First, find how many ounces are in a half-gallon. Since a half-gallon is two quarts, multiply 2 by 32 ounces (1 quart):
32 × 2 = 64 oz in a half-gallon
Then, divide by 8 to find how many 8-ounce glasses there are in 64 ounces:
64 ÷ 8 = 8 eight-ounce glasses
Divide 96 cents by 8 to find out how much each eight-ounce glass costs:
96 ÷ 8 = 12
Each eight-ounce glass of milk costs 12 cents.

10. First, find how many feet are in 2 miles: Change 2 miles (a larger unit) to feet (a smaller unit). Multiply 2 by the number of feet in a mile (1 mi = 5280 ft):
5280 × 2 = 10,560
Then, divide that by 15 feet to find the number of shrubs needed:
10,560 ÷ 15 = **704 shrubs**

Exercise 2: Basic Operations with Measurement
page 625

1. **6 ft 7 in**
$$\begin{array}{r} 9\text{ ft } 4\text{ in} \\ -2\text{ ft } 9\text{ in} \end{array} = \begin{array}{r} 8\text{ ft } 16\text{ in} \\ -2\text{ ft } 9\text{ in} \\ \hline 6\text{ ft } 7\text{ in} \end{array}$$

2. **4 hr 20 min**
$$\begin{array}{r} 1\text{ hr } 20\text{ min} \\ +3\text{ hr} \\ \hline 4\text{ hr } 20\text{ min} \end{array}$$

3. **121 lb 12 oz**
$$\begin{array}{r} 130\text{ lb} \\ -8\text{ lb } 4\text{ oz} \end{array} = \begin{array}{r} 129\text{ lb } 16\text{ oz} \\ -8\text{ lb } 4\text{ oz} \\ \hline 121\text{ lb } 12\text{ oz} \end{array}$$

4. **37.1 in or 3 ft 1.1 in**
$$\begin{array}{r} 5.3\text{ in} \\ \times\quad 7 \\ \hline 37.1\text{ in} \end{array}$$

5. **7 ft 6 in**
$$\begin{array}{r} 7\text{ ft}\quad 6\text{ in} \\ 3\overline{)22\text{ ft}\quad 6\text{ in}} \\ 21\text{ ft} \\ \hline 1 = +12\text{ in} \\ \hline 18\text{ in} \\ 18\text{ in} \\ \hline 0 \end{array}$$

6. **40 min**
$$\begin{array}{r} 0\text{ hr}\quad 40\text{ min} \\ 8\overline{)5\text{ hr}\quad 20\text{ min}} \\ 0 \\ \hline 5\text{ hr} = +300\text{ min} \\ \hline 320 \\ 320 \\ \hline 0 \end{array}$$

7. **7 oz**
$$\begin{array}{r} 1\text{ lb } 4\text{ oz} \\ -\quad 13\text{ oz} \end{array} = \begin{array}{r} 20\text{ oz} \\ -13\text{ oz} \\ \hline 7\text{ oz} \end{array}$$

8. **1 ft 8 in**
$$\begin{array}{r} 1\text{ ft}\qquad 8\text{ in} \\ 4\overline{)6\text{ ft}\qquad 8\text{ in}} \\ 4\text{ ft} \\ \hline 2\text{ ft} = +24\text{ in} \\ \hline 32\text{ in} \\ 32\text{ in} \\ \hline 0 \end{array}$$

9. **(3) $3.25**
First, find the number of inches needed:
45 × 4 = 180 in
Then, find the number of yards in 180 inches (36 in = 1 yd):
180 ÷ 36 = 5 yd
Then, find the cost of 5 yards:
5 × $.65 = $3.25

10. **(4) 19($415)**
1 lb 3 oz = 16 oz + 3 oz = 19 oz

11. **(5) $107.50**
First, find the total number of hours:
$$\begin{array}{r} 2\text{ hr } 30\text{ min} \\ 3\text{ hr} \\ 4\text{ hr } 45\text{ min} \\ 7\text{ hr } 15\text{ min} \\ +\ 4\text{ hr} \\ \hline 20\text{ hr } 90\text{ min} \end{array} = 21\text{ hr } 30\text{ min} = 21\tfrac{1}{2}\text{ hr}$$
Then, find the total pay:
$$21\tfrac{1}{2}\text{ hr} \times \$5 = \frac{43}{2} \times \frac{5}{1} = \$107.50$$

Exercise 3: Metric Measurement
page 628
This chart will help you follow the solutions below:

kilo hecto deca	basic unit	deci centi milli

1. 500 meters to centimeters: Move the decimal point 2 places right.
500.00 m = **50,000 cm**

2. 7423 milligrams to grams: Move the decimal point 3 places left.
7423 mg = **7.423 g**

3. 50.3 centimeters to millimeters: Move the decimal point 1 place right.
50.3 cm = **503 mm**

4. .027 kilograms to grams: Move the decimal point 3 places right.
.027 kg = **27 g**

5. First, 1 kiloliter to liter: Move the decimal point 3 places right.
1.000 kl = 1000 l
Second, add 47 liters to 1000 liters = **1047 liters**

6. First, 42 centimeters to meters: Move the decimal point 2 places left.
42 cm = .42 m
Second, add 6 meters + .42 meters = **6.42 m**

7. First, add
400 cm + 15 cm + 1285 cm + 15 cm
= 1715 cm
Second, 1715 centimeters to meters:
Move the decimal point 2 places left.
1715 cm = **17.15 m**

8. First, one week = 7 days
857 mg × 7 = 5999 mg
Second, 5999 milligrams to grams: Move
the decimal point 3 places left.
5999 mg = **5.999 g**

9. 1000 meters to kilometers: Move the
decimal point 3 places left.
1000 m = 1.000 = **1 km**

10. $\dfrac{1\,km}{.621\,mi} = \dfrac{80\,km}{n}$

$\dfrac{.621 \times 80}{1} = 49.68$ mph in Canada

The U.S. allows 55 mph, and Canada
allows 49.68 mph.
The U.S. allows a faster speed.

11. (2) .75 × $6.40

12. (3) 91
.91 × 100 = 91

Exercise 4: Money Problems
pages 630–631

1. (4) $101.33
First: $49.95 + $29.90 + $14.85 =
$94.70 subtotal
Second: $94.70 × .07 = $6.63 tax
Third: $94.70 + $6.63 = $101.33 total

2. (3) $200
First, find the number of pounds in
two tons.
$\dfrac{1\,T}{2000\,lb} = \dfrac{2\,T}{n\,lb}$

$\dfrac{2000 \times 2}{1} = 4000$ lb

Then, find the total number of bags:
4000 lb ÷ 50 lb = 80 bags
Then, find the profit:
$5.95 × 80 = $476 income
2 × $138 = $276 expenses
$476 − $276 = $200 profit

3. (2) $15.68
First, find the number of yards in 48
feet:
$\dfrac{1\,yd}{3\,ft} = \dfrac{n\,yd}{48\,ft}$

$\dfrac{1 \times 48}{3} = \dfrac{48}{3} = 16$ yd

Then, find the total cost:
16 × $.98 = $15.68

4. (4) $8\dfrac{1\,qt}{4\,c} = \dfrac{3\,qt}{n\,c}$

$\dfrac{4 \times 3}{1} = \dfrac{12}{1} = 12$ cups

$12 \div 1\frac{1}{2} = 8$ servings

5. (1) Happy Bran
Happy Bran:
$\dfrac{\$1.79}{25\,oz} = \dfrac{n}{1\,oz}$

$\dfrac{1.79 \times 1}{25} = \$.0716 = \$.07$

Wheatos:
$\dfrac{\$1.49}{12\,oz} = \dfrac{n}{1\,oz}$

$\dfrac{1.49 \times 1}{12} = \$.1242 = \$.12$

Friendly Flakes:
$\dfrac{\$2.19}{29\,oz} = \dfrac{n}{1\,oz}$

$\dfrac{2.19 \times 1}{29} = \$.0755 = \$.08$

Sugar Snaps:
$\dfrac{\$2.39}{20\,oz} = \dfrac{n}{1\,oz}$

$\dfrac{2.39 \times 1}{20} = \$.1195 = \$.12$

6. (2) 12¢
$\dfrac{\$6.48}{36} = \$.18$ per capsule

$.18 × 2 = $.36 per dose
$\dfrac{\$4.32}{36} = \$.12$ per capsule

$.12 × 2 = $.24 per dose
$.36 − $.24 = $.12

7. (4) $.29 + 3($.23)

Exercise 5: Time Problems
pages 632–633

1. (2) 3
75¢ ÷ 5¢ = 15¢
15 × 12 min = 180 min
$\dfrac{1\,hr}{60\,min} = \dfrac{n}{180\,min}$ $\dfrac{180 \times 1}{60} = 3$ hr

2. (3) $4\frac{1}{2} \times 8 \times 5 \times 4$

First: 10 A.M.
to noon = 2 hr
noon to
2:30 P.M. = + $2\frac{1}{2}$ hr
$4\frac{1}{2}$ hr each day

Second: Multiply $4\frac{1}{2}$ hours per day by
$8 per hour by 5 days per
week by 4 weeks.

3. (1) 362.5
8:30 A.M. to noon = $3\frac{1}{2}$ hrs
noon to 3:45 P.M. = + $3\frac{3}{4}$ hrs
Total time $7\frac{1}{4}$ hrs
$7\frac{1}{4}$ hrs × 50 = 362.5 miles

4. (5) $4\frac{3}{4}$

5/20	8 hr
5/21	$9\frac{1}{2}$ hr
5/22	$10\frac{3}{4}$ hr
5/23	8 hr
5/24	+ $8\frac{1}{2}$ hr
Total	$44\frac{3}{4}$ hr

$44\frac{3}{4} - 40 = 4\frac{3}{4}$ hr overtime

5. (4) **$371**

$40 \times \$7.85 = \quad \$314$
$4\frac{3}{4} \times \$12 \quad = + \quad 57$
Total $\quad\quad\quad \$371$

6. (4) **$248.57**

$1\% + 25\% + 7\% = 33\%$
$33\% \times \$371 = \$122.43$ deductions
$\$371 - \$122.43 = \$248.57$ take-home pay

7. (2) $960 \times \frac{1}{3}$

$d = rt$ $\quad\quad$ (20 min = $\frac{1}{3}$ hr)

$\quad = 960(\frac{1}{3})$ or $960 \times \frac{1}{3}$

8. (5) $75 \div 2\frac{1}{2}$

75 miles $\div 2\frac{1}{2}$ hr

Exercise 6: Scales and Meters
page 636

1. (4) $2\frac{1}{2}$ in

$\frac{1 \text{ in}}{180 \text{ mi}} = \frac{n \text{ in}}{450 \text{ mi}}$

$\frac{1 \times 450}{180} = 2\frac{1}{2}$ in

2. (3) **1 in = 200 mi**

$\frac{2000 \text{ mi}}{10 \text{ in}} = \frac{n \text{ mi}}{1 \text{ in}}$

$\frac{2000 \times 1}{10} = 200$ miles

3. (1) **$113.63**

New reading $\quad$ 4752 kwh
Old reading $\quad - 3843$ kwh
difference $\quad\quad$ 909 kwh

$\frac{\$.125}{1 \text{ kwh}} = \frac{n \text{ dollars}}{909 \text{ kwh}}$

$\frac{\$.125 \times 909}{1} = \$113.625$ or $\$113.63$

4. (4) **$77.89**

First, find the cost of 100 cu ft:
$\quad \$.3065 \times 173 = 53.0245 = \$53.02$
Then, find the subtotal:
$\quad \$53.02 + \$19.16 + \$2.00 =$
$\quad \$74.18$ subtotal
Find the 5% tax and add it to the subtotal:
$\quad \$74.18 \times .05 = 3.709 = \$3.71$
$\quad \$74.18 + \$3.71 = \$77.89$ total

CHAPTER 7: GRAPHS, STATISTICS, AND PROBABILITY

Exercise 1: Mean and Median
pages 638–639

1. **$3,713.14**
$4300 + 5600 + 1875 + 4250 + 2876 + 4108$
$\quad + 2983 = 25,992$
$25,992 \div 7 = 3,713.142 = \$3,713.14$

2. **44 points**
$37 + 63 + 42 + 24 + 44 + 51 = 261$
$261 \div 6 = 43.5 = 44$ points

3. **61 points**
Find the middle numbers:

45 $\quad$ 48 $\quad$ | 53 $\quad$ 68 | $\quad$ 72 $\quad$ 74

Find the average: $53 + 68 = 121$
$\quad\quad\quad\quad\quad\quad 121 \div 2 = 60.5,$
$\quad\quad\quad\quad\quad\quad$ or 61 points

4. **60 points**
$48 + 45 + 53 + 72 + 68 + 74 = 360$
$360 \div 6 = 60$ points

5. **$44.80**
Arrange from smallest to largest and find the middle number:

$39.95 $\quad$ $42.88 $\quad$ | $44.80 | $\quad$ $48.95 $\quad$ $52.25

Exercise 2: Circle Graphs
page 640

1. **$68,383.33**
Find the total expenses for 3 years:
$\quad 92,000 + 156,000 + 125,000 = 373,000$
Find the average for one year:
$\quad 373,000 \div 3 = \$124,333.33$
Find 55% of this:
$\quad \$124,333.33 \times .55 = \$68,383.33$

2. **$4800**

$\frac{n}{32,000} \times \frac{15}{100} = \frac{32,000 \times 15}{100} = \$4800$

3. **$666.67**
First, find the yearly expenses for rent:

$\frac{n}{32,000} \times \frac{25}{100} = \frac{32,000 \times 25}{100} = \$8000$

Then, find the monthly expenses for rent:
$\quad \$8000 \div 12 = \$666.67$

4. (5) **not enough information is given**
$\quad$ Nothing is said about clothing on the graph.

5. (1) **1 to 10**

$\frac{\text{savings}}{\text{total}} = \frac{10\%}{100\%} = \frac{10}{100} = \frac{1}{10}$

Exercise 3: Bar Graphs
page 641

1. **$17,000**

2. **$19,750**
First, find the total:
$\quad 13,000 + 20,000 + 21,000 + 25,000 =$
$\quad \$79,000$
Then, find the average:
$\quad \$79,000 \div 4 = \$19,750$

3. (4) **1993**

4. (2) **$2,000**
$\quad \$23,000 - \$21,000 = \$2,000$

**Exercise 4: Line Graphs
pages 642–643**
1. sales; 1990; 1993
2. ten thousands of dollars
3. months of the year
4. $60,000
5. $90,000
6. higher

**Exercise 5: Mixed Graph Practice
pages 643–644**
1. $\frac{3}{100}$

$$\frac{\text{savings}}{\text{earnings}} = \frac{3\%}{100\%} = \frac{3}{100}$$

2. **$600**
First, find the yearly take-home pay:
$$\frac{n}{12,000} = \frac{60}{100} \qquad \frac{12,000 \times 60}{100} = 7200$$
Then, find the monthly pay:
$7200 \div 12 = \$600$

3. **$1750**
$$\frac{n}{25,000} = \frac{7}{100} \qquad \frac{25,000 \times 7}{100} = \$1750$$

4. **$33,333.33**
$$\frac{20,000}{n} = \frac{60}{100} \qquad \frac{20,000 \times 100}{60} = \$33,333.33$$

5. **$15,120**
First, find the total deductions:
$27\% + 7\% + 3\% = 37\%$
$$\frac{n}{24,000} = \frac{37}{100} \qquad \frac{24,000 \times 37}{100} = \$8880$$
Now, subtract to find Mike's take-home pay.
$\$24,000 - 8880 = \$15,120$

6. **200 ft** $\quad 1450 - 1250 = 200$ ft
7. **1557 ft** $\quad 1450 + 107 = 1557$ ft
8. **2.45 times as tall**
$$\frac{\text{World Trade Center}}{\text{Washington Monument}} = \frac{1350}{550} = 2.45$$
9. **31%**
$$\frac{\text{Notre Dame Cathedral}}{\text{Sears Tower}} = \frac{450}{1450} = \text{approximately } 31\%$$
10. **$1008\frac{1}{3}$ ft**
$450 + 550 + 1000 + 1250 + 1350 + 1450 = 6050$
$6050 \div 6 = 1008\frac{1}{3}$ ft
11. **1125 ft**
$1000 + 1250 = 2250$
$2250 \div 2 = 1125$ ft
12. **111 floors**
$1450 \div 13 = 111.5$ or 111 floors
13. **7500 people**
$4500 + 3000 = 7500$ people
14. April and July
15. **$69,750**
Youth: 4000 at $5.75 = $23,000
Adults: 5500 at $8.50 = $\underline{46,750}$
$69,750

**Exercise 6: Probability
pages 645–646**
1. $\frac{1}{52}$ $\quad \dfrac{1 \text{ ace of spades}}{52 \text{ cards}} = \frac{1}{52}$

2. 25% $\quad \dfrac{13 \text{ hearts}}{52 \text{ cards}} = \frac{1}{4} = 25\%$

3. $\frac{1}{13}$ $\quad \dfrac{4 \text{ kings}}{52 \text{ cards}} = \frac{1}{13}$

4. (1) $\frac{1}{6}$ $\quad \dfrac{1 \text{ possibility}}{6 \text{ faces}} = \frac{1}{6}$

5. (4) $33\frac{1}{3}\%$
$$\frac{2 \text{ possibilities}}{6 \text{ faces}} = \frac{1}{3} = 33\frac{1}{3}\%$$

6. (5) 50%
$$\frac{3 \text{ possibilities}}{6 \text{ faces}} = \frac{3}{6} = 50\%$$

7. (1) 0 $\quad$ This is not possible.

8. (5) $66\frac{2}{3}\%$
$$\frac{4 \text{ possibilities}}{6 \text{ faces}} = \frac{2}{3} = 66\frac{2}{3}\%$$

9. (5) 100%
10. (2) $\frac{1}{12}$ $\quad \dfrac{\text{March}}{12 \text{ months}} = \frac{1}{12}$

11. (2) $\frac{1}{10}$ $\quad \dfrac{1 \text{ digit}}{\text{the numbers } 0\text{–}9} = \frac{1}{10}$

12. (3) $\frac{1}{2}$ $\quad \dfrac{1 \text{ head}}{2 \text{ possibilities}} = \frac{1}{2}$

13. (4) $\frac{3}{4}$
$960 - 240 = 720$ $\quad \dfrac{720 \text{ good pots}}{960 \text{ pots}} = \frac{3}{4}$

**Exercise 7: Dependent Probability
pages 647–648**
1. $\frac{1}{13}$ $\quad \dfrac{4 \text{ aces}}{52 \text{ cards}} = \frac{1}{13}$

2. $\frac{1}{17}$ $\quad \dfrac{3 \text{ aces}}{51 \text{ cards}} = \frac{1}{17}$

3. $\frac{4}{51}$ $\quad \dfrac{4 \text{ aces}}{51 \text{ cards}} = \frac{4}{51}$

4. $\frac{4}{17}$ $\quad \dfrac{12 \text{ spades}}{51 \text{ cards}} = \frac{12}{51} = \frac{4}{17}$

5. $\frac{3}{10}$ $\quad \dfrac{3 \text{ women}}{10 \text{ people}} = \frac{3}{10}$

6. $\frac{2}{3}$ $\quad \dfrac{6 \text{ men}}{9 \text{ people}} = \frac{6}{9} = \frac{2}{3}$

7. $\frac{1}{8}$ $\quad \dfrac{1 \text{ woman}}{8 \text{ people}} = \frac{1}{8}$

8. $\frac{2}{9}$ $\quad \dfrac{2 \text{ quarters}}{9 \text{ coins}} = \frac{2}{9}$

9. $\frac{1}{4}$ $\quad \dfrac{2 \text{ quarters}}{8 \text{ coins}} = \frac{1}{4}$

10. $\frac{1}{7}$ $\quad \dfrac{1 \text{ nickel}}{7 \text{ coins}} = \frac{1}{7}$

CHAPTER 8: NUMERATION

Exercise 1: Powers
page 650

1. **25** $5 \times 5 = 25$
2. **$\frac{1}{4}$** $\frac{1}{2} \times \frac{1}{2} = \frac{1}{4}$
3. **729** $9 \times 9 \times 9 = 729$
4. **$\frac{27}{64}$** $\frac{3}{4} \times \frac{3}{4} \times \frac{3}{4} = \frac{27}{64}$
5. **.09** $.3 \times .3 = .09$
6. **1**   1 to any power is 1.
7. **16** $2 \times 2 \times 2 \times 2 = 16$
8. **1.44** $1.2 \times 1.2 = 1.44$
9. **1**   Any number to the 0 power is 1.
10. **10,000** $10 \times 10 \times 10 \times 10 = 10,000$
11. **625** $25 \times 25 = 625$
12. **.008** $(.2)(.2)(.2) = .008$
13. **$\frac{4}{9}$** $\left(\frac{2}{3}\right)\left(\frac{2}{3}\right) = \frac{4}{9}$
14. **27** $3 \times 3 \times 3 = 27$
15. **0** $0 \times 0 = 0$

Exercise 2: Simplifying Square Roots
page 650

1. **$3\sqrt{2}$** $\sqrt{18} = \sqrt{9 \cdot 2} = 3\sqrt{2}$
2. **$4\sqrt{3}$** $\sqrt{48} = \sqrt{16 \cdot 3} = 4\sqrt{3}$
3. **$2\sqrt{2}$** $\sqrt{8} = \sqrt{4 \cdot 2} = 2\sqrt{2}$
4. **$6\sqrt{2}$** $\sqrt{72} = \sqrt{36 \cdot 2} = 6\sqrt{2}$
5. **$3\sqrt{3}$** $\sqrt{27} = \sqrt{9 \cdot 3} = 3\sqrt{3}$

Exercise 3: Square Roots
page 651

1. 9
2. 1
3. 5.3 (approx.); $\sqrt{4 \cdot 7} = 2\sqrt{7}$ (simplified)
4. 3
5. 12
6. 7.2 (approx.); $\sqrt{4 \cdot 13} = 2\sqrt{13}$ (simplified)
7. 3.2 (approx.)
8. 4
9. 11
10. 9.5 (approx.); $\sqrt{9 \cdot 10} = 3\sqrt{10}$ (simplified)
11. 15
12. 20
13. 5.7 (approx.); $\sqrt{16 \cdot 2} = 4\sqrt{2}$ (simplified)
14. 8
15. 0

Exercise 4: Order of Operations
page 652

1. **0** $\dfrac{7-5}{2} + 3 - 5$
   $2 + 3 - 5 = 0$
2. **29** $\dfrac{8 \times 3}{24} + 5$
   $24 + 5 = 29$
3. **23** $8 + \dfrac{3 \times 5}{15}$
   $8 + 15 = 23$
4. **8** $6 + \dfrac{21 \div 3}{7} - 5$
   $6 + 7 - 5 = 8$
5. **5** $\dfrac{40 \div 2}{20} - \dfrac{5 \times 3}{15} = 5$

6. **28** $3 + 5^2$
   $3 + 25 = 28$
7. **20** $15 - 3 + 2^3$
   $15 - 3 + 8 = 20$
8. **33** $4 + 3^3 + 3 \times 2 - 2^2$
   $4 + 27 + 3 \times 2 - 4$
   $4 + 27 + 6 - 4 = 33$

Exercise 5: More Order of Operations
page 653

1. **83** $2 + 3^2 \times (4 + 5)$
   $2 + (9 \times 9) = 83$
2. **15** $\dfrac{(12 - 5)}{7} + \dfrac{(14 - 6)}{8} = 15$
3. **40** $49 - (28 - 19)$
   $49 - 9 = 40$
4. **44** $8 + 6 \times (10 - 2^2)$
   $8 + 6 \times (10 - 4)$
   $8 + 6 \times 6$
   $8 + 36 = 44$

Exercise 6: Evaluating Formulas
page 654

1. **144 sq in** $A = s^2$
   $A = 12^2 = 144$
2. **125 cu in** $V = s^3$
   $V = 5^3 = 125$
3. **\$288** $i = prt$
   $i = (800)(.12)(3) = \$288$
4. **28.26 sq in** $A = \pi r^2$
   $A = (3.14)(3^2)$
   $A = (3.14)(9) = 28.26$
5. **76 miles** $d = rt$
   $d = (38)(2) = 76$
6. **1130.4 cu in** $V = \pi r^2 h$
   $V = (3.14)(6^2)(10)$
   $V = (3.14)(36)(10)$
   $= 1130.4$
7. **54 sq cm** $A = \frac{1}{2}bh$
   $A = \dfrac{(12)(9)}{2} = \dfrac{108}{2} = 54$
8. **40 ft** $P = 2l + 2w$
   Change 2 yards to 6 feet:
   $P = 2(14) + 2(6)$
   $P = 28 + 12 = 40$

Exercise 7: Scientific Notation
page 656

1. 8.2×10^{-3}
2. 5×10^2
3. 3.82×10^4
4. 5.8×10^{-1}
5. $1.624 \times 1000 = \mathbf{1624}$
6. $3.12 \times .10 = \mathbf{.312}$
7. $8.24 \times 1 = \mathbf{8.24}$
8. $7.13 \times 1000 = \mathbf{7130}$

CHAPTER 9: GEOMETRY

Exercise 1: Pairs of Angles
pages 658–659

1. **38°**   because $\angle DBC$ and $\angle ABD$ are supplementary angles.
   $180° - 142° = 38°$
2. **38°**   because $\angle ABE$ and $\angle DBC$ are vertical angles.
3. **142°**   because $\angle EBC$ and $\angle ABD$ are vertical angles.
4. **38°** $90° - 52° = 38°$
5. **105°** $180° - 75° = 105°$

Exercise 2: Angles in Triangles
page 660

1. $\angle B = 70°$
Add the two known angles:
$70° + 40° = 110°$
Subtract that sum from 180°:
$180° - 110° = 70°$

2. $\angle Q = 125°$
Add the two known angles:
$30° + 25° = 55°$
Subtract that sum from 180°:
$180° - 55° = 125°$

3. $\angle X = 90°$
Add the two known angles:
$30° + 60° = 90°$
Subtract that sum from 180°:
$180° - 90° = 90°$

4. $\angle E = 60°$
Add the two known angles:
$60° + 60° = 120°$
Subtract that sum from 180°:
$180° - 120° = 60°$

Exercise 3: Types of Triangles
pages 660–661

1. (a) Scalene triangle—because all three sides have different lengths
(b) Right triangle—because the triangle has one right angle
(c) Isosceles triangle—because two sides and two angles of the triangle are equal
(d) Equilateral triangle—because all three sides of the triangle are equal
(e) Right triangle—because $\angle C$ is a right angle

2. $\triangle RST$ is a right triangle.
Add the two given angles:
$70° + 20° = 90°$
Subtract from the number of degrees in a triangle:
$180° - 90° = 90°$

3. 76°
Find the total of the base angles:
$52° \times 2 = 104°$
Subtract from the total degrees in a triangle:
$180° - 104° = 76°$

4. 30°
Find the total of the known angles—you are told that this is a right triangle (one angle of 90°) and that there is a 60° angle.
$90° + 60° = 150°$
Subtract from the total degrees in a triangle:
$180° - 150° = 30°$

Exercise 4: Similar Triangles
pages 662–663

1. 9 in $\dfrac{DF}{AC} = \dfrac{DE}{AB}$

$\dfrac{DF}{15} = \dfrac{6}{10}$

$\dfrac{15 \times 6}{10} = \dfrac{90}{10} = 9$ in

2. 12 ft $\dfrac{t}{8} = \dfrac{18}{12}$

$t = \dfrac{18 \times 8}{12} = \dfrac{144}{12} = 12$ ft

3. (a) First recognize two similar triangles and draw them. Set up a proportion:
$\dfrac{d}{b} = \dfrac{c}{a}$

(b) 150 ft
$\dfrac{d}{6} = \dfrac{50}{2}$
$d = \dfrac{50 \times 6}{2} = \dfrac{300}{2} = 150$ ft

4. $31\frac{1}{2}$ ft

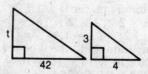

(Remember: a yardstick is 3 feet long.)
$\dfrac{t}{3} = \dfrac{42}{4} = \dfrac{42 \times 3}{4} = \dfrac{126}{4} = 31\frac{1}{2}$ ft

Exercise 5: The Pythagorean Theorem
pages 665–666

1. (a) $c = 15$ $c^2 = a^2 + b^2$
$c^2 = 9^2 + 12^2$
$c^2 = 81 + 144$
$c^2 = 225$
$c = \sqrt{225} = 15$

(b) $3 = a$ $c^2 = a^2 + b^2$
$5^2 = a^2 + 4^2$
$25 = a^2 + 16$
$25 - 16 = a^2$
$9 = a^2$
$\sqrt{9} = a$
$3 = a$

(c) $c = 26$ $c^2 = a^2 + b^2$
$c^2 = 10^2 + 24^2$
$c^2 = 100 + 576 = 676$
$c = \sqrt{676} = 26$

2. $c = 25$ in $c^2 = a^2 + b^2$
$c^2 = 15^2 + 20^2$
$c^2 = 225 + 400 = 625$
$c = \sqrt{625} = 25$

3. Yes, the triangle is a right triangle.
Side 1 is 20 in; $20^2 = 400$ $a^2 = 400$
Side 2 is 21 in; $21^2 = 441$ $b^2 = 441$
Side 3 is 29 in; $29^2 = 841$ $c^2 = 841$
$a^2 + b^2 = c^2$
$400 + 441 = 841$

4. (3) 100 $c^2 = a^2 + b^2$
$c^2 = 60^2 + 80^2$
$c^2 = 3600 + 6400 = 10,000$
$c = \sqrt{10,000} = 100$ meters

5. (5) 75

First draw a sketch of the problem. A television antenna is perpendicular to the flat roof. There are three guy wires, but draw only one and then multiply the answer by 3 to find out how much wire is used on the antenna.

$c^2 = a^2 + b^2$
$c^2 = 7^2 + 24^2$
$c^2 = 49 + 576 = 625$
$c = \sqrt{625} = 25$
$3 \times 25 = 75$ feet of wire

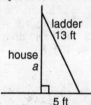

antenna wire
24 ft c
hook
roof
7 ft

6. (2) 12

First draw a sketch of the problem.

$c^2 = a^2 + b^2$
$13^2 = a^2 + 5^2$
$169 = a^2 + 25$
$169 - 25 = a^2$
$144 = a^2$
$\sqrt{144} = a$
$12 = a$

ladder
13 ft
house
a
5 ft

Exercise 6: Perimeter
pages 668–669

1. 360 ft $P = 4s$
$P = 4 \times 90 = 360$ ft

2. $3\frac{1}{4}$ ft

First, find the number of inches:
$P = 2l + 2w$
$P = 2\left(8\frac{1}{2}\right) + 2(11) = 2\left(\frac{17}{2}\right) + 22$
$P = 17 + 22 = 39$ inches
Then, change inches to feet:
$39 \div 12 = 3\frac{3}{12} = 3\frac{1}{4}$ feet

3. 49.9 in $P = a + b + c$
$P = 16.5 + 12.4 + 21 = 49.9$ in

4. $2691

First, find the total perimeter:
$P = 2l + 2w$
$= 2(400) + 2(224)$
$= 800 + 448 = 1248$ yd
Then, convert to feet:
$1248 \times 3 = 3744$ ft
Then, find the number of 8-foot sections:
$3744 \div 8 = 468$ sections
Finally, find the total cost:
$468 \times 5\frac{3}{4} = \frac{468}{1} \times \frac{23}{4} = 117 \times 23 = \$2691$

5. 70 m

First, find the lengths of the sides that are not labeled:
$20 - 15.3 = 4.7$
$10.8 + 4.2 = 15.0$
Then, add all of the sides together:
$20 + 4.2 + 4.7 + 10.8 + 15.3 + 15 = 70$ m

6. 194 ft

Find the perimeter:
$P = 2l + 2w$
$= 2(70) + 2(48) = 236$
Subtract the length of the house:
$236 - 42 = 194$ feet

7. 8 times

First, find the perimeter of the block:
$P = 2l + 2w$
$= 2\left(\frac{1}{4}\right) + 2\left(\frac{1}{8}\right)$
$= \frac{2}{4} + \frac{2}{8} = \frac{4}{8} + \frac{2}{8} = \frac{6}{8} = \frac{3}{4}$ mile

Then, find how many times around the block equals 6 miles:

$6 \div \frac{3}{4} = \frac{6}{1} \times \frac{4}{3} = \frac{24}{3} = 8$ times

8. 97.68 m

The perimeter of the rink includes two sides of 30 meters and the circumference of two half-circles (or one full circle). Find the circumference of the circle:
$C = \pi d$
$= 3.14(12) = 37.68$ meters
Add the given sides to the circumference:
$30 + 30 + 37.68 = 97.68$ meters

Exercise 7: Area
pages 670–671

1. 128.7 m² $A = lw$
$= 14.3 \times 9$
$= 128.7$ m²

2. 75.09 sq in

This figure consists of two shapes.
Square: $A = s^2$
$= 4.7 \times 4.7$
$= 22.09$ sq in
Rectangle: $A = lw$
$= 5.3 \times 10$
$= 53$ sq in
Add together for total area:
$53 + 22.09 = 75.09$ sq in

10 in
4.7
10 in
5.3 in
5.3 in

3. $\frac{11}{14}$ sq in $A = \pi r^2$
$= \frac{22}{7} \times \left(\frac{1}{2}\right)^2$
$= \frac{22}{7} \times \frac{1}{4}$
$= \frac{11}{7} \times \frac{1}{2} = \frac{11}{14}$ sq in

4. 50 sq yd

First, find the area of the room:
$30 \times 15 = 450$ sq ft
Then, divide by 9 to get the number of square yards:
$450 \div 9 = 50$ sq yd

5. $345

First, find the area of the room:
$15 \times 20 = 300$ sq ft
Then, find the cost of the office:
$300 \times \$1.15 = \$345$

6. 78.5 sq ft

The largest possible diameter for this rug is 10 feet, so the radius is 5 feet.

The area is: $A = \pi r^2$
$= 3.14\,(5^2)$
$= 78.5$ sq ft

7. 200 sq ft
$A = lw$
$= 20 \times 10$
$= 200$

8. 10%
Find the area of the pool:
$A = \pi r^2$
$= 3.14 \times 9^2 = 254.34$ sq ft
Find the area of the yard:
$A = lw$
$= 45 \times 58 = 2610$ sq ft
Round the area of the pool and make a ratio:
$$\frac{\text{area of pool}}{\text{area of yard}} = \frac{254}{2610}$$
$$\frac{254}{2610} = \frac{n}{100} = \frac{254 \times 100}{2610}$$
$$\frac{25,400}{2610} = 9.7; \text{ rounds to } 10\%$$

9. 22.22 sq yd
First, find the area of the patio:
$A = lw = 20 \times 10 = 200$ sq ft
Then, divide by 9 (number of square feet in a square yard):
$200 \div 9 = 22.22$ sq yd

10. 4 times larger
First, find the area of the pool:
$A = \pi r^2 = 3.14 \times 9^2 = 254.34$
Then, find the area of the garden:
$A = s^2 = 8^2 = 64$
Then find $\frac{\text{pool}}{\text{garden}}$
$\frac{254}{64} = 3.97 = 4$ times larger

Exercise 8: Volume
page 672

1. 72 cu ft $V = lwh$
$= (6)(3)(4)$
$= 72$ cu ft

2. 45 gallons
Find the volume of the fish tank:
$V = (18)(12)(48)$
$= 10,368$ cu in
Find how many gallons will fit in this tank:
$10,368 \div 231 = 44.9 = 45$ gallons

3. 500 cu ft
Convert 6 inches to $\frac{1}{2}$ foot:
$V = (25)(40)(\frac{1}{2})$
$= 500$ cu ft

4. $\frac{1}{8}$
Find the volume of each cube:
$V = 2^3 = 8$ cu in
$V = 4^3 = 64$ cu in
Compare the two with a ratio:
$\frac{\text{small cube}}{\text{large cube}} = \frac{8}{64} = \frac{1}{8}$

5. 25,872 cu ft
$V = \pi r^2 h$
$= \frac{22}{7}(14^2)(42)$
$= 22(196)(6) = 25,872$ cu ft

Exercise 9: Review of Geometry
pages 673–674

1. (3) 33
First, find the perimeter of each window.
Window A:
$2l + 2w = 2(36) + 2(54) = 180$ in
Window B:
$2l + 2w = 2(60) + 2(48) = \underline{216 \text{ in}}$
Total $= \overline{396 \text{ in}}$
Then, find how many feet this is:
$396 \div 12 = 33$ feet

2. (4) 230 $V = lwh$
$= 11\frac{1}{2} \times 8 \times 2\frac{1}{2}$
$= \frac{23}{2} \times \frac{8}{1} \times \frac{5}{2}$
$= 23 \times 2 \times 5 = 230$ cu in

3. (1) $(3.14)(1.5)^2(4)$
This represents substitution in the formula $V = \pi r^2 h$. The radius, r, which is $\frac{1}{2}$ the diameter (3), is 1.5.

4. (2) 8 $\quad c^2 = a^2 + b^2$
$17^2 = 15^2 + b^2$
$289 = 225 + b^2$
$289 - 225 = b^2$
$64 = b^2$
$8 \text{ in} = b$

5. (3) 1386 $A = \pi r^2$
$= (\frac{22}{7})(21)^2$
$= (\frac{22}{7})(\frac{21 \times 21}{1})$
$= (22)(63) = 1386$ sq mi

6. (5) not enough information is given
To find this, you would need the radius of the half-circle. The radius is not given.

7. (3) 60 $A = \frac{1}{2}bh$
$= \frac{1}{2}(15)(8) = 60$ sq ft

8. (3) 400 m $\quad \frac{d}{40} = \frac{250}{25}$
$d = \frac{250 \times 40}{25} = 400$ meters

9. (1) 30° $\quad 90° + 60° = 150°$
$180° - 150° = 30°$

10. (1) $t = \frac{s \times b}{a}$
This represents the solution to the proportion that can be used to find a side of a similar triangle.
$\frac{t}{b} = \frac{s}{a}$
$t = \frac{s \times b}{a}$

11. (1) $17\frac{1}{2}$ $\quad \frac{\text{height}}{\text{shadow}} = \frac{\text{height}}{\text{shadow}}$
$\frac{5}{12} = \frac{n}{42}$
$\frac{42 \times 5}{12} = \frac{210}{12} = 17\frac{1}{2}$

12. (2) 10 feet $\quad c^2 = a^2 + b^2$
$c^2 = 8^2 + 6^2 = 100$
$c = 10$ feet

13. (3) 108°
Find the angles being compared:
$180° - 57° = 123°$
$90° - 75° = 15°$
Find the difference:
$123° - 15° = 108°$

14. (2) 96
Cargo area = lwh
$\qquad = 8 \times 8 \cdot 12 = 768$ cu ft
Boxes = $s^3 = 2^3 = 8$ cu ft
Find how many boxes will fit:
$\qquad 768 \div 8 = 96$ boxes

15. (1) 100
$$C = \pi d$$
$$628 = 3.14d$$
$$\frac{628}{3.14} = d$$
$$200 = d$$
$$100 = \tfrac{1}{2}d \text{ or } r$$

CHAPTER 10: ALGEBRA

Exercise 1: Terms
page 676

1. 4 and $+x$
2. $8x$ and $+7y$ and -5
3. $2x^2$ and $-\dfrac{3}{x}$
4. $8ab$ and $+12$

Exercise 2: Equations
page 677

1. 5 added to 7 times a number (y) equals 19.
2. 9 times a number (y) is 27.
3. A number (a) minus 5 equals 23.
4. 10 divided by a number (y) minus 5 equals 0.
5. A number (y) divided by 8 equals 9.

Exercise 3: Eyeballing
page 678

1. 2 **3.** 5 **5.** 13 **7.** 2
2. 10 **4.** 5 **6.** 3 **8.** 4

Exercise 4: One-Step Equations
page 679

1. $x = 4$
$$3 + x = 7$$
$$3 - 3 + x = 7 - 3$$
$$\underbrace{}_{0}$$
$$x = 4$$

2. $x = 36$
$$\frac{x}{3} = 12$$
$$\frac{3}{1} \cdot \frac{x}{3} = 12 \cdot 3$$
$$x = 36$$

3. $x = 3$
$$2x = 6$$
$$\frac{2x}{2} = \frac{6}{2}$$
$$x = 3$$

4. $x = 8$
$$x - 8 = 0$$
$$x \underbrace{- 8 + 8}_{0} = 0 + 8$$
$$x = 8$$

5. $x = 15$
$$5x = 75$$
$$\frac{5x}{5} = \frac{75}{5}$$
$$x = 15$$

6. $x = 64$
$$\frac{x}{4} = 16$$
$$\frac{4}{1} \cdot \frac{x}{4} = 16 \cdot 4$$
$$x = 64$$

7. $x = 15$
$$x - 3 = 12$$
$$x \underbrace{- 3 + 3}_{0} = 12 + 3$$
$$x = 15$$

8. $x = 28$
$$\frac{1}{2}x = 14$$
$$\frac{2}{1} \cdot \frac{1}{2}x = 14 \cdot 2$$
$$x = 28$$

Exercise 5: Translating English to Algebra
page 681

1. $6 - x$
2. $14x$
3. $\dfrac{x - y}{3}$
4. $x^2 + y^2$
5. $4(x + 10)$
6. $2x - 7$
7. $x^2 + 12$
8. $\dfrac{x^3}{4}$
9. $(x + y) - 4$
10. $\dfrac{5x}{2x}$

Exercise 6: Translating Sentences to Equations
pages 682–683

1. $\frac{1}{4}x = 18$ or $\frac{x}{4} = 18$
2. $x - 2 = 40$
3. $3x + 1 = 25$
4. $9 + \frac{1}{2}x = 13$
$\quad$ or $9 + \frac{x}{2} = 13$
5. $6x = 35$
6. $x - y = 8$
7. $18 + 2x = 22$
8. $\frac{x}{4} = 18$
9. $2x - 3 = 5x + 9$
10. (3) $x - 48 = 75$
11. (1) $x - 5 = 19$
12. (4) $\frac{x}{7} = 5$
13. (3) $22 + 12h = 64$
14. (1) $x + 6 = \frac{7}{6}x$

Exercise 7: Solving One-Step Algebra Word Problems
page 684

1. $x = 15$
$$x - 7 = 8$$
$$x \underbrace{- 7 + 7}_{0} = 8 + 7$$
$$x = 15$$

2. 18 baseballs
$$2.25x = 40.50$$
$$\frac{2.25}{2.25}x = \frac{40.50}{2.25} = 18$$

3. $x = \$20$
$$\frac{1}{8}x = 2.50$$
$$\frac{8}{1} \cdot \frac{1}{8}x = 2.50 \cdot 8$$
$$x = \$20$$

4. $x = \$192$
$$72 = x - 120$$
$$72 + 120 = x \underbrace{- 120 + 120}_{0}$$
$$\$192 = x$$

5. $x = 12$ ft
$$x - 5\tfrac{1}{2} = 6\tfrac{1}{2}$$
$$x \underbrace{- 5\tfrac{1}{2} + 5\tfrac{1}{2}}_{0} = 6\tfrac{1}{2} + 5\tfrac{1}{2}$$
$$x = 12$$

6. $x = 158$ lbs

$$x + 14 = 172$$
$$x + \underbrace{14 - 14}_{0} = 172 - 14$$
$$x = 158$$

7. $x = 36$ years

$$x + 12 = 48$$
$$x + \underbrace{12 - 12}_{0} = 48 - 12$$
$$x = 36$$

8. $x = \$5793.75$

$$927 = .16x$$
$$\frac{927}{.16} = \frac{.16x}{.16}$$
$$927 \div .16 = x$$
$$\$5793.75 = x$$

Exercise 8: Combining Like Terms
page 685

1. $15x$
2. $3y$
3. $9x + 9y$
4. $7x^2 + 5x$
5. $13x - 3$
6. $5x^2 + 7x + 9$
7. $3a$
8. $x + y$
9. $12a^2 + 5a$
10. $9xy + 6x - 3y$

Exercise 9: Removing Grouping Symbols
page 686

1. $5(3x + 2) = 15x + 10$
2. $4(7x - 8) = 28x - 32$
3. $6x + 2(12x - 7) = 6x + 24x - 14$
$$= 30x - 14$$
4. $2(x - 1) = 2x - 2$
5. $3(2x + 4 - 3y) = 6x + 12 - 9y$
6. $-6(5x - 12) = -30x + 72$
7. $x - 2(9 + 6x) = x - 18 - 12x$
$$= -11x - 18$$
8. $2(x - y) = 2x - 2y$

Exercise 10: Solving Multi-Step Equations
page 687

1. $x = 2$

$$3x + 9 = 15$$
$$3x + 9 - 9 = 15 - 9$$
$$3x = 6$$
$$x = 2$$

2. $x = 14$

$$2x - 26 = 2$$
$$2x - 26 + 26 = 2 + 26$$
$$2x = 28$$
$$x = 14$$

3. $x = 15$

$$\frac{x}{3} + 4 = 9$$
$$\frac{x}{3} + 4 - 4 = 9 - 4$$
$$\frac{x}{3} = 5$$
$$x = 15$$

4. $x = 21$

$$\frac{4x}{3} - 14 = 14$$
$$\frac{4x}{3} - 14 + 14 = 14 + 14$$
$$\frac{4x}{3} = 28$$
$$4x = 84$$
$$x = 21$$

5. $x = 4$

$$8(x - 4) = 0$$
$$8x - 32 = 0$$
$$8x - 32 + 32 = 0 + 32$$
$$8x = 32$$
$$x = 4$$

6. $x = 1$

$$2(5x - 11) + 12x = 0$$
$$10x - 22 + 12x = 0$$
$$22x - 22 + 22 = 0 + 22$$
$$22x = 22$$
$$x = 1$$

Exercise 11: Setting Up and Solving Multi-Step Equations
pages 688–690

1. (4) $3(x + 32) = 123$
2. (1) $\$9$
3. (4) $2x + 24 = 56$
4. (1) 16
5. (4) $(2x - 6) + x = 42$
6. (2) 16
7. (5) $4800 + 36x = 10,200$
8. (2) $\$150.00$
9. (5) not enough information is given
You do not know how many attendees were contest winners.
10. (5) not enough information is given

Exercise 12: Number Line
page 692

1. $1\frac{1}{2} > -1$
2. $-4 < -2\frac{1}{2}$
3. $-2 > -3$
4. $-6 < 0$

Exercise 13: Signed Numbers
page 692

1. $-\$12$
2. $-15°F$
3. -3 yd
4. $+\$75$
5. $+4\frac{1}{2}$ pt
6. $7 < 11$
7. $-9 < -4$
8. $-3 < 1$
9. $0 > -4$
10. $-6 < 2.4$
11. $-\frac{1}{4} > -\frac{1}{2}$
12. 9
13. $\frac{1}{2}$
14. $2\frac{1}{3}$
15. 3

Exercise 14: Combining Signed Numbers
page 694

1. 15
2. -1
3. -17
4. -2
5. -5
6. -33
7. -96
8. -3
9. 35
10. -19
11. 3.8
12. -7.7

Exercise 15: Eliminating Double Signs
page 694

1. $-6 - (-2) = -6 + 2 = -4$
2. $-6 + (-2) - (-9) =$
$$-6 - 2 + 9 = 1$$
3. $3 - (+8) = 3 - 8 = -5$
4. total gain of 22 yd

$$\begin{array}{ll} +23 & -4 \\ +8 & -6 \\ \underline{+3} & \underline{-2} \\ 34 & -12 \end{array}$$

$$+34 - 12 = +22$$

5. $3\frac{2}{3}$ yd $\quad 22 \div 6 = 3\frac{2}{3}$
6. $19°$ $\quad 12 - (-7) = 12 + 7 = 19$
7. $\$158$

$$\begin{array}{ll} +140 & -14 \\ +56 & -32 \\ \underline{+26} & \underline{-18} \\ +222 & -64 \end{array}$$

$$+222 + (-64) = +158$$

Exercise 16: Multiplying and Dividing Signed Numbers
page 696

1. 40	5. 225	9. −5
2. −144	6. 36	10. 3
3. −30	7. −84	11. −4
4. −88	8. 0	12. 5

13. $-1\frac{1}{2}$ or a drop of $1\frac{1}{2}$ pt

$$(-\tfrac{3}{8})(4) = -\tfrac{12}{8} = -1\tfrac{1}{2}$$

14. **−$22,284**

$$(-\$2476)(9) = -\$22,284$$

Exercise 17: One-Step Inequalities
page 697

1. $x > -2$
$$x - 3 > -5$$
$$x - 3 + 3 > -5 + 3$$
$$x > -2$$

2. $x < 2$
$$5 + x < 7$$
$$5 - 5 + x < 7 - 5$$
$$x < 2$$

3. $x < -7$
$$-3 + x < -10$$
$$-3 + 3 + x < -10 + 3$$
$$x < -7$$

4. $x > -36$
$$\frac{x}{-3} < 12$$
$$-3 \cdot \frac{x}{-3} > 12 \cdot (-3)$$
$$x > -36$$
Note change in direction.

5. $x \geq 4$
$$x - 5 \geq -1$$
$$x - 5 + 5 \geq -1 + 5$$
$$x \geq 4$$

6. $x < -2$
$$-4x > 8$$
$$\frac{-4x}{-4} < \frac{8}{-4}$$
$$x < -2$$
Note change in direction.

7. $x \leq 7$
$$x - 7 \leq 0$$
$$x - 7 + 7 \leq 0 + 7$$
$$x \leq 7$$

8. $14 > x$
$$70 > 5x$$
$$\frac{70}{5} > \frac{5x}{5}$$
$$14 > x$$

9. $x < 4$
$$-4x > -16$$
$$\frac{-4x}{-4} < \frac{-16}{-4}$$
$$x < 4$$
Note change in direction.

Exercise 18: Multiplying Algebraic Expressions
page 699

1. $24x^3$ $8x \cdot 3x^2 =$
$$8 \cdot 3 \cdot x \cdot x^2 = 24x^3$$

2. $-28x^2y$ $7xy(-4x) =$
$$7 \cdot (-4) \cdot x \cdot x \cdot y = -28x^2y$$

3. $-18a^3b^2$ $(-6ab^2)(3a^2) =$
$$-6 \cdot 3 \cdot a \cdot a^2 \cdot b^2 =$$
$$-18a^3b^2$$

4. $-15x^3y^3$ $(-5x^2y)(3xy^2) =$
$$-5 \cdot 3 \cdot x^2 \cdot x \cdot y \cdot y^2 =$$
$$-15x^3y^3$$

5. $2x^3 + 2x$ $2x(x^2 + 1) =$
$$2x \cdot x^2 + 2x \cdot 1 =$$
$$2x^3 + 2x$$

6. $6y^3 - 12y^2 - 21y$
$$3y(2y^2 - 4y - 7) =$$
$$3y(2y^2) + 3y(-4y) + 3y(-7) =$$
$$6y^3 - 12y^2 - 21y$$

Exercise 19: The Greatest Common Factor
page 700

1. $7x^2(3x - 2)$
$$21x^3 - 14x^2 =$$
$$7x^2(3x) + 7x^2(-2) =$$
$$7x^2(3x - 2)$$

2. $4a^2(25a^2 - 4)$
$$100a^4 - 16a^2 =$$
$$4a^2(25a^2) + 4a^2(-4) =$$
$$4a^2(25a^2 - 4)$$

3. $11p^4(11p - 3)$
$$121p^5 - 33p^4 =$$
$$11p^4(11p) + 11p^4(-3) =$$
$$11p^4(11p - 3)$$

4. $4(2x^2 - 1)$
$$8x^2 - 4 =$$
$$4(2x^2) + 4(-1) =$$
$$4(2x^2 - 1)$$

5. $9x^2y^2(x + 4y)$
$$9x^3y^2 + 36x^2y^3 =$$
$$9x^2y^2(x) + 9x^2y^2(4y) =$$
$$9x^2y^2(x + 4y)$$

6. $50x^2(2x^3 - x + 2)$
$$100x^5 - 50x^3 + 100x^2 =$$
$$50x^2(2x^3) + 50x^2(-x) + 50x^2(2) =$$
$$50x^2(2x^3 - x + 2)$$

7. $5x^2(x^2 + 5x - 4)$
$$5x^4 + 25x^3 - 20x^2 =$$
$$5x^2(x^2) + 5x^2(5x) + 5x^2(-4) =$$
$$5x^2(x^2 + 5x - 4)$$

8. $9x(x^2 - 1)$
$$9x^3 - 9x =$$
$$9x(x^2) + 9x(-1) =$$
$$9x(x^2 - 1)$$

Exercise 20: Factoring by Grouping
page 700

1. $(x + 4)(x + 3)$
$$x^2 + 4x + 3x + 12$$
$$x(x + 4) + 3(x + 4)$$
$$(x + 4)(x + 3)$$

2. $(x - 2)(x + 5)$
$$x^2 - 2x + 5x - 10$$
$$x(x - 2) + 5(x - 2)$$
$$(x - 2)(x + 5)$$

3. $(4y + 3z)(2y + 3z)$
$$8y^2 + 6yz + 12yz + 9z^2$$
$$2y(4y + 3z) + 3z(4y + 3z)$$
$$(4y + 3z)(2y + 3z)$$

4. $(x - 4)(2y^2 + 1)$
$$2xy^2 - 8y^2 + x - 4$$
$$2y^2(x - 4) + 1(x - 4)$$
$$(x - 4)(2y^2 + 1)$$
Notice 1 is the common factor of the second pair of terms.

Exercise 21: Ordered Pairs
page 702
1. $A\,(2,2)$ 4. $D\,(0,0)$ 7. $G\,(0,-2)$
2. $B\,(0,3)$ 5. $E\,(-5,0)$ 8. $H\,(1,-1)$
3. $C\,(-3,1)$ 6. $F\,(-1,-4)$ 9. $I\,(3,0)$

Exercise 22: Distance by Counting
page 704
1. 9   2. 9   3. 3   4. 5   5. 6

Exercise 23: Distance Between Two Points
page 704

1. 5 $(x_1,y_1) = (0,-2)$
$(x_2,y_2) = (4,-5)$
$$d = \sqrt{(4-0)^2 + (-5-(-2))^2}$$
$$= \sqrt{4^2 + (-3)^2}$$
$$= \sqrt{16 + 9}$$
$$= \sqrt{25} = 5$$

2. 13 $(x_1,y_1) = (6,3)$
$(x_2,y_2) = (-6,-2)$
$$d = \sqrt{(-6-6)^2 + (-2-3)^2}$$
$$= \sqrt{(-12)^2 + (-5)^2}$$
$$= \sqrt{144 + 25}$$
$$= \sqrt{169} = 13$$

3. 6 E and F are on the same vertical line.
Count the units from $(1,4)$ to $(1,-2)$;
$d = 6$

4. $5\sqrt{2}$ $(x_1,y_1) = (-2,3)$
$(x_2,y_2) = (-1,-4)$
$$d = \sqrt{(-1-(-2))^2 + (-4-3)^2}$$
$$= \sqrt{(-1+2)^2 + (-7)^2}$$
$$= \sqrt{1^2 + (-7)^2}$$
$$= \sqrt{1 + 49}$$
$$= \sqrt{50} = \sqrt{25 \cdot 2} = 5\sqrt{2}$$

5. 6   The distance can be counted;
$d = 6$

Exercise 24: The Slope of a Line
page 706

1. $\dfrac{4}{3}$ $\dfrac{4-0}{3-0} = \dfrac{4}{3}$

2. $\dfrac{1}{11}$ $\dfrac{0-(-1)}{6-(-5)} = \dfrac{1}{11} = \dfrac{1}{11}$

3. 0 $\dfrac{3-3}{9-(-9)} = \dfrac{0}{18} = 0$

4. -1 $\dfrac{-1-(-2)}{-2-(-1)} = \dfrac{-1+2}{-2+1} = \dfrac{1}{-1} = -1$

5. 1 $\dfrac{2-3}{-1-0} = \dfrac{-1}{-1} = 1$

6. $\dfrac{1}{2}$ $\dfrac{-6-(-3)}{-3-3} = \dfrac{-3}{-6} = \dfrac{1}{2}$

7. 0   The line is parallel to the x-axis; the slope is 0.

8. $\dfrac{3}{7}$ $\dfrac{5-8}{0-7} = \dfrac{-3}{-7} = \dfrac{3}{7}$

Exercise 25: Algebra Review
pages 707–710

1. (2) $1400 - 120x$
Let $120x$ = depreciation in x years
$1400 - 120x$ = value at end of x years

2. (5) $\frac{1}{3}x + 70 = \frac{1}{2}x$

Let x = monthly salary
$\frac{1}{3}x = \frac{1}{3}$ salary and $\frac{1}{2}x = \frac{1}{2}$ salary
$\frac{1}{3}x + 70 = \frac{1}{2}x$

3. (3) 9 in   Let x = shortest piece
$x + 6$ = second piece
$2x$ = third piece
$$x + (x+6) + 2x = 42$$
$$4x + 6 = 42$$
$$4x + 6 - 6 = 42 - 6$$
$$4x = 36$$
$$x = 9$$

4. (2) $2x + 2(x+5) = 78$
Let x = width
$x + 5$ = length
$P = 2l + 2w$
$78 = 2(x+5) + 2x$

5. (2) $20°$ $-12 + 25 + 7 = -12 + 32 = 20$

6. (1) -3 Let x = the number
$$10x - 6x = 2x - 6$$
$$10x - 6x - 2x = 2x - 2x - 6$$
$$2x = -6$$
$$x = \frac{-6}{2} = -3$$

7. (1) 240 ft $h = 128t - 16t^2$
$$= 128(3) - 16(3)^2$$
$$= 384 - 16(9)$$
$$= 384 - 144 = 240$$

8. (1) -4
$$3x + 2(4-x) = x - (3x+1) - 3$$
$$3x + 8 - 2x = x - 3x - 1 - 3$$
$$x + 8 = -2x - 4$$
$$x + 2x + 8 = -2x + 2x - 4$$
$$3x + 8 = -4$$
$$3x + 8 - 8 = -4 - 8$$
$$3x = -12$$
$$x = -4$$

9. (3) $x < 8$
$$x + 5 < 13$$
$$x + 5 - 5 < 13 - 5$$
$$x < 8$$

10. (3) 20

Let x = number of hours at 55 mph
$x + 2$ = 2 more hours

$$55x = 45(x + 2)$$
$$55x = 45x + 90$$
$$55x - 45x = 45x - 45x + 90$$
$$10x = 90$$
$$x = 9$$
$$x + x + 2 = 9 + 9 + 2 = 20 \text{ hr}$$

11. (2) 37 yd $+17 - 4 - 4 + 28 =$
$$+45 - 8 = +37$$

12. (3) $24x = 672$

Let x = number of gallons
miles per gallon × gallons = miles
$24x = 672$

13. (4) \$32 x = today
$\quad\quad\quad 2x$ = yesterday
$$x + 2x = 48$$
$$3x = 48$$
$$\frac{3x}{3} = \frac{48}{3}$$
$$x = 16 \quad 2x = 32$$

14. (5) not enough information is given

You are not able to set up an equation because you do not know how much she originally needed.

15. (3) 8 x-axis to (4,4) is 4
$\quad\quad\quad\quad$ x-axis to (4,−4) is 4
$$4 + 4 = 8$$

16. (3) +376

chocolate sundae = +560 calories
three sets of tennis =
$3(-200) = -600$
one glass of orange juice = +96
six cookies = 2(160) = +320
$+560 - 600 + 96 + 320 =$
$976 - 600 = +376$

17. (4) 4

slice of cheesecake = 478
2 12-oz bottles of soda =
$\quad 2(105) = 210$
$478 + 210 = 688$ calories
$688 \div 172 = 4$ miles

18. (1) $-\dfrac{1}{9}$

$$m = \frac{y_2 - y_1}{x_2 - x_1}$$
$$= \frac{2 - 3}{5 - (-4)} = \frac{2 - 3}{5 + 4}$$
$$= \frac{-1}{9} = -\frac{1}{9}$$

Post-Tests

Since you began your study in this book, you have been moving closer to your goal—the actual GED Tests. To find out how ready you are, you should take the Post-Tests on the following pages. These tests will indicate how well you understood the subjects you studied in each of the five test areas presented earlier in this book. These Post-Tests will give you an idea of what the real ones are like. They are based on the real GED Tests with the same kinds and number of questions.

We recommend the following approach to the Post-Tests.

1. Take only one Post-Test at a time. Try to finish the test within the allotted time so that you can see how you will do on the actual GED Tests. If you are not done within that time period, mark where you were when the time was up and finish the test. You want to finish the entire Post-Test so that you can make use of the Evaluation Charts.

Time Allowed for Each Test		
Writing Skills	Part 1	75 minutes
	Part 2	45 minutes
Social Studies		85 minutes
Science		95 minutes
Literature and the Arts		65 minutes
Mathematics		90 minutes

2. After you have finished each of the Post-Tests, check the answers in the answer key and fill in the Evaluation Charts. The answer keys and Evaluation Charts follow each test. Be sure to read the explanations for all of the questions that you missed.

3. If the Evaluation Charts indicate that you still need work in a certain area, refer to the review pages given in the charts.

4. Although these are Post-Tests, you should give them your best effort. If an item seems difficult, mark it and come back later. Always answer every question—even if you have to make an "educated guess." Sometimes you may know more than you give yourself credit for. Also, on the real GED Tests a blank counts as a wrong answer. It's always wise to answer every question as best you can.

POST-TEST 1: WRITING SKILLS
Part 1: Conventions of English

The following items are based on paragraphs that contain numbered sentences. Some of the sentences may contain errors in sentence structure, usage, or mechanics. A few sentences, however, may be correct as written. Read the paragraph and then answer the items based on it. For each item, choose the answer that would result in the most effective writing of the sentence or sentences. The best answer must be consistent with the meaning and tone of the rest of the paragraph.

When you are finished with the test, check your answers and turn to the Evaluation Charts on pages 753 and 755. Use the charts to evaluate whether or not you are ready to take the final Practice Test and, if not, in what areas you need more work.

POST-TEST 1: WRITING SKILLS ANSWER GRID

1 ① ② ③ ④ ⑤	15 ① ② ③ ④ ⑤	29 ① ② ③ ④ ⑤	43 ① ② ③ ④ ⑤
2 ① ② ③ ④ ⑤	16 ① ② ③ ④ ⑤	30 ① ② ③ ④ ⑤	44 ① ② ③ ④ ⑤
3 ① ② ③ ④ ⑤	17 ① ② ③ ④ ⑤	31 ① ② ③ ④ ⑤	45 ① ② ③ ④ ⑤
4 ① ② ③ ④ ⑤	18 ① ② ③ ④ ⑤	32 ① ② ③ ④ ⑤	46 ① ② ③ ④ ⑤
5 ① ② ③ ④ ⑤	19 ① ② ③ ④ ⑤	33 ① ② ③ ④ ⑤	47 ① ② ③ ④ ⑤
6 ① ② ③ ④ ⑤	20 ① ② ③ ④ ⑤	34 ① ② ③ ④ ⑤	48 ① ② ③ ④ ⑤
7 ① ② ③ ④ ⑤	21 ① ② ③ ④ ⑤	35 ① ② ③ ④ ⑤	49 ① ② ③ ④ ⑤
8 ① ② ③ ④ ⑤	22 ① ② ③ ④ ⑤	36 ① ② ③ ④ ⑤	50 ① ② ③ ④ ⑤
9 ① ② ③ ④ ⑤	23 ① ② ③ ④ ⑤	37 ① ② ③ ④ ⑤	51 ① ② ③ ④ ⑤
10 ① ② ③ ④ ⑤	24 ① ② ③ ④ ⑤	38 ① ② ③ ④ ⑤	52 ① ② ③ ④ ⑤
11 ① ② ③ ④ ⑤	25 ① ② ③ ④ ⑤	39 ① ② ③ ④ ⑤	53 ① ② ③ ④ ⑤
12 ① ② ③ ④ ⑤	26 ① ② ③ ④ ⑤	40 ① ② ③ ④ ⑤	54 ① ② ③ ④ ⑤
13 ① ② ③ ④ ⑤	27 ① ② ③ ④ ⑤	41 ① ② ③ ④ ⑤	55 ① ② ③ ④ ⑤
14 ① ② ③ ④ ⑤	28 ① ② ③ ④ ⑤	42 ① ② ③ ④ ⑤	

Choose the best answer to each question that follows.

Questions 1–11 refer to the following passage.

(1) Many people own and operate microwave ovens, but they were not really aware of exactly how a microwave oven cooks their food. (2) A magnetron tube in the oven convert electrical energy to microwave energy and directs that energy to a fanlike stirrer. (3) The stirrer evenly channels into the oven the short radio waves who penetrate food and cause the molecules in the food to vibrate. (4) This vibration or friction creating the heat that cooks the food. (5) Glass, paper, and most types of china are used in microwave cooking becuase the microwaves can pass through these containers; however, the microwaves do not pass through metal. (6) The microwaves penetrated the food to a depth of ¾ to 1½ inches. (7) As cooking continues, the heat spreads to the interior of the food. (8) When the microwaves stop, the friction action continues, slows, and it stops.

(9) Most microwave ovens have settings such as warm, defrost, simmer medium-high, and high so that a person can choose the speed at which the food cooks. (10) The time needed to cook food depends on the amount of food being cooked. (11) One hot dog may cook in one minute, while four hot dogs take about two minutes, and six hot dogs take about four minutes. (12) Microwave ovens vary in features, and size, but owners can safely and effectively use this household appliance by following instructions carefully.

1. Sentence 1: **Many people own and operate microwave ovens, but they were not really aware of exactly how a microwave oven cooks their food.**

   What correction should be made to this sentence?

   (1) change *own* to *owns*
   (2) remove the comma after *ovens*
   (3) replace *they* with *he or she*
   (4) replace *were* with *are*
   (5) replace *their* with *they're*

2. Sentence 2: **A magnetron tube in the oven convert electrical energy to microwave energy and directs that energy to a fanlike stirrer.**

   What correction should be made to this sentence?

   (1) insert a comma after *oven*
   (2) change *convert* to *converts*
   (3) insert a comma after *microwave energy*
   (4) change *directs* to *direct*
   (5) no correction is necessary

3. Sentence 3: **The stirrer evenly channels into the oven the short radio waves who penetrate food and cause the molecules in the food to vibrate.**

   What correction should be made to this sentence?

   (1) insert a comma after *oven*
   (2) change *waves* to *waves'*
   (3) replace *who* with *that*
   (4) insert a comma after *food*
   (5) no correction is necessary

4. Sentence 4: **This vibration or friction <u>creating</u> the heat that cooks the food.**

   Which of the following is the best way to write the underlined portion of this sentence? If you think the original is the best way, choose option (1).

   (1) creating
   (2) may create
   (3) creates
   (4) then creating
   (5) create

5. Sentence 5: **Glass, paper, and most types of china are used in microwave cooking becuase the microwaves can pass through these containers; however, the microwaves do not pass through metal.**

   What correction should be made to this sentence?

   (1) remove the comma after *Glass*
   (2) replace *china* with *China*
   (3) replace *are* with *is*
   (4) change the spelling of *becuase* to *because*
   (5) replace *containers; however* with *containers, however*

6. Sentence 6: **The microwaves penetrated the food to a depth of ¾ to 1½ inches.**

   Which of the following is the best way to write the underlined portion of this sentence? If you think the original is the best way, choose option (1).

   (1) penetrated
   (2) penetrates
   (3) penetrate
   (4) had penetrated
   (5) will penetrate

7. Sentence 7: **As cooking continues, the heat spreads to the interior of the food.**

   What correction should be made to this sentence?

   (1) change *continues* to *continuing*
   (2) remove the comma after *continues*
   (3) change *spreads* to *spread*
   (4) insert a comma after *interior*
   (5) no correction is necessary

8. Sentence 8: **When the microwaves stop, the friction action continues, slows, and it stops.**

   Which of the following is the best way to write the underlined portion of this sentence? If you think the original is the best way, choose option (1).

   (1) it stops
   (2) they stop
   (3) stops
   (4) to stop
   (5) stopped

9. Sentence 9: **Most microwave ovens have settings such as warm, defrost, simmer medium-high, and high so that a person can choose the speed at which the food cooks.**

   What correction should be made to this sentence?

   (1) change *have* to *has*
   (2) insert a comma after *simmer*
   (3) replace *a person* with *you*
   (4) change *choose* to *chose*
   (5) change *cooks* to *cooking*

10. Sentences 10 and 11: **The time needed to cook food depends on the amount of food being cooked. One hot dog may cook in one minute, while four hot dogs take about two minutes, and six hot dogs take about four minutes.**

    The most effective combination of sentences 10 and 11 would include which of the following groups of words?

    (1) cooked, one hot dog
    (2) cooked, but one hot dog
    (3) cooked; however, one hot dog
    (4) cooked; for example, one hot dog
    (5) cooked although one hot dog

11. Sentence 12: **Microwave ovens vary in features, and size, but owners can safely and effectively use this household appliance by following instructions carefully.**

What correction should be made to this sentence?

(1) change *vary* to *varies*
(2) remove the comma after *features*
(3) remove the comma after *size*
(4) insert a comma after *safely*
(5) change the spelling of *carefully* to *carfully*

Questions 12–23 refer to the following passage.

(1) Americans have been jogging for several years, and most of us were aware of the many physical and psychological benefits of running or walking outdoors. (2) For many people, however, hectic schedules make it difficult to find the time to go out and run around the neighborhood. (3) Some people do not want to be seen perspiring and jiggling along their neighbors sidewalks, and others are afraid to jog after sundown, the only time they have to exercise. (4) A good alternative to outdoor jogging are staying inside one's room, apartment, or house and running in place. (5) Although some joggers enjoy the privacy of this form of exercise, its main advantage is convenience. (6) A person who does not relish the idea of jogging outdoors in the heat of summer or the cold of Winter can find a spot on the floor and run in place. (7) Experts state that they should jog for at least fifteen minutes and run more vigorously than they would outside. (8) Knees and feet should be raised high off the floor the runner must be careful of wearing the carpet thin! (9) Wearing good running shoes and running on a thick carpet or folded throw rug may reduce stress on feet and ankles. (10) Indoor runners can relieve the boredom by watching television, listening to music, or including children in the exercise time. (11) If parents have to stay home alone with small children who need supervision, indoor jogging be a good way for them to keep fit.

(12) Indoor runners may not breath fresh air or appreciate nature, but those who would otherwise be sitting in front of their televisions are better off jogging.

12. Sentence 1: **Americans have been jogging for several years, and most of us were aware of the many physical and psychological benefits of running or walking outdoors.**

What correction should be made to this sentence?

(1) replace *years* with *year's*
(2) remove the comma after *years*
(3) change *were* to *are*
(4) change the spelling of *benefits* to *bennefits*
(5) no correction is necessary

13. Sentence 2: **For many people, however, hectic schedules make it difficult to find the time to go out and run around the neighborhood.**

Which of the following is the best way to write the underlined portion of this sentence? If you think the original is the best way, choose option (1).

(1) people, however, hectic
(2) people. However, hectic
(3) people; however, hectic
(4) people however, hectic
(5) people however hectic

14. Sentence 3: **Some people do not want to be seen perspiring and jiggling along their neighbors sidewalks, and others are afraid to jog after sundown, the only time they have to exercise.**

What correction should be made to this sentence?

(1) change *do* to *does*
(2) replace *their* with *there*
(3) replace *neighbors* with *neighbors'*
(4) remove the comma after *sidewalks*
(5) change the spelling of *exercise* to *exercize*

15. Sentence 4: **A good alternative to outdoor jogging are staying inside one's room, apartment, or house and running in place.**

What correction should be made to this sentence?

(1) change *are* to *is*
(2) replace *one's* with *ones*
(3) remove the comma after *room*
(4) insert a comma after *house*
(5) no correction is necessary

16. Sentence 5: **Although some joggers enjoy the privacy of this form of exercise, its main advantage is convenience.**

If you rewrote sentence 5 beginning with

While the main advantage of this form of exercise is convenience,

the next word should be

(1) so
(2) although
(3) enjoy
(4) before
(5) some

17. Sentence 6: **A person who does not relish the idea of jogging outdoors in the heat of summer or the cold of Winter can find a spot on the floor and run in place.**

What correction should be made to this sentence?

(1) replace *who* with *which*
(2) insert a comma after *outdoors*
(3) change *summer* to *Summer*
(4) change *Winter* to *winter*
(5) insert a comma after *floor*

18. Sentence 7: **Experts state that they should jog for at least fifteen minutes and run more vigorously than they would outside.**

Which of the following is the best way to write the underlined portion of this sentence? If you think the original is the best way, choose option (1).

(1) they
(2) the experts
(3) you
(4) a person
(5) indoor joggers

19. Sentence 8: **Knees and feet should be raised high off the floor the runner must be careful of wearing the carpet thin!**

Which of the following is the best way to write the underlined portion of this sentence? If you think the original is the best way, choose option (1).

(1) floor the
(2) floor, the
(3) floor, and the
(4) floor; and the
(5) floor, to the

20. Sentence 9: **Wearing good running shoes and running on a thick carpet or folded throw rug may reduce stress on feet and ankles.**

If you rewrote sentence 9 beginning with

To reduce stress on feet and ankles,

the next word should be

(1) wearing
(2) joggers
(3) running
(4) should
(5) to

21. Sentence 10: **Indoor runners can releive the boredom by watching television, listening to music, or including children in the exercise time.**

    What correction should be made to this sentence?

    (1) replace *runners* with *runners'*
    (2) change the spelling of *releive* to *relieve*
    (3) replace *listening* with *they can listen*
    (4) change *including* to *include*
    (5) no correction is necessary

22. Sentence 11: **If parents have to stay home alone with small children who need supervision, indoor jogging be a good way for them to keep fit.**

    What correction should be made to this sentence?

    (1) change *have* to *has*
    (2) insert a comma after *alone*
    (3) remove the comma after *supervision*
    (4) replace *who* with *which*
    (5) change *be* to *is*

23. Sentence 12: **Indoor runners may not breath fresh air or appreciate nature, but those who would otherwise be sitting in front of their televisions are better off jogging.**

    What correction should be made to this sentence?

    (1) change the spelling of *breath* to *breathe*
    (2) change the spelling of *appreciate* to *apreciate*
    (3) remove the comma after *nature*
    (4) replace *but* with *or*
    (5) no correction is necessary

Questions 24–34 refer to the following passage.

(1) Mars, a small rocky planet is about half the size of Earth. (2) Transmitted by an unmanned Mariner IV space probe, we on Earth first saw close-range photos of Mars in 1965. (3) In view was cratered landscapes, deserts, and mountains. (4) The highest mountain on Earth, Mt. Everest, is 5.5 miles high, one mountain on Mars reaches a height of 15 miles. (5) In 1976, Vikings I and II orbited and landed on Mars, produsing more high-quality, close-up photographs. (6) The additional photos will reveal huge mountains, deep holes, and sandy dunes on Mars. (7) Another feature revealed by the photos was large cracks in the surface of the planet one crack is larger than our Grand Canyon. (8) Dried-up riverbeds suggested that water once may have flowed on the Planet. (9) Also noticeable in the photos was that Mars looked red. (10) Looking for the source of the red color, scientists tested samples of Mars atmosphere and soil. (11) In the future, scientists will continue to study this planet that may tell us more about Earth's origins, development, and what may be ahead.

24. Sentence 1: **Mars, a small rocky planet is about half the size of Earth.**

    What correction should be made to this sentence?

    (1) remove the comma after *Mars*
    (2) insert a comma after *planet*
    (3) change *is* to *are*
    (4) change *Earth* to *earth*
    (5) no correction is necessary

25. Sentence 2: **Transmitted by an unmanned Mariner IV space probe, <u>we on Earth first saw close-range photos of Mars in 1965</u>.**

Which of the following is the best way to write the underlined portion of this sentence? If you think the original is the best way, choose option (1).

(1) we on Earth first saw close-range photos of Mars in 1965
(2) Mars was first seen by us on Earth in close-range photos in 1965
(3) Mars was first seen close-range by us in photos on Earth in 1965
(4) Mariner IV photos of us on Mars were first seen in 1965
(5) the first close-range photos of Mars were seen by us on Earth in 1965

26. Sentence 3: **In view <u>was</u> cratered landscapes, deserts, <u>and</u> mountains.**

Which of the following is the best way to write the underlined portion of this sentence? If you think the original is the best way, choose option (1).

(1) was
(2) were
(3) are
(4) is
(5) have been

27. Sentence 4: **The highest mountain on Earth, Mt. Everest, is 5.5 miles <u>high, one</u> mountain on Mars reaches a height of 15 miles.**

Which of the following is the best way to write the underlined portion of this sentence? If you think the original is the best way, choose option (1).

(1) high, one
(2) high, so one
(3) high; in contrast, one
(4) high; consequently, one
(5) high one

28. Sentence 5: **In 1976, Vikings I and II orbited and landed on Mars, produsing more high-quality, close-up photographs.**

What correction should be made to this sentence?

(1) replace *Vikings* with *vikings*
(2) change the spelling of *orbited* to *orbitted*
(3) change *landed* to *land*
(4) change the spelling of *produsing* to *producing*
(5) no correction is necessary

29. Sentence 6: **The additional photos will reveal huge mountains, deep holes, and sandy dunes on Mars.**

What correction should be made to this sentence?

(1) replace *photos* with *photo's*
(2) change *will reveal* to *revealed*
(3) replace *mountains* with *Mountains*
(4) insert a comma after *dunes*
(5) no correction is necessary

30. Sentence 7: **Another feature revealed by the photos was large cracks in the surface of the <u>planet one</u> crack is larger than our Grand Canyon.**

Which of the following is the best way to write the underlined portion of this sentence? If you think the original is the best way, choose option (1).

(1) planet one
(2) planet, one
(3) planet. One
(4) planet and one
(5) planet; however, one

31. Sentence 8: **Dried-up riverbeds suggested that water once may have flowed on the Planet.**

What correction should be made to this sentence?

(1) change *riverbeds* to *Riverbeds*
(2) change *suggested* to *suggests*
(3) change *flowed* to *flown*
(4) change *Planet* to *planet*
(5) no correction is necessary

32. Sentence 9: **Also noticeable in the photos was that Mars looked red.**

If you rewrote sentence 9 beginning with

The fact that Mars looked red

the next word should be

(1) was
(2) being
(3) noticeable
(4) and
(5) photos

33. Sentence 10: **Looking for the source of the red color, scientists tested samples of Mars atmosphere and soil.**

What correction should be made to this sentence?

(1) remove the comma after *color*
(2) replace *scientists* with *scientist's*
(3) replace *Mars* with *Mars's*
(4) add a comma after *atmosphere*
(5) no correction is necessary

34. Sentence 11: **In the future, scientists will continue to study this planet that may tell us more about Earth's origins, development, and <u>what may be ahead.</u>**

Which of the following is the best way to write the underlined portion of this sentence? If you think the original is the best way, choose option (1).

(1) what may be ahead
(2) what may lie ahead
(3) days ahead
(4) years ahead
(5) future

Questions 35–44 refer to the following.

(1) Consumers are constantly warned about the dangers of eating foods that may contribute to obesity, cavities, diabetes, heart disease, stress, or cancer. (2) We were told to avoid junk food, but that term means different things to different people. (3) To some people, junk food is fast food. (4) Other people think junk food is any food available in vending machines, such as potato chips, candy, cookies, ice cream bars, and soda pop. (5) Many of us are not quiet sure why we should not eat hot dogs, but we know they are also on the list of junk foods. (6) Lack of nutritional value, as well as negative health effects, are characteristic of junk food, say nutritionists. (7) Especially bad for us are sugar, salt, refined flour, and chemical additives. (8) Additives artificially improve the color, flavor, and shelf life of foods. (9) Refined sugar, which can be found in about one-fourth of the foods we eat, can affect us badly; in fact, though giving a boost of energy, stress can be caused by too much sugar. (10) So if our lunchboxes contains a sandwich made of cold cuts and slices of processed cheese on white bread, potato chips, and packaged pudding, nutrition is lacking. (11) Wanting quick and easy-to-prepare meals, you may be sacrificing nutrition for convenience. (12) By learning more about junk food and it's damaging effects, we may be healthier for years to come.

35. Sentence 1: **Consumers are constantly warned about the dangers of eating foods that may contribute to obesity, cavities, diabetes, heart disease, stress, or cancer.**

What correction should be made to this sentence?

(1) insert a comma after *warned*
(2) insert a comma after *to*
(3) remove the comma after *obesity*
(4) change *disease* to *disese*
(5) no correction is necessary

36. Sentence 2: **We were told to avoid junk food, but that term means different things to different people.**

What correction should be made to this sentence?

(1) change *were* to *are*
(2) insert a comma after *told*
(3) remove the comma after *food*
(4) replace *but* with *so*
(5) change the spelling of *different* to *differant*

37. Sentences 3 and 4: **To some people, junk food is fast food. Other people think junk food is any food available in vending machines, such as potato chips, candy, cookies, ice cream bars, and soda pop.**

The most effective combination of sentences 3 and 4 would include which of the following groups of words?

(1) fast food, but other people
(2) fast food or any food available
(3) fast food in vending machines
(4) junk food is available
(5) fast food; therefore, other people

38. Sentence 5: **Many of us are not quiet sure why we should not eat hot dogs, but we know they are also on the list of junk foods.**

What correction should be made to this sentence?

(1) replace *us* with *them*
(2) replace *quiet* with *quite*
(3) replace *hot dogs* with *Hot Dogs*
(4) remove the comma after *dogs*
(5) replace *they are* with *it is*

39. Sentence 6: **Lack of nutritional value, as well as negative health effects, are characteristic of junk food, say nutritionists.**

Which of the following is the best way to write the underlined portion of this sentence? If you think the original is the best way, choose option (1).

(1) are
(2) is
(3) were
(4) was
(5) being

40. Sentences 7 and 8: **Especially bad for us are sugar, salt, refined flour, and chemical additives. Additives artificially improve the color, flavor, and shelf life of foods.**

The most effective combination of sentences 7 and 8 would include which of the following groups of words?

(1) additives; in fact, all these ingredients
(2) additives that artificially improve
(3) additives artificially improve
(4) additives, or they
(5) additives' artificial color

41. Sentence 9: **Refined sugar, which can be found in about one-fourth of the foods we eat, can affect us badly; in fact, though giving a boost of energy, stress can be caused by too much sugar.**

Which of the following is the best way to write the underlined portion of this sentence? If you think the original is the best way, choose option (1).

(1) stress can be caused by too much sugar
(2) too much sugar can cause stress
(3) too much stress can be caused by sugar
(4) stress is a result of eating too much sugar
(5) sugar can cause too much stress

42. Sentence 10: **So if our lunchboxes contains a sandwich made of cold cuts and slices of processed cheese on white bread, potato chips, and packaged pudding, nutrition is lacking.**

What correction should be made to this sentence?

(1) replace *our* with *your*
(2) change *contains* to *contain*
(3) remove the comma after *bread*
(4) remove the comma after *pudding*
(5) no correction is necessary

43. Sentence 11: **Wanting quick and easy-to-prepare meals, you may be sacrificing nutrition for convenience.**

What correction should be made to this sentence?

(1) change the spelling of *prepare* to *prepair*
(2) remove the comma after *meals*
(3) replace *you* with *we*
(4) insert a comma after *nutrition*
(5) change the spelling of *convenience* to *conveniance*

44. Sentence 12: **By learning more about junk food and it's damaging effects, we may be healthier for years to come.**

What correction should be made to this sentence?

(1) insert a comma after *food*
(2) replace *it's* with *its*
(3) replace *effects* with *affects*
(4) change the spelling of *healthier* to *healthyer*
(5) no correction is necessary

Questions 45–55 refer to the following passage.

(1) Leasing a car can be a useful alternative to the high price tag of ownership. (2) In the last decade, the price of automobiles have risen greatly, and you can expect to spend over $15,000 for a car that cost $7,000 ten years ago. (3) An alternative to the high cost of new cars is buying a used car, but consumers have found that inflation also has effected the price of used cars. (4) Leasing a car can be a wise economic decision just as leasing a home has some advantages over buying. (5) Recently, the concept of leasing a car grew more popular. (6) Before leasing a car, you should shop around to see the variety of cars and lease agreements available. (7) You may have to pay a security deposit before you can sign a lease agreement, the monthly payments are usually lower than a typical monthly loan payment on a new car. (8) Some leasing business's allow you to apply all of your payments to the eventual purchase of the car, much like renting with an option to buy a home. (9) Other companies simply rent by the month and do not wish to sell its rental cars. (10) You should study carefully any leasing agreement before signing it. (11) Issues to consider before signing include responsibility for maintenance and insurance. (12) Before completing the deal, the car should be examined by all potential drivers.

45. Sentence 1: **Leasing a car can be a useful alternative to the high price tag of ownership.**

What correction should be made to this sentence?

(1) change *can be* to *was*
(2) change the spelling of *useful* to *usefull*
(3) insert a comma after *alternative*
(4) insert a comma after *tag*
(5) no correction is necessary

46. Sentence 2: **In the last decade, the price of automobiles have risen greatly, and you can expect to spend over $15,000 for a car that cost $7,000 ten years ago.**

Which of the following is the best way to write the underlined portion of this sentence? If you think the original is the best way, choose option (1).

(1) have risen
(2) has risen
(3) have rose
(4) has rose
(5) has rised

47. Sentence 3: **An alternative to the high cost of new cars is buying a used car, but consumers have found that inflation also has effected the price of used cars.**

What correction should be made to this sentence?

(1) change *is* to *are*
(2) remove the comma after *car*
(3) replace *found* with *finded*
(4) replace *effected* with *affected*
(5) no correction is necessary

48. Sentence 4: **Leasing a car can be a wise economic decision just as leasing a home has some advantages over buying.**

If you rewrote sentence 4 beginning with

Leasing a home has some advantages over buying; similarly,

the next word should be

(1) leasing
(2) cars
(3) can
(4) a
(5) just

49. Sentence 5: **Recently, the concept of leasing a car grew more popular.**

Which of the following is the best way to write the underlined portion of this sentence? If you think the original is the best way, choose option (1).

(1) grew
(2) has grew
(3) has grown
(4) will grow
(5) grows

50. Sentence 6: **Before leasing a car, you should shop around to see the variety of cars and lease agreements available.**

Which of the following is the best way to write the underlined portion of this sentence? If you think the original is the best way, choose option (1).

(1) you should shop
(2) one should shop
(3) you shop
(4) you should have shopped
(5) he or she should shop

51. Sentence 7: **You may have to pay a security deposit before you can sign a lease agreement, the monthly payments are usually lower than a typical monthly loan payment on a new car.**

Which of the following is the best way to write the underlined portion of this sentence? If you think the original is the best way, choose option (1).

(1) agreement, the
(2) agreement the
(3) agreement but the
(4) agreement, but the
(5) agreement and the

52. Sentence 8: **Some leasing business's allow you to apply all of your payments to the eventual purchase of the car, much like renting with an option to buy a home.**

What correction should be made to this sentence?

(1) replace *business's* with *businesses*
(2) change *allow* to *allows*
(3) replace *you* with *one*
(4) replace *your* with *you're*
(5) no correction is necessary

53. Sentence 9: **Other companies simply rent by the month and do not wish to sell its rental cars.**

What correction should be made to this sentence?

(1) change the spelling of *companies* to *companys*
(2) replace *month* with *Month*
(3) add a comma after *month*
(4) change *do* to *does*
(5) replace *its* with *their*

54. Sentences 10 and 11: **You should study carefully any leasing agreement before signing it. Issues to consider before signing include responsibility for maintenance and insurance.**

The most effective combination of sentences 10 and 11 would include which of the following groups of words?

(1) signing issues such as
(2) signing it and considering issues
(3) signing it and considering responsibility
(4) signing it to be responsible
(5) signing it, considering such issues as

55. Sentence 12: **Before completing the deal, the car should be examined by all potential drivers.**

Which of the following is the best way to write the underlined portion of this sentence? If you think the original is the best way, choose option (1).

(1) Before completing the deal
(2) Before the deal is completed
(3) Before the deal has been completed
(4) Before you complete the deal
(5) Before completing your deal

Answers begin on page 752.

Part 2: The Essay

Directions: This part of the test is designed to find out how well you write. The test has one question that asks you to present an opinion on an issue or explain something. In preparing your answer for this question, you should take the following steps:

1. Read all of the information accompanying the question.

2. Plan your answer carefully before you write.

3. Use scratch paper to make any notes.

4. Write your answer on a separate sheet of paper.

5. Read carefully what you have written and make any changes that will improve your writing.

6. Check your paragraphing, sentence structure, spelling, punctuation, capitalization, and usage and make any necessary corrections.

Take 45 minutes to plan and write on the assigned topic. Write legibly and use a ballpoint pen.

Topic

The invention of the television brought about many changes in American life. It provided us with a whole new way of receiving information, and it quickly became a new form of entertainment.

Write a composition of about 200 words describing the effects of television on American life. You may describe the positive effects, the negative effects, or both. Be specific and use examples to support your view.

Information on evaluating your essay is on page 755.

POST-TEST 1: WRITING SKILLS ANSWER KEY

Part 1: Conventions of English

1. **(4)** The verb *are* is consistent with the present tense of this sentence.

2. **(2)** The verb form *converts* agrees with the singular subject *tube*.

3. **(3)** The relative pronoun *who* is never used to refer to things. The relative pronoun *that* can refer to either things or people.

4. **(3)** The original sentence is a fragment because *creating* requires a helping verb. The verb form *creates* does not.

5. **(4)** The correct spelling is *because*.

6. **(3)** *Penetrate* agrees with the rest of the passage, which is written in the present tense.

7. **(5)** No correction is necessary.

8. **(3)** Each of the parts of the series should have parallel structure: *continues, slows, stops*.

9. **(2)** Always separate the items in a series with commas.

10. **(4)** The new sentence would read, "The time needed to cook food depends on the amount of food being cooked; for example, one hot dog may cook . . ."

11. **(2)** No comma is needed to separate only two items.

12. **(3)** The verb *are* is consistent with the present tense of the sentence and of the passage as a whole.

13. **(1)** There is no error.

14. **(3)** The plural possessive *neighbors'* shows that several neighbors have sidewalks.

15. **(1)** The verb *is* agrees with the singular subject *alternative*.

16. **(5)** The new sentence would read, "While the main advantage of this form of exercise is convenience, some joggers enjoy its privacy."

17. **(4)** The names of seasons are not capitalized.

18. **(5)** In the original sentence, *they* incorrectly refers to *experts*. Substituting *indoor joggers* makes the meaning clear.

19. **(3)** The original sentence is a run-on. Using the conjunction *and* joins the two independent clauses correctly.

20. **(2)** The new sentence would read, "To reduce stress on feet and ankles, joggers should wear good running shoes and run on a thick carpet or folded throw rug."

21. **(2)** The spelling of *relieve* follows the general "I before E" rule.

22. **(5)** The correct present-tense form of *be* for the singular subject *indoor jogging* is *is*.

23. **(1)** *Breathe* is a verb, the action of taking air into the lungs. *Breath* is a noun.

24. **(2)** The phrase *a small rocky planet* is a renaming phrase and should be set off by commas.

25. **(5)** The modifying phrase *Transmitted by an unmanned Mariner IV space probe* is misplaced. It describes the first photos, not we on Earth.

26. **(2)** The plural compound subject *landscapes, deserts, and mountains* requires the verb *were*.

27. **(3)** The original sentence contains a comma splice. This choice joins the two independent clauses correctly.

28. **(4)** Even though *producing* sounds like it contains an *s*, it is spelled with a *c*.

29. **(2)** The past tense *revealed* should be used to be consistent with the rest of the passage.

30. **(3)** This run-on can be corrected by dividing the independent clauses into two separate sentences.

31. **(4)** *Planet* is not a specific name and should not be capitalized.

32. **(1)** The new sentence would read, "The fact that Mars looked red was also noticeable in the photos."

33. **(3)** The possessive *Mars's* shows that the atmosphere and soil were of Mars.

34. **(5)** The noun *future* is in parallel form with *origins* and *development*.

35. **(5)** No correction is necessary.

36. **(1)** Use the verb *are*, present tense, to be consistent with the rest of the passage.

37. **(1)** The new sentence would read, "To some people, junk food is fast food, but other people think junk food is any food available in vending machines, such as potato chips, candy, cookies, ice cream bars, and soda pop."

38. **(2)** *Quiet* means "still"; *quite* means "very."

39. (2) The singular subject *value* requires the verb *is*. The phrase *as well as negative health effects* is not part of the subject.

40. (2) The new sentence would read, "Especially bad for us are sugar, salt, refined flour, and chemical additives that artificially improve the color, flavor, and shelf life of foods."

41. (2) The modifier *though giving a boost of energy* should describe *too much sugar*, not *stress*.

42. (2) The verb *contain* agrees with the plural subject *lunchboxes*.

43. (3) Throughout the passage, the pronouns *we*, *us*, and *our* are used.

44. (2) The correct possessive pronoun is *its*.

45. (5) No correction is necessary.

46. (2) The verb *has risen* agrees with the singular subject *price*.

47. (4) *Affected*, meaning "influenced," is the correct verb.

48. (1) The new sentence would read, "Leasing a home has some advantages over buying; similarly, leasing a car can be a wise economic decision."

49. (3) The word *recently* shows that the present perfect tense is needed.

50. (1) There is no error.

51. (4) The original sentence contains a comma splice. This choice joins the two complete thoughts correctly.

52. (1) The plural form, *businesses*, not the possessive, is needed.

53. (5) The possessive pronoun *their* is plural and correctly refers to *companies*.

54. (5) The new sentence would read, "You should study carefully any leasing agreement before signing it, considering such issues as responsibility for maintenance and insurance."

55. (4) The original sentence implies that the car will be completing the deal. The modifier, *Before completing the deal*, dangles. Changing it to an independent clause with the subject *you* makes the meaning clear.

Use the answer key on pages 752–753 to check your answers to the Post-Test. Then find the item number of each question you missed and circle it on the chart below to determine the writing content areas in which you need more practice. Pay particular attention to areas where you missed half or more of the questions. The page numbers for the content areas are listed below on the chart. For those questions that you missed, review the pages indicated.

POST-TEST 1: WRITING SKILLS EVALUATION CHART

Content Area	Item Number	Review Pages
Nouns	14, 33, 52	60–64
Verbs	6, 22, 29, 36, 49	65–76
Subject-Verb Agreement	2, 15, 26, 39, 42, 46	76–79
Pronoun Reference	3, 18, 43, 53	82–92
Sentence Fragments	4	93–95
Sentence Combining	10, 16, 19, 20, 27, 30, 32, 37, 40, 48, 51, 54	95–107
Sequence of Tenses	1, 12	109–110
Misplaced/Dangling Modifiers	25, 41, 55	111–112
Parallel Structure	8, 34	112–116
Capitalization	17, 31	117–119
Punctuation	9, 11, 13, 24	119–125
Spelling	5, 21, 23, 28, 38, 44, 47	126–141
No Error	7, 35, 45, 50	

Important Note

On the actual GED Writing Skills Test, you will be given one score, which is a composite of your scores from Part 1 and Part 2 of the test. This score is determined by grading your essay holistically, giving it a score, then combining this score with your score from Part 1 in a proportion determined by the GED Testing Service.

Because you are not able to score your essay holistically, it is not possible for you to determine a valid composite score for your performance on this Writing Skills Test. Instead, it is wise to look at your performance on each part of the test separately. In this way, you will be able to determine whether you need additional work in one part of the test or the other.

The following chart gives you a general idea of how you might do on Part 1 of the GED Writing Skills Test, given your performance on Part 1 of this Post-Test and your performance on Part 1 of the Practice Test that starts on page 832.

Fewer than 20 items correct: You are probably not ready to take the GED Writing Skills Test. Even with a good score on Part 2, you are unlikely to receive a passing composite score. Work through the Writing Skills section of this book again, or consult Contemporary's *GED Test 1: Writing Skills* for further instruction.

20–35 items correct: With a good score on Part 2 of this Post-Test, you are probably ready to take the GED Writing Skills Test. To prepare further, look at the evaluation chart on page 753 and determine the areas in which you need more work.

More than 35 items correct: You have done very well on Part 1 of this Post-Test, and you are certainly ready to take the GED Writing Skills Test if you also do well on Part 2 of this test (see page 755). You may want to review the explanations for items you missed in order to be as well prepared as possible.

Part 2: The Essay

If possible, give your essay to an instructor to evaluate. That person's opinion of your writing will be useful in deciding what further work you need to write a good essay.

If, however, you are unable to show your work to someone else, you can try to evaluate your own essay. If you can answer *yes* to the five questions in the Essay Evaluation Checklist, your essay would *probably* earn an upper half score (4, 5, or 6) on Part 2 of the Writing Skills Test. If you receive any *no* answers on your evaluation checklist, you should read your essay carefully to see how it could be improved and review Chapter 4 of the Writing Skills section.

Essay Evaluation Checklist

YES   NO

____   ____   **1.** Does the essay answer the question asked?

____   ____   **2.** Does the main point of the essay stand out clearly?

____   ____   **3.** Does each paragraph contain specific examples and details that help prove the main point?

____   ____   **4.** Can you follow how the writer has arranged and linked ideas in sentences and paragraphs?

____   ____   **5.** Is the writer's control of grammar and usage effective enough so that you were able to read the essay easily and smoothly?

POST-TEST 2: SOCIAL STUDIES

This Social Studies Post-Test will give you an opportunity to evaluate your readiness for the actual GED Social Studies Test.

This test contains 64 questions. Some of the questions are based on short reading passages, and some of them require you to interpret a chart, map, graph, or an editorial cartoon.

You should take appproximately 85 minutes to complete this test. At the end of 85 minutes, stop and mark your place. Then finish the test. This will give you an idea of whether or not you can finish the real GED Test in the time allotted. Try to answer as many questions as you can. A blank will count as a wrong answer, so make a reasonable guess for the answers to questions you are not sure of.

When you are finished with the test, check your answers and turn to the Evaluation Chart on page 778. Use the chart to evaluate whether or not you are ready to take the final Practice Test and, if not, in what areas you need more work.

POST-TEST 2: SOCIAL STUDIES ANSWER GRID

1 ① ② ③ ④ ⑤	17 ① ② ③ ④ ⑤	33 ① ② ③ ④ ⑤	49 ① ② ③ ④ ⑤
2 ① ② ③ ④ ⑤	18 ① ② ③ ④ ⑤	34 ① ② ③ ④ ⑤	50 ① ② ③ ④ ⑤
3 ① ② ③ ④ ⑤	19 ① ② ③ ④ ⑤	35 ① ② ③ ④ ⑤	51 ① ② ③ ④ ⑤
4 ① ② ③ ④ ⑤	20 ① ② ③ ④ ⑤	36 ① ② ③ ④ ⑤	52 ① ② ③ ④ ⑤
5 ① ② ③ ④ ⑤	21 ① ② ③ ④ ⑤	37 ① ② ③ ④ ⑤	53 ① ② ③ ④ ⑤
6 ① ② ③ ④ ⑤	22 ① ② ③ ④ ⑤	38 ① ② ③ ④ ⑤	54 ① ② ③ ④ ⑤
7 ① ② ③ ④ ⑤	23 ① ② ③ ④ ⑤	39 ① ② ③ ④ ⑤	55 ① ② ③ ④ ⑤
8 ① ② ③ ④ ⑤	24 ① ② ③ ④ ⑤	40 ① ② ③ ④ ⑤	56 ① ② ③ ④ ⑤
9 ① ② ③ ④ ⑤	25 ① ② ③ ④ ⑤	41 ① ② ③ ④ ⑤	57 ① ② ③ ④ ⑤
10 ① ② ③ ④ ⑤	26 ① ② ③ ④ ⑤	42 ① ② ③ ④ ⑤	58 ① ② ③ ④ ⑤
11 ① ② ③ ④ ⑤	27 ① ② ③ ④ ⑤	43 ① ② ③ ④ ⑤	59 ① ② ③ ④ ⑤
12 ① ② ③ ④ ⑤	28 ① ② ③ ④ ⑤	44 ① ② ③ ④ ⑤	60 ① ② ③ ④ ⑤
13 ① ② ③ ④ ⑤	29 ① ② ③ ④ ⑤	45 ① ② ③ ④ ⑤	61 ① ② ③ ④ ⑤
14 ① ② ③ ④ ⑤	30 ① ② ③ ④ ⑤	46 ① ② ③ ④ ⑤	62 ① ② ③ ④ ⑤
15 ① ② ③ ④ ⑤	31 ① ② ③ ④ ⑤	47 ① ② ③ ④ ⑤	63 ① ② ③ ④ ⑤
16 ① ② ③ ④ ⑤	32 ① ② ③ ④ ⑤	48 ① ② ③ ④ ⑤	64 ① ② ③ ④ ⑤

Choose the best answer to each question that follows.

Questions 1 and 2 are based on the following passage.

. . . The Monroe Doctrine of 1823 was largely an expression of the vibrant post–1812 nationalism suffusing the United States. . . . While giving vent to a spirit of patriotism, it simultaneously deepened the illusion of isolation. Many unthinking Americans falsely concluded, then and later, that we were in fact isolated from European dangers simply because we wanted to be, and because, in a nationalistic outburst, we had publicly proclaimed that we were going to be.

1. In the passage, the phrase "illusion of isolation" refers to the

    (1) guarantee that the United States will not become involved in European affairs
    (2) false belief that the United States can stay out of European affairs
    (3) promise that the United States will fight for its allies worldwide
    (4) mistaken belief that Americans want the United States to be a world power
    (5) view that the United States and Europe will be allies in all future crises

2. The passage about the Monroe Doctrine addresses only *one* of *two* aspects of the proclamation—neutrality in European affairs. Which of the following describes the other aspect of the doctrine not mentioned in the quote?

    (1) containment of communism in the Americas
    (2) prohibition against further European intervention in the Americas
    (3) announcement of American imperialist intentions throughout the world
    (4) declaration of American support of all free peoples resisting domination
    (5) a drive to extend the U.S. borders to the Pacific Ocean

Questions 3 and 4 are based on the following map and definitions.

plains—extensive areas with little or no change in elevation

hills—elevations of 500 to 1,000 ft. that have sides sloping up to flat or rounded tops

plateaus—elevations of less than 500 ft. with sides that rise sharply to broad flat tops

trenches—steep-sided valleys usually associated with plateaus

mountains—elevations of over 1,000 ft., usually with steep rocky inclines on all sides and a pointed or rounded top

3. Based on the land elevations indicated on the map, the dominant topographical feature consists of

   (1) plateaus
   (2) plains
   (3) hills
   (4) mountains
   (5) trenches

4. The topography shown on this map would most likely apply to which of the following states?

   (1) Ohio
   (2) Mississippi
   (3) Kentucky
   (4) West Virginia
   (5) Iowa

5. "The price of the 'melting pot' theory is self-annihilation. While the foreign groups are permitted to contribute to the life of a nation, they do so by losing their own existence." The author of this quote holds the position that immigrants

   (1) must give up their own customs and traditions in order to become Americans
   (2) are more likely to die in America than in their native lands
   (3) are really not welcome in the United States
   (4) must give up all of their wealth in order to gain permission to live in America
   (5) are openly accepted into American life

Questions 6 and 7 are based on the following passage.

More than thirty years ago, anthropologist Jane Goodall went to Africa to begin her study of chimpanzees. She has since witnessed chimps working together to kill baboons and pigs, and she has seen them use sticks to find and eat termites.

6. These behaviors can lead to the conclusion that chimpanzees

   (1) are cruel and vicious animals
   (2) have the instinctive behavior to kill
   (3) are capable of making tools and cooperating with one another
   (4) are a selfish and greedy species
   (5) have exactly the same behaviors as humans

7. Jane Goodall believes her studies have given scientists some clues about human behavior because chimpanzees

(1) and humans have similar cultures
(2) and humans both live in a variety of environments
(3) are the most intelligent species in the world
(4) can be taught the behavior of humans
(5) and humans are believed to have evolved from a common ancestor

Question 8 is based on the following passage.

Walk into a factory in the year 2000 and chances are you'll see teams of robots at work. The number of robots performing heavy and routine chores in manufacturing is expected to increase to 200,000—10 times the number there were in 1979. That increase will probably lower the demand for factory workers. The BLS (Bureau of Labor Statistics) expects that manufacturing will claim only one tenth of the 16 million new jobs that will be created by 1995. Some experts predict that the portion of U.S. workers in manufacturing, 17.4 percent in 1991, will decline to 10 percent by the year 2000.

8. The impact that the increased use of robots will have on the job market is likely to be

(1) an increase in the number of people employed in factories
(2) a lowered demand for factory workers
(3) a reduced number of people who will rely on goods manufactured in factories
(4) increased individual salaries to make up for employment changes
(5) a decrease in the number of people employed in service industries

Questions 9 and 10 are based on the following passage.

Quite often, underdeveloped or developing countries are referred to collectively as the *Third World*. The term originated in France in the 1950s as a comparison to the third estate, or class, of the population. The third class in France was made up of commoners who had little material wealth and who wanted more. So, the Third World has little of the world's wealth and seeks more of its share. To get more, social scientists agree that the Third World will have to strive for

• good communication systems
• good transportation networks
• a healthy and employable population
• political stability
• adequate raw materials, especially fuels for power and manufacturing

9. Which of the following would most likely fit the description of a Third World nation?

(1) Japan
(2) West Germany
(3) Great Britain
(4) Australia
(5) Zimbabwe

10. The islands of the South Pacific enjoy a mild climate, a disease-free environment, long-running governments, and even modern telephones, televisions, and airports. But they are small, widely dispersed, and lacking in the production of goods essential to their economic development. So, their biggest drawback to development is their not having

(1) good communication systems
(2) good transportation networks
(3) a healthy and employable population
(4) political stability
(5) adequate raw materials, especially fuels for power and manufacturing

Questions 11 and 12 are based on the following graph.

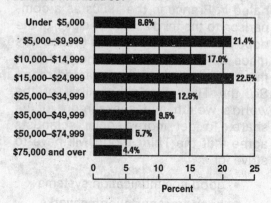

PERCENT DISTRIBUTION BY INCOME: 1991

Families with head 65+

Income	Percent
Under $5,000	8.8%
$5,000–$9,999	21.4%
$10,000–$14,999	17.0%
$15,000–$24,999	22.5%
$25,000–$34,999	12.8%
$35,000–$49,999	8.5%
$50,000–$74,999	5.7%
$75,000 and over	4.4%

Percent

Source: U.S. Bureau of the Census

11. Based on the facts in the graph, which of the following can you conclude about families headed by individuals 65 years or older?

   (1) A greater percentage are very poor than are very wealthy.

   (2) Twice as many had incomes of $15,000 or more than had incomes of less than $10,000.

   (3) The percentages of very poor and very wealthy are equal.

   (4) Elderly women are more likely to be poor than elderly men.

   (5) There are more households comprised of single senior citizens than couples.

12. If the official poverty level was designated to be $7,905 for elderly couples in 1990 and $6,268 for individuals, which of the following is supported by the information in the graph?

   (1) 6.6 percent of all families 65+ live below the poverty level.

   (2) 28 percent of all families 65+ live below the poverty level.

   (3) 21.4 percent of all families 65+ live below the poverty level.

   (4) The total percentage of families 65+ living below the poverty level cannot be determined from the graph.

   (5) The percentage of families 65+ who live below the poverty level can be determined only for individuals and not for couples.

13. In the Dani culture of New Guinea, pigs are raised by the children and considered a sign of wealth among the community members. In India, cows are sacred and are symbols of worship. The importance of animals in these two countries is based on

   (1) cultural universals

   (2) cultural relativity

   (3) ethnocentrism

   (4) values and customs

   (5) cultural diffusion

14. In 1974 and again in 1986, the U.S. Congress established committees to investigate alleged wrongdoings by the president and his staff. This congressional action is an example of

   (1) amending the Constitution

   (2) overriding a veto

   (3) passing a bill

   (4) applying checks and balances

   (5) approving a treaty

Questions 15 and 16 are based on the following passage.

During the early 1980s, the IRS had 87,000 employees. By 1990, that number had risen to 116,425, an increase of 33 percent. But the number of taxpayers' returns has climbed from 137.4 million to 201.7 million, a jump of 46 percent. The IRS has attempted to handle the rising workload by reducing by 20 percent the staff members who handle taxpayer inquiries, process returns and get refunds in the mail. The personnel remaining in these jobs have had to pick up the slack and have faced unrealistic work quotas. Overwhelming workloads led to large-scale foul-ups. Clearly, massive tax reform is needed on several fronts. The income tax must be simplified and made as fair as possible for all. But on top of that, the IRS must clean up its own house so that it can do its work with accuracy and precision. Until the code is simplified and until the computer works, more help must be hired.

15. Which of the following is an opinion suggested, but not directly stated, by the author of the editorial?

(1) More than 116,000 IRS workers processed more than 200,000 tax returns in 1990.
(2) The number of tax returns to be processed rose by 46 percent from the early 1980s to 1990.
(3) Workloads should be lightened to avoid major mistakes in tax processing.
(4) Twenty percent of the IRS's staff were reassigned in an attempt to remedy problems.
(5) Remaining personnel have had to face unrealistic workloads.

16. What does the writer believe to be the cause of the major foul-ups by the IRS?

(1) computer errors
(2) heavy workloads
(3) complicated tax forms
(4) unskilled workers
(5) unfair tax laws

---

17. In recent years, the top two manufacturers of soft drinks, Coca-Cola and PepsiCo, each sought to purchase the number three and four soft drink producers, Dr. Pepper and Seven-Up. However, the Federal Trade Commission prevented the takeover. The FTC refused the companies' attempts because the takeovers would

(1) interfere with free competition in the soft drink industry among its four largest manufacturers
(2) create a monopoly, concentrating merchandising power in the hands of a single company
(3) reduce the quality and variety of the product offered
(4) drive the prices up, forcing consumers to buy fewer soft drinks
(5) force the other smaller, independent bottlers to merge with one of the two giants

Questions 18 and 19 are based on the following map.

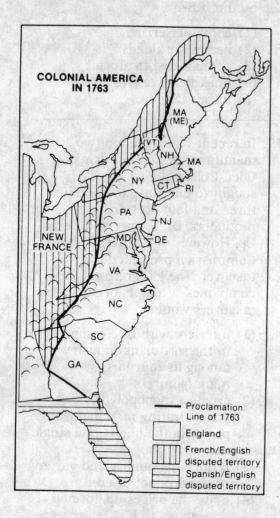

COLONIAL AMERICA IN 1763

MA (ME)
VT
NH
MA
NY
CT
RI
PA
NJ
NEW FRANCE
MD
DE
VA
NC
SC
GA

—— Proclamation Line of 1763
England
French/English disputed territory
Spanish/English disputed territory

18. Vermont, admitted to the Union in 1791, was the subject of a territorial dispute during colonial times. Based on the map, which bordering states can you conclude were rivals for the Vermont territory before it obtained statehood?

    (1) Maine and New Hampshire
    (2) New Hampshire and Rhode Island
    (3) New York and Rhode Island
    (4) Connecticut and New York
    (5) New York and New Hampshire

19. The Proclamation Line of 1763 resulted from a treaty between France and England for control of colonial America. What was the intended effect of the Line of Proclamation?

    (1) to separate the country geographically into east and west
    (2) to grant freedom to portions of the thirteen colonies lying east of the line
    (3) to establish a mountain pass connecting the northeast with the southeast
    (4) to separate French from English territory in the New World
    (5) to prevent colonists from escaping into New France

20. The United States has put quotas (limits) on the number of automobiles that foreign countries can export to America. Which one of the following explanations would be an acceptable justification for the quotas?

    (1) American manufacturers must be protected from unfair competition.
    (2) Automobiles are the highest-costing products to export.
    (3) More cars are exported than any other product.
    (4) The dollar amount of trade between other car-manufacturing countries and the United States is very low.
    (5) There is no demand for foreign cars by American consumers.

21. In an attempt to try to reduce the trade deficit, the United States should limit its trade with which one of the following trade partners from which it imports more than it exports?

    (1) Eastern Europe
    (2) Latin America
    (3) Australia and Oceania
    (4) Spain
    (5) Japan

Questions 22 and 23 are based on the following passage.

So many issues now receiving attention in the media and in the political arena are really family issues—drug abuse, teen suicide, teen pregnancy, the crisis in education. If we can redirect our discussions of these issues to an exploration of what can be done early in a child's life to help families create a healthy environment in which to grow and develop, we can lessen both the likelihood and the extent of many subsequent personal and societal crises.

We place great stock in the importance and effectiveness of preventive measures, and research and practical experience are behind us. We know, for example, the following:

Children who do not receive regular preventive health care from an early age are likely to suffer from undetected health problems and disabilities.

Children without supportive adult care are likely to lack confidence, feel alienated and distrustful, and suffer from learning and behavioral problems.

Children who are not stimulated and encouraged to develop through activities appropriate to their age are likely to experience problems in school.

22. A child grows and develops within the environment in which he or she is raised. This learning process is known as

(1) heredity
(2) socialization
(3) conditioning
(4) programming
(5) trial-and-error learning

23. Which one of the following statements would likely be inconsistent with the author's beliefs?

(1) Attitudes and behaviors of adults result from childhood experiences.
(2) Families can be affected by a variety of governmental programs and policies.
(3) Many problems in society can be solved by providing a healthy family environment.
(4) Schools are the only place children can be taught discipline and proper attitudes.
(5) Children from good family environments are less likely to find themselves in trouble.

Question 24 is based on the following.

"The conjunction of an immense military establishment and a large arms industry . . . new in American experience, exercises a total influence . . . felt in every city, every state house, every office of the federal government. . . . In the councils of government, we must guard against the acquisition of unwarranted influence by the military-industrial complex."

General Dwight Eisenhower,
34th President of the United States,
Farewell Address, 1961

24. Which of the following opinions is supported by this statement?

(1) An overgrown military establishment could pose a threat to democracy.
(2) Industrial influence on the military has made our government more democratic.
(3) Only the military-industrial complex can safeguard our liberties.
(4) The military should be allowed more influence in government affairs.
(5) Civilian control of the military should never be allowed.

Questions 25 and 26 are based on the graph and information below.

FEDERAL DEFICIT
(In Billions of Dollars Per Fiscal Year)

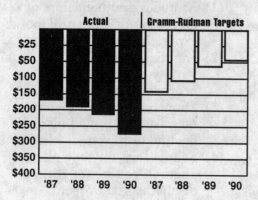

Source: Office of Management and Budget

In 1985, the Congress passed a law known as the Gramm-Rudman-Hollings Act. Its purpose was to achieve a balanced budget by 1991 by yearly cuts in the budget deficit. The graph shows the planned implementation of the law.

25. A budget deficit refers to the

(1) taxes collected in a given year
(2) money spent on domestic programs
(3) funds allocated to pay the national debt
(4) money the government has left over for special projects
(5) money spent that exceeds the amount received in taxes

26. Assuming the graph is accurate, which of the following should have resulted from the Gramm-Rudman-Hollings legislation?

(1) The Congress would have spent more money than it received in taxes.
(2) Government programs would have been established to control private enterprise.
(3) The national debt gradually would have been reduced.
(4) The Gramm-Rudman-Hollings Act would have been repealed.
(5) The business cycle would no longer be part of the American economy.

Questions 27 and 28 are based on the graph below.

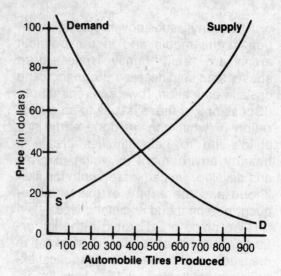

27. According to the graph, what would be the market price of the tires?

(1) $20
(2) $40
(3) $60
(4) $80
(5) $100

28. What would a producer probably do to increase demand if the price of the tires rose above the market price shown on the graph?

(1) increase production
(2) put 800 tires on the market to sell
(3) raise the price even more
(4) lower the cost of the tires
(5) reduce the quality of the tires but keep the prices the same

Questions 29–31 are based on the following definitions.

Economic systems may be categorized in several different ways. Defined below are five categories of economic systems that operate throughout the world.

pure communism—an economic system in which there is no government control with each individual working for the good of all

Marxian socialism—an economic system in which the government owns all the means of production and controls all aspects of the citizens' economic life

democratic socialism—an economic system in which the government owns the basic industries such as steel, textiles, and energy while permitting some private enterprise and greater consumer freedom

American capitalism—an economic system in which individuals rather than government own the means of production and, along with consumer demand, determine what will be produced

pure capitalism—an economic system in which there is no government regulation or influence, with each individual working for his or her own success

29. Which economic system maintains that decisions about the production and distribution of goods must be determined by a central authority?

(1) pure communism
(2) Marxian socialism
(3) democratic socialism
(4) American capitalism
(5) pure capitalism

30. Biologist Charles Darwin believed that the species that was better able to adapt would continue to exist—survival of the fittest. Under which one of the following economic and social policies did the belief in and application of survival of the fittest thrive?

(1) Franklin Roosevelt's New Deal and government-funded work programs
(2) Teddy Roosevelt's progressivism and regulation of big business activities
(3) Herbert Hoover's conservatism and noninterference in the affairs of business
(4) Dwight Eisenhower's policies of moderation
(5) Lyndon Johnson's Great Society and generous spending for social programs

31. An economic system is designed to meet the needs of the people by establishing production priorities and allocating the limited resources. In which one of the following economic systems would there be the most coordinated use of production facilities while still permitting individual consumer choice?

(1) pure communism
(2) Marxian socialism
(3) democratic socialism
(4) American capitalism
(5) pure capitalism

Questions 32 and 33 are based on the following passage.

Virginia Louisa Minor was the first woman in Missouri to take a public stand in favor of women's suffrage. Her husband, Francis Minor, was a lawyer, and he was the first person to argue that women were enfranchised by the equal protection clause of the Fourteenth Amendment. In 1872 Mrs. Minor and her husband filed suit against a St. Louis registrar who had refused to allow her to register. The lower court held against the Minors, who then appealed to the Supreme Court of the United States. In 1875 the court handed down a unanimous decision holding that suffrage was not coextensive with citizenship and that the political rights of women were to be decided by the states. The opinion did say, "If the law is wrong, it ought to be changed," but added that "the power for that is not with us." After this ruling the National Woman Suffrage Association felt it had no alternative but to propose an amendment to the U.S. Constitution.

32. Which one of the following conclusions best summarizes the Supreme Court's decision in this case?

(1) Women should not have the right to vote because they do not own property.

(2) The government is a male domain, and women have no place in it.

(3) Virginia Minor did not meet the age or residency requirements to register to vote.

(4) The Equal Rights Amendment was being considered by the state legislature.

(5) The Supreme Court cannot interfere with the states' right to determine voter requirements.

33. A *precedent* is a legal decision that may serve as a reason or justification for a later case. Using the Minor case as such, what would the U.S. Supreme Court decide in a case appealed by a seventeen-year-old male citizen who claims that under the state criminal code he is considered an adult and, therefore, should be treated as an adult and given the right to vote? The U.S. Supreme Court would probably

(1) permit seventeen-year-olds to vote to make the laws more consistent

(2) deny the appeal because the law must be changed by the state

(3) refuse to hear the case because the issue was previously decided

(4) allow only seventeen-year-old males to vote since women were already denied the vote

(5) require the states to amend their law to allow seventeen-year-olds to vote

---

34. A presidential primary election is *chiefly* different from a general election in that

(1) a presidential primary is usually of local interest only

(2) a person does not have to be a registered voter to vote in a primary

(3) a primary election does not determine who will be the president of the United States

(4) a primary election determines the number of electoral college votes a particular candidate gets

(5) a primary election must have only two opposing candidates on the ballot

Questions 35 and 36 refer to the following illustration.

VIOLENT CRIMES:
THE FUNNEL EFFECT

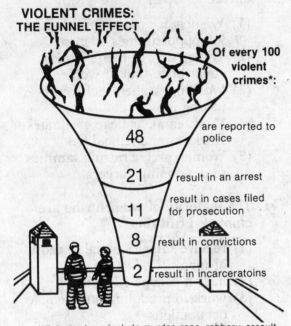

Of every 100 violent crimes*:

48 are reported to police

21 result in an arrest

11 result in cases filed for prosecution

8 result in convictions

2 result in incarceratoins

*Violent crimes include murder, rape, robbery, assault.

Source: National Crime Survey, Bureau of Justice Statistics

35. The term "funnel effect" refers to the

   (1) idea that all crimes are put into the same criminal justice system

   (2) belief that every criminal gets caught and is punished

   (3) concept that most suspects who go through the criminal justice process are actually guilty

   (4) idea that only a very few suspects arrested for committing a crime are actually punished

   (5) belief that crime is under control in the United States

36. Which one of the following statements about the criminal justice system is *not* based on the illustration?

   (1) Over half of violent crimes go unreported.

   (2) Less than one-fourth result in an arrest.

   (3) Most violent crimes occur in instances in which the victim knows the criminal.

   (4) The states' criminal justice system has a low conviction rate.

   (5) About 10 percent of the violent crimes are actually prosecuted.

Questions 37 and 38 refer to the following passage.

WE, THEREFORE, the Representatives of the UNITED STATES of AMERICA, in General Congress, Assembled, appealing to the Supreme Judge of the world for the rectitude of our intentions, do, in the Name, and by Authority of the good People of these Colonies, solemnly publish and declare, That these United Colonies are, and of Right ought to be, FREE AND INDEPENDENT STATES. . . .

37. This statement was proclaimed by members of which group?

   (1) Constitutional Convention
   (2) Boston Tea Party
   (3) Pilgrims
   (4) Second Continental Congress
   (5) the first House of Representatives

38. Which of the following statements supports the author's opinion?

   (1) All people should be free from government control.

   (2) The United States should be free from outside control.

   (3) All wealthy countries have the right to control the weaker countries of the world.

   (4) The people shall have the right to vote for their leaders.

   (5) The United States needs a strong federal government.

39. The fact that the U.S. Constitution can be amended is the basis for the conclusion that the authors

   (1) made many mistakes in the original writing

   (2) did not really know what they wanted to say

   (3) took into account future changes in the needs and values of the people

   (4) were required by the Supreme Court to include this power

   (5) considered all possible circumstances and situations and included them in the original Constitution

Questions 40 and 41 refer to the following passage.

Despite the attention afforded female astronauts or Supreme Court justices, statistics show that women's occupations have remained "remarkably traditional."

So writes Nancy Barrett in "The American Woman 1987: A Report in Depth." Women still "are overwhelmingly concentrated in low-paying female occupations," according to Barrett. "In 1985, 70 percent of all full-time employed women were working in occupations in which more than three-quarters of the employees were female. Among those occupations were receptionist, child-care worker, bank teller, data-entry keyer, and cashier. More than one-third of all employed women work in clerical jobs.

"Where they have moved into formerly male domains, they remain on the bottom rungs of the job ladder or are tracked into predominantly female 'ghettos'—relatively low-paying subcategories of jobs with higher-paying occupations dominated by men," Barrett says.

According to 1991 Bureau of Labor statistics, the situation had improved only slightly in six years. The number of women in professional and administrative positions had increased only a few percentage points.

40. With which one of the following conclusions would Barrett likely agree?

   (1) Women are not given the same job opportunities as men.

   (2) The quality of men's work is superior to that of women's.

   (3) Working women seek lower-paying jobs.

   (4) Most female college graduates work in the medical field.

   (5) Women prefer raising families to developing careers.

41. The majority of women who are employed full-time

   (1) receive salaries equal to those of men

   (2) have a college education

   (3) work in predominantly female occupations

   (4) fill executive and administrative positions

   (5) prefer clerical work

---

42. In the 1930s, England and France followed a policy of appeasement toward German territorial expansion. Germany took over all of Czechoslovakia and threatened Poland and Austria. Many experts in international relations claim that appeasing German expansionism led to World War II.

Based on this description, you could infer that appeasement is

   (1) refusing to allow European nations to interfere in American affairs

   (2) taking in unlimited numbers of immigrants from other countries

   (3) the right to use land that belongs to someone else

   (4) compromising in the face of aggression

   (5) German domination of international politics

Questions 43 and 44 are based on the following map.

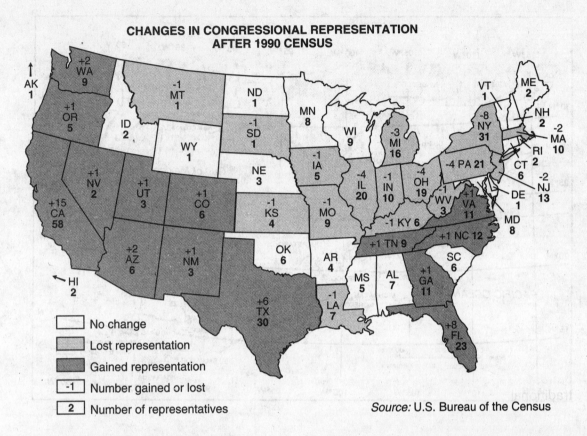

**CHANGES IN CONGRESSIONAL REPRESENTATION
AFTER 1990 CENSUS**

☐ No change

▨ Lost representation

▨ Gained representation

-1 Number gained or lost

2 Number of representatives

Source: U.S. Bureau of the Census

43. Which one of the following statements is supported by the information in the map?

(1) More states lost representatives than gained them.

(2) New York has more representatives than any other state.

(3) More states experienced no change in representation than gained representatives.

(4) States that lost representatives are concentrated in the South.

(5) States that gained representatives are concentrated in the North.

44. A candidate for president needs a majority of electoral votes to be elected. Which group of states would have the largest number of electoral votes?

(1) Nebraska, North Carolina, California

(2) Texas, Ohio, Minnesota

(3) Pennsylvania, Tennessee, Oregon

(4) Wisconsin, Mississippi, Connecticut

(5) Florida, Virginia, New York

Questions 45–47 are based on the map below.

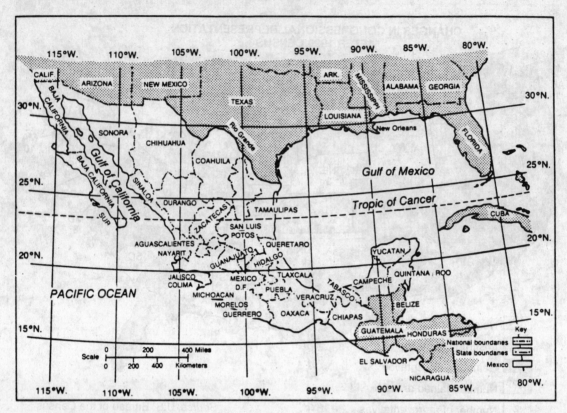

45. Durango, Mexico, is located at 25 degrees north and 105 degrees west. A pilot traveling from Durango to the country of Guatemala would have to follow which instructions as he leaves Durango and travels?

(1) 15 degrees north and 90 degrees west
(2) 10 degrees north and 15 degrees east
(3) 10 degrees south and 90 degrees west
(4) 10 degrees north and 15 degrees west
(5) 10 degrees south and 15 degrees east

46. This map would be most useful in

(1) identifying political boundaries
(2) developing a highway map
(3) identifying topographical formations
(4) recognizing historical landmarks
(5) identifying population centers

47. Looking from west to east on the map, for every 15 degrees an hour is added. If it is 9:00 P.M. in eastern Arizona, what time would it be on the eastern coast of Florida?

(1) 11:00 P.M.
(2) 10:00 P.M.
(3) 9:00 P.M.
(4) 8:00 P.M.
(5) 7:00 P.M.

Questions 48–50 are based on the following passage.

Never in history have the interests of all the people been so united in a single economic problem. . . . Danger to one is danger to all. . . .

What do the people of America want more than anything else? To my mind, they want two things: work, with all the moral and spiritual values that go with it; and with work, a reasonable measure of security. . . .

Our Republican leaders tell us economic laws—sacred, inviolable, unchangeable—cause panics which no one could prevent. But while they prate [talk] of economic laws, men and women are starving. We must lay hold of the fact that economic laws are not made by nature. They are made by human beings. . . .

48. Based on this quote, you can infer that the speaker would *not* support which of the following?

(1) laissez-faire business policies
(2) progressive social legislation
(3) government-funded public works programs
(4) government-funded welfare programs
(5) wage-price controls

49. The statement "economic laws are made by human beings" implies that

(1) Americans are the only people to have an economic system
(2) Republican leaders said that man could not control economics
(3) economic laws are based upon moral and spiritual values not controlled by man
(4) nations throughout the world can select and control their own economic system
(5) laws of economics are "sacred, invaluable, unchangeable"

50. The preceding quote could accurately be attributed to

(1) Harry S Truman
(2) Franklin D. Roosevelt
(3) Herbert C. Hoover
(4) Dwight D. Eisenhower
(5) Ronald W. Reagan

51. Ethnocentrism refers to the practice of judging another culture by one's own standards and beliefs. Which of the following represents ethnocentric behavior?

(1) a student who tutors an immigrant in English
(2) a tourist who lectures his foreign hosts on the "uncivilized" nature of their marriage customs
(3) a Peace Corps volunteer who helps dig wells in Central Africa
(4) a Russian Jewish immigrant who insists that his children learn English and Hebrew
(5) a Hispanic community group that demands that public aid forms be published in English and Spanish

52. Liberals believe that the problems of the country should be solved by a strong federal government. They support funding for social programs, limiting military spending, and negotiation as the basis for American foreign policy. Which one of the following federal programs would liberals in America be likely to oppose?

(1) guaranteed government loans to college students
(2) a national health insurance program
(3) stricter pollution laws
(4) Star Wars space defense system
(5) job training for the handicapped

Questions 53–55 are based on the following cartoon.

53. Which of the following best describes the man in the cartoon?

   (1) an average citizen
   (2) an elected official
   (3) a political poll taker
   (4) a political candidate
   (5) a behavioral scientist

54. What information is the man trying to get from the woman?

   (1) how her feelings about the present election compare with her feelings about the 1988 election
   (2) what it takes to make her happy
   (3) why she is happy the election is over
   (4) why she was unhappy about the 1988 election
   (5) how she voted in the 1992 and 1988 elections

55. The cartoonist is expressing which of the following opinions?

   (1) Americans should feel happier about elections.
   (2) Poll takers don't know when to quit asking questions.
   (3) Political polls are getting too personal.
   (4) Ordinary people don't care enough about political analysis.
   (5) Public opinion polls don't do any good.

56. In 1993, the Army recommended that the Pentagon consider shutting down undersized and outdated Fort Riley. But the base was not included on the Pentagon's list of possible closings. After all, Fort Riley was located in Kansas, the home state of a powerful senator. The information in this passage supports which of the following conclusions?

   (1) Politics can influence military decisions.
   (2) Military decisions are based solely on standards of efficiency.
   (3) The Army is not in favor of any more base closings.
   (4) Politics has no effect on military decisions.
   (5) Fort Riley will be closed in spite of the Pentagon's decision.

Questions 57 and 58 are based on the following table.

COMPARISON OF AVERAGE TEMPERATURE AND RAINFALL IN EASTERN ASIA AND EASTERN NORTH AMERICA												

Shanghai (Lat. 31°11'N.)

	Jan.	Feb.	Mar.	Apr.	May	Jun.	Jul.	Aug.	Sep.	Oct.	Nov.	Dec.	Year
Temperature (in Fahrenheit)	37.8°	39.4°	46.0°	56.1°	65.5°	73.4°	80.4°	80.2°	73.0°	63.5°	52.0°	42.1°	59.1°
Rainfall (in inches)	2.0	2.3	3.5	3.7	3.5	7.2	6.0	5.7	4.4	3.2	2.1	1.4	45.0

Charleston, S.C. (Lat. 32°47'N.)

Temperature (in Fahrenheit)	49.8°	51.2°	57.5°	63.9°	72.1°	78.1°	80.6°	80.0°	76.2°	67.0°	57.8°	51.0°	65.4°
Rainfall (in inches)	3.1	3.3	3.4	2.9	3.4	4.8	7.1	6.6	5.0	3.6	2.4	2.9	48.5

57. Using the table as a basis, which one of the following conclusions is *most* valid?

(1) On a day-to-day basis, the weather in both cities is the same.
(2) The summer months in Shanghai and Charleston show the least variation in temperature.
(3) Heavy rainfall makes Shanghai uninhabitable.
(4) While it is winter in Charleston, it is summer in Shanghai.
(5) Eastern Asia and eastern North America experience the same jet stream patterns.

58. Which one of the following statements is an *opinion* rather than a fact?

(1) Weather conditions in Charleston are better than those in Shanghai.
(2) Charleston, S.C., has a greater amount of annual rainfall than does Shanghai.
(3) Both cities are north of the equator.
(4) The greatest amount of rainfall in both cities occurs in the summer months.
(5) January is the coldest month in Charleston and Shanghai.

59. In 1972, eighteen-year-olds were given the right to vote through which one of the following methods?

(1) a Supreme Court decision
(2) a law passed by Congress
(3) an amendment to the Constitution
(4) an executive order from the president
(5) a consensus vote of the fifty states

60. "Government should do for the people only what the people cannot do for themselves" best describes the philosophy of which of the following forms of government?

(1) dictatorship
(2) authoritarianism
(3) democracy
(4) totalitarianism
(5) monarchy

Questions 61 and 62 are based on the following cartoon.

61. According to the cartoon, what effect does the abortion debate have on Illinois legislators?

   (1) It makes them angry.
   (2) It makes them nervous.
   (3) It makes them think about philosophy.
   (4) It makes them feel confused.
   (5) It makes them think about other important issues.

62. The cartoon supports which of the following conclusions about Illinois legislators?

   (1) They don't believe the abortion debate is a valid political issue.
   (2) They have already taken sides on the abortion issue.
   (3) They enjoy controversial issues.
   (4) They want to avoid making a decision about such a controversial issue.
   (5) They are willing to protest against procrastination.

63. Political parties in America are a significant part of the electoral process. If the political parties no longer existed

   (1) democratic elections would no longer be held
   (2) the number of candidates would probably be unlimited
   (3) election campaigns would be unnecessary
   (4) elected officials would not have a constituency
   (5) issues would be more clearly defined and identifiable

64. Sociologists define "classical conditioning" as behavior that is maintained after a stimulus has been introduced several times. Which of the following is an application of classical conditioning in child rearing?

   (1) getting the child to consistently associate the time that "Sesame Street" ends with naptime
   (2) becoming irritable with a child who will not be toilet trained
   (3) giving a child a bicycle for his seventh birthday
   (4) keeping a child with chicken pox away from school
   (5) giving young girls gifts of cars and trucks instead of dolls

Answers begin on page 775.

POST-TEST 2: SOCIAL STUDIES ANSWER KEY

1. (2) An illusion is a false belief. The passage says that "Americans falsely concluded . . . that we were in fact isolated from European dangers simply because we wanted to be. . . ."

2. (2) The only choice listed that represents the other aspect of the Monroe Doctrine is the prohibition against further European colonization in the Americas.

3. (4) Mountains are land elevations of over 1,000 feet. Most of the land shown is over 1,000 feet above sea level.

4. (4) West Virginia is the only mountainous state listed among the choices.

5. (1) Giving up one's customs and traditions is a restatement of the quote from the passage "losing their own existence."

6. (3) Working together to kill other animals and using sticks to find and eat termites are examples of cooperating with each other and making tools.

7. (5) The study of chimpanzees is important to understanding human behavior because it is believed that both species have a common ancestor.

8. (2) The passage states that the portion of U.S. workers in manufacturing is predicted to fall to 10 percent by the year 2000.

9. (5) Of the choices listed, only Zimbabwe meets the criteria of having little material wealth and wanting more. The other choices represent industrialized nations.

10. (5) The passage states that the South Pacific islands lack the production of goods essential for their economic development.

11. (2) The combined total percentage of families headed by persons 65+ earning less than $10,000 is 28 percent; the combined total for those earning more than $15,000 is 55 percent.

12. (4) The information on the graph is not broken down into these two categories—those earning less than $6,268 and those earning less than $7,905.

13. (4) Values and customs determine what practices a culture follows.

14. (4) Congressional investigations into the actions of the president are an example of the checks and balances built into the Constitution.

15. (3) Choice (3), which contains the word *should*, represents an opinion. Choices (1), (2), (4), and (5) are facts stated in the passage.

16. (2) The passage refers to a rising workload and a reduction of staff as well as to overwhelming workloads.

17. (1) The takeover would result in the two major soft drink manufacturers controlling the third- and fourth-largest companies.

18. (5) New York and New Hampshire are states that border Vermont; therefore, you can conclude that a territorial dispute involved these two states.

19. (4) The Proclamation Line divided New France from the English colonies; the other choices are not supported by the map.

20. (1) Quotas would limit the number of foreign cars that could be placed on the market to compete with American-made automobiles.

21. (5) Currently, Japan is the only area or nation given that exports more to the United States than it imports from the United States.

22. (2) The process by which an individual learns the ways of the culture is called *socialization*.

23. (4) The author clearly believes that many institutions in society, especially the family, play a key role in children's development.

24. (1) This is the only statement that reflects Eisenhower's concern about "an immense military establishment and a large arms industry."

25. (5) A budget deficit occurs when the government spends more money than it receives in taxes.

26. (3) The goal of the Gramm-Rudman-Hollings Act was to eliminate further budget deficits through gradual reductions in government spending.

27. (2) The market price is $40 because that is the equilibrium point (the point at which the demand and supply curves intersect).

28. (4) The producers would lower the price of the tires to encourage consumers to buy the tires.

29. (2) Marxian socialism is the only economic system in which these decisions are made by the government.

30. (3) Herbert Hoover's policies of government noninterference in business encouraged the strongest businesses to survive, sometimes at the expense of the weakest.

31. (3) Democratic socialism permits individual consumers choice while maintaining government control over the means of production.

32. (5) The Supreme Court decided that the states had the right to determine voter requirements, and therefore the laws of the state would have to be changed.

33. (2) Based upon precedent, the state law would have to be changed to allow seventeen-year-olds to vote. Choice (5) is incorrect because the Supreme Court cannot require a state to amend its laws.

34. (3) In a general election, the president of the United States is elected; a primary election determines which candidate from each party will run in the general election.

35. (4) Of all the crimes committed and reported to the police, only about 2 percent result in incarceration.

36. (3) The illustration does not indicate that most violent crimes occur in instances in which the victim knows the criminal.

37. (4) The Second Continental Congress met in order to declare the colonies' independence from England.

38. (2) The authors of the Declaration of Independence believed that the colonies should be free and independent states.

39. (3) An article for amending the Constitution was included so that the document could be altered to reflect the needs and values of the people in the future.

40. (1) Barrett believes that women do not have the same job opportunities as men, and she cites statistics that show that in 1985, 70 percent of all full-time employed women were working in occupations in which more than three-quarters were female.

41. (3) Women who are employed full-time tend to be in the traditionally female-oriented occupations of receptionist, child-care worker, bank teller, data-entry keyer, and cashier.

42. (4) The passage points out that England and France followed a policy of appeasement in the face of Germany's aggression. This means that appeasement is compromise in the face of aggression.

43. (3) A greater number of states are white on the map; this indicates that those states experienced no change in congressional representation.

44. (1) Of the states shown, Nebraska, North Carolina, and California would have the largest total number since they are the most populous.

45. (5) To travel from Durango to Guatemala, one would have to travel 10 degrees south then 15 degrees east.

46. (1) This map identifies the political boundaries within and surrounding Mexico.

47. (1) Traveling east from Arizona to the eastern coast of Florida, you go from 110 degrees west to 80 degrees west, resulting in a gain of two hours. Therefore, it would be 11:00 P.M. in Florida.

48. (1) *Laissez-faire* means letting business operate on its own without government interference. The speaker's words suggest that it is government's responsibility to help its citizens cope with economic hardships.

49. (4) Each nation has an economic system that best reflects the values of the people in that culture.

50. (2) Franklin D. Roosevelt, a Democrat, was best known for the federal programs his administration began that helped provide jobs and security for Americans during the Great Depression.

51. (2) To call the practices of another culture "uncivilized" is judgmental and therefore ethnocentric.

52. (4) The "Star Wars" space defense system is a military program that would be opposed by liberals.

53. (3) The questions the man asks and the clipboard he carries identify him as a political poll taker rather than any of the other choices.

54. (1) The man's first question is clearly about a recent election. His second question asks the woman to compare her degree of happiness to how she felt in 1988, another election year.

55. (2) By having the woman respond "Aaah" to the second question, the cartoonist is saying that the poll taker has asked one question too many.

56. (1) The passage supports the conclusion that the Pentagon omitted Fort Riley from its list of closings because the base was located in the home state of a powerful senator. Closing the base would hurt the state's economy and offend the senator, a politician with influence.

57. (2) The temperatures for the months of June, July, August, and September show the least variation.

58. (1) It is an opinion to say that one city has better weather conditions than another since the term *better* is relative.

59. (3) The Twenty-sixth Amendment to the Constitution gives eighteen-year-olds the right to vote.

60. (3) In a democracy, the government is there to help the people, but the people do most things for themselves.

61. (2) The figure representing the legislature is pulling at his collar, sweating, and gulping—all signs of nervousness. There are no visible signs that suggest the other choices.

62. (4) By delaying action on the abortion debate, the legislature hopes that the issue will go away before they have to make a decision about it. Only the pro-life and pro-choice protestors appear to have clearly taken sides (2). The legislature is avoiding controversy and is in favor of procrastination, or putting off the vote.

63. (2) Without political parties to reduce the number of candidates, any number of candidates could run for public office.

64. (1) The only example of a conditioned response is the child who learns to associate taking a nap with the end of "Sesame Street."

Use the answer key on pages 775–777 to check your answers to the Post-Test. Then find the item number of each question you missed and circle it on the chart below to determine the reading skill and content areas in which you need more practice. Pay particular attention to areas where you missed half or more of the questions. The reading skills are covered on pages 187–243. The page numbers for the content areas are listed below on the chart. Knowledge of reading skill and content area–based questions is absolutely essential for success on the GED Social Studies Test. The numbers in boldface are questions based on graphics. For those questions that you missed, review the skill pages indicated.

POST-TEST 2: SOCIAL STUDIES EVALUATION CHART

Skill Area/ Content Area	Comprehension (pages 189–195)	Application (pages 195–199)	Analysis (pages 200–210)	Evaluation (pages 211–222)
Behavioral Sciences (pages 247–262)	22, 41	13, 51, 64	6, 40	5, 7, 23
U.S. History (pages 263–300)	1, 37	24	2, **18**, 42, 50	**19**, 38, 39
Political Science (pages 301–318)	34, **35, 55, 57, 58**	14, 52, 56, 60, **61**	15, 16, 32, 59	33, **36, 62**, 63
Economics (pages 319–332)	**25, 27**, 49	21, 29, 30, 31	**11**, 17, **26, 28**	8, **12**, 20, 48
Geography (pages 333–342)	3, **44**	**4**, 9, **45, 46, 47**	10, **54**	**43, 53**

POST-TEST 3: SCIENCE

This Science Post-Test will give you the opportunity to evaluate your readiness for the actual GED Science Test.

This test contains 66 questions. Some of the questions are based on short reading passages, and some require you to interpret a chart or diagram.

You should take approximately 95 minutes to complete this test. At the end of 95 minutes, stop and mark your place. Then finish the test. This will give you an idea of whether or not you can finish the real GED Test in the time allotted. Try to answer as many questions as you can. A blank will count as a wrong answer, so make a reasonable guess for answers to questions you are not sure of.

When you are finished with the test, check your answers and turn to the Evaluation Chart on page 799. Use the chart to evaluate whether or not you are ready to take the final Practice Test and, if not, in what areas you need more work.

POST-TEST 3: SCIENCE ANSWER GRID

1 ① ② ③ ④ ⑤	18 ① ② ③ ④ ⑤	35 ① ② ③ ④ ⑤	51 ① ② ③ ④ ⑤
2 ① ② ③ ④ ⑤	19 ① ② ③ ④ ⑤	36 ① ② ③ ④ ⑤	52 ① ② ③ ④ ⑤
3 ① ② ③ ④ ⑤	20 ① ② ③ ④ ⑤	37 ① ② ③ ④ ⑤	53 ① ② ③ ④ ⑤
4 ① ② ③ ④ ⑤	21 ① ② ③ ④ ⑤	38 ① ② ③ ④ ⑤	54 ① ② ③ ④ ⑤
5 ① ② ③ ④ ⑤	22 ① ② ③ ④ ⑤	39 ① ② ③ ④ ⑤	55 ① ② ③ ④ ⑤
6 ① ② ③ ④ ⑤	23 ① ② ③ ④ ⑤	40 ① ② ③ ④ ⑤	56 ① ② ③ ④ ⑤
7 ① ② ③ ④ ⑤	24 ① ② ③ ④ ⑤	41 ① ② ③ ④ ⑤	57 ① ② ③ ④ ⑤
8 ① ② ③ ④ ⑤	25 ① ② ③ ④ ⑤	42 ① ② ③ ④ ⑤	58 ① ② ③ ④ ⑤
9 ① ② ③ ④ ⑤	26 ① ② ③ ④ ⑤	43 ① ② ③ ④ ⑤	59 ① ② ③ ④ ⑤
10 ① ② ③ ④ ⑤	27 ① ② ③ ④ ⑤	44 ① ② ③ ④ ⑤	60 ① ② ③ ④ ⑤
11 ① ② ③ ④ ⑤	28 ① ② ③ ④ ⑤	45 ① ② ③ ④ ⑤	61 ① ② ③ ④ ⑤
12 ① ② ③ ④ ⑤	29 ① ② ③ ④ ⑤	46 ① ② ③ ④ ⑤	62 ① ② ③ ④ ⑤
13 ① ② ③ ④ ⑤	30 ① ② ③ ④ ⑤	47 ① ② ③ ④ ⑤	63 ① ② ③ ④ ⑤
14 ① ② ③ ④ ⑤	31 ① ② ③ ④ ⑤	48 ① ② ③ ④ ⑤	64 ① ② ③ ④ ⑤
15 ① ② ③ ④ ⑤	32 ① ② ③ ④ ⑤	49 ① ② ③ ④ ⑤	65 ① ② ③ ④ ⑤
16 ① ② ③ ④ ⑤	33 ① ② ③ ④ ⑤	50 ① ② ③ ④ ⑤	66 ① ② ③ ④ ⑤
17 ① ② ③ ④ ⑤	34 ① ② ③ ④ ⑤		

Choose the best answer to each question that follows.

Questions 1–4 are based on the following passage.

Cancer is one of the leading causes of death in our society. *Cancer* is a disease in which a cell in the body loses its sensitivity to factors that regulate cell growth and division. The cell begins to multiply without restriction, creating a growing mass called a *tumor*, which interferes with the structure and functioning of the organ in which it is located.

Frequently, cancer cells become *metastatic*, meaning that they travel, settling in a number of places and giving rise to secondary tumors. Much of medical research is devoted to finding ways of preventing, controlling, and curing cancer.

1. The passage above indicates that cancer cells usually

   (1) are of only one type
   (2) may be eradicated by radiation
   (3) are not restricted to one body area
   (4) are caused by viruses
   (5) look just like normal cells

2. Because of the metastatic trait of cancer cells, we can judge a cancer treatment to be effective only if

   (1) the entire body has been proven free of tumors over a period of time
   (2) the highest possible levels of treatment have been used
   (3) the original-source tumor has been identified
   (4) no new cancer cells are found in two weeks
   (5) the complete tumor is removed

3. Based on the information in the passage, you can conclude that

   (1) some specific body sites are more susceptible to cancer than others
   (2) the cure for cancer will be found in the near future
   (3) understanding the factors that affect cell growth is critical to finding a cure for cancer
   (4) secondary tumors are of greater danger than the original tumor
   (5) cancer is known only in our society

4. We would be correct in rejecting any proposed cure for cancer that

   (1) did not alter cancer cells' ability to metastasize
   (2) was based on research that was done on a variety of experimental subjects
   (3) was done for a period of time, with frequent checks and controls
   (4) was based on radiation therapy
   (5) was based on a drug therapy approach

Questions 5–8 are based on the following passage.

Although most animals and some plants detect and respond to sound vibrations, the precise sensitivity that we call *hearing* is rare in the living world. It is highly developed only in birds and mammals, and the same operational system applies in all vertebrate auditory systems.

Sound waves cause a liquid within the organism's auditory apparatus to vibrate. These vibrations are picked up by receptors that transmit signals to nerve cells. These cells then communicate the sound to the brain. Humans can hear vibrational frequencies of 20 to 20,000 cycles per second; cats respond to frequencies of up to 50,000 cycles per second; and porpoises and bats pick up frequencies of 100,000 cycles per second.

5. According to the passage, we can infer that one nonhearing organism is the

   (1) eagle
   (2) orangutan
   (3) opossum
   (4) cricket
   (5) whale

6. According to the information in the passage, auditory systems are based on the principle of

   (1) acoustical waves striking the bones of the outer ear
   (2) sound waves vibrating solid masses
   (3) sound waves setting a liquid in motion
   (4) sound waves bouncing off the eardrum
   (5) sound waves traveling through the ear canal

7. The passage supports the statement that

   (1) humans have the best hearing of all animals
   (2) cats and porpoises are especially adapted to hearing low frequencies
   (3) ears are damaged by high frequencies
   (4) some frequencies are beyond the hearing range of humans
   (5) invertebrates have better "hearing" systems than vertebrates

8. If subjected to sound frequencies of 25,000 to 100,000 cycles per second, which of the following animals would be least affected?

   (1) a porpoise
   (2) a house cat
   (3) a cheetah
   (4) a bat
   (5) a human being

Questions 9–12 are based on the following passage.

Fat can be defined loosely as a source for energy storage in the human body. The human anatomy is designed to carry food reserves to ensure the body's survival when food becomes scarce. However, in our slim-conscious society, many people go to great lengths to keep fat from accumulating on their bodies, sometimes with harmful effects.

Fat is more efficient in storing energy than carbohydrates for several reasons. One, fat is a highly concentrated energy source. Two, fat weighs less than the same energy amount of carbohydrates. Three, fat is much more efficient to carry as an energy source because it does not hold water as do carbohydrates. For example, an average 70 kg human male normally has about 11 kg of fat in his body. This fat represents enough stored energy to keep him alive for a month without eating. The same amount of energy stored as starch would double his body weight.

9. According to the passage, humans store energy in the form of fat because

   (1) fat keeps our bodies from drying out
   (2) fat is difficult to burn off
   (3) fat is used as a protective covering
   (4) body definition requires fat acquisition
   (5) it is nature's way of providing an auxiliary food source

10. If humans stored energy as carbohydrates instead of fat, they would

    (1) be in a constant search for food
    (2) eliminate many potential food sources
    (3) weigh much more than normal
    (4) maintain the same body structure
    (5) require a much higher liquid intake

11. The passage supports the opinion that

    (1) being obese is healthier than being underweight
    (2) reserves of fat serve no purpose in the human body
    (3) excessive dieting can be detrimental to one's health
    (4) fats lead to high cholesterol levels
    (5) one's physical appearance is more important than the storage of fat

12. The passage indicates that fat makes up approximately what fraction of body weight in a normal person?

    (1) none
    (2) $\frac{1}{7}$
    (3) $\frac{1}{2}$
    (4) $\frac{2}{3}$
    (5) $\frac{3}{4}$

Questions 13–15 are based on the following diagram.

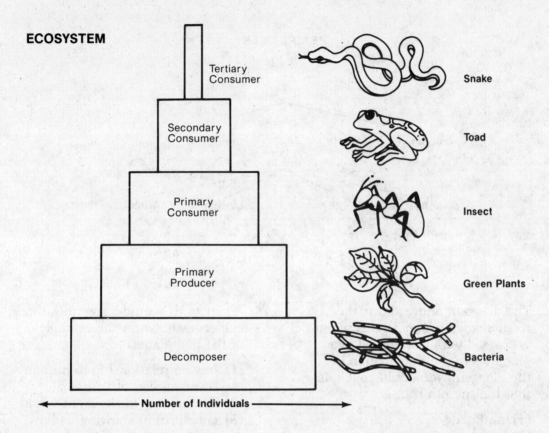

13. According to the ecosystem diagram above, which member is the most populous?

    (1) snakes
    (2) toads
    (3) insects
    (4) green plants
    (5) bacteria

14. The illustration best proves which well-known fact about the animal world?

    (1) Amphibians are the largest group known.
    (2) Insects form the largest group.
    (3) Mammals form the largest group.
    (4) Birds form the largest group.
    (5) Reptiles are nearly extinct, as they represent the smallest group shown.

15. The South American boa constrictor, which eats amphibians, would be categorized in this ecosystem as a

    (1) decomposer
    (2) primary producer
    (3) primary consumer
    (4) secondary consumer
    (5) tertiary consumer

Questions 16–19 are based on the following diagram.

PEA PLANTS

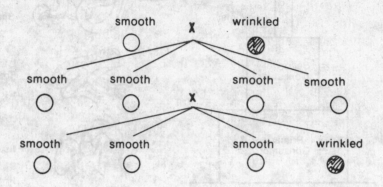

16. The diagram above shows the results when a smooth pea plant is crossed with a wrinkled pea plant. From the information in the diagram, you could conclude that the smooth trait is

    (1) mutated
    (2) recessive
    (3) dominant
    (4) hidden
    (5) incomplete

17. From the information in the diagram, you could conclude that the wrinkled trait is

    (1) mutated
    (2) recessive
    (3) dominant
    (4) hidden
    (5) incomplete

18. A geneticist would agree that the evidence shown in the example of the pea plants

    (1) has no relationship to human transmission of traits
    (2) is true only in the plant world
    (3) is helpful in showing us how traits are transmitted from parents to offspring
    (4) is too dated to have application in today's world
    (5) is based purely on chance

19. Based on the diagram, when the middle two smooth peas are crossed, the percentage of the offspring that is likely to be wrinkled is

    (1) 33 percent
    (2) 50 percent
    (3) 25 percent
    (4) 10 percent
    (5) 75 percent

Questions 20–25 are based on the following information.

One way in which organisms are classified is by how they obtain their food for energy use. Listed and defined below are five categories that describe the food-getting habits of organisms.

herbivore—an organism that feeds directly on plant matter

carnivore—an organism that feeds on the flesh of other organisms

omnivore—an organism that includes both plant and animal matter in its diet

parasite—an organism that obtains its nourishment by attaching itself to another organism, called a *host*

decomposer—an organism that usually lives in soil and obtains food by breaking down the wastes and remains of other organisms

20. A giant manatee that spends its day in a Florida river consuming water hyacinths would be categorized as a(n)

   (1) herbivore
   (2) carnivore
   (3) omnivore
   (4) parasite
   (5) decomposer

21. A consumer of fast-food fare such as a hamburger and french fries would be categorized as a(n)

   (1) herbivore
   (2) carnivore
   (3) omnivore
   (4) parasite
   (5) decomposer

22. A flea that attaches itself to a dog's skin and feeds on its blood would be categorized as a(n)

   (1) herbivore
   (2) carnivore
   (3) omnivore
   (4) parasite
   (5) decomposer

23. The Kodiak bear of Alaska feeds on various food items during the year. If the bear eats salmon in the fall, berries in the summer, and small animals year-round, the bear would be categorized as a(n)

   (1) herbivore
   (2) carnivore
   (3) omnivore
   (4) parasite
   (5) decomposer

24. The harpy eagle of Central America subsists exclusively on monkeys, sloths, and other small mammals. Based on this information, you would judge the harpy eagle to be a(n)

   (1) herbivore
   (2) carnivore
   (3) omnivore
   (4) parasite
   (5) decomposer

25. Based on the information above, the relationship between a biting mosquito and its human victim would be

   (1) prey-predator
   (2) organism-decomposer
   (3) parasite-host
   (4) herbivore-carnivore
   (5) omnivore-carnivore

Questions 26 and 27 are based on the following passage.

Insectivorous (insect-eating) plants are among the most fascinating members of the plant kingdom. They combine the characteristics of a plant with those of an animal. These plants have highly specialized leaves that capture and digest insects. The proteins of the digested insect supply the plant with nitrogen, which is usually unavailable in the poor soils in which these plants grow.

The Venus's flytrap of North and South Carolina is an example of an insectivorous plant. The leaves of this plant are hinged along the middle and swing upward and inward. An insect landing on the leaf triggers a sensitive motor mechanism that closes the leaf blades. The captured insect is then slowly digested by enzymes secreted by cells in the leaves.

26. According to the passage, what would probably result if insectivorous plants grew in richer soils?

  (1) They would grow to a much larger size.
  (2) It would be possible for the plants to take larger insects.
  (3) They would be able to obtain nitrogen from sources other than insects.
  (4) The plants would bloom more often.
  (5) The plants would be able to grow deeper roots.

27. Insectivorous plants such as the Venus's flytrap demonstrate best which of the following scientific principles?

  (1) the law of action and reaction
  (2) the law of conservation of energy
  (3) the theory of natural selection
  (4) the law of periodicity
  (5) the theory of evolution

Questions 28–30 are based on the following passage.

A plant stem's two main functions are to support the leaves and to transport materials between roots and leaves. As a stem develops, it possesses three types of permanent tissues: surface tissue, ground tissue, and vascular tissue. The surface and ground tissues support and give structure to the plant. The vascular tissues are the transport systems of the plant. The vascular tissues usually exist in one of three patterns and are known as the *phloem* and *xylem*.

Both the xylem and phloem are made up of several different types of cells that make up transport tubes for needed nutrients. In general, xylem nutrients, or "sap," travel from the roots to the rest of the plant. Phloem sap is derived from photosynthesizing leaves and from there is carried throughout the plant.

28. You can predict that a cut made through the stem of a plant would

  (1) cause the plant to bud
  (2) not affect the xylem and phloem
  (3) destroy a plant's material transportation systems
  (4) rejuvenate (restore) a plant
  (5) not be critical to a plant's survival

29. Which generalization can we make about the transport functions of xylem and phloem?

  (1) Xylem sap flows "from the bottom up"; phloem sap flows "from the top down."
  (2) Phloem sap flows "from the bottom up"; xylem sap flows "from the top down."
  (3) Both xylem and phloem handle two-way sap transport.
  (4) The transport functions of the xylem and phloem are secondary to those of the pith and cortex.
  (5) The transport functions of the xylem and phloem are exactly the same in all cases.

30. By injecting a nutrient dye into the root of a plant, we would be able to study

 (1) phloem sap transport
 (2) all vascular tissues
 (3) xylem sap transport
 (4) pith and cortex cells
 (5) total plant photosynthesis

Questions 31–36 are based on the following definitions.

Plants can propagate, or reproduce themselves, by one of five different methods. Listed and described below are five parts of plants out of which new plants are known to grow.

bud—a protuberance of a plant that can be cut off and planted, resulting in a new plant

runner—a horizontal offshoot from a plant that runs above or below ground and that can develop root systems to start new plants

bulb—an underground fleshy bud that multiplies and whose leaves store food; bulbs can be separated to grow a new plant

seed—a grain or ripened ovule of a mature plant that, when planted in moist soil, sprouts a new plant

stem cutting—a section of a plant that, when placed in a moist environment, develops roots and grows into a new plant

31. New peonies, perennial plants that produce showy flowers, can be propagated from the parent plant by dividing corms that grow undergound. This reproductive form described most closely resembles a

 (1) bud
 (2) runner
 (3) bulb
 (4) seed
 (5) stem cutting

32. Strawberries produce stolons that crawl along the ground and produce new plants when the tips of the stolons take root. This form of vegetative propagation is a

 (1) bud
 (2) runner
 (3) bulb
 (4) seed
 (5) stem cutting

33. Ferns grow from spores, one-celled structures that grow in cases on the undersides of the leaves. When the cases split, the spores fall to the ground, resulting in new plants when the soil conditions are right. A spore is most like a

 (1) bud
 (2) runner
 (3) bulb
 (4) seed
 (5) stem cutting

34. Potatoes have eyes that, when cut out from the fleshy tuber, can be planted to grow a new plant. This form of propagation is a

 (1) bud
 (2) runner
 (3) bulb
 (4) seed
 (5) stem cutting

35. We can propagate certain varieties of fruit trees by grafting—joining recently cut parts from two different trees. The method of vegetative propagation that this is most similar to is

 (1) bud
 (2) runner
 (3) bulb
 (4) seed
 (5) stem cutting

36. Potato plants are usually grown from buds, not seeds. The most likely explanation for this is that

(1) seeds germinate only in Idaho soil

(2) buds are more likely to duplicate the qualities of the parent plant

(3) buds are not as subject to blight as seeds are

(4) potatoes cannot be grown from seeds

(5) buds represent a form of asexual reproduction and seeds represent sexual reproduction

Questions 37–41 are based on the diagram and the information below.

Mechanical energy is classified in two ways: energy waiting to be used and energy causing action. When an object is at rest at a place from which it can move, it is said to have potential energy, such as the rock illustrated in the diagram. An idling car has this stored energy, as does a ball in one's hand or a cocked pistol. The higher the rock sits on the hill, the greater potential energy it has.

The other type of energy is kinetic energy, or the energy of motion. Once an object is upset from its position and set into motion—the accelerator of a car is depressed, a ball thrown, or a pistol fired—the potential energy is converted to kinetic energy.

37. The purpose of this passage is to describe

(1) the two types of mechanical energy

(2) how kinetic energy becomes potential energy

(3) the relationship of mass and kinetic energy

(4) how height can be changed into power

(5) the dissipation of energy

38. In the diagram, the rock in the resting position at the top of the hill is said to have

(1) mechanical force

(2) mechanical advantage

(3) no energy

(4) kinetic energy

(5) potential energy

39. The energy of motion is called

(1) kinesthetic energy

(2) fuel-burning energy

(3) kinetic energy

(4) hydraulic energy

(5) potential energy

40. In order for an object to have kinetic energy, there must be

(1) elevation

(2) motion

(3) a storage mechanism

(4) a starting gun

(5) conversion

41. A pendulum at the top of its swing represents

(1) potential energy

(2) kinetic energy

(3) no energy

(4) hydraulic energy

(5) mechanical energy

Questions 42–44 are based on the following passage.

The orderly pattern of the atoms in a crystal influences many properties apart from its external appearance. One of these properties is cleavage. *Cleavage* refers to the ability of a crystal to split in a certain direction along its surface. The direction of the cleavage is always parallel to a possible crystal face. Cleavage planes are dependent on the atomic structure, and they pass between sheets of atoms in well-defined directions.

How easily a mineral cleaves and the effect of the cleavage vary from one mineral to another. A crystal whose cleavage results in exceptionally smooth surfaces is said to show *eminent cleavage*; other types of cleavages are classified as *distinct* or *poor*. All crystalline gemstones undergo cleavage before they can be mounted in a setting. This cutting process may also be easy or difficult. A diamond cleaves easily despite its great hardness and may be cut into many different forms.

42. The passage indicates that the type of cleavage that a crystal exhibits is dependent upon the crystal's

(1) direction of cleavage
(2) eminent cleavage
(3) molecular makeup
(4) arrangement of atoms
(5) elemental mass

43. According to the passage, we can conclude that

(1) all crystals demonstrate good cleavage
(2) some crystals may not be used for gemstones because of poor cleavage
(3) eminent cleavage is inherent in all crystals of the quartz family
(4) cleavage of diamonds is a random property and differs from stone to stone
(5) cleavage improvement depends upon the location of mineral excavation

44. Based upon the knowledge that cleavage is characteristic of crystals, which of the following gems would *not* have this property?

(1) ruby
(2) emerald
(3) pearl
(4) diamond
(5) sapphire

Questions 45 and 46 are based on the following passage.

Off the coast of Chile and Peru, ocean currents and winds cause a rising of cold, nutrient-laden water. This enrichment of the ocean's surface layer results in an abundant plankton crop, which in turn supports large fish and seabird populations.

El Niño is the name for a set of oceanographic conditions that occurs every five to eight years, causing disturbances in Earth's biological and weather systems. El Niño (Spanish for "Christ child") gets its name from the fact that it usually happens around Christmas.

El Niño occurs when trade winds that drive the currents weaken and fail. In the ocean, the supply of nutrients is cut off, and rather sterile warm water kills off the plankton. The fish and seabirds starve.

Dramatic changes also take place in the world's weather. As the trade winds subside, the wind patterns around the globe are disrupted. For example, the normally cool European continent may experience prolonged periods of torrid temperatures as its normal wind patterns change. El Niño's effects may be felt for as long as two years at a time.

45. According to the passage, a resumption of the trade winds off the coast of South America would likely result in

(1) a major anchovy and tuna migration
(2) an end to El Niño
(3) further weather disruptions
(4) continued high European temperatures
(5) a condition known as El Aguaje

46. A spokesman states, "El Niño will have no effect on world food prices." The speaker is probably in error because

(1) food consumption goes up during El Niño
(2) food production increases because of El Niño
(3) new food sources are constantly being found
(4) the loss of fish as well as variable weather conditions reduce the availability of food
(5) the Northern Hemisphere makes up the Southern Hemisphere's food losses

Questions 47–49 are based on the following passage.

Quasars are recent additions to our body of knowledge about the physical universe. *Quasars* (quasistellar objects) are astronomical objects that are starlike in appearance and emit nonthermal radiation, usually more ultraviolet and infrared radiations than stars.

Quasars were first discovered in the early 1960s when telescopes picked up mysterious radio-wave emission sources that, at the time, couldn't be explained. Since then, thousands of radio-emitting and radio-quiet quasars have been located.

One interesting feature of quasars is that their energy output can change by great amounts in a short period of time. To date, scientists have not been able to account for these energy changes.

47. The information in the passage supports the belief that

(1) we really know nothing about our physical universe
(2) scientists hold the key to all knowledge about outer space
(3) scientists are baffled by new discoveries in outer space
(4) often, significant discoveries are made by accident
(5) at some point we will know all there is to know about our physical universe

48. The information in the passage supports the opinion that

(1) quasars are a threat to life on Earth
(2) the radio emissions of quasars are signs of communication from aliens
(3) quasars are restricted to the Milky Way galaxy
(4) there is still much to learn about the behavior of quasars
(5) the nearest quasar is 4.2 light-years away from Earth

49. Forms of life similar to those on Earth could not sustain themselves near quasars because of

(1) the distance of quasars from Earth
(2) the changes in the energy that quasars emit
(3) the blinding light that quasars emit
(4) the nearness of quasars to black holes
(5) an overabundance of radio waves in space

Questions 50–52 are based on the following illustration and caption.

CHEMICAL CELL

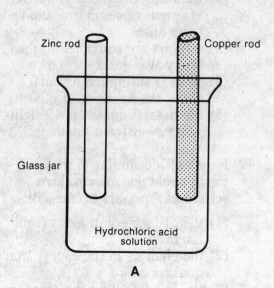
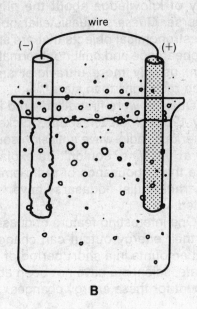

The model above illustrates the components of a chemical cell in A
and its operation in B.

50. When a zinc rod and a copper rod are connected by a wire and immersed in a hydrochloric acid solution, an electrical current is generated. Unless it is disconnected, the circuit will continue until

(1) the hydrochloric acid evaporates
(2) the glass jar breaks
(3) the zinc rod disintegrates
(4) the copper rod disintegrates
(5) the wire breaks

51. An electrolyte is a substance that when dissolved in a liquid will conduct an electric current. The electrolyte in this battery is the

(1) zinc rod
(2) glass jar
(3) wire
(4) water
(5) hydrochloric acid

52. A substance is oxidized when it loses electrons and reduced when it gains electrons. Which of the following is true in the above experiment?

(1) The zinc rod loses electrons and is oxidized.
(2) The zinc rod gains electrons and is reduced.
(3) The copper rod loses electrons and is reduced.
(4) The hydrochloric acid reduces the copper.
(5) The hydrochloric acid oxidizes the copper.

Questions 53 and 54 are based on the following passage.

The science of producing and transmitting sound waves in materials has become widespread with many practical applications. *Ultrasonics*, as this science is called, was first developed during World War II as a method of detecting enemy submarines. Today ultrasonics has many applications. When the waves used are of a low amplitude, ultrasonics can be used to map the ocean's depths, detect flaws in materials, locate cancers in the human body, and scan fetuses for deformities.

Higher-amplitude waves are used in cleaning, in manufacturing materials, and in fatigue tests for metals. The destruction of bacteria and the use of tightly focused ultrasound as a surgical knife are biological applications of high-amplitude waves.

53. The passage indicates that the uses of ultrasonics are dependent upon the

   (1) frequency of the sound waves
   (2) amplitude of sound waves used
   (3) type of ultrasonic generator employed
   (4) medium to be investigated
   (5) wattage available to the user

54. According to the passage, a low-amplitude ultrasonic scanning of the human body would be able to

   (1) give a clear picture of interior body details
   (2) remove cancerous materials without radiation
   (3) remove bacteria painlessly
   (4) serve as an antiviral agent in infectious cases
   (5) aid the body's immune system

Questions 55 and 56 are based on the following passage.

Nuclear scientists have determined that a fourth state of matter exists: plasma. The state of plasma is reached when matter acquires a temperature so high that some of the molecules and atoms are broken down into ions and electrons. Stellar and interstellar matters are mostly forms of plasma.

On Earth, plasma exists in the ionosphere, in flames, and in chemical and nuclear explosions. Matter in a controlled thermonuclear reactor also exists in a plasma state.

Plasma is most like a gas. However, it differs from un-ionized gas in that it is a good conductor of electricity and heat.

Scientists hope to understand the occurrence of plasma in nature and to harness it as an inexpensive energy source.

55. Based upon the passage, we can infer that

   (1) plasma is a by-product of human research
   (2) plasma exists in nuclear reactions only
   (3) the plasmatic state of matter exists when a hydrogen bomb is detonated
   (4) the dangers of plasma research are not worth the risk to human life
   (5) fusion power would never be shared with developing countries

56. Based on the passage, the cost of developing thermonuclear power can be defended because

   (1) it is applicable to all technologies
   (2) plasma is the source of power that can be used without special equipment
   (3) it provides cheap power
   (4) it is almost perfected already
   (5) current nuclear power is too dangerous

Questions 57–59 are based on the following passage.

Chemists have determined that elements with atomic numbers greater than 92 are all radioactive. In general, their half-lives are much shorter than the age of the universe. This means that they no longer exist in nature and have all been artificially produced by scientists in nuclear reactions.

Elements 93 through 105 in the periodic table have been created and named, and scientists have claimed discovery of elements 106 and 107. The transuranium elements, as they are called, become less stable as the atomic number and mass increase. For example, element number 93, neptunium, has a half-life of two million years, while element number 104, kurchatovium, has a half-life of seventy seconds.

The transuranium elements are the heaviest elements that exist and are readily fissionable when subjected to a nuclear bombardment. Chemists studying these elements and the periodic table predict that stable elements may be found around atomic numbers 114 or 126.

57. According to the passage, we would predict that the half-life of element number 105 would be

   (1) measured in days or weeks
   (2) less than seventy seconds
   (3) incalculable (not capable of being determined)
   (4) greater than the other transuranium elements
   (5) greater than two million years

58. From the information listed, we can conclude that

   (1) all newly discovered elements will probably be radioactive
   (2) scientists are in extreme danger in carrying out transuranium research
   (3) half-lives of newly discovered elements will all be very long
   (4) there is an end limit to the discovery of new elements
   (5) new elements will be named after the planets

59. Based on the information in the passage, which of the following relationships appears to be true?

   (1) The greater the atomic number, the higher the half-life.
   (2) The greater the atomic number, the lower the half-life.
   (3) The greater the radioactivity, the greater the half-life.
   (4) The greater the half-life, the greater the radioactivity.
   (5) The greater the atomic number, the greater the element's stability.

Questions 60 and 61 are based on the following passage.

Although water is the most common hydrogen-oxygen compound, hydrogen and oxygen form another compound called *hydrogen peroxide*, H_2O_2. Hydrogen peroxide was first obtained by treating barium peroxide with an acid. Very small quantities of hydrogen peroxide are present in dew, rain, and snow because of the action of ultraviolet light upon oxygen and water vapor.

Hydrogen peroxide has many different applications, depending upon its concentration. A 3 percent solution is used in the home as a mild antiseptic and germicide. A 30 percent solution is used in industry as a bleaching agent because of the permanency of the whiteness it produces. Concentrations of 90 percent are used as oxidizing agents in rockets and high explosives.

60. According to the information in the passage, we could predict that adding water to an industrial-strength hydrogen peroxide solution could result in

    (1) an explosion
    (2) a new substance
    (3) an antiseptic
    (4) a rocket fuel
    (5) a bleaching agent

61. The main idea of the passage is that hydrogen peroxide has

    (1) the same characteristics as water
    (2) different uses in different concentrations
    (3) all of the molecular characteristics of a peroxide
    (4) characteristics atypical of a peroxide
    (5) the chemical characteristics of barium

Questions 62–64 are based on the following illustration.

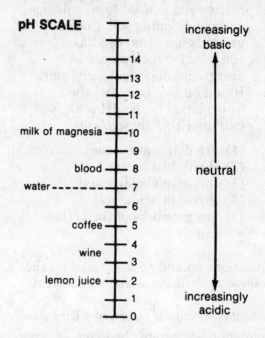

62. According to the scale above, a substance that registers 2.5 on the pH scale would be categorized as a(n)

    (1) base
    (2) neutral substance
    (3) alkali
    (4) acid
    (5) hydroxide

63. According to the scale, a substance that registers 7 on the pH scale would be categorized as a(n)

    (1) base
    (2) neutral substance
    (3) alkali
    (4) acid
    (5) hydroxide

64. Compost is a mixture that consists of decayed organic matter and is used for fertilizing and conditioning soil. Coffee grounds are often used as a compost for such plants as evergreens and rhododendrons. Based on this fact, and the information in the pH scale, you can infer that these plants

(1) are deficient in iron
(2) thrive in alkaline soil
(3) thrive in clay-like soil
(4) thrive in acidic soil
(5) are members of the coffee family

Questions 65 and 66 are based on the following definitions and illustration.

reflection—angular return of a light wave

refraction—apparent bending of light waves through different mediums

diffraction—bending of light waves near an obstacle

interference—altering of brightness of light waves

polarization—restriction of light waves to one plane

RAYS OF LIGHT

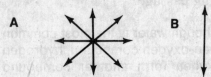

A   B

65. A certain type of lens changes the direction of light rays from A to B. This illustrates the property of

(1) deflection
(2) diffraction
(3) reflection
(4) refraction
(5) polarization

66. In the illustration, which rays are being screened out?

A. vertical rays

B. diagonal rays

C. horizontal rays

(1) A
(2) B
(3) C
(4) A and B
(5) B and C

Answers begin on page 797.

POST-TEST 3: SCIENCE ANSWER KEY

1. (3) Cancer cells metastasize and travel to various regions in the body.

2. (1) Since cancer can spread so widely, only long-term scans of the body that indicate an absence of cancer can indicate that the cancer has been cured.

3. (3) Until the mechanisms of cell growth are known completely, the variables that cause cancer cannot be identified.

4. (1) A cure for cancer would likely include preventing cancer from metastasizing or spreading to other sites in the body.

5. (4) The cricket is an insect—the only animal form listed for whom hearing is not possible.

6. (3) The passage says that vibrations in a liquid are translated into signals, which serve as the basis for auditory systems.

7. (4) Human hearing range extends to only 20,000 cycles per second, thus making higher frequency levels inaudible.

8. (5) Human beings are not capable of hearing frequencies of 25,000 cycles per second and more.

9. (5) The passage says that the human anatomy is designed to carry food reserves to ensure the body's survival when food becomes scarce.

10. (3) The passage states that the storage of carbohydrates would double a person's body weight.

11. (3) The passage states that in our society, people go to great lengths to keep fat from accumulating, sometimes with harmful effects. This suggests that excessive dieting can be detrimental to one's health.

12. (2) You can estimate that 11 out of 70 kg of weight is approximately $^{10}/_{70}$, or $^1/_7$.

13. (5) The label at the bottom of the ecosystem pyramid shows the number of individuals in that category. The longest bar is for the category labeled **bacteria**.

14. (2) Of the animals listed, insects form the largest group.

15. (5) A boa constrictor is a snake that eats amphibians. The chart shows snakes that eat toads (a kind of amphibian) as tertiary consumers.

16. (3) Since the number of offspring having smooth skins outnumbers the number with wrinkled skins, you can conclude that the trait for smooth skin is dominant.

17. (2) Since only one of the offspring is wrinkled, you can infer that the trait is recessive.

18. (3) By studying heredity in pea plants, geneticists have learned how plants and animals transmit traits to their offspring.

19. (3) One-fourth, or 25 percent, of the pea plants are wrinkled.

20. (1) Water hyacinths are plants; an animal that lives on plants is classified as a herbivore.

21. (3) A hamburger is beef—the flesh of a steer—and french fried potatoes belong to the vegetable family.

22. (4) The definitions classify a parasite, such as a flea, as an organism that feeds itself by attaching itself to another organism, such as a dog.

23. (3) An animal that feeds on plant and animal matter is categorized as an omnivore.

24. (2) Because the harpy eagle subsists on monkeys, sloths, and other small mammals, it is categorized as a carnivore.

25. (3) The mosquito lives on humans' blood; therefore, the relationship would be described as parasite-host.

26. (3) From the information given, the only choice that can be made is that the plants may become less dependent on insects for nitrogen.

27. (3) The Venus's flytrap demonstrates the theory of natural selection. In a nitrogen-deficient environment, the plant developed specialized leaves to trap insects from which it obtains nitrogen to survive.

28. (3) A cut made through the stem of a plant would kill the plant by severing its food transport system.

29. **(1)** Xylem absorbs nutrients through the roots and transports the nutrients upward. Phloem nutrients created from the process of photosynthesis are sent from the leaves down to the rest of the plant.

30. **(3)** The dye would be absorbed by the xylem at the root level and would be distributed throughout the plant.

31. **(3)** A corm is similar to a bulb, which grows underground and stores food for the plant's usage. Corms and bulbs multiply and can be divided to start new plants.

32. **(2)** A strawberry plant produces stolons, or runners, that trail along the surface of the soil, take root, and start new plants.

33. **(4)** A spore is most similar to a seed—a grain or ripened ovule that sprouts when planted in moist soil.

34. **(1)** A bud from a potato can be planted and can develop into a new plant.

35. **(5)** Sap running from both cuts creates a moist environment that enables the parts to grow together. This is most similar to the process described as stem cutting.

36. **(2)** The only plausible explanation for the effectiveness of a potato bud over a potato seed is the possibility that a bud is more likely to duplicate the qualities of the parent plant than a seed is.

37. **(1)** The entire passage describes the differences between the two forms of mechanical energy.

38. **(5)** The rock is not in motion, so it has potential energy.

39. **(3)** Kinetic energy is defined in the passage as energy in motion.

40. **(2)** The second paragraph of the passage states that in order for an object to have kinetic energy, there must be motion.

41. **(1)** A pendulum at the top of its swing represents potential energy because it pauses to change direction and is not in motion. As it begins to swing again, the energy becomes kinetic.

42. **(4)** According to the passage, cleavage is dependent on the atomic structure of crystal.

43. **(2)** A crystal must have good cleavage in order to be cut into a gemstone.

44. **(3)** Although considered by many to be a gemstone, a pearl is not a crystal and would not have the property of cleavage.

45. **(2)** A resumption of the trade winds would reverse the condition that caused El Niño.

46. **(4)** El Niño affects fishing and agricultural harvests, leading to reduced food supplies.

47. **(4)** According to the passage, quasars were discovered when astronomers picked up mysterious wave emissions from planetary objects. This fact suggests that the discovery of quasars was an accident.

48. **(4)** Since much of the information about quasars is hypothetical, there is still much to be learned about them.

49. **(2)** Life is dependent upon a steady, stable flow of energy. Energy flowing from quasars is described as being changeable. Therefore, life could not be sustained near quasars.

50. **(3)** Illustration B shows the zinc rod being used up by the electrical current in the chemical cell.

51. **(5)** The electrolyte is the hydrochloric acid, which conducts the current.

52. **(1)** A substance is oxidized when it loses electrons. In the experiment, the negatively charged zinc rod is oxidized.

53. **(2)** The uses of ultrasonics are divided into two broad categories as defined by wave amplitude—low-amplitude and high-amplitude ultrasonics.

54. **(1)** The passage states that low-amplitude ultrasonics can be used to pinpoint the location of potential deformities in the unborn.

55. **(3)** The passage says that plasma exists in nuclear explosions; the detonation of a hydrogen bomb is an example of a nuclear explosion.

56. **(3)** The passage states that scientists hope to harness plasma as an inexpensive energy source.

57. **(2)** The passage says that element 104 has a half-life of seventy seconds. The half-life decreases as the atomic number increases; therefore, element 105 would have a shorter half-life.

58. (1) Since all transuranium elements are radioactive, we can assume that newly discovered elements will also be radioactive.

59. (2) According to the information in the passage, the transuranium elements become less stable as their atomic numbers increase. This means that the greater the atomic number, the lower the half-life.

60. (3) Diluting an industrial hydrogen peroxide solution with water could reduce it to a concentration level suitable for use as an antiseptic.

61. (2) Hydrogen peroxide is used in one concentration as an oxidizing agent for rocket fuels, in another as a bleach, and in a third concentration as an antiseptic.

62. (4) An acid registers below 7 on the pH scale.

63. (2) The number 7 represents neutrality on the pH scale.

64. (4) On the pH scale, coffee has a reading of 5, indicating that it is an acid. Therefore, you can infer that evergreens and rhododendrons thrive in acidic soil.

65. (5) Polarization of light rays is the restriction of reflected rays to one plane.

66. (5) Horizontal and diagonal rays are being screened out, and vertical rays are allowed to penetrate the lens.

Use the answer key on pages 797–799 to check your answers to the Post-Test. Then find the item number of each question you missed and circle it on the chart below to determine the reading skill and content areas in which you need more practice. Pay particular attention to areas where you missed half or more of the questions. The reading skills are covered on pages 187–243. The page numbers for the content areas are listed below on the chart. Knowledge of reading skill and content area–based questions is absolutely essential for success on the GED Science Test. The numbers in boldface are questions based on graphics. For those questions that you missed, review the skill pages indicated.

POST-TEST 3: SCIENCE EVALUATION CHART

Skill Area/ Content Area	Comprehension (pages 189–195)	Application (pages 195–199)	Analysis (pages 200–210)	Evaluation (pages 211–222)
Biology (pages 355–374)	1, 6, 9, 10, 12, **13**, **19**	8, **15**, 20, 21, 22, 23, 24, 25, 27, 30, 31, 32, 33, 34, 35	3, 5, **16**, **17**, 26, 28, 29, 36	2, 4, 7, 11, **14**, **18**
Earth Science (pages 375–398)			45, 49	46, 47, 48
Chemistry (pages 399–418)	**51**, **52**, 53, 54, 61	**62**, **63**	**50**, 57, 58, 60, 64	59
Physics (pages 419–440)	**37**, **39**, 42	**38**, **41**, 44, **65**	**40**, 43, 55, **66**	56

POST-TEST 4:
LITERATURE AND THE ARTS

The Literature and the Arts Post-Test will give you the opportunity to evaluate your readiness for the actual GED Literature and the Arts Test.

This test contains 45 questions. Most of the questions are based on excerpts from novels, short stories, plays, and speeches; some questions are based on a complete poem, essay, or review.

You should take approximately 65 minutes to complete this test. At the end of 65 minutes, stop and mark your place. Then finish the test. This will give you an idea of whether or not you can finish the real GED Test in the time allotted. Try to answer as many questions as you can. A blank will count as a wrong answer, so make a reasonable guess for answers to questions you are not sure of.

When you are finished with the test, check your answers and turn to the Evaluation Chart on page 813. Use the chart to evaluate whether or not you are ready to take the final Practice Test and, if not, in what areas you need more work.

POST-TEST 4: LITERATURE AND THE ARTS ANSWER GRID

1 ① ② ③ ④ ⑤   13 ① ② ③ ④ ⑤   25 ① ② ③ ④ ⑤   36 ① ② ③ ④ ⑤

2 ① ② ③ ④ ⑤   14 ① ② ③ ④ ⑤   26 ① ② ③ ④ ⑤   37 ① ② ③ ④ ⑤

3 ① ② ③ ④ ⑤   15 ① ② ③ ④ ⑤   27 ① ② ③ ④ ⑤   38 ① ② ③ ④ ⑤

4 ① ② ③ ④ ⑤   16 ① ② ③ ④ ⑤   28 ① ② ③ ④ ⑤   39 ① ② ③ ④ ⑤

5 ① ② ③ ④ ⑤   17 ① ② ③ ④ ⑤   29 ① ② ③ ④ ⑤   40 ① ② ③ ④ ⑤

6 ① ② ③ ④ ⑤   18 ① ② ③ ④ ⑤   30 ① ② ③ ④ ⑤   41 ① ② ③ ④ ⑤

7 ① ② ③ ④ ⑤   19 ① ② ③ ④ ⑤   31 ① ② ③ ④ ⑤   42 ① ② ③ ④ ⑤

8 ① ② ③ ④ ⑤   20 ① ② ③ ④ ⑤   32 ① ② ③ ④ ⑤   43 ① ② ③ ④ ⑤

9 ① ② ③ ④ ⑤   21 ① ② ③ ④ ⑤   33 ① ② ③ ④ ⑤   44 ① ② ③ ④ ⑤

10 ① ② ③ ④ ⑤   22 ① ② ③ ④ ⑤   34 ① ② ③ ④ ⑤   45 ① ② ③ ④ ⑤

11 ① ② ③ ④ ⑤   23 ① ② ③ ④ ⑤   35 ① ② ③ ④ ⑤

12 ① ② ③ ④ ⑤   24 ① ② ③ ④ ⑤

Read each excerpt and choose the best answer to each question that follows.

Questions 1–5 refer to the following excerpt from a short story.

WHAT MADE THE TEACHER CRY?

The day Mr. DePalma came out into the cold and asked us to line up in front of him was the day that President Kennedy was shot. Mr.
5　DePalma, a short, muscular man with slicked-down black hair, was the science teacher, P.E. coach, and disciplinarian at P. S. 13. He was the teacher to whose homeroom you
10　got assigned if you were a trouble-maker, and the man called out to break up playground fights, and to escort violently angry teenagers to the office. And Mr. DePalma was the
15　man who called your parents in for a "conference."

That day, he stood in front of two rows of mostly black and Puerto Rican kids, brittle from their
20　efforts to "keep moving" on a No-vember day that was turning bitter cold. Mr. DePalma, to our complete shock, was crying. Not just silent adult tears, but really sobbing.
25　There were a few titters from the back of the line where I stood shivering.

"Listen," Mr. DePalma raised his arms over his head as if he were
30　about to conduct an orchestra. His voice broke, and he covered his face with his hands. His barrel chest was heaving. Someone giggled behind me.
35　"Listen," he repeated, "some-thing awful has happened." A strange gurgling came from his throat, and he turned around and spat on the cement behind him.

40　"Gross," someone said, and there was a lot of laughter.

"The President is dead, you idi-ots. I should have known that wouldn't mean anything to a bunch
45　of losers like you kids. Go home."

—Judith Ortíz-Cofer, excerpted from "American History," 1992

1. Where does the action of the story take place?

　(1) in the gym of a
　　　community center
　(2) on the front steps of a
　　　federal courtroom
　(3) on the playground of a
　　　public school
　(4) in the yard of a federal prison
　(5) in front of a detention home

2. Mr. DePalma might best be described as

　(1) softhearted
　(2) funny
　(3) conceited
　(4) strict
　(5) bookish

3. Mr. DePalma cried because he was

　(1) hurt that people were making
　　　fun of him
　(2) upset about the death of
　　　the president
　(3) in pain after a fight with a
　　　violent young man
　(4) sick to his stomach and
　　　unable to breathe
　(5) frightened that war was about
　　　to be declared

4. How does Mr. DePalma feel about the speaker and her friends?

　(1) indifferent
　(2) proud
　(3) fearful
　(4) affectionate
　(5) disgusted

5. The author develops the character of Mr. DePalma in all of the following ways except

(1) revealing what Mr. DePalma says to other characters
(2) disclosing what Mr. DePalma secretly thinks
(3) showing how Mr. DePalma interacts with others
(4) describing what Mr. DePalma looks like
(5) having the narrator (speaker) summarize what Mr. DePalma is like

Questions 6–11 refer to the following excerpt from a play.

WHAT HAS HAPPENED TO D.J.?

DOCTOR [*Reads from folder*]: "An anonymous soldier standing in front of him, the barrel of his AK-47 as big as a railroad tun-
5 nel, his finger on the trigger slowly pressing it."

D.J.: That's the one.

DOCTOR: Who is that anonymous soldier?

10 D.J.: You know who that is.

DOCTOR: No, I don't.

D.J.: Ain't you done your homework? [*Pointing to folder*]

DOCTOR: My memory is shaky. . . .
15 Please?

D.J.: That's the dude who should have killed me.

DOCTOR: "Should have"?

D.J.: Would have.

20 DOCTOR: What happened?

D.J.: He misfired.

DOCTOR: And?

D.J.: And that's it.

DOCTOR: That's what?

25 D.J.: That's it, man. What do you want—a flag that pops out of his rifle and says "Bang"?

DOCTOR: They say you then beat him to death with the butt of
30 your weapon. . . . In combat, near—Dakto.

D.J.: That's what they say.

DOCTOR: That is what they say.

D.J.: So I have heard.

35 DOCTOR: What else have you heard?

D.J.: That I showed "conspicuous gallantry."

DOCTOR: You're quoting to me?

40 D.J.: That is what they say, at banquets given in my honor.

DOCTOR: It's part of the citation. Is it not?

D.J. [*Quoting; far-away look*]: Con-
45 spicuous gallantry, above and beyond the call of duty. . . . [*With Texas accent*] "Ouah hearts and ouah hopes are turned to peace . . . as we as-
50 semble heah . . . in the East Room . . . this morning . . ."

DOCTOR: Lyndon B. Johnson?

D.J.: You got it.

DOCTOR: What did you feel?

55 D.J.: Nothing.

DOCTOR: But when he hung the medal around your neck, you were crying.

D.J.: See, you *done* your homework!

—Tom Cole, excerpted from *Medal of Honor Rag*, 1977

6. D.J. had received a medal for his part in

(1) World War II
(2) the Korean conflict
(3) the Vietnam War
(4) riots at Kent State University
(5) American invasion of Grenada

7. The action of this excerpt centers around

(1) a police inquiry into the actions of D.J.
(2) a doctor attempting to learn more about a patient
(3) an interview for a military promotion
(4) an inquiry about drug use in the military
(5) a newspaper interview about a soldier

8. Lines 14, 15, and 18, "My memory is shaky. . . . Please?" and "Should have?" suggest that the doctor is

(1) probing for more information
(2) very confused about D.J.
(3) old and incompetent
(4) young and inexperienced
(5) not very interested in D.J.'s feelings

9. D.J.'s attitude toward the doctor can be described best as

(1) playful and coy
(2) respectful and appreciative
(3) extremely hostile and violent
(4) cooperative and cordial
(5) guarded and sarcastic

10. Which of the following *best* characterizes the tone of this excerpt?

(1) friendly exchanges between the doctor and D.J.
(2) sarcastic comments made by the doctor
(3) humorous responses given by D.J.
(4) short, rapid-fire exchanges between D.J. and the doctor
(5) angry outbursts by the doctor

11. Based on the excerpt, this play would most likely fall within the category of

(1) farce, an exaggerated form of comedy
(2) situation comedy
(3) slapstick, or highly physical comedy
(4) melodrama
(5) allegory, or highly symbolic drama

Questions 12–19 refer to the following poem.

WHAT CONFLICT TAKES PLACE ON THE LAWNS?

Suburban Prophecy

On Saturday, the power-mowers' whine
Begins the morning. Over this neighborhood
Rises the keening, petulant voice, begin
Green oily teeth to chatter and munch the cud.

5 Monsters, crawling the carpets of the world,
Still send from underground against your blades
The roots of things battalions green and curled
And tender, that will match your blades with blades
Till the revolted throats shall strangle on
10 The tickle of their dead, till straws shall break
Crankshafts like camels, and the sun go down
On dinosaurs in swamps. A night attack
Follows and by the time the Sabbath dawns
All armored beasts are eaten by their lawns.

—Howard Nemerov, 1977

12. In the first stanza, the poet uses words such as *whine, voice, teeth, chatter,* and *munch* to suggest that the power-mowers are

(1) alive
(2) green
(3) in need of repair
(4) like cows
(5) very powerful

13. The imagery in the first stanza most appeals to the reader's sense of

    (1) sight
    (2) touch
    (3) hearing
    (4) taste
    (5) smell

14. The phrase "your blades" in line 8 refers to

    (1) grass
    (2) roots
    (3) gardeners
    (4) lawnmowers
    (5) monsters

15. The action of the poem takes place in the time period of

    (1) an afternoon
    (2) a morning
    (3) twenty-four hours
    (4) a week
    (5) one sunset; a few hours

16. The events and imagery of the second stanza create an atmosphere in which

    (1) the lawns are overrun with crabgrass
    (2) suburbanites use their lawnmowers against each other
    (3) the people pushing the mowers are completely exhausted
    (4) the smell of freshly cut grass lingers in the air
    (5) lawns and lawnmowers are battling

17. Throughout the poem, Nemerov creates an interesting image of lawnmowers by comparing them to

    (1) other machines
    (2) people
    (3) animals
    (4) plants
    (5) swamps

18. The poet is ridiculing

    (1) suburbanites who turn into monsters
    (2) suburbanites who keep perfect lawns
    (3) lawnmowers and other modern machines
    (4) realtors who sell houses without lawns
    (5) neighbors who borrow from each other

19. In one description, Nemerov makes a comparison using the word *like* (a simile) and uses repetition of a beginning consonant (alliteration). Which of the following descriptions represents both of these techniques?

    (1) "crawling the carpets of the world"
    (2) "Green oily teeth to chatter and munch the cud"
    (3) "Crankshafts like camels"
    (4) "and the sun go down / on dinosaurs in swamps"
    (5) "All armored beasts are eaten by their lawns"

Questions 20–25 refer to the
following essay.

WHAT IS HARRIS'S IDEA
OF REALISM?

Narrow "Realism" Misses the Point
of Real Vision

One of the half-dozen most difficult words in the world to define or
to understand is *realism*; and yet
people use it all the time to make
5 judgments about many things, including the arts.

What does a man really mean
when he says he likes realistic painting? He means, in most cases, that
10 he likes a picture to represent objects the way the eye sees them. But
the eye does not see reality.

When we look at a chair, we do
not see the real chair, but an optical
15 illusion. The real chair is a mass of
particles moving at incredible
speeds with ceaseless energy.

When we look at a person, we
see the face, the limbs, the clothes.
20 Are these the real person? Nobody
would deny that it is the character,
the spirit, the emotional structure
beneath the bone that makes the
real person.

25 A telescope sees big things
more "realistically" than the eye; a
microscope sees little things more
"realistically" than the eye. If we do
not expect the scientist to look at
30 the world with our naive realism,
why should we expect the artist to
do so?

What we call reality is merely
the surface of things, the appear-
35 ance of objects. There is no truth to
be found in this, and both the scientist and the artist seek a truth not
visible to the naked eye.

Actually, we do not even believe
40 in our own realism; we do not believe that the Earth is flat, as it
seems to be; we do not believe that
the man who looks kind is kind, as
he seems to be. We ourselves apply

45 more critical, more sophisticated,
and (to use a dirty word) more intellectual yardsticks to everyday things
around us.

The artist goes us one further.
50 He accepts *nothing* as it seems to
be, for it is his task to throw a
searchlight on the caverns and labyrinths of life. Now, his searchlight
may be weak, or soiled, or focused
55 in the wrong way, and the art he
gives us will then be dim or
defective.

But whether he is a good or bad
artist, we cannot ask him to look at
60 the world the way we do, for then he
would see nothing more than we do.
If anything, history shows that the
mass of mankind spend their todays
in trying to catch up to the artists of
65 yesteryear. We have just barely
begun to come to an appreciation of
[William] Blake's visions.

There is an amusing story
about realism and [Pablo] Picasso.
70 A sailor once complained to him
that his paintings were not realistic,
and then took out a tiny snapshot of
his child for the painter to see. Picasso squinted seriously at the
75 snapshot and handed it back to the
father, merely saying, "Small, isn't
she?"

—Sydney J. Harris, 1982

20. According to the author, the main
problem with defining realism in
art is that

(1) everything is real
(2) we cannot see what is real
(3) artists dislike the term
(4) science is real, but art is not
(5) only art of this century
is realistic

21. The author sees the artist as someone who

    (1) looks deeper into life than the rest of us
    (2) sees everything as real
    (3) tries to see the world as the majority of us do
    (4) searches for the most realistic presentation
    (5) ignores the opinions of critics and does as he or she pleases

22. The story about Picasso illustrates that realistic, if taken literally, means that

    (1) a photograph is realistic art
    (2) photography is not art
    (3) the sailor's daughter was actually the size in the photo
    (4) the sailor did not have a daughter
    (5) the artist will always reject the work of others

23. If you saw a four-star action-packed movie and said you liked the film because it was realistic, you described the movie that way because it was

    (1) real to everyone
    (2) lifelike, according to the way you see life
    (3) set in a believable location
    (4) based on someone's life story
    (5) easy to understand

24. In the essay, Harris draws comparisons between the artist and the scientist. This technique is effective because both the artist and the scientist

    (1) use quite different skills
    (2) follow the scientific method of inquiry
    (3) exercise the same skills
    (4) suffer from a lack of respect
    (5) work in fields that have a longer history than most other fields

25. For gifted artists whose works are more widely appreciated after their deaths, Harris would likely have agreed that

    (1) their art wasn't real enough to the average person in the street
    (2) they hadn't perfected their craft during their lifetime
    (3) they were too far behind the public in the minds of the critics
    (4) they were visionaries who saw far beyond what the public was able to understand
    (5) their work was too abstract for anybody to appreciate

Questions 26–30 refer to the following excerpt from a novel.

WHO IS CAROL MILFORD?

On a hill by the Mississippi where Chippewas camped two generations ago, a girl stood in relief against the cornflower blue of
5 Northern sky. She saw no Indians now; she saw flour-mills and the blinking windows of skyscrapers in Minneapolis and St. Paul. Nor was she thinking of squaws and por-
10 tages, and the Yankee fur-traders whose shadows were all about her. She was meditating upon walnut fudge, the plays of Brieux, the reasons why heels run over, and the
15 fact that the chemistry instructor had stared at the new coiffure which concealed her ears.

A breeze which had crossed a thousand miles of wheatlands bel-
20 lied her taffeta skirt in a line so graceful, so full of animation and moving beauty, that the heart of a chance watcher on the lower road tightened to wistfulness over her
25 quality of suspended freedom. She lifted her arms, she leaned back against the wind, her skirt dipped and flared, a lock blew wild. A girl on a hilltop; credulous, plastic,
30 young; drinking the air as she longed to drink life. The eternal aching comedy of expectant youth.

It is Carol Milford, fleeing for an hour from Blodgett College.

35 The days of pioneering, of lassies in sunbonnets, and bears killed with axes in piney clearings, are deader now than Camelot; and a rebellious girl is the spirit of that bewil-
40 dered empire called the American Middlewest.

—Sinclair Lewis, excerpted from *Main Street*, 1920

26. Carol Milford is
  (1) an Indian squaw
  (2) a pioneer
  (3) a college student
  (4) a princess
  (5) a chemistry instructor

27. The setting of this passage is the state of
  (1) Mississippi
  (2) Iowa
  (3) Illinois
  (4) New York
  (5) Minnesota

28. The author's style is characterized by
  (1) concise wording
  (2) descriptive images
  (3) the use of suspense
  (4) exciting plot events
  (5) short sentences

29. The author uses the character of Carol Milford to represent
  (1) traditional women
  (2) female teachers
  (3) the future of immigrants
  (4) the spirit of the Midwest
  (5) the shallowness of young girls

30. The writing style of this passage would probably *not* be effective in a(n)
  (1) biography
  (2) textbook
  (3) poem
  (4) short story
  (5) opening scene of a play

Questions 31–38 refer to the following speech.

WHAT IS THE SPEAKER'S GOAL?

FRIENDS AND FELLOW CITI-ZENS—I stand before you to-night under indictment for the alleged crime of having voted at the last
5 presidential election, without having a lawful right to vote. It shall be my work this evening to prove to you that in thus voting, I not only com-mitted no crime, but, instead, simply
10 exercised my *citizen's rights*, guar-anteed to me and all United States citizens by the National Constitu-tion, beyond the power of any State to deny.
15 The preamble of the Federal Constitution says:

"We, the people of the United States, in order to form a more per-fect union, establish justice, insure
20 *domestic* tranquillity, provide for the common defense, promote the gen-eral welfare, and secure the bless-ings of liberty to ourselves and our posterity, do ordain and establish
25 this Constitution for the United States of America."

It was we, the people; not we, the white male citizens; nor yet we, the male citizens; but we, the whole
30 people, who formed the Union. And we formed it, not to give the bless-ings of liberty, but to secure them; not to the half of ourselves and the half of our posterity, but to the
35 whole people—women as well as men. And it is a downright mockery to talk to women of their enjoyment of the blessings of liberty while they are denied the use of the only
40 means of securing them provided by this democratic-republican gov-ernment—the ballot.

—Susan B. Anthony, excerpted from "On Woman's Right to Suffrage," 1873

31. The speaker emphasizes the term "citizen's rights" (line 10) because she believes that

(1) no citizens have any rights in this country
(2) all men have the right to vote
(3) as a woman, she should be allowed to vote
(4) only Native Americans are truly citizens
(5) no one really cares about the meaning of citizenship

32. The speaker quotes from the Preamble of the Constitution to illustrate

(1) the principles on which voting laws should be based
(2) that men wrote the Constitution
(3) the contrast between the rights of men and women
(4) the basis of the women's rights movement
(5) that voting is not mentioned in the document

33. What the speaker believes to be "downright mockery" is to

(1) speak to women in public places
(2) treat women as if they were really free
(3) insist that women respect the Constitution
(4) place women on trial for crimes
(5) live by the principles set forth in the Constitution

34. The speaker uses the term "this democratic-republican govern-ment" (lines 41–42) to refer to

(1) America's two-party system
(2) the advantage that Democrats have over Republicans
(3) the liberty of men and lack of freedom of women
(4) a system that is led by males
(5) a system in which the people govern

35. The theme of this passage is that

(1) black men as well as white men should be allowed to vote
(2) both men and women should be allowed to vote
(3) the U.S. Constitution is out-of-date
(4) only those who founded the Union should be allowed to vote
(5) only women should be allowed to vote

36. The speaker's tone can best be described as

(1) polite and reserved
(2) weak and without support
(3) rude and abusive
(4) confident and forceful
(5) radical and too emotional

37. The speaker's use of the term "alleged crime" (lines 3–4) reveals that she

(1) has been found guilty by a jury
(2) finds humor in her arrest
(3) does not believe she has committed a crime
(4) does not respect the U.S. Constitution
(5) has a long history of criminal activity

38. Because of her beliefs expressed in this passage, the speaker would support which of the following?

(1) a nuclear test ban treaty
(2) an amendment outlawing capital punishment
(3) anti-handgun legislation
(4) the Equal Rights Amendment
(5) a right to life amendment

Questions 39–45 refer to the following review of a musical.

WHAT IS THE CRITIC'S OPINION OF *SMILE*?

"Beauty Marks"
Review of *Smile*
Music by Marvin Hamlisch
Book and Lyrics by Howard Ashman

This season's first four new American musicals all closed the week they opened, continuing a daunting three-year run of almost
5 unrelieved financial failure for what used to be Broadway's mainstay. Staged with varying degrees of artistry, the ill-fated shows shared one disabling presumption: musicals
10 must be "about" something beyond melody and romance. . . . All suffocated under the weight of their ambition.

One might expect the same fate to befall *Smile*, adapted from a 1975
15 Michael Ritchie film that satirized beauty pageants. The narrative, centering on girls who are strangers, inevitably lacks complex
20 relationships and love interest. Moreover, it is difficult to write a parody much funnier than the real Miss America proceedings. And it is hard to keep audiences interested in
25 the climax—which entrant will win— after repeatedly telling them it shouldn't matter. Curiously, *Smile* works. It is a swift-paced, skillfully performed and thoroughly profes-
30 sional entertainment that balances amusement at the shallow ambitions of the characters with respect for the depth of their feelings. Composer Marvin Hamlisch (*A Chorus*
35 *Line*) and Author-Lyricist Howard Ashman (*Little Shop of Horrors*) have written touching songs for the stars, Anne Marie Bobby as a sweet, awkward A student who realizes she

40 is out of her element at the pageant
and Jodi Benson as a wanderer who
is prematurely wise in the ways of
selling herself, including a talent-
show "dramatic reading" that turns
45 into a strip-tease. *Smile* may not be
a landmark, but it is a pleasure.

—William A. Henry III,
Time, December 8, 1986

39. According to the critic, musicals
were, at the time,

(1) as popular as ever
(2) unsuccessful on Broadway
(3) gaining popularity each year
(4) successful only when the
subjects were serious
(5) not as popular as films

40. Lines 11–13 state that "All
suffocated under the weight of
their ambition." The critic
includes this descriptive language
to suggest that

(1) there was not time to breathe
between scenes
(2) the directors and actors were
not experienced
(3) the musicals relied too much
on light humor
(4) producers were too concerned
with winning awards
(5) the musicals tried to make a
statement as well as entertain

41. The critic states that the musical
"balances amusement at the
shallow ambitions of the
characters with respect for the
depth of their feelings" (lines
30–33). This expresses a contrast
between the audience's

(1) feelings about Miss America
and patriotism
(2) depth of understanding of the
two main characters
(3) mixed emotions about the
characters' struggles
(4) favorable opinion of *Smile*
(5) impatience with the
characters and weak plot

42. The critic believes the music is

(1) too humorous for the theme
(2) shallow and without purpose
(3) appropriate for the characters
(4) outstanding and destined to
be popular
(5) inappropriate for the topic

43. Which of the following statements
best describes the critic's opinion
of *Smile*?

(1) Although *Smile* is not a great
musical, it is enjoyable.
(2) *Smile* is an example of why
musicals are no longer
popular.
(3) *Smile* unjustly criticizes the
Miss America pageant.
(4) Since *Smile* is about women,
it will surely be popular.
(5) *Smile* is the best musical of
the year.

44. According to the experience of
Broadway shows for three years
running, the type of production
that would have been most likely
to fail would be a

(1) comedy about marriage
(2) drama about Nazi Germany
(3) satire on college life
(4) musical about a person's
personal triumph
(5) one-woman concert

45. The statement "Curiously, *Smile*
works" reveals the critic's

(1) total disgust
(2) dislike of the musical
(3) lack of faith in the audience
(4) surprise at the
musical's success
(5) belief that all musicals are
worth watching

Answers begin on page 811.

POST-TEST 4: LITERATURE AND THE ARTS ANSWER KEY

1. (3) The first paragraph makes reference to "P.S. 13" (a public school), teachers, homeroom, and parent-teacher conferences. In the second paragraph, references to the cold let readers know that the action takes place outdoors, probably on a playground.

2. (4) In the first paragraph, Mr. DePalma is described as a "disciplinarian" (line 8) and "the man who called . . . parents in for a 'conference' " (lines 14–16).

3. (2) In paragraphs 3 and 4, Mr. DePalma is choked by sobs as he tries to tell the students that President Kennedy has been assassinated.

4. (5) In the last paragraph, Mr. DePalma says, "I should have known that [Kennedy's death] wouldn't mean anything to a bunch of losers like you kids."

5. (2) Because the story is told in the first person by a former student, rather than Mr. DePalma or an outside narrator, Mr. DePalma's unspoken thoughts cannot be disclosed.

6. (3) Clues in the passage that refer to the Vietnam War are "Dakto" and Lyndon B. Johnson, who was president during the latter years of the Vietnam War.

7. (2) The doctor refers to a folder and asks D.J. questions in order to learn more about D.J. This suggests a doctor-patient relationship.

8. (1) The doctor wants D.J. to give more details and explanations.

9. (5) D.J. does not volunteer information; the doctor has to ask for it. D.J. also makes sarcastic remarks such as "Ain't you done your homework?"

10. (4) The exchanges between the doctor and D.J. are short and to the point. Choices (1), (2), (3), and (5) cannot be supported by the excerpt.

11. (4) The serious circumstances under which the questioning takes place suggest that the play would be a melodrama and not a form of comedy or an allegory.

12. (1) The poet uses characteristics of living things.

13. (3) Sound words such as *whine, keening, petulant voice,* and *munch* appeal to hearing.

14. (4) The poem is about lawnmowers. The phrase "Monsters . . . send from underground against your blades" implies that blades of grass fight the blades of lawnmowers.

15. (3) The time referred to in the poem is Saturday morning until the dawn of Sabbath (Sunday).

16. (5) References in the poem that suggest war or battle are *battalions, blades, strangle, attack,* and *armored beasts.*

17. (3) Phrases that suggest the imagery of animals include "munch the cud," "crankshafts like camels," "dinosaurs in swamps," and "armored beasts."

18. (2) Suburbanites are often ridiculed for the care they lavish upon their lawns. The poem pokes fun by suggesting the lawns will someday fight back.

19. (3) A simile is a comparison between two unlike things using the word *like.* Alliteration is the repetition of a beginning consonant. The phrase "Crankshafts like camels" represents both.

20. (2) The essay states that "the eye does not see reality." This means that we cannot see what is real.

21. (1) The passage says that it is the task of the artist "to throw a searchlight on the caverns and labyrinths of life" and that "we cannot ask him to look at the world the way we do." These lines indicate that the artist is someone who looks deeply into life.

22. (3) Picasso describes the sailor's daughter as being small to show that if reality is the way things appear to be, then in real life the daughter would be as small as she is in the picture.

23. (2) The passage says that reality is judged by how an individual sees things in life.

24. (1) The comparison between the artist and the scientist is effective because each is perceived as representing different skills. The artist is perceived to be dreamy and impractical, and the scientist is perceived to be logical and practical.

25. (4) The passage says that "the mass of mankind spend their todays in trying to catch up to the artists of yesteryear." This suggests that artists see far beyond what the public is able to understand.

26. (3) The excerpt included references to a chemistry instructor and Carol's "fleeing for an hour from Blodgett College."

27. (5) Minneapolis and St. Paul are in Minnesota.

28. (2) The first sentence of the excerpt uses words to paint a picture. The rest of the passage describes the setting and character.

29. (4) The last sentence states that "a rebellious girl is the spirit" of the Midwest.

30. (2) Textbook writing is generally factual and objective, not excessively descriptive.

31. (3) According to Susan B. Anthony, *citizen* includes men and women.

32. (1) Anthony quotes the Preamble to the Constitution to support her purpose: to show why she felt she should have been able to vote.

33. (2) Anthony states "to talk to women of their enjoyment of . . . liberty while they are denied . . . the ballot" is "downright mockery." This suggests that a gap exists between what is practiced and what is proclaimed.

34. (5) The term refers to the U.S. government—of, by, and for the people.

35. (2) The entire speech is based on the argument that women should not be denied the right to vote.

36. (4) From the words used, Anthony's speech expresses confidence and forcefulness.

37. (3) The word *alleged* means "supposed." Anthony does not feel she has broken a law.

38. (4) The only choice shown that is closely related to Susan Anthony's suffragist movement is the Equal Rights Amendment—an amendment that was drafted to end discrimination on the basis of sex.

39. (2) According to the review, musicals had failed on Broadway for three years.

40. (5) The critic's words suggest that the musicals tried to do too much by being entertaining and making a social statement at the same time.

41. (3) The words *amusement* and *respect* suggest competing feelings, which can be described as mixed emotions.

42. (3) The critic says the songwriters "have written touching songs for the stars." This suggests that the music is appropriate for the characters.

43. (1) The last sentence states that "*Smile* may not be a landmark, but it is a pleasure." This suggests that the musical is enjoyable although it is not great.

44. (4) The review begins by reporting the failures of Broadway musicals. Therefore, of the choices listed, choice (4), a musical about a person's personal triumph, would have been likely to fail.

45. (4) Considering the fate of the other musicals on Broadway that year and the problems with *Smile*, the musical is suprisingly enjoyable according to the critic.

Use the answer key on pages 811–812 to check your answers to the Post-Test. Then find the item number of each question you missed and circle it on the chart below to determine the reading skill and content areas in which you need more practice. Pay particular attention to areas where you missed half or more of the questions. The reading skills are covered on pages 187–243. The page numbers for the content areas are listed below on the chart. Knowledge of reading skill and content area–based questions is absolutely essential for success on the GED Literature and the Arts Test. For those questions that you missed, review the skill pages indicated.

POST-TEST 4: LITERATURE AND THE ARTS EVALUATION CHART

Skill Area/ Content Area	Comprehension (pages 189–195)	Application (pages 195–199)	Analysis (pages 200–210)
Prose Fiction (pages 453–482)	1, 2, 3, 4, 26, 27	30	5, 28, 29
Poetry (pages 483–502)	14, 15, 18		12, 13, 16, 17, 19
Drama (pages 503–518)	6, 7, 8, 9	11	10
Nonfiction Prose (pages 519–536)	20, 21, 22, 25, 31, 33, 34, 37	23, 38	24, 32, 35, 36
Commentaries (pages 537–546)	39, 40, 42, 43, 45	44	41

POST-TEST 5: MATHEMATICS

This Mathematics Post-Test will give you the opportunity to evaluate your readiness for the actual GED Mathematics Test.

The test contains 56 questions and should take approximately 90 minutes to complete. At the end of 90 minutes, stop and mark your place. Then finish the test. This will give you an idea of whether or not you can finish the real GED Test in the time allotted. Try to answer as many questions as you can. A blank will count as a wrong answer, so make a reasonable guess for answers to questions you are not sure of.

When you are finished with the test, check your answers and turn to the Evaluation Chart on page 830. Use the chart to evaluate whether or not you are ready to take the final Practice Test and, if not, in what areas you need more work.

You may find the formulas on page 815 useful for some of the problems.

POST-TEST 5: MATHEMATICS ANSWER GRID

1 ① ② ③ ④ ⑤	15 ① ② ③ ④ ⑤	29 ① ② ③ ④ ⑤	43 ① ② ③ ④ ⑤
2 ① ② ③ ④ ⑤	16 ① ② ③ ④ ⑤	30 ① ② ③ ④ ⑤	44 ① ② ③ ④ ⑤
3 ① ② ③ ④ ⑤	17 ① ② ③ ④ ⑤	31 ① ② ③ ④ ⑤	45 ① ② ③ ④ ⑤
4 ① ② ③ ④ ⑤	18 ① ② ③ ④ ⑤	32 ① ② ③ ④ ⑤	46 ① ② ③ ④ ⑤
5 ① ② ③ ④ ⑤	19 ① ② ③ ④ ⑤	33 ① ② ③ ④ ⑤	47 ① ② ③ ④ ⑤
6 ① ② ③ ④ ⑤	20 ① ② ③ ④ ⑤	34 ① ② ③ ④ ⑤	48 ① ② ③ ④ ⑤
7 ① ② ③ ④ ⑤	21 ① ② ③ ④ ⑤	35 ① ② ③ ④ ⑤	49 ① ② ③ ④ ⑤
8 ① ② ③ ④ ⑤	22 ① ② ③ ④ ⑤	36 ① ② ③ ④ ⑤	50 ① ② ③ ④ ⑤
9 ① ② ③ ④ ⑤	23 ① ② ③ ④ ⑤	37 ① ② ③ ④ ⑤	51 ① ② ③ ④ ⑤
10 ① ② ③ ④ ⑤	24 ① ② ③ ④ ⑤	38 ① ② ③ ④ ⑤	52 ① ② ③ ④ ⑤
11 ① ② ③ ④ ⑤	25 ① ② ③ ④ ⑤	39 ① ② ③ ④ ⑤	53 ① ② ③ ④ ⑤
12 ① ② ③ ④ ⑤	26 ① ② ③ ④ ⑤	40 ① ② ③ ④ ⑤	54 ① ② ③ ④ ⑤
13 ① ② ③ ④ ⑤	27 ① ② ③ ④ ⑤	41 ① ② ③ ④ ⑤	55 ① ② ③ ④ ⑤
14 ① ② ③ ④ ⑤	28 ① ② ③ ④ ⑤	42 ① ② ③ ④ ⑤	56 ① ② ③ ④ ⑤

FORMULAS

Description	Formula
AREA (A) of a:	
square	$A = s^2$ where s = side
rectangle	$A = lw$ where l = length, w = width
parallelogram	$A = bh$ where b = base, h = height
triangle	$A = \frac{1}{2}bh$ where b = base, h = height
circle	$A = \pi r^2$ where $\pi \cong 3.14$, r = radius
PERIMETER (P) of a:	
square	$P = 4s$ where s = side
rectangle	$P = 2l + 2w$ where l = length, w = width
triangle	$P = a + b + c$ where a, b, and c are the sides
circle—circumference (C)	$C = \pi d$ where $\pi \cong 3.14$, d = diameter
VOLUME (V) of a:	
cube	$V = s^3$ where s = side
rectangular container	$V = lwh$ where l = length, w = width, h = height
cylinder	$V = \pi r^2 h$ where $\pi \cong 3.14$, r = radius, h = height
Pythagorean theorem	$c^2 = a^2 + b^2$ where c = hypotenuse, a and b are legs of a right triangle
distance (d) between two points in a plane	$d = \sqrt{(x_2 - x_1)^2 + (y_2 - y_1)^2}$ where (x_1, y_1) and (x_2, y_2) are two points in a plane
slope of a line (m)	$m = \frac{y_2 - y_1}{x_2 - x_1}$ where (x_1, y_1) and (x_2, y_2) are two points in a plane
mean	$mean = \frac{x_1 + x_2 + \ldots + x_n}{n}$ where the xs are the values for which a mean is desired and n = number of values in the series
median	$median$ = the point in an ordered set of numbers at which half of the numbers are above and half of the numbers are below this value.
simple interest (i)	$i = prt$ where p = principal, r = rate, t = time
distance (d) as function of rate and time	$d = rt$ where r = rate, t = time
total cost (c)	$c = nr$ where n = number of units, r = cost per unit

Solve each problem.

1. If Tom pays $10.56 every two months for his newspaper home delivery, how much does he pay in one year?

   (1) $9.36
   (2) $10.56
   (3) $36.72
   (4) $63.36
   (5) $126.72

2. Wesley willed his estate to Margaret, Betty Jo, and Johnny. He gave Margaret $2000. Betty Jo got $2\frac{1}{2}$ times as much as Margaret. Johnny got $3\frac{1}{2}$ times as much as Margaret. What was the total value of the estate?

   (1) $8000
   (2) $12,000
   (3) $14,000
   (4) $122,000
   (5) not enough information is given

3. Of the following, which is the nearest in value to 8?

   (1) 8.1
   (2) 8.001
   (3) 7.998
   (4) 8.01
   (5) 7.09

4. José has 2 boards. One board is $2\frac{3}{4}$ feet and the other is $2\frac{1}{3}$ feet. To make them equal, how many *inches* must he cut from the longer piece?

   (1) $\frac{1}{3}$

   (2) $\frac{5}{12}$

   (3) $\frac{1}{2}$

   (4) 2

   (5) 5

5. Valentina needs $3\frac{1}{2}$ yards of nylon at $2.40 per yard. Excluding tax, how much change should she get back from a $20 bill?

   (1) $2.40
   (2) $5.90
   (3) $8.40
   (4) $11.60
   (5) $11.95

Questions 6 and 7 are based on the information below.

John worked as a waiter on Friday nights to supplement his income. He kept a list of the tips he received for 8 weeks and the number of hours he worked each Friday night.

WEEK	1	2	3	4	5	6	7	8
TIPS	$48	$65.25	$20	$73	$60	$62.50	$70.25	$53
HOURS	6	6	3	6	4	5	6	4

6. To the nearest dollar, what was the average amount of John's weekly tips?

(1) $50
(2) $57
(3) $60
(4) $227
(5) $452

7. In addition to his tips, John was paid $2 per hour by his employer. How much did he actually earn per hour, including his wages and his tips, during week 5?

(1) $2
(2) $4
(3) $8
(4) $17
(5) $68

Questions 8 and 9 are based on the drawing below.

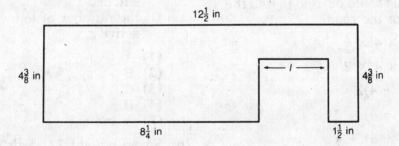

8. Find the missing length (l) in inches.

(1) $2\frac{3}{4}$

(2) $3\frac{1}{4}$

(3) $4\frac{1}{4}$

(4) $9\frac{3}{4}$

(5) not enough information is given

9. How many inches of molding would be needed to frame the figure above?

(1) $16\frac{7}{8}$

(2) $26\frac{5}{8}$

(3) $33\frac{3}{4}$

(4) 37

(5) not enough information is given

10. School District #105 has 450 employees. There are 35 administrators, 40 clerical staff, and 15 custodians. If the remainder are instructors, what is the ratio of instructors to the total number of employees?

    (1) $\frac{1}{5}$

    (2) $\frac{1}{4}$

    (3) $\frac{4}{5}$

    (4) $\frac{5}{4}$

    (5) $\frac{4}{1}$

11. A semiprofessional baseball player hits 9 home runs in the first 12 games of the season. At the same rate, how many can he expect to hit in the entire 28-game season?

    (1) 18
    (2) 20
    (3) 21
    (4) 22
    (5) 27

12. On a scale drawing, $\frac{1}{2}$ inch = 10 miles. If the length of a road on this scale is 4 inches, which of the following could be used to find the length of the road?

    (1) $10 \times 4 \times \frac{1}{2}$

    (2) $10 \times 4 \times 2$

    (3) $(10 + 4)2$

    (4) $(10 + 4) \div 2$

    (5) $(10 + 4) \div \frac{1}{2}$

13. Brenda earns $1840 a month. Her employer deducts 18% for federal income tax, 7% for social security tax, and 3% for state income tax. What is her *take-home pay* for the month?

    (1) $515.20
    (2) $1320.80
    (3) $1324.80
    (4) $2355.20
    (5) not enough information is given

14. A salesman at Daniel's Jewelers is paid $350 per week plus 15% commission on sales. If he sells jewelry items for $42, $126, $785, and $384 during the week, which expression below best describes his pay for the week?

    (1) $350 + 15(1337)$
    (2) $350 + .05(1337)$
    (3) $.05 + 350(1337)$
    (4) $.05 + 350 + 1337$
    (5) $350 + .15(1337)$

15. Mrs. Caille is buying a school jacket for her son. She wants his name stitched on the front and his favorite school activity printed on the back. The basic cost of a jacket is $32.95 plus $2.50 to stitch his name on the front. It will cost an additional $.80 per letter to print the activity on the back. What other information does Mrs. Caille need to figure the cost of the jacket?

    A. the basic cost of the jacket
    B. the number of letters in her son's name
    C. the cost of having his name stitched
    D. the number of letters in his activity

    (1) A
    (2) B
    (3) C
    (4) D
    (5) A and C

16. Susan bought 12 yards of terry cloth. How many towels, each 24 inches long, can be cut from this length of material?

    (1) 2
    (2) 4
    (3) 6
    (4) 18
    (5) 108

17. At six candy bars for 89¢, what will 2 dozen candy bars cost?

    (1) $.45
    (2) $2.76
    (3) $3.56
    (4) $5.34
    (5) $10.68

18. The scale on a map is 1 inch equals 65 miles. How many miles apart are two towns that are $2\frac{1}{2}$ inches apart on the map?

(1) 97.5
(2) 135
(3) 145
(4) 150
(5) 162.5

19. If Sarah and her 2 roommates share their apartment rent evenly, what is Sarah's portion of their $300 per month rent?

(1) $50
(2) $100
(3) $150
(4) $175
(5) $275

Questions 20–22 are based on the information below.

BARNES FAMILY BUDGET – 1993

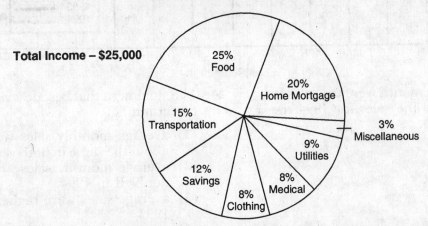

Total Income – $25,000

20. Housing costs include home mortgage payments and utilities. How much were the housing costs in 1993 for the Barnes family?

(1) $725
(2) $2250
(3) $5000
(4) $7250
(5) not enough information is given

21. If the money is spent equally, how much is allocated to each person in the Barnes family for clothing in 1993?

(1) $500
(2) $800
(3) $1000
(4) $2000
(5) not enough information is given

22. If the Barnes family's income rose 10% in 1994 and the family followed the same budget, how much money was put into savings in 1994?

(1) $250
(2) $330
(3) $2500
(4) $3300
(5) not enough information is given

Questions 23 and 24 are based on the graph below.

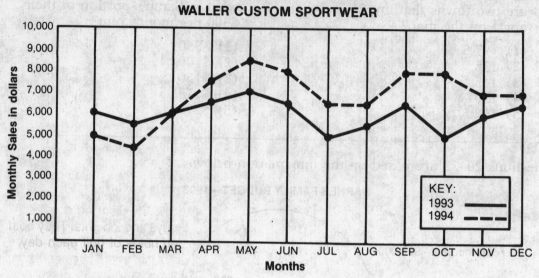

WALLER CUSTOM SPORTWEAR

KEY:
1993 ———
1994 ‑ ‑ ‑

23. In which month were the sales for 1993 and the sales for 1994 the closest?

(1) JAN
(2) FEB
(3) MAR
(4) AUG
(5) DEC

24. The statement that best describes the graph is

(1) average monthly sales were about the same in both years
(2) average monthly sales doubled in 1994
(3) average sales were higher in 1993
(4) average sales were higher in 1994
(5) sales were always higher in the summer than in the rest of the year

25. The ten finalists in the local beauty pageant include 3 blonds, 4 brunettes, 1 redhead, and 2 black-haired women. What is the probability that the winner will be a brunette?

(1) $\frac{1}{9}$
(2) $\frac{1}{10}$
(3) $\frac{2}{5}$
(4) $\frac{4}{9}$
(5) $\frac{2}{3}$

26. Arrange the following numbers in order from the *smallest value to the greatest*: 1^5, 2^3, 4^1, and 6.

(1) 6, 4^1, 1^5, 2^3
(2) 1^5, 4^1, 6, 2^3
(3) 1^5, 2^3, 4^1, 6
(4) 6, 4^1, 2^3, 1^5
(5) 2^3, 4^1, 6, 1^5

27. Many calculators express very large or very small numbers in scientific notation. If the number 4.32×10^4 appears in the display of a calculator, what is the value of this number?

(1)   .0432
(2)   4.0032
(3)   432
(4)   43,200
(5)   4,320,000

28. Evaluate the expression
$3z + 3(x + y)$, if $x = 6$, $y = 2$, and
$z = 5$.

(1) 13
(2) 20
(3) 24
(4) 31
(5) 39

29. Choose the point that is closest to
the value $-\frac{3}{4}$.

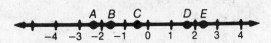

(1) A
(2) B
(3) C
(4) D
(5) E

30. On the highway, Albert always
drives at 55 mph. Colleen always
drives at 65 mph. If they start
together, driving in the same
direction, which expression below
tells how far apart they will be at
the end of a 4-hour drive?

(1) $4(65 + 55)$
(2) $4 \times 65 - 55$
(3) $65 - 55 \times 4$
(4) $\frac{65 + 55}{4}$
(5) $4(65 - 55)$

31. A store had received a supply of 8
dozen calculators, which it sold
for $9.99 each. If the store sold all
but 2 dozen of the calculators,
approximately how much money
did it make?

(1) $72
(2) $100
(3) $172
(4) $720
(5) $1000

32. Katy's age is 14 years less than
Sarah's age, x. The sum of their
two ages is 22. Choose the
equation that can be solved to find
the girls' ages.

(1) $2x - 14 = 22$
(2) $2(x - 14) = 22$
(3) $2x - 14 + x = 22$
(4) $x^2 - 14 = 22$
(5) not enough information is
given

Questions 33 and 34 are based on the
information below.

Manny and Judy went on a golfing
vacation for 2 days and 2 nights. They both
played eighteen holes of golf each day.
Eighteen holes of golf cost $18 per person.
The total bill for the weekend including golf
and their hotel room (including meals) was
$182.

33. Which equation best describes the
situation above?

(1) $x + 18 = 182$
(2) $2x + 18 = 182$
(3) $2x + 36 = 182$
(4) $2(x + 36) = 182$
(5) $x + 36 = 182$

34. What is the daily room rate
(including meals)?

(1) $55
(2) $73
(3) $82
(4) $146
(5) $164

35. Find the value of x in the equation
$\frac{2x}{3} = 12$.

(1)   2
(2)   4
(3)   9
(4)   18
(5)   108

36. What is the point of intersection of the line $x + y = 5$ with the line $y = -2$?

    (1) $(2,3)$
    (2) $(7,-2)$
    (3) $(-2,7)$
    (4) $(-2,3)$
    (5) $(3,-2)$

37. Emily was notified by her bank that she is overdrawn $187. If the bank charged her account $15 for correcting the overdraft and she deposited $350, what would be her new balance in the account?

    (1) $148
    (2) $178
    (3) $522
    (4) $552
    (5) not enough information is given

38. In the equation $x^2 + 7x = 0$, the equation will be true if x is

    (1) only -7
    (2) only 7
    (3) only 0
    (4) 0 or -7
    (5) 0 or 7

39. A social club has 20 members. There are 6 more men than women in the club. How many men and women are in the club?

    (1) 6 women and 14 men
    (2) 14 women and 6 men
    (3) 7 women and 13 men
    (4) 13 women and 6 men
    (5) not enough information is given

40. One winter day in the Rocky Mountains, the thermometer read 12°F at 9:00 A.M. The temperature dropped $3\frac{1}{2}$ degrees per hour for the next four hours, then rose one degree during the next hour. What was the temperature at the end of that hour?

    (1) $-1°$
    (2) $0°$
    (3) $1°$
    (4) $6°$
    (5) $15°$

41. Which of the following shows how the expression $4x^2 - 36x$ should be factored?

    (1) $4(x^2 - 36)$
    (2) $4x(x - 36)$
    (3) $4x(x - 9x)$
    (4) $4x(x - 9)$
    (5) $4x(x^2 - 9)$

42. In the expression $x + 2 > 13$, which of the following could be the value of x?

    (1) 2
    (2) 9
    (3) 11
    (4) 13
    (5) not enough information is given

43. In the figure below, find the distance between point A and point B.

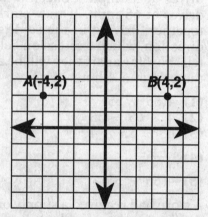

    (1) -4
    (2) 0
    (3) 2
    (4) 4
    (5) 8

WEEKLY MUTUAL FUND REPORT

Company	High	Low	Close	Change
Faith Investments	13.16	12.91	13.61	+.38
Hatton Group	15.13	14.77	15.13	+.14
Mary Link Services	12.01	11.94	11.97	−.09
Selected Funds	14.56	14.29	14.56	+.09
American Mutuals	17.26	16.94	17.26	+.08

44. The weekly investment report above shows each company's stocks with its high bid, low bid, closing bid prices, and the net change from last week's closing bid. What is the average net change for all five companies listed?

(1) .02
(2) .06
(3) .6
(4) .12
(5) 1.2

45. Which statement best describes the relationship between lines *M* and *N*?

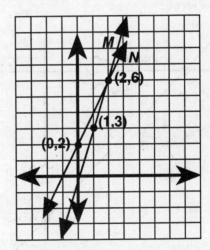

(1) Line *M* and line *N* both have positive slopes.
(2) Line *M* and line *N* both have negative slopes.
(3) Line *M* has a positive slope, and line *N* has a negative slope.
(4) Line *M* has a negative slope, and line *N* has a positive slope.
(5) There is not enough information to calculate the slopes of line *N* and line *M*.

46. Opposite sides of the figure below are parallel. Find the measure of angle x in the parallelogram shown here.

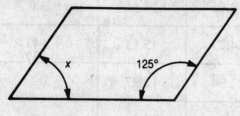

(1) 35°
(2) 55°
(3) 90°
(4) 180°
(5) 235°

47. According to the map below, how many miles is it from Jackson to Pierce?

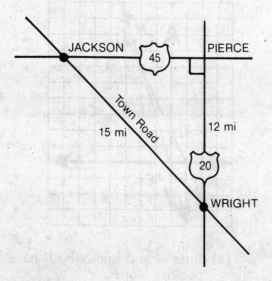

(1) 3
(2) 8
(3) 9
(4) 15
(5) 21

48. Two angles of a triangle are equal, and the third angle is 38°. Which expression below describes the relationship among the three angles if one of the equal angles is x?

(1) $x + 38° = 90°$
(2) $2x + 38° = 90°$
(3) $x + 38° = 180°$
(4) $2x + 38° = 180°$
(5) $2x + 38° = 360°$

49. To estimate the height of the tall evergreen on his farmland, Doug used the measurements of a small pine tree and the lengths of the shadows of the evergreen and the pine tree. What is the height in feet of the evergreen?

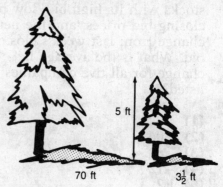

(1) 49
(2) $71\frac{1}{2}$
(3) 75
(4) 100
(5) 105

50. According to the Pythagorean theorem, the length of the side *BD* can be found by solving which of the expressions below the figure?

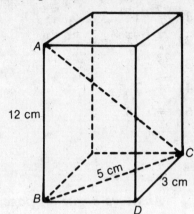

(1) $5^2 + 3^2 = BD^2$
(2) $3^2 + BD^2 = 5^2$
(3) $5^2 + BD^2 = 3^2$
(4) $\sqrt{5^2 + 3^2} = BD^2$

(5) not enough information is given

51. Britton wants to cut material for a flag she is making. The diagram below shows 4 triangular sections. Each triangle will be cut from a different cloth. She must be sure that each angle has the correct measure. If $\angle AEC$ is 110°, what is the measure of $\angle CED$?

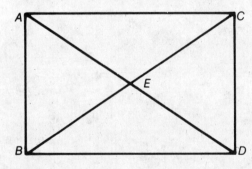

(1) 35°
(2) 55°
(3) 70°
(4) 125°
(5) 250°

52. How many square inches larger is the area of $\triangle ABC$ than $\triangle CDE$ shown in the figure?

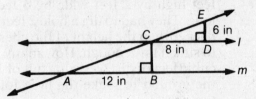

(1) 9
(2) 24
(3) 30
(4) 54
(5) 78

53. How many inches long is the radius of the largest circle that can fit inside a rectangle 18 inches long and 12 inches wide?

(1) 3
(2) 6
(3) 9
(4) 12
(5) 18

54. The Lytle family plans to install indoor-outdoor carpeting to cover their patio with the dimensions shown below. At $8.00 per *square yard*, how much will it cost them to do this?

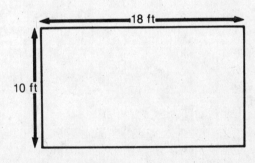

(1) $28
(2) $160
(3) $180
(4) $1440
(5) not enough information is given

55. The pirates buried their treasure chest in the ground. The dimensions of the chest were 3 feet high by 2 feet wide by 4 feet long. They had to dig a hole 2 feet deeper than the height of the chest to sink it low enough. How many cubic feet of dirt were dug out of the ground to make the hole for the chest?

(1)   9
(2)   11
(3)   24
(4)   40
(5) 120

56. A circle has a diameter of 14 inches. Which of the following could be used to find the area of the circle?

(1) $\frac{22}{7} \cdot 14^2$

(2) $\frac{22}{7} \cdot 7^2$

(3) $\frac{22}{7} \cdot 14$

(4) $\frac{22}{7} \cdot 7$

(5) $\frac{22}{7} \cdot 28$

Answers begin on page 827.

POST-TEST 5: MATHEMATICS ANSWER KEY

1. (4) $63.36

Find the number of 2-month payments in a year:
   $12 \div 2 = 6$
Find how much Tom pays in a year:
   $10.56 \times 6 = \$63.36$

2. (3) $14,000

Find each part of the estate:
Margaret = $2000
Betty Jo = $2000 $\times 2\frac{1}{2}$ = $5000
Johnny = $2000 $\times 3\frac{1}{2}$ = $7000
Add to get the total estate:
$2000 + $5000 + $7000 = $14,000

3. (2) 8.001

Give all the same number of decimal places:
   8.100; 8.001; 7.998; 8.010; 7.090
   8.001 is the closest to 8.

4. (5) 5

Find the difference between the two boards:

$$2\frac{3}{4} = 2\frac{9}{12}$$
$$-2\frac{1}{3} = 2\frac{4}{12}$$
$$\frac{5}{12} \text{ ft} = 5 \text{ in}$$

5. (4) $11.60

Find the cost of the nylon:
   $2.40 $\times 3\frac{1}{2}$ = $8.40
Subtract to determine the amount of change:
   $20.00 − $8.40 = $11.60

6. (2) $57

Find the average:
   $48 + $65.25 + $20 + $73 + $60
   + $62.50 + $70.25 + $53 = $452
   $452 $\div$ 8 = $56.50 to the nearest dollar is $57

7. (4) $17

Find John's salary in week 5:
   4 hr $\times$ $2 = $8
Add that to his tips:
   $60 + $8 = $68
Divide by the number of hours:
   $68 $\div$ 4 = $17

8. (1) $2\frac{3}{4}$

Add the given sides that are parallel to the top:

$$8\frac{1}{4} + 1\frac{1}{2} = 9\frac{3}{4}$$

Subtract from the length of the top side:

$$12\frac{1}{2} - 9\frac{3}{4} = 2\frac{3}{4}$$

9. (5) not enough information is given

Since you cannot find the two interior sides, you cannot find the perimeter of the drawing.

10. (3) $\frac{4}{5}$

Find the number of instructors:
   $35 + 40 + 15 = 90$ noninstructors
   $450 - 90 = 360$ instructors
Write the ratio of instructors to employees:
   $\frac{360}{450} \div \frac{90}{90} = \frac{4}{5}$

11. (3) 21

$$\frac{9 \text{ home runs}}{12 \text{ games}} = \frac{x \text{ home runs}}{28 \text{ games}}$$
$$x = \frac{28 \times 9}{12} = 21$$

12. (2) $10 \times 4 \times 2$

$$\frac{\frac{1}{2} \text{ in}}{10 \text{ mi}} = \frac{4 \text{ in}}{x \text{ mi}}$$
$$x = \frac{10 \times 4}{\frac{1}{2}} = 10 \times 4 \div \frac{1}{2}$$
$$\text{or } 10 \times 4 \times 2$$

13. (3) $1324.80

Find the total percent of tax deductions:
   $18\% + 7\% + 3\% = 28\%$
Find the amount deducted:
$$\frac{x}{\$1840} = \frac{28}{100}$$
$$x = \frac{28 \times \$1840}{100} = \$515.20$$
Subtract to find Brenda's take-home pay:
   $1840 − $515.20 = $1324.80

14. (5) $350 + .15($1337)

First find the total in sales:
   $42 + $126 + $785 + $384 = $1337
Identify the expression for the salesman's salary plus 15% commission on sales:
   $350 + .15($1337)

15. (4) D only

Since she already knows the basic cost of the jacket (A) and the cost of getting his name stitched on the coat (C), she needs the number of letters in his activity to multiply by $.80.

16. (4) 18

Find the number of inches in 12 yards:
   $12 \times 36 = 432$ in
Divide to find how many 24-inch towels can be cut:
   $432 \div 24 = 18$

17. (3) $3.56
2 dozen candy bars = 24 candy bars
$$\frac{6 \text{ candy bars}}{\$.89} = \frac{24 \text{ candy bars}}{x}$$
$$x = \frac{24 \times \$.89}{6} = \$3.56$$

18. (5) 162.5
$$\frac{1}{65} = \frac{2\frac{1}{2}}{x}$$
$$x = 2\frac{1}{2} \times 65$$
$$x = 162.5$$

19. (2) $100
*Divide the rent by the number of
people sharing the apartment:*
$300 \div 3 = \$100$

20. (4) $7250
Find the total in housing costs:
$20\% + 9\% = 29\%$
Find 29% of total income:
$$\frac{x}{\$25,000} = \frac{29}{100}$$
$$x = \frac{\$25,000 \times 29}{100} = \$7250$$

21. (5) not enough information is given
You do not know how many people
are in the Barnes family.

22. (4) $3300
Find 10% of the income:
$$\frac{x}{\$25,000} = \frac{10}{100}$$
$$x = \frac{\$25,000 \times 10}{100}$$
$$= \frac{\$250,000}{100} = \$2500$$
Find the total income for 1994:
$\$25,000 + \$2500 = \$27,500$
Find 12% to be put into savings:
$$\frac{x}{\$27,500} = \frac{12}{100}$$
$$x = \frac{\$27,500 \times 12}{100} = \$3300$$

23. (3) MAR
In the month of March, sales are the
same.

24. (4) average sales were higher in 1994
The graph shows the overall sales
were higher in 1994 than in 1993.

25. (3) $\frac{2}{5}$
$$\frac{4 \text{ brunettes}}{10 \text{ finalists}} = \frac{2}{5}$$

26. (2) $1^5, 4^1, 6, 2^3$
$1^5 = 1 \times 1 \times 1 \times 1 \times 1 = 1$
$4^1 = 4$
$6 = 6$
$2^3 = 2 \times 2 \times 2 = 8$

27. (4) 43,200
$4.32 \times 10^4 = 4.3200 = 43,200$

28. (5) 39
$3z + 3(x + y) =$
$3(5) + 3(6 + 2) = 15 + 24 = 39$

29. (3) C
$-\frac{3}{4}$ is between 0 and -1.

30. (5) $4(65 - 55)$
Using $d = rt$, this expression shows
the difference in their distances
assuming the same amount of time
but different rates of speed.

31. (4) $720
*Find how many dozen calculators
were sold:*
8 dozen − 2 dozen = 6 dozen
Approximate the total sales:
72(6 dozen) × $10(approximately
$9.99) = $720

32. (1) $2x - 14 = 22$
Let x = Sarah's age
$x - 14$ = Katy's age
The sum of the ages is
$x + x - 14 = 22$ or
$2x - 14 = 22$

33. (4) $2(x + 36) = 182$
Let x = room rate
Golf cost $2 \times 18 = \$36$ per day
Two days cost $2(x + \$36)$

34. (1) $55
$$2(x + \$36) = \$182$$
$$2x + \$72 = \$182$$
$$2x = \$110$$
$$x = \$55$$

35. (4) 18
$$\frac{2x}{3} = 12$$
$$2x = 12 \cdot 3$$
$$2x = 36$$
$$x = 18$$

36. (2) $(7,-2)$
Substitute -2 for y.
$x + y = 5$
$x + (-2) = 5$
$x + 2 - 2 = 5 + 2$
$x = 7$
$x = 7$ and $y = -2$ so the point of
intersection is $(7,-2)$

37. (1) $148
$-\$187$ overdrawn
$\underline{-\ \$15}$ charge
$-\$202 + \$350 = \$148$

38. (4) 0 or −7
$x^2 + 7x = 0$
For 0: $0^2 + 7(0) = 0$
For −7: $(-7)^2 + 7(-7) =$
$\quad\quad\quad\quad 49 - 49 = 0$

39. (3) 7 women and 13 men
Let x = number of women
$x + 6$ = number of men
$x + x + 6 = 20$
$2x = 20 - 6$
$2x = 14$
$x = 7$ women
$x + 6 = 13$ men

40. (1) $-1°$
$-3\frac{1}{2}° \times 4 = -14°$
$12° - 14° = -2°$ at the end of 4 hours
$-2° + 1° = -1°$ at the end of 5 hours

41. (4) $4x(x - 9)$
$$4x^2 - 36x =$$
$$\boxed{4 \cdot x} \cdot x - 9 \cdot \boxed{4 \cdot x} =$$
$$4x(x - 9)$$

42. (4) 13
$x + 2 > 13$
$x + 2 - 2 > 13 - 2$
$x > 11$
Since x must be greater than 11, the only possible value of those given is 13.

43. (5) 8
Since both points are on the horizontal line $y = 2$, you can count the units:
-4 to $0 = 4$; 0 to $4 = 4$
$4 + 4 = 8$

44. (4) .12
Find the total:
$+.38 + .14 - .09 + .09 + .08 = .60$
Find the average:
$.60 \div 5 = .12$

45. (1) Line M and line N both have positive slopes.

46. (2) 55°
Subtract to find the supplement of 125° since x *is equal to that supplementary angle:*
$180° - 125° = 55°$

47. (3) 9
$$c^2 = a^2 + b^2$$
$$15^2 = 12^2 + b^2$$
$$225 = 144 + b^2$$
$$225 - 144 = b^2$$
$$81 = b^2$$
$$9 = b$$

48. (4) $2x + 38° = 180°$
The angles of a triangle equal 180°. Two equal angles ($2x$) plus 38° equal 180°.

49. (4) 100
Set up a proportion:
$$\frac{height}{70 \text{ ft shadow}} = \frac{5 \text{ ft}}{3\frac{1}{2} \text{ ft shadow}}$$
$$h = \frac{70 \times 5}{3\frac{1}{2}}$$
$$h = \frac{350}{1} \div \frac{7}{2} = \frac{350}{1} \times \frac{2}{7} = 100$$

50. (2) $3^2 + BD^2 = 5^2$
Side BD is one side of a right triangle, $\triangle BCD$. Substitute the given values in the Pythagorean theorem as follows:
$$a^2 + b^2 = c^2$$
$$3^2 + BD^2 = 5^2$$

51. (3) 70°
$\angle CED$ is the supplement of $\angle AEC$.
$180° - 110° = 70°$

52. (3) 30
Set up a proportion to find side BC:
$$\frac{x}{12} = \frac{6}{8}$$
$$x = \frac{6 \times 12}{8} = 9$$
Find the area of both triangles:
$$\triangle ABC = \frac{1}{2} \cdot \frac{9 \cdot 12}{1} = 54 \text{ sq in}$$
$$\triangle CDE = \frac{1}{2} \cdot \frac{6 \cdot 8}{1} = 24 \text{ sq in}$$
Find the difference:
$54 - 24 = 30$ sq in

53. (2) 6
The width of the rectangle would be the diameter of the circle, $d = 12$.
Radius $= \frac{1}{2}d$
$$r = \frac{1}{2} \cdot \frac{12}{1} = 6 \text{ in}$$

54. (2) $160
Find the area of the patio:
$A = lw$
$A = 18 \times 10 = 180$ sq ft
Find the number of square yards (there are 9 square feet in a square yard):
$180 \div 9 = 20$ sq yd
Find the total cost:
$20 \times \$8 = \$160$

55. (4) 40
Find the depth of the hole (height):
$3 + 2 = $ height
Find the volume of dirt:
$V = lwh$
$V = (4)(2)(5)$
$V = 40$ cu ft

56. (2) $\frac{22}{7} \cdot 7^2$
Choose the correct formula for area:
$A = \pi r^2$ where $\pi \cong \frac{22}{7}$
$A = \frac{22}{7} \cdot r^2$
Since the diameter is 14, the radius is 7.
$A = \frac{22}{7} \cdot 7^2$

Use the answer key on pages 827–829 to check your answers to the Post-Test. Then find the item number of each question you missed and circle it on the chart below to determine the mathematics skill and content areas in which you need more practice. Pay particular attention to areas where you missed half or more of the questions. The page numbers for the content areas are listed below on the chart. The numbers in boldface are questions based on graphics. For those questions that you missed, review the pages indicated.

POST-TEST 5: MATHEMATICS EVALUATION CHART

Skill Area/ Content Area	Item Number	Review Pages
Whole Numbers & Problem Solving	**7**, 15, 19, **21**, 30, 31, 37	559–572
Decimals	1, **6**	573–586
Fractions	2, 4, 5	587–604
Ratio & Proportion	10, 11, 17	605–610
Percent	13, 14, **20**, **22**	611–620
Measurement	12, 16, **18**	621–636
Graphs, Statistics, & Probability	**23**, **24**, 25	637–648
Numeration	3, 26, 27	649–656
Geometry	**8**, **9**, **46**, **47**, 48, **49**, **50**, **51**, **52**, **53**, **54**, 55, 56	657–674
Algebra	28, **29**, 32, 33, 34, 35, 36, 38, 39, 40, 41, 42, **43**, **44**, **45**	675–710

Practice Tests

Realizing that practice makes perfect, we've added Practice Tests as final indicators of your readiness for the real GED Test. These tests are just like the Post-Tests in terms of format, level of difficulty, and percentages found on the real test. After you have completed the Practice Tests, you will be able to finally determine whether you are ready to take the GED Test and, if not, what areas you need to review. As with the Post-Tests, Evaluation Charts are included to help you judge your performance. We recommend the following approach to the Practice Tests.

1. Take only one Practice Test at a time. Try to finish the test within the allotted time so that you can see how you will do on the actual GED Tests. If you are not done within that time period, mark where you were when the time was up and finish the test. You want to finish the entire Practice Test so that you can make use of the Evaluation Charts.

Time Allowed for Each Test

Writing Skills	Part 1	75 minutes
	Part 2	45 minutes
Social Studies		85 minutes
Science		95 minutes
Literature and the Arts		65 minutes
Mathematics		90 minutes

---

2. After you have finished each of the Practice Tests, check the answers in the answer key and fill in the Evaluation Charts. The answer keys and Evaluation Charts follow each test. Be sure to read the explanations for all of the questions that you missed.

3. If the Evaluation Charts indicate that you still need work in a certain area, refer to the review pages given in the charts.

4. When you have finished all of the tests, checked your answers, and filled out the Evaluation Charts, transfer your test scores from the Evaluation Charts to the GED Readiness Worksheet on page 927. Use the Worksheet to determine whether you are ready for the actual GED Tests.

5. Although these are Practice Tests, you should give them your best effort. If an item seems difficult, mark it and come back later. Always answer every question—even if you have to make an "educated guess." Sometimes you may know more than you give yourself credit for. Also, on the real GED Tests a blank counts as a wrong answer. It's always wise to answer every question as best you can.

Good luck on the Practice Tests and on the GED!

PRACTICE TEST 1: WRITING SKILLS
Part 1: Conventions of English

The following items are based on paragraphs that contain numbered sentences. Some of the sentences may contain errors in sentence structure, usage, or mechanics. A few sentences, however, may be correct as written. Read the paragraph and then answer the items based on it. For each item, choose the answer that would result in the most effective writing of the sentence or sentences. The best answer must be consistent with the meaning and tone of the rest of the paragraph.

When you are finished with the test, check your answers and turn to the Evaluation Charts on page 848. Use the charts to evaluate whether or not you are ready to take the actual GED Test and, if not, in what areas you need more work.

PRACTICE TEST 1: WRITING SKILLS ANSWER GRID

1 ① ② ③ ④ ⑤	15 ① ② ③ ④ ⑤	29 ① ② ③ ④ ⑤	43 ① ② ③ ④ ⑤
2 ① ② ③ ④ ⑤	16 ① ② ③ ④ ⑤	30 ① ② ③ ④ ⑤	44 ① ② ③ ④ ⑤
3 ① ② ③ ④ ⑤	17 ① ② ③ ④ ⑤	31 ① ② ③ ④ ⑤	45 ① ② ③ ④ ⑤
4 ① ② ③ ④ ⑤	18 ① ② ③ ④ ⑤	32 ① ② ③ ④ ⑤	46 ① ② ③ ④ ⑤
5 ① ② ③ ④ ⑤	19 ① ② ③ ④ ⑤	33 ① ② ③ ④ ⑤	47 ① ② ③ ④ ⑤
6 ① ② ③ ④ ⑤	20 ① ② ③ ④ ⑤	34 ① ② ③ ④ ⑤	48 ① ② ③ ④ ⑤
7 ① ② ③ ④ ⑤	21 ① ② ③ ④ ⑤	35 ① ② ③ ④ ⑤	49 ① ② ③ ④ ⑤
8 ① ② ③ ④ ⑤	22 ① ② ③ ④ ⑤	36 ① ② ③ ④ ⑤	50 ① ② ③ ④ ⑤
9 ① ② ③ ④ ⑤	23 ① ② ③ ④ ⑤	37 ① ② ③ ④ ⑤	51 ① ② ③ ④ ⑤
10 ① ② ③ ④ ⑤	24 ① ② ③ ④ ⑤	38 ① ② ③ ④ ⑤	52 ① ② ③ ④ ⑤
11 ① ② ③ ④ ⑤	25 ① ② ③ ④ ⑤	39 ① ② ③ ④ ⑤	53 ① ② ③ ④ ⑤
12 ① ② ③ ④ ⑤	26 ① ② ③ ④ ⑤	40 ① ② ③ ④ ⑤	54 ① ② ③ ④ ⑤
13 ① ② ③ ④ ⑤	27 ① ② ③ ④ ⑤	41 ① ② ③ ④ ⑤	55 ① ② ③ ④ ⑤
14 ① ② ③ ④ ⑤	28 ① ② ③ ④ ⑤	42 ① ② ③ ④ ⑤	

Choose the best answer to each question that follows.

Questions 1–9 refer to the following passage.

(1) Is you stressed out by work or school or life in general? (2) One popular way to cope with stress the practice of meditation. (3) Many people spend ten minutes meditating quietly. (4) Meditating lets them get back to their day feeling refreshed and energetic. (5) First, sit comfortably in a chair with your back straight but not stiff. (6) Relax, place your hands in your lap, and your feet flat on the floor. (7) Close your eyes feel your abdomen expand when you breathe in and collapse when you breathe out. (8) If the worries of the day keep intruding, don't fight it off. (9) Just let them go gently, out of your mind. (10) Concentrating on your breathing. (11) Once you got the hang of it, ten minutes of meditating can leave you feeling as rested as a night's sleep.

1. Sentence 1: **Is you stressed out by work or school or life in general?**

   What correction should be made to this sentence?

   (1) change *Is* to *Are*
   (2) insert a comma after *work*
   (3) change *school* to *School*
   (4) change the spelling of *general* to *genral*
   (5) change the question mark to a period

2. Sentence 2: **One popular way to cope with stress the practice of meditation.**

   Which of the following is the best way to write the underlined portion of this sentence? If you think the original is the best way, choose option (1).

   (1) with stress the practice of
   (2) with stress is to practice
   (3) with stress, the practice of
   (4) with stress, practice
   (5) with stress. The practice of

3. Sentences 3 and 4: **Many people spend ten minutes meditating quietly. Meditating lets them get back to their day feeling refreshed and energetic.**

   The most effective combination of sentences 3 and 4 would include which of the following groups of words?

   (1) After meditating quietly for ten minutes,
   (2) Before meditating quietly for ten minutes,
   (3) Meditating quietly for ten minutes, therefore,
   (4) To spend ten minutes meditating quietly,
   (5) While meditating quietly for ten minutes,

4. Sentence 6: **Relax, place your hands in your lap, and your feet flat on the floor.**

Which of the following is the best way to write the underlined portion of this sentence? If you think the original is the best way, choose option (1).

(1) lap, and your feet
(2) lap, and you're feet
(3) lap, and put your feet
(4) lap and your feet
(5) lap; and your feet

5. Sentence 7: **Close your eyes feel your abdomen expand when you breathe in and collapse when you breathe out.**

What correction should be made to this sentence?

(1) change *Close* to *Closed*
(2) insert a semicolon after *eyes*
(3) insert a comma after *eyes*
(4) change *expand* to *expands*
(5) insert a comma after *in*

6. Sentence 8: **If the worries of the day keep intruding, don't fight it off.**

What correction should be made to this sentence?

(1) change *If* to *Because*
(2) insert a comma after *day*
(3) change *keep* to *keeps*
(4) change *don't* to *dont*
(5) change *it* to *them*

7. Sentence 9: **Just let them go gently, out of your mind.**

Which of the following is the best way to write the underlined portion of this sentence? If you think the original is the best way, choose option (1).

(1) let them go gently,
(2) lets them go gently,
(3) let it go gently,
(4) let them goes gently,
(5) let them go gently

8. Sentence 10: **Concentrating on your breathing.**

What correction should be made to this sentence?

(1) change *Concentrating* to *Concentrate*
(2) change the spelling of *Concentrating* to *Consentrating*
(3) insert a comma after *Concentrating*
(4) change *your* to *you're*
(5) no correction is necessary

9. Sentence 11: **Once you got the hang of it, ten minutes of meditating can leave you feeling as rested as a night's sleep.**

What correction should be made to this sentence?

(1) change *you* to *you'll*
(2) change *got* to *get*
(3) change *it* to *them*
(4) change *leave* to *left*
(5) change the spelling of *night's* to *nite's*

Questions 10–19 refer to the following passage.

(1) Vultures have the worst reputation of all birds but make an important contribution to our world. (2) They cleans up dead bodies. (3) Road kills and other animal carcasses can infectious diseases. (4) When vultures eat this meat, they protect humans and other animals from getting infected. (5) Some vultures even have eaten bones. (6) The lammergeier vulture which can be found in Africa and Eurasia drops bones from a great height onto a rocky surface. (7) The bones land with enough force to split open, and then the vulture consumes it. (8) These Trash Collectors of the skies do their work efficiently. (9) They find carcasses through sharp eyesight, alertness, and they work as a team. (10) A vulture swoops down, and it's a signal to other vultures that a meal is on the table. (11) They sped toward the scene on their massive wings and devour even a large animal in minutes.

10. Sentence 1: **Vultures have the worst reputation of all birds but make an important contribution to our world.**

Which of the following is the best way to write the underlined portion of this sentence? If you think the original is the best way, choose option (1).

(1) reputation of all birds but
(2) reputation, of all birds, but
(3) reputation of all birds and
(4) reputation. Of all birds but
(5) reputation of all birds so

11. Sentence 2: **They cleans up dead bodies.**

What correction should be made to this sentence?

(1) change *They* to *He*
(2) change *cleans* to *clean*
(3) insert a comma after *up*
(4) change the spelling of *bodies* to *bodys*
(5) no correction is necessary

12. Sentence 3: **Road kills and other animal carcasses can infectious diseases.**

Which of the following is the best way to write the underlined portion of this sentence? If you think the original is the best way, choose option (1).

(1) carcasses can
(2) carcass can
(3) carcasses can carry
(4) carcasses. They can carry
(5) carcasses can carries

13. Sentence 5: **Some vultures even have eaten bones.**

What correction should be made to this sentence?

(1) change *vultures* to *vulture*
(2) insert a comma after *vultures*
(3) change *have eaten* to *eat*
(4) change *have eaten* to *ate*
(5) change *have eaten* to *eats*

14. Sentence 6: **The lammergeier vulture which can be found in Africa and Eurasia drops bones from a great height onto a rocky surface.**

Which of the following is the best way to write the underlined portion of this sentence? If you think the original is the best way, choose option (1).

(1) vulture which can be found in Africa and Eurasia
(2) vultures which can be found in Africa and Eurasia
(3) vulture, which can be found in Africa and Eurasia,
(4) vulture what can be found in Africa and Eurasia
(5) vulture which can be found in africa and eurasia

15. Sentence 7: **The bones land with enough force to split open, and then the vulture consumes it.**

What correction should be made to this sentence?

(1) change *land* to *lands*
(2) insert a comma after *land*
(3) change *vulture* to *vultures*
(4) change *it* to *them*
(5) no correction is necessary

16. Sentence 8: **These Trash Collectors of the skies do their work efficiently.**

What correction should be made to this sentence?

(1) change *These* to *This*
(2) change *Trash Collectors* to *trash collectors*
(3) insert a comma after *skies*
(4) change *their* to *there*
(5) change the spelling of *efficiently* to *eficiently*

17. Sentence 9: **They find carcasses through sharp <u>eyesight, alertness, and they work as a team.</u>**

Which of the following is the best way to write the underlined portion of this sentence? If you think the original is the best way, choose option (1).

(1) eyesight, alertness, and they work as a team
(2) eyesight alertness, and they work as a team
(3) eyesight, alertness, and it works as a team
(4) eyesight, alertness, and they work like a team
(5) eyesight, alertness, and teamwork

18. Sentence 10: **A vulture swoops down, and it's a signal to other vultures that a meal is on the table.**

If you rewrote sentence 10 beginning with

Swooping down,

the next words should be

(1) a vulture
(2) a signal
(3) other vultures
(4) a meal
(5) on the table

19. Sentence 11: **They sped toward the scene on their massive wings and devour even a large animal in minutes.**

What correction should be made to this sentence?

(1) change *They* to *It*
(2) change *sped* to *speed*
(3) change the spelling of *scene* to *seen*
(4) change *on* to *under*
(5) change *their* to *they're*

Questions 20–28 refer to the following passage.

(1) Times are tough it's harder than ever to live within your income. (2) A lot of people are looking for ways to live more cheaply than he or she used to. (3) Even people who used to have money, are trading in their BMWs for sensible, high-mileage compact cars. (4) One of the best ways to save money is to stop buying on credit. (5) The interest is so high. (6) You might also have skipped one meat-based meal each week. (7) Pasta, rice, and to eat other grains are much cheaper than meat. (8) Avoid buying everything from food to clothes to compact discs on impulse, you'll be surprised at how much you save. (9) Finally, don't throw things out until their really worn out. (10) Americans throwed away almost 1,500 pounds of garbage per person per year. (11) Getting a few more wearings out of those jeans and re-using grocery bags is good for both your wallet and the environment.

20. Sentence 1: **Times are tough it's harder than ever to live within your income.**

    Which of the following is the best way to write the underlined portion of this sentence? If you think the original is the best way, choose option (1).

    (1) are tough it's
    (2) is tough it's
    (3) are tough, it's
    (4) are tough, and it's
    (5) are tough its

21. Sentence 2: **A lot of people are looking for ways to live more cheaply than he or she used to.**

    What correction should be made to this sentence?

    (1) change the spelling of *people* to *poeple*
    (2) change *are* to *is*
    (3) change *are looking* to *looked*
    (4) change *ways* to *way*
    (5) change *he or she* to *they*

22. Sentence 3: **Even people who used to have money, are trading in their BMWs for sensible, high-mileage compact cars.**

    What correction should be made to this sentence?

    (1) change *who* to *what*
    (2) change the spelling of *sensible* to *sensable*
    (3) remove the comma after *money*
    (4) change *are* to *is*
    (5) change *their* to *they're*

23. Sentences 4 and 5: **One of the best ways to save money is to stop buying on credit. The interest is so high.**

    The most effective combination of sentences 4 and 5 would include which of the following groups of words?

    (1) credit, even if the interest
    (2) credit because the interest
    (3) credit, although the interest
    (4) credit; however, the interest
    (5) credit, and the interest

24. Sentence 6: <u>**You might also have skipped**</u> **one meat-based meal each week.**

Which of the following is the best way to write the underlined portion of this sentence? If you think the original is the best way, choose option (1).

(1) You might also have skipped
(2) One might also have skipped
(3) You might also, have skipped
(4) You might also skip
(5) You might also skips

25. Sentence 7: **Pasta, rice, and to eat other grains are much cheaper than meat.**

What correction should be made to this sentence?

(1) remove the comma after *pasta*
(2) remove *to eat*
(3) change *to eat* to *eating*
(4) change *are* to *is*
(5) change *than* to *then*

26. Sentence 8: **Avoid buying everything from food to clothes to compact discs on <u>impulse, you'll be surprised</u> at how much you save.**

Which of the following is the best way to write the underlined portion of this sentence? If you think the original is the best way, choose option (1).

(1) impulse, you'll be surprised
(2) impulse you'll be surprised
(3) impulse. You'll be surprised
(4) impulse, youll be surprised
(5) impulse, you'll be surprized

27. Sentence 9: **Finally, don't throw things out until their really worn out.**

What correction should be made to this sentence?

(1) change *don't* to *dont*
(2) change *throw* to *threw*
(3) insert a comma after *out*
(4) change *their* to *they're*
(5) change *their* to *there*

28. Sentence 10: **Americans throwed away almost 1,500 pounds of garbage per person per year.**

What correction should be made to this sentence?

(1) change *Americans* to *americans*
(2) change *throwed* to *threw*
(3) change the spelling of *almost* to *allmost*
(4) change *garbage* to *Garbage*
(5) no correction is necessary

Questions 29–37 refer to the following passage.

(1) The average person catches four colds a year and miss about seven days of work, according to a medical study. (2) Young children get colds more often and spread them more rapidly. (3) So it's not surprising that the parents of young children take more sick days than anyone else. (4) Not only do they have to stay home to take care of their sick kids, but they're also likely to get sick from their kids. (5) The best way to stay healthy, is to avoid exposure to cold germs. (6) Colds are usualy passed on by hand-to-hand contact. (7) This could include shaking hands with a sick person which has just rubbed his eyes or even using the phone of a sniffling co-worker. (8) While a cold virus can't penetrate skin, it can penetrate mucous membranes in your mouth, nose, and eyes. (9) All colds are caused by germs. (10) That myth you're mother told you about the dangers of catching cold from sitting in a draft or getting your feet wet is just a myth. (11) If one is unlucky enough to come down with a cold, your best cures are resting, eating right, and avoiding stress.

29. Sentence 1: **The average person catches four colds a year and miss about seven days of work, according to a medical study.**

    What correction should be made to this sentence?

    (1) change *catches* to *catch*
    (2) change the spelling of *four* to *for*
    (3) change *miss* to *misses*
    (4) change *days* to *days'*
    (5) no correction is necessary

30. Sentences 2 and 3: **Young children get colds more often and spread them more rapidly. So it's not surprising that the parents of young children take more sick days than anyone else.**

    The most effective combination of sentences 2 and 3 would include which of the following groups of words?

    (1) If young children
    (2) Since young children
    (3) Although young children
    (4) But young children
    (5) While young children

31. Sentence 5: **The best way to stay healthy, is to avoid exposure to cold germs.**

    Which of the following is the best way to write the underlined portion of this sentence? If you think the original is the best way, choose option (1).

    (1) to stay healthy, is
    (2) too stay healthy, is
    (3) to stay helthy, is
    (4) to stay healthy is
    (5) to stay healthy, are

32. Sentence 6: **Colds are usualy passed on by hand-to-hand contact.**

    What correction should be made to this sentence?

    (1) change *are* to *is*
    (2) change the spelling of *usualy* to *usually*
    (3) insert a comma after *usualy*
    (4) insert a comma after *on*
    (5) no correction is necessary

33. Sentence 7: **This could include shaking hands with a sick person which has just rubbed his eyes or even using the phone of a sniffling co-worker.**

Which of the following is the best way to write the underlined portion of this sentence? If you think the original is the best way, choose option (1).

(1) person which has just rubbed his eyes
(2) person, which has just rubbed his eyes
(3) person who has just rubbed his eyes
(4) person which will rub his eyes
(5) person which has just rubbed their eyes

34. Sentence 8: **While a cold virus can't penetrate skin, it can penetrate mucous membranes in your mouth, nose, and eyes.**

If you rewrote sentence 8 beginning with

A cold virus can't penetrate skin,

the next word should be

(1) since
(2) therefore
(3) and
(4) but
(5) so

35. Sentence 9: **All colds are caused by germs.**

What correction should be made to this sentence?

(1) change *All* to *Every*
(2) change *colds* to *Colds*
(3) insert a comma after *colds*
(4) change *are* to *were*
(5) no correction is necessary

36. Sentence 10: **That myth you're mother told you about the dangers of catching cold from sitting in a draft or getting your feet wet is just a myth.**

Which of the following is the best way to write the underlined portion of this sentence? If you think the original is the best way, choose option (1).

(1) myth you're mother told you
(2) myth, you're mother told you
(3) myth your mother told you
(4) myth you're Mother told you
(5) myth you're mother will tell you

37. Sentence 11: **If one is unlucky enough to come down with a cold, your best cures are resting, eating right, and avoiding stress.**

What correction should be made to this sentence?

(1) change *If* to *Because*
(2) change *one is* to *you are*
(3) change *your* to *you're*
(4) change *cures* to *cure*
(5) change *avoiding* to *to avoid*

Questions 38–46 refer to the following passage.

(1) Did you know their are people who work as garbologists? (2) Study garbage to learn more about our society and how to help the environment. (3) They have learned that almost none of the garbage buried in landfills breaks down into useful soil. (4) Garbologists have found 40-year-old hot dogs and old newpapers that are still readable. (5) Paper is the single biggest part of any landfill. (6) It accounts for almost half of the garbage thrown away. (7) A year's subscription, to the *New York Times*, takes up as much space as 19,000 crushed aluminum cans. (8) Potato peels take up more room in landfills than any other fresh food. (9) Garbologists have found that most people eat both Health Foods and junk foods. (10) When they find the remains of lettuce and high-fiber bread, he knows the Twinkies wrappers aren't far behind. (11) The contents of landfills varies depending on the geographic region and local income level.

38. Sentence 1: **Did you know their are people who work as garbologists?**

    What correction should be made to this sentence?

    (1) change *Did* to *Does*
    (2) change *know* to *knew*
    (3) change *their* to *there*
    (4) change *are* to *were*
    (5) change *garbologists* to *Garbologists*

39. Sentence 2: **Study garbage to learn more about our society and how to help the environment.**

    Which of the following is the best way to write the underlined portion of this sentence? If you think the original is the best way, choose option (1).

    (1) Study garbage
    (2) You study garbage
    (3) We study garbage
    (4) I study garbage
    (5) They study garbage

40. Sentence 3: **They have learned that almost none of the garbage buried in landfills breaks down into useful soil.**

    Which of the following is the best way to write the underlined portion of this sentence? If you think the original is the best way, choose option (1).

    (1) They have learned
    (2) They will learn
    (3) One has learned
    (4) They has learned
    (5) They will be learning

41. Sentence 4: **Garbologists have found 40-year-old hot dogs and old newpapers that are still readable.**

    What correction should be made to this sentence?

    (1) change *have* to *has*
    (2) change the spelling of *newpapers* to *newspapers*
    (3) insert a comma after *newpapers*
    (4) change *are* to *is*
    (5) no correction is necessary

42. Sentences 5 and 6: **Paper is the single biggest part of any landfill. It accounts for almost half of the garbage thrown away.**

If you rewrote sentences 5 and 6 beginning with

The single biggest part of any landfill,

the next word should be

(1) accounting
(2) paper
(3) almost
(4) half
(5) garbage

43. Sentence 7: **A year's <u>subscription, to the *New York Times*, takes up</u> as much space as 19,000 crushed aluminum cans.**

Which of the following is the best way to write the underlined portion of this sentence? If you think the original is the best way, choose option (1).

(1) subscription, to *The New York Times*, takes
(2) subscription, to *The New York Times*, take
(3) subscription, to *the new york times*, takes
(4) subscription to *The New York Times* takes
(5) subscription, to *The New York Times*, took

44. Sentence 9: **Garbologists have found that most people eat both Health Foods and junk foods.**

What correction should be made to this sentence?

(1) change *have* to *has*
(2) insert a comma after *found*
(3) change *eat* to *were eating*
(4) change *Health Foods* to *health foods*
(5) change *junk foods* to *Junk Foods*

45. Sentence 10: **When they find the remains of lettuce and high-fiber bread, he knows the Twinkies wrappers aren't far behind.**

What correction should be made to this sentence?

(1) change *When* to *Until*
(2) change *they find* to *he finds*
(3) remove the comma after *bread*
(4) change *he knows* to *they know*
(5) change *aren't* to *weren't*

46. Sentence 11: **The contents of landfills varies depending on the geographic region and local income level.**

What correction should be made to this sentence?

(1) change *geographic region* to *Geographic Region*
(2) change *varies* to *veries*
(3) change *depending* to *depends*
(4) change *varies* to *vary*
(5) insert a comma before *and*

Questions 47–55 refer to the following passage.

(1) Is you're job a pain in the neck? (2) If you works at a computer all day, it may be a pain in the wrists. (3) Millions of americans suffer from something called repetitive stress injuries. (4) For example, suppose you keystroke day after day. (5) Eventually your wrists may start to hurt because the small muscles are repeating the exact same movement again and again. (6) The pain can be intense enough to keep you from keyboarding for weeks. (7) There were ways to protect against repetitive stress. (8) Stand up every half hour or so and shake out your arms, and hands. (9) Make the tightest fists you can and rotate them to work your mussels in different directions. (10) Better yet, if your keyboard has a tilt adjustment, adjusting it to the same height as your elbows while you work. (11) That way your wrists won't have to tilt, and his muscles won't be subjected to repetitive stress.

47. Sentence 1: **Is you're job a pain in the neck?**

What correction should be made to this sentence?

(1) change *Is* to *Are*
(2) change *you're* to *your*
(3) insert a comma after *job*
(4) change *job* to *jobs*
(5) no correction is necessary

48. Sentence 2: **If you works at a computer all day, it may be a pain in the wrists.**

Which of the following is the best way to write the underlined portion of this sentence? If you think the original is the best way, choose option (1).

(1) If you works
(2) Although you works
(3) If one works
(4) If you work
(5) If you worked

49. Sentence 3: **Millions of americans suffer from something called repetitive stress injuries.**

What correction should be made to this sentence?

(1) change the spelling of *millions* to *millyuns*
(2) change *americans* to *Americans*
(3) change *suffer* to *suffers*
(4) insert a comma after *something*
(5) no correction is necessary

50. Sentences 4 and 5: **For example, suppose you keystroke day after day. Eventually your wrists may start to hurt because the small muscles are repeating the exact same movement again and again.**

The most effective combination of sentences 4 and 5 would contain which of the following groups of words?

(1) If you keystroke day after day,
(2) Before you keystroke day after day,
(3) Despite keystroking day after day,
(4) Then you keystroke day after day,
(5) Unless you keystroke day after day,

51. Sentence 7: **There were ways to protect against repetitive stress.**

What correction should be made to this sentence?

(1) change *There* to *Their*
(2) change *were* to *are*
(3) change *ways* to *way*
(4) insert a comma after *protect*
(5) change the spelling of *against* to *aganst*

52. Sentence 8: **Stand up every half hour or <u>so and shake out your arms,</u> and hands.**

Which of the following is the best way to write the underlined portion of this sentence? If you think the original is the best way, choose option (1).

(1) so and shake out your arms,
(2) so, and shake out your arms,
(3) so but shake out your arms,
(4) so and shake out you're arms,
(5) so and shake out your arms

53. Sentence 9: **Make the tightest fists you can and rotate them to work your mussels in different directions.**

What correction should be made to this sentence?

(1) change *Make* to *Makes*
(2) change *rotate* to *rotated*
(3) change *them* to *it*
(4) change the spelling of *mussels* to *muscles*
(5) change the spelling of *different* to *differnt*

54. Sentence 10: **Better yet, if your keyboard has a tilt adjustment, adjusting it to the same height as your elbows while you work.**

What correction should be made to this sentence?

(1) change *has* to *had*
(2) change *adjusting* to *adjust*
(3) change *keyboard* to *keybord*
(4) change *work* to *worked*
(5) no correction is necessary

55. Sentence 11: **That way your wrists won't have to tilt, <u>and his muscles won't</u> be subjected to repetitive stress.**

Which of the following is the best way to write the underlined portion of this sentence? If you think the original is the best way, choose option (1).

(1) and his muscles won't
(2) if his muscles won't
(3) and your muscles won't
(4) and his muscles wouldn't
(5) and his muscles wont

Answers begin on page 846.

Part 2: The Essay

Directions: This part of the test is designed to find out how well you write. The test has one question that asks you to present an opinion on an issue or explain something. In preparing your answer for this question, you should take the following steps:

1. Read all of the information accompanying the question.

2. Plan your answer carefully before you write.

3. Use scratch paper to make any notes.

4. Write your answer on a separate sheet of paper.

5. Read carefully what you have written and make any changes that will improve your writing.

6. Check your paragraphing, sentence structure, spelling, punctuation, capitalization, and usage and make any necessary corrections.

Take forty-five minutes to plan and write on the assigned topic. Write legibly and use a ballpoint pen.

Topic

Movies are increasingly available on videocassettes for use on a VCR, and many people have less and less reason to go to movie theaters. These changes are profoundly affecting the entire motion picture industry, which is losing money as never before.

Write a composition of about 200 words describing the effects of these changes on your life. You may write about the positive and negative aspects of the video revolution, as well as the way you prefer to watch movies and why. Be specific and use examples to support your view.

Information on evaluating your essay is on page 848.

PRACTICE TEST 1: WRITING SKILLS ANSWER KEY

Part 1: Conventions of English

1. **(1)** Even though this sentence is inverted, the verb still agrees with the subject, *you.* So it should be *Are.*

2. **(2)** This sentence needs a verb (*is*) to make it complete.

3. **(1)** The original sentences have a time order relationship. Starting the new sentence with *After* best expresses this relationship.

4. **(3)** The three parts of the sentence that are separated by commas should all be in the same form, so the second one needs to have a verb added: *Relax, place, ... and put. ...*

5. **(2)** The original sentence contains two independent thoughts run together. A semicolon separates them.

6. **(5)** The antecedent is *worries,* so the pronoun should be plural: *them.*

7. **(5)** The prepositional phrase *out of your mind* should not be separated from the main sentence with a comma.

8. **(1)** The original sentence is a fragment. Change the verb to *Concentrate.*

9. **(2)** To agree with the rest of the paragraph, the verb form should be in the present tense: *get.*

10. **(1)** This sentence is correct as written.

11. **(2)** The pronoun *they,* referring to the vultures, is plural, but the verb *cleans* is singular. Change *cleans* to *clean* to make the subject agree with the verb in number.

12. **(3)** The sentence needs a verb. The verb must agree with the subject (*road kills and ... carcasses*) in number. That plural verb is *carry.*

13. **(3)** The passage is written in the present tense, but the original verb here is a present perfect verb. Option (3), *eat,* is present tense.

14. **(3)** The nonrestrictive clause *which can be found in Africa and Eurasia* must be set off with commas.

15. **(4)** The object refers to *bones,* so the pronoun should be *them.*

16. **(2)** The term *trash collectors* is a common noun, not a proper name, so it should not be capitalized.

17. **(5)** The three parts of the sentence that are separated by commas should all be nouns. *Teamwork* is a noun, but *they work as a team* is a clause.

18. **(1)** The phrase *Swooping down* modifies the sentence's subject, so the subject must be *a vulture.* The word modified by such a phrase should always be placed as close to the modifying phrase as possible.

19. **(2)** *Sped* is a past tense verb form. For consistency with the rest of the paragraph, the verb should be present tense: *speed.*

20. **(4)** This sentence is complex, with two subject-verb combinations: *Times are* and *it's* (*it is*). The two parts should be separated with the conjunction *and* and a comma.

21. **(5)** The pronoun refers to *people,* so it should be plural: *they.*

22. **(3)** Never separate the main parts of a sentence, the subject and predicate, with a comma.

23. **(2)** The original sentences have a cause-and-effect relationship. This is best expressed by *because.*

24. **(4)** To agree with the rest of the paragraph, the verb form should be in the present tense: *skip.*

25. **(2)** The three parts of the sentence that are separated by commas should all be in the same single-item form: *Pasta, rice, and grains.* In the original sentence, the third item is in the form of an infinitive phrase (*to eat other grains*).

26. **(3)** The original sentence contains two complete thoughts run together. Choice (3) correctly divides the two complete thoughts into separate sentences.

27. **(4)** Test the contraction *they're* by replacing it with *they are.* This makes sense. The possessive pronoun *their* does not.

28. **(2)** The correct past tense form of this irregular verb is *threw.*

29. **(3)** The subject is singular (*person*). So the verb must be singular to agree with it: *misses.*

30. (2) The original sentences have a cause-and-effect relationship. Starting the new sentence with *Since* expresses this relationship. (*Because* would also work.) The new sentence might read, "Since young children get colds more often and spread them more rapidly, it's not surprising that their parents take more sick days than anyone else."

31. (4) Never separate the main parts of a sentence, the subject and predicate, with a comma.

32. (2) You may need to memorize the spelling of this tricky word.

33. (3) Always use the relative pronoun *who* to refer to a person. *Which* is the correct relative pronoun for a thing.

34. (4) The main part of the sentence is an exception to the fact stated in the introductory clause. The conjunction *but* expresses this relationship. The new sentence would read, "A cold virus can't penetrate skin, but it can penetrate mucous membranes in your mouth, nose, and eyes."

35. (5) This sentence is correct as written.

36. (3) Substitute the words *you are* for the contraction *you're*. *You are mother* doesn't make sense, so the contraction must be wrong. Change it to the possessive pronoun *your*.

37. (2) To agree with the rest of the paragraph, the pronoun should be in the second person: *you*, not *one*. *You* takes a plural verb, so change the verb from *is* to *are*.

38. (3) The possessive pronoun *their* has nothing to modify in this sentence. The correct word is the adverb *there*.

39. (5) To agree with the rest of the paragraph, the subject of this sentence should be the third person plural: *They*. This pronoun refers to the garbologists.

40. (1) This sentence is correct as written.

41. (2) You may need to memorize the spelling of this word.

42. (2) The subject of the first sentence is *paper*. The subject of the second sentence is a pronoun that refers to *paper*. Therefore, when the first sentence is turned into an introductory clause modifying the subject, that subject is still *paper*.

43. (4) "To the *New York Times*" is a prepositional phrase. Prepositional phrases should not be set off by commas.

44. (4) The term *health foods* is a common noun, not a proper noun, so it should not be capitalized.

45. (4) The subject of the sentence must agree with the subject of the introductory clause, *they*. The plural form also makes this sentence agree with the rest of the passage.

46. (4) *Contents* is a plural noun, so the verb should be *vary* to agree in number with the subject.

47. (2) *You're* is a contraction for *you are*. However, *you are job* makes no sense. Change the contraction to the possessive pronoun *your*.

48. (4) *You* is the subject, so for agreement, it requires the verb *work*. The second person *you* is also consistent with the rest of the paragraph.

49. (2) *Americans* is a proper noun, so it should be capitalized.

50. (1) The original sentences have a cause-and-effect relationship. Starting the new sentence with *If* expresses this relationship. The new sentence would read, "If you keystroke day after day, eventually your wrists may start to hurt because the small muscles are repeating the exact same movement again and again."

51. (2) To agree with the rest of the paragraph, this sentence should be in the present tense: *are*. *Were* is a past tense verb.

52. (5) *Arms and hands* is part of a compound predicate. It should not be interrupted by a comma.

53. (4) You may need to memorize the spelling of this word.

54. (2) *Adjusting* is a participle, not a verb, so Sentence 10 is a fragment, since there is no verb in the main clause. Change *adjusting* to *adjust* to make this fragment a complete sentence.

55. (3) The rest of the sentence (and the paragraph) is written in the second person: *your* wrists. For consistency, change the third-person *his* to *your*.

Use the answer key on pages 846–847 to check your answers to the Practice Test. Then find the item number of each question you missed and circle it on the chart below to determine the writing content areas in which you need more practice. Pay particular attention to areas where you missed half or more of the questions. The page numbers for the content areas are listed below on the chart. For those questions that you missed, review the pages indicated on the chart.

PRACTICE TEST 1: WRITING SKILLS EVALUATION CHART

Content Area	Item Number	Review Pages
Nouns, Pronouns	27, 36, 37, 38, 47, 55	60–64, 80–92
Verbs	2, 12, 28	65–76
Subject-Verb Agreement	1, 11, 29, 46, 48	76–79
Pronoun Reference	6, 15, 21, 33, 45	82–92
Sentence Fragments	5, 8, 20, 26, 39, 54	93–98
Sentence Combining	3, 23, 30, 34, 42, 50	95–107
Sequence of Tenses	9, 13, 19, 24, 51	109–110
Misplaced/Dangling Modifiers	18	111–112
Parallel Structure	17, 25	112–116
Capitalization	16, 44, 49	117–119
Punctuation	4, 7, 14, 22, 31, 43, 52	119–125
Spelling	32, 41, 53	126–141
No Error	10, 35, 40	

Part 2: The Essay

If possible, give your essay to an instructor to evaluate. That person's opinion of your writing will be useful in deciding what further work you need to write a good essay.

If, however, you are unable to show your work to someone else, you can try to evaluate your own essay. If you can answer *yes* to the five questions in the Essay Evaluation Checklist, your essay would *probably* earn an upper half score (4, 5, or 6) on Part 2 of the Writing Skills Test. If you receive any *no* answers on your evaluation checklist, you should read your essay carefully to see how it could be improved and review Chapter 4 of the Writing Skills section.

Essay Evaluation Checklist

YES NO

____ ____ 1. Does the essay answer the question asked?

____ ____ 2. Does the main point of the essay stand out clearly?

____ ____ 3. Does each paragraph contain specific examples and details that help prove the main point?

____ ____ 4. Can you follow how the writer has arranged and linked ideas in sentences and paragraphs?

____ ____ 5. Is the writer's control of grammar and usage effective enough so that you were able to read the essay easily and smoothly?

PRACTICE TEST 2: SOCIAL STUDIES

This Social Studies Practice Test will give you an opportunity to evaluate your readiness for the actual GED Social Studies Test.

This test contains 64 questions. Some of the questions are based on short reading passages, and some of them require you to interpret a chart, map, graph, or an editorial cartoon.

You should take appproximately 85 minutes to complete this test. At the end of 85 minutes, stop and mark your place. Then finish the test. This will give you an idea of whether or not you can finish the real GED Test in the time allotted. Try to answer as many questions as you can. A blank will count as a wrong answer, so make a reasonable guess for the answers to questions you are not sure of.

When you are finished with the test, check your answers and turn to the Evaluation Chart on page 874 and the GED Readiness Worksheet on page 927. Use the chart and worksheet to evaluate whether or not you are ready to take the actual GED Test and, if not, in what areas you need more work.

PRACTICE TEST 2: SOCIAL STUDIES ANSWER GRID

1 ① ② ③ ④ ⑤	17 ① ② ③ ④ ⑤	33 ① ② ③ ④ ⑤	49 ① ② ③ ④ ⑤
2 ① ② ③ ④ ⑤	18 ① ② ③ ④ ⑤	34 ① ② ③ ④ ⑤	50 ① ② ③ ④ ⑤
3 ① ② ③ ④ ⑤	19 ① ② ③ ④ ⑤	35 ① ② ③ ④ ⑤	51 ① ② ③ ④ ⑤
4 ① ② ③ ④ ⑤	20 ① ② ③ ④ ⑤	36 ① ② ③ ④ ⑤	52 ① ② ③ ④ ⑤
5 ① ② ③ ④ ⑤	21 ① ② ③ ④ ⑤	37 ① ② ③ ④ ⑤	53 ① ② ③ ④ ⑤
6 ① ② ③ ④ ⑤	22 ① ② ③ ④ ⑤	38 ① ② ③ ④ ⑤	54 ① ② ③ ④ ⑤
7 ① ② ③ ④ ⑤	23 ① ② ③ ④ ⑤	39 ① ② ③ ④ ⑤	55 ① ② ③ ④ ⑤
8 ① ② ③ ④ ⑤	24 ① ② ③ ④ ⑤	40 ① ② ③ ④ ⑤	56 ① ② ③ ④ ⑤
9 ① ② ③ ④ ⑤	25 ① ② ③ ④ ⑤	41 ① ② ③ ④ ⑤	57 ① ② ③ ④ ⑤
10 ① ② ③ ④ ⑤	26 ① ② ③ ④ ⑤	42 ① ② ③ ④ ⑤	58 ① ② ③ ④ ⑤
11 ① ② ③ ④ ⑤	27 ① ② ③ ④ ⑤	43 ① ② ③ ④ ⑤	59 ① ② ③ ④ ⑤
12 ① ② ③ ④ ⑤	28 ① ② ③ ④ ⑤	44 ① ② ③ ④ ⑤	60 ① ② ③ ④ ⑤
13 ① ② ③ ④ ⑤	29 ① ② ③ ④ ⑤	45 ① ② ③ ④ ⑤	61 ① ② ③ ④ ⑤
14 ① ② ③ ④ ⑤	30 ① ② ③ ④ ⑤	46 ① ② ③ ④ ⑤	62 ① ② ③ ④ ⑤
15 ① ② ③ ④ ⑤	31 ① ② ③ ④ ⑤	47 ① ② ③ ④ ⑤	63 ① ② ③ ④ ⑤
16 ① ② ③ ④ ⑤	32 ① ② ③ ④ ⑤	48 ① ② ③ ④ ⑤	64 ① ② ③ ④ ⑤

Choose the best answer to each question that follows.

Questions 1 and 2 are based on the following pie charts.

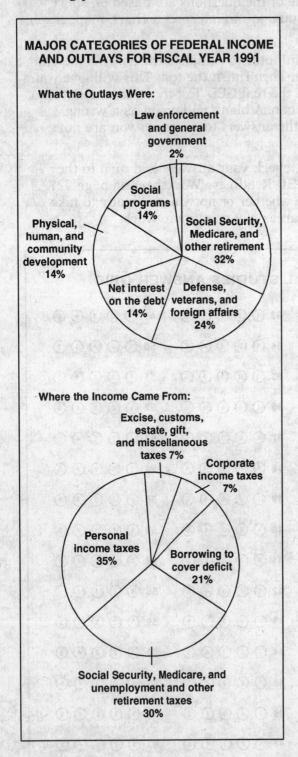

MAJOR CATEGORIES OF FEDERAL INCOME AND OUTLAYS FOR FISCAL YEAR 1991

What the Outlays Were:

- Law enforcement and general government 2%
- Social programs 14%
- Physical, human, and community development 14%
- Social Security, Medicare, and other retirement 32%
- Net interest on the debt 14%
- Defense, veterans, and foreign affairs 24%

Where the Income Came From:

- Excise, customs, estate, gift, and miscellaneous taxes 7%
- Corporate income taxes 7%
- Personal income taxes 35%
- Borrowing to cover deficit 21%
- Social Security, Medicare, and unemployment and other retirement taxes 30%

1. Based on these charts, from which of the following sources does the federal government derive most of its income?

   (1) a variety of taxes on individuals
   (2) business taxes
   (3) income tax alone
   (4) taxes on goods
   (5) trade with other countries

2. According to the pie charts, which of the following was true about federal spending in 1991?

   (1) More was spent on social programs than on physical, human, and community development.
   (2) More was spent on social security, Medicare, and other retirement benefits than was taken in through taxes.
   (3) More was spent on deficit interest than was taken in through borrowing.
   (4) Seven percent of borrowed money was actually spent on paying off the deficit.
   (5) Defense spending accounted for the largest expenditure.

Questions 3 and 4 are based on the following passage.

Humans share two methods of learning with the other animals. One is *individual situational learning*, in which individuals learn from their own experience. For example, both a person and an animal learn that standing out in the rain will make them wet. The second shared method is *social situational learning*, in which behavior is learned from other members of a social group through observation. Kittens learn to catch mice by imitating their mothers, and children learn to play tag by watching other children. A third method of learning is uniquely human. *Cultural learning* relies on concepts and values to guide behavior. For example, mothers tell children to share their toys, and people learn that certain behaviors are thought of as right or wrong. No other animal has been observed to learn in this manner.

3. Which of the following is an example of cultural learning?

    (1) avoiding fire
    (2) saying thank you after receiving a gift
    (3) making a snowman
    (4) standing in line in the supermarket
    (5) doodling

4. Which of the following is a conclusion that the author draws?

    (1) Cultural learning is uniquely human.
    (2) Cultural learning is based on concepts and values.
    (3) Mothers teach children to share.
    (4) People learn that some behavior is right and some is wrong.
    (5) No other animals learn about concepts and values.

Questions 5–7 are based on the following passage.

The Bill of Rights, which most Americans take for granted, was not unanimously accepted by the thirteen original colonies. Federalist delegates to the Constitutional Convention in 1787 didn't think that a Bill of Rights was needed. They argued that most of the states already provided enough protection for citizens. Anti-Federalists believed that a national Bill of Rights was important to protect the people from an overly powerful central government. The argument lasted for four years, with a three-fourths approval vote by the states in 1791. One hundred and fifty years later, Massachusetts, Georgia, and Connecticut finally ratified the Bill of Rights.

5. The Federalists' argument was based on which of the following assumptions?

    (1) A central government might override states' rights.
    (2) The states were powerful enough to protect the rights of their citizens.
    (3) Citizens' rights were unimportant.
    (4) Citizens' rights were too important to be ignored.
    (5) A Bill of Rights would take too long to be ratified.

6. Which of the following conclusions is supported by the information in the passage?

　(1) The Bill of Rights wasn't really necessary.
　(2) The Bill of Rights was never ratified by the original states.
　(3) The Founding Fathers had differing views about the role of the central government.
　(4) Members of the Constitutional Congress all agreed about political issues.
　(5) The federal government is too powerful.

7. According to the passage, the Bill of Rights became law by approval of the states in which of the following years?

　(1) 1776
　(2) 1787
　(3) 1791
　(4) 1900
　(5) 1939

Question 8 is based on the following cartoon.

© 1986 WASSERMAN—BOSTON GLOBE

8. The cartoonist is expressing which of the following opinions?

　(1) Working women should be given maternity leave.
　(2) Businesses would rather treat working women like men than like women.
　(3) Women should be at home instead of at work.
　(4) Business women should be wives.
　(5) Workers and management can never come to an agreement.

Questions 9–12 are based on the following passage.

"Yesterday, December 7, 1941—a date which will live in infamy—the United States of America was suddenly and deliberately attacked by naval and air forces of the Empire of Japan.

The United States was at peace with that nation and, at the solicitation of Japan, was still in conversation with the government and its emperor looking toward the maintenance of peace in the Pacific.

. . . . It will be recorded that the distance of Hawaii from Japan makes it obvious that the attack was deliberately planned many days or even weeks ago. During the intervening time, the Japanese government has deliberately sought to deceive the United States by false statements and expressions of hope for continued peace.

. . . . As commander in chief of the Army and Navy, I have directed that all measures be taken for our defense.

. . . . No matter how long it may take us to overcome this premeditated invasion, the American people in their righteous might will win through to absolute victory.

I believe I interpret the will of the Congress and of the people when I assert that we will not only defend ourselves to the uttermost but will make very certain that this form of treachery will never endanger us again."

—from President Franklin Roosevelt's message to Congress after the invasion of Pearl Harbor

9. According to the passage, which of the following is true about President Roosevelt?

   (1) He wanted to avoid war at all costs.
   (2) He felt that Japan was in the right.
   (3) He had not expected to go to war with Japan.
   (4) He had little faith in the American people.
   (5) He was willing to ignore the attack on Pearl Harbor.

10. Roosevelt was offended by Japan's action because he placed a high value on which of the following?

    (1) freedom of speech
    (2) honesty
    (3) military strength
    (4) patriotism
    (5) good planning

11. According to the passage, Japan's action led to

    (1) American isolationism
    (2) America's entrance into World War II
    (3) Roosevelt's conflict with Congress
    (4) Hawaii's admittance to the Union
    (5) a peace treaty between the United States and Japan

12. According to this message, Roosevelt made which of the following assumptions?

    (1) Congress was unwilling to declare war.
    (2) Americans would sympathize with Japan.
    (3) Americans would support going to war with Japan.
    (4) Japan's army and navy were stronger than America's.
    (5) Japan would be willing to return to peace negotiations.

13. Clearing of forest lands for timber and pasture has been blamed for soil erosion. Cattle grazing on newly cleared land tends to leave the earth bare. The small root systems of shrubs and weeds can't anchor the soil, so topsoil is blown or washed away. Which of the following is most likely to result in prevention of soil erosion?

(1) bringing in sheep instead of cattle
(2) letting nature take its course
(3) watering the land intensively
(4) immediate replanting of trees and grasses
(5) clearing more forest land

Questions 14 and 15 are based on the following table.

14. According to the table below, which circuit court handles the highest number of burglary, robbery, and auto theft cases?

(1) the First
(2) the Fourth
(3) the Sixth
(4) the Seventh
(5) the Tenth

15. Which of the following statements is supported by the information in the table?

(1) The sentence imposed for each type of crime is standardized throughout the court system.
(2) The sentence imposed for each type of crime varies from court to court.
(3) The sentence imposed for each type of crime depends on the number of cases handled in that court.
(4) Burglary is the same as robbery.
(5) Auto theft is the most recurrent crime.

MEDIAN SENTENCE IMPOSED BY JUDICIAL COURTS
(In Years)

	Burglary		Robbery		Class 2 Auto Theft	
	Median	Number of Cases	Median	Number of Cases	Median	Number of Cases
Circuit						
1st	4.0	51	5.5	6	7.0	3
2nd	4.0	29	0.0	0	3.0	2
3rd	4.0	65	3.5	8	3.0	18
4th	4.0	82	4.0	1	4.0	8
5th	4.0	46	3.0	2	4.0	4
6th	4.0	130	4.0	17	6.0	3
7th	4.0	71	4.8	6	3.5	3
8th	3.5	32	0.0	0	3.0	1
9th	4.0	35	6.0	1	3.5	2
10th	4.0	97	3.8	116	4.0	6

Questions 16–19 are based on the following information.

To sociologists, crowds are groups of people who get together temporarily with a common focus. There are five general types of crowds.

casual crowd—people who share a brief interest on an unplanned basis and have little to do with one another

conventional crowd—people who gather as a result of deliberate and formal planning but have little to do with one another

expressive crowd—people who gather informally to share an emotional or entertaining experience

acting crowd—people who, after gathering for any reason, commit violent and destructive acts

protest crowd—people who intentionally gather to perform actions to promote a political goal

16. A group of people gather on a city street to watch a firefighter rescue a child from a burning building. This is an example of

    (1) a casual crowd
    (2) a conventional crowd
    (3) an expressive crowd
    (4) an acting crowd
    (5) a protest crowd

17. A group of people gather in front of City Hall with picket signs. They want to stop the rezoning of a residential area. This is an example of

    (1) a casual crowd
    (2) a conventional crowd
    (3) an expressive crowd
    (4) an acting crowd
    (5) a protest crowd

18. A group of people gather in a large tent to hear a traveling preacher. This is an example of

    (1) a casual crowd
    (2) a conventional crowd
    (3) an expressive crowd
    (4) an acting crowd
    (5) a protest crowd

19. A group of people who had gathered to watch a hockey game became upset by a ruling. The people began to throw things into the rink and then started climbing over the barricades and attacking the players. This is an example of

    (1) a casual crowd
    (2) a conventional crowd
    (3) an expressive crowd
    (4) an acting crowd
    (5) a protest crowd

20. Psychologists believe that social play is an important part of a child's development. One study shows that riddling builds language and logic skills. In addition to telling traditional riddles, a child will often experiment by creating new riddles based on already-learned patterns. This information supports the conclusion that

(1) verbal play is more than simply a way for children to amuse each other
(2) a child who does not create riddles will not develop properly
(3) a child who tells only traditional riddles does not understand the underlying pattern
(4) psychologists are wrong to place importance on social play
(5) language and logic skills cannot be learned from social play

Question 21 is based on the following graph.

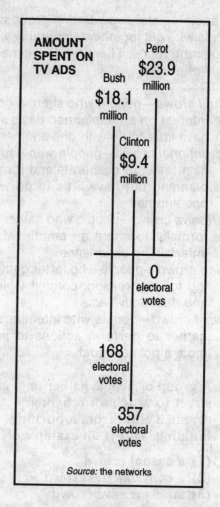

Source: the networks

21. The main idea of this graph is that

(1) the more a candidate spends on ads, the better the chances of getting elected
(2) presidential candidates spend too much on their campaign ads
(3) the Democratic party is opposed to spending excessively on political campaigns
(4) spending a lot on political ads does not guarantee election
(5) political ads have no effect on an election

Questions 22–25 are based on the following information.

The president of the United States is often advised by members of his Cabinet, most of whom are heads or secretaries of one of fourteen executive government departments. The executive departments help regulate and serve many aspects of American life. For example, funeral services for ex-military personnel are provided by the National Cemetery System, an agency administered by the Department of Veterans Affairs. The general services provided by five of the executive departments are as follows:

Department of Agriculture—responsible for improving farms and farm income and reducing poverty, hunger, and malnutrition

Department of Commerce—responsible for encouraging international trade and economic growth and preventing unfair trade

Department of the Interior—responsible for the conservation of public lands and natural resources, including wildlife and historic places

Department of State—responsible for formulating and carrying out foreign policy and protecting American overseas interests

Department of Transportation—responsible for the planning and safety of highways, mass transit, railroads, aviation, and waterways

22. An agency builds merchant ships for the federal government and provides aid to private shipbuilders. Which Cabinet member heads this agency's department?

    (1) secretary of commerce
    (2) secretary of agriculture
    (3) secretary of the interior
    (4) secretary of state
    (5) secretary of transportation

23. An agency helps the establishment and development of businesses owned by minorities. Which Cabinet member heads this agency's department?

    (1) secretary of commerce
    (2) secretary of agriculture
    (3) secretary of the interior
    (4) secretary of state
    (5) secretary of transportation

24. An agency administers the standardization, grading, and classing of over six hundred farm products. Which Cabinet member heads this agency's department?

    (1) secretary of commerce
    (2) secretary of agriculture
    (3) secretary of the interior
    (4) secretary of state
    (5) secretary of transportation

25. An agency protects and maintains the nation's system of national parks and recreation areas. Which Cabinet member heads this agency's department?

    (1) secretary of commerce
    (2) secretary of agriculture
    (3) secretary of the interior
    (4) secretary of state
    (5) secretary of transportation

26. A monarchy that had been under native rule since 1795, the Hawaiian Islands began to attract American missionaries during the late nineteenth century. In addition to the opportunity to save souls, Hawaii offered new agricultural and military resources. Despite anti-imperialist objections, Hawaii became an American territory in 1898. Which of the following assumptions prompted the first missionaries to go to the Hawaiian islands?

   (1) The native monarchy was failing.
   (2) Americans would soon develop a taste for tropical fruit.
   (3) Native Hawaiians would welcome the opportunity to become the fiftieth American state.
   (4) Native Hawaiians would welcome the opportunity to become Christians.
   (5) The American government would welcome new sites for military bases.

27. One factor in the law of supply and demand is the ratio of sellers to buyers. The more sellers of a product, the greater the choices a buyer has. This principle of supply and demand has a special effect on the real estate market. When there have been more houses on the market for a long period than there have been buyers, which of the following is likely to happen?

   (1) A buyer will offer more than the seller's asking price.
   (2) A seller will refuse to consider an offer lower than the stated asking price.
   (3) A seller will accept an offer lower than the asking price.
   (4) More people will put up their homes for sale.
   (5) Potential buyers will wait until house prices go down.

28. *Acculturation* refers to the process by which members of one culture adopt the customs and tastes of the culture into which they have moved. But firsthand contact between two cultures can also influence the dominant culture. Chinese-Americans have adopted many American ways. Which of the following is the best example of how Americans have adapted to Chinese culture?

   (1) trade with Hong Kong
   (2) Nixon's diplomatic trip to China
   (3) the use of Chinese lanterns at pool parties
   (4) the use of bicycles as inner-city transportation
   (5) the acceptance of Chinese cuisine as a popular American food

Questions 29 and 30 are based on the following graph.

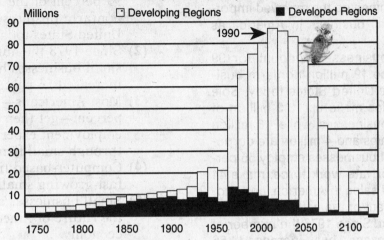

**WORLD POPULATION: AVERAGE ANNUAL INCREASE
FOR EACH DECADE, 1750–2100 (PROJECTED)**

Millions   ☐ Developing Regions   ■ Developed Regions

1990 →

Source: "World Population in Transition," *Population Bulletin,*
by Thomas W. Merrick and PRB Staff

29. According to the graph, which of the following is true about the population of developed and developing regions of the world?

  (1) The populations of both developed and developing regions have already reached their peak.

  (2) The population of developed regions will drop in the future while the population of developing regions will continue to grow.

  (3) A sharp rise in world population will not begin until the year 2000.

  (4) The population of developed regions and developing regions grow and decline at about the same rate.

  (5) The population of developed regions will continue to grow, while the population of developing regions will drop in the future.

30. Which of the following is the most probable cause of the change in the population in developing regions between 1950 and 1990?

  (1) Developing regions began using effective forms of birth control.

  (2) Residents of developing nations migrated in large numbers to developed regions.

  (3) Improved health care and agricultural practices had been adopted by developing regions.

  (4) The pregnancy rate in developed regions began to drop.

  (5) Women in developing regions realized the economic value of having large families.

Questions 31–33 are based on the following passage.

The writers of *The Universal Almanac* have summed up the renewed importance of small business in America as follows:

"Small businesses account for 99 percent of the 19 million nonfarm businesses in the United States today. Sole proprietorships make up 13.2 million of these small businesses, while 1.8 million are partnerships and 4 million are corporations. Small businesses employ 55 percent of the private work force, make 44 percent of all sales in America, and produce 38 percent of the nation's gross national product. Since 1978 the number of small businesses has increased 56 percent.

"Most Americans—nearly 67 percent—get their first employment experience through small firms. Small businesses lead the way in the creation of new jobs in the American economy. Between 1981 and 1986, small businesses with fewer than 500 employees created 62 percent of the 8.9 million new jobs in the country. Between September 1987 and 1988 alone, 2.3 million new jobs were generated in small-business-dominated industries.

"Among the fastest-growing small businesses today are eating and drinking establishments, trucking firms, doctors' offices, computer and data services, and amusements and recreation services."

Small businesses are clearly the future of America's economy. The role they play is too important to be ignored. Anyone who starts a small business today is guaranteed financial success.

31. According to the passage, which of the following is the most important economic function of small businesses?

(1) hiring high school students
(2) creating new jobs
(3) providing fast food
(4) adding to the GNP
(5) competing with large corporations

32. Which of the following is an opinion expressed in this passage?

(1) Small businesses account for 99 percent of the 19 million nonfarm businesses in the United States today.
(2) Since 1978 the number of small businesses has increased 56 percent.
(3) Most Americans—nearly 67 percent—get their first employment experience through small firms.
(4) Computer-based firms are fast-growing small businesses.
(5) Small businesses are clearly the future of America's economy.

33. Which of the following is wrong with the logic of the conclusion "Anyone who starts a small business today is guaranteed financial success"?

(1) It falsely assumes that small businesses are economically important.
(2) It ignores the role of large companies.
(3) It falsely equates any small business with the small businesses that have actually succeeded.
(4) It falsely assumes that America needs more small businesses.
(5) It ignores the problem of small business insurance.

Questions 34–36 are based on the following passage.

The first post office mail deliveries to the American West went by steamship to Panama, crossed to the Pacific by rail, and then traveled again by ship to San Francisco. The process took at least a month, and letters arrived in huge, unsorted bundles.

Official overland delivery began in 1858, with John Butterfield's stagecoach company bringing the mail over a 2,800-mile route in only twenty-four days. The short-lived Pony Express further reduced the time to ten days. But the effort had its dangers. The ad for riders read, "Wanted: Young, skinny, wiry fellows not over 18. Must be expert riders, willing to risk death daily. Orphans preferred."

The completion of the transcontinental railroad in 1869 changed mail delivery to the West forever. Letters and packages began to arrive in cities and small towns alike, quickly and presorted.

34. Which of the following was the major obstacle to efficient mail delivery in the early days of the American West?

(1) lack of willing riders
(2) unreliability of stagecoaches
(3) the distance to be covered
(4) the post office red tape
(5) the sorting process

35. California residents requested improved overland mail delivery in 1856. They took this action because they placed a high value on which of the following?

(1) support of the government
(2) communication with friends and family
(3) employment of orphans
(4) the hardships of frontier life
(5) railroad travel

36. The major change in mail service to the West is comparable to which of the following?

(1) the gradual settlement of the Midwestern states
(2) the increase in postal rates between the 1960s and 1990s
(3) the development of small telephone companies because of demonopolization of AT&T
(4) the growing competition between personal computer companies
(5) the improvement of international telephone communication because of the laying of the transatlantic cable

---

37. In April 1993, the passage of President Clinton's short-term job-stimulus package was prevented by Republicans' filibustering. The rule of unlimited debate allows a senator to keep the floor by filibustering, or talking long enough to force the withdrawal of the bill under discussion. By engaging in a filibuster, the Republicans made it clear that they

(1) could talk longer than the Democrats
(2) objected to the contents of the bill
(3) wanted the bill to pass
(4) wanted to embarrass President Clinton
(5) believed that America had enough jobs

Questions 38–40 are based on the following cartoon.

38. Which of the following best states the main idea of this cartoon?

    (1) Improved technology is causing problems for mapmakers.
    (2) Mapmaking is simpler now than ever before.
    (3) The changes in national politics are difficult for mapmakers to keep up with.
    (4) Maps do not reflect changes in political boundaries.
    (5) Rand McNally is involved in a war.

39. The cartoon supports the statement that major changes are occurring in which of the following areas?

    (1) Canada and the United States
    (2) Western Europe
    (3) Latin America
    (4) the Middle East
    (5) Eastern Europe

40. Which of the following best expresses the artist's opinion about mapmakers?

    (1) Making accurate maps today is as complicated as going to war.
    (2) Mapmakers depend too much on secondhand reports.
    (3) Mapmakers don't try hard enough to keep up with world changes.
    (4) Mapmakers should be more concerned about political geography.
    (5) Mapmakers take their job too seriously.

Questions 41–43 are based on the following information.

Lobbyists work to affect foreign policy and to influence domestic issues. There are five general types of lobbyists:

economic lobby groups—representatives of American businesses and industries who attempt to influence domestic and international policy in their own favor
ethnic lobby groups—associations based on common national or cultural background
foreign government lobby groups—representatives of foreign countries who attempt to influence legislation in favor of their own nation's business and national interests
public-interest lobby groups—representatives working to protect the welfare of most or all of the American public
single-issue lobby groups—representatives working to promote legislation that affects only one issue, usually not related to economics

41. A group works to promote laws that protect the environment. This is an example of a(n)

(1) economic lobby
(2) ethnic lobby
(3) foreign government lobby
(4) public-interest lobby
(5) single-issue lobby

42. A group works to promote legislation that outlaws abortions. This is an example of a(n)

(1) economic lobby
(2) ethnic lobby
(3) foreign government lobby
(4) public-interest lobby
(5) single-issue lobby

43. A group works to promote legislation that allows off-shore oil exploration and drilling. This is an example of a(n)

(1) economic lobby
(2) ethnic lobby
(3) foreign government lobby
(4) public-interest lobby
(5) single-issue lobby

44. The term *melting pot* was coined by Israel Zangwell in 1907 to express the idea that immigrants from many countries came to America to form one nation. Zangwell had a vision of people sharing their traditions to become one united people. Fifty years later, Jesse Jackson said that the United States was more like a "vegetable soup." Jackson expressed a vision of the American people in which

(1) many types of people live together but do not give up their distinct identities
(2) all Americans look and act alike
(3) Americans would never be able to live together in peace
(4) Americans are more concerned with food than with cultural ideas
(5) people from other cultures are no longer accepted as true Americans

Question 45 is based on the following graph.

PROJECTED FEDERAL DEFICIT
(in billions of dollars)

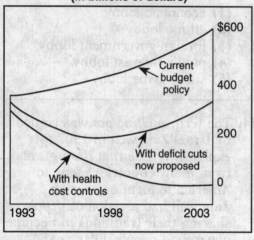

45. According to the graph, health cost controls will result in

   (1) a continued rise in the federal deficit

   (2) a higher federal deficit than would occur with the current budget policy

   (3) the same decrease in the federal deficit as would occur with the deficit cuts now proposed

   (4) a dramatic decrease in the federal deficit

   (5) little or no change in the federal deficit

Questions 46 and 47 are based on the map below.

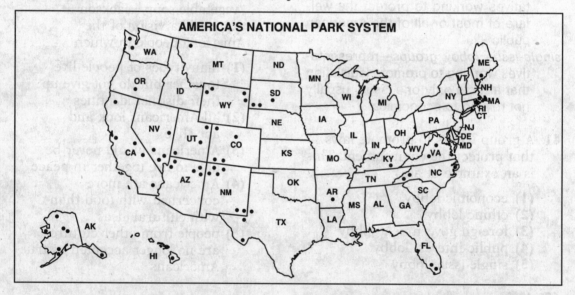

In 1872, the U.S. government began to set aside and conserve unusually scenic and natural areas as national parks. The most recent parks were established in Alaska and Nevada between 1980 and 1986. The map shows the general location of America's national parks.

46. According to the map, where are the majority of national parks located?

   (1) in the Northeast
   (2) in the Southeast
   (3) in the West
   (4) in Alaska and Hawaii
   (5) in most of the states

47. Which of the following best accounts for the locations of many of the national parks?

   (1) These areas were still undeveloped for residential or agricultural use.

   (2) These areas couldn't be used for anything else.

   (3) These areas were difficult to reach.

   (4) These areas were rich in natural resources such as oil, gold, and timber.

   (5) These areas could be bought cheaply by the government.

48. As cities grew in the twentieth century, so did their social problems. Overcrowding, traffic jams, crime, pollution, and unemployment became commonplace. Faced with decaying downtowns and "white flight" to the suburbs, city planners began to incorporate social programs in their plans for economic and physical urban renewal. Efforts to rehabilitate low-income inner-city neighborhoods are based on which of the following assumptions?

(1) Downtown areas are not worth saving.
(2) Suburbanites can be tempted back into the cities.
(3) Low-income families won't be willing to move to the suburbs.
(4) Government intervention can correct and prevent social problems.
(5) Low-income neighborhoods won't cost much to improve.

49. Acid rain is a toxic by-product of coal and oil-burning industries, power plants, and automobile exhaust. Because of the natural water cycle, acid rain can travel as far as 2,500 miles from its source. This information supports which of the following conclusions?

(1) Acid rain cannot be considered a localized pollution problem.
(2) Acid rain is a natural phenomenon.
(3) The effects of acid rain can easily be contained to industrial areas.
(4) Acid rain is limited to cities.
(5) Rural areas are free from the effects of acid rain.

Questions 50 and 51 are based on the following table.

EFFECTIVE FEDERAL MINIMUM HOURLY WAGE RATES, 1950–1992			
In effect	Minimum rate for nonfarm workers	Percent of avg. earnings[1]	Minimum rate for farm workers[2]
1950	$0.75	54%	N.A.
1956	1.00	52	N.A.
1961	1.15	50	N.A.
1963	1.25	51	N.A.
1967	1.40	50	$1.00
1968	1.60	54	1.15
1974	2.00	46	1.60
1975	2.10	45	1.80
1976	2.30	46	2.00
1978	2.65	44	2.65
1979	2.90	45	2.90
1980	3.10	44	3.10
1981	3.35	43	3.35
1989	3.35	32	3.35
1991	4.25[3]	39	4.25[3]

Note: N.A. = not applicable. 1. Percent of gross average hourly earnings of production workers in manufacturing. 2. Not included until 1966. 3. In effect June 1, 1992. Source: U.S. Dept. of Labor.

50. The information in the table supports the conclusion that

(1) The minimum wage doubled between the mid-seventies and the early nineties.
(2) Wages for farm workers always lag behind wages for nonfarm workers.
(3) The minimum wage in the fifties was too low.
(4) The minimum wage will not increase until 1999.
(5) More people than ever before are earning the minimum wage.

51. Which of the following is the most probable cause of the increase in the minimum wage?

(1) the increase in the number of women in the workforce
(2) the increase in the national debt
(3) a recognition of the importance of unskilled workers
(4) an attempt to decrease unemployment
(5) a continued rise in the cost of living

Questions 52–54 are based on the following information.

Any new business faces many challenges and obstacles. There are five major barriers to new businesses entering into economic competition:

previous patent on a product—A patent guarantees the right of its owner to be the sole producer of a product for seventeen years. If a patent for a product already exists even if it has not been put on the market, the inventor of a similar product cannot manufacture the product until the previous patent expires or is purchased from the patent holder.

government licensing—federal, state, and local governments can restrict the number of similar businesses in an area by issuing a limited number of licenses

control of raw materials—limited access to materials needed to produce a product

limited market size—a market needs to be large enough to provide enough consumers for the product or service

large capital outlay—the amount of money needed to begin and sustain operation of a business, including equipment, raw materials, and wages

52. A new restaurant in town wanted to begin serving alcoholic drinks with dinner to attract a broader clientele. But the owners discovered that the city issued only a certain number of liquor permits, and none would be available until an existing business gave up its permit. This situation describes which barrier to competition?

    (1) patent on a product
    (2) government licensing
    (3) control of raw materials
    (4) limited market size
    (5) large capital outlay

53. A recent college graduate came up with a totally new design for a kitchen product. Her research showed that no one else had thought of the same design even though there would be a good market for it. But because of her large college debt and her lack of business experience, the bank would not grant her a loan to begin manufacturing the product on her own. Which barrier to competition is the young inventor facing?

    (1) patent on a product
    (2) government licensing
    (3) control of raw materials
    (4) limited market size
    (5) large capital outlay

54. A couple who had run a video rental store moved to a new neighborhood. They wanted to open a similar store in their new area, but they found that two video stores were already operating there. Which barrier to competition is the couple facing?

    (1) patent on a product
    (2) government licensing
    (3) control of raw materials
    (4) limited market size
    (5) large capital outlay

55. Bill Clinton's first nomination for attorney general, Zoe Baird, was rejected because she once had hired undocumented workers as household help without paying taxes on their wages. Congress later approved the appointment of Janet Reno, the first woman to hold this important position. These events support which of the following conclusions about the American people?

(1) They did not want a woman as attorney general.
(2) They wanted the attorney general to obey the laws.
(3) They did not trust the president's judgment.
(4) They believed that undocumented workers should not be discriminated against.
(5) They preferred Baird to Reno.

56. Post-traumatic stress disorder is a random recurrence of a horrifying event in the mind of the person who experienced it. PTSD victims also suffer from depression, nightmares, memory loss, or delayed feelings of isolation, guilt, and rage. Which of the following might be a cause of this disorder?

(1) watching a violent movie
(2) being in a massive traffic accident
(3) witnessing a fire
(4) hearing that a friend has been murdered
(5) reading about a rape in the newspaper

Question 57 is based on the following political cartoon.

"WE BELIEVE PRESIDENT-ELECT CLINTON'S CABINET APPOINTMENTS DO NOT REFLECT AMERICA'S DIVERSITY... THEY'RE ALL HUMANS!"

© 1992 JORGENSEN—EXTRA NEWSPAPER FEATURES

57. The artist intended this cartoon as a comment on the demands for political appointments by

(1) animal-rights activists
(2) space aliens
(3) Republicans
(4) Democrats
(5) minority groups

Questions 58 and 59 are based on the following passage.

"Aristotle said it was the reward of an active life lived with sweet reason. Sigmund Freud said it was mostly a matter of work and love. Charles Shultz, the cartoonist-philosopher, claimed it was really a warm puppy. So just what is this thing called happiness? For centuries, people were too busy pursuing it to spend much time analyzing it. Now a pioneering band of researchers has finally bagged the elusive quarry—or at least taken its measure. . . . And their answer to the age-old mystery is that it all depends.

"Happiness, that is, depends on what makes you feel happy, which is why psychologists often call it 'subjective well-being.' But from studies of various age and population groups in the United States and abroad, they have reached some objective conclusions on the makings of happiness. What comes up consistently at the top of the charts is not, as many might expect, success, youth, good looks or any of those enviable assets. The clear winner is relationships. Close ones. Followed by a happy marriage. Next comes religious faith, of almost any kind. 'Supportive, intimate connections with other people seem tremendously important,' says psychologist David Myers, whose book *The Pursuit of Happiness* is one of the cluster of recent publications in the field."

58. According to the passage, what is the *primary* cause of happiness?

   (1) success
   (2) youth
   (3) good looks
   (4) close relationships
   (5) religious faith

59. The information in the passage supports which of the following conclusions about the definition of happiness?

   (1) Happiness was best defined by early philosophers.
   (2) Happiness is easy to define.
   (3) There is no one clear definition of happiness.
   (4) There is only one clear definition of happiness.
   (5) Psychologists have finally defined happiness.

Questions 60–62 are based on the following map.

Allies Reply to Saddam, 1991

After Saddam Hussein violated international agreements by sending Iraqi troops into Kuwait and missiles into other neighboring countries, the Allies responded with military action.

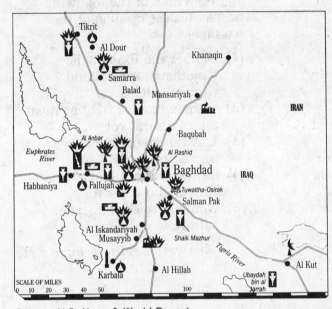

Source: U.S. News & World Report

60. Which part of the Allied action is detailed on the map?

(1) the ground war in the desert
(2) the air campaign in the Baghdad area
(3) the battle on the Kuwait-Iraq border
(4) the Allied bases in Saudi Arabia
(5) the movement of Allied troops into Iraq

61. The information on the map supports which statement about the Allied attack?

(1) Its purpose was to destroy oil refineries.
(2) It was unable to penetrate Iraqi defenses.
(3) It was focused on Iraq's military centers.
(4) It underestimated Iraq's military strength.
(5) It was poorly planned and unorganized.

62. The strategy of this attack was based on which of the following assumptions?

(1) The action would totally destroy Iraq's economy.
(2) Saddam Hussein would be killed during the attack.
(3) Saddam Hussein would be forced to renew his offensive.
(4) Residents of Baghdad would join forces with the Allies.
(5) Destruction of major military centers would help bring a quick end to the conflict.

63. *La Linea* is the Hispanic name for America's 1,950-mile southern border. It draws thousands of jobless migrants from Mexico's interior. To them, La Linea represents much more than a national boundary. The crossing of the muddy waters of the Tijuana River and Rio Grande River by these families is similar to which of the following?

   (1) the crossing of the Atlantic by Columbus
   (2) the crossing of the Atlantic by enslaved Africans
   (3) the ocean crossings by the ancestors of Irish, Polish, and Chinese-Americans
   (4) the crossing of the Delaware River by Washington's troops
   (5) the crossing of the English Channel by American soldiers

64. Women's roles differ widely from culture to culture. The Yanomamo female is dominated by her husband and brothers. Her life is spent doing endless labor on tasks thought too menial for men. The independent Ibo woman is much luckier. She has economic freedom and enjoys high social status. Which of the following best states the opinion of the passage?

   (1) Neither the Ibo nor the Yanomamo understand women's rights.
   (2) Women have to fight against their cultural roles.
   (3) The Yanomamo women are treated properly.
   (4) Ibo women are luckier than Yanomamo women.
   (5) Women's roles vary from culture to culture.

   Answers begin on page 871.

PRACTICE TEST 2: SOCIAL STUDIES ANSWER KEY

1. **(1)** The chart for income shows that 30 percent comes from social security and other personal taxes, 35 percent comes from income tax, and 7 percent comes from other taxes that apply to individuals.

2. **(2)** The amount taken in for social security, etc., was 30 percent, but the amount expended was 32 percent. None of the other choices are supported by the figures shown.

3. **(2)** Expressing thanks is an act of politeness, a learned value. Choices (1) and (5) are examples of individual situational learning. Choices (3) and (4) are learned through observation.

4. **(1)** Choice (2) is a definition of cultural learning. Choices (3) and (4) are examples of cultural learning by humans. Choice (5) is a fact about the other animals. They are all supporting statements that lead to the conclusion that only humans use cultural learning.

5. **(2)** The Federalists assumed that the Federal government had no power over what had already been decided by the states. Choice (1) refers to the Anti-Federalist position.

6. **(3)** The Founding Fathers were split into two groups over the Bill of Rights. The split was based on their ideas about the rights and powers of a central government.

7. **(3)** The passage states that a three-fourths approval vote occurred in 1791, making the Bill of Rights law. None of the other dates affected its acceptance as law.

8. **(2)** By having the employer suggest that the women need wives instead of benefits, the artist is saying the employer wants the women to be more like men. None of the other choices apply to the cartoonist's drawing.

9. **(3)** Roosevelt's expectation that war with Japan would not happen is found in paragraph 2, "looking toward the maintenance of peace in the Pacific."

10. **(2)** Roosevelt emphasized that Japan had "deliberately sought to deceive the United States." Although he placed importance on the other choices, it was this betrayal that offended the president.

11. **(2)** Based on the date of the message and Roosevelt's call to military action, the result of the invasion of Pearl Harbor was America's entrance into the war. None of the other choices would have resulted from the Japanese invasion.

12. **(3)** Roosevelt believed the American public was willing to defend themselves and so would support going to war. He expected no opposition from Congress (1) nor any Japanese renegotiation (5).

13. **(4)** Replanting of trees whose roots would hold the soil would be a practical solution. Sheep (1) would be even more destructive than cattle. The natural process (2), further watering (3), or clearing (5) would result in further soil erosion.

14. **(5)** The highest total for all three sentencing rates can be found on the table for the tenth circuit court.

15. **(2)** The table shows that the median years of sentences changes from court to court, rather than being standardized (1). None of the other choices is supported by the table.

16. **(1)** The group described came together by accident and have only a brief interest in the rescue in common.

17. **(5)** The group described have come together with an intentional political purpose.

18. **(3)** The group described have gathered informally, each person coming as a result of personal interest. But the intent is to share a spiritual experience.

19. **(4)** The group described began as an expressive crowd, sharing an entertaining experience. But emotions got out of hand and turned the crowd into an acting group.

20. (1) According to the passage, riddling, a form of verbal play, helps children develop language and logic skills in addition to being an amusement, so choice (5) is wrong. Pyschologists are right to see social play as important, so choice (4) is incorrect. There is no evidence for choices (2) or (3).

21. (4) The graph shows how much each of the three 1992 presidential candidates spent on TV ads and the number of electoral votes they received. It demonstrates that there is no direct relationship between the amount of money spent and the number of electoral votes attained, since Perot spent the most and got the fewest electoral votes.

22. (5) The secretary of transportation would oversee an agency that dealt with maritime vessels.

23. (1) The secretary of commerce would oversee an agency that helped promote new businesses.

24. (2) Anything to do with farm products would belong to an agency under the secretary of agriculture.

25. (3) Because national parks are public lands, this agency would be governed by the secretary of the interior.

26. (4) Missionaries originally went to the island to "save souls," so they expected that the Christian religion would be welcome. None of the other choices would have been assumptions that influenced the missionaries' decision.

27. (3) With more houses on the market, the seller would realize that a buyer could choose another house and so would likely accept a lower offer. Choices (1) and (2) apply to a situation in which there are more buyers than sellers. With many homes on the market, homeowners would be discouraged from putting their houses up for sale. Choice (5) indicates a buyer who knows little about the housing market.

28. (5) Chinese food is popular as shown by the number of Chinese restaurants. Choices (1) and (2) are not examples of acculturation. Chinese lanterns are a fad, not a cultural adaptation. Bicycles are not used as often as alternative means of transportation in inner cities as they could be.

29. (1) The highest point of population for both developed countries and developing countries occurs at or before 1990. After that period, both figures are projected to decline.

30. (3) The graph shows that the population of developing nations increased sharply between 1950 and 1990. Improved health care and nutrition would mean that more babies would be carried to term, more children would live to be adults, and more adults would live to bear children, thus increasing the population. Improved birth control would be more likely to influence a decrease rather than an increase in population. The same is true of migration from developing to developed regions. The pregnancy rate in developed regions would not affect developing regions.

31. (2) The passage emphasizes the economic importance of new jobs generated by small businesses. None of the other choices are as important to the economy.

32. (5) Speculation about the future is an opinion. The other choices are established facts backed up with figures.

33. (3) There is no evidence that any specific small business will be a financial success. In fact, the contrary is true. Small businesses have a high failure rate. The evidence supports only the conclusion that small business in general is important in the economy.

34. (3) Mail had to travel 2,800 miles to reach the West. The other choices might have been minor problems but were much less important than the distance to be traveled.

35. (2) Improved delivery would mean better communication. The other choices would not influence a decision about mail delivery.

36. (5) The transatlantic cable linked two distant places through improved technology. None of the other changes improved communication or involved a major technological advance.

37. (2) By forcing the withdrawal of the bill, Republicans showed their disapproval of it, which is the opposite of choice (3). Choice (1) might be true, but there is no evidence of how long Democrats could talk if they wanted to. There is no evidence that choices (4) or (5) are true.

38. (3) The mapmakers are tracing rapidly changing political events in order to update the map.

39. (5) The only countries mentioned in the cartoon are in Eastern Europe.

40. (1) The artist compares mapmaking to war by using the setting of a "situation room," a term for a place used for planning military strategies.

41. (4) Protection of the environment is in the public interest.

42. (5) This group is concerned with a single law.

43. (1) Off-shore drilling and exploration are economic issues and could benefit specific businesses.

44. (1) Vegetable soup is made up of a variety of ingredients that retain their own characteristics and are not blended together into a single taste, choice (2), or at odds with each other, choice (3).

45. (4) The line for the effect of health control costs dips down to 0 by the year 2003. The other lines both show a continued federal deficit.

46. (3) Only a few of the marked areas are in the Northeast (1) or Southeast (2). The map shows an uneven distribution of parks, with most marked areas in the West and a few in Hawaii and Alaska (4).

47. (1) By 1872, much of the East and Midwest was already settled while large areas in the West were still unspoiled and unclaimed even though they were rich in natural resources.

48. (4) By renovating inner-city neighborhoods, modern city planners assume they can eliminate the sources of many social problems. This assumption is also applied to downtown areas, choice (1), but is definitely not cheap, choice (5).

49. (1) The passage states that acid rain spreads miles from its source, so it is not a local problem. People cannot control the natural water cycle, so acid rain is difficult to contain to specific areas.

50. (1) The figures for the minimum wage in 1974 and 1975 are $2.00 and $2.10, and in 1991 the figure is $4.25, just over twice the amount. By 1978, farm wages equaled nonfarm wages. There are no figures to support the other choices.

51. (5) The government realizes that a rise in the cost of living requires higher wages in order for workers to keep up. Increases in the type of people in the work force or the amount of government spending would not affect wages.

52. (2) The owners are limited by the number of licenses available. Until they can get one, they cannot compete with other businesses that serve alcohol.

53. (5) The inventor cannot raise the necessary cash to make her product even though she has no problem with a patent or market size.

54. (4) The other two video stores are already serving the market and would limit the number of customers available to the couple.

55. (2) Baird had broken a law. As a candidate for the highest legal position in the land, she would set a poor example for the American people. Another woman was appointed, so (1) is incorrect. The other choices have no support.

56. (2) The traffic accident is the only horrifying event that the person actually experienced. The other events are reports or observations.

57. (5) The characters' demands refer to "America's diversity," a phrase that is used to include all minority groups.

58. (4) According to the passage, relationships are top on the list of the makings of happiness. Faith comes in third. The others are not included as causes of happiness.

59. (3) The first paragraph gives several definitions of happiness but ends with the statement that happiness "all depends." The information does not support the other conclusions.

60. (2) The symbol in the map legend specifies the targets of air strikes.

61. (3) The targets indicated on the map are mainly missile sites, air bases, and weapons-research complexes. The Allied attack did get through Iraq's defenses and showed no evidence of underestimating Iraq or of being disorganized.

62. (5) By focusing on destruction of military centers, the Allies could expect that Iraq's defense would be weakened to the point of surrender.

63. (3) Immigrants who crossed the oceans to America came in search of better jobs and a better life for their families; these are the same goals as those of migrant Mexicans. Columbus crossed the water for economic reasons. Enslaved Africans came to America involuntarily. The other two choices refer to military events.

64. (4) The author is making a judgment by saying the Ibo women are luckier. Such a description of the contrast is opinion, not fact. The author's opinions about women's rights and what women should do are not expressed. Choice (5) is a fact, not an opinion.

Use the answer key on pages 871–874 to check your answers to the Practice Test. Then find the item number of each question you missed and circle it on the chart below to determine the reading skill and content areas in which you need more practice. Pay particular attention to areas where you missed half or more of the questions. The reading skills are covered on pages 187–243. The page numbers for the content areas are listed below on the chart. Knowledge of reading skill and content area–based questions is absolutely essential for success on the GED Social Studies Test. The numbers in boldface are questions based on graphics. For those questions that you missed, review the pages indicated.

PRACTICE TEST 2: SOCIAL STUDIES EVALUATION CHART

Skill Area/ Content Area	Comprehension (pages 189–195)	Application (pages 195–199)	Analysis (pages 200–210)	Evaluation (pages 211–222)
Behavioral Sciences (pages 247–262)	3, 4	16, 17, 18, 19, 28	8, 56, 58, 64	20, 59
U.S. History (pages 263–300)	7, 9, 34, **60**	36, 44	5, 11, 12, 26, 48, **62**	6, 10, 35, **61**
Political Science (pages 301–318)	**14**, 37, **57**	22, 23, 24, 25	**21**, 41, 42, 43	**15**, 55
Economics (pages 319–332)	2, 31	52, 53, 54	27, 32, **45**, **51**	1, 33, **50**
Geography (pages 333–342)	**29**, **38**, **46**	13, 63	**30**, **40**, **47**	**39**, 49

PRACTICE TEST 3: SCIENCE

This Science Practice Test will give you the opportunity to evaluate your readiness for the actual GED Science Test.

This test contains 66 questions. Some of the questions are based on short reading passages, and some require you to interpret a chart or diagram.

You should take approximately 95 minutes to complete this test. At the end of 95 minutes, stop and mark your place. Then finish the test. This will give you an idea of whether or not you can finish the real GED Test in the time allotted. Try to answer as many questions as you can. A blank will count as a wrong answer, so make a reasonable guess for answers to questions you are not sure of.

When you are finished with the test, check your answers and turn to the Evaluation Chart on page 897 and the GED Readiness Worksheet on page 927. Use the chart and worksheet to evaluate whether or not you are ready to take the actual GED Test and, if not, in what areas you need more work.

PRACTICE TEST 3: SCIENCE ANSWER GRID

1 ① ② ③ ④ ⑤	18 ① ② ③ ④ ⑤	35 ① ② ③ ④ ⑤	51 ① ② ③ ④ ⑤
2 ① ② ③ ④ ⑤	19 ① ② ③ ④ ⑤	36 ① ② ③ ④ ⑤	52 ① ② ③ ④ ⑤
3 ① ② ③ ④ ⑤	20 ① ② ③ ④ ⑤	37 ① ② ③ ④ ⑤	53 ① ② ③ ④ ⑤
4 ① ② ③ ④ ⑤	21 ① ② ③ ④ ⑤	38 ① ② ③ ④ ⑤	54 ① ② ③ ④ ⑤
5 ① ② ③ ④ ⑤	22 ① ② ③ ④ ⑤	39 ① ② ③ ④ ⑤	55 ① ② ③ ④ ⑤
6 ① ② ③ ④ ⑤	23 ① ② ③ ④ ⑤	40 ① ② ③ ④ ⑤	56 ① ② ③ ④ ⑤
7 ① ② ③ ④ ⑤	24 ① ② ③ ④ ⑤	41 ① ② ③ ④ ⑤	57 ① ② ③ ④ ⑤
8 ① ② ③ ④ ⑤	25 ① ② ③ ④ ⑤	42 ① ② ③ ④ ⑤	58 ① ② ③ ④ ⑤
9 ① ② ③ ④ ⑤	26 ① ② ③ ④ ⑤	43 ① ② ③ ④ ⑤	59 ① ② ③ ④ ⑤
10 ① ② ③ ④ ⑤	27 ① ② ③ ④ ⑤	44 ① ② ③ ④ ⑤	60 ① ② ③ ④ ⑤
11 ① ② ③ ④ ⑤	28 ① ② ③ ④ ⑤	45 ① ② ③ ④ ⑤	61 ① ② ③ ④ ⑤
12 ① ② ③ ④ ⑤	29 ① ② ③ ④ ⑤	46 ① ② ③ ④ ⑤	62 ① ② ③ ④ ⑤
13 ① ② ③ ④ ⑤	30 ① ② ③ ④ ⑤	47 ① ② ③ ④ ⑤	63 ① ② ③ ④ ⑤
14 ① ② ③ ④ ⑤	31 ① ② ③ ④ ⑤	48 ① ② ③ ④ ⑤	64 ① ② ③ ④ ⑤
15 ① ② ③ ④ ⑤	32 ① ② ③ ④ ⑤	49 ① ② ③ ④ ⑤	65 ① ② ③ ④ ⑤
16 ① ② ③ ④ ⑤	33 ① ② ③ ④ ⑤	50 ① ② ③ ④ ⑤	66 ① ② ③ ④ ⑤
17 ① ② ③ ④ ⑤	34 ① ② ③ ④ ⑤		

Choose the best answer to each question that follows.

1. Which of the following facts is the *best evidence* that helium gas is lighter than air?

   (1) Helium will not burn when exposed to flame in the presence of oxygen.
   (2) By volume, helium makes up only 0.0005 percent of air.
   (3) Helium atoms do not combine with other air atoms.
   (4) Helium-filled balloons rise in air.
   (5) Helium has the lowest boiling point of all known elements.

2. Tides, caused by the moon's gravity, create a frictional force that is gradually slowing down Earth's rotation speed. One million years from now, scientists may discover that, compared to today, Earth's

   (1) day is longer
   (2) day is shorter
   (3) year is longer
   (4) year is shorter
   (5) day has stayed the same

3. To fight the effects of acid rain, scientists in many countries dump large quantities of calcium carbonate into polluted lakes. You can infer from this action that calcium carbonate is

   (1) an acid
   (2) a base
   (3) a neutral substance
   (4) a powdered substance
   (5) not harmful to fish

4. The source of energy responsible for life on Earth is

   (1) the moon
   (2) the Sun
   (3) the wind
   (4) water
   (5) plant life

Questions 5 and 6 refer to the following passage.

When a green plant cell is exposed to sunlight, a chemical reaction called photosynthesis takes place. During photosynthesis, carbon dioxide gas (CO_2) reacts with water (H_2O) to produce three compounds: a type of sugar called glucose ($C_6H_{12}O_6$), oxygen gas (O_2), and water. The chemical equation for photosynthesis is written as follows:
$$6CO_2 + 12H_2O \rightarrow C_6H_{12}O_6 + 6O_2 + 6H_2O$$

5. In the equation for photosynthesis, how many molecules of oxygen gas are produced in the formation of one molecule of glucose?

   (1) one
   (2) two
   (3) six
   (4) seven
   (5) twelve

6. Which of the following must be present in order for photosynthesis to take place?

   (1) glucose
   (2) oxygen
   (3) nitrogen
   (4) water
   (5) soil

7. An advertisement for a new diet drink claims that an eight-ounce serving

   A. contains only 240 calories
   B. contains two ounces of protein
   C. tastes better than other leading brands
   D. costs only 14 cents per ounce

   Which of the above claims is (are) based on opinion?

   (1) A
   (2) B
   (3) C
   (4) D
   (5) C and D

8. Precipitation is the process by which atmospheric water vapor returns to Earth's surface in one form or another. Each of the following is an example of precipitation *except*

   (1) rain
   (2) sleet
   (3) dust
   (4) snow
   (5) hail

9. Self-preservation is a natural reaction shown by an animal for the purpose of avoiding serious harm. Which of the following is the best example of self-preservation?

   (1) a young man decides to quit smoking
   (2) a salmon swims back to the place of its birth to lay eggs
   (3) a bee spreads pollen as it flies from flower to flower
   (4) a dog barks when it sees its owner
   (5) a mouse runs when it sees a cat

Questions 10–14 are based on the following passage.

Organisms vary greatly in complexity. Single-celled organisms, such as bacteria, are much less complex than multicellular organisms such as flowers. In bacteria, all functions needed to sustain life are carried out by the one cell. In a flower, each life function is carried out by a group of cells working as a unit. Flowers, like other complex organisms, show several levels of structural organization. Here are five of the most common levels:

organelle—An organized structure found in a cell's cytoplasm. Each organelle takes part in carrying out some cellular function. Plant cells, for example, contain chloroplasts that absorb and use light energy to make the cell's food.

cell—The basic structural and functional unit of life. A cell uses energy, moves, grows, responds to changes in its environment, and reproduces. In a multicellular organism, a cell performs a specific function. For example, a human nerve cell relays messages to different parts of the body.

tissue—A group of structurally similar cells that are organized to perform the same activity. In a plant cell, vascular tissue carries water and nutrients to all parts of the cell.

organ—A structural unit composed of several tissues that work together to perform a specific function. The heart is an example of a human organ whose function is to pump blood throughout the body.

organ system—An association of several organs that work together to perform one or more functions. The muscular system, made up of groups of muscles, is an example of a human organ system.

10. In a plant, the epidermis is a special layer of cells that covers and helps protect roots, stems, leaves, flowers, and seeds. This layer of specialized cells is best classified as a(n)

   (1) organelle
   (2) cell
   (3) tissue
   (4) organ
   (5) organ system

11. Mitochondria are rod-shaped structures in a cell's cytoplasm. Mitochondria are the centers of cellular respiration and are a type of

   (1) organelle
   (2) cell
   (3) tissue
   (4) organ
   (5) organ system

12. When Derek reached forty-three years of age, his pancreas no longer produced sufficient insulin, a hormone that controls sugar levels in the blood. As a result, Derek was diagnosed as having diabetes, a condition that often can be controlled through proper diet. Because it is made up of several types of specialized tissues, the pancreas is best classified as a(n)

   (1) organelle
   (2) cell
   (3) tissue
   (4) organ
   (5) organ system

13. As soon as you put food in your mouth, saliva breaks the food down into a form your cells can use. This process is further carried out in your stomach and small intestine. Your mouth, stomach, and small intestine work together as a(n)

    (1) organelle
    (2) cell
    (3) tissue
    (4) organ
    (5) organ system

14. An amoeba is a microscopic organism that has a complete life cycle. As a single-celled organism, an amoeba reproduces by fission, dividing itself into two new amoebas. The highest level of organization exemplified by an amoeba is that of a(n)

    (1) organelle
    (2) cell
    (3) tissue
    (4) organ
    (5) organ system

15. Which of the following shows that sunlight can be changed to heat energy?

    A. a magnifying glass can focus a beam of sunlight
    B. you feel warmer in sunlight than in shade
    C. the surface of a car gets hot when sitting in direct sunlight
    D. sunlight reflects off a mirror without noticeably warming the mirror

    (1) A and B
    (2) A and C
    (3) A and D
    (4) B and C
    (5) B and D

Questions 16–20 refer to the following passage.

Celery has long been used in Asian countries to help in the treatment of high blood pressure. Recently, researchers at the University of Chicago have found a possible explanation for this medical benefit of celery. They discovered that celery contains a chemical called 3-n-butyl phthalide. They believe that this phthalide compound causes muscles that line blood vessels to relax, allowing the vessels to widen, lowering blood pressure.

In an experiment with rats, these researchers found that a dose of the phthalide compound equivalent to four stalks of celery for humans lowered blood pressure by 13 percent. The hope is that further studies may lead to the development of a safer, more effective drug treatment of high blood pressure than is now available.

The statements in questions 16–20 can be classified into one of the five categories defined below:

an experiment—a procedure used to investigate a problem

a finding—an experimental result obtained or a conclusion reached as part of the investigation

a hypothesis—a reasonable, but not proved, explanation of an observed fact

a prediction—an opinion about something that may occur in the future

a nonessential fact—a fact that does not help the researcher understand the problem being investigated

16. Researchers believe that eating celery helps lower blood pressure by causing muscles that line blood vessels to relax.

This is best classified as a(n)

(1) experiment
(2) finding
(3) hypothesis
(4) prediction
(5) nonessential fact

17. Celery is a biennial plant, living for two years before it produces seeds and dies. You should classify this statement as a(n)

(1) experiment
(2) finding
(3) hypothesis
(4) prediction
(5) nonessential fact

18. Researchers gave rats a dose of 3-n-butyl phthalide and measured changes in the rats' blood pressure.

This statement is best classified as a(n)

(1) experiment
(2) finding
(3) hypothesis
(4) prediction
(5) nonessential fact

19. With further research, scientists may find that other stalky vegetables such as carrots also help lower blood pressure.

This statement is best classified as a(n)

(1) experiment
(2) finding
(3) hypothesis
(4) prediction
(5) nonessential fact

20. Researchers discovered that the chemical 3-n-butyl phthalide can lower the blood pressure of rats.

You should classify this statement as a(n)

(1) experiment
(2) finding
(3) hypothesis
(4) prediction
(5) nonessential fact

Questions 21–25 are based on the following passage.

In recent years, scientists have discovered that Earth's temperature is slowly increasing. In fact, scientists believe that today's average temperature is several degrees higher than the average at the beginning of the industrial revolution in the late 1700s. This warming is thought to be caused by a phenomenon known as the greenhouse effect.

In a greenhouse, sunlight passes through a glass roof and provides energy to the plants growing inside. The glass prevents heat in the greenhouse from escaping. Similarly, sunlight passes through our atmosphere and warms Earth's surface. Much of the surface heat is prevented from escaping because it is absorbed by greenhouse gases in the atmosphere. As long as the average level of greenhouse gases does not increase, Earth's temperature stays in a comfortable range.

Two main greenhouse gases are carbon dioxide and carbon monoxide. Since the industrial revolution, humans have increased the amount of atmospheric carbon dioxide by burning fossil fuels (wood, coal, and oil) both for the production of electricity and for home heating. By driving cars, humans have increased the amount of atmospheric carbon monoxide, present in car exhaust.

Scientists point out that further increases in Earth's average temperature could result in the melting of the polar ice caps and in the changing of weather patterns worldwide.

21. Which of the following is the best definition of a greenhouse gas?

   (1) any gas that is commonly present in automobile exhaust
   (2) any gas that absorbs heat radiating off of Earth's surface
   (3) any gas that reflects sunlight
   (4) any gas that is commonly present in a greenhouse
   (5) any gas that is given off by the burning of fossil fuels

22. Which of the following best demonstrates the greenhouse principle?

   (1) a kettle-type barbecue grill
   (2) a heated aquarium
   (3) a car with rolled-up windows
   (4) a solar battery–powered calculator
   (5) a microwave oven

23. Which of the following would most likely result from a gradual increase in Earth's average temperature?

   (1) a gradual decrease in the length of a day
   (2) a gradual increase in the length of a year
   (3) a lowering of ocean levels
   (4) a gradual increase in the number of active volcanos
   (5) a gradual rise in ocean levels

24. Each of the following contributes to the greenhouse effect *except*

   (1) a forest fire
   (2) a bus that runs on diesel fuel
   (3) soil bacteria that release carbon dioxide gas
   (4) a gas-powered lawn mower
   (5) a hydroelectric power plant

25. Scientists predict that if something is not done to stop the increase in atmospheric greenhouse gases, the average temperature of Earth may increase 6°F to 10°F in the next fifty years. Which of the following actions would be *most effective* toward helping solve the greenhouse effect?

   (1) reducing human dependence on all types of fossil fuels
   (2) raising the gas tax on cars
   (3) restricting the use of fireplaces to wintertime only
   (4) developing efficient electric cars to replace gasoline-powered cars
   (5) recording changes in Earth's average temperature during the next fifty years

Questions 26 and 27 refer to the following table.

COMPOSITION OF PURE DRY AIR

Gas	Symbol or Formula	Percent by Volume
Nitrogen	N_2	78.1%
Oxygen	O_2	20.9%
Argon	Ar	0.9%
Carbon dioxide	CO_2	0.03%
Neon	Ne	
Helium	He	
Krypton	Kr	very
Xenon	Ze	small
Hydrogen	H_2	amounts
Nitrous Oxide	N_2O	
Methane	CH_4	

---

26. According to the table, the third most abundant gas in pure dry air is

(1) helium
(2) carbon dioxide
(3) krypton
(4) oxygen
(5) argon

27. Which of the following can be determined from information given on the table above?

A. the difference in percent of helium and oxygen present in pure dry air
B. the volume of oxygen present in a one cubic foot sample of pure dry air
C. the difference in the percent of argon and carbon dioxide present in pure dry air
D. the volume of water vapor present in 100 percent humid air

(1) A and B
(2) A and C
(3) B and C
(4) B and D
(5) C and D

Questions 28 and 29 refer to the following passage.

Temperature and pressure affect the amount of gas that can be dissolved in a liquid. An increase in temperature decreases the amount of dissolved gas. An increase in pressure increases the amount of dissolved gas.

28. Soda pop has a fizz because of dissolved carbon dioxide gas. If a cold bottle of soda is left open on a kitchen counter, which of the following will occur?

(1) The amount of dissolved carbon dioxide gas will remain the same.
(2) The amount of dissolved carbon dioxide gas will increase.
(3) The amount of dissolved carbon dioxide gas will decrease.
(4) The temperature of the soda will decrease.
(5) The pressure that the soda exerts on the bottle will increase.

29. In a stream, fish tend to swim in shaded areas along the river bank or in regions of deep water. The reason for this is most likely that water in these places

(1) contains the largest number of insects close to the surface
(2) has the least amount of dissolved carbon dioxide gas
(3) has the greatest amount of dissolved carbon dioxide gas
(4) has the least amount of dissolved oxygen gas
(5) has the greatest amount of dissolved oxygen gas

Questions 30–33 are based on the following passage.

What does an aluminum rowboat have in common with a helium-filled balloon? Both the rowboat and balloon exhibit buoyancy—the tendency of an object to float in liquid or to rise in gas.

The rowboat and balloon each have two forces acting on them: a downward gravitational force (equal to the object's weight) and an upward buoyancy force. The buoyancy force is equal to the weight of liquid or gas that the object displaces (takes the place of).

- A rowboat floats in water because the upward buoyancy force exactly balances the downward gravitational force. A 500-pound rowboat sinks just to the point where it displaces 500 pounds of water.
- A rock sinks in water because the gravitational force is greater than the buoyancy force.
- A helium-filled balloon rises in air because it displaces a volume of air that weighs more than the weight of the helium gas–filled balloon—in other words, the upward buoyancy force is greater than the downward gravitational force.

30. According to the passage, buoyancy refers to the tendency of an object to

    A. have weight
    B. float in liquid
    C. move when pushed
    D. rise in air

    (1) A
    (2) A and C
    (3) B
    (4) B and D
    (5) A, B, C, and D

31. An iceberg floats with about 11 percent of its ice above the water's surface. From the passage we know that the weight of the water displaced by the iceberg is

    (1) 11 percent greater than the weight of the iceberg
    (2) 11 percent less than the weight of the iceberg
    (3) equal to the weight of that part of the iceberg rising above the surface
    (4) equal to the weight of that part of the iceberg lying below the surface
    (5) equal to the weight of the iceberg

32. Each of the following objects is designed to employ the buoyancy principle *except* a

    (1) submarine
    (2) life preserver
    (3) hot-air balloon
    (4) kite
    (5) canoe

33. When Erin swims, she notices that if she takes a deep breath, she floats. If she exhales all the air in her lungs, she sinks. Which of the following is the best explanation of Erin's discovery? After exhaling, but not before, Erin displaces an amount of water that

    (1) weighs less than her body
    (2) weighs more than her body
    (3) is equal to her body weight
    (4) has more volume than her body volume
    (5) has less volume than her body volume

Questions 34 and 35 refer to the following drawing.

NORMAL DAYTIME CONDITIONS

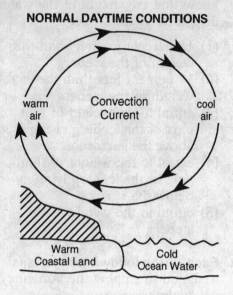

Convection
Current

warm
air

cool
air

Warm
Coastal Land

Cold
Ocean Water

34. The best definition of a convection current is movement of

(1) air caused by elevation differences
(2) air caused by differences in distance from the ocean
(3) air caused by temperature differences
(4) water caused by the presence of land
(5) water caused by elevation differences

35. In normal nighttime conditions, the wind next to Earth's surface blows toward the water from the land. From this fact, you can deduce that usually at night

(1) ocean currents are not as strong as during the day
(2) ocean temperature changes more quickly than land temperature
(3) the sun is not warming either the land nor the ocean
(4) the temperature of the land is higher than that of the ocean
(5) the temperature of the land is lower than that of the ocean

Questions 36 and 37 refer to the following passage.

Respiration takes place in the body cells and provides a source of energy. During respiration, oxygen (O_2) reacts with the sugar glucose ($C_6H_{12}O_6$). The products of this reaction are carbon dioxide (CO_2), water (H_2O), and energy. The chemical equation for respiration is written as follows:
$$C_6H_{12}O_6 + 6O_2 \rightarrow 6CO_2 + 6H_2O + energy$$

36. For each molecule of oxygen (O_2) that is used during respiration, how many molecules of carbon dioxide (CO_2) are produced?

(1) one
(2) two
(3) four
(4) six
(5) twelve

37. Which of the following is most likely considered a waste product of cellular respiration?

(1) glucose
(2) oxygen
(3) carbon dioxide
(4) nitrogen
(5) energy

Questions 38–40 refer to the following information.

An electric circuit can be either a series circuit or a parallel circuit. In a series circuit there is only one path for the electric current to take. A break anywhere in this circuit stops all of the current flow.

In a parallel circuit, there is more than one electric current path. A break in one part of the circuit does not stop current from flowing in a second (or third) path.

SERIES CIRCUIT

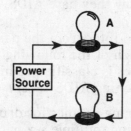

If bulb A burns out,
bulb B also goes out.

PARALLEL CIRCUIT

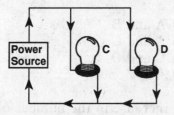

If bulb C burns out,
bulb D stays lit.

38. Four wall sockets are wired in series with an emergency shutoff switch. If the shutoff switch is opened, what happens to the wall sockets?

(1) Only the socket closest to the switch goes out.
(2) All four wall sockets go out.
(3) All four wall sockets stay on.
(4) Two wall sockets go out, one on each side of the switch.
(5) Only the socket farthest from the switch goes out.

39. What is most likely the main advantage of buying a string of Christmas tree lights that are wired in a parallel circuit rather than in a series circuit?

(1) Parallel circuits cost less to make.
(2) Different colored lights can be used in a parallel circuit.
(3) A parallel circuit uses less electricity.
(4) A burned-out bulb is found more easily in a parallel circuit.
(5) The bulbs are closer together in a parallel circuit.

40. Which statement is true about the circuit drawn below?

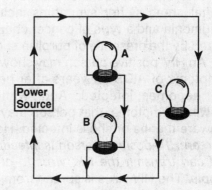

(1) If bulb B burns out, bulb A and bulb C will stay lit.
(2) If bulb C burns out, bulb A and bulb B will go off.
(3) If bulb A burns out, bulb B will go off, but bulb C will stay lit.
(4) If bulb B burns out, bulb A and bulb C will go off.
(5) If bulb A burns out, bulb B will stay lit, but bulb C will go off.

Questions 41–44 are based on the following passage.

AIDS (acquired immunodeficiency syndrome) is a serious, contagious disease for which there is no cure as yet. AIDS is a disease of the human immune system, the system that enables the body to destroy germs that cause infections and illness. With an AIDS-weakened immune system, a patient may develop life-threatening infections and cancers that usually don't affect healthy people.

AIDS is caused by a virus known as HIV, the human immunodeficiency virus. Once infected, a person is called "HIV positive." The first symptoms of AIDS include weight loss, swollen lymph nodes, body weakness, persistent cough, and chronic yeast infections of the mouth or genital areas. Other symptoms include pneumonia and a type of cancer characterized by the presence of purplish spots.

An HIV-positive person may show no symptoms of AIDS for years after he or she becomes infected. And, without showing symptoms, that person may be unaware that he or she is infected. However, *an HIV-positive person is infectious and can transmit the HIV virus to other people.* The HIV virus is spread from the blood of an infected person to the blood of an uninfected one. Because blood cells are present in sexual fluids, the HIV virus can spread from one person to another during sexual activity.

AIDS is spread in one of three main ways:

- by having unsafe sex with an infected person
- by sharing a needle with an infected drug user
- from an infected mother to the fetus during pregnancy, or to the baby during delivery or breast feeding

Although AIDS is not curable, AIDS is preventable. People can protect themselves from AIDS by engaging in safe sex and by staying away from drugs.

41. AIDS is a disease of the

(1) reproductive system
(2) digestive system
(3) nervous system
(4) skeletal system
(5) immune system

42. Which of the following is true about all HIV-positive people?

All HIV-positive people

(1) show AIDS symptoms
(2) caught AIDS from drug use
(3) can transmit AIDS
(4) are single adults
(5) know they have AIDS

43. You can infer from the passage that each of the following activities is classified as high risk for catching AIDS *except*

A. sharing needles for drug use
B. having multiple sex partners
C. swimming in a community pool
D. playing with an HIV-positive child

(1) A
(2) A and B
(3) A and C
(4) C and D
(5) D

44. An increase in the number of reported HIV-positive people is occurring in the U.S. This increase is most likely due to each of the following reasons *except*

(1) an increasing awareness by doctors of the symptoms of AIDS
(2) an increasing effort to educate U.S. citizens about the AIDS problem
(3) an increase in the spread of AIDS
(4) an increase in testing to determine who has the HIV virus
(5) an influx of HIV-positive people into the United States from foreign countries

45. Two important processes performed for plants by leaves are photosynthesis and transpiration. During photosynthesis, leaves produce glucose, a form of sugar. During transpiration, plants release water by evaporation from the leaf surfaces. What is the most likely reason that a desert plant has few or no leaves?

(1) to increase photosynthesis
(2) to decrease photosynthesis
(3) to keep photosynthesis at a constant level, day and night
(4) to increase transpiration
(5) to decrease transpiration

Questions 46–48 are based on the following drawing and passage.

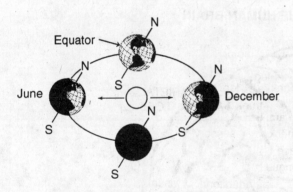

Earth's rotation axis is tilted with respect to the direction of the Sun's rays. This tilt remains constant as Earth rotates on its axis and as it moves around the Sun. The tilt leads to two important consequences for Earth:

• Summer occurs in the hemisphere that is tilted toward the Sun, while winter occurs in the hemisphere that is tilted away from the Sun.
• The hemisphere that is tilted toward the Sun has longer days and shorter nights than the hemisphere that is tilted away from the Sun.

46. During summer in the northern hemisphere, the North Pole experiences

(1) twenty-four hours of darkness each day
(2) twenty-four hours of daylight each day
(3) twelve hours of daylight each day
(4) twelve hours of darkness each day
(5) eighteen hours of daylight each day

47. During December, which location will have most nearly twelve hours of daylight and twelve hours of darkness?

A town that is located

(1) close to the North Pole
(2) close to the South Pole
(3) halfway between the equator and North Pole
(4) halfway between the equator and the South Pole
(5) close to the equator

48. Which of the following would be true if Earth's rotation axis did not tilt?

A. Days and nights would be the same length everywhere on Earth.
B. There would be no hours of darkness on points along the equator.
C. Earth would have no seasons.
D. Each part of Earth would have the same daily temperature pattern.

(1) A
(2) A and C
(3) A and D
(4) B
(5) B and C

49. Malaria is a disease caused by *parasitic protozoans*, one-celled animals that feed upon the cells of the host—the body of the person they invade. Malaria can be spread by the bite of the *Anopheles* mosquito. Knowing this, you can deduce that protozoans that cause malaria are present in the host's

(1) lungs
(2) stomach
(3) bone tissue
(4) liver
(5) blood

50. Which of the following is the best evidence that light travels at a greater speed than sound?

(1) Humans have separate sense organs for vision and hearing.
(2) Light travels through outer space, but sound doesn't.
(3) Light passes easily through thick glass, but sound doesn't.
(4) You see lightning before you hear thunder.
(5) The frequency of visible light is much greater than that of sound.

Questions 51–54 refer to the following drawing and passage.

CEREBRUM OF THE HUMAN BRAIN

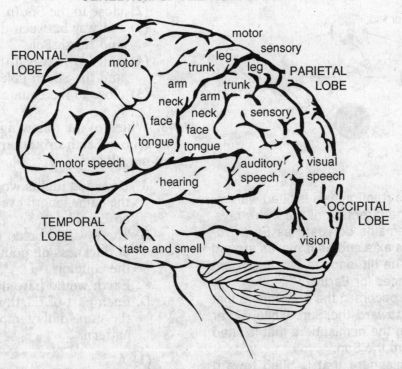

The largest region of the human brain is the cerebrum, or forebrain. The cerebrum consists of two halves, or hemispheres, joined through the center by a bundle of nerve fibers known as the corpus callosum. Each hemisphere is made up of four parts, or lobes, that control specific motor (voluntary movement) and sensory (sensation) functions.

Scientists have long known that the left hemisphere (shown above) controls the right side of the human body and the right hemisphere controls the left side. In recent years, scientists have also discovered that each hemisphere is specialized for specific learning activities. The left hemisphere seems best suited for written language, scientific skills, math, and logical reasoning. The right hemisphere seems more specialized for art, music, insight, and imagination.

51. An elderly woman suffered a stroke—a restriction of blood flow to the brain. If the stroke caused the right side of her body to become temporarily paralyzed, she most likely experienced a decreased blood flow to

    (1) the left side of her body
    (2) the right side of her body
    (3) the front of her brain
    (4) the left side of her brain
    (5) the right side of her brain

52. Which two of the following people are most likely to be referred to as "left-brained"—showing skills most often associated with the left side of the human brain?

    A. a mathematician
    B. a portrait painter
    C. a chess player
    D. a storyteller

    (1) A and B
    (2) A and C
    (3) B and C
    (4) B and D
    (5) C and D

53. Which area of the brain controls feeling on the left side of a person's face?

    (1) the right occipital lobe
    (2) the left parietal lobe
    (3) the left temporal lobe
    (4) the right frontal lobe
    (5) the right parietal lobe

54. Which facts below represent the best evidence that brain size is not the main cause for differences in intelligence?

    A. An adult's brain is larger than a baby's brain.
    B. A human being's brain is larger than a cat's.
    C. All adult human brains are about the same size.
    D. An elephant's brain is larger than a human being's.

    (1) A and B
    (2) A and D
    (3) B and C
    (4) B and D
    (5) C and D

Questions 55 and 56 refer to the graph below.

PERCENT OF CARBOHYDRATES IN SELECTED FOODS

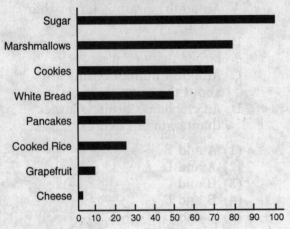

55. Which of the following foods has a carbohydrate content of 50 percent or more?

A. grapefruit
B. rice
C. marshmallows

(1) A
(2) B
(3) C
(4) A and C
(5) B and C

56. Which statement is best supported by information given on the graph?

(1) Cooking increases the carbohydrate content of food.
(2) Sugar is not a form of carbohydrate.
(3) The carbohydrate content of food increases as its sugar content increases.
(4) A food that does not contain sugar has zero carbohydrate content.
(5) All foods contain some amount of sugar.

57. Many people feel that while it is all right to raise animals such as cows for slaughter, it is not all right to kill more intelligent animals such as whales or chimpanzees. What value concerning intelligence is reflected by this position?

(1) Food production for human consumption is more important than animal rights.
(2) Humans should have a higher regard for animals of high intelligence than for animals of low intelligence.
(3) Animals should not be harmed when used for medical research.
(4) The only justification for killing an animal is for use as a source of food.
(5) Animals that are physically similar to people ought to be treated differently than animals that aren't.

Question 58 is based on the following graph.

MAIN SUBSTANCES IN SEA WATER
(by weight)

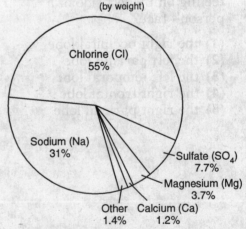

58. From information given on the graph, you can deduce that the main substance dissolved in sea water is

(1) magnesium oxide (MgO)
(2) sulfuric acid (H_2SO_4)
(3) calcium chloride ($CaCl_2$)
(4) potassium chloride (KCl)
(5) sodium chloride (NaCl)

Question 59 refers to the following drawing.

BAR MAGNET

| S | | N |

CUT IN HALF

| S | N | | S | N |

59. You can infer from the drawing above that

   (1) a bar magnet has more than one north pole and one south pole
   (2) cutting a bar magnet in half produces two weaker bar magnets
   (3) cutting a bar magnet in half produces two shorter bar magnets
   (4) cutting a bar magnet in half doubles the magnetic strength available
   (5) to produce two bar magnets, a larger bar magnet must be cut exactly in half

Question 60 is based on the following drawing.

←Olive Oil

←Water

←Mercury

60. You can infer from the drawing above that the density of water

   A. is less than the density of olive oil
   B. is less than the density of mercury
   C. is greater than the density of ice
   D. is greater than the density of olive oil

   (1) A and B
   (2) B
   (3) B and D
   (4) C and D
   (5) D

Questions 61 and 62 are based on the following drawing.

REFRACTION OF WHITE LIGHT BY A GLASS PRISM

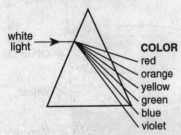

white light → COLOR
red
orange
yellow
green
blue
violet

61. The refraction of white light through a glass prism shows that

(1) white light travels in a straight line as it passes through a glass prism
(2) white light consists of several types of colored light
(3) white light cannot pass through glass without being separated into its color components
(4) glass absorbs white light but allows colored light to pass through
(5) red light refracts more than violet light when passing through a glass prism

62. What is the *best evidence* that sunlight is a form of white light (light that looks white but consists of many colors)?

(1) a clear blue sky
(2) white moonlight
(3) a color television
(4) a rainbow
(5) a color photograph

Questions 63 and 64 are based on the following drawing and information.

MUSCLES THAT CONTROL EYE MOVEMENT

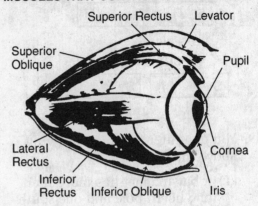

Superior Rectus Levator
Superior Oblique
Pupil
Lateral Rectus
Cornea
Inferior Rectus Inferior Oblique Iris

Each eye muscle controls eye movement by contracting (shortening) and pulling the eye.

63. As you look at a picture, the lateral rectus muscle in your right eye allows your eye to

(1) sweep from the top of the picture to the bottom
(2) sweep from the bottom of the picture to the top
(3) sweep from right to left across the picture
(4) sweep from left to right across the picture
(5) close the eyelid to rest the eye when it is tired

64. If a woman has a detached superior rectus muscle in her left eye, what symptom will she most likely show?

(1) an inability to raise her left eye
(2) an inability to see through her left eye
(3) an inability to shut her left eye
(4) an inability to blink with her left eye
(5) an inability to move her left eye from right to left

Question 65 is based on the drawing below.

PROPANE MOLECULE

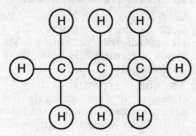

65. The drawing above shows the molecular structure of propane. Each H stands for one hydrogen atom and each C stands for one carbon atom. The formula for a propane molecule is written as

 (1) 3C8H
 (2) $3C_8H$
 (3) C_3H_8
 (4) C_8H_3
 (5) C_8H_8

Question 66 is based on the drawing below.

SIMPLE REFLEX ARC

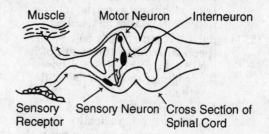

66. A reflex reaction, such as pulling your hand back from a hot stove, does not immediately involve the brain. The nerve impulse that controls the reaction takes place in a simple reflex arc as shown above. In a simple reflex arc, an interneuron

 (1) starts the nerve impulse at the sensory receptor
 (2) transmits the nerve impulse to a motor neuron
 (3) transmits the nerve impulse to the brain
 (4) transmits the nerve impulse to the spinal cord
 (5) transmits the nerve impulse to the muscles that react

Answers begin on page 894.

PRACTICE TEST 3: SCIENCE ANSWER KEY

1. (4) Although all five choices are facts, only choice (4), that helium-filled balloons rise, involves a relationship between the relative weights of helium gas and air.

2. (1) Earth's rotation (spin on its axis) speed determines the length of its day. As the rotation speed slows, the length of an Earth day will lengthen.

3. (2) A base neutralizes an acid. Choice (1) would increase acidity. Choice (3) is incorrect because a neutral substance such as water would have no effect. Neither choice (4) nor (5) can be inferred from the action of the scientists.

4. (2) All life on Earth is possible because of sunlight, which is the primary source of energy for all activity (including life) on Earth's surface.

5. (3) The products of the reaction are shown on the right side of the arrow. The formula $6O_2$ shows that six molecules of oxygen gas (O_2) are formed.

6. (4) Besides sunlight, both carbon dioxide and water must be present for photosynthesis to take place. Only water is given as one of the choices. Glucose, choice (1), is a product of photosynthesis; oxygen, choice (2), is a by-product of the process; and nitrogen gas, choice (3), does not exist in a free state.

7. (3) Only choice (3) is an opinion. Choices (A) and (B) can be checked by chemical analysis. Choice (D) can be checked by going to a store that sells the drink.

8. (3) Dust is the only choice that is not a form of water.

9. (5) Of all the examples, only choice (5), a mouse running when it sees a cat, represents a natural reaction intended to avoid harm. Choice (1) is based on an intelligent decision, not on a natural reaction. None of the other choices is an example of self-preservation.

10. (3) The epidermis is a layer of cells, each of which is organized to perform the same activity, leading to its classification as a tissue.

11. (1) Mitochondria are organelles, structures found within a cell's cytoplasm.

12. (4) Because the pancreas is a structural unit containing several types of tissues, it is best classifed as an organ.

13. (5) The question describes the digestive process, which involves several organs working together to perform a specific function.

14. (2) An amoeba is a single-celled organism that carries on all the major life processes.

15. (4) Choices (A) and (D) are facts but neither shows that sunlight can be changed to heat energy.

16. (3) This statement is a hypothesis because it gives a reasonable but untested explanation of why celery helps lower blood pressure.

17. (5) The life cycle of celery has nothing to do with the attempt to determine the medicinal characteristics of celery.

18. (1) Giving rats the phthalide compound was part of the experiment described in the passage.

19. (4) This is a prediction because it is an opinion about something that might happen in the future.

20. (2) Any experimental result or discovery is classified as a finding.

21. (2) A greenhouse gas is defined by its ability to absorb heat that radiates from Earth's surface, preventing it from radiating into space.

22. (3) A car with its windows rolled up is almost identical to a greenhouse. The glass lets light energy in but prevents heat energy from escaping.

23. (5) As Earth's temperature rises, the polar ice caps will likely melt. The water from the melting ice will cause a rise in ocean levels.

24. (5) A hydroelectric plant converts the energy of flowing water to electricity. No greenhouse gases are emitted in the process.

25. (1) Reducing our dependence on all types of fossil fuels would reduce the atmospheric greenhouse gases released.

26. (5) Nitrogen is most abundant, followed by oxygen, and argon is the third most abundant.

27. (3) Choice (A) is incorrect because the percent of helium is not listed. Choice (D) is not correct because the table refers to pure dry air only.

28. (3) The amount of carbon dioxide gas will decrease as the temperature of the pop increases. The soda will then taste flat.

29. (5) Cold water has a greater amount of dissolved oxygen gas than warm water, which explains why fish tend to swim in shaded areas or in deep water, where the temperature is lower.

30. (4) Choices (B) and (D), an object's tendency to float in water or rise in air, demonstrate the principle of buoyancy, as described in the first paragraph of the passage.

31. (5) The weight of water displaced by any floating object is equal to the weight of the whole object, regardless of how much of the object is floating above the water level.

32. (4) A kite rises in air because of the pressure of the wind against its surface, not because of buoyancy.

33. (1) After exhaling, Erin sinks, which means that her weight is greater than the buoyancy force. Therefore, the weight of the water she displaces is less than her body weight.

34. (3) As the drawing shows, a convection current is air movement caused by temperature differences. Water convection currents occur in the ocean.

35. (5) In normal nighttime conditions, the land is colder than the ocean. As a result, the air over the ocean rises and causes a breeze to flow from the land.

36. (1) The chemical equation shows that six molecules of O_2 are used up while six molecules of CO_2 are created. The same number are created that are used up: one used up, one created.

37. (3) The energy and water that are created by cellular respiration are used by the body. The CO_2 (carbon dioxide) is expelled by the lungs as a waste product.

38. (2) Since the switch and wall sockets are wired in series, if one goes out they all go out. Opening the switch breaks the circuit, and all sockets go out.

39. (4) If the bulbs are wired in a parallel circuit, the burned-out bulb does not affect the other good bulbs, making the burned-out one easy to find.

40. (3) Only choice (3) is true. Lights A and B are part of the same series circuit, and if one goes out, so will the other. Light C, though, will stay lit no matter what happens to lights A and B.

41. (5) The first paragraph of the passage states that AIDS is a disease of the human immune system.

42. (3) All HIV-positive people can transmit AIDS, and this makes the spread of AIDS difficult to stop. Many HIV-positive people don't know they are infected, and they infect others.

43. (4) As far as is known, no one has ever caught AIDS in a community swimming pool or from playing with an HIV-positive child. Choices (A) and (B) are the two most high-risk activities known.

44. (2) Increasing efforts to educate citizens about AIDS can only help in the worldwide effort to conquer this dreaded disease.

45. (5) Cacti and other desert plants can survive in the desert only by conserving water. As a result, desert plants have evolved little or no leaf surface through which transpiration can take place.

46. (2) During summer months, the North Pole is tilted toward the sun and receives sunlight twenty-four hours each day.

47. (5) Actually, a town that is located just south of the equator will have twelve hours of daylight and twelve hours of darkness during December. During June, a town that is just north of the equator will have equal day and night hours.

48. (2) As the passage states, the tilt of Earth's axis is responsible for differences in day and night hours and for seasonal differences.

49. (5) A mosquito can transmit the blood of one person to the blood of a second person. Therefore, you can correctly conclude that malaria is transmitted by the blood.

50. (4) An electrical discharge in a cloud causes both thunder and lightning. You see the lightning before you hear the thunder because light travels faster than sound.

51. (4) According to the passage, the left side of the brain controls the right side of the body. Problems on the right side of the body indicate a decreased blood flow to the left side of the brain.

52. (2) Of the four choices listed, mathematician and chess player are the two whose skills most depend on math and logical reasoning—"left-brain" skills.

53. (5) The left side of the face is controlled by the right side of the brain. The parietal lobe controls facial sensations.

54. (5) Choices (A) and (B) would seem to indicate that a larger brain implies greater intelligence. Choices (C) and (D) suggest that brain size is not a determining factor for differences in intelligence.

55. (3) Marshmallows have a carbohydrate content of about 80 percent; the other choices contain less than 50 percent of carbohydrates.

56. (3) The list when read from bottom to top indicates that as the sugar content increases, the carbohydrate content increases.

57. (2) Many people feel that more intelligent species should be preserved from slaughter, possibly because of their value in research on intelligence.

58. (5) The two major substances in sea water are chlorine (Cl) and sodium (Na), the two elements that make up sodium chloride (NaCl), most often called table salt.

59. (3) You can infer only that two shorter magnets are created. However, you can't tell from the drawing what the strength of these magnets are.

60. (3) When liquids don't freely mix, the one with the greatest density sinks to the bottom. The liquid with least density floats on top.

61. (2) Each color component of white light refracts (changes direction) a different amount as it enters and leaves the prism. This is how a prism separates white light into its color components.

62. (4) A rainbow forms because suspended rain drops act as tiny prisms and cause sunlight (natural white light) to separate into its color components.

63. (4) When the lateral rectus contracts it pulls the front of the eye to the right, sweeping the eye from left to right across the picture.

64. (1) The superior rectus contracts to pull the eye upward. If this muscle is detached (or severely weakened) the woman would be unable to raise the eye.

65. (3) The correct way to show three carbon atoms and eight hydrogen atoms is with the formula C_3H_8.

66. (2) As the drawing shows, the interneuron receives the nerve impulse from the sensory neuron and transmits the impulse to the motor neuron.

Use the answer key on pages 894–896 to check your answers to the Practice Test. Then find the item number of each question you missed and circle it on the chart below to determine the reading skill and content areas in which you need more practice. Pay particular attention to areas where you missed half or more of the questions. The reading skills are covered on pages 187–243. The page numbers for the content areas are listed below on the chart. Knowledge of reading skill and content area–based questions is absolutely essential for success on the GED Science Test. The numbers in boldface are questions based on graphics. For those questions that you missed, review the pages indicated.

PRACTICE TEST 3: SCIENCE EVALUATION CHART

Skill Area/ Content Area	Comprehension (pages 189–195)	Application (pages 195–199)	Analysis (pages 200–210)	Evaluation (pages 211–222)
Biology (pages 355–374)	41, 42, 43, **53**, 55, **63**	9, 10, 11, 12, 13, 14, 16, 17, 18, 19, 20, 52	45, 49, **51**, **64**, 66	44, **54**, **56**, 57
Earth Science (pages 375–398)	21, **34**, **46**	8, 22, 24, **47**	2, 23, **35**, 48	25, 27
Chemistry (pages 399–418)	5, **26**, **27**, 36, **65**	3, 28	6, 7, 29, 37, **58**	1
Physics (pages 419–440)	4, 30, **59**, **60**, **61**	31, 32, **38**	15, **39**, **40**	33, 50, **62**

PRACTICE TEST 4:
LITERATURE AND THE ARTS

The Literature and the Arts Practice Test will give you the opportunity to evaluate your readiness for the actual GED Literature and the Arts Test.

This test contains 45 questions. Most of the questions are based on excerpts from novels, short stories, plays, and speeches; some questions are based on a complete poem, essay, or review.

You should take approximately 65 minutes to complete this test. At the end of 65 minutes, stop and mark your place. Then finish the test. This will give you an idea of whether or not you can finish the real GED Test in the time allotted. Try to answer as many questions as you can. A blank will count as a wrong answer, so make a reasonable guess for answers to questions you are not sure of.

When you are finished with the test, check your answers and turn to the Evaluation Chart on page 913 and the GED Readiness Worksheet on page 927. Use the chart and worksheet to evaluate whether or not you are ready to take the actual GED Test and, if not, in what areas you need more work.

PRACTICE TEST 4: LITERATURE AND THE ARTS ANSWER GRID

1 ① ② ③ ④ ⑤	13 ① ② ③ ④ ⑤	25 ① ② ③ ④ ⑤	36 ① ② ③ ④ ⑤
2 ① ② ③ ④ ⑤	14 ① ② ③ ④ ⑤	26 ① ② ③ ④ ⑤	37 ① ② ③ ④ ⑤
3 ① ② ③ ④ ⑤	15 ① ② ③ ④ ⑤	27 ① ② ③ ④ ⑤	38 ① ② ③ ④ ⑤
4 ① ② ③ ④ ⑤	16 ① ② ③ ④ ⑤	28 ① ② ③ ④ ⑤	39 ① ② ③ ④ ⑤
5 ① ② ③ ④ ⑤	17 ① ② ③ ④ ⑤	29 ① ② ③ ④ ⑤	40 ① ② ③ ④ ⑤
6 ① ② ③ ④ ⑤	18 ① ② ③ ④ ⑤	30 ① ② ③ ④ ⑤	41 ① ② ③ ④ ⑤
7 ① ② ③ ④ ⑤	19 ① ② ③ ④ ⑤	31 ① ② ③ ④ ⑤	42 ① ② ③ ④ ⑤
8 ① ② ③ ④ ⑤	20 ① ② ③ ④ ⑤	32 ① ② ③ ④ ⑤	43 ① ② ③ ④ ⑤
9 ① ② ③ ④ ⑤	21 ① ② ③ ④ ⑤	33 ① ② ③ ④ ⑤	44 ① ② ③ ④ ⑤
10 ① ② ③ ④ ⑤	22 ① ② ③ ④ ⑤	34 ① ② ③ ④ ⑤	45 ① ② ③ ④ ⑤
11 ① ② ③ ④ ⑤	23 ① ② ③ ④ ⑤	35 ① ② ③ ④ ⑤	
12 ① ② ③ ④ ⑤	24 ① ② ③ ④ ⑤		

Read each excerpt and choose the best answer to each question that follows.

Questions 1–6 refer to the following excerpt from an autobiography.

HAS SHE CHANGED?

For four days I waited on the curious in the Store, and let them look me over. I was that rarity, a Stamps girl who had gone to the
5 fabled California and returned. I could be forgiven a few siditty airs. In fact, a pretension to worldliness was expected of me, and I was too happy to disappoint.

10 When Momma wasn't around, I stood with one hand on my hip and my head cocked to one side and spoke of the wonders of the West and the joy of being free. Any lis-
15 tener could have asked me: if things were so grand in San Francisco, what had brought me back to a dusty mote of Arkansas? No one asked, because they all needed to
20 believe that a land existed some-where, even beyond the Northern Star, where Negroes were treated as people and whites were not the all-powerful ogres of their experience.

25 For the first time the farmers acknowledged my maturity. They didn't order me back and forth along the shelves but found subtler ways to make their wants known.

30 "You all have any long-grain rice, Sister?"

The hundred-pound sack of rice sat squidged down in full view.

"Yes, ma'am, I believe we do."

35 "Well then, I'll thank you for two pounds."

"Two pounds? Yes, ma'am."

I had seen the formality of black adult equals all my youth but had
40 never considered that a time would come when I, too, could participate. The customs are as formalized as an eighteenth-century minuet, and a child at the race's knee learns the
45 moves and twirls by osmosis and observation.

Values among Southern rural blacks are not quite the same as those existing elsewhere. Age has
50 more worth than wealth, and reli-gious piety more value than beauty.

There were no sly looks over my fatherless child. No cutting in-sinuations kept me shut away from
55 the community. Knowing how closely my grandmother's friends hewed to the Bible, I was surprised not to be asked to confess my evil ways and repent. Instead, I was
60 seen in the sad light which had been shared and was to be shared by black girls in every state in the coun-try. I was young, yes, unmarried, yes—but I was a mother, and that
65 placed me nearer to the people.

I was flattered to receive such acceptance from my betters (se-niors) and strove mightily to show myself worthy.

—Maya Angelou, excerpted from
Gather Together in My Name, 1974

1. The young woman in the excerpt has just returned from living in

   (1) San Francisco, California
   (2) Greensboro, North Carolina
   (3) Northern Star, Mississippi
   (4) Stamps, Arkansas
   (5) New York City, New York

2. When the woman returned home, she pretended to be

(1) rich
(2) religious
(3) sophisticated
(4) married
(5) famous

3. The town where the excerpt takes place can best be described as

(1) wealthy and exclusive
(2) rural and small
(3) mysterious and threatening
(4) exciting and bustling
(5) cold and impersonal

4. Which of the following words best describes how the townspeople feel about the woman?

(1) ashamed
(2) angry
(3) resentful
(4) accepting
(5) proud

5. In lines 30–37, the author quotes a conversation between herself and a townsperson to

(1) help readers picture how badly store clerks were treated
(2) let readers know what kinds of food were popular in the town
(3) show what kind of job she held when she returned home
(4) poke fun at the way the people in the town spoke
(5) give an example of the townspeople's idea of good manners

6. Imagine that you're taking a poll. Which of the following individuals would you expect to top the town's Most Admired People list?

(1) an Oscar-winning actor
(2) the head of the nation's largest corporation
(3) a local religious leader
(4) the wealthiest person in the county
(5) the winner of a state beauty pageant

Questions 7–11 refer to the following excerpt from an article.

IS HER FUTURE IN BASEBALL?

"I'm going to be the first woman playing in the major leagues." The speaker is my daughter, Casey, age 10. She is convinced of her future as
5 a first baseman for the Red Sox. "Baseperson sounds stupid," she tells me, looking at me evenly. "If a woman has the same athletic skills as a man, why shouldn't she play
10 baseball in the major leagues?" This much has changed in 14 years.

We sit in the stands, mother and daughter. There have been hundreds of women sportswriters since
15 I was in Boston. I would like to be able to say that Casey and I talk baseball stats but the truth is her father, a scholar of Red Sox history, has infected her with his love of the
20 game. As a 10-year-old girl, she understands the mechanisms: She has a feel for the individual players, a sense of their capabilities and the benighted baseball fate of her be-
25 loved team.

She has thoughts about the 1993 Red Sox and is filled with judgments on the skills of Ivan Calderon, Roger Clemens and Frank Viola.
30 Baseball cards clog her room. At spring training batting practice, as always, young fans push baseballs at the players, begging for autographs. "Mr. Clemens!" "Mr. Cal-
35 deron!" "Mr. Dawson, pul-leese." I look down at the crowd of kids. Half of them are girls. This is new. During a game against the Minnesota Twins, I noticed that the bat boy was
40 a girl.
—Marie Brenner, excerpted from "Girls of Summer," *New York Times*, April 5, 1993

7. Casey, the ten-year-old girl, would like to become a

(1) sportswriter
(2) sports announcer
(3) baseball historian
(4) bat girl
(5) first baseman

8. Casey is a collector of

    (1) sports stars' autographs
    (2) signed baseballs
    (3) baseball cards
    (4) sports statistics
    (5) books about sports

9. The excerpt is mainly about how

    (1) females are becoming more
        and more involved in
        professional sports
    (2) a father helped his daughter
        develop an intense interest
        in sports
    (3) the daughter of a female
        sportswriter shares her love
        of sports
    (4) girls make up a large part of
        the audience for a typical Red
        Sox game
    (5) major league baseball is
        making an effort to attract
        female fans

10. The purpose of the last sentence
is to

    (1) make the article more
        interesting by giving
        specific details
    (2) prove that the team does not
        discriminate against females
    (3) give an example of how the
        Red Sox are preparing for
        the future
    (4) support the idea that females
        are taking a more active role
        in sports
    (5) convince girls to become
        participants in major league
        baseball

11. Which of the following statements
would the author of the excerpt
be most likely to make?

    (1) "A woman's place is at
        home plate."
    (2) "It's a man's world."
    (3) "The more things change, the
        more they stay the same."
    (4) "Anything men can do,
        women can do better."
    (5) "Girls don't have the same
        interests as boys."

Questions 12–16 refer to the following
excerpt from a short story.

WHO'S LISTENING?

In the living room the voice-
clock sang, *Tick-tock, seven o'clock,
time to get up, time to get up, seven
o'clock*! as if it were afraid that no-
5 body would. The morning house lay
empty. The clock ticked on, repeating and repeating its sounds into the
emptiness. *Seven-nine, breakfast
time, seven-nine!*

10 In the kitchen the breakfast
stove gave a hissing sigh and
ejected from its warm interior eight
pieces of perfectly browned toast,
eight eggs sunnyside up, sixteen
15 slices of bacon, two coffees, and
two cool glasses of milk.

"Today is August 4, 2026," said
a second voice from the kitchen
ceiling, "in the city of Allendale, Cal-
20 ifornia." It repeated the date three
times for memory's sake. "Today is
Mr. Featherstone's birthday. Today
is the anniversary of Tilita's marriage. Insurance is payable, as are
25 the water, gas, and light bills."

Somewhere in the walls, relays
clicked, memory tapes glided under
electric eyes.

*Eight-one, tick-tock, eight-one
30 o'clock, off to school, off to work,
run, run, eight-one!* But no doors
slammed, no carpets took the soft
tread of rubber heels. It was raining
outside. The weather box on the
35 front door sang quietly: "Rain, rain,
go away; rubbers, raincoats for today . . ." And the rain tapped on the
empty house, echoing.

Outside, the garage chimed
40 and lifted its door to reveal the waiting car. After a long wait the door
swung down again.

At eight-thirty the eggs were
shriveled and the toast was like

45   stone. An aluminum wedge scraped them into the sink, where hot water whirled them down a metal throat which digested and flushed them away to the distant sea. The dirty
50   dishes were dropped into a hot washer and emerged twinkling dry.

     —Ray Bradbury, excerpted from "There Will Come Soft Rains," 1950

12. The house in the excerpt is best described as

(1) messy
(2) deserted
(3) dirty
(4) haunted
(5) aging

13. How are the details in the excerpt organized?

(1) order of importance (least significant details presented first)
(2) flashback (past events interspersed with events currently happening)
(3) general to specific (a general statement followed by specific details)
(4) time order (events presented in the order in which they might actually happen)
(5) main idea and example (a major point followed by specific instances)

14. The tone, or mood, of the excerpt can best be described as

(1) humorous
(2) cheerful
(3) sarcastic
(4) bitter
(5) lonely

15. Given the details in the excerpt, you can tell that the family

(1) liked doing housework
(2) enjoyed cooking breakfast together
(3) thought it was important to be well organized
(4) hated to be told what to do
(5) was unemployed and out of money

16. Which of the following TV programs would be the most likely to include an episode based on the excerpt?

(1) "Science Fiction Stories," which features dramas showing the interaction of people and technology of the future
(2) "The Model Home," which takes prospective home buyers on tours of houses that have the latest in home gadgets
(3) "Tomorrow Is Here," which presents documentaries on scientific innovations that are sweeping the United States
(4) "Comedy Showcase," which specializes in funny skits on subjects that are currently in the news
(5) "Tell Me How," which takes new inventions and explains to children how they work and who developed them

Questions 17–21 refer to the following excerpt from a short story.

LIKE FATHER, LIKE SON?

The last time I saw my father was in Grand Central Station. I was going from my grandmother's in the Adirondacks to a cottage on the
5 Cape that my mother had rented, and I wrote my father that I would be in New York between trains for an hour and a half, and asked if we could have lunch together. His sec-
10 retary wrote to say that he would meet me at the information booth at noon, and at twelve-o'clock sharp I saw him coming through the crowd. He was a stranger to me—my
15 mother divorced him three years ago and I hadn't been with him since—but as soon as I saw him I felt that he was my father, my flesh and blood, my future and my doom.
20 I knew that when I was grown I would be something like him; I would have to plan my campaigns within his limitations. He was a big, good-looking man, and I was terri-
25 bly happy to see him again. He struck me on the back and shook my hand. "Hi, Charlie," he said. "Hi, boy. I'd like to take you up to my club, but it's in the Sixties, and if you
30 have to catch an early train I guess we'd better get something to eat around here." He put his arm around me, and I smelled my father the way my mother sniffs a rose. It was a
35 rich compound of whiskey, after-shave lotion, shoe polish, woolens, and the rankness of a mature male. I hoped that someone would see us together. I wished that we could be
40 photographed. I wanted some rec-ord of our having been together.

—John Cheever,
excerpted from "Reunion," 1952

17. The father responded to his son's invitation by

(1) calling him on the telephone
(2) having his secretary write a note
(3) asking the boy's mother to call
(4) sending a messenger
(5) ignoring the boy's request

18. How did the son feel about seeing his father?

(1) angry and hostile
(2) nervous and hopeful
(3) happy and proud
(4) suspicious and wary
(5) bored and uninterested

19. What does the son mean when he says, "I knew that when I was grown I would be something like him [the father]; I would have to plan my campaigns within his limitations" (lines 20–23)?

(1) In the future, his father will try to tell him what to do.
(2) Like his father, he will have limited funds.
(3) As a man, he will have some of the same faults as his father.
(4) As an adult, he will support the same political party as his father.
(5) When he is grown, he will plan his life around his father's activities.

20. The fact that the father and son meet in a train station shows that the

(1) father is living in the streets
(2) two do not have a close relationship
(3) son has an unusually busy schedule
(4) rest of the family dislikes the two
(5) mother fears the father will hurt the son

21. Which of the following books would the father be most likely to read?

   (1) *The Frantic Father: How to Juggle Work and Family*
   (2) *Making a Killing: Your Guide to Increasing Business Profits*
   (3) *A Man's Right: You Can Win Custody of Your Child*
   (4) *Husband and Wife: Improving Communication with Your Spouse*
   (5) *Back to Work: How to Survive Unemployment and Find a Good Job*

Questions 22–27 refer to the following excerpt from a short story.

IS HE HIS MOTHER'S FAVORITE?

Life was very hard for the Whipples. It was hard to feed all the hungry mouths, it was hard to keep the children in flannels during the
5   winter, short as it was: "God knows what would become of us if we lived north," they would say: keeping them decently clean was hard. "It looks like our luck won't never let up
10 on us," said Mr. Whipple, but Mrs. Whipple was all for taking what was sent and calling it good, anyhow when the neighbors were in earshot. "Don't ever let a soul hear us com-
15 plain," she kept saying to her husband. She couldn't stand to be pitied. "No, not if it comes to it that we have to live in a wagon and pick cotton around the country," she said,
20 "nobody's going to get a chance to look down on us."
       Mrs. Whipple loved her second son, the simple-minded one, better than she loved the other two chil-
25 dren put together. She was forever saying so, and when she talked with certain of her neighbors, she would even throw in her husband and her mother for good measure.
30   "You needn't keep on saying it around," said Mr. Whipple, "you'll make people think nobody else has any feelings about Him but you."

35   "It's natural for a mother," Mrs. Whipple would remind him. "You know yourself it's more natural for a mother to be that way. People don't expect so much of fathers, some way."
40   This didn't keep the neighbors from talking plainly among themselves. "A Lord's pure mercy if He should die," they said. "It's the sins of the fathers," they agreed among
45 themselves. "There's bad blood and bad doings somewhere, you can bet on that." This behind the Whipples' backs. To their faces everybody said, "He's not so bad off. He'll be all
50 right yet. Look how He grows!"
       Mrs. Whipple hated to talk about it, she tried to keep her mind off it, but every time anybody set foot in the house, the subject always
55 came up, and she had to talk about Him first, before she could get on to anything else. It seemed to ease her mind. "I wouldn't have anything happen to Him for all the world, but
60 it just looks like I can't keep Him out of mischief. He's so strong and active, He's always into everything; He was like that since He could walk. It's actually funny sometimes, the
65 way He can do anything; it's laughable to see Him up to His tricks."

—Katherine Anne Porter, excerpted from "He," 1935

22. The second son suffers from

   (1) a dangerous blood disease
   (2) stunted growth
   (3) the effects of malnutrition
   (4) a severe learning disability
   (5) a crippling muscular disorder

23. Which of the following phrases best describes the Whipple family?

   (1) poor and struggling
   (2) isolated and feared
   (3) popular and admired
   (4) arrogant and conceited
   (5) open and honest

24. You learn about the Whipple family mainly through

   (1) descriptions made by the person telling the story

   (2) Mrs. Whipple's unspoken thoughts

   (3) dialogue between the Whipples and their neighbors

   (4) Mr. Whipple's comments to the reader

   (5) the interaction between the parents and their children

25. Mrs. Whipple fears that

   (1) she will have to become a migrant farm worker to earn a living

   (2) the second son's problems are God's punishment for being sinful

   (3) her husband and children think she doesn't love them

   (4) her family is angry with her for complaining too much

   (5) the neighbors might look down on her and the rest of the family

26. Imagine that you are planning to make a film version of the excerpt. Which of the following places would make the best setting for the story?

   (1) an urban neighborhood of high-rise apartments

   (2) a wealthy resort community in the mountains

   (3) a white-collar suburb of a large eastern city

   (4) an oceanside retirement village on the west coast

   (5) a small town in a southern state

27. That the Whipples refer to their second son as "He" instead of by name shows that they

   (1) think of the child as someone important

   (2) did not give much thought to their children's names

   (3) do not want the child to know when they are talking about him

   (4) view the child as different from their other children

   (5) want to draw people's attention to the child

Questions 28–30 refer to the following poem.

DID THESE FORMER CLASSMATES ENJOY THEIR REUNION?

25th High School Reunion

We come to hear the endings
of all the stories
in our anthology
of false starts:
5   how the girl who seemed
as hard as nails
was hammered into shape;
how the athletes ran
out of races;
10   how under the skin
our skulls rise
to the surface
like rocks in the bed
of a drying stream.
15   Look! We have all
turned into
ourselves.

—Linda Pastan, 1978

28. According to the speaker in the poem, the former classmates attend their twenty-fifth high school reunion to

(1) see what kind of physical shape everyone is in
(2) find out how people's lives have turned out
(3) reminisce about their school experiences
(4) cheer on the school's former athletic stars
(5) compare how much they all have aged

29. What is the meaning of the following comparison "under the skin / our skulls rise / to the surface / like rocks in the bed / of a drying stream" (lines 10–14)?

(1) The former students' facial features are as sharp and pointed as the rocks a person might find in a stream.
(2) Rocks that are located beneath the surface of a stream become visible when the water dries up.
(3) Just as rocks become prominent when a stream begins to dry up, so the skulls of the ex-classmates have become more prominent with age.
(4) The once-young students are now as old and shriveled as a stream that is losing its water supply.
(5) The manner in which the sun has dried out the skin of the former classmates is similar to the manner in which the sun dries out rocks in a stream.

30. The language used in the poem might best be described as

(1) flowery and poetic
(2) complex and hard to understand
(3) formal and scholarly
(4) unusual and original
(5) simple and conversational

Questions 31–34 refer to the following excerpt from a play.

DO THIS MOTHER AND SON SHARE IN THE AMERICAN DREAM?

DOLORES: I'll never be okay until I go home again.

JAVIER: [*Crossing to chair*]: Oh Mom . . .

5 DOLORES: What's wrong with you? The first sky you saw was a Puerto Rican sky. Your first drink of water was Puerto Rican water. But you don't re-
10 member. You were just a baby! But I remember. Son, I want to see chickens run across my yard, all year round. I want to hear my language spoken by
15 everyone I meet, even little children. Spanish is so beautiful when children speak it. I left everything I cared about when I left Puerto Rico.

20 JAVIER: Hasn't this ever been home?

DOLORES: Never. This place has never been any good to any of us—

25 JAVIER: It's been good to me. I think I can go far here. [*He crosses to Dolores and takes her hand.*]

DOLORES: I don't doubt that for a moment. But Ramon is not
30 you.

JAVIER: Is that why you can't accept this as your home?

DOLORES [*Crosses to her altar*]: This "home" took away my lit-
35 tle girl . . .

JAVIER: Mom, you've got to let her go. You've got to bury her. You can't blame this house for—

DOLORES: Yes I can!

40 JAVIER: It would have happened down there. She would have died down there—

DOLORES: For six days she lived
here! This cold house killed
45   her!

JAVIER: She was born sickly, Mom;
anything could've—

DOLORES: She was strong. I could
feel how strong she was. I
50   could feel it in her hands. I
could see it in her busy, red
face. I heard it when she cried.
[*Trying not to cry*] I came to
her. I warmed her. I held her
55   against me, keeping her from
the cold air in this dying house.
For six days Ramon worked on
the furnace, trying to make it
start, but it wouldn't start. One
60   day, as I was making the coffee, while Ramon was at work,
she died. I . . . stood by that
window for a whole day, facing
Puerto Rico. And poor Ramon.
65   He almost went crazy. [*She
starts to cry openly.*]

JAVIER: Oh Mom, don't do that.

—Jose Rivera, excerpted from
The House of Ramon Iglesia, 1983

31. In the excerpt, Dolores is
experiencing an inner conflict, or
psychological struggle, over the

(1) negative attitude her son
has developed toward his
new home
(2) difficulty of speaking
Spanish in an English-
speaking community
(3) difference between life in
Puerto Rico and life in the
United States
(4) inability of her husband,
Ramon, to find a job with
a future
(5) family's move to a
chicken farm in a
Hispanic community

32. Dolores blames her daughter's
death on

(1) Ramon
(2) a birth defect
(3) Javier
(4) the cold air
(5) dirty water

33. Read the stage directions for the
character of Javier in line 3 and
lines 26–27. The character's
actions and his conversation with
Dolores reveal him to be

(1) nervous
(2) explosive
(3) rigid
(4) shy
(5) caring

34. How does Javier feel about his
future?

(1) confident
(2) worried
(3) depressed
(4) angry
(5) confused

Questions 35–40 refer to the following
excerpt from a review of a play.

WHAT IS THE PLAY ABOUT?

Fifty years ago, a struggle
erupted in Munich that sadly seems
timely today also: Five brave university students published and distrib-
5   uted throughout Germany and Austria anonymous anti-Nazi leaflets
entitled "The White Rose." Their
propaganda was a rare public act of
defiance against the vicious Third
10   Reich.
Arrested by the Gestapo on
February 22, 1943, the freedom
fighters of the White Rose were
quickly put on trial for high treason
15   and denied the defense of a jury,
press coverage or the opportunity
to appeal. The punishment was
grimly predictable.

Honoring these young idealists
and chronicling the moral struggle
of the security officer who must decide their fate, "The White Rose," . . .
written by Lillian Garrett-Groag, . . .
is inspired in part by the experience
of the playwright's father, an Aus-
trian who fled Vienna in 1938 to
avoid the Nazis' takeover.

Even more relevantly, the play
reminds us how history can repeat
itself, as in the recent resurgence of
neo-Nazi intolerance at home and
abroad.

Director Russell Vanden-
broucke believes that this history
play speaks to the present. "The
playwright uses the story not so
much to talk about the kids, who
were educated and cultured idealists, but about the man in whose
hands their fate lies. Unlike many
today, they put their ideas to action
and they had the audacity to believe
the things their teachers taught
them about free thinking and
justice.

"What's hard is for the audience
to see themselves, not in these cou-
rageous students, but in the policeman, a man who is also forced to
take a stand. In reality, the Gestapo
officer gave Sophie Scholl, a member of the White Rose, a chance to
escape; she refused."

—Lawrence Bommer,
" 'White Rose' Celebrates Anti-Nazi
Heroes," *Chicago Tribune*,
March 5, 1993

35. According to the excerpt, the
playwright was inspired to write
The White Rose as a result of her

(1) arrest by the Gestapo in
Nazi Germany
(2) experiences as a World War II
journalist in Munich
(3) father's escape from the Nazis
in Vienna
(4) friendship with anti-Nazi
artists in Berlin
(5) participation in the trial of
freedom fighters in Austria

36. The white rose of the play's title
refers to

(1) the main character of the play
(2) a group of students and the
leaflets they published
(3) the European village where
the play takes place
(4) a German officer and his
special force of soldiers
(5) the flower the townspeople
presented to their slain leader

37. The primary purpose of the first
three paragraphs of the excerpt
is to

(1) let readers know whether the
play is worth seeing
(2) give background information
about events dramatized in
the play
(3) publicize the play and
generate interest in seeing it
(4) summarize the content of the
first act of the play
(5) describe the strengths and
weaknesses of the play's plot

38. According to the excerpt, on
which of the following aspects of
the play does the director focus?

(1) the idealism of the upper class
in Germany
(2) Sophie Scholl's refusal
to escape
(3) neo-Nazism in the United
States and Europe
(4) the difficult moral decision
made by the Gestapo officer
(5) the punishment that the
government inflicted on
its enemies

39. The central situation of the play is similar to which of the following more recent world events? The

    (1) Chinese government's execution of young people who protested in Tiananmen Square for government reform

    (2) disbanding of the Union of Soviet Socialist Republics (U.S.S.R.) after the collapse of the communist government

    (3) United Nations relief mission into Somalia to maintain order and distribute food and medical supplies

    (4) conflict between people of different ethnic groups in the formerly communist state of Yugoslavia

    (5) trial and acquittal in Israel of "Ivan the Terrible," a retired autoworker accused of murdering prisoners in a Nazi death camp

40. The reviewer's writing style is characterized by the

    (1) reliance on slang and other informal language

    (2) lack of description and other vivid words

    (3) development of a bitter, negative tone

    (4) use of long, flowing sentences

    (5) large number of witty puns

Questions 41–45 refer to the following excerpt from a book review.

WHAT IS THE BOOK *IN MY PLACE* ABOUT?

[Charlayne] Hunter-Gault, now a well-known television correspondent, was one of the two black students whose entrance to the University
5 of Georgia in 1961 desegregated that institution—with much national attention and local uproar. Her graceful and unpretentious memoir, however, is concerned less
10 with that civil-rights triumph than with what it was like to grow up as the daughter of a distinguished dynasty of preachers in a generally self-sufficient minority community.
15 The Hunters were not poor—her father was an Army chaplain—and unpleasant collisions with neighboring whites were either unknown or have been omitted. The brick-throwing
20 that greeted the author at the university is described without rancor, as her commitment to the cause of civil rights is described without heat. One learns about segregated
25 schools (poor equipment, dedicated teachers), visits to farming relatives with lavish tables, prom dresses, and Ms. Hunter-Gault's early addiction to journalism by way of the
30 *Brenda Starr* comic strip. Most of these amiable recollections—including the compulsory home-economics class in which she learned "how to make white sauce"—parallel
35 white experience. Perhaps the implication of similarity was precisely Ms. Hunter-Gault's intention. It is only in the book's final chapter, containing her address to the graduat-
40 ing class of 1988 at the University of Georgia, that she speaks bluntly of the need for "acknowledging the guiding principles of fundamental human decency and then living by
45 them" in "a waiting and needful world."

—Review of *In My Place*,
The Atlantic, December 1992

41. According to the review, Hunter-Gault grew up

   (1) on a prosperous farm
   (2) near a university campus
   (3) by the ocean
   (4) in a poor neighborhood
   (5) in a minority community

42. Hunter-Gault was a victim of racism when she

   (1) went to her father's church
   (2) visited relatives who farmed
   (3) enrolled at the University of Georgia
   (4) walked into her home economics class
   (5) spoke at a graduation ceremony

43. Hunter-Gault might describe her childhood as

   (1) happy
   (2) violent
   (3) insecure
   (4) tragic
   (5) lonely

44. Most of the review focuses on

   (1) persuading readers that Hunter-Gault's book is badly written
   (2) making suggestions on how the book might be improved
   (3) pointing out and correcting factual errors in the book
   (4) giving an overview of the contents of the book
   (5) providing background information on Hunter-Gault's TV career

45. According to the review, Hunter-Gault's book consists mainly of

   (1) her impressions of what it was like to grow up in her family and community
   (2) an explanation of how the civil rights movement developed in the United States
   (3) her recollections of racist acts committed by whites in her neighborhood
   (4) an account of the profound difference between black and white life experiences
   (5) her descriptions of life as the first African-American TV anchor

   Answers begin on page 911.

PRACTICE TEST 4:
LITERATURE AND THE ARTS ANSWER KEY

1. (1) In lines 14–18, the author says, "Any listener could have asked me: if things were so grand in San Francisco, what had brought me back to a dusty mote of Arkansas?"

2. (3) The author states in lines 7–9, "a pretension to worldliness was expected of me, and I was too happy to disappoint."

3. (2) The author refers to the town as "a dusty mote" and makes reference to "Southern rural blacks," and all the people in the town seem to know each other.

4. (4) In the last sentence of the excerpt, the author states that she was "flattered to receive such acceptance."

5. (5) Just before quoting the conversation, the author says, "the farmers acknowledged my maturity" and "found subtler ways to make their wants known." The conversation illustrates the subtler, more polite ways. In addition, the author says directly after the conversation, "I had seen the formality of black adult equals all my youth but had never considered that a time would come when I, too, could participate." This statement sums up the purpose of the conversation—to show proper etiquette among adults in her community.

6. (3) The excerpt states that in the value system of rural southern African-Americans, "age has more worth than wealth, and religious piety more value than beauty" (lines 49–51).

7. (5) Lines 4–5 state that Casey expects to become a first baseman for the Red Sox.

8. (3) According to line 30, "baseball cards clog her [Casey's] room."

9. (1) Throughout the excerpt, the author gives examples of women's and girls' participation in baseball. She mentions female sportswriters, fans, and a bat girl.

10. (4) In lines 30–37, the author says, "At spring training batting practice . . . I look down at the crowd of kids. Half of them are girls. This is new." The final sentence gives a specific example of another new development—the traditionally male job of bat boy now being filled by a female.

11. (1) Throughout the excerpt, the author is supportive of her daughter's and other females' interest in baseball.

12. (2) Lines 5–6 state that the house is empty.

13. (4) Details are arranged chronologically. At the beginning of the excerpt, it is 7:00 in the morning. The next major actions occur at 7:09, 8:01, and 8:30.

14. (5) Note the repetition of the words *empty* and *emptiness* and descriptions such as the following: "the rain tapped on the empty house, echoing" (lines 37–38).

15. (3) Given the number of electronic-voice messages that remind the family of important dates (a birthday, an anniversary, payments due), one can infer that the family valued being well organized.

16. (1) The excerpt is primarily about the interaction of people and technology of the future—more specifically, the absurdity of technology divorced from humanity.

17. (2) In lines 9–11, the son says, "His secretary wrote to say that he would meet me."

18. (3) The son expresses happiness when he says, "He was a big, good-looking man, and I was terribly happy to see him again" (lines 23–25). The son expresses pride when he says, "I hoped that someone would see us together. I wished that we could be photographed. I wanted some record of our having been together" (lines 37–41).

19. (3) In lines 17–19, the son says, "as soon as I saw him I felt that he was . . . my future and my doom." The use of the word *doom* indicates that the son expects to display some of the same weaknesses or failings as his father.

20. (2) Had the father and son shared a close relationship, it is likely that they would have met in a more intimate setting. The psychological distance between the two characters is underscored by the fact that they meet in a train station—an impersonal place where strangers sit side-by-side without communicating.

21. (2) The father's life appears to revolve around his job.

22. (4) Line 23 states that the son is "simple-minded," an old-fashioned way of saying that the child has a severe learning disability.

23. (1) According to the first two sentences of the excerpt, "Life was very hard for the Whipples. It was hard to feed all the hungry mouths, it was hard to keep the children in flannels during the winter, short as it was. . . ."

24. (1) Throughout the excerpt, the narrator, or person telling the story, describes what the Whipples are like. Note, for example, the first two sentences of the excerpt, all of the second paragraph, and the first two sentences of the last paragraph.

25. (5) Lines 10–17 state that "Mrs. Whipple was all for taking what was sent and calling it good, anyhow when the neighbors were in earshot. . . . She couldn't stand to be pitied."

26. (5) According to the excerpt, the story takes place in a location where the winters are short (line 5) and it is possible to pick cotton for a living (lines 18–19). These details point to a small southern town.

27. (4) By referring to the child only by pronoun, the parents set him apart from their other children.

28. (2) In the first two lines of the poem, the speaker says, "We come to hear the endings / of all the stories."

29. (3) This complex comparison rests on two analogies. The first similarity is between a stream that is drying up and an aging person whose life is "drying up." The second similarity is between rocks jutting out from a stream that is drying out and the increasing prominence of the facial bones of a person who is aging. Note that all the comparisons in the poem develop the idea of people changing and "turning into themselves" over the course of time.

30. (5) Typical of the poem's language is the vocabulary of the last three lines—"Look! We have all / turned into / ourselves." Note that the vocabulary in these lines is commonplace, easy to understand, and could be heard in an informal conversation between friends.

31. (3) Dolores's inner conflict is expressed in the first line of the excerpt—"I'll never be okay until I go home again."

32. (4) In lines 44–45, Dolores says, "This cold house killed her!"

33. (5) Javier shows a caring attitude toward his mother when he crosses the room to be closer to her, takes her hand in his, and tries to calm her by saying, "Oh Mom, don't do that."

34. (1) Javier displays confidence in his future when he says, "I think I can go far here" (lines 25–26).

35. (3) Lines 24–27 explain that the playwright was inspired to write the play because her father had fled Vienna to escape the Nazi takeover.

36. (2) The first sentence of the excerpt refers to the anti-Nazi leaflets as "The White Rose." Later, in lines 51–52, the reviewer quotes the director of the play as saying that Sophie Scholl was "a member of the White Rose." His statement indicates that the group of student freedom fighters took its name from the leaflets it published.

37. (2) Because the play is based on actual incidents involving people who are not well known, the reviewer needs to provide background information at the beginning of the review.

38. (4) In lines 35–40, the reviewer states, "The playwright uses the story not so much to talk about the kids, who were educated and cultured idealists, but about the [Gestapo officer] in whose hands their fate lies."

39. (1) In each incident—that which involved the White Rose and that which took place in Tiananmen Square—university students were executed for protesting against a government that they viewed as immoral.

40. (4) The sentence structure of the review tends to be sophisticated. Most of the sentences are complex, and even simple sentences contain many qualifying phrases.

41. (5) Line 14 states that Hunter-Gault grew up in a "self-sufficient minority community."

42. (3) The first sentence of the excerpt refers to Hunter-Gault's enrollment in the University of Georgia and the part she played in desegregating the school. Lines 19–21 mention that campus racists threw bricks at Hunter-Gault.

43. (1) The anecdotes that Hunter-Gault chose to include—recollections of attending dinners at relatives' farms, shopping for prom dresses, and reading newspaper comic strips—exemplify a happy and normal childhood. Note that the reviewer characterizes Hunter-Gault's recollections as "amiable" (line 31).

44. (4) The excerpt is primarily informational, focusing on the content of the book rather than on criticism. Note that the reviewer never makes mention of the quality of the writing or of the strengths and weaknesses of the book.

45. (1) The second sentence of the excerpt says, "[Hunter-Gault's] memoir . . . is concerned less with that civil-rights triumph [the desegregation of the University of Georgia] than with what it was like to grow up as the daughter of a distinguished dynasty of preachers in a generally self-sufficient minority community."

Use the answer key on pages 911–913 to check your answers to the Practice Test. Then find the item number of each question you missed and circle it on the chart below to determine the reading skill and content areas in which you need more practice. Pay particular attention to areas where you missed half or more of the questions. The reading skills are covered on pages 187–243. The page numbers for the content areas are listed below on the chart. Knowledge of reading skill and content area–based questions is absolutely essential for success on the GED Literature and the Arts Test. For those questions that you missed, review the pages indicated.

PRACTICE TEST 4: LITERATURE AND THE ARTS EVALUATION CHART

Skill Area/ Content Area	Comprehension (pages 189–195)	Application (pages 195–199)	Analysis (pages 200–210)
Prose Fiction (pages 453–482)	12, 15, 17, 18, 19, 20, 22, 23, 25, 27	16, 21, 26	13, 14, 24
Poetry (pages 483–502)	28		29, 30
Drama (pages 503–518)	31, 32, 34		33
Nonfiction Prose (pages 519–536)	1, 2, 3, 4, 7, 8, 9	6, 11	5, 10
Commentaries (pages 537–546)	35, 36, 38, 41, 42, 43, 44, 45	39	37, 40

PRACTICE TEST 5: MATHEMATICS

The Mathematics Practice Test will give you the opportunity to evaluate your readiness for the actual GED Mathematics Test.

The test contains 56 questions and should take approximately 90 minutes to complete. At the end of 90 minutes, stop and mark your place. Then finish the test. This will give you an idea of whether or not you can finish the real GED Test in the time allotted. Try to answer as many questions as you can. A blank will count as a wrong answer, so make a reasonable guess for answers to questions you are not sure of.

When you are finished with the test, check your answers and turn to the Evaluation Chart on page 926 and the GED Readiness Worksheet on page 927. Use the chart and worksheet to evaluate whether or not you are ready to take the actual GED Test and, if not, in what areas you need more work.

You may find the formulas on page 815 useful for some of the problems.

PRACTICE TEST 5: MATHEMATICS ANSWER GRID

1 ① ② ③ ④ ⑤	15 ① ② ③ ④ ⑤	29 ① ② ③ ④ ⑤	43 ① ② ③ ④ ⑤
2 ① ② ③ ④ ⑤	16 ① ② ③ ④ ⑤	30 ① ② ③ ④ ⑤	44 ① ② ③ ④ ⑤
3 ① ② ③ ④ ⑤	17 ① ② ③ ④ ⑤	31 ① ② ③ ④ ⑤	45 ① ② ③ ④ ⑤
4 ① ② ③ ④ ⑤	18 ① ② ③ ④ ⑤	32 ① ② ③ ④ ⑤	46 ① ② ③ ④ ⑤
5 ① ② ③ ④ ⑤	19 ① ② ③ ④ ⑤	33 ① ② ③ ④ ⑤	47 ① ② ③ ④ ⑤
6 ① ② ③ ④ ⑤	20 ① ② ③ ④ ⑤	34 ① ② ③ ④ ⑤	48 ① ② ③ ④ ⑤
7 ① ② ③ ④ ⑤	21 ① ② ③ ④ ⑤	35 ① ② ③ ④ ⑤	49 ① ② ③ ④ ⑤
8 ① ② ③ ④ ⑤	22 ① ② ③ ④ ⑤	36 ① ② ③ ④ ⑤	50 ① ② ③ ④ ⑤
9 ① ② ③ ④ ⑤	23 ① ② ③ ④ ⑤	37 ① ② ③ ④ ⑤	51 ① ② ③ ④ ⑤
10 ① ② ③ ④ ⑤	24 ① ② ③ ④ ⑤	38 ① ② ③ ④ ⑤	52 ① ② ③ ④ ⑤
11 ① ② ③ ④ ⑤	25 ① ② ③ ④ ⑤	39 ① ② ③ ④ ⑤	53 ① ② ③ ④ ⑤
12 ① ② ③ ④ ⑤	26 ① ② ③ ④ ⑤	40 ① ② ③ ④ ⑤	54 ① ② ③ ④ ⑤
13 ① ② ③ ④ ⑤	27 ① ② ③ ④ ⑤	41 ① ② ③ ④ ⑤	55 ① ② ③ ④ ⑤
14 ① ② ③ ④ ⑤	28 ① ② ③ ④ ⑤	42 ① ② ③ ④ ⑤	56 ① ② ③ ④ ⑤

Solve each problem.

1. Compact discs are on sale at Super Sounds for $6.89 each. Which of the following is closest to the price of five discs?

   (1) $25
   (2) $35
   (3) $40
   (4) $45
   (5) $49

2. Gonzalo is a brick mason. Let x stand for the hourly wage he pays his apprentice. Gonzalo makes $5 more than three times the wage of his apprentice. Which of the following expresses Gonzalo's hourly wage?

   (1) $3x + 5$
   (2) $3(x + 5)$
   (3) $3x + 3$
   (4) $x + 5$
   (5) $3x$

3. Assuming no waste, how many boards each $1\frac{1}{2}$ feet long can be cut from a board that is 12 feet long?

   (1) 6
   (2) 8
   (3) 9
   (4) 15
   (5) 18

4. The figure below shows the plan of the living room and the dining room of a house. What is the area in square feet of the floors of both rooms?

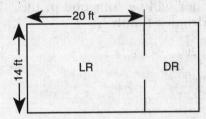

   (1)   68
   (2) 140
   (3) 280
   (4) 420
   (5) not enough information is given

5. What is the perimeter of the figure pictured below?

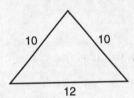

   (1) 20
   (2) 22
   (3) 32
   (4) 40
   (5) 44

6. Each of the four members of the Rodriguez family bought a ticket for a music festival. A total of 360 tickets were sold. If one ticket holder will win the grand prize, what is the probability that the winner will be someone in the Rodriguez family?

   (1) $\frac{1}{200}$

   (2) $\frac{1}{100}$

   (3) $\frac{1}{90}$

   (4) $\frac{1}{36}$

   (5) $\frac{1}{4}$

7. When Abdul was 20 years old, he weighed 150 pounds. When he was 40, he weighed 180 pounds. By what percent did his weight increase in those years?

   (1) 10
   (2) 20
   (3) 30
   (4) $33\frac{1}{3}$
   (5) 40

8. If $3m + 6 = 30$, what is the value of m?

   (1) 4
   (2) 6
   (3) 8
   (4) 10
   (5) 12

9. In a recent year, 327,000 Americans were employed as fire fighters. What is this number rounded to the nearest 10,000?

   (1) 320,000
   (2) 325,000
   (3) 327,000
   (4) 328,000
   (5) 330,000

Use the following information to answer questions 10 and 11.

A man's shirt is listed in a catalog for $30. Below is a list of prices for the same shirt at several stores.

Clyde's Clothes	$24
Sam's Supply	$32
Florence's Fashion	$33
Dave's Duds	$27
Alma's Apparel	$35

10. For which store is the price of the shirt *10% less* than the catalog price?

    (1) Clyde's Clothes
    (2) Sam's Supply
    (3) Florence's Fashion
    (4) Dave's Duds
    (5) Alma's Apparel

11. For a Labor Day sale, Florence's Fashion has all clothes marked $\frac{1}{3}$ off the regular price. What will be the price of the shirt during the sale?

    (1) $11
    (2) $22
    (3) $27
    (4) $30
    (5) $32

12. Below is a plan of a rectangular vegetable garden. Which of the following represents the number of feet of fencing required to enclose the garden?

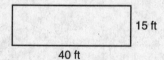

15 ft

40 ft

    (1) 40×15
    (2) $40 + 15$
    (3) $2(40) + 15$
    (4) $(40 + 15)^2$
    (5) $2(40) + 2(15)$

13. What is the value of $20^2 + 2^3$?

    (1)   46
    (2)   48
    (3) 392
    (4) 408
    (5) 484

14. What is the ratio of the width to the height of the door illustrated below?

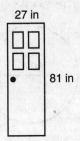

27 in

81 in

    (1) 2:3
    (2) 1:2
    (3) 1:3
    (4) 2:7
    (5) 1:8

15. For the rectangle pictured below, which side is parallel to *AB*?

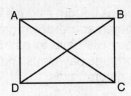

    (1) *AC*
    (2) *AD*
    (3) *BC*
    (4) *BD*
    (5) *CD*

The graph below shows the percent of the U.S. population living in each of the four major areas in the continental United States. Use the graph to answer questions 16 and 17.

DISTRIBUTION OF U.S. POPULATION

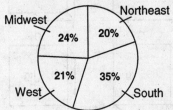

16. What fraction of the population lives in the South?

    (1) $\frac{1}{5}$
    (2) $\frac{1}{4}$
    (3) $\frac{1}{3}$
    (4) $\frac{7}{20}$
    (5) $\frac{13}{20}$

17. The population of the United States is about 250,000,000. Approximately how many people live in the Northeast?

    (1) 15 million
    (2) 20 million
    (3) 25 million
    (4) 35 million
    (5) 50 million

18. Arrange the packages pictured below in order from *lightest to heaviest*.

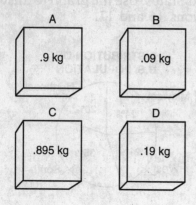

(1) A, D, C, B
(2) D, B, C, A
(3) B, D, C, A
(4) A, B, D, C
(5) B, A, C, D

Use the figure below to answer questions 19 and 20.

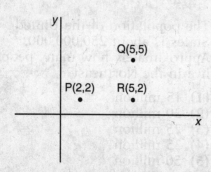

19. What is the distance between *P* and *R*?

(1) 1
(2) 2
(3) 3
(4) 4
(5) 5

20. What is the distance between *P* and *Q*?

(1) 3
(2) $\sqrt{3^2 + 3^2}$
(3) 5
(4) 3^2
(5) 5^2

21. If $4n - 9 = 31$, then

(1) $n = 4$
(2) $n = 5$
(3) $n = 8$
(4) $n = 10$
(5) $n = 12$

22. The figure below shows the plan of a pool. Which of the following is closest in feet to the distance around the pool?

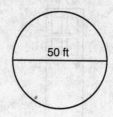

(1) 1.57
(2) 15.7
(3) 157
(4) 314
(5) 1963

Use the following information to answer questions 23–25.

The Martins bought a house that cost $80,000. They made a down payment of $12,000. They will have to pay $420 a month in mortgage payments and $700 a year in real estate taxes.

23. The down payment was what percent of the total cost of the house?

(1) 9
(2) 10
(3) 12
(4) 15
(5) 20

24. Which expression represents the Martins' yearly mortgage payments and real estate taxes?

(1) $\frac{\$420}{12}$
(2) $\frac{\$700}{12}$
(3) 12($420)
(4) 12($700)
(5) 12($420) + $700

25. The difference between the total cost of the house and the down payment is the amount of the mortgage. How much is their mortgage?

(1) $63,000
(2) $68,000
(3) $73,000
(4) $85,000
(5) $92,000

---

26. A team can assemble 15 machine parts in two hours. How many parts can it assemble in a 40-hour workweek?

(1) 180
(2) 200
(3) 240
(4) 300
(5) 360

27. What is the diagonal distance *JL* for the rectangle pictured below?

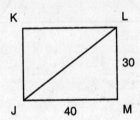

(1) 30
(2) 40
(3) 50
(4) 60
(5) 70

28. Find the distance in meters around a monument whose base is a square measuring 4.5 meters on each side.

(1) 4(4.5)
(2) $\frac{2.5}{2}$
(3) 2(4.5)
(4) $(4.5)^2$
(5) 4.5 + 4.5

29. The Greek letter π (pi) is defined as the ratio of the circumference (*C*) divided by the diameter (*d*) of a circle. Which of the following represents π?

(1) $\frac{C}{d}$
(2) $\frac{(C + d)}{2}$
(3) $\frac{d}{C}$
(4) $\frac{Cd}{2}$
(5) $\frac{(C - d)}{2}$

30. Which of the following represents the volume in cubic inches of the rectangular box pictured below?

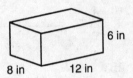

(1) 12 × 8
(2) 12 + 8
(3) 12 × 8 × 6
(4) 2(12 + 8)
(5) 6(8 + 12)

31. If $12a - 5 = 4a + 11$, then $a =$

(1) 2
(2) 3
(3) 5
(4) 8
(5) 12

32. The choices below list the price of an 8-ounce package of fish sticks at five different stores. Which is least expensive?

(1) 2 for $3
(2) $1.29 each
(3) 10 for $9
(4) $4.49 for 4
(5) $3.99 for 3

33. The expression $3a - 12$ is the same as which of the following?

    (1) $3(a - 4)$
    (2) $3(a - 12)$
    (3) $12(a - 3)$
    (4) $3(4a)$
    (5) $3a(12)$

34. Find the number of degrees in $\angle C$ of the triangle pictured below.

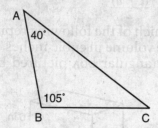

    (1) 25
    (2) 35
    (3) 60
    (4) 70
    (5) 90

Use the number line below to answer question 35.

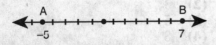

35. How many units apart are points A and B?

    (1) 2
    (2) 5
    (3) 7
    (4) 12
    (5) 35

36. If $y = 2x - 5$, what is the value of y when $x = 3$?

    (1) -1
    (2) 0
    (3) 1
    (4) 3
    (5) 7

37. Which of the following equals $(1.5)^2$?

    (1) .75
    (2) 2.25
    (3) 3
    (4) 4.5
    (5) 15

38. Which of the following represents the area of the figure below?

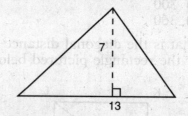

    (1) $2 \times 13 \times 7$

    (2) 13×7

    (3) $2(13) + 2(7)$

    (4) $\frac{1}{2}(13 + 7)$

    (5) $\frac{1}{2} \times 13 \times 7$

39. Giorgos drove for three hours at an average speed of 55 mph and then for another two hours at 40 mph. Which of the following represents the total distance that he drove?

    (1) 5×45

    (2) 5×95

    (3) $55 \times 3 + 2$

    (4) $55 \times 3 + 40 \times 2$

    (5) $\frac{(55 + 40)}{5}$

40. For the figure below, $QR = 120$. What is the length of PQ?

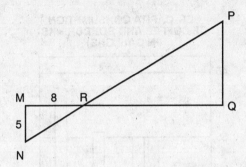

    (1)   15
    (2)   24
    (3)   64
    (4)   75
    (5) 100

41. If $x - 6 > 24$, then

    (1) $x > 4$
    (2) $x > 6$
    (3) $x > 24$
    (4) $x > 28$
    (5) $x > 30$

42. At the rate of $9 an hour, how much does Shirley make in $1\frac{1}{2}$ hours?

    (1) $4.50
    (2) $11.50
    (3) $13.50
    (4) $18
    (5) not enough information is given

43. Find the slope of the line that passes through the two points indicated on the graph below.

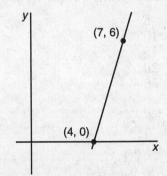

    (1) 2
    (2) 3
    (3) 4
    (4) 6
    (5) 7

44. The scale on a map is 1 inch = 60 miles. Two towns are 80 miles apart. Find the distance in inches between the towns on the map.

    (1) $1\frac{1}{3}$
    (2) $1\frac{3}{4}$
    (3) 2
    (4) $2\frac{1}{3}$
    (5) $2\frac{2}{3}$

45. Sam bought 2 brushes for $8 each and 3 gallons of paint for $15 each. Which of the following represents the total dollar cost of the purchases?

    (1) $2(8) + 3(15)$
    (2) $2(15) + 3(8)$
    (3) $5(23)$
    (4) $(2 + 3) \times (8 + 15)$
    (5) $\frac{(2 + 8 + 15)}{3}$

46. The diameter of the cylinder pictured below is 10. What is the volume of the cylinder?

    (1)   10
    (2)   100
    (3)   314
    (4) 3140
    (5) not enough information is given

47. If 7 more than 6 times a number is 19, what is the number?

    (1) 1
    (2) 2
    (3) 3
    (4) 6
    (5) 9

Use the illustration below to answer question 48.

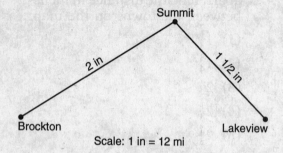

48. What is the distance in miles from Brocton to Lakeview by way of Summit?

    (1) 18
    (2) 24
    (3) 30
    (4) 36
    (5) 42

---

49. Which of the following expresses "3 less than a number squared?"

    (1) $2x - 3$
    (2) $x^2 - 3$
    (3) $x^3 - 2$
    (4) $3x - 2$
    (5) $2(x - 3)$

50. Maxine is 20 years older than her daughter Pilar. Let y stand for Maxine's age. Which equation expresses the sum of Maxine's and her daughter's ages if the sum of their ages equals 58?

    (1) $y + 20 = 58$
    (2) $y - 20 = 58$
    (3) $2y - 20 = 58$
    (4) $20y = 58$
    (5) $\frac{y}{20} = 58$

51. Simplify the expression $7s - 4s$.

    (1) $28s$
    (2) $11s$
    (3) $11s^2$
    (4) $3s$
    (5) s

Use the graph below to answer questions 52 and 53.

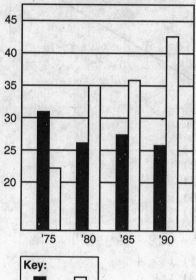

52. Approximately how many gallons of coffee were consumed per capita in 1975?

    (1) 22
    (2) 27
    (3) 31
    (4) 35
    (5) 42

53. By approximately how many gallons did the yearly consumption of soft drinks increase from 1975 to 1990?

    (1) 5
    (2) 10
    (3) 15
    (4) 20
    (5) 25

54. In a recent year, the U.S. government received $98,000,000,000 in corporate income tax. Which of the following expresses that number in scientific notation?

(1) 98×10^6
(2) 9.8×10^6
(3) 9.8×10^8
(4) 9.8×10^{10}
(5) 9.8×10^{12}

55. At a cost of $.90 per linear foot, what is the price of a board that is 78 inches long?

(1) $4.95
(2) $5.40
(3) $5.85
(4) $7.02
(5) $7.20

56. Which of the following expresses the relationship among the sides of the figure below?

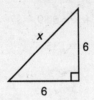

(1) $x = 6 + 6$
(2) $x = 2(6)$
(3) $x = 2(6) + 2(6)$
(4) $x = \dfrac{(6 + 6)}{2}$
(5) $x^2 = 6^2 + 6^2$

Answers begin on page 924.

PRACTICE TESTS

PRACTICE TEST 5: MATHEMATICS
ANSWER KEY

1. (2) $35

$c = nr$ $r = \$6.89 \cong \$7$
$c = 5 \times \$6.89$ $c \cong 5 \times \$7$
$c = \$34.45$ $c \cong \$35$
The closest is $35.

2. (1) $3x + 5$

3. (2) 8

$12 \div 1\frac{1}{2} =$
$\frac{12}{1} \div \frac{3}{2}$
$\frac{12}{1} \times \frac{2}{3} = \frac{24}{3} = 8$

4. (5) not enough information is given
You do not know the width of the dining room.

5. (3) 32

$P = a + b + c$
$P = 10 + 10 + 12$
$P = 32$

6. (3) $\frac{1}{90}$

$\dfrac{\text{family members}}{\text{total tickets}} \quad \dfrac{4}{360} = \dfrac{1}{90}$

7. (2) 20%

$\begin{array}{r} 180 \\ -\ 150 \\ \hline 30 \end{array}$ $\dfrac{30}{150} = \dfrac{x}{100}$

$150x = 3000$
$x = 20\%$

8. (3) 8

$3m + 6 = 30$
$\quad\ -\ 6 \quad -\ 6$
$\dfrac{3m}{3} = \dfrac{24}{3}$
$m = 8$

9. (5) 330,000
3̲27,000 to the nearest 10,000 is 330,000.

10. (4) Dave's Duds

$\dfrac{x}{\$30} = \dfrac{10}{100}$

$\begin{array}{r} \$30 \\ -\ \$3 \\ \hline \$27 \end{array}$

$100x = \$300$
$x = \$3$

11. (2) $22

$\dfrac{1}{3} \times \dfrac{33}{1}$ $\begin{array}{r} \$33 \\ -\$11 \\ \hline \$22 \end{array}$

12. (5) $2(40) + 2(15)$

$P = 2l + 2w$
$P = 2(40) + 2(15)$

13. (4) 408

$20^2 + 2^3 =$
$20 \times 20 + 2 \times 2 \times 2 =$
$400 + 8 = 408$

14. (3) 1:3
width:height = 27:81 = 1:3

15. (5) CD

16. (4) $\frac{7}{20}$

$35\% = \dfrac{35}{100} = \dfrac{7}{20}$

17. (5) 50 million

$20\% = \dfrac{1}{5}$

$\dfrac{1}{5} \times 250,000,000 = 50,000,000$

18. (3) B, D, C, A
A = 0.9 = 0.900
B = 0.09 = 0.090
C = 0.895
D = 0.19 = 0.190

19. (3) 3
R is 3 units to the right of P.

20. (2) $\sqrt{3^2 + 3^2}$

$d = \sqrt{(x_2 - x_1)^2 + (y_2 - y_1)^2}$
$d = \sqrt{(5 - 2)^2 + (5 - 2)^2}$
$d = \sqrt{3^2 + 3^2}$

21. (4) $n = 10$

$\begin{array}{rcr} 4n - 9 & = & 31 \\ +9 & & +9 \\ \hline \dfrac{4n}{4} & = & \dfrac{40}{4} \\ n & = & 10 \end{array}$

22. (3) 157

$C = \pi d$
$C = 3.14 \times 50$
$C = 157$

23. (4) 15

$\dfrac{\$12,000}{\$80,000} = \dfrac{3}{20}$

$\dfrac{3}{20} = \dfrac{x}{100}$

$20x = 300$
$x = 15\%$

24. (5) $12(\$420) + \$700$

25. (2) $68,000

$\begin{array}{lr} \text{total cost} & \$80,000 \\ \text{down payment} & -\$12,000 \\ \hline \text{mortgage} & \$68,000 \end{array}$

26. (4) 300

$\dfrac{\text{parts}}{\text{hours}} \quad \dfrac{15}{2} = \dfrac{x}{40}$

$2x = 600$
$x = 300$

27. (3) 50

$c^2 = a^2 + b^2$
$c^2 = 40^2 + 30^2$
$c^2 = 1600 + 900$
$c = \sqrt{2500}$
$c = 50$

28. (1) $4(4.5)$

$P = 4s$
$P = 4(4.5)$

29. (1) $\dfrac{C}{d}$

30. (3) $12 \times 8 \times 6$

$V = lwh$
$V = 12 \times 8 \times 6$

31. (1) 2

$$12a - 5 = \quad 4a + 11$$
$$\underline{-4a} \qquad \underline{-4a}$$
$$8a \;\; -5 = \qquad 11$$
$$\underline{+5} \qquad \underline{+5}$$
$$\frac{8a}{8} = \qquad \frac{16}{8}$$
$$a = \qquad 2$$

32. (3) 10 for $9

Choice (1) is $3 \div 2 = \$1.50$ each.
Choice (2) is $1.29 each.
Choice (3) is $9 \div 10 = \$.90$ each.
Choice (4) is $4.49 \div 4 = \$1.12$ each.
Choice (5) is $3.99 \div 3 = \$1.33$ each.

33. (1) $3(a - 4)$

Divide each term by 3:
$3a - 12 = 3(a - 4)$

34. (2) 35

$$\begin{array}{cc} 105° & 180° \\ \underline{+\;40°} & \underline{-145°} \\ 145° & 35° \end{array}$$

35. (4) 12

Point A is 5 units to the left of 0.
Point B is 7 units to the right of 0.
The points are $5 + 7 = 12$ units apart.

36. (3) 1

$$y = 2(3) - 5$$
$$y = 6 - 5$$
$$y = 1$$

37. (2) 2.25

$(1.5)^2 = 1.5 \times 1.5 = 2.25$

38. (5) $\frac{1}{2} \times 13 \times 7$

$$A = \tfrac{1}{2}bh$$
$$A = \tfrac{1}{2} \times 13 \times 7$$

39. (4) $55 \times 3 + 40 \times 2$

40. (4) 75

$$\frac{MR}{MN} = \frac{QR}{PQ}$$
$$\frac{8}{5} = \frac{120}{x}$$
$$8x = 600$$
$$x = 75$$

41. (5) $x > 30$

$$x - 6 > 24$$
$$\underline{+6} \quad \underline{+6}$$
$$x > 30$$

42. (3) $13.50

$$1\tfrac{1}{2} \times \$9 =$$
$$\frac{3}{2} \times \frac{\$9}{1} = \frac{\$27}{2}$$

43. (1) 2

$$\frac{\text{change in } y}{\text{change in } x} \qquad \frac{6}{3}$$

44. (1) $1\frac{1}{3}$

$$\frac{1}{60} = \frac{x}{80}$$
$$60x = 80$$
$$x = \frac{80}{60} = 1\tfrac{1}{3}$$

45. (1) $2(8) + 3(15)$

46. (5) not enough information is given

You do not know the height of the cylinder.

47. (2) 2

$$6x + 7 = 19$$
$$\underline{-7} \quad \underline{-7}$$
$$\frac{6x}{6} = \frac{12}{6}$$
$$x = 2$$

48. (5) 42

$$\begin{array}{cc} 2 & 3\tfrac{1}{2} \times 12 = \\ \underline{+\;1\tfrac{1}{2}} & \tfrac{7}{2} \times \tfrac{12}{1} = 42 \\ 3\tfrac{1}{2} & \end{array}$$

49. (2) $x^2 - 3$

50. (3) $2y - 20 = 58$

Maxine $= y$
Pilar $= y - 20$
sum: $y + y - 20 = 58$
$\qquad 2y - 20 = 58$

51. (4) $3s$

$7s - 4s = 3s$

52. (3) 31

53. (4) 20

$$\begin{array}{ll} 1990 & 42 \text{ gal} \\ 1975 & \underline{-\;22} \\ & 20 \text{ gal} \end{array}$$

54. (4) 9.8×10^{10}

55. (3) $5.85

$$6\tfrac{1}{2} \times \$.90 =$$
$$\frac{13}{2} \times \frac{\$.90}{1} = \$5.85$$

56. (5) $x^2 = 6^2 + 6^2$

$$c^2 = a^2 + b^2$$
$$x^2 = 6^2 + 6^2$$

Use the answer key on pages 924–925 to check your answers to the Practice Test. Then find the item number of each question you missed and circle it on the chart below to determine the mathematics content areas in which you need more practice. Pay particular attention to areas where you missed half or more of the questions. The page numbers for the content areas are listed below on the chart. The numbers in boldface are questions based on graphics. For those questions that you missed, review the pages indicated.

PRACTICE TEST 5: MATHEMATICS EVALUATION CHART

Skill Area/ Content Area	Item Number	Review Pages
Whole Numbers & Problem Solving	1, 9, 25, 26, 32, 39, 44, 45, 48	559–572
Decimals	37, 42, 55	573–586
Fractions	3, 11, **16**	587–604
Ratio & Proportion	**14**	605–610
Percent	7, 10, **17**, 23	611–620
Measurement	**35**	621–636
Graphs, Statistics, & Probability	6, **52**, **53**	637–648
Numeration	**18**, 47	649–656
Geometry	**4**, **5**, **12**, 13, **15**, **22**, **27**, 28, 29, 30, **34**, **38**, **40**, **46**, **56**	657–674
Algebra	2, 8, 19, 20, 21, 24, 31, 33, 36, 41, 43, 49, 50, 51, 54	675–710

GED READINESS WORKSHEET

Congratulations! You have finished the five Practice Tests, checked your answers, and filled out the Evaluation Charts at the end of each test. At this point, it's important to know if you are ready to take the actual GED Tests. Use the chart and the directions below to help you make that decision.

You will use the number of correct answers to estimate what is called your standard score. Every GED examinee's test results are reported as a *standard score*, so it is important to see how your numbers relate to the standard scores.

TEST	Number Correct	STANDARD SCORES									Standard Score	Required Score
		25	30	35	40	45	50	55	60	65		
Writing Skills	← See page 848 for evaluation, and then refer to the Important Note on page 754 for final scoring. →											
Social Studies		12	15	20	27	35	44	50	55	58		___ / ___
Science		13	15	20	28	35	43	49	54	57		___ / ___
Literature and the Arts		8	10	15	20	26	32	36	38	40		___ / ___
Mathematics		11	13	18	24	32	39	43	48	50		___ / ___
										Average		

1. **Fill in the number of answers that you got correct** in the column labeled **Number Correct**. Do this for all of the tests except Writing Skills. (Because evaluation of the writing sample makes this test more complicated, consult pages 754 and 848 to determine your readiness for the Writing Skills Test.)

2. **Figure your approximate standard score for each test.** Look across each row and find the number that is closest to your number of correct answers. The number in bold type at the top of that column will be your **Standard Score**.

   For example, Henry got 19 questions right on the Social Studies Test. This is closest to the given number of 20 correct answers. Now look at the top of the column that 20 falls in. This represents a standard score of 35. Henry would fill in 35 as his standard score in Social Studies. On Science, Henry got 37 right. This is closest to the given number of 35, which corresponds to the standard score of 45, so Henry would fill in 45 as his standard score for Science. As this example shows, you may estimate up or down, depending on which given number of correct answers you are closest to.

   Following this example, estimate your standard scores for Tests 2–5.

3. **Compare your standard scores to those required by your state, province, or territory.** There are two scores that you must look at: the *minimum score per test* and the *minimum average score*. To find out the scores required in your area, consult the listing on page 929. Write the minimum and minimum average numbers for your area in the column titled **Required Score**.

Are You Ready?

Here are some guidelines to help you decide whether or not you are ready to take any or all of the GED Tests.

If any of your standard scores are at or below the first minimum score that is given on page 929, you need more review before you take the GED Tests. (In most cases, the minimum score is a 35 or 40.) Any score below the minimum will keep you from passing that test and from getting the average score needed for all of the five tests.

If this is the case, use the Evaluation Charts following each Practice Test to determine which areas of the book you need to study more.

If all of your scores exceed the first minimum score that is given and are around the second score (in most cases this is 45), you are probably ready to take the GED Tests. Some scores can be a little higher and some can be a little lower because the second score given is really an average.

Be sure to consult your evaluation of the Writing Skills Practice Test before making any final decisions.

Remember, if you try the GED Tests and do not pass the first time, you will have the opportunity to study some more and retake all or some of the tests. (See page xvii for advice on this.)

Minimum Score Requirements for Award of the GED Credential*

The following are the minimum score requirements for the award of the GED credential in the United States, the territories, and the Canadian Provinces. When two numbers are given, the **first** is the **minimum score required on each test**, and the **second** is the **minimum average score for all five GED Tests**.

Each Test	Combined Average	
40 or 45		Louisiana, Marshall Islands, Northern Mariana Islands, Mississippi, Nebraska, Texas, Micronesia
40 or 50		New Mexico
35 and 45		Alabama, Alaska, Arizona, Connecticut, Georgia, Hawaii, Illinois, Indiana, Iowa, Kansas, Maine, Massachusetts, Michigan, Minnesota, Montana, Nevada, New Hampshire, North Carolina, Ohio, Pennsylvania, Rhode Island, South Carolina, Tennessee, Vermont, Virginia, Wyoming, Guam, Kwajalein Island, Puerto Rico, Virgin Islands
40 Minimum		American Samoa
40 and 45		Arkansas, California, Colorado, Delaware, District of Columbia, Florida, Idaho, Kentucky, Maryland, Missouri, New York, North Dakota, Oklahoma, Oregon, South Dakota, Utah, Washington, West Virginia, Panama Canal Area, Newfoundland, Republic of Palau
40 and 46		Wisconsin
45 Minimum		Alberta, British Columbia, Manitoba, New Brunswick, Northwest Territories, Nova Scotia, Ontario, Prince Edward Island, Saskatchewan, Yukon Territory
42 on Test 1, 40 on Tests 2–4, 45 on Test 5 and 45 Average		New Jersey

*As of April 1996

As of January 1997 the minimum score on each test will be 40 with a minimum average of 45. States, territories, and the Canadian Provinces may require scores higher than these minimums. It is important to verify the score requirements in your area by contacting your local GED testing center.

INDEX